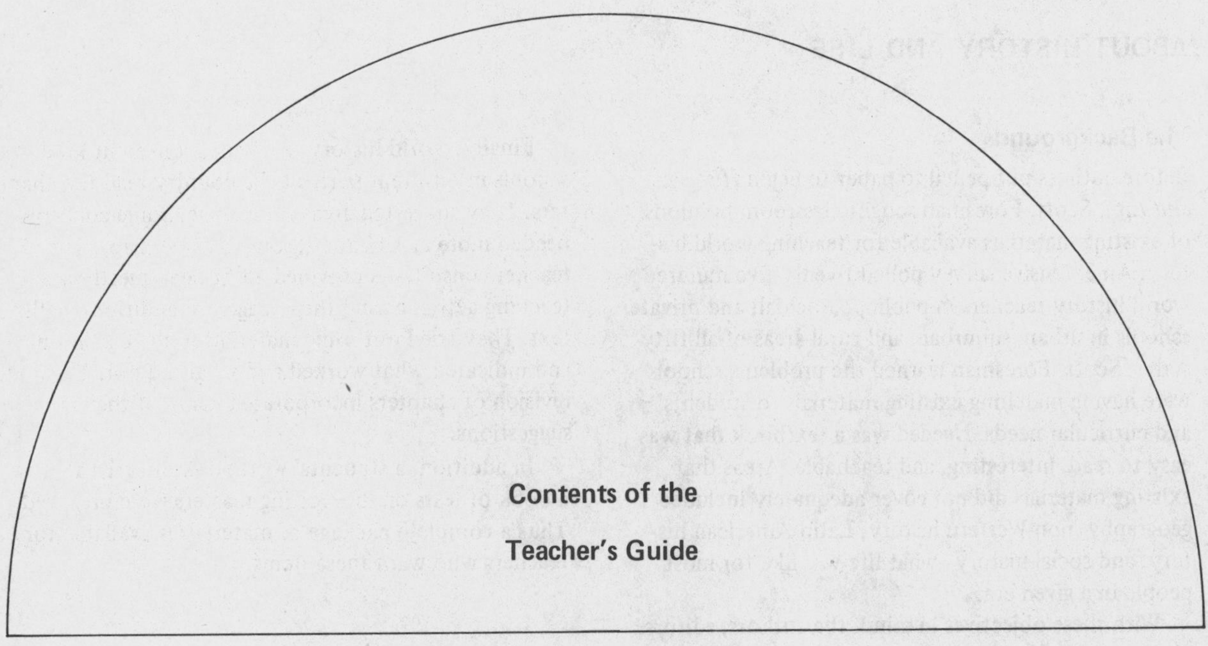

Contents of the Teacher's Guide

ABOUT HISTORY AND LIFE

The Background

Before authors put pencil to paper to begin *History and Life,* Scott, Foresman sought classroom opinions of existing materials available for teaching world history. An extensive survey polled twenty-five hundred world history teachers in public, parochial, and private schools in urban, suburban, and rural areas of all fifty states. Scott, Foresman learned the problems schools were having matching existing materials to students' and curricular needs. Needed was a textbook that was easy to read, interesting, and teachable. Areas that existing materials did not cover adequately included geography, non-Western history, Latin American history, and social history–what life was like for most people in a given era.

With these objectives in mind, the authors, editors, illustrators, cartographers, and teacher consultants began to work to develop *History and Life.* (1) To make it easy and interesting to read, they wrote lively prose at an appropriate reading level; they included definitions and pronunciations in the text; they used a large, bold print; they illustrated the book with full-color pictures, photographs, and maps; and they included features dealing with movies and mysteries in history. (2) To make it teachable, they organized the book into 9 units and 36 chapters to accommodate the school year; they developed a solid pedagogical framework and tested it with practicing classroom teachers; they included section and chapter reviews, chapter and unit tests, and a wide variety of activities emphasizing skills; and they provided practical helps in the form of a teacher's annotated edition. (3) To include the content desired by most teachers, authors devised a well-balanced presentation of Western, non-Western, and Latin American history; they included substantial material on cultures and everyday life as well as on political and economic history; and they added geography essays at regular intervals throughout the book to serve students as keys to history.

Finally, world history teachers in different kinds of schools in different parts of the country read the chapters. They suggested areas for change. Some concepts needed more clarification; some needed maps. The teacher consultants provided additional questions and teaching activities and they suggested additions to the text. They tried out some materials in the classroom and indicated what worked and what did not. The final revision of chapters incorporated many of their suggestions.

In addition, a students' workbook of activities and a book of tests on duplicating masters were prepared. Thus a complete package of materials is available for teachers who want these items.

Teacher's Annotated Edition

by Patricia Gutierrez

for

HISTORY and LIFE

The World and Its People

T. Walter Wallbank
University of Southern California

Arnold Schrier
University of Cincinnati

Donna Maier-Weaver
University of Texas at Dallas

Patricia Gutierrez
Roberto Clemente High School
Chicago, Illinois

Scott, Foresman and Company • Glenview, Illinois

Dallas, Tex. • Oakland, N.J. • Palo Alto, Cal. • Tucker, Ga.

ISBN: 0-673-11683-2

2345678910-RRC-85848382818079

Teachable Organization

The Units Each unit corresponds to a well-defined area of historical study. Each begins with a four-page introduction and ends with a one-page unit test. The introduction includes a poster-like collage, text, and time lines. The collage is made up of period symbols and represents an underlying theme of the unit. A short caption calls students' attention to the theme. The text puts forth the main ideas of the unit. Then, horizontal time lines, one for each chapter in the unit, let students examine the chronological relationships among events in the unit. The unit test is a multiple-choice or short-answer test that requires students to demonstrate they can relate the people, events, and ideas of the different chapters to each other.

The Chapters The first page of every chapter gives students the time period covered, the title, and an illustration and caption that together make a statement about a person, artifact, event, or movement of major significance. Then begins a brief anecdote to capture students' interest and introduce the major ideas of the chapter. These ideas make up the sections of the chapter, and they are listed at the end of the chapter introduction.

The Sections Each chapter is divided into three to six sections, which are identified in the table of contents as well as in the chapter introductions. Each section is introduced by a full-sentence heading. It is further broken down into subsections, which also have full-sentence headings. Students can skim these headings to preview the chapter and, after reading it, to review the main ideas. Each section ends with a number of questions that require students to identify the major people and events in the section and recall the relationships among them. Often these questions also require students to make comparisons between material studied earlier and material in the section.

Chapter Reviews Two pages at the end of each chapter provide a variety of ways of reviewing the material. The text is summarized section by section. Questions called "Who? What? When? Where?" let students check the people, places, events, and chronology of the chapter. "Questions for Critical Thinking" invite students to evaluate evidence, draw comparisons, make predictions, and make value judgments. "Activities" include a number of suggestions that lead beyond the text. Finally, a short-answer, objective "Chapter Test" concludes the chapter. It is organized section-by-section for ease in use.

ABOUT THE TEACHER'S ANNOTATED EDITION

The Teacher's Guide

The first forty-eight pages, numbered G1-G48, make up the Teacher's Guide. This guide includes introductory material, lesson material, and a bibliography. The Table of Contents for the Teacher's Guide is located on page G3.

Lesson material for each chapter is located on a separate page to make it easy to find. Objectives, stated in behavioral terms, are given. A list is given of all the words defined in the chapter. To make *History and Life* easy to read, difficult words and words that have a special social studies meaning are defined for students right on the page where they are first used. (Also, words that may be hard to pronounce are respelled in the phonetic symbols used in Thorndike-Barnhart dictionaries. A pronunciation key is given on page 701.) Some teachers may choose to use the list of defined words to present these words to students before discussing a chapter.

Motivational Activities are included for a teacher to use in introducing a chapter and in helping students see relevance in their study of world history.

Skill Exercises, each labeled with the skill it is designed to reinforce, provide for the development of a variety of social studies skills. These include:

Vocabulary skills
Map skills
Research skills
Developing a sense of chronology
Classifying
Drawing inferences
Synthesizing information
Evaluating evidence
Distinguishing between fact and opinion
Identifying propaganda techniques
Forming hypotheses
Making predictions
Making value judgments

The Annotations

The main body of the Teacher's Annotated Edition consists of the students' pages of *History and Life* with additional teaching suggestions and answers overprinted in blue. Annotations are keyed to symbols in the margin of the text. For example, if a page has two notes on it, one will be keyed with a ● and the other with a ■. At the bottom of the page, the notes will bear matching symbols.

Answers to Section Review questions are cross-referred. As you read along, you will find annotations in the margins that read **ans. 1**, **ans. 2**, and so forth. These annotations point to places in the text where answers to Section Review questions can be found. When you come to a Section Review, each question will be annotated with the page number where the answers are found. For example, on page 30 the first question in Section Review 1 asks: *How did the farming methods of the early Egyptians lead to the beginnings of local governments?* In the margin appears the annotation **p. 22** (in blue); on page 22, the annotation **ans. 1** appears at the beginning of a paragraph that gives the answer.

For chapter and unit tests, the answers are underlined in the Teacher's Edition. Where short answers will not fit on the lines provided, a ● or a ■ keys a note at the bottom of the page. See Chapter Test 2 on page 46 for examples.

Unit 1 CIVILIZATION BEGINS, page 2

Chapter 1 EARLY HUMANS, page 6-19

Objectives

Upon completion of this chapter, the student should be able to:

1. Describe or identify from descriptions the work of anthropologists, archaeologists, geologists, and paleontologists.
2. List the stages in the development of life forms from one-celled plants and animals to mammals as described by scientific theories; understand the length of time involved and factors in the survival or extinction of different forms of life.
3. Explain the processes in the development of early humans as they progressed from food gatherers to more advanced ways of life from the Stone Ages to the Bronze Age.

Words Defined

culture	*Homo sapiens*	awl
civilization	Australopithecines	domesticated
prehistoric	*Homo erectus*	nomads
anthropologist	Paleolithic	nomadic
archaeology	Mesolithic	flax
excavate	Neolithic	prevailing winds
geologist	glacier	potter's wheel
paleontologist	microlith	commerce

Motivational Activities

1. To help students conceptualize the length of time under discussion, draw a clock face on the board. If the earth's life is shown taking place in one revolution of the clock's hands, there is no life for the first 8 hours. From 8 to 10 o'clock, plants, and very primitive animals evolve. At 11 o'clock mammals appear. *Homo erectus* develops between 40 and 50 seconds to midnight, half of which time is spent in the Stone Ages. Civilization, from the first farming community to the present Nuclear Age, occurs in the last millisecond.
2. To explain B.C. and A.D., draw a long time line on the board. Start from a center point and number the years backward for the years B.C. and forward for A.D. Explain that these terms came into use when Pope Gregory XIII (1502-1585) reformed the Christian calendar then in use in Europe. B.C. denotes years before Christ, A.D. comes from *anno domini,* Latin for "in the year of our Lord." On the time line place important dates from Chapter 1 and other years suggested by students.

Skill Exercises

1. **Research skills**: Have students (individually or in groups) make "comic books" of the lives and adventures of prehistoric people. Clothes, tools, food, and physical appearance should be authentic for the period. Different groups could do Old, Middle, and New Stone Ages, and the Bronze Age. Encourage library use and require that all sources be cited.
2. **Classifying**: On the board or on small slips of paper write the concepts, events, and other items taught. Have students rearrange the items into either chronological order or under headings such as inventions, customs, and discoveries.
3. **Developing a sense of chronology**: Have students draw time lines representing their own lives. Have them put points on the line marking important events and experiences they've had. (Birth, started school, moved, baby sister or brother born, etc.) If they want to, you might allow comparison and conversation. (This is one way of helping students get to know each other.)

Notes

Students are usually very interested in prehistoric times. Unfortunately, in the usual World History course there is too little time to cover everything a teacher would like to. This chapter can help give the students an idea of the length of the life of the earth and a beginning understanding, and respect, for the accomplishments of people who were struggling under very difficult conditions.

Chapter 2 THE FIRST CIVILIZATIONS, pages 20-46

Objectives

After studying Chapter 2, students should be able to:

1. Define civilization and state what aspects of each culture made it a true civilization.
2. Describe the accomplishments of the various river valley peoples.
3. Describe some ways in which geography influenced the development of each civilization.
4. Analyze the types of government that developed, the class structure, and the role of religion in each civilization.

Words Defined

civilization	polytheism	class
loess	hieroglyphic	despot
administrator	papyrus	despotism
dynasty	cuneiform	stylus
pharaoh	clan	alabaster
empire	tribe	citadel
theocracy	monotheism	millet
scribe	city-state	paddies

Motivational Activities

1. Discuss what students' ideas of these concepts are: civilization; government; religion.

Ask: What do these words mean to you?
Why are they important?
How did they begin?

Explain that these important ideas were developed by the peoples students will study in Chapter 2. Ask students to suggest ways that Stone Age people could have developed civilizations.

2. Discuss the ways a system of writing may have been invented. Discuss the importance of written communication. Have students "invent" symbols to communicate ideas by working in groups that exchange "writings" to see if other groups can decipher them.

3. Hold a brainstorming session to determine best geographic area for civilization to begin in. List people's basic needs on the board as class members mention them. Help students determine the pros and cons of various geographic areas in enabling people to meet those needs.

Skill Exercises

1. **Research skills**: Using dictionaries, encyclopedias, and books on ancient cultures, have students make charts showing the development of the letters of the alphabet.
2. **Map skills**: Supply, or have students draw, maps of the Middle East and Asia (or use world maps). Have students show possible trade routes by which early civilizations may have contacted each other. If a globe or atlas is available that shows currents and winds, students can find other areas that might have been contacted. (North and South America?) Be sure students read the geography essay on the Etesian winds, page 27.
3. **Evaluating evidence and summarizing**: Have students each write a paragraph about the archaeological evidence found at one of the sites mentioned in their text. They should describe the evidence and tell what inferences about how the people lived can be drawn from it. If students use sources outside the text, be sure they cite them.
4. **Additional synthesizing skills**: Exercises are provided for in the Activities section of the Chapter Review, page 46.

Notes

In addition to the general objectives stated above, this chapter also can be used to introduce important concepts (see the word list) and to teach the role of men and women in early societies.

The relationship of religion to government is an important concept stressed in Section 1. This concept is further developed in following material.

It might be helpful to discuss with the students why religion was so important in the lives of early peoples. Students should realize that these people were trying to understand the forces of nature, sickness, and disasters. They were probably often frightened by what seemed to them mysterious or magical events. Polytheistic beliefs formed as the people felt forces all around them that were beyond their understanding. People tried to control their environment and their lives through offerings to these forces, or gods. The people who became important in government were those priests and rulers who seemed to be able to influence the gods.

Unit 2 CLASSICAL CIVILIZATIONS, page 48

Assign a notebook to be compiled on the civilizations studied in this unit. Suggested contents: maps of each culture's area and of routes of contact among them; time lines of each culture's chronology; outside research on a specific area comparing the different civilizations' contributions, such as art, literature, or religion.

Chapter 3 THE GOLDEN AGE OF INDIA, pages 52–68

Objectives

Studying this chapter should enable the student to:
1. Describe India's geography and climate and evaluate the effect they have had on the history and ethnic make-up of its people.
2. Discuss the caste system, family structure, and religious beliefs of ancient Indian society that persist today.
3. Analyze the importance of cross-cultural contact in the development of classical civilizations and the role of strong rulers in providing that contact.
4. Name some of the contributions India made to the world during its Golden Age and identify the reasons for its decline.

Words Defined

classical	(mountain) passes
viceroy	caste system
subcontinent	reincarnation
Indo-Aryan	religious toleration
monsoons	nirvana
rajah	monks
Brahmans	Gandharan art
pariahs	junks

Motivational Activities

1. After a class reading of the unit introduction, discuss what aspects of our society have been influenced by classical civilizations.
2. Before beginning to study the chapter, have students survey the material by looking at the pictures, captions, headings, and maps. Make sure students know where India is. Refresh students' memories if necessary by quick rereading of Chapter 2, Section 3.

Skill Exercise

Research skills: Have students do outside research on the Mauryan or Gupta empires to find out more about how the people lived. Require students' papers be written in their own words.

Notes

Important concepts of classical Indian civilization treated in this chapter are the development of the caste system; the beginnings of Hinduism and Buddhism; empire building and cultural contacts with Greece and Rome; and the accomplishments of India's Golden Age.

The teacher might like to do additional research on the Hindu and Buddhist philosophies since only a general overview can be given here. These philosophies developed five centuries before Christ and are among the world's great religions today. The *Life* series on religion, almanacs, and encyclopedias can be helpful. Students could be asked to find out what religions have the most followers and in what countries today.

Chapter 4 THE GREAT AGE OF CHINA, pages 69-84

Objectives
Chapter 4 should enable the student to:
1. Describe how China's geography aided its rulers in keeping the country isolated from the outside world.
2. Name the major developments in class structure, economy, philosophy, and art that took place during the 800 years of the Chou dynasty.
3. Describe the attempts of the Ch'in and Han dynasties to extend and secure China's borders; list the achievements made in China during this time and point out the results of contact with the West and other Asians.
4. Tell in what ways the period of the Tang dynasty was China's Golden Age and in what ways long-term harmful effects began then.

Words Defined

levee	feudal	jade
yoke	civil service	block printing

Motivating Activities
1. Project a map of China on the chalkboard and trace (or have a student prepared to) a line representing the Great Wall. Have students read the introductory section and point out that the Wall is the only man-made structure visible from space. Discussion can follow about the usefulness in early times of building a wall to keep the enemy out and the conditions necessary for undertaking such a project—long period of peace, large numbers of people not needed for farming, the wealth and power of the government, and others.
2. Explain to the class that the developments in this chapter describe the formation of a great culture that changed very little until the 20th century. For 2000 years, China's rulers voluntarily isolated the country from the rest of the world. Today we are beginning to learn about a nation that contains one-quarter of the world's population and that is taking its place as one of the great powers. We will need to know more about the Chinese people in the future and in order to understand their culture we should begin by trying to understand their past.

Skill Exercises
1. **Map and research skills**: Have students superimpose a traced outline of China over an outline of the United States. Tables or charts showing the resources, climate, or population of each country can be assigned. Students can add these tables and charts to their notebooks on classical civilizations.
2. **Making comparisons**: Have students do outside reading to compare the basic ideas of Confucius and the Buddha.
3. **Developing a sense of chronology**: Have students make time lines for the different dynasties and show the important events that took place. These time lines can be expanded when Chapters 16 and 33 are studied.

Notes
This chapter deals with 2000 years of Chinese history from the fall of the Shang Dynasty in 1027 B.C. through the Tang in the 10th century A.D. A major point is the isolation of China from contact with the outside world, the culture that developed here was entirely Asian. Also important was the ability of the society to endure despite cyclical periods of war and peace as dynasties rose and fell. Confucianism developed during this period. The teachings of Confucius stressed correct behavior as crucial in finding happiness on earth. Unlike the religions already studied, life after death was not offered as a reward for a good life.

During China's Golden Age Confucianism formed the basis of the civil service exams. Scholars were brought into government on every level according to their ability to memorize the classics. This emphasis on the past accounts for the unchanging quality of Chinese society, but it also served to keep China from being prepared to deal with outsiders when the need arose in the 19th century.

Chapter 5 GREEK CIVILIZATION, pages 85-108

Objectives

After completing this chapter, students should be able to:

1. Name the reasons for the rise and fall of the Minoan and Mycenaean cultures.
2. Describe the development of democracy in Athens and compare that government with Sparta's.
3. Describe the importance of the Persian Wars in Athens' rise to leadership and evaluate Athenian democracy and its decline.
4. Analyze the accomplishments of Philip of Macedonia and Alexander the Great.
5. Identify the major contributions of the Greeks in philosophy, science, historiography, and drama.

Words Defined

democracy	oligarchy	spartan
propaganda	infantry	Socratic method
minotaur	cavalry	pure, or direct, democracy
labyrinth	tyrant	representative democracy
strait	ostracism	republic
polis	helots	funeral oration

Motivational Activities

1. Remind the class that this is the third of the classical civilizations to be studied in this unit and explain that the early Greeks were the first to experiment with giving the people a part in running their government. This form of government is one reason ancient Greece is called a "classical" civilization, since many countries, including the United States, are using that form of government today. Discuss what the students know about "democracy" or the system of government in the U.S.
2. Read the story of Socrates from page 102 of the text. Discuss the importance of obedience to the law.
3. Using the pictures and other materials from this text or other sources, demonstrate the contributions of ancient Greece that have made it among the most respected of early cultures.

Skill Exercises

1. **Map skills**: Assign maps to be drawn (or filled in) showing Greek colonization; Greek-Persian Wars; Alexander's conquests.
2. **Drawing inferences**: Have students write letters, pretending they are either Athenians or Spartans, that describe their life-styles.
3. **Distinguishing between fact and opinion**: Ask students to bring in examples of news articles that serve as examples of the way either Herodotus or Thucydides might write if he were living today.
4. **Research skills**: Have students visit a travel agency to pick up brochures or posters on Greece. Have them research what remains of ancient Greece a traveler could still find today.

Notes

Activities in the Chapter Review (page 108) include suggestions for using research skills, writing in students' own words, debating, and role playing.

Chapter 6 THE ROMAN EMPIRE, pages 109–128

Objectives

This chapter is designed to enable the student to:

1. List the conquests the early Romans made in their mastery of the Italian peninsula; list the basic reasons for the strength of the early republic and its culture.
2. Describe the steps of Rome's rise as a world power including both foreign conquests and the internal changes in people and government.
3. Identify the factors in the survival of the Roman Empire, the problems that weakened it, and the different attempts to save it.
4. Evaluate the contributions of the Romans to world civilization and state to what extent the Romans preserved Greek culture.

Words Defined

Pax Romana	legion	despotism
senate	company	frescoes
patricians	tribunes	legal interpretations
plebeians	veto	codified
republic	forum	vernacular
consul	tribute	aqueducts
dictator	Fabian policy	vaults
Pyrrhic victory	ratify	

Motivational Activities

1. Have class read *A Mystery in History* on page 122. Allow time for questions and discussion. Additional material on Pompeii, including beautiful pictures, can be found in "Part IV: The *Whispers of Pompeii," Life* magazine, March 25, 1966. This article is one of a series called "The Romans" that was published in 1966.
2. Have students read Gibbon's and Toynbee's conflicting views of the Roman Empire in the chapter introduction, pages 109–110. Ask students what their own feelings are about Rome—discuss what they already know. (Repeat this discussion after finishing the chapter to see if their attitudes have changed.)

Skill Exercises

1. **Research skills**: Suggested topics for papers: Role of Women in Ancient Roman Society; The Military Strength of the Roman Empire; The Gods of Ancient Rome.
2. **Research skills**: Have students add specific material (maps, time lines, etc.) to their notebooks on classical civilizations.
3. **Vocabulary skills**: Choose a short paragraph from any book. Have students use a dictionary to look up the origins of the words. Ask them to classify them under Latin Origin, Greek Origin, Others. Have them show both the modern English word and the original from which it is derived.
4. **Vocabulary skills**: Have students research the origins of the names of the months of the year. A dictionary is a good source.
5. **Synthesizing information**: Organize students into teams to debate:
Julius Caesar was correct in believing a dictatorship could do more for a society than a representative form of government could.

Notes

Encourage students to see things around them that can be traced back to the Romans. (Examples: Roman numerals, architecture, languages, specific words, laws, government.) A visit to a travel agency can provide pictorial information on Roman ruins in Italy and Spain.

As a follow-up activity to this unit have class discussions about the four civilizations studied: Which did they like best? Why? What aspects of each culture, if any, did they not like or feel were wrong? What were the most important contributions of each? How were the four cultures similar—different? How were they like or unlike us?

Unit 3 THE WORLDS OF CHRISTENDOM AND ISLAM, page 130

Chapter 7 THE RISE OF CHRISTIANITY, pages 135-150

Objectives

Upon completion of this chapter the student should be able to:

1. Describe the origins and growth of Christianity.
2. List some causes of the decline of the Roman Empire and give some reasons why the Eastern Empire remained strong.
3. List and evaluate the contributions of the early Christian Church in providing needed services and in civilizing the Germanic invaders.
4. Tell how the Frankish kings were important in preserving culture and religion in western Christendom.

Words Defined

catacombs	theology	monasteries
Messiah	presbyter	illuminated
Christ	diocese	papacy
heretics	patriarch	counties
Gentiles	pope	missi dominici
epistles	sanctuary	marks

Motivational Activities

1. Use the unit introduction to begin the study of the chapters on Christianity and Islam. Explain that these are two of the world's major religions and that there were two main divisions in the Christian Church after the fall of Rome. Have students examine the time line to get an idea of when the events they will study happened. Have students look over the maps and illustrations to see where events occurred and what the people of that time considered important enough to record in their art forms. Students should note that most of the art is religious–this shows the preoccupation of the age with things of the spirit.
2. Allow students to discuss this material as it is gone through in class. Many will have some knowledge of early Christian traditions, and the experience of sharing their information–being listened to and listening to others with consideration–can be valuable.
3. Have students read the Sermon on the Mount (Matthew: 5, 6, and 7). List on the board phrases students recognize as familiar. Invite discussion of the kind of life Jesus was preaching about.

Skill Exercises

1. **Making comparisons**: Have students compare Jesus' teachings with the teachings of other religious leaders they have studied. (The Ten Commandments of the Jews are in the Old Testament, Exodus: 20. The Buddha's teachings are summarized in *History and Life* on page 60, Confucius's on page 75.) Encourage students to go beyond the text to find out about religious teachings.
2. **Research skills**: Have students read about the life of an early Christian missionary from those named on pages 144-145. Students should report their findings to the class.
3. **Synthesizing information**: Have students list the various Germanic tribes that settled in areas of Europe. Have them compare the map on page 142 with the map of modern Europe on page 692 to see which nations were settled by which tribes.

Notes

Religious developments and beliefs are an important part of history. This is one chapter of a unit which deals in religion. Students can be assigned notebooks on the Teachings and Lives of Great Religious Leaders.

Chapter 8 WESTERN CHRISTENDOM IN THE MIDDLE AGES, pages 151-169

Objectives
In completing this chapter students will be asked to:
1. Show that they understand the concept of feudalism and know where and why it began.
2. Describe the medieval manor and the class system that developed in the Middle Ages.
3. Evaluate the strength of the Church in the 11th and 13th centuries and the purposes and results of the crusades.
4. Explain the effect of newly increased trade on medieval society.
5. List the scientific advances of medieval scholars; discuss the origins and development of modern languages.

Words Defined

feudalism	tithe	manorial system
lords	sacraments	manor
ladies	baptism	keep
vassal	confirmation	burghers
fief	penance	bourgeoisie
feud	Holy Eucharist	dowry
serf	extreme unction	universities
steward	matrimony	Romance languages
reeve	Holy Orders	morality plays
bailiff	excommunication	

Motivational Activities
1. Have students read the "Mystery in History" on page 166. Point out the early English quotation that begins this mystery and ask if students can translate it into modern English. Some might wish to find other examples of early English writings in the library for translation. Suggest Chaucer.
2. Use the illustrations that accompany this chapter to discuss what can be seen of the daily life of medieval society. Types of buildings, clothing, goods sold in shops, farming methods, upper- and lower-class activities are some examples.
3. Numerous films on the period are available; one especially good one is *The Middle Ages: A Wanderer's Guide to Life and Letters* (27m.C.). The film follows a student through scenes from the literature of the day in 14th-century England.

Skill Exercises
1. **Research and classifying skills**: Have students find and rank according to status the various titles used in England during the Middle Ages. These could be displayed in chart form (on a large poster perhaps) to show the relationship between land ownership and title. If some students research titles for a different country, they will find there is some overlap of titles.
2. **Developing a sense of chronology**: Have students place the events in "Who? What? When? Where?" 1, page 168, on a time line. Ten events are given. Ask students to choose five more they consider important.
3. **Research skills**: Suggest that an "old document" be made of the rules a knight had to follow during the Age of Chivalry. The document should be written in old English script on a large piece of white paper, charred at the edges, "aged" at very low heat in an oven and rolled to resemble a scroll. (Onion juice makes good old-looking ink.) A poem might be written in this way also.

Notes
1. Section 1 raises the possibility of conflicting loyalties when a vassal owed service to more than one lord. A vassal pledged liege homage to the lord from whom he received his first fief. This obligation would take precedence over later ones to other lords.
2. In German towns, a serf who escaped from the manor and lived in town for one year and a day became free.

Chapter 9 BYZANTINE CIVILIZATION AND THE FORMATION OF RUSSIA, pages 170–184

Objectives

Upon completion of this chapter, students should be able to:

1. Describe the multi-cultural aspects of Byzantine civilization; name two events that formalized the split between Roman and Greek Catholicism; and enumerate the causes of the eventual collapse of the Byzantine Empire.
2. Compare Byzantine culture with that of the earlier classical civilizations and of contemporary western Christendom; cite four factors in the strength and endurance of Byzantine civilization.
3. Identify the ethnic background of the Russians; describe what contacts existed between Constantinople and Russia; evaluate some effects of Orthodox Christianity on Russian culture.
4. Tell what effect Mongol rule had on the history of Russia, give examples of Russian resistance to invasion, give examples of the strength of the Moscow princes.

Words Defined

Byzantine	*Rús*
patriarch	Eastern Orthodox Church
bezant	Cyrillic alphabet
mosaics	icons

Motivational Activities

1. Use the geography essay "Strategic Straits" on page 173 to motivate a discussion of the importance of location in a city's history. Have students find the areas shown on the map on a globe or wall map. If possible, project a map of Eastern Europe on the board and invite students to trace trade routes with chalk.
2. Bring in small samples of some of the items traded between Europe and the East. Point out that even ordinary items like fish and honey were valued by advanced eastern peoples. Have students act out a bartering session using the trade items.
3. Assign groups of students to use your school and/or local libraries to compile bibliographies of books on Byzantine culture, art and architecture, Russian history, or Mongol culture. These lists can be used by the other students in preparing reports or extra-credit assignments.

Skill Exercises

1. **Vocabulary skills**: Have students, in groups, prepare glossaries by looking up words in particular sections that they feel are difficult. Ask one student from each group to type the words and relevant definitions on a ditto master so that copies can be run off for the entire class.
2. **Synthesizing information**: Have students summarize in their own words the events described in this chapter. Selected students can then tell the class what happened in each section. This works best when students are seated in a circle.
3. **Evaluating evidence**: Using pictures on pages 176 and 181, have students write papers comparing Byzantine and Russian daily life.

Note

Additional map skill activities are included at the end of Chapter 9, page 184.

Chapter 10 THE RISE OF ISLAM AND THE MUSLIM EMPIRE, pages 185–200

Objectives

After completing this chapter students should have successfully:

1. Identified the basic beliefs and traditions of Islam.
2. Described the relationship between religion and government in the Muslim world as well as those areas conquered by 750.
3. Explained the major reasons for the break up Muslim political unity.
4. Described the rise to power of Seljuk and Ottoman Turks and the relationship between Muslims and Christians during the period of the crusades.

Words Defined

Hijra	Ramadan	Moors
Islam	Hajj	Amir
Muslims	ulema	harems
Allah	Imam	Sultan
Kaaba	mosque	Janissary corps
Koran	caliphs	

Motivational Activities

1. Read the chapter introduction pointing out sentences regarding the size of Islam. Ask students what they know about the religion and write all responses on one side of chalkboard. Ask what questions about Islam they would like to have answered and write these on the other side of the chalkboard. Have students write these questions in their notebooks to be answered as chapter is studied. Any questions not answered in text should be assigned as outside research work.
2. Have students add information on Mohammad to their notebooks on the leaders of the world's religions.
3. Read poems on page 188 and assign papers, charts, or oral reports on visions of heaven and hell as held by the world's major religions.

Skill Exercises

1. **Map skills:** Have students prepare a set of maps for possible classroom display showing the areas controlled by Muslims at various times including the present.
2. **Map and research skills:** On a map of the world have students show by using color-coding the predominant religions of the world today. This information can be found in encyclopedias or almanacs.
3. **Developing a sense of chronology**: Have students place the most important events in the history of Islam on a time line. Have students compare each other's work.

Notes

Be sure students understand the terms used to describe the followers of a religion as well as the religion itself. For example, the religion founded by Mohammad is called Islam; those who are members are Muslims. Others are easier: Christ, Christianity, Christian; Hinduism, Hindu; Buddha, Buddhism, Buddhist.

Additional discussion question: If Charles Martel had lost the battle at Tours in 732 and the Muslims had conquered western Europe, how might history have been different? Would the United States be a Muslim nation today?

Chapter 11 ISLAMIC CIVILIZATION, pages 201-217

Objectives

After finishing this chapter, students should be able to:
1. Describe some major effects of the Islamic theocracy on the lives of the people in the empire and compare its culture with that of western Christendom.
2. Explain the importance of trade in the Muslim Empire.
3. Give examples of the scientific and cultural achievements of the Muslims.

Words Defined

Hajji	optics
joint-stock company	alchemy
damask	patrons
letters of credit	minarets

Motivational Activities

1. Use the chapter introduction to motivate a discussion of the advanced culture of Islamic civilization. Emphasize the time span covered by this chapter and, if necessary, refer back to Chapter 8 to point out the contrasts between the two cultures between the 9th and 12th centuries.
2. Type up and hand out selections chosen from the *Arabian Nights* or *The Rubáiyát.* Have questions based on the readings ready for class discussion or as a written assignment.

Skill Exercises

1. **Map and research skills:** In conjunction with Section 2, which discusses the extensive trade that went on in the Muslim world, have students show on a map the route taken by some imported items they may have. Store managers can be interviewed and package labels and shipping labels used for additional information. There are, of course, many examples of imported goods today: shoes, clothing, cars, radios, cameras, and so forth.
2. **Classifying:** Assign charts (possibly poster size) to be made showing the various scientific advances of the Muslims. "Who? What? When? Where?" 3, on page 215 has possible headings that can be used. Students should indicate if particular contributions were based on knowledge learned from other cultures.
3. **Research skills:** Have students find out, through library or newspaper sources, whether Muslims still make the pilgrimage to Mecca and, if so, how many make the journey each year and what ceremonies and traditions are followed.

Note

The prohibition of the representation of humans or animals in Islamic art originated with Mohammad's destroying the idols in the Kaaba. Point out the beautiful geometric and floral designs included in the illustrations in Chapters 10 and 11. Formal Arabic script was used as decoration also.

This is the final chapter in Unit 3; review what students have learned by using the Unit Review Test, page 217.

Unit 4 THE WORLDS OF AFRICA AND THE AMERICAS, page 218

Chapter 12 THE LANDS AND PEOPLE OF AFRICA, pages 222-237

Objectives

Upon completion of this chapter, students should be able to:

1. Name the ecological regions of Africa, tell where they are found, and describe the changing conditions of the region of the Sahara.
2. Describe some aspects of the cultures of the rain forest peoples and of the Rift Valley people.
3. Identify some of the agricultural problems of Africa, tell the importance of cattle in a pastoral society, and explain the possible origins of iron working.
4. Evaluate the importance of lineage relationships in African society; describe two methods used in choosing leaders; enumerate the functions of griots; and describe the lost-wax process of casting bronze statues.

Words Defined

savanna	lineage	griots
oasis	Bantu migrations	lost-wax process
caravans	compound	yam
pastoral	plantain	tsetse fly

Motivational Activities

1. Have the class read the unit and chapter introductions, pages 219-223. Allow time for students to express opinions and ask questions. Ask what students already know about Africa and list their responses on the board. Tell students some of their ideas may change as they study Chapters 12 and 13. For example: Students may believe Africa is mostly jungles and wild animals; Section 1 points out that most of Africa is desert and grasslands. Due to recent urban growth, conservationists today are concerned about the dwindling numbers of wildlife species.
2. After reading about the problems of the Kulango in adjusting to another life-style (pages 222-223) have students discuss similar problems faced by people today in moving to new areas.

Skill Exercises

1. **Comparing historical sources**: Ask students to read "A Mystery in History," page 229, and compare it with the version in the Bible. Oral reports would be a good way to discuss what they find. (Bibles are available in libraries, if students do not have them at home.)
2. **Research skills**: Have students prepare reports giving additional information on pastoral culture. The Masai, of modern Kenya and Tanzania, are the people whose praise song appears on page 231. Some students may wish to report on their culture.
3. **Developing a sense of chronology**: Events listed in Chapters 12 and 13 should be combined on one time line to show the full scope of Africa's early development.

Note

Emphasize the point made in the unit introduction that our lack of information about Africa is due to the failure of Western cultures to make contact with Africans not because there is any lack in African culture itself.

Chapter 13 AFRICAN CIVILIZATIONS SOUTH OF THE SAHARA, pages 238-256

Objectives

After finishing this chapter, students should be able to:
1. Describe the trade and sources of power of the empire of Ghana and compare its culture and government with that of the Mali Empire.
2. Explain the importance of location on the development of the city-states of East Africa; explain the role of the Portuguese in Africa in the late 15th century.
3. State the sources from which we have learned about Zimbabwe and describe its culture and decline.
4. Explain the spread of Islam to south Africa and the ways in which Africa's history was affected by it.
5. Describe the growth of the forest states and the effect of European trade and slavery on African culture.

Words Defined

silent trade	kola
mansa	*jihad*
Guinea gold	oba
Swahili	cassava

Motivational Activities

1. Students should have a good grasp of the existence of strong African cultures from working on Chapter 12. In class, look through this chapter's illustrations, reading and discussing the captions. Pause at pages 252-253 to allow students to express opinions about slavery. Ask what students think might have been the effect of slavery on the areas of Africa where it was carried on. What might have been the attitudes of the people involved, black and white? Can any present-day racial attitudes be traced back to slavery?
2. Use the illustrations from this chapter to reinforce the main idea from the chapter introduction, that highly developed civilizations existed in Africa.

Skill Exercises

1. **Research skills**: Assign papers, using additional sources, on these topics: The Effects of the Slave Trade on African Culture, Natural Resources of Africa, African Poetry or Folk Tales, Archaeological Sites in Africa.
2. **Map skills**: On a world map have students show routes by which cultural contacts were made within Africa and between Africa and Asia, America, and Europe. Students should label each route with the correct year and the names of some items traded. (Students can use their texts as a source for this exercise.)
3. **Classifying**: Have students chart the achievements of each of the governments mentioned in the text. The area controlled by each ruler and the correct time span of each should be shown.

Note

African history is continued in the following parts of the book:

Chapter 22	The Formation of Latin America
Section 3	Indians and Africans were the main source of labor, pages 409-412
Chapter 28	The Building of Empires
Section 5	Africa was carved into many colonies, pages 531-534
Chapter 35	Nation-Building in the Middle East, Africa, and Latin America
Section 2	Black Africa changed rapidly, pages 655-661
Chapter 36	The Changing World
Section 3	The gap between rich and poor countries widened, pages 678-683

Chapter 14 EARLY CULTURES IN THE AMERICAS, pages 257-274

Objectives

After completing this chapter, students should be able to:

1. Explain the origins of the American Indians and the term *Indian* and compare four Indian cultures.
2. Tell where Mayan civilization began and describe the daily life and accomplishments of its people.
3. Describe the major attributes of Aztec culture and religious beliefs, showing an understanding of the reasons for those beliefs.
4. State the evidence for our knowledge of the Tiahuanaco and Inca people; describe their government and major accomplishments.
5. Evaluate the importance of social classes in some Indian societies.

Words Defined

Indian	cacao beans	coca
totem pole	codex	Acllacuna
potlatch	Inca	cochineal
adobe	quipus	henequen
ideographic writing	llama	chicle
maguey cactus		

Motivational Exercises

1. Make up and duplicate a set of mathematical problems for students to solve using the Mayan number system as described on page 264. These can be either in Arabic numbers for students to change to Mayan or in Mayan for students to rewrite in Arabic.
2. Give students blank maps of North America on which they are to label states, cities, rivers, and lakes that have names of American Indian origin. This text contains some examples; others can be found in books on American Indian tribes.
3. Project a transparency of the world and/or Western Hemisphere and with markers show the route by which the first humans are thought to have migrated here across the Bering Strait. Allow time for questions. Fill in areas where the Indian cultures lived as mentioned in text. Have students fill in desk copies of maps with the same information.

Skill Exercises

1. **Research skills**: As an extra reading assignment for students especially interested in American Indian culture, Hal Borland's *When the Legends Die* is highly recommended. Available in paperback, Bantam Books.
2. **Making comparisons**: Have students make charts or collages showing the different achievements of specific Indian cultures. These could be made up for classroom display.
3. **Developing a sense of chronology**: Assign time lines to be drawn showing events in the Americas, Asia, Europe, Africa, at the times treated in this chapter. This can be a group project—one group per area. Results should be discussed.

Notes

There is a great deal of material available in libraries or paperback books on early American culture. Students are usually interested in these groups and should welcome the opportunity to learn about the first Americans.

See the teaching notes for Chapter 22, page G28, for an outline showing the further treatment of Latin American history in *History and Life.*

Unit 5 THE WORLDS OF ASIA, page 276

Chapter 15 INDIA UNDER MUSLIM RULE, pages 280-293

Objectives

After completing this chapter, students should be able to:

1. Describe the conquest of India by the Muslims and explain why the Hindu and Muslim cultures did not blend into one.
2. Analyze the importance of family structure, religion, and caste on Hindu culture.
3. Explain the Mughul conquest of India and compare the reigns of Akbar and Shah Jahan.
4. Evaluate the rule of Aurangzeb and give reasons for the decline of the Mughul Empire.

Words Defined

infidel	minaret	suttee
sultanate	joint family	caste
purdah	cremated	Mughul

Motivational Activities

1. Have students read the unit and chapter introductions noting that these chapters bring the history of Asia up to the point of contact with the West. The religious conflict mentioned in the introduction to Chapter 15 laid the basis for the many serious present-day problems of the Indian subcontinent.
2. Project a map of the Eastern Hemisphere sketching in the areas conquered by the Muslims in the Middle East, Africa, and Asia (see maps on pages 191, 192, 198, 206, and 282). Follow with a reading and discussion of Section 1.
3. If necessary, refresh students' memories by rereading the last section of Chapter 3, which describes the apathy and self-satisfaction of Hindu rulers in India that left them vulnerable to Muslim conquest.

Skill Exercises

1. **Drawing inferences from textual material**: (a) Have students write reports on Hindu culture as seen by a Muslim official advising the Sultan on occupation policy. (b) Write the views of a Hindu or Buddhist regarding their attitudes toward the Muslim invaders. (c) Give the views of an untouchable toward the Muslims. (It was often the lower castes who converted to Islam because they felt hopelessly trapped in the cycle of reincarnation; Islam offered them hope and escape from suffering.)
2. **Developing a sense of chronology**: Have students arrange the events in "Who? What? When? Where?" 1, page 292, on a time line. Have students add a specified number of events.
3. **Map skills, research skills, and making comparisons**: Other suggestions are included in the Activity section at the end of Chapter 15 (page 293).

Notes

The name *Mughul* (sometimes *Mogul*) is a corruption of *Mongol,* a word much dreaded in India because of its association with Tamerlane, the destroyer of Delhi. It has been suggested that *Mongol* was converted to *Mughul* through a common mispronunciation or through a wish on the part of the Indians to conceal the fact the Mughuls were in truth Mongols.

The history of India continues in Chapter 28, The Building of Empires, and is brought up to the present in Chapter 34, The Assertion of Asian Independence.

Chapter 16 CHINA FROM THE SUNG THROUGH THE MANCHUS, pages 294–309

Objectives

Upon completion of this material, the student should be able to:

1. Interpret events in China in the light of two basic themes of Chinese history (the dynastic cycle and continuity) and describe the advances and art of the Sung period.
2. Describe the trade, business, family, and class structure of Sung China.
3. Identify the Mongols and Marco Polo and tell the importance of each in China's history; describe the effects of nomadic life on the assimilation of the Mongols into Chinese culture.
4. Compare Ming and Manchu rule in China and tell the effect of isolation on the country's history.

Words Defined

dynastic cycle	Mongols
continuity	steppes
moldboard	assimilation
seismograph	Ming
abacus	Forbidden City
porcelain	isolation
china	queues
foot binding	thermoluminescence
graduated income tax	

Motivational Activities

1. Use the quotations from primary sources found on pages 301 and 307 to stimulate discussion about the attitudes of the Chinese peasant and emperor toward their environment.
2. Follow a reading of the chapter introduction with handouts of selections from the diary of Marco Polo (available in most libraries or paperback). Discuss why his travels and writings meant so much to a Europe still in the Middle Ages.
3. Read the "Mystery in History" on page 300. Discuss the significance of finding the bronze pots in Southeast Asia.

Skill Exercises

1. **Classifying**: Have students chart the accomplishments of the six dynasties treated in this chapter, the years of each should be given as well as the high and low points of each.
2. **Research skills**: Assign papers or posters to be made on the contributions of China. Extra reading in other sources would be helpful.
3. **Synthesizing information and making hypotheses**: Ask students to list aspects of Chinese culture that were affected by the Chinese policy of isolation. Then have them think about their own lives in those same areas. How would their lives be different if the United States followed a policy of isolation? Have students write a fictional account of life in the United States after two hundred years of isolation. Students with weak writing skills could put their ideas in the form of a drawing or song; some might choose to present their ideas in a dramatization or dialogue.

Chapter 17 THE EMERGENCE OF JAPAN, pages 310–324

Objectives

Upon completion of this chapter, students should be able to:

1. Describe Japan's grographical location and evaluate the importance of the sea and nature in Japanese culture.
2. Explain the origins of the Japanese people, the beliefs of Shintoism, and list aspects of Japanese culture that have been adopted from China.
3. Identify the importance of the shogun and the samurai, and compare developments that took place during the Ashikagawa and Tokugawa Shogunates.
4. Describe the development of the role of women in Japanese society and some aspects of daily life in Japan.

Words Defined

samurai	shogun
seppuku	hereditary
hara-kiri	Bushido
Nippon	Kamikaze
Shinto	daimyo
Kuroshio	No drama
kana	Kabuki
tanka	hibachi
haiku	

Motivational Exercises

1. After reading the chapter introduction, discuss: (a) Should people be concerned about the loss of old customs and traditions? (b) Why did Mishima's plea meet with no response from the people? (c) In what ways was Mishima's death an honorable one?
2. Discuss the Japanese poetry offered in this chapter and additional selections you provide on handout sheets. Point out the concise simplicity and emphasis on things from nature.
3. Explain that although Japan at one time borrowed many ideas from China, the two cultures are not identical. Spoken Japanese is completely different from the Chinese language. Written Japanese is a combination of Yamoto and Chinese. The written language is ideographic—each idea or object has its own symbol (ideogram); originally the ideograms were simplified pictures. There are tens of thousands of ideograms—one must know 3,000 to read a Japanese newspaper. A child spends six years learning to read and write about 1,000 ideograms.
4. If possible, a visit to a Japanese restaurant would be an excellent way to motivate the students to learn about Japan. Most students should enjoy tempura, teriyaki, or sukiyaki. Perhaps the students could prepare some of these dishes at home for the class to enjoy.

Skill Exercises

1. **Drawing inferences**: Have students design the garden and floor plan of a Japanese home. Outside resources can be consulted and some may wish to build a three-dimensional model.
2. **Research skills and making evaluations**: Assign a paper on the history, meaning, and methods of the martial arts. This might be interestingly presented as an oral report, especially if one of the students is involved in these sports.
3. **Research skills**: A suggestion for an outside reading assignment is: *Why the Japanese Are the Way They Are,* Benjamin Appel; Little, Brown, 1973, a short, very readable, thorough survey of Japanese history and culture. One of a series: Russia and China are the other subjects.

Note

Japanese shogunates were not the same as dynasties in China. Shoguns were succeeded by chosen heirs not necessarily related by blood. Talented men would be named—much as the Roman Caesars adopted men to succeed them on the throne.

Unit 6 THE RISE OF THE WEST, page 326

This unit brings the areas of study back to Europe at the time when it began its rapid rise to world power. Use the unit introduction to make the points that Europe changed rapidly after 1200 and that the new nations were able to dominate the world because non-Europeans did not organize into strong states. Use the collage in the introduction to have students identify paintings illustrated in the rest of the unit.

Chapter 18 THE DEVELOPMENT OF NATIONS, pages 330–344

Objectives

On completing this chapter, students should be able to:
1. Evaluate the reasons for the end of the feudal period; describe the growth of national power.
2. List the steps by which England became a nation.
3. Describe the development of the French state; give reasons for the Hundred Years' War and France's victory.
4. Compare the national growth in Spain and Portugal with that of France and England; identify the problems Russia, Germany, and Italy had in becoming nations.

Words Defined

mercenaries	Parliament
nation	sheriffs
nationalism	borough
patriotism	burgesses
common law	representative body
circuit court	redress of grievances
grand jury	acts, statutes, bills
petit jury	Reconquista
Magna Charta	tsar
	Electors

Motivational Activities

1. Project map transparencies, if available, or use the book maps of Europe during the Middle Ages (page 332) and after the growth of national states (page 355) to note the changes in political boundaries. Refer to these maps as students discuss the steps in each nation's development from the text.
2. List on the board the factors in the decline of feudalism and rise of centralized power as students suggest them from the text. Check to make sure that students grasp the cause and effect relationship.

Skill Exercises

1. **Developing a sense of chronology**: Have students make separate time lines to show events in the development of each nation.
2. **Vocabulary skills**: Have students write paragraphs using the defined words to describe events in this chapter. Emphasize that (except for vocabulary words) these paragraphs must be in their own words.
3. **Classifying**: Have students make charts that compare feudal methods of warfare with more modern methods.

Chapter 19 THE EUROPEAN RENAISSANCE, pages 345–361

Objectives

After completing this chapter, the student should be able to:

1. Identify the geographical and political factors that made northern Italy the birthplace of the Renaissance.
2. Discuss the importance of Greek and Roman classics on Renaissance thought and on the works of Petrarch and Boccaccio; select the characteristics that made da Vinci a Renaissance man.
3. Compare Renaissance art with that of the Middle Ages; describe the work of five Renaissance artists.
4. Explain the results of the invention of movable type; evaluate the work of northern Renaissance humanists, artists, and writers.

Words Defined

condottieri	Renaissance
humanism	perspective
frescoes	parchment
	vellum

Motivational Activities

1. Assign different students to bring one of the spices listed in Section 1 to class. Use the map of trade routes on page 347, a globe of the world if possible, and the information in the first section to explain how the wealth of the East was brought to Europe. Point out the geographical importance of Italy as a stopping point between the Muslim Empire and western Europe.
2. Use da Vinci's sketches on pages 350–351 and the text material about him to motivate an interest in the men of the Renaissance. If possible bring in a book of additional plans and drawings made by da Vinci and allow students to look through it and discuss it.
3. Have students compare the artwork illustrated in Chapters 7 and 8 with that in this chapter. Discuss the differences and ask what changes can be seen in subject matter, life-styles, attitude of the artists.

Skill Exercises

1. **Research and vocabulary skills**: Have students find a specified number of examples of uses of this chapter's vocabulary words. Students should look either in the textbook alone or in outside sources as well.
2. **Synthesizing information**: Ask students to write a diary of a caravan merchant carrying goods from an eastern city to an Italian city-state. The diary should give details of the journey, the types of terrain traveled, methods of transportation used, cities stopped at, and kinds of people met. All of this information can be found in the textbook. Geography essays should be used also.
3. **Synthesizing information and making comparisons**: Have abler students write papers comparing Medieval, Renaissance, and modern attitudes toward individualism.

Note

The value of spices lay in their ability to make the often partially spoiled meat and otherwise bland foods of Europe more palatable. The nobles of Europe, who were then becoming wealthier because of taxes they collected from the emerging middle class, bought more and more jewels with their wealth.

Chapter 20 THE REFORMATION AND NATIONAL POWER, pages 362-382

Objectives

Upon completion of this chapter, students should be able to:

1. Describe the weaknesses and problems of the 14th-century Catholic Church and some of the early attempts at reform.
2. Compare the main features of the Reformation with those of the Counter Reformation and evaluate the effects of both on Europe.
3. Show the attempts of European rulers to maintain the balance of power; explain the role of religion in two wars.
4. Describe the attempts of French rulers to strengthen France; show how the balance of power was restored in 1713.
5. Evaluate the reigns of Peter the Great and Catherine the Great in Russia.
6. Analyze the roles of Prussian rulers in the strengthening of that country and explain the involvement of overseas colonies in the War of the Austrian Succession.

Words Defined

simony
justification by faith
Protestant
papal indulgences
predestination
Huguenots
balance of power

Motivational Activities

1. Refer to the time line in the unit introduction to show that some of the events of the Reformation occurred during the later Renaissance period and were another aspect of the questioning spirit of the times.
2. Discuss the map on page 364. Have students name the religions of various nations. Remind students that the people of an area had to belong to the same religion as their ruler.

Skill Exercises

1. **Developing a sense of chronology**: In incorrect order, list events of the Reformation and Counter Reformation on a time line on the board. Then have students rearrange the events in the correct order.
2. **Research skills**: Have students use the school library resources, such as encyclopedias, to write biographies of a Protestant leader, such as Calvin, Knox, or Zwingli. Have the best biographies read aloud in class.
3. **Evaluating evidence and synthesizing information**: Compare the balance of power in Europe of the 1600's and 1700's with that of today.

Note

Points to emphasize are that the reformers at first were trying to return the Church to its traditional practices and broke away only after being rebuffed by the Church hierarchy.

Chapter 21 THE AGE OF EXPLORATION, pages 383-400

Objectives

After completing this chapter, students should be able to:

1. Discuss the motivations and efforts of early explorers.
2. Identify the explorations of various European seafarers.
3. Describe the founding of overseas empires by European powers.
4. Evaluate the social, political, and ecological changes brought about by the Age of Exploration.

Words Defined

papal line of demarcation
joint-stock company
Commercial Revolution
capitalism
mercantilism
inflation

Motivational Activities

1. Use "A Mystery in History: Who Really Discovered America?" (page 386) to introduce a new aspect of a topic that students are probably familiar with. Read and discuss the mystery in class. Then have students make a chart on the board listing the early explorers of America, the dates of their trips, and the areas each explored. Finally, hold a class discussion on the reliability of the evidence for each trip.
2. Have students bring to class examples of the items that Europeans got from their various colonies, such as table dishes from China, peanuts from Africa, and sweet potatoes from the Americas. Ask students to speculate aloud on how these and other imports must have changed everyday life in Europe.
3. On a globe, have students trace Columbus's planned voyage to India. Point out his error in not knowing about the Western Hemisphere. Emphasize to students that sailors of Columbus's time had no doubts that the world was round, that ancient Greek scholars had written about the world being round.

Skill Exercises

1. Making value judgments: Discuss with students the procedure by which European powers "claimed" various territories as their colonies. Ask students what gave European governments the right to claim these lands and how present-day thinking might be different than what went on during the Age of Exploration. Also ask students whether they think that colonialism was a good or bad thing overall. Make students give reasons for their opinions.
2. Research skills and synthesizing information: Have students write biographical essays on their favorite explorers. Suggest they use encyclopedias as resources. More able students might be assigned to write diaries about life during one of the voyages. Information might include (1) problems–such as lack of drinking water, scurvy, and fear of the unknown; or (2) daily life information–such as details of ship construction, the routines of standing watch, changing the rigging for a wind shift; or (3) ship discipline.

Chapter 22 THE FORMATION OF LATIN AMERICA, pages 401–417

Objectives

After completing this chapter, students should be able to:

1. Describe the methods used by Cortés and Pizarro in their conquests; compare the methods of colonization used in Spain and Portugal.
2. Identify the methods used by and problems of Spain in governing its colonies.
3. Describe the effects of colonialism on the Spaniards, the Indians, and the Africans.
4. Describe the major factors involved in the development of Latin American culture.

Words Defined

conquistadores
viceroy
peninsulares
creoles
mestizos
encomienda

Motivational Activities

1. Use the chapter introduction to help students realize the extent to which Aztec culture had developed before the Spaniards arrived. It is important to stress the significance of the first contact between the two cultures.
2. Point out and discuss the different attitudes of the Spanish colonialists toward the Indians: conquistadores saw them as people to be conquered, landowners used them as laborers, missionaries wanted to protect them from abuse and to save their souls, government officials were supposed to enforce laws written to protect the Indians and at the same time ensure a steady flow of Indian-produced wealth back to Spain. Discuss what the students feel might have been the Indians' feelings toward the Spanish.

Skill Exercises

1. **Research skills**: Have students find examples of Spanish colonial religious art and pre-Columbian art. What are some similarities? What are the differences? (Facial features, design, materials.)
2. **Map skills**: On a map of the Western Hemisphere, have students show all of the territory once claimed by Spain and tell what parts of the United States are included in this area. Spanish place names in the present-day United States should be especially noted.
3. **Research skills**: Assign students to find examples of the blending of cultures in Latin American food, music, art, language, and customs. The extent to which that blended culture is part of the culture of the United States could also be included.

Note

This is the last chapter of Unit 6. Have students review what has been learned by rereading the Section Summaries at the end of each chapter. The Unit Review can be assigned as an independent review for students to test themselves or as an end-of-the-week quiz.

Latin American history is continued in the following parts of the book:

Chapter 24 The Age of Democratic Revolutions
Section 5 Latin American colonies became independent nations, pages 451–456
Chapter 25 The Growth of Liberalism, Nationalism, and Democracy
Section 2 Continental Europe was politically changed, pages 462–466
Chapter 28 The Building of Empires
Section 6 Imperialism grew in Latin America, pages 534–538
Chapter 35 Nation-Building in the Middle East, Africa, and Latin America
Section 3 Latin America faced many challenges, pages 661–667

Unit 7 REVOLUTIONARY CHANGES IN THE WEST, page 418

Discuss the concept of revolution. Briefly state that all the chapters in this unit continue the basic theme of change.

Chapter 23 SCIENCE AND THE AGE OF REASON, pages 422-437

Objectives

After completing this chapter, students should be able to:

1. Describe contributions to scientific knowledge made by Copernicus, Bacon, Galileo, and Newton and explain the attitudes of the Church toward the new theories.
2. Discuss the importance of new discoveries and inventions in the 17th and 18th centuries.
3. Describe the work of Vesalius, Harvey, Janssen, and Van Leeuwenhoek in the field of medicine.
4. Describe the development of the political and social reforms of the Enlightenment.

Words Defined

revolution	physiology
scientific revolution	political science
geocentric theory	Enlightenment
heliocentric theory	social contract
scientific method	deism
element	atheist
rehabilitation	neoclassic
	ellipse

Motivational Activities

1. Explain the conflict between the heliocentric and geocentric theories and why the Church resisted the heliocentric theory so strongly. Allow students to look out the window to observe what ancient Greek thinkers based their theory of the movement of the planets on. Discuss that the Church felt it was so important not to change its long-accepted teachings because people might have begun to question other Church teachings.
2. Go through Chapter 23 listing the discoveries, inventions, and new ideas. List and discuss the ways in which people's lives have been changed by each.

Skill Exercises

1. **Research skills**: Have students find newspaper and magazine articles or pictures that show examples of the advances discussed in this chapter.
2. **Research and communication skills**: Have students interview their math, science, or English teachers about the important advances made in these areas during the Age of Reason. Then have a class discussion for students to share what they have learned with each other.
3. **Making value judgments**: Have students read part of *Robinson Crusoe* or *Gulliver's Travels* or listen to part of the *Messiah* or a Mozart composition and then write essays on their likes and dislikes about the selections. Require students to define their likes and dislikes with examples.

Chapter 24 THE AGE OF DEMOCRATIC REVOLUTIONS, pages 438-456

Objectives

Upon completing this chapter, the student should be able to:

1. Describe the causes of problems of the Stuart kings and Parliament, the Restoration, the Glorious Revolution, and the results of the Act of Settlement.
2. Discuss some of the causes and results of the American Revolution.
3. Describe the social structure of the Old Regime; describe the developments of the French Revolution.
4. List some of the effects of Napoleon's actions on the rest of Europe.
5. Describe the internal and external causes of revolution in Latin America and identify that area's problems in establishing stable democracies.

Words Defined

petition	prime minister
First Estate	federal
Second Estate	Whig
Third Estate	bourgeoisie
cabinet	Tory
Code Napoleon	guillotine

Motivational Activities

1. Divide the class into groups and have the groups make lists of the causes of resentment and conflict in each of the revolutions discussed in the chapter. Allow students to use their textbooks and talk among themselves while making the lists. Now bring the class back together and compare the lists that have been made.
2. Simulate the trial of Charles I. To do this, students should first research the procedure followed in a British trial. Witnesses should be called from the groups in English society mentioned in the text to give their testimony as to whether the king was guilty of treason and if so, should be executed.
3. Have students role-play random interviews with members of French, English, North American, or Latin American societies at the time of their revolutions to get the citizens' viewpoints. As homework, have students write compare-and-contrast essays on the varying viewpoints expressed.

Skill Exercises

1. **Classifying and developing a sense of chronology:** Have students list under the correct heading (English Revolution, American Revolution, or French Revolution) the specific causes, events, and results of each. Each cause should be a short phrase; events and results should be listed in chronological order.
2. **Drawing inferences and synthesizing information:** With books closed and after completing the study of this chapter, have students write paragraphs on each revolution summarizing the ways in which each was a "revolution."
3. **Map skills:** On a world map, have students label the areas in which each revolution took place and the years of its occurrence.

Chapter 25 THE GROWTH OF LIBERALISM, NATIONALISM, AND DEMOCRACY, pages 457-475

Objectives

After completion of this chapter, students should be able to:

1. Describe the conflicts that arose between the European governments that resisted change and the liberals and nationalists who tried to achieve change.
2. Describe the Crimean War as an example of Realpolitik; discuss the political changes in France, Italy, and Prussia.
3. Describe the growth of democracy in Britain, France, and Germany.
4. Explain why reforms were slow to develop in Spain, Portugal, Austria-Hungary, and the Ottoman Empire.

Words Defined

liberalism	self-determination
nationalism	Realpolitik
democracy	Reichstag
Zollverein	Risorgimento
	Bundesrat

Motivational Activities

1. Before students begin to read this chapter, have them go through it as a class and discuss the illustrations, especially the political cartoons.
2. Compare the map of Europe 1815, page 459, with that of Europe 1721, page 376, and Napoleon's Empire, page 449. Have students identify differences and list them on the board under the headings: Europe in 1721, Europe in 1810, and Europe in 1815.
3. Stress the meanings of the political terms used in this chapter. Use the chapter introduction to define the three 19th-century movements, point out instances in the text that deal with them, and emphasize the ways in which these terms are used today.

Skill Exercises

1. **Research and drawing inferences**: In newspapers and magazines, have students find examples of uses of the words *liberal, conservative,* and *self-determination.* Then hold a class discussion on how and why these terms are used today.
2. **Map skills**: Have students compare the map of Europe 1815, page 459, with the map of Contemporary Europe, page 692. Note not only the changes in national boundaries but also the countries that now exist.
3. **Drawing inferences and evaluating evidence**: Have students list what they feel are important social or political issues today. Students should describe their attitudes toward these issues and give some solutions. Have students vote to decide whether they, as a group, are liberal, conservative, or moderate.

Notes

In dealing with the political terminology discussed in this chapter it is important to point out that what liberals want today is not the same as what liberals of the 1800's wanted. Have students suggest why they think these attitudes have changed.

Skill Exercise 3 should bring out the fact that an individual is usually not wholly liberal on every issue nor wholly conservative. Discuss the reasons for this variance in a person's beliefs.

Chapter 26 THE INDUSTRIAL REVOLUTION, pages 476-494

Objectives

After completing this chapter, students should be able to:

1. Describe ways in which the Industrial Revolution changed methods of production, agriculture, transportation, and business.
2. Identify and evaluate some scientific and medical advances of the 19th century.
3. Analyze three artistic styles (romanticism, realism, and impressionism) and describe the architectural development of the period.

Words Defined

realism	romanticism
Industrial Revolution	factory system
corporation	atoms
industrial capitalism	molecules
capital	pasteurization
puddling	genes
domestic system	psychology
	impressionism

Motivational Activities

1. To illustrate the differences between the domestic and factory systems, have students "manufacture" items using two methods of assembly. In the first, have one student perform all the operations required to make the product; in the second, have an assembly line share the work. Examples of items that can be "produced" are: stringing beads, assembling and stapling multi-paged tests, filing cards, or filling boxes with cookies. Discuss which system is best for speed, quality, efficiency, and worker-satisfaction. Allow time for necessary evaluation and discussion during this activity. Encourage students to suggest more efficient methods to manufacture the product.
2. Use "Geography: A Key to History—Resources and Industrial Development" (page 479) to introduce industrial development. Follow up by reading the list of conditions on page 478 that explain the reasons for industrialization in England. Reinforce these concepts with Skill Exercise 1.

Skill Exercises

1. **Research skills**: Have students use the current *Minerals Yearbook* to find the production of specific resources by different areas and report to the class on what they find.
2. **Research skills**: Have students report on the beginnings and growth of a company that is well known. Selections should include both small local companies and large national ones.
3. **Evaluating evidence and forming hypotheses**: Have students discuss the importance today of discoveries such as anesthetics, radium, and vaccines for smallpox and rabies.

Note

The Activities in the Chapter Review contain suggestions relating to the artistic and literary aspects of the Industrial Revolution.

Chapter 27 SOCIAL PROTEST AND MASS SOCIETY, pages 495-513

Objectives

Upon completing this chapter, students should be able to:

1. List some social problems caused by rapid urbanization and the improvements suggested by reformers.
2. Discuss the programs of early socialists and the beliefs of Karl Marx.
3. Describe four changes in 19th-century society caused by an increased number of voters; explain why Marxism was more radical in eastern than in western Europe.
4. List some of the ways in which the new mass society affected education, sports, government services, and the views of the middle class toward government.

Words Defined

laissez-faire	classes
socialism	class struggle
subways	yellow journalism
scientific socialism	labor theory of value
proletariat	trade unions
	progressive income tax

Motivational Activities

1. Point out how the changes introduced in previous chapters culminated in a new mass society that demanded far-reaching governmental and social reforms. Using the text if necessary, have students review the ideas of the Enlightenment and French Revolution which, when combined with the growth of urbanism and industrialism, produced the events brought out in this chapter.
2. Have students read selections from Dickens's *Hard Times* and Studs Terkel's *Working.* Choose sections from both books that describe the working conditions in factories. Ask questions about the readings such as: What changes have been made in factory conditions in 100 years? What has remained the same? What were the problems of the 19th-century factory worker? The 20th-century worker?
3. Use the illustrations in this chapter to motivate class discussion. Ask students what they can tell about what life was really like during the Industrial Revolution. Write comments on the board.

Skill Exercises

1. **Research skills and evaluating evidence**: Use almanacs or news articles to find out the changes in the cost of living in America in the past decade. Ask students to decide if the rich are getting richer and the poor poorer as Marx predicted. Is the middle class better off or in worse condition than in the past?
2. **Identifying propaganda techniques**: Clarify and discuss the idea of "yellow journalism." Have students find examples from the media of sensationalized reporting techniques.
3. **Research skills and synthesizing information**: Have the class study the evolution of the campaign for women's voting rights. Some students might do biographical papers on leaders such as Susan B. Anthony and Emmeline Pankhurst. Better students could study the campaign for the acceptance of women's voting rights in a single country, such as Norway or the United States.

Unit 8 THE WORLD IN UPHEAVAL, page 514

Read the unit introduction and survey the titles and illustrations of the five chapters that make up the study of The World in Upheaval. Refer to the time line to point out the years that will be studied and discuss any events with which students may be familiar.

Chapter 28 THE BUILDING OF EMPIRES, pages 518–538

Objectives

After completing this chapter, students should be able to:

1. Describe the events that led to British rule of India; analyze the effects of that rule on the Indian subcontinent.
2. Discuss the exploitation of China by foreign powers; describe the Chinese reaction to the presence of foreigners.
3. List the background causes of Japanese acceptance of Western ideas and tell some of the results of that Westernization.
4. List the areas of Asia that came under Russian, British, French, Dutch, and United States control.
5. Tell how Africa came under foreign control and list results of that imperialism.
6. Discuss conditions in Latin America that led to European attempts at control; tell what role the United States played in Latin American affairs in the 1890s and after the Spanish-American War.

Words Defined

suttee	condominum
extraterritoriality	concessions
spheres of influence	dollar diplomacy
	Roosevelt Corollary

Motivational Activities

1. List on the board the areas of Asia and Africa controlled by the United States and specific European countries and have students find and name the reasons for these imperialistic ambitions.
2. Select two students, one to role-play the part of a European colonist and one a colonial native. Have them debate the moral legitimacy of imperialism.

Skill Exercises

1. **Evaluating evidence and forming hypotheses**: Have students write short paragraphs explaining why Japan did not fall under the control of an imperialistic country and instead itself became an imperialistic power.
2. **Research skills**: Have students write reports on present-day uses of the Monroe Doctrine and/or dollar diplomacy.
3. **Research skills and evaluating evidence**: Have students write reports about the extent to which Christian missionaries were successful in converting the peoples with whom they worked. Concluding paragraphs of these reports should give the student's opinion of the success or failure of the missions.

Note

When finished with this chapter, have a short discussion period reviewing the material and pointing out problems that caused conflicts between European countries or between European nations and their colonies.

Chapter 29 WORLD WAR I, pages 539–556

Objectives

Upon completing this chapter, the student should be able to:

1. Describe the problems that drove European nations to form alliances before World War I; tell why these alliances caused additional problems.
2. Compare the efforts at peaceful cooperation with the conditions that made war more likely.
3. Describe the tensions in eastern Europe that touched off World War I.
4. Discuss the course of World War I; and give the importance of the Fourteen Points.
5. Describe the Paris Peace Conference, the treaty, and the effect of the war on the old empires of Europe.

Words Defined

Entente Cordiale	Polish Corridor
blank check	self-determination
neutral	mandates
	unrestricted submarine warfare

Motivational Activities

1. Have the class read the chapter introduction carefully and analyze and discuss the political cartoons on pages 539 and 541. Stress that this was the first war to involve so many people over so great an area. Encourage students to discuss what they learned in Unit 7 about the growing world tensions that led to World War I.
2. On a large map of the world, have students place colored markers to show the shifting patterns of alliances and overseas empires that were involved in World War I. Small soldiers, submarines, and battleships can be used to recreate specific battles. Extra research to find out more information on these will be necessary.
3. Use role-play to help students realize the various viewpoints of the countries involved in World War I. It is important that students see there are more than just good and bad sides to most conflicts. Have students play Nicholas II, Grey, Berchtold, Kaiser William II, Francis Joseph I, Lloyd George, Wilson, and Clemenceau. The actors should each make a speech to convince the rest of the class what each did was the "right" thing. After the speeches, hold a class discussion stressing the ideas of national self-interest and balance of power.

Skill Exercises

1. **Synthesizing information and forming hypotheses:** Have students list the steps that led to war, the nation or nations involved, and what could have been done at what point to avoid war.
2. **Identifying propaganda techniques:** Have students find examples of political cartoons, editorials, headlines, and posters from the World War I era and report on the methods used in gaining the desired effect. In addition, students could draw and write their own examples. Class discussion should bring out the purpose of each propaganda technique.

Notes

Finish the study of this chapter with a round-table discussion at which students state the most important point they have learned about World War I. Students should consider which problems were left unresolved or were created by the war and which made the postwar years unstable.

Chapter 30 AN UNSTABLE WORLD, pages 557-572

Objectives

Upon completing this chapter, students should be able to:

1. List the problems in Europe that were caused by or remained after World War I.
2. Discuss some of the factors that led to the 1929 stock market crash and the effects of the depression on events in the United States and Europe.
3. Compare two forms of dictatorship; describe the rise to power of three fascist groups.

Words Defined

reparations	coalition
Nazi	fascist
Il Duce	Führer
benevolent	Reich
credit financing	Lebensraum
dictator	gentiles
dictatorship	master race
	totalitarianism

Motivational Activities

1. To enlarge upon the events of the depression years, have students read newspaper and magazine articles of the period to find out what people felt at the time and more about what daily life was like.
2. Supply students with copies of articles about Hitler, Mussolini, and Ataturk from newspapers or magazines of the 1930s. Select articles that deal with terrorism, both *pro* and *con*.

Skill Exercises

1. **Map skills:** Have students prepare maps of the British Empire before and after World War I, showing especially the areas that became independent countries after the war.
2. **Making value judgments and identifying propaganda techniques:** Study movies of the 1930s which were designed to show poverty-stricken audiences that happiness couldn't be bought. Discuss how these films told audiences what they wanted to hear. Examples are "You Can't Take It With You," "My Man Godfrey," "Topper," and "It Happened One Night."
3. **Drawing inferences and making value judgments:** Select portions of James Hilton's *Lost Horizon* for the class to read. Concentrate on the theme of utopia and what Hilton viewed as worth preserving.

Notes

An excellent filmstrip series to use on the Depression Era is "The Great Depression" from Educational Audio Visuals, Pleasantville, New York. It comes in four parts: "Causes," "Effects," "Solutions," and "Economics" and is accompanied by records.

Chapter 31 THE RISE OF COMMUNISM IN RUSSIA, pages 573–590

Objectives

After completing this chapter, students should be able to:

1. Compare 19th-century Russia with other European nations; discuss the end of serfdom and results of the 1905 revolution.
2. List events in Russia from the March, 1917, revolution to Stalin's rise to power.
3. Discuss Stalin's rule in the 1930s.
4. Describe relations between Russia and the West in the 1920s and 1930s.

Words Defined

mir	NEP
zemstvo	Duma
pogroms	war communism
soviets	Stalinization
	Comintern

Motivational Activities

1. If necessary, review material on Marxism in Chapter 27. Compare Marx's views with those of Lenin. For example, Marx had foreseen a republic of workers. Lenin's dictatorship of the proletariat was composed of a highly centralized despotism whose word was law.
2. Provide handouts to the class of the "Stalin Constitution." Have students analyze its ideas as examples of an ideal democracy.
3. Have students find reasons in other chapters to explain why Marx's ideas led to revolutions not in highly industrialized nations such as England or Germany but in Russia where industrialism was just beginning. Point out that masses of confused, illiterate peasants were moving to cities to work in factories where they were being cruelly exploited.

Skill Exercises

1. **Drawing inferences**: Have students write reports as spokespersons for the serfs in tsarist Russia. They should prepare lists of demands, including the reasons for making those demands.
2. **Distinguishing between fact and fiction and identifying propaganda techniques**: Have students watch the 1939 movie *Ninotchka* starring Melvyn Douglas and Greta Garbo. Ask them to evaluate the film as an anti-communist statement and as a statement on the problems of the 1930s.
3. **Synthesizing information and evaluating evidence**: Have students make time lines showing the history of Russia from the formation of the country during the Byzantine Empire to the present. Students should include what they consider to be the most important events.

Notes

Much of the material in this chapter may be difficult for slower students to grasp. The important aspects to stress are the type of government Russia has and the effect this government has on the people.

Chapter 32 WORLD WAR II, pages 591-607

Objectives

Upon completion of this chapter, students should be able to:

1. Describe the actions of fascist governments that led to increased tensions in the 1930s.
2. List Hitler's actions in the late 1930s and evaluate the reactions of Britain, France, and Russia.
3. Identify the steps by which the war became world-wide.
4. Describe what happened inside Germany during the war and tell how the fighting was ended.

Words Defined

Axis powers	annex
appeasement	New Order
Gestapo	genocide
blitzkrieg	Loyalists

Motivational Activities

1. Probably the most effective way to introduce this chapter on World War II would be a thorough examination of the illustrations that accompany it. Allow time for the students to express their feelings freely in discussing the pictures. Follow up with a reading of the chapter introduction.
2. For additional information, interested students could read John Hersey's *Hiroshima* and report on what effects the atomic bomb had on the Japanese people and on the American soldiers who dropped it.
3. Discuss the wartime problem of an individual's moral judgment versus the necessity for following orders. Point out that conflicts since World War II have put similar choices upon the combatants. Example: My Lai, Vietnam.
4. Show the class examples of Bill Mauldin's cartoons from World War II. Discuss why the cartoons were so popular and the different ways in which they express the spirit of the times.

Skill Exercises

1. Research skills, synthesizing information, and making value judgments: Have students report on how World War II affected civilians. Begin the lesson by reading parts of Harrison E. Salisbury's *The 900 Days* to the class. Then assign groups to research: the United States, Japan, Germany, Britain, Russia, and Italy. (A special report might be the internment of Japanese Americans.)
2. Developing a sense of chronology and synthesizing information: Have students prepare time lines showing the steps leading to war and the progress of the fighting in the Atlantic and the Pacific theaters.
3. Research skills: Assign biographical reports on Roosevelt, Churchill, Hitler, Mussolini, or Stalin.

Unit 9 THE CONTEMPORARY WORLD, page 608

Review the material in the chapters that make up this unit by looking through them; use the unit test as a pre-test.

Chapter 33 THE SEARCH FOR STABILITY, pages 612-629

Objectives

After completing this chapter, the student should be able to:

1. List the factors in the continuing conflicts that followed World War II.
2. Describe the postwar Soviet Union, its achievements, shortcomings, and reaction to dissent.
3. Describe some international efforts at coexistence since the war.

Words Defined

denazified
satellite
Cold War
Truman Doctrine
containment
armistice

Motivational Activities

1. List some of the "firsts" of our times and have students suggest others.
2. Assign one student to report on the capacity of the superpowers to destroy the world in an atomic war. Then have a class discussion on the necessity for peace and various ways to achieve it.
3. Supply students with copies of news releases or speeches by government officials that give various viewpoints about the relationship between the United States and the Soviet Union. Allow students to evaluate these views through discussion or opinion papers.

Skill Exercises

1. **Research skills and developing a sense of chronology**: Have students show the development of space technology, illustrated perhaps with drawings or pictures from magazines of the various space equipment.
2. **Research and synthesizing information**: Have students study how voting blocks in the United Nations have changed as the membership has changed. Discuss the effect this change has had on United States influence.
3. **Research skills and evaluating evidence**: Using newspapers and magazines, students are to select articles or pictures illustrating either the concepts of Cold War or coexistence.

Notes

Check the progress and comprehension of students by having them define, in their own words, but using information from text, the vocabulary terms listed in this section.

Chapter 34 THE COMING OF ASIAN INDEPENDENCE, pages 630-648

Objectives
After completing this chapter, students should be able to:
1. Identify the ways in which Indian and Chinese leaders worked for the independence of their nations.
2. State some problems and some reforms that were factors in the relationships between Muslims and Hindus on the Indian subcontinent.
3. Describe the background causes of nationalism in Southeast Asia; list the results of Sukarno's policies in Indonesia and of the United States in Vietnam.
4. Discuss results of the Chinese revolution and of the American occupation of Japan.

Words Defined

mahatma	communes
untouchables	agricultural collectives
jute	Kashmir
Viet Cong	Red Guards

Motivational Activities
1. This chapter as well as the others in this unit deal with the time span from 1945 to the present. Point out that most of the events mentioned in these chapters took place within the lifetimes of the students' parents and some of the students themselves. See Skill Exercise 1 for a related assignment.
2. Supply students with information on the lives of the people mentioned in the text. Gandhi, Chiang Kai-shek, Ho Chi Minh, and Chou En-lai are some examples. Students are to determine which of these leaders showed admirable qualities from the viewpoint of that leader's own people. Also discuss the reactions of colonial powers to these leaders' works.
3. Have students name the reasons for the conflict between Hindus and Muslims in India. Ask students to find out, from text, the history of this problem.

Skill Exercises
1. **Developing a sense of chronology**: Students are to make time lines of their parents' or their own lives and include the major world events that took place within that time.
2. **Research skills and evaluating evidence**: Ask students to find news reports about events in Asia today. Then discuss with the class which of these events may have lasting effects and why.
3. **Research and map skills**: Show on a map of Asia which nations are communist states and which are democracies, monarchies, or dictatorships. (Almanacs or encyclopedia yearbooks will have this information.)

Note
If some activities seem too difficult for slower students to complete on their own, have them work in assigned groups or teams. Another method is to do the activity as a class with different students going to the board to complete a chart, map, or time line while the teacher helps students see that all can contribute.

Chapter 35 NATION-BUILDING IN THE MIDDLE EAST, AFRICA, AND LATIN AMERICA, pages 649–667

Objectives

After completing this chapter, students should be able to:

1. List the ways in which the nations of the Middle East achieved independence; describe background causes of the Arab-Israeli conflict.
2. Discuss some of the problems that faced black Africa after independence.
3. Describe some of the problems and some of the solutions in Latin America's attempts at modernization.

Words Defined

nationalism
protectorate
mandates
extractive economy
apartheid
trade embargo

Motivational Activities

1. Emphasize the concept of nationalism by having the class read the poem that opens this chapter. Ask students to tell why these areas wanted their independence. List responses on the board. Compare this chapter's map of Africa (page 657) with the one in Chapter 28 (page 520). Point out the similar boundaries.
2. Write out, in short phrases on slips of paper, the specific factors involved in the development of nationalism in the areas discussed. Then have the class match the factors with the proper nation.
3. Have students bring in news articles on world affairs. Using the textbook, ask them to find out the origins of the problems or news developments. This will coordinate the textbook with what is happening currently and show the importance or role of the past in the present.

Skill Exercises

1. Vocabulary skills: Have students write definitions in their own words for the terms in the vocabulary list.
2. Making predictions and evaluating evidence: Have students write out solutions to specific problems listed in the chapter. Then have students evaluate each other's solutions. Evidence must be cited to prove why a solution won't work. (Include the geography essay as a source of information on the problems of Africa.)

Notes

If Questions for Critical Thinking, 4, page 667, is assigned or discussed, ask students to consider what the attitude of the United States should be toward communism in developing countries. Should we fight it or ignore it? How can we persuade developing nations to support our views? Is it important that they do so? Why?

Chapter 36 THE CHANGING WORLD, pages 667-688

Objectives

Upon completion of this chapter, students should be able to:

1. Give two reasons for the increase in scientific advances in this century; describe some of the advances made in science and technology.
2. List recent innovations in art and music.
3. Discuss some differences between rich and poor countries and reasons for the growth of these differences.
4. Discuss the increased urbanization of this century; describe some of the problems of city living.

Words Defined

automation	concrete music
synthetics	synthesizer
realia	megalopolis

Motivational Activities

1. For contrast, begin this chapter by reading the essay on the Tasaday (page 671). If possible, there are films and a number of books on these people which can be shown to the class. Discuss: Should the Tasaday be civilized? What would they gain or lose if they became "just like us"? Students should realize that the question is hypothetical. One of the Tasaday men has been quoted as wanting to see where the "great bird" (airplane) comes from.
2. Play selections of jazz, blues, and rock music. Have students research the major musicians of each type of music and the instruments used.
3. Play selections by Ravi Shankar and "Within You, Without You" by the Beatles found on the record album "Sgt. Pepper's Lonely Hearts Club Band." Discuss the similarities in sounds. Also discuss the lyrics to the Beatles' song and how they reflect Indian philosophy.

Skill Exercises

1. **Making predictions and evaluating evidence**: Have students prepare notebooks titled "20th-century History" or something similar of their own choice. In it, they are to compile information about what they feel are the most important events, discoveries, and problems of today. Things included should be those that students feel will be included in the history books of the future. Allow students to see each other's work and discuss why they have included or excluded particular items.
2. **Research skills and making predictions**: Have students gather information about problems of today and where experts say these problems are leading us. Sources might include Alvin Toffler's *Future Shock* or Muriel Moulton's *What About Tomorrow?* (SF 1974).

Notes

Culminating activities for the end of the year might include papers on the most memorable person learned about or why things are the way they are in a specific area such as India, Africa, or Latin America.

List the names of the different periods studied during the year on the board. Have students give the approximate time span and write short paragraphs describing what happened during that time. Or, mix up the names of the periods, have students rearrange them, and then proceed with the exercise above.

BIBLIOGRAPHY OF RECOMMENDED BOOKS AND AUDIO-VISUAL MATERIALS FOR TEACHERS AND STUDENTS

Teaching World History

Bureau of Secondary Curriculum Development. *Teaching World History*. New York State Education Department.

Fraser, Dorothy M., and West, Edith. *Social Studies in Secondary Schools: Curriculum and Methods.* Ronald.

Kenworthy, Leonard S. *Social Studies for the Seventies.* Ginn.

Logasa, Hannah, comp. *Historical Fiction.* 7th ed. rev. and enl. McKinley.

Mallory, David. *Teaching About Communism, a Definition of the Problem and a Description of Some Practices.* National Assn. of Independent Schools.

National Council for the Social Studies, NEA. *Controversial Issues in the Social Studies: A Contemporary Perspective,* ed. by Raymond Muessig. 45th Yearbook. The Council.

National Council for the Social Studies, NEA. *How to Develop Time and Chronological Concepts.* (How to Do It Series, No. 22) The Council.

National Council for the Social Studies, NEA. *New Perspectives in World History,* ed. by Shirley H. Engle. 34th Yearbook. The Council.

Webster's Biographical Dictionary. rev. ed. Merriam.

General Histories

Brinton, Crane, and others. *A History of Civilization.* 2 vols., 2nd ed. Prentice-Hall.

Davies, Herbert A. *An Outline History of the World.* 3rd ed. Oxford.

Toynbee, Arnold J. *The World and the West.* Oxford.

Wallbank, T. Walter, and others. *Civilization–Past and Present.* 1 vol. ed. Scott, Foresman.

Wells, H. G. *The Outline of History.* 4 vols., Somerset.

UNIT ONE

For the Teacher

Glob, P. V. *The Bog People, Iron-Age Man Preserved.* Cornell U. Press.

Lissner, Ivar. *The Living Past: 7000 Years of Civilization;* tr. by J. Maxwell Brownjohn. Capricorn.

McBurney, C. B. *The Stone Age of Northern Africa.* Penguin.

Mellersh, Harold E. *Story of Early Man: Human Evolution to the End of the Stone Age.* Viking.

Wilson, John A. *The Culture of Ancient Egypt.* Phoenix.

For Students

Bruckner, Karl. *The Golden Pharaoh;* tr. by Frances Lobb. Pantheon.

Coolidge, Olivia. *Egyptian Adventures.* Houghton.

De Camp, L. Sprague. *The Dragon of Ishtar Gate.* Doubleday.

Huxley, Julian, ed. *The Doubleday Pictorial Library of World History; Civilization from Its Beginnings.* Doubleday.

Waltari, Mika. *The Egyptian.* Putnam.

Audio-Visual Materials

Films

The Ancient Egyptians. (IFF) 27 min.; Color.

Ancient Mesopotamia. (Coronet) 11 min.; B&W; Color.

Cave Dwellers of the Old Stone Age. (EBF) 18 min.; B&W; Color.

Filmstrip

The Epic of Man. (EAV) Color. The story of man, in 13 filmstrips.

Tapes

Digging Up the Past. (WNAD Radio, Univ. of Okla.) 15 min.

Egyptian Gods. (National Gallery of Art) 9 min.

Millions of Years Ago. (WNAD Radio, Univ. of Okla.) 15 min. A description of the earth and its inhabitants millions of years ago.

UNIT TWO

For the Teacher

Bury, John B. *The Invasion of Europe by the Barbarians.* Russell.

Creel, H. G. *Chinese Thought from Confucius to Mao Tse-tung.* Mentor.

Daniel-Rops, Henry. *Daily Life in the Time of Jesus;* tr. by Patrick O'Brian. Hawthorn.

De Selincourt, Aubrey. *The World of Herodotus.* Little, Brown.

Dillon, Eilis. *Rome Under the Emperors.* Thomas Nelson Pub..

Gibbon, Edward. *The Portable Gibbon: The Decline and Fall of the Roman Empire,* ed. by Dero A. Saunders. Viking.

Hamilton, Edith. *The Greek Way to Western Civilization.* Mentor.

Lin Yutang, *The Wisdom of China and India.* Modern Library.

Wheeler, R. E. M. *Early India and Pakistan.* Praeger.

For Students

Duggan, Alfred. *Winter Quarters.* Ace. A novel of the triumphant days of the Roman Empire.

Faulkner, Nancy. *The Traitor Queen.* Doubleday. Ancient Crete is the setting for this story.

Komroff, Manuel. *Julius Caesar.* Messner.

Nehru, Jawaharlal. *The Discovery of India;* abr. by Robert I. Crane. Anchor.

Ritchie, Rita. *The Year of the Horse.* Dutton. An adventure story set in the time of Genghis Khan.

Sutcliff, Rosemary. *The Silver Branch.* Oxford. A novel of Rome's weakening power in Britain.

Audio-Visual Materials

Films

The Ancient Orient: The Far East. (Coronet) 13½ min.; B&W; Color.

The Assassination of Julius Caesar. (McGraw) 27 min.; B&W.

The Death of Socrates. (McGraw) 27 min.; B&W.

Rise of the Roman Empire. (Coronet) 13½ min.; B&W; Color.

Roman Life in Ancient Pompeii. (Sutherland) 16 min.; Color.

The Roman Wall. (Coronet) 11 min.; B&W; Color.

The Triumph of Alexander the Great. (McGraw) 27 min.; B&W.

India's History: Early Civilizations. (Coronet) 11 min.; B&W; Color.

Filmstrip

The Classical Age. (SVE) Color. Four filmstrips showing the Hellenistic Greeks, the Roman Republic, and the Roman Empire.

Tape

Wonders of the Ancient World. (National Gallery of Art) 11 min.

UNIT THREE

For the Teacher

Diehl, Charles. *Byzantium: Greatness and Decline;* tr. by Naomi Walford. Rutgers.

Holmes, Urban T., Jr. *Daily Living in the Twelfth Century.* Univ. of Wis.

Hitti, Philip K. *Islam and the West: A Historical Cultural Survey.* Anvil.

The Koran. *The Meaning of the Glorious Koran;* tr. by Mohammed Marmaduke Pickthall. Mentor.

McDonald, Lucile. *The Arab Marco Polo: Ibn Battuta.* Thomas Nelson Pub.

Rice, David T. *The Byzantines.* Praeger.

Ross, James B., and McLaughlin, Mary M. eds. *The Portable Medieval Reader.* Viking.

For Students

Bagley, J. J. *Life in Medieval England.* Putnam.

Mitchison, Naomi. *The Young Alfred the Great.* Roy.

Ritchie, Rita. *Secret Beyond the Mountains.* Dutton. The story of a young cadet with Genghis Khan.

Serraillier, Ian. *Beowulf, the Warrior.* Walck.

Scott, Sir Walter. *Ivanhoe.* Signet.

Treece, Henry. *The Golden One.* Criterion. The story of a young boy and his sister during the battle for Constantinople in 1204.

Audio-Visual Materials

Films

Middle Ages–Sword and Sickle. (Indiana Univ. Radio and TV Service) 14½ min.

Selections from "The Rubaiyat." (Oregon School of the Air, Radio Station KOAC) 15 min.

Filmstrips

The Crusades. (EAV) Color.

Medieval Europe. (EBF) Color.

The Middle Ages. (SVE) Color.

UNIT FOUR

For the Teacher

Bingham, Hiram. *Lost City of the Incas: The Story of Machu Picchu and Its Builders.* Atheneum.

Coe, Michael. *Mexico.* Praeger. From approximately 7000 B.C. to the conquest of Cortés.

Davidson, Basil. *The Lost Cities of Africa.* Little, Brown.

Desai, Ram. *African Society and Culture.* M. W. Lads Publishing.

Hyams, Edward, and Ordish, George. *The Last of the Incas: the Rise and Fall of an American Empire.* Simon and Schuster.

Kubler, George. *The Art and Architecture of Ancient America: the Mexican, Mayan, and Andean People.* Pelican, dist. by Houghton.

Murdock, George P. *Africa: Its People and Their Culture History.* McGraw-Hill.

Schiffers, Heinrich. *The Quest for Africa: 2,000 Years of Exploration;* tr. from the German by Diana Pyke. Putnam.

For Students

Baity, Elizabeth C. *Americans before Columbus.* Rev. ed. Viking.

Chu, Daniel, and Skinner, Elliott. *A Glorious Age in Africa.* Zenith Books.

Davidson, Basil. *A Guide to African History.* Zenith Books.

Macgowan, Kenneth. *Early Man in the New World.* Anchor.

Von Hagen, Victor W. *The Sun Kingdom of the Aztecs.* World Pub. An interesting reconstruction of Aztec life.

Audio-Visual Materials

Films

The Aztecs. (Coronet) 11 min.; B&W.

Early American Civilizations. (Coronet) 13½ min.; B&W; Color.

The Incas. (Coronet) 11 min.; B&W; Color.

Indians of Early America. (EBF) 22 min.; B&W; Color.

The Lost World of the Maya. (NOVA) 45 min.; Color.

The Mayas. (Coronet) 11 min.; B&W; Color.

Filmstrip

The Mayas of Central America and Mexico. (EyeGate) Color.

Tapes

America Before Columbus. (WNAD Radio, Univ. of Okla.) 15 min.

The African Peoples. (British Information Services) 15 min.

UNIT FIVE

For the Teacher

Carroll, David. *The Taj Mahal in History.* Newsweek.

Fitzgerald, Charles P., and Horizon Editors. *The Horizon History of China.* McGraw.

Fréderic, Louis. *Daily Life in Japan at the Time of the Samurai, 1185–1603.* trans. by Eileen M. Lowe. Praeger.

Reischauer, Edwin. *Japan: The Story of a Nation.* Knopf.

Seegar, Elizabeth. *The Pageant of Chinese History.* Longmans.

Spear, Percival. *A History of India.* Vol. 2. Penguin.

Storry, Richard. *History of Modern Japan.* Penguin.

For Students

Leonard, Jonathan. *Great Ages of Man: Early Japan.* Silver Burdett.

Schulberg, Lucille. *Great Ages of Man: Historic India.* Silver Burdett.

Webb, Robert. *Genghis Khan: Conqueror of the Medieval World.* Franklin Watts Inc.

Audio-Visual Materials

Filmstrip

Japanese Cultural Heritage. (Bailey)

UNIT SIX

For the Teacher

Burckhardt, Jacob. *The Civilization of the Renaissance in Italy,* ed. by Irene Gordon. Mentor.

Bainton, Roland H. *Here I Stand: A Life of Martin Luther.* Mentor.

Cheyney, Edward P. *The Dawn of a New Era: 1250–1453.* Torchbooks.

Cortez, Hernando. *Conquest;* abr. by Irwin Blacker. Universal Library.

Davies, R. Trevor. *The Golden Century of Spain, 1501–1621.* New ed. St. Martin's.

Durant, Will. *The Reformation.* Simon and Schuster. (Story of Civilization Series)

Durant, Will, *The Renaissance.* Simon and Schuster. (Story of Civilization Series)

Las Casas, Bartolomeo de. *History of the Indies.* Harper-Row.

Perroy, Edouard. *The Hundred Years' War.* Indiana Univ.

For Students

Barnes, Margaret C. *The Tudor Rose.* Macrae Smith. The story of Elizabeth of York, wife of Henry VII and mother of Henry VIII.

Barr, Gladys H. *The Master of Geneva.* Holt. A novel about John Calvin.

Duggan, Alfred. *Growing Up in the 13th Century.* Pantheon.

Gladd, Arthur A. *Galleys East!* Dodd. An adventure story set in the Mediterranean of the 16th century.

Tey, Josephine, pseud. *The Daughter of Time.* Berkeley. A mystery story about the murder of two little princes in the Tower of London.

Audio-Visual Materials

Filmstrips

Discovery, Exploration and Colonization. (SVE) Color.

The Renaissance. (EAV) Color. Series of four filmstrips.

Spanish Explorers of the New World. (EAV) Color. A series of six filmstrips.

UNIT SEVEN

For the Teacher

Anderson, Matthew S. *Europe in the Eighteenth Century, 1713–1783.* Holt.

Armitage, Angus. *The World of Copernicus.* Mentor.

Brinton, Crane. *A Decade of Revolution: 1789–1799.* Torchbooks.

Bruun, Geoffrey. *Europe and the French Imperium, 1799–1814.* Torchbooks.

Burke, Edmund. *Reflections on the Revolution in France,* ed. by William B. Todd. Holt.

Day, Clive. *Economic Development in Europe.* Rev. ed. Macmillan.

Hazard, Paul. *The European Mind: 1680–1715.* Meridian.

Marx, Karl. *The Living Thoughts of Karl Marx, Presented by Leon Trotsky.* Premier.

Mumford, Lewis. *The Story of Utopias.* Compass.

Neal, Harry E. *The Hallelujah Army.* Chilton.

Nussbaum, F. L. *The Triumph of Science and Reason, 1660–1685.* Torchbooks.

Toynbee, Arnold. *Industrial Revolution.* Beacon.

For Students

Davenport, Marcia. *Mozart.* Rev. ed. Scribner.

Farmer, Laurence. *Master Surgeon: A Biography of Joseph Lister.* Harper.

Komroff, Manuel. *Napoleon.* Messner.

McLean, Allan Campbell. *Ribbon of Fire.* Harcourt. A rebellion of the farmers of the Isle of Skye.

Scherman, Katharine. *Catherine the Great.* Random. (World Landmark Books)

Audio-Visual Materials

Films

English History: 19th Century Reforms. (Coronet) 13 min.; B&W; Color.

The French Revolution. (Coronet) 16 min.; B&W; Color.

Galileo. (Coronet) 13½ min.; B&W; Color.

The Meaning of the Industrial Revolution. (Coronet) 11 min.; B&W; Color.

The Napoleonic Era. (Coronet) 13½ min.; B&W; Color.

Strange Sleep. (NOVA) 60 min.; Color. The discovery of anesthesia, with its often bitter and tragic payoffs for the pioneers.

Filmstrips

The 1848 Revolutions. (EAV) Color.

The French Revolution and Napoleon. (Pictor) B&W.

The Industrial Revolution in England. (EAV) B&W. A series of 11 filmstrips.

Nineteenth-Century Nationalism. (EAV) Color.

The Victorian Age. (Guidance) Color.

UNIT EIGHT

For the Teacher

Baldwin, Hanson. *World War I.* Black Cat.

Falls, Cyril. *The Great War, 1914–1918.* Capricorn.

Florinsky, Michael T. *The End of the Russian Empire.* Collier.

Lawrence, T. E. *Seven Pillars of Wisdom.* Dell.

Pares, Sir Bernard. *Russia Between Reform and Revolution.* Schocken.

Purcell, V.W.W.S. *The Boxer Uprising: A Background Study.* Cambridge.

Rowse, A. L. *Appeasement.* Norton.

Shirer, William L. *The Rise and Fall of the Third Reich: A History of Nazi Germany.* Crest.

Thomas, Hugh. *The Spanish Civil War.* Colophon.

Tuchman, Barbara (Wertheim). *The Guns of August.* Dell. The story of the Western Front in World War I.

Tuchman, Barbara. *The Proud Tower.* Dell. A story of Europe to 1914.

For Students

American Heritage. *D-Day: The Invasion of Europe,* by the Editors; narrative by Al Hine. Dist. by Meredith.

Falls, Cyril. *The Great War, 1914–1918.* Capricorn.

Grey, Elizabeth. *Friend Within the Gates.* Houghton. An excellent biography of the British nurse, Edith Cavell.

Hall-Quest, Olga. *With Stanley in Africa.* Dutton.

Morris, Edita. *The Flowers of Hiroshima.* Pocket Books.

Ryan, Cornelius. *The Longest Day: June 6, 1944.* Crest. The allied invasion of Normandy.

Audio-Visual Materials

Films

Ataturk, the Father of Modern Turkey. (McGraw) 26 min.; B&W.

The Battle of Britain. (McGraw) 27 min.; B&W.

D-Day. (McGraw) 27 min.; B&W.

Dec. 7, 1941. (McGraw) 27 min.; B&W.

From Kaiser to Fuehrer. (McGraw) 26 min.; B&W.

Imperialism and European Expansion. (Coronet) 13½ min.; B&W; Color.

Mahatma Gandhi. (EBF) 19 min.; B&W.

The Rise of Adolf Hitler. (McGraw) 27 min.; B&W.

Soviet Russia: From Revolution to Empire. (McGraw) 15 min.; B&W.

Turn of the Century. (McGraw) 27 min.; B&W. A picture of the European world and way of life which was destroyed by the First World War, and the personalities and forces which led to that war.

War in China: 1932–1945. (McGraw) 26 min.; B&W.

War in Spain. (McGraw) 26 min.; B&W. The Spanish Civil War.

World War I: The Background. (Coronet) 13½ min.; B&W.

World War I: The War Years. (Coronet) 13½ min.; B&W.

Filmstrips

Fascist Dictatorships. (EAV) Color.

The Great Depression. (EAV) Color.

Video Cassette

The Lysenko Affair. (PTL) 60 min.; Color. Lysenko's effect on Soviet science during the Stalin era.

UNIT NINE

For the Teacher

Dickson, Mora. *New Nigerians.* Rand McNally.

Erikson, Erik H. *Gandhi's Truth: On the Origins of Militant Nonviolence.* Norton.

Fein, Leonard J. *Israel: Politics and People.* Little, Brown.

FitzGerald, Frances. *Fire in the Lake: The Vietnamese and the Americans in Vietnam.* Little, Brown.

Lukacs, John A. *A New History of the Cold War.* Rev. and enl. Anchor.

Ridgway, General Matthew B. *The Korean War.* Popular Library.

Rivkin, A. *Nation-Building in Africa: Problems and Prospects.* Rutgers Univ.

Schoenbrun, David, and Szekely, Lucy. *The New Israelis.* Atheneum.

Shepherd, George W., Jr. *The Politics of African Nationalism.* Praeger.

Ward, Barbara, and Dubos, Rene. *Only One Small Earth: The Care and Maintenance of a Small Planet.* Norton.

For Students

Archer, Jules. *African Firebrand: Kenyatta of Kenya.* Messner.

Archer, Jules. *Ho Chi Minh: Legend of Hanoi.* Crowell.

Elegant, Robert S. *Mao's Great Revolution.* World Pub.

Gillon, Diane, and Gillon, Meir. *The Sand and Stars: The Story of the Jewish People.* Lothrop.

Goode, Stephen. *The Prophet and the Revolutionary.* Franklin Watts Inc.

Grant, Neil. *The German-Soviet Pact.* Franklin Watts Inc.

Hall, Elvajean. *The Land and People of Czechoslovakia.* Rev. ed. Lippincott.

Henderson, Larry. *Egypt and the Sudan: Countries of the Nile.* Nelson.

Hey, Nigel. *How Will We Feed the Hungry Billions: Food for Tomorrow's World.* Messner.

Marchus, Rebecca. *Survivors of the Stone Age.* Hastings House.

Millard, Reed. *How Will We Meet the Energy Crisis: Power for Tomorrow's World.* Messner.

Paton, Alan. *The Land and People of South Africa.* Rev. ed. Scribner.

Piper, H. Beam. "Omnilingual" in *The Days After Tomorrow.* H. H. Santesson, ed. Little, Brown. An archaeologist learns to read a Martian language with the aid of the periodic table of elements.

Audio-Visual Materials

Films

Apartheid: Twentieth Century Slavery. (McGraw) 37 min.; B&W.

The Arab Middle East. (McGraw) 16 min.; B&W; Color.

Berlin–Outpost of Freedom. (Alemann) 20 min.; Color.

The Other Way. (NOVA) 45 min.; Color. A scientist argues for less complicated technology.

The People of Hungary. (AV-ED) 20 min.; B&W.

People Problem. (Films) 17 min.; Color.

The Philippines: Land and People. (EBF) B&W; Color.

The Plutonium Connection. (NOVA) 60 min.; Color.

The Rise of Nationalism in Southeast Asia. (McGraw) 16 min.; B&W.

Filmstrips

Living in the Iron Curtain Countries Today. (SVE) Color.

Nature of Democracy. (Curriculum) rev.; Color. A series of seven filmstrips.

The Seventies: Decade for Decision. (NY Times) B&W.

Tapes

Malaya Today. (British Information Services) Parts I and II, 15 min. each.

Portrait of Canada. (Canadian Broadcasting Corporation) 13½ min.

Video Cassette

Take the World from Another Point of View. (PTL) 60 min.; Color. Two prominent scientists present their differing methods and concerns.

Audio-Visual Sources

(Alemann) Alemann Films, P.O. Box 76244, Los Angeles, Calif. 90005

(AV-ED) AV-ED Films, 7934 Santa Monica Boulevard, Hollywood, Calif. 90028

(Bailey) Bailey Film Associates, 11559 Santa Monica Boulevard, Los Angeles, Calif. 90025

(Coronet) Coronet Films, 65 E. South Water Street, Chicago, Ill. 60601

(Curriculum) Curriculum Materials Corporation, 1319 Vine Street, Philadelphia, Pa. 19107

(EAV) Educational Audio Visual, Inc. 29 Marble Avenue, Pleasantville, N.Y. 10570

(EBF) Encyclopaedia Britannica Educational Corporation, 425 N. Michigan Avenue, Chicago, Ill. 60611

(EyeGate) Eye Gate House, Inc., Filmstrip Dept., 146-01 Archer Avenue, Jamaica, N.Y. 11435

(Guidance) Guidance Associates, 41 Washington Avenue, Pleasantville, N.Y. 10570

(IFF) International Film Foundation, 475 Fifth Avenue, New York, N.Y. 10017

(McGraw) McGraw-Hill Text Films, 330 W. 42nd Street, New York, N.Y. 10036

(NOVA) Time-Life Films, Rockefeller Center, New York, N.Y. 10020

(NYTimes) New York Times, Office of Educational Activities, 229 W. 43rd Street, New York, N.Y. 10036

(Pictor) Pictorial Events, 220 Central Park South, New York, N.Y. 10019

(PTL) Public Television Library, 485 L'Enfant Plaza West, S.W., Washington, D.C. 20024

(Sutherland) Sutherland Learning Associates, 8425 W. Third St., Los Angeles, Calif. 90048

(SVE) Society for Visual Education, Inc., 1345 Diversey Parkway, Chicago, Ill. 60614

All tape recordings listed in this bibliography can be ordered directly from:
National Tape Repository
Bureau of Audio Visual Instruction
Stadium Building, Room 348
University of Colorado
Boulder, Colorado

HISTORY and LIFE

The World and Its People

T. Walter Wallbank

Arnold Schrier

Donna Maier-Weaver

Patricia Gutierrez

HISTORY and LIFE

The World and Its People

T. Walter Wallbank
University of Southern California

Arnold Schrier
University of Cincinnati

Donna Maier-Weaver
University of Texas at Dallas

Patricia Gutierrez
Roberto Clemente High School
Chicago, Illinois

Scott, Foresman and Company
Glenview, Illinois
Dallas, Tex. • Oakland, N.J. • Palo Alto, Cal. • Tucker, Ga. • Brighton, England

About the Authors

T. Walter Wallbank is the author of numerous articles and books in the field of world history. He pioneered the development of civilization and world history courses in high schools and colleges and has studied and taught extensively in Europe, Africa, and Asia.

Arnold Schrier has written extensively in the field of European and world history. He is an authority on Russian history and does research and teaching on the subject in this country and abroad. He also works with public high schools in the development of social studies curriculum.

Donna Maier-Weaver has served as an African studies consultant for encyclopedia and trade book publishers. She has traveled and studied in Africa and Europe. She is the author of a number of articles dealing with African culture and is presently lecturing in African history and oral history.

Patricia Gutierrez has participated widely in the formation of curriculum materials for urban schools and students. She has been a social studies teacher in several Chicago high schools and is presently teaching world history and Latin American history.

Teacher Consultants

Sue May
Social Studies Teacher
Jackson Public Schools
Jackson, Mississippi

Joyce L. Stevos
Human Relations and Cultural Studies Planner
Providence School Department
Providence, Rhode Island

Richard L. Tucker
Chairperson, Social Studies Department
Longmont High School
Longmont, Colorado

David A. Varela
World History Teacher
Anderson High School
Austin Independent School District
Austin, Texas

The section entitled "Acknowledgments," pages 698–700, is an extension of this page.

ISBN: 0-673-11682-4

2345678910-RRW-85848382818079

Contents

UNIT 2 Classical Civilizations 48

UNIT 4 The Worlds of Africa and the Americas 218

UNIT 7 Revolutionary Changes in the West 418

How to Use This Book

History and Life has been organized to make it easy to use. Chapters follow a regular structure you can depend on. Special features—Geography: A Key to History, History in the Movies, and A Mystery in History—occur in each unit. The Table of Contents, Map List, and Index can help you find what you want to know.

The Units

The nine units of *History and Life* correspond to well-defined historical periods. The art at the beginning of each unit was done especially for this book and is made up of visual images of the period. The unit introduction gives an overview of the main ideas in the unit. Time lines show you the chronology of events in the chapters within a unit; you can see when events in one chapter happened in relation to events in the other chapters. At the end of each unit is a test you can use to check your understanding of the material in the unit.

The Chapters

Below are the first and last pages of a typical chapter, "The First Civilizations." All chapters have the same elements: **A** a chapter numeral, title, and time span of events, **B** a chapter introduction, **C** a list of the sections of the chapter, **D** section headings, and **E** subsection headings. The section and subsection headings together make a sentence outline of the main ideas in a chapter. By skimming a chapter and reading the headings, you can get a good idea of what you will be studying.

World history includes many foreign place names and proper names. Wherever one occurs in text, it will be followed by its pronunciation. Page 21 below gives pronunciations for Cairo [kī′rō], Tigris [tī′gris], and Euphrates [yü frā′tēz]. In addition, world history has its own vocabulary—words that have specific meanings related to concepts under discussion. On page 21, *civilization* and *loess* are defined. Vocabulary words are defined in text right after their first use. If you look up a word in the index, you can find the page on which it is defined and the pronunciation given.

End-of-Chapter Material

Every chapter ends with two pages like the ones shown here. In **F,** paragraphs summarize the chapter, section by section; **G** asks you to recall the important terms, people, events, and dates in

20

A CHAPTER **2** 5,000–500 B.C.

The First Civilizations

Excavations at Mohenjo-Daro in the Indus River Valley revealed a 2,500-year-old city. The streets formed blocks similar to those in modern cities. On this residential street, people lived in two-story houses with indoor plumbing.

The first civilizations developed along rivers in Egypt, the Middle East, India, and China. The rivers were so important to the lives of the people who lived along them that they were worshiped as gods. The following lines from a hymn to the Nile were sung over 4,000 years ago. B

> Praise to thee, O Nile, that issueth from the earth, and cometh to nourish Egypt. Of hidden nature, a darkness in the daytime . . . .
>
> That watereth the meadows, he that [the sun god] hath created to nourish all cattle. That giveth drink to the desert places, which are far from water: it is his dew that falleth from heaven.

Egypt is a model birthplace for civilization. If you were to head south into the countryside from Cairo [kī′rō], the modern capital of Egypt, you would soon be in a narrow valley. You would see fields vivid green with fine crops. You would also see the vast expanse of dry, golden brown desert that borders this river valley. The Nile River makes this contrast possible. Without the river, all would be desert. Every September, the Nile floods, bringing huge amounts of water that can be used for irrigation. At the same time, the soil is made richer by deposits of Nile mud and silt, the fine particles of earth and sand that are carried by moving water. These conditions have been the same for thousands of years. This fertile soil gave rich harvests.

In times past, the amount of food available was enough to let the population grow. Everyone did not have to work at getting food; some people were free to spend their lives in other kinds of work. In this kind of situation, over hundreds of years, people developed what we call civilization.

Civilization is the advanced stage of human life in which people have cities and organized governments. The people have different occupations. Some are merchants, some are soldiers. Some are farmers, some are weavers. Most civilized people have writing to communicate with and a calendar to keep track of time. They have numbers to keep track of how much is spent, how much is paid, and how much is owed. History really begins with civilization, and civilization began in Egypt.

The same favorable conditions for human progress existed in Mesopotamia, the land between the Tigris [tī′gris] and Euphrates

21

[yü frā′tēz] rivers. In what is today Pakistan and western India, the Indus River performed the same services as the Nile, bringing water and enriching the soil.

In China, around the Hwang Ho (Yellow River), conditions were also favorable for human progress. But the Chinese conditions were different from those in the other river valleys. Here, strong winds from Central Asia had deposited rich dust or light soil, called *loess* [les], forming a great plain. The area was excellent for farming. The people were able to improve their ways of living, and civilization advanced. This chapter tells how:

1. Civilization first developed in Egypt.
2. City-states and empires flourished in Mesopotamia. C
3. An ancient city revealed early Indus civilization.
4. Chinese civilization developed along the Hwang Ho.

1 Civilization first developed in Egypt D

By 5000 B.C., New Stone Age people living along the Nile had learned to farm and to raise cattle. From this rather primitive culture developed one of the first civilizations in the world.

Egyptian farmers took the first steps toward civilization. The farmers of ancient Egypt relied on the September flood of the Nile to bring new soil and water to their fields. During other months, farmers dug irrigation ditches to bring water from the Nile into their fields. E the chapter; **H** gives questions that call for in-depth thinking about the main ideas; **I** suggests activities to help you learn the material and sometimes to lead beyond the chapter to a deeper study; and **J** is a short chapter test, organized section by section.

The Map Program

Most of the 85 maps are historical maps. They show the places under discussion as they appeared at the time being discussed. On pages 690–697 is an Atlas of the Contemporary World; there you will find modern maps. Color on maps is used in a special way. Gray is used for areas that are not part of the subject matter of a map. On maps that show growth, such as The Growth of the Ottoman Empire, colors go from light to dark. The lightest color shows the earliest spread of territory; the progressively darker colors represent areas that were added at later periods. All maps have a scale of miles and kilometers, so you can estimate the distance between points. All maps have a north arrow, grid, or reference point at the North Pole.

Geography: A Key to History

In order to understand why civilization developed in a certain way in a certain place, it is often necessary to understand geographic aspects of the place. In each unit, a one-page essay with a map explains some aspect of geography that has affected history.

A Mystery in History

Historians are somewhat like detectives. They piece together the story of what happened by finding and analyzing clues. The clues are government records, diaries, newspaper accounts, ruins, tombs, ballads, paintings, old books, and artifacts found in the ground. Sometimes there is so much evidence, historians can agree about what happened. But there are puzzles too. In each unit, an illustrated essay sets forth a historical mystery with its clues and some interpretations.

History in the Movies

Filmmakers have found that history has all the elements of a good movie. Adventure stories, love stories, mysteries, comedies, and musicals have come out of history books and onto the screen. In each unit, you will find an example of a movie that was made from the material you are studying. Most of these films turn up from time to time on the television; you might want to watch for them.

18

CHAPTER REVIEW 1

F

SECTION SUMMARIES

1. Life began on ancient Earth. According to geologists, the earth was formed about 4.5 to 5 billion years ago from a flaming mass of gas and vapor. Seas and oceans formed, and gradually early forms of life appeared in them. As living things developed from simple to more complex forms, land plants and animals appeared. This took millions of years. Scientists believe that *Homo sapiens* came quite late in the long span of the development of life on Earth. From skeletal remains, anthropologists have learned about the changes that occurred from Australopithecines and *Homo erectus* to Cro-Magnon, the first modern type of human.

2. People developed basic skills in the Old Stone Age. Because people could think and could talk, they were able to make advances in their ways of living. During the Old Stone Age, which lasted from about 2 million B.C. to about 8000 B.C., people learned to make stone tools and weapons by chipping one stone against another. They discovered uses for fire. Neanderthal people learned to live in caves and to make clothing of skins, thereby adapting themselves to living in the cold of the Ice Age. Cro-Magnon people made advances in tools and weapons and carved and painted pictures on the walls of caves.

3. People made great advances in the Middle Stone Age and the New Stone Age. About 8000 B.C., the Middle Stone Age began, following the end of the Ice Ages. During this period, people made microliths, tamed the dog, made the first pottery from sunbaked clay, and hollowed out logs to make crude boats. In the New Stone Age, which began about 6000 B.C., people learned to make sharper stone tools, to spin and weave, and to fire clay to make pots. They became food producers by domesticating animals and growing plants from seed. When people began to farm, some settled down to live in one place. They formed towns for protection, made laws, created governments, and developed more elaborate forms of religion than had earlier people.

4. Important inventions appeared during the Bronze Age. Bronze Age people learned to make metal tools and weapons, to improve farming with methods of water control and with plows drawn by harnessed animals, to transport goods in wheeled carts and sailboats, and to make pottery on a potter's wheel. Such improvements brought about specialization in work and the beginnings of trade.

G

WHO? WHAT? WHEN? WHERE?

1. Match the items below with the correct time period: a. Paleolithic, b. Mesolithic, c. Neolithic, d. Bronze Age

Neanderthal	spinning and weaving
tools sharpened by grinding not chipping	invention of wheel
specialization of labor	Cro-Magnon
first permanent settlements	domesticated animals
Australopithecines	Ice Ages

2. Important skeleton finds were made at these sites: Java; Peking; Heidelberg; the Neander Gorge; the Cro-Magnon cave; the Olduvai Gorge. In what modern country is each site located?

3. Name at least seven countries of modern Europe whose lands were partly or completely covered by glaciers during the greatest extent of the Ice Age.

4. Use each of these terms in a sentence that explains its meaning. Example: A geologist is a scientist who studies the crust of the earth.

geologist	microlith
anthropologist	domesticated
archaeologist	irrigate
Ice Age	potter's wheel
Homo sapiens	culture

H

QUESTIONS FOR CRITICAL THINKING

1. Explain how specialization of labor began. Why did this make important changes in the lives of people? Are people today becoming more specialized in the work that they do? Give examples.

2. Explain the inventions of primitive people that have helped civilization to progress.

3. Why did some groups of prehistoric people remain hunters while others went on to become herders or farmers? Why are there a few areas today where people are still living in the Stone Age?

4. Why were many plants and animals unable to survive when their living conditions changed? Why have people survived through many changes in their environment?

I

ACTIVITIES

1. Rearrange the following in the order in which scientific theories say they took place:

a. great reptiles, such as dinosaurs, lived
b. clouds appeared, and rain fell
c. jellyfish, worms, snails, crabs, and fish developed
d. modern humans *(Homo sapiens)* developed
e. the earth was a flaming mass of gas and steam
f. simple, one-celled, water-dwelling plants and animals appeared
g. the earth cooled and hardened
h. birds and more complex animals developed
i. rain collected in oceans and seas

2. Draw a picture showing the different developments listed in the activity above as they took place. Or make a time line showing the amount of time it took for each development.

3. Describe: Australopithecines, *Homo erectus*, *Homo sapiens* (Cro-Magnon and Neanderthal). What did they eat? What tools did they use? What could Neanderthal people do that their ancestors could not? How was Cro-Magnon more advanced than Neanderthal?

19

CHAPTER TEST 1

J

SECTION 1

1. Scientists who excavate the remains of ancient cultures are called: a. geologists, b. anthropologists, c. archaeologists

2. The earliest forms of life began in the: a. deserts, b. oceans, c. atmosphere

3. Modern humans belong to which of these groups: a. Australopithecines, b. *Homo sapiens*, c. *Homo erectus*

SECTION 2

4. Two qualities that make humans superior to other animals are their abilities to ________ and ________.

5. Food found in ancient graves suggests that early people believed in: a. heaven and hell, b. life after death, c. reincarnation

6. True or false: The last Ice Age ended during the Mesolithic period.

7. Cro-Magnon people painted on ________.

SECTION 3

8. An achievement of the New Stone Age was: a. use of fire, b. bow and arrow, c. farming

9. In places where there was little rain, farmers learned to ________ their fields.

10. An important invention of the Middle Stone Age was: a. use of fire, b. wheel, c. microlith

11. True or false: Nomadic farmers in the New Stone Age used hoes.

SECTION 4

12. The first metal used by most early peoples was: a. iron, b. copper, c. bronze

13. An invention of the Bronze Age was: a. bow, b. potter's wheel, c. hoe

14. True or false: The digging stick was an example of the improved tools made during the Bronze Age.

15. Tin and copper melted together in the right amounts make ________.

Map List

About History: An Introduction

Why study history? What is it about; what is it good for? Opinions vary. The following statements are some of these opinions. Although the statements disagree, they are all worth thinking about.

. . . if one suspects that the 20th century's record of inhumanity and folly represents a phase of [hu]mankind at its worst, . . . it is reassuring to discover that the human race has been in this box before—and emerged.

Barbara W. Tuchman, 1912–
American historian

Those who cannot remember the past are condemned to repeat it.

George Santayana, 1863–1952,
American philosopher

History is . . . the record of what one age finds worthy of note in another.

Jakob Burckhardt, 1818–1897,
Swiss historian

The history of all hitherto existing society is the history of class struggles.

Karl Marx and Friedrich Engels,
The Communist Manifesto, 1848

History repeats itself, says the proverb, but that is precisely what it never really does. It is the historians (of a sort) who repeat themselves.

Clement F. Rogers, 1866–1949,
English theologian

It is a great pity that every human being does not, at an early stage of . . . life, have to write a historical work. He [or she] would then realize that the human race is in quite a jam about truth.

Dame Rebecca West, 1892–
British writer

History is made out of the failures and heroism of each insignificant moment.

Franz Kafka, 1883–1924,
Czech novelist

History is the witness of the times, the light of truth, the life of memory, the teacher of life, the messenger of antiquity.

Marcus Tullius Cicero, 106–43 B.C.,
Roman statesman

The subject of history is the life of peoples and of humanity.

Count Leo Tolstoy,
War and Peace, 1865–1872

Human history is in essence a history of ideas.

H. G. Wells,
Outline of History, 1920

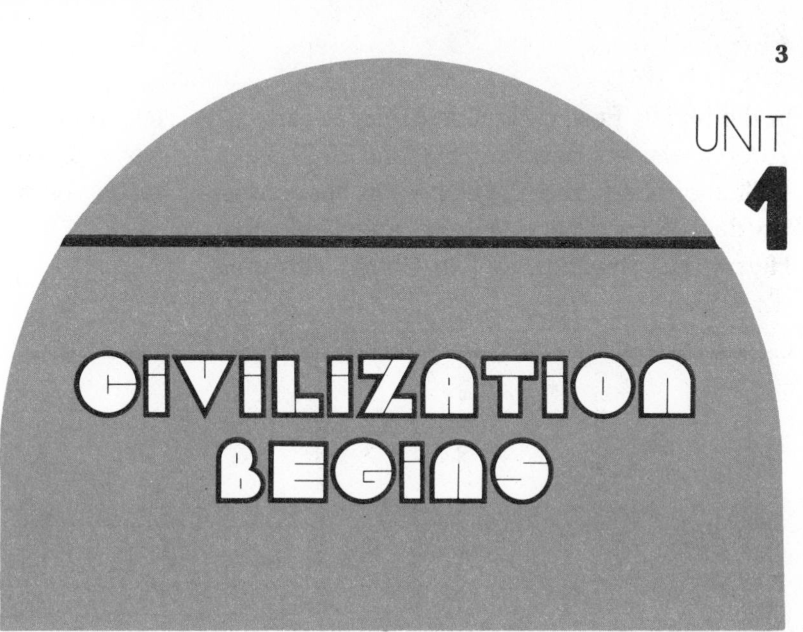

UNIT 1

CIVILIZATION BEGINS

How did it all come about? Today we see and read about many nations and all kinds of people with different ways of life and different forms of government. Scattered over the world are great cities. In each, there are different industries and various ways of making a living. Television programs show quarrels among people and wars between nations. How did people come to be this way? For an explanation, we must look at history—at the story of how people lived, what they did and said, how they tried to solve their problems, and what ideas and customs they developed.

Scientists believe that the earth is perhaps 5 billion years old. ● They think that the oldest humanlike creatures lived some 3 million years ago and that the first fully human people appeared about 300 thousand years ago. For these people, life was difficult. Their problems were how to make shelter, get food, protect themselves from wild animals, and build societies that would make group living possible. The way in which people live and work to satisfy these basic needs is called their *culture.*

A great advance in people's culture came when they began farming, formed governments, began to use metals, lived in cities, and invented writing. This kind of human living is called *civilization.* People who lived before writing was invented are said to be *prehistoric,* because they left no written records of their time.

Civilization first began in four river valleys. Along the valleys of the Nile and the Tigris [tī′gris]-Euphrates [yü frā′tēz] rivers

Farming was the first step toward civilization.

● The special pages of the Teacher's Guide in the front of this book give additional teaching suggestions. Ideas for helping students understand time (B.C. and A.D.) and use time lines are included.

in the Middle East, civilization began as early as 7,000 years ago. Between 2500 and 2000 B.C., civilization had also developed in the Indus [in′dəs] River Valley in India and along the Hwang Ho [hwäng′ hō′] in China. This unit tells how humans survived and improved their ways of living in the Stone Age and finally reached civilization.

4,000,000 B.C.
3,750,000 B.C.
3,500,000 B.C.
3,250,000 B.C.
3,000,000 B.C.
2,750,000 B.C.
2,500,000 B.C.
2,250,000 B.C.

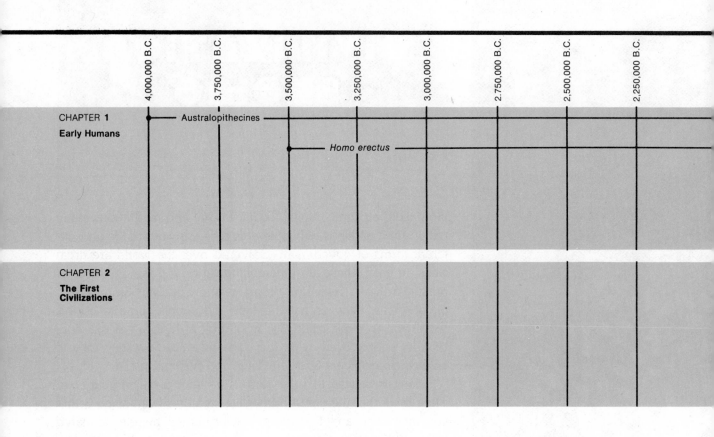

CHAPTER **1**
Early Humans

Australopithecines

Homo erectus

CHAPTER **2**
The First Civilizations

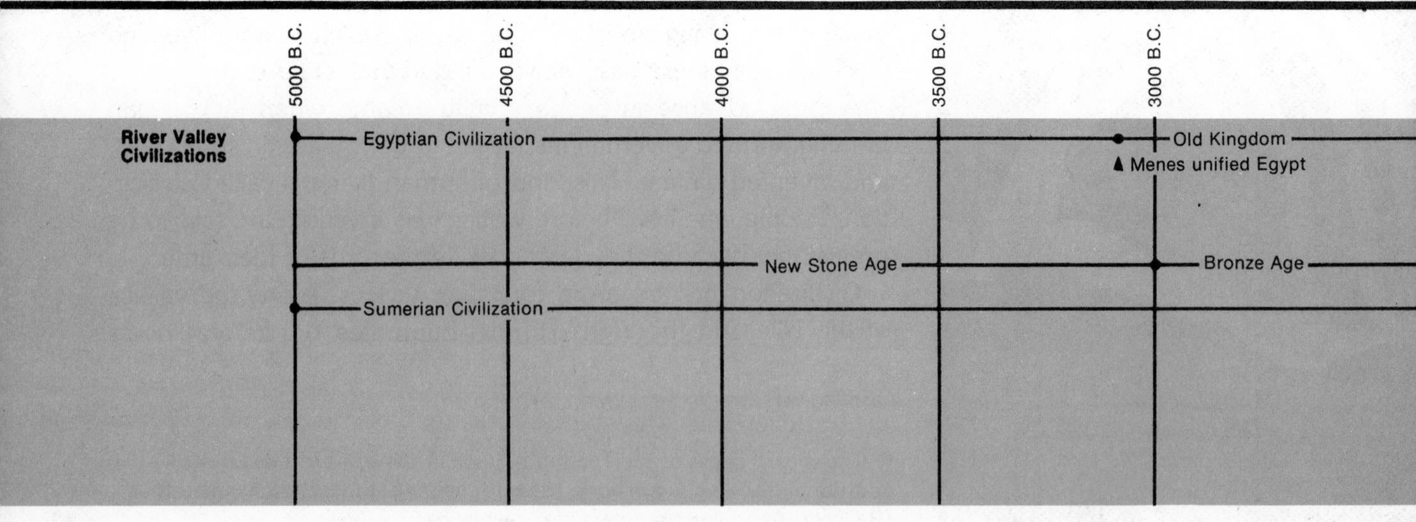

The Time Line. The time lines below give an indication of the very long periods of time between different stages in human progress toward civilization. The first two green areas show the events discussed in the two chapters of this unit. The orange area at the far right represents just 5 thousand years in the 4 million-year story. In order to show the events in those years, the orange time line at the bottom uses a different scale.

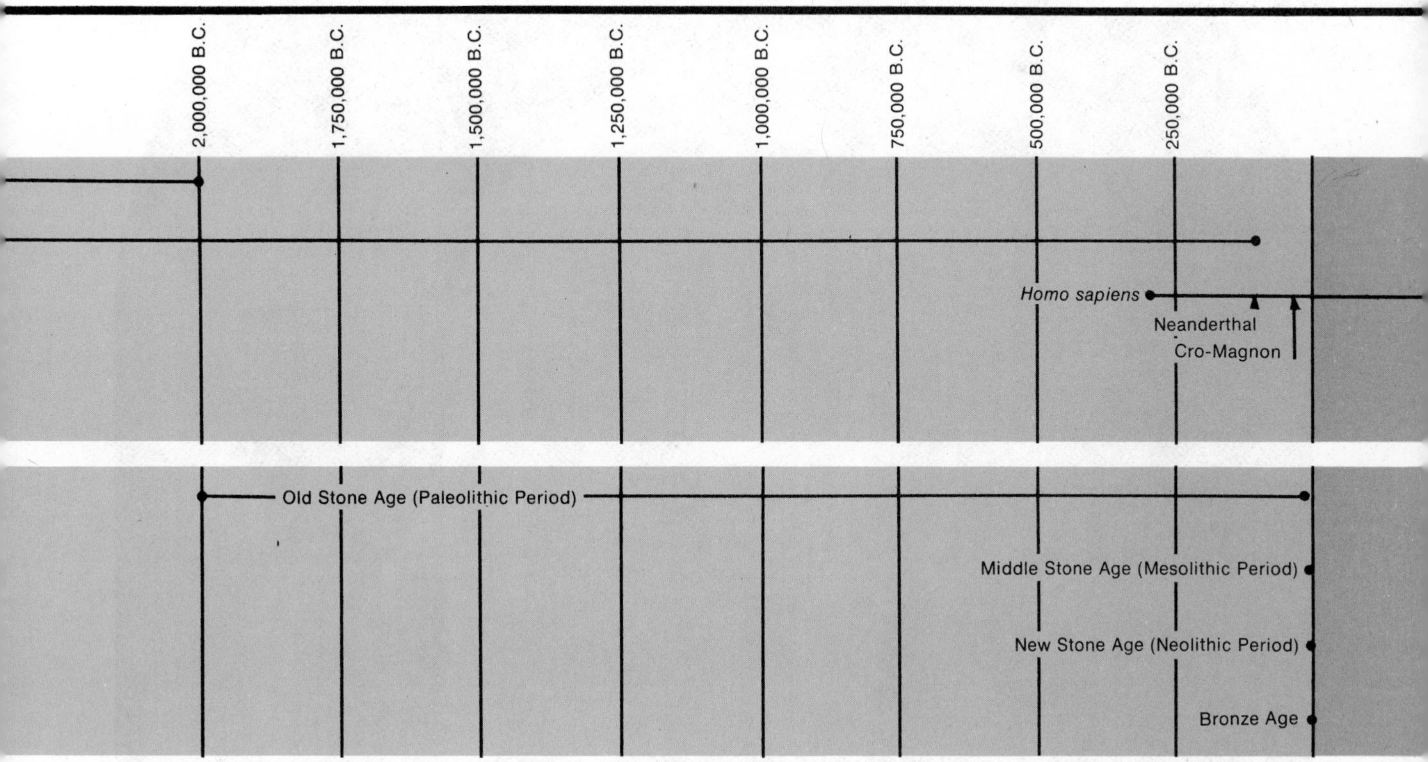

2,000,000 B.C.
1,750,000 B.C.
1,500,000 B.C.
1,250,000 B.C.
1,000,000 B.C.
750,000 B.C.
500,000 B.C.
250,000 B.C.
Homo sapiens
Neanderthal
Cro-Magnon
Old Stone Age (Paleolithic Period)
Middle Stone Age (Mesolithic Period)
New Stone Age (Neolithic Period)
Bronze Age

2500 B.C.
2000 B.C.
1500 B.C.
1000 B.C.
500 B.C.
Middle Kingdom
New Kingdom
Hyksos ruled Egypt
Thutmose III
Akhenaton
Tutankhamon (King Tut)
Hittite Empire
Era of Small States
Assyrian Empire
Persian Empire
Chaldean Empire
Hammurabi ruled Mesopotamia
Phoenicians
Hebrews
Cyrus the Great
Darius I
Indus River Valley Civilization
Yellow River Valley Civilization

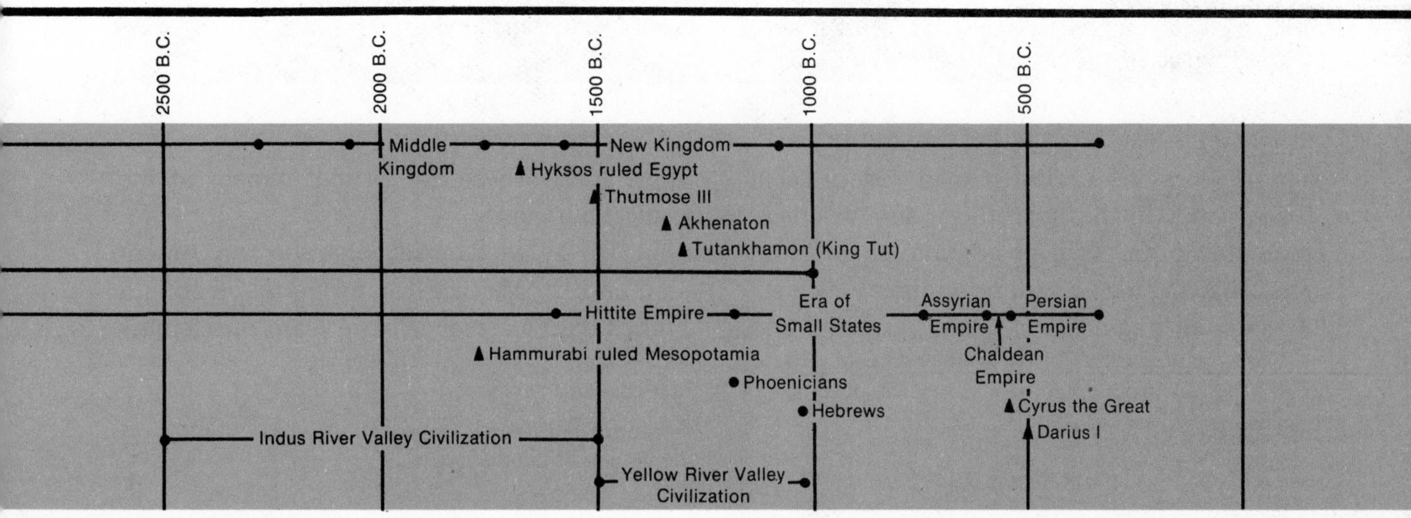

CHAPTER
1

4,000,000–■
2,000 B.C.

Early Humans

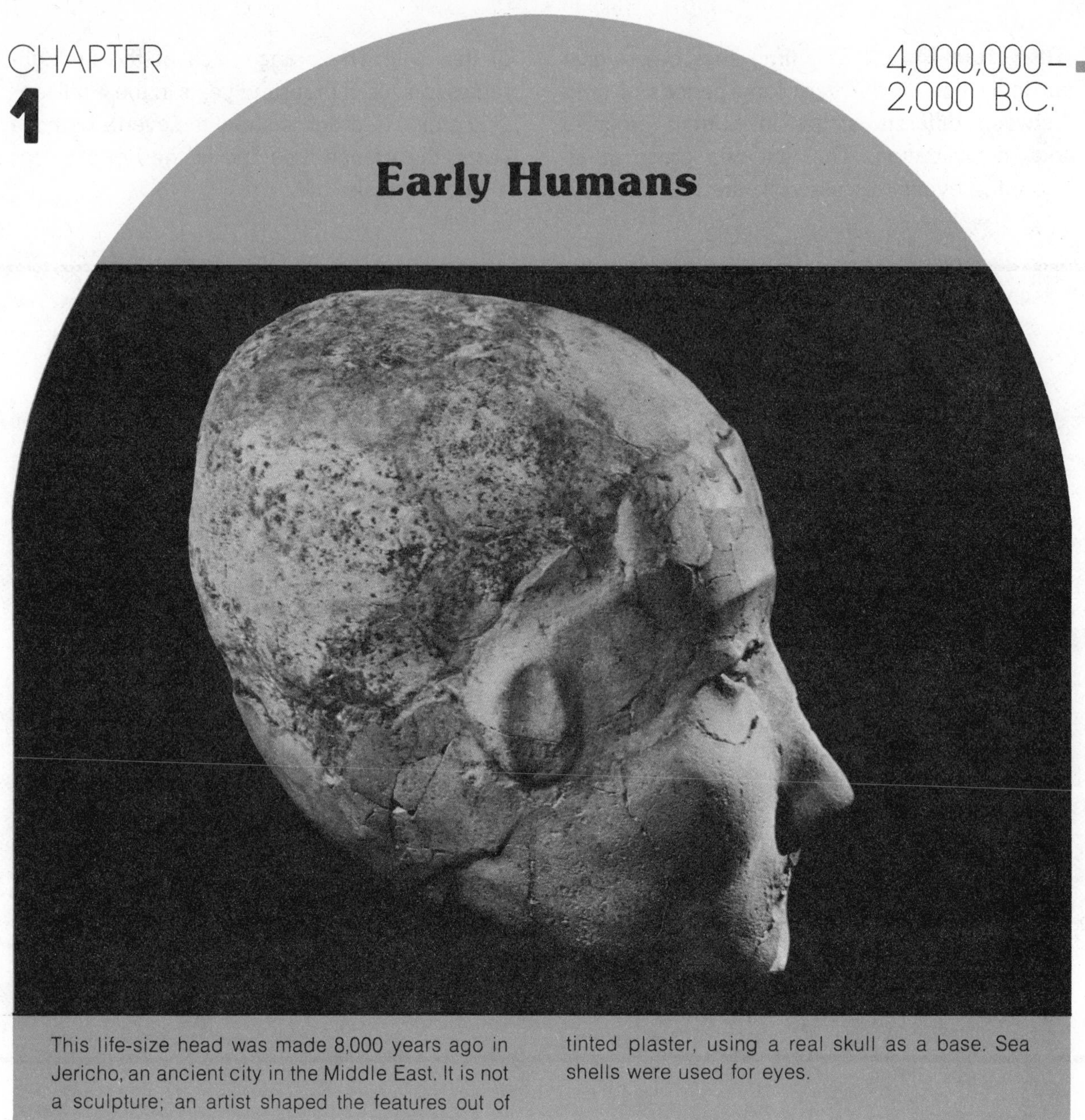

This life-size head was made 8,000 years ago in Jericho, an ancient city in the Middle East. It is not a sculpture; an artist shaped the features out of tinted plaster, using a real skull as a base. Sea shells were used for eyes.

The clues to the earliest human history lie in ● the ground. In the hot African sun, scientists measure off an old river bed into square meters. They dig it up a square at a time. They sift the dust for fragments of bones and teeth and stone tools. These are all that remain of the earliest humans.

In 1974, Dr. Donald Johanson, an American, and Dr. Maurice Taieb [mō rēs′ tī eb′], a ● Frenchman, were directing a team of scientists

● The 52-minute film *The Manhunters,* M.G.M. (1970) is an effective introduction to the work of archaeologists.

■ The years covered by each chapter are given on the first page of the chapter.

● Phonetic pronunciation guides are given for most names and unfamiliar words.

digging at a site in Ethiopia [ē thē ō′pē ə], a country in East Africa. The site, called the Afar site, was near the Awash River. The scientists were digging under a layer of lava more than 3 million years old, and so they knew that any bones they found had to be at least that old.

On November 25, 1974, Dr. Johanson was looking over the site for a new place to dig. "I was returning to the Land Rover, glanced down and noticed a bit of an arm bone. It was
● small but definitely hominid [humanlike]. As I knelt down to pick it up, I spotted skull fragments nearby. Immediately to the left we saw a half mandible [jaw bone] and part of a thigh bone right on the surface. A dream had been realized—never before had such a complete skeleton of so ancient a [person] been discovered."

In all, Dr. Johanson and his team found 40 percent of a female skeleton. The Americans on the team named her Lucy. The Ethiopians called her Denkenesh [dink′nesh], which means "you are wonderful." She was the oldest humanlike creature any scientist had as yet found. By studying her remains and those found at other sites, scientists try to learn about the beginnings of human life.

The teams of scientists who study early people include workers with different specialities.
■ *Anthropologists* study the origins, races, and customs of people, both ancient and modern. One branch of anthropology is called *archaeology* [är′ kē ol′ə jē]. Archaeologists *excavate,* or dig out, the remains of ancient cultures. They classify and study their finds. *Geologists* study the earth's rocky crust and figure out how old Earth is. *Paleontologists* [pā′lē on tol′ə jists] study *fossils,* the hardened remains of life forms. All of these specialists may be included in a scientific team. Together they work out theories about what early people were like and how they lived. This chapter tells how:

1. Life began on ancient Earth.

2. People developed basic skills in the Old Stone Age.

3. People made great advances in the Middle Stone Age and the New Stone Age.

4. Important inventions appeared during the Bronze Age.

1 Life began on ancient Earth

How old is the earth? How long have people lived on it? In the past few years, scientists have found much to help answer these questions.

The earth was formed. Geologists believe that the earth is approximately 4.5 to 5 billion ans. 1
years old. According to scientific theories, the earth began as a flaming mass of gas and steam that slowly cooled and hardened. For millions of years, clouds dropped rain onto the hot surface of the earth. The heat turned the rain to steam, which rose to become part of the overhanging clouds. As the earth cooled still more, the fallen water filled hollows and became deep oceans and shallow seas that covered most of the earth.

It was in these oceans and seas that living things first appeared. And with them begins the story of life on Earth.

Living things developed from simple to more complex forms. Most scientists be-

● Definitions are supplied in text for many terms which may be new to students.

■ Clarify the differences between these two fields of science.

● Answers to Section Review questions will be indicated in the margins of the text where they can be found.

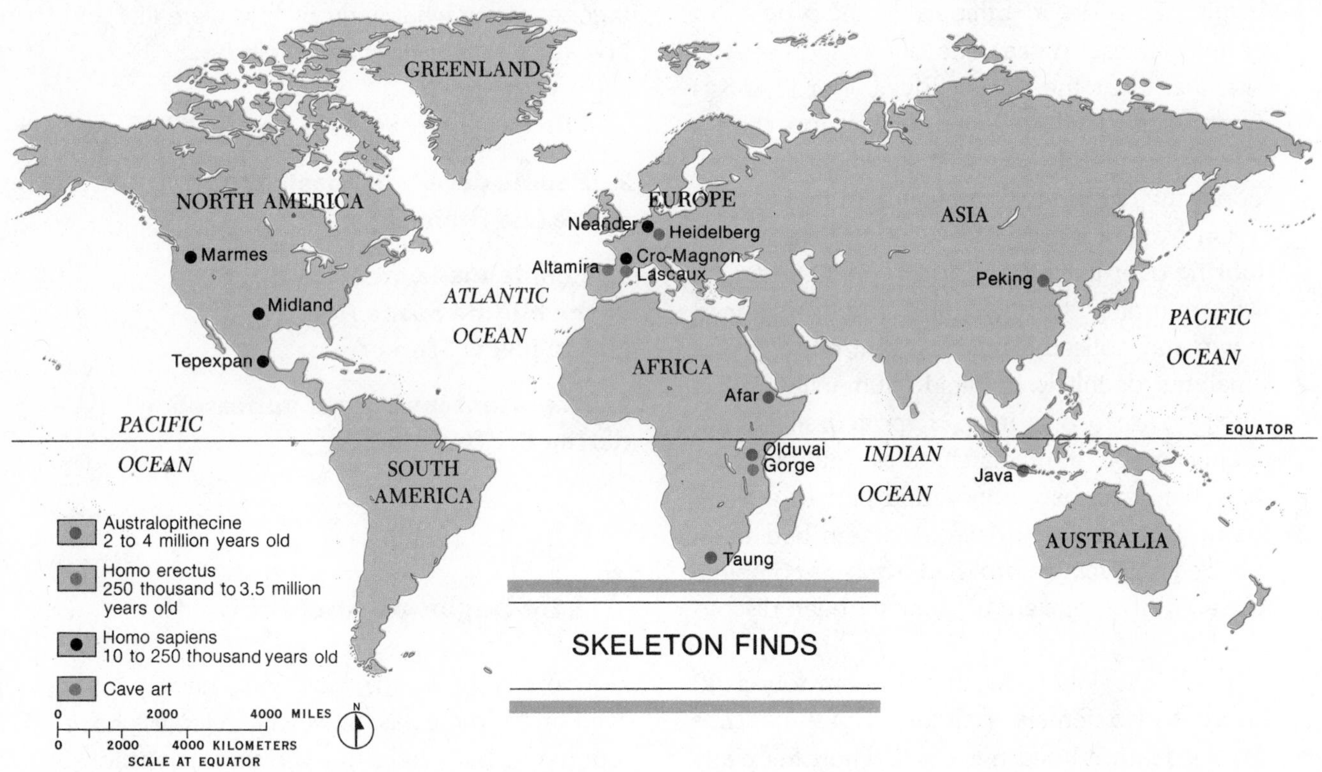

lieve that the first living things—which existed at least 1 billion years ago—were simple, one-
ans. 2 celled, water-dwelling plants and animals. These tiny bits of living matter had no bony structures. As advanced life forms developed, they were composed of more than one cell. Jellyfish, worms, snails, crabs, and then fish appeared in the water.

All the earliest animal life forms lived in water. From them developed amphibians, which could live on land as well as in the water. Later, such reptiles as snakes and lizards appeared. And, after a long time, birds and more complex animals developed. Each of these stages of animal development took millions of years.

Conditions were not easy for these early life forms. To survive, they had to struggle against other living things and against the strong forces of nature. Many plants and animals could not survive. Others became stronger as new generations changed to meet conditions on the earth. Some animals changed a great deal. For example, millions of years ago horses were only about 1 foot (30 centimeters) high, and they had four-toed front feet and three-toed hind feet. Today, horses are from 5 to 6.5 feet (150 to 195 centimeters) tall and have only one toe on each foot.

Skeletons gave clues to the appearance of early humans. There are many theories about the origin of human beings. However, scientists believe that *Homo sapiens* [hō′mō sā′pē enz], modern human beings, came into being quite late in the long development of life on Earth—about 300 thousand years ago. Other humanlike creatures lived on Earth before this time. Ancient skeletons give important clues to what the earliest humans and near-humans looked like. Anthropologists can put together the probable shape of an entire body from the bony parts they have found. They can also find out about a creature's diet and culture from the plant and animal remains and tools they find with skeletal remains.

Scientists have called one group of early near- ● humans *Australopithecines* [ô′strə lō pith′ə-sēns]. Remains of these near-humans have been found in Africa. The first of these fossils was found in 1924 at Taung [tä ůng′] in South Africa. Then in 1959, a British husband-and-wife team of anthropologists, Louis and Mary Leakey, pieced together a complete skull from fragments found at the Olduvai [ōl′dů vā] Gorge in Tanzania. This ans. 3 near-human was low-browed and long-faced, with large, deep jaws. Since then, the skeletal remains of many Australopithecines have been found. Scientists who studied the pelvic and leg bones think these creatures walked upright. Lucy, the fossil described earlier, was a 3-foot (90 centimeter) tall Australopithecine who probably ate crabs, turtle and crocodile eggs, and plants.

Living at the same time as some of the later Australopithecines were creatures more like modern humans. Scientists call them *Homo erectus* [hō′mō ə rek′təs]. The word *Homo,* from the Latin word for *man,* is the scientific term for humans. The word *erectus* means they walked upright.

The first remains of *Homo erectus* were found in 1891 and 1892 by Eugene Dubois [ʏzhen′ dʏ bwä′], a Dutch surgeon and anthropologist. He found the top of a skull, three teeth, and a left thighbone in a dry river bed on the island of Java. From these remains, and others found in China, Africa, and Europe, anthropologists suggest that *Homo erectus* was ans. 3 shorter than the average person today is. The head hung forward on the chest, and the strong teeth and jaws stuck outward. The skull was small and very thick, and the forehead sloped back. The oldest known *Homo erectus* fossil, found in Java and presumed to have lived 1.9 million years ago, is the skull of a 2- or 3-year-old baby. Other important discoveries were made in China near Peking and in Germany near Heidelberg [hī′dl bėrg′]. ■

The study of skeletal finds shows the changes that took place over thousands of years. The brain became larger, the teeth became smaller, ans. 3 the legs became longer and straighter, and more erect posture was developed. Finds from the Neander Gorge in Germany and the Cro-Magnon [krō mag′nən] cave in France show these changes. Scientists label these finds *Homo sapiens,* which means "thinking man."

Anthropologist Donald Johanson and Lucy, the 3-million-year-old skeleton

● Australopithecines—this term is a combination of Latin: *austral* (southern) and Greek: *pithecus* (ape). They were not ancestors of *Homo sapiens,* but an early 'branch' that became extinct.

■ Point out various sites on map and if possible on a globe. No pre - *Homo sapiens* have been found in the Western Hemisphere.

REVIEW 1

p. 7 **1.** According to geologists, how old is the earth? How was it formed?

2. According to scientists, what stages did living
p. 8 things go through to develop from simple to more complex forms?

3. How were Australopithecines and *Homo erectus*
p. 9 different from modern human beings? What physical changes took place in human development?

2 People developed basic skills in the Old Stone Age

Generally, the time from about 2 million B.C. to about 3000 B.C. is called the Stone Age. During this time, people made most of their weapons and tools of stone. Archaeologists divide the Stone Age into three periods according to the kinds of stone-working done in each period. The earliest is called the Old Stone Age, or *Paleolithic* [pā′lē ə lith′ik] period. It lasted until about 8000 B.C. The Middle Stone Age, or *Mesolithic* [mes′ə lith′ik] period, lasted from about 8000 B.C. to 6000 B.C. The New Stone Age, or *Neolithic* [nē′ə lith′ik] period lasted from about 6000 B.C. to 3000 B.C.

During these very long stone ages, humans progressed more than all other living things.
● One important quality that made humans superior to other animals was their capacity to
ans. 1 learn from experience and to devise ways of doing things—in short, the ability to think. Another important quality was the ability to exchange ideas with others—to talk. Such capacities have helped humans rise far above the level of the wild beasts and make steady advances in their ways of living.

● Key Concept: Humans are superior to other animals. Human qualities, should be stressed.

Early people developed tools and skills. The earliest humanlike creatures probably did not know how to make or use tools or weapons. It is likely that they lived on insects, fish, and animals that they caught with their bare hands. They gathered roots and wild plants for food. At this early stage, people's way of living was like that of the beasts.

One of the first advances was the development of crude tools and weapons. People found ways of shaping rocks to sizes and forms
that were helpful to them. They made the fist ans. 2 ●
hatchet, an early tool and weapon, by using one rock to chip another. One end of a rock was left thick so that it would fit into one hand, and the other end was chipped to a point or edge that could be used for striking or cutting. With such weapons, people could hunt animals larger than those they could kill with their hands and teeth alone.

People found uses for fire. Anthropologists believe that it took thousands of years
for people to learn to use fire. People knew ans. 3 ●
of fire because they saw leaves, grass, or forests burning where lightning struck. If the fire was small, they were not afraid of it. They picked up burning sticks and used them to frighten off dangerous animals. This gave people another weapon for use against their natural enemies. After a few thousand years, people learned to keep a fire burning by adding wood or leaves. They learned to cover the fire with ashes at night so there would be coals glowing in the morning for rekindling new flames. An even longer time passed before people learned to start a fire.

Glaciers affected people's way of living. Fire became very important to people in regions affected by *glaciers*. These giant masses of ice covered much of the Northern Hemisphere during four different periods in the Old Stone Age. In each period, called an Ice Age, the polar ice caps expanded; glaciers gradually moved toward the equator and eventually melted, retreating toward the poles. The map below shows the greatest extent of land covered by ice during the Ice Ages of the Old Stone Age.

Ice covered much of northern and central Europe, Siberia, and North America. As the ice moved south, it pushed tons of gravel, boulders, and stones ahead of it. In America, glaciers gouged out what became the Great Lakes, and melting waters formed the Ohio and Missouri rivers. About 50 thousand years ago, the glaciers stopped moving; about 20 thousand years ago, the glacial ice began melting. Many scientists think that modern times are the middle of an interglacial period.

During the Ice Ages, many people and animals died from exposure or starvation. Others moved to warmer areas. Still others adapted themselves to the cold. Some animals developed thick hides or coats of fur. Among these were the woolly mammoth and the woolly rhinoceros.

Some people were also able to adapt to living in a cold world. They lived in caves and ans. 4
learned to wear animal skins for warmth. To make such clothing, they had to invent new tools—stone knives for skinning and bone tools for scraping the flesh and fat from the inner side of animal skins. They invented the bow and arrow, which served hunters and fighters until the gun came into use about 1300 A.D.

Neanderthal people advanced beyond their ancestors. Neanderthal [nē an′dər täl] people were one Old Stone Age type that ad-

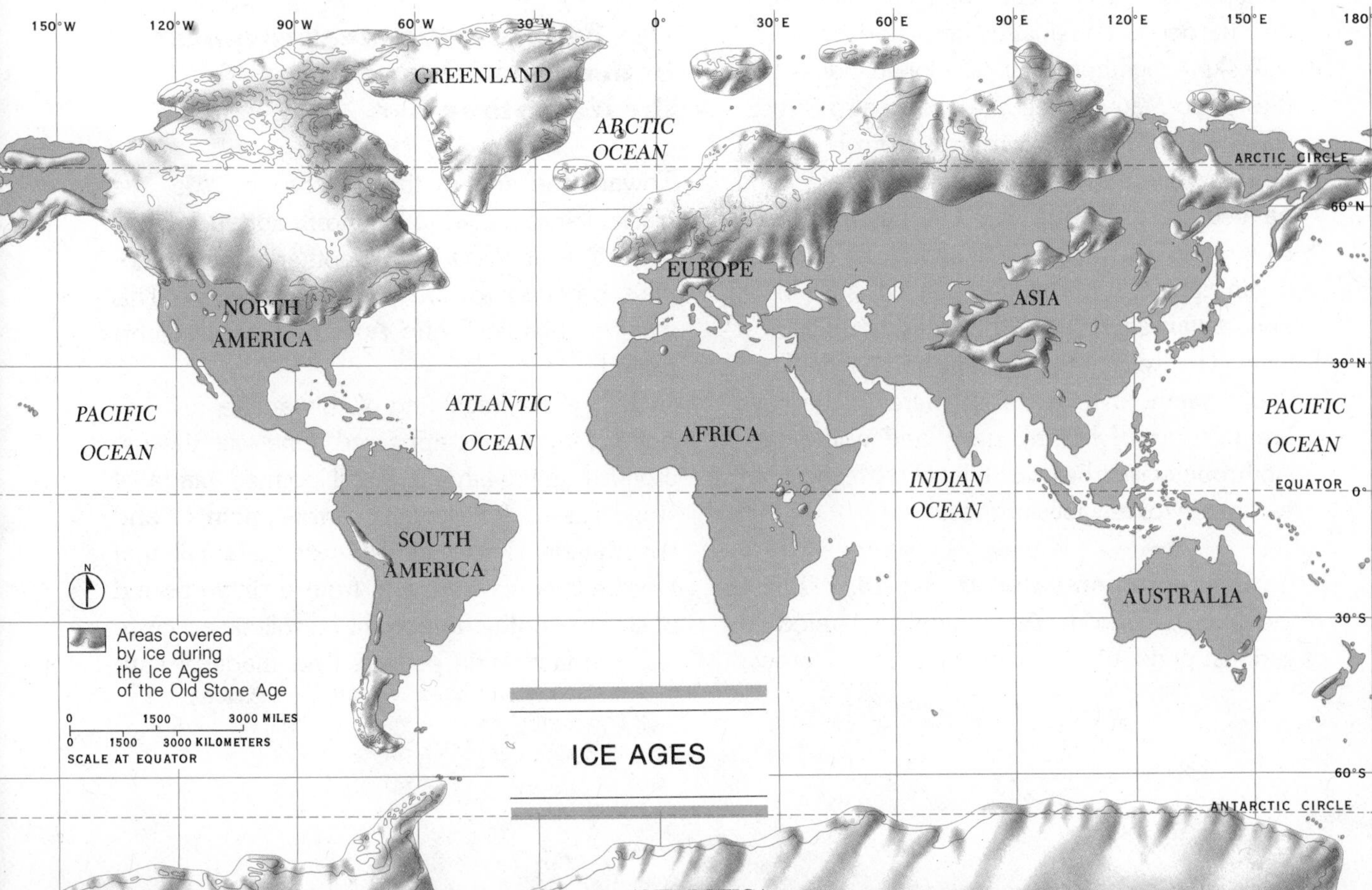

e cold. They used fire, lived in caves ossible, and made their clothing of skins. By studying the tools and weapons that Neanderthal people used, anthropologists know that these people learned to fasten handles to chipped stones to make crude knives and spears. They also began to form religious beliefs. Remains of food and weapons found in the graves of their dead show that they may have believed in some kind of life after death.

Cro-Magnon people developed art. Late in the last Ice Age, about 30 thousand years ago, a group of people lived near the Cro-Magnon cave in southern France. They did not have the chinless head, receding skull, and slouching posture of earlier types. The remains of Cro-Magnon people show they had the features of modern humans.

ans. 5 Cro-Magnon people invented better tools and weapons than did Neanderthals. Cro-Magnon people made spears with fine flint points and harpoons of reindeer horn and bone. To sew skins together, they developed bone needles. Cro-Magnon people were also artists. They carved figures of animals from horn and bone, molded statues in clay, and carved and painted the walls of caves. On the ceiling of a cave called Altamira [äl′ tə mir′ə], in northern Spain, are bison, painted in red and black and drawn so skillfully that they seem almost alive. Their eyes bulge in rage and terror. Their flanks seem to heave. Elsewhere in the cave are pictures of horses, deer, and wild boars. Anthropologists believe this Cro-Magnon art was made for religious purposes.

Early people populated the world. During the long Old Stone Age, people migrated to various parts of the world. Little is known about this travel. By 30,000 B.C., however, ■ modern humans lived in Europe, Australia, Asia, and Africa, and were crossing the Bering Strait into the Americas.

SECTION REVIEW **2**

1. What are the two important qualities that helped humans progress faster than other animals? p. 10

2. What kinds of tools and weapons did people make in the Old Stone Age? How did these new weapons and tools change people's lives? p. 10

3. How did people probably learn about fire? How did fire change their way of living? p. 10

4. About when did the first Ice Age begin? The last end? List three ways Neanderthal people adapted to living in the Ice Age. p. 11

5. Name three advances Cro-Magnon people made over their ancestors. p. 12

3 People made great advances in the Middle Stone Age and the New Stone Age

Toward the end of the Old Stone Age, the glacial ice retreated to the north and the forests grew. About 8000 B.C., another stage in people's progress toward civilization began. This was the Middle Stone Age, or the Mesolithic period.

Before the beginning of this age, a few important inventions appeared. One was the *microlith* [mī′krə lith], a small pointed blade of stone used for knives, arrow points, and spearheads. The microlith was so small that hundreds could be made from a single pound of stone. Another important Mesolithic advance was the first crude pottery. Pots made of sun- ans. 1

ans. 1 (beside "microlith")

■ Point out by 30,000 B.C. all continents were inhabited. Different chapters in this book deal with each area's people and their cultures.

Prehistoric Life The art and tools of ancient people tell much about their life. *Above:* This Paleolithic cave painting in Spain shows archers in a war dance. *Center:* Many early peoples worshiped an Earth Mother goddess. This one, found in France, is only as big as a thumb. *Below:* This stone scraper, found in North America, was used to skin animals and scrape hides. *Far left:* Neolithic people traded across great distances. This decorated bronze awl (a tool used to punch holes in leather) was made by people in Italy whose products have been found in Spain, Britain, and Scandinavia. *Center left:* This Paleolithic spear thrower was carved from an antler. A thong was strung through the hole in the handle, the spear tucked in the notch under the bird's tail. When a hunter swung the thrower around his head, he gained force and distance for his throw.

baked clay were used to store food and water. ● Since many Mesolithic peoples lived along the shores of rivers, lakes, and seas, fish was their main food. Middle Stone Age people invented ans. 1 the fishhook and many types of nets and learned how to hollow out logs to make boats.

During Mesolithic times, people tamed the ans. 1 wild dogs, such as jackals, that followed groups of humans. Dogs became valuable for hunting and for guarding property.

About 6000 B.C., the Middle Stone Age gradually gave way to the New Stone Age. New Stone Age peoples learned to sharpen ans. 2 stone tools and weapons by grinding them against gritty stones instead of by chipping or flaking them. However, this is only one of many advances that made New Stone Age peoples different from those of the Old Stone Age.

People began to farm. New ways of getting food were among the most important discoveries of the New Stone Age. Neolithic people ans. 2 learned to tame such wild animals as sheep, goats, pigs, and cattle so they could have meat when they needed it. When herds and flocks of these *domesticated,* or tamed, animals ate most of the grass supply near a camping place, the people and animals moved to fresh grazing lands. This way of life is called *nomadic* [nō mad′ik], and the people who wander from pasture to pasture are called *nomads.*

About this same time, one of the greatest discoveries of all time was made. People ■ found that a seed planted in the earth would grow into a plant that would furnish food and many more seeds. In this way, people learned to grow food—to farm.

With this new knowledge of herding animals and raising plants, people could produce their food supply. They no longer had to depend on luck in hunting animals or in finding edible ans. 3 fruits, roots, and seeds. People became less likely to starve. With a reliable food supply, people could turn their attention to improving other ways of living.

New Stone Age people developed other skills. During the New Stone Age, people learned to spin and weave. Goats' hair was woven directly into cloth. Later, people learned to spin the fleece from sheep and the fibers of *flax,* a plant, to make thread. Then they learned to weave threads into cloth. During this period, people also learned to press and roll animal hairs together to make felt blankets.

Important discoveries were made at an ever faster rate. Farming led to the invention of hoes and other stone tools for cultivating the soil. Milling stones were invented for grinding grain. Pottery-making was improved by heating the clay in a fire, so that the pots were stronger. In time, potters learned to make a wide variety of cups, bowls, and plates and to decorate them with paint.

People learned to live in communities. Far back in the Paleolithic period, people had learned to help each other in hunting and fishing. Groups of families joined together for this purpose and formed a simple type of community. When farming began, many people established permanent settlements. ans. 4 Some farmers began to think of the land they farmed as belonging to them or their group. To protect their fields and animals, groups of New Stone Age farmers formed villages or small towns for safety against enemies.

As people began to live together in larger groups, they began to realize the need for rules. These rules served as laws to protect in-

● Point out this example of the effect of environment on life-styles.

■ Key Concept: Control of food supply. Discuss ways farming may have begun and its importance to human development.

● Key Concept: Origins of government and law.

dividual life, the community's food and water supplies, and important property. People developed governments to enforce these laws. Historians believe that in the earliest food-producing societies, the government was controlled by a small group of armed men, each of whom had a voice in the government.

In the more advanced food-producing societies, irrigation was very important. The government was controlled by members of the families who lived closest to the river. These families could become powerful because they could control the water supply for the entire community and for the crops. Often, the people looked to an important member of such a family to serve as the ruler and make decisions for the entire group.

This man was dug out of a peat bog in Denmark where he had lain for 2,000 years. Scientists do not know whether he was hanged as a criminal or a human sacrifice.

Anthropologists believe that behavior among Stone Age people was governed by custom. Different groups of Stone Age people developed their own ways of arranging marriages, bringing up children, distributing food, and showing respect for different members of the group. Anyone who broke these rules was considered a wrongdoer.

Stone Age people probably punished most wrongdoers by humiliating them. Anyone who cheated or injured another person was scorned ■ and ridiculed by all the members of the group. People living in small groups were very dependent on each other for survival; unpopularity was a severe form of punishment. Even within small groups, however, some offenses, such as murder or treason, were punished in more formal ways. After the group decided a person was guilty, the wrongdoer could be banished from the group and made to try to live alone or be executed. As people began to farm and groups became larger, more offenses were punished formally. Laws included the punishment to be given for each offense.

Religion, too, became more elaborate as people learned to live in groups. People turned to certain men and women in their group who seemed to be skilled at praying and understanding what others needed. These special persons often became kinds of priests. It was their job to pray and try to keep droughts, famines, floods, and plagues from happening. To gain favor with the spirits of nature, people of the New Stone Age developed religious ceremonies, particularly dances. These ceremonies often were carried out for the purpose of producing good crops. In some groups, the powers of nature were believed to be gods. To gain favor with the gods, people prayed to them and offered them gifts.

■ Humiliation is an effective punishment where the individual knows all members of the community and values their good opinion. Also, outcasts would find it extremely difficult to survive without the group.

SECTION REVIEW 3

p. 12, **1.** What advances did people make in the Mesolith-
14 ic period?

p. 14 **2.** What improvements did New Stone Age people make in their tools and weapons? What new skills did they develop?

p. 14 **3.** Why was the herder safer from starvation than the hunter? Why was the knowledge of how to grow plants from seed an important discovery?

p. 14 **4.** How did farming change people's way of living?

4 Important inventions appeared during the Bronze Age

As long as people were dependent upon stone tools, they were limited in the kinds of work they could do. Stone tools and weapons broke easily. To make better tools, people needed a longer-lasting material that could be molded more easily into different sizes and shapes.

People learned to make tools and weapons of metal. Toward the end of the New Stone Age, people in the Middle East found that they could use copper in an almost pure metallic state to make tools and weapons. At first, they hammered the copper to shape it. Later, they learned that they could melt it, pour the liquid metal into molds, and make tools and weapons of any desired size or shape.

Early metalworkers made another advance when they discovered that tin and copper melted together in the right amounts made a metal
ans. 1 called bronze. Bronze was easier to shape, was harder, and gave a sharper cutting edge than copper alone. Because it was the chief metal for about 2,000 years, the period in which it was used is called the Bronze Age. This age began about 3000 B.C.

Progress was made in farming, transportation, and commerce. Along with metal
tools came other inventions. One of these was ans. 2
the plow drawn by animals. At first, farmers had planted seeds in holes made with a digging stick. Then they had made a simple hoe that they pulled through the earth with a rope. The next step was to harness animals, such as the ox, to an improved hoe that became a plow. This invention enabled farmers to cultivate large fields instead of small plots. Another aid to farming was the development of better ways to control and use water for crops. In places where there was little rainfall, farmers learned
to irrigate, that is, to bring water to their fields ans. 2
by digging ditches to lakes and streams. They also learned to build dikes to protect their fields from floods.

One problem for early people was finding ways to transport heavy loads. Middle Stone Age people used a crude sled. Later, an ox was used to pull the sled. Someone may have learned that a sled could be pulled more easily if poles or logs were put under it so that it moved forward as the logs rolled along the ground. Many experiments were made before
people invented the wheel. ans. 2

Just as early people found easier ways to move heavy loads on land, they also found easier ways to carry these loads safely across water. One of the most important early inventions was the sailboat. Sailors discovered how ans. 2
to take advantage of the winds that always blew in the same direction, called *prevailing winds.* They also learned the shortest sea routes from one place to another.

This painting was done about 14,500 B.C. in a cave in present-day France.

Bronze Age people also learned to build a
ans. 2 *potter's wheel.* This small, flat wheel was set on top of a vertical axle, called a spindle. The potter threw a lump of wet clay onto the wheel and then, while turning the wheel, shaped the clay with his or her hand. The potter's wheel made possible the production of a larger number of pots of a more uniform shape and size than before.

● All of these new discoveries called for specialized services. No longer were all people hunters, herders, or farmers. Some became metalsmiths, sailors, potters, or tradespeople. *Commerce,* or trade, began when people turned to one another for certain goods and services.

● Key Concept: specialization of labor, the result of surplus food freeing workers for other jobs.

Different peoples passed through the prehistoric ages at different times. People around the world did not advance from one stage of prehistoric development to the next at the same time. Some people remained hunters while others became herders and farmers. Today, there are a few isolated areas where people are still living in the Stone Age. ■

SECTION REVIEW 4

1. In what ways was bronze better than copper for making tools and weapons? p. 16

2. What improvements in farming, transportation, and pottery-making took place during the Bronze Age? p. 16, 17

■ Explain the importance of opportunity and environment on cultural developments. See also the mystery on the Tasaday in Unit 9.

CHAPTER REVIEW 1

SECTION SUMMARIES

1. Life began on ancient Earth. According to geologists, the earth was formed about 4.5 to 5 billion years ago from a flaming mass of gas and vapor. Seas and oceans formed, and gradually early forms of life appeared in them. As living things developed from simple to more complex forms, land plants and animals appeared. This took millions of years. Scientists believe that *Homo sapiens* came quite late in the long span of the development of life on Earth. From skeletal remains, anthropologists have learned about the changes that occurred from Australopithecines and *Homo erectus* to Cro-Magnon, the first modern type of human.

2. People developed basic skills in the Old Stone Age. Because people could think and could talk, they were able to make advances in their ways of living. During the Old Stone Age, which lasted from about 2 million B.C. to about 8000 B.C., people learned to make stone tools and weapons by chipping one stone against another. They discovered uses for fire. Neanderthal people learned to live in caves and to make clothing of skins, thereby adapting themselves to living in the cold of the Ice Age. Cro-Magnon people made advances in tools and weapons and carved and painted pictures on the walls of caves.

3. People made great advances in the Middle Stone Age and the New Stone Age. About 8000 B.C., the Middle Stone Age began, following the end of the Ice Ages. During this period, people made microliths, tamed the dog, made the first pottery from sunbaked clay, and hollowed out logs to make crude boats. In the New Stone Age, which began about 6000 B.C., people learned to make sharper stone tools, to spin and weave, and to fire clay to make pots. They became food producers by domesticating animals and growing plants from seed. When people began to farm, some settled down to live in one place. They formed towns for protection, made laws, created governments, and developed more elaborate forms of religion than had earlier people.

4. Important inventions appeared during the Bronze Age. Bronze Age people learned to make metal tools and weapons, to improve farming with methods of water control and with plows drawn by harnessed animals, to transport goods in wheeled carts and sailboats, and to make pottery on a potter's wheel. Such improvements brought about specialization in work and the beginnings of trade.

WHO? WHAT? WHEN? WHERE?

1. Match the items below with the correct time period: a. Paleolithic, b. Mesolithic, c. Neolithic, d. Bronze Age

Neanderthal	spinning and weaving
tools sharpened by grinding not chipping	invention of wheel
specialization of labor	Cro-Magnon
first permanent settlements	domesticated animals
Australopithecines	Ice Ages

2. Important skeleton finds were made at these sites: Java; Peking; Heidelberg; the Neander Gorge; the Cro-Magnon cave; the Olduvai Gorge. In what modern country is each site located?

3. Name at least seven countries of modern Europe whose lands were partly or completely covered by glaciers during the greatest extent of the Ice Age.

4. Use each of these terms in a sentence that explains its meaning. Example: A geologist is a scientist who studies the crust of the earth.

geologist	microlith
anthropologist	domesticated
archaeologist	irrigate
Ice Age	potter's wheel
Homo sapiens	culture

WHO? WHAT? WHEN? WHERE?

1. a., c., d., c., a., c., d., a., c., b.

2. Java, China, Germany, Germany, France, Tanzania

3. Norway, Sweden, Finland, Russia, Belgium, Germany, France, England

4. Answers will vary. Students should use their own words.

QUESTIONS FOR CRITICAL THINKING

1. Explain how specialization of labor began. Why did this make important changes in the lives of people? Are people today becoming more specialized in the work that they do? Give examples.

2. Explain the inventions of primitive people that have helped civilization to progress.

3. Why did some groups of prehistoric people remain hunters while others went on to become herders or farmers? Why are there a few areas today where people are still living in the Stone Age?

4. Why were many plants and animals unable to survive when their living conditions changed? Why have people survived through many changes in their environment?

ACTIVITIES

1. Rearrange the following in the order in which scientific theories say they took place:

7 a. great reptiles, such as dinosaurs, lived
3 b. clouds appeared, and rain fell
6 c. jellyfish, worms, snails, crabs, and fish developed
9 d. modern humans *(Homo sapiens)* developed
1 e. the earth was a flaming mass of gas and steam
5 f. simple, one-celled, water-dwelling plants and animals appeared
2 g. the earth cooled and hardened
8 h. birds and more complex animals developed
4 i. rain collected in oceans and seas

2. Draw a picture showing the different developments listed in the activity above as they took place. Or make a time line showing the amount of time it took for each development.

3. Describe: Australopithecines, *Homo erectus*, *Homo sapiens* (Cro-Magnon and Neanderthal). What did they eat? What tools did they use? What could Neanderthal people do that their ancestors could not? How was Cro-Magnon more advanced than Neanderthal?

QUESTIONS FOR CRITICAL THINKING
1. Answers will vary. Possible answers may include: Surplus food freed some people to do other work, crafts, etc. Today in medicine, doctors are specializing in many areas.
2. Student's opinion should be supported with evidence.

CHAPTER TEST 1

SECTION 1

1. Scientists who excavate the remains of ancient cultures are called: a. geologists, b. anthropologists, c. archaeologists

2. The earliest forms of life began in the: a. deserts, b. oceans, c. atmosphere

3. Modern humans belong to which of these groups: a. Australopithecines, b. *Homo sapiens*, c. *Homo erectus*

SECTION 2

4. Two qualities that make humans superior to other animals are their abilities to __think__ and __talk__.

5. Food found in ancient graves suggests that early people believed in: a. heaven and hell, b. life after death, c. reincarnation

6. True or false: The last Ice Age ended during the Mesolithic period.

7. Cro-Magnon people painted on __cave walls__.

SECTION 3

8. An achievement of the New Stone Age was: a. use of fire, b. bow and arrow, c. farming

9. In places where there was little rain, farmers learned to __irrigate__ their fields.

10. An important invention of the Middle Stone Age was: a. use of fire, b. wheel, c. microlith

11. True or false: Nomadic farmers in the New Stone Age used hoes. Farmers aren't nomadic.

SECTION 4

12. The first metal used by most early peoples was: a. iron, b. copper, c. bronze

13. An invention of the Bronze Age was: a. bow, b. potter's wheel, c. hoe

14. True or false: The digging stick was an example of the improved tools made during the Bronze Age.

15. Tin and copper melted together in the right amounts make __bronze__.

3. Environmental factors, isolation.
4. Possible answers: Conditions changed too quickly, correct changes were not made. People had intelligence to make necessary choices.
ACTIVITIES
3. Outside research can be done to find additional information.

CHAPTER
2

5,000–500 B.C.

The First Civilizations

Excavations at Mohenjo-Daro in the Indus River Valley revealed a 2,500-year-old city. The streets formed blocks similar to those in modern cities. On this residential street, people lived in two-story houses with indoor plumbing.

The first civilizations developed along rivers in Egypt, the Middle East, India, and China. The ● rivers were so important to the lives of the people who lived along them that they were worshiped as gods. The following lines from a hymn to the Nile were sung over 4,000 years ago.

● Asks students to name reasons why rivers were so important. Examples: to provide water for drinking, washing, watering crops, transportation, sometimes as barriers to invaders.

Praise to thee, O Nile, that issueth from the earth, and cometh to nourish Egypt. Of hidden nature, a darkness in the daytime . . . .

That watereth the meadows, he that [the sun god] hath created to nourish all cattle. That giveth drink to the desert places, which are far from water: it is his dew that falleth from heaven.

Egypt is a model birthplace for civilization. If you were to head south into the countryside from Cairo [kī′rō], the modern capital of Egypt, you would soon be in a narrow valley. You would see fields vivid green with fine crops. You would also see the vast expanse of dry, golden brown desert that borders this river valley. The Nile River makes this contrast possible. Without the river, all would be desert. Every September, the Nile floods, bringing huge amounts of water that can be used for irrigation. At the same time, the soil is made richer by deposits of Nile mud and silt, the fine particles of earth and sand that are carried by moving water. These conditions have been the same for thousands of years. This fertile soil gave rich harvests.

● In times past, the amount of food available was enough to let the population grow. Everyone did not have to work at getting food; some people were free to spend their lives in other kinds of work. In this kind of situation, over hundreds of years, people developed what we call civilization.

Civilization is the advanced stage of human life in which people have cities and organized governments. The people have different occupations. Some are merchants, some are soldiers. Some are farmers, some are weavers. Most civilized people have writing to communicate with and a calendar to keep track of time. They have numbers to keep track of how much is spent, how much is paid, and how much is owed. History really begins with civilization, and civilization began in Egypt.

The same favorable conditions for human progress existed in Mesopotamia, the land between the Tigris [tī′gris] and Euphrates [yü frā′tēz] rivers. In what is today Pakistan and western India, the Indus River performed the same services as the Nile, bringing water and enriching the soil.

In China, around the Hwang Ho (Yellow River), conditions were also favorable for human progress. But the Chinese conditions were different from those in the other river valleys. Here, strong winds from Central Asia had deposited rich dust or light soil, called *loess* [les], forming a great plain. The area was excellent for farming. The people were able to improve their ways of living, and civilization advanced. This chapter tells how: ■

1. Civilization first developed in Egypt.
2. City-states and empires flourished in Mesopotamia.
3. An ancient city revealed early Indus civilization.
4. Chinese civilization developed along the Hwang Ho.

1 Civilization first developed in Egypt

By 5000 B.C., New Stone Age people living along the Nile had learned to farm and to raise cattle. From this rather primitive culture developed one of the first civilizations in the world.

Egyptian farmers took the first steps toward civilization. The farmers of ancient Egypt relied on the September flood of the Nile to bring new soil and water to their fields. During other months, farmers dug irrigation ditches to bring water from the Nile into their fields.

● This passage explains how specialization of labor began. The idea of civilization is an important one. Point out that while civilized people are not necessarily *better* than less advanced people, they do have advantages which make life easier for more people.

■ Point out difference in development of China's civilization due to geographical and climatic conditions.

Review concepts of B.C. and A.D. if necessary. Refer to time line in Unit Introduction.

ans. 1 In order to dig the ditches, keep them in repair, and build dams for the benefit of all, the farmers formed groups. Each group had a leader, or *administrator,* who directed the work and made rules for the workers to follow. In time, as the work became more complicated and larger numbers of people were in each group, the leader grew more important and more powerful. He directed the work of planting and harvesting crops, and he decided whether to store or distribute crop surpluses. These early cooperative efforts, accompanied by the rise of an administrative class, probably were the earliest form of local government in Egypt. ●

Because the farmers needed to keep track of the passage of time in order to plan for planting and harvesting, they counted the days between the Nile floods. They studied the paths of the sun, moon, and stars to learn when to expect the spring planting season. Their studies led to the invention of a calendar that first came into use around 4000 B.C.

The Egyptians noticed that on one day each year about floodtime a bright star—now known as Sirius [sir′ē əs]—appeared in the eastern sky before sunrise. By counting the days between appearances of this star, they figured that the length of a year is 365 days. They divided the year into twelve months and gave each month thirty days, with five days added at the end of the year. Although a year is actually one-quarter day longer than 365 days, the calendar served the Egyptians well. ■

The development of irrigation, the rise of local governments, and the invention of a calendar took place between 5000 and 3100 B.C. During this time, the Egyptians also developed a system of writing and discovered how to make copper tools. They invented the plow, which greatly increased crop production, and much later,

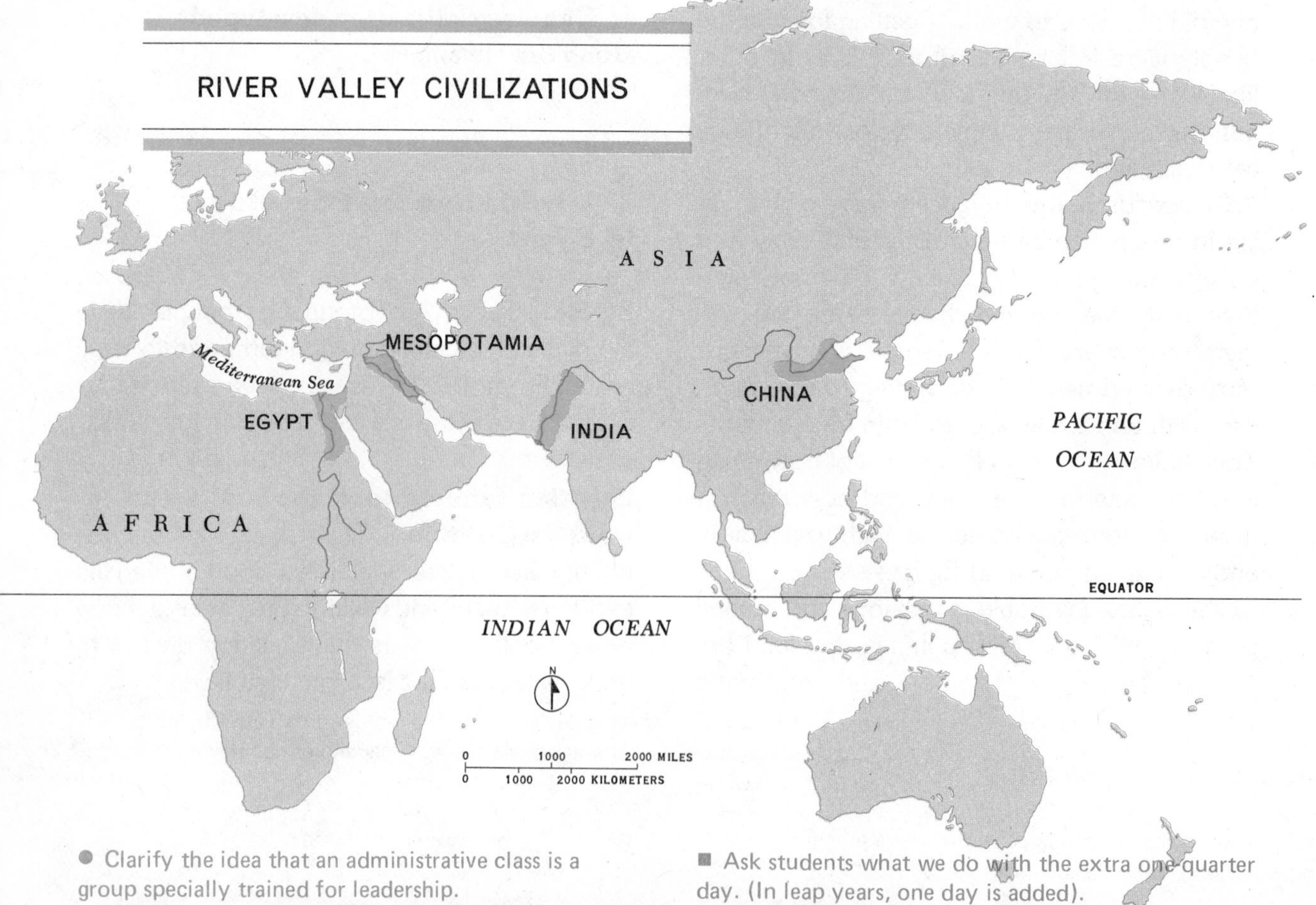

● Clarify the idea that an administrative class is a group specially trained for leadership.

■ Ask students what we do with the extra one-quarter day. (In leap years, one day is added).

around 2000 B.C., they learned to make bronze by combining copper and tin.

The Old Kingdom began with the unification of Egypt (3100–2270 B.C.). At first, Egypt simply consisted of a number of independent, separate villages. In time, local rulers won control over nearby villages and then over larger areas. By 3100 B.C., two separate kingdoms had developed. King Menes [mē′nēz], the ruler of one, united Egypt and made Memphis the capital city.

The reign of King Menes marked the first time in history that a strong government ruled so large an area. He also founded the first Egyptian ● *dynasty* [dī′nə stē], that is, the first series of rulers belonging to the same family. With the unification of Egypt, a great period called the *Old Kingdom* began.

During the Old Kingdom, trading ships sailed ■ up and down the Nile, and expeditions left the Nile Valley to trade with peoples in other parts of Africa and the Mediterranean. Artisans carved fine statues, wove soft linen cloth, and made pottery with the use of a potter's wheel. Workers continued to use stone tools, but they also made some tools from copper.

As generations passed, a ruling class of nobles and princes emerged. Perhaps because these nobles lived in large and luxurious houses, the Egyptian word *pharaoh* [fer′ō], which means "great house," also became the word for king.

The Pyramids were built during the Old Kingdom as tombs for the pharaohs. The largest pyramid, built at the town of Giza [gē′zə] for Pharaoh Cheops [kē′ops], is about 450 feet (135 meters) high. Each of its four sides measures 756 feet (226.8 meters) long at the base. It is said that it took twenty years and the work of 100 thousand men to build this pyramid. The largest stone blocks weigh several tons (megagrams) each. To quarry, transport, and raise these huge blocks into place with almost no machinery was a remarkable engineering feat.

● Important term. Explain hereditary rule, if necessary.

■ More information on trade is in Geography essay on p. 27.

The Middle Kingdom arose (2060–1785 B.C.). In 2270 B.C., civil war brought an end to the Old Kingdom. For more than 200 years, rival leaders fought among themselves for wealth and power. Eventually princes from the city of Thebes [thēbz] reunified the kingdom. This period is known as the Middle Kingdom. The princes from Thebes became the new pharaohs, and they made Egypt strong and prosperous. They encouraged art and literature. They began new irrigation projects that greatly increased the crop area. Pharaohs of the Middle Kingdom built a canal that joined the business centers of the Nile Valley with the trade routes of the Red Sea.

About 1680 B.C., while weak from internal disorder, Egypt was conquered by invaders from Asia called the Hyksos [hik′sos]. An ancient record speaks of them savagely burning cities, destroying Egyptian temples, and treating the people with great cruelty. The Hyksos ruled Egypt harshly for about 100 years. However, the Egyptians learned how to fight wars with horses and chariots that the Hyksos had brought to Egypt. This knowledge proved useful to the Egyptians in the next period of their history.

Egypt freed itself during the New Kingdom and became an empire (1580–1085 B.C.). Thebes provided leaders who drove the Hyksos out and restored Egyptian rule to Egypt. This victory marked the beginning of the New Kingdom, or Empire. During this period, the pharaohs created an empire that extended

Daily Life in Egypt *Left bottom:* Both men and women used make-up. This wood and ivory cosmetic box belonged to a butler in the Middle Kingdom. It held a mirror, perfumed oils, and pots of make-up. *Center:* These good-luck charms, or *scarabs,* were made during the reign of Queen Hatshepsut (1503–1483 B.C.). The hieroglyphs [hieroglyphs] spell her royal name. *Above:* The orchestra and dancer in this tomb painting were believed to come alive and entertain in the afterlife. *Opposite top:* New Kingdom furniture looks modern. A board game is set up on the table. A wine goblet and bowl of fruit sit on a stool of wood and woven reeds. *Opposite below:* This two-panel painting "reads" from right to left. Above, some vineyard workers on a noble estate pick grapes; others crush them underfoot to make wine. Below, servants bring home the wild birds a noble family has caught during a hunting party. Other servants pluck the birds and hang them up to dry.

Paintings and artifacts from Egyptian tombs give a wealth of information about daily life. You might use this page to motivate outside research.

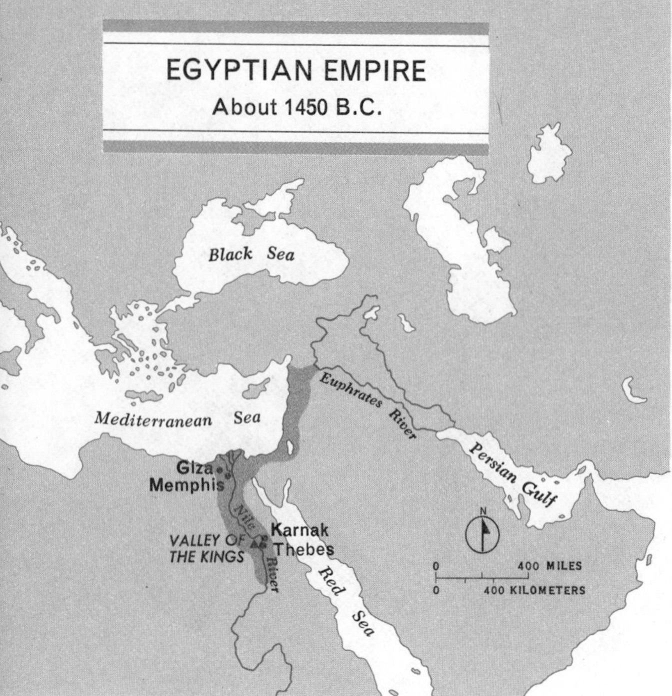

Egyptian rule into western Asia, far beyond the Nile River Valley. When a group of people conquers other very different groups of peoples and rules these new lands and peoples, we call this expanded nation an *empire*.

For about 450 years, increased trade and • booty from conquered countries made Egypt rich. The capital, Thebes, became a city of statues, temples, and palaces. Egyptian ships carried products, such as wheat and linens, across the Mediterranean to Europe and Asia. The ships returned with lumber and metal weapons, which Egypt needed but did not produce.

By 1100 B.C., Egypt had again grown weak from quarrels among its leaders, rebellion among its conquered peoples, and costly battles with foreign enemies. Years of civil war and foreign invasions followed.

The power of the pharaohs was absolute.
ans. 3 The pharaohs had absolute power over their subjects—partly because most of these rulers governed justly, but primarily because the people believed that the pharaohs were descended from a god and were gods themselves. A government in which the religious leader rules the state as a god's representative is called a *theocracy* [thē ok′ rə sē]. In theory, the pharaoh owned all the land, commanded the army, and controlled the irrigation system. Since no one person could administer such a huge kingdom, the pharaoh appointed officials to assist him. However, he was personally responsible for making all the important decisions of government. Beginning with the Old Kingdom, Egyptians created a complicated but efficient government that supported the absolute power of the pharaoh.

Egyptian society was divided into three classes. ■ The upper class of people was made up of priests, court nobility, and landed nobility. The men and women who were priests performed religious ceremonies, especially those having to do with the burial of the dead. The court nobles advised the pharaoh and the queen and carried out their orders. The landed nobility managed their great estates. Women of this class were especially important because land and property were passed from mother to daughter.

The middle class included men and women who became rich through trade. Skilled artisans, who made furniture and jewelry, worked with leather and cloth, and directed the building of tombs and palaces, were also in the middle class. So were professional people such as teachers, artists, doctors, and scribes. *Scribes,* who wrote letters and documents for a living, held an important place in Egyptian life because few people could read or write.

The lower class, to which the great mass of Egyptians belonged, was made up of two

• *Booty* is treasure taken from conquered peoples.

■ Concepts of class, class structure, and social nobility are introduced here.

Geography: A Key to History

Nile Currents and Etesian Winds

About 5,000 years ago, the ancient Egyptians learned how to use the regular summer winds to move sailboats. As a result, they were able to greatly expand trade and travel along the Nile River.

Etesian [ē tē′shən] is the name given to the winds that blow across the Mediterranean Sea into Egypt each summer. These winds form because the air over the desert in the south is much hotter than air near the sea in the north.

Great desert lands extend from northwestern India clear across Egypt. In the summer, the air above these deserts becomes very hot. As the air is heated, it expands, becomes lighter, and rises. The cooler air in the north stays near the ground, because it is heavier. It flows south to replace the hot air rising from the desert. This flow of air toward the desert forms the Etesian winds.

The Etesian winds begin in about the middle of May and continue until mid-October. During the day, the winds blow at speeds from 10 to 30 miles an hour, sometimes reaching speeds of 40 miles an hour. During the cooler nights, the Etesian winds die down, for not as much hot air rises from the desert.

By using sailboats to harness the winds' power, the ancient Egyptians were able to carry on a two-way trade along the Nile. The river current carried boats north (downstream) toward the Mediterranean. The Etesian winds pushed huge sailboats south (upstream) toward Thebes and Karnak. The Egyptians had found a way to solve the problem that faces all river-traders: how to move goods upstream, against the current.

For the times, the boats offered a quick and easy way to travel. The system allowed Egyptian traders to do business all up and down the river. As trade increased, many villages along the Nile became centers of business and government. The growth of these villages helped develop civilization in ancient Egypt.

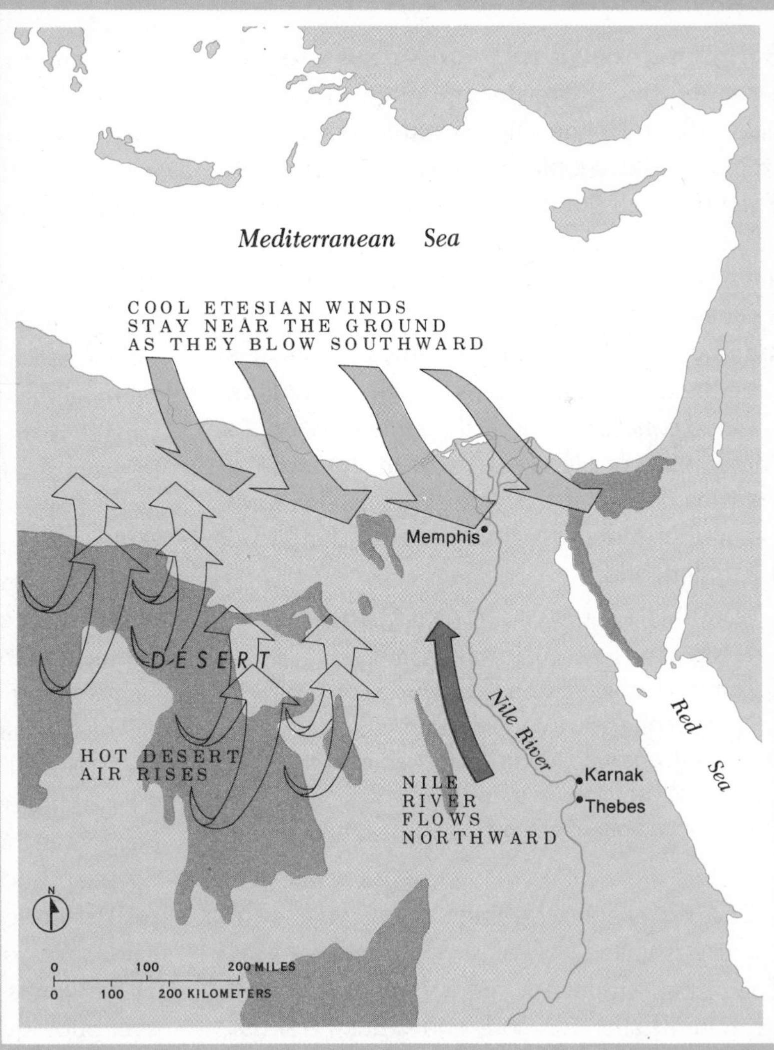

groups—slaves and free laborers. The slaves were usually prisoners of war. Like the free laborers, they worked on farms, irrigation systems, roads, and building projects. The free laborers, heavily burdened by taxes, had few political rights. They lived poorly in small, mudbrick homes with few furnishings. However, it was possible for smart and ambitious young Egyptians to rise to higher rank. Sometimes loyal and able slaves were given their freedom. On a few occasions, a talented slave rose to become a government official.

Religion in Egypt was concerned with life after death. Egyptians reasoned that just as plants decline in the autumn and reappear in the spring, so also people must have life after death. They believed that the human body should be preserved after death, as a mummy, in order for the soul to live on. Preserving the body became a highly skilled art. Beliefs about the afterlife led the Egyptians to build large tombs in which to keep the mummified bodies of their dead rulers.

Good conduct was also thought necessary for immortality, or life after death. In the *Book of the Dead,* one of the early Egyptian writings, the soul of a deceased man says to the god of the underworld:

> Here am I: I come to thee; I bring to thee
> Right and have put a stop to wrong.
> I am not a doer of wrong to men.
> I am not one who slayeth his kindred.
> I am not one who telleth lies instead of truth.
> I am not conscious of treason.
> I am not a doer of mischief.

The Egyptians worshiped many gods. This practice is called *polytheism* [pol′ē thē′iz′əm]. The most important gods were Amon-Re [ä′mən rā], the sun god, and Osiris [ō sī′ris], the god of the underworld and lord of the afterlife. However, during the reign of Pharaoh Akhenaton [ä′kə nä′tn] in the New Kingdom, a new faith was born. Akhenaton, who ruled from 1379 to 1362 B.C., believed in one supreme god, rather than in many gods. The supreme god, Akhenaton thought, was Aton [ä′ton], the sun. Akhenaton outlawed the worship of all gods but Aton and took government support away from the priests of other gods.

● Key Concept: discuss reasons why early peoples might have believed natural forces had supernatural powers.

Yet the priests were many and powerful. They succeeded in terrifying the already fearful people into believing that if they obeyed Akhenaton they would suffer the anger of the gods. While Akhenaton lived, his orders were not openly disobeyed. After his death, however, the priests persuaded Egyptians to return to the worship of many gods.

Hieroglyphic writing was developed. Between 4000 and 3000 B.C., the Egyptians developed a kind of picture writing known as *hieroglyphics* [hī′ər ə glif′iks]. The first writings consisted of pictures of objects. Gradually, picture signs came into use for ideas as well as objects. For example, a picture of an eye could mean *sight* or *eye.* In time, writers also used picture signs to indicate sound. These developments were only the beginnings of an alphabet. A true alphabet is a complete set of letters, each representing a sound.

The first Egyptian books were written as early as 4000 B.C. on the material made from the *papyrus* [pə pī′rəs] plant, a kind of reed. Papyrus is the origin of the English word *paper.* Egyptian books consisted of long rolls of papyrus pasted together. Most books were about religion, but some adventure stories were written. These works were probably the first storybooks ever published.

King Tut's Tomb

The date was November 26, 1922. Archaeologist Howard Carter chipped through the door of the tomb and held a candle into the darkness. At first, Carter was speechless. Then his partner asked, "Do you see anything?" "Yes," said Carter, "wonderful things!"

What Carter had found was the Egyptian burial tomb of a relatively unimportant boy king named Tutankhamen [tü′tängk ä′mən]. Tut, as he has been nicknamed, became pharaoh about 1361 B.C., when he was only 10. At age 18, he died. Other tombs had been found by archaeologists before Carter's discovery. What made King Tut's tomb so important was that it was still in almost the same condition as when the king had died 3,275 years before.

In the 1800s, archaeologists busily carried out their digs, looking for clues to Egypt's past. They were most interested in the west bank of the Nile River in Upper Egypt, near the modern town of Luxor. Here, in what is now called the Valley of the Kings, were many temples that had been carved into the face of the valley cliffs. Many tombs had been discovered, but grave robbers had been there ahead of the archaeologists. By 1900, it was generally believed that all the tombs had been discovered and robbed.

Howard Carter did not agree. After three years of digging, he was rewarded with what has been called "the world's most legendary treasure." Tut's tomb contained hundreds of things, many of them from the king's brief life. His bow, checkerboard, boomerang, and childhood chair were all there. Also found were chariots, statues, a golden throne, and a golden couch. Everywhere there was gold. A gold shrine showed scenes from Tut's everyday life. His mummified body was found in a solid gold casket. Most spectacular of all was Tut's solid gold funeral mask. It was slipped over his head and shoulders to preserve his god-like beauty forever. The calm face of the mask gazes at the world with wide-open eyes of bright blue lapis lazuli. Today, experts put the value of the mask alone at 50 million dollars.

The tomb also told archaeologists many things about Tut as a person. He was very fond of hunting and of flowers. He had a pet lion. He was happily married. The gold shrine shows Tut on a hunting trip, with his queen handing him arrows. Another scene shows the queen tying Tut's collar before some important festival.

But of most importance to history is the fact that King Tut's tomb was never robbed. There had been an unsuccessful robbery attempt, after which the tomb was sealed up again. Then, when the tomb of a later ruler was built higher up in the same cliff, huge amounts of stone and rubbish were thrown down. These completely covered the entrance to Tut's tomb. Thus a twist of fate made the boy ruler much more important in death than in life. The Egyptian belief in a wonderful afterlife for their rulers came true in this case. As one burial saying goes, "You come in your former shape, as on the day you were born."

What of the powerful pharaohs? What riches did their tombs contain? These are gone. Only the riches of a boy king remain as a hint of the unimaginable riches of others.

This mystery can be used to motivate outside research.

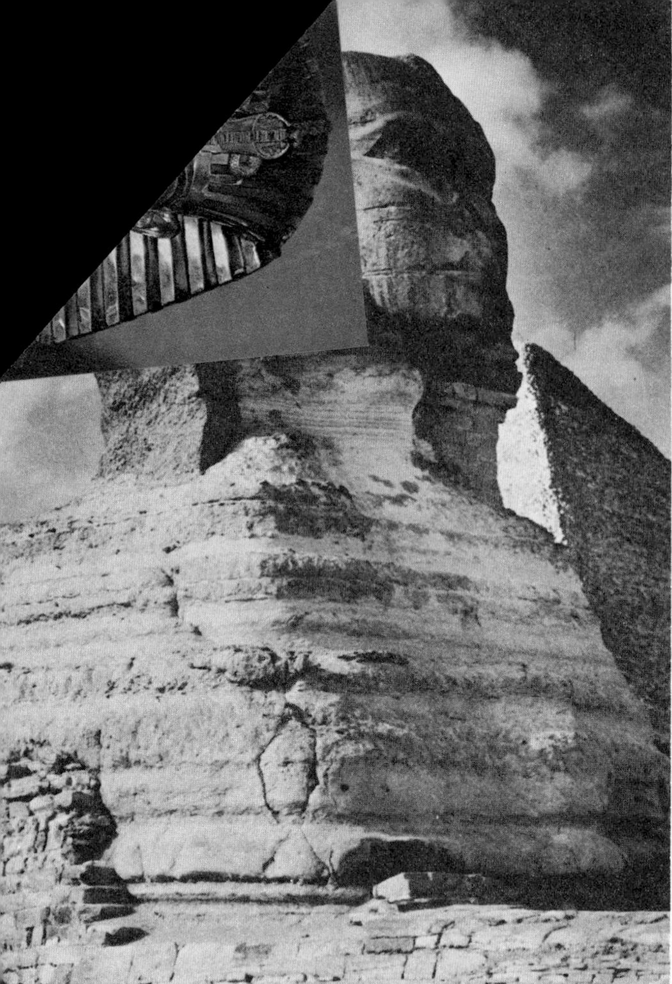

● The Great Sphinx, with a man's head and lion's body, guards the pyramid behind it.

Mathematics and medicine advanced. Because Nile floods washed away markers for land boundaries, the Egyptians surveyed the land often and used practical geometry in measuring the boundaries. Their engineers also used mathematics to work out the precise measurements necessary in the construction of the Pyramids and temples. The Egyptians were good builders in stone, and both sculptors and engineers liked to think big. Religion inspired the building of Egyptian tombs and temples. The most famous temple was that of the god Amon-Re, at Karnak [kär′nak], built between 1290 and 1224 B.C. Part of this great temple still stands. Its hall is larger than a football field and 80 feet (24 meters) high. The roof was supported by rows of giant columns.

Egyptian doctors were familiar with the anatomy of the human body and the healing properties of certain herbs. They also knew how to set broken bones and how to cure wounds.

● The Sphinx was carved from remaining rock in the quarry after the pyramid in the background was built.

SECTION REVIEW 1

1. How did the farming methods of the early Egyptians lead to the beginning of local governments? p. 22
2. Compare the definition of a civilization in the introduction of this chapter with the description of ■ Egypt before 3100 B.C. What elements of civilization did the Egyptians have by that time?
3. Why was the pharaoh able to have absolute p. 26 power over his people? Give two reasons.
4. What was the most important accomplishment ● of the Old Kingdom? The Middle Kingdom? The New Kingdom?

2 City-states and empires flourished in Mesopotamia

About the same time that civilization arose in Egypt, it also was emerging in the valley of the Tigris and Euphrates rivers. This region is known as Mesopotamia, or "land between the rivers." Mesopotamia was a part of the Fertile Crescent, a large area that extends in an arc from the southeastern end of the Mediterranean Sea to the Persian Gulf (see map on page 33). Many of the peoples in the Fertile Crescent were nomadic herders. They lived, with their flocks, in family groups, or *clans*. When several clans recognize ties with other clans of the same ancestry, this large group is called a *tribe*. A tribe is made up of the people of the clans, their slaves,

■ 2. Answers may vary.

● 4. Answers may vary. See p. 23, 26.

and some adopted strangers. All the people of a tribe share the same language, religion, and customs. Much of life in the Fertile Crescent was tribal. However, during the years covered in this Section (4000–300 B.C.), some of these tribes settled and built up cities.

This book deals mainly with civilized groups whose activities had some influence on the way people live today. But it is important to remember that there were other groups of people busy pursuing other ways of living.

Civilized living in the Fertile Crescent first emerged in a small area of lower Mesopotamia in what is now Iraq [i rak′]. The area extended about 500 miles (800 kilometers) northwest from the Persian Gulf. The Bible calls this area the Plain of Shinar [shī′när]. Some authorities ● believe that the earliest civilization in the world began here.

The Sumerians lived in city-states (4000–2500 B.C.). About 4000 B.C., a tribe known as the Sumerians [sü mir′ē əns] moved down from the hill country of the northeast into the fertile area of the Tigris and Eu-
ans. 1 phrates rivers. Like the Egyptians, the Sumerians dug canals to control the spring floods and to irrigate the land.

Unlike the Egyptians, who formed a unified nation under the Old Kingdom, the Sumerians created a number of *city-states.* Each city-state included a city and the farmlands and villages around it. The city-states were most prosperous from 2900 to 2400 B.C. During this time, Sumerian farmers raised barley, oats, and dates. Some city dwellers were skilled in crafts, and their products were traded as far away as India and Egypt.

Each city-state was a theocracy. The local god, believed to be the real ruler of the city-state, was represented by an earthly ruler who served as high priest and city governor. The city ruler performed administrative duties, such as supervising the irrigation system. Like the Egyptian pharaoh, he was an all-powerful ruler with absolute authority over the people, but he was not considered a god himself, as the Egyptian pharaoh was.

The Sumerians made several important contributions to the civilization of Mesopotamia. One was a form of writing. The Sumerians did not have paper. They used a *stylus,* or pointed stick, to make impressions on soft clay bricks or tablets. The tablets were then baked to give them permanent form. The Sumerians' type of writing is called *cuneiform* [kyü nē′ə fôrm], meaning "wedge-shaped," because of marks made by their stylus. Each combination of marks stood for a syllable. Sumerian cuneiform writing was later used by other peoples of the Fertile Crescent.

The Plain of Shinar lacked stones for building, but clay was everywhere. The Sumerians used it to build their houses and temples. And their invention of the arch continues to be important to architecture, because an arch can support very heavy structures even over the openings of doorways and windows. The Sumerians probably were the first to make wheeled vehicles (although the wheel was invented earlier), and they taught the Egyptians to do the same.

The Sumerian people of each city-state worshiped their own local god as well as gods brought in by other peoples. Sumerian literature tells of their religious beliefs. The epic poem *Gilgamesh* [gil′gə mesh′] is their most important piece of literature. One of its sections tells a fascinating story of a flood like the story of Noah and the Ark, explained perhaps by the ever present possibility of river floods.

● Point out that historians do not always agree. There is a difference of opinion on this point.

Hammurabi wrote a code of laws. Mesopotamia had no natural barriers against invasion. Furthermore, the individual city-states were easy to attack. However, in spite of invasion, Sumerian civilization lasted because the conquerors took on Sumerian ways.

About 2500 B.C., the city-states were united by Sargon I, an invader from the north. Later, about 1760 B.C., Hammurabi [ham′ ů rä′bē], who came from what is now Syria, brought all of lower Mesopotamia under one rule. His capital was the city of Babylon [bab′ə lən], and all of lower Mesopotamia became known as Babylonia [bab′ə lō′nē ə].

Hammurabi's most important gift to civilization was his written code of law. It was discovered in 1901 by a team of French archaeologists digging at Susa [sü′sə], Iran [i ran′]. They found three pieces of black stone with a long series of writing on them. Put together, the stones made one block nearly 8 feet (2.4 meters) high. The discovery of this block of stone excited archaeologists and historians because the writing gave the earliest record of laws set down by a government. The Code had nearly 300 sections and covered in detail the everyday relations of the people who lived in Hammurabi's empire. The following laws show that in Babylonia, human life was considered to be of less value than personal property.

> If a man has stolen goods from a temple or house, he shall be put to death; and he that has received the stolen property from him shall be put to death.
>
> If a man has broken into a house, he shall be killed in front of the place where he broke through and buried there.
>
> If a man has committed highway robbery and has been caught, that man shall be put to death.

● Discuss: rivers, mountains, deserts, etc. as natural barriers.

■ This material may be used to motivate a discussion on the importance of law in all societies.

Penalties varied according to the social position of the injured: "If a man has knocked out the eye of a noble, his eye shall be knocked out," whereas if the same man knocked out the eye of a commoner, he was only required to pay a fine. There are other parts of the Code that are more like modern justice. They bear out Hammurabi's claim that the Code would "prevent the strong from oppressing the weak." Slavery for debt was limited to four years, and dishonest business practices were punished. Laws governing the fees of doctors and veterinarians allowed poor people to pay less for medical and surgical services than the rich. A woman's right to keep her marriage dowry and to control slaves was guaranteed.

Hammurabi's Code was not the first of its kind. He used existing laws and revised another code that was then 300 years old. But his Code became the basis for other legal systems long after his death. Since law is one of the main ans. 2 ■

Sargon's bronze head shows proud features and curly beard. The jeweled eyes have been stolen.

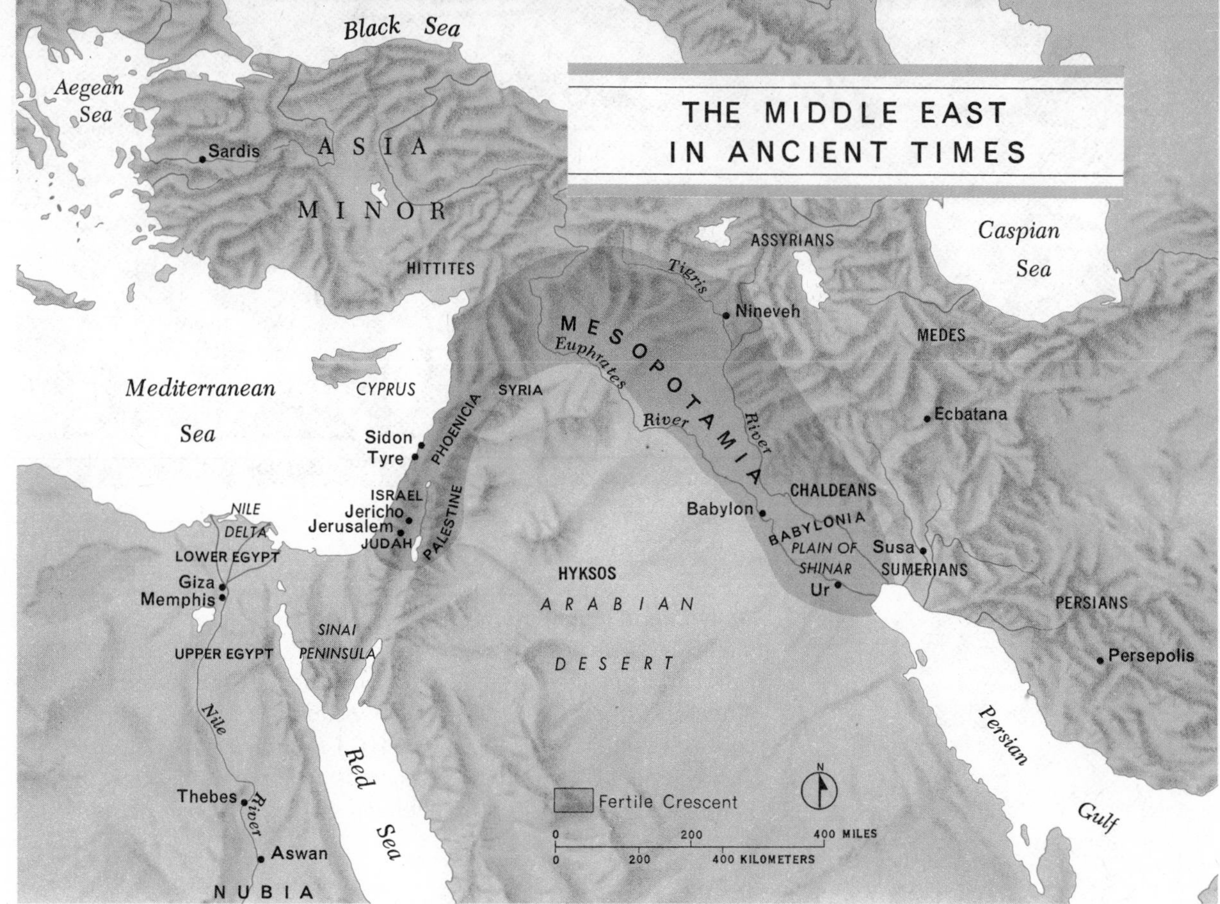

ways that people establish and keep social order, the Code represents a large step forward in the journey toward an advanced stage of civilization.

After Hammurabi's death, mountain tribes invaded his kingdom from the east and north. The Hittites [hit′īts], one of these invading tribes, became powerful in the Fertile Crescent.

The Hittites ruled a powerful empire with iron weapons (1600–1200 B.C.). The Hittites lived in an area to the northwest of Babylonia, in what is now Turkey. They had just and humane laws, and their architecture was notable. Their most important gift to civilization, however, was the knowledge of how to work iron. They refined iron ore and used it to make tools and weapons.

● The use of iron was spread throughout the Middle East during this time.

Armed with their iron weapons, which were harder and stronger than those made of bronze, the Hittites moved southward into Syria, in the western part of the Fertile Crescent. Shortly after 1600 B.C., they conquered Babylonia and became rulers of the area once governed by Hammurabi.

These conquests alarmed the Egyptian pharaohs, who sent armies north to challenge the Hittites. Thus began a long struggle that weakened both the Hittite and Egyptian empires. ●

Civilization advanced during an era of small states (1200–750 B.C.). By 1200 B.C., the Hittite kingdom was beginning to collapse, and Egypt had also lost much of its power. In this situation, several small states were able to develop and maintain their freedom.

Daily Life in Mesopotamia *Above:* Wearing helmets and cloaks, Sumerian soldiers went to war in horse-drawn chariots (about 2600 B.C.). *Left:* Details of furniture, hair, and clothes show in the seated Babylonian harpist (about 1900 B.C.) and *left bottom* the spinner being fanned by a slave, from Susa (about 1200 B.C.). *Directly below:* Seals pressed in clay were used for signatures. Here is an imprint and, below, the seal that made it. *Below right:* Sumerians worshiped many gods. This is Ningal, the moon god's wife.

Two, the Phoenicians and the Hebrews, made important contributions to civilization.

The Phoenicians [fə nish′ənz] had been desert nomads who moved westward into an area of the Fertile Crescent bordering the eastern Mediterranean. There they became sea traders and built the great trading cities of Tyre [tīr] and Sidon [sīd′n]. Their ships sailed to Greece, Italy, North Africa, Spain, the west coast of Africa, and possibly even to faraway ● Britain. The Phoenicians set up many distant trading colonies, the greatest of which was Carthage, in North Africa.

To keep track of their trading operations, the Phoenicians developed a more advanced system of writing than that used by the Egyptians or Sumerians. They used letters or signs that ■ represented sounds to make an alphabet. The word *alphabet* comes from their first two letters—*aleph* and *beth.* The Phoenician alphabet was made up of twenty-two consonant symbols. Later, when the Greeks adopted the alphabet, they introduced vowel signs. From this combination of consonant and vowel signs came the alphabet we use today.

In Palestine was the country of the Hebrews, or Jews. Much of the history of this people is told in the Old Testament of the Bible. It tells how the Hebrews, under their leader Abraham, came from the eastern part of the Plain of Shinar. They searched for a "Promised Land" in which to settle, and after years of wandering came to Canaan [kā′nən], or Palestine. The Book of Exodus in the Bible tells how some of the Hebrew tribes were enslaved by the Egyptians. After a long captivity, a great Hebrew leader named Moses led his people back to Palestine. Jewish scriptures relate how Moses gave the Jews the Ten Commandments that God had revealed to him on Mount Sinai [sī′nī].

● Some historians believe they may have reached the Americas.

■ Egyptian, Sumerian, and Chinese styles of writing are shown on p. 77.

According to the Old Testament, the Hebrews had to fight the Canaanites and later the Philistines [fil′ə stēnz′] for possession of Palestine. Around 1025 B.C., Saul became their first king. He was followed on the throne by David who, scriptures say, had killed the Philistine giant, Goliath, with a stone hurled from a slingshot. After defeating the Philistines, David established a kingdom with Jerusalem as its capital.

The Hebrew kingdom reached its height under David's son, Solomon, who reigned from about 977 to 937 B.C. In Jerusalem he built a temple to God and sent his ships to trade in distant countries. His expenses caused such high taxes that the Hebrew tribes in the north grew unhappy with Solomon's reign. After his death, they set up an independent kingdom. The land of the Hebrews divided into two parts: the Kingdom of Israel in the north and the Kingdom of Judah in the south. Thus weakened, the Hebrews were open to invaders. Between 722 B.C. and 66 A.D., the Jews were conquered by different peoples..

In 66 A.D., the Jews staged a revolt against their Roman rulers. The Romans destroyed Jerusalem and drove many of the Jews from Palestine, and they scattered to many different parts of the world. In spite of this *Diaspora* [dī as′pər ə], or "scattering," the Jews clung to their religion and customs and dreamed of someday returning to the Promised Land.

Compared with the Egyptian, Babylonian, and Hittite empires, the Hebrews were an unimportant state. It is in the areas of religion and justice that they made lasting contributions to civilization. The religion that the Hebrews developed ans. 3 is called *Judaism* [jü′dē iz′əm]. With its *monotheism,* or belief in one god, and teachings of the Old Testament, Judaism formed the base of two other great religions of the world—Chris-

THE TEN COMMANDMENTS

Down from the mountain, Moses (Charlton Heston) shows the ten commandments to the awe-struck Hebrew people. This powerful event has captured the imaginations of people for centuries. Epic director Cecil B. De Mille made a 1926 silent version and this hugely successful 1956 sound version of *The Ten Commandments.*

tianity and Islam. From an early worship of many gods, the Hebrews developed the idea of one god for their own tribe. This idea, in time, developed into the idea of one loving Father who ruled over the whole universe. Building upon the Ten Commandments, prophets developed some of the noblest rules of human behavior, as shown in the following passage from the Holy Scriptures (Micah 6:8).

> It hath been told thee, O man, what is good,
> And what the Lord doth require of thee: Only to do justly, and to love mercy, and to walk humbly with thy God.

The Assyrians ruled the largest empire the world had seen (750–605 B.C.). The era of small states ended with the rise of the Assyrians [ə sir′ē ənz]. Their original homeland was a highland region north of the upper Tigris River. Shortly before 1000 B.C., they began a series of attacks on their neighbors. Babylonia fell to them in 729 B.C. and Israel in 722 B.C. By 700 B.C., the Assyrians had created the largest empire yet. It included the Fertile Crescent, the area surrounding it, and Egypt.

The Assyrians ruled their empire by developing an advanced system of political administration and by building a well-trained army equipped with iron weapons. First, Assyrian bowmen weakened the enemy, using bows with vicious iron-tipped arrows as their main weapon. Then came attacks by horsemen and charioteers wearing helmets and breastplates. Bearing iron spears, swords, and bows, they smashed the ranks of the enemy and drove them from the field.

● A regular feature in each unit, these movie stills show students that events in history inspired the imaginations of film makers.

Few conquerors in history have been so cruel and heartless in war. The Assyrians terrorized conquered peoples and forced them to bow to Assyrian will, frequently burning them alive or cutting off their heads. However, their fine library of clay tablets in their capital, Nineveh [nin′ə və], helped preserve much of the knowledge of their day.

In 612 B.C., Nineveh was captured by the Chaldeans [kal dē′ənz] from Babylonia and the Medes from Persia. Everywhere in the empire, the people rejoiced when their cruel Assyrian masters were overthrown.

A new Babylonian empire arose (605–550 B.C.). With the fall of Nineveh, Babylonia became powerful for the first time since Hammurabi. The Chaldeans, guided by their strong king Nebuchadnezzar [neb′yə kəd nez′ər], built the Chaldean Empire by conquering the Fertile Crescent. Nebuchadnezzar rebuilt Babylon. Its marvels included the hanging gardens built on rooftops.

The Chaldeans, building on the work of earlier peoples, studied the stars, as well as the sun, the moon, and the planets. Without any telescopes or accurate time-recording instruments they used mathematics to work out detailed tables of the movements of these bodies and thus made an important contribution to the science of astronomy.

A fierce lion decorates this Persian gold drinking cup (5th or 6th century B.C.).

The Chaldeans believed it was possible to tell the future through a study of the stars. They used charts of the movements of stars to help them make important decisions. Thus they began the study of astrology.

With Nebuchadnezzar's death in 562 B.C., the Chaldean Empire began to decay. It was eventually succeeded by the Persian Empire.

The Persians built a vast empire (525–331 B.C.). Among the different peoples of the Assyrian Empire were two related groups, the Medes and the Persians. After the Medes had helped the Chaldeans defeat the cruel Assyrians, they built a prosperous kingdom that included the Persians. The capital of this kingdom was at Ecbatana [ek bat′ə nə].

In 550 B.C., a Persian general named Cyrus the Great led the Persians in a successful attack against the Medes. His troops captured Ecbatana, then the neighboring kingdoms, and finally the entire Chaldean Empire. At the time of Cyrus' death in 529 B.C., Persian rule extended east to the borders of India, west to the Aegean Sea, and south to Egypt. Cyrus' successors conquered Egypt in 525 B.C. and even won land in southeastern Europe. Unlike the Assyri- ans. 4
ans, however, the Persian kings sought to give the different peoples in their empire equal rights and responsibilities. They allowed conquered peoples to worship their own gods, to use their own languages, and to keep their own customs.

The Persian government, like the Assyrian and Chaldean governments, was a *despotism*, or rule of a king, called a *despot*, having unlimited power. Under Darius I, who ruled from 521–486 B.C., the Persian Empire reached its ●

● Compare Persian and Assyrian methods. Explain how both were despotic governments.

greatest size. Four capitals—Susa, Ecbatana, Babylon, and Persepolis [pər sep′ə lis]—were set up in different parts of the empire. The whole empire was divided into districts, each governed by a representative of the king. To keep himself informed on how well his officials governed, Darius employed inspectors, called "The Eyes and Ears of the King," who traveled from district to district, reporting their findings personally to him.

To improve communications throughout the huge empire, the Persian kings maintained a network of fine roads. Along these highways galloped the king's messengers, changing horses every 14 miles (22 kilometers). Relays of these horsemen could cover 1,500 miles (2,400 kilometers) in a little more than a week; ordinary travelers took three months to travel the same distance.

The Persian kings protected farming and helped trade in the whole empire, partly because they wanted all districts to be able to pay taxes. The tax burden, however, was not heavy. Throughout the empire, a money system of gold and silver coins was used.

The fair treatment of other peoples by the Persian kings was partly due to the Persian religion. Founded by the teacher Zoroaster [zôr′ō as′tər] in the 7th century B.C., this religion asks its followers to choose Ahura Mazda [ä′hu̇r ə maz′də], the god of good, over Ahriman [är′i mən], the god of evil. In time, the Zoroastrians believed, the world would come to an end. Ahura Mazda would win over Ahriman. At that time, there would be a last judgment, and the righteous would go to heaven and the wicked to hell. In describing one of his victories, Darius I showed how he was influenced by the Persian religion:

> . . . Ahura Mazda bore me aid . . . because I was not an enemy, I was not a deceiver, I was not a wrong-doer, neither I nor my family; according to justice and rectitude I ruled.

SECTION REVIEW 2

1. In what ways was Sumerian civilization like that of Egypt? In what ways was it different? p. 31

2. What is important about Hammurabi's code of laws? In what ways were the laws different from modern laws? p. 32

3. What is the religion of the Hebrews? Name the other two great religions based on its beliefs. p. 35 36

4. In what ways was Persian rule different from Assyrian rule? (Name at least two.) p. 37 38

Mighty warriors decorated the public buildings in Persepolis.

3 An ancient city revealed early Indus civilization

Over 4,000 years ago, people living in the Indus River Valley in what is now Pakistan and India had a highly organized way of life. Yet practically nothing was known about this early river valley civilization until recent times.

Archaeologists discovered a lost city. In the 1850s, engineers began to build a railroad in the Indus Valley. As workers prepared the area, ans. 1 they uncovered large numbers of bricks. These they promptly used in laying the railroad bed. They also uncovered many ornaments and small figures, which were mostly ignored or carried off as mementos by the local villagers. Little did they know that they were destroying the evidence of an ancient way of life.

No one thought much about these discoveries for 70 years. Then in the 1920s, the British government began to study the area. Archaeologists discovered enough remains to learn that there, where the railroad workers had found bricks, had once been the city of Harappa [hə rap′ə]. They found red limestone sculpture and delicate jewelry, graveyards, pottery, and tools. The ans. 3 people of this city had developed an advanced civilization at about the same time as the Egyptians and Sumerians. This civilization covered a huge area from the Arabian Sea to the city of Delhi [del′ē].

In the years since Harappa was discovered, British, American, and Indian archaeologists have learned much about this ancient culture. Remains of 60 villages and towns have been found. The best source of information is Mohenjo-Daro [mō hen′jō dä′rō], a city 400 miles (640 kilometers) southwest of Harappa. (See map on page 54.)

Life in Mohenjo-Daro was highly organized. The city of Mohenjo-Daro was laid out in blocks. The streets were paved with bricks ● and lined with shops. The windows of houses faced interior courtyards, not the street. Light and fresh air came through window grills made of red clay or *alabaster,* a white marble-like stone. Staircases led to the roof, where the family enjoyed the cool night air. Most houses had ans. 4 indoor toilets, and some of the larger houses had baths. Neat brick-lined sewers along the streets carried off bath and rain water.

In the center of the city was a thick-walled, mud-brick fort, or *citadel* [sit′ə del], that guarded the city. Inside the citadel were public buildings: a great bath, probably used for religious bathings, and a granary where carts could drive right up to deposit the harvest.

Life for members of the upper-class was luxu- ans. 4 rious. Their two-story houses had rooms for servants and guests. Waterproof tiles lined their bathtubs. Their wooden furniture, long since ■ disintegrated, was decorated with bone, shell, and ivory inlays. They also had ornate pottery, bronze tools, silver pitchers, and gold jewelry.

Numerous toys and stamp seals have been found. Toy birds, animals, bulls tethered to small carts, marbles, balls, and rattles amused the children of Mohenjo-Daro. The stamp seals were small pieces of stone with carefully detailed carvings. It is thought they were pressed into soft material—wax or clay—to show ownership. Most had small rings on the back and could be worn on thongs as ornaments.

The people of Mohenjo-Daro had an elaborate religion. Many female statues have been found, showing that the people worshiped a goddess. She is shown adorned with necklaces, bracelets, and a *girdle,* or belt, around her exaggerated hips. Sculpture and carvings on the

● See illustration, p. 20.

■ The wood disintegrated, but the inlays did not, and were found on the floor where the chair had been.

Daily Life in the Indus Valley *Left:* This toy pottery bull has a head that goes up and down. Toy carts have also been found at Mohenjo-Daro, evidence that the Indus Valley people used wheels and animals to pull heavy loads. *Center:* This stamp seal, with a design of goats and a tree, has characters that may have spelled the owner's name. Goods marked with Indus Valley seals have been found in cities along the ancient caravan route to Mesopotamia. *Bottom left:* This haughty figure with barbered hair and beard is believed to have been a high priest. *Bottom right:* Grain was stored in jars like this to keep it dry and safe from pests. The design on the jar is a row of peacocks and a row of leaves. Because they believed that peacock flesh never decayed, the Indus Valley people considered peacocks a symbol of eternal life.

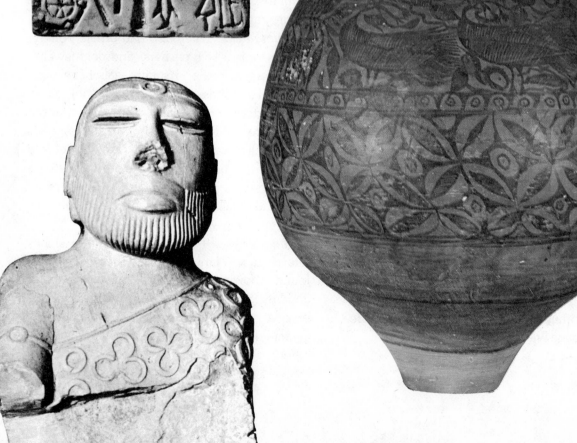

seals also show that the people burned incense or candles to their goddess and that animals were included in their religion. The great bath house, with its huge public bathing area surrounded by smaller private baths, also had living quarters. These suggest that a priest class lived ● in luxury and celebrated ritual bathings.

Farming and some trade formed the economy of this ancient civilization. Farming was the basis of life. There were huge round platforms in the city where an organized labor force pounded grain. Trade was important, too. Quartz weights, many of them exactly the same size, have been found. These indicate that the people used standard weights to measure goods in their business deals. Some weights are so small they must have been used to weigh gold. Others were used by grocers who sold spices. The largest ones, made of stones so heavy they had to be hauled into place by ropes, may have been used to weigh large amounts of grain.

The ancient Indus Valley civilization had two port cities, recently excavated. Today, these
ans. 2 cities are 30 miles inland from the Arabian Sea. However, huge piers and warehouses indicate that the cities must have once sat right on the water. The shape of the Indian subcontinent has been changing. Layers of rock deep in the earth's surface have shifted, raising up mud to become land where it was once coastline.

The port cities received ships from the Sumerians. Sailboats of the Indus Valley people traveled the Arabian Sea. Camels and ox-drawn carts carried goods overland.

History is silent about the end of these people. The people of this ancient Indus culture had writing, but scholars have not yet learned to read it. Little is known about what happened to these people. The city of Mohenjo-Daro seems to have been slowly overrun by mud from a nearby lake, formed from the earth's shifting surface. Over and over, houses were rebuilt on platforms raised to higher, safer levels. Some archaeologists believe this constant work reduced the will and energy of the people. We do know that the oldest buildings, found 40 feet (12 meters) below the mud surface, were much better built than those above. Dikes and banks seem to have been neglected, and prosperity declined.

Then disaster struck. About 1500 B.C., some terrible misfortune hit Mohenjo-Daro and possibly all the Indus River people. Skeletons were found in groups, some showing axe or sword cuts, as though these long-dead people had huddled together for comfort in the face of a terrible catastrophe. But what happened is still a mystery. The name Mohenjo-Daro means "the place of the dead."

SECTION REVIEW 3

1. Why were scientists able to learn more about Mohenjo-Daro than about Harappa? p. 39

2. What evidence shows that the shape of the Indian subcontinent has changed in the last 4,000 years? p. 41

3. Name two other river valley civilizations that existed at the same time as that in the Indus Valley. p. 39

4. In what ways did the people of Mohenjo-Daro have an advanced way of life? p. 39

4 Chinese civilization developed along the Hwang Ho

The Chinese have many myths and legends about ancient times. They are very tall stories that have to be taken with several grains of salt.

● Hindus today bathe for a religious purpose, to wash away sin and suffering.

ans. 1 One tells of the first man, P'an Ku, who used a hammer and chisel for 18 thousand years to make the universe. The job was finished 2,229,000 years ago!

More definite information tells us that from 2205 to 1766 B.C., princes, called the Hsia [hə sī′] ruled over a number of little kingdoms. Yu, the first prince, is remembered as brave and strong. He is said to have fought a mighty river to save his people from floods. According to an early Chinese saying, the people claimed that, "But for Yu, we should all have been fishes." Such legends are unreliable, but it is true that people of a New Stone Age culture settled in the Hwang Ho Valley. (See map on page 71.)

Neolithic Chinese were farmers. The early people of China were farmers. In the cold, dry areas of northern China were great plains of fertile loess. The Hwang Ho ran through these plains carrying large amounts of coffee-colored silt. It continually built up the river bed until its banks became higher than the surrounding plain. From time to time the river overflowed, causing tragic floods, so that the river came to be called "China's Sorrow." In spite of this, its waters brought life to the valley. Forests did not grow in the plains and the land did not need to be cleared for farming. It was on these plains ans. 2 that the Chinese "invented" farming.

As long ago as 4500 B.C., Chinese farmers • were growing *millet* [mil′it]. (This grass, with tufts that look like fuzzy caterpillars, is eaten today by about one third of the world's population.) A thousand years later, soybeans were cultivated, and pigs were raised for food and farm work.

By 3500 B.C., Chinese women were raising silkworms, spinning the unraveled cocoons into fine silk thread, and weaving silk cloth. Throughout history, people have considered Chinese silk among the best in the world.

About 3000 B.C., the people in the southern, semitropical climate at the mouth of the Yangtze [yang′tsē] River learned to grow rice. Because ans. 2 rice needs to have its roots underneath water, these people developed the elaborate farming methods still used in much of Southeast Asia today. They made artificial pools, called *paddies,* by building dikes around low-lying land and diverting water from nearby streams. Then, they sowed the rice seeds in dry land and transplanted them to the paddies by hand, a plant at a time, when the shoots were about a foot high. (Later, as the low-lying land became used, they learned to build paddies on hillsides.)

These early Chinese lived in villages near their farmland. Walls of pounded earth protected their villages. Their houses were mud-and-grass walled cones placed over circular areas dug out of the ground. The roof was supported by six posts cut from tree trunks and it was made of wooden beams covered with straw and earth. The structure was between 12 and 17 feet (3.6 to 5.0 meters) in diameter. The doorway was in the roof.

Shang kings were religious leaders (1500–1027 B.C.). The written history of China begins about 1500 B.C. with the rise of the Shangs, whose capital was located north of the lower part of the Hwang Ho, near the present city of Anyang. The Shang kings controlled only a small area around their capital, while strong nobles ruled the more distant parts of the kingdom. However, the nobles recognized the Shang king as the head of the armies and as the religious leader. They believed that he governed ans. 3 by command of heaven. As high priest, he paid homage to his ancestors and made animal

• Examples of these grains could be brought to class so students could see what they look like.

Daily Life in China *Top left:* The Chinese believed that the tiger had special powers to drive off demons. This bronze container was used to hold wine in religious ceremonies. It was cast in the shape of a tiger protecting a man. Its whole surface was decorated with figures that stand for demons. *Top right:* A 4-thousand-year-old earthenware pot, made on a potter's wheel, was buried as part of a funeral ceremony. *Opposite:* One of the earliest examples of Chinese writing (written about 1766–1123 B.C.) is found on this bone. The cracks were made when the bone was heated. Chinese priests interpreted the spirits' answers by placing importance on which words were interrupted by the cracks. *Below:* This jade tiger (late Shang or early Chou) used to guard a grave.

sacrifices to gods to bring about good harvests.

Much of the knowledge of Shang history comes from excavations, begun in 1928, of sites near Anyang. Archaeologists here found no great monuments or palaces. Stone was scarce in China, and buildings were made from perishable wood and packed earth. A poem from the *Book of Odes,* the oldest collection of Chinese poetry, tells how the people built:

> He called upon his overseer of public works,
> He called upon his Minister of Education,
> And charged them to build dwellings.
> They levelled all the land by skillful measuring,
> They built wooden frames which rose straight
> and high,
> The temple of our ancestors grew mightily.
> Armies of men brought earth in baskets
> And, shouting joyfully, poured it into the
> frames.
> They rammed it in with great ringing blows,
> They leveled off the walls and these resounded
> mightily,
> They built up five thousand cubits at once,
> And so well did they labour
> That the rolling of the great drum
> Would not cover the noise thereof.

One important source of information about the early Chinese is the writing on pieces of animal bones and tortoise shells. Priests wrote questions about the future on the bones and shells. Then they heated the bones and interpreted the cracks that appeared as answers from gods or ancestors. Questions were asked on many subjects, and they tell us much about the Shang civilization. The bones ask about what to sacrifice to the spirits, when will be a good day for an important journey, and when will be a good time for the army to attack. Priests asked about the harvest and the weather, about when the time was good to go hunting or fishing. Also, the priests told the spirits about their enemies' misdeeds, about how many people had been killed or taken prisoner, so the spirits could punish their enemies. The inscriptions show that Chinese writing was well advanced at this time. Shang writing had about 2,000 symbols. In addition to writing on bones and shells, the people kept records on tablets of wood or bamboo.

● Pictured on p. 43.

The people of the Shang period are best known for their fine bronze work. Artisans made bronze vases of different shapes for different purposes. A slender, rectangular vase, the *ting* vase, stood on four legs and was used for honoring ancestors. Another vase stood on three legs and had large, hollow feet. Another was built in two sections, like a modern double-boiler, with space for water in the bottom part and food in the top. These vases were beautifully shaped and elaborately decorated with scrolls, spirals, and the faces of dragons and other fabulous creatures. ans. 4

In addition to the bronze work, pieces of carved ivory and jade, marble sculptures, dagger-axes, and chariot fittings have been found at Shang sites. These discoveries show a high level of technology. The Shang people, however, were conquered in 1027 B.C. by a less civilized group of nomads who invaded the country from the northwest.

SECTION REVIEW 4

1. What is the ancient Chinese legend of the origin of the universe? p. 42

2. Name the three crops grown by early farmers in China. Tell the year by which each was being used. p. 42

3. Why did the strong nobles accept the Shangs as kings? p. 42

4. What are the people of the Shang period best known for? p. 44

CHAPTER REVIEW 2

SECTION SUMMARIES

1. Civilization first developed in Egypt. Farmers in the Nile Valley formed local governments to control irrigation. They developed a calendar and the plow. By 3100 B.C., a strong king, Menes, unified Egypt, marking the beginning of the Old Kingdom. Egyptian religion involved many gods, pharaoh-worship, good conduct, and belief in afterlife. The Pyramids were built; trade flourished; society was divided into different classes. Princes from Thebes ruled during the Middle Kingdom, and a canal was built to join the Nile Valley with the Red Sea. Following 100 years of Hyksos rule, the New Kingdom began, and Egyptian power grew into a great empire. Books were written on papyrus rolls. Mathematics, medicine, and architecture advanced.

2. City-states and empires flourished in Mesopotamia. The Sumerians were the first nomadic tribe to build cities in the Tigris-Euphrates Valley. Like the Egyptians, their government was a theocracy. They developed cuneiform writing, invented the arch, and used wheeled vehicles.

When Hammurabi conquered lower Mesopotamia and ruled from Babylon, he wrote a code of laws and made the government responsible for enforcing them. The Hittites conquered Babylonia with iron weapons and ruled so large an empire that Egypt engaged them in a lengthy war that weakened both empires. Then followed an era of small states. Two lasting achievements, the Phoenician alphabet and the Hebrew religion, developed in this time. Next, large empires ruled by despots followed. The Assyrian Empire was held together by efficient administration, an excellent army, and terrorism. The Chaldeans were noted for their developments in astronomy and astrology. Finally, the Persians built a vast empire run by a highly organized government. Zoroastrian beliefs led the Persians to rule with consideration and justice.

3. An ancient city revealed early Indus civilization. Excavations at Mohenjo-Daro revealed a civilization based on farming and trade. Port cities connected Indus people with the Red Sea. Indus people were divided into classes. They worshiped a goddess and some animals. How this civilization ended is not known.

4. Chinese civilization developed along the Hwang Ho. Early Chinese civilization was based on farming. Millet, soybeans, and rice were early crops. Silk worms were domesticated, and the silk trade was begun. Hsia princes ruled over small kingdoms. The first Chinese dynasty was the Shang. Shang kings were high priests recognized by nobles in the Hwang Ho Valley. Priests interpreted spirits' answers on bones and shells, and guided everyday life. Ancestors were honored. The Shang people are known for their cast bronze pottery.

WHO? WHAT? WHEN? WHERE?

1. Find the time during which each of the following events took place:

4000–3001 B.C. b, i
1500–1001 B.C. c, f
3000–2001 B.C. a
1000–501 B.C. e
2000–1501 B.C. d, g, h

a. Civilization began in the Indus Valley.
b. The Egyptian calendar came into use.
c. The written history of China began.
d. Hammurabi ruled Babylonia.
e. Solomon ruled the Hebrew kingdom.
f. Mohenjo-Daro came to an end.
g. The Egyptians learned to make bronze.
h. The Hittites fought with iron weapons.
i. Millet, soybeans, pigs, and oxen were being used in China.

2. Name the civilization that:

a. built the pyramid at Giza
b. asked questions on bones and tortoise shells
c. believed P'an Ku made the universe

2. a. Egyptian, b. Chinese, c. Chinese

d. used cuneiform writing
e. invented the arch
f. brought horses and chariots to Egypt
g. developed an alphabet
h. taught the Egyptians to use the wheel
i. wrote the Old Testament
j. first used columns in architecture

3. Write sentences about the people in this chapter to show you understand these terms:

civilization	polytheism
monotheism	despotism
dynasty	empire
theocracy	class

4. What archaeological evidence is there for each of the following:
a. the ways buildings were made in China during the Shang period
b. religious practices of the Indus people
c. Egyptian belief in life after death
d. property valued more highly than life in Mesopotamia

QUESTIONS FOR CRITICAL THINKING

1. What does Hammurabi's Code tell about how people lived in ancient Mesopotamia?
2. What did the Egyptians learn from the Sumerians? From the Hittites? Why is it important that people have contact with others not like themselves?
3. In what ways are civilized people better off than primitive people? What might be some advantages to having a simpler, less civilized life-style?

ACTIVITIES

1. Draw time lines showing the important events in each of the four river valleys.
2. Make charts comparing the accomplishments of six of the different peoples discussed.
3. Draw a detailed city-map showing Mohenjo-Daro, Thebes, or Babylon.

d. Sumerians, e. Sumerians, f. Hyksos, g. Phoenicians, h. Sumerians, i. Hebrews, j. Egyptians
3. Answers will vary.
4. a. Book of Odes, b. statues, baths, c. pyramids, prayers, mummies, d. Hammurabi's Code of Laws

CHAPTER TEST 2

SECTION 1

1. Writing, cities, metals, and trade are signs of a civilization.
2. The beginning of government in Egypt was helped by: a. religion, b. despotism, c. irrigation projects
3. The Old Kingdom was famous for its pyramids.
4. The name of the pharaoh who believed in only one god was Akhenaton.
5. True or false: When an Egyptian woman died, her husband inherited her property.

SECTION 2

6. True or false: The Sumerians lived in city-states.
7. A code of laws was developed by: a. the Hittites, b. the Hyksos, c. Hammurabi
8. After Solomon's death, the Hebrew kingdom was divided into the ________ and the ________. ●
9. Which city was *not* a Persian capital: a. Nineveh, b. Babylon, c. Ecbatana, d. Persepolis

SECTION 3

10. Mohenjo-Daro was in which river valley, the: a. Hwang, b. Indus, c. Nile
11. True or false: Mohenjo-Daro had indoor plumbing, baths, and sewers.
12. People of the Indus Valley used stamp seals to mark their property.
13. True or false: The Indus Valley people had no contact with other early civilizations.

SECTION 4

14. Millet, soybeans, rice, and silk were grown in China by: a. 4500 B.C., b. 3500 B.C., c. 3000 B.C.
15. The first Chinese dynasty was the Shang.
16. The rich soil of the great plain in China is made of: a. silt, b. loam, c. loess
17. True or false: Shang kings had absolute power over everyone in the kingdom.

● 8. Kingdoms of Israel and Judah

UNIT REVIEW 1 TEST YOURSELF

1. Choose the letter to show when the following events took place:

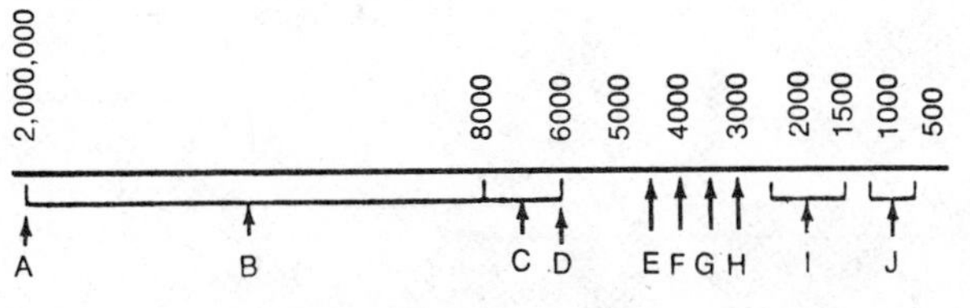

G Silk was being woven in the Hwang Ho Valley
D The New Stone Age began
I A civilization developed in the Indus River Valley
B The years of the Old Stone Age
F A calendar was being used in Egypt
J The years of the era of small states
A Australopithecines lived in Africa
C The years of the Middle Stone Age
H The Bronze Age began
E Farming began in the Hwang Ho Valley

2. Match the cultural contributions with the name of the people that developed them:

K wheel	A Cro-Magnons
H microliths	B Hebrews
D calendar	C Chaldeans
I iron	D Egyptians
B Old Testament	E Neanderthals
J silk, rice, millet	F Phoenicians
C astronomy and astrology	G Old Stone Age people
L code of law	H Middle Stone Age people
D hieroglyphic writing	I Hittites
E first belief in afterlife	J Chinese
J bronze vases	K Sumerians
G fire	L Hammurabi
F alphabet	
A beautiful cave art	

3. Match these terms with the correct meanings from the list below:

F fossils	polytheism C
O monotheism	Paleolithic G
I anthropologists	microliths N
D despotism	Mesolithic P
J irrigation	theocracy H
L empire	Ice Ages K
Q *Homo sapiens*	culture A
E civilization	prehistoric B
R domesticated	geologist M

A The way people live and satisfy their needs
B Before the invention of writing
C A belief in more than one god
D A government ruled by one person with absolute power
E Stage of human life with cities, metals, writing, government
F The hardened remains of ancient plants or animals
G Scientific term for the Old Stone Age
H A government in which the ruler is also the head of the official religion
I Scientists who study ancient and modern peoples
J The supplying of water to farmland
K Four periods when glaciers covered large parts of the earth
L Different peoples under the rule of a strong nation
M Scientists who study the earth's crust and its layers
N Small, pointed stone blades for spears or knives
O Belief in one, all-powerful, god
P Scientific term for the Middle Stone Age
Q Modern human beings; thinking man
R Animals that have been tamed for use by people

UNIT 2

CLASSICAL CIVILIZATIONS

Human life has certain things in common. People are born; most ● grow up and learn to work and communicate with each other. People raise families, build societies, and organize governments. They develop rules of conduct and create beautiful art and architecture. They find ways to explain the mysteries of nature and the purpose of life. And most people leave written records that future generations can read. No other creatures on earth can do all the things humans can.

However, human beings pursue these activities in different ways. All peoples have customs, but they do not all have the same customs. From family organization to government organization, the different peoples of the world have found different ways to shape society. There seems to be no limit to human imagination; people are creative. No matter where or how they live, people make cultures for themselves. Civilizations have developed in widely separated parts of the world.

Around 1000 B.C., at least four major civilizations began to emerge in India, China, Greece, and Italy. The peoples in each of those areas had their own ideas about religion, government, family life, art, and literature. The civilizations they developed have gone through many changes in the past 3,000 years. However, these ancient civilizations are still thought of as a kind of standard, ■ or ideal, by many modern peoples. That is why they are called *classical*.

Ships carried culture along with trading goods.

● Students should be encouraged to realize that the similarities among people outnumber the differences.

■ Key Concept: classical civilizations.

Each of the four classical civilizations made important contributions. India was the birthplace of two of the world's great religions, Hinduism and Buddhism. During India's classical times, customs developed that still shape Indian village life. Important cities flourished in both north and south India. Trade with both the Roman civilization to the west and the Chinese civilization to the east brought a healthy interchange of ideas. Indian religion and architecture spread throughout Southeast Asia.

In China's classical period, China became a vast empire. The religions of Confucianism and Taoism had their beginnings there. A civil service system and governmental units were formed that served China until the 1900s. Basic ideas about how people should behave toward one another were developed and recorded, and a tradition of reverence for things of the past was begun.

Greece was the home of democracy. Western ideals of freedom, equality before the laws,

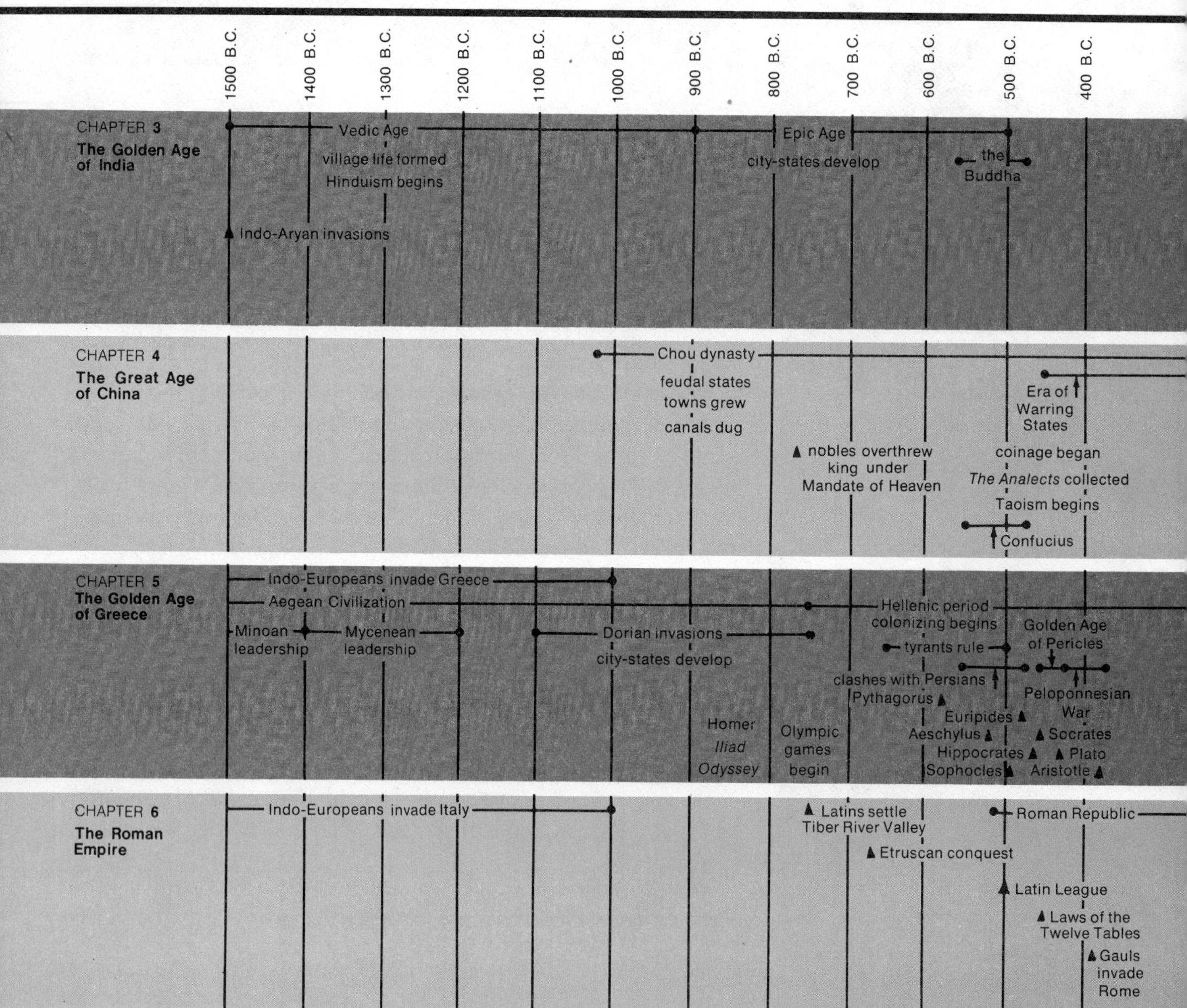

individualism, and public involvement in government have their roots in the thinking of the classical Greeks. Modern science, mathematics, and medicine began with the writings of the ancient Greeks. And classical standards of harmony and balance have dominated all the arts in the West until the twentieth century.

The great Roman Empire, which began in Italy, preserved Greek culture and spread it from Britain in the northwest to the eastern shores of the Mediterranean Sea. Roman military strength and governmental genius served as models for European rulers of many later centuries. And the Roman legal system is the foundation of the legal systems in much of the modern Western world.

In addition, all four civilizations made contributions to science and technology. Professional schools began during these classical times. And some of the finest art and architecture in all human history was produced.

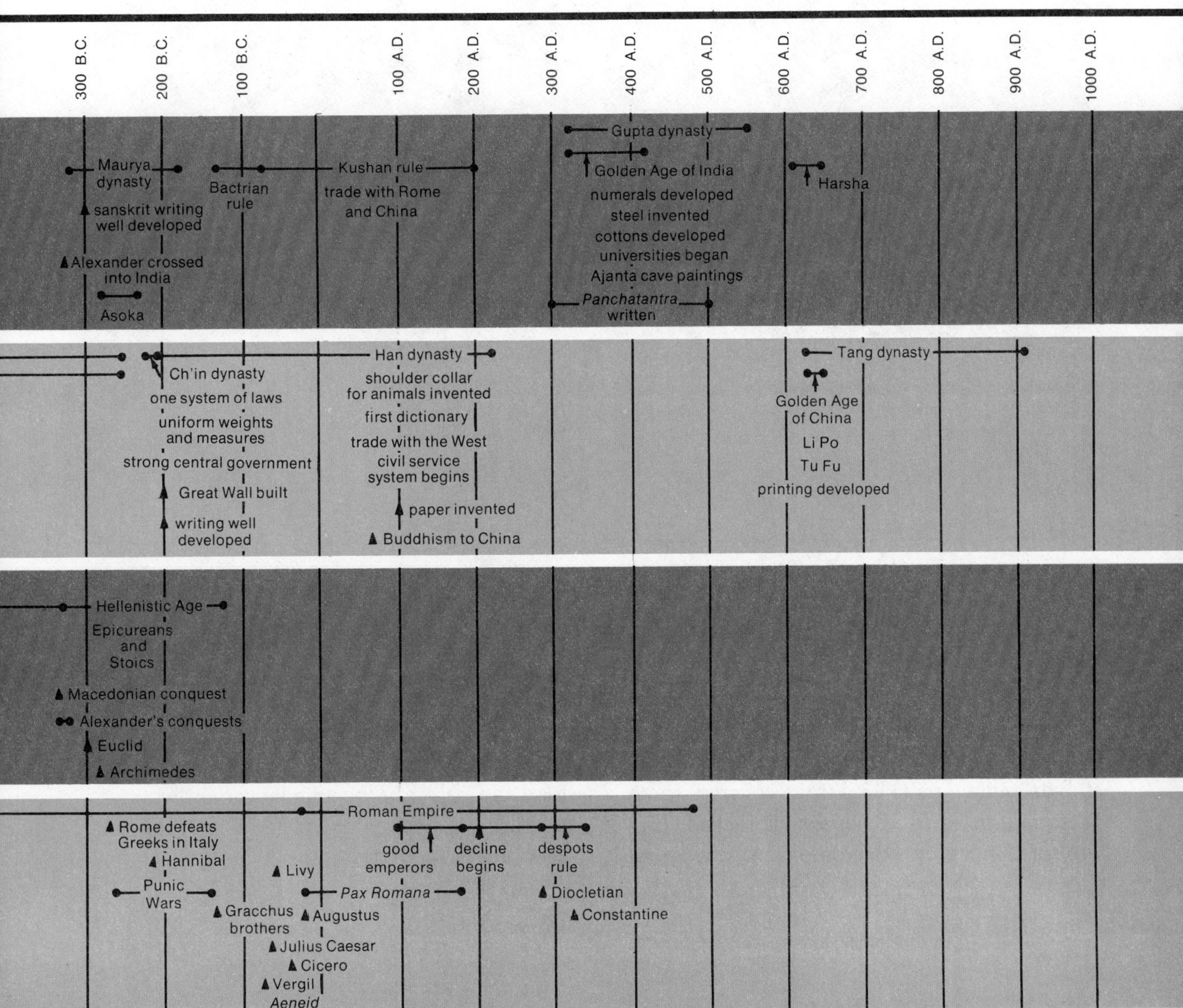

CHAPTER **3**

1500 B.C.–1000 A.D.

The Golden Age of India

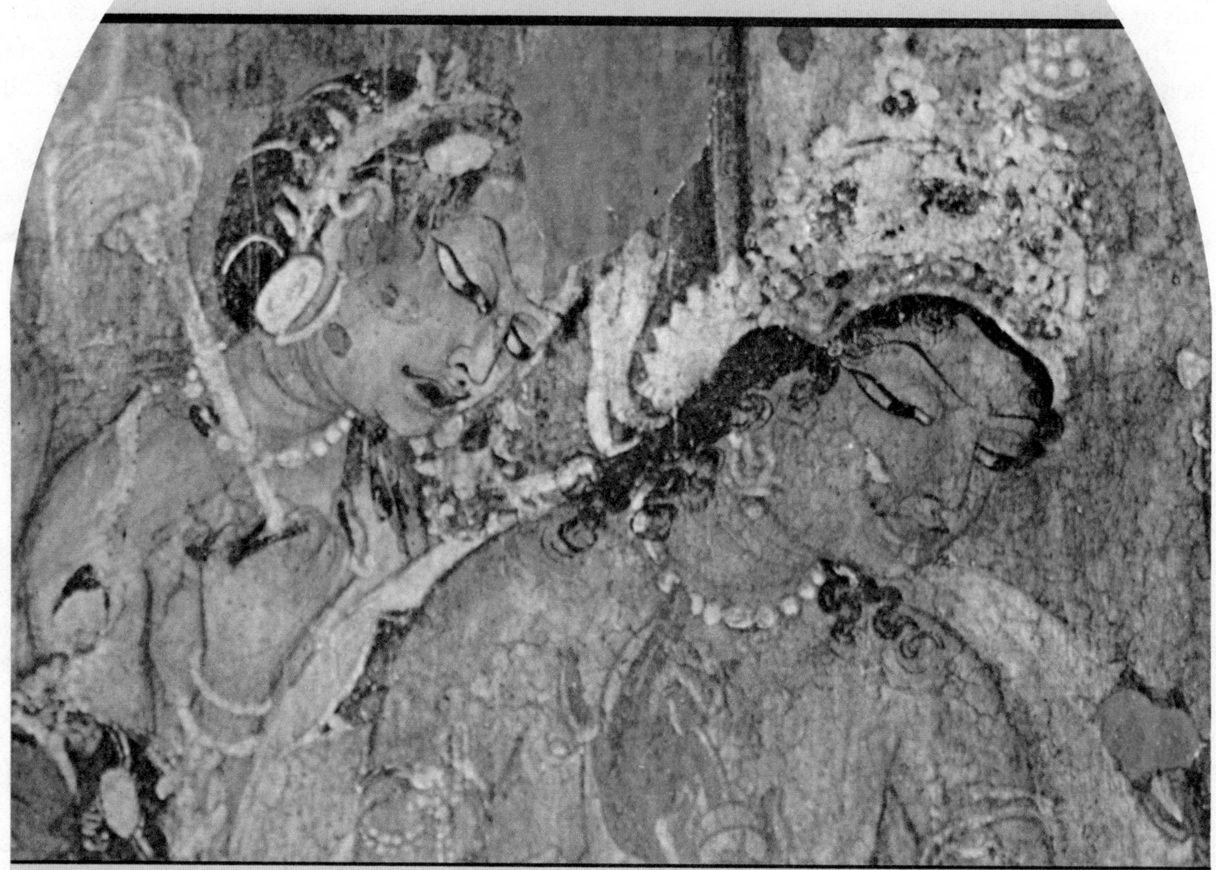

Huge temples were carved into the rocks at Ajanta in western India (4th century A.D.). The interior walls were covered with paintings of scenes from Buddhist literature. The rich colors, calm expressions, and graceful postures express religious peace.

In the 4th century B.C., the mighty Mauryan [mä′ür yən] Empire flourished in the Ganges River Valley in northeastern India. The capital, at Pataliputra [pä′tə li pü′trə], covered some 18 square miles (46.8 square kilometers) and was surrounded by a deep moat and a wooden wall. Sixty-four gates gave entrance to the city, and 572 towers guarded it. Streets were laid out in an orderly way. At the heart of the city stood the palace, a beautifully carved wooden structure. Its pillars were plated with gold and silver and covered with intricate designs.

Chandragupta Maurya [chun′drə gu̇p′tə mä′u̇r yə], the king, rarely left his palace. But on special holidays he toured the capital city. A Greek visiting in 302 B.C. described one such colorful procession. First came the monarch, riding an elephant.

> Then came a great host of attendants in holiday dress, with golden vessels, such as huge basins and goblets six feet broad, tables, chairs of state, drinking and washing vessels, all of Indian copper, and many of them set with jewels, such as emeralds, beryls, and Indian garnets. Others wore robes embroidered in gold thread and led wild beasts, such as buffaloes, leopards and tame lions, and rare birds in cages.

The visitor was favorably impressed by the prosperity and wealth of the empire. All land belonged to the state, and a tax on farm products was the chief source of government income. Farmers irrigated their fields and rotated their crops to increase their yield. Famine was almost unknown in the land. Trade and handicraft industries thrived. Artisans made textiles, cutlery, and farm tools for export. Products from southern India, China, Mesopotamia, and Asia Minor were sold in markets in Pataliputra, Taxila [tak si′lə], and other cities of the empire.

The Mauryan Empire was one of the first large, well-protected, and well-run states in history. It was divided into three provinces. Each was governed by a *viceroy*, the king's representative in the province, who had his own staff of civil servants. In Pataliputra, government committees guarded the rights of craft workers, recorded all births and deaths, regulated the quality of goods for sale, and collected taxes. The Mauryan army had 600 thousand infantrymen and 30 thousand cavalrymen. They used 9 thousand war elephants in much the same way that modern armies use tanks. Excellent roads, with markers showing distances, connected the many villages and towns. One road extended for 1,200 miles (1,920 kilometers) from Taxila to Pataliputra.

● Have students find the areas mentioned in this section on map, p. 54. Compare with the map of Asia in the Modern World Atlas at the back of this book.

After the fall of the Mauryas in the 2nd century B.C., influences from outside India helped bring about changes in the way of life. Five hundred years passed before the Gupta [gup′tə] Empire began. Chapter 3 shows how:

1. Geography shaped history in India.

2. Many features of Indian life began in early times.

3. Strong rulers built empires in India.

4. Gupta rule launched a golden age.

1 Geography shaped history in India

Geography has greatly influenced the history and lives of people in India. Ancient India in- ans. 1
cluded the land that is now India, Pakistan, and ●
Bangladesh. This area of 1.6 million square miles (4.2 million square kilometers) is about half the size of the United States. It is called a *subcontinent*, because it is so large and is so isolated from the rest of the continent of Asia. India is shaped like a triangle, with its eastern and western sides on the sea. Its third side, on
the north, is a great mountain wall formed by ans. 2
the Himalayas [him′ə lā′əz] and the Hindu Kush [hin′dü ku̇sh′] Mountains.

Mountain passes are doorways into India. The Himalayas make up the largest part of the mountain wall. The Hindu Kush Mountains, which are in the northwest, have openings, called *passes,* through them. For 4,000 years, invaders have pushed through these passes into India. Best known is the Khyber [kī′bər] Pass. While the mountains did not give complete protection from invasion, they helped set India apart from the rest of the world.

India's history is a story of succeeding invasions of people through the passes. As each group came, it gradually mingled with the people who had come before. The modern people of India are so intermixed it is difficult to distinguish the different races. However, the people of India can be divided into groups according to the languages they speak.

The largest group speak Indo-Aryan [in′dō er′ē ən] languages. Another major ans. 4
group speak Dravidian [drə vid′ē ən] languages. Members of this group lived in India before the Indo-Aryans came. Some historians believe they may be descendants of the people of Mohenjo-Daro. Another group is made up of people who speak Tribal languages. The ancestors of these hardy people once lived all over

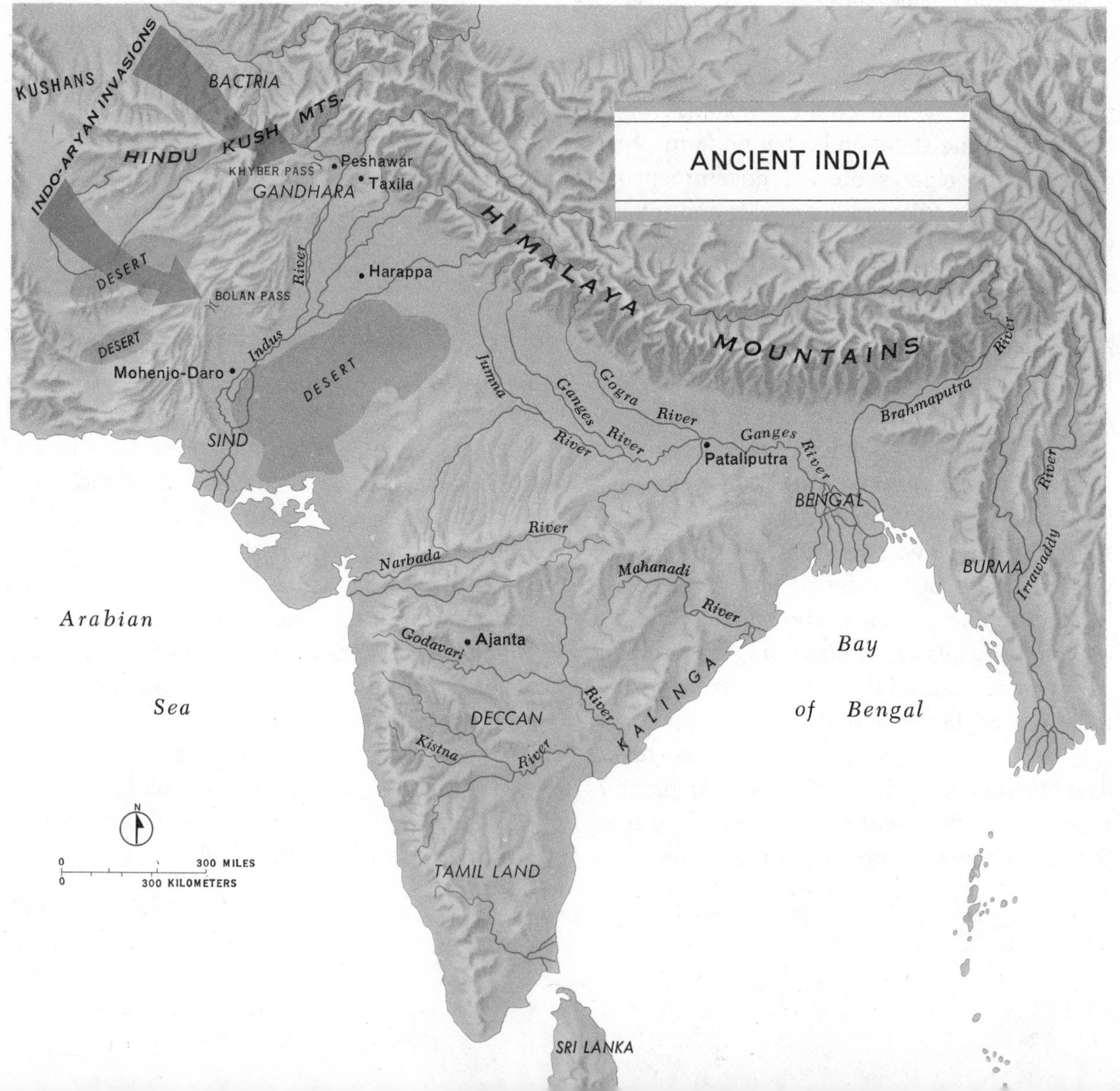

● India. Some of these people were absorbed in advancing civilizations. Others were pushed into the hills and jungles. Modern Tribal people continue to follow the fishing and food-gathering cultures their ancestors began thousands of years ago. A fourth group is made up of Mongoloids [mong′gə loidz], who live in the mountains in the far north. Their ancestors came to India from central Asia, bringing a Mongol language with them. Of these four main groups, the Indo-Aryan and the Dravidian are most important to the history of India.

Rivers and monsoons bring life-giving water. Two great river systems that cross India have also been important to Indian history.
ans. 3 On their banks most of India's history has happened. In the northwest is the Indus, where one of the first civilizations began. The Ganges [gan′jēz′] River, in the east, is sacred to the Indians, who call it "Mother." These rivers offer the only water to be found in some of the desert areas.

The climate has been as important as the physical features in shaping the lives of the people. Generally, India is an extremely hot land. The south is warm year-round; the average monthly temperature is always above 65° F. (18°C.). Rain, not temperature, distinguishes one season from another. Summer is the wet season; winter, the dry. In the northern plains, temperatures are more extreme. Summer highs of 125°F. (51°C.) have been recorded. In the winter, the temperature may reach the freezing point (32°F., 0°C.).

Above all, life in India has been dependent ■ upon its seasonal winds, called *monsoons* [mon sünz′]. The summer monsoons blow from the Arabian Sea and carry heavy moisture. If these monsoons fail, crops do not grow well and famine results. Lack of water has caused terrible crop failures and famines throughout Indian history, and much suffering and death have resulted. Great efforts have been made to guard water supplies. Thousands of ponds have been made to hold rainfall for use during the dry season.

All in all, India's geography is a picture of contrasts. There are dry deserts and heavy rainfalls. There are lands of permanent snow and the baking plains of the south. There are the highest mountains in the world with flat plains at their base. The Indian landscape is interesting, even beautiful, but the climate has been difficult to live with. This fact has influenced all aspects of Indian life.

SECTION REVIEW 1

1. Name the modern countries that make up what was once ancient India. p. 53

2. What two mountain ranges divide India from the rest of Asia? Describe two effects these mountains have had on Indian history. p. 53, 54

3. What are the two major river systems in India? p. 55

4. What makes the people of the four major groups different from each other? p. 54, 55

2 Many features of Indian life began in early times

In the period from 1500 to 500 B.C., the Indian people developed ways of living that are still ans. 1
followed today. Strict rules of social behavior and two great religions, Hinduism and Buddhism, developed then. The people began following customs that still influence how villagers make a living, worship, dress, and eat.

● Explain how a people can become part of a larger group and so lose their own culture.

■ See geography essay, p. 59.

Modern farmers in southern India use planting methods from the Vedic Age.

Indo-Aryans invaded from the northwest. About 1500 B.C., tribes of invaders began pouring through the mountain passes into northwest India. These were the Indo-Aryans, groups of people who spoke *Indo-European* languages. The Indo-Europeans came originally from central Asia. In ancient times, one branch of this large group moved westward into Greece, Italy, and western Europe. Others, such as the Hittites and Persians, moved into Asia Minor.

The Indo-Aryans were hearty eaters and drinkers who fought hard and led simple lives. They did not have writing or cities. They lived mainly by herding cattle and by farming small plots of ground. The richest families were those who had the most cattle. (The Indo-Aryan word for *war* meant "a desire for more cows.") Usually, the richest man in a tribe was the ruler, or *rajah* [rä′jə].

When the Indo-Aryans came into India, they found the Dravidians already living there. The Dravidians had created a strong, well-organized society in India, especially in the south. They had built large cities and castles, and they traded with Babylonia. Although the Indo-Aryans defeated the Dravidians, they took on many Dravidian customs and ideas, including certain parts of the Dravidian religion.

Village life took shape in the Vedic Age
ans. 2 **(1500–900 B.C.).** The first Indo-Aryan civilization lasted some 600 years, and this period is called the *Vedic* [vā′dik] (meaning "knowledge") *Age.* Information about the Indo-Aryans is found in the *Vedas,* which are collections of writings on religion, philosophy, and magic.

● Indian village life then followed much the
ans. 1 same pattern as it does today. There was a village leader, called the *headman.* Sometimes he inherited the post. Sometimes he was elected to it. An elected council of village men and women distributed land and collected taxes. The villagers were farmers or craft workers, or both. Their houses had mud walls, clay floors, and thatched roofs. A man's chief garment was a wraparound skirt, the end of which he threw over his shoulder. A woman wore a similar garment, usually wrapped tightly under her arms. Another piece of cloth covered her head.

● Indian society has been based on three factors: the independent village, the joint family, and the caste system. The rajah's government was mainly concerned with collecting taxes from the villages. The joint-family system was important in maintaining a secure society.

The family was the center of social and religious life. Families were often large. When the older sons married, they brought their wives into the family home. The grandfather was the head of the family. All males of a family group were consulted on serious matters, because property belonged to the family group as a whole. Marriage was very important, because it joined families and their property. Each person's wishes were thought to be less important than the family's interests. For thousands of years, the interests and safety of the family group dominated the life of India's villagers.

ans. 3 **Indo-Aryans set up the basis of the caste system.** At the time of their first invasions, some Indo-Aryans married Dravidians. Soon, however, the invaders began to feel that if they continued to intermarry, in a few generations they would be indistinguishable from the Dravidians. In addition, they feared that Dravidians might enter into the high government positions that the Indo-Aryans wanted for themselves. To prevent this, the Indo-Aryans developed a system of rigid social groups. Dravidians were not allowed to marry Indo-Aryans or even to associate closely with them.

For some time, the system was just a simple division between the two groups of peoples. Gradually, however, five distinct groups appeared among the Indo-Aryans: ● (1) *Brahmans,* who were priests and their families; (2) warriors and their families; (3) traders and landholding farmers; (4) serfs, and (5) *pariahs* [pə rī′əz], also called the *untouchables.* Other Indians believed that the touch, or even shadow, of a pariah would contaminate them. For a long time, the warriors ranked first. But as warfare declined and religion became more important, the Brahmans became most important.

From this beginning, the people of India developed even more rigid and complex divisions called the *caste* [kast] *system.* Hundreds of divisions were based on skin color, politics, place in society, kind of work, wealth, and religion. The members of each caste had to follow its rules for marriage, work, and religious rites. There were even rules for eating and drinking. People had to marry within their own caste. No amount of success or achievement would allow a person to move from one caste to another.

Indian writing developed. Over a period of a thousand years, the Indo-Aryans in India developed a written language called *Sanskrit* [san′skrit], which had its own alphabet. By 300 B.C., spoken Sanskrit had become different from the written forms of the language used by priests and poets.

Knowledge of Sanskrit did not reach Europe until more than 3,000 years later, in the 18th century. It then became the basis for a comparative study of languages. Many words in Greek, Latin, English, German, Persian, and other languages are also found in Sanskrit. The Sanskrit word *mata,* for example, became *mater* in Latin, *mutter* in German, and *mother* in English. The English words *brother, sister, daughter,* and *son* are directly related to the Sanskrit words *bhrata, svasir, duhita,* and *sunu.* ■

The most important Sanskrit literature is the *Rig-Veda* [rig vā′də], meaning "Hymns of Knowledge." It has 1,028 hymns of praise to different gods that were passed down by word of mouth from generation to generation. Scholars wrote many notes and explanations about the *Vedas,* called the *Upanishads* [ü pan′ə shadz]. This collection of religious writings deals with the beginning of the world and the meaning of life.

Hinduism began. The Indian religion of Hinduism had its beginnings in the Vedic Age. The early Indo-Aryans sacrificed animals to a number of gods. The *Rig-Veda* verses tell of the greatest god, Indra, who—like the main god in other religions at the time—threw thunderbolts, ate bulls by the hundred, and drank lakes of wine. But the *Rig-Veda* hymns tell about something more than the gods; they tell about a moral law that rules both gods and people. Hinduism gradually moved to a belief that the universe and everything in it was God, or *Brahma.* The many gods were like different

● The non-Aryans were at the bottom of society as serfs and outcasts.

■ This shows the relationships among Indo-European languages referred to on p. 56. The language of northern India today, Hindi, developed from the spoken languages of the 4th century B.C.

faces of Brahma. During the Vedic Age, three gods emerged as the most important: Brahma (the creator), Siva (the destroyer), and Vishnu (the preserver).

City-states developed during the Epic Age (900–500 B.C.). The Indo-Aryans had been gradually pushing east to the valley of the Ganges River and south toward the Narbada [när bä′də] River. Settlement reached these river banks about 900 B.C., marking the beginning of the 400-year-long *Epic Age.* Our knowledge of this time comes from the long poems, or epics, which were written during the period.

By the beginning of the Epic Age, the Indo-Aryans had formed many city-states. These states were almost always at war with each other. Cities of this time were protected by moats and walls. Each city had its own rajah, who had much greater power than any village headman. The rajah lived in a palace in the center of the city. He kept an army and consulted a royal council made up of relatives and other nobles. His power extended over the villages in the countryside beyond the city walls. Villages paid taxes to the rajah.

A new social class began to develop as some city people became rich through trade. They formed a middle class between the villagers and the nobles. As trade increased, people needed some form of money and credit. Copper coins came into use, and by the end of the Epic Age, banking had developed.

Literature was developed. The Epic Age produced two great epic poems, the *Mahabharata* [mä hä′bə rä′tə] and the *Ramayana*
ans. 4 [rä′mä yä′nə]. Unlike the *Vedas,* which were religious, the epics tell about the adventures of heroes of the early wars. The *Mahabharata* tells of a great war, and is probably the work of many poets. Its most famous part is a long poem, the *Bhagavad-Gita* [bug′ə vəd gē′tə], meaning "The Lord's Song," which emphasizes that one must never shirk duty nor fear death. The *Ramayana* tells of a hero's wanderings and the patient wait of his faithful wife.

Hinduism stressed rebirth. Much can be learned about Hinduism from the epics. Verses tell of the religious wish to escape from the physical world into a world of the spirit. True happiness and peace come when a person's soul is taken by the "world-soul" and becomes a part of it. The following lines from the *Bhagavad-Gita* show how Hindus see little difference between life and death. To them, the end of life is like going to a new place. They believe that after death they will be born into a new body. This belief is called *reincarnation* [rē′in kär nā′shən].

All that doth live, lives always! To man's frame
As there come infancy and youth and age,
So come there raisings-up and layings-down
Of other and of other life-abodes
Which the wise know and fear not.

By the Epic Age, Hinduism had been developing for 1,000 years. The ideas expressed in the *Bhagavad-Gita* continue to have a profound effect on peoples' lives, and Hinduism has made many great contributions to world culture. Because Hinduism recognizes many paths to truth, it has encouraged *religious toleration,* that is, the freedom to follow one's own beliefs. Hinduism has encouraged scholarship, work, love, meditation, and civic responsibility. And it has developed a deep appreciation for art and beauty.

● The caste system has become the way in which a soul proceeds from the lowest to the highest levels of the life-cycle.

■ Modern Indian leaders have often based their actions on this ancient poem. Sometimes to justify war; others have used its ideals in developing the political techniques of non-violence and passive resistance. The ancient stories of the Mahabharata and Ramayana are known to millions of Indians today. At feasts and other ceremonies these stories are chanted by holy men to crowds of listeners.

Geography: A Key to History

Monsoon Winds and Indian History

Like most other parts of southern Asia, India has been greatly affected by the seasonal winds called *monsoons.* As early as 300 B.C., people in India were writing about the monsoons.

The summer monsoon winds are mainly caused by seasonal changes in air pressure. From March to June, extremely hot air accumulates above the Deccan Plateau, forming a low-pressure area. From June through September, cooler air from the Indian Ocean sweeps across the subcontinent into this low-pressure area.

The cooler air brings heavy rains. The heaviest rains fall in the northeast corner of the subcontinent. There the clouds drop their remaining moisture before they reach the Himalayas. The rainwaters often flood the lands of the Ganges River Valley.

India gets about 90 percent of its yearly rainfall from the summer monsoons. The people rejoice at the sight of the first great drops of rain. Without the rains, crops wither and die, and the people may starve. In good years, the summer monsoons bring the right amount of rain at the right time. In bad years, the monsoon rains wash away the crops or come too early or too late. The monsoon rains are so important that in many of the Indian languages the most common words for "year" also mean "rain" or "rainy season."

From October through January, the winter winds move across India, blowing southwest from the Himalayas to the Indian Ocean. The winter monsoons are the trade winds, which blow throughout the tropical part of the Northern Hemisphere. The winter winds are cool and dry.

The monsoons have affected more than farming. During the 1st century A.D., a sea captain named Hippalus discovered that the winds in the Indian Ocean regularly blew in certain directions. By using the summer winds, ships could sail directly across the Indian Ocean from the Persian Gulf or Africa, rather than sailing along the coast. This route cut the sailing time from twelve months to two months. The winter monsoons enabled ships to make a rapid return journey. With this discovery, sea trade between India and the Mediterranean countries increased.

The monsoons have also affected warfare. Invaders have waited for the dry season before attacking. The muddy conditions that exist during the wet season bring fighting to a halt.

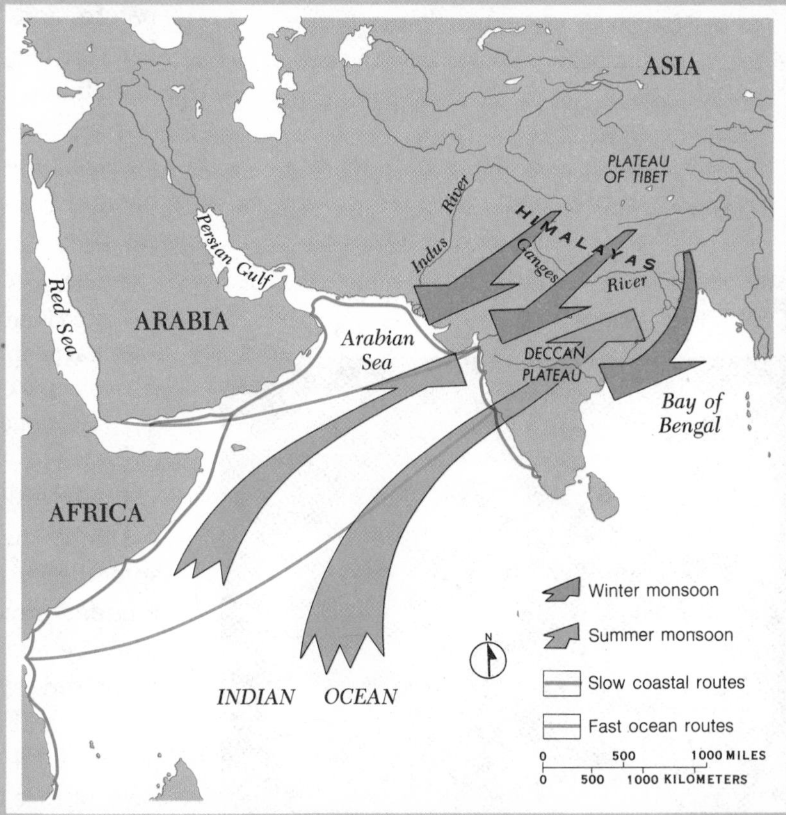

Buddhism originated in India. Some Indian thinkers disagreed with the elaborate rites of Hinduism and with the caste system. One of these was Siddhartha Gautama [sid′är′thə gô′tə mə], who lived from 563 B.C., to 483 B.C. Gautama was the son of a king whose land lay close to the Himalayas. When Gautama was twenty-nine, he left his wife and child and his easy life to search for an answer to the question, Why do people suffer pain and sorrow? He lived with holy men, fasted, and tortured himself. Then, one day as he sat meditating under a sacred tree, he felt that the truth had come to him. Thereafter, he was known as the Buddha [bü′də], a name meaning "The Enlightened One." He taught and preached for the rest of his life, and formulated these beliefs, the Four Noble Truths:

1. Human life—from birth, through old age, sickness, and death—is full of pain and sorrow.

2. Pain is caused by a longing for life, passion, and pleasures.

3. Pain can be stopped.

4. The way to stop longing and thus to end pain, is to travel the *Eightfold Path.* One must practice (a) right belief, (b) right intention, (c) right speech, (d) right action, (e) right livelihood, (f) right effort, (g) right thinking, and (h) right meditation.

The Buddha believed that by following these rules the soul would finally be freed of the bondage of rebirth and would enter *nirvana* [nir vä′nə]. Nirvana, according to the Buddha, cannot be defined, but it is the end of all earthly desires when the soul finds perfect peace.

As a reformer of the Hinduism of his time, the Buddha preached against the teachings of [ans. 5] the priests and broke with their rules of caste by treating all people alike. He also attacked the extremes of some holy men who tortured their own bodies in order to deny their physical nature and heighten their spiritual life. The Buddha taught the Middle Way, or moderation in all things.

This simple and humble teacher claimed no godlike powers. He left some of the most noble and beautiful rules for right conduct among people:

> Hatred is never ended by hatred at any time; hatred is ended by love.
>
> Let people overcome anger by love, let them overcome evil by good.
>
> Everyone trembles at punishment, everyone loves life. Remember that you are like unto them, and do not cause slaughter.

During the Buddha's lifetime, his teachings spread over all central and northern India. He founded several orders of *monks,* holy men who live apart from society. These monks built monasteries [mon′ə ster′ēz] that became centers of learning. The Buddha's followers continued his work after his death. The religion called Buddhism is based on his teachings. ●

● Gautama reformed and purified Hinduism. He accepted many of its basic principles. After his death many things he had attacked were incorporated into his teachings as his followers came to think of him as a god.

The robe and the pose of this Buddha show Greek influence in Indian art.

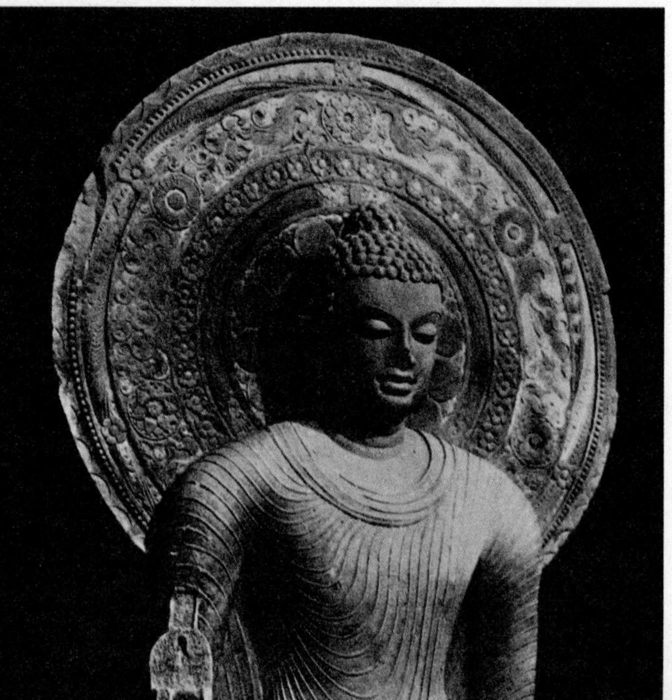

Asoka had thousands of Buddhist shrines, called *stupas* [shtu̇′pəz] built. This one holds the bones of two saints.

SECTION REVIEW 2

p. 55, 56 **1.** List at least 6 features of modern Indian life that had their beginnings between 1500 and 500 B.C. Which 3 do you think are the most important.

p. 56 **2.** What are the years of the Vedic Age? Why is the early Indo-Aryan period called the Vedic Age?

p. 57 **3.** What were the reasons behind the origin of the caste system? What changes took place in the system?

p. 58 **4.** What was the main subject of the *Vedas?* Of the epics?

p. 60 **5.** What Hindu beliefs and practices did the Buddha attack? What beliefs and practices did he encourage?

3 Strong rulers built empires in India

Shortly after the end of the Epic Age, India was threatened by a new attack from the northwest. These attackers were led by Alexander the Great, a Greek general who became one of the great conquerors of the world. He had defeated Persia in 328 B.C. Two years later, hoping to conquer still more land, he crossed the Indus River into India. He defeated an Indian army and pushed on toward the east. However, his soldiers refused to go farther, and he had to turn back.

● This was India's first empire.

The Mauryan dynasty brought unity and peace (321–184 B.C.). Alexander is said to have met and influenced a young Indian named Chandragupta Maurya [chun′drə gu̇p′tə mä′u̇r yə]. In 321 B.C., Chandragupta seized an Indian kingdom and made himself ruler from its capital, Pataliputra [pä′tə li pu′trə]. His power grew, and in the years following, he conquered all of northern India. He was the first of the Mauryan dynasty. ●

In 273 B.C., Chandragupta's grandson, Asoka [ə sō′kə], became emperor. He led a military campaign that enlarged the Mauryan Empire to include all but the southern tip of

India. But the cruelty of battle horrified him, ans. 1 and he never fought again. Asoka explained how he came to this decision. He had the following words carved on a rock for all to see:

> Kalinga was conquered by his Sacred and Gracious Majesty [Asoka] when he had been consecrated eight years. 150,000 persons were thence carried away captive, 100,000 were slain, and many times that many died. . . . Thus arose [Asoka's] remorse for having conquered the Kalingas because the conquest of a country previously unconquered involves the slaughter, death, and carrying away captive of the people.

Asoka determined to give his people peace rather than war.

At about this time, he became a Buddhist. His new religion may well have helped turn him away from warfare. Asoka commanded his people to be kind and truthful. He had rules of conduct carved on stone pillars 30 or 40 feet (9 to 12 meters) high. Some of these still stand ● today. A strong believer in not hurting people or animals, Asoka stopped the religious sacrifice of animals in Pataliputra. He encouraged nobles to make holy trips to Buddhist shrines instead of going on hunting parties. Asoka ate no meat and encouraged his people to be vegetarians. Although a devout Buddhist, he allowed other religions in his empire.

Asoka sent Buddhist missionaries north to the lands of the Himalayas, to the southern tip of India, east to Burma, and west across Syria and Egypt to Cyrene in North Africa. As a result, Buddhism became the religion of a large part of the world.

Asoka, one of the outstanding rulers in history, gave India unity and peace. But soon after his death in 232 B.C., his empire began to fall apart. The last Mauryan emperor was assassinated in 184 B.C., and a series of attacks brought northern India under foreign rule.

Greek kings ruled in India (183–130 B.C.). In the eastern part of Alexander's ans. 2 empire, bordering northern India, was the Greek kingdom of *Bactria.* Demetrius [də mē′trē əs], a Bactrian ruler, conquered part of northern India in 183 B.C. He ruled an area stretching from Persia to the middle of the Ganges Valley, including Pataliputra. Demetrius believed in joining East and West on an equal basis. Coins during his rule had Greek writing on one side and Indian on the other.

An important development that came from this mixing of cultures is seen in the religious art, called Gandharan [gand här′ən]. Because ■ the Buddha had taught against the worship of idols, artists up to this time had never shown him in human form. In Gandharan art, the Buddha is shown in a beautiful form; his face is graceful and peaceful.

In 130 B.C., Bactria, with its majority of Indian people and a ruling Greek class, was attacked by nomads from central Asia. Greek rule in India was over.

Kushan rulers (78–200 A.D.) helped spread Buddhism. A period of many wars and different rulers followed the fall of Bactria. But by the 1st century A.D., an Asian tribe called the Kushans [ku̇ shanz′] had proved themselves to be the most important of the invading tribes.

The most powerful Kushan king, Kanishka [kə nish′kə], became ruler about 78 A.D. He ruled over a large area of Asia, including what is now Afghanistan and northwestern India. He pushed his boundaries south, perhaps as far as the Narbada River. He built fine buildings in his

● These inscriptions show that writing was highly developed at that time and also that it was commonly used throughout the empire.

■ Ask students if they can see the Greco-Roman influence in the Gandharan art shown on p. 60. Refer to Chapters 5 & 6 for pictures of Greco-Roman art.

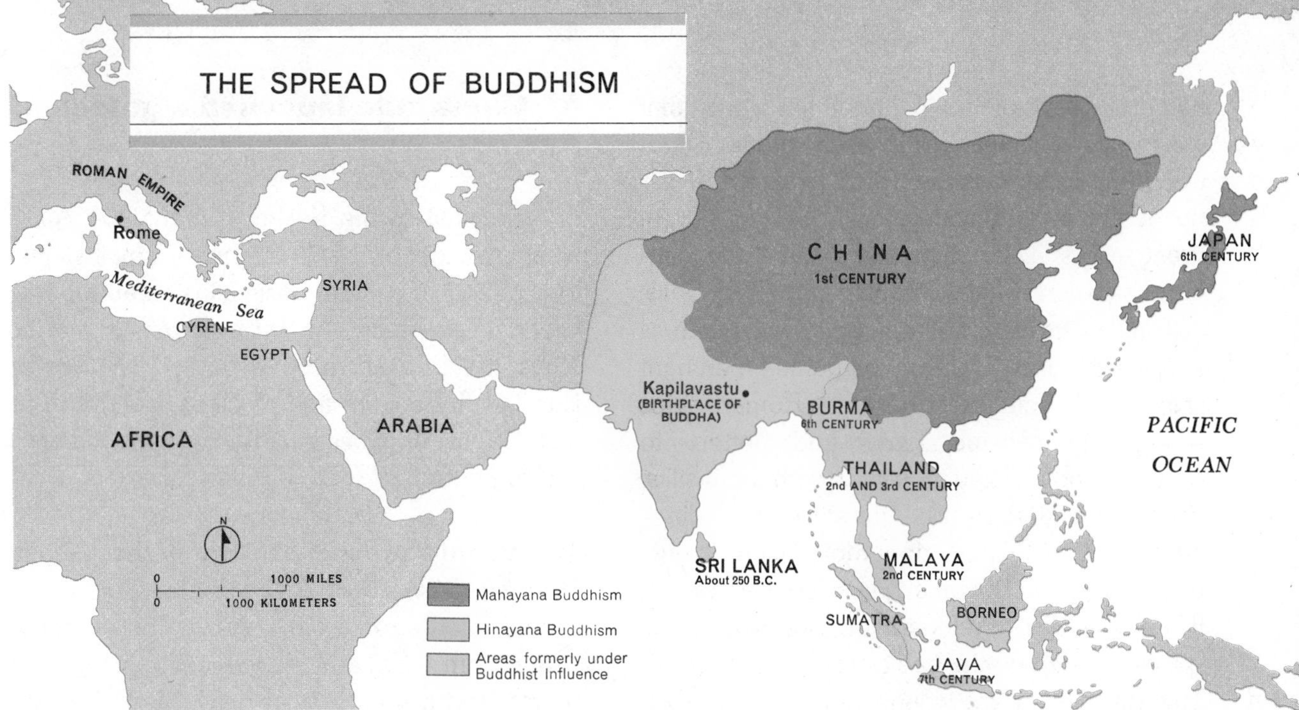

capital, Peshawar [pə shä′wər]. One of his best-remembered buildings was an immense wooden tower, said to be 600 feet (180 meters) high. It was decorated with many figures of Buddha and was still standing as late as the 6th century A.D. Foreign visitors thought of it as one of the wonders of the world.

Kanishka was a patron of Buddhism. During his reign, Gandharan art flourished. Many statues were carved to honor Buddha. In a secluded valley of what is now Afghanistan, carvings were made on the face of a rock cliff. One image of Buddha is 115 feet (30 meters) high, another is 170 feet (51 meters). A person standing by the second carving only comes up to the toe of the image.

Kanishka called together a great council of 500 monks. They developed what is known as
ans. 3 the Mahayana [mä′hə yä′nə] school of Buddhism. The believers of this school added to the original Buddhist traditions. One difference is that they believe in a great number of minor gods who help people reach nirvana. Mahayana Buddhism spread through much of northern Asia, China, Mongolia, Tibet, and Japan. The traditional, or Hinayana [hē′nə yä′nə] Buddhism, was strongest in Burma, Thailand, and Malaya, and also on the island of Sri Lanka (formerly Ceylon).

Southern India traded with Rome. During the Kushan period, India carried on a flourishing trade with the western world. By this time, the enormous Roman Empire had grown up along the Mediterranean Sea. With its capital at Rome, it included the northern coast of Africa, Spain, Europe to the Rhine River, and many of the eastern lands that Alexander had conquered. There was a great exchange of goods between the Kushan and Roman empires. Most of it passed through the ports of southern India.

The people of the south, the *Tamils* [tam′əlz], were descendants of the Dravidians. They

● See map of the Roman Empire, p. 111.

had built several independent kingdoms that were often at war with each other. Especially important was the Tamil kingdom at the tip of the Indian peninsula. The Tamils were great sailors. Their ships could travel the dangerous waters of the Arabian and Red Seas.

Tamil ports were well-equipped with wharves and warehouses. Lighthouses guided merchant
ans. 4 ships safely into their harbors. Roman ships brought gold, wine, glass, and pottery to
● southern India. They took back with them silks, pearls, rice, and spices. The spices of India—pepper, ginger, and cinnamon—were highly valued by the Romans. Food spoiled fast in those days before refrigeration, and rich-tasting spices covered up the bad taste of spoiling food. The silks that went in and out of these ports came either by a long journey overland across central Asia or by sea in Chinese ships, called *junks*.

Harbors on the west coast of Tamil land were crowded with merchants, caravan leaders, and sailors. There were so many outsiders that special settlements were built to house them. With this incoming population came a number of Arabs, Jews, and Christians whose descendants live in south India today.

SECTION REVIEW **3**

p. 62 **1.** Why was Asoka's first military campaign also his last? How did he encourage Buddhism?

p. 62 **2.** During what years did Greeks rule a part of India? What effect did this rule have on Indian religious art?

p. 63 **3.** What is the name of the new form of Buddhism that grew up under Kanishka? Where is it practiced today?

p. 64 **4.** How do we know that Indians traded with the Roman Empire? What goods were traded by the Indians and the Romans?

● Excavations have uncovered large amounts of Roman coins in southern India, as well as pieces of pottery inscribed with the names of Italian craftsmen. An ivory statuette of an Indian goddess was found in the ruins of Pompeii.

■ Some Buddhist teachings were adopted by Hindus.

4 Gupta rule launched a golden age

After the fall of the Kushans about 200 A.D., northern India broke up into many small states. This period of cultural decline lasted about 100 years. Then in the 4th century, a new line of kings, the *Guptas,* came to power. Their reign is called the golden age of Hindu culture. The first Gupta king became ruler of the Ganges Valley about 320 A.D.

The people prospered during the Gupta Empire (320–500 A.D.). The Gupta emperors ruled strongly and fairly. Their income came from port duties, the royal lands and mines, and a tax on farm produce. Trade and manufacturing flourished. So good was life in the Empire that a Chinese Buddhist who went to India wrote:

> . . . The people are many and happy. They do not have to register their households with the police. There is no death penalty. Religious groups have houses of charity where rooms, couches, beds, food, and drink are supplied to travelers.

Buddhism, however, was no longer one of
the chief religions. In time, it almost entirely ■
disappeared from the land of its founder. As foreign invaders, such as the Greeks and Kushans, took to Buddhism, its Indian followers
became fewer. People began to feel that ans. 1
Hinduism was a more truly Indian religion. Gupta rulers also aided Hinduism by supporting its priests.

Learning and art flourished. Learning and science grew under the Guptas. The astronomer and mathematician, Aryabhata [är′yə-

Dancers in the temple inspired this Gupta sculpture.

ans. 2 but′ə], wrote verses about the value of pi (π), and the rotation and spherical shape of the earth. Other Indian astronomers calculated the size of the moon and wrote on gravitation.

● The contributions of Indian mathematicians to world civilization are among the greatest of any people. They developed the number symbols that served as the basis for our own numerals. (It is because these symbols were adopted and carried westward by Arab traders that they are called Arabic numerals.) Gupta scholars also worked out the decimal system and were among the first—along with the Maya Indians of Yucatan—to use the zero.

Indians found new uses for chemistry in manufacturing. Their steel was the best in the world. They were the first to make cashmere and such cotton fabrics as calico and chintz. Gupta doctors were among the best doctors of the time. In special schools begun during this time, physicians learned to clean wounds, do surgery, and treat snake bites.

Gupta literature is famous for its fairy tales and fables. The most famous storybook of the time is the Panchatantra [pan′chə tan′trə]. This collection of eighty-seven stories was written between 300 and 500 A.D. Other Indian writings included the world-famous story of Sinbad that finally found its way into *The Arabian Nights.* Some Indian fables were later translated into European languages and were used by such authors as Chaucer, the Grimms, and Kipling in their tales. Much good poetry and drama also belongs to the Gupta period.

● Students from all over Asia attended India's university at Nalanda. Founded in the fifth century, it had an enrollment of 10,000 students.

During the time of the Gupta Empire, Indian painters and sculptors freed themselves from Greek influences to create a distinctly Indian art. Artists, inspired chiefly by Hinduism, produced dignified and restrained work. The Ajanta cave paintings are well known for their beauty.

Indian culture influenced other peoples. From about the 2nd to the 10th centuries, Indian emigrants, traders, and armies carried their way of life to all of Southeast Asia. The influences were gradual but eventually reached as far away as Madagascar and Taiwan.

Indian influence was strongest in such places ans. 3
as Sri Lanka, Burma, and what is now central Thailand. Here the cultures became almost entirely Indian. In more distant places such as Java, Cambodia, and southern Indochina, Indian influence was not so strong, and Indian culture blended with local customs.

Indian art, however, made a strong impression on all of Southeast Asia. In central Java, the world's largest Buddhist shrine shows Indian influence. About the same time, Hindus in Cambodia began one of the greatest religious buildings in the world, the temple of Angkor Wat [ang′kōr wät′].

Centuries of disunity followed Gupta decline. Gupta power began to decline after Chandragupta II died in 413 A.D. The Huns, a fierce people from the central Asian plains, invaded northwestern India near the end of the 5th century. By the middle of the 6th century, the Gupta Empire was ended.

Small states continued to make war on one another until early in the 7th century when a ruler named Harsha brought order. He made himself master of most of the area of the Gupta Empire between 606 and 612. Harsha was a patron of the arts, a poet, and a good military leader and administrator. He was a despot, though a kindly one. When he died in 647, he left no one trained to take his place. All of northern India again fell into warfare.

Not only was there no strong government, but other areas of life also suffered. There was no progress in learning or thinking. The Hindus
ans. 4 had become satisfied with what they had and what they were. As a 10th-century visitor to India wrote:

> The Hindus believe that there is no country but theirs, no nation like theirs, no religion like theirs, no sciences like theirs. . . . If they traveled and mixed with other nations they would soon change their mind, for their ancestors were not so narrow-minded as the present generation.

This Indian attitude not only halted progress, it also weakened the country. Their self-imposed isolation kept them from learning of new methods of warfare. Because of this weakness, the Indians could not defend themselves against a new wave of attacks.

SECTION REVIEW 4

1. Why did Buddhism lose most of its followers in India? p. 64

2. What contributions did Gupta scholars make in science, technology, mathematics, and literature? p. 65

3. In what areas of Southeast Asia was Indian influence strongest? Where did it have less effect? p. 65

4. What weakened India after 647 A.D.? p. 66

Angkor Wat in Cambodia is one of the most beautiful examples of Hindu building.

CHAPTER REVIEW 3

SECTION SUMMARIES

1. Geography shaped history in India. Surrounded on two sides by water, India traded with both east and west. The mountains on the north protected it, but there are passes through which warring tribes attacked. Two great river systems provided fertile soil for the development of civilization. A hot climate, wet and dry seasons, and the monsoons have influenced the way Indians farm, trade, and wage war.

2. Many features of Indian life began in early times. Indo-Aryan invaders defeated the Dravidians and pushed them towards the south. But the mingling of cultures produced some basic features of Indian culture. Among the most important were the village community, the caste system, and the Hindu religion. In the first stage of this development, the Vedic Age, Sanskrit writing became well developed and religious writings were produced. In the following Epic Age, city-states grew strong, a middle class developed through trade, and great poems were produced. Another Eastern religion, Buddhism, was also begun in India at this time. Its founder, Gautama Buddha, wanted to reform Hinduism. Instead, his followers made a religion of his teachings after his death.

3. Strong rulers built empires in India. Shortly after an invasion by Alexander the Great, northern India was united under the Mauryan dynasty. Asoka, an important ruler of this dynasty, brought peace and spread Buddhism. The decline of the Mauryas in the 2nd century B.C. was followed by other invasions. Rule by Greeks from Bactria gave rise to an important Buddhist art style, called Gandharan, which began then and spread to parts of Asia. The Kushans, who controlled northern Indian areas for 200 years, also aided the growth of Buddhism. During the Kushan period, a lively trade with the West moved through Tamil ports.

4. Gupta rule launched a golden age. The Gupta Empire was a prosperous time. Many contributions were made to the world, including the numerals now used in most of the world, the decimal system, and advances in astronomy and medicine. Writers and artists also made important contributions to the civilization of India. Indian influence in art and religion reached the people of Southeast Asia. However, because Gupta rulers favored Hinduism, Buddhism almost disappeared from the land of its birth.

After the Guptas, India was thrown into discord. During a brief period in the 7th century, Harsha provided strong rule. Following his death, there was a 800-year-long period of isolation and decline.

WHO? WHAT? WHEN? WHERE?

1. Why is each of these names important in Indian history?

Chandragupta Maurya	Demetrius
Siddhartha Gautama	Kanishka
Alexander the Great	Harsha
Asoka	Aryabhata

2. What is the importance of these terms to the Hindu religion: *Rig Veda,* Brahma, Siva, Vishnu, reincarnation?

3. What question was Gautama trying to find the answer to when he left his family?

4. In which of these time periods did each of the following events occur:

f	1500–1001 B.C.	1–500 A.D.	c, h
g, i	1000–501 B.C.	501–1000 A.D.	a
b, d, j	500–1 B.C.	1001–1500 A.D.	e

a. Harsha brought peace to India.
b. Gautama Buddha died.
c. Gupta rule began.
d. Alexander the Great crossed the Indus River into India.

1. Answers will vary. Encourage students to express their ideas in their own words.
2. From pp. 57, 58.
3. Why do people suffer?

e. The Cambodian temple, Angkor Wat, was finished.
f. The Vedic Age began.
g. The *Mahabharata* was written.
h. Kaniska built great monuments to Buddha.
i. Indo-Aryan settlements reached the Ganges and Narbada rivers.
j. Gandharan art began.

5. Locate the areas covered by each of the following at the time given:
a. Mauryan Empire, about 270 B.C.
b. Bactrian Empire, in 183 B.C.
c. Mahayana Buddhism, about 100 A.D.
d. Tamils, about 100 A.D.
e. Spread of Indian culture, 2nd to 10th centuries

QUESTIONS FOR CRITICAL THINKING

1. Compare Indian family life and marriage with that in the United States. In what ways are they alike? Different?

2. What are some of the original sources of information about early Indian life mentioned in this chapter? Why were they written? When?

3. What is your opinion of the caste system? Was there any opposition to that system in early times? Explain.

4. What usually happened when an important leader, such as Asoka, or Harsha, died?

5. How are Hinduism and Buddhism alike? How are they different? If you were an Indian ruler, which would you choose to follow? Why?

ACTIVITIES

1. Pretending you are a visitor to India during the Gupta Empire, write a letter home describing your experiences.

2. Read one or both of the excerpts from the *Bhagavad-Gita* and Buddha's *Four Noble Truths;* write a paragraph telling what these writings mean to you.

5. a. pp. 61–62, capital Pataliputra p. 54, b. see map p. 63, c. See the map p. 63 d. See the map p. 54 e. All of Southeast Asia.
QUESTIONS FOR CRITICAL THINKING
1. Answers will vary.
2. Examples are given throughout chapter.

CHAPTER TEST 3

SECTION 1

1. The mountains to the north of India are the Himalayas.

2. The people of India are divided into groups by their: a. height, b. language, c. race

3. True or false: The two great rivers of India are the Gupta and the Ganges.

4. One of the passes through which invaders have entered India is the: a. Khyber, b. Tamil, c. Harsha

SECTION 2

5. The first group to live in India were the: a. Indo-Aryans, b. Tamils, c. Dravidians

6. In Indian family life, which is most important? a. family unit, b. individual, c. children

7. The Vedic and Epic ages of Indian history are named for written works

8. The three most important Hindu gods are Brahma, Siva, and Vishnu.

SECTION 3

9. True or false: Alexander the Great conquered India in 330 B.C.

10. True or false: The peace and unity of Asoka's empire lasted 100 years.

11. The first art form to show Buddha as a human was: a. Malayan, b. Gandharan, c. Mahayanan

SECTION 4

12. In the 10th century, Indians had become weak because they were: a. trying to conquer other nations, b. ill from diseases, c. too satisfied with their way of life

13. Write *T* if the statement is *true* about the Gupta Empire; *F* if it is *false;* and *N* if no evidence is given for the statement.
T a. Arabic numerals were developed
N b. algebra and geometry were invented
F c. Buddhism reached its peak
T d. Indian culture influenced all of Southeast Asia

3. Buddha is one example.
4. Empires distintegrated because of dependence on one-person rule.
5. Answers will vary. Both accept reincarnation. Buddhism teaches moderation.

1027 B.C.–
900 A.D.

CHAPTER
4

The Great Age of China

The Great Wall of China extends for miles across the mountains to protect the Chinese from invaders. Troops and traders have traveled along the stone walkway. Soldiers have guarded the borders from the watchtowers.

Astronauts in orbit looking down at Earth can see little evidence that the planet is inhabited. Only two features of human existence can be seen: smog over major cities and the Great Wall of China. It is the longest wall in the world. It extends for 1,500 miles (2,400 kilometers), crossing mountains and blocking narrow valleys. The building of the Wall was begun in the 3rd century B.C. A Chinese ruler decided that the empire needed a defensive barrier against the Huns, tribal nomads who periodically attacked China's northern borders.

Building the wall was an amazing undertaking. The forced labor of thousands of men was used. Huge blocks of stone had to be cut and moved from quarries and then fitted into the wall. Many men were killed in accidents. It is said that every block cost a human life.

When it was completed, the wall was 40 to 50 feet (12 to 15 meters) high, and its base measured 15 to 30 feet (4.5 to 9 meters) in width. In some places, it consisted of three different walls, built one behind the other for better defense. Every few miles there were tall watch towers, where guards could look across the countryside for signs of invaders. Behind the Wall were permanent camps for soldiers.

The Wall gave the Chinese long periods of safety. Only a handful of invaders have been able to break through it. The Wall has been called one of the wonders of the world. It is to China what the Pyramids are to Egypt. Over the years various rulers have repaired or improved the wall.

The course of Chinese history described in this chapter covers about 2,000 years. During this long period, China profited from important inventions, such as printing and the making of paper. It developed the first civil service system in the world, and it gained from the wisdom of fine philosopher-teachers. Great poetry and matchless painting were produced. In this chapter, you will find that:

1. Geography helps explain the Chinese story.

2. The Chou dynasty ruled longest in China.

3. Two dynasties united China.

4. The Tang dynasty gave China a golden age.

● Have students locate the geographical features mentioned in this section on the map on p. 71, paying special attention to the natural barriers which have isolated China.

1 Geography helps explain the Chinese story

In every country, geography has some influence on how people live. However, different aspects of geography are important in different countries. In India, for example, climate is the most important geographic influence. In China, the land itself is most important.

Natural borders isolated China. China covers an area a little larger than that of the 50 United States. China's borders of sea, jungles, mountains, and deserts are natural barriers that have hampered invaders from other parts of the world. Until the 19th century, the wide salt marshes on the seacoast and the lack of harbors stopped invaders from the east. To the south, mountains and the thick jungles of Indochina also made a natural border. At the west, the rugged Plateau of Tibet, more than 10 thousand feet (3,000 meters) above sea level, and the towering Himalayas protected China.

ans. 1 ●

Only at the north and northwest have outsiders been periodically successful at invading China. There, the Gobi (gō′bē) – the huge desert of Mongolia (mong gō′lē ə) – and other parts of central Asia have been home to nomadic tribes called the Huns for thousands of years. In these dry regions, there was little farming. The Huns moved their settlements each season as their herds grazed on the vast but scanty grasslands. In dry years, there would be little grass for the herds. Then the tribes would begin to push south into the fertile valleys of China.

The isolation of China, and the fact that many of the neighboring peoples lived as nomads rather than as farmers or as city people,

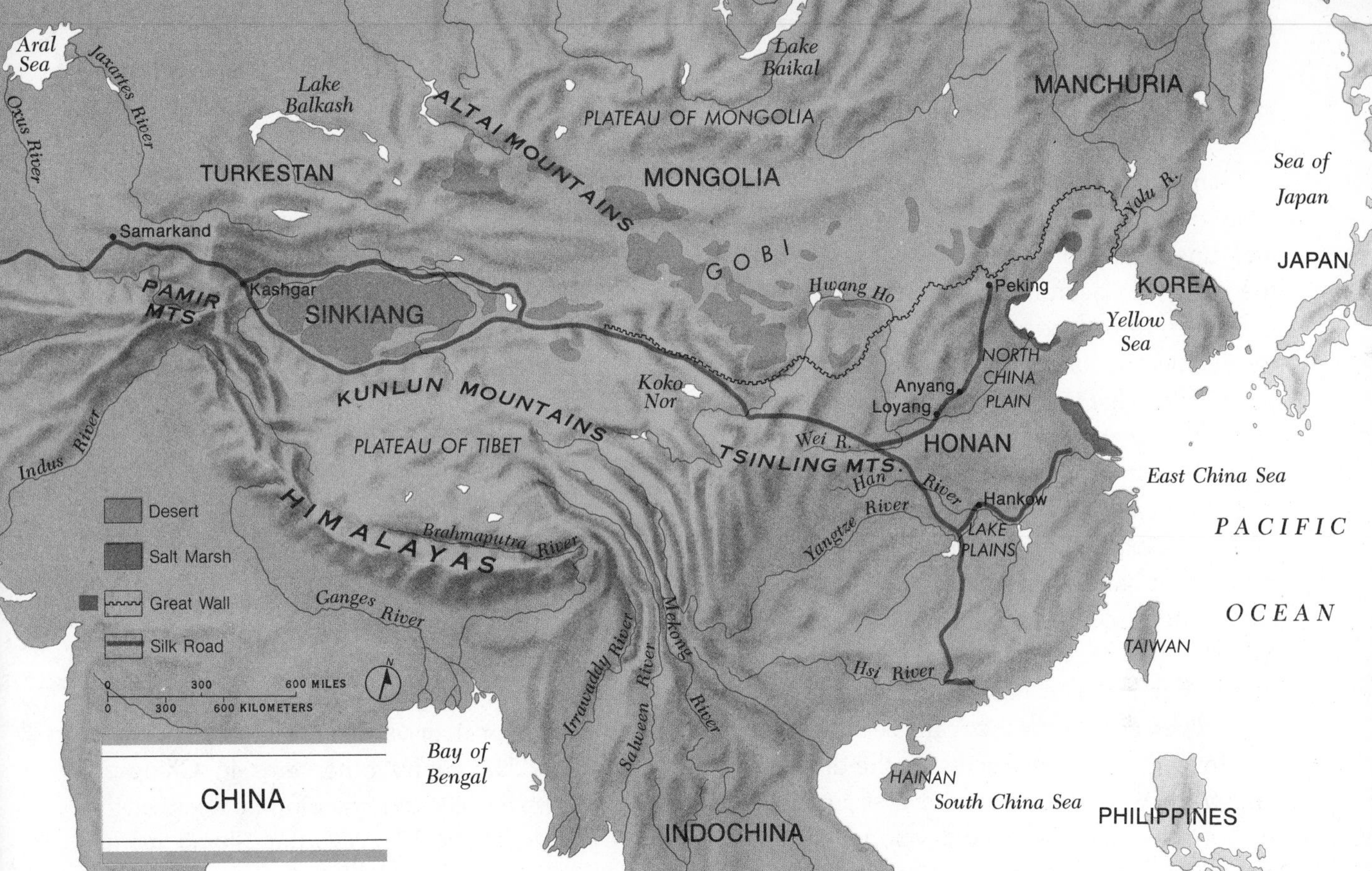

ans. 2 led the Chinese to think of themselves as superior. They spoke of their country as the Middle Kingdom and considered it to be the center of the world. The people who lived in the barren wastes of central Asia were said to live in the Outer Kingdoms.

Within China itself, natural features isolated different parts of the country from each other. The rough, hilly land made it difficult to build roads across China. The Tsinling (ching′ling′) Mountains naturally separate northern China from southern China. Northern China is relatively dry and has seasonal changes in temperature similar to those in the northeastern United States. Southern China is relatively wet, because monsoon winds from the Pacific Ocean bring large amounts of rain. The temperatures are similar to those in the southeastern United States.

■ The Great Wall is shown on the above map as it is today. By comparing this map with that on page 74, students can see evidence that the wall has been added to and changed over the centuries.

Fertile valleys aided the growth of civilization. High in the western mountains, fewer than 100 miles apart, are two streams. One flows northeast, the other, southeast. These streams are the headwaters of the two biggest river systems of China — the Hwang Ho and the Yangtze [yang′tsē]. Both rivers carry rich silt as well as water. Chinese civilization developed in the fertile valleys formed by these rivers. The valley of the Hsi [shē] River, in the south, has also been important in Chinese history.

The Hwang Ho meanders through the loess-filled plains of northern China. Because the river often floods, through the centuries the Chinese have built dikes, or *levees,* to keep it within its banks. In the process, they also created irrigation systems. Governments developed in part because of the need to control the dikes and irrigation systems. ●

● Remind students that similar developments occurred in ancient Egypt.

Chinese civilization developed first in the Hwang Ho Valley. Since the river is shallow and unsuitable for navigation by large boats, the valley has been more important as a millet- and wheat-growing area than as a trading center. As the population grew, people moved past the hills to settle in the Yangtze Valley.

The Yangtze flows through the rough, hilly land of southern China. Much of its course lies in the so-called lake plains. Here small rivers and lakes expand and contract, depending on the season and the amount of rainfall. The small bodies of water ultimately flow into the Yangtze, making it a river that varies greatly in width. For instance near Hankow, where the Han River flows into the Yangtze, the river is 3/4 mile (1 kilometer) across in the dry season and 5 miles (8 kilometers) across in the wet season. The Chinese have developed irrigation systems that use this water to grow rice.

The culture of southern China is quite different from that of the north. Food, language, clothing, housing—all reflect the isolation of the two areas and the differences in climate and land. The Yangtze is navigable for 600 miles (960 kilometers) inland, and it was an early trade route.

In the southernmost part of China is the Hsi Valley, which is farmable year-round. It is isolated from the rest of China by rough hills. The point where the river empties into the South China Sea is one of the few natural harbors in China. The villages near the river's mouth developed as trading centers.

SECTION REVIEW **1**

p. 70 **1.** Name the four types of geographic barriers that have kept China separated from other parts of the world. Tell where each barrier is found.

2. How did the Chinese think of themselves and their neighbors? How would this attitude add to their isolation from non-Chinese peoples? p. 71

3. Name three ways the geography of southern p. 71
China affected the people's lives. Give two ways 72
in which life in northern China was different from ●
life in southern China.

2 The Chou dynasty ruled longest in China

The Shang dynasty had flourished in the region of the Hwang Ho Valley—the most northern of the three major river valleys in China. This period ended, like many other eras in Chinese history, with a successful invasion by a less civilized people. In 1027 B.C., the Shang were conquered by a group of people who lived on the northern edge of the Shang territory. The leader of this less civilized group was known as *Chou* [jō]. The dynasty named after him lasted until 256 B.C.—almost 800 years.

Strong nobles ruled feudal states. During the first 250 years or so of the Chou dynasty, the kingdom was made up of more than 1,000 *feudal* [fyü′dl] states. (A feudal state is ruled by a noble who gets his authority from the king. In return, he owes the king soldiers to keep order and to extend the borders of the kingdom.) At first, the nobles were loyal to the king. Toward the end of this period, however, ans. 1 the nobles used their soldiers to fight among themselves and increase the size of their own states. Finally in 771 B.C., some of the nobles joined together and marched on the Chou capital at Loyang [lō′yäng′] in the province of Honan [hō′nan′]. There they killed the king.

● Answers will vary.

A new Chou king was allowed to take the throne, but he had little power. He became hardly more than a high priest who performed state religious rituals and tried to keep peace among the nobles. During this period, the Chinese moved into and settled the richly fertile river valley of the Yangtze [yang′tsē]. The stronger nobles gained control over the land of the weaker nobles. As a result, the number of feudal states decreased, but those that survived increased in power.

The last 200 years of the Chou period are sometimes called the Era of Warring States. During this time, the strong nobles were constantly battling with one another. They invented catapults to break down the mud walls of enemy towns. For the first time, small groups of archers riding on horses were used to make sudden attacks. ●

Life for the rich merchants and nobles was luxurious and elegant. This was in sharp contrast to the poverty among the peasants and unskilled workers. The poor lived in mud huts with thatched roofs of straw. The rich had homes that were groups of buildings with courtyards, gardens, and tiled roofs. In the north, the poor lived on a food grain called millet. In the south, they ate rice. Everywhere, rich people had huge banquets using the "five flavors"—sweet, sour, salty, spicy, and bitter.

The rich developed an elaborate social code in the nobles' courts. They took part in archery contests that were accompanied by music and were more like ballets than sporting events. In their free time, the rich played checkers, gambled with dice, hunted, fenced, and trained horses and dogs. The peasants had few comforts, paid taxes to the rich, served as soldiers, and had no political rights. The nobles were separated from the peasants by land ownership and family descent—a system that did not change for hundreds of years.

Jade symbol of heaven (late Chou), for 3,000 years an important religious medal

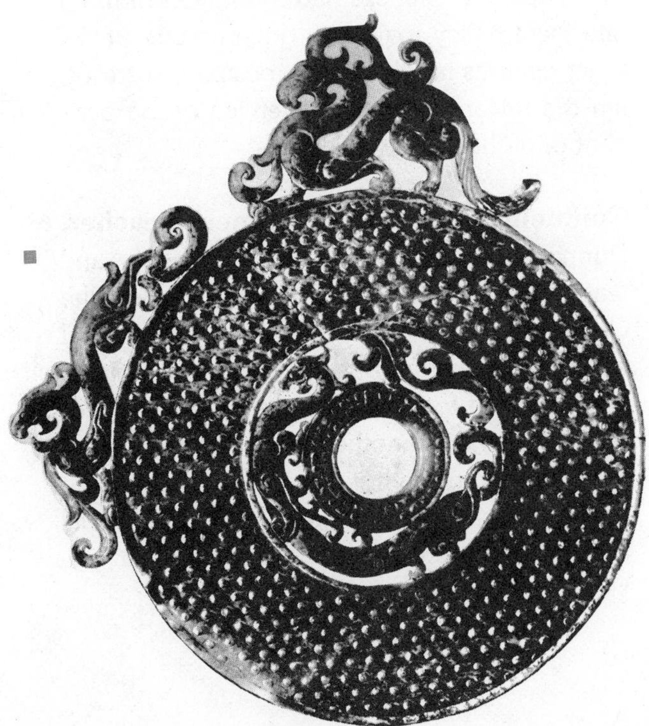
■

The Chou period made lasting achievements. Even though there was much confusion and fighting among the nobles, the 800 years of Chou rule were perhaps the most important in Chinese history. This time is often called the *classical* period because many basics of Chinese civilization were formed at that time.

During the Chou period, economic life in China changed greatly. Towns grew in size and number as many people became merchants or artisans. Skilled workers who had the same trade started organizations to help each other and to improve the quality of their work. Canals were dug to move goods more easily, and better ways of irrigating the land were found.

Even though farming methods improved, many farmers found it hard to make a living. The farms were often too small to produce

● Horseback riding was learned from the nomads of Central Asia who were enemies of the Chinese.

■ This symbol was as well known to the Chinese as the cross is to Christians.

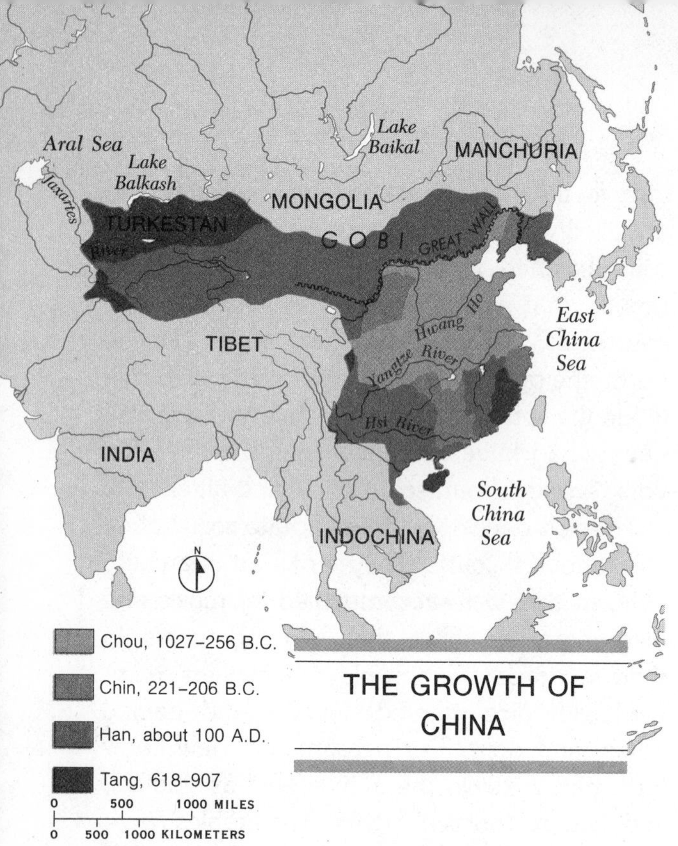

THE GROWTH OF CHINA

crop surpluses to be stored for use at times when the harvests were bad.

Because the family unit was very important in Chinese culture, family members stayed together. As the population grew, more and more people had to be supported from the harvests of farms that were already too small. This problem, which began during the Chou dynasty, remained until the Chinese communist government in the 20th century broke up farm holdings and redistributed the people to where their work was needed.

Trade grew during the Chou dynasty, although most of it took place within the Chou kingdom itself. The goods traded included jade ornaments, bronze mirrors and vessels, iron tools, silks, furs, and furniture. During the Chou period, small coins with square holes were being made and used in trade. These continued as the basic coinage until late in the 19th century.

The Chou era was also an important time for the government of China. The Chinese, like the Egyptians, believed that their ruler was divine. Beginning with the Chou period, the Chinese called their king the *Son of Heaven.* Unlike the Egyptians, however, the Chinese limited the power of their kings. When the Chous came to power, they said that they were right in taking over because the Shangs had not ruled well and therefore had lost the support of the gods. In this theory, called the *Mandate of Heaven,* all rulers were expected to govern justly and to look after the well-being of the people. If a king did not do this, he would no longer have the support and favor of the gods and could be overthrown by his people. This belief made people feel that revolution was sometimes necessary and right.

The king was aided by a chief minister and six department heads. They were chosen for their intelligence rather than their birth. They headed the departments of agriculture, public works, war, religious affairs, finance, and justice. Thus, the Chinese had a tradition of using intelligent policy makers in government, unlike other cultures in which such positions were often the reward for military service or the accident of birth.

Confucius was a great Chinese teacher. During the Chou period, great thinkers and teachers drew up rules of conduct for the Chinese people. These leaders decided what should be worn for special occasions, how to serve and eat food, and the way in which people talked to one another. Even the conduct of a son toward his father, a wife toward her husband, a friend toward a friend, and other social relationships were regulated. This code of politeness changed little until recent times.

One of the greatest Chinese teachers, Kung-fu-tze, is better known in the West today as Confucius [kən fyü′shəs]. He is the most honored and revered person in all of Chinese history.

Confucius was born in 551 B.C., only a few years after the Buddha. He began to teach when he was 22 years old. One story about him tells that when he was 52 years old, he was so famous that the prince of his state asked him to become governor of a province. Confucius gave the people good government, but a jealous neighboring governor forced him to resign. Confucius tried to get other princes to use his plans of government. When this did not work, he went back to teaching.

Confucius did not think of himself as an inventor of new ideas. He thought of himself as one who passed on the ideas of others. He is believed to have preserved the literature of China for later times. Because he lived during a troubled era, Confucius feared that the literature would be lost. Therefore, he gathered earlier writings together into what are called the "Five Classics."

Unlike the Buddha, Confucius did not seek
ans. 2 to escape from the world. Instead, he wanted to find a way for people to be happy on Earth. Confucius taught that human nature is good, not bad. If people would think and act properly, he believed, most evils would disappear. His teachings held that individuals should be tolerant and kind and have respect for older people and ancestors. In government, he believed that the ruler was like the father in a family. The ruler directed the government, but was responsible for the welfare of his people. Confucius also stressed the importance of education, good manners, and respect for the ways of the past.

Many of the sayings of Confucius are in a book called the *Analects*. These samples show his wisdom and understanding of human nature:

> A man who has committed a mistake and doesn't correct it is committing another mistake.
>
> A man who brags without shame will find great difficulty in living up to this bragging.
>
> He was asked, "What do you think of repaying evil with kindness?" Confucius replied, "Then what are you going to repay kindness with? Repay kindness with kindness, but repay evil with justice."
>
> A gentleman blames himself, while a common man blames others.
>
> To know what you know and know what you don't know is the mark of one who knows.

The teachings of Confucius gave a useful standard of correct behavior for the people of China and had a great influence on them. His followers combined his teachings with their religious ideas about ancestor worship to make a religion called *Confucianism* [kən fyü′shə niz′əm], which continues today.

The Chinese religion, unlike that of the people of India, has little to do with the mystery of the afterlife. As Confucius once said, "While you do not know life, what can you know about death?" The main concern of the Chinese since the days of the Chou has been how to have a happy, well-balanced life in this world. They have always respected learning and have given top position to the scholar and philosopher.

Great as Confucius was, he may not have ans. 3
been altogether good for China. He loved tradition and the past. He stimulated in the Chinese a strong dislike for change that had serious consequences in later years.

Taoism grew out of Lao-tse's teachings. Chou China produced another great teacher, Lao-tse [lou′ tse′]. Very little is known about him as a person, but his teachings make up a religion known as *Taoism* [dou′iz′əm]. It has had a great influence on China. This religion holds that the best way to live is according to nature. The word *Tao* means "way." Taoists believe that those who follow this way, as taught by Lao-tse, will learn the meaning of the universe. The religion holds that people should be kind, free from pride, humble, thrifty, and should return an injury with a great kindness. Confucius had stressed the importance of good government. Lao-tse, however, believed that the less people are governed, the better off they are.

Over the centuries, simple Taoism became buried under a great deal of superstition and magic. Many Taoist teachers claimed they had supernatural powers. They could foretell the future and prolong life "through breathing exercises and diets of powdered dragon bones, moonbeams, and mother of pearl." Sorcery, fortune telling, and charm selling eventually became important activities of Taoist believers. But early Taoists, because of their stress on nature and inner peace, made important contributions to Chinese thought. Taoism provided a simple, acceptable philosophy to the Chinese people that greatly strengthened social order and internal peace.

Art and literature flourished. Especially in
ans. 4 painting, some of the most beautiful art the world has ever seen has been produced by Chinese artists. A large amount of the art produced in the Chou period has been excavated. This includes handsome bronze vases used in religious ceremonies, many pieces of carved jade, and lacquer and pottery ware. Chou artists carved jade and ivory very well. *Jade* is a ● semiprecious stone that is usually whitish or soft green in color. However, the most prized stones are emerald green or pure white. Once, when Confucius was asked why the Chinese liked jade so much, he said:

> It is because, ever since the olden days, wise men have seen in jade all the different virtues. It is soft, smooth, and shining, like kindness; it is hard, fine, and strong, like intelligence; its edges seem sharp but do not cut, like justice . . . the stains in it, which are not hidden and which add to its beauty, are like truthfulness.

The Chinese developed writing. Chinese writing has been in use for over 3,500 years and is the oldest living language in the world. Long before the Chous rose to power, the Chinese had a system of writing. By the end of ■ Chou rule, this system was so well developed that it has come down to the present with few changes.

The Chinese have a very complicated language, although Chinese words have only one syllable each. A single word may have several meanings. For example, the word *fu* can mean "rich," "store up," or "not." The speaker's tone of voice gives the meaning. As a result, spoken Chinese varies in tone and has a rhythmic quality.

Chinese writing, like that of the Egyptians, developed from picture writing. But unlike the Egyptians, the Chinese continued to use one symbol for each word or idea. Today, there are about 50,000 Chinese word symbols. Only a few scholars learn all of them. For many centuries, the great majority of Chinese people never learned to read or write because there were too many word-symbols to memorize.

● An example of a jade carving is shown on p. 73.

■ A well-educated Chinese can read works written twenty centuries ago. The spoken language, however, has split into different dialects. There are from four to nine tones for each word depending on the dialect.

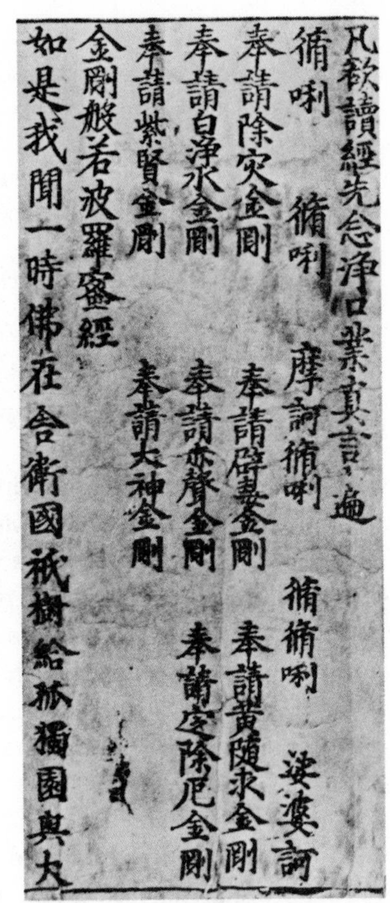

凡欲讀經先念淨口業真言遍
脩唎 脩唎 摩訶脩唎 脩脩唎 娑婆訶
奉請除災金剛 奉請辟毒金剛 奉請黃隨求金剛
奉請白淨水金剛 奉請赤聲金剛 奉請定除災金剛
奉請紫賢金剛 奉請大神金剛
金剛般若波羅蜜經
如是我聞一時佛在舍衛國祇樹給孤獨園與大

History of Writing These examples show some of the earliest written forms people developed. The oldest forms are the cuneiform writing of the Middle East *(above left)* and Egyptian hieroglyphics *(bottom right)*, both developed around 4000 B.C. The Chinese characters were probably next, about 3500 B.C. This example *(above right)* is from the world's oldest printed book—9th century A.D. Sanskrit *(above center)*, though not the earliest writing of India, is the basis of many modern languages. Greek letters (the water-clock *below left*) are the basis of the English alphabet.

SECTION REVIEW 2

p. 72 **1.** Why did the Chou rulers have trouble keeping peace in their kingdom?

p. 75 **2.** What was the goal of Confucius' teachings?

p. 75 **3.** Why might Confucius' teachings have been bad for the Chinese?

p. 76 **4.** What types of art were produced in China?

This painted pottery model shows what houses looked like in Han China.

3 Two dynasties united China

In the last years of the Chou dynasty, many of the feudal states were at war with one another. The king of Ch'in [chin], one of these states, emerged as the most powerful ruler. The Chou dynasty fell in 256 B.C. After a power struggle among several states, the Ch'in ruler seized
ans. 1 control in 221 B.C. He began a new dynasty, and it is from this dynasty that China got its name.

A Ch'in emperor centralized the government. Ch'in rule lasted only until 206 B.C., but its control was absolute. The ruler had complete authority over all the people. Only a very able, strong man could have brought about such a state of affairs. This man was called Shih Huang Ti [shir′ hwäng′ tē′], which means "first emperor."

Shih Huang Ti extended China's boundaries south. He united the country by making Ch'in laws the laws of the whole nation. He set up a uniform system of weights and measures and built a network of tree-lined roads. Most important, he strengthened the central government by ending the power of the nobles. He then divided China into 36 military provinces, each governed by an appointed official. With a few changes, this basic form of government lasted for more than 2,000 years until 1912 A.D.

To bolster his rule, Shih Huang Ti tried to ans. 2
erase the ideas of Confucius from the minds of the Chinese. He ordered all Confucian literature burned because it favored tradition and called the old Chou system good and just. However, many books survived and were later collected and saved.

Trading caravans stopped at villages on the Silk Road to buy and sell goods. This model is made from pottery funeral figures of the Han Dynasty.

Han Dynasty sundial was more accurate than any Western one until the 1200s A.D.

Shih Huang Ti wanted to protect the northern and western border areas from the frequent invasions of the Huns. To do this, he added to and joined together several protective walls to make the Great Wall of China.

The Han dynasty extended the boundaries of China. Civil war broke out in China shortly after the death of Shih Huang Ti in 210 B.C. After eight years of fighting, a new dynasty gained control. It took the name *Han* because its first ruler had once led an army on the Han River. The Han dynasty was one of the most outstanding in Chinese history. Some Chinese still call themselves "sons of Han." The Hans ruled for more than 400 years—from 202 B.C. to 220 A.D. During Han rule, China grew as large and prosperous as the Roman Empire of the same period.

ans. 3 The greatest Han ruler was Wu Ti [wü′ dē′], who lived between 140 and 87 B.C. He drove the Huns back from the Great Wall and took over part of Korea. He extended the empire south to Indochina and west to central Asia and brought an era of peace to all of central and eastern Asia. Later Han rulers pushed the boundaries to the borders of India and Persia.

During Han rule, the Chinese made several cultural advances. They invented the first *yoke*, or shoulder collar, for draft animals. This made it possible for animals to pull heavier loads. [Europeans did not have a similar device for another 1,400 years.) By 100 A.D., the Chinese had invented paper. They also wrote the world's first dictionary and the first scholarly history of China.

China met other civilizations. The expansion of China during Han rule brought the country into contact with other peoples. Trade did well, especially along the so-called "Silk Road." This route ran from China through central Asia, crossing deserts and mountains, to the edges of the Middle East. Along the way, probably in Chinese Turkestan, merchants from the West met Chinese trade caravans. The Chinese had luxury goods—silks, spices, and furs—that were highly prized by the merchants from the West. The two groups traded ideas as well as goods and exchanged much information.

People of the West learned about such fruits ans. 4
as peaches, apricots, and rhubarb from the Chinese. Western influence led the Chinese to take a more lifelike approach to art and design and possibly learn new ideas about music and chemistry. From central Asian peoples, the Chinese learned about grapes and alfalfa.

Chinese contact with India led to the introduction of Mahayana Buddism in China. A

This Buddha praying under the Tree of Enlightenment was painted on silk (Tang).

Chinese mission went to the Kushan Empire and brought back the religion about 67 A.D. After that, Buddhism spread rapidly in China.

SECTION REVIEW 3

p. 78 **1.** What dynasty gave China its name? Name some of the accomplishments of that period. How did these accomplishments help unite China?

p. 78 **2.** Why did Shih Huang Ti try to destroy Confucianism?

p. 79 **3.** What were the accomplishments of Wu Ti? Name four cultural advances of the Han dynasty.

p. 79 **4.** What did the West learn from the Chinese? What did the Chinese learn from other peoples?

● Point out that in Europe however, Greco-Roman civilization did not recover its former political power.

■ The Tang government was a model for the cultures which rose in Korea, Japan, and Vietnam.

4 The Tang dynasty gave China a golden age

The glory of the Hans faded in the third century A.D. Strong nobles seized parts of the empire, and the last of the Hans was overthrown in 220 A.D. China broke up into little warring kingdoms. Barbarians broke through the Great Wall. Science, art, invention, and trade stood
still or declined. China, like Europe at the same ans. 1
time, went through a period of darkness and
confusion. Chinese recovery began in 618, ●
when the Tangs [tängs], came to power.

For almost 300 years the Tangs gave China ans. 2
a golden age. The country was prosperous and free from invasion. Its people made progress in education, literature, and the arts. New canals were built, and foreign trade grew. The population grew to 50 million. At its height, the Tang Empire was the strongest, most advanced, and best governed in the world.

A great emperor governed wisely. A great Tang ruler, T'ai Tsung [tī′ dzung′], became emperor in 627, when he was only 21 years
old. He pushed back invaders and enlarged ■
the borders of China.

After several wars, T'ai Tsung concentrated on the peaceful internal development of China. He strengthened the government, stopped the growth of large estates, and tried to make taxes more equal. He valued history and once said: "By using the past as a mirror, you may learn to foresee the rise and fall of empires."

T'ai Tsung did not believe harsher laws were the way to stop crime. He explained that to "diminish expenses, lighten the taxes, and employ only honest officials . . . will do more to abolish robbery than the employment of the severest punishments." He knew that he owed

● it to his people to govern wisely. One day, when in a boat with his son, he said: "The water bears up the boat, but it can also overturn it. So with the people—they uphold the prince but they can also overthrow him!"

Education strengthened Chinese government. The Chinese were the first to fill *civil service* jobs, that is, government jobs, by public examination. The system, which began during Han rule, was strengthened by the Tangs.

Education had an important place. Good students were sent from local schools to the colleges of their provinces. The best students then went to the imperial school in the capital, where several thousand of them studied for the civil service. This system gave China intelligent and well-trained officials. They were highly thought of and had many duties. They collected taxes, kept order, punished wrongdoers, conducted tests for government service, and ran the postal service. Other countries of Asia also sent their young men to China to be educated. As a result, Chinese influence spread beyond the borders of China.

Thousands of officials of the Chinese government belonged to the civil service. They were chosen after taking written tests that were given every three years. Each candidate sat in a small, separate room, like a phone booth. In some towns, there were acres of these booths in long rows. The test took three days. Food was brought in by servants. Officials watched from high towers to see that no one cheated. The test was so important that some candidates went mad or even died of exhaustion. The final examination tested knowledge of current events, Confucian classics, creative writing, law, and math. Candidates could take the tests many times.

● Discuss these quotations with the class to make sure they understand them. Ask if they feel the statements are relevant today.

Bright young men from very poor families could take the easiest test. If successful, they could enter the lowest civil service rank. With more study and experience, they could be promoted to the highest posts. Thus, in Chinese government there was the kind of "log cabin to White House" idea that is found today in the United States.

This Chinese system of selecting government workers lasted until the early 1900s. Although ans. 3
it was more advanced than any other such system in the world, it did have a serious fault. The candidates were tested mainly on the old classics. Not enough attention was paid to new ideas. Therefore, civil servants chose to support old ways rather than to prepare their country for change. This weakness became very serious in modern times, when China was not able to meet the challenges of a rapidly changing world.

Many poets wrote during the Tang period. A common saying about the Tang period held that "Whoever was a man was a poet." One of the greatest and certainly one of the most carefree of the Tang poets was Li Po [lē′ bô′]. One of his poems, called "The Moon over the Mountain Pass," reads:

The bright moon soars over the Mountain of
  Heaven,
Gliding over an ocean of clouds.
A shrill wind screaming ten thousand li away,
And a sound of whistling from Yu-men pass.
The imperial army marches down White
  Mound Road.
The Tartars search the bays of the Blue Sea.
The warriors look back to their distant homes:
Never yet has one been seen to return.
Tonight, on the high towers she is waiting.
There is only sorrow and unending grieving.

Pottery figures show dancers and musicians entertaining a princess. Such entertainment in the Tang court often began after dinner—a sumptuous feast of tortoise, duck, and other delicacies. The cart and trader *(below)* are also funeral figures.

The Chinese invented printing. Literature flourished under the Tangs. This was not only because the people were prosperous and the government stable, but also because of the invention of printing. Ink had been used as early as 1200 B.C., and paper made from wood pulp had been invented during the Han dynasty.

ans. 4 Early Chinese printing done during the Tang era is called *block printing.* The printer carved raised characters on a block of wood, wet the surface of the characters with ink, and pressed sheets of paper against them. Chinese printers in the 11th century invented movable type made of baked clay. These characters could be rearranged to form different words and so be used over and over again. But because of the difficulty of making the nearly 50 thousand characters in the Chinese alphabet, most Chinese printers continued to use block printing.

Most early Chinese books were really printed on rolls of paper. Gradually, however, the Chinese made books with pages and covers. They also invented paper money and printed playing cards.

SECTION REVIEW **4**

1. After the fall of the Han dynasty, what did China have in common with Europe of the same period? p. 80

2. In what ways were the years of the Tang Empire a golden age in China? p. 80

3. What was the major fault of the Chinese civil service system? p. 81

4. What two kinds of printing were invented in China? Which was used more? Why? p. 82

CHAPTER REVIEW 4

SECTION SUMMARIES

1. Geography helps explain the Chinese story. Natural barriers have isolated China from other centers of civilization. Within China, the Tsinling Mountains have separated the peoples of the north and south. Different ways of life developed in these two regions. The Yangtze River provided a good trade route with the interior. The Hsi River promoted year-round farming, and a port city developed at its mouth.

2. The Chou dynasty ruled longest in China. In the history of China, the Chou period, from 1027 to 256 B.C., is called *classical.* This is because many basics of Chinese civilization were formed at this time. A group of fine thinkers, especially Confucius, wrote lessons that guided personal actions and behavior for the next 2,000 years. Taoists followed another "way." Also, during this time, a feudal government that limited the king's power was built. Towns and trade grew. Fine art was designed. Social customs were formed.

3. Two dynasties united China. In the 3rd century B.C., the Ch'in dynasty united the feudal states. Under Shih Huang Ti, laws were standardized and the country was divided into 36 provinces. The Great Wall was built as a barrier against invaders. After the Ch'in dynasty, the Hans ruled China from 202 B.C. to 220 A.D. They won control of eastern and central Asia and provided an era of peace. Contact with the world beyond the borders of China led to increased trade with the West and brought Buddhism from India.

4. The Tang dynasty gave China a golden age. The emperor T'ai Tsung expanded China and ruled with wisdom and justice. For 300 years, Tang emperors held the empire together. Education and a civil service system were improved, great poetry was written, and printing was developed.

2. Chou: c, h, k, n; Ch'in: d, f, i, p; Han: a, j, m, o; Tang: b, e, g, l.
3. The Great Wall. Nomadic invaders from Central Asia, the Huns
4. Answers will vary. Examples: Culture, government, language.

WHO? WHAT? WHEN? WHERE?

1. Match each dynasty with the years of its rule and arrange in chronological order.

Han	623 A.D. – 900 A.D.	Tang
Chou	1027 B.C. – 256 B.C.	Chou
Tang	221 B.C. – 206 B.C.	Ch'in
Ch'in	202 B.C. – 220 A.D.	Han

2. Match the correct dynasty (Han, Chou, Tang, or Ch'in) with the statements below:

a. This dynasty was named after a river.
b. Li Po lived then.
c. The last years of this dynasty are called the Era of Warring States.
d. The "First Emperor" built the Great Wall.
e. Printing was invented.
f. It ruled only fifteen years.
g. This was China's "golden age."
h. This dynasty lasted for almost 800 years.
i. Shih Huang Ti tried to destroy the works of Confucius.
j. Ideas and goods were traded with the West.
k. Confucius began his teaching.
l. The civil service system was greatly improved.
m. This dynasty was as large and prosperous as the Roman Empire.
n. The "classical" period of Chinese history
o. Mahayana Buddhism was introduced in China.
p. This dynasty gave China its name.

3. What barrier did the Chinese build to keep out strangers? Who were these strangers?

4. In what ways did Chinese life change very little for 2,000 years?

5. Give evidence to prove that Shih Huang Ti was not able to completely destroy the ideas of Confucius.

6. Name some Chinese improvements or inventions in these areas: government, farming, transportation, warfare, and writing.

5. One possible answer is the fact that civil service candidates during the Tang dynasty were tested on Confucian classics.
6. Answers will vary.

CHAPTER TEST 4

QUESTIONS FOR CRITICAL THINKING

1. China was weakened by not changing for 2,000 years. Why didn't the leaders realize that they were hurting themselves?

2. A common saying in the Tang period was: "Whoever was a man was a poet." How does this idea fit in with our society's ideas of manliness? Why?

3. How did trade help the Romans and the Chinese improve their lives? Why is contact between people with different ideas and life-styles important?

4. List some ways in which our lives have been improved by inventions of the Chinese.

5. For what common reason did different Chinese dynasties rise and fall?

ACTIVITIES

1. Compare the teachings of Confucius and Lao-tse. Use quotations from the test to show how the two are alike and how they are different. Which one do you prefer? Why?

2. In everyday language, explain the sayings of T'ai Tsung. Was T'ai Tsung a wise leader?

3. Discuss the *Mandate of Heaven.* Is there any way in which it is like our ideas about government today?

4. Describe the different types of Chinese art mentioned in this chapter. What materials were used? What were some subjects shown by the artists? What outside influences changed Chinese art styles? How?

5. On a map of China, sketch in and label the ocean, jungle, mountain, and desert areas that have protected it from the rest of the world. Add the great rivers, and show where various crops are grown. Indicate the "Outer Kingdoms" of Mongolia and Sinkiang, and draw arrows representing invasions.

SECTION 1

1. The Huns invaded because: a. they needed new grazing lands for their herds, b. they needed more farmland to feed a growing population, c. they hated the Chinese

2. The Chinese built ______ to control the Hwang Ho floods: a. levees, b. the Great Wall, c. canals

3. True or false: The Hwang Ho is not a trade route.

SECTION 2

4. The Chou dynasty ruled from __1027__ B.C. to __256__ B.C., a period of __771__ years. ●

5. True or false: There was a sharp contrast between the lives of the rich and the poor.

6. Write "T" for true, "F" for false, or "N" if no evidence is given for these statements:

T a. Large families on small farms were a problem until the 20th century in China.

F b. The Chinese government was exactly like that of the Egyptians.

N c. Jade is found only in China.

7. Who gathered earlier writings together into what are called the "Five Classics"? a. Wu Ti, b. Li Po, c. Confucius

SECTION 3

8. The religion that is not native to China is: a. Confucianism, b. Buddhism, c. Taoism

9. True or false: Chinese today call themselves "Sons of Ch'in."

10. True or false: Shih Huang Ti was a firm believer in Confucianism.

SECTION 4

11. The population of China reached 50 million during the __Tang__ dynasty.

12. Civil service officials were chosen by: a. election, b. family name, c. ability

13. True or false: Chinese printers preferred movable-type printing.

QUESTIONS FOR CRITICAL THINKING:

1. They did not realize because of their attitude that China was the center of the world and all outsiders were 'barbarians'.
2. Answers will vary.
3. Each culture benefited by learning new ways of doing things and by getting products not grown in its area.
4. Paper, ink, printing, etc. have improved our lives.
5. The dynasties fell due to power struggles between warring states.

● Accept an approximation of 800 years.

1600 – 31 B.C.

CHAPTER 5

The Golden Age of Greece

Greece's greatest contribution to civilization was its example as a workable democratic government. This painting on a cup (490 B.C.) shows warriors casting ballots as Athena, the patron goddess of Athens, looks on.

● In ancient Greece, it was thought an honor to be able to die in battle. A famous speech given in honor of the war dead has come down to us from a historian named Thucydides [thü sid′ə dēz′], who wrote in the 400s B.C. This speech, or *funeral oration,* is remembered because it describes not the soldiers, but the way of life they fought to preserve.

● This introduction can be useful in motivating the study of Greek Civilization, the third in this unit on Classical Civilizations.

> Our government is not copied from our neighbors. We are an example to them. Our constitution is called a *democracy* because power is in the hands not of the few but of the whole

people. When it is a question of settling private disputes, everyone is equal before the law. No talented man is kept out of public service because he is poor or from the wrong class. We have no dark words or angry looks for our neighbor if he enjoys himself in his own way. We are open and friendly in our private, day-to-day relations with each other. In our public affairs we keep strictly to the law.

Our city is so large and powerful that all the wealth of all the world flows in, and our own products seem no more homelike to us than the works of other nations. The gates of our city are flung open to the world. We let visitors see or discover anything, even though it might help an enemy, because we trust not in military equipment, but in our own good spirit in battle.

The speaker was Pericles [per′ə klēz′], a famous general and statesman of the Greek city-state Athens. The speech was what we call today *propaganda,* that is, its main purpose was to spread ideas or beliefs. In it, Pericles described effectively the things that he felt made the Athenians better than their enemies, the Spartans. Of more importance to us, his praise for his native city described the contributions of ancient Greece to civilization. These contributions include the following:

● 1. The Greek government, in which citizens were equal before the law, became a model for Western democracy.

2. Public service was thought to be an honorable and necessary part of every citizen's life.

3. Individuals were free to live their own lifestyles, to come and go as they pleased, to speak their minds openly.

4. An awareness of beauty enhanced Greek life. As Pericles said: "Our love of what is beautiful does not lead to extravagance; our love of the things of the mind does not make us soft."

● Encourage students to express their thoughts on these aspects of Greek culture and their effect on our own.

■ After completing the study of this chapter, you might have students return to these questions for a closing exercise.

5. Public debates were held before the state took action. As Pericles also said: ". . . we decide or debate carefully and in person all matters of policy. We do not think there is an incompatibility between words and deeds. The worst thing is to rush into action before the consequences have been properly debated."

These five qualities of the best in Athenian society make up what is often described as the Greek view of life.

Western civilization owes even more to the Greeks. The classic forms of architecture and sculpture, history, philosophy, drama, and poetry come from Greek originals. Modern science began with the study of Greek writings on physics, mathematics, biology, and medicine.

How was it that these talented people were able to leave such magnificent gifts to civilization? Historians cannot agree on any one answer. There are many points to consider: the origin of the Greeks, the relative isolation of their individual city-states, the freedom and individualism fostered by their society, the competition and rivalry among themselves, and their conflicts with outsiders. This chapter discusses these points in the following sections: ■

1. Aegean civilization depended on sea trade.

2. The Greeks established the basic principles of democracy.

3. The Greeks were threatened by Persia and by city-state rivalries.

4. The Macedonians united Greece and the Hellenistic Age began.

5. Greek civilization formed the basis for Western culture.

1 Aegean civilization depended on sea trade

To early people, the sea meant mystery and danger. In their small boats, they ventured upon it with caution. They stayed close to the shoreline by day and took refuge in harbors at night. Little by little, the sea became more important as a highway for trade. The Phoenicians were among the early traders who dared to sail the open waters. Others who met the challenge of the deep were the people who lived on the islands of the Aegean [i jē′ən] Sea and along its shores.

Crete developed a flourishing culture. It is believed that the island of Crete [krēt] was settled as early as 6000 B.C. by Neolithic peoples from southwest Asia. About 3100 B.C., Egyptians also immigrated to Crete. Between 1600 and 1400 B.C., Crete became a power in the ancient world. The island served as a stop ans. 1
on the trade routes between Europe and Africa and between Africa and Asia. The civilization that developed on Crete is called *Minoan* [mi nō′ən] for King Minos [mī′nəs]. According to mythology, he ruled Crete.

Ancient Greek legends include a number of references to Minoan civilization. One of the best-known stories concerns the Minotaur [min′ə tôr], a monster with the head of a bull and the body of a man. The Minotaur was an object of worship and was kept beneath the royal palace in a *labyrinth* [lab′ə rinth′], an intricate and bewildering series of passageways. Every year, the Minotaur was offered a human sacrifice of seven boys and seven girls from Athens. Finally, it was killed by the Greek hero,

ANCIENT GREECE
about 480 B.C.

Theseus [thē'sē əs]. He escaped from the labyrinth by following a thread given him as a guideline by Minos' daughter.

Until the end of the 1800s, little was known about Minoan civilization. But in 1894, Sir Arthur Evans, an English archaeologist, began excavations on Crete. He found inscribed clay tablets and jewelry. These showed that the
ans. 2 Minoans had a system of writing. Copper and bronze tools and weapons showed an advanced stage of technology. An important find was the ruin of the royal palace at Knossos [nos'əs], the capital city. It was an amazing building, covering 6 acres (1.4 hectares). Like a giant labyrinth, it had many living quarters, corridors, tunnels, storerooms, and an ingenious underground plumbing system.

Crete became rich from its overseas trade and metalworking industries. Minoan manufactured goods included decorated clay vases, bronze weapons, and locks and keys. These were traded for gold, silver, and grain.

Egyptian influences can be found in much Minoan art, but the island people also had their own forms of architecture, painting, and sculpture. Their art reveals their love of athletics and the world of nature. Many of the wall paintings show the dangerous sport of "bull dancing." The idea of this sport was to meet the bull head-on, grab his horns, and somersault over his back to safety. Women as well as men participated in these events.

About 1900 B.C., people from the area around the Caspian [kas'pē ən] Sea invaded the Greek peninsula. The newcomers are known as Mycenaeans [mī'sə nē'ənz]. They spoke an early form of Greek. The Mycenaeans built fortified cities and began to engage in trade and manufacturing. They did especially well at the cities of Mycenae [mī sē'nē] and Tiryns [tī'rinz]. About 1500 B.C., the Mycenaeans captured Knossos. During the following century, they attacked and destroyed other cities on Crete. However, in 1400 B.C., the Minoans succeeded in driving the Mycenaeans off the island. Minoan trade and city life revived somewhat, but commercial leadership in the Aegean had passed to Mycenae. The island of Crete no longer was the main center of trade.

Mycenae and Troy became centers of Aegean civilization. From 1400 to 1200 B.C., Mycenae was the most important power in the Aegean community. During this time, all the people of the Aegean area developed a
feeling of fellowship. They spoke a common ans. 3
language and believed in the same gods. Zeus [züs], the strongest god, ruled over a family of gods and goddesses who were believed to live on Mt. Olympus.

Aegean civilization also included parts of Asia Minor. The city of Troy was especially important. It was strategically located on the Helles- ans. 4
pont [hel'i spont], a *strait,* or narrow channel, connecting two major bodies of water. (The Hellespont is now called the Dardanelles [därd'n elz'].) Because of its location, Troy controlled the trade between the two seas.

After about 1300 B.C., Mycenaean trade began to decline. The reasons for this decline are still not fully understood. Trade contacts with Egypt and the east coast of the Mediterranean were cut. This time of crisis is revealed in the *Iliad* [il'ē əd] and the *Odyssey* [od'ə sē], two epic poems thought to have been written in the 800s B.C. by the blind poet Homer.

The *Iliad* tells of the siege of Troy. Probably the most familiar part of the poem is the story of how Troy was taken. The Mycenaean invaders built a huge wooden horse outside the city

● Students might be interested in finding out more about Greek mythological figures by doing library research. Ask them to "rewrite" some of these stories in modern language.

■ See picture of bull-dancing, top, facing page. This activity probably had religious significance.

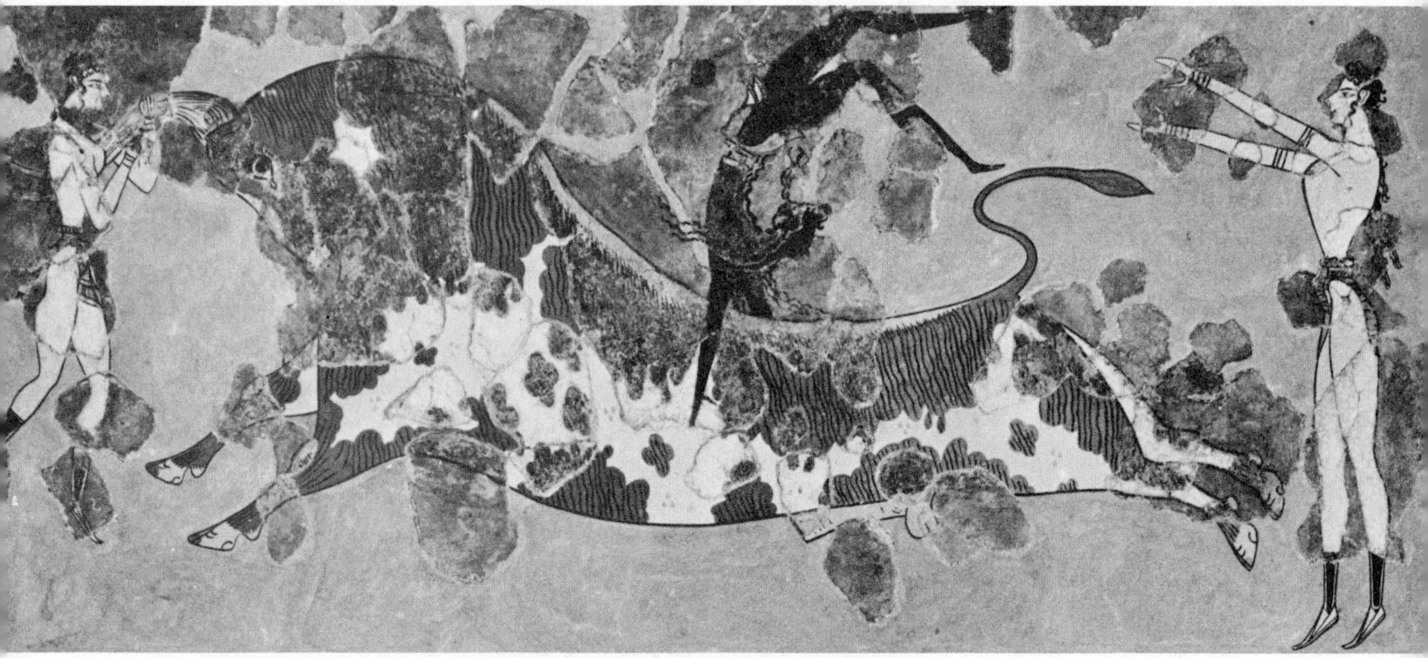

Bull dancers from a restored wall painting at the Palace at Knossos (1550 B.C.)

Minoan priests carry sacrificial offerings in a royal funeral procession.

gates and then went away. The Trojans were impressed with this statue. They moved it into their city only to discover—too late—that enemy soldiers were hidden inside this Trojan horse. The *Odyssey* describes the many adventures of the soldier Odysseus [ō dis′ē əs] on his 20-year trip home after the Trojan War.

SECTION REVIEW 1

p. 87 **1.** Tell why Crete's geographical location made it a power in the ancient world.

p. 88 **2.** List three items that show that the Minoans were civilized.

p. 88 **3.** What did the peoples of the Aegean community have in common? Why was this important to their feeling of unity?

p. 88 **4.** Where was Troy? Why was this an important location for a city?

2 The Greeks established the basic principles of democracy

Throughout its existence, the Aegean civilization had been threatened by invaders. About 1100 B.C., the warlike Dorian people from the north began moving into the Greek peninsula. The Mycenaeans were driven from their cities. Many of the survivors fled east and settled in and around the city of Athens [ath′ənz]. Others moved to the islands of the Aegean and the strip of seacoast in Asia Minor known as Ionia [ī ō′nē ə]. But in time, a peaceful mingling began to take place. From this mixture of different groups emerged the Greeks. During this time of transition—from the first invasions to about the middle of the 700s B.C.—the basis for Greek civilization was made.

Little is known about this time. Trade stopped and people lived in small farming communities. Slowly, the people of Athens and other cities began to cooperate with each other for protection and for religious festivals. From these contacts came the famous Olympic games, beginning in the 8th century B.C. They were held every four years in honor of Zeus. Little by little, the people reestablished the feelings of cultural unity, or *brotherhood,* that had existed when Mycenaean power was at its height.

The Greeks called themselves *Hellenes* [hel′ēns] after Hellas, an area in the northern and western part of Greece. The great era that followed the time of transition is called the *Hellenic* [he len′ik] *period.* It lasted from about 750 to 338 B.C.

Independent city-states were formed on the Greek peninsula. Early Greek society was simple. The people grouped into clans ruled by a king or tribal chief. Each clan founded a settlement, known as a *polis* [pō′lis], where the people would be safe from attack. The country around the polis was used for farming and grazing. The geographic isolation of these settlements led to the growth of small, independent city-states. The members of the city-state were proud of their home city. The city-states were jealous of their independence. They did not often cooperate with each other except when invaders threatened. ans. 1 ●

■ One of the greatest contributions of the city-states to civilization was democratic government. However, only male landowners born in the city-state could become full citizens. Democratic government evolved gradually. The first step was most often the formation by the nobility of an *oligarchy* [ol′ə gär′kē], or govern-

● This was a weakness that would later lead to the end of Greek independence.

■ Four major types of government were known to and named by the Greeks: Monarchy, oligarchy, tyranny, and democracy.

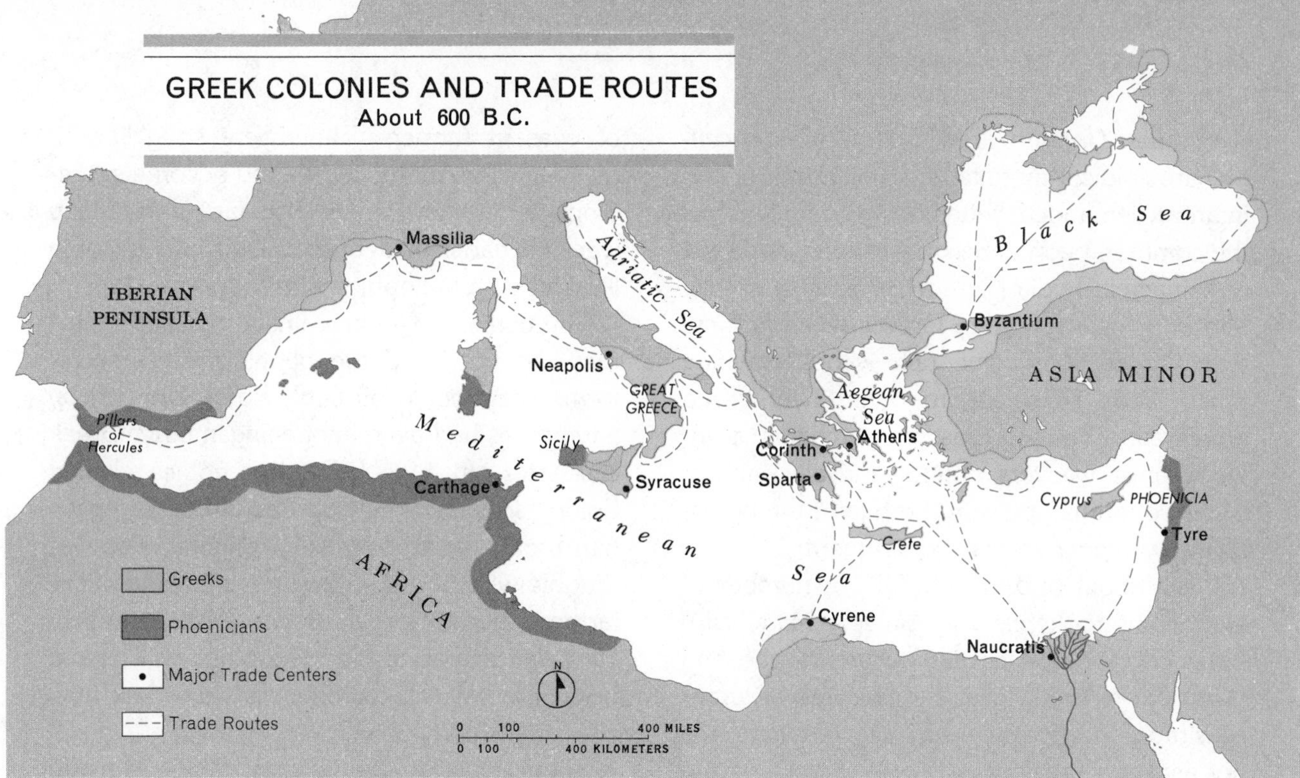

ment by the few, that replaced the ruling king or tribal chief. With their increased power, the nobles wrote law codes. No longer was justice a matter of whim or guess. Penalties were set by law rather than by a judge, and the laws were available for all to see. In this way the common people also benefited from the law codes.

Greek traders set up colonies and trade routes. By the middle of the 700s B.C., the nobles who ran the Greek world had so much power that they became corrupt. They had increased their wealth through control of the farmland. Small farmers had been forced to mortgage their land or sell themselves into slavery to pay their debts. Many farmers gave up the land in favor of small-scale manufacturing. Poor soils and a lack of good land also led to the decline of farming.

The making of pottery, textiles, and bronze weapons and tools developed rapidly. It was not long before the Greeks needed more markets for their goods and new sources of food. A growing population put even greater demands on the available food. Migration would give the people a chance to get rich or have more political freedom. For these reasons, the Greeks began to set up colonies. ●

Each new colony was bound by social and religious ties to its parent city-state. Thus the city-states became less isolated. Colonies were established in the north Aegean and the Black Sea areas, and in Egypt, Sicily, Italy, and southern France. ■

The power of the nobility was challenged by tyrants. The colonies did not end the discontent in Greece, however. A number of trends brought about the fall of the nobility. The first was the growth of a heavily armed infantry of citizens. The power of this *infantry* grew until they were a match for the *cavalry* of

● "When men who have nothing, and are in need of food, ... follow their leaders in an attack . . . on the rich – these . . . are sent away by the [ruler] in a friendly spirit as far as he is able; and this . . . is termed a colony." Plato

■ Despite these ties, the colonies were politically independent.

the nobles. (*Infantry* are foot soldiers, and *cavalry* are soldiers mounted on horseback.) The infantry demanded better living conditions for the common people. Second, the development of coinage in Lydia [lid′ē ə], a country in Asia Minor, quickly spread to Greece. With money, a family could become rich without owning much land. Third, an important new group appeared: a business class of merchants, owners of ships, weavers, potters, and blacksmiths. They were unhappy with the rule of the nobility and wanted a voice in government.

From about 650 to 500 B.C., a number of revolutions took place in Greece. Many city-states came under the rule of *tyrants* who had taken power unlawfully. To the Greeks, tyranny simply meant one-man rule. A tyrant was not always a cruel or oppressive ruler—as the word means today. Often he was a noble who had become democratic in outlook and to whom the people turned for leadership. In Greece, the rise of tyrants was the first step toward government by the people.

The first democracy grew in Athens. On the dusty coastal plain of Attica [at′ə kə] in southeast Greece lay the city of Athens. The city hugged the slopes of a hill known as the Acropolis [ə krop′ə lis]. It was here that the Athenians built their forts and temples. Sailors and merchants from far-away countries brought money and many different ideas to Athens.

From the 700s to the 500s B.C., the government in Athens was controlled by a council of nobles. The most important public official was the chief magistrate, who was elected every year from among the nobles. During these two centuries, different groups of citizens in Athens became more and more unhappy with their conditions. One of these groups was made up of peasant farmers. They were struggling to make a living on the hills or had become sharecroppers on the nobles' rich farmland. Many were so badly in debt that they had become like slaves to the nobles who supported them.

The council of nobles finally realized that if they did not heed the people's cries for reforms, they would probably be overthrown by a tyrant, as had been happening in other Greek city-states. In 594 B.C., the nobles elected Solon [sō′lən] to be chief magistrate and gave him broad powers to make changes. Solon was a noble who had both an understanding of the farmers' needs and a strong sense of justice. He made middle-of-the-road reforms. His name has come down in history as a byword for wise statesmanship.

Solon canceled the farmers' debts. He outlawed the practice of debt slavery. However, he resisted the farmers' demands to redistribute the land. He enlarged the council and included not only the nobles but also rich property owners. This Council of 400 drew up new laws, and an assembly of all citizens voted on them. Solon offered citizenship to craftsmen who had not been born in Athens if they and their families would settle there. He encouraged trade. Solon did not create democracy, but his rule opened a new chapter in the history of Athens. ans. 2

However, there was still discontent in Athens. The shepherds were unhappy because they owned no land. They found a leader in Pisistratus [pī sis′trə təs], a distant relative of Solon. Pisistratus took over in 560 B.C. and ruled as tyrant for over thirty years. He solved the economic problems by banishing many nobles and distributing their lands among the poor. He encouraged trade and the arts.

The next important tyrant in Athenian history was Cleisthenes [klīs′thə nēz], who came to power in 508 B.C. Under Cleisthenes, *ostracism* was begun. Ostracism was a system that gave the 6,000 citizens a chance once a year to banish any officials they thought were dangerous to the Athenian state. Cleisthenes strengthened the growth of democracy. He set up new political districts and increased the number of members in the council to 500. These changes allowed more people to take part in politics and a greater variety of local interests to be represented in government. •

Solon, Pisistratus, and Cleisthenes were champions of the people. With their reforms, Athens took large steps toward becoming a democracy. Other city-states followed the lead of Athens. By 500 B.C., democratic governments were being set up in most city-states.

Sparta became a warrior state. The city-state of Sparta was an important exception to the trend toward popular government. Sparta lay on the Peloponnesus [pel′ ə pə nē′səs], the peninsula that makes up the southern part of Greece. When the ancestors of the Spartans came to the Peloponnesus, they subdued the natives, whom they called *helots.* Allowed to remain on the land as farmers, the helots grew food for the conquerors. In the 700s B.C., the Spartans took over neighboring Messenia [mə sē′nē ə]. Sparta then had enough land and was not attracted by colonization and trade. Of greatest importance in shaping the Spartan government was the never-ending threat of rebellion by the Messenians and the ans. 3
helots.

This bronze statue pays tribute to the brave soldiers who fought off the Persian threat. (pages 96–97)

In about 600 B.C., the Spartans set up a constitution. Its purpose was to keep up the military strength of the state. An assembly of citizens was created, but it had little power. Control of the state was held by a small group of citizens called the Council of Elders. The council made laws for the assembly to vote on and appointed magistrates.

Sparta was set up much like a military camp. To keep up high health standards, all weak or deformed children were killed. Only the strong

• Key Concept. Democracy grew gradually as the numbers of people allowed to participate in politics grew.

Greek Daily Life Artists of ancient Greece were interested in the details of ordinary life. The statues and vases they made show a great deal about how they lived. *Below left:* A painted terra cotta figurine shows two friends talking. Hair and clothing styles are carefully shown. *Above left:* Men are bathing in a public bath house; the water comes from animal-head spouts on the wall. *Above center:* A weaver is spinning thread before she weaves it

into cloth. *Above right:* At dinner parties, men reclined on couches and amused themselves with singing, dancing, and playing instruments. The bearded man is holding a shallow bowl, which he drinks from. His friend is playing a tune on double pipes. *Below right:* A scene in a cobbler's shop decorates a large vase. The shoemaker on the left is cutting leather to fit his customer's foot.

Point out to students that archaeologists learn much about ancient peoples from fragmentary remains such as are shown here. Ask students to discuss what they can discover about early life-styles before reading explanatory captions.

ans. 3 and healthy were allowed to live. At age seven, boys were taken from their homes and sent to real military camps. There they got strict training in gymnastics and military exercises. Each year, they were flogged to test their powers of physical endurance. At age 20, the young men became field soldiers, and were then allowed to marry, but they continued to live in the barracks. At age 30, men were admitted to the assembly and given various government posts. Girls were trained to be strong, healthy mothers of warriors. As their men marched off to war, Spartan women said goodby with the following words: "Come back with your shield or on it." To this day, the English word *spartan* means sternly disciplined.

The helots were looked upon as state property and were little better than slaves. They could not be citizens and were governed harshly. To spy on them and to stop revolt, the Spartans set up a secret police force. Once a year, war was declared on the helots. That way, the government made it legal to wipe out possible troublemakers.

The highly trained Spartan army was used against its neighbors with some success. But it was diplomacy, backed by force, that allowed Sparta to extend its influence. In the 500s B.C., Sparta formed the Peloponnesian League, a military alliance with nearby states in the south of Greece, that increased Sparta's power.

SECTION REVIEW 2

p. 90 **1.** Why did the early peoples of Greece settle in isolated city-states?

p. 92, 93 **2.** What reforms of Solon, Pisistratus, and Cleisthenes helped bring Athens closer to democracy?

p. 93, 96 **3.** Why was it important to the Spartans to have a strong army? How did they make sure they would stay strong?

3 The Greeks were threatened by Persia and by city-state rivalries

The Greeks came into contact with other peoples as they expanded their colonies and their power. The Persian Empire was the most dangerous enemy. Bad feelings between the Persians and the Greeks began when Cyrus [sī'rəs] of Persia attacked and defeated Croesus [krē'səs], the king of nearby Lydia, in 546 B.C. Cyrus stayed on the attack until he had beaten most of the Ionian Greeks in Asia Minor.

The next Persian ruler to threaten the Greeks was Darius I, who came to power in 522 B.C. One of his most important acts—the reorganization of the empire into administrative districts—made the Ionian Greeks very angry. Although they were a part of one of these districts, they felt they had been given a lesser role in the empire. In 499 B.C., the Ionian Greeks attacked the Persians. Athens sent ships to help the Ionians, but the Greeks were defeated decisively at the naval battle of Miletus [mī lē'təs] in 494 B.C. The city of Miletus was burned by the Persians. This act of revenge made the Athenians angry. They began to build a navy to protect their city. However, Darius was determined to take the Greek mainland and punish the Athenians for helping the Greeks in Asia Minor.

The Greeks were victorious at Marathon and Salamis. In 492 B.C., Darius tried to crush the people of Thrace [thrās], an area north of Greece. At the same time, he tried to punish Athens, but his navy was almost destroyed by a storm. Two years later, a Persian army and navy crossed the Aegean Sea to the Bay of Marathon, about 25 miles (40 kilometers) from Athens. The Greeks were ready for this move. Athens and Sparta had earlier agreed to an alliance to fight the Persians. But when the Athenians sent a runner to Sparta to tell of the Persians' approach, the superstitious Spartans refused to march until the next full moon. Without aid from Sparta, the Athenians were outnumbered by the Persians two to one. The Greek historian, Herodotus [hə rod′ə təs], described the battle:

> So when the battle was set in array, and the victims showed themselves favorable, instantly the Athenians . . . charged the barbarians at a run. Now the distance between the two armies was a little short of a mile. The Persians, therefore, when they saw the Greeks coming on at speed, made ready to receive them, although it seemed to them that the Athenians [had lost] their senses, and [were] bent upon their own destruction; for they saw a mere handful of men coming on at a run without either horsemen or archers . . . the Athenians in close array fell upon them, and fought in a manner worthy of being recorded. . . .

● The success of the battle of Marathon in 490
ans. 1 gave the Greeks confidence and touched off
rebellions in other parts of the Persian Empire.

Ten years later, Xerxes [zėrk′sēz′], the son of Darius, attacked Greece. Athens and the Peloponnesian League took on the main job of defense. The Persians defeated the Spartan army at Thermopylae [thər mop′ə lē] in 480 B.C. Next, Xerxes took Athens and burned the Acropolis. The Athenians were not so easily defeated. They took to their ships and fought the enemy in the harbor of the island of Salamis [sal′ə mis]. This sea battle was a disaster for the Persians. Xerxes returned to Asia Minor.

The Greeks had proved themselves the masters of the Aegean. A major result of their victory was that the budding city-states had a chance to develop their democratic systems of government.

Athens became the leading city in Greece. After the defeat of the Persians, Athens took the lead in holding many of the city-states together in a loose federation called the Delian [dē′lē ən] League. The power and wealth of Athens was based on a thriving trade, supremacy at sea, and prestige. Led by Pericles, Athens reached the high point of its democracy. His rule from 460 to 429 B.C. is called the Golden Age of Pericles. During this time, the Parthenon [pär′thə non]—a beautiful temple to the goddess Athena—was built, and the arts and literature flourished.

The real power of government lay in the as- ans. 2
sembly. All male citizens over 18 years old were members. The assembly passed laws, decided important issues, and elected an executive board of ten generals. The generals were controlled by the assembly. It could reelect them, exile them, or put them to death. Pericles was president of the board of generals.

The Council of 500, which drew up laws for the assembly to pass on, was divided into committees dealing with matters such as public buildings and street repair. Everyone serving the state was paid for his work. This meant that even poor men were able to serve. The juries of the court were also paid. The juries were made up of as many as 2,001 jurors, too many for anyone to bribe. To prevent corruption, judges and juries were chosen by lot.

Athenian democracy was based on the principle that all citizens were equal. This made it
possible for nearly every citizen to hold one or ■
more public offices during his life. The mass participation of citizens in political life is known

● This victory destroyed the belief that the Persians could not be defeated and in the words of Herodotus, demonstrated that . . ." free men fight better than slaves."

■ The number of adult male citizens was not much more than 50,000.

as *pure* or *direct democracy.* Governments in which the citizens elect representatives to act for them are called *representative democracies* or *republics.*

Not all people in Athens could be citizens, however. Women, foreigners, and slaves could not be, and these groups far outnumbered the citizens. Therefore, limits to the idea of equality did exist.

The Athenians either bought their slaves or captured them as prisoners of war. The slaves who worked in the silver mines did so in chains and suffered horribly. House slaves, however, were often treated well, almost as members of the family. Some slaves even became free noncitizens. There were about 100,000 slaves in Athens. This huge number made possible the Hellenic idea of leisure. While slaves did most of the work, citizens had time to cultivate their minds and beautify their environment.

A liberal education was stressed. Education in Athens was important in keeping up a healthy democratic government. The aim of Athenian education was to help students develop fine bodies and an appreciation for the arts, to learn to think for themselves, and to become good Athenians.

By law, parents had to educate their sons. ans. 3
However, the state did not provide schools, so parents hired tutors to teach their sons. Most tutors taught large groups of children. Even so, tutors were poorly paid. Athenian boys started school when they were 6 years old and continued until they were 16 or older. Most boys learned to play musical instruments, such as the flute or lyre [līr], an ancient stringed instrument, somewhat like a small harp. Then, at age 14, boys began going to a gymnasium. Here they were trained in running, wrestling, boxing, and other athletic skills. Here, too, they studied

HELEN OF TROY

In Greek mythology, Helen was the world's most beautiful woman. Married to Sparta's king, she was persuaded by Paris, a Trojan prince, to go to Troy. This led to the Trojan War. Helen, seen in this 1956 movie version, has been described as both a betrayer of her country and family and as an innocent victim of her own beauty.

geometry, astronomy, natural history, geography, and public speaking.

Women in Athens did not take part in political affairs, so the training of girls was more limited. Women did not have any standing in court. If a woman wanted the protection of the law, she had to find a male citizen to represent her in court. Girls did not attend school as the ● boys did. However, girls were taught in their homes to read, write, and play a musical instrument. Girls were also taught many skills, such as weaving and pottery making. Athenian homes were often self-sufficient workshops run by women.

ans. 4 **City-state rivalries undermined Greek power.** Athens kept the Delian League from becoming a true union of Greek states. City-states in the Delian League were forced to pay taxes to Athens. And farmers in other city-states were often forced off their land by Athenian settlers. Athenian traders kept the best commercial advantages for themselves.

During the last years of Pericles' rule, the other city-states tried to bring about the downfall of Athens. In addition, corruption crept into the government of Athens. Pericles' successors did not have his intellect or high morals. They used the ruling bodies for their own gain.

In 431 B.C., the resentment of the other city-states brought open war. With Sparta in the lead, the city-states fought Athens in the Peloponnesian [pel′ ə pə nē′shən] War. In 404 B.C., after a long and costly struggle, Sparta defeated Athens. Wars among the city-states went on, however, and brought about the collapse of Spartan leadership. The disastrous Peloponnesian War left the Greeks weakened and divided. Meanwhile, to the north, a new power was gaining strength.

● Women were also not allowed to watch or participate in the Olympic games, so they organized athletic contests of their own.

SECTION REVIEW 3

1. Why were the battles of Marathon and Salamis important? p. 97
2. In what ways was Athenian government democratic? Undemocratic? p. 97, 98
3. Why did the training of an Athenian boy differ from that of a Spartan boy? p. 98
4. What caused the decline of Athens? p. 99

4 The Macedonians united Greece and the Hellenistic Age began.

To the north of Greece lay Macedonia [mas′ ə dō′nē ə], which was inhabited by hardy mountain people. Philip, their king, was an excellent military strategist. When Philip came to power in 359 B.C., he organized a standing army of professional soldiers. They were drilled in cavalry and infantry tactics and kept in trim through a rigorous program of athletics. Philip was also a ruthless leader. He was willing to use bribery, lies, and other treacherous ways to reach his goals. He was determined to unite the Greeks under his rule. Little by little, he brought outlying Greek areas under his control. Yet Philip wanted the friendship of the Greeks and at first avoided the use of force. As a youth he had been a hostage in the Greek city, Thebes [thēbz], and had learned to respect Greek culture.

Philip's conquest of the Greeks ended the Hellenic period. Early in 338 B.C., Athens and Thebes formed an alliance to protect themselves from the Macedonian threat. In (ans. 1) the summer, they attacked Philip. But the Macedonian king almost destroyed the Greek army. This fight marked the end of the power of the city-states. All of the Greek peninsula except Sparta quickly came under Philip's rule.

Within a year, Philip called together delegates from the major city-states of Greece (except Sparta) at Corinth. There the so-called Hellenic League was formed. The city-states got a large degree of self-government, but agreed to give Philip military support against any of them who threatened the general peace. ● Then, in 336 B.C., Philip died suddenly.

ans. 2 Fortunately, Philip was one of the few kings of ancient times who had prepared his successor for the task of ruling. His son, Alexander, had been given the finest education available. This included tutoring by the famous Greek philosopher, Aristotle [ar′ə stot′l]. While Alexander was still in his early teens, Philip had shared state secrets with him. At age 16, Alexander took command of an elite guard. On taking the throne at age 20, he proved himself a strong leader by crushing a revolt by Thebes.

Alexander conquered the Persian Empire. The young Alexander decided to carry out his father's plan to conquer Persia. He admired Hellenic civilization and wanted to spread it abroad. Also, he believed that it was his destiny to rule the world. In 334 B.C., with more than 30 thousand infantry and 5 thousand cavalry, he marched east. It was a journey from which Alexander would never return.

In 334 B.C., Alexander won a great triumph at the battle of Granicus. This victory encouraged the Greeks in Asia Minor to revolt against their Persian masters. The next year, Alexander's forces met the armies of the Persian ruler, Darius III at Issus [is′əs]. Though outnumbered three to one, Alexander's army defeated the Persians roundly. Darius fled from the field of battle and cheated Alexander of the chance to defeat him once and for all. Then Alexander made a successful trip to Egypt, where he founded the city of Alexandria. After this, he swung north to face Darius again. In 331, in the battle of Arbela [är bē′lə], Alexander again defeated Darius's troops, and Darius again got away. It was clear, however, that the Persian ruler could no longer rally his forces against Alexander's army, and Darius was later murdered by one of his own men. Alexander marched on to Babylon and then Persepolis, where he took his seat on the throne of Persia. So ended almost two hundred years of Persian threats to the Mediterranean world.

Alexander then moved east through Persia ■ to India. However, his homesick, weary soldiers made him turn back. In 323 B.C., he died in Babylon, a victim of fever. Many of his military successes were due in part to the disorganized state of the Persian Empire. But Alexander in his own right was a skillful general and a gallant leader of men.

To later generations, Alexander's idea of ans. 3 "one world" was of great importance. He planned a blend of Greek and Persian culture with the Greek language and Greek law as strong bonds. Marriages between his soldiers and native women were encouraged. Alexander himself married two Persian princesses. One system of money was used throughout the lands he conquered. The Persian system of administrative districts was kept almost the same. Over seventy new cities were founded. Their governing bodies were staffed by Persians as well as Greeks and Macedonians. In short, Alexander believed in the creation of a strong world government in which all peoples were equal.

● He was assassinated by a noble with a personal grudge.

■ The breadth of Alexander's conquests can be seen most effectively on a world globe.

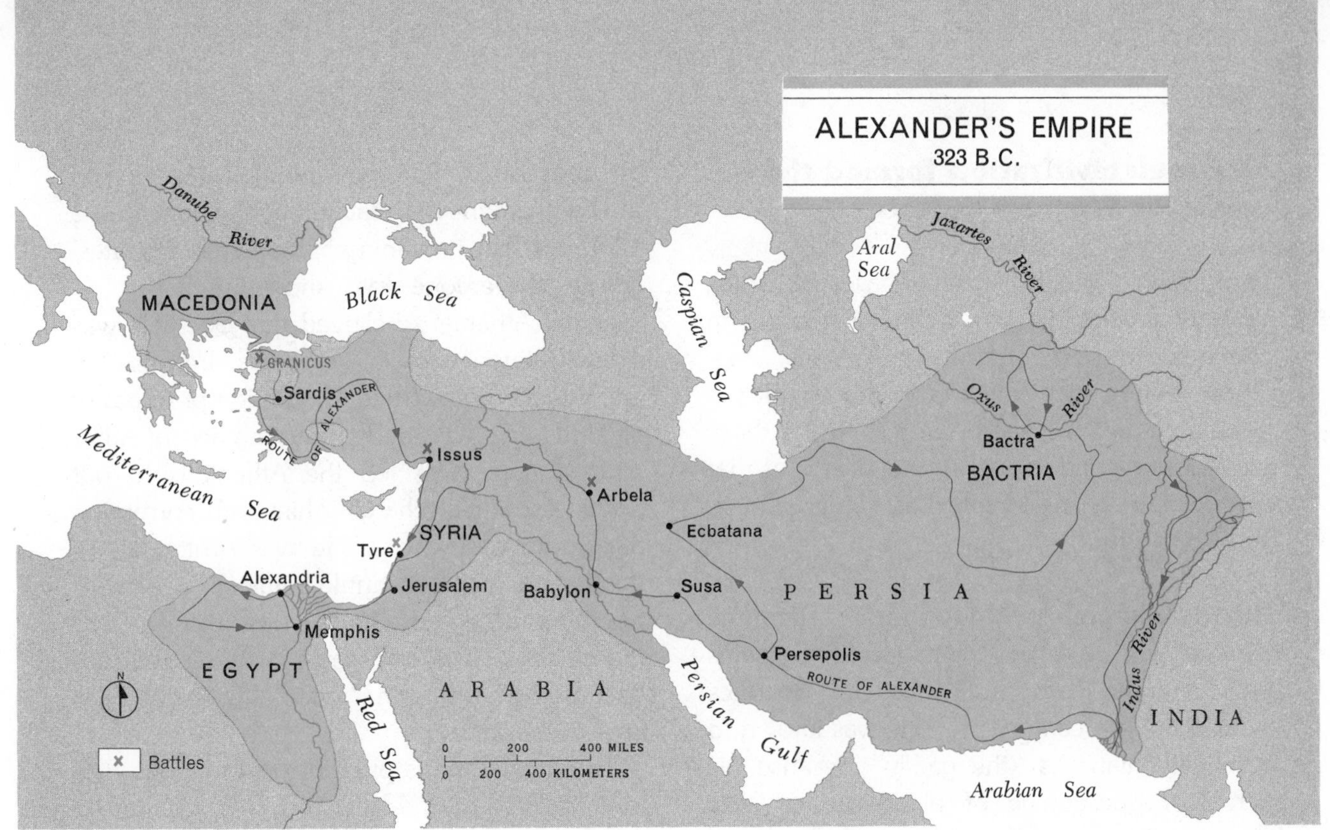

Commerce and culture spread during the Hellenistic Age. With the death of Alexander, the empire was left with no heirs to govern it. As a result, it was divided into three parts, each ruled by one of Alexander's generals. Antigonus [an tig′ ə nəs] ruled the kingdom of Macedonia, which had partial control over Greece. Egypt was ruled by Ptolemy [tol′ə mē]. Syria and Persia were ruled by Seleucus [sə lü′kəs]. Dynasties were established in these kingdoms, and the three parts made up what was called the *Hellenistic world.* The period of these kingdoms, called the *Hellenistic Age,* lasted for almost two hundred years after Alexander's death. ●

The Hellenistic Age was a time of great economic growth and of cultural exchange between East and West. The network of cities founded by Alexander made new markets for a variety of goods and acted as centers for the spread of Greek culture. The greatest city of all was Alexandria, Egypt, with a population of over half a million people. The city had wide, beautiful streets and a great library of 750 thousand books. A lighthouse nearly 400 feet (120 meters) high was judged by the Greeks to be one of the Seven Wonders of the World.

● It lasted until the Roman defeat of the last Ptolemy in 30 B.C.

SECTION REVIEW 4

1. Why was Philip able to conquer the Greek city-states? What was the result of his victory? p. 99, 100

2. What was unusual about Alexander's early training in leadership? Name the areas included in his empire. How was his empire divided after his death? p. 100, 101

3. How did Alexander try to form a "one world" culture in the areas he conquered? p. 100

5 Greek civilization formed the basis for Western culture

The Hellenic and Hellenistic phases of Greek civilization were different from each other in one basic respect. During the Hellenic Age, Greek culture was confined to the Greek peninsula. In the Hellenistic Age, it spread to those parts of the world known to the Greeks at that time, especially the Middle East, India, China, and North Africa.

● **Athens had great philosophers.** The three greatest Greek philosophers were Socrates [sok′rə tēz′], Plato, and Aristotle. Socrates lived in the 5th century B.C. He was known to other Athenians as "the gadfly" because his
ans. 1 persistent questioning of all ideas and acts stung his listeners into thinking. In fact, the so-called Socratic method consisted of asking questions and then carefully analyzing the answers to try to arrive at truth. Socrates might begin by asking the question, What is the beautiful and what is the ugly? Each answer would be questioned. Further questions were asked until agreement was reached by the participants about the exact meaning of the terms. Socrates' advice to everyone was "know thyself."

Some Athenians believed that Socrates was a bad influence on his students, because he encouraged young men to question practices of all kinds. He even questioned the acts of Athenian leaders. This led the Athenians to put Socrates on trial, charging him with corrupting the youth of the city. He was sentenced to death and made to drink hemlock, a poison. Socrates accepted the verdict calmly. His friends urged him to escape. Socrates refused, because he insisted that people must obey the laws of the state.

The most famous pupil of Socrates was Plato, who lived from 430 to 347 B.C. He started the Academy, a famous school in Athens that existed for almost nine hundred years. His best ans. 2
known work is *The Republic.* It is a book that describes an imaginary land in which each person does the work that suits that individual best. All young people would be given twenty years of education, and no job would be closed to women. Plato believed that there should be three classes of people. One class would be the workers who would produce the necessities of

Greece had a black population that came from its African colonies. This statue was modeled after a black youth.

● Point out to students that philosophers try to find out such things as the meaning of life, what is good, evil, etc.

life. Another class would be the soldiers who would guard the state. The final class would be the philosophers who would rule in the interests of all. Private property would be ended, and education would be set up for the benefit of the rulers. Today, Plato's ideas of communal life and a rigid class system seem harsh and much like Spartan ideas. However, *The Republic* is an important work because it was the first attempt to devise a planned society.

Plato's most famous pupil was the 4th-century philosopher, Aristotle. He was a brilliant thinker with wide interests. He wrote about biology, astronomy, physics, ethics, and politics. However, he is best known for his studies in logic.

Like most Athenians, Aristotle believed that a person could be happy by being moderate in most things. He taught that people should strike a balance, or mean point, between rash action and inactivity. According to this Doctrine of the Mean, the best way to meet danger is through brave action—brave action being the mean between foolhardiness and cowardice. In his *Politics,* Aristotle wrote about the good and bad features of different kinds of governments: monarchy, aristocracy, and democracy. Unlike Plato, he did not describe an imaginary state, nor did he find a single ideal system. *Politics* serves to point out an important difference between Plato and Aristotle. Plato often appears to deal only with abstract ideas. Aristotle seems more down-to-earth.

Hellenistic philosophers sought the good
ans. 2 **life.** Two major schools of Greek philosophy came out of the Hellenistic Age. These were Epicureanism [ep′ ə kyů rē′ə niz′ əm] and Stoicism [stō′ə siz′ əm]. The first was developed by Epicurus, a man who believed that a life free of extremes was best for lessening pain and increasing pleasure. Some of his followers misunderstood his ideas about pleasure. They thought he meant that one should only eat, drink, and be merry. For this reason, Epicureanism is often misinterpreted as meaning that pleasure, instead of the mental activity that Epicurus emphasized, is a way of gaining inner peace.

Zeno [zē′nō] developed a philosophy known as Stoicism. He taught that true happiness, or inner peace, can be reached by people when they find their proper places in nature. His followers were called *Stoics,* because they often met on a *stoa,* or porch. Believing all nature to be good, the Stoics thought that people must accept poverty, disease, and even death as the will of God. This philosophy led them to an indifference toward all kinds of experience, good or bad. Today, the word *stoic* means a person who does not show feelings or emotions.

The Greeks made many advances in science. In the Hellenic Age, Aristotle contributed to the development of the natural sciences. Other Greeks made important discoveries also.
Pythagoras [pə thag′ər əs], a philosopher, set ans. 3
up the geometric rule that bears his name, the Pythagorean [pə thag′ ə rē′ən] theorem. Hippocrates [hi pok′rə tēz′] founded a medical school. "Every disease has a natural cause," he said. His work helped end some of the superstitions and belief in magic that had stood in the way of the study of disease. Physicians today swear an oath based on one that Hippocrates drew up for the ethical conduct of doctors. It is called the Hippocratic oath.

During the Hellenistic Age, Euclid [yü′klid] wrote his textbook, *The Elements.* It is still the

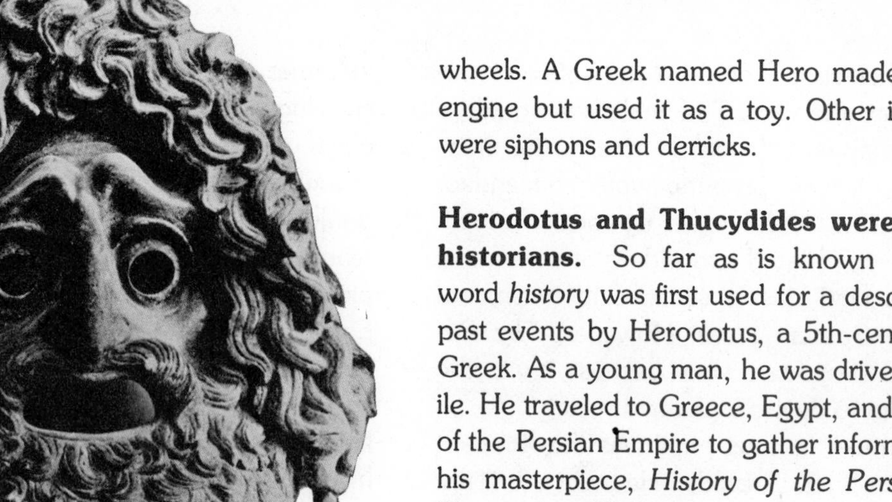

Masks used in Greek drama helped the audience see and hear the actors. They worked like megaphones.

basis for the study of plane geometry, and Euclid is often called "the father of geometry." Archimedes [är′ kə mē′dēz] figured out a way to measure the circumference of a circle. He also discovered the rule of specific gravity. He noticed that the water in his bathtub overflowed when he lowered himself into it. From this experience, he wrote what is known as Archimedes' law: "A body floating in a liquid is held up by a force equal to the weight of the liquid displaced." Another scientist, Aristarchus [ar′ is tär′ kəs] discovered that the earth rotated and revolved around the sun. Eratosthenes [er′ ə tos′thə nēz] made a fairly good estimate of the circumference of the earth. He also drew the first longitudes and latitudes on a map of the world. Thus, more than 1,700 years before • Columbus, Hellenistic scientists had learned that the earth is round.

Scientists of the Hellenistic Age made many machines that used levers, cranks, and geared wheels. A Greek named Hero made a steam engine but used it as a toy. Other inventions were siphons and derricks.

Herodotus and Thucydides were famous historians. So far as is known now, the word *history* was first used for a description of past events by Herodotus, a 5th-century B.C. Greek. As a young man, he was driven into exile. He traveled to Greece, Egypt, and the lands of the Persian Empire to gather information for his masterpiece, *History of the Persian War.* The work is filled with anecdotes, legends, and ans. 4
many entertaining bits of odd information that are not always reliable as historical evidence. However, Herodotus let the reader know when he was describing events that he could not verify. This allowed his readers to decide whether the events were fact or fiction. Herodotus' basic belief was that the gods punish people who have excessive pride. To his mind, the Persians were guilty of great pride and were destroyed by the gods. In spite of its rambling style, the *History* has caused Herodotus to be called "the father of history."

Like Herodotus, Thucydides lived in the 5th century B.C. and was also an exile. Also like Herodotus, Thucydides wrote only one book, the *History of the Peloponnesian War.* Here, however, the similarities between the two men end. Thucydides only used material that he felt was important to the history. He judged evidence and only used facts he had carefully checked. He said:

> Of the events of the war I have not ventured to speak from any information, nor according to any notion of my own; I have described nothing but what I either saw myself or learned from others of whom I made the most careful and particular inquiry.

• Emphasize this point. So many students still believe Columbus was trying to prove the world was round.

Thucydides looked for the human causes of the Greek wars. He did not believe that human events could be explained as fate or as acts of the gods. *History of the Peloponnesian War* has become a model for other historians.

ans. 5 **The Greeks invented drama.** Greek drama began as part of religious rites that were held at festivals honoring the god of wine, Dionysus [dī′ ə nī′səs]. A chorus of men chanted hymns and performed stately dances in praise of the god. In the 6th century B.C., changes in the rites eventually led to the development of drama. Individual actors were separated from the chorus and given roles to play. Dialogue was used. Most important was the use of new themes based on heroic tales not related to Dionysus.

Greek tragedy often expressed religious ideas, and poetic language was thought to be the proper form. The chorus was a basic part of the play, commenting on the action as it took place. Both men's and women's roles were played by men. Most important, tragedy dealt with serious matters—people's destinies and the problems of good and evil. The most famous authors of tragedies were three Athenian poets who lived in the 5th century: Aeschylus [es′kə ləs], Sophocles [sof′ə klēz′], and Euripides [yü rip′ə dēz′].

Comedy also began in the festivals of Dionysus. The greatest comic author was Aristophanes [ar′ə stof′ə nēz′], another 5th-century Greek. Since no laws protected Athenians from false or damaging statements, Aristophanes often ridiculed important citizens in his plays.

Now in ruins, the Theater of Dionysus dates from the 5th century B.C.

The Parthenon, on the Acropolis, has inspired many architects for centuries.

The open-air theater of Dionysus sat on the slopes of the Acropolis. It was semi-circular in shape and seated 14 thousand people. Various devices were used to make a play understandable to the large audiences. The actors wore thick-soled shoes to make them taller. They carried painted masks showing grief, horror, and other strong emotions. Speaking tubes were used to make the actors' voices louder.

Greek architecture and sculpture were widely copied. Most Greeks, even those who were rich, lived in simple clay-brick homes. However, they built beautiful temples of marble for their gods. The finest of these temples was the Parthenon. It is judged to be one of the most beautifully proportioned buildings of all time. Many modern buildings use features created by the Greeks.

Early Greek sculptors made bronze and marble figures that were stiff and formal. But later workers, including the famous Phidias [fid′ē əs] of the 5th century used the natural lines of the human body. In the 4th century B.C., Praxiteles [prak sit′l ēz′] carved figures that equaled or surpassed those of Phidias in grace and poise.

SECTION REVIEW 5

1. How did Socrates try to teach his students to think for themselves? Why was he put on trial? Why did he refuse to escape? p. 102

2. What were the contributions of Plato and Aristotle? How did the Stoics differ from the Epicureans? p. 102 103

3. What were the scientific contributions of Pythagoras, Hippocrates, Archimedes, Euclid, Aristarchus, and Erastosthenes? p. 103 104

4. What is the difference between history as written by Herodotus and by Thucydides? p. 104 105

5. How did Greek drama originate? What was the purpose of the chorus? What were the tragic dramas about? p. 105

CHAPTER REVIEW 5

SECTION SUMMARIES

1. Aegean civilization depended on sea trade. The first civilization, the Minoan, developed on Crete. Later Mycenae and Troy became important centers. In time, this civilization fell to a warlike people, the Dorians. They settled in the Peloponnesus and drove the Mycenaeans into Attica and Ionia. Gradually, the Dorians and the original inhabitants intermarried to become the Greeks.

2. The Greeks established the basic principles of democracy. Though the Greeks had a common language and customs, they formed city-states rather than one nation. The two most important city-states were Athens and Sparta. From a council of nobles and a weak assembly, Athens developed a democratic government. Sparta developed a militaristic state to prevent the downtrodden Messenians and helots from uprising. Athens and many other city-states set up colonies and trade routes in the Mediterranean region.

3. The Greeks were threatened by Persia and by city-state rivalries. During the Hellenic Age, 750–338 B.C., the Greeks beat off invasions of the Persians. Athens became the most powerful city-state, and the head of the Delian League. Athens reached its height during the Golden Age of Pericles. Then jealousy and fear of Athens led to the Peloponnesian War.

4. The Macedonians united Greece and the Hellenistic Age began. Weakened by wars among themselves, the city-states were prey to Philip of Macedonia. His conquest of Greece ended the Hellenic Age. Philip's son Alexander surpassed his father in military and political achievements. Using Greek and Macedonian forces, Alexander conquered the Persian Empire. He then spread Greek culture throughout his lands. His death was followed by the division of his empire.

WHO? WHAT? WHEN? WHERE?
2. 750-338 B.C.; 323 B.C.-123 B.C.
3. Answers will vary. See map p. 91.
4. Answers will vary. See map p. 101.

5. Greek civilization formed the basis for Western culture. The Greeks of the Hellenic Age left magnificent examples of sculpture, architecture, drama, and poetry. Outstanding contributions to philosophy and science were made. The Greeks' democratic government inspired democratic movements the world over. In the Hellenistic Age, new centers of Greek culture arose in the Middle East, especially in Alexandria. The chief contributions of this time were in science and technology, mathematics, and the philosophies of the Stoics and Epicureans.

WHO? WHAT? WHEN? WHERE?

1. Match the items below with the correct years:

2000–1501 B.C. k. 500–401 B.C. a., f., h., l.
1500–1001 B.C. c., i. 400–301 B.C. b., d.,
1000–501 B.C. e,. g., j., m., n.

a. The Golden Age of Pericles
b. Philip of Macedonia conquered Greece
c. The Dorians drove the Mycenaeans into Attica
d. Alexander began his attacks on the Persians
e. The first Olympic Games were held
f. The Parthenon was built
g. Cyrus attacked the Ionian Greeks
h. Plato wrote *The Republic*
i. The Mycenaeans captured Knossos
j. Sparta set up a military state
k. Crete became an important Aegean trade center
l. Athens won the battle of Marathon
m. Solon canceled debt slavery
n. Greek city-states set up colonies

2. Give the years of the Hellenic Age. Of the Hellenistic Age.

3. Name four modern countries and three islands where Greek colonies were located.

4. Name at least six modern countries, or parts of countries, in the area conquered by Alexander.

p. 96, 97 **5.** Explain the importance of the battles of Marathon and Salamis: Who was fighting? Who won? What were the results of the war?

p. 97 -99 **6.** Describe Athenian government in the Golden Age of Pericles: How did a citizen help run the government? Who made the laws and decided important issues? How were the generals controlled? Who received an education in Athens? Why? What groups were not allowed citizenship?

● **7.** Name the author and tell what each of these books is about:

Politics	*The Republic*
History of the Persian Wars	*Iliad*
History of the Peloponnesian War	*Odyssey*

QUESTIONS FOR CRITICAL THINKING

1. Compare Athenian democracy with democracy in the United States. How are they alike? Different? Could Americans have a pure democracy? Why or why not?

2. What do you think are the greatest things accomplished by the Greeks? Tell why you think so. Why were the Greeks able to do so much?

3. Why weren't the Greeks able to avoid being conquered by Macedonia? What should they have done?

ACTIVITIES

1. Find the Hippocratic Oath and report on its meaning.

2. Find out what the English word *marathon* means and why.

3. Write "historical" paragraphs in your own words using the methods of Herodotus or Thucydides.

4. Debate the good and bad points of Athenian democracy or Spartan militarism.

5. Act out the life of Socrates, his teaching, arrest, trial, and death. Discuss whether he should have escaped.

● *Politics*, Aristotle, analysis of government; *History of the Persian Wars,* Herodotus, rambling account of those wars; *History of the Peloponnesian War,* Thucydides, objective account of that war; *The Republic,* Plato, an ideal society; *Illiad* and *Odyssey,* Homer, the seige of Troy and travels of Ulysses.

CHAPTER TEST 5

SECTION 1

1. The earliest civilization on Crete is called _Minoan_.

2. True or false: The story of the fall of Troy is told in the *Iliad.*

3. True or false: There is evidence that shows there was contact between Egypt and Crete.

4. According to legend, a monster named _Minotaur_ lived in a _maze_ under the royal palace in Crete.

SECTION 2

5. The Greeks called themselves: a. Aegeans, b. Minoans, c. Hellenes

6. The Greeks were the first to develop _democracy_.

7. The Spartans valued: a. beauty, b. strength, c. freedom

SECTION 3

8. True or false: At the battles of Marathon and Salamis, the Greeks defeated the Phoenicians.

9. At the end of the Peloponnesian Wars, _Athens_ became the leading city in Greece.

10. The period from _460_ to _429_ B.C. is called the Golden Age of Pericles.

SECTION 4

11. The leader who dreamed of "one world" was: a. Philip, b. Alexander, c. Pericles

12. True or false: Greek culture spread throughout the known world during the *Hellenic* period.

13. True or false: At the death of Alexander, his empire was passed on to his son.

SECTION 5

14. The philosopher who refused to escape death was: a. Aristotle, b. Plato, c. Socrates

15. A person who does not show his or her feelings is called a _stoic_.

750 B.C.–
395 A.D.

CHAPTER
6

The Roman Empire

The mighty Roman army conquered an empire that extended from the Atlantic Ocean to Persia and included over 100 million people. Here four infantrymen and a standardbearer are shown from a large column made as a war memorial.

To Edward Gibbon, the 18th-century English historian and author of *Decline and Fall of the Roman Empire,* "the period in the history of the world during which the condition of the human race was most happy and prosperous" was the 2nd century A.D. It was during this century that the Roman Empire reached its greatest extent and was, according to Gibbon, "governed by absolute power, under the guidance of virtue and wisdom." A Roman subject

● This introduction begins with a series of quotations from a variety of sources giving conflicting points of view about the greatness of the Roman Empire. After students read, ask what they feel might account for these differences of opinion.

of the 2nd century had this to say about the era in which he lived:

> . . . The whole world keeps holiday; the age-long curse of war has been put aside; mankind turns to enjoy happiness. Strife has been quieted, leaving only the competition of cities, each eager to be the most beautiful and the most fair. Every city is full of gymnastic schools, fountains and porticos, temples, shops, and schools of learning. The whole earth is decked with beauty like a garden.

There were those who would disagree. Some thought Roman rule was a mixed blessing at best. Others felt it was oppressive and tyrannical. The famous modern-day historian, Arnold J. Toynbee, has called the 2nd century A.D. a time of stalemate when the world "lay more or less passive under the pall" of Roman power. The 2nd-century Roman historian Tacitus [tas′ə təs] agreed: "They [the Romans] make desolation, which they call peace."

A difference of opinion is a good point at which to begin to look at Roman history. In truth, military conquest made Rome a world state. The boundaries of the empire expanded as the Roman armies scored victory after victory. Yet force alone was not enough to maintain a unified state. Skillful diplomacy and effective government, a flexible system of law, a widespread network of roads and commercial towns—all these factors helped bring together a great number of peoples of varying customs and races. For over two centuries, from 27 B.C. to 180 A.D., the Romans maintained the *Pax Romana*, or "Roman Peace," throughout their far-flung domain.

The story of how Rome grew from a small city-state on the central Italian peninsula to a vast empire is told in this chapter as follows:

1. The Roman Republic arose on the Italian peninsula.

2. The republic became a world state.

3. The empire lasted for five centuries.

4. The Romans preserved Greek culture.

1 The Roman Republic arose on the Italian peninsula

Between 2000 and 1000 B.C., about the time that the Greek-speaking tribes were moving into their future homeland, another branch of Indo-Europeans moved south through the Alps • into the Italian peninsula. Most important were the Latins, a group of tribes who settled along the west coast of the central Italian peninsula in the lower valley of the Tiber [tī′bər] River. About midpoint in the 8th century B.C., they built a small settlement on the Palatine, a hill near the Tiber. The city of Rome grew from this modest beginning.

Early Rome was ruled by the Etruscans. In the 7th century B.C., the Latin tribes were conquered by their powerful neighbors to the north, the Etruscans. Little is known about the Etruscans. It is thought that they came originally from Asia Minor. They drained the marshes around Rome, encouraged trade, and taught the Latins to use arches in their buildings

Many important features of Roman government developed under Etruscan rule. A king of Etruscan descent ruled the state and was elect-

• Remind students that the Indo-Aryans who entered India at the same time (Chapter 3) were of the same language group.

ed to his office by the Latin tribal chieftains. He served as high priest as well as chief magistrate. The king chose a group of nobles known as the *senate* to advise him. These high-ranking freemen were usually large landowners and were known as *patricians* [pə trish′əns], or fathers of the state. The common people—small farmers and tradespeople—were known as *plebeians* [pli bē′əns].

The Roman Republic was established. In 509 B.C., the patricians led a revolt against their harsh Etruscan king, Tarquin the Proud. ans. 1 They then set up a *republic,* a state in which the citizens elected representatives to run the government. As in the early oligarchies of Greece, power in the Roman Republic was not in the hands of the people but was held tightly by the men at the top of the social scale.

The new republic was governed by two chief magistrates, called *consuls,* and the senate. The consuls could serve for only one year. This provision kept them from becoming too powerful. In wartime or other emergencies, a *dictator,* or absolute ruler, could rule in place of the consuls, but his term of office was limited to six months. The senate was made up of 300 members who were appointed for life by the consuls. The senate proposed the laws and nominated the consuls for office. Only patricians could become consuls or serve in the senate.

The plebeians had their own assembly that passed laws for their class. At first, however, it was not very important in Roman government.

Rome expanded within the Italian peninsula. Soon after Tarquin was overthrown,

Rome and the nearby Latin tribes got together to form the Latin League. By the beginning of the 4th century B.C., Rome and the league controlled the central Italian peninsula.

Two setbacks to Roman expansion occurred. The first was the invasion in 390 B.C. by the Gauls. These fierce, fair-haired warriors came from what is now France and northern Italy. The Gauls burned Rome to the ground. Although they left after they were paid a tribute, the damage to Roman prestige was serious. The second setback took place in 340 B.C., when other members of the Latin League, jealous of Rome, revolted. Two years later, Rome defeated them, dissolved the league, and forced each tribe to sign a separate treaty. The Romans then turned north and conquered the
ans. 2 Etruscans, who were weak from repeated attacks by the Gauls. A defensive line on the Arno River was set up to stop future attacks.

The only serious rivals to Roman rule left on the Italian peninsula were the Greeks in southern Italy. They had settled colonies there and on the island of Sicily [sis′ə lē] during the 8th century B.C.

ans. 2 The Greeks became alarmed at the growing power of Rome. They called upon Pyrrhus [pir′əs], a relative of Alexander the Great and an ambitious military leader from northern Greece, to help them. In 280 B.C., with an army of 25 thousand men and twenty elephants, he defeated the Romans in battle. He then invited the former members of the Latin League to join forces with him against Rome. They refused. Stunned, he made a peace offer to Rome. It was rejected. Pyrrhus then launched a second successful attack. But his losses were so great that he exclaimed, "Another such victory and we are lost." To this day, a costly victory is known as a *Pyrrhic victory*.

Pyrrhus returned to Greece, and the Romans quickly conquered the Greek holdings on the
Italian peninsula. By 270 B.C., less than 250 ans. 2
years after the founding of the republic, Rome was master of all the central and southern Italian peninsula.

The values of the early Romans helped strengthen the republic. Most of the early Romans were farmers. They lived simply,
worked hard, and fought well. The Roman ans. 3
family was a close-knit group. It was held together by affection, the necessities of a frugal life, and the strict authority of parents. Both parents played important roles in family activities. (See picture below.) They taught their children the virtues of loyalty, courage, and self-control. Most Romans took their civic and religious duties seriously. They strengthened the laws and customs of the republic.

The stern virtues prized by Roman family life were a source of strength to the early republic. In later years, when increasing power and wealth began to undermine Roman family life, some people were unhappy about the passing of the old order. "Rome stands built upon the ancient ways of life," warned a poet of the 3rd century B.C.

This tomb sculpture shows scenes in the life of a child to school age.

Military strength was combined with wise rule. The success of the Roman conquests was due largely to the well-trained army of citizen-soldiers. The basic military unit was the legion [lē′jən]. This infantry force had 6,000 men at full strength. The legions were divided into groups of 120 men each called *companies*. As Rome expanded, the need for soldiers increased. Conquered tribes were forced to supply troops for the Roman army.

The Romans had great talents for organization. They gave full privileges of Roman citizenship to some of the conquered. These conquered could vote and hold political office in Rome. Others were given less important rights, such as the right to own property in Rome.

Rome granted a large measure of independence to the peoples it conquered. They were free to run their own affairs, set up their own assemblies, and elect their own magistrates. Rome controlled the administration of justice and handled city-to-city affairs.

The plebeians wanted equal rights within Rome. Soon after the founding of the republic, the plebeians began to demand a greater role in government. As Rome's need for loyal and well-trained citizen-armies grew, the plebeians were able to gain a greater voice.

ans. 4 In 494 B.C., two plebeian officials, called *tribunes,* were appointed to protect the members of their class from injustice. Anyone, even a consul, who tried to harm a tribune, could be killed. In time, the number of tribunes was increased to ten. The tribunes sat in on senate discussions. They could not take part in the debates or vote. But if they felt the laws under discussion would not be in the plebeians' favor they could cry out *"Veto,"* that is, "I forbid." At first, the veto did not stop the senate from passing laws, but it encouraged senators to rethink unpopular legislation.

About 450 B.C., the plebeians won the right to have laws put in writing. This prevented judges from making different decisions on similar cases. These written laws were called the Laws of the Twelve Tables. They were carved on twelve bronze tablets hung in the *forum,* an open-air meeting place. One of the laws prohibited marriage between plebeians and patricians, but by 440 B.C., intermarriage had become legal.

Little by little, the plebeians made more gains. The veto power of the tribunes became effective. By the 4th century B.C., one of the consulships was held by a plebeian. At the end of that century, plebeians could become members of the senate. In 287 B.C., a law made ● the plebeian assembly into a popular assembly for the entire state. The old distinctions between patrician and plebeian were wiped away. However, the struggle for political power and social equality did not come to an end. In the centuries ahead, differences in wealth and status played an important part in the story of the internal affairs of Rome.

● This Tribal Assembly passed laws that were binding on all citizens, patricians as well as plebeians.

SECTION REVIEW 1

1. Describe the government of the early Roman Republic. p. 111

2. Name four enemies defeated by the Romans in their conquest of the Italian peninsula. In what year did Rome become master of the central and southern Italian peninsula? p. 112

3. Describe early Roman family life. How did the Roman family help keep the government strong? p. 112

4. Tell the steps by which the plebeians won more rights in the republic. p. 113

2 The republic became a world state

The story of Roman expansion turns next to Carthage, on the north African coast. The city of Carthage had been founded in 814 B.C. by Phoenicians. Carthage had grown rich from the sea trade in the western Mediterranean. The Carthaginian domain included territory in north Africa and the Iberian peninsula (present-day Spain) and important trading centers on the islands of Sardinia, Corsica, and Sicily. The strong Carthaginian navy blocked Roman expansion in the Mediterranean region.

Between 264 and 146 B.C., Carthage and Rome fought three wars, known as the *Punic* [pyü′nik] *Wars.* (The word *Punici* is Latin for Phoenicians.)

ans. 1 **The Punic Wars strained the resources of Rome.** Sicily was the prize of the First Punic War. The contest was clearly unequal. The odds favored Carthage, which was rich in gold, manpower, and ships. The Romans were not a seafaring people, but they realized that Carthage could be defeated only if its navy were smashed. With amazing determination, the Romans built up a navy. While the ships were being built, the Romans trained their soldiers as oarsmen on shore. Several Roman fleets were ● destroyed with great loss of life. Finally, the Romans were able to defeat the Carthaginians off the coast of Sicily in 241 B.C.

Sicily became the first Roman province. It was made to pay an annual tribute, or tax, of grain to Rome. Three years after the end of the war, Sardinia was conquered; later, Corsica. In 227 B.C., both were made into a single province. No longer was Roman power restricted to the Italian peninsula. The Roman navy was the strongest in the western Mediterranean. Although the First Punic War had exhausted Rome and Carthage, both made ready for another struggle.

The Second Punic War has been called a "conflict between the nation Rome and the man Hannibal." Hannibal was a Carthaginian general whose military genius has been rated as equal to that of Alexander the Great. Hannibal began the war in 219 B.C. by attacking a Roman ally, the city of Sagento in the Iberian peninsula. With cavalry, war elephants, and about 40 thousand infantrymen, Hannibal then crossed through southern Gaul and over the Alps into the Italian peninsula. The difficult journey cost him about half of his men, much of his equipment, and all but one elephant. With the Gauls of the northern Italian peninsula as allies, Hannibal began to march south.

To meet the emergency, the Romans made Fabius Maximus dictator. He was a cautious leader who refused to risk an all-out battle. His so-called *Fabian policy* of watchful waiting frustrated Hannibal. However, it was unpopular with many Romans. They wanted a face-to-face battle with Hannibal. It came at Cannae [kan′ā] in the southern Italian peninsula. There, in 216 B.C., the Carthaginian general encircled the Romans and wiped out a force at least a third larger than his own. But Hannibal dared not lay siege to Rome without reserves of manpower and supplies. He was cut off from these by Roman armies in the Iberian peninsula and on Sicily.

Finally, the Romans decided to open up another front. Under the leadership of Scipio the Elder, Roman forces invaded north Africa. Hannibal had to return home to defend Carthage. At Zama [zā′mə] in 202 B.C., Hannibal was defeated. He fled to the east to save his ■

● The Romans lost 200,000 men in these first naval battles.

■ Hannibal continued anti-Roman activities and in 182 B.C. committed suicide to escape capture by the Romans.

life. The peace terms dictated by the Romans were harsh. Carthage gave up its navy, lost its freedom in foreign affairs, paid annual tribute to Rome, and surrendered the Iberian peninsula. Still, the Romans were afraid Carthaginian power would grow again.

This fear was well founded. In 150 B.C., the Carthaginians attacked a Roman ally. The Romans replied by attacking North Africa one year later. They laid siege to Carthage and kept food from coming into the city. Most of the people starved to death. When the Romans entered Carthage, they burned the city to the ground. Then they destroyed the fertility of the soil by throwing salt into the plowed land outside the city. The Carthaginians who were left were sold into slavery. Thus, in 146 B.C. the Third Punic War ended. Rome made the former Carthaginian holdings in north Africa into the Roman province of Africa.

ans. 2 **Roman armies were victorious in the east.** Shortly after the end of the Second Punic War, the Roman legions turned eastward. After a series of wars, they defeated the Macedonians. In 146 B.C., Macedonia became a Roman province. In the same year, the Romans burned Corinth and made the other Greek city-states subject to Rome.

When the king of Pergamum in Asia Minor willed his kingdom to Rome in 133 B.C., the Romans began to take over lands in the Middle East. Egypt and other countries allied themselves with Rome and later became Roman territories. By 100 B.C., all land bordering the Mediterranean was under Roman control.

Roman expansion led to changes within the republic. During the Punic Wars and the conquest of Mediterranean lands, changes were taking place in the republic. These changes made the years from 150 to 31 B.C. stormy ones.

As Rome became increasingly involved in ans. 3
foreign affairs, the senate grew in power and prestige by conducting state negotiations. The popular assembly had the power to *ratify* treaties, that is, to approve them, and to declare war. However, this body acted merely as a rubber stamp for the decisions of the senators. The tribunes became yes-men of the senate. Political power had become concentrated in the senate. Corruption in government increased, particularly in the provinces. ● Officials sent to the provinces often took advantage of their jobs to make themselves rich. The senate decided whom the army would buy supplies from and who could collect taxes in the provinces. Men who wanted these jobs often bribed senators to get them.

The wars hurt farming in the Italian peninsula. The southern peninsula had been devastated by Hannibal's army. The farmers from this region drifted to Rome in search of jobs. But there were none. The big landowners used slaves captured in wars to work their land, and there was no large-scale industry to give these farmers jobs. An unhappy, out-of-work mob ■ was created that could easily be made to riot.

As the riches of war poured into Rome, some people became rich for the first time. This new wealth changed Roman attitudes toward the state. The traditions of public duty and self-discipline gave way to greed and soft living.

Civil War weakened the republic. Two brothers, Tiberius [tī bir′ē əs] and Gaius [gī′yəs] Gracchus [grak′əs], came to the support of the masses. In 133 B.C., Tiberius was elected tribune. He proposed a law that would

● It may be necessary to define the term *corruption.*

■ The disappearance of the small land-owner was one of the basic causes of the decline of the Roman Republic.

MAZICINVS

Roman Daily Life *Opposite page, top left:* Contests between gladiators were a popular form of entertainment. This mosaic shows the winner Alumnus waving his sword over the dead, upside down Mazicin. *Opposite page, top right:* When a patrician went out in the streets, he or she might ride in a litter. Strong servants, identically dressed, would lift the corner poles onto their shoulders. A cushion and curtains made the ride comfortable. *This page right:* This water heater made hot water available for washing and cooking. *Opposite page, bottom:* The many products of the empire were sold in the cities. Here men and women bargain for pillows. *Below:* Here actors dress for a comedy. Roman masks were more caricatured, less formal, than the Greek.

divide the farmlands gained in war among the out-of-work farmers. He also wanted to make it against the law for any person to own more than a certain amount of land. His proposal would have taken away land from some of the richest families. To stop him, a group of rich men had him murdered. They also had 300 of his followers killed, saying these followers were public enemies.

Ten years later, Gaius was elected tribune. He was able to pass a land reform bill, and the wealthy were again alarmed. Many of Gaius' supporters were attacked and killed. Gaius committed suicide.

Rome was now the scene of bitter rivalry between the People's party, supported by the plebeians and the masses, and the senate, the agent of the rich patricians. The country was divided by violence and civil war. Hundreds of Romans were killed. Finally, Sulla [sul′ə], a victorious general, restored order. He doubled the size of the senate and limited the power of the veto. Sulla's changes wiped out many of the gains made by the plebeians in their long struggle for equality. In 79 B.C., Sulla retired. He had brought peace to Rome, but his changes were not to last.

Julius Caesar became dictator of Rome. During the time of civil strife, the army had changed. Traditionally, the Roman army had been made up of citizens who fought because of duty to the state. Now the army included volunteers from the landless class. These soldiers expected to get rich from the gains of war. They were willing to serve for long periods of time and were loyal to their leader. It was easy to see that a popular general could use his military power to gain political power. Such a man was the brilliant general Julius Caesar [sē′zər].

● He also reformed the calendar using Egyptian knowledge; with minor changes, this calendar of 365¼ days is still in use today.

After a successful military career in the Iberian peninsula, Julius Caesar joined with Pompey, another military hero, and Crassus, one of the wealthiest men in Rome. Their support made it possible for Caesar to become consul. In 60 B.C., the three men formed a union, called the First Triumvirate [trī um′və rāt′], to rule the state jointly.

From 58 to 51 B.C., in the Gallic Wars, Caesar conquered Gaul and extended Roman borders northward to include most of modern France and Belgium. He also led his legions across the English Channel to invade Britain. These accomplishments made Caesar popular with the Roman masses. But the jealous senate, fearing his growing power, ordered him to return to Rome without his army. Caesar knew that to obey meant imprisonment or death. Crassus was dead, and Pompey, he knew, had conspired with the senate to ruin him. ans. 4

On January 10, 49 B.C., Caesar brought his army across the Rubicon River into the northern part of the Italian peninsula. Afraid of the legions who were friendly to Caesar, Pompey and most of the senators fled to Greece. Caesar followed and defeated them. When Caesar returned to Rome, he became dictator.

During his five years of rule, Caesar made moderate reforms. He weakened the power of the senate, but at the same time increased its membership to 900. Roman citizenship was extended to persons living outside the Italian peninsula. In the provinces, taxes were adjusted and the administration improved. ●

The senate became afraid that Caesar meant to make himself king and begin a dynasty. A group of men, including Marcus Brutus, one of his best friends, joined in a plot to murder Caesar. On March 15, 44 B.C., a day known as the "Ides of March," the plotters surrounded Caesar on the floor of the senate building and stabbed him to death.

Augustus became the first Roman emperor. Before his death, Julius Caesar had made his grandnephew and adopted son, Octavian, his heir. The eighteen-year-old Octavian joined with Mark Antony, Caesar's chief lieutenant to restore order in Rome and to punish the murderers. They attacked Brutus and his fellow conspirators, defeating them in the Battle of Philippi in 42 B.C.

For the next ten years, Octavian and Antony shared absolute power in the republic. Octavian ruled Rome and the western part of the empire. Antony ruled Egypt and the eastern part. While Octavian was shrewdly increasing his power in Rome, Antony had fallen in love with Cleopatra, the glamorous queen of Egypt. Word reached Rome that Antony had given Roman territory to Cleopatra and was plotting to seize the whole empire. Octavian persuaded the Romans to declare war on Egypt.

In 31 B.C., at Actium, a cape on the western coast of Greece, Octavian's fleet clashed with that of Antony and his queen. When Cleopatra fled the battle, Antony deserted his men and followed her to Egypt. The following year, Octavian landed in Egypt. Antony and Cleopatra, unable to get a navy to fight him, committed suicide. Egypt became a Roman province.

ans. 5 Octavian returned to Rome and proclaimed that he would return the government from a dictatorship to a republic. Although he was careful to observe the forms of republican government, he kept the final power in his own hands, largely through his control of the army. He was called *imperator* from which the word "emperor" comes. In 27 B.C., the senate gave Octavian the honorary title of Augustus, meaning "The Majestic." From then on, he was known by that name. After a century of civil war, Rome at last had been united under one ruler. The reign of Augustus ushered in the Roman Empire.

SECTION REVIEW 2

1. Give the years of the Punic Wars and the lands p. 114,
won in each war. 115

2. How and when did Rome get control of the eastern Mediterranean areas of Macedonia, Greece, Pergamum, and Egypt? p. 115

3. What changes in government, farming, city life, and attitudes of the people took place as Rome became a world power? Why did these changes happen? p. 115

4. Why was Julius Caesar popular with the Roman people? Why did the senate fear him? p. 118

5. How did Octavian become the supreme ruler of Rome? p. 119

3 The empire lasted for five centuries

Augustus ruled a mighty world state. The empire extended east to the Euphrates River and west to the Atlantic Ocean, north to the Rhine and Danube rivers and south across the Mediterranean to north Africa and the sands of the Sahara. By the 2nd century A.D., the empire included 100 million people of different races, faiths, and customs.

Generally speaking, the first two and one half centuries of the empire were peaceful and prosperous. This period, from 27 B.C. to 180 A.D., is known as the *Pax Romana*, or "Roman Peace." Within the empire, business grew as conditions for trade improved. Bandits and pirates were hunted down. Roads and sea lanes were cleared for commerce. Ostia, at the mouth of the Tiber River, served as a seaport for the city of Rome. Egypt, North Africa, and Sicily furnished grain for the entire empire. Timber and various farm products came from Gaul and central Europe. The Iberian peninsula supplied gold, silver, and lead; Britain, tin; Cyprus, copper; the Balkans, iron ore and gold. Outside the empire, Rome carried on a thriving trade with distant lands, such as India and China.

Augustus was the architect of the Pax Romana. Augustus proved to be a wise ruler. He improved the government of the prov-
ans. 1 inces and did away with corruption there. A census was taken and tax rates were adjusted. A program of public works was begun; and roads, bridges, and aqueducts were built.

Augustus was not successful in his attempts to restore the old ideas of Roman simplicity and home life. Laws were passed to encourage large families and to limit luxurious living—but with little lasting effect. He made the old religious rituals again a part of the affairs of state. In time, worship of the emperor began, and as the years went by, served as a bond for all peoples within the empire.

Both bad and good rulers followed Augustus. When Augustus died in 14 A.D., the senate voted the title of imperator to his stepson, Tiberius. It was during his reign, which lasted until 37 A.D., that Jesus was crucified in Palestine. From the time of Tiberius to the end of the empire in 476 A.D., Rome was ruled by a wide variety of emperors, some improved the government and some thought only of selfish interests. Nero, judged the most wicked and worthless ruler ever to mount the throne, murdered his wife and his mother. He was accused ● of setting fire to Rome in 64 A.D. This nine-day catastrophe destroyed half the city.

In spite of incompetent rulers, the empire held together. Efficient administrators at many ans. 2
levels of responsibility kept justice and order. Commercial strength helped keep the empire stable. Only when economic decline and social unrest set in did the lack of good leadership at the top harm the empire.

During the 2nd century A.D., the empire enjoyed the rule of a group of good emperors. Trajan, who ruled from 98 to 117, was an ambitious military leader. Before his death, the ■ empire reached its greatest extent. His successor, Hadrian, ruled from 117 to 138. Hadrian made it his policy to strengthen the frontiers. Traveling throughout the empire, he supervised the building of many public works. One of the most famous projects was Hadrian's Wall in Britain. This wall was built as a protection against the unfriendly tribes living in what is now Scotland. Marcus Aurelius, who ruled from 161 to 180, won both the respect and admiration of his people. His volume of essays, called *Meditations,* is one of the best expressions of the Stoic philosophy ever written. It is one of the ironies of history that this scholarly, bookish man was forced to spend most of his rule as a soldier, defending the frontiers of the empire in the north and east.

Economic decline and political instability weakened the empire. By the end of the ans. 3
2nd century A.D., attacks on the frontiers came more and more often. To meet these threats, the empire doubled the size of its army. The drain on the supply of men and resources brought on an economic crisis that

● Nero may or may not have been responsible for the fire. He did, however, use the disaster as an excuse for terrible persecutions of the Christians whom he blamed for starting the fire.

■ The empire at that time consisted of more than 1¼ million square miles and 100 million people of various ethnic groups.

was made more severe by other factors. Poverty and unemployment were on the rise. Trade started to fall off. In an attempt to save valuable metals, the emperors reduced the gold and silver content of the money in circulation. Because money was worth less, people charged higher prices. Thus inflation and further hardship came about.

Business was hurt by crime of all kinds which, in turn, was caused by political instability. Meetings of the senate and the popular assembly had become formalities. These two groups were no longer effective in governing the state. Political power was held by the emperor, who himself was often at the mercy of the army. Peaceful succession to the imperial throne was rare. The death of an emperor signaled a free-for-all struggle. Of the twenty-nine emperors who ruled between 180 and 284 A.D., only four died of natural causes. The others were murdered by army officers or by rivals for the throne. The soldiers had the real power to select the new emperor. As a result, emperors often followed the cynical advice of Emperor Septimius Severus, who is said to have told his sons, "Make the soldiers rich and don't trouble about the rest." To keep the legions at full strength, barbarians were recruited and war captives were forced to enlist. These new legionnaires cared for the empire only so long as they were paid.

Two emperors tried despotism to save Rome. After a century of decline and civil disorder, two emperors were able to halt the disintegration of the empire. The first was Diocletian [dī ə klē′shən], who reigned from 284 to 305 A.D. He set up a full-fledged *despotism,* or government by a ruler with unlimited power. Harsh laws controlled all business.

● Constantine, in 313, legalized Christianity.

To style hair, curling irons, dyes, hair nets, wigs, and hairpins were used.

Constantine was the next emperor and he enforced even more despotic control over his subjects. He also moved the capital of the empire from Rome to Byzantium, which he renamed Constantinople after himself. ●

Diocletian and Constantine halted civil war and economic decline for a time. Yet, as a cure-all, despotism proved worse than the ills from which the empire suffered. State regulation of business killed individual initiative. The secret police choked off reform. Trade came to a standstill in many places, and the amount of wealth available for taxation decreased. After the death of Constantine in 337, rivals for the throne butchered one another. The last ruler of a united Roman Empire was Theodosius I. At his death in 395, the empire was divided between his two sons: one son ruled the western half, the other son ruled the east. ans. 4

Time capsules on planet Earth

Time capsules are usually buried in the ground or in the cornerstone of a building. Some time capsules have been in place for a hundred years or more. Inside the time capsule, which is usually a hollow cylinder or block, are things people have put there to show future generations what their way of life was like. What might you find in a time capsule? Could an entire city be put in a time capsule? In a way, that's what happened to Pompeii, in southern Italy, some 1,700 years ago.

Until August 24, 79 A.D., the city of Pompeii [pom pā′] was a bustling, fun-loving place. It was bounded on one side by mountains and on the other by the sea. In between were gently curving streets and gracious houses. Cool interior gardens and fountains in the houses gave pleasure to their owners. Beautiful wall paintings, called *frescoes*, decorated the inside walls of many buildings.

Streetside was another story. Graffiti covered the blank outside walls of buildings. Children wrote the alphabet up as high on the walls as they could reach, and boys scribbled their girlfriends' names. Pompeians even left messages for each other: "Samius to Cornelius – Go hang yourself!"

The city had a huge sports arena where the government staged free entertainment. Gladiatorial contests were the favorites. And Pompeii did well in business. Trade in wine, olive oil, and clothing were all very successful.

Founded about 800 years earlier, this city of nearly 20,000 people prospered. They never paid much attention to Vesuvius, the volcanic mountain that loomed over them. Then suddenly Vesuvius blew up. Volcanic cinders and ash began to fall in the streets and on the houses like rain. By August 26, Pompeii was buried under 20 feet (6 meters) of lava chunks and ash. More than 75 percent of the people were dead.

The volcano was a good preserver. It made a time capsule that was not opened until 1748. In that year, archaeologists found Pompeii. They found hollows in the ash where Pompeians had fallen, dying from the poisonous fumes or the rocks that Vesuvius shot out. Plaster was poured into the hollows, and casts were obtained, some of pet dogs and their owners. Coins were recovered from cafe counters where they had been dropped. Surgical instruments, a little pig in a roasting oven, and brushes in the bath lay where they were abandoned by fleeing citizens.

Are there other time capsules like Pompeii? Very likely. One of them may be the "lost continent" of Atlantis that Plato wrote about in 355 B.C. Others may lie buried deep in the earth and long forgotten. Our planet may be full of time capsules waiting to be discovered.

SECTION REVIEW 3

p. 120 1. How did Augustus improve the government and economy of the provinces?

p. 120 2. Why was the empire able to survive during periods when there were bad rulers?

p. 120 121 3. What problems weakened the empire between 180 and 284 A.D.?

p. 121 4. What did Diocletian and Constantine do to stop the empire from falling apart? Why was despotism not the answer to Rome's problems?

4 The Romans built on Greek culture

The roots of Western civilization can be traced to the blend of Greek and Roman culture, known as *classical culture,* that flourished during the *Pax Romana.* The Romans admired Hellenic culture and borrowed widely from the Greeks. In the process, certain elements of the culture were changed. For example, Roman sculpture became more lifelike than the Greek; Roman architecture, more elaborate. In addition, the Romans themselves made many contributions of their own that, when added to the Greek heritage, helped form a truly Greco-Roman culture. Perhaps the greatest single achievement of the Romans was the creation of a body of laws suitable for governing a world state.

ans. 1 **Roman law held the peoples of the empire together.** In modern-day Italy, France, Spain, and Latin America, law codes based on Roman legal principles are still in use. Law in the modern English-speaking countries was also greatly influenced by Roman law.

Roman law developed from the Laws of the Twelve Tables—those written laws won by the plebeians so that they would know how they would be ruled. As Rome expanded, laws governing noncitizens were added. The decisions of different magistrates in the provinces were kept, and these *legal interpretations* helped other judges decide cases. Sometimes, the existing laws of a conquered place influenced the magistrate's decision. In this way, local rules and customs became a part of the larger body of Roman law. Roman laws became international, particularly the laws dealing with commerce. When Augustus was emperor, professional law schools were established to teach the law. Later, in the 6th century A.D., Justinian, emperor of the eastern empire, had this huge body of laws *codified,* that is, organized into a system that could more easily be used.

The Latin language was a lasting gift to civilization. The Romans spoke a language called Latin. It is one of the Indo-European languages, as are German, Slavic, Greek, and Sanskrit. The Romans did not develop writing until the 7th century B.C., when they adopted an alphabet used by the Etruscans. Writing with an alphabet is much easier than writing with picture forms, as in Chinese, the oldest system of writing still in use. Today, the so-called Roman alphabet is the most widely used alphabet in the world.

During the years of Roman civilization, two forms of Latin developed. One was literary Latin, the form used in writing. The second was the *vernacular* [vər nak′yə lər], or simplified, spoken language used in people's everyday dealings with each other. Literary Latin continued to be more formal and is highly prized for its logic and exactness.

ans. 4 Latin was the official language of business, education, government, and the arts throughout the empire. It formed the basis of the modern Spanish, Portuguese, Romanian, French, and Italian languages and contributed many words to English. All of these languages are written in the Roman alphabet, as are German, Dutch, Polish, Czech, Hungarian, Finnish, Swedish, and Turkish. Literary Latin was preserved for centuries after the end of the Roman Empire because it was the official language of the Roman Catholic Church. Today, it still uses Latin for all official documents, but the vernacular is no longer spoken.

The Romans were great engineers and architects. A network of roads knit together the Roman realm. They were built to help speed the movement of armies and military supplies, but the roads were free to the public for travel and commerce. Built of several layers of stone, the Roman roads were superior to any highways constructed in Europe until the 1800s. Roman engineering skill was used throughout the empire in the construction of numerous dams, bridges, drainage systems, and *aqueducts*—bridgelike structures that held water pipes.

From the Etruscans, the Romans learned ans. 2
how to build arched constructions called *vaults*. Little by little, the Romans improved vault forms so that large interior spaces could be enclosed. To roof these areas, domes were often used. To make the structures solid and lasting, Roman architects used cement and concrete as basic materials. Exteriors were faced with marble or stucco and decorated with sculpture. The Romans preferred decoration to the simplicity of Greek architecture.

Roman public buildings were both magnificent and practical. The public baths were multilevel structures that included steam rooms, different bathing and swimming pools, gardens, gyms, and libraries. The Roman baths, which were like modern athletic clubs, served as popular meeting places for social and business purposes. By the 4th century A.D., the city of Rome boasted 1,000 public baths. The huge Colosseum in Rome seated 50 thousand persons and was the scene of bloody gladiatorial combats and even mock naval battles. At the Circus Maximus, a stadium in Rome that seated 150 thousand, chariot races were held.

The Romans are justly famous for city planning. Provincial cities and towns were usually built around a central public square, called a

The aqueduct *(left)*, atrium *(center)*, and apartment building *(right)* show off Roman construction skill. Aqueducts carried drinking water for miles across rivers and valleys. The atrium was an interior courtyard graced with fountains and plants onto which the doors and windows of a townhouse opened. Apartment buildings were sometimes five stories high.

forum, that was close to the crossing of two main roads. The main civic buildings and the marketplace were centrally located in the forum area, and building codes were enforced to keep architectural styles uniform. The logical planning in the provinces was in strong contrast to the capital city of the empire. Rome had narrow, winding streets, a poor drainage system, and was overcrowded. In the 2nd century A.D., the city's population of over a million persons was jammed into 9 square miles (23.4 square kilometers). Augustus claimed that he had found the city of brick and had left it of marble. However, the splendid public buildings built or repaired under his direction were often flanked by dark and flimsy tenement houses. Throughout the lifetime of the empire, Rome remained a sprawling, bustling city of magnificence and squalor.

The Romans used Greek models for literature. Throughout the history of Rome, Greek literature remained the most important influence on Latin literary works. An educated Roman was expected to know Greek as well as Latin. Wealthy families often owned Greek slaves who served as tutors for the children of the household. With Greek models to imitate, the Romans developed a literature of the first rank. While it was the Greek genius to speculate brilliantly about destiny and the universe, the Romans had a gift for describing less high-flown ideas, using literature to point out important ethical concepts.

The wealth and leisure resulting from Roman conquests provided a growing audience for literature. From about 100 B.C. to 14 A.D.—the years from the last century of the republic through the reign of Augustus—Latin literature was at its best. This period has been called the Golden Age of Latin literature.

One of the leading writers of the Golden Age ans. 4
was the master statesman and polished orator, Cicero [sis′ə rō′]. His speeches, letters, and essays showed a wide-ranging intellect and nobility of character. The respect he commanded as spokesman for the senate made Mark Antony jealous. Antony had Cicero put to death in 43 B.C. Julius Caesar contributed to Latin literature. His military history, *Commentaries on the Gallic Wars,* is famous for its careful descriptions and vigorous style.

The greatest poet of the Golden Age was Vergil [vėr′jəl]. He has been called the "Homer of Rome" because the *Iliad* and the *Odyssey* served as models for his epic, the *Aeneid*

[i nē′id]. The chief character in Vergil's work was Aeneas, a legendary Trojan hero who overcame many obstacles before founding the city of Rome. The most outstanding aspect of the *Aeneid* is Vergil's patriotism; the glories of Rome were praised in poetry. Another patriotic writer was Livy [liv′ē], whose history of Rome was called *From the Founding of the City.* By picturing the past greatness of Rome in glowing terms, he hoped to convince his readers to return to the simple ways of their ancestors.

The Roman historian Tacitus [tas′ə təs] is best known for *Germania,* his study of the German tribes that lived north of the imperial frontiers in central Europe. Like Livy, Tacitus urged a return to traditional Roman values. His work contrasts the strength and simplicity of the Germans with the weakness and immorality of upper-class life in Rome.

A second important writer was the Greek biographer Plutarch [plü′tärk]. His masterpiece, *Parallel Lives*, paired forty-six biographies of Greek and Roman statesmen, orators, or warriors whose careers and talents were similar. Plutarch did not flatter the Greeks at the expense of the Romans. His accounts were well balanced and his judgments of character sound. His descriptions of people and events are so colorful that *Parallel Lives* proved to be an invaluable source for later writers. The famous English playwright Shakespeare drew heavily on Plutarch's biographies when writing *Julius Caesar* and *Antony and Cleopatra.*

Greeks in the empire made important scientific discoveries. During Roman times, most of the noted men of science were Greeks. Alexandria, Egypt, the former Greek colony, was a center for research and experimentation, with its famous museum and library. One famous Greek scholar was the astronomer Ptolemy [tol′ə mē]. Between 127 and 151 A.D., he brought together in one book all that was then known about astronomy. For 1,500 years, Ptolemy's views were generally accepted by educated people. Unlike Aristarchus before him, he believed that the sun revolved around the earth. Also a map maker, Ptolemy was the first to draw the earth as round. ●

The Greek physician Galen [gā′lən], who lived in the 2nd century A.D., also studied in Alexandria. Next to Hippocrates, he was the most famous doctor of ancient times. He discovered that arteries contain blood. Up to that time, they were thought to be filled with air.

The Romans themselves made few contributions to scientific knowledge. However, they were skillful in applying Greek findings in medicine and public health. The Romans built the first hospitals, some of which gave free medical care to the poor. About 14 A.D., the first school of medicine was established in Rome, and it was there that Celsus [kel′səs], a Roman-born physician, wrote and taught. One of his books describes surgical procedures for removing tonsils and cataracts, as well as the steps involved in elementary plastic surgery.

SECTION REVIEW 4

1. In what countries of the world today are the laws based on Roman law? p. 123

2. What types of buildings did the Romans erect? What materials were used? How was Roman architecture different from that of the Greeks? p. 124

3. Who were the greatest writers of the Golden Age of Latin literature? Name their works. p. 125 126

4. What language did the Romans speak? In what ways did it continue to be used after the end of the empire? p. 124

● Unfortunately he exaggerated the size of Asia, influencing Columbus to believe the Atlantic Ocean was smaller than it is and to set sail from Spain in search of Asia.

CHAPTER REVIEW 6

SECTION SUMMARIES

1. The Roman Republic arose on the Italian peninsula. Conquered by the Etruscans in the 7th century B.C., the Romans overthrew their Etruscan king in 509 B.C. and set up a republic that lasted until 31 B.C. After a long struggle for equal rights with the high-born patricians, the plebeians got some control over the government. From 509 to about 100 B.C., the Roman state expanded. By 270 B.C., the Italian peninsula was conquered.

2. The republic became a world state. Rome defeated Carthage in the Punic Wars. Further military campaigns in the Middle East resulted in Roman control by 100 B.C. over lands bordering the Mediterranean. Although conquest brought wealth to Rome, it also created serious problems for the republic. Graft and corruption increased. Rich officials bought up the land of the little farmers, who then went to Rome vainly seeking work. The population became divided into the many poor and the few very rich. The tribunes Tiberius and Gaius Gracchus were unsuccessful in their attempts to reform the state, and civil wars broke out, lasting for about 100 years. Finally, after the Battle of Actium in 31 B.C., Octavian (later known as Augustus) became ruler of Rome. He was a strong ruler whose reign marked the beginning of the Roman Empire.

3. The empire lasted for five centuries. The first 250 years of the empire were peaceful and prosperous, and the *Pax Romana* was extended from Britain to the Euphrates, from the Rhine to North Africa. By the 3rd century A.D., the Roman Empire had begun to show signs of decay. Poverty increased, business activity declined, and the authority of the central government weakened. Diocletian and Constantine chose despotism as a way to strengthen the government, but civil wars followed their reigns.

2. Answers will vary.

3. pp. 115-116. Gracchus Bros. tried land reform Sulla increased the power of the Senate, ending civil war between the common people and the Senate. Caesar reformed taxes, citizenship requirements, and

4. The Romans preserved Greek culture. The Romans developed a legal system that was effective in holding together the many different peoples and customs of the empire. Engineers and architects built excellent roads, bridges, aqueducts, and massive public buildings. Literature flourished, particularly during the last century of the republic and the reign of Augustus. The Romans admired Hellenistic culture and blended it with their own achievements to form a truly Greco-Roman culture.

WHO? WHAT? WHEN? WHERE?

1. Give the dates for each of these events, and arrange the events in chronological order:

3 The Roman Republic was begun. 509 B.C.
9 Diocletian set up a despotic government. 284-305 A.D.
8 Octavian defeated Antony in the Battle of Actium. 31 B.C.
1 Rome was founded. 8th Cent. B.C.
2 The Latins were conquered by the Etruscans. 7th cent. B.C.
7 Caesar became dictator of Rome. 49 B.C.
10 Constantine moved the capital to Byzantium. 309-395 A.D.
4 Tribunes were created to protect the plebeians. 494 B.C.
6 The Romans destroyed Carthage. 146 B.C.
5 Pyrrhus won a costly victory over Rome. 280 B.C.

2. Using the map of the Roman Empire in the book on page 111 and modern maps of the world, name at least 10 countries today that are in areas that were once part of the empire.

3. Name three problems that led to the end of the Roman Republic. Tell how each of these men tried to deal with the problems: Tiberius and Gaius Gracchus, Sulla, Julius Caesar.

4. Name one important contribution to literature or science made by each of these men: Julius Caesar, Tacitus, Livy, Vergil, Celsus, Marcus Aurelius, Cicero, Galen, Plutarch, Ptolemy.

provincial government in response to continuing clashes between landless peasants and the rich.

4. See p. 125, 126.

CHAPTER TEST 6

QUESTIONS FOR CRITICAL THINKING

1. Is there any relationship between the strength and unity of the family and that of the country? Explain what effect the breakdown of family life can have on a country. What caused family ties to become weak in Rome? What is the state of family life in the United States today?

2. What were the greatest accomplishments of the Romans? What mistakes did they make? List two of each.

3. How much responsibility for the end of the Roman Republic is Julius Caesar's? Why was he killed? Why didn't his death save the republic?

4. Describe the increases in the plebeians' power during the republic. What happened to increase the conflicts between the rich and poor? What kinds of reform were needed?

5. In Greco-Roman culture, which contributions were Greek and which Roman? Give specific examples. Why is it significant today that the Romans preserved Greek culture?

ACTIVITIES

1. Choose a short paragraph from any book. Use a dictionary to look up the origins of the words. How many are of Latin origin? Greek? Other origins? Show the original forms for the words you look up.

2. Make a time line of the development of Roman power from the early Latin tribes to the death of Emperor Theodosius in 395 A.D. Show important events, such as the dates of the Punic Wars, when Caesar crossed the Rubicon, the crucifixion of Jesus, and others that you feel should be included.

3. Report or discuss how life must have changed for a people when their land became part of the Roman Empire. Think of the conquered people's language, government, law, transportation, food and other goods, etc.

4. Research the origins and meanings of the names for the months of the year.

● QUESTIONS FOR CRITICAL THINKING

1. This question asks the student to think about the result of affluence on the family as well as the responsibility of the parents to uphold respect for authority.

■ Gracchus

SECTION 1

1. The tribal group from which the Romans developed were the: a. Etruscans, b. Gauls, c. Latins

2. Pyrrhus is the powerful Greek general who regretted his defeat of the Romans. To this day, a Pyrrhic victory means a victory that cost more than it is worth.

3. Upper-class Romans were called: a. plebeians, b. patricians, c. *Punici*

4. The officials who protected the plebeians were the: a. tribunes, b. patriarchs, c. consuls

SECTION 2

5. The Punic Wars were fought between Rome and: a. Sicily, b. Carthage, c. Corinth

6. Tiberius and Gaius were brothers who ■ became tribunes and proposed land reforms that would have given land to the poor.

7. The Roman army during the time of civil strife was made up of: a. citizens, b. foreigners, c. professional soldiers

8. The first Roman emperor was: a. Octavian, b. Julius Caesar, c. Antony

SECTION 3

9. Hadrian's Wall was built in: a. Britain, b. Gaul, c. the Iberian peninsula

10. When some emperors reduced the amount of gold and silver in the coins, this caused: a. despotism, b. inflation, c. increased trade

11. From 180 to 284 A.D., real power was in the hands of the: a. senate, b. emperor, c. army

SECTION 4

12. The blend of Greek and Roman culture is known as Greco-Roman culture.

13. True or false: The laws in many countries today are based on Roman legal ideas.

14. True or false: Ptolemy believed the earth was round.

UNIT REVIEW 2

TEST YOURSELF

1. Match the name of the person with the correct identifying phrase.

Buddha c
Ptolemy a
Gracchus brothers j
Wu Ti g
Herodotus i
Asoka b
Julius Caesar d
Solon e
Confucius f
Socrates h

a. The first to make a map showing the earth was round
b. A ruler who turned against war
c. He taught a way to find peace through the Four Noble Truths
d. A great military leader, also the author of a history of the Gallic Wars
e. A wise statesman, he made middle-of-the-road reforms in his city
f. His teachings gave his people a standard of behavior and a deep respect for the past
g. The greatest of the Han rulers, he brought peace to central and eastern Asia.
h. A great teacher, he asked questions to arrive at the truth
i. The "Father of History," he wrote a rambling account of the Persian Wars.
j. He tried to pass land reform laws to help the poor.

2. Julius Caesar ruled the Roman Republic in the same century that: a. Confucius lived and taught, b. Asoka ruled India, c. Wu Ti ruled in China

3. Which of these great men lived at the same time? a. Buddha, Socrates, Confucius, b. Buddha, Confucius, Cleisthenes, c. Pericles, Asoka, Cicero

4. Which developed first? a. *Pax Romana,* b. Golden Age of India, c. Golden Age of China, d. Golden Age of Pericles

5. The Great Wall of China was built during: a. India's Vedic Age, b. Hellenic Period in Greece, c. the days of the Roman Republic

6. The *Iliad* and the *Odyssey* were composed when: a. India was in its Epic Age, b. Hannibal crossed the Alps, c. coinage came into use in China

7. Choose the letter of the civilization associated with these inventions or developments: a. India, b. China, c. Greece, d. Rome

democracy c
Arabic numerals a
Great Wall b
hospitals d
geometry c
Hadrian's Wall d
Stoicism c
printing b
aqueducts d
steel a
paper b
highways d
drama c
cotton cloth a
civil service system b
theory of natural causes of disease d

8. Match the letter of the civilization with the statement below that describes that civilization:

a. India, b. China, c. Greece, d. Rome

". . . The whole world keeps holiday; the age-long curse of war has been put aside." d

"[to] diminish expenses, lighten taxes, and employ only honest officials will do more to abolish robbery than . . . the severest punishments." b

". . . power is in the hands not of the few but of the whole people." c

". . . The people are many and happy. They do not have to register . . . with the police. There is no death penalty." a

UNIT 3

the worlds of Christendom and Islam

We now turn to two major civilizations that were largely shaped by religion—the world of Christendom and the world of Islam. Both had their origins in the Mediterranean area. They were often enemies, but there was also a great deal of interchange between them.

Christianity was the religion that united the peoples from Ireland to Russia and from Scandinavia to Sicily. Although there were people of other faiths who lived in this vast area, Christian laws and customs governed the way of life. Christendom was divided into two parts. Western Christendom looked to the head of the Church in Rome for leadership. Latin was the language of religion and governments. Eastern Christendom looked to Constantinople, and Greek was the official language.

The 1,000 years of western Christendom were called by later people the "medieval period," or "middle ages." From the fall of Rome to the fourteenth century, it seemed that nothing important had happened. There were no great empires, very little trade. Cities shrank into towns, and people lived in isolation on large, but separate estates. But important things did happen. Universities began. And great art, architecture, and literature were produced.

In eastern Christendom, the Byzantine Empire flourished. Its capital, Constantinople, was a far more brilliant center of culture

These banners show the Christian cross and Muslim star and crescent.

than Rome. So great was Byzantine influence, that at the end of the tenth century, Greek Orthodox Christianity was adopted by the Slavic rulers of the Black Sea. From that time onward, Orthodox Christianity played a major role in the formation of Russia.

The world of Islam arose in the seventh century when nomadic Arabs adopted the Muslim faith and created a powerful empire. From the Fertile Crescent, the world of Islam moved across North Africa and into southern Spain. It spread east across Asia Minor to the

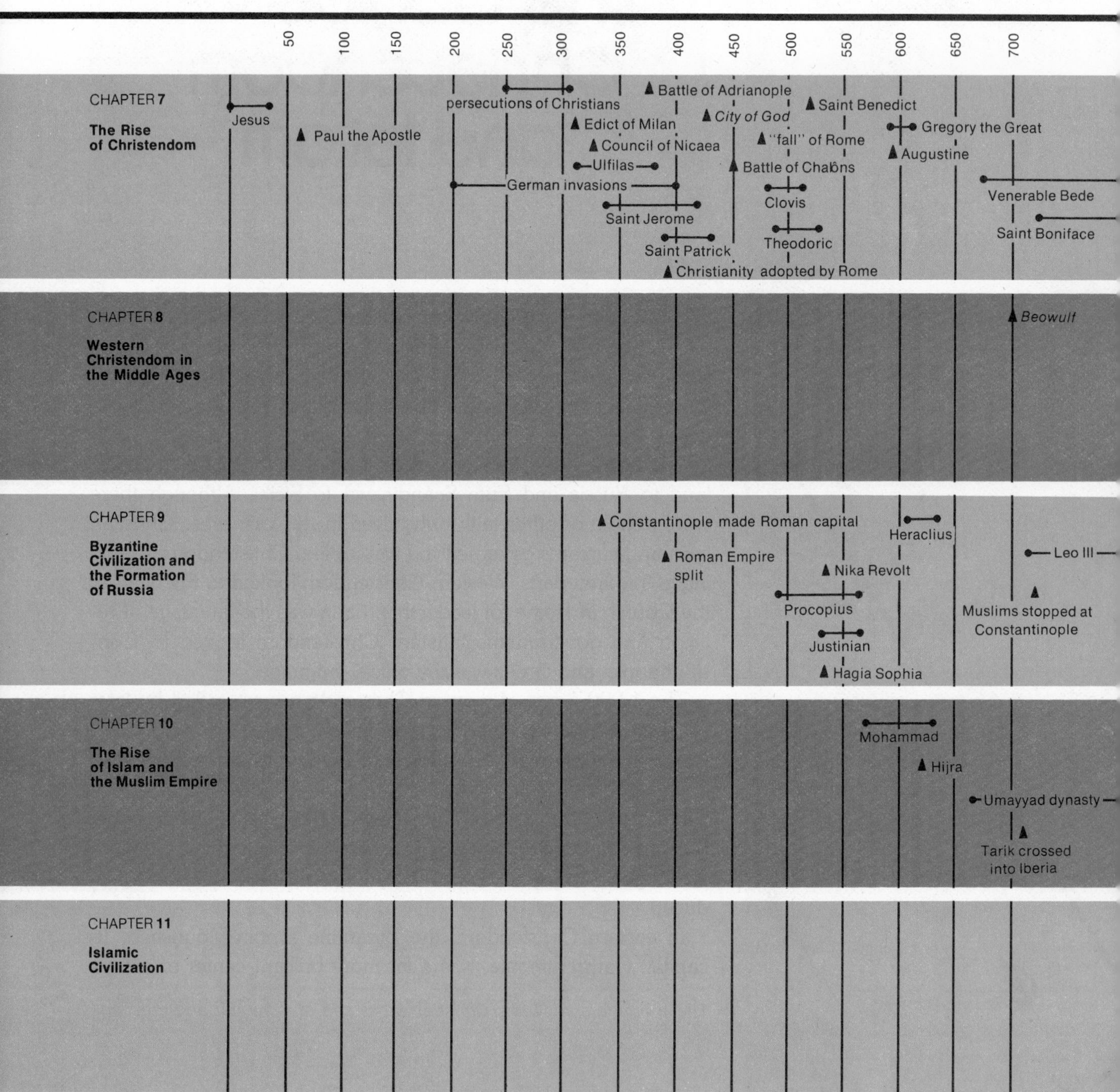

Indus River. Held together by a common religion and language, Muslim civilization was based on widespread trade. In Muslim cities, people could buy silks from China, gold from Africa, and glass from Spain. Ideas were exchanged. And great advances in science, medicine, mathematics, literature, and architecture took place. In both worlds, religious buildings reached their steeples, spires, or domes into the sky. And religion affected both the daily lives of individuals and the activities of governments.

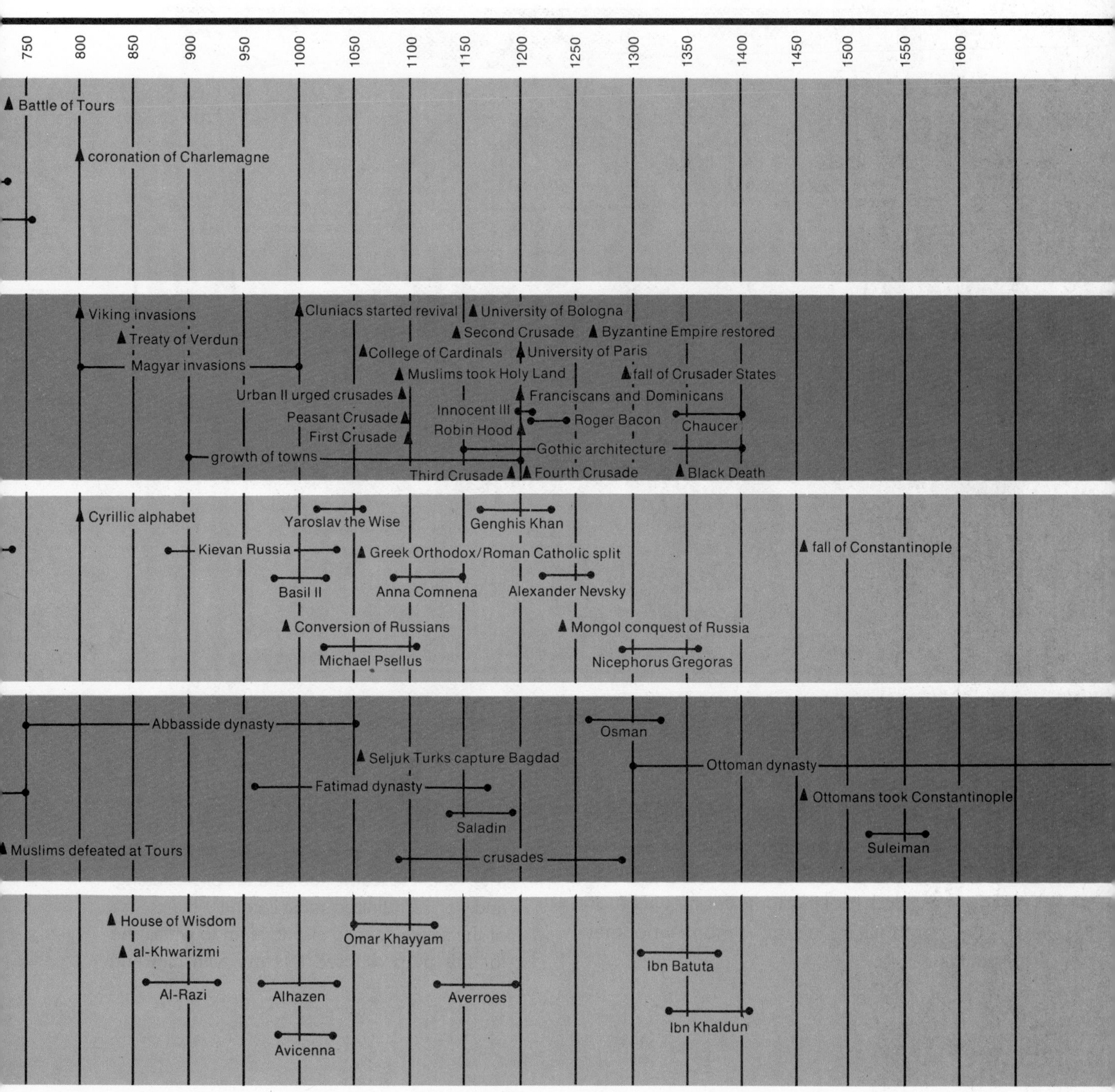

CHAPTER
7

1 A.D. –
800 A.D.

The Rise of Christendom

Early Christians buried their dead in underground tombs, called *catacombs*, outside Rome's city walls. Later, when Christians were persecuted, the catacombs became secret meeting and worship places. Art, such as this 4th-century painting of Jesus, decorated the walls.

The king of the Franks was an unusual man. Like other rulers in the 8th century, he had to spend much time fighting fierce battles to defend or expand his kingdom, yet he was more than a great military leader. A monk who knew him well wrote:

Charles spent much time and labour in learning rhetoric and [logic], and especially astronomy. . . . He learnt, too, the art of reckoning, and . . . scrutinized most carefully the course of the stars. He tried also to learn to write, and for this purpose used to carry with him and keep under the pillow of his couch tablets and writing-sheets that he might in spare moments accustom himself to the formation of letters. But he made little advance in this strange work, which was begun too late in life.

Six-feet, four-inches tall, with massive shoulders and "great-chested like a steed," the king of the Franks was a giant among men. In the 8th century, he was the conqueror of a realm that was the largest empire of western Christendom. He was a steadfast defender of Christianity who carried the word of Jesus into the wilds of his vast empire. Thus he became known as Charlemagne [shär′lə mān], that is, Charles the Great.

Charlemagne made contributions to government and law, learning, and the arts. He was also the hero of many legendary tales. In legend, he was shown as an extraordinary king who was capable of superhuman and incredible deeds. As king of the Franks, one of the Germanic tribes, and later as head of a large empire, he served as the symbol of political unity. In addition, as a Christian warrior-king of German blood who admired the culture of the Roman Empire, he represented the forces that would reshape western Christendom. This chapter traces the rise of Christendom by describing how:

1. Christianity became a strong religion in the Roman world.

2. German tribes attacked the Roman Empire.

3. The Church became the preserver of civilization.

4. An alliance of popes and Franks aided western Christendom.

● The destruction of the empire is discussed in Section 2.

1 Christianity became a strong religion in the Roman world

By the middle of the 4th century, the once powerful and prosperous Roman Empire showed unmistakable signs of decay. The government was riddled by corruption. Barbarian tribes threatened the imperial frontiers. Heavy taxes burdened the citizens. And city mobs shouted for bread as food production continued to drop off. In the face of these problems, many Romans turned to their old gods—Mars, Jupiter, and Minerva. Other Romans looked to the teachings of Greek philosophy, chiefly Stoicism, which taught people to accept their fate with quiet courage. Still others turned to Mesopotamian religions. ans. 4 ●

Of greater significance in the history of Western civilization was the rise of a new faith that had been founded in Palestine in the 1st century A.D. This faith—Christianity—was the religion based on the teachings of a Jew named Jesus.

Christianity began with the teachings of Jesus. Solid historical information about Jesus is extremely scanty. Most of what is known about him comes from the Gospels, the first four books of the New Testament of the Bible. The Gospels were written years after Jesus's death, and despite much agreement, there are points on which they seem to disagree. According to the Gospels, Jesus was born in Bethlehem and reared in the village of Nazareth. He apparently stopped working as a carpenter at the age of thirty and began to travel throughout Palestine, preaching his doctrines.

The teachings of Jesus had their roots in Judaism. Like other Jews, Jesus condemned

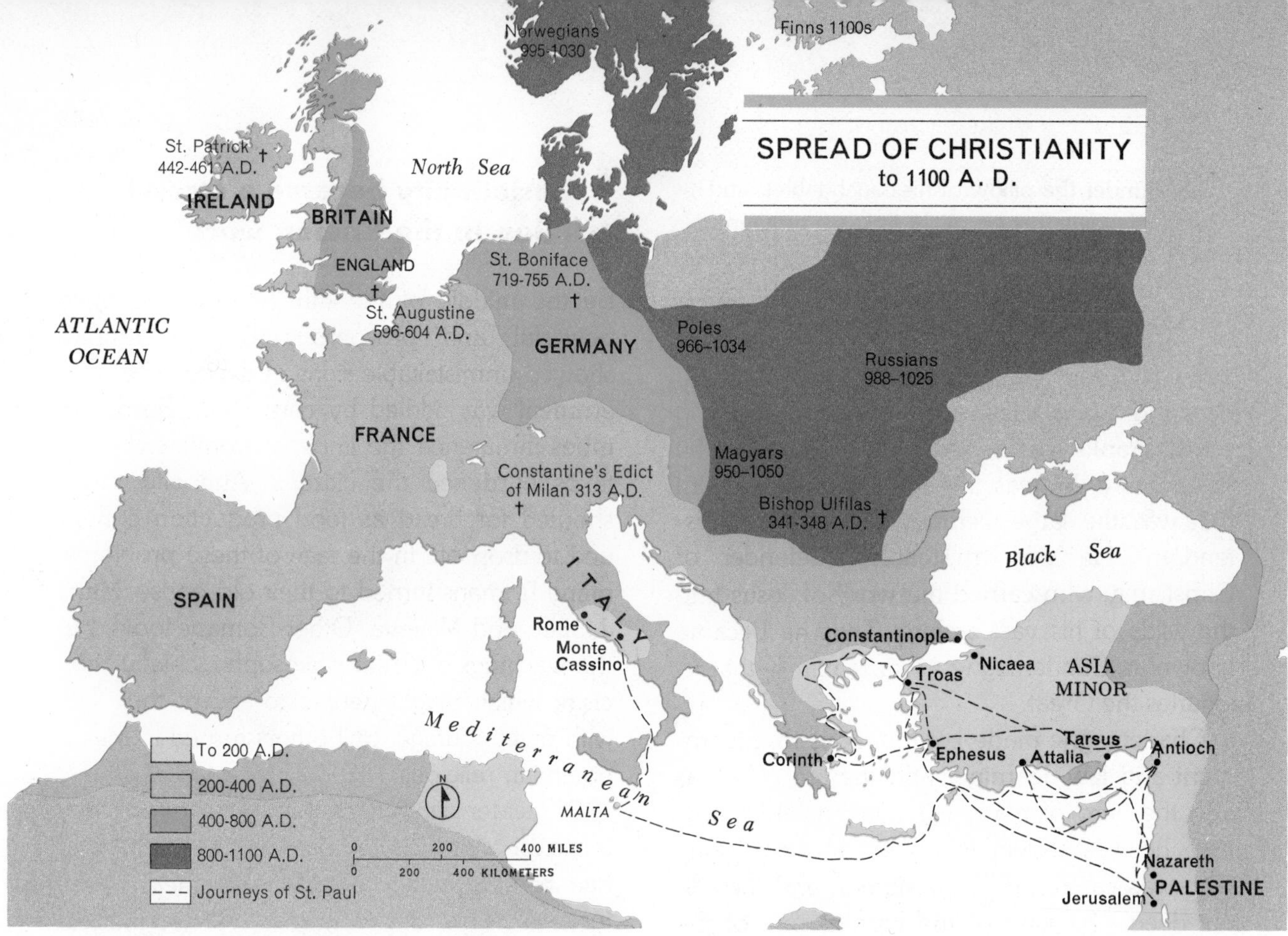

violence and selfishness and taught doctrines based on brotherhood. Most Jews, however, did not accept Jesus's claim that he was the Messiah, the leader who was divinely chosen to usher in the great judgment at the end of time. (*Messiah* is a Hebrew word; in Greek it is *Christ.*)

The Gospels report that Jesus attracted crowds of people wherever he went. Both
ans. 1 Roman rulers and Jewish authorities reacted against his preaching. To Jewish authorities, proclaiming oneself the Messiah was blasphemy [blas′fə mē]. To the Romans, concerned about political discontent in Palestine, it appeared to be a call to overthrow the government. Historians differ as to exactly what happened next. But in 33 A.D., Jesus was put to death by crucifixion by the order of Pontius Pilate [pon′shəs pī′lət], the Roman governor of Judea.

The New Testament tells how Jesus reappeared to his disciples following the crucifixion and confirmed his teachings of eternal life. A few followers set about to spread the news of the Resurrection. They became missionaries of the new faith. They called themselves "brethren," brothers, of "the way." Later, believers in "the way" were called Christians and their faith Christianity.

Paul spread the teachings of Jesus. The most important missionary was Paul, a well-educated Jew from the Hellenistic city of Tarsus in Asia Minor. As a young man, Paul believed that Christian teachings went against Judaism, and he took part in the persecutions

of Christians. According to the Acts of the Apostles (9:1-5) in the New Testament, Paul was on his way to arrest any men or women whom he found to be followers of "the way," when a vision of Jesus appeared to him. After this experience, Paul became dedicated to Christianity. Immediately, he set out to bring Jesus's teachings to as many people as possible—to Jews and Gentiles, non-Jews, alike.
ans. 2 From about 37 A.D. until his death in the year 67, he journeyed to many cities around the eastern Mediterranean, spreading the Christian gospel. His great contribution helped Christianity grow from a small Jewish sect in Palestine to a world religion.

Christianity triumphed over persecution. Officials of the Roman government allowed many different religions to exist in the empire as long as the people accepted government
ans. 3 authority. The Christians, however, refused to obey many of the Roman laws—particularly that of emperor worship. Roman officials, therefore, looked upon Christians as enemies of the state.

Nero blamed the Christians for the burning of Rome in 64 A.D. and punished them severely. Other emperors, seeking excuses for bad conditions during their reigns, used the Christians as scapegoats. They crucified Christians, threw them to wild beasts and to mad dogs in arenas, or had them burned alive.

The first widespread persecution was carried on from 249 to 251 A.D. The last was ordered in 303. During these years, Christians lived a hunted existence. But the religion could not be wiped out. In fact, the courage with which Christians met death inspired a Roman writer of the 2nd century to say that "the blood of the martyrs became the seed of the Church."

In 311 A.D., Christianity was made a legal religion in the eastern Roman Empire. About two years later, Emperor Constantine in the western empire issued the Edict of Milan, which legalized Christianity throughout the empire. In 395, the emperor Theodosius made Christianity the official religion.

Christianity was strengthened by a common creed. Because Jesus left no written messages, Christians disagreed about their beliefs. To resolve this conflict, the Emperor Constantine called the Council of Nicaea [nī sē′ə] in 325. This body put together a creed which

Saints Savin and Cyprian were two early martyrs who were tortured and killed by the Romans. This painting, showing them brought before a Roman official, is from a French church where their relics are preserved.

said that God and Christ were of the same substance. All members of the council agreed to the Nicene [nī sēn′] Creed except a priest named Arius and his few followers. They maintained that God and Christ were of different substances. Arius and his followers were therefore banished from the Church as *heretics* (persons who hold a belief different from the accepted view). However, many people continued to cling to Arian beliefs. As the years passed, the Nicenes and the Arians struggled for leadership in the Church. The Nicenes were finally victorious.

In addition to the Nicene Creed, the early Church developed an official book of sacred writings. To the holy writings of the Jews, which the early Christians called the Old Testament, were added religious writings collected after the death of Jesus. Twenty-seven of these collections, or books, were selected to make the New Testament. In his travels from place to place, Paul had kept in touch with Christians through letters of encouragement and advice. These letters, or *epistles,* make up some of the most important books of the New Testament.

The official teaching, or *theology,* of the Christian Church was systematized by a group of men known as the Church Fathers. Saint Jerome, one of the most famous, lived from about 340 to 420 A.D. From the Hebrew original, he made a Latin translation of the Bible, called the Vulgate, which is still used as the official version in the Roman Catholic Church. In 426, another of the Church Fathers, Saint Augustine finished *The City of God.* This book provided much of the foundation of Christian theology.

This eight-foot-high marble head of the emperor Constantine was once part of an enormous statue.

● Key Concept: the Christian Church developed an organization that was able, later, to provide governmental services.

The Church established a well-knit organization. At first, Christians met in small groups, often in their homes. As time went by and more people became Christians, an organization developed, based on Roman governmental units.

Presbyters [prez′bə tərz], later known as priests, were ordained, officially consecrated, to conduct the services and business of village churches. Several villages made up a diocese [dī′ ə sis], which was placed under the direction of a bishop, a priest who administered the religious affairs of a church district. A number of dioceses made up a province under the authority of an archbishop. And a group of provinces made up a patriarchate. The title of patriarch [pā′trē ärk] was given to the bishop of a large city, such as Rome, Constantinople, or

Alexandria. Gradually the Bishop of Rome assumed leadership as *pope*, from a Greek word meaning father.

ans. 5 Church leadership developed in Rome partly because it was the capital of the empire. In addition, with the decline of the western part of the empire, the Roman bishops took on governmental leadership as it slipped from the hands of the weak emperors. Finally, the popes • claimed supremacy through the Petrine Theory. This doctrine held that the Roman church had been founded by Peter, leader of Jesus's Apostles and was therefore the most important church. By the year 600, Rome was thought of as the capital of the Church and the pope as head of the Church.

Christians from very early times regarded Jesus's mother, Mary, as an important figure. This catacomb painting shows her holding her infant son.

• The patriarch of the Eastern Empire opposed the Petrine Theory; this material is discussed in Ch. 9.

SECTION REVIEW 1

1. Why did the Roman rulers and Jewish authorities in Jerusalem disapprove of Jesus's teachings? p. 136

2. How did Paul the Apostle help spread the Christian religion? p. 137

3. Why were early Christians "enemies of the Roman state"? What effect did the persecutions have on the number of followers of the Christian religion? p. 137

4. Name four problems of the Roman Empire in the 4th century and explain why Christianity became stronger at that time. p. 135

5. Why did Rome become the capital city of Christianity? By what year had this happened? What was the title of the leader of the Church? p. 139

2 German tribes attacked the Roman Empire

While the Church was growing stronger, the once mighty government of the Caesars was crumbling. Added to its many difficulties was a final crushing blow—attack by Germanic tribes.

German tribes pressed against the Roman frontier. In the 4th century A.D., most Germanic peoples in Europe were living east of the Rhine and north of the Danube. To the west and north of the Black Sea, were the East Goths (Ostrogoths) and the West Goths (Visigoths). To the west of these tribes and extending over a large area east of the Rhine were the Vandals, Lombards, Alemanni, Burgundians, and Franks. In and near present-day Denmark lived the Jutes, Angles, and Saxons (see map on page 142).

These groups were partly nomadic, herding their flocks and tilling the soil. Large and vigorous, the people prized strength and courage in battle. They worshiped many gods, including Tiw, the god of war; Wotan, the chief of the gods; Thor, the god of thunder; and Freya, the goddess of fertility. (Their names are preserved in the English words Tuesday, Wednesday, Thursday, and Friday.)

● The Germans governed themselves with tribal assemblies made up of voting freemen. Their laws were based on long-established customs of the tribe. These political practices had a strong influence later in medieval England, where they laid a foundation for parliamentary government and English common law.

For hundreds of years, the Germans had fought the Romans on the borders of the empire. Long periods of war alternated with periods of peace. During the peaceful periods, the Roman and Germanic peoples mixed with each other. Some Germans entered the Roman Empire and settled on vacant lands. Others, captured in war, became slaves on Roman estates, and still others became soldiers in the legions. If this mixing had been allowed to continue, the Germans might have been gradually absorbed into the empire. However, outside forces suddenly turned the gradual infiltration into a rushing invasion.

German tribes forced their way into all parts of the western Roman Empire. In Asia, during the 4th century, fierce nomads called Huns were on the march from the East. Mounted on swift horses, they attacked with lightning ferocity all tribes in their path. Crossing the Dnieper River, they conquered the Ostrogoths in eastern Europe. The Visigoths, ans. 1 fearing that the Huns would attack them also, begged Roman authorities for safety in the empire. The Roman officials agreed, promising the Visigoths lands to settle if they came unarmed.

Neither side lived up to the agreement. The Visigoths, without land and facing starvation, began to attack Roman settlements. In 378 A.D., the Roman emperor Valens led a great army against the Visigoths at the Battle of Adrianople. To everyone's surprise, the Visigoths defeated the Romans, the imperial force was scattered, and the emperor killed. This battle is ans. 2 considered to be one of the decisive battles in world history because it left the Roman Empire defenseless. German tribes outside the empire began to round up their cattle, mobilize their fighting men, and move toward the Roman borders.

The German general Alaric led the Visigoths southwest. They reached Rome in 410 A.D. and looted the city. By that time, other German tribes—the Franks, Vandals, and Burgundians—were moving into the empire. And about 450 A.D., Germans from northwest Europe—the Angles, Saxons, and Jutes—sailed to Britain, where they killed or enslaved the Britons they found there and forced others to retreat into Wales and Scotland.

To add to the confusion, the Huns, led by Attila, had also invaded the empire and were threatening to enslave or destroy both Romans and Germans. Forgetting their own differences for a while, the Romans and Germans united against a common enemy. They fought together in Gaul (present-day France) and defeated Attila at the Battle of Châlons in 451. Shortly afterward, Attila died in Italy and his savage cavalry drifted apart.

● Key Concept: Germanic tribal assemblies were a basis for the development of democratic traditions in Europe.

Germanic Daily Life

To the Romans, with their advanced civilization, the Germanic peoples seemed like barbarians. They did not have a vast empire, great marble buildings, nor cities bustling with trade. But the Germanic peoples had their own cultures. They had religions, literature, laws, trading ships, and powerful armies. The drawing to the *right* shows the forts of nine noble Saxon families. *Below right* are a king's helmet and a purse lid, both found at Sutton Hoo in Britain. A complete ship was buried there with the treasure and equipment of a 7th-century Saxon king. The purse is gold and enamel decorated with garnets and colored glass; obviously the Saxons were skilled artisans. *Below left* is a scene from a Roman column showing the fierce fighting that frequently broke out on the empire's borders. Here the Romans attack a German village.

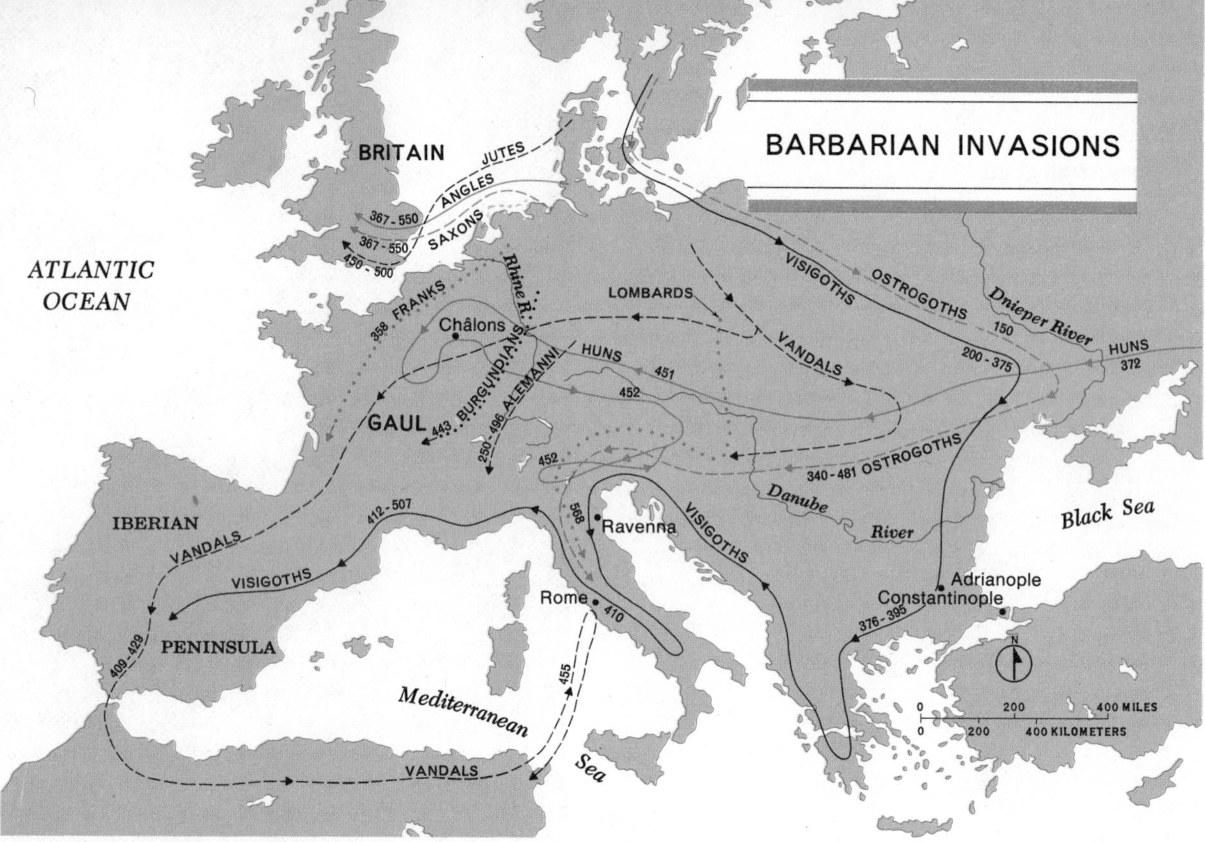

The western empire collapsed. Meanwhile, the emperors in Rome had become so weak that they were mere puppets of the
ans. 3 army. Many of the soldiers were of German birth, and one, Odoacer [ō′dō ā′sər], became a commander of the Roman armies. In 476, he deposed the last of the Roman emperors and became the first German ruler of Rome. This date—476—is often given as the date for the
● "fall" of Rome. In a strict sense, there was no "fall." The decline of Roman imperial power was slow and complicated. Weak emperors, corrupt officials, and the admission of German soldiers into the legions all played a part.

Since the early decades of the 4th century, emperors at Rome had sensed the growing weakness of the empire in the west. In the year 330 A.D., Emperor Constantine had moved his capital to the city of Byzantium, in the eastern part of the empire. By the end of the century, the Roman Empire had become permanently divided. One emperor ruled in the west and another in the east. Although separated, the two sections of the empire continued to be thought of as one.

● The idea of a slow, gradual "fall" may need explaining for some students.

However, the western part of the empire was breaking up. By the year 476, when Odoacer came to the throne, German kingdoms had been established in many former Roman provinces. The Anglo-Saxons were in England. The Visigoths had moved into the Iberian peninsula. In north Africa, the Vandals had built up a kingdom, and by 486, the Franks controlled Gaul. The Italian peninsula was the scene of much warfare, and near the end of the 5th century, it fell under the rule of the Ostrogoths.

The Ostrogoths had been freed from the Huns after the death of Attila in 453. The Ostrogoths then built a settlement within the Roman Empire south and west of the Danube.

In 471, they elected Theodoric their king, and soon afterward he led a march toward the eastern part of the empire.

The emperor in the east tried to stop the Ostrogoths from moving into his lands. He encouraged Theodoric to invade the Italian peninsula instead and to overthrow Odoacer, who had ruled there since 476. Theodoric did so and established his capital at the city of Ravenna, in the northeast part of the Italian peninsula. His rule brought prosperity and peace to his kingdom, but at his death in 526, civil war began again. In the middle of the 6th century, a strong emperor at Constantinople, Justinian, won back Italian lands for a few years. Then the Lombards, another German tribe, conquered the Italian peninsula in 568 and stayed there for 200 years.

ans. 4 The eastern part of the empire, however, did not give way to internal decay and barbarian invasions. With its capital at Constantinople, it endured, carrying on the imperial tradition for a thousand years more. It preserved much of Greco-Roman culture and served as a buffer for western Europe against invasions from the Middle East.

SECTION REVIEW **2**

p. 140 **1.** Why did the semipeaceful relationship between Romans and Germans change suddenly in the 4th century?

p. 140 **2.** How did the Battle of Adrianople in 378 affect the Roman Empire?

p. 142 **3.** What happened in 476 that is called the "fall" of Rome?

p. 143 **4.** How long did the eastern part of the empire remain strong? Give two reasons why the eastern empire was important to western Europe after the fall of Rome.

● Help students to understand why people left the cities as government services declined. People turned to farming and were protected by the landowners. As these farmers fell behind in their rent payments, Roman law bound them to the land.

3 The Church became the preserver of civilization

As the Roman Empire declined, a new pattern of civilization developed. This pattern combined the old Roman culture with the vigor of the Germanic tribes. The Christian Church became the main force in shaping this new pattern—preserving culture and civilizing the Germans.

Although services provided by the Roman government were gradually dropped, and pop- ● ulations of cities shrank during the German invasions, most persons saw little change in their daily lives. About two-thirds of the land changed ownership, but usually only the wealthy landowners were affected. In a few regions, the Germans outnumbered the old inhabitants, but the newcomers soon took on the customs of the Romans. The blending of peoples that had been going on before the invasions continued. The Germans made use of ans. 1 some of the old Roman political forms and kept Latin as the official language.

Many of the invaders had been Christianized by missionaries. They respected the Church and were impressed and awed by the ritual of the Christian service.

The Church provided protection and order. During the invasions, Roman law was not enforced. The Church took over the task of ans. 2 protecting the helpless and punishing the criminal. Persons fleeing for their lives could find safety, called *sanctuary*, in any church building.

As the Roman emperors became weaker, popes and their assistants took over governmental powers. They set up Church courts and took over the right to collect taxes. The governmental power of the Church was especially evident from 590 to 604, when Gregory the Great was pope. He supervised the police, directed the generals of the army, coined money, and kept aqueducts in repair.

ans. 3 **Missionaries spread Christianity.** As early as the 3rd century, fearless missionaries had carried the teachings of the Christian Church beyond the frontiers of the Roman Empire. One of the most important of these missionaries was Ulfilas [ul′fi ləs], an Arian Christian, who preached among the Gothic peoples. He invented a Gothic alphabet, which he used in translating the Bible. Another famous missionary, Saint Patrick, was born in Britain about 389. He journeyed to Ireland to convert the Celtic peoples to the faith and founded many monasteries that became famous as centers of learning. In 596, Pope Gregory sent a Roman monk, Augustine, as missionary to England. Augustine later became the first Archbishop of Canterbury.

In the early part of the 8th century, a young priest named Winfrid was sent to preach in Germany. He later changed his name to Boniface and became famous as the Apostle of Germany. There he founded churches and monasteries until his death in 755.

Monks helped preserve culture. During the years of the Roman persecutions, a few Christians went into the wilderness, giving up worldly interests and living alone. Others lived in groups, dedicating themselves to the service of God. Christian *monasteries,* places where groups of monks lived apart from the world, were first set up in Egypt. Later, monasteries appeared in the eastern part of the Roman

Empire. About the middle of the 4th century, monasteries also sprang up in the west.

When men went out to live a holy life alone, they were often too hard on themselves. Monasteries gave these men a way to live apart from society, to dedicate their lives to God, and yet live useful lives. About the year 520, Saint Benedict set up a monastery in Italy at Monte Cassino and drew up rules for the monks to live by. His rules required obedience and poverty, daily prayers, and at least six hours of useful work each day. The rules of the Benedictine order were widely adopted by other monasteries in western Christendom.

ans. 4 In German lands beyond the old frontiers, where life was rough, monks not only spread the teachings of Christianity but also advanced civilization. In wild and forested lands, monks often cleared the forests, drained the swamps, and introduced new crops. The few schools that existed in Europe during the early Middle Ages were run by monks. The monasteries also served as inns for travelers and as hospitals.

At a time when libraries were neglected and precious manuscripts were destroyed or lost in looting, copies of the Scriptures and some of the classics were made by monks and preserved in monasteries. Nearly all the important monasteries had a writing room where monks copied manuscripts by hand. These they illustrated, or *illuminated,* with decorative designs, borders, and initials done in gold and brilliant colors. The monks also kept historical records, called *Chronicles.* One, *The Ecclesiastical History of the English Nation,* written by Saint Bede in the early 8th century, is the best account available of nearly two hundred years of English history.

From the 4th century on, Christianity spread rapidly throughout the Roman Empire and the Germanic peoples on its borders. The picture *far left* is a fragment of an illustrated, 5th-century Bible, written in Greek, and probably made in the Roman colony in Egypt. *Left* shows Saint Matthew writing the Gospel from Charlemagne's illustrated copy of the Bible. *Right* are cast-bronze figures of Jesus and angels made in Ireland in the 8th century for a book cover. *Far right* is a Frankish tombstone showing Jesus carrying a spear and surrounded by a halo.

SECTION REVIEW 3

p. 143 **1.** Tell three ways in which the German tribes became like the Romans they invaded.

p. 143 **2.** What services were provided by the Church after the collapse of Roman law?

p. 144 **3.** Describe the work of the Christian missionaries.

p. 145 **4.** How did the monks bring civilization to the German lands outside the empire?

4 An alliance of popes and Franks aided western Christendom

In the last part of the 5th century, the Franks, a German tribe, began to build a nation in the north and east of Gaul. This nation became the greatest empire of early medieval times.

Clovis united the Franks and extended the power of the Church. Clovis began his remarkable career as the ruler of a small Frankish kingdom. By 486 A.D., he had overcome the last remains of Roman authority in Gaul. He then turned against the other Frankish kings and crushed their forces. In 507, the Visigothic kingdom in southern Gaul was conquered, and the Visigoths fled to their relatives in the Iberian peninsula.

Clovis was converted to Christianity when he won a victory in battle after an appeal to the Christian God. As a result, not only Clovis but all his warriors were baptized into the Christian faith.

Clovis became one of the most powerful rulers in western Europe. He was the first important Germanic king to become a Roman Catholic. All other Germanic rulers and their subjects—except those in England—were Arian Christians. The pope considered them to be heretics. This gave Clovis an excuse to attack his Arian neighbors. He said, "I cannot endure that those Arians should possess any part of Gaul. With God's aid we will go against them and conquer their lands." He whipped the Arians, extending his lands and the authority of the pope at the same time. ans. 1

Clovis died in 511, and his kingdom was divided among his four sons. They pushed Frankish authority into lands north and east of the Rhine, but their four kingdoms were poorly governed. The kings that followed were immoral, weak drunkards who were nicknamed the Do-Nothing Kings.

The Carolingian family won control of the Franks. Since the Frankish kings did not perform their duties, the office of Mayor of the Palace became politically important. One mayor, Pepin, took control of all Frankish lands and actually became the sole ruler. He also cooperated with the Christian church and supported missionaries sent by the pope. In 714, his son Charles inherited the office of mayor. Charles's greatest success was at the Battle of Tours in 732. Pitted against an army of Muslim invaders from the Iberian peninsula, he won a victory that saved the northern European continent for Christianity. After that, he was known as Charles Martel, or Charles the Hammer.

When Charles Martel's son, Pepin the Short, became Mayor of the Palace, he asked the pope to decide whether he or a Do-Nothing King should be considered the legal ruler of the Franks. The pope approved Pepin, and thus began the Carolingian [kar′ ə lin′jē ən] line of kings. In return, Pepin led an army against the Lombards, who were threatening the *papacy*, that is, the office and government of the pope. ans. 3

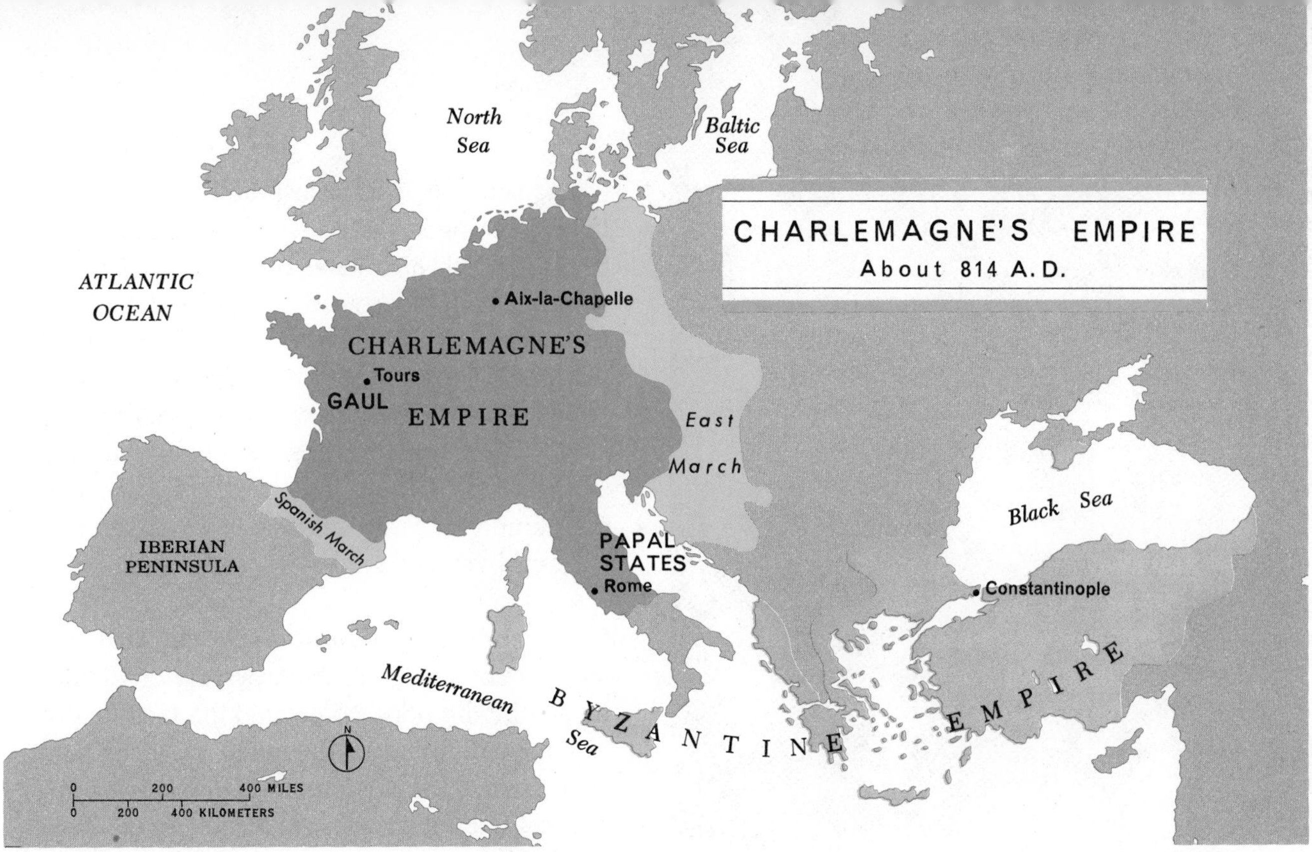

In 756, Pepin turned over to the pope a part of the territory the Lombards had controlled. This Donation of Pepin came to be known as the Papal States.

Charlemagne built an empire. In 768, Pepin's sons Charles and Carloman inherited the throne. Charles became the sole ruler in 771. He was called Charles the Great, or Charlemagne. Charlemagne too led an army to protect the pope's interests. This time, the Lombards were completely beaten. In 774, Charlemagne took the title of King of the Lombards. He went on to win other battles against different German tribes. Eventually, he governed an empire stretching from the Danube to the Atlantic Ocean, from Rome to the Baltic and North seas. Priests traveled with his armies. While the armies made conquests for Charlemagne, the priests made converts for the Church.

Charlemagne appointed counts to run the *counties,* or districts, into which he divided his empire. He kept law and order through agents called *missi dominici,* or "messengers of the lord." The *missi,* traveling in pairs, visited every county annually, checked on the local courts, and reported their findings to Charlemagne. On the borders, he set up defense districts called *marks,* or marches.

Charlemagne modeled his capital at Aix- ans. 2
la-Chapelle (present-day Aachen, West Germany) on Roman cities and imported statues and marble from the Italian peninsula to improve the beauty of his city. Aix-la-Chapelle [āks′ lä shä pel′] was also famous for the revival of learning, often called the Carolingian Renaissance. Charlemagne urged priests to study and improve their education. He also sponsored a refinement of the system of handwriting then in use and generously supported Church schools. There boys were taught Chris- ●

● Earlier styles of handwriting were replaced by an easier-to-read method using small letters. (The Romans had used only capitals.)

When Pope Leo III crowned Charlemagne, the idea of a new Roman Empire was born.

tian doctrine, arithmetic, grammar, and singing. The rebirth of learning during Charlemagne's rule helped preserve Roman culture and continue the development of civilization in western Christendom.

Charlemagne was crowned by both Church and state. In the year 800, Charle-
ans. 3 magne traveled to Rome. While he was attending Church services on Christmas Day, the pope placed a crown on the king's head and declared, "To Charles Augustus crowned of God, great and pacific Emperor of the Romans, long life and victory." Whether the pope planned this action with Charlemagne's knowledge is unknown. However, the ceremony proved that the idea of the Roman Empire was still alive, and that there was a strong desire to bring back the political unity of imperial Rome.

The coronation also illustrated another great theme of medieval history: the struggle between Church and state. By crowning Charlemagne, the pope showed his approval of Charlemagne's rule. Charlemagne was emperor by the grace of God, with the Church on his side. However, it was not all a positive gain for the king. The coronation also showed that the Church had the right to say who was the Roman emperor. From that time on, popes and kings each claimed to have the highest authority.

Christendom emerged as a civilization. Most important of all, the crowning of Charlemagne by the pope completed the blending of two major ideas after a period of some 400 years. One of those ideas was the concept of political unity that was represented by the old Roman Empire. The other was the idea of religious unity that was represented by the new Christian Church. The mixture of the two ideas resulted in a civilization that can best be described as Christendom.

The world of Christendom was one in which Christianity was the single most powerful force that influenced the way people behaved and what they believed. People who lived in that world thought of themselves as Christians, not Romans. The religious unity of western Christendom was to last for more than 700 years.

SECTION REVIEW **4**

1. Why did Clovis's victories have religious impor- p. 146
tance?

2. How did Charlemagne preserve Roman culture p. 147
and civilization in western Europe?

3. Give two examples from this section of a pope p. 146,
approving a king's right to rule. What does this 148
show about the power of the Church?

CHAPTER REVIEW 7

SECTION SUMMARIES

1. Christianity became a strong religion in the Roman world. The Christian religion grew from the teachings of Jesus. Although he was crucified and his followers harshly persecuted, the small group of "believers" gathered strength through the work of missionaries, especially that of Paul. At first, the Romans outlawed the practice of the religion and put many of its followers to death. But Christianity grew in strength and finally became the official religion in the empire.

2. German tribes attacked the Roman Empire. German invasions, which had begun as early as the 2nd century B.C., increased in the 4th century A.D. At that time, Huns from Asia forced the German tribes to seek safety in the empire. Once inside, they increased their power and landholdings at the expense of the Romans. After the Visigoth defeat of the Roman army in 378 A.D., many German tribes moved onto Roman lands. In time, a German ruler, the general Odoacer, became the Roman emperor, and German kingdoms took hold in many former Roman provinces.

3. The Church became the preserver of civilization. As the western part of the Roman Empire crumbled, the Church at Rome, having become the head of all Christian churches, took over leadership in civil government. Church missionaries carried the Christian religion and Roman culture to the German tribes. In the monasteries, culture was preserved and education continued.

4. An alliance of popes and Franks aided western Christendom. In Gaul, about the year 500, the Frankish king Clovis grew powerful and extended his lands in the name of his new religion. The Do-Nothing Kings who followed Clovis allowed the Carolingian family to gain control. The greatest member of this royal house was Charlemagne, who expanded the Frankish Empire still farther. His reign was noteworthy for good government, for the encouragement of education, and for the extension of the power of the Christian church. When the pope crowned him emperor in 800, a tradition was established that would affect the relationships of popes and kings for many centuries. It also symbolized the completion of the process that resulted in the rise of Christendom.

WHO? WHAT? WHEN? WHERE?

1. Why are these dates important in the Christian religion?

a. 33 A.D.
b. 37–67
c. 311
d. 313
e. 395
f. 325
g. 600

2. What effect did each of these people have on the growth of the Church?

a. Paul p. 136
b. Theodosius p. 137
c. Nero p. 137
d. Saint Jerome p. 138
e. Saint Patrick p. 144
f. Pope Gregory the Great p. 137
g. Constantine p. 138, 144
h. Saint Augustine p. 144

3. When did Christianity spread to the following countries? (Use the map in this chapter.)

a. Spain 200–400 A.D.
b. France 200–400 A.D.
c. Germany 400–800 A.D.
d. England 200–800 A.D.
e. Ireland 200–400 A.D.
f. Norway 400–800 A.D.

4. Using the map showing Saint Paul's journeys (p. 136) and maps of Europe and the Middle East from the Atlas of the Contemporary World at the back of this book, name nine cities and six modern countries that Paul visited.

5. Give the years and the importance of:

a. the Battle of Adrianople 378 A.D. (p. 140)
b. the Battle of Châlons 451 A.D. (p. 140)
c. the Battle of Tours 732 A.D. (p. 146)

1. a, the crucifixion of Christ; b, the travels of Paul the Apostle; c, Christianity became legal in eastern Roman Empire; d, Christianity was legalized in the western Empire; e, Theodosius made Christianity the official religion of the empire; f, the Council of Nicea met; g, the pope in Rome was accepted as head of the Roman Catholic Church.

4. Answers will vary.

QUESTIONS FOR CRITICAL THINKING

● **1.** Why is it not correct to say that Rome "fell" in 476?

2. What problems was the Roman Empire suffering from in the 4th century? Why do some people turn to religion in times of trouble? Give examples from this chapter and from the present.

3. Why did the Germanic invaders take on so many of the ways of the peoples whose lands they invaded?

4. Why did men enter monasteries such as the one set up by Saint Benedict in 520? Consider what life was like at that time in the outside world.

5. Why didn't the persecutions of the early Christians by the Romans destroy the Christian religion?

ACTIVITIES

1. Discuss how the early missionaries were able to convince people to become Christians.

2. Discuss how the collapse of the Roman Empire could have been avoided.

3. Study the pictures and their captions in this chapter. Write a few sentences on three of the pictures explaining what the subject of the picture is, what material the picture is made of, and (where possible) how old the picture is.

4. Describe the routes of the Germanic invasions, telling which countries the various tribes traveled through, the years of the invasions, and where the tribes settled.

5. Make a chart showing the way that Church government was set up. Which areas were run by priests, bishops, archbishops, patriarchs, and the pope?

6. Look over some of Saint Paul's epistles in the Bible. How do they begin? What are some of the things he wrote to the early Christians about? Write a letter such as Paul might have written, encouraging your friends to lead a religious life.

CHAPTER TEST **7**

SECTION 1

1. Most of what is known about Jesus is found in: a. the Old Testament, b. the Gospels, c. Petrine Theory

2. The word *Christ* is from the ______ language. a. Greek, b. Hebrew, c. Latin

3. The member of the Council of Nicaea who did not agree with the Nicene Creed is: a. Arius, b. Petrarch, c. Ulfilas

4. The capital city of the Christian religion was: a. Jerusalem, b. Rome, c. Alexandria

SECTION 2

5. Attacked by the ______, the Germanic tribes pushed into the Roman Empire. a. Muslims, b. Norsemen, c. Huns

6. The first German ruler of Rome was: a. Attila, b. Odoacer, c. Theodoric

7. The capital city of the eastern empire was: a. Constantinople, b. Ravenna, c. Damascus

SECTION 3

8. After the fall of Rome, some civil government services were provided by the: a. Germans, b. Church, c. army

9. People looking for personal protection could find ______ in any church building. a. monasteries, b. libraries, c. sanctuary

10. An important Arian Christian missionary was: a. Ulfilas, b. Patrick, c. Benedict

SECTION 4

11. The first important German king to become a Roman Catholic was: a. Charlemagne, b. Pepin, c. Clovis

12. The Carolingian kings took over from the: a. weak Roman emperors, b. Arians, c. Do-Nothing Kings

13. The crowning of Charlemagne showed the strength of the: a. Church, b. emperor, c. army

● QUESTIONS FOR CRITICAL THINKING

1. See p. 142
2. Answers will vary.
3. Possible answer: superior lifestyle of Roman culture.
4. Monks were looking for a peaceful, more orderly way of life.
5. Good discussion topic. Some possible answers may be that people admired the Christian martyrs; Pagan religions did not have so strong a hold on the person's mind.

800 – 1300

CHAPTER **8**

Western Christendom in the Middle Ages

In the towns of the Middle Ages, stores opened directly onto the street. Here we can see tailors working in the shop on the left, a barber giving a shave in the center, and a grocer with pies and a large, white loaf of sugar on the right. The shopkeepers lived above their stores.

"In the name of God, Saint Michael, and Saint George, I dub thee knight. Be valiant." To a young man of the Middle Ages, these words, along with the tap of a sword blade on his neck or shoulder, meant that he had become a knight.

Knighthood reached its greatest importance in western Christendom during the Middle Ages, when law was in the hands of the nobility. Nobles, called *lords,* owned much of the land and ruled through a system called *feudalism,* which lasted from the 9th through the 13th centuries.

The great unifying force in western Christendom was the Church. The Church held vast areas of land, and clergymen were involved in feudal rivalries. Also, the Church urged Christians to fight in religious wars called *crusades*.

In the early Middle Ages, most people lived and worked on manors in the countryside. In the 11th century, trade began to expand beyond the local markets of the manor, and town life revived. A middle class of people made up of carpenters, weavers, people in other crafts, and merchants began to develop.

Some members of the middle class grew so rich and powerful that they became rivals of the feudal lords. Many people of this middle class used their wealth to advance education, learning, and the arts. By the late Middle Ages, the civilization of western Christendom was at its highest cultural level. This chapter explains how:

1. Feudalism arose in western Christendom.

2. The manor was the center of economic life.

3. The Church unified Christendom.

4. Town life revived in the later Middle Ages.

5. Education, learning, and the arts advanced.

1 Feudalism arose in western Christendom

The kings who followed Charlemagne were not able to hold the reigns of power. Strong nobles forced Charlemagne's weak successors to give them special rights. As a result, strong local governments, which had begun to form during the decline of Rome, again became important.

Division weakened the Carolingian Empire. In 843, Charlemagne's grandsons signed the Treaty of Verdun, which divided the empire into three parts. Charles the Bald got lands west of the Rhone River, called West ans. 2
Frankland. This land later became France. Louis ●
the German got lands east of the Rhine, called East Frankland, which became modern Germany. A narrow strip of land between these two kingdoms was given to the eldest grandson, Lothair. Ever since, the ownership and government of this land have been the cause of many wars between Germany and France.

The three kingdoms were still thought of as ans. 3
parts of one great empire, but none of the three brothers had any real authority. Government and economic life were run by hundreds of local counts, dukes, and other nobles.

Vikings, Magyars, and Muslims attacked the empire. During and after Charlemagne's rule, the empire was invaded by bands of Scandinavian warriors. These people were known as Vikings, Northmen, or Norsemen. They sailed ■
to Russia, England, the shores of western Europe, and into the Mediterranean. They set fire to towns, seized all movable riches, and sacked churches.

Some Vikings settled on the coast of West Frankland. They were known as Normans, and the area became known as Normandy. They developed a well-governed, Christian state.

At the end of the 9th century, another group, the nomadic Magyars from Asia, attacked eastern Europe. By the late 10th century, they had

● Emphasize the point that it was hundreds of years before these areas developed into what may be called modern nations. These developments are explained in Chapter 18.

■ The Vikings also sailed as far as North America.

formed settlements, adopted Christianity, and built a new state known as Hungary.

Meanwhile, another very powerful group was building an empire to the south. These were the Muslims, Arab followers of the religion of Islam. They pushed into the southern Italian peninsula and the southern coast of West Frankland. They sacked towns and sold their captives in the slave markets of North Africa. They built bases on most of the important islands in the Mediterranean and drove Christian traders out.

During these invasions, the Carolingian kings gave little protection to their people. In fact, no central government worthy of the name existed.

Feudalism, a new system of government, emerged. With the disappearance of a central government, a new system based on land ownership and personal service gave government services to the people of western Christendom. ■ This system is called *feudalism* [fyü′dl iz′ əm]. Landowning nobles became ● almost independent of kings and princes. They settled legal disputes, kept armies, controlled the food supply and collected taxes.

Feudalism had its beginnings during the ans. 1
decline of Rome. Cities no longer gave good law enforcement, and small landowners turned over their property to larger landowners in return for protection. An early German tribal custom also contributed to the development of feudalism. German chiefs divided the spoils of war among their companions in return for pledges of loyalty and military service. These warriors became lords and passed out their lands for the same pledges. This process continued until at the bottom were land divisions just large enough to support one knight.

The person who received land from a lord was called a *vassal* and the land called a *fief* [fēf] or a *feud* [fyüd]. A feudal contract between the lord and the vassal laid out the rights ans. 4
and duties of each. The lord had to protect the vassal and his family, defend their honor, and give them justice in his court. The vassal had to provide military service, pay taxes, and sometimes give shelter, entertainment, and food to his lord.

Feudalism became complicated and clumsy because it divided western Christendom into thousands of local governments. For example, one lord might be the vassal of several other lords. Sometimes a king, with many vassals of his own, might also become a vassal of another king. For instance, King John of England, who held lands in France, was a vassal of the French king, Philip.

The Church entered into feudal contracts. Gifts of land to the Church often carried feudal obligations. The result was that a clergyman

● Neither Charles Martel nor Charlemagne had standing armies. They raised armies by giving land to mounted knights in return for their services in war. This practice helped the growth of a powerful class of nobles.

■ Key Concept: feudalism was the governmental system of the Middle Ages.

holding a fief was at the same time a servant of the pope and a vassal of a lord. Often he had to decide to whom he owed first loyalty. When a Church official died, the Church still held the land. Church lands increased in size until the Church owned about a third of the land in western Christendom.

Medieval society had fixed classes: nobility, clergy, and peasants. The nobility was made up of the kings, their vassals, and lesser lords. Their status was inherited.

Generally speaking, clergymen, or churchmen, were the only group educated in subjects other than warfare. Bishops and high-ranking clergy lived on a level as high as that of the rich lords. However, village priests came from the lower class and had only a little education.

The peasants were on the bottom of the social scale. Nearly all of them were *serfs,* peasants who by law had to work the land they were born on. They depended on the nobles for their livelihood. A peasant could never become a noble. But a man from the peasant class might become a clergyman; he could even become a bishop or pope.

A very small group of people were freemen. They rented their lands from the lord. They could hire someone to do their work. Or, they could leave if they found a new tenant.

SECTION REVIEW 1

p. 153 **1.** List three steps in the development of feudalism in western Christendom.

p. 152 **2.** Name two modern nations that began during this period.

p. 152 **3.** How did the Treaty of Verdun weaken the Carolingian Empire?

p. 153 **4.** How was feudalism a form of government?

● The size of a manor varied from about 350 acres, containing perhaps a dozen families, to 5000 acres, supporting fifty families.

2 The manor was the center of economic life

The economic system of the Middle Ages was the *manorial system.* Almost all the goods and ans. 1
services necessary for life were produced on the ■
manors, or estates, of the nobles. The manorial system developed at a time when towns in Europe had become few and small. Trade, which had flourished between different centers during the Roman Empire, had almost stopped. Throughout a great part of western Europe, most people lived on the manors of nobles.

Farming formed the basis of the manorial system. The fief of a large landowner might include several hundred manors that were widely separated from each other. The fief of a small landowner might be only one manor. ● Each manor was the center of the social and economic life of the people who lived on it. Just as the peasants depended on the lord for protection and provisions, so also the lord's power and wealth depended on the peasants who worked his estates.

The manor house was the heart of a manor. In many cases, the manor house was a large fortified building, even a castle. The lord's barns, stables, mill, bakehouse, and cookhouse were also on the estate. Nearby were the church, the priest's house, and the village where peasants' huts lined a narrow street. The lord divided up meadows and woodlands as he pleased. But he made a pasture available to everyone.

All the people of the manor shared the farmland. The lord usually took the best and let the peasants raise food for their families on the poorer land. The farmland was divided into long strips, most often separated only by dirt ridges. The peasants pooled their oxen and plows and

■ Key Concept: the manorial system was the economic system of the Middle Ages.

worked all the fields together. By planting only some of the fields each year, they kept the farmland from being overworked.

Because the lord could live on only one of his estates, and also because he was often busy ans. 2 fighting, the day-to-day running of the manors was left to certain officials. In England, these people were known as the *steward*, the *bailiff*, and the *reeve*.

The steward had the highest rank. He was a legal adviser to the lord and ran the manor court. He traveled from one manor to another, checking on conditions.

The bailiff supervised the work of the peasants and the farming of the land. He also checked the financial accounts and the collection of rents, dues, and fines.

The reeve helped the bailiff supervise farm work. A large manor might need many reeves just as a large factory today needs many foremen. The reeves oversaw the growing and storage of hay, the care of bees and herds, and the harvesting of crops. It was also the reeve's job to tell the lord of any complaints the peasants had about his officials.

Serfs had to work two to three days a week on the lord's land. Even more time was required during planting and harvest. In addition, they had to pay part of their own harvest in taxes. Most of the flour, bread, and wine made by the serfs in the lord's mill, oven, or wine press had to be given to the lord. Serfs could not leave the manor of their own free will. Nobles considered them to be property not much above cattle. They could not hunt in the woods, for the woodlands belonged to the lord, nor could they fish in his streams.

Literature of the times is filled with references to peasant ugliness, stupidity, and filthiness. Peasants had no education and believed in witches, magic, and ogres. Only from time to time were their dull lives brightened up by folk dances, church festivals, or rough athletic contests.

15th-century scene of the year in a farmer's life: planting, apple-picking, cutting wood for fuel

Women worked hard on the manor. Most women in the Middle Ages were housewives and mothers. They took care of the home and raised large families of children. They also worked on the estate.

Peasant women did every kind of farm work except heavy plowing. They planted and harvested grain. They sheared sheep, milked cows, and took care of chickens. They thatched roofs by joining together many bunches of straw or rushes to form a solid covering.

Noble women, called *ladies,* inherited land and held honors and offices. Because there were so many wars, lords were often absent and the ladies ran the manor and defended it if it were attacked. If a lord were taken prisoner, his wife raised the ransom needed to save him. And noble women performed the medical services needed on the manor, as there were very few doctors.

Women of all classes married young, often by the time they were fourteen. Their fathers set up the marriages, sometimes while the girls were still babies. Every father tried to have a *dowry* for his daughter, some amount of money, land, or goods, that she took to her marriage. Without a dowry, it was almost impossible for a girl to marry. Letters and diaries of the time indicate that arranged marriages in the Middle Ages turned out well.

Living conditions in the castle were crude. The lord's manor house or castle was built mainly for defense against enemies. The great stone tower, or *keep,* provided a safe place during a seige. Other buildings—holding stables and supplies—were near the keep.

A high wall, often several feet thick, surrounded all the buildings. During a battle, defenders could stand on dirt walks near the top of the wall. Then they poured burning oil or dropped heavy rocks on the enemy below. A moat [mōt], or ditch filled with water, ran around the outside of the wall. Entrance to the castle was controlled by a drawbridge that was lowered across the water from inside a gate in the wall. A heavy iron grating that could be dropped quickly protected the drawbridge gate.

By modern standards, the castle had few comforts. Rooms were dark, cold, and musty. In winter, hearth fires warmed only small areas. Since chimneys did not come into use until the 14th century, large rooms were often full of smoke. When eating in the great hall, nobles sat at boards placed on sawhorses. They threw food scraps over their shoulders to the dogs. Rushes, which were spread over the floor to lessen the cold, became filthy and evil smelling from the garbage that collected in them. Carpets were not used to cover floors until late in medieval times.

The nobles' huge, heavy beds were often built on platforms. There were canopies on top and heavy curtains around the sides for privacy and protection from drafts. Falcons, dogs, and even farm animals slept in the same room as the family.

During the evenings, jesters and clowns entertained the nobility. Travelers were welcome, for they brought news and gossip from places beyond the manor. Welcome also were the traveling musicians who moved from one castle to another, bringing their poems and music of heroic deeds, love, and great adventures.

SECTION REVIEW 2

1. In what ways was a manor self-supporting? p. 154
2. Who ran the manor? What were the different duties of different officials? p. 155
3. What were some differences between the lives of the serfs and the lives of the nobles? ●

● Answers will vary.

Daily Life of Medieval Nobles

There were colorful moments in the lives of medieval lords and ladies. Hunts *(left)* brought both food and amusement as the lords gave chase on horseback to the sounds of barking dogs and the horns of the men who kept the group together and the animal in view. When there were no battles to fight, knights kept in shape by jousting in tournaments. The picture *center* shows a parade of contestants at a tournament in which three French knights faced 36 foreign challengers in one week. Such bloody contests were considered fine entertainment. Instead of dating, lords and ladies "courted," as this tapestry *(right)* shows. In addition to being decorative, tapestries hung on castle walls to keep in warmth and cut down on noise and drafts.

3 The Church unified Christendom

The Church was the unifying force in the Middle
ans. 1 Ages; most Europeans believed that only the
● Church could give eternal salvation. Church influence was so strong that Europe was referred to as Christendom. Many government services were provided by the Church. Church laws crossed political borders and reached into every part of life.

The Church had also grown very wealthy. Its income was more than that of all the important kings and princes put together. The Church constantly received large gifts of land in addition to the *tithe,* or tenth part of a person's income, that each member had to pay to the Church.

People looked to the Church for salvation. The Church had developed a body of beliefs that all Christians accepted. Most important were the seven sacraments: (1) baptism, (2) confirmation, (3) penance, (4) the Holy Eucharist, (5) extreme unction, (6) matrimony, and (7) holy orders. The *sacraments* were ceremonies believed to be necessary for salvation, though no one received all seven.

In *baptism,* a person—usually an infant—became a Christian. In *confirmation,* the individual crossed over from childhood to become an adult member of the Church. In *penance,* the individual confessed his or her sins and was forgiven. In the *Holy Eucharist,* a priest reenacted Jesus's Last Supper with his disciples and the people received consecrated bread and wine. *Extreme unction* was given by a priest to a dying person. All Church members received these five sacraments. Of the two others, *matrimony* was the marriage ceremony, and *holy orders* were for men who became priests.

The Church enforced its rules. The Church had courts to help protect the weak and to punish those who had done wrong. It also tried clergymen and others for religious offenses. These people were judged by canon law—the law of the Church.

Heresy was the most horrible of all crimes. It was thought to be a crime against God, because it denied religious teachings. The Church looked for and punished *heretics* [her′ə tiks].
One of the main weapons it used against of- ■
fenders was *excommunication.* When a person was excommunicated, he or she was no longer a member of the Church and therefore could never go to heaven. So the Church usually tried to persuade heretics to give up their beliefs. If a heretic refused, he or she was usually burned at the stake.

The Church became stronger and more independent. During the 10th century, the papacy depended upon a German king for protection against feudal abuses, unruly Italian nobles, and Roman mobs. This arrangement led German kings to interfere in Church affairs, even in the election of popes.

During the 11th century, a great religious revival was begun by the monks at Cluny [klü′nē]. ans. 2
They spoke out against kings and princes who interfered in Church affairs. They started a reform program to remove all civil control over the pope, to forbid the sale of Church jobs, and to stop kings and nobles from choosing bishops. In 1059, the College of Cardinals was created. Its job was to elect a successor to the pope who would be the choice of the Church, not of a king or Roman mob.

The power of the Church grew under the reign of Pope Innocent III (1198 to 1216). Innocent claimed that his authority was above

● The point might be made that the church offered the peasants hope in a happier life after death.

■ Another weapon used by the Church was the interdict which stopped all Church services (except Baptism and Extreme Unction) in the land of a disobediant noble in order that his subjects would protest and make him obey Church law.

that of any other ruler and that the word of the Church was final. He forced King John to give England to the papacy and then take it back as a fief. This made John a vassal of the pope. Innocent also made vassals of other rulers.

During the 12th and 13th centuries, two religious groups, the Franciscans and the Dominicans, were begun. Unlike other groups, these two worked among the people. They preached in the towns and countryside to spread the gospel and fight heresy. Both groups became famous as university teachers. They had an important influence at a time when many people criticized the Church for being too interested in power and wealth.

The Church urged crusaders to save the Holy Land for Christians. For hundreds of years, Christians had visited the Holy Land to worship at places associated with the life of Je-
ans. 3 sus. In the 11th century, Muslim Seljuk Turks swept into Palestine. By 1089, they had taken Jerusalem and were threatening Constantinople, the capital of the Byzantine Empire. The Byzantine emperor asked the pope for help.

In 1095, Pope Urban II called a meeting where he urged thousands of knights to become *crusaders,* a word that means "marked with the cross." Urban promised the crusaders forgiveness for their sins, freedom from their creditors, and a choice of fiefs in the land to be conquered. His stirring speech created great enthusiasm. As Urban finished speaking, the audience roared, "God wills it!"

While the knights began to organize an army, preachers in France and Germany urged peasants to join the crusade. Thus aroused, mobs of poor, ignorant peasants started to Jerusalem, killing and pillaging thousands. Many victims were Jews, who were singled out as nonbelievers in Christianity. The peasants also murdered 4,000 Hungarians, mostly Christians. The peasants reached Constantinople in 1096 and began to burn and steal. After leaving Constantinople, they were attacked by the Turks; few ever got to Jerusalem.

Unlike the Peasant Crusade, the First Crusade was an organized army. Led by Frankish princes and nobles, it included 3,000 knights and 12,000 infantry. In 1099, the army got to Jerusalem and mercilessly slaughtered Muslims, Jews, and some Christians. The crusaders seized land and created the Crusader States on a strip of land along the Mediterranean. Nearly fifty years later, Muslims attacked the Crusader States. A Second Crusade was begun in 1147. Again, after Jerusalem was taken by the Muslim leader, Saladin, a Third

The Gothic cathedral at Amiens shows typical pointed arches, round rose window, and triple doors.

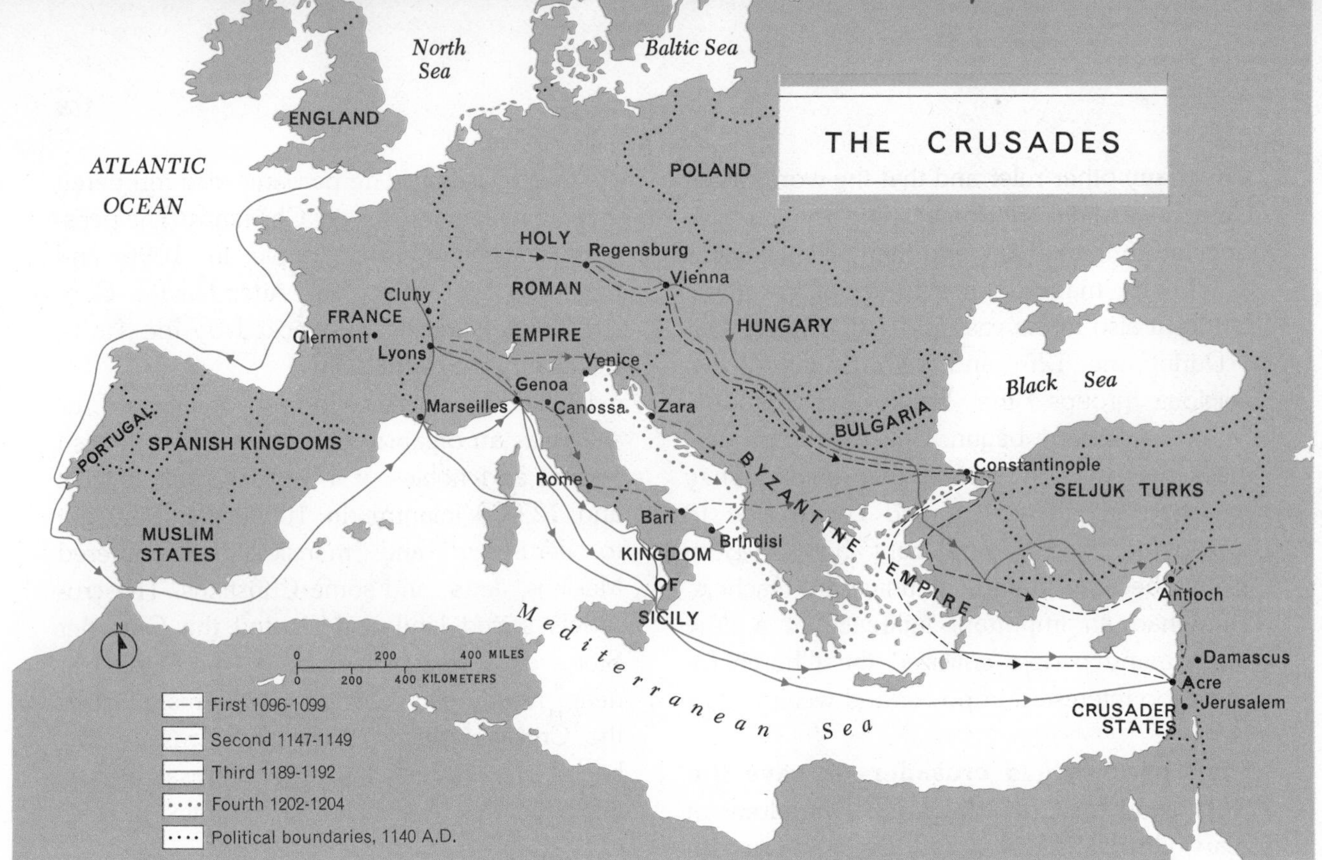

Crusade started in 1189. Both failed; Christians merely won the right to visit Jerusalem. But to gain that right the Third Crusade cost the lives of 300 thousand soldiers and countless civilians.

In 1202, a Fourth Crusade began. Instead of fighting the Muslims, however, the crusaders captured and sacked Constantinople. They set up their own government, the Latin Empire. In 1261, they were thrown out, and the Byzantine Empire was restored. But it never wholly recovered from the blow dealt it by the Fourth Crusade. Thirty years later, Acre, the last Christian stronghold in the Middle East, fell to the Muslims. This marked the end of the crusades.

The Holy Land was lost to Christendom.
ans. 4 However, contact with the Middle East ended the isolation of Europe. Christendom had been exposed to a civilization that in many ways was superior to its own.

The crusades helped spread commerce and indirectly led to the growth of great ports and cities. Knowledge of the Middle East enriched Christendom's culture. New foods and fabrics were brought back to Europe.

In addition, the crusades reduced the number of Christian nobles. This weakened feudalism and thereby indirectly led to the rise of royal power in western Europe.

SECTION REVIEW **3**

1. Why did most people of western Christendom, from serfs to kings, obey the rules of the Church? p. 158

2. Give two examples of how the strength of the Church increased from the 11th to 13th centuries. p. 158

3. What was the main reason for the crusades? p. 159
What military gains were made? 160

4. How did the crusades benefit western Christendom? p. 160

4 Town life revived in the later Middle Ages

During the 10th and 11th centuries, new towns and cities began to appear in Christendom and old cities began to revive. However, the fastest growth was in the 13th century when trade increased. The cities were places where new classes of people grew in wealth and power. Cities also became centers for education, literature, and the arts.

ans. 1 **Trade increased between Italian cities and the Middle East.** The Fourth Crusade ended in 1204. Then trade grew between the Middle East and Italian city-states such as Venice. People in western Christendom, especially the nobility, wanted to buy the spices and silks that Arab sea merchants brought back from Asia.

Large fleets of ships from Venice, Genoa, and other Italian cities sailed the Mediterranean, bringing luxury goods to England and northern Europe. As international trade grew, towns grew; as cities grew, trade expanded.

The use of money replaced barter. During the early Middle Ages, barter had been a common practice. Serfs bartered farm products or homemade goods in the local market. They traded a wooden spoon, for example, for some eggs. Local markets were held each week in the open squares near castles or churches.

ans. 2 As nonlocal trade increased, feudal lords set up annual fairs. These became meeting ● places for merchants from all over Christendom. The lords rented space and levied fines and taxes for income. People at the fairs used money, but they had different coins. So money changers set up booths and, for a small fee, exchanged different coins.

Soon, merchants and traders found that it was safe to leave large sums of money with the money changers. They, in turn, lent money to borrowers and charged interest. A merchant could also deposit money in one city, get a receipt, and collect the money in another city. This was a safe way to transfer money. In Europe, these simple forms of banking and credit developed first in northern Italy. The use of money helped break down the isolation of the era.

Many factors helped the growth of towns. The recovery of trade was very important in causing towns to grow. But there were also other reasons towns grew. Changes in farming ans. 3 had a marked effect on town growth. New farm methods and technology yielded bigger crops, bettered living standards, and led to an increase in population. At the same time, fewer people were needed to do the work on the manors. Three inventions—the tandem harness, the horse collar, and horseshoes—helped transportation and farming methods.

At the beginning of the 11th century, more land became available for farming as forests were cleared, swamps drained, and land reclaimed from the sea. The lords who developed many of these wilderness lands needed workers to dig ditches, build dikes, cut timber, and uproot tree stumps. To get workers for these new lands, the lords promised serfs their freedom and the right to rent land at fixed fees. The peasant with a little money could now choose to remain on the manor or move to the town. ■

Towns gained independence and grew in political stability. City living became increasingly desirable, and serfs continued to leave the manors. This exodus lasted for hundreds of years and was one of the great social, political, and economic revolutions of history.

● Both goods and ideas were exchanged. People met and discussed new methods of industry, agriculture and transportation.

■ In town, the former serf could become a wealthy craftsman or merchant, completely changing his way of life. Many serfs ran away from the manor to the more inviting towns.

Daily Life in Medieval Towns

Surrounded by thick walls like the one being built *above,* towns gave protection to merchants and provided a lively atmosphere for the exchange of ideas. Artists and scholars no longer lived in monasteries, but benefited from the contacts of urban living. Artisans in town belonged to guilds that protected their crafts. Through their guilds they made and enforced rules about the making of goods and the training of apprentices. *Below left* a guild warden inspects textile dyers. *Below right* artisans work in their workshop, probably a room in their home.

Town life had good and bad features. In their early stages, towns were rural in character. To leave the country and live in a city did not mean giving up fresh air. Even in the country, houses were built close together for protection and warmth. In the cities, rows of houses served as a protective wall, and the gardens they surrounded became space for playing games and growing food. A middle-class home might house the shop, workrooms, and family living space.

Opportunities to make money and gain personal freedom in the cities were more important than the discomforts and dangers of large populations. As cities grew larger, public health and safety laws to lessen these dangers began to appear. Over a period of about two hundred years, some cities began to have paved streets. Fireproof roofing was required in some cities. England forbade people to throw waste into ditches and rivers.

In 1347, an epidemic of bubonic plague began in Constantinople. In 1348 and 1349, it spread all over Europe, following the trade routes. The people of the times called it the Black Death, because the corpses of its victims turned a dark color. The Black Death struck hardest in the cities. Some records say that half the city population died from it.

Despite the Black Death, the cities recovered. Populations began to increase. By the middle of the 15th century, London had a population of 40 thousand and Brussels, 35 thousand. Paris had grown to 300 thousand.

ans. 4 **New classes of people arose in western Christendom.** With the rise of towns and the expansion of trade and industry, a powerful class of people had developed in Christendom. Unlike the nobility, their interest was in business rather than war. They were referred to as men of the burg, that is, *burghers* [bėr′gərz], or the *bourgeoisie* [bůr′ zhwä zē′]. At the top of the scale were the prosperous merchants and bankers. Their sons attended the universities and became important professional men, even advisers to kings. Feudal lords looked down their noses on the middle class as mere upstarts, but the bourgeoisie continued to prosper. They became patrons of the arts and established a kind of nobility of their own. In turn, they looked down on those beneath them on the social scale, such as the skilled workers. Thus, class distinctions were developing along lines of wealth rather than birth.

The economic life of skilled workers was regulated by organizations called guilds. Merchants and craftspeople had separate guilds. A guild strictly controlled its number of members and the quality of goods produced. Guild courts settled disputes and judged members. The guilds assisted needy members, built homes for the poor, and held banquets and other social events.

The bourgeoisie were the city landholders. They hired former serfs, but they did not let them own land in the cities, hold political office, or vote.

SECTION REVIEW 4

1. How did the increased trade between the Middle East and western Christendom help the growth of towns? p. 161

2. What was the purpose of the fairs? How did they encourage the use of money? p. 161

3. What reasons other than trade helped towns become larger? p. 161

4. Describe the new classes of people that lived in towns: what was the name of the class; what kinds of work did they do? p. 163

5 Education, learning, and the arts advanced

By 600, formal education had almost ended in western Christendom. The few schools that did exist were run by the Church to train men to become monks. This situation lasted for 500 years. Then new conditions created a need for people with other kinds of training and education.

Universities were begun all over Christendom. During the 1100s, three things helped
ans. 1 the growth of learning in Christendom: (1) the rise of cities and a rich middle class, (2) Church reforms, and (3) contact with other cultures. Both the Church and civil governments needed trained lawyers for courts, for drawing up documents, and for government. To meet these demands, teachers and students formed groups called *universities.* They had no set courses of study, no permanent buildings, and few rules. Students were granted rights, such as freedom from military service and from the jurisdiction of town officials.

One famous university was begun at Bologna [bə lō′nyə] about 1158. Another started at Paris about 1200. Bologna gained a reputation for the study of law. Student groups controlled the administration, hired teachers, and made the rules for the school. At Paris, the university was run by the administration and faculty, not the students. Other universities patterned themselves on one of these two systems.

Classrooms were cold in winter. Students wore heavy gowns and hoods and sat on floors covered with straw for warmth. They went to one or two classes every day, each class being several hours long. Once darkness fell, studies were stopped, for candles were expensive.

The most famous scholar of the Middle Ages was Saint Thomas Aquinas [ə kwī′nəs]. He lived from about 1225 to 1274. He joined the Dominicans as a youth and became a brilliant lecturer and writer. During his lifetime, a scholarly controversy over conflicts between faith and reason reached its height. Saint Thomas disagreed with both sides. He taught that a person's reason and faith are both gifts of God, that certain truths can be understood by powers of reasoning, while other truths, basic to Christianity, can be understood only by faith. So convincing were his arguments that his work *Summa Theologica* (The Highest Theology) is still an authority for the Roman Catholic Church.

Scientific knowledge made some progress in the later Middle Ages. Greek and Arab ans. 2
works flowed into Christendom, particularly after the beginning of the 12th century. Algebra from the Arabs, trigonometry from the Muslims, and Euclid's *Geometry* added to the scope and accuracy of math.

In the 1100s, the sailor's compass was invented, followed by the development of a better rudder for larger ships in about 1300. The 1300s also saw the introduction of the blast furnace and progress in iron-working. Greek and Arab writings on biology were popular among doctors and improved their techniques.

Roger Bacon, an English monk of the 1200s, advanced scientific knowledge. He felt that learning should be based not on faith, but on observation and experience. As a result, he was attacked by many of the learned men of his day. Toward the end of his life, he was put in prison for 15 years, and his works were condemned. But it was Roger Bacon who predicted the coming of power-driven ships, cars, and flying machines.

Popular languages replaced Latin. Among educated people, Latin was an international means of communication. Almost all the writings of the Church, the governments, and the schools were in Latin. However, most of the people in western Christendom could not speak or understand it, even though they came in contact with Latin in the Church. They spoke different local languages.

ans. 3 After the fall of the Roman Empire, changes in the spoken Latin developed that varied from geographic area to area. Latin-based languages now known as *Romance languages* appeared in Italy, France, Spain, and Portugal during the early Middle Ages. Several hundred Germanic words became part of the Romance languages from the time of the earliest barbarian invasions. Contact with the Middle East brought in words from the Greek, Persian, and Arabic languages as well.

Native German became the base of the Dutch and Scandinavian languages, as well as modern German. The major influence on English was Germanic, but hundreds of English words come from Latin. The Latin original and its variations can be seen clearly in the English words *study, letter,* and *city:*

LATIN	ITALIAN	FRENCH	SPANISH
studiare	studiare	étudier	estudiar
littera	lettera	lettre	letra
civitas	città	cité	ciudad

Literature of the Middle Ages took many forms. Latin was used both for serious works and for the saucy poetry written by university students. Traveling students sang happy, irreverent verses about the joys of wine, love, and song in exchange for food and housing.

The earliest form of native literature was the epic, a long poem that told of the adventures of

DRACULA

In the mid-1400s, Count Dracula ruled part of present-day Romania. The real Count's deeds were even more horrible than the movie stories about him. During a war with the Turks, Dracula butchered 20 thousand of his capital's population. When the Turks got there several months later, they found the rotting bodies. Overwhelmed that Dracula could treat his own subjects in such a terrible manner, the Turks retreated.

Did Robin Hood Really Exist?

Lithe and lysten, gentylmen,
That be of frebore blode:
I shall you tell of a good yeman.
His name was Robyn Hode.

So begins "A Lytell Geste [story in verse] of Robyn Hode" from an old manuscript preserved in the library at Cambridge University in England. Hundreds of these four-line stanzas tell of the courteous outlaw and his Merry Men who lived in Sherwood Forest. They stole from the rich and gave to the poor. And they were heroes of ballads at least as long ago as the 13th century.

Was Robin Hood a real person? Who was he and when did he live? The answers are clouded in mystery.

A poem of the late 14th century speaks of the "rymes of Robyn Hode." *Rymes* were popular ballads based on legend. Since it takes time for a legend to become the subject of a ballad, if there really was a Robin Hood, he must have lived in the early 1200s.

Not until the 16th century did two historians try to prove he really existed. They had little to go on but early versions of the ballads and various graves that the people of the countryside had always believed to be the grave of Robin Hood—but there was more than one!

One historian suggested that Robin Hood was really a nobleman who had come on hard times. His theory became very popular. Today almost all films and stories about Robin Hood show him to be a knight or earl who lost his wealth. But medieval documents do not support this interpretation.

Several 19th-century historians tried to prove that a man named Robert Hood, who bought a plot of land in 1316, was the real Robin Hood. They had many impressive pieces of evidence to support their case. But the date is too late. In fact, a charter in 1322 makes it clear that Robin Hood was already a legendary figure by that time.

Historians will go on searching for the real Robin Hood because uncovering the past is what history is all about. But even if they never find him, the ballads will always be important for history.

They express the peasant discontent that raged in 13th- and 14th-century England. It was a time when English peasants bitterly resented the harsh demands of the landowners and sheriffs who protected them. The peasants wanted social justice. Robin Hood was their ideal of someone who could give it to them.

great heroes. *Beowulf,* written in the Anglo-Saxon language in the 8th century, is an example of an early epic.

With the rise of the city and the influence of the middle class, a short story form became popular. These stories were comical, often scandalous. Also popular were animal stories, such as *Reynard the Fox,* and ballads, such as those about Robin Hood.

Dante and Chaucer were two great poets. Dante Alighieri [dän′tā ä′lē gyer′ē] was an Italian poet, philosopher, and student of politics. Born in Florence in 1265, he wrote a poem that later admirers called the *Divine Comedy.* This work shows the religious spirit of the times, telling of a mythical journey through hell, purgatory, and paradise. His writings in Latin and in the local Tuscan dialect were an inspiration for many poets who came after him.

Geoffrey Chaucer was born about 1340 in
ans. 4 London, the son of a wine merchant. His best known work is *The Canterbury Tales,* which tells the story of thirty pilgrims on their way to Canterbury cathedral. It offers a vivid picture of England in Chaucer's time. The Midland dialect Chaucer used was the base from which English developed.

The arts served the needs of the Church. Most music in the Middle Ages was written for the Church. Church services were sung or chanted. Musicians used various instruments—organs, violins, dulcimers, and lutes.

ans. 5 Dramatizations of Bible stories and religious teachings were performed in the churches. At first, these stories were sung by the choir. Later, they developed into plays. In time, plays were performed in local languages and in public places outside of church buildings. But the plays kept their religious character and were called *morality plays.*

Artists and sculptors of the day were hired to decorate churches and cathedrals. Both the outside and inside walls were covered with pictures showing events in the life of Jesus, the saints, and scenes from Bible stories. The use of stained-glass windows, which dated from ancient times, became a fine art in the medieval period.

Gothic architecture was developed by the middle of the 12th century. Gothic churches used pointed arches for the roof. Outside supports, called *buttresses,* made it possible for these buildings to be taller than those built before. Throughout the 13th century, towns competed in building the highest cathedral in the area. Walls, no longer needed to support the roof, were thinner and were covered with stained-glass windows. In some churches, such as Sainte Chapelle in Paris, the sides of the building served mainly as a framework for the beautiful jewellike windows.

SECTION REVIEW **5**

1. Why was there an increased need for educated men in Europe during the 1100s? Who ran the university at Bologna? At Paris? p. 164

2. Name some of the scientific advances made in Europe during the Middle Ages. Which were based on ideas from the Greeks? From the Arabs? p. 164

3. How did the different peoples of western Christendom come to speak different languages? Name three languages that developed from Latin. Name two Germanic languages. p. 165

4. What medieval literature gives an example of the English dialect of the Middle Ages? What was this dialect called? p. 167

5. How did medieval music, drama, and art help people learn about their religion? p. 167

CHAPTER REVIEW 8

SECTION SUMMARIES

1. Feudalism arose in western Christendom. With no protection from a central government, and in the face of repeated attacks by invaders, local governments became strong throughout Europe. Feudal contracts described the relationships among kings, nobles, knights, and peasants. The Church, too, was involved in feudal arrangements. Society was divided into fixed classes, and there was little social mobility.

2. The manor was the center of economic life. Self-sufficient manors supplied most of life's necessities for the people who lived on them—and the majority of people lived on manors. Supervised by officials, the peasants produced food and drink, clothing, and building materials. The manor house was the center of the manor and was built to withstand attacks. Life inside these houses or castles was crude by modern standards.

3. The Church unified Christendom. Almost all people in western Europe during the Middle Ages were Christians who believed the seven sacraments of the Church were necessary for salvation. This fact gave the Church enormous control over people's daily lives. In addition, the Church was the largest landowner of its day. The Church had its own laws and courts, and excommunication was its severest penalty. A religious revival, begun by monks at Cluny, helped to strengthen the Church. It became even more independent of civil authority. During the 11th century, the Church urged its members to fight for Christian lands in Palestine. A series of holy wars, called the crusades, were marred by senseless killing and destruction. No permanent gains were made. However, the crusades brought Christendom into contact with the Arab world, and trade increased.

2. Answers will vary. See sections 1 and 2.

3. a, Barbarians were converted and civilized; b, Law and order were based on religious teachings; c, The lives of the poor were eased somewhat through their hopes for salvation. They were also expected to tithe and accept their lives and the teachings of the Church uncomplainingly.

4. Town life revived in the later Middle Ages. As a result of increased trade and a new group of free peasants, towns began to grow. Money and banking replaced barter. And new classes, the bourgeoisie and skilled workers, developed.

5. Education, learning, and the arts advanced. Universities began to supply learned men for governments and the Church. Advances in mathematics, navigation, iron-working, and medicine took place. Popular languages developed, and literature was written in them, rather than in Latin. Music, theater, and architecture were used to enhance church services, and these art forms progressed.

WHO? WHAT? WHEN? WHERE?

1. Give the years in which these events or developments took place:

a. The Black Death spread throughout Europe. 1348–9
b. Muslim Turks captured Jerusalem. 1089
c. The Treaty of Verdun divided Charlemagne's empire. 843
d. Saint Thomas Aquinas lived. 1225–74
e. The College of Cardinals was created. 1059
f. Pope Innocent III was supreme overlord in Europe. 1198–1216
g. Vikings, Magyars, and Muslims invaded Europe. 750–1050
h. Universities were founded in Bologna and Paris. ●
i. Pope Urban II urged thousands of knights to become crusaders. 1095
j. The last crusade was undertaken. 1202–4

2. Explain how each of these fit into the feudal system: a. king, b. nobles, c. vassals, d. fief, e. manor, f. knights

3. Give examples of the influence of religion on: a. barbarian invaders in the 9th and 10th centuries, b. law and order in medieval society, c. the lives of the poor during the Middle Ages

● 1158, 1200

• **4.** What effect did each of the following have on the growth of towns in Christendom? a. crusades, b. trade with the Middle East, c. fairs

5. Name one achievement of each of the following: a. Saint Thomas Aquinas, b. Dante Alighieri, c. Roger Bacon, d. Innocent III, e. Geoffrey Chaucer, f. Urban II

QUESTIONS FOR CRITICAL THINKING

1. Why did the feudal system develop? What were some good and bad effects of feudalism on people's lives?

2. How did the Church make up for the lack of central government during the feudal period?

3. Why did Latin die out as the language of western Europe? How do languages change? Give some examples from this chapter and from your own experience with language today.

ACTIVITIES

1. Use material in this chapter, including the pictures, to draw or write a description of a medieval manor. Show how the manor was self-sufficient. Include a castle, with its different parts, and the other buildings necessary for life on the manor.

2. Write a diary for a week in the life of a person during the Middle Ages. How would the lives of these people differ: a. noblewoman, b. village priest, c. knight, d. serf (man and woman)?

3. Look up pictures of medieval architecture in this book and in the library. Find out the differences between Romanesque and Gothic church styles. What problems did architects have in the Middle Ages? What materials did they use? Name some churches that were built during the Middle Ages that can be visited today.

4. Make a piece of art that illustrates some part of modern life that comes from the Middle Ages.

• 4. a, The Crusades made Christendom aware of the riches of the East; b, Trade between East and West was channeled through towns; c, Many towns grew at sites of trade fairs.

5. Answers will vary.

CHAPTER TEST **8**

SECTION 1

1. Which of the following was not a reason for the breakdown of central governments? a. weak rulers, b. barbarian invasions, c. crusades

2. Power during the feudal period was based on: a. land, b. money, c. education

3. In exchange for land, a lord received ______ from his vassals. a. ransom, b. money, c. military service

SECTION 2

4. True or false: Each fief consisted of only one manor.

5. The ______ supervised the peasants' work and collected rents. a. reeve, b. bailiff, c. steward

6. True or false: Most of the food and clothing for the peasants had to be brought in from other parts of the country.

SECTION 3

7. Dominicans and Franciscans were: a. hermits, b. teachers, c. farmers

8. The crusades were formed to save: a. the Turks, b. Constantinople, c. Jerusalem

9. The Church became very important because it offered salvation to its followers.

SECTION 4

10. The use of money replaced the ______ system. a. barter, b. fair, c. bank

11. The power of the bourgeoisie was based on: a. land, b. money, c. education

12. Cities first appeared in: a. England, b. France, c. Italy

SECTION 5

13. During the Middle Ages, education was kept alive by the: a. nobles, b. governments, c. Church

14. During the Middle Ages, scientific knowledge came from Greeks and Arabs.

CHAPTER
9
330–1453

Byzantine Civilization and the Formation of Russia

Russia became Christian in the 900s, after repeated contact with the Byzantine Empire. This cathedral, built in Novgorod between 1045 and 1052, is similar to many Byzantine churches. But the onion-shaped domes are distinctively Russian. Novgorod also had paved streets and a *kremlin*.

● While western Christendom went through a long period of decline, Christian civilization in the east flourished. This eastern Christendom was known as the Byzantine Empire. Constantinople was its capital, and its wealth and culture attracted many visitors. One of those visitors was Rabbi Benjamin ben Jonah, a Jew from the Iberian peninsula, who visited Constantinople in 1161. He was wide-eyed with wonder, as we can see from this excerpt from his diary:

● Some students may be unfamiliar with the idea of 'eastern' and 'western' Christian churches and will require help in understanding this material. The map and material on p. 174 should be helpful.

> It is a busy city, and merchants come to it from every country by sea or land, and there is none

like it in the world except Bagdad, the great city of Islam. . . .

The Greek inhabitants are very rich in gold and precious stones, and they go clothed in garments of silk with gold embroidery, and they ride horses, and look like princes. Indeed, the land is very rich in all cloth stuffs, and in bread, meat, and wine.

Wealth like that of Constantinople is not to be found in the whole world. Here also are men learned in all the books of the Greeks, and they eat and drink every man under his vine and his fig-tree.

The Byzantine Empire lasted for 1,000 years, produced new forms of art and architecture, and preserved the great contributions of ancient Greece and Rome.

Byzantine influence reached beyond the empire's borders and was felt by the Slavs living north of the Black Sea. Those Slavs, ancestors of the present-day Russians, adopted from the Byzantines their religion (Orthodox Christianity) and their written literature.

The early Russians did not build a state as strong as that of the Byzantines. The first Russian political organization was really a grouping of city-states under the leadership of the city of Kiev. For two centuries, Kiev had close ties with Christendom and it was through Kiev that Christianity spread to the rest of Russia. When civil war broke out among the ruling princes, the Kievan state became internally weak and was conquered by Mongols from Asia in the early 13th century.

The Mongols ruled Russia for more than two centuries. Their hold on the country was finally broken when a series of strong princes in Moscow, a city in central Russia, defeated them in battle and began to form a new Russian state. This chapter tells how:

● The essay on Constantinople, on p. 173 can be used to motivate students.

1. The eastern empire survived the fall of Rome.

2. The Byzantines made important contributions in many fields.

3. Kiev became the first Russian state.

4. The Mongols conquered and ruled Russia.

1 The eastern empire survived the fall of Rome

In southeastern Europe, on a peninsula between the Black and Aegean seas, lies the modern-day city of Istanbul. On its site, a Greek colony called Byzantium [bi zan′tē əm] was begun in the 7th century B.C. This colony fell under Roman control in 196 A.D.

Constantine, emperor of Rome from 306 to 337 A.D., ordered a new city built on the site of this Greek colony. In 330, it became the second capital of the Roman Empire. Known as Constantinople, or the city of Constantine, it became a thriving metropolis and the center of a new civilization, usually called *Byzantine* [biz′n tēn′] after the original Greek settlement. ●

The Byzantine Empire was the continuation of the Roman Empire. After the death of Emperor Theodosius in 395, two emperors ruled the Roman Empire—one in the east at Constantinople and one in the west at Rome. While Germanic tribes invaded the western empire, the eastern empire stood firm.

Justinian restored Roman greatness. The eastern emperor Justinian, who ruled from

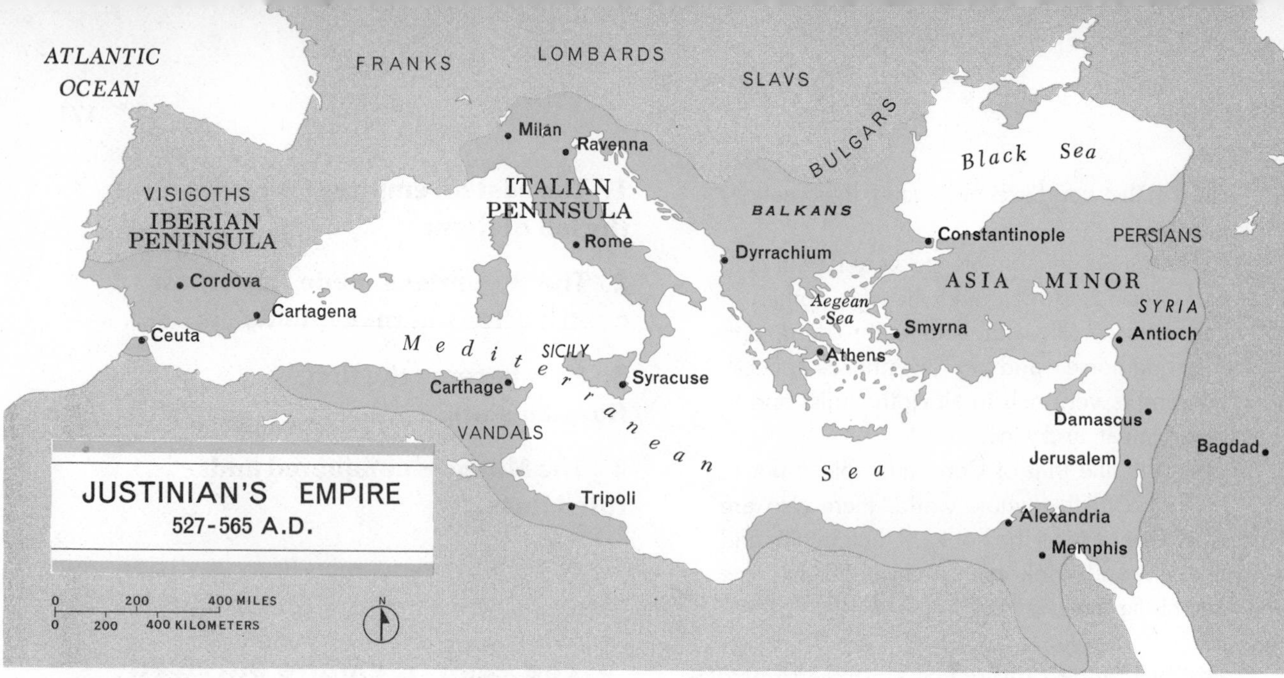

527 to 565, took back some of the crumbling western empire from the Germanic tribes. In a brilliant campaign, Justinian's army destroyed the Vandal kingdom in North Africa and gained a foothold on the Iberian peninsula. He then fought the Ostrogoths on the Italian peninsula. After many years of desperate fighting, the Byzantines won. In the process, however, the Italian peninsula was devastated. Fields lay untilled, cities fell into ruin, and famine and disease were everywhere. Justinian's triumphs were a hollow mockery to the people he had "rescued" from Germanic domination.

ans. 1 Justinian's most lasting contribution to western civilization was his organization of Roman law into a systematic form. A commission of lawyers revised and codified the laws.

Justinian also lavished money on roads, aqueducts, and other public projects. He helped make Constantinople one of the wonders of the Middle Ages, far larger and more beautiful than any city in western Europe.

At his death, Justinian left a realm that was dangerously weakened by his extravagant ambitions. The treasury was empty, and the western borders of the overextended empire were hard to defend. In reclaiming the lost territories of Rome, Justinian had neglected the eastern provinces of his own empire. Persians, Slavs, Bulgars, and others periodically attacked the eastern borders.

● Compare the map (above) of Justinian's empire with the map of the Roman empire at its height, p. 111. Draw attention to Justinian's near success in restoring the lands once ruled by Rome.

The eastern empire became Byzantine. After Justinian's death, the western empire was sliced away by further Germanic conquests. The idea of a united Roman Empire was never entirely discarded. However, by the 8th century, the eastern empire had developed a civilization that was more Greek and Middle Eastern than Roman.

The Byzantine population was largely Greek, ans. 2 but it included Slavs, Syrians, Jews, and others. Greek was the national tongue. The Greek classics formed the basis of Byzantine literature. (Latin was used for state documents until the 7th century when it was completely discarded.)

The Middle Eastern traditions in the Byzantine Empire came from the ancient empires of Persia and Mesopotamia. Eastern customs were reflected in the elaborate etiquette at the royal court and the lavish ceremonies associated with the semi-divine status of the emperor. Roman

Geography: A Key to History

Strategic Straits

A body of water can both divide people and bring them together. If the body of water is wide, deep, or unnavigable, it separates people. If it can be navigated and easily crossed, it can help bring them together. The straits and small sea that separate Asia from Europe are of the latter kind. They have helped human contact and trade more than they have hindered.

The Bosporus, Sea of Marmara, and the Dardanelles separate Europe from Asia. But they also link the Black Sea to the Mediterranean. For the last 2,500 years, some important city has controlled one or the other of the straits. Troy controlled the Dardanelles (which was called the Hellespont in ancient Greek times). Byzantium and then Constantinople controlled the Bosporus. Indeed, control of the Bosporus helped make Constantinople great.

When Constantine founded Constantinople in 330 A.D., he chose the best site he could find. He built the city on a point of land above a natural harbor called the Golden Horn. The Golden Horn has such a narrow (yet deep) entrance that in the past a chain could be stretched across it to prevent enemy ships from entering. The Bosporus itself was so narrow that trade caravans could easily cross it by ferry.

Constantinople became the most important trading center between Europe and the East. From Russia by way of the Black Sea came furs, fish, and honey. They were exchanged for wines, silks, fruits, glassware, and other luxuries. From Persia and East Asia came spices, perfumes, jewels, and other costly goods.

Constantinople's wealth made it a place that many people wanted to control. Arabs, Russians, Europeans, and Turks—all attacked Constantinople between the 7th and 15th centuries. The city's geographic location helped it withstand these attacks. The city was protected on three sides by water. Enemies approaching by water could easily be spotted. On its land side, the city was protected by fortified walls.

Eventually, Constantinople fell to the Turks. But the desire to control the straits has continued to the present. Today, western European countries, the United States, and Russia have treaties to keep the straits open.

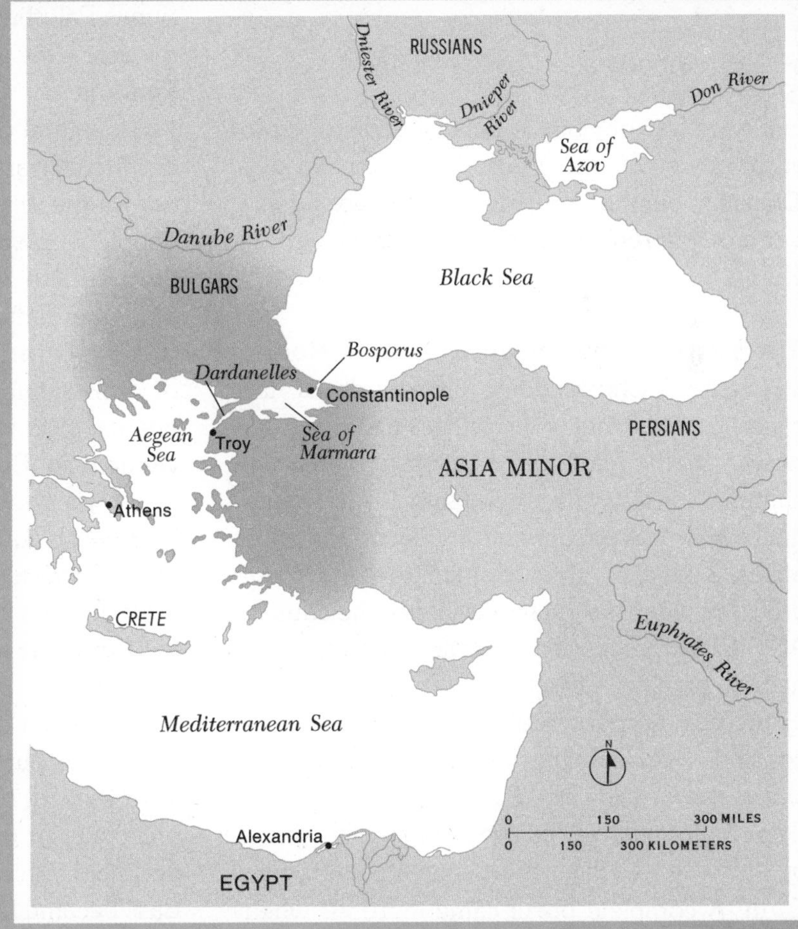

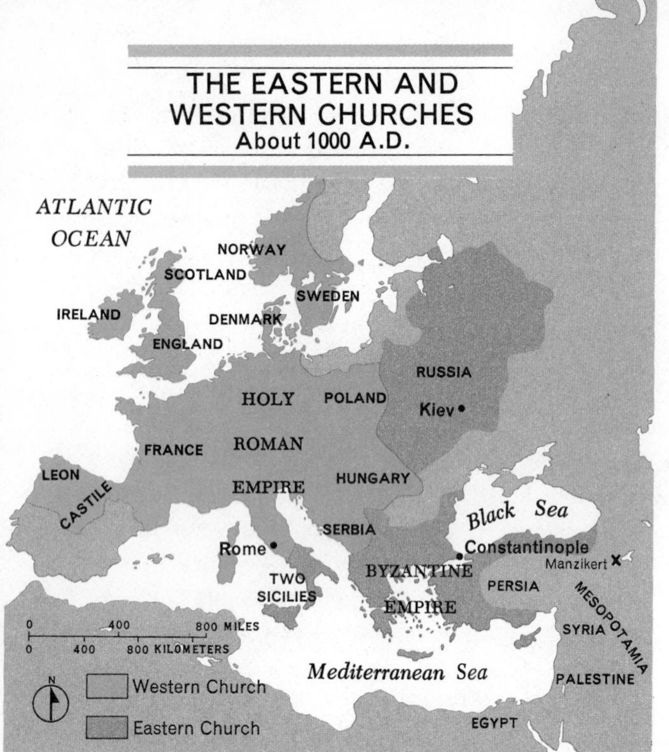

influence was obvious in the law and in the political power of the emperor. The empire was Christian, but the Byzantine church evolved in a pattern different from that of the church in Rome.

The Eastern Church split off from Rome. In western Christendom, the power of the church grew as that of the princes and kings declined. In the east, the relationship between church and state was not the same. The Byzantine emperor was supreme in church and state affairs. However, he customarily let the *patriarch,* the highest church official, run the church. And the emperor left the details of civil government to his chief advisers.

Increasingly poor feelings strained the relationship between the eastern and western
ans. 3 churches. As early as 381 A.D., the church in Constantinople rejected the theory that the bishop of Rome was the highest church authority on Earth. A complete break came in 1054, when Pope Leo IX and Patriarch Michael Cerularius [ser′ū ler′ē əs] excommunicated each other. Then, after the crusaders plundered Constantinople in the Fourth Crusade, the Eastern (Orthodox) Church and the Roman Catholic Church went their separate ways.

● The map above shows the lands of the Eastern and Western Churches at the time of Basil II's rule. The Holy Roman Empire had been founded by the German king, Otto the Great, in 962. (Ch. 18)

The Byzantines withstood many invaders. Periods of imperial instability and economic decline alternated with periods of strength and prosperity. For ten centuries, the Byzantine capital fought off numerous attempts to destroy it. The outer provinces were sometimes taken. In the 7th century, the emperor Heraclius [her′ə klī′ əs] beat the Persians and took back Syria, Palestine, and Egypt. However, a new menace—the Muslim Arabs—soon replaced the Persians. By the end of the 7th century, the Muslims had conquered North Africa, the eastern Mediterranean lands, and parts of Asia Minor. In the 7th century, the Bulgars, a nomadic people who spoke a Finnic language, attacked the northern Balkans. They overpowered the Slavs and settled what is now Bulgaria.

A Muslim army was repulsed at the very gates of Constantinople (717–718), and the Byzantine navy drove off the invader's fleet. A major element in Byzantine naval success over the years was the use of "Greek fire." This was a flammable liquid containing lime, sulfur, and other chemicals that set fire to the enemy ships.

Under Leo III, who ruled from 717 to 741, the Byzantine Empire regained its strength. Leo increased the power of the emperor by weakening the power of the provincial governors.

Another outstanding emperor, Basil II, ruled from 976 to 1025. He revived the power and prosperity of the empire after a long period of decline. For his ruthless conquest of the Bulgars, Basil became known as the "Bulgar Slayer." On one occasion, Basil had thousands of Bulgars blinded and only a handful left with a single eye each to guide the rest home. The Bulgarian king is said to have died of shock when this sightless multitude returned. However, once the fighting was over, Basil gave the Bulgars self-rule within the Byzantine Empire.

After Basil's death, the empire fell into another era of decay. The city-state of Venice and ● other newly emerging centers offered serious competition to Byzantine trade in the eastern Mediterranean. And the Muslim Turks, a foe more powerful than any the Byzantines had faced to that time, appeared from central Asia. After the Turks beat a Byzantine army at Manzikert in 1071, the whole of Asia Minor was overrun by these hardy invaders.

Turks overwhelmed the Byzantine Em-
ans. 4 **pire.** The Byzantine Empire never fully recovered from the attack on Constantinople made by the crusaders of the Fourth Crusade. Even after they were thrown out in 1261, the empire did not have peace. Civil war broke out as different princes fought to become emperor. Religious differences divided the people. And the economy of the empire was in poor shape. Peasants were overtaxed. Repeated warfare had been costly. And trade had been hurt. Onto this sorry scene came the Ottoman Turks.

The Ottomans, former subjects of the Muslim Turks, by-passed the Byzantine capital and crossed the Bosporus into Europe in 1354. By 1445, Constantinople was all that remained of the once-mighty Byzantine Empire. Eight years later, the end came. Barely 8,000 defenders—many of them foreign-born troops serving only for their pay—were left to fight the besieging Turkish army of 160 thousand men. After eight heroic weeks, the city fell. Emperor Constantine IX died with his men. As the Turks stormed the walls of the city, the emperor rushed to meet them, crying out as he was cut down, "God forbid that I should live an Emperor without an ■ Empire! As my city falls, I fall with it."

● These Italian city-states were among the first to revive in the later Middle Ages. Some historians suggest it was merchants from these city-states who incited the Fourth Crusaders to attack Constantinople.

■ This quotation may be useful in stimulating a discussion of what constitutes bravery.

SECTION REVIEW 1

1. Name three of Justinian's accomplishments. p. 172

2. In what ways was Byzantine civilization Greek? p. 172
Middle Eastern? Roman?

3. What were the causes of the conflict between p. 174
the Byzantine church and the Roman popes? What names are used by the two religions?

4. What problems weakened the empire and led to p. 175
its final collapse in 1453?

2 The Byzantines made important contributions in many fields

Byzantine civilization was superior to the civiliza- ans. 1
tion that existed in medieval Europe. Not until the 1300s were Byzantine standards of art and scholarship reached by the peoples of western Christendom. The amazing strength and endurance of Byzantine civilization was due to several factors: a centralized government and a well-trained bureaucracy; an efficient and well-led army and navy; the strength and leadership of the Orthodox Church; and a high standard of living due to a strong economy.

Industry and trade thrived. With its strong commercial life, the Byzantine Empire was able to survive civil war and the steady attacks of foreign enemies. Sitting at the crossroads of Europe and Asia, Constantinople was the greatest center of trade at that time. In an era when the

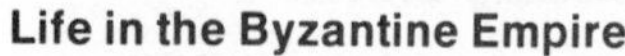

Life in the Byzantine Empire

The Byzantine court blended Greco-Roman traditions with those of Persia and the Middle East. The ivory carving *above* shows a Byzantine empress in a stiff, Middle Eastern pose, with Roman columns beside her. The capital, Constantinople, was one of the best protected cities of its day. The map *above left* shows the 13 miles (20 kilometers) of city wall that were built in the 5th century to keep out the Huns and Goths. Princess Olga of Kiev, in Russia, visited the court in 957, *below*. She turned down the Emperor's marriage proposal but returned to Kiev with rich gifts—a sign of friendship between two Christian rulers.

commerce of western Europe had almost stopped, the Byzantine capital was filled with merchants from many lands. A stable money system based on gold greatly helped the empire's economic position. Because money was scarce in the west, the gold *bezant* coin became a basis for international exchange.

The government acted as a stern watchdog over all parts of the economy. Industry was rigidly controlled. Wages, prices, and working conditions were set. The quality of products was checked, and exports were subject to strict regulation. Jeweled ornaments, magnificent tapestries, carved ivory, and exquisite leather work were the pride of Constantinople. Cloth was the chief industrial product. About 550 A.D., silkworms were smuggled out of China. Thereafter, splendid silk fabric and clothing were made in Constantinople. The silk industry became a profitable state monopoly.

The lower classes did not share in the general prosperity. However, their standard of living, meager as it was, would have been envied by the peasants in western Christendom. The Byzantine economy was relatively stable. And the lives of peasants were improved by governmental supervision of the great estates.

ans. 2 **Rulers maintained a centralized government.** Unlike the feudal system of western Europe, the Byzantine state was centralized. In theory, the emperor was a despot; however, custom and tradition limited his use of power. The weaker emperors were often overshadowed by strong governmental ministers or church patriarchs. An army of civil servants was responsible for the actual workings of government. Despite corruption and bribery, the administrative officials were generally conscientious and efficient.

● Some students may need the term "legal succession" defined. You might ask if any student can explain it to the class.

As with the empire in Rome, a serious defect ans. 2
marred Byzantine political life. This defect was the lack of legal succession to the throne. Any ● upstart might become emperor. Many did so, and the story of the rise and fall of Byzantine emperors is a record of intrigue and violence. Of the 107 emperors who ruled between 395 A.D. and 1453, only 40 died a natural death in office.

The excitable city population of Constantino- ans. 2
ple added to the hazards of government. Popular uprisings were apt to break out at any time. The most famous of these was the terrible Nika Revolt in 532, during the reign of Justinian. Named for the rallying cry of the rebels (*nika* means "victory"), the revolt lasted for seven days. Before it was over, some 30 thousand people had died. Empress Theodora's bravery inspired her husband to stay in the city and crush the rebellion. She said to Justinian:

> If . . . it is your wish to save yourself, O Emperor, there is no difficulty. For we have much money, and there is the sea, here the boats . . . as for myself, I approve a certain ancient saying that royalty is a good burial-shroud.

Byzantine civilization spread throughout Europe. ● The Slavic peoples of Russia and the Balkans were the most deeply influenced by the Byzantine Empire. Missionaries carried Christianity to these tribes in the 9th century. Today, the Orthodox faith is the major religion in Russia, Yugoslavia, Greece, and Bulgaria. The Cyrillic [si ril′ik] alphabet, used in the Russian, Serbian, and Bulgarian languages, is taken from the modified Greek letters of Byzantium. And much of the literature of early Russia, especially the lives of the saints, is Byzantine in origin.

Scholars preserved classical learning. Byzantium inherited the intellectual treasures of

● Key Concept: Byzantine civilization is the base of many modern-day Eastern European cultures.

ancient Greece. The works of Plato and Aristotle were studied with deep respect. The most outstanding Byzantine scholar was Michael Psellus [sel′əs], an 11th-century professor who wrote widely on many subjects. Yet his writings had little originality, for, like other learned men of the time, he preferred to comment on the ancient classics rather than to think in untried areas. Only in the fields of history and theology did the empire produce works of real excellence. Anna
● Comnena [kom nē′nə], daughter of the 11th-century emperor Alexius, wrote an important work on the life and times of her father. In the 1300s, Nicephorus Gregoras [nē′se fôr′əs greg′ə rəs] wrote movingly of the declining empire. Probably the best-known historian, however, is Procopius [prō kō′pē əs]. His notorious *Secret History* is a biased but fascinating account of Justinian's reign.

The libraries of the empire were rich in the masterpieces of Greek philosophy and literature. Even though priceless manuscripts were lost in the plunders of Constantinople, the works that did survive were important to cultural revival.

Architects and artists created domes, mosaics, and paintings. The creativity of the empire in art and architecture is in direct contrast to the imitativeness of its scholarship. In the church of Hagia Sophia, Byzantine genius in the arts came to full flower. It was a church, wrote Procopius, "the like of which has never been seen since Adam, nor ever will be." Built in the shape of a Greek cross, which is about as long as it is wide, the church was surmounted by a huge dome suspended 179 feet (53.7 meters) above the floor. Hagia Sophia was both an artistic and engineering triumph.

In the decorative arts, Byzantines are best known for their use of *mosaics*—small bits of colored glass or stone formed into patterns and pictures. Mosaics were usually placed on the walls and ceilings of churches. Most of the designs were scenes of religious importance. Wall paintings and *icons,* images of sacred figures, usually painted, also added richness to church interiors.

The nonreligious art in the royal palaces was also done on a dazzling scale. Polished marble, inlaid bronze, rich fabrics, gold and silver dishes, and jeweled ornaments were all representative of the Byzantine genius.

SECTION REVIEW **2**

1. How did Byzantine civilization compare with that of Greece and Rome? With that of western Christendom? ■

2. What strengths of the Byzantine Empire helped it last so long? What were the two most serious problems that caused trouble in the empire? p. 177

3 Kiev became the first Russian state

The original homeland of the Slavs is unknown. It is thought that they were one of many peoples who migrated from Asia long before the Christian era. Three distinct groups eventually emerged: the southern or Balkan Slavs; the western Slavs, including the Czechs and the Poles; and the eastern Slavs, who much later became known as Russians, Ukrainians, and Belorussians. ans. 1 By the early 700s, the eastern Slavs had settled between the Baltic and Black seas. In the more isolated areas, they lived by farming, hunting, and fishing. In the growing towns they led an active commercial life. The Slavs did

● This chapter is especially useful in showing the role of women in history. The Empress Theodora, Anna Comnena, and Olga of Russia are included here.

■ Chapters 5 & 6; pp. 175–178

ans. 1 not have a central government, but were organized in city-states. In these, the ruling class was made up of wealthy merchants.

Viking invaders ruled the first Russian state. Viking raids along the coasts and inland waterways of Europe in the 800s also reached Slavic settlements. According to tradition, in 862 A.D., a Viking chief named Rurik [růr′ik] became ruler of Novgorod [nôv′gə rot′], an important city in the northwestern part of Russia. In 882, his successor, Oleg, captured Kiev [kē′ef], a city to the south. Later on, Oleg took Smolensk [smō lensk′], another city, and formed the first Russian state. The Vikings and Slavs intermarried, and their cultures mixed. The name *Russia,* which came into use much later, probably comes from *Rus′,* a term once used by foreigners to describe both the Slavs and their Viking rulers.

ans. 2 For three centuries, Kiev was the capital of a loose confederation of city-states. Its site on the Dnieper [nē′pər] River made it a major stop on the trading route with the Byzantine Empire. Sometimes, the Russian traders were badly treated by the Byzantines. In 907, Oleg led a successful attack against Constantinople. Four years later, the Byzantine emperor agreed to a treaty giving Russian traders favorable treatment.

Russia adopted some of Byzantine culture. In 954 or 955, Olga, the ruling princess of Kiev and the first female ruler in Russian history, was converted to Christianity by Byzantine missionaries. Olga did not try to convert her people to Christianity. That was done in 988 by her grandson Vladimir [vlad′i mir]. In trying to ans. 3
decide which faith to choose, Vladimir sent out ten men to observe the Muslim Bulgarians, the Catholic Germans, and the Orthodox Byzantines. When they returned, they reported:

> we journeyed among the Bulgarians. . . . there is no happiness among them, but instead only sorrow and a dreadful stench. . . . Then

> we went among the Germans . . . but we beheld no glory there. Then we went on to Greece . . . to the buildings where they worship their God, and we knew not whether we were in heaven or on earth. For on earth there is no such splendor or such beauty, and we are at a loss how to describe it. We know only that God dwells there among men, and their service is fairer than the ceremonies of other nations.

Vladimir officially adopted the Orthodox faith for all his people. He ordered that the idols of the former gods be destroyed and that the whole population be baptized. However, it took ● several hundred years for Christianity to be accepted by the common people.

The adoption of Orthodox Christianity was the single most important event in Russia's early history. Through the Church, Byzantine culture influenced the literature, art, law, manner, and customs of Kievan Russia. Orthodoxy also helped unify the country with a common religion. In addition, Russia stayed outside the Roman Catholic Church and was isolated from the Latin civilization of western Christendom.

Yaroslav was the Charlemagne of Russia. Kievan Russia reached the top of its power during the rule of Yaroslav [yu ru slaf′] the Wise, from 1019 to 1054. Kiev became the religious and cultural center of Russia as well as the political capital. It also became one of the wealthiest cities of Christendom and was richer and more brilliant than Paris or London. Yaroslav founded schools and libraries to support scholars and artists. With the help of Byzantine architects, he had a copy of the cathedral of Hagia Sophia built in Kiev. The Byzantine patriarch sent a bishop to head the Kievan Church.

Yaroslav extended his domain by defeating the Lithuanians [lith′ü ā′nē əns] to the west, the Finns and Estonians [e stō′nē əns] to the north, and the Pechenegs [pech′ə negz′] to the south. In 1036, the Pechenegs were decisively beaten. Never again did they bother Kiev or block the river road to Constantinople.

The empire of Yaroslav has been compared to that of Charlemagne. Russian unity was broken by civil war among Yaroslav's heirs. It was regained only briefly during the twelve-year rule of Vladimir Monomakh, 1113–1125.

● Question for Critical Thinking number 2 deals with this material and asks students to conjecture as to what might have been the result of Russia's adopting western Christianity.

SECTION REVIEW 3

1. Which of the three Slavic groups were ancestors of the Russian people? What kind of government organization did they have? Who were their rulers? p. 178 179
2. How did trade take place between the Russians and Constantinople? What articles were traded? p. 179
3. Why did Vladimir choose Orthodox Christianity for his people? How did it affect Russian culture? p. 179 180

4 The Mongols conquered and ruled Russia

From the time of the Huns in the 5th century, periodic waves of invaders from Asia had swept into Europe. The Russians always managed to hold off the invaders and stay independent. But in the 1200s, a more powerful conqueror appeared. Led by Genghis Khan [jeng′gis kän′], these Mongol horsemen overran parts of China, Persia, and Russia. In 1240, Genghis Khan's grandson, Batu, captured Kiev and the other Russian states.

The Mongols created fear and terror. ans. 1
These horsemen were a fierce tribe who showed their enemies no mercy. Their savagery can be

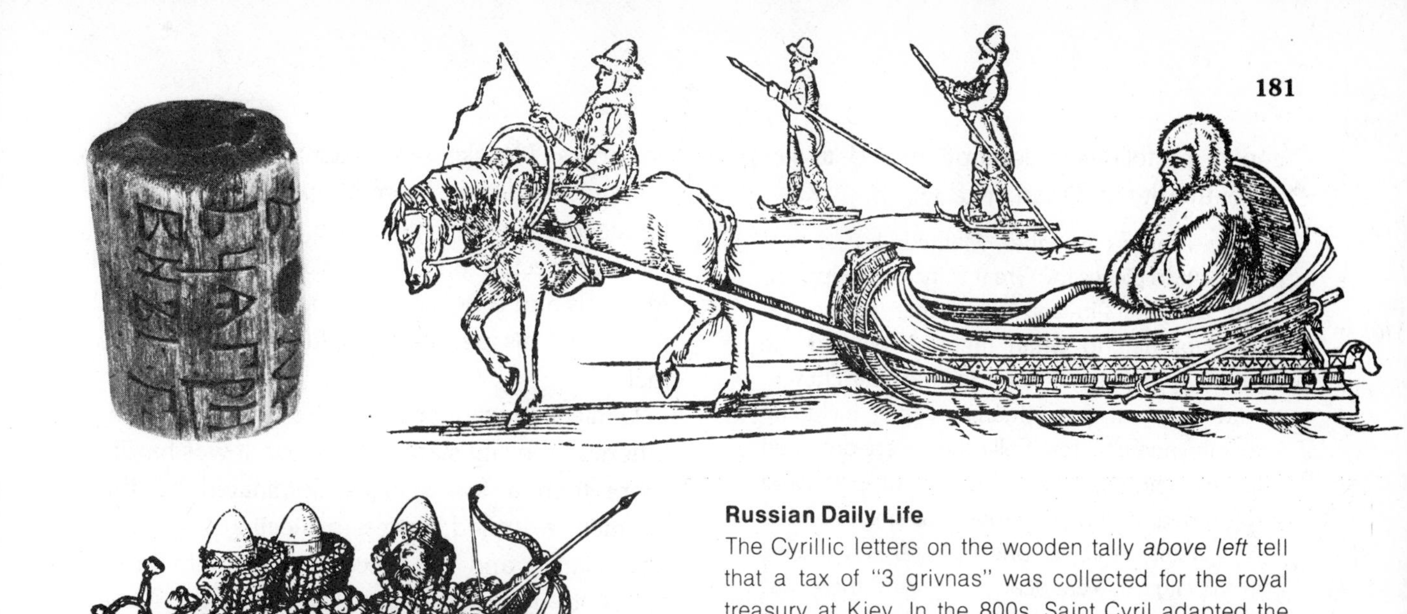

Russian Daily Life

The Cyrillic letters on the wooden tally *above left* tell that a tax of "3 grivnas" was collected for the royal treasury at Kiev. In the 800s, Saint Cyril adapted the Greek alphabet to use in writing the Bible in Slavic for the inhabitants of the Balkans, whom he was converting. The Russians adopted this alphabet in the 10th century for writing their language, and modern Cyrillic has developed from this ancient form. *Above right:* Horse-drawn sleds and skis were the main methods of transportation during the harsh Russian winters. Such harnesses, sleds, and skis can still be seen in Russia today. The Russian archers *opposite* were mounted and dressed in a style they copied from their Mongol conquerors. The Mongol armies included whole families. While the men engaged in combat, the women kept camp *(below)* and did the work of modern mess sergeants and supply officers.

seen in the following description of Batu's capture of the city of Riazan in 1237:

> They came to the Cathedral . . . and they cut to pieces the Great Princess Agrippina, her daughters-in-law, and other princesses. They burned to death the bishops and the priests and put the torch to the holy church. And they cut down many people, including women and children. Still others were drowned in the river. . . . And churches of God were destroyed, and much blood was spilled on the holy altars. And not one man remained alive in the city. All were dead. . . . And there was not even anyone to mourn the dead.

Mongol rule influenced Russian history. So widespread was the destruction in Russia and so great were the tributes, that some historians estimate that Mongol rule held back the development of Russia by 150 or 200 years. The Mongols also cut Russia off from Byzantium and in part from western Christendom for about 250 years. Russia's isolation increased.

ans. 1 The Mongols made very few positive contributions to Russian civilization. As the Mongols had adopted the Muslim faith, they kept apart from the Russians. They did not interfere with the Orthodox Church, but the Church had to support the Mongol power. The Mongols deserve some credit for bringing a postal system and a census to Russia, but they brought nothing important in philosophy or science.

Russian princes gradually grew stronger.
ans. 2 Russia's national hero during the early years of Mongol rule was Prince Alexander of Novgorod. Known as Alexander Nevsky [nev′skē] for his defeat of a Swedish army on the Neva River in 1240, he also fought off other attacks from the west. His most notable victory was in 1242 over the Teutonic Knights, a German group of crusaders. Nevsky never dared challenge the ● Mongols, however. From his capital at Vladimir, he led the Russian nation from 1252 to 1263. His rule rested on the formal consent of the Mongols and a peace agreement he negotiated to protect his people from further Mongol attack.

Daniel, Alexander Nevsky's youngest son, inherited the city-state of Moscow. It was hardly more than a few villages dominated by the Kremlin, a walled fortress protecting the inner city. Daniel and his successors built up Moscow's strength and gained control of the Moscow River, their road to the Volga and to the trade routes. Moscow became the new center of the Russian church when the bishop moved there in 1328.

The princes of Moscow were obedient and ans. 3
reliable servants of the Mongols. In return, they were put above the other Russian rulers. After the Mongol Empire began to disintegrate in the late 1300s, Russian forces under Moscow's leadership crushed a huge Mongol army at Kulikovo in 1380. The victory was short-lived, however. Mongol power was revived under Timur the Lame (Tamerlane). Moscow was sacked in revenge, and regular tribute was again exacted from the Russian princes. Not until 1480 was the Mongol threat ended forever. Then Moscow began to take over leadership of the Russian land.

SECTION REVIEW 4

1. Who were the Mongols, and what effect did they ■ have on Russia's history?
2. What are two examples of successful battles of p. 182 the Russians against western invaders?
3. How did the princes of Moscow become p. 182 stronger than the other Russian princes?

● At times Nevsky received Mongolian aid in fighting western attackers.

■ p. 180, 181

CHAPTER REVIEW 9

SECTION SUMMARIES

1. The eastern empire survived the fall of Rome. Christendom in the east became the Byzantine Empire. It inherited its territory and much of its political tradition from the Roman Empire. In costly warfare, the Byzantines fought to take back lands that the Romans had once ruled. The eastern empire was more Greek and Oriental than Roman. The break between the churches strengthened this division. The Byzantines withstood many invaders, but finally fell to the Turks in 1453.

2. The Byzantines made important contributions in many fields. Constantinople, the strategically placed Byzantine capital, was a prosperous city that kept the best of Greco-Roman culture. Rulers maintained a strong central government that acted as a stern watchdog over all parts of the economy. Byzantine scholars tended to be imitative rather than creative. However, artists and architects created magnificent domes, mosaics, and paintings.

3. Kiev became the first Russian state. The eastern Slavs and their Viking rulers created the foundation of a new state—Russia. For three centuries, Kiev was the capital of a loose confederation of city-states. The single most important event of this era was the adoption of Orthodoxy by Vladimir in 988 for himself and all his people. Yaroslav the Wise, who ruled from 1019 to 1054 and has been compared to Charlemagne, brought Kievan Russia to the peak of its power. After his death, civil war broke out. Unity was regained only briefly during the rule of Vladimir Monomakh.

4. The Mongols conquered and ruled Russia. In the 13th century, the Mongol yoke was fastened upon the Russian people. Mongol rule seriously delayed Russia's development. The Mongols brought terror and destruction to Russia, along with demands of heavy taxes. Alexander Nevsky was the national hero of the time, although he never tried to drive off the Mongols. During the next hundred years, the principality of Moscow slowly grew in strength. In 1380, Russian forces under Moscow's leadership beat a huge Mongol army at Kulikovo. However, Timur the Lame sacked Moscow in revenge. Two centuries passed before the princes in Moscow were able to win independence for Russia.

WHO? WHAT? WHEN? WHERE?

1. Find the correct time for each event: a. 301–600, b. 601–900, c. 901–1200, d. 1201–1500

Tartar rule ended in Russia. d.
Justinian ruled the Byzantine Empire. a.
Muslim Turks deated the Byzantine army. c.
Oleg captured Kiev. b.
Basil II crushed the Bulgar forces. c.
Russia adopted Orthodox Christianity. c.
The Fourth Crusade looted Constantinople. d.
The Mongols captured Kiev. d.
The final collapse of the Byzantine Empire occurred. d.
Roman Catholic and Eastern Orthodox leaders excommunicated each other. c.
Yaroslav the Wise ruled Kiev. c.
Leo III restored the power of the Byzantine Empire. b.
The Russians got favorable trade agreements with Constantinople. c.

2. Give one event in Byzantine or Russian history that involved each of these peoples:

Muslim Turks p. 175 | Mongols p. 180 | Pechenegs p. 180
Ottoman Turks p. 175 | Vikings p. 179 | Teutonic Knights p. 182
Lithuanians p. 180 | Bulgars p. 174,

3. Why was each of these persons important in Byzantine history?

Procopius p. 178 | Anna Comnena p. 178
Empress Theodora p. 177 | Justinian p. 172
Leo III p. 174 | Nicephorus Gregoras p. 178

4. Give one accomplishment or event from Russia's history for each of these leaders:

Vladimir Monomakh p. 180 | Oleg p. 179
Alexander Nevsky p. 182 | Olga p. 179
Rurik p. 179 | Vladimir p. 179

5. Why was each of the following important in Byzantine history?

Hagia Sophia p. 178 | icons p. 178
mosaics p. 178 | "Greek fire" p. 174

QUESTIONS FOR CRITICAL THINKING

1. What were the successes and failures of Justinian's rule? What should he have done that he did not do?
2. How might the world be different today if Russia had become Roman Catholic instead of Eastern Orthodox in 988?
3. Why did the common people in Russia continue to practice their old religious customs for hundreds of years after the official conversion to Christianity?

ACTIVITIES

1. Discuss how the people in the United States might react if the government were to make all people follow a new religion. What steps might a government take to change its people's religious beliefs?
2. On a map of Europe (you could trace one in the back of this book), show where the enemies of the Byzantine Empire came from. Label these enemies and give the years of their attacks. Draw a line around the empire at its greatest extent. Label Constantinople.
3. Using maps, do research on the importance of the geographic location of six cities around the world. Why was Constantinople in a good location? Consider defense, transportation, trade, communication within the country and with other nations.

CHAPTER TEST 9

SECTION 1

1. The language of the Byzantine population was: a. Latin, b. Greek, c. Oriental
2. In the 5th century, the Byzantine Empire was all that remained of the: a. Roman Empire, b. Germanic kingdoms, c. Greek colonies
3. In the Eastern Church, the __b.__ was supreme in church affairs. a. pope, b. emperor, c. patriarch
4. A serious problem of the Byzantine government was: a. disease, b. religion, c. power rivalries

SECTION 2

5. True or false: Byzantine civilization was more advanced than that of western Christendom.
6. The Byzantine Empire helped keep __c.__ armies out of western Christendom. a. Russian, b. German, c. Muslim
7. Byzantine merchants traded with Russia across the __c.__ Sea. a. Red, b. North, c. Black

SECTION 3

8. The ancestors of the Russian people were the __b.__ Slavs. a. southern, b. eastern, c. western
9. The term *Rus'* was used by foreigners to describe the Slavs and the: a. Mongols, b. Byzantines, c. Vikings
10. The religion of the Russians was officially changed by: a. Vladimir, b. Olga, c. Yaroslav

SECTION 4

11. The __b.__ cut Russia off from the rest of the world for more than 200 years. a. Byzantines, b. Mongols, c. Vikings
12. During Mongol rule in Russia: a. the invaders became Christian, b. the Russian people became Muslim, c. each group kept its own religion
13. Alexander Nevsky won a great victory over the: a. Mongols, b. German crusaders, c. Russian traders

● QUESTIONS FOR CRITICAL THINKING

1. (pp. 171–172) Justinian's Code was a revival of Roman law. He also built many public works and made Constantinople the most beautiful European city of that time. His expenses weakened the empire.—Opinion.
2. Russia's culture would have been more like that of western Europe and relations between Russia and the U.S. might be friendlier today.
3. Answers will vary. One reason is that people are usually very hesitant to give up their religious traditions.

622-1700

CHAPTER

10

The Rise of Islam and the Muslim Empire

It was a holy duty of every Muslim who could to make a pilgrimage to Mecca, the birthplace of the prophet Mohammad. The painting above shows the caravan of a wealthy woman. She is riding inside the golden tent on top of a camel. Her attendants assure her a safe, and joyous, trip.

The three men hid in the cave as their pursuers searched the hillside. At last, the searchers gave up, mounted their camels, and rode away. Mohammad, his faithful father-in-law, Abu Bakr, and their guide remained in the cave for three more days. Then, when they were certain it was safe to leave, they led their camels quietly out of the stuffy cavern. Although the city of Medina was their destination, they rode off in the opposite direction. For ten days, they wound about the hot Arabian desert, zig-zagging back and forth to make sure that no one was following them. Finally, the three tired men rode into Medina and sank down in the shade of a tree. It was 622, and this was the end of the *Hijra*, the "migration" of the prophet of a new religion called *Islam*.

Within a few years, this new faith from Arabia spread far and wide. Today, more people are followers of Islam than of any other religion in the world except Christianity.

Mohammad and his first followers were Arabs. After Mohammad's death, his followers conquered huge territories beyond Arabia and converted many people to Islam. Because followers of Islam are called *Muslims*, the empire they established is known as the Muslim Empire. At its height, the Muslim Empire was larger than either the Byzantine or Roman empires had ever been.

By the 8th century, the empire included peoples of very different backgrounds and needs. As there was no government strong enough to hold the entire empire together, some smaller states broke away. Nevertheless, Islam and its culture gave unity to the Muslim world.

Eventually, the Arab dynasties that first ruled the empire were replaced by Turks, who were also Muslims. Turkish rule was long; a part of the empire continued to be ruled by Turks up to the early 1900s. This chapter tells of the growth of Islam and the spread of the Muslim Empire:

1. Islam was based on Mohammad's teachings.

2. Arab caliphs conquered a huge empire.

3. The Muslim Empire divided.

4. Turks assumed leadership of the Muslim world.

1 Islam was based on Mohammad's teachings

The Arabian peninsula is a land of deserts that was inhabited in early times by nomadic peoples. These nomads had no organized government but lived in small family groups, or clans, and depended on their flocks of sheep for food and clothing. Their religion consisted of worshiping the spirits that they believed lived in trees and rocks.

By the 7th century, prosperous trading cities flourished on the Arabian coasts of the Red Sea and the Persian Gulf. Many caravans traveled the trade routes that connected India and China with the Byzantine Empire. The city of Mecca, near the Red Sea, was a busy caravan stop. It was in Mecca that Mohammad was born, and it was to Mecca that he returned triumphant. Mecca was to become a holy city for all his followers from the prosperous merchants to the nomadic shepherds to the people in lands beyond Arabia as well. (See map on page 191.)

Mohammad gained many followers in his lifetime. About the year 570, Mohammad was born in Mecca. Little is known of his early life except that he was orphaned as a child and was raised by relatives. As a young man, he went to work for a wealthy widow who was engaged in the caravan trade through Arabia. He traveled with the caravans to manage his employer's transactions. In his travels he met many people of different cultures, including Jews and Christians. These contacts were to have a profound influence on the religion he later developed.

As Mohammad grew older, his employer's respect and love for him grew. Eventually, she married him, in spite of the fifteen years' differ-

ence in their ages. They had four children. Mohammad's marriage brought him economic security and social prestige. It also gave him leisure time, which he spent in meditation and prayer. By the time he was about 40, he began to have visions in which God and the Angel Gabriel were speaking to him. Mohammad be-
● came convinced that he was the appointed prophet of the one true God, called *Allah* in the Arabic language. At first, Mohammad made few converts beyond his own family.

ans. 1 As Mohammad's teachings became more widely known, he aroused opposition from the wealthy merchants who dominated Mecca. They feared that if many were converted to Mohammad's new religion, they would lose money. Mecca held a most important Arab shrine, the Kaaba (meaning cube). The Kaaba was a cube-shaped building that housed a sacred black stone and the images of several hundred tribal gods. Every year, many Arabs made pilgrimages to the Kaaba, and the money they spent in Mecca was an important source of income to the local merchants. These merchants also suspected that Mohammad wanted to become the ruler of their city, and they proceeded to make life miserable for him and his small band of followers.

In 622, Mohammad fled Mecca for a more promising field for his missionary work, the trade city of Medina. His departure is known as the *Hijra* [hi′jər ə], meaning flight. It is so
■ important to Muslims that it marks the beginning of the Muslim calendar, just as the birth of Jesus marks the first year of the Christian calendar.

Mohammad soon became Medina's political and religious leader. He formed an army and launched a holy war against his enemies. It was successful, and in 630 he returned to Mecca in triumph. The idols were taken out of the Kaaba, and it was preserved as a sacred temple of the Muslim faith. Two years later, at the time of Mohammad's death, Islam had spread to most of the Arabian peninsula.

The Koran was the Bible of the Muslims. The teachings and sayings of Mohammad were set down in the Koran, the Muslim holy book. The official version was prepared by Mohammad's followers soon after his death. They believed that the words of the Koran were inspired by Allah.

The Koran included laws on personal behavior. It described five duties of a good Muslim. These are sometimes known as the Five Pillars ans 2
of Islam. The first, and most important, was to believe and state publicly that there is only one God, Allah, and Mohammad is his prophet. The second duty was to pray five times daily, facing toward Mecca. Giving money to the poor and fasting during the daylight hours of the holy month, *Ramadan*, were the third and fourth duties. The fifth duty was to make a Hajj [haj],

A Christian monk bows before the young Mohammad as an angel anoints the prophet's head.

● Explain the terms *prophet* and *convert* if necessary.

■ This idea may need to be explained to some students, perhaps by drawing a time line on the board and pointing out both events.

or pilgrimage, to Mecca. Many Muslims who lived far away from Mecca could never afford the trip. They were not punished, for it was only important that they wanted to go.

In addition to describing what good Muslims must do, the Koran stated those things which they must not do. Worshiping idols, gambling, drinking liquor, and eating pork were forbidden.

The Koran taught that there is a life after death. The faithful will be rewarded with the eternal joys of heaven; unbelievers will be condemned to the fire of hell. In the Koran, it is said that believers are:

In a high garden
Where they hear no idle speech,
Wherein is a gushing spring,
Wherein are couches raised
And goblets set at hand
And cushions ranged
And silken carpets spread.

The foundations of Islam are pictured here. *Left:* a page from a Koran illustrates its beautiful script. The scribes' devotion to Mohammad's words shows in the care with which they executed them. *Center:* an illustration from an early Islamic manuscript shows Mohammad preaching to his disciples. *Right:* is a drawing of Mecca; the square building in the center is the Kaaba.

The Koran also told what will happen to those in hell. They will be:

Toiling, weary,
Scorched by burning fire,
Drinking from a boiling spring.
No food for them save the bitter thorn-fruit
Which doth not nourish nor release from hunger.

Mohammad taught that all Muslims were equal. In the sight of Allah, there were no differences among believers. For this reason, there was no racism in the Muslim world. Arab, black, and European converts mingled freely in the mosques and marketplaces. Equality, however, extended only to Muslims. The ancient Arab custom of slavery continued, but one Muslim could not enslave another. It was considered a good deed to free a slave, but in practice, Arab culture depended on a large number of slaves. ans. 3

While Muslim women had equal rights to the joys of heaven, their lives on Earth were dominated by men. Mohammad's teachings limited men to four wives (there had been no limit previously), and Arab customs dictated that women's activities were restricted to the home. Arab women inherited property, however, which meant that some women became wealthy and influential in their communities. But, like a modern executive in a penthouse office, a

wealthy Arab woman conducted business through others she appointed, all of whom were men.

Mohammad taught that an individual should communicate directly with God; no human could intervene between God and the individual. Therefore, no organized or privileged priesthood developed in the Muslim world. However, there were learned teachers, known as the *ulema* [ü′ lə mä], who explained religious doctrine. Also, in each community a certain man, known as the *Imam* [i mam′] led the prayers. Praying together was especially important for the noon prayer on Fridays, the holy day of Islam.

Mosques were the churches of Islam. A mosque [mosk] was the place of prayer. It could be as simple as a circle of stones, or a vast, beautiful building decorated with fountains and mosaics. Mosques dominated the skylines of cities in the Muslim Empire just as churches did in Christendom.

Islam borrowed from many sources. The influence of Judaism and Christianity on Islam was great. Many figures in both the Old and New Testaments, including Moses and Jesus, are accepted as prophets. However, Mohammad is considered the last, and most important, prophet.

SECTION REVIEW 1

1. Why did Mohammad leave Mecca in 622? How is this event remembered by Muslims today? p. 187

2. What are the Five Pillars of Islam? p. 187

3. What was Mohammad's teaching about equality of individuals? Give two effects of this teaching on the development of Islamic society. What peoples in the Muslim Empire did not receive equal rights? p. 188

2 Arab caliphs conquered a huge empire

Mohammad's successors, called caliphs [kā′lifs], led Muslim armies in a series of holy wars. Mohammad had left the commandment to spread the faith, by the sword if necessary. This, and a growing population's need for new lands to settle, spurred the Arab conquerors. Within 100 years of the Prophet's death, most of the peoples in the area from the Iberian peninsula through North Africa to India were living under Muslim rule.

Mohammad established a theocracy. Mohammad was the religious and political ruler ans. 1

of Medina, Mecca, and much of the Arabian peninsula. He controlled an army and made laws. He negotiated peace treaties with surrounding peoples and settled legal disputes. Many of the rules in the Koran deal with trade, taxation, slavery, and such military matters as war booty and prisoners.

When Mohammad died, he left no son to inherit his rule. Leadership passed to his companion on the Hijra, Abu Bakr. Abu Bakr took the title of Caliph, which means deputy (of the Prophet). The caliph was Mohammad's successor ● in every way except that he could not change the religious laws. However, Muslims swore to obey the caliph, which was the same to them as obedience to Mohammad and to God.

The caliphs continued Mohammad's work of spreading the faith. Religious fervor was only one reason for Arab expansion. The Arabian deserts could not support large numbers of people. Yet, with the prosperity that trade through Mecca brought, the population of the peninsula grew. New places to settle and farm were needed, as well as new land to tax for revenue.

Arabs conquered much of the Byzantine and Persian empires. The weaknesses of the only other important states—the Byzantine and Persian empires—contributed to the early success of Arab armies. The Byzantines and Persians had been fighting each other for a long time, and the conquered peoples in these two empires were tired of the warfare and heavy taxes. They put up little resistance to Arab attack.

One of the first places the Arabs attacked was
ans. 2 Syria, at that time part of the Byzantine Empire. Its capital, Damascus, was easily conquered. From Syria, the Arab armies moved west to Egypt and took Alexandria. The Nile River Valley gave the Muslims a base from which to conquer all of North Africa.

At the same time, Arab armies moved northeast into the Persian Empire and took Iraq. They repeatedly defeated the weak Persian army. And within ten years of Mohammad's death, they completely destroyed the Persian Empire.

The many peoples under Arab rule were given the choice of either becoming Muslims or paying a head tax. Jews and Christians were ■ tolerated because the Muslims believed that they worshiped the same God, although in a different way. Nevertheless, they had to pay the head tax. As time passed, these heavy taxes caused many persons to convert to Islam. For the first hundred years of the empire, converts who were not Arabs were a kind of second-class citizen who did not have equal rights. Gradually, Mohammad's teaching of equality for believers came to be extended to all converts.

The Umayyad dynasty increased Arab lands (661–750). The first four caliphs were elected by the Muslims in Mecca and had all been associated with Mohammad. However, the expansion of Muslim territory yielded a new kind of ruler. The generals and governors of the new provinces became more powerful than the caliphs in Mecca. In 661, the Muslim governor of Syria declared himself caliph and made Damascus the capital of Muslim lands. This new caliph founded the Umayyad [ü mī′yad] dynasty, which lasted until 750. Under the Umayyad caliphs, Arab conquests continued.

Along the northwest coast of Africa, in northern parts of present-day Morocco, Algeria, and Tunisia, lived a nomadic tribal people, the Berbers. Arab armies, under Umayyad leadership, moved into this area, conquered the people,

● Explain that the caliph could not change any religious beliefs or laws.

■ A head tax is a tax levied on each person.

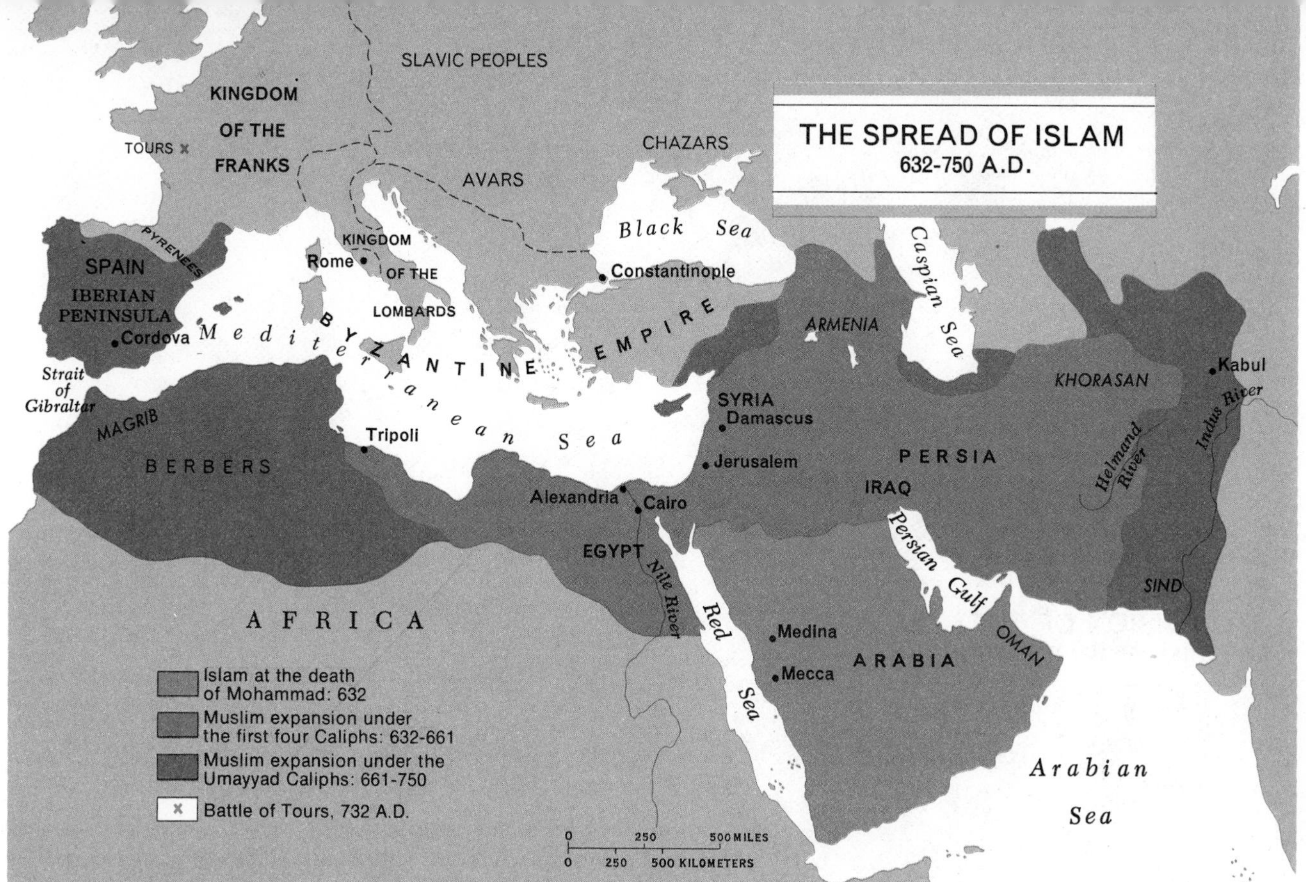

and converted them to Islam. In 711, a Muslim army of Arabs and Berbers, led by the able Berber commander Tarik, crossed the Strait of Gibraltar into the Iberian peninsula. In less than ten years, Muslims crushed the Visigothic forces there. By 719, the Muslim army had crossed the Pyrenees [pir′ə nēz] Mountains that form the border between modern Spain and France.

The southwest area of France was at that time a Christian stronghold, and its people feared a Muslim conquest. But in 732, the Frankish leader Charles Martel (grandfather of Charlemagne) defeated the Muslims at Tours. Muslim losses were heavy, and the remaining troops retreated during the night.

Muslim rule in Spain continued for over 700 years. The people of mixed Arab and Berber ancestry are known as Moors, and they developed a Moorish civilization in Spain. Islamic influences, especially in architecture, have remained strong in Spain down to the present.

The furthest eastern extent of the Arab empire was the region of Sind in the northwestern Indian subcontinent in what is now Pakistan. From 637 to 644, the Arabs sent several small naval expeditions to Sind. These the ruling Indian chiefs turned back. Next, between 650 and 700, Arab armies attacked Kabul, the Helmand Valley, and Sind. They succeeded in capturing Sind in 712.

At first Arab control was loose, and local chiefs retained their power. But by 724, the Arab governor Junayad ruled as the caliph's representative. The people of the area were converted to Islam and have remained so.

The Muslim navy and armies repeatedly attacked the Byzantine capital of Constantinople. In a famous siege in 717–718, Constantinople

Use the map of the spread of Islam (above) to reinforce the idea of the rapid growth of the Muslim empire.

● Spanish culture retains customs begun during Moorish conquest. Example: relative seclusion of women.

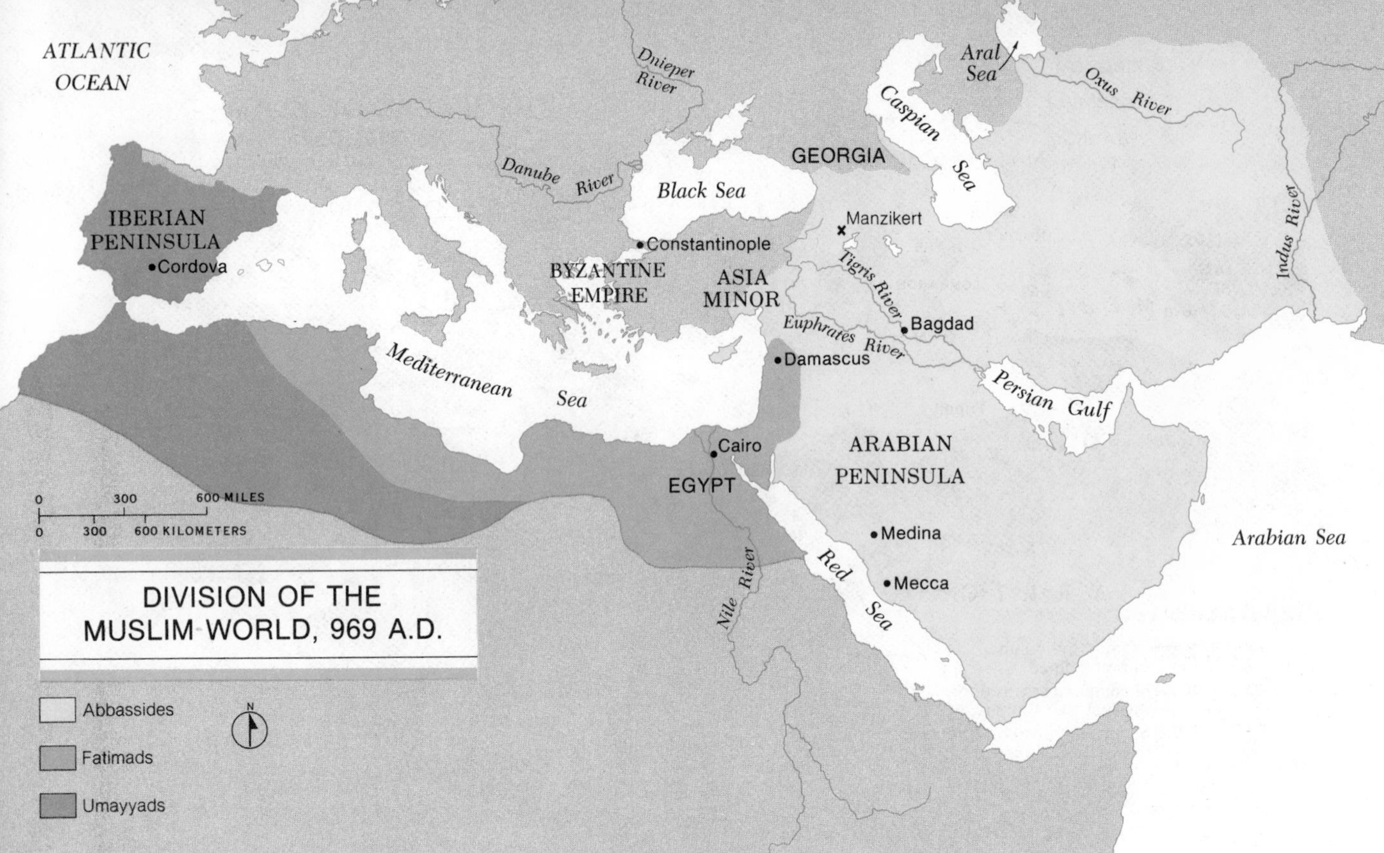

held off the Arab navy by stretching a great chain across the narrow entrance to the Black Sea. The Umayyads were never able to take Constantinople.

For many centuries, the Pyrenees Mountains in the west and Constantinople in the east were the borders between the Islamic and Christian worlds. The Indus Valley was the border between the Islamic and Hindu worlds. The Muslim Empire thus included a vast group of peoples with different cultures, languages, and religions.

SECTION REVIEW **2**

p. 189 190 **1.** In what ways was Muslim government a theocracy? How did the Koran support the idea that religion and government are the same?

p. 190 191 **2.** What peoples came under Arab rule during the first four caliphs?

● Have you covered the meaning of *theocracy?* The concept was first mentioned in Ch. 2.

3 The Muslim Empire divided

The vast Muslim Empire was difficult to rule. Communication and transportation were slow, and the peoples of different regions had very different problems. For efficient administration, regional governors were given the power to make many decisions on their own. As these regional governors grew in power, some refused to obey the caliph at Damascus. Eventually, three regions broke political ties with the empire.

The Abbassides overthrew the Umayyads. The Umayyad rulers and governors primarily occupied themselves with military affairs and left matters of trade and agriculture to the local peoples. As the Arab expansion halted, the Umayyads and their armies became less important. A government was needed that took an ans. 1

interest in the expansion of trade and agriculture.

The peoples of the empire were also ready for new rulers. Many of the non-Arab peoples in the empire were treated as second-class citizens by their Arab conquerors. This caused much dissatisfaction; these peoples felt they were just as good as the Arabs and many had become Muslims in hopes of receiving better treatment. They wanted to take part in the government, but the Umayyad dynasty would not allow it.

In 750 A.D., a revolution took place. It was very carefully planned and had been preceded by much propaganda: speeches, pamphlets, protests, and even such acts of terror as political murders. The Umayyads were overthrown, and new rulers called the Abbassides [ab′ə sīdz] came to power. Like the Umayyads, the Abbassides were Muslim Arabs, but the Abbassides promised that all Muslims—Arab and non-Arab alike—would be treated as equals. Many non-Arabs were made part of the new government.

The most famous Abbasside caliph was the 8th-century ruler Harun al-Rashid [hä rün′ al ra shēd′]. His legendary deeds were recorded in the tales of the *Arabian Nights*, which include the popular stories of "Aladdin and His Lamp" and "Ali Baba and the Forty Thieves." Harun al-Rashid lived at the same time as Charlemagne, and the two exchanged gifts to encourage peace between their lands. The Muslim sent the Christian rich fabrics, perfumes, and even an elephant named Abu-Lababah, meaning the father of intelligence. Harun al-Rashid's relationship with the Byzantine emperor was not so cordial, and border conflicts between their empires erupted periodically.

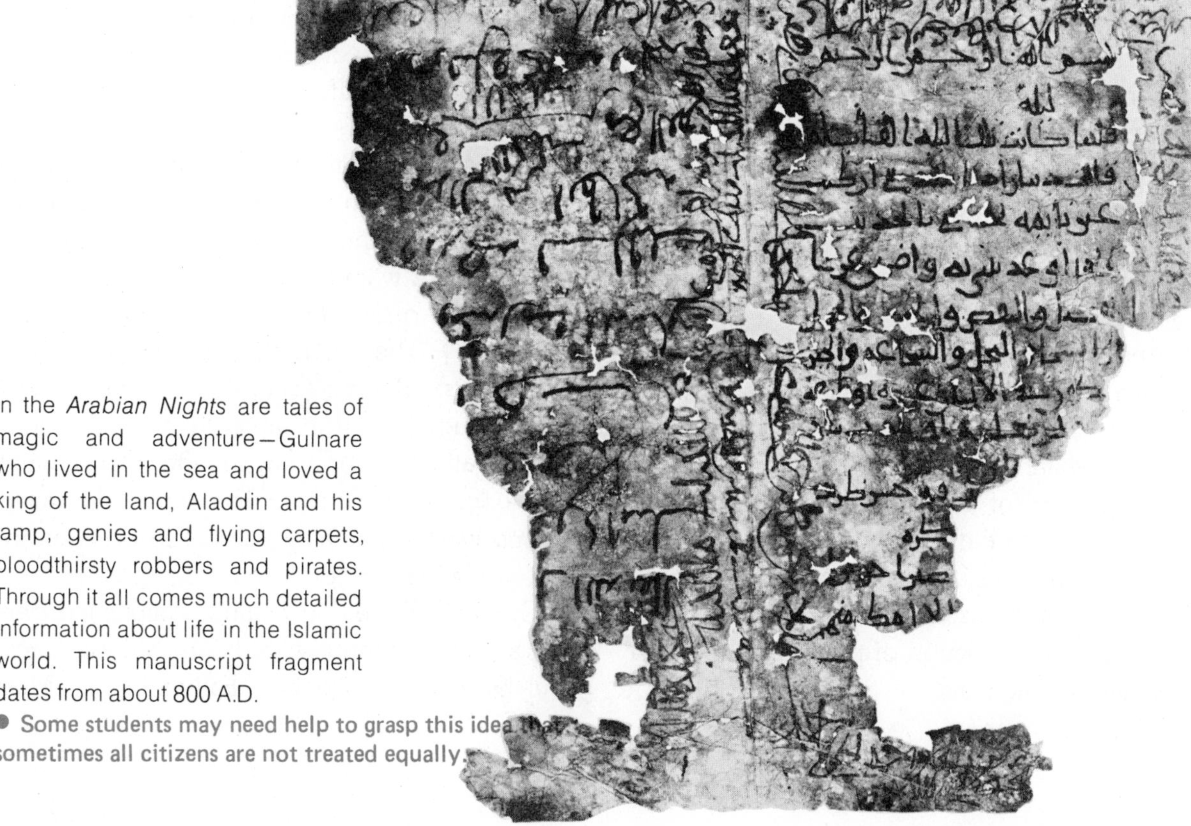

In the *Arabian Nights* are tales of magic and adventure—Gulnare who lived in the sea and loved a king of the land, Aladdin and his lamp, genies and flying carpets, bloodthirsty robbers and pirates. Through it all comes much detailed information about life in the Islamic world. This manuscript fragment dates from about 800 A.D.

● Some students may need help to grasp this idea that sometimes all citizens are not treated equally.

The first Abbassides moved the capital from Damascus to a new city to the east, called Bagdad. Over 100 thousand workers labored for four years on the banks of the Tigris River to build Bagdad. Many trade routes crossed there, and fertile farm land surrounded the new capital. In Bagdad, the Abbasside rulers surrounded themselves with luxury, pomp, ceremony, and a culture with strong Persian influences. Bagdad became a world center of ideas, trade, wealth, and government.

Moving the capital to Bagdad meant less control of North Africa and the Iberian peninsula by the Abbassides. Soon, the Muslim Empire split into several separate regions.

Iberian and North African Muslims broke with the Bagdad caliphate. During the
ans. 2 revolution, the Abbassides had tried to kill all members of the Umayyad family. However, a young prince named Abd al-Rahman [ab′ däl rə män′] escaped by swimming across the Euphrates River. In a journey filled with danger, and pursued by Abbasside spies, he made his way to the Iberian peninsula. Once there, Abd al-Rahman gathered an army from among those who believed him to have a true claim to power. He took over leadership of the Iberian peninsula in 756, and Umayyad rule continued until 1031.

Abd al-Rahman did not claim to be caliph but contented himself with the title *Amir* [ə mir′], meaning leader. Nevertheless, his Muslim state, with its capital at Cordova, refused to recognize the authority of the Abbassides in Bagdad. Thus, it became the first part of the Muslim Empire to break away. Under the rule of Abd al-Rahman and his descendants, the Iberian peninsula enjoyed a period of peace and splendor that rivaled Bagdad's.

The Abbasside government became corrupt. In the luxury of their palaces at Bagdad, Abbasside rulers began to neglect the business of the empire. Court standards of morality lowered, and many rulers cared only about eating, drinking, and being merry. Throughout the empire, taxes rose to support the rich living of the caliph's court. These taxes were not collected fairly. The caliphs did nothing to protect the trade routes from bandits, nor to assure farmers a fair price for their produce.

Another result of the Abbaside life-style was ans. 4
the changing status of women. In the early years of Abbasside rule, many upper-class women had political influence. Some were educated and respected for their poetry, musical talent, and storytelling. Other women rode horses splendidly and even led troops to war. Under the later Abbassides, however, women were secluded in *harems*—rooms of palaces where only women were allowed. This custom never took hold in the villages in the empire. Women were needed to work in the fields and thus villagers could not afford to keep women out of men's sight.

In the early 10th century, small resistance movements began all over the Muslim Empire.
The major resistance was in North Africa. The ans. 3
people there wanted a ruler who was a direct descendant of Mohammad's daughter, Fatima [fə tē′mə]. The Fatimads opposed the Abbasside rulers, whose relationship to Mohammad was through his uncle Abbas. In 908, a member of the Fatimad dynasty was made ruler of what is modern-day Tunisia. The Fatimads called themselves caliphs and claimed to be rulers of the whole Islamic world.

One after the other, Fatimad caliphs led Berber armies in conquests of North African states. By 969, the reigning Fatimad, Al Muiz [äl mü iz′], had succeeded in adding all of Egypt to the Fatimad Empire. Al Muiz founded Cairo and made it the capital of an empire that extended from Morocco to Syria. The Fatimads were never able to overthrow the Abbassides, but neither were the Abbassides able to put down the Fatimad dynasty. Fatimad rule lasted until 1171.

Thus by 969, almost 300 years after its beginning, the Muslim Empire had split into three major sections: one centered in Bagdad, one centered in Cordova, and one in Cairo. All three, however, had similar governmental forms; a single religion, Islam; one written language, Arabic; and one legal system. There were periods of insecurity, but the advancements in culture, trade, and farming that occurred under the Umayyads, Abbassides, and Fatimads were significant.

SECTION REVIEW 3

p. 192 193 **1.** Give two reasons the Umayyads lost power.

p. 194 **2.** Why did the Muslims on the Iberian peninsula break away from the Abbasside Empire?

p. 194 **3.** Why did North Africa become dissatisfied with Abbasside rule?

p. 194 **4.** How did the role of women in Muslim society change during Abbasside rule?

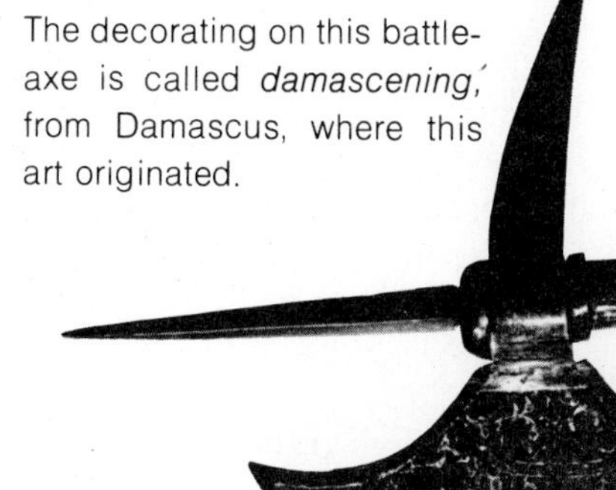

The decorating on this battle-axe is called *damascening,* from Damascus, where this art originated.

4 Turks assumed leadership of the Muslim world

About 1000 A.D., Turkish nomads from central Asia migrated into Abbasside territory in Persia. A great chieftain, Seljuk [sel′jûk], led these warring nomads, who became known as the Seljuk Turks. They became Muslims and before the end of the century dominated the world of Islam from the Mediterranean to China. ans. 1

The Seljuk Turks ruled from Bagdad. In 1055, Bagdad was captured by the Turks. Although the Seljuk Turks could not read or write, they appreciated the high level of Abbasside civilization. Bagdad continued to be the center of Muslim culture in the east for another three centuries. The Seljuk rulers did not depose the Abbasside caliphs, instead they took the title *Sultan.* Although caliphs continued to reign, sultans were the real power in the Muslim Empire.

The Seljuks embraced Islam and Muslim culture whole-heartedly. They built mosques and libraries wherever they went and reconquered large areas.

The second Seljuk sultan, Alp Arslan [äl′ pär slan′], was a brilliant general. He conquered Georgia (on the east coast of the Black Sea), Armenia (south of Georgia), and most of Asia Minor. Alp Arslan defeated the Byzantine emperor at the Battle of Manzikert (Syria) in 1071. It was these Seljuk advances that prompted the First Crusade.

The Seljuks fought the crusaders. Both religious and economic reasons spurred the crusades. Christendom had watched with dismay as the Seljuk army captured Jerusalem from the easygoing Abbassides and swept into the By- ans. 2

● The map on p. 192, shows these divisions.

■ Key Concept: the world of Islam had cultural unity, not political unity.

Daily Life in the Islamic World For the most part, the Islamic world was a man's world. At the age of seven, young boys left the harems, where they had been cared for by women, and went to the mosque school to learn to read and write and behave like gentlemen. Their fathers reviewed their lessons in the evenings. In the picture *opposite,* one boy is reciting for his teacher; another is pulling the ceiling fan. The men in the *top left* picture are enjoying the luxuries of wealth: hours spent in conversation in a well-kept garden, waited on by servants, dancers, and musicians. *Above right:* in a tile-lined bath, servants give a shampoo, bring more water, and distribute towels.

zantine Empire. The Byzantine emperor wrote to the pope and princes of western Christendom for help in regaining his lost provinces and their holy land. But he did not expect the army of crusaders. When they arrived in Constantinople in 1096, he quickly turned them toward the Turks. The First Crusade was the most successful. The Seljuks, split by rivalries and jealousies, were very weak, and the Christians succeeded in establishing the Crusader States in Syria and Palestine. The Muslims recaptured Jerusalem in 1187 and the last of the Crusader States in 1291. (See map on page 160.)

One of the greatest Seljuk leaders was the able soldier, Saladin [säl′ə dən]. Sultan of Egypt and Syria, he ended the Fatimad dynasty and founded his own. In 1187, Saladin attacked the Crusader States. This provoked the Third Crusade, led by three of the most famous medieval knights—Frederick Barbarossa of Germany, Richard the Lion-Hearted of England, and Philip Augustus of France. Frederick was drowned in Asia Minor. And after many quarrels with Richard, Philip returned home leaving Richard to challenge the Turks. Saladin and Richard grew to admire each other's statesmanship. Eventually, a truce was worked out, but it merely gave Christian pilgrims free access to Jerusalem, something Saladin would have granted at any time. By Saladin's death in 1193, the Crusader States were nearly destroyed.

Mongols broke up the eastern Muslim Empire. In the 1200s, the Mongols, under
ans. 3 their famous leader Genghis Khan, swept into the Middle East. In 1258, his successors captured Bagdad, killed the caliph, and ended the Abbasside dynasty. The new invaders did not convert to Islam. The center of the Muslim world shifted to Egypt. There, in 1260, a powerful, professional army, the Mamluks, stopped the westward movement of Mongols.

Ottoman Turks made new conquests for Islam. The Ottoman Turks had once been vassals of the Seljuk Turks. Their fief was in Asia Minor, on the border of the weak Byzantine Empire. Through repeated attacks across the border, the Ottomans grew in wealth and power. Under their leader Osman, who lived from 1259 to 1326, the Ottomans took over from the Seljuks and moved west. They beat the ans. 4
Mamluks in Egypt and put a final stop to Mongol invasion in the Middle East.

The Ottomans also conquered the Muslim lands of Iraq, much of the Arabian peninsula, Egypt, and all of the North African coast. The areas now known as Tunisia and Algeria became bases for Turkish pirates who preyed on ships from Europe. Not since the Umayyads had this entire area been unified under one Muslim leader.

For two centuries, Ottoman power grew. In 1453, the Ottomans finally succeeded in capturing the Byzantine capital of Constantinople, the object of Muslim attacks for 750 years. They changed the city's name to Istanbul and from there pressed on into southeastern Europe.

The Ottoman Empire reached its height during the reign of Suleiman [sü lā män′] the Magnificent (1520–1566). In 1529, Suleiman led the Ottoman armies in an attack on Vienna. But it became difficult to continue to provide food and ammunition for his troops, and Suleiman was forced to withdraw. In 1683, the Ottomans again attacked Vienna. They were defeated by the more powerful weapons and gunpowder of the Viennese. However, the Muslims had sent a chill of fear through all of western Christendom.

● This date marks the end of the eastern, Byzantine, empire, almost 1000 years after the fall of Rome.

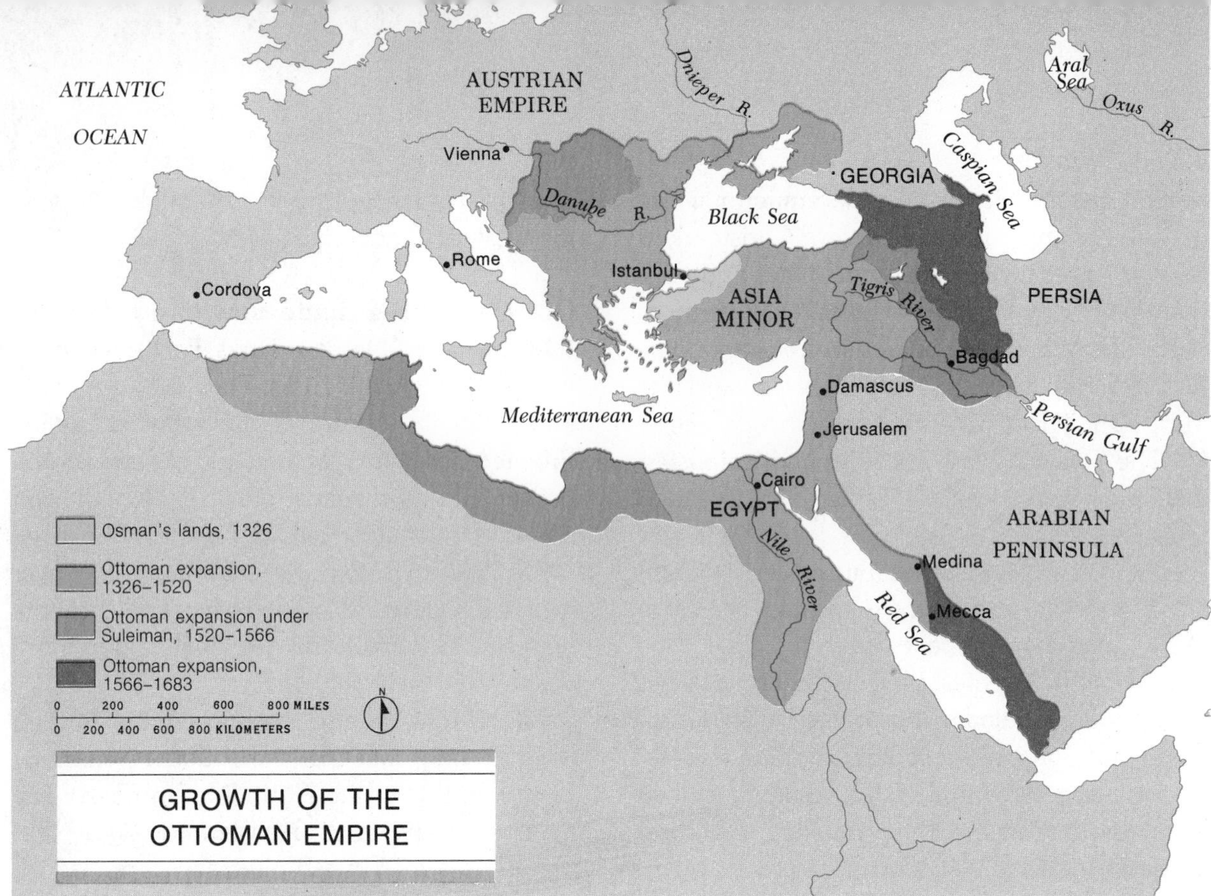

GROWTH OF THE OTTOMAN EMPIRE

ans. 5 **The Ottoman Empire lasted for many centuries.** One of the strengths of the Ottoman Empire was its governmental organization. Every five years, thousands of young non-Muslim boys were chosen from among the conquered peoples of the empire and taken as slaves to Istanbul. The boys were educated, converted to Islam, and trained to become military and governmental leaders. The brightest and most industrious slaves could hope to become advisers to the sultan himself. This elite group, called the Janissary corps, became fanatically devoted to the Ottoman Empire and to Islam. With this efficient slave system, the Ottomans ruled their large empire for a long time.

In the 18th century, European states such as Austria and Russia grew stronger and overran the frontiers of the Ottoman Empire. At the same time, Ottoman provinces such as Egypt claimed independence. In the 19th and 20th centuries, there were attempts to reform the old, tottering empire, but without success. In World War I, the Ottoman Empire lost its many provinces and became the nation of Turkey. Despite weakness in the last years, Ottoman rulers led the Muslim world from the 13th to early 20th centuries.

SECTION REVIEW **4**

1. Where did the Seljuk Turks come from? How did they strengthen Islamic civilization? p. 195

2. What encouraged western Christendom to invade Muslim lands? What did they hope to gain? Were the Christians successful? p. 195 197

3. When and why did the center of the Muslim world move from Bagdad to Egypt? p. 197

4. What areas did the Ottoman Turks conquer? p. 197

5. What was the Janissary corps? How was it recruited? What did it do for the Ottoman Empire? p. 198

CHAPTER REVIEW 10

SECTION SUMMARIES

1. Islam was based on Mohammad's teachings. During the 7th century A.D., an Arab named Mohammad inspired the religion of Islam. In 622, Mohammad's opponents forced him to flee from Mecca to Medina. He became the political and religious leader of Medina, launched a holy war against his enemies, and began a series of conquests that was to become an empire. Mohammad's teachings, recorded in the Koran, spell out the religious duties of a good Muslim. The Koran also includes rules for governing the Islamic world. Mohammad taught that all Muslims are equal.

2. Arab caliphs conquered a huge empire. Mohammad had established a theocracy. The caliphs who came after him continued to rule as heads of both the religion and the empire. Overpopulation of the Arabian peninsula and religious zeal led the Muslims to spread Islam. They first took Damascus in the Byzantine Empire. After the first four caliphs, power moved to the Umayyads. The empire was extended west to take in vast regions of North Africa. Arab armies moved east into the Persian Empire up to the Indus Valley. In 711, Tarik led an army into the Iberian peninsula. Six years later, it was conquered. The Muslim move into western Christendom was halted at Tours by Charles Martel. But a Moorish civilization was established that lasted 700 years. An 8th-century siege of Constantinople failed.

3. The Muslim Empire divided. The peoples of the empire grew dissatisfied with Umayyad rule. In a carefully planned revolution, the Abbassides overthrew the Umayyads. Bagdad became the capital of the empire. In the 8th century, Harun al-Rashid kept peace with Charlemagne's Christian empire. Border disputes marred relations with the Byzantine Empire. Abd al-Rahman took control of the Iberian peninsula, and his descendants ruled for several centuries. In North Africa, the Fatimads took control. By 969, the empire was divided into three parts. One religion, one written language, and one legal system continued to unite the world of Islam.

4. Turks assumed leadership of the Muslim world. In 1055, the Seljuk Turks captured Bagdad and ruled as sultans, allowing Abbasside caliphs to continue in title only. The Seljuks became Muslims and preserved Islamic culture. They reunited much Islamic land under one rule. Seljuk advances brought on the crusades. Saladin, the sultan of Egypt and Syria, ended the Fatimad dynasty. He fought the crusaders and regained most of the lands they won. Then, in 1258, new invaders, the Mongols, took Bagdad and put a final end to the Abbassides. The center of Islam moved to Egypt where it was protected by the Mamluks. Ottoman Turks took over from their former lords, the Seljuks, and stopped the Mongol attacks. The Ottoman Turks built up a huge empire. In 1453, they took Constantinople and changed its name to Istanbul. The Ottoman Empire lasted for many centuries and was finally broken up in the 20th century.

WHO? WHAT? WHEN? WHERE?

1. Give the years in which the following events took place:

Mohammad was born c. 570
the Hijra 622
Muslims landed in the Iberian peninsula 711
Battle of Tours 732
Abbasside takeover 750
Seljuks took Bagdad 1055
Ottomans took Constantinople 1453

2. How did each of these persons influence Muslim history?

Tarik p. 191	Abd al-Rahman p. 194	Saladin p. 197
Harun al-Rashid p. 193	Al Muiz p. 194, 195	Suleiman p. 197

3. Tell how each of these terms applies to Islam:

Allah God	Koran holy book	ulema religious teachers
Muslim a believer	Ramadan holy month	caliph ruler
Hijra pp. 185-187	theocracy 189-90	Kaaba p. 187
Imam prayer leader	mosque church	Sultan p. 195

4. What was the most important accomplishment of each of these?

Umayyads p. 191	Seljuks p. 195	Ottomans p. 197
Abbassides p. 193	Mongols p. 197	Fatimads p. 194

5. What happened at each of these cities during Muslim history? When? In what modern-day country is each city?

Mecca Saudi Arabia	Damascus Syria	Vienna Austria
Medina Saudi Arabia	Cordova Spain	Cairo Egypt

QUESTIONS FOR CRITICAL THINKING

1. Was there any relationship between the life-style of the early Muslims and their ideas of heaven and hell as expressed in the Koran?
2. Why did Mohammad use the Kaaba as a holy place for Muslims after he returned to Mecca?
3. What reasons explain the rapid spread of Islam?
4. Was religion more important to people in the Muslim Empire than it is today? Defend your answer with specific examples.

ACTIVITIES

1. Compare the basic teachings of Christianity and Islam. In what ways are they alike and different?
2. Write a report on the Muslim world today. What is its importance in world political affairs? Its resources? Use news articles for your report.
3. Draw (or trace) a map showing the areas controlled by Muslims from 650 to 1450. Label the areas held by the Umayyads, Abbassides, Seljuks, Mongols, and Ottomans.

QUESTIONS FOR CRITICAL THINKING

1. Heaven is like an oasis and hell like a desert, both basic ingredients in the desert nomads' lives.

CHAPTER TEST 10

SECTION 1

1. The correct name of the religion begun by Mohammad is: a. Mohammadanism, b. Islam, c. Muslim
2. Muslims date their calendar using the ______ as the year one. a. Kaaba, b. mosque, c. Hijra
3. True or false: Once a year, Muslims fast during the feast of Fatima.
4. The holy book of the Muslims is called the: a. Kaaba, b. Allah, c. Koran

SECTION 2

5. True or false: Mohammad passed on his rule to his only son.
6. Islam was spread to other countries by: a. missionaries, b. teachers, c. holy wars
7. Christians and Jews in Muslim territories were: a. made to pay a special tax, b. treated badly, c. forced to leave the country
8. True or false: Tours and Constantinople were important Arab cities.

SECTION 3

9. The Umayyad and Abbasside dynasties were: a. Mongol, b. Arab, c. Turkish
10. True or false: The Abbasside dynasty made many non-Muslims part of the government.
11. The first area to break away from Abbasside control was: a. Tunisia, b. Egypt, c. the Iberian peninsula
12. True or false: When the Abbasside Empire split up, those who broke away were no longer Muslims.

SECTION 4

13. True or false: The Ottomans changed the name of Constantinople to Istanbul.
14. True or false: Before their conquest of Bagdad, the Turks had been Muslims.
15. The empire that lasted until World War I was: a. Ottoman, b. Seljuk, c. Abbasside

2. Accept answers that recognize the tradition of the Kaaba and a desire to convert a population.
3. Possible answers—Holy war; advantages to converts; existing trade routes; need for better land.
4. Answers will vary.

700 – 1400

CHAPTER 11

Islamic Civilization

Muslim achievements in architecture often combined the best elements from the cultures that came under Islamic rule. The Royal Mosque in Isfahan (Persia) had a Byzantine-type dome decorated with mosaic tiles, a large central court that surrounded a pool, and floors of blue tiles.

● There is a story in the *Arabian Nights* about a beautiful slave girl named Towaddud. She had a good master, but he was very poor. As a solution to his problems, she suggested he sell her to the caliph, Harun al-Rashid, for 100 thousand pieces of gold. Her master reluctantly agreed and together they went to the palace. Harun al-Rashid was amused by their suggestion. He asked why they thought she was worth such an enormous price. Towaddud replied that she could prove herself to be as wise and knowledgeable as all the caliph's most intelligent ad-

● Students may be interested in reading some of these stories to get a feeling of eastern culture.

visers. Her boast intrigued him; Harun al-Rashid sent for the most learned scientists, teachers, and scholars of the land.

For days, Towaddud was questioned about everything the learned people knew. They asked her questions about the Koran and about grammar, about poetry, history, mathematics, philosophy, astronomy, geography, law, and medicine. All were amazed to find that she could answer anything they asked. In addition she was talented at playing music and composing poetry. She even defeated the champion chess player of the empire three times.

Impressed by her many talents, the caliph agreed to pay Towaddud's price. Then he asked her if there was any favor she wished, but she only wanted to be restored to her master. So Harun al-Rashid made him an official at the palace, and Towaddud and her master no longer had to live in poverty.

The story of Towaddud's knowledge is obviously an exaggeration. But it was not unusual for slave girls and boys to receive some education when the Muslim Empire was at its height of culture, 900–1100. Those two hundred years are often called the golden age of Muslim learning. Poor children learned to read and write a little by memorizing the Koran. Wealthy persons received an extensive education and often devoted their adult lives to scientific study, writing, observation, and experimentation. Others pursued the arts by writing poetry, playing music, painting, weaving, or designing buildings. Throughout the Muslim world, scholars, scientists, and artists made outstanding contributions in their fields.

Chapter 10 dealt with political developments in the world of Islam from 622 to about 1700. This chapter concentrates on Islamic cultural activities of that time in three sections:

● This point deserves emphasis in helping students to appreciate the accomplishments of Islamic Civilization.

1. Religion and government encouraged prosperity.

2. Vigorous trade spread Islamic culture.

3. Science and the arts flourished.

1 Religion and government encouraged prosperity

Religion and government in the Islamic Empire were inseparable. The caliph was the head of both, and the Koran, the holy book, dealt with both people's religious activities and governmental ways of ruling. Holy pilgrimages brought many different people in contact with each other. Agriculture advanced with the caliphs' support. Industry grew as artisans in the cities made their wares for trade.

Arabs preserved the cultures of the peoples they conquered. Often the Arab armies conquered regions in which the armies and governments were weak. Most of these places were not occupied by poor or primitive peoples; the Arabs conquered much of the finest territory of the Byzantine and Persian empires. The peoples in these lands had their own long traditions of culture. They had beautiful towns with thriving markets. They had poems and ballads, industries and productive farms. The Arabs had ans. 1
much to learn from the peoples they conquered, for the Arab armies were made up of simple ●
nomads who had become warriors. They appreciated the cultures they encountered, and did much to preserve them. The Arabs translated many of the classical works of the Greco-Roman culture into Arabic. Persian and Indian classics

too were translated into Arabic. Huge libraries made these documents available to Muslim scholars.

Whenever a person converted to Islam, he or ● she learned Arabic in order to say prayers and read the Koran. All the laws and official correspondence of the Muslim world were in Arabic even in areas where the language of the majority of the people was Persian or Greek. Although some civilizations have developed without writing, Arabic was definitely important to the development of the high level of learning achieved in the Muslim world.

Islamic civilization was made up of the contributions of a vast variety of peoples of different races, backgrounds, and religions. Muslims, Christians, Jews, Arabs, Persians, Indians, Ber- ■ bers and other Africans—each group brought its special crafts, customs, and ideas to the empire.

The pilgrimage encouraged the exchange of ideas. Each Muslim was supposed to make ● a pilgrimage to Mecca at least once in a lifetime. To a sincere Muslim, this was one of the high points of his or her life. When pilgrims set out from their home towns, large celebrations and feasts provided a proper send-off. The journey took as much as eight years as pilgrims traveled over land and sea, on camels, donkeys, in tiny boats, or on foot. Some travelers never returned home.

A Muslim could not make the pilgrimage to Mecca at any time, but had to be there during the special pilgrimage month. During that month, Mecca was filled with hundreds of thousands of believers from all over the world. All the pilgrims in Mecca were dressed exactly the same, in a seamless white cloth. Thus rich and poor, kings and farmers, men and women could hardly be told apart. All the pilgrims prayed at the same time and performed the same devotions for 10 days.

The pilgrimage, called the Hajj, was so inspiring for Muslims that it frequently caused them to reform their lives. Chiefs and kings were known to retire from ruling after performing the Hajj. Upon return from Mecca, a Muslim was called Hajji [hä′ jē] for the rest of his or her life, a term of great respect.

For centuries people came together during ans. 2
the pilgrimage. They exchanged ideas and learned of the differences and similarities among all peoples. Pilgrims acquired a tolerance for differences and an openness to new ideas, and these attitudes were strengths for the Islamic world. As pilgrims returned to their home communities, they brought new ideas with them. Because people in the community respected a pilgrim for having made a significant religious act, they were willing to listen to the new things the Hajji spoke about.

●● These were extremely important factors in unifying peoples of different cultures under one rule.

■ Key Concept: Islamic civilization was a pluralistic society. Help students see the parallels with society in the United States today.

Arab traders traveled the seas in boats manned by slaves. From a 13th-century manuscript.

The caliphs improved farming methods and crop yields. The centuries of the Umayyad and Abbasside reigns were generally ones of peace within the empire. Islam provided a tie which helped prevent Muslims from fighting each other. The caliphs in Bagdad were usually successful at keeping civil wars and revolts from breaking out within their realm. This peace made it possible for agriculture and trade to expand without disruption.

The caliphs built vast irrigation projects. They extended the canals of ancient Mesopotamia and encouraged such scientific farming methods as crop rotation and the use of fertilizer. The arid regions of the Middle East and North Africa blossomed as never before. Wheat and other grains were grown in the valley of the Nile. Cotton, flax, and sugar cane were cultivated in North Africa. Olives, fruits, and fine wines were produced in Spain.

Stock breeding flourished in Asia Minor, Persia, and Syria. New varieties of sheep furnished raw material for fine woolen cloth. Arabian horses, famous for their speed and endurance, were brought to full development. The camel, the "ship of the desert," became the chief means of land transportation across the Sahara.

Food for the empire was produced on great estates, which were worked by tenant farmers and serfs. Though slavery was common, most slaves were personal or household servants; slaves were not used for plantation labor. Small landholdings were very common; although the peasants seldom became rich, they had more independence than the serfs of Christendom.

Artisans made a variety of products. Muslim industry centered around the great cities of the empire, most of which specialized in the manufacture of certain products. Bagdad

This pitcher of brass inlaid with silver is decorated with astrological signs.

was noted for glassware, jewelry, silks, and luxury goods; Damascus for strong, tempered steel and "damask," or embossed linen; Cordova for leather products; and Toledo for fine steel.

Beautiful, durable, hand-woven carpets, known today as "Oriental" carpets, were made from the wool of sheep raised in Syria and Persia. Papermaking was introduced from China, and some of the secrets of Byzantine metalworking in gold, silver, and bronze were learned by Muslim artisans. Workers in the different crafts formed guilds which protected their rights, supervised the training of new artisans, and controlled most of the production and sale of goods.

Cities enjoyed a high standard of living. ans. 3
The heavily populated and well-planned urban centers of Islamic civilization had fountains, li-

braries, teeming markets, and proper drainage. They were in sharp contrast to the smaller, less healthy wooden villages and crude, cold stone castles surrounded by serfs' and peasants' huts in western Christendom.

Daily life for city people in the Muslim Empire was far better than that in western Christendom. Muslims enjoyed a large variety of fruits and vegetables, the result of extensive agriculture and irrigation projects. In the cities, people learned to eat a variety of differently prepared foods from the many peoples who lived in the empire. Fashions in clothing, such as baggy trousers, and new games, such as polo, chess, and backgammon, became popular. New conveniences like ovens, frying pans, and porcelain dishes made the work of servants in a Muslim household less dreary.

The common people as well as the aristocracy had some leisure, which was often spent in listening to lute players or in reciting poetry. Public taverns and restaurants for men, and special hours at the public baths for women, were opportunities for social gathering. While Bagdad boasted thousands of public baths, in Christendom it was common for people to go a whole year without bathing.

SECTION REVIEW 1

p. 202 **1.** How did the conquering Arabs react to the more advanced cultures they met?

p. 203 **2.** How did the pilgrimage to Mecca help to unify the Muslim Empire?

p. 204 205 **3.** Compare life in Muslim cities about 1000 A.D. with life in feudal Christendom. Consider the variety of products available, the comforts of warmth and ● cleanliness, the freedom of religious beliefs, the level of education. What people in Christendom knew how to read? In the world of Islam?

● Students should refer to Ch. 8, if necessary, for information about Christendom.

2 Vigorous trade spread Islamic culture

Islam had begun in Mecca, the major trade center of Arabia. Mohammad and his wife had been ans. 1
part of the caravan trade. Mohammad had traveled with the camel trains to trade in distant towns. Thus Muslims considered trading to be an honorable profession. Commerce was a bigger business than either industry or agriculture.

Many factors helped trade. Within the empire there were no trade barriers, such as taxes or import duties, between regions. Business terms such as *bazaar, tariff, traffic, check,* and *caravan* have come into English from Arabic. Gold and silver coins were used in trade. Moneychangers and moneylenders were in every market.

A complex banking system grew in the Islamic world three centuries before it did in Christendom. Central banks were formed with branches in distant cities of the empire. The Muslims used a variety of business and banking practices, such ans. 2
as the use of receipts, checks, and letters of credit. This meant that a merchant who placed money in the care of a banker in Bagdad could draw on that money from the banker's relative or employee when he arrived in Damascus, or Tunis, far from his home bank.

The Muslims also formed trade associations and developed joint-stock companies. These associations made it possible for several persons to pool their money and finance large trading expeditions. An expedition might take five or ten years to send goods to markets in a distant country and return with the profits. No single member of the association would have been able to afford such a large, long-term expense alone.

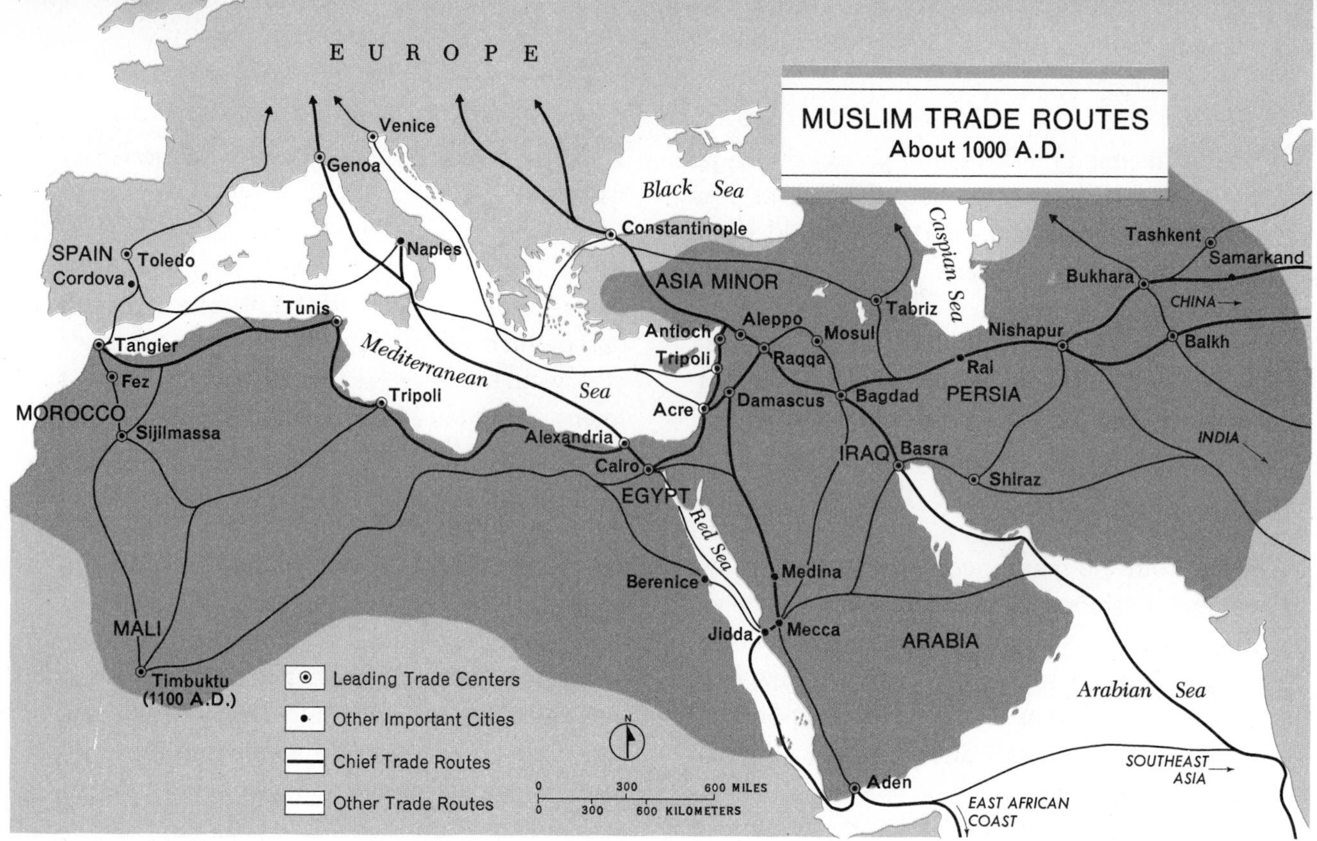

Muslim trade spread culture to foreign lands. Trade flourished beyond the borders of the empire to China, India, Europe, Russia, and Central Africa. Daring explorers opened up new overland routes to East Asia. Sea voyages to India and China by way of the Persian Gulf, the Red Sea, and the Indian Ocean were undertaken by Muslim traders centuries before Western navigators discovered the Atlantic route to the East. New inventions—the compass and the astrolabe—helped sailors find their way.

Along with their goods, Muslim merchants carried their religion. And Islam spread to East and West Africa, India, parts of China, and Indonesia. Peaceful and energetic Muslim traders made converts in lands where the battles and swords of Islam had long ago failed.

The traders also acquired and passed on much new knowledge. Muslim traders learned about the numerals *1* through *9* from the Hindus in India and devised the important zero, later teaching these to the Europeans. These so-called "Arabic numerals" became the basis for all modern mathematics. From China, Muslim traders carried the secrets of making paper throughout the empire.

This map of Muslim trade routes will be helpful to the students in working on Activity 2.

Ibn Batuta traveled widely. Perhaps no single person saw as much of the Muslim world as did Ibn Batuta [ib′ ən ba tü′ tä]. He was a living example of the cultural unity of Islamic civilization. Ibn Batuta was born in Morocco, North Africa. In 1325, when he was 21, he set out for the pilgrimage to Mecca. He was already highly educated and trained to be a judge in Islamic law; but by the time he reached Egypt, Ibn Batuta knew he wanted to learn more about the peoples and places of the world. He decided to

The Arab Marketplace
Slaves were just another product in the Islamic markets. *Opposite* a Muslim gentleman chooses among black and white slaves. The dealer, on the platform above, is a careful businessman. He weighs another customer's money to be sure he is getting full value from the gold pieces. *Below* is another trade item: a donkey bag made of carpeting. Nomads hung such bags over their animals' backs, the pockets filled with food, clothing, and sometimes children. Today, such items are prized as art objects.

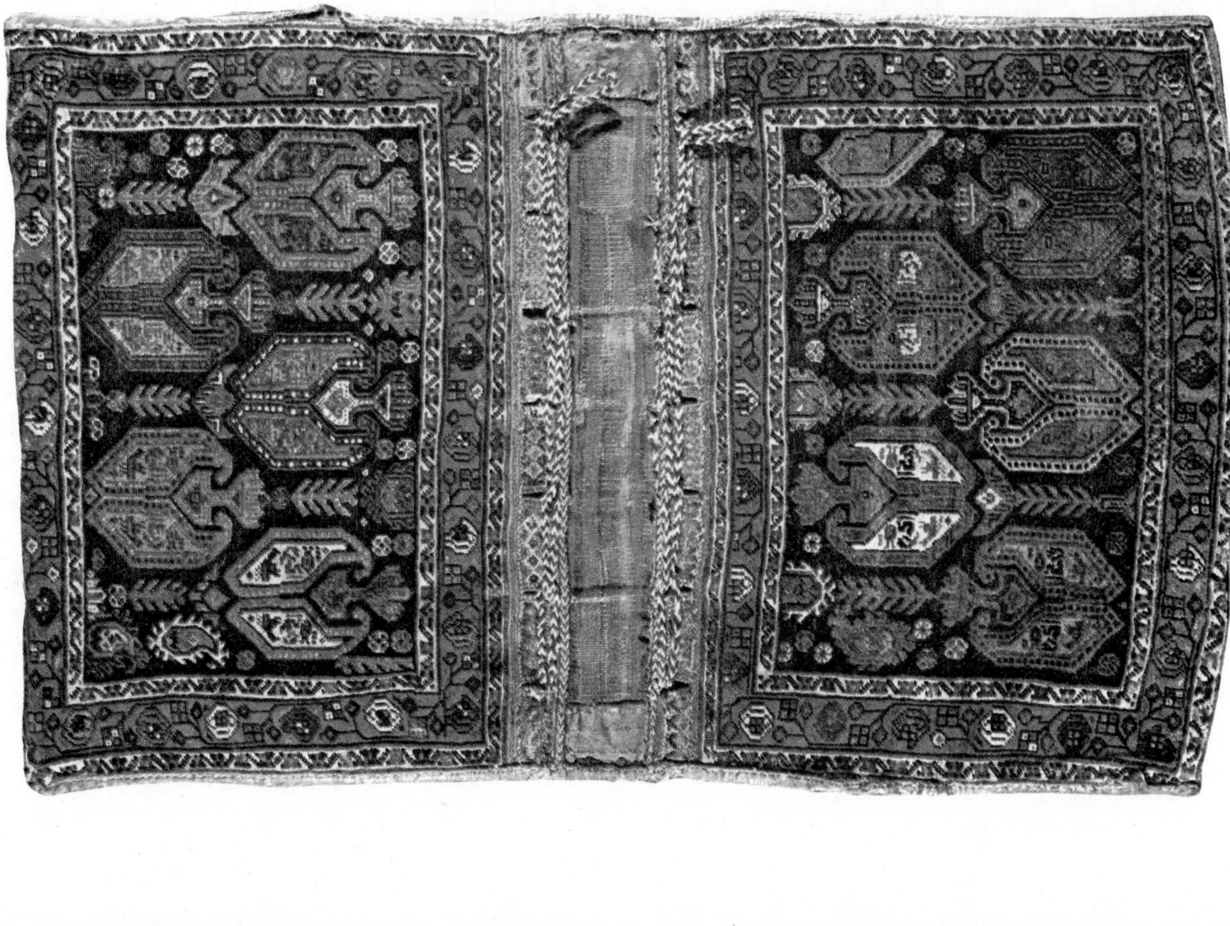

travel and set himself the rule "never to travel any road a second time." By the end of his life, Ibn Batuta is said to have traveled more than 75,000 miles.

Ibn Batuta journeyed through Arabia, Syria, Persia, Iraq, and Asia Minor. He went from Samarkand to India. In India he worked two years as a judge in the employ of a Muslim sultan. Then, in 1342, the sultan sent Ibn Batuta on an official mission to China. Travel was dangerous in those days, and it took Ibn Batuta several years to reach China. Robbery and shipwreck accompanied his trip. Pirates attacked his ship in the Indian Ocean, and all his notes and diaries were lost. His mission was finally successful. From China he returned by sea to Bagdad and then home to Morocco.

But Ibn Batuta was still not content, for he wished to visit every Muslim country. So he set off for Spain. From Spain he journeyed south, across the Sahara to West Africa and visited the thriving Muslim African state of Mali in 1352. His account of Mali, describing everything from the advanced scholarship of the capital, Timbuktu, to the curious hippopotamuses in the Niger River, is one of the most valuable and unique sources for the history of Africa at that time. After traveling in Africa, Ibn Batuta returned to Morocco to live out the rest of his life and write his great book *Travels*.

ans. 3 Ibn Batuta was able to travel so far because the Islamic world at that time was large and peaceful. He was able to stop and work as a judge wherever he went because Islamic law was in use in most of the places he visited. He was always received with respect and was considered a most learned and religious man. As he traveled, he learned from others and spread his own knowledge. Ibn Batuta was an ambassador of Islamic culture.

SECTION REVIEW **2**

1. Why did Muslims consider trade an honorable profession? Did trade strengthen their culture? p. 205

2. Name three business practices that helped trade. Explain how they worked. p. 205

3. Why was Ibn Batuta able to travel so far and to find work wherever he went? In what ways was he an "ambassador of Islamic culture"? p. 208

3 Science and the arts flourished

The Arabs before the time of Mohammad had little knowledge of the physical and natural sciences. However, their desire for trade and their increased traveling promoted a need for more understanding of mathematics and astronomy. The Umayyad and Abbasside rulers were tolerant of new ideas. Early Abbasside caliphs encouraged and paid for the systematic translation of books. The science and philosophy of the Greeks were eagerly studied and the works of Aristotle, Euclid, Ptolemy, Archimedes, and Galen were translated into Arabic. The people of Europe rediscovered these classics in Muslim Spain and, during the Crusades, in Syria and Palestine. But, in addition to preserving Greek knowledge, Muslims contributed much original information and theory of their own. In medicine, mathematics, astronomy, chemistry, and physics, Muslim achievements were particularly noteworthy.

Muslim works on medicine were the most advanced of the time. Islamic medicine is perhaps the best known of the Muslim achievements, partly because it was only a century ago that Western schools of medicine stopped including Islamic medical practices and books as part of their requirements.

ans. 1 Well-equipped hospitals, usually associated with medical schools, were located in principal cities throughout the Muslim Empire. At a time when superstition still hampered the practice of medicine in Christendom, Muslim physicians were basing their practices on careful observation of the patient, the symptoms, and the effect of treatment. They diagnosed diseases, prescribed cures, and performed surgery. Pharmacies were common and druggists had to pass an examination in order to practice. Doctors also had to be licensed and they were trained in medical schools and hospitals.

Caliphs were willing to pay for medical services to poor rural areas. They also supported the examinations and license system that made medicine and health care so highly developed in the Muslim world. The first hospital in Bagdad was established by Harun al-Rashid.

Probably the greatest of all Muslim physicians was the 9th-century figure, al-Razi, known in the West as Rhazes [rā′ zēz]. He was the author of many scientific works, including a

Mountain goat, from a book that described its curative powers: goat's bile for fear, dung for baldness and burns, fat for bee and scorpion stings.

A Persian portrait of a physician studying. Christian doctors learned of Muslim medical practices when they cared for the wounded in the Crusades.

An illustration of the constellation of Perseus, from a 10th-century book on astronomy

comprehensive medical encyclopedia and a pioneering handbook on smallpox and measles. Other Muslim doctors developed an early method of vaccinating against smallpox. It was first observed by Europeans in the early 18th century in Istanbul and was used in Europe and America until a better method was developed in England in the early 19th century. A 10th-century physician, Avicenna [av′ə-sen′ə], wrote a huge *Canon of Medicine,* which was considered the standard guide in Muslim and European medical circles until the late 17th century. The portraits of Rhazes and Avicenna are in the great hall of the School of Medicine of the University of Paris today.

Muslim physicists founded the science of optics, the study of sight. Al-Hazen [al hä′zen] who lived from 965 to 1039, challenged the Greek view that the eye sends rays to the object it sees. Al-Hazen said that one sees because the object sends rays of light to the eye.

Related to the field of medicine was that of ans. 2
alchemy [al′kə mē], an Arabic word that means "the art of mixing metals." Alchemy was an ancient study that went back to early Egypt and early China. Its followers melted and mixed different metals to make stronger or more beautiful objects.

Muslim alchemists searched for a way to change less valuable metals into more precious ones such as gold. Although they were never successful, in trying, they developed ways of analyzing materials that became the basis of modern chemistry. Such carefully controlled methods as distillation and crystallization, which include melting, boiling, evaporating, and filtering, were invented by Muslim alchemists. Through their experiments, they also discovered new substances such as alum, borax, nitric and sulfuric acids, carbonate of soda, cream of tartar, antimony, and arsenic.

Astronomy and mathematics advanced.
Pilgrims, traders, and sailors needed good ways ans. 3
of finding directions. Arab travelers provided geographers and map makers with a wealth of information. Muslim scholars made atlases of the heavens and the earth. The great poet Omar Khayyám [ō′mär kī yäm′] worked out a calendar so accurate that it contained an error of only one day in 3770 years compared to an error of one day in 3330 years in the Gregorian calendar, now used in the Western world.

Calculations for determining the position of the planets, distances across land, and complex calendars, as well as the advanced Muslim banking system, gave rise to the need for better mathematics. Although the Arabs learned about numerals from the Hindus in India, scholars credit the development of the indispensable zero to Muslim mathematicians. Important advances were made in algebra, analytical geometry, and plane and spherical trigonometry.

The "Father of Arithmetic" was a Muslim by the name of al-Khwarizmi [al′kwə riz′mē] who lived in the mid-9th century in Bagdad. He wrote a large number of books on mathematics and invented algebra, which comes from an Arabic word. In addition to scholarly books, al-Khwarizmi wrote a simplified book on calculation for people to use in everyday trade, in determining inheritances, and in surveying lands.

The caliphs encouraged scholars. Throughout history, scholars, philosophers, and poets have found it difficult to earn a living from their work. Today, such people often teach to earn money and write or paint in their spare time. In the past this was also true, but often rulers or wealthy upper- and middle-class people who enjoyed music, books, and works of art supported scholars and artists. These people who gave approval and support are called *patrons*.

The early Umayyad caliphs were patrons of the arts and scholarship. They encouraged
ans. 4 people to write down the early nomadic poetry that up to that time had been passed on orally. In 830, the Abbasside caliph al-Mamun
ans. 4 [al′mä mün′] established a House of Wisdom in Bagdad for the translation of the Greek classics. Here also was a library, a museum, and an academy where scholars taught students. Al-Khwarizmi lived and worked at the House of Wisdom. Avicenna was often in the employ of various lesser rulers and governors. But the palaces of the Muslim rulers were best known for their support of poetry, literature, and art.

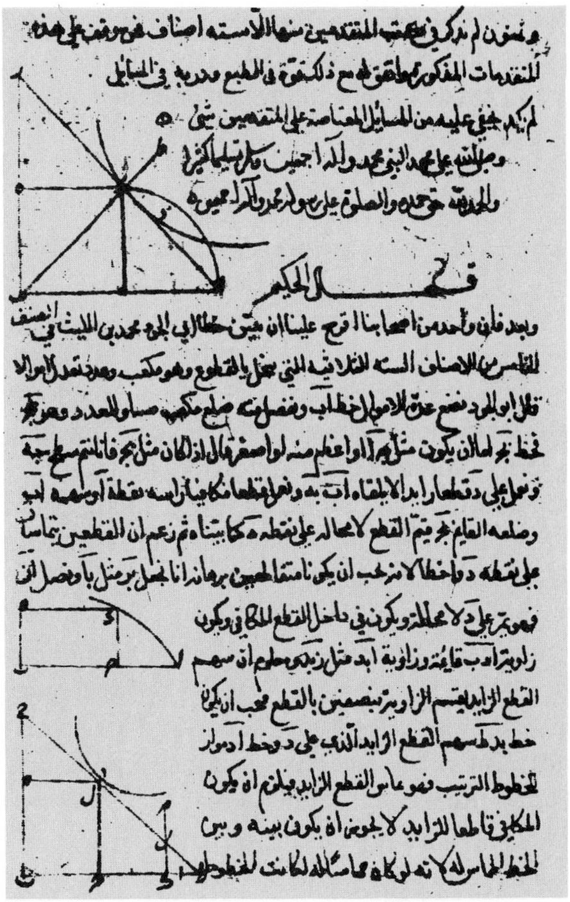

From Omar Khayyam's *Algebra*, showing his method of solving cubic equations using conic sections

Poetry was highly esteemed among Muslims. The Arab poets of the nomadic desert tribes had held positions of respect. They had been entertainers, historians, and mental record-keepers of political and judicial events. As a result they often had great political influence.

During the early Muslim Empire, poets began to write down poems. These works often reflected social situations and problems. A famous young poet, who was the wife of an early Umayyad caliph, expressed what many of the Arabs must have felt after they left their life in the desert to settle and govern in Damascus:

A tent with rustling breezes cool
Delights me more than palace high,
And more the cloak of simple wool
Than robes in which I learned to sigh.

Poetry was not just for the rich. Muslims enjoyed hearing poetry recited much as Americans enjoy listening to songs on the radio or watching a movie, for the verses told a story and were often accompanied by music. People who could compose good poems and recite them well were famous and popular in the Muslim world.

By the time of the Abbasside caliphs, Arabic poetry and literature were strongly influenced by Persian sources. The *Arabian Nights,* written in Arabic, includes many Persian and Indian stories. One of the most famous Persian poets was Omar Khayyám, who wrote the *Rubaiyat* [rü bī ät′] in the 12th century. Khayyám's poems, and those of many Muslims, were often full of the romance and leisure that surrounded the caliphs' courts, as these popular lines from the *Rubaiyat* show:

A Book of Verses underneath the Bough,
A Jug of Wine, a Loaf of Bread—and Thou
  Beside me singing in the Wilderness—
Oh, Wilderness were Paradise enow!

A Muslim in the time of the Abbassides would have declared that poetry and literature were the most important Islamic contributions and the marks of true civilization.

Philosophy was a common theme in Islamic books. Muslims, with their interest in religious matters, considered it necessary for every scholar to know philosophy. The Muslim thinkers, including the physician Avicenna, valued the works of the ancient Greek philosophers, such as Plato, and compared what the Greeks said with the teachings of Islam.

A century before Saint Thomas Aquinas tried to reconcile the teachings of Aristotle with those of Christianity, the most distinguished Muslim philosopher, Averroes [ə ver′ō ēz′], tried to bring together the principles of Aristotle and the faith of Islam. Averroes lived in Cordova, in Muslim Spain, in the 12th century. He was the personal doctor of the caliph there. Averroes is another example of the Muslim belief that every great scientist or scholar is also a philosopher. His books on Aristotle's works were read in Christendom long before the original Greek texts were available.

Muslims also wrote excellent histories and biographies. Ibn Khaldun [ib′ən kal dün′] of Tunis, applied philosophical ideas to history. He produced a lengthy history of the Arab states, emphasizing Spain and North Africa. In this work he showed history as an evolutionary process in which societies and institutions change continually. Historical development depends on a number of things, according to Ibn Khaldun, including geography, climate, economics, and personalities, as well as moral and spiritual forces. Such ideas do not seem so new today, but in Ibn Khaldun's time they had never been stated before. Because of his attempt to see history in this broad, evolutionary way, Ibn Khaldun is often said to be the first modern historian and the founder of social science.

Muslim cities had beautiful buildings. The Arabs had originally lived in tents in the desert. As they conquered lands, they built mosques wherever they went. In the Byzantine

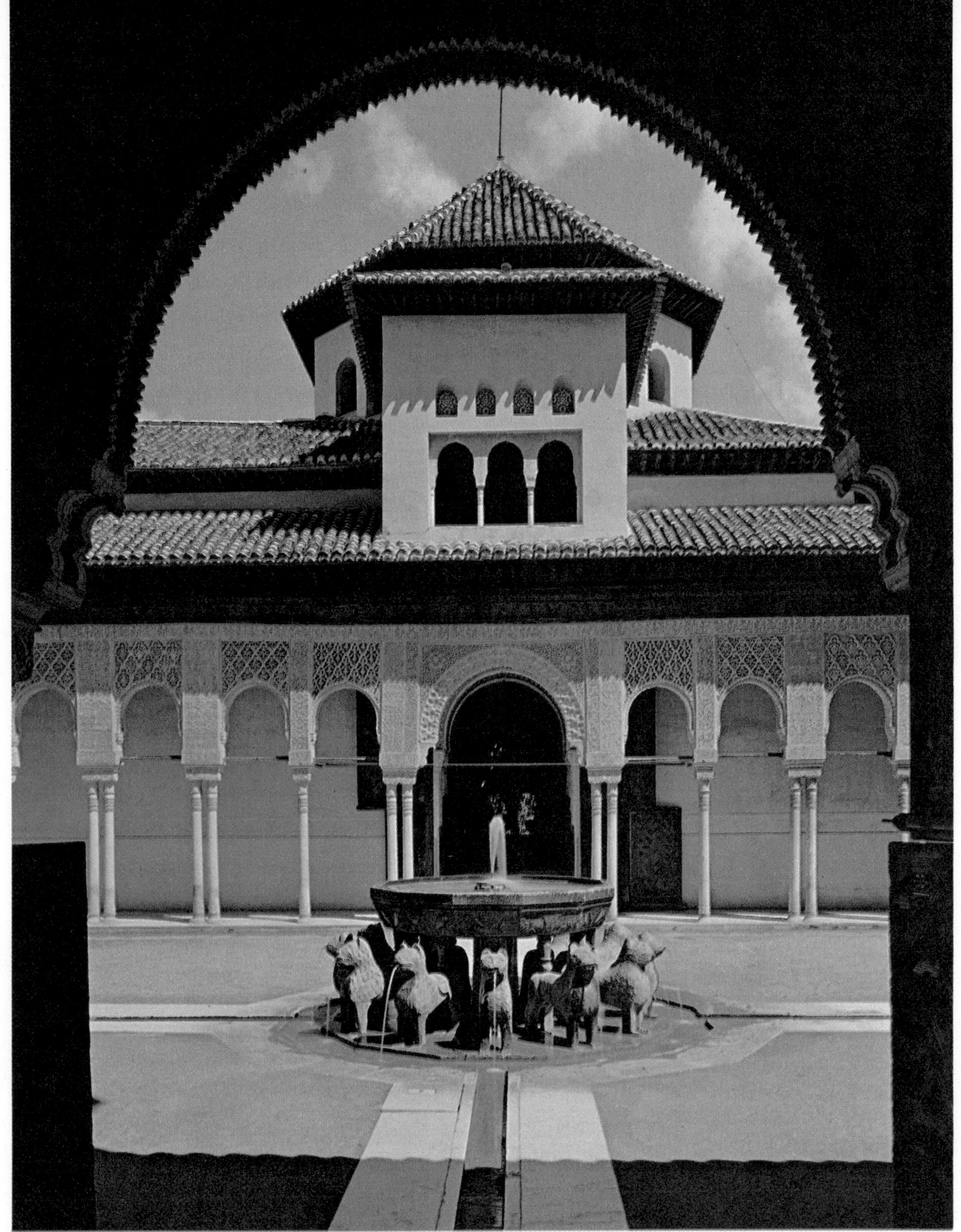

Graceful columns and arches frame this courtyard, called the Court of the Lions, in the center of the Alhambra palace in Granada, Spain. Sultans ruled southern Spain from this palace until 1492.

territories they often built on the sites of old Christian churches. In time a distinctive Muslim
ans. 5 style developed. This style used domes that had been used in Byzantine churches and added minarets [min′ə rets′]—slender towers from which the faithful were called to prayer. The arcade and the horseshoe arch are other graceful features of Muslim architecture.

Soon the caliphs and wealthy Muslim citizens began to build beautiful palaces and homes for themselves. Great care was taken to make whole cities attractive and convenient for everyone. Damascus, for example, had a city water supply that is still in use today. Bagdad, constructed from builders' plans, led the Muslim world in beauty, wealth, and services.

ans. 6 Second only to Bagdad was Cordova, the capital of Muslim Spain. By the 11th century, Cordova had paved streets with public lights, hot and cold running water in some homes, 80,000 shops and perhaps as many as 3,000 mosques. It had 113,000 homes, many suburbs, and a population of more than a million people. There were libraries, schools, and a university. A bridge with 15 arches spanned the river that ran through town. The royal palace, with quarters for thousands of slaves and guards, was surrounded by gardens with rare fruit trees, fountains, shade trees, and flowers. Other gardens were located throughout the city.

A typical middle-class home in Cordova was located on a narrow clean street. Its wooden doors and windows were usually shut to keep out street noise. Inside, a long archway led into a sunlit central courtyard. The mosaiclike tile floor was easy to keep washed. In the center, beside some lemon trees or some flower plants, was a large clay pot filled with cool water and a cup for the thirsty to drink from. All the rooms of the house opened onto the courtyard.

In the far corner of the first floor was the kitchen. Bread was baked in brick ovens and meat was cooked over charcoal fires. Another cooler room was used for storing fruits, vegetables, milk, and yogurt. Colorful plates and dishes were arranged on the shelves. On the second story, sleeping rooms opened onto a balcony overlooking the courtyard. Each one had feather mattresses laid on the floor and numerous pillows, linen sheets, and carefully embroidered wool blankets.

Muslims enjoyed luxurious furnishings and elaborate designs. The decorative handicrafts of rug weaving, pottery making, jeweled metal work, and tiled mosaics showed exquisite workmanship. These products adorned the interiors of Muslim buildings. Because the followers of Islam believed that the representation of human and animal figures was a form of idol worship, Muslim artists concentrated on intricate geometric and floral designs in their architecture and crafts. Arabic script was used a great deal as decoration in art and on household objects too.

SECTION REVIEW **3**

1. Give four or five examples showing how Muslim p. 209
medical practice was advanced.

2. What was the goal of alchemy? What new p. 210
methods and discoveries were made by alchemists?

3. Name four activities that led the Muslims to de- p. 210
velop a better system of mathematics. What were 211
some Muslim advances and what did they learn from others?

4. Give an example of how Muslim government p. 211
encouraged knowledge and culture.

5. What feature of Byzantine architecture was used p. 214
by the Muslims? What are three Muslim contributions to architecture?

6. In what ways was Cordova like a modern city? p. 214
What made a middle-class home comfortable?

CHAPTER REVIEW 11

SECTION SUMMARIES

1. Religion and government encouraged prosperity. The large empire which the Arabs conquered in the 7th century soon became the foundation of a remarkable civilization and a surge of prosperity which lasted several centuries. The religion of Islam, the central government provided by caliphs, and the Arabic language gave a unity to the many varied peoples of the Muslim Empire. The Hajj helped spread ideas throughout the empire. Improvements in agricultural methods provided abundant harvests, and trade brought variety to the dinner tables in Muslim cities.

2. Vigorous trade spread Islamic culture. Trade was an honorable profession in the Muslim world and many factors encouraged its growth. No taxes hindered its activity; coins and banking practices eased the way; joint stock companies made large, lengthy trade ventures possible. Islamic religion and culture went wherever Muslim traders went.

3. Science and the arts flourished. Muslim scholars of Damascus and Bagdad were very interested in science. They preserved and studied the ancient Greeks' works and added their own ideas and observations. Al-Razi, al-Khwarizmi, Avicenna, and al-Hazen made names for themselves in medicine and mathematics. The study of geography, philosophy, and history interested Muslim scholars too. Caliphs and wealthy governors were patrons of poets, scholars, and artists.

The cities of Bagdad, Damascus, and Cordova were unequaled in wealth and splendor. Middle-class people enjoyed many comforts.

WHO? WHAT? WHEN? WHERE?

1. What contributions did these people make to Muslim culture?

Ibn Batuta p. 206. 208	al-Hazen p. 210
al-Razi p. 209, 210	al-Mamun p. 211
Avicenna p. 210	Harun al-Rashid p. 209
Omar Khayyám p. 210, 212	Averroes p. 212
al-Khwarizmi p. 211	Ibn Khaldun p. 212

2. How was Muslim culture enriched by knowledge learned from:

The Byzantine Empire p. 214	China p. 206
Persia p. 212	India p. 206

3. Give specific examples of how civilization has benefited from Arabic contributions in:

chemistry p. 210	literature p. 212
mathematics p. 210, 211	language p. 205
astronomy p. 210	business p. 205

4. a. Give the meanings of these words: *bazaar, tariff, traffic, caravan;* b. What are *polo, chess,* and *backgammon?* c. What is the importance of the Arabic terms *Hajj* and *Hajji?* ●

QUESTIONS FOR CRITICAL THINKING

1. Why are math and science important to civilization? What is the importance of poetry and literature? Explain why you agree or disagree with the Muslim view that poetry and literature are the marks of a true civilization.

2. How did the life-styles of the Arab people change after they became Muslims? How much of this change was due to Mohammad? Explain whether or not they would have advanced as far if he had not been born.

3. Describe the ties that unified the Muslim peoples. Is the United States today a unified country? What are some factors that separate Americans today? What brings them together? What could be done to make the United States a more unified country?

● 4. a. Have students use dictionaries; b. Possible class activities; c. p. 203.

QUESTIONS FOR CRITICAL THINKING
1. Suggest students think of the uses and importance of these fields in their own lives.
2. Answers will vary. (p. 202)
3. Some factors are religion, language, government. Opinions will vary. Good for class discussion.

CHAPTER TEST 11

ACTIVITIES

● **1.** On a map draw the route of Ibn Batuta's travels. Label the cities he visited.

2. With a group of students, form a joint stock company to finance a caravan from one city in the Muslim Empire to a distant city. Where will your caravan go? Draw a map showing the route. How many miles does the route cover? Will someone from the company go with the caravan? Why? Will the caravan bring back goods? What ones? Make out the bill of lading you receive when the caravan reaches its destination.

3. Based on information in the chapter, draw a typical middle-class house in Cordova. Make a floor plan for the house. Find, or design yourself, a geometric pattern for decorating the courtyard floor.

4. Describe the goods and activities that would be found in a bazaar in Bagdad about 1000 A.D. Where would the products have come from? What might the people at the bazaar be doing?

■ 

● If possible, give students blank outline maps of the Middle East and Asia drawn on the same scale.

■ The tile design on this page is a modern design based on Islamic motifs. Use it to motivate students' own designs.

SECTION 1

1. True or false: The Arab armies brought civilization and culture to the areas they conquered.

2. Muslim civilization was unified by trade, religion, and: a. nationality, b. language, c. race.

3. The official language of the world of Islam was: a. Muslim, b. Arabic, c. Persian.

4. After a pilgrim made the trip to Mecca, he or she was called Hajji.

SECTION 2

5. Because Mohammad had been one, many Muslims became: a. teachers, b. farmers, c. traders.

6. Which of the following inventions did not guide traders' journeys: a. arcade, b. astrolabe, c. sextant?

7. The system of numbers we use today originated with the: a. Arabs, b. Persians, c. Hindus.

8. True or false: Ibn Batuta was shipwrecked on his way to China.

9. Ibn Batuta's account of 12th-century ________ is an important historical record. a. Mali, b. Morocco, c. Bagdad.

SECTION 3

10. Muslim scholars preserved the classic works of the ancient: a. Christians, b. Greeks, c. Arabs.

11. Muslim medicine was based on: a. superstition, b. observation, c. alchemy.

12. Artists and scholars of the Muslim Empire were supported by: a. the caliphs, b. their own work, c. their relatives.

13. Name the modern nation in which each Muslim city is located: You might suggest using an atlas.

Cordova	Spain	Mecca	Saudi Arabia
Damascus	Syria	Toledo	Spain
Bagdad	Iraq	Samarkand	Morocco
Tunis	Tunisia	Timbuktu	Mali

UNIT REVIEW 3 — TEST YOURSELF

● **1.** Write a sentence for each of the following places. Tell its importance in history.

Rome	Red Sea
Constantinople	Persian Gulf
Crusader States	Mecca
Italian city-states	Iberian peninsula
Baltic Sea	Pyrenees Mountains
Black Sea	Indus Valley

2. Place these events in chronological order:

15 Muslims captured Constantinople.	"Fall" of Rome 4
5 Mohammad's birth	The First Crusade 10
7 *Beowulf*	Vladimir chose Christianity. 9
1 Jesus' crucifixion	Hijra 6
8 Charlemagne's coronation	Black Death 14
3 *City of God*	Alexander Nevsky's rule 12
13 Ibn Batuta's birth	University of Bologna founded. 11
2 Roman Empire split	

3. Match the letter of the correct answer with the description: a. feudal Christendom, b. Byzantine Empire, c. Russia, d. Muslim Empire

d The Umayyads, Abbassides, and Fatimads were important dynasties.
c Olga was the first female ruler.
b Justinian had Hagia Sophia built.
c Conquest of the area by Mongols held back its progress by 150 to 200 years.
b The capital was captured by Muslims in 1453.
b The population was mostly Greek, and Greek was the national language, but there were many Slavs, Jews, Syrians, and others.
a Gothic architecture developed.
d Trade was an honored profession, and no taxes hindered its growth; coins, banks, and joint-stock companies helped its spread.
c Vikings ruled the Slavs.
a Stewards, bailiffs, and reeves helped run manors.
d Ibn Batuta was a famous traveler.

● 1. Answers will vary but must be geographically correct.

4. Fill in the following statements with the letter representing the person described: a. Saint Patrick, b. Theodora, c. Genghis Khan, d. Roger Bacon, e. Jesus, f. Odoacer, g. Yaroslav, h. Mohammad

The New Testament tells how ___e___ reappeared to his disciples following the crucifixion.

In 476, ___f___ deposed the last Roman emperor and became the first Germanic ruler of Rome.

___a___ journeyed to Ireland to convert the Celtic peoples to Christianity and began many monasteries.

Although he was imprisoned for his teachings, it was ___d___ who predicted power-driven cars, ships, and flying machines.

Refusing to escape during the Nika Revolt, ___b___ said, "I approve a certain ancient saying that royalty makes a good burial-shroud."

During the rule of ___g___, Kiev became the religious and cultural center of Russia.

Led by ___c___, Mongol horsemen overran north China, central Asia, Persia, and southern Russia.

___h___ became convinced that he was the appointed prophet of the one true God.

UNIT 4

THE WORLDS OF AFRICA AND THE AMERICAS

Throughout the centuries that cultures and civilizations were rising and falling in the Mediterranean and Asian worlds, people were creating important civilizations and empires in the worlds of Africa and the Americas. People in these civilizations also lived and died, fought wars and planted crops, struggled to be successful, and built great buildings. For the most part, the rest of the world knew nothing about these peoples.

From the 9th century on, Muslim traders and travelers came in contact with African empires such as Mali, Songhai, and the East African city-states. In the 15th century, Portuguese traders made contact with the African coasts. Arab and Portuguese records have shed light on civilizations whose own records have not yet been deciphered by scholars.

In the Americas too, documentary evidence is scanty or undeciphered for the centuries before the Spanish conquerors came. But ruined buildings and the sites of cities give archaeologists much evidence with which to piece together the story of the great Maya, Aztec, and Inca civilizations.

In places where people did not build with materials that last as long as stone, where people did not write, and where people were not met by other people who did, historians have difficulty discovering the past. Even where records exist, they more often tell what rulers did than what the common people did. It is our lack of knowledge that makes the worlds of Africa and the Ameri-

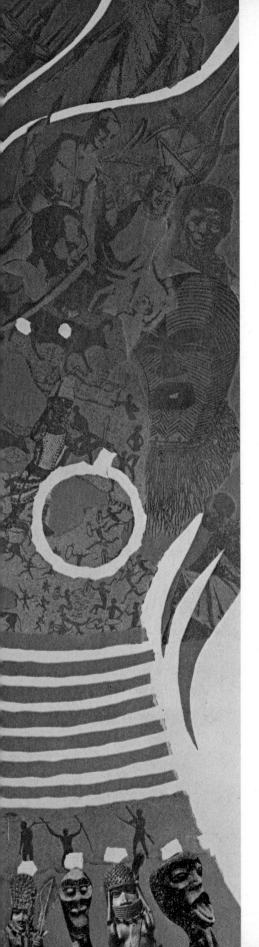

Wearing ceremonial headdresses, a native American and an African face each other.

cas seem remote, not a lack of vitality on the part of the people who lived in these cultures. To know something about the history of all these peoples is to widen our understanding of the human experience.

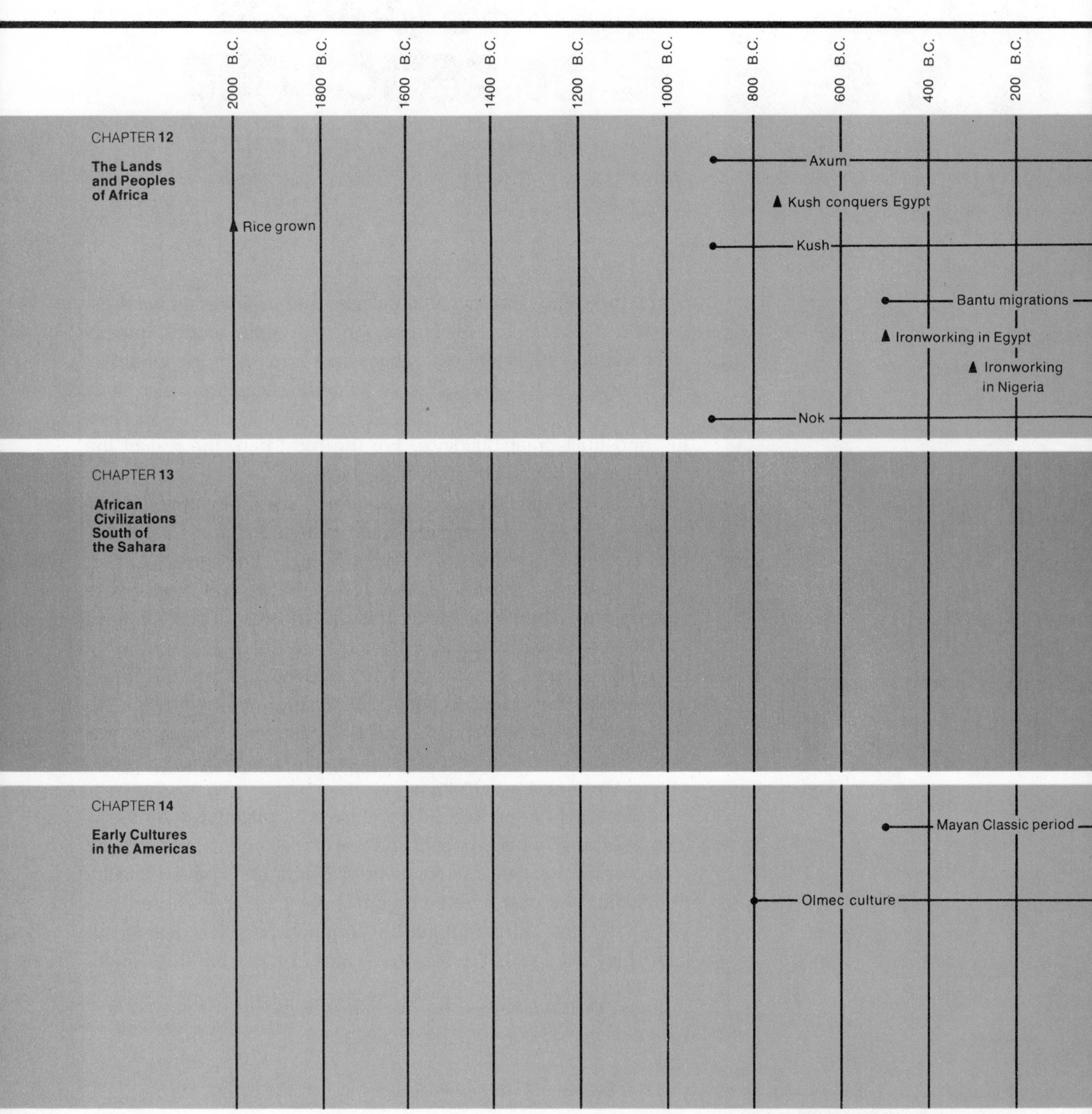

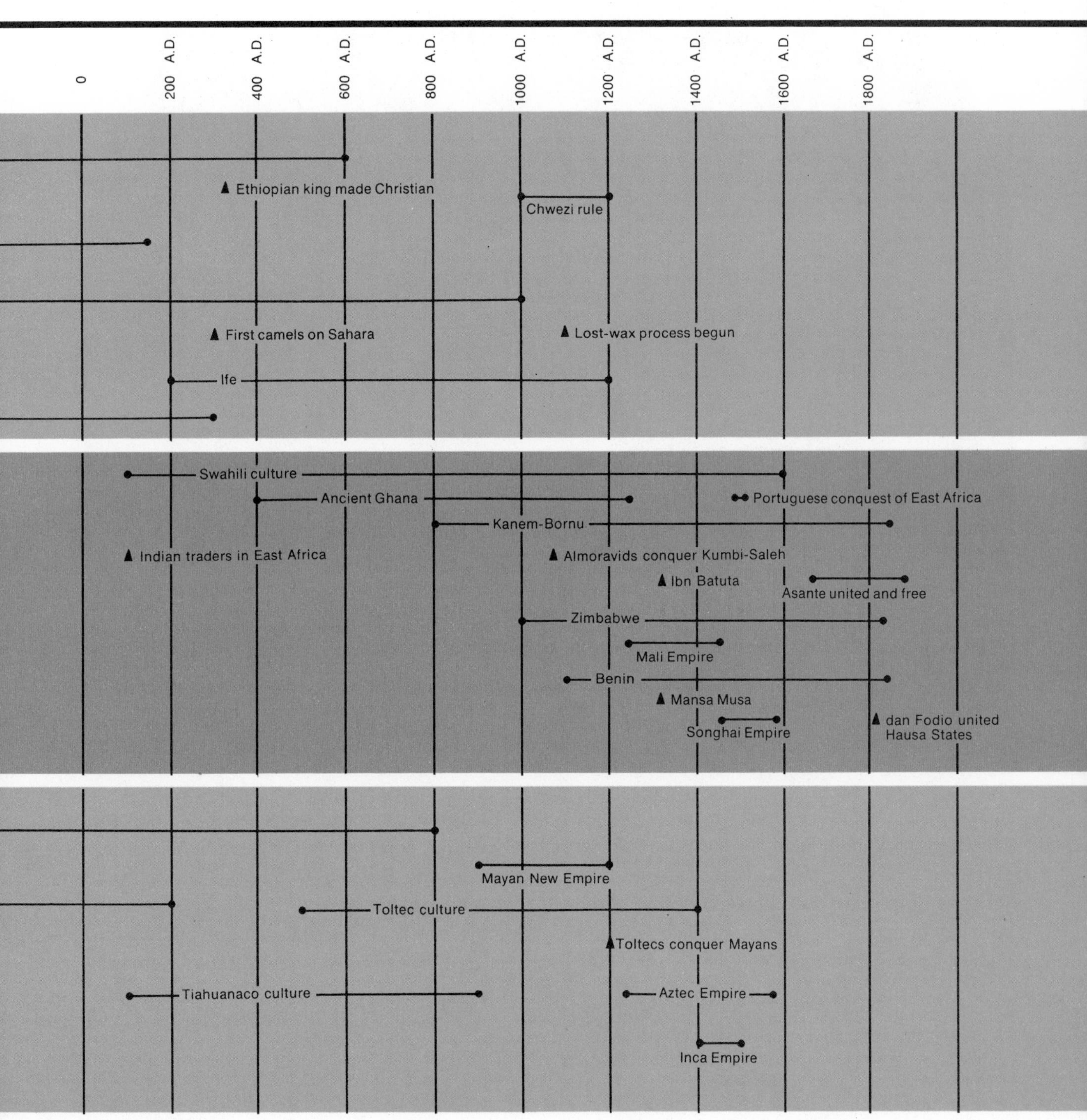
0
200 A.D.
400 A.D.
600 A.D.
800 A.D.
1000 A.D.
1200 A.D.
1400 A.D.
1600 A.D.
1800 A.D.
Ethiopian king made Christian
Chwezi rule
First camels on Sahara
Lost-wax process begun
Ife
Swahili culture
Ancient Ghana
Portuguese conquest of East Africa
Kanem-Bornu
Indian traders in East Africa
Almoravids conquer Kumbi-Saleh
Ibn Batuta
Asante united and free
Zimbabwe
Mali Empire
Benin
Mansa Musa
Songhai Empire
dan Fodio united Hausa States
Mayan New Empire
Toltec culture
Toltecs conquer Mayans
Tiahuanaco culture
Aztec Empire
Inca Empire

CHAPTER
12

2000 B.C.–
1400 A.D.

The Lands and Peoples of Africa

From the 11th to the 16th centuries, the kingdom of Benin flourished in West Africa, in what is today southern Nigeria. Much of Benin history was recorded on bronze plaques, like this one showing a king and his attendants.

● In the 18th century, a small group of people called the Kulango lived in the *savanna*, or grasslands, of West Africa. They had few possessions other than their houses, clothing, and cooking utensils. Life was a struggle because they did not always have enough rain for their crops. But in the forest to the south of them was a wealthy country called Asante [ə sän′tē]. Some of the Kulango wanted to move there. The land was better, and rainfall was plentiful in Asante, they said. And the Kulango could benefit from the wealth in the capital city of Kumasi.

● This anecdote might help students to more fully understand the difficulties in attempting to change people's way of life. Some students may be able to identify with the Kulango and their problems. See Activity number 4 in QUESTIONS FOR CRITICAL THINKING before assigning this chapter.

Some Kulango families went to Kumasi to beg the king, Opoku Ware, to give them a place to live. Pleased that the Kulango had heard of his wealth and power and wanted to settle in his kingdom, Opoku Ware gave them good land in his forest.

For several years, the Kulango lived in the Asante forest. They made farms and built houses. But try as they would, they could not adjust to life in the forest. It was simply too different from their savanna home. True, Asante was a wealthy kingdom with much trade and plenty of food. But the Kulango could not grow the same crops in the forest as they had grown in the savanna. They had to eat foods they were not used to and get along without donkeys and horses to carry their goods to market. Some of the Kulango people even died because they were not used to the food and climate.

Naturally, the Asante people, who had lived in the forest all their lives, liked the food and knew how to grow forest crops. They were very healthy. The Asante thought that the Kulango had very strange habits and tastes.

Finally, the Kulango went back to King Opoku Ware and explained to him that they could not adjust to forest living. He listened sympathetically and suggested that they move to a different part of Asante where there were grassy plains. This they did. They made new houses and farms like those they had had in the savanna, and they settled down once again to the way of life they knew.

In Africa, there are many different climates and land formations. Each of the many regions has its own unique forms of plant and animal life. Over the centuries, the many different peoples of Africa have learned to adapt their ways of living to the climate, crops, and animal life available in their own regions. Some of these ways of living have developed so differently from others that the people of one region cannot adjust to living in a different region.

In ancient Africa (from about 2000 B.C. to about 1000 A.D.), the people learned basic skills that helped them live in their sometimes harsh environment. These skills included ironworking, farming, animal breeding, house construction, and political organization. The skills provided firm foundations upon which African societies grew. This chapter explains that:

1. Much of Africa is desert and savanna.

2. Other features of geography made Africa a land of variety.

3. The peoples of ancient Africa developed many practical skills.

4. Ancient Africans made advances in their societies and cultures.

1 Much of Africa is desert and savanna

Africa is the second largest continent in the world. It has four major ecological regions: coast, desert, savanna, and rain forest. At the very north and south of Africa are two narrow regions of fertile coast. A relatively short distance inland, these areas give way to deserts—the huge Sahara in the north and the Kalahari in the south. Where the deserts end, the savanna begins. Near the deserts, the savanna's bushes and grasses are short. Nearer the equator, the grasslands of the savanna give way to a lush rain forest.

ans. 1

● This chapter deals with the basic geographic and cultural development of ancient Africans. Chapter 13 contains a historical treatment of the peoples south of the Sahara and the effects of contact with Europeans and Muslims.

■ Key Concept: Africa is more than jungle and desert.

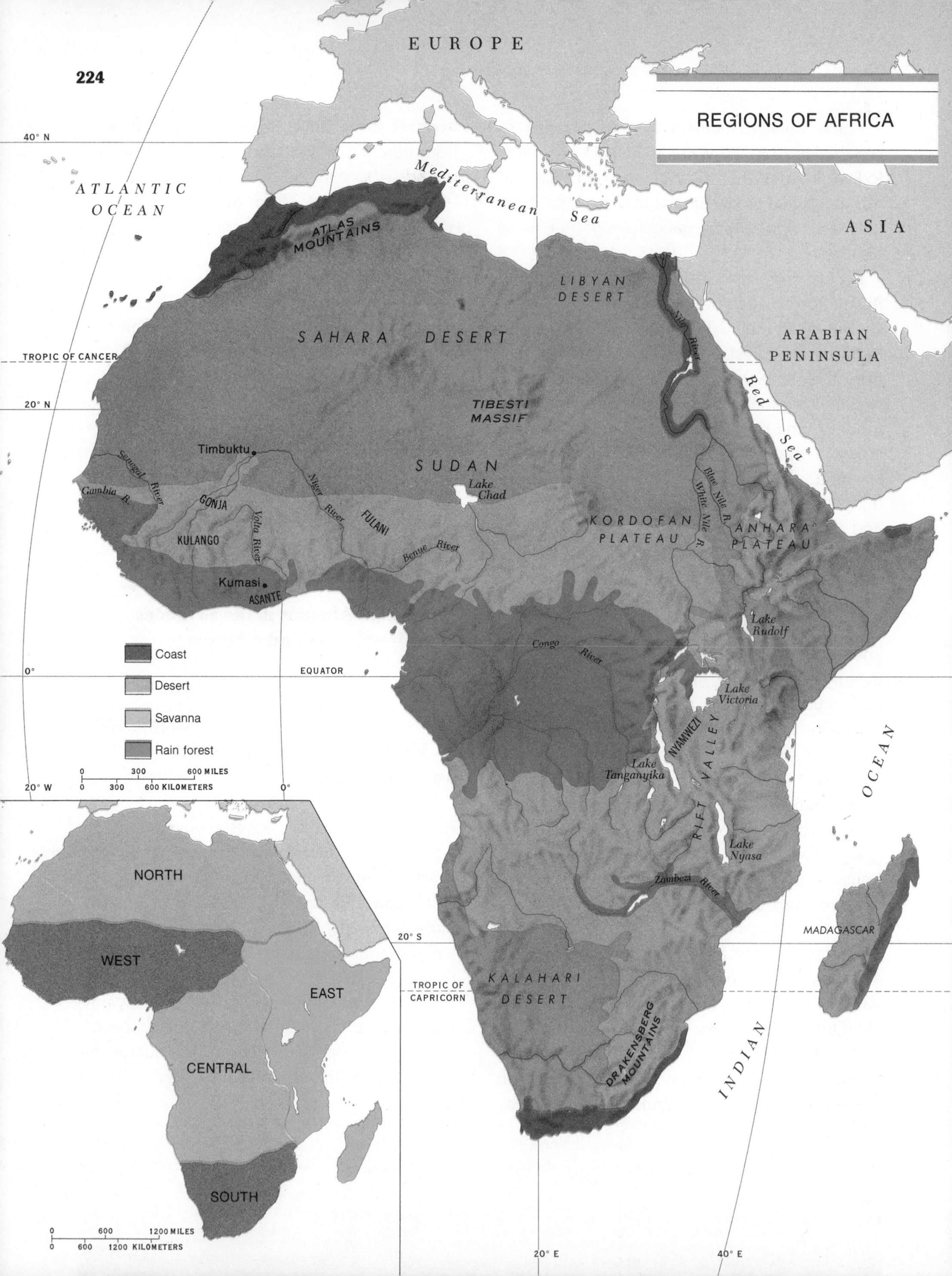
REGIONS OF AFRICA
EUROPE
ASIA
ATLANTIC OCEAN
Mediterranean Sea
ATLAS MOUNTAINS
LIBYAN DESERT
SAHARA DESERT
ARABIAN PENINSULA
Red Sea
Nile River
TIBESTI MASSIF
Timbuktu
Senegal River
Gambia R.
GONJA
Niger River
SUDAN
Lake Chad
FULANI
KULANGO
Volta River
Benue River
Kumasi
ASANTE
KORDOFAN PLATEAU
Blue Nile R.
White Nile R.
AMHARA PLATEAU
Lake Rudolf
Congo River
Lake Victoria
NYAMWEZI
RIFT VALLEY
Lake Tanganyika
Lake Nyasa
Zambezi River
MADAGASCAR
KALAHARI DESERT
DRAKENSBERG MOUNTAINS
INDIAN OCEAN
40° N
TROPIC OF CANCER
20° N
0°
EQUATOR
20° W
20° S
TROPIC OF CAPRICORN
20° E
40° E
Coast
Desert
Savanna
Rain forest
0 300 600 MILES
0 300 600 KILOMETERS
NORTH
WEST
EAST
CENTRAL
SOUTH
0 600 1200 MILES
0 600 1200 KILOMETERS

The Sahara was not always the vast wasteland that it is today. The Sahara (which means "desert" in Arabic) is nearly as large in area as the United States. It covers about a fourth of the African continent and is the world's largest desert. Many areas of the Sahara are barren of plants, uninhabited, and unexplored. Spectacular sand dunes dominate the western and eastern thirds of the desert. However, much of the Sahara is hard dirt and rocky sand that supports patches of scrubby plants. These areas are lightly populated. Small groups of people live as nomadic herders, moving each week from one place to another in search of fresh grazing lands.

The Sahara was not always this way. Until about 2000 B.C., regular rainfall made it possible for plants, animals, and people to live there easily. Paintings in caves and on rocky sides of mountains show what life must have been like between 6000 and 1500 B.C. In these Mesolithic paintings, horses pull carts. Hunters give chase to giraffes, elephants, and hippopotamuses. People gather wild grain. And musicians play for women who wear elaborate hair styles and long robes and capes.

What happened to the nameless people whose artists decorated the Sahara caves? Scientists believe that about 2000 B.C., the Sahara became dry. Over the years, rainfall gradually stopped, and the people died or moved to more fertile areas. Some moved to the Nile Valley, some to North Africa, and some south to the savanna.

Travel across the deserts was dangerous. Although most of the Sahara was no longer habitable, travel across it never stopped. It has always been a link between the Mediterranean world and the parts of Africa that are to the south. Through the ages, travelers followed trails across the Sahara, carrying goods, moving armies, and exchanging ideas. Many oases [ō ā′sēz′] helped keep the trails open. An *oasis* is a place in the desert where an underground spring comes close to the surface. People kept the oases habitable by digging wells and irrigating nearby land. Traders and travelers stopped at oases to rest and water their animals.

Just as the Sahara was sometimes called an ocean of sand, so the camel was called the "ship of the desert." Beginning about 300 A.D., people used camels to cross the Sahara. Camels were much better suited to the hot, dry climate than were donkeys or horses. They could travel fully loaded in the desert for four days without

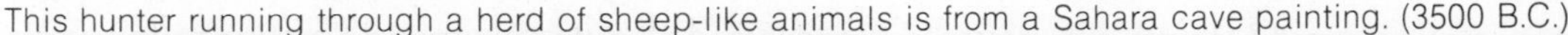

This hunter running through a herd of sheep-like animals is from a Sahara cave painting. (3500 B.C.)

water. Traders, soldiers, travelers, statesmen, desert nomads—all used camels.

To guard against becoming lost and as protection against bandits, people crossed the Sahara in large groups, called *caravans.* Long lines of camels, sometimes as many as 10,000, carried the heavy goods, including leather bags of water. Caravans journeyed from Morocco or Tunisia in the north to large trading cities along the Niger [nī′jər] River, such as Timbuktu. The journey usually took two months. A skilled guide always led the caravan. He knew his way across the desert by following the stars and by watching for landmarks such as large rocks. No one dared leave the caravan, for to do so would probably mean death.

ans. 3 Despite the dangers and hardships, caravans made great profits by guiding passengers across the desert and by selling the caravan's goods. Salt, copper, and cloth brought good prices in the cities on the Niger River. And such valuable items from the savanna and forests as gold, ivory, and hides were prized by merchants.

The life of the people in the Kalahari Desert was quite different from that in the Sahara. They lived as hunters, often traveling great distances when stalking game. They also gathered roots, leaves, and seeds for food. They had no permanent homes and no draft animals like the camel. Entire hunting groups would camp wherever they had killed an animal; when the food supply ● was gone, they would move on. To survive in their hostile environment, they had to become highly skilled hunters and gatherers.

Large populations have flourished in the savanna. South of the Sahara the savanna starts at the Atlantic coast and extends across the continent to the Indian Ocean. In the east, the grassland pushes south to the tip of southern

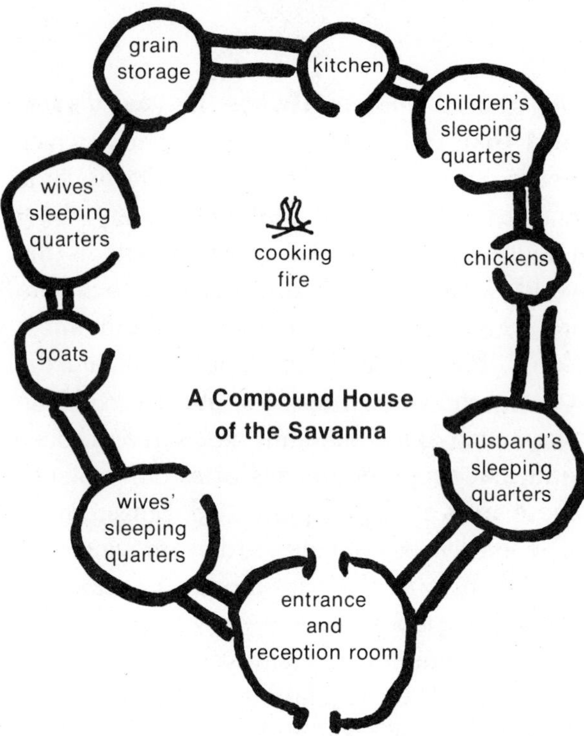

A Compound House of the Savanna

Africa and thus covers almost half the continent. In the savanna, a dry season alternates with a rainy season. Prairie grass and scrub trees grow.

The savanna has supported large populations. For the past 2,000 years, farming villages and some large cities and towns have been scattered all over the savanna. Livestock were kept, and many crops such as millet and rice were grown. Most Africans lived in the savanna, and many African states were located there.

Few trees grew in the savanna. Savanna peoples used all available wood for supporting roofs and for making fires, tools, and weapons. The walls of buildings were made of a strong plaster of mud and straw. Sometimes, the mud and straw mixture was baked into bricks.

People built one-room houses and topped them with thatched straw roofs. Several of these one-room houses formed a circle, and a wall or fence around the houses gave protection and privacy. The many little buildings thus connected formed a bigger living area called a *com-*

● Students may not realize the degree of skills necessary for survival by 'primitive' peoples. Ask what equipment modern campers use, contrast with few tools used by early hunters and gatherers.

pound. A courtyard in the center provided an area for cooking and visiting. The straw roofs and thick mud walls of the houses kept out the sun, and the inside was as cool as modern air-conditioning might have made it. Houses are still being built in the savanna in the same way as they have been for the past 2,000 years.

Domesticated animals were important in the savanna. In ancient Africa, some people in the savanna were nomadic herders who raised cattle, sheep, and goats. These herders moved their homes whenever their livestock needed new places to graze and drink. The
ans. 4 herders' cattle and sheep provided much-needed meat for the farmers of the savanna. The farmers in turn sold grains to the herders for making bread and porridge.

The donkey was an important domesticated animal in the grasslands. While camels were vital for crossing the desert, they were not well suited to the savanna, for their soft hooves rotted in the wetter climate. Therefore, when a caravan reached the southern edge of the Sahara, the camels were unloaded, and donkeys were used for the trip across the grasslands.

The savanna was also the breeding ground of fine horses. Some of the savanna states had large cavalries. The powerful armies of these states controlled large areas inhabited by farming peoples, who had no way to defend themselves against the mounted soldiers.

SECTION REVIEW 1

p. 223 **1.** Name the four major ecological regions of Africa. In what parts of Africa are these regions found?

p. 225 **2.** What evidence is there that more people once lived in the Sahara? When and why did the region become a desert?

3. What items were carried by the caravans that crossed the Sahara? p. 226

4. How did herders and farmers help each other? p. 227

2 Other features of geography made Africa a land of variety

Some people believe Africa to be covered with "jungles." In fact, however, the rain forests
cover only about 20 percent of the African con- ans. 1
tinent. Yet the forests have played a significant role in African history. Rivers, too, have presented opportunities and challenges to the peoples of Africa. And long, long ago, earthquakes left fertile land for the people of the Rift Valley to develop. The people of Africa acquired special skills to use these natural features.

The heavy rains influenced life in the forests. The rain forests begin along the southern coast of West Africa and push east and south into the savanna. Rainfall is heavy in all seasons; sometimes more than 7 feet (2.1 meters) of rain fall in a year. The rain and constant warmth make the forests places of thick green vegetation and towering trees. But the forests are not impassable jungles. The tall trees block out the sun's rays, and only a few shade-loving plants grow on the wet floor of the forest. "Jungles" of dense, entangling underbrush appear only where the trees have been cleared by nature or by people. There the sun's rays hit the ground, and many, many low plants grow.

The peoples who developed civilizations in ●
the forest had to acquire special skills to overcome the difficulties of living there. They built villages and cultivated small farm plots. Some

● Key Concept: Living in the rain forests has required a high degree of skill.

crops could be grown in the forests that would not grow in the drier savanna. Plantain (a very nutritious type of banana) and yam (a kind of sweet potato) are good examples. Many kinds of fruit also grew in the forests.

The tsetse [tset′sē] fly affected life in the forest. This insect carries a disease known as African sleeping sickness. It kills cattle, horses, and sometimes people. The tsetse fly probably has been present in the African forests for thousands of years. It thrives in the trees and shrubs of the rain forest.

ans. 2 The tsetse fly also affected transportation in the forests. Donkeys could not be used because they fell victims to African sleeping sickness. Horses could not survive either the disease or the forest climate. Therefore, in forest regions, goods were carried by people. Africans found that the easiest way to carry a large bundle of heavy goods was by balancing it on their heads. In this way, the entire body, not just the arms or shoulders, supported the weight of the load. Wealthy traders or important chiefs of the forest regions often traveled with many porters who had large boxes or baskets balanced on their heads. This was also the only way that farm produce got to markets in the African forest.

The forest affected communication and warfare. Because the use of donkeys and horses was impossible, the African forest kingdoms had to rely on foot soldiers in times of war. The soldiers fought hand-to-hand combat among trees and across rivers. They were disciplined and ready to act in case of a sudden change in the battle. They had to rely on their wits since messages reached them slowly.

Drums were sometimes used to send messages in the forest. These drums had strings on their sides which, if pressed in and out, changed the tension of the drumhead and made the sound of the drum higher or lower. The drums did not actually make the sound of a word, but worked more as a bugle does in modern armies. Everyone knew that certain patterns of sounds meant certain things, such as to advance, retreat, or prepare for the arrival of the king.

Great states developed among the isolated forest peoples. In the forest, large roads quickly became overgrown with vegetation. This meant that many small groups of people in the forest were isolated from each other. Villages were seldom visited by travelers, traders, or even tribute collectors.

However, large kingdoms were able to repair roads and make large clearings in the forest for their towns. The forest provided wood for strong houses, furniture, and tools. And the regular rainfall yielded good crops. As a result, for hundreds of years, many Africans have lived in the forest. Powerful kingdoms such as Asante and Benin [bə nēn′] developed.

Four rivers have been important to Africa's economic history. Four great rivers, the Niger, the Nile, the Zambezi [zam bē′- ans. 3
zē], and the Congo, flow through the savanna and forest regions. Towns, farms, and markets dot the river valleys. Farmers settled near rivers because the yearly flooding renewed the fertility of the soil. Fishermen used the rivers to earn a living; traders used them for traveling.

Canoes were used for transportation on the rivers, and large barges carried loads of goods, animals, and people for long distances, especially on the Nile and the Niger. Flat-bottomed boats holding up to 100 tons of goods transported items for hundreds of miles along the Niger River. In other parts of Africa, rivers do

Who Was the Queen of Sheba?

A story in the Bible (I Kings 10: 1–13) tells of the visit of the beautiful Queen of Sheba to King Solomon of Israel.

The Queen wanted to see if Solomon was as wise and rich as people said he was. She found that he was more wise and wealthy than all the rumors had claimed, so she stayed and visited with him for several months. Solomon, the Bible says, enjoyed her company. When she was ready to return to her own country, he gave her many gifts and granted all her requests.

But where was the country of the Queen of Sheba? No one is certain. Some scholars say it was in the southern Arabian peninsula. But the people of Ethiopia in Africa believe it was their country and that the Queen of Sheba was their queen.

Ethiopian documents dating from the 4th century A.D. tell the story of Solomon and the Queen almost as the Bible does. But they add something. They say that the Queen's name was Makeda [mə kā′də], and that while she was in Jerusalem, Solomon fell in love with her. He asked her to marry him, but Makeda refused. Solomon then agreed not to marry her unless he could find her guilty of taking something from his palace. Makeda consented to this arrangement, confident she would never take anything from Solomon.

But Solomon was very clever. That same night he served Makeda a very spicy, salty dinner. During the night she became so thirsty that she got up and took a drink of water. Solomon was watching. He leaped up and claimed his right to marry her immediately because she had taken water that was his. When Makeda later returned to her own country, she gave birth to a son of Solomon.

This son, the Ethiopians claim, was their first king, called Menelik I [me′nə lik]. When he grew up, he is said to have ruled justly and to have introduced the laws of Judaism into Ethiopia. All the kings of Ethiopia, even into the 20th century, have claimed direct descent from Solomon and the Queen of Sheba, Makeda.

In about 330 A.D., the king of ancient Ethiopia converted to Christianity. After that, the story of Solomon and the Queen of Sheba became even more popular with the Ethiopian Christians. They believed the story provided an important link between themselves and the Jewish people and Jesus.

Could the details of the story be true? Could the Queen of Sheba have come from Ethiopia? There was a very powerful kingdom in Ethiopia from about 500 B.C. to 600 A.D. It was called Axum. Axum conquered many states, including Kush, traded with India, made its own gold coins, and had its own written language. An early queen of Axum could have traveled to visit the famous King Solomon in 900 B.C. Whether she did or not, historians may never know, but Ethiopians have been convinced of it for centuries.

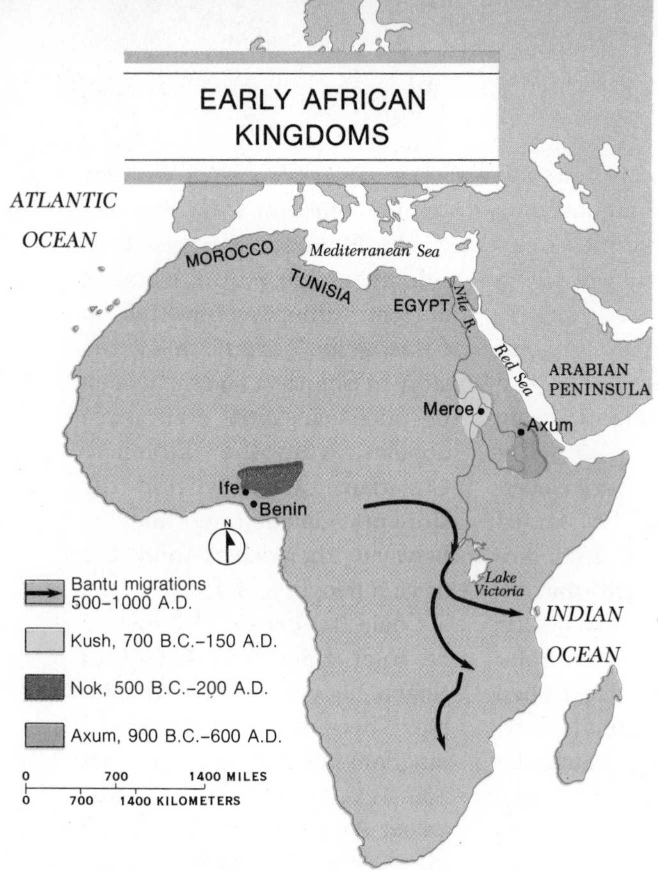

not provide long, smooth stretches of water for boat travel. Rapids, waterfalls, and rocks interrupt their streams. Goods transported on these rivers had to be unloaded frequently and carried overland.

Civilization developed in the Rift Valley. In East Africa, a region called the Rift Valley was formed by earthquakes and volcanoes millions of years ago. High mountains tower over this deep valley that extends for hundreds of miles. So high are the mountains that snow and ice stay on them all year-round, even though
ans. 4 they are located on the equator. In the valley, the soil is very fertile and the climate is pleasant. Large lakes provide a ready source of water year-round, as well as good fishing.

The large variety and quantity of foods available on the shores of Lake Victoria contributed to the growth of a healthy population. Legends tell about the people who were ruled by warrior kings called the Chwezi [chə wā′zē]. As long ago as 1000 A.D., say the legends, the Chwezi kings, more than 8 feet (2.3 meters) tall, ruled the land without fear. It was said you could not look a Chwezi in the face, because his eyes were so bright that it was like looking at the sun.

SECTION REVIEW 2

1. What percentage of Africa's land is covered by forests? What crops were grown there? p. 227

2. What effect did the tsetse fly have on the transportation methods of the forest peoples in Africa? p. 228

3. What were three occupations of people who lived near rivers? Name the four major rivers of Africa. Why were many other rivers unsuitable for travel? p. 228

4. Why were many people able to live good lives in the Rift Valley? p. 230

3 The peoples of ancient Africa developed many practical skills

Early peoples of Africa hunted, fished, and gathered wild grain. The artists of the Sahara, whose rock-paintings show these ways of life, lived before the development of farming. However, after the Sahara dried up and some of the peoples moved south into the savanna, they developed farming methods and other skills.

African farmers learned to grow different crops in different areas. Farming probably began in Africa in the Nile Valley. However, wheat and barley, which were good crops along the Nile, did not grow well in the savanna. The savanna people of the Niger River Valley had to

experiment to find plants they could cultivate.
ans. 1 Beginning about 2000 B.C., they grew African rice, which does not need large amounts of water, and millet. None of these crops, however, grew well in the forest. By 500 B.C., the forest peoples had learned to grow yams. About 100 A.D., Indian sailors landed small boats in East Africa. They brought with them the plantain, which added more nutrition to the African diet. These new foods made it possible for larger numbers of people to live in Africa.

The soil in the savanna and forests of Africa was not very fertile, because the rain and sun removed many of the nutrients that helped plants grow. African farmers observed this and learned to let the land lie fallow to regain the nutrients needed for another good crop. Also, African farmers had to find and clear new land continually.

For the past 3,000 years, farms in most of Africa were cultivated by hoes, not plows. Farming with hoes required much more work, but the plow was not suitable for the poor African soils, because it cut too deeply. A plow turned up unfertile soil and increased erosion.

Herders brought domesticated animals to Africa. Cattle, sheep, and goats were not native to Africa. These animals were imported to northern Egypt and then south along the Nile River. By 2000 B.C., the people in East Africa
ans. 2 had become herders. Some societies that developed were based entirely on herding and raising cattle. The life of people in such a society was *pastoral,* that is, it revolved around the care of the cattle.

Pastoral children learned at an early age to watch and tend cattle. They learned every animal in their family's herd by name. The children sang songs of praise to the animals, much as cowboys of the American West sang songs to quiet their herds of cattle. One of these, sung today by African children, calls God the finest white cow who must protect the herd:

White cow of heaven, you have fed in rich pastures
And you who were small have grown great.
White cow of heaven, your horns have curved full circle
And are joined as one.
White cow of heaven, we throw at you the dust
Which your feet have trampled in our kraals [corrals]
White cow of heaven, give your blessing on the kraals
Which you have overseen
So that the udders of our cows may be heavy
And that our women may rejoice.

Adults in pastoral societies measured their wealth by how many cattle they owned. Cattle were important for milk and were considered too valuable to butcher regularly. But the occasional sick or aged animal was killed for meat.

The use of iron changed the lives of many Africans. About 500 B.C., ironworking became common in Egypt, where it had been introduced by the Hittites. Historians are not certain how Africans far away from Egypt learned
to make iron. Perhaps the knowledge spread ans. 3
from Egypt along ancient trade routes. However, in what is today Nigeria, in western Africa, archaeologists have found ironworking sites that date from about 300 B.C.—almost the same time that iron became common in Egypt. It is possible that the skill of ironmaking developed independently in western Africa about the same time that the Egyptians learned about it.

The use of iron caused major changes in Africa. Iron tools were stronger and longer-lasting than stone or wood ones. These stronger tools made it possible to grow more food and feed more people. Better hunting weapons meant more meat for the community. And strong weapons meant that people were not as afraid to venture into strange lands, because they could protect themselves. Between 500 B.C. and 1000 A.D., great migrations into central and southern Africa took place as population expanded. These are called the *Bantu migrations,* from the name of the group of languages that most of these people spoke.

Kush was an important ironworking center. The kingdom of Kush flourished from about 700 B.C. to 150 A.D. It was located south of Egypt on the Nile River, in what is today the country of Sudan. The Kushites had been Egyptian subjects. About 750 B.C., they invaded and conquered Egypt. The Kushite kings made themselves the 25th dynasty of the pharaohs of Egypt. By about 630 B.C., the Kushites were no longer able to defend Egypt against outside attacks and were driven back to their own land of Kush. There they continued to rule independently from their capital of Meroe [mə rō′]. Around Meroe were valuable iron ore deposits that the Kushites learned to use. Meroe carried on a lively iron trade with Egypt, Arabia, India, what is now Ethiopia, and portions of Africa farther south.

Today, Meroe is uninhabited. However, the extensive heaps of iron refuse and ruins of brick palaces, pyramids, temples, and homes attest to Kush's greatness. Lovely jewelry and iron tables and chairs have been found in the ruins. Kush kings and queens were buried with iron weapons and artifacts. Kush had its own hieroglyphics, which modern-day scholars have been unable to decode. This makes it difficult to know exactly what happened in Kush during the centuries of power and what brought this kingdom to an end. However, Kush's importance as an ironworking center is certain.

SECTION REVIEW 3

1. When were rice, yams, and plantains first grown in Africa? What two natural forces destroyed the fertility of African soil? p. 231

2. What is the importance of cattle in a pastoral society? p. 231

3. Give two possible explanations for the first use of iron in Africa. Why is little known about the details of the kingdom of Kush? p. 231 232

4 Ancient Africans made advances in their societies and cultures

The increasing use of iron and the advances in tools, farming, food, and trade laid the foundations for African civilizations over the centuries. In Africa, as in other parts of the world, im-

proved farming meant more food; more food meant that everyone in the community did not need to work at getting food; other occupations could be pursued full-time. Specialists such as miners, potters, metalsmiths, and political and religious leaders could devote all their time to serving their communities with new skills.

Lineage was the basis of tribal organization. Government in African tribal societies ans. 1 was a matter of custom based on family relationships. Persons in a tribe belonged to subsections, called lineages [liń ē ə jəz]. It was through a person's lineage that he or she had a place in tribal society.

A lineage is several generations of a people who are all descended from the same person—usually a great-great-great-great-grandfather. Most people in Africa belonged to the lineage of their father, although in some societies, people belonged to the lineage of their mother's brother instead.

A lineage took care of its own members. It gave food and money to those who were in trouble. If a person committed a crime, it was the responsibility of the lineage to pay the fine and make certain that the criminal was punished. Widows, orphans, the old, and the sick were taken care of by their lineage. Individuals knew their own status in the lineage and treated older members with respect. Tribes recognized a few of the oldest members, called elders, as their leaders. The kings, chiefs, and elders in a tribe often had to come from certain lineages.

A village in Africa was usually composed of several lineages. People in the same lineage lived in different houses. Most households were made up of small family groups. Especially in farming communities, a husband, his wife or wives, and their unmarried children lived together in one house. Each of these households worked their own farm separately. Special activities, such as house-building and some harvests, required other members of the lineage to help.

Religion, politics, and law became important. As African societies increased in size and skills from the 1st century A.D. on, the need for political organization, accepted rules of behavior, and an official religion increased. Among ans. 2 some peoples, such as the early Gonja in West Africa, certain priests gained influence. The priests who prayed for rain and good crops came to control the distribution of land in the community. They advised the proper time for planting crops and even decided which crops should be planted.

In other communities, such as the many Nyamwezi [nī′ am wē′zē] groups who lived in what is now Tanzania, a chief with political duties was more important than the priests. The chief's power came from such activities as raising armies, collecting taxes, and settling court cases. Cases about taxes and trade were very

Kush noblemen were part of a parade of his subjects that decorated Pharaoh Seti I's tomb (3100 B.C.).

common. Although the laws of the community were not written down, everyone knew the laws and agreed to them. These laws were remembered, and much care was taken to pass them on from generation to generation. A chief, although he was very powerful, had to conform to the laws of the community. Eloquent debating in court cases was a skill practiced by many young Africans who wanted to be leaders.

Historians were respected in West Africa.
ans. 3 Knowledge of events and laws of the past became more important as societies grew larger and more complicated. Kings wanted to know who their ancestors had been and what brave deeds they had done. Other people wanted to know how land had been divided and how taxes had been paid so they would not be cheated. In most of Africa, however, local languages were not written. Although the Arabic language was both written and spoken in Africa, most of Africa's peoples did not use it. As a result, history and laws were memorized.

In West Africa, a special group of people called griots [grē′ōz] were the professional record keepers, historians, and political advisers to chiefs. Griots were living libraries of information about their society's past.

To become a griot, a young man underwent a long, careful education. He traveled from village to village, studying under famous griots, learning all they had to teach, memorizing everything. Kings and other important people in West Africa always had a griot attached to their families. He was given food, clothing, and shelter in exchange for poems about the family. Having a griot insured that the family's name and deeds would be remembered. The griot also entertained the family with poems and stories of the tribe's history. If a noble family fell on hard times, the members often would sell their horses and all their belongings before they would dismiss the family griot.

Through griots, history has been passed on from generation to generation for at least the last eight centuries. Some griots today can remember detailed family histories that go back more than 200 years and can recite the brave deeds of famous kings who lived 700 years ago.

Early Africans made outstanding sculpture. Sculpture and wood carvings depicting people and animals were the most common art form in ancient Africa. Sometimes, the carvings were decorated with ivory and were very realistic. Others showed people with exaggerated faces and bodies. Statues of kings and queens were sometimes covered with symbols of their reign; these were especially common in the area now called Zaïre.

Unfortunately, wood does not last long in the African climate. As a result, the oldest remaining wood carvings were made only 400 years ago. Clay, on the other hand, lasts much longer. Some clay sculptured heads have been found near the town of Nok, Nigeria. These sculptures were made as early as 500 B.C. The heads were made in a uniform style with exaggerated lips and eyes. But there is no doubt that they represented human faces and that they were made by very skilled artists, probably for religious purposes.

Around 1100 A.D., sculptors in the kingdom of Ife [ē′fā], in present-day Nigeria, began making beautiful bronze sculptures. These sculptors developed a method of bronze casting known as
the *lost-wax process.* In this process, the artist ans. 4
made a model of the sculpture in wax. Because the wax was soft, it could be sculpted in delicate detail. The wax model was then covered with

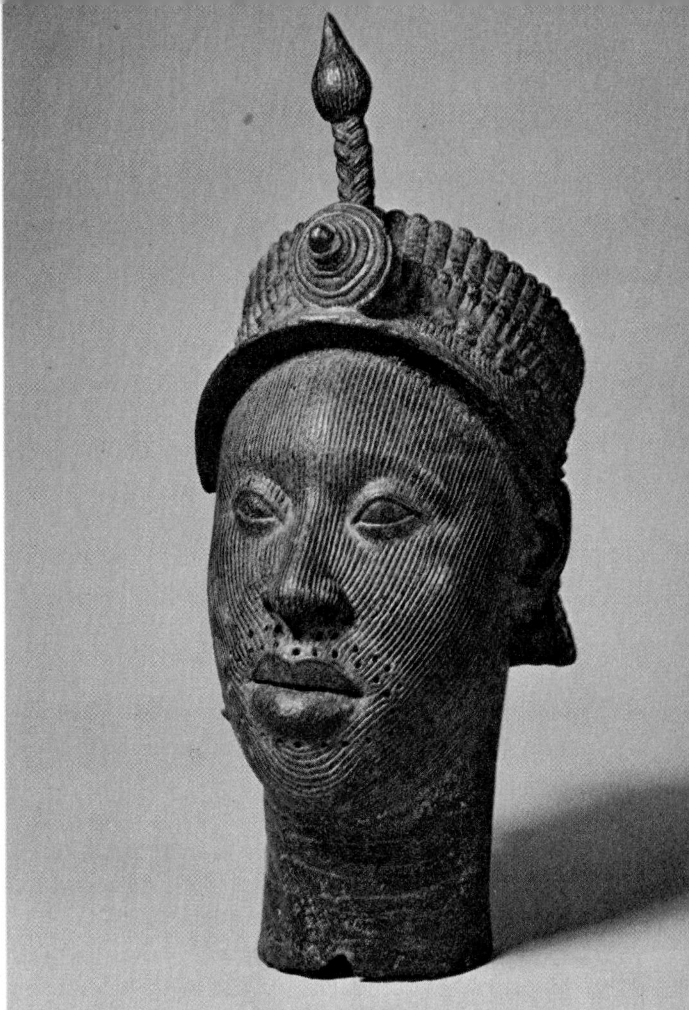

West African Sculpture
These two heads are outstanding examples of the high level of sculpture reached by ancient Nigerians. *Above* is a stylized, terra cotta head from the Nok culture; *left*, the bronze head of a king of Ife.

clay and heated. As the wax melted away, its form was left in the clay. Then, melted bronze was poured into the clay form. When the bronze cooled, the clay was washed away and an exact bronze copy of the wax original remained. The bronze sculptures of Ife, made by this lost-wax process, are considered to be some of the best sculpture in the world.

The people of Benin learned the lost-wax process from the people of Ife. By the 15th century, the Benin people were not only making beautiful sculptures of peoples and animals, but also wall plaques, hundreds of which have been found. These plaques show military and historical events from Benin's past. Great heroes, famous battles, the coronations of kings, and wealthy traders who became prominent citizens were portrayed on the plaques.

These early African art objects are sought and prized by art collectors all over the world today. The stylized form of African art influenced such famous European artists as Pablo Picasso.

SECTION REVIEW **4**

1. How were lineage relationships important in African society? p. 233
2. From what group of people did leaders come in the Gonja community? In the Nyamwezi? p. 223
3. Why did West African kings need griots? p. 234
4. Describe the three steps in the lost-wax method of sculpture. p. 234

CHAPTER REVIEW 12

SECTION SUMMARIES

1. Much of Africa is desert and savanna. The continent of Africa has several different ecological regions. In the north and south are narrow regions of fertile coast. Farther inland are deserts—the Sahara in the north and the Kalahari in the south. Camels have ensured African trade and contact across the Sahara. The deserts of Africa merge into large regions of savanna where populations have prospered because of the farming and pastoralism that are possible there.

2. Other features of geography made Africa a land of variety. In the west-central section of the continent is the rain forest. Fruits and vegetables grow well here, but the tsetse fly has prevented the raising of cattle and horses. The rivers of Africa connected the villages and cities that dot the valleys. Canoes and barges carried trading goods on the rivers. In East Africa, ancient earthquakes and volcanoes formed a mountain, valley, and lake region called the Rift Valley. Legends of the glorious Chwezi kings demonstrate that peoples have benefited from this pleasant and fertile region for centuries.

3. The peoples of ancient Africa developed many practical skills. Useful farming methods, specialized cattle-raising, and ironworking helped Africans grow more food and control their environment. The Bantu migrations populated central and southern Africa. One of the earliest ironworking centers in Africa gave rise to the ancient kingdom of Kush.

4. Ancient Africans made advances in their societies and cultures. Tribal groups and lineages formed the basis of social organizations. Every person was expected to know his or her position in the lineage and to act in a way proper for that role. Priests became important in some groups, while in other groups political chiefs became powerful. Law and history were memorized and passed from generation to generation. Griots in West Africa had the job of studying history and remembering it for the whole community. Cultural advances were also made in early Africa. Some societies had a long tradition of art, particularly sculpture. The clay heads of Nok and the bronze sculpture of Ife and Benin are considered to be some of the best sculpture in the world.

● You may want to require students to write in their own words when doing these items.

WHO? WHAT? WHEN? WHERE? ●

1. Write an identifying sentence for each of the following groups:

Kulango p. 222, 223
Asante p. 222, 223
Chwezi p. 230
Ethiopians p. 229
Kushites p. 232
Gonja p. 233
Nyamwezi p. 233
Bantu p. 232

2. Explain the importance of these terms to African culture:

compound p. 226
caravan p. 226
oases p. 225
lineage p. 233
tribe p. 233
tsetse fly p. 228
fallow p. 231
plantain p. 228
griots p. 234
cattle p. 231

3. Find the years of these events and place them on a timeline:

farming began in the Niger River Valley 2000 B.C.
ironworking began in Nigeria 300 B.C.
the kingdom of Kush flourished 700 B.C.–150 A.D.
bronze sculpture was made in Ife 1000 A.D.
people lived where the Sahara is now 6000–1500 B.C.
the Chwezi ruled 1000 A.D.
plantain was brought from India 100 A.D.
the Bantu migrations took place 500 B.C.–1000 A.D.
the people of Nok made clay sculpture 500 B.C.

4. List the four ecological areas of Africa and name • the modern countries that are in each.

QUESTIONS FOR CRITICAL THINKING

1. Why were the Kulango unable to adjust to life in Asante? Can you think of any difficulties people might be having today in trying to start life again in a new place? Explain.
2. What might be some reasons little has been known about African history and culture until recently?
3. In what ways do people of different occupations exchange goods today similar to the cooperation between farmers and herders of the African savanna?
4. How has studying this chapter changed your ideas about Africa?
5. How does the geography of an area make people develop special skills? Give specific examples from African history and from life today.

ACTIVITIES

1. Do research to find out what is happening in the countries near the borders of the Sahara today. Is the size of the desert still changing? Why? What effect is this having on the people who live there?
2. Show the four ecological areas of Africa on a map. Find pictures illustrating the different ways of life followed in these areas.
3. Make a chart showing the lineage relationships of your family. Discuss in class the responsibilities of families toward their members today and compare with the traditional African system.
4. Write an African folk tale based on the ways of life explained in this chapter.
5. Find pictures of different examples of African sculpture and wood carving. How are they different from examples of European art? Modern art?

• This item may be done on an outline map of Africa. Students should refer to map in Atlas.

QUESTIONS FOR CRITICAL THINKING:
1. Students may be familiar with problems faced by immigrants in the U.S.
2. Lack of writing is one reason. Geographical factors also isolated Africa from the outside world.
3. Answers will vary.
4. Suggest students begin by writing their ideas about Africa before chapter is studied.
5. Answers will vary.

CHAPTER TEST 12

SECTION 1

1. The largest area of African geography is: a. jungle, b. desert, c. grassland
2. True or false: The Sahara has been an impassable boundary between North and South Africa.
3. The _______ was an important animal to the people of the savanna. cow, horse, or donkey
4. Most African people have lived in the: a. desert, b. savanna, c. forest

SECTION 2

5. Cattle cannot be raised in the African forest because of: a. lions, b. tsetse flies, c. custom
6. _______ was an important forest kingdom. a. Niger, b. Benin, c. Masai
7. The Rift Valley was formed _______ of years ago. a. millions, b. thousands, c. hundreds
8. True or false: Plantain and yams were important crops to forest people.

SECTION 3

9. The people of the savanna grew: a. wheat, b. millet, c. yams
10. A pastoral society is one whose culture is based on: a. herding, b. farming, c. fishing
11. True or false: Archaeologists have learned much about the Kushites by studying their hieroglyphics.
12. Farmlands in Africa were cultivated with: a. hoes, b. plows, c. shovels

SECTION 4

13. In African society, a group of people who are descended from the same person is: a. a tribe, b. a lineage, c. a compound
14. The people who were trained to remember and pass on tribal history were called griots.
15. The lost-wax process was used to make: a. candles, b. iron tools, c. bronze sculptures
16. True or false: The priests were the most important leaders in all African societies.

CHAPTER
13

400–1900

African Civilizations South of the Sahara

Gold has played an important part in Africa's history. Africans used it to pay for goods bought from foreigners. They worked it into religious ornaments and symbols of power and wealth. They kept secret its sources in the ground. This dazzling pendant mask was made by the Asante people.

Dixon Denham did not know what to expect. He had heard contradictory stories about the kingdom of Kanem-Bornu, but no European had seen this part of Africa. It was 1823, and he would be the first.

Denham rode ahead of his companions toward the African kingdom. Suddenly, in front of him appeared several thousand cavalry. The soldiers were dressed in chain mail, and their horses were decorated with quilted cloth and metal coverings. The African cavalry remained steady until Denham's fellow travelers caught up with him. Then a shout rang out from the leaders of the force. Trumpets blew. And the cavalry charged to welcome them:

> There was an appearance of tact and management in their movements which astonished me: Three separate small bodies, from the centre of each flank, kept charging rapidly towards us, to within a few feet of our horses' heads, without checking the speed of their own until the moment of their halt, while the whole body moved onwards. These parties . . . [were] mounted on small very perfect horses who stopped and wheeled from their utmost speed with great precision and expertness, shaking their spears over their heads, exclaiming "Barka! Barka! [that is] . . . Blessing, Blessing!"

Denham and his party were surprised to find so powerful a cavalry and so well-administered an empire in the interior of Africa. Europeans for ● centuries had had only wisps of information about Africa. Sometimes, it was hinted that there were cities of gold. Other rumors told of vast stretches of uninhabited rain forest. Yet, large empires had been rising and falling and replacing each other in Africa for centuries. These empires featured trade, education, effective governments, and well-developed cities.

Long trade routes across the desert had been tapping the gold supplies of West Africa. And great empires flourished on this trade. Sea routes across the Indian Ocean kept East Africa in constant communication with India and China. Islam spread across West Africa in waves of religious revival that were both violent and inspiring. Powerful states developed in the rain forest. This chapter describes some of the highly developed civilizations that arose in Africa south of the Sahara:

● Key Concept: African empires have come and gone without the Europeans knowing of them.

■ Ask students *why* gold is valuable. Is it because it is scarce and beautiful? Or has it more to do with the acceptance of its value by rulers.

1. Famous empires grew in the West African savanna.

2. City-states flourished along the East African coast.

3. The kingdom of Zimbabwe developed in the interior.

4. Islam stimulated new states in West Africa.

5. The forest states developed strong governments.

1 Famous empires grew in the West African savanna

The Sahara can be compared to an ocean. It is crossed by the "ship of the desert," the camel. And, just as cities grow up on ocean coasts, cities grew up on the edge of the desert. The towns in the Sudan (a name for the northern savanna of Africa that should not be confused with the modern nation of that name) were much like port cities. For more than eight centuries, they took their turn as capitals of three powerful empires: Ghana, Mali, and Songhai.

Gold was exchanged for salt across the Sahara. A rich gold-mining area lay in a wide forest region called Wangara [wäng gä′rə] near the sources of the Niger, Senegal, and Gambia rivers. Gold from Wangara was the basis for ■ profitable trade as far back as ancient Roman times because it was prized by the rich and powerful of many nations.

Traders brought the gold through the forests to the savanna. There, they were met by other traders from the cities of the North African coast who exchanged goods for the gold and carried it across the Sahara to the coastal cities. From there, much of the gold was shipped for sale in Europe and Asia.

One important item the North Africans had to trade for the West Africans' gold was salt. Salt is an essential item in people's diets; without it they will die. In hot climates, the people need even more salt than those who live in cooler places. There were very few salt deposits in West Africa. But on the coasts and in places in the Sahara that once must have been the sites of salt lakes, there are large salt deposits.

A place named Taghaza [tə gä′zə] developed near a salt deposit in the Sahara. It became a major stop on the trade routes. The gold mines of Wangara are exhausted, but there is still plenty of salt near Taghaza. Even today, caravans of camels and jeeps come to Taghaza to buy salt for the people in the savanna.

The 10th-century Arab geographer al-Masudi described what has come to be called the "silent trade." He said that traders from the north ans. 1
crossed the desert and came to a certain place in the Sudan, possibly on the banks of the Niger River. At this place every year, they laid their goods — salt, cloth, and copper — on the ground. Then, they beat their drums to let the people of the savanna know the market was ready, and withdrew a half-day's journey away.

Next, the savanna people came and placed piles of gold beside the goods in as large a quantity as they thought them worth. Then, they too went a half-day's journey away, beating drums to signal merchants from the north.

The North Africans returned, and, if they thought the price was right, they took the gold and left. If not, they withdrew again to wait for the savanna traders to put down more gold. The exchange went on for several days until both groups were satisfied with the price. Neither group of traders ever saw or spoke with the other.

The silent trade took place in other parts of Africa as well. The 4th-century Greek histori-

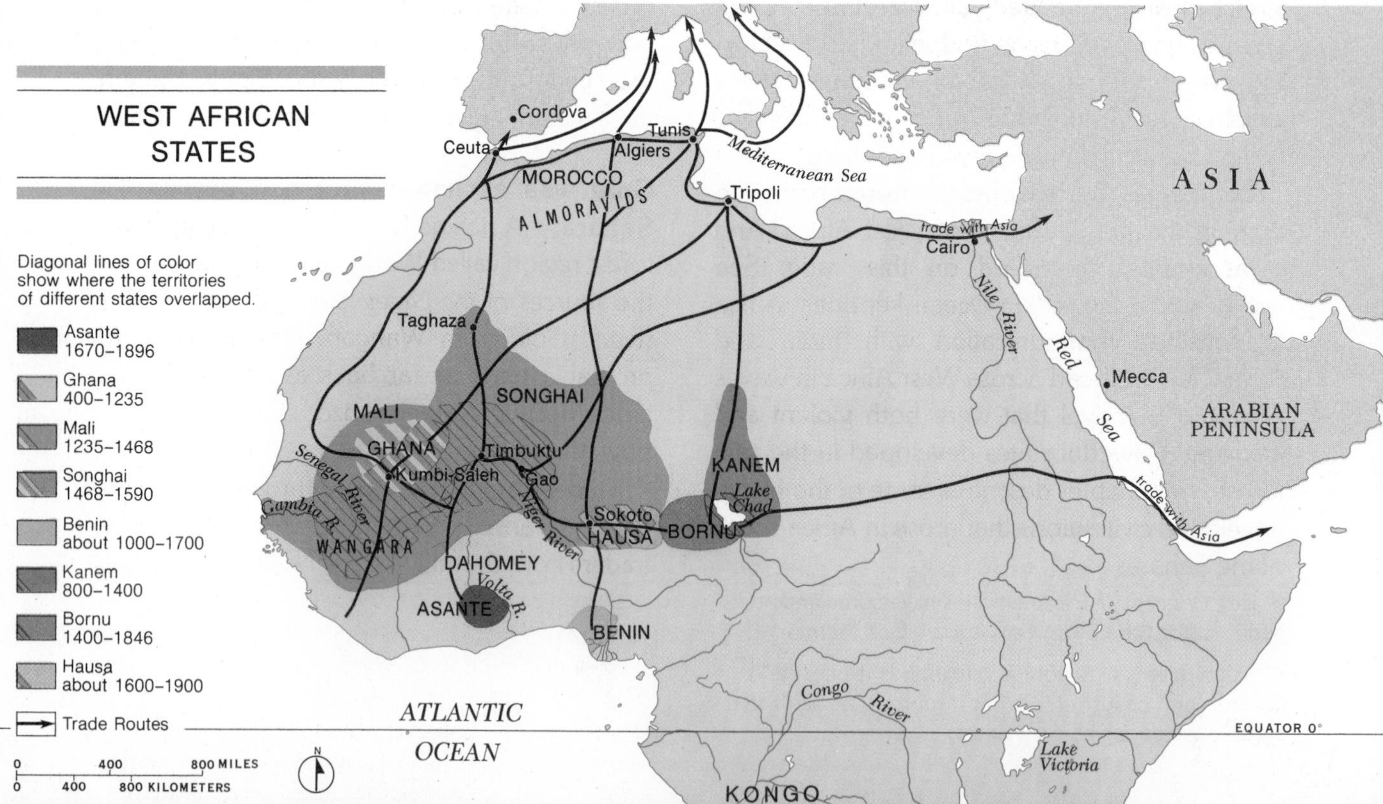

This picture of a warrior in Bornu's cavalry is from Denham's own account, published in 1827.

an Herodotus described it going on in the northwest coast of Africa. And a 6th-century Greek trader saw it in East Africa.

Ancient Ghana controlled the gold trade (400–1235). In about 400 A.D., the kingdom of Ghana [gä′nə] began to develop in the Sudan. It should not be confused with the modern country of the same name, which is far to the south of ancient Ghana. Ancient Ghana grew near the marketplace of the gold traders, and its power came from its location.

By the end of the 7th century, the people of the Muslim world began to write about Ghana as the spread of Islam brought Arabs in contact with North Africans. From the writings of Arab geographers, we know that by this time Ghana was a large empire based on trade and
● agriculture. Its strong central government was ruled by a king who appointed the different officers of the kingdom and who was the final judge of all court cases. Ghana's government was a
ans. 2 theocracy; the ruler was believed to be partly divine and able to talk with the gods for the good of the empire.

● African governments were not usually despotic, rulers had to obey traditional rules of behavior.

The king claimed the right to own all the gold nuggets that came from the mines of Wangara. Other people could trade only in gold dust. With this right, the king of Ghana could control the economy. He could prevent inflation by holding back gold nuggets from trade if the price was not right. In addition to owning all the gold nuggets, the empire taxed all goods, including salt and gold, entering and leaving Ghana.

A powerful army protected the kingdom and helped the king control the large variety of peoples within its boundaries. In 1067, the Arab writer al-Bakri wrote that the army was made up of 200 thousand warriors.

The twin cities of Kumbi-Saleh [kům′- ans. 3
bē sä′lə] made up the capital of ancient Ghana. In one town lived the king and his officers; in the other lived merchants and strangers. The towns, located on the edge of the Sahara, were about 6 miles (10 kilometers) apart. Between the two towns were the small mud houses of the people who grew food to support the inhabitants of the capital.

The king's town was built like a fortress. Whenever the king appeared in public, he was surrounded by servants carrying gold swords. The princes and advisers of the empire, in splendid dress, accompanied him. Horses with gold cloth blankets and dogs with gold and silver collars were also part of his parade.

The traders' town was made up of two-story stone houses and public squares. After the 7th century, mosques were built there because many of the traders were Muslim. The kings and farmers of Ghana, however, kept their traditional religious customs.

In the 11th century, a group of Muslim Berbers, the Almoravids [al′ mə rä′ vidz] lived

A 1347 map of West Africa shows the Atlas Mountains as a wall. The king wearing a gold crown is Mansa Musa.

northwest of Ghana. The Almoravids believed in living a very strict religious life. And they believed it was their mission to stamp out wickedness and convert people to Islam. In 1076, they attacked Kumbi-Saleh in order to make the people there better Muslims. The Almoravids occupied the capital for about ten years, and then the people of Ghana won it back.

Ghana never recovered from the occupation. Great damage had been done. The many provinces of Ghana no longer obeyed the weak Ghana government. Many merchants moved from Kumbi-Saleh to other trading towns on the edge of the desert. Within fifty years, an army from one of Ghana's provinces conquered Ghana, and a new empire emerged that became larger and more prosperous than Ghana had been.

● Some students may need help with this analogy. Remind students of the griot's role (Ch. 12).

Trade and learning flourished in Mali (1235–1468). Sundiata [sůn′dē ä′tə] was the leader of a province of Ghana called Mali [mä′ lē]. The king of Ghana had had eleven of Sundiata's brothers murdered so that the province would not be a threat to Ghana. But these measures did not stop Mali's ambitions. In 1235, Sundiata led his people to victory over the last king of Ghana.

During the years of his rule, Sundiata conquered vast territories and Mali became an empire. He brought the gold- and salt-mining areas under his control. From his time forward, traders met face to face, and after nearly a thousand years, the silent trade was no longer used. ● Sundiata became a hero to his people much as George Washington is to the people of the United States.

One of the most famous *mansas*, or kings, of Mali was Sundiata's nephew Mansa Musa [män′sə mü′sə]. His rule began in 1307. Mansa Musa was a believer of Islam, for by this time the rulers of Mali were Muslim. Most of the common people, however, were not Muslim. It is said that the gold miners in Wangara once threatened to strike when Mansa Musa tried to force them to become Muslims.

In 1324, Mansa Musa set out on his pilgrimage to Mecca. It was an amazing journey. Records tell of thousands of servants, gifts of gold and ivory, and a caravan of camels, horses, and slaves. When his caravan reached Cairo, Egypt, it brought so much gold, spent so much, and gave so much to the poor that the value of gold in Cairo dropped for at least twelve years.

The gold trade brought Mali great wealth. The empire was the supplier of gold to Europe, though many Europeans did not know that this was where the gold was coming from. *Guinea* [gin′ē] gold was used for the coins of the Italian city-states of the fourteenth century. (*Guinea* is an old word for West Africa.)

ans. 3 The city of Timbuktu, located on the bend in the Niger River, was the cultural center of Mali. Scholars from the Muslim world came to study the manuscripts stored in its huge library. The conversion to Islam had brought the kings of Mali in contact with Arabic, both spoken and written. Mansa Musa's pilgrimage had served as an advertisement of the wealth of his country. And scholars and travelers came to Timbuktu to see Mali for themselves.

The globe-trotting Muslim traveler, Ibn Batuta, visited Timbuktu in 1352 and stayed in Mali for eight months. He found that the people had a strong sense of justice; wrongdoers were quickly punished. Both the city streets and countryside were safer places than any he had noted in his wide travels. He also wrote about the women of Mali. Unlike many other places in the Islamic world, women here were not kept out of public sight and were not required to obey their husbands. He met Mali women who were educated. Ibn Batuta was impressed by the wealth, comfortable living, and great amount of trade that he saw.

The map on p. 240 should be used to clarify where the place names mentioned in this section were located.

The Songhai Empire (1468–1590) replaced Mali. After Mansa Musa's death, Mali had a series of rulers who were not able to control the huge empire. Many provinces struggled to seize power. One was Songhai [song′hī] with its capital Gao [gow] not far from Timbuktu.

In 1468, Sonni Ali [son′ē ä lē′], the king of Songhai, attacked and captured Timbuktu. He then went on to capture many other cities of Mali. Sonni Ali ruled for thirty-five years. They were years of persecutions and warfare. At his death, one of his generals became head of the empire.

Askia [äs kē′yə] Mohammad, Sonni Ali's successor, came to power in 1493. During his thirty-five-year reign, the empire grew to include most of the grasslands of West Africa. It reached from the Atlantic Ocean halfway across Africa to Lake Chad, from what is today the southern border of Algeria south to the edge of the rain forest. He was an able administrator who gave the empire an improved system of government. ans. 4

Sonni Ali had been a man of the countryside. He had failed to understand or help the people of the towns. He had judged their dissatisfaction as disloyalty and had been ruthless in his treatment of them. His reaction to a revolt in Timbuktu had been such widespread slaughter that he gained a permanent reputation as a ruthless tyrant. Askia Mohammad reversed this policy.

Askia Mohammad understood the wealth and commerce that the towns brought the empire. He set up a fair system of taxation and good communication with the provinces. He encouraged the Muslim religion (most of the townspeople, especially the traders, were Muslims). Timbuktu reached new heights as a center for scholarship. A visitor in the early 16th century wrote this description:

> The rich king of Timbuktu has many plates and sceptres of gold, some whereof weigh 1300 pounds; and he keeps a magnificent and well-furnished court. . . . Here are a great store of doctors, judges, priests and other learned men, that are bountifully maintained at the king's cost and charges. And hither are brought divers manuscripts of written books out of Barbary [North Africa] which are sold for more money than any other merchandise.

Songhai was probably the most highly organized and efficient of all the early West African states. Its wealth and power aroused the jealousy of Morocco in North Africa. The Songhai rulers who came after Askia Mohammad were not as powerful as he had been. In 1590, the king of Morocco equipped an army of about 5,000 men to cross the Sahara and attack Songhai. Only about 1,000 of the Moroccan soldiers survived the crossing. But they had brought with them guns and gunpowder, which were superior to the swords and spears of the Songhai army. The Moroccans were able to beat the Songhai army, but they were not able to hold the empire together. During the following years, large numbers of provinces, cities, and small groups broke away and began to govern themselves. This large and powerful empire in West Africa came to an end.

In this 1853 German engraving, a caravan approaches Timbuktu, the intellectual and trading center of Songhai.

SECTION REVIEW 1

p. 240 **1.** What was the silent trade? What goods were traded? Who was involved? Why was it silent?

p. 241 **2.** Name three sources of the king of Ghana's power. How did the empire of Ghana fall?

p. 243 **3.** How was life in Timbuktu, during the Mali Em-
241 pire, different from life in the capital of Ghana? Name at least three ways. Think about religion, education, the layout of the cities.

p. 243 **4.** In what ways was Askia Mohammad a different
244 kind of ruler than Sonni Ali?

2 City-states flourished • along the East African coast

ans. 1 More than 2,000 years ago, people from India and Arabia sailed westward looking for new sources of trade. The monsoon winds, or trade winds, of the Indian Ocean blew steadily toward East Africa for months and then steadily back toward India for months giving sailors a safe, direct route. By about 120 A.D., a guide published in Egypt told where ports were to be found along the East African coast.

The 7th-century expansion of Islamic trade caused the East African and Indian Ocean trade to boom. A distinctive culture developed in East African city-states. Then, in the 16th century, Portuguese traders nearly destroyed the economic life of the coast. But the culture survived to the present.

ans. 2 **International trade was the basis of East African civilization.** As in West Africa, there were large supplies of gold in East Africa. Ivory, which came from the tusks of the African elephant, was another valuable trade item. It was strong but soft enough to be carved into objects that were both beautiful and useful. Chessmen and even thrones were carved from African ivory. Ivory was in great demand in the Muslim Empire, India, and China. A third item of export was East African iron, considered of high quality and carried to all the markets of Asia where it was made into strong, sharp weapons.

Asian and Arab traders brought cotton cloth and porcelain utensils to sell in East Africa. Chinese porcelain was especially prized; East Africans built small niches in the walls of their homes to display the finer pieces. Along the coasts of modern-day Kenya and Tanzania, broken pieces of very old Chinese cups, saucers, and vases lie in the sand, evidence of the trade that took place many centuries ago.

City-states developed from East African ports. In response to the centuries-old trade, coastal marketplaces developed into large cities. Traders from Africa and the Middle East built homes and settled in the port cities to act as agents for distant traders.

One of the richest was the city of Kilwa. South of most of the other cities, Kilwa was closer to the gold fields of the kingdom of Zimbabwe [zim bä′bwā]. Zimbabwe was in what is today Rhodesia. The merchants of Kilwa controlled much of the gold trade and grew wealthy by imposing taxes on its sale.

Ibn Batuta visited Kilwa in 1331 and wrote that it was one of the most beautiful and well-constructed towns he had seen. Today, stone ruins of enormous palaces, mansions, mosques, arched walkways, town squares, and public fountains hint at what Kilwa once was. Coral and wood were used to make carved arches,

• The map on p. 246 locates these areas.

doors, and windows. The main palace of Kilwa was built on the very edge of a cliff overlooking the ocean. It had over one hundred rooms and an eight-sided bathing pool in one of its many courtyards.

Kilwa was only one of several important trading towns. Each had its own ruler, government, laws, taxes, and small police force. The influence of each of these city-states spread a certain distance from the city itself, sometimes all along a trade route to the interior. Each city-state was in fierce competition with the others.

Swahili culture thrived in the city-states. ● The African, Indian, and Arab traders who had settled in the port cities intermarried and had large families. Eventually a way of living called *Swahili culture* grew up. Swahili [swä hē′lē] is the name of the language the coastal peoples spoke. It is a combination of many African and Indian languages, along with Arabic. Swahili was written in Arabic script until modern times. (Today it is sometimes written in the English alphabet.) The Swahili people wrote poetry and stories in both Arabic and Swahili.

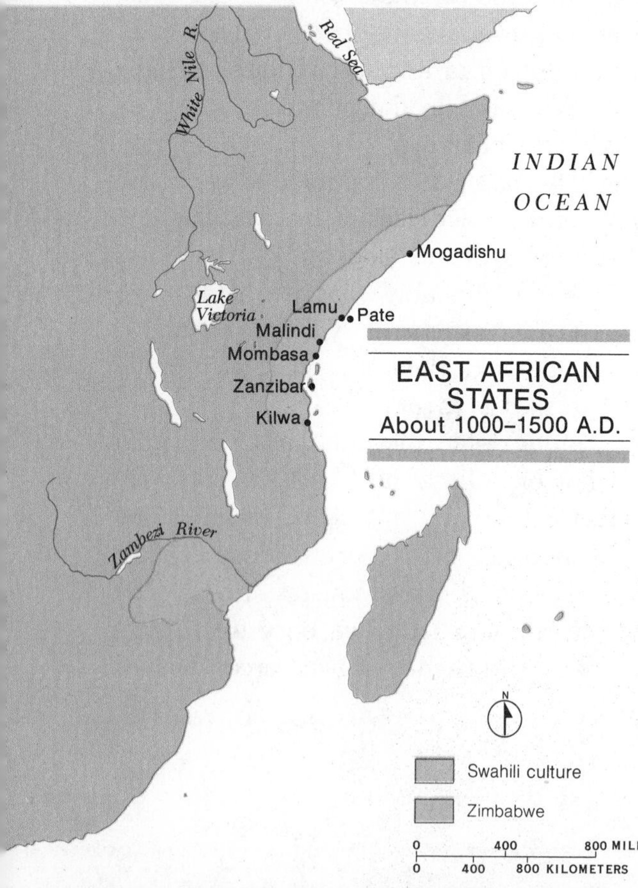

Life in the city-states was comfortable. People were free to practice the religious beliefs of their choice. The Arab influence caused some to convert to Islam. But most Swahili people kept to traditional African religions.

Swahili peoples kept in touch with distant lands seeking good trade relations. A Chinese painting shows a giraffe brought to the emperor of China in 1415 by the people of Malindi [mä lin′dē]. Malindi was one of the smaller city-states. Writing on the picture tells of the emperor's pleasure with the gift. He sent a fleet and thousands of Chinese sailors with numerous gifts to accompany the Malindi traders back to their country.

EAST AFRICAN STATES
About 1000–1500 A.D.

The Portuguese destroyed much of the East African trade. By the 12th century, the Christian kingdom of Portugal was established on the west coast of the Iberian peninsula. The Portuguese were a seafaring people. In the 15th century, Prince Henry the Navigator encouraged Portuguese sailors to seek new trade routes to Asia. In 1498, Vasco da Gama ■ [väs′kō də gä′mə] sailed around the southern tip of Africa. For the first time, the Portuguese saw the East African coast. ans. 3

They were eager for gold and wealth and were delighted to find the thriving city-states. Their descriptions give a picture of life in Kilwa as even more prosperous than when Ibn Batuta visited. The common people dressed in imported cottons and silks. The wealthy wore gold, silver, and jeweled ornaments. Freshwater streams, orchards, and fruit gardens surrounded the town.

● Key Concept: Note the creativity of a pluralistic society, a recurring phenomenon throughout history.

■ Additional information on the early European explorers may be found in Ch. 21.

Benin sculpture, made of terra cotta, or mud, is a former king who was a great warrior.

The Portuguese wanted to participate in the rich trade, but they were scorned by the Swahili. The Swahili thought the Portuguese had bad manners, unclean habits, and cheap trading goods. But the Portuguese had something few Swahili had – guns.

Most of the Indian Ocean trade was fairly peaceful at that time. The East African city-states had few defenses. With the power of their muskets and cannon, the Portuguese began a campaign of piracy and looting. They burned Kilwa in 1505. After capturing the town of Mombasa further north, Da Gama ordered it to be looted. Portuguese sailors, swinging axes, broke into the houses and killed anyone who had not escaped before the attack. A Swahili poet later wrote of the ruin of his city:

> Where once the porcelain stood in the wall niches,
> Now wild birds nestle their fledglings

The Portuguese built their own trade fort at Mombasa. But just as the Moroccans had been unable to hold the Songhai Empire together, the Portuguese could not replace the functioning governments and trade networks of East Africa. The destruction, insecurity, and fear that they caused led to a decline in trade. Swahili culture, however, managed to survive. And today, Swahili language and poetry are an important part of life in Tanzania and Kenya.

SECTION REVIEW **2**

1. How did geography help the economy of East African city-states? p. 245

2. What items did Arabs, Indians, and East Africans trade with each other? p. 245

3. How was Vasco da Gama's trip around the tip of Africa important for the Portuguese? What was its effect on Swahili culture? p. 246 247

3 The kingdom of Zimbabwe developed in the interior

In 1868, a European hunter stumbled across the massive stone ruins of a group of palaces, fortresses, and houses in the interior of Rhodesia. The buildings were made from oblong slabs of granite. The elaborately patterned walls were not held together by mortar. Instead, each one of the rocks had been shaped to fit together exactly.

At first, white settlers in the area refused to believe that these buildings, with walls 10 feet (3 meters) thick and 30 feet (9 meters) high, had been the work of Africans. They thought that Africans were not capable of making ans. 1 sophisticated structures. But the impressive stone buildings of Zimbabwe, which means "royal dwelling," were built entirely by Africans from the 10th through the 18th centuries.

Zimbabwe grew from an iron-working settlement. The builders of Zimbabwe were descended from the iron-working peoples of the Bantu expansion. Historians believe that the Bantu probably originated in the Congo forest and migrated from there. By the 11th century, some Bantu peoples, called the *Shona* [shō′nə], had crossed the Zambezi River and pushed back or conquered any hunting and gathering peoples that lived there.

The Shona people found gold deposits near Zimbabwe. They mined the gold and traded it with the Swahili city-states. They imported such Asian goods as cotton, brass, and porcelain. By the 15th century, Zimbabwe was a powerful state with a large population, much wealth, and a centralized government.

Gold formed the basis of Zimbabwe's economy. The Portuguese never saw Zim-

This aerial photograph gives a sense of the size of the massive walled compound at Zimbabwe.

babwe itself. But in the 16th century, they recorded conversations with the descendants of
ans. 2 the Shona people. From these Portuguese re-
● cords and from archaeologists' study of the stone ruins, historians have learned what Zimbabwe was like at its height in the 1400s.

Zimbabwe was ruled by a king who was believed to be semi-divine. His health was important for the welfare of the kingdom. If he became ill, he was supposed to commit suicide so that a healthy king could take his place and keep the country strong. The king made the necessary decisions, but only his closest advisers were allowed to see him.

One of the major stone buildings at Zimbabwe is thought to have been the palace where the king lived with his royal wives, advisers, and officers. About 1,000 people lived at the palace at one time. Cooks, servants, farmers, and soldiers lived with their families in smaller stone buildings surrounding the palace. Ruined buildings of this type have been found not only at Zimbabwe but all over the region. The larger sites were probably the homes of provincial chiefs.

Many of the common people were involved in gold mining. The mines were pits dug into the earth; some were as much as 50 feet (15 meters) deep. Men and women both worked in the gold mines and along the streams, where even more gold washed out of the ground.

In the early 1500s, the Portuguese tried to gain control of the gold regions, but the rulers of Zimbabwe prevented them from reaching even the capital. The Zimbabwe kings dictated to the Portuguese all rules concerning trade and taxes.
ans. 3 Gradually, Zimbabwe's trade with the East African coast dropped off as a result of the destructive Portuguese actions there. Internal quarrels among brothers who all wanted to be king further weakened Zimbabwe. However, the kingdom survived until 1830. Then, it was attacked by Zulu [zü′lü] peoples from the south who were seeking land on which to settle. The great stone buildings were abandoned and large hordes of gold were left to be found and carried off by European prospectors in the 19th century.

● Students might be interested in this material on how we know about ancient Africa.

SECTION REVIEW 3

1. Who built Zimbabwe? Where did they come from? During what years were the stone buildings built? p. 248
2. From what two sources do we get our knowledge of 15th-century Zimbabwe? p. 249
3. Give three causes of the decline of Zimbabwe. p. 249

4 Islam stimulated new states in West Africa

When Songhai collapsed in the Moroccan invasion, the center of trade and political power in West Africa shifted south and east. The Muslim state of Kanem-Bornu emerged as the most powerful military state of the central Sudan. Fierce religious wars converted the people of the ans. 1
Hausa [hou′sə] states to Islam, and religious warfare continued in West Africa until the early 19th century.

Kanem-Bornu had a long history (800–1846). The rich empires of Ghana, Mali, and Songhai overshadowed the lesser states of the Sudan before 1600. Yet, the history of these states goes back for centuries. About the year 800 A.D., a centralized state with a king emerged in Kanem [kä′nem] east of Lake

Chad. This first king, Saif [sef], began a dynasty that ruled for a thousand years.

In 1085, the king of Kanem was converted to Islam. The kingdom continued to grow in strength, and Islam became firmly established among its rulers. Most of the agricultural population, however, continued traditional religions.

Like other states of the Sudan, Kanem engaged in trade across the Sahara. The people of Kanem exchanged cloth and leather goods for the salt of the north.

By 1400, civil war and attacks from the east had weakened Kanem. The king and his court moved west of Lake Chad to Bornu [bôr′nü], and the new state was called Kanem-Bornu.

After the fall of Songhai in 1591, Kanem-Bornu became the strongest state in the central Sudan. Its most famous ruler was Idris Alooma [id′ris ə lü′mə], who ruled from 1580 to 1617. He spread Islamic law throughout his territories and forced the common people to become Muslims, something which had never been done in Ghana, Mali, or Songhai.

ans. 2 Idris Alooma built up the cavalry of Kanem-Bornu until it was the terror of the central Sudan. Both riders and horses wore chain mail and padded cloth coverings, like the knights and horses of western Christendom. Experts from Egypt and Asia Minor trained the army in the use of guns imported from North Africa. Idris Alooma personally led the cavalry. Thus, the horse became one of the basic requirements for any state in the Sudan that wanted to be strong. Many rulers of smaller states imitated Kanem-Bornu's cavalry. So important a state was Kanem-Bornu that ambassadors were sent to create good relations between Kanem-Bornu

This modern-day Hausa tribesman is wearing the chain mail of a 13th-century ancestor.

and the Ottoman Empire and to confirm that Kanem-Bornu was part of the Muslim world.

The rulers who followed Idris Alooma were not as strong as he had been. The state gradually weakened. The last king of Kanem-Bornu was killed in 1846 in the religious wars.

Trade flourished in the Hausa states. A people called the Hausa lived in trading cities in what is now northern Nigeria. The Hausa city-states did not unite with each other but remained individual states. Each had its own government, laws, and taxes.

The Hausa city-states were small and weak until the 15th century when Islam was introduced. After that, these cities enjoyed a lively trade with Mali, and later Songhai, as well as with the lesser states in the African forest.

ans. 3 The Hausa engaged in trade and manufacture. From the forest, they collected ivory, hides, and kola nuts to trade with North Africa. The kola nut was very popular with the Muslims, who chewed it like gum or tobacco. The kola nut contains caffeine, which not only keeps one awake, but also helps one to go long periods of time without food or water. To Muslims, who were not supposed to drink alcoholic beverages, the kola was a popular stimulant. (Many modern soft drinks are made from this same nut.) The development of such handicraft industries as leather manufacture and cloth weaving made several Hausa cities prosperous.

Uthman dan Fodio united the Hausa states. Living in the Sudan and the Hausa cities were a people called the Fulani [fü lä′nē]. As the Hausa cities became more wealthy and powerful, the Fulani began to resent the control the Hausa people had over them. After years of discontent and minor uprisings, a leader arose in the early 1800s to lead the Fulani in a revolution against the Hausa.

Uthman dan Fodio [u̇th′mən dan fō′dē ō] ans. 4
was a devoted Muslim who claimed that his revolution was a Holy War, or *jihad* [jə häd′], fought to please God and to reform the lax behavior of the Muslim Hausa peoples. His writings are full of criticisms of the Hausa's careless religious practices as well as their high taxes, forced military service, and neglect of the rural peoples under Hausa control.

Uthman dan Fodio's revolution was successful. By the time of his death in 1817, he had established an empire over the disunited Hausa city-states. The capital was at Sokoto [sə kō′-tō], and its ruler took the title of Sultan, as Muslim rulers of large territories were called all over the Islamic world. The Sultan of Sokoto believed in fair rule with no special privileges.

The *jihad* against the Hausa was not the only holy war in the Sudan. Earlier Muslim wars had spread across the western Sudan from the Senegal and Gambia river valleys to the valley of the Niger. New states formed wherever the Muslims were successful. Hundreds of thousands of people were converted to Islam in these *jihads,* and others who were already Muslim became increasingly devout. Uthman dan Fodio's *jihad* was one of the last and most successful. The warfare of this completely African revolution did not end until the late 19th century.

SECTION REVIEW **4**

1. How did Islam spread to the peoples of Kanem-Bornu? To the Hausa? p. 249
2. What was unusual about Idris Alooma's army? p. 250
3. Name five items traded by the Hausa. p. 251
4. What were Uthman dan Fodio's reasons for leading his people against the Hausa? p. 251

5 The forest states developed strong governments

The forest states of Benin, Dahomey, Kongo, and Asante flourished on agriculture and trade. One kind of trade, the trade in human beings, became a great source of wealth for these states. As the demand for cheap labor on the plantations of the West Indies increased, slave raids in Africa took an enormous toll. Eventually, the slave trade was stopped. Efficient governments continued to keep the forest states strong until the European conquests of the 19th century.

Strong kings helped Benin grow wealthy and powerful. The forest state of Benin, located in what is now southern Nigeria, had kings, called *Obas*. The first Oba [ō′bə] lived some time in the 11th century. Oba Ewedo
ans. 1 [yü wā′dō], who ruled in the 14th century, strengthened the position of the Oba by weakening the power of the council of elders who helped him rule. Ewedo built a new capital, which he called Benin.

A 15th-century Oba, Eware [yü wä′rē] the Great, increased the strength of the Benin army. With this more powerful army, he expanded the state by conquering many villages in the area. He fortified the city of Benin with high wooden walls.

The Obas of Benin were religious rulers. They
ans. 1 were responsible for all religious ceremonies and prayed to the gods for Benin's welfare. The reigns of the Obas were recorded on cast bronze plaques that were hung on the palace walls. Many of these have been preserved, and they give historians details about Benin's past.

Europeans arrived in West Africa. In the late 15th century, sailors from Portugal came to the coasts of West Africa looking for places to ans. 2
trade their country's manufactured goods. They brought muskets and metal utensils in exchange for gold and spices. The first visit of a Portuguese ship to Benin was in 1472.

By 1500, the English, French, and Dutch were also trading with Benin. Benin regulated trade with the Europeans. The foreign traders had to pay port taxes and import duties. They could only trade with chosen representatives of the Oba. Europeans were not allowed to live in Benin. They could visit it for a short time, but had to live on their ships anchored off the coast.

The Europeans brought new foods to Africa. ans. 2
The Portuguese brought corn and cassava (a plant from which tapioca is made) from their colonies in the Americas. These foods grew so well in the African forest that within fifty years they had become staple items in the forest peoples' diet. The population increased as a result.

Many small forest states close to the coast traded with the Europeans. Through this trade, these forest states grew rich and powerful.

Slave trade produced wealth for the cities and terror in the countryside. African states had always had a form of domestic slavery based on prisoners of war, debtors, and convicts. In addition, there was some international trade in slaves in the Muslim cities. But this slave trade was not based on race; both light- and dark-skinned people were offered for sale in slave markets. And slaves were not used as the basis of plantation labor. Slaves were usually treated well, though often underfed. And some were able to gain freedom through hard work and marriage into free families. Some slaves even became advisers to kings.

By the 16th century, the Europeans had ans. 3
begun sugar plantations in the West Indies.

Armed with rifles, African slave traders wipe out a village's defenses and capture the population.

They needed large numbers of slaves to work these plantations. These slaves were treated very cruelly and had almost no chance of gaining freedom. The Europeans came to the markets of West Africa to buy their slaves.

Many West African states, such as Benin, Dahomey [də hō′mē], and Asante [ə sän′tē] kept strict control over the slave trade in their countries. They made certain the Europeans did not leave the coast and capture slaves for themselves. These states grew very rich from the sale of captives from the interior.

African merchants raided isolated villages and kidnaped anyone they could find. Most of the peoples who fell victim to the slave raiders did not have centralized governments to help protect them. Villages posted children in trees to act as lookouts for slave raiders.

● Encourage students to express their feelings about what is shown in the picture and the slave trade itself.

● The slave trade was made illegal in the U.S. and in Britain's colonies in 1807. Slavery was abolished in Britain's colonies in 1833, the U.S. in 1865, in Brazil by 1888.

In some regions, such as the Kongo, so many people were enslaved and taken to the Americas that the population became dangerously small. In Benin, the slave merchants bought guns and challenged the Oba's army. The power of the Oba began to lessen. The people grew frightened. Taxes did not come in regularly. And laws could not be enforced. Not until early in the 19th century was anti-slavery sentiment in America and Europe strong enough to finally put a stop to the slave trade. ■

ans. 4

Trade, taxes, and good government made Asante a strong state. About 1670, two great leaders united the many small clans who lived in the Asante forest. They were Osei Tutu [ô′sā tü′tü], the first king of Asante and his friend the priest Okomfo Anokye [ō kōm′fō ə nō′chē]. Together they persuaded the clans to settle their differences and form a union. The union was then represented by a Golden Stool that Okomfo Anokye brought out and said had been sent from God.

The Golden Stool, a low wooden seat covered with gold, was a state symbol much like flags are to modern nations. It was displayed on official occasions. No one was allowed to sit on it except the king at a festival once a year. Kings could die or be removed from office, but the Golden Stool remained to represent the collective nation of Asante.

To further cement the new union, Okomfo Anoyke introduced certain laws and customs. One famous rule stated that no Asante could talk about the place his or her relatives came from. Thus, all Asantes would remember that they were Asante first and persons of a certain town or clan second. An idea of citizenship was formed.

A well-organized army helped Asante expand. All men could be called up for military service. And every clan and village had its assigned place in the army. There were orderly ranks for officers and systematic methods for giving orders in the field. Under the leadership of two kings, Opoku Ware (1710–1750) and Osei Bonsu (1801–1824), Asante conquered a large empire covering almost the same area as the modern nation of Ghana. The newly conquered peoples were expected to pay taxes to the Golden Stool in return for the benefits of law courts, protection, and good roads that the Asante government provided.

Trade in gold, kola nuts, and slaves gave Asante a good tax base. A bureaucracy of officials chosen for ability rather than noble birth or wealth managed the governing of the empire. This system had two advantages over government by an all-powerful king: (1) government could continue to operate even when the king died or was removed from office; (2) the bureaucratic departments accomplished more jobs than one king could do by himself. One department made certain that taxes were paid. Another was responsible for seeing that messages got through. A different department saw that appeals from court cases were heard. Yet another enforced trade regulations with foreigners. One department kept the roads throughout the empire clear and safe for travelers. It enforced a law in the capital city of Kumasi [kü mä′sē] requiring persons to burn their garbage behind their houses every morning.

Asante was eventually conquered by the British in 1896 after several wars and the loss of many lives on both sides. But Asante was never destroyed. There is still a king who appears publicly with his court and the Golden Stool. He has his own judicial court and is influential in the politics of modern Ghana.

SECTION REVIEW **5**

1. How was the government of Benin strengthened in the 14th and 15th centuries? How was Benin's history recorded? p. 252

2. What new products were brought to Africa by European traders? Name at least four. What four European countries traded with the West African coast? p. 252

3. Why did the Europeans want slaves? How did the slave trade affect the forest states with strong governments? What happened in the isolated villages in the interior? p. 252 253

4. What differences in the governments of Benin and Asante might account for one of them growing weaker after the slave trade and the other continuing in strength? p. 253 254

CHAPTER REVIEW 13

SECTION SUMMARIES

1. Famous empires grew in the West African savanna. Ancient Ghana, Mali, and Songhai were three empires in the western savanna from the 9th through the 16th centuries. They were based on the gold and salt trade across the Sahara. They were wealthy empires, and their armies and governments controlled large areas. Cities of these empires, such as Timbuktu, became centers of scholarship in the 14th and 15th centuries.

2. City-states flourished along the East African coast. From the 7th through the 14th centuries, trading ships from Arabia, India, and China carried on a lively trade with the East African coast. Thriving city-states grew up there. These cities were inhabited by Africans and Asians. The combination of peoples gave rise to Swahili culture, which had its own language and tolerated many religions and lifestyles. The Portuguese destroyed much of the East African trade after 1500.

3. The kingdom of Zimbabwe developed in the interior. In the interior of East Africa, other states were developing from the 11th century on. One was Zimbabwe. The extensive ruins of large stone buildings are evidence of the power and sophistication of this kingdom was based on gold.

4. Islam stimulated new states in West Africa. Islam had a strong effect on West Africa as well as the Middle East. The rulers of Mali, Songhai, and Kanem-Bornu had been Muslims. In the 17th and 18th centuries, waves of Muslim reform movements spread over West Africa. Large numbers of the common people were converted to Islam, and small Islamic states were formed. Uthman dan Fodio united the Hausa states in one of these holy wars in 1801.

5. The forest states developed strong governments. States such as Benin had begun to grow in the forests by the 11th century. The arrival in the 1400s of the Europeans in search of trade and slaves, and the foods brought from the Americas by the Portuguese, caused more states to expand and grow rich. However, the slave trade did much damage to many African communities until it was stopped in the 19th century. Complex governments like that of Asante developed in spite of the slave trade.

WHO? WHAT? WHEN? WHERE?

1. Make timelines charting the development of these African empires:

Ghana p. 241	Zimbabwe p. 248, 249
Mali p. 242	Kanem-Bornu p. 249
Songhai p. 243	Benin p. 252

2. Explain the importance of these groups in Africa's history:

Bantu p. 248	Muslims 249, 251	Fulani p. 251
Hausa p. 249	Portuguese p. 246	Asante p. 253, 254
Swahili p. 246	Zulu p. 249	Almoravids p. 241

3. Write identifying sentences for these individuals:

Sundiata p. 242	Askia Mohammad p. 243
Mansa Musa p. 243	Vasco da Gama p. 246
Ibn Batuta p. 243	Idris Alooma p. 250
Sonni Ali p. 243	Uthman dan Fodio p. 251
Okomfo Anokye p. 254	Opoku Ware p. 254

4. What did these terms mean to early Africa?

silent trade p. 240	Oba p. 252
Guinea gold p. 243	Golden Stool p. 254
jihad p. 251	monsoon p. 245

5. Describe the trading systems of early Africa: list the items traded, the states involved in the trade, the effect of the trade on the peoples of Africa.

QUESTIONS FOR CRITICAL THINKING

1. Why were gold and salt so important in early African trade? What do you feel are the most im-

5. Answers will vary.

QUESTIONS FOR CRITICAL THINKING:

1. Gold has always been valued by people and their governments as a symbol of wealth. Salt is a vital element in people's diet. The rest of this question asks for students' opinions.

portant items of trade today? What nations or regions are involved in this trade?
2. In what way was Swahili an international culture? What are some cultures today that are international? Explain your ideas.
3. Why and how did the Portuguese destroy East African trade? Do you think this was right?
4. In what ways was the slave trade harmful to some African states? Which ones?
5. Why do you think African kings cooperated with European slave traders?

ACTIVITIES

1. Draw a map of the African continent. Outline and label the modern nations of Africa. Show where these ancient states were located: Ghana, Mali, Songhai, Kanem-Bornu, Sokoto, Kilwa, Malindi, Mombasa, Zimbabwe, Benin, Asante, Dahomey, and Kongo. Show important rivers.
2. If Uthman dan Fodio were a member of your community, what would he find to criticize? Give a speech he might make telling why a religious war is necessary.
3. Suppose you were the king of a country that controlled a resource (like gold) wanted by people in other nations. What rules would you make for trade? Why? What would be the effect of those rules on the growth and wealth of your nation?
4. Use magazines and newspapers to do research on your country's trade relations with the oil-producing nations of Africa and the Middle East. How are modern trade regulations similar to ancient ones? How are they different?
5. Pretend you are Ibn Batuta visiting your town. Write a page in your diary telling what you see. Include things that make outstanding impressions, such as strange customs you observe. Is it a rich place? A poor place? What do you think of the manners and food of the people you meet?

2. Swahili culture was a combination of cultures from different countries, India, Arabia and southern Africa. Likewise the cultures of the Americas are international.

3. and 4. In addition to the factual information asked for encourage students to make value judgments on the slave trade as practiced by the Portuguese and traders.

5. Answers will vary.

CHAPTER TEST 13

SECTION 1

1. True or false: The ancient Romans knew that gold was mined in West Africa.
2. The silent traders exchanged salt for gold.
3. Mansa Musa's religion was: a. Christian, b. tribal, c. Muslim

SECTION 2

4. Indian travelers to Africa were helped by winds called monsoons or trade winds
5. True or false: Chinese homes displayed very old African dishes.
6. The culture that is a blend of African, Indian, and Arab is called: a. Benin, b. Swahili, c. Hausa

SECTION 3

7. True or false: Portuguese traders were frequent visitors to Zimbabwe.
8. The buildings at Zimbabwe were built by the: a. Shona, b. Swahili, c. Benin
9. Zimbabwe was destroyed in the year: a. 1865, b. 1885, c. 1830

SECTION 4

10. True or false: Idris Alooma was famous because he allowed freedom of religion in his kingdom.
11. The army of Kanem-Bornu was trained by experts from: a. India, b. Turkey, c. China
12. Many Africans were converted to Islam through: a. *jihads,* b. missionary work, c. bribery

SECTION 5

13. The history of Benin can be seen on: a. rock paintings, b. bronze plaques, c. stone carvings
14. True or false: White Europeans entered African villages and captured many slaves.
15. True or false: Slavery had harmful consequences everywhere in Africa.

3000 B.C.–
1500 A.D.

CHAPTER
14

Early Cultures in America

The ruins of Machu Picchu stand on a ridge between two mountains in the Andes, silent testimony to a once-mighty empire. This Inca city was built after an earthquake in 1440 destroyed the original city. Other engineering feats of the Incas included paved roads and suspension bridges.

High in the Andes Mountains in Peru, almost always shrouded in cold mist, stands Machu Picchu [mä′chü pēk′chü], the deserted ruins of the last center of Inca civilization. This mountain fortress is believed to have been the last hiding place of the Inca nobles who fled the Spanish conquerors in the sixteenth century. No one knows how long the Inca nobles or their descendants might have remained there. Machu Picchu lay hidden away and forgotten for centuries, until it was discovered in 1911 by the North American archaeologist Hiram Bingham.

Who were the Incas? Before the Spanish conquest, they ruled over the largest empire in all the Americas. At its height, the Inca Empire stretched from Ecuador to central Chile—more than 2,500 miles (4,167 kilometers).

How did the Incas keep control over so vast an area? The secret of their success is partly revealed in the following excerpt, written by a Spaniard who traveled widely in Peru in the 1530s and 1540s and interviewed many Incas.

> So great was the veneration that the people felt for their [Inca] princes, throughout this vast region, that every district was as well regulated and governed as if the lord was actually present to chastise those who acted contrary to his rules. This fear arose from the known valour of the lords and their strict justice. It was felt to be certain that those who did evil would receive punishment without fail, and that neither prayers nor bribes would avert it. At the same time, the Incas always did good to those who were under their sway, and would not allow them to be ill-treated, nor that too much tribute should be exacted from them.

Besides the Incas, there were many other Indian cultures in North and South America. Most cultures north of the Rio Grande (now the border between Mexico and the United States) were based on hunting, fishing, and food gathering and did not develop cities. South of the Rio Grande, two major civilizations in addition to that of the Incas developed—that of the Mayas in the Yucatan region and that of the Aztecs in central Mexico. This chapter tells how:

Olmec civilization (Mexico, 800 B.C.—A.D. 200) produced this jade *werejaguar* (half jaguar, half human).

1. American Indian cultures developed over many centuries.

2. The Mayas achieved a most complex civilization.

3. The Aztecs conquered much of central Mexico.

4. The Incas controlled a vast empire in South America.

5. Indians had distinctive customs.

1 American Indian culture developed over many centuries

When Columbus reached the Caribbean islands at the end of the 15th century, he mistakenly called the people he met "Indians," because he thought he had landed in the Indies in Asia. But the lands and people he found were not a part of the "Old World." Columbus had landed in a "New World" that had a long and complex history of its own. ans. 1

We know very little of this history. Most of the Indian cultures were destroyed or greatly weakened by contact with Europeans. For example, the Spanish conquerors of Latin America killed ● many of the Indian leaders, tore down their temples, and burned their books. Very few Indian writings have survived. From these and from the not-always-trustworthy accounts of Indian life written by European conquerors has come knowledge of 16th-century American cultures. Archaeologists know about earlier periods by studying the many artifacts left by early cultures. Of course, archaeologists are constantly uncovering evidence. Knowledge of ancient ■ American cultures is constantly being revised.

● The Spanish conquerors were convinced that the idols and writings of the Indians were works of the devil.

■ Key Concept: The destruction of Indian cultures has left us with an incomplete knowledge of pre-Columbian America.

EARLY GOVERNMENTS
IN THE AMERICAS
ESKIMO
Bering Strait
NORTH PACIFIC
COAST TRIBES
1300s–1800s A.D.
PLAINS
INDIANS
IROQUOIS
1000s–1600s A.D.
NORTH AMERICA
Mesa Verde
PUEBLOS
about 500—1690 A.D.
Rio Grande
MEXICO
TOLTECS
about 700—1200 A.D.
Chichen Itza
YUCATAN
MAYAS
about 500 B.C.—1200 A.D.
Tenochtitlan
AZTECS
1200s–1520 A.D.
OLMEC
CENTRAL
AMERICA
Caribbean Sea
ATLANTIC
OCEAN
TROPIC OF CANCER
EQUATOR
PACIFIC
OCEAN
ANDES MTS.
SOUTH AMERICA
INCAS
1000s–1532 A.D.
Machu Picchu
Cuzco
Lake Titicaca
Tiahuanaco
100–900 A.D.
TROPIC OF CAPRICORN
0 250 500 1000 MILES
0 250 500 1000 KILOMETERS
45°
30°
15°
0°
15°
30°
45°
120°
105°
90°
75°
60°
45°
30°

The first American Indians probably came from Asia. Archaeologists believe that people have been living in the Americas as long as ans. 1 10 to 30 thousand years. The first Americans probably came from Asia in many separate migrations over a long period of time. They may have come over the Bering Strait between Siberia and Alaska. The prehistoric people of the Americas had fire, stone tools, skin clothing, and the domesticated dog. Most of them lived as hunters or gatherers. During the centuries before the coming of the Europeans, descendants of these people settled in most areas of North and South America.

Most evidence indicates that the American Indians were isolated from the civilizations of the Old World. Some scholars believe, however, that daring seafarers crossed the Pacific or Atlantic oceans to America centuries before the Vikings or Columbus. (See page 386.) Other authorities believe that the Indians developed their cultures independently. They maintain that similar inventions in the Eastern and Western Hemispheres indicate only that peoples often hit upon similar ideas when they face the same kinds of problems.

Farming changed Indian life. Perhaps as early as 7000 B.C., some Indians learned to ans. 2 grow crops. As time passed, the people developed new varieties of plant life. The most important of these was corn, which was developed about 3000 B.C. in Central America. Corn became as important in the Western Hemisphere as wheat was in the Eastern Hemisphere. Farming made it possible for people in America to settle in communities, to develop such skills as weaving and pottery making, and to set up a division of labor. These skills spread slowly throughout the Americas.

North American Indians had a variety of cultures. As people everywhere had done, the Indians of North America learned to live with

North American Indians produced widely differing styles in art and architecture. *Left* are the remains of an 8-story Pueblo city at Mesa Verde; *below:* a painted wooden mask of the Northwest Indians.

their environment. Since the climate and geography of the huge North American continent is so varied, Indians in different parts of the continent developed different cultures.

ans. 3 Eskimos lived in the frozen lands of the extreme north. The short growing season made it impossible to grow crops. Instead, the Eskimos fished and hunted for food, particularly walrus, whales, seals, small fish, and caribou. They used the bone and ivory of some of these animals to make tools such as needles, knives, fishhooks, and harpoons. With the skins they made clothing and tents. They also learned to build houses out of snow and ice. Eskimos lived in small family groups and never needed to develop a central government. The resources of the extreme north were not great enough to support a large, centralized population.

Farther south, in a heavily forested area that reached from southern Alaska to the present state of Washington, lived the North Pacific coast Indians. Like the Eskimos, they hunted and fished for food. But they also gathered wild berries from the forest. And, unlike the Eskimos, these Indians lived in villages. From the many woods available in the forests, they built wooden houses.

In front of their home, each family put up a *totem pole.* These wooden poles were carved with the figures of an animal whose spirit was considered special to the family. The totems identified families as belonging to the Beaver people, the Bear people, and so on. Strangers with the same totem were always welcome.

North Pacific tribes were divided into nobles, common people, and slaves, whom they captured from other tribes. One important custom of the nobles was a ceremony called *potlatch.* On major occasions, particularly those marking events in their children's lives, such as the day a daughter gathered her first berries, noble families would give a great feast. At the feast, the family would give away its most prized and beautiful possessions because it was considered a greater virtue "to give rather than to receive."

In the eastern part of the continent in the northeast woodlands, the Indians were not only hunters but also farmers. They lived in villages and built long, oval-shaped houses called wigwams out of poles covered with bark and skins.

Five Woodland tribes—the Seneca, Cayuga, Onondaga, Oneida, and Mohawk—formed a ans. 4
confederation called the League of the Iroquois, or the Five Nations. Through this political organization, the five tribes acted together on matters of common interest. Rivalry among them was strong and frequently erupted in war. By the 1700s, the League controlled an area from Lake Michigan to the Atlantic and from the St. Lawrence River to the Tennessee River.

Before the 1600s, most of the Indians who lived on the Great Plains in the central part of the North American continent made a living as farmers. After the Spanish brought horses to America, the Indians, such as the Sioux and the Cheyenne, became buffalo hunters.

Pueblo Indians lived in cities. One of the oldest and most complex cultures north of the Rio Grande was that of the Pueblo tribes in what is now the southwestern United States. They used adobe [ə dō′bē], or sun-dried clay, to build several-storied houses that have been •
called the first American apartment buildings. In the Pueblo form of government, the people chose their own chiefs. These chiefs, in turn, were advised by a council of elders. No action could be taken unless all these leaders agreed.

Pueblo Indians were master farmers who developed a complex system of irrigation ca-

• See the picture on the facing page.

nals. Their main crop was corn. But they also gathered seeds and berries. As a safeguard against drought, each family carefully built up a supply of food that was held in reserve. The Pueblo Indians produced excellent pottery, beautifully decorated blankets with geometric designs, and finely woven baskets.

Pueblo Indians, which included the Hopi and Zuni, were peaceful people. They fought wars rarely and only when necessary for survival. ● Returning warriors had to go through a long ritual to get rid of their "madness." The religion of the Pueblo Indians taught that people should live in harmony with nature, that they should respect the life of others and the traditions of the past, and that they should do things in moderation.

SECTION REVIEW 1

p. 260 **1.** Where did the American Indian peoples originate?
p. 258 Why is the term "Indian" not correct when used to describe the first people of the Americas?

p. 260 **2.** When was farming started by early Americans?

p. 261 **3.** What were some differences between the cultures of the Eskimo and North Pacific Coast Indians? What did geography have to do with their cultural differences?

p. 261 **4.** How were the people of the Five Nations different from those of the Pueblo?

2 The Mayas achieved a most complex civilization

Indians in Mexico and in Central and South America built more complex civilizations than their neighbors to the north. They began their development at about the time the Hans of China and the Romans were building their empires thousands of miles away. The Mayas in the Yucatan Peninsula, the Aztecs of central Mexico, and the Incas in Peru had civilizations that in many respects rivaled those of ancient Egypt and Mesopotamia.

● Ask students what they think is meant by this statement. Could this practice have value today after wars?

These cultures of the south developed further than those of the north probably because they had learned earlier how to raise corn. As a result, they had lived in one place for longer periods than the northern Indians. This allowed for more time to develop skills.

Mayan culture had two main periods. Beginning about 500 B.C., the Mayan Indians developed a high culture located chiefly in the ans. 1
peninsula of Yucatan (present-day southeastern Mexico, Belize, and Guatemala). By 1 A.D., the Mayas had writing, a system of numbers, and a very accurate calendar. These were impressive cultural achievements. By 300 A.D., in Honduras, north Guatemala, and nearby areas of Mexico, the Mayas had established a distinctive civilization. Its early phase, which lasted until the 9th century, is called the *Classic* period, or *Old Empire.* During this time, the Mayas built several cities and perfected their arts, science, and learning. Then, in the 800s, the people began to abandon these centers. Why they left remains a mystery. Some scholars have guessed that the population grew too great for the food supply. Others have suggested that epidemics and wars may have killed off many people.

After the Old Empire crumbled, large numbers of Mayas evidently moved northward and built new cities in the northern tip of the Yucatan Peninsula. Around these new centers grew up city-states somewhat similar to those of ancient Greece. Some scholars believe that the Mayan governments were theocratic since Mayan life

Mayan astronomers studied the stars and planets from observatories like this one at Chichen Itza.

Mayan weavers were specially trained and protected by a goddess. It was a solemn occupation.

seems to have been dominated by priests. This later Mayan phase, usually called the *Post-Classic* period or *New Empire*, flourished from about 900 to 1200 A.D. It is characterized by new cultural influences, particularly the worship of a a feathered serpent god that probably began with a northern tribe called the Toltecs. (ans. 1)

Toltec warriors conquered the Mayas of Yucatan in the 12th century and remained in control for about 200 years. During this time, the Mayan city-states seem to have gone into a long period of decline. Certainly, their cities were not as well built or as beautifully decorated as they had been in earlier times. But some scholars think the Maya were simply focusing their attention on economic activities such as trade rather than on religious affairs. At any rate, when the Spanish came to America in the early 16th century, most of the great Mayan cities of the Post-Classic period were no longer occupied and had long been covered by the rain forest.

● Ask students if they can see the relationship between the astronomical observatories and their other achievements, for example, their calender.

Mayan cities were trade and religious centers. Most Mayas were corn farmers who lived in thatched huts on the outskirts of cities. These cities were chiefly religious centers with huge stone pyramids, astronomical observatories, temples, and monuments. When a religious ceremony was to be held, the people would come in from the nearby farm villages and gather in the great stone buildings. (ans. 2) ●

Each city usually had a market square. There merchants and shoppers carried on business. People made cotton cloth and pottery at home and then brought their products to the central market to sell. Traders set up booths to display carved jade, jewelry made of shells, and brilliant feather headdresses to be used for special ceremonies. Women ran restaurant stalls where they served hot tortillas [tôr tē′yəs] and beans.

Mayan cities also had large stone ballcourts. In these courts, a very serious game was played by two teams. Players had to hit a large rubber ball with their elbows, hips, or knees and try to get it through vertical stone or wooden rings twenty feet above the ground. Some scholars believe the ball represented the sun and that the two teams fought a symbolic struggle between the forces of light and darkness, or life and death. There is some evidence that the losing team was offered up as a sacrifice to the Mayan gods.

The Mayas excelled in many fields. In the
ans. 3 field of the arts, Mayan architecture and sculpture were outstanding. The commonest type of building looked like a pyramid but had a flat top. The whole structure was faced with limestone. On top was a temple. All over the building were carved stone figures. Inside it were brightly colored murals.

ans. 3 The Mayas developed an *ideographic* system of writing in which symbols stood for ideas. Scholars have not yet learned to read it except for some of the symbols that stand for gods, stars, and dates. The Mayas produced paper from bark or tough fibers of the maguey [mag′wā] cactus and used it to make folding books. But the Spanish conquerors destroyed all but three of these.

ans. 3 Perhaps the Mayas' greatest accomplishment was their calendar. Mayan astronomers discovered that the year was slightly less than 365¼
● days long.

ans. 3 The Mayas were also skilled in mathematics. They worked out a system of numbers that included the idea of zero. The Mayan zeros looked like this: [zero symbol] Numbers up to nineteen were made by adding ones and fives. For example:

•	•••	—	•• —	•••• ≡
1	3	5	7	19

The number system was based on the number *20.* That is, zero at the end of a number meant twenty times the number before it.

Twenty is [• over zero symbol] or 1 x20 = 20   Two hundred is [= over zero symbol] or 10 x20 = 200

● In the 12th century the Arabs had a calendar more accurate than the one we use today.

SECTION REVIEW 2

1. Where did the Mayan civilization develop? What do scholars call its major phases? p. 262, 263
2. Describe three activities that took place in Mayan cities. Where did most of the people live? What was their main occupation? p. 263
3. Name four accomplishments of the Mayan civilization. p. 264

The Aztec god Xolotl, shown as a skeleton, guided the dead on their dangerous journey.

3 The Aztecs conquered much of central Mexico

North of the Mayas lived other Indian peoples. Some of them gradually extended their power and influence through military conquest. Among these were the early Toltecs, who laid a cultural foundation upon which the Aztecs later built a large empire.

The Toltecs preceded the Aztecs. At the time of the Mayan Old Empire, the Toltec Indians began to develop a culture of their own in central Mexico, near present-day Mexico City. They had come from the north about the 1st century A.D. By 700, the Toltecs were building great pyramids. Between 900 and 1200, the Toltecs were at the height of their development.

The Aztecs built a great city. In the 13th century, a warlike Indian people swept into central Mexico from the northwest. They called themselves Aztecs, which probably refers to their original name, *Aztlan,* meaning "White Land." Scholars think Aztlan may be what is now New Mexico or Arizona.

The Aztecs eventually conquered the Toltecs and many other neighboring tribes. Since the Aztecs also called themselves *Mexica* people, the lands they conquered eventually came to be known as Mexico. Aztec power reached its height during the 15th and early 16th centuries.

ans. 1 The center of the Aztec empire was their city of Tenochtitlan [tä nōch′tē tlän′], which was probably built about 1325. According to legend, the Aztecs decided to locate their capital where they saw a heaven-sent eagle, with a snake in its beak, sitting on a cactus growing from a rock in a lake. (This scene is pictured on the flag of modern-day Mexico, and Mexico City now stands on the ancient site of Tenochtitlan and the vanished lake.)

Tenochtitlan prospered and probably had a population of 400,000 by the early 15th century. The setting of this city was magnificent. It lay out in the water, on islands and land reclaimed from the shallow lake. There were canals between the islands. A visitor could enter the heart of the city either by canoe or by walking over one of the long stone causeways that connected the central city to the mainland.

Striking features of Tenochtitlan were the great temples and pyramids that stood in the city square. Near the temples were ball courts, where the Aztecs played a ball game of religious significance similar to that of the Mayas. Most of the people lived in adobe houses, which they painted white and then trimmed in bright colors.

There were several great marketplaces in Tenochtitlan. In one section fruits and vegetables were for sale, in other cloth and ready-to-wear clothing. There were also booths that sold delicate jewelry made of jade, shell, and turquoise. Customers either traded items by barter or paid for them with cacao [kə kä′ō] beans—the source of chocolate—which were used as a kind of money.

The Aztecs ruled an empire. The Aztecs did not destroy the tribes they conquered. Instead, they ruled over them and forced them to pay tribute. Payments were made in cacao beans, deer hides, conch shells, and bolts of cotton cloth. A kind of picture writing was used to record these payments. By 1500, the city of Tenochtitlan was the center of an empire that included at least 5 million people. Most of these people were farmers.

The head of the Aztec government was called the Chief of Men. At the time the Spanish ar-

In a blood sacrifice to the gods, an Aztec priest cuts out the heart of a prisoner.

rived, the Aztec leader was Montezuma. Although the Chief of Men was looked upon almost as a god, many nobles, merchants, and leaders had nearly as much power.

● **Young people were strictly educated.** At the age of 15, the sons of nobles and rich merchants began to study at the "house of youth."
ans. 2 They trained to become warriors or priests, the two most important professions in Aztec life. At these schools, they learned how to use weapons, studied religious rites and duties, learned Aztec history, and were trained in arts and crafts. Aztec history was written on long strips of paper. These were folded like a fan to make a book called a *codex*. Priests also taught the boys Aztec rules of good conduct, such as "never tell lies" and "console the poor and unfortunate." Even boys from poor Aztec families had a chance to become army officers, landholders, or government officials.

● This material can help in discussing the values of these early native Americans.

Some young women were trained to become ans. 2
priests and to take part in temple ceremonies. Others took charge of booths in the markets, watched over the production and sale of crops, or ran households. Aztec mothers taught their girls to be respectful daughters and faithful wives. One Aztec mother advised her daughter to "take care that your garments are decent and proper; and . . . do not adorn yourself with much finery, since this is a mark of vanity and folly."

Aztec girls married at 16 and the boys at 20. Parents arranged the marriage and at the time of ceremony a feast was held. There were many presents and much drinking and dancing.

Religion and war dominated Aztec life. ans. 3 The Aztecs had many gods. Huitzilopochtli [wēt′zēl ō potch′tlē], the god of the sun and god of war was one. Another important one was Tlaloc [tlä′lok], the rain god. A third important god was Quetzalcoatl [ket′säl kō′ə tl], represented in the form of a feathered snake. The Aztec believed the world had been created and destroyed four times. The fifth and present creation of the world was the result of Quetzalcoatl's sacrifice of his own blood. To keep the universe ● alive, then, the Aztecs believed that it was necessary to make continual human sacrifices.

The Aztecs needed large numbers of prisoners for these sacrifices. This was one reason they were almost always at war with other Indian tribes. There was deep bitterness among the subject peoples from whom the Aztecs constantly demanded victims to be sacrificed on the temple-pyramids of Tenochtitlan.

By the time a small band of Spaniards landed in Mexico in 1519 in search of gold, many conquered Indian tribes were ready to turn against their Aztec masters.

SECTION REVIEW 3

p. 267 **1.** When was Tenochtitlan built? What city now stands there?

p. 267 **2.** What was the purpose of the education of Aztec boys and girls? What opportunities were available to Aztec boys from poor families?

p. 268 **3.** What kinds of gods did the Aztecs have? Why did the Aztecs sacrifice humans?

■ **4.** What were two major cultural achievements of the Aztecs?

● Help students to understand that the Aztecs really believed the sacrifices were necessary to keep the universe alive.

■ Answers may vary. The cities, writing, government, education, are some possible answers.

4 The Incas controlled a vast empire in South America

Far to the south of the Mayas and Aztecs, various groups of Indians lived in the Andes Mountains and Pacific Coast regions of South America. Between 100 A.D. and 400 A.D., some of these people began to develop high cultures.

The Tiahuanaco culture developed in the Andes Mountains. High in the Andes, near the shores of Lake Titicaca [tit′i kä′kä], lies a mass of gigantic stones—the ruins of Tiahuanaco [tē′ə wä nä′kō]. Like Mohenjo-Daro in India, the name of this site means "the place of the dead." Evidence indicates that this was a religious center.

Little is known about the people who lived in ans. 1 the Tiahuanaco region. But they were skillful builders. Some of the stone slabs they worked at the Tiahuanaco site weigh 200 tons (180 megagrams or metric tons). These blocks were fitted together tightly without mortar.

Archaeologists do not know what caused the end of the Tiahuanaco culture. It apparently died out around 900 A.D. Some of its cultural achievements, however, were not forgotten and were evidently passed on to later peoples.

The Incas unified an extensive empire. A few centuries after the decline of Tiahuanaco, a people of the Peruvian mountains began to develop a distinctive way of life. The ruler of these people was known as the *Inca*. This term has since been applied to the entire group.

Around the 11th century, the Incas settled in a valley of the Andes. They eventually conquered the Indians there and set up a capital city called Cuzco [küs′ko], which means "navel of the Earth." The Incas soon expanded their rule

Geography: A Key to History

Climate and Population in South America

Before 1500, most of the people of South America lived in highland settlements. The climate in the hills and mountains was generally more attractive than that in the lowlands. The highlands favored the development of agriculture, which is necessary to civilization.

Most of South America lies near the Equator or the Tropic of Capricorn. In general, the lowlands in such latitudes are hot all year because they get a great deal of direct sunlight every day. In the highlands, however, the heat of the sun's rays is offset by the altitude. The higher the elevation, the cooler the air.

The most important highlands in South America are the Andes. These mountains parallel the Pacific Coast in an almost unbroken chain from north to south.

Among the mountain ranges of the Andes are valleys, basins, and plateaus. In some of these areas, the combination of sun, rain, and temperature was just right for the growing of staple crops. No wonder these places have been inhabited for thousands of years.

By contrast, the lowlands of South America were only lightly populated until about 300 years ago. Muggy rain forests of the Amazon River Basin cover most of the northern third of the continent.

Like the rain forests of Africa, those of the Amazon Basin are lush with plant growth. It is not easy to farm in these areas, however. They are too wet for such crops as corn. Clearing the forest is a difficult task. And heavy rains rapidly wash away nutrients in the soil.

The people who first settled in the rain forest lived by hunting and gathering, not by farming. Tropical diseases and the limits of their food production kept the population small.

It has been said that in the rain forest, it is the small animals, not the large ones, that make life miserable. Mosquitoes and other insects are not just pests. They carry diseases, such as malaria and yellow fever, that either kill or greatly weaken humans. These pests are active year-round, since the tropical forest never has a frost that will kill them.

By contrast, the most heavily populated parts of the highlands have just enough cold weather to kill most of the pests. The highlands also have enough hot weather to produce two crops of farm products each year.

to neighboring mountain valleys. By 1400—like the Aztecs far to the north—they were conquering distant regions. By the 16th century, the Incas were ruling an empire of more than 12 million people who spoke 20 different languages and belonged to more than 100 different ethnic groups.

Unlike the Aztecs, the Incas absorbed those they conquered into their own culture. They brought the sons of conquered chiefs to Cuzco and educated them in the Inca schools. In addition, they sent colonies of loyal subjects to live in conquered areas, where they showed the new subjects the Inca way of life.

The Incas held the empire together with highly organized systems of government, communications, and transportation. One great Inca road ran from one end of the empire to the other along the Pacific Coast. Another ran along the crest of the Andes Mountains. Many sections of the roads were paved, and suspension bridges hung over gorges and rivers. These bridges were marvels of engineering for the age in which they were built. Over these roads and bridges, relays of Indian runners rushed messages from one part of the empire to another.

Inca life was carefully regulated. At the head of the Inca government was the emperor, or Inca. He claimed to be a descendant of the sun god and while he lived, he was worshiped. His rule was absolute. As the Inca ruler Atahualpa [ā′tə wäl′pä] said to the Spanish conqueror Francisco Pizarro [pi zär′ō], "In my kingdom no bird flies, no leaf quivers if I do not will it."

The Inca government owned and controlled all means of making and distributing goods. Land belonged to the state and not to those who lived on it. Government officials in Cuzco ans. 3

ROYAL HUNT OF THE SUN

Greedy for Inca gold and silver, ambitious fortune-hunter Francisco Pizarro (Robert Shaw) and his troops clashed with the Incas and their haughty emperor, Atahualpa (Christopher Plummer). Based on Peter Schaffer's play of the same name, the film focuses on the confrontation between these two strong personalities.

kept records of the number of people in every area of the empire. All persons were classified according to their age and ability to work. Most men had to serve in the army and to spend a certain amount of time working on government projects.

ans. 3 The government also regulated the private lives of individuals. If a young man were unmarried by a certain age, he had to choose a wife or take one selected by lot. Every so often, all engaged couples were married at huge state ceremonies held in the name of the Inca. Unlike the Mayas and Aztecs, the Incas had no written language. They kept records on knotted strings called quipus [kē'püz]. Using various kinds and colors of knots, they recorded crop production and other data needed by the Inca government. Only specially trained people could inter-
ans. 2 pret the quipus. Inca history and legends were learned by heart, and then passed down from generation to generation. Most of our information about the Incas comes from this memorized poetry, which was later written down in Spanish.

Incas worked at many occupations. Most Incas were farmers. In the mountainous landscape, they learned to raise crops on terraced hillside plots. Low stone walls kept the dirt from slipping. To water their crops, they built complex irrigation systems. As beasts of burden, the Inca farmers used the llama [lä'mə], a member of the camel family. The chief food crops were corn, white and sweet potatoes, and peanuts. For meat, they raised guinea pigs and ducks. Along the coast, fishing was important.

Some Incas were weavers who made fine ans. 4
cloth. Others made excellent pottery. Incas also worked as miners, digging for gold, silver, and copper. They smelted the ore and designed jewelry for priests and noble families. They also made decorations for temples. The Incas had specially trained surgeons who knew how to set broken bones, perform amputations, and even do brain surgery. For an anesthetic they probably gave the patients coca [kō'kə], a plant from which the drug cocaine is made.

The Incas had no formal schools. But they did train young men of the noble class in warfare and religion. Some were taught how to build. Like the people of Tiahuanaco the Incas were great builders. Some of their temples still stand despite centuries of devastating earthquakes.

Inca ceremonial jugs show a seated god *(left)* and warriors in battle *(center)*. The Inca farmer in the 1580 calendar picture *(right)* irrigates her fields with water from a small stone reservoir.

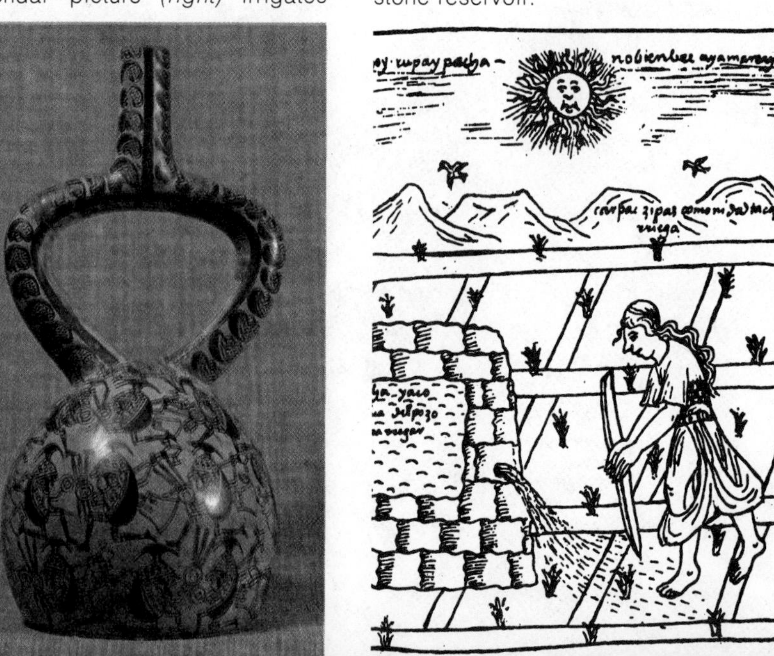

A small number of young women were selected to be Acllacuna [äk′lä kü′nä], "Chosen Women." They were especially trained in religion, weaving, and cooking. Some of them became wives of nobles and others served in the temples.

Like the Aztecs and various other peoples of the Americas, the Incas used human sacrifice. But they limited it to special occasions, for example, when a new emperor was installed or in times of great crisis such as plague or military defeat.

SECTION REVIEW **4**

p. 268 **1.** What is known about the people of Tiahuanaco?
p. 270 **2.** How has Inca history come down to us?
p. 269 **3.** Describe four ways the Incas regulated their
270 empire.
p. 270 **4.** List three major accomplishments of the Incas.

5 Indians had distinctive customs

Out of the thousands of different customs practiced by the many groups of American Indians, some are of special interest. Indian religious beliefs, for example, reveal a great deal about the people who held them. Achievements in various fields indicate their cultural levels and help explain the nature and extent of the Indian contributions to Western civilization.

ans. 1 **Religious practices were important.** Religion was an important influence in the lives of most Indians, and among the Mayas, Aztecs, and Incas, the priests exercised great power. Many American Indians worshiped the sun. Several tribes had other gods that represented something in daily life, such as agriculture or an aspect of nature. Religious ceremonies took place constantly. They were an important part of everyday life.

One of the most important features of Indian religion was human sacrifice. This custom had grown out of the widespread Indian belief that people must give something of great value to the gods in order to receive favors in return. As nothing was more valuable than human life itself, sacrifice took on a noble and holy quality.

Indians stressed group living. Indian life ans. 2
among most groups centered around the tribe
or the clan and not around the individual. Often, ●
the tribe owned all the land and individuals did not own land privately.

Among Indians who farmed for a living, the land was often given out to the people on a more or less equal basis. Upon marriage, every man usually received a plot of land. But this land could be redistributed at any time. For example, the land of an Aztec farmer might, and probably would, be worked by his son after the father's death. Neither the father nor son, however, had the right of private ownership. They could not prevent the village council from giving the land to someone else.

Indian achievements varied. In the field of ans. 3
writing and literature, the Mayas and Aztecs created a system of writing. All American Indian peoples had literature. It was passed on by word of mouth from generation to generation. Most of the literature took the form of poetry and often expressed religious ideas or tribal traditions. Indians also like to tell myths and legends about animals and war.

In arts and crafts, Indians produced very beautiful basketry, weaving, embroidery, metal-

● Students may need help in grasping this idea.

work, painting, sculpture, and architecture. Sculpture decorated temples and palaces. Low-relief carvings adorned walls, illustrating historical events or religious ceremonies. Indians also made fine pottery, especially in what is now the southwestern United States and in Peru. Several of the Latin American tribes excelled in metalwork with gold, silver, and copper.

One serious obstacle to progress in such fields as science and technology was the lack of draft animals. Llamas could only carry light loads, and there were no horses or cattle in America before the coming of Europeans. As a result, Indians had to rely on human power for many difficult and time-consuming tasks. Probably because of the lack of draft animals, the early peoples of America did not develop use of the wheel. We know that they knew about this important principle, for ancient Indian toys with wheels have been found.

Indian contributions enriched world culture. Indian influences are seen in several aspects of American life. Indian names occur throughout the Western Hemisphere. They have been given to countries, provinces, states, towns, cities, rivers, and lakes throughout Canada, the United States, and Latin America. For example, Alaska, Mississippi, Illinois, and Wyoming are among states in the United States that have Indian names.

Some Indian words were adopted into English. For example, *avocado, chocolate, tomato, chili, ocelot,* and *coyote* were all originally Aztec words. Indians also are credited with many im-
ans. 3 portant inventions still in use today. They invented the snowshoe, toboggan, and canoe. In medicine, they first used quinine, cocaine, and the bulb syringe. They first discovered the properties of rubber, developed adobe for building, and invented the game of lacrosse. Indian ingenuity also provided such technical contributions as cochineal [koch′ə nēl′] dye, a red dye made from the dried bodies of an insect, and henequen [hen′ə kin], a fiber from the leaves of a desert plant used for making rope.

The most important contributions of the early ans. 3
peoples of the Americas, however, were in the field of agriculture. Although most of the early Europeans who conquered the Indians had eyes only for the gold and silver they could carry home, it was the humble farm products they took back that made the most lasting impression on world civilization. The Indians were the first to grow corn, potatoes, tomatoes, squash, pumpkins, avocados, and several kinds of beans. From them other peoples of the world also learned about pineapples, strawberries, vanilla, cinnamon, tapioca, and chocolate. Indians were also the first to make maple sugar and to develop chicle [chik′əl], the main ingredient of chewing gum.

All these products greatly increased the quantity and variety of the food supply in Europe and Africa. In Ireland and much of northern Europe, for example, the white potato became a major food crop. And when Europeans began settling in the New World, it was these foods, as well as the farming techniques that the Indians taught them, that made it possible for the European colonists to survive and flourish.

SECTION REVIEW **5**

1. Which social group in Maya, Aztec, and Inca society was probably most important? Why? p. 271

2. In what way was the tribe more important than the individual in Indian life? p. 271

·3. Name at least six contributions Indians made to world civilization. p. 271 272

CHAPTER REVIEW 14

SECTION SUMMARIES

1. American Indian cultures developed over many centuries. The first peoples of North and South America probably came from Asia and spread gradually over two continents. There were many different Indian cultures. Each reflected the way Indians learned to live with their environment, and included Eskimos in the extreme north who were hunters and fishermen, as well as Pueblo Indians in the southwestern United States who were farmers. After the Indians learned to grow corn, they established permanent settlements and developed new skills.

2. The Mayas achieved a most complex civilization. In the Mayan Old Empire, writing was developed, a system of numbers came into use, and a very accurate calendar was invented. Several cities were centers of learning. In the New Empire, city-states were ruled by priests. Toltec warriors conquered the Mayas.

3. The Aztecs conquered much of central Mexico. The Aztecs ruled a vast empire from their capital city of Tenochtitlan. Religion dominated Aztec life, and the Aztecs were frequently at war, capturing victims for their sacrifices.

4. The Incas controlled a vast empire in South America. Tiahuanaco culture developed in the Andes Mountains. The Inca was king, and a highly centralized government took care of all the people's needs.

5. Indians had distinctive customs. The different Indian cultures developed differently. But there are some customs that are similar among them. Religion was important in most cultures. Most Indians valued the group above the individual. And Indian achievements in the arts and handicrafts are among the most beautiful of the world. World culture has been enhanced by Indian contributions, especially in the areas of language and agriculture.

4. The modern nations of the New World are those on the continents of North and South America. Refer students to the modern map on pp. 696–697. Europeans called America the New World because these continents were not part of the world as they knew it. Then they referred to the world they had originally known as the Old World.

WHO? WHAT? WHEN? WHERE?

1. Find the years for these events:

The first people lived in North America 32,000–12,000 B.C.
Wild corn was domesticated 3000 B.C.
The Sioux hunted buffalo 1600s A.D.
The Mayan Old Empire 1–800 A.D.
Mayan cities were abandoned 800s A.D.
The Mayan New Empire 900–1200 A.D.
Aztecs moved into Mexico 1200s A.D.
Toltec culture reached its peak 900–1200 A.D.
Tenochtitlan was built 1325 A.D.
Spaniards landed in Mexico 1519 A.D.
Incas settled in an Andes valley 1000s A.D.
Inca Empire was established 1400–1600 A.D.

2. Write sentences identifying each of these terms with the correct Indian culture:

totem pole p. 261	feathered serpent p. 263, 268
potlatch p. 261	maguey p. 264
wigwam p. 261	pyramid p. 264, 267
Five Nations p. 261	Mexica p. 265
codex p. 267	quipus p. 270

3. To which modern nation or nations would you go to visit the remains of these cultures or cities?

Maya Mexico, Belize, Guatemala	Tenochtitlan Mexico
Cuzco Peru	Pueblo United States
Tiahuanaco Peru	Aztlan United States

4. What are the modern nations of the New World? Why is that term used? What was the Old World?

QUESTIONS FOR CRITICAL THINKING

1. Do you feel that the early Americans developed their cultures on their own? What Indian achievements are so similar to Old World ones that people could believe there was contact between the two "worlds"?

2. What effect has environment had on the development of the cultures of the Eskimo, Maya, Aztec, and Inca peoples? What effect has environment had on your culture?

3. Which do you feel were the most important Indian achievements? Why?

4. Compare the Aztec and Inca methods of controlling their empires. How were the conquered peoples treated in each? What are some advantages and disadvantages of each system?

5. Why do you think the Spanish conquerors destroyed the Mayan writings?

6. How was the Indian system of land-holding different from others? What does the Indian system tell you about their attitude toward the tribe and toward the individual?

ACTIVITIES

1. On a map of the Western Hemisphere, show the territories of the cultures studied in this chapter.

2. Prepare a chart listing contributions of Indians to world culture. Illustrate it with pictures you find in magazines or draw yourself.

3. Write 37 using Mayan numerals. Try writing some others. Can you add or subtract using Mayan numerals? How might you write this equation: 23−3=20?

4. Prepare a menu for a meal using only foods available to the American Indians before 1500.

5. On a map of the world, trace the spread of the use of different foods.

6. Imagine you were an Aztec when the Spanish came. Write a diary account of the actions of the Spanish and the reactions of the Aztec people. Be sure to include your own personal reactions.

QUESTIONS FOR CRITICAL THINKING

1. Opinion.
2. Environment helps determine foods, government, religion; opinion.
3. Opinion.
4. Aztecs kept their conquered peoples separate, demanding tribute, the Incas 'absorbed' theirs; opinion.

CHAPTER TEST **14**

SECTION 1

1. The first people to live in the Americas came from ____Asia____.

2. True or false? Wheat was domesticated in the New World perhaps as early as 4000 B.C.

3. The wooden poles used to identify the spirit belonging to a North Pacific Coast Indian family was called: a. a potlatch, b. a wigwam, c. a totem

SECTION 2

4. The Mayan city-states were like those of ancient: a. Rome, b. Greece, c. China

5. The ball game played in Mayan cities was: a. a religious ceremony, b. a national spectator sport, c. child's play

6. Which of these was not an invention of the Mayas? a. a calendar, b. the codex, c. zero

SECTION 3

7. Mexico City stands where _______ once was: a. Teotihuacan, b. Cuzco, c. Tenochtitlan

8. ___cacao beans___ were used as money in Aztec marketplaces.

9. The Aztecs made many human sacrifices because: a. they did not value human life, b. they believed the gods demanded it, c. they enjoyed killing

SECTION 4

10. True or false? *Tiahuanaco* means "White Land."

11. Inca records were kept by means of: a. a number system based on 20, b. picture writing, c. knotted ropes

SECTION 5

12. Which was most important to Indians: a. the family, b. the individual, c. the tribe

13. The American contribution that changed European life the most was: a. foods, b. gold, c. medicine

5. The Spanish considered them works of the devil.
6. Indian land belonged to the community which had more importance than the individual.

UNIT REVIEW 4 — TEST YOURSELF

1. Match the cultural group with the statement that describes it:

Ghana G	Aztec J
Mali D	Inca C
Songhai F	Maya I
Zimbabwe A	Five Nations B
Kanem-Bornu E	Pueblo H

A. The Portuguese traded for gold with these people but were never allowed to enter their territory.
B. They controlled the area from Lake Michigan to the Atlantic Ocean and from Canada to Tennessee.
C. This empire was carefully regulated by the ruler who used runners to carry messages to any part of it.
D. Italian city-states used "Guinea gold" from this empire for their coins.
E. Experts from Egypt and Turkey trained the army of this state to use guns.
F. Although very well organized, this empire was destroyed by wars with Muslim armies that had guns.
G. This empire's power came from its location near the "silent trade."
H. These people fought only when necessary; their warriors had to be cleansed of their "madness."
I. Among this group's accomplishments were the calendar and the number zero.
J. A warlike people from the northwest, they built a beautiful city on a lake.

2. Match the area with the description of how people lived there:

desert C
savanna E
northwest woodlands A
extreme north D, C
rain forest B

A. People lived in villages, used wood for houses and totem poles, and hunted and fished.
B. Since the climate was unsuitable for pack animals, people carried goods in large bundles on their heads.
C. Skilled hunters traveled great distances to search for food.
D. Since farming was unknown, animals and fish had to provide everything the people needed.
E. Houses made of mud were as cool inside as if they were air-conditioned.

3. People trained to remember important historical events were: a. North Africans and Mayas, b. West Africans and Aztecs, c. West Africans and Incas, d. East Africans and Pueblos

4. Plows were not used for farming in African rain forests because: a. iron was not used in Africa, b. only the top layer of soil was fertile, c. plots of land were too small to be plowed, d. there were no animals to pull the plows

5. American Indians did not use wagons to carry loads because: a. there were no animals to pull the wagons, b. they did not know what wheels were, c. their wagons were too wide for their roads

6. The Portuguese explorers who reached the east coast of Africa: a. found only primitive tribal groups, b. brought items needed by the Africans, c. were welcomed by the Africans who thought the Portuguese were gods, d. destroyed a thriving trading culture

7. The African slave trade: a. was the first time people had made slaves of other people, b. was a partnership between Europeans and African rulers, c. was controlled and run by Europeans, d. destroyed civilizations in all parts of Africa

8. Human sacrifice was practiced by some American Indian cultures because they: a. found it was a good way to get rid of enemies, b. enjoyed killing, c. valued human life and believed it was the best gift for the gods, d. did not value human life

UNIT 5

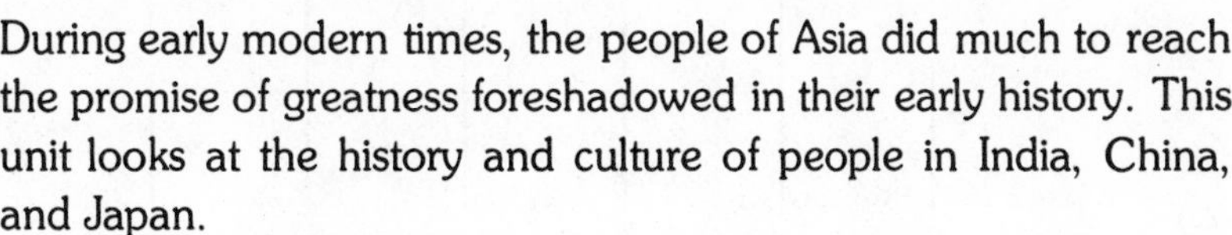

THE WORLD OF ASIA

During early modern times, the people of Asia did much to reach the promise of greatness foreshadowed in their early history. This unit looks at the history and culture of people in India, China, and Japan.

In India, during the 500 years following their invasion and conquest, Muslim rulers generally gave their Hindu subjects good government. They were also great patrons of art and learning. The most famous was the Mughul emperor Akbar, who is regarded as one of the wisest statesmen in world history.

About the same time that Muslim leaders began to push into India (the 13th century), nomadic northern people became a constant threat to China. From 906 to the end of the 1700s, four great dynasties governed this land: Sung, Mongol, Ming, and Manchu. While two were foreign invaders, the Mongol and Manchu, Chinese civilization persisted. It produced great art in ceramics, painting, and poetry. Important advances were also made in science.

Off the Asian mainland was a group of islands whose people became known as the Japanese. Their legendary beginnings go back to a first emperor in the 7th century B.C. Much of Japanese history was shaped by its system of feudalism. Its actual ruler was called the shogun; the emperor had no power. The backbone of the system was the samurai, or warrior, who resembled the knights of feudal Europe. The Japanese developed a rich and dis-

A seated Buddha symbolizes all of Asia.

tinctive civilization. A strong love of nature can be seen in many aspects of Japanese culture. No other people have excelled them in landscape gardening and the artistic arrangement of flowers. Great skill was also reached in poetry, drama, and painting.

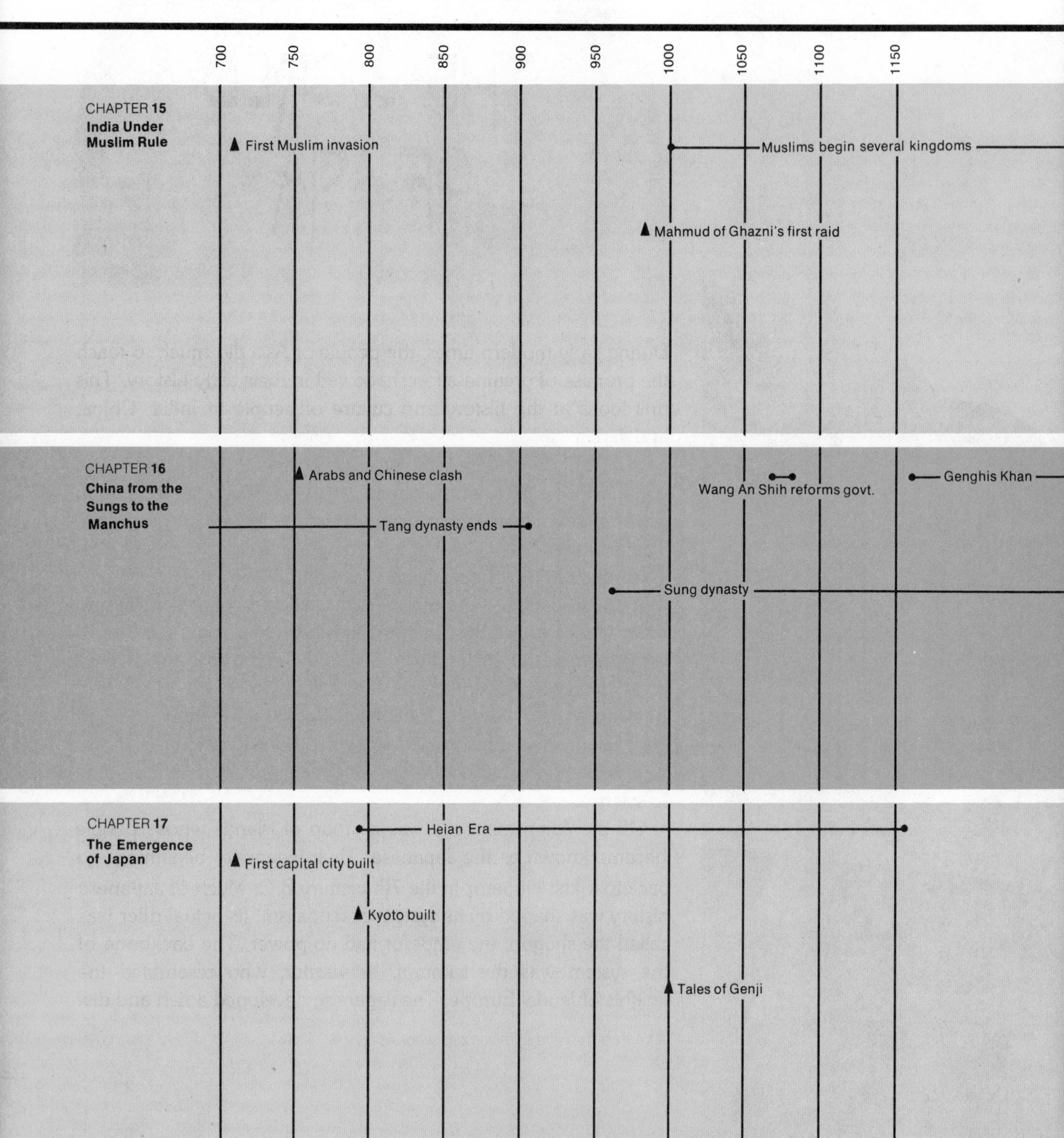

All three of these Asian civilizations developed serious political weaknesses by the 18th century. In the cases of India and China, the weaknesses made possible control and conquest by Europeans.

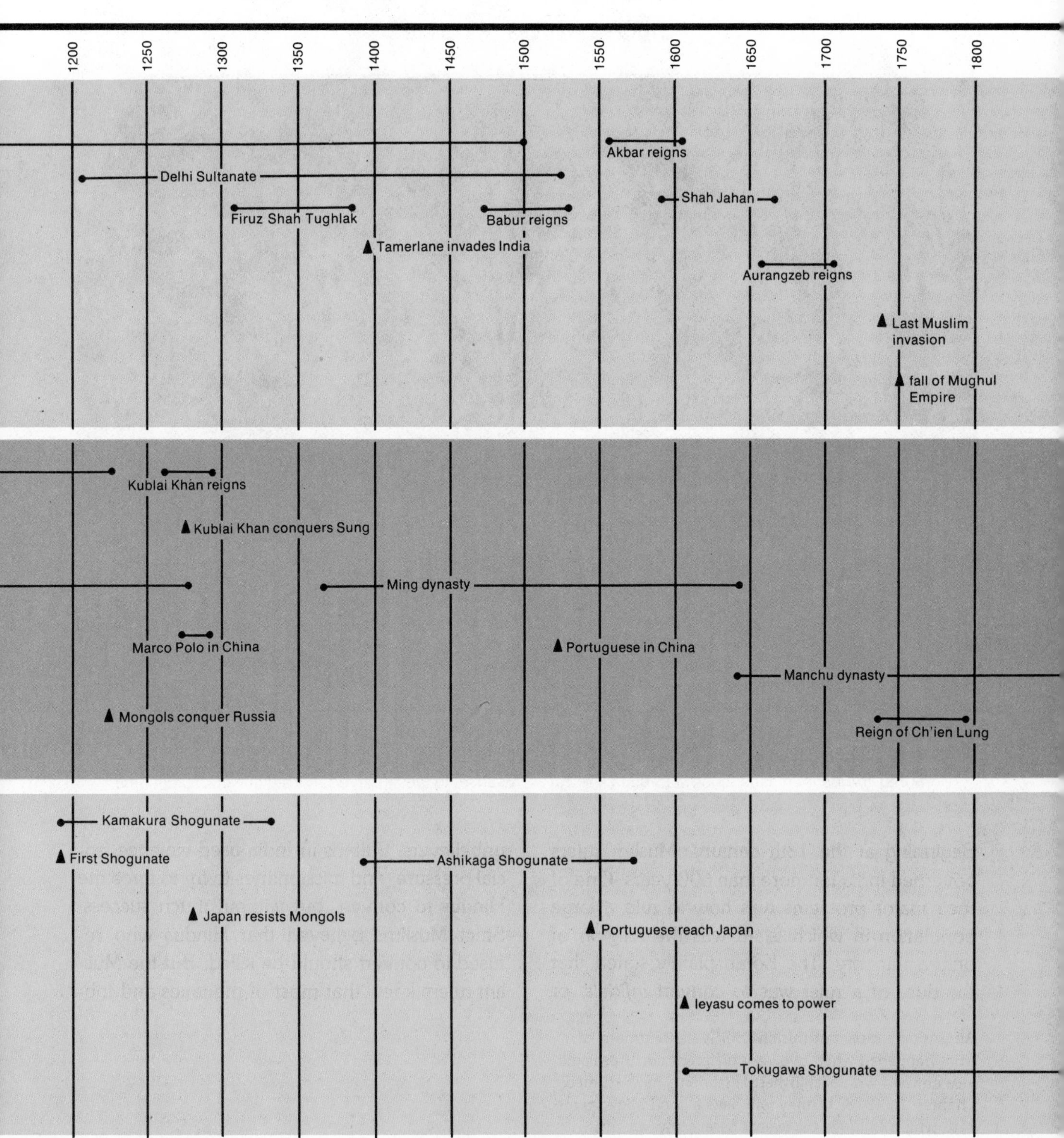

CHAPTER **15** 1206 - 1750

India under Muslim Rule

When his beautiful young wife Mumtaz Mahal died, the emperor Shah Jahan was heartbroken. He ordered the best artisans in India to build the Taj Mahal, a huge marble building for her tomb. Everything about it, from the dome that turns pink at sunset to these carved marble flowers, is feminine.

Beginning at the 13th century, Muslim rulers governed India for more than 600 years. One of their major problems was how to rule a large population in which Islam was the religion of only a minority. The Koran plainly stated that the duty of a ruler was to convert *infidels,* or unbelievers. Sultans in India used violence, social pressure, and missionaries to try to force the Hindus to convert, but without much success. Strict Muslims believed that Hindus who refused to convert should be killed. But the Muslim rulers knew that most of the taxes and trib-

An important part of this chapter is its treatment of what happened when two very different cultures came into contact with each other. If students have studied Chapters 3, 10, & 11 they will have a good background with which to judge the events here. However, this chapter can be used alone.

ute came from Hindu subjects; it would not have made good sense to kill all the Hindus.

How, then, should India be governed? In the early 1300s, a sultan discussed this problem with a Muslim scholar. The scholar suggested,

> When the revenue officer demands silver from the Hindus, they should, without question and with all humility and respect, [give] gold. If the officer throws dirt into their mouths, they must without reluctance open their mouths wide to receive it. By doing so they show respect for the officer. . . . To keep the Hindus in abasement is especially a religious duty, because they are the most inveterate enemies of the Prophet, and because the Prophet has commanded us to slay them, plunder them, and make them captive.

Then the sultan said,

> Oh, doctor, thou art a learned man, but thou hast had no experience; I am an unlettered man, but I have seen a great deal; be assured then that the Hindus will never become submissive and obedient till they are reduced to poverty. I have, therefore, given orders that just [enough] shall be left to them from year to year, of corn, milk, and curds, but that they shall not be allowed to accumulate hoards and property.

Many sultans followed this harsh policy. They were able to do so because they had a strong military force. Even though the Hindus greatly outnumbered the Muslims, the Hindus were not united. India therefore was ruled by Muslims, but Hindu life in the villages continued unchanged.

Not all Muslim rulers in India were cruel and brutal. Some governed with fairness and justice and were considered the greatest of all Muslim rulers. Others were strong supporters of art, literature, and architecture. During their reigns, masterpieces were produced that are among the finest ever. In this chapter you will read how:

1. Muslims controlled India for centuries.

2. Hindus lived and worked under Muslim rule.

3. The Mughuls united and ruled most of India.

4. The Mughul Empire declined quickly.

1 Muslims controlled India for centuries

Arab Muslims invaded and established a foothold in the southern Indus Valley as early as the year 711, but India rulers prevented them from expanding. Then, 300 years later, another Muslim force came to India. The sultanate of the city of Delhi [del′ē] was the most important Muslim power until 1526.

Muslim invaders came from the north. During the 11th and 12th centuries, warlike Muslim invaders came from the mountainous country of Afghanistan through the passes into northwest India. Some were Afghans and some were Turks from Turkestan in central Asia (see map on page 74), but all of them believed in the religion of Islam, the faith of the Prophet Mohammad. They were firm believers in one God and looked down on the Hindus as heathen worshipers of many idols. In the Islamic religion, all followers were equal in the eyes of Allah; Muslims could not understand the inequalities of the Hindu caste system. They believed that India was to be conquered and plundered. ●

ans. 3

● Key Concept: The idea of superiority based on religion, race or culture has often been the reason given for conquests.

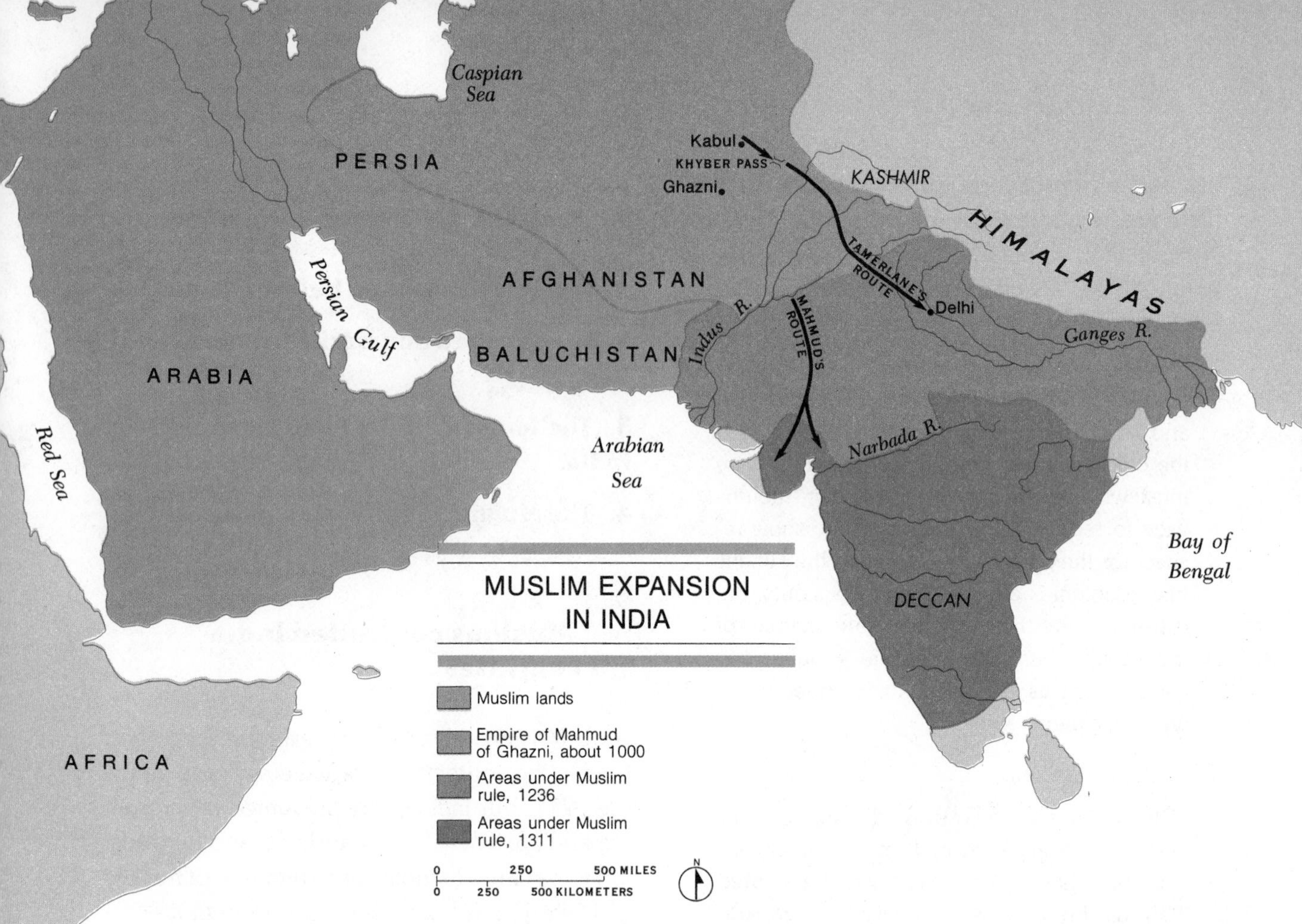

At first, the invaders came as robbers to loot the gold and jewels of Indian cities and to destroy Hindu temples and shrines. Mahmud of Ghazni, who made his first raid on the India plains in 986, believed it was his duty to kill Hindus and his right to get a good profit of treasure from a holy war. He usually left his cool mountain country in the fall of the year, returning home with his plunder as the hot season began in India. In all, he made seventeen raids. Terrible battles were fought in which the Hindu forces were usually defeated. Cities were attacked and their populations massacred.

ans. 1 The victory of the invaders can be explained by several factors. First, the Hindu fighting tactics were quite out of date. Second, although the Hindus had huge armies, the jealous commanders did not work well together to plan and carry out a consistent defense. Third, the many elephants used by the Hindus usually bolted in panic once the fighting began. Fourth, the Hindus used only one warrior caste for defense; in ● the Muslim forces every man was a soldier. Fifth, the invaders were physically bigger and stronger, and once they had passed through the mountains there was no easy retreat. They had to win or die.

The Muslim leaders created kingdoms. Once it was clear how rich and weak India was, Muslim leaders began setting themselves up as kings and princes. Between the years 1000 and 1500 they established many sultanates, or independent Muslim kingdoms.

● Caste was introduced on p. 57.

The Delhi Sultanate was the most powerful (1206 to 1526). The most important Muslim kingdom was centered around the great ans. 2 city of Delhi. It lasted from 1206 to 1526. During this time, much of northern India and part of the Deccan region in southern India was governed from Delhi.

The history of the Delhi Sultanate is not a pleasant one. Its rulers were an amazing mixture of opposite qualities—cruelty, harshness, generosity, and often a keen interest in learning and art. One such sultan obtained his throne by murdering his father and getting rid of a number of close relatives whom he regarded as rivals. This ruler varied his actions from handsome gifts for those who had his favor to executions for those who earned his displeasure. It was said that at his door one could always see either some poor person on the way to wealth or on the way to execution.

Firuz Shah Tughlak [fē rüz′ shä′ təg lak′] was the best of the Delhi sultans. He stopped the torture of criminals and built towns, dams, bridges, and hospitals. He had little use for Hinduism and destroyed some of its temples, but he gave the country a prosperous reign.

Following Tughlak's death in 1388, civil war broke out. Taking advantage of the confusion, ● the Muslim conqueror Timur the Lame (Tamerlane) brought an army of 90 thousand horsemen into India in 1398. He came to find treasure and to kill as many infidel Hindus as possible. He met an Indian army outside the gates of Delhi. The defenders had 120 huge war elephants protected with armor. However, by skillful tactics, Tamerlane's army managed to stampede the elephants.

Delhi was captured and plundered. Most of its people fled or were massacred. It was said that "For two whole months not a bird moved a wing in the city." In 1450, the Delhi Sultanate was revived, but its rulers had little authority. In 1526 the rulers, like their victims before them, were destroyed by an invasion from the north.

The Delhi sultans brought new ways of life to India. Up to the time of the Muslim invasions, the Hindus had always been able to absorb invaders who took on Indian ways. However, this absorption did not happen during the Delhi Sultanate. There was very little mixing ans. 4 between the two peoples. The Muslims thought of themselves as a superior race. Muslim women were secluded in harems or veiled in public. The Muslims ate meat, which angered the Hindus. In ■ addition, the Muslims created much bitterness by their brutal methods of conquest and the destruction of many Hindu temples.

However, there was some contact between the two peoples. Some Hindus were employed as officials in the Muslim government, and others were converted to Islam. Intermarriage of Muslim men and Hindu women, while not ● common, did take place. Various habits of living were exchanged. Some Hindus adopted the Muslim custom of *purdah* [pėr′də], the seclusion of women, and Muslim dress was also copied. Most of the Muslims lived in cities, and their rule had little effect on village life. They were a governing minority in a foreign land.

Muslim rulers, though often cruel, were great lovers of art. They left many beautiful buildings and introduced a new style of architecture that blended both Indian and Islamic features. The arch, dome, and minaret (tower) were especially featured. Many fine examples, such as mosques, still stand in the modern city of Delhi. Most mosques had a minaret from which an official called Muslims to prayer several times a day. (Today, in large Muslim cities such as Cairo,

● Referred to in Ch. 9 where his invasion of Russia is dealt with.

■ The basic philosophy of the Hindu religion is covered in Ch. 3.

● Check to see if students understand why marriages between Muslim women and Hindu men would have been almost impossible. (Because of the seclusion of Muslim women.)

Egypt, loudspeakers are used.) One of the most famous of these minarets at Delhi is the great tower of Kutb Minar [küb mə när′]. It is 238 feet (71.4 meters) high, decorated with beautiful carving, and is unrivaled anywhere in the Muslim world.

SECTION REVIEW 1

p. 282 **1.** Give five reasons that explain the victory of the Muslims over the Hindu armies. Which were Hindu weaknesses? Which were Muslim strengths?

p. 283 **2.** What parts of India were conquered by the Muslims? Where was the Muslim capital?

p. 281 **3.** What were some reasons for the cruelty of the sultans?

p. 283 **4.** Why weren't the Muslims absorbed into Hindu culture as other invaders had been?

2 Hindus lived and worked under Muslim rule

During the period of the Delhi Sultanate, the
ans. 1 masses of Hindus had to bear heavy taxes and were made to feel that they were a conquered people. Village life, however, was little touched by Muslim government. The village was really a small self-governing unit, free to manage its own affairs.

Most Hindus were farmers. India has always been a farming country. The great majority of the people made their living on the land. Indian farmers grew crops such as wheat, barley, cotton, sugar cane, rice, and millet. The peasant in medieval India, like many today, had few and simple farming tools: plows, hoes, and water-lifts for irrigating. Oxen helped with the heavy work—pulling plows and carts and raising large buckets of water from wells.

Indian peasants were bound by ancient rules of landholding and taxes. There were always two parties: the ruler and the tenant farmer. The farmer worked the land and gave the ruler a share of what was produced. The ruler, in turn, gave protection. While rulers might come and go, the role of farmer peasants changed very little as long as they paid their taxes. No matter who was the ruler, the peasants usually had very little left over after taxes.

The village was self-sufficient. Just as India's economic life depended on agriculture, so its social and family life centered around the vil- ans. 2
lage. In medieval times, nearly 90 percent of the people lived in the country. There was very little migration to other villages or to cities. People were born, lived, and died in their villages. The village was made up of various families who had lived there for centuries.

Villages were relatively isolated from one another, since roads were very poor. Each little community had to be responsible for its food and equipment. In the village, therefore, lived the artisans—the carpenters, ironworkers, potters, weavers, and leather workers—whose work produced what the community needed. The village people had no money and so they paid for supplies in produce or work.

Life in the village was busy. Barbers and washermen carried on their trades. The potter made jars, pitchers, cooking pots, and cups. The carpenter built chests, boxes, and bed frames. The blacksmith hammered out iron tips for plows and tools for the carpenter and the tailor.

Sometimes, entertainers came to the marketplace. They traveled from village to village, performing as jugglers, ropedancers, and acrobats.

Two Religions in India

India's Muslim conquerors brought their religion, Islam. The mosques they built had Islamic features, even when they were built by Hindu artisans. At *right* is the ruins of the first mosque at Delhi (1193). Note the shape of the arch and the dome in the distance. These are typical of Muslim architecture. The minaret is the Kutb Minar, begun in 1199.

In constant conflict with the Muslim invaders were various Indian princes, some of them very rich and powerful. They too built great buildings to glorify their religion, Hinduism, and serve as cultural centers. The Hindu temple *below* was built in 1002.

▼ Crown Copyright, Victoria and Albert Museum

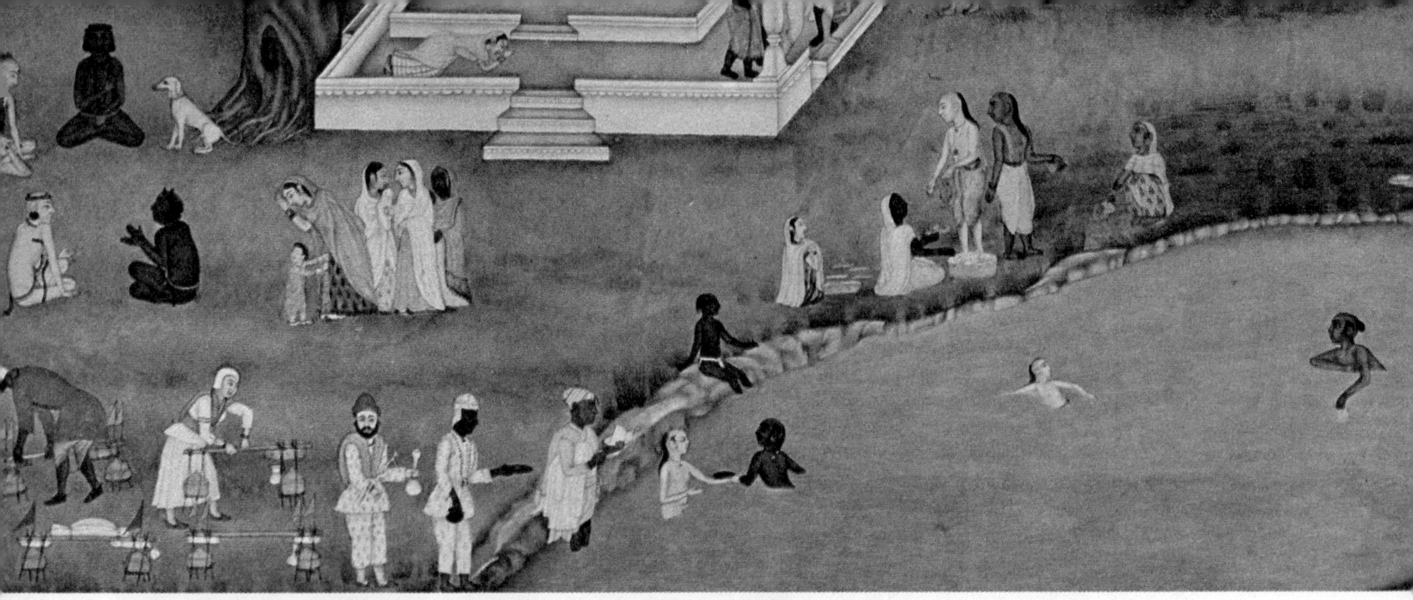

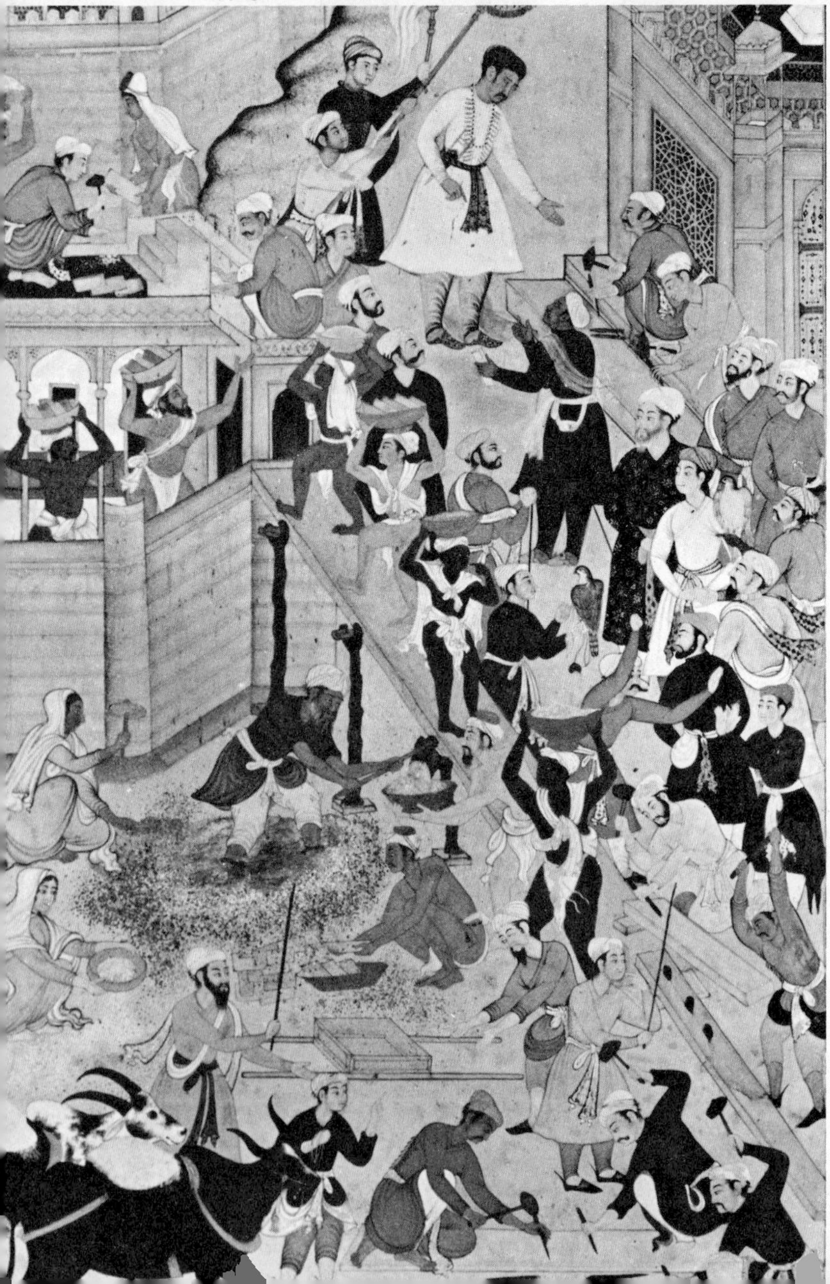

Daily Life under Mughul Rule

The Mughul rulers were patrons of building and the arts. Their court was magnificent. Thousands of people were employed in providing them with luxuries to wear, eat, and gaze at, as well as in entertaining them. The painting *left* shows the ruler Akbar overseeing the building of his new capital (1569). *Below* a Mughul ruler listens to the request of one of his subjects as others wait their turn. In the scene *above*, Hindu pilgrims bathe at a shrine of the god Siva.

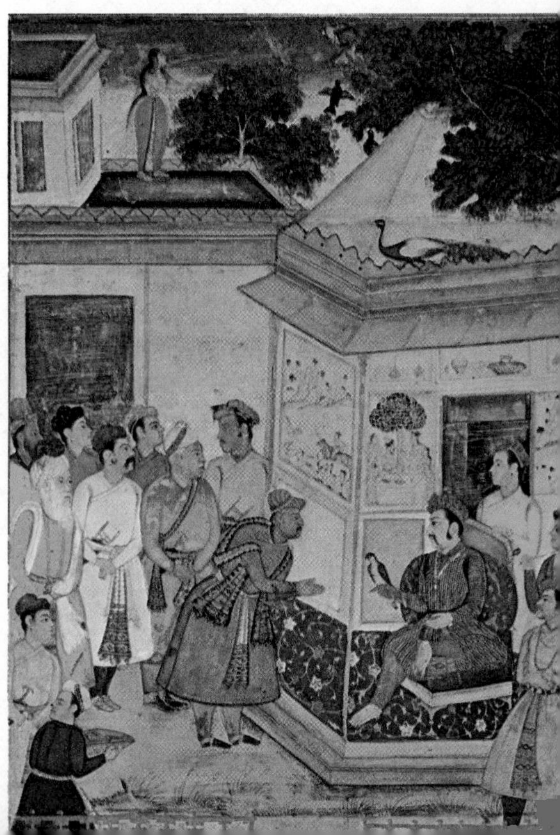

Snake charmers sat cross-legged on the ground. Each played a flute, causing a deadly cobra to swing and sway as it came out of a jar in front of him.

The houses in the village were small mud cottages with thatched roofs and dark, windowless rooms. These cottages were crowded together on narrow streets that were very dirty. A ditch in front of the houses served as the kitchen garbage pail. All the waste from the house was dumped out the door.

The family was the most important force in an Indian villager's life. Hindus had a
ans. 3 joint-family system that has come down to the present. The joint family consisted of father and mother, their sons, grandsons, and the wives and daughters of all who were married. The joint family was controlled by the father while he was alive. After the father's death, the eldest son took charge. All males of the group were consulted on important matters. All land and income belonged to the group as a whole.

Within the family Hindu women had inferior
ans. 3 status. The most important event in a Hindu woman's life was marriage. Families arranged the marriages of their children, picking out prospective husbands and wives when they were very young. Dating, as it is known in the United States, did not exist. Wives treated their husbands with great respect. A wife called her husband, "My master, my lord." However, he often treated her with little politeness.

ans. 3 The role of a widow was special. She could not remarry and had to live with her dead husband's family. She could not attend family feasts and was expected to get by on one small meal a day. Often she had to shave her head.

If a widow did not obey these harsh rules, Hindus believed that she would have an unhappy rebirth in her next life. When the body of her dead husband was *cremated* [krē′mātəd], or burned, on a funeral pyre, it was considered most honorable for the wife to throw herself on the fire with her mate. This custom, called *suttee* [su′tē′], was not declared illegal until the early part of the 19th century.

Hindu India was very religious. India was always a land of religion. Religious shrines and temples dotted the entire landscape. Indian villagers were Hindus who worshiped many gods and believed people were born into new lives after death (reincarnation). Many villages had several religious processions every year. The statue of a god was placed on a huge wooden cart and pulled through the streets.

Hindus were rigidly divided into castes, or ans. 4
classes, that strictly controlled all features of village life. A person's caste regulated what one's job could be, who one's friends could be, whom one could eat with, and whom one could marry. There were thousands of different castes. Some were considered to be very high while others were thought to be barely human. A person was born into his or her caste. Good behavior was rewarded in the next life, when it was believed a worthy person would be born into a higher caste. Caste is still very strong in rural India. ●

● Key Concept: The belief in the caste system has had a lasting hold on all Indian castes.

SECTION REVIEW 2

1. How did Muslim rule affect Indian life? p. 284
2. Why were the small villages so important to Indian society? p. 284
3. Who were the members of the joint family? Name two ways the joint family controlled the lives of its members. p. 287
4. Give examples of how religion and caste controlled villagers' lives. p. 287

3 The Mughuls united and ruled most of India

ans. 1 By the early 1500s, the Delhi Sultanate had grown too weak to rule north India. New Muslim conquerors came through the mountain passes and established a rule, called Mughul [mu̇′gu̇l] rule, in India. Mughul rulers expanded the territories under their control to include all but the southern tip of India.

Babur invades India. A young ruler named Babur [bä′bər] started his career as the ruler of a little kingdom in central Asia. He was an adventurer and a fighting man, a Muslim descendant of the dreaded Mongol conquerors Tamerlane and Genghis Khan. In 1504, Babur captured the important city of Kabul, in what is now Afghanistan.

The riches of India aroused his ambition. He made several raids into the country. In 1526, ans. 1 he completely defeated the weak Muslim sultan at Delhi. A group of Hindu chiefs formed an army to try to regain control of northern India, but Babur defeated them too. Mughul (from the Persian word for Mongol) rule was begun.

Babur had little time to organize his new government. He died only five years after his conquest. However, he is regarded as one of India's great leaders. Not only a brave soldier and a wise statesman, he also was interested in the beauty of fine gardens, poetry, and art. His *Memoirs* are considered to be great literature.

Akbar became emperor. For about twenty years after Babur's death, rival groups weakened Mughul control. Then Babur's grandson, Akbar, became ruler at Delhi in 1556. Though only thirteen years old, he defeated a strong Hindu army. By 1576, he had extended his rule eastward by conquering Bihar and Bengal. Ten years later, Kabul and Kashmir in the north were added. By 1595, when Baluchistan became a part of his empire, Akbar was the undisputed ruler of northern India.

Akbar created an excellent governmental system. ans. 2 His empire was divided into a dozen provinces and placed in the hands of well-paid and efficient civil servants. Well-educated men from various parts of central Asia came into his service. Seventy percent were from outside India, the rest were Hindu or Muslim Indians. These officials throughout the country formed a network that carried out the Mughul orders from Delhi. In addition, Akbar had many soldiers in the provinces and twelve thousand horsemen ready for any emergency.

Law was also administered. ans. 2 In each village, the headman was responsible for keeping law and order. In the cities, special officials decided law cases. Akbar himself often acted as judge; everyone under his rule had the right to appeal to him personally. He tried to outlaw the practice of suttee and allowed widows to remarry. Child marriages were also made illegal.

Akbar accepted all religions. Unlike the Delhi sultans, he was not hostile toward Hindus. He had been raised as a Muslim, but he had doubts about this faith and searched for a religion that all people in his empire could accept. Akbar enjoyed debates and discussions about religion. He invited several Catholic priests to visit him and explain the doctrine of Christianity. Finally, he created his own religion, called the Divine Faith, which borrowed from several religions. It did not, however, make many converts.

As emperor, Akbar's goal was to unite all Muslims and Hindus under a common loyalty to Mughul rule. He accepted Hindu chiefs into his government and also married several Hindu princesses, giving them an honored place in the royal household. He tried to give all his subjects justice, religious freedom, and relief from unfair taxes.

Akbar was one of the greatest and most interesting rulers in history. He had many gifts. He enjoyed the sport of hunting and the excitement of battle and could ride for hours without tiring. He was also interested in architecture, painting, and good books. When he died in 1605, his empire was perhaps the best governed and most prosperous in the world.

Rulers after Akbar had serious faults. Akbar's successors continued the peace and prosperity that began during his rule. Generally, however, they did not have his wisdom. Bloody feuds often took place between contestants for the throne. Akbar's grandson, Shah Jahan [shä′ jə hän′], became emperor in 1628 after a bitter quarrel in which most of his male relatives were murdered. His reign was the high point of Mughul power, a kind of golden age. ans. 4
The royal treasury is estimated to have had a value of more than one billion dollars. The emperor's court was famous for its luxury and splendor. Great palaces and forts were built; artists and musicians were supported.

But the people did not live as well as they had ans. 3
under Akbar. They were taxed too heavily. In addition, Shah Jahan began to end the religious freedom allowed by his grandfather. Hindu temples were destroyed, and Islam was restored as the official state religion.

The Mughuls were great builders. The Mughul emperors were very interested in the arts: painting, literature, music, and architecture.

Akbar was a great builder of forts, tombs, and palaces. His most famous work was the capital city of Fatehpur Sikri [fät′ə per si′krē]. Within it there were many beautiful buildings, such as a great mosque and a huge gateway made of delicate rose-colored sandstone.

The first Mughul emperor, Babur, stops to consider his choice of words as he writes on a hillside.

Akbar was noted for his wisdom and compassion. These qualities are easily seen in this drawing.

The all-powerful emperor, Jahangir, had Nur Mahal's husband murdered so he could marry her.

Under Shah Jahan, architecture reached its height. When his empress died, the sorrowing ruler built an exquisite tomb to her memory, the Taj Mahal [täj′ mə häl′]. It took fifteen years, the labor of 20 thousand workers, and millions of dollars to build. With its decorated marble, minarets, formal gardens, and fountains, the Taj Mahal has been called "the miracle of miracles, the final wonder of the world."

At Delhi, Shah Jahan built fifty-two new palaces. One famous hall had ceilings of solid gold and silver. In it was the emperor's Peacock Throne, decorated with costly jewels.

Painting was not neglected by the Mughuls. Their artists developed an unusual style combining Persian, Hindu, and European methods. Literature also flourished, the official language being Persian. Valuable memoirs were written, and there were important poets and historians.

SECTION REVIEW 3

1. Why were the Mughuls able to conquer India? p. 288
2. Give four examples of the excellence of Akbar's government. p. 288
3. How did the rule of Shah Jahan harm India? p. 289
4. In what ways was Shah Jahan's rule a "golden age"? p. 289

4 The Mughul Empire declined quickly

When the aged Shah Jahan became ill and was unable to rule, rivalries broke out among his heirs. These ended in 1658, when one of his sons, Aurangzeb [ôr′əng zeb′], gained the throne after killing three of his brothers, as well as a son and a nephew. He also threw his father, Shah Jahan, into prison, where he died. Aurangzeb's rule was the beginning of the end of Mughul rule in India.

Aurangzeb tried to unite all of India. Once on the throne, Aurangzeb proved to be a ans. 1
stern and devout Muslim with a will of iron. He raised the taxes of Hindus, got rid of the Hindus in his government, and destroyed Hindu temples and schools. He came to think of himself as the ruler of a Muslim nation, not the ruler of all people of any faith. He was also opposed to most forms of recreation and the arts. Musicians and artists were dismissed from his service.

Aurangzeb's main ambition was to unite all India under Muslim rule, and this aim ended in disaster. He spent the last twenty-six years of his life trying to conquer the Hindu kingdoms in the Deccan and south India. Aurangzeb assembled great armies. In one huge tent city, 30 miles

(48 kilometers) around, the army and servants totaled 500 thousand persons. In addition, there were 30 thousand elephants and 50 thousand camels.

By 1690, Aurangzeb claimed his authority extended from north India to its very tip in the far south. However, the conquest was never complete. Revolts continually broke out. Hindu forts, captured after hard fighting and several years of effort, were lost again to the Hindu armies.

ans. 2 Aurangzeb, tired and ill from directing his armies, left south India in 1705. He was now an old man. His pro-Islam policies and attempt to conquer all of India had failed. Despite the great amounts of money that had been spent, rebellions were taking place not only in the south but also in north India. The last of the great but misguided Mughul emperors died in 1707, at the age of eighty-eight. ●

Conditions in India were miserable. During the next fifty years, law and order broke down in India. There were feuds between rival armies. Local governors set up independent kingdoms. And the peasants were the victims of this lack of leadership. No law or power protected them from any prince or army in the area.

ans. 4 In 1739, a final Muslim invasion was led by the king of Persia. Delhi was captured and plundered. The crown jewels, the royal treasure, and the Peacock Throne were taken to Persia. The Mughuls never recovered from this blow.

ans. 3 Many reasons have been given for the fall of the Mughuls. For one, the old Mughul nobility, once so strong, had been wiped out in the bloody wars of succession. New nobles from central Asia were no longer recruited. Another reason was that the Mughuls were really an alien minority in a foreign land. Only Akbar's policies

● Discuss: in what ways were the Mughul rulers great? Misguided?

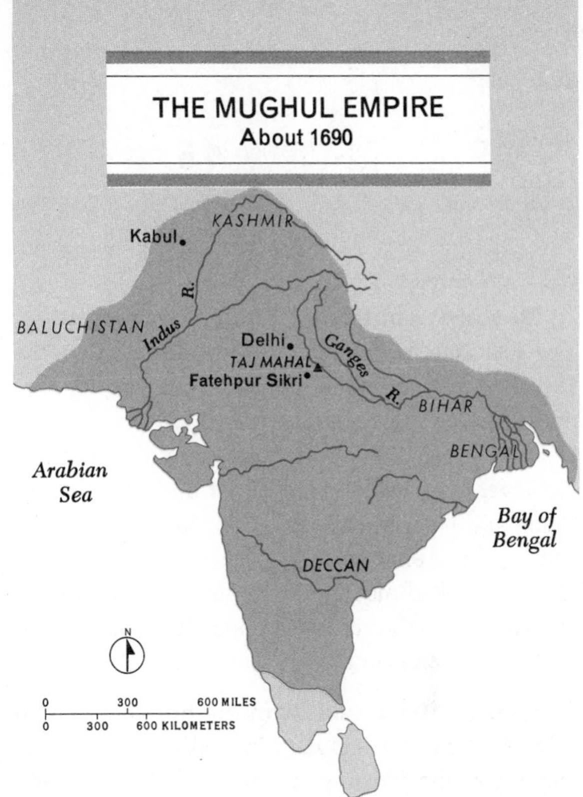

could have solved this weakness. There were also economic reasons, such as the corruption of officials and their stealing of tax money, the oppression of the peasants, and the waste of money in costly wars.

By 1750, the Mughul Empire had split apart. The emperor still had his title but no power. India was now weak and open to new conquerors. This time they came not from across the mountains, but from across the seas, from Britain.

SECTION REVIEW 4

1. In what ways was Aurangzeb as a ruler similar to his father? How was Aurangzeb's rule different from Shah Jahan's? p. 290

2. Why was Aurangzeb unable to complete his conquest of India? p. 291

3. Give five reasons for the fall of the Mughuls. p. 291

4. When was the last Muslim invasion of India? What happened? p. 291

CHAPTER REVIEW 15

SECTION SUMMARIES

1. Muslims controlled India for centuries. The first Muslim invaders came into India in the 11th and 12th centuries. They set up kingdoms in north India. The most powerful of these was the Delhi Sultanate. The Delhi sultans were often cruel. However, they were lovers of art and architecture. Delhi rule was interrupted at the turn of the 15th century by Tamerlane. His fierce army captured Delhi and killed most of the population. The sultanate was rebuilt, but its rulers had little power, and in 1526, they were conquered by Babur.

2. Hindus lived and worked under Muslim rule. Muslim rule had very little effect on the vast majority of the Indian population, who were Hindu peasant farmers. Indian villages were small, isolated, and self-sufficient. Indian daily life was controlled by the joint-family system, the caste system, and the Hindu religion.

3. The Mughuls united and ruled most of India. After Babur's conquests, the first and greatest Mughul ruler was Akbar. He provided efficient government, uniform administration of justice, and religious toleration. He brought educated people into government service from within India and from central Asia. Akbar's grandson Shah Jahan is remembered for the luxury and magnificence of his reign. His buildings, such as the Taj Mahal, were fine pieces of architecture. He was a patron of the arts.

4. The Mughul Empire declined quickly. During Aurangzeb's reign, large amounts of money were spent on wars to bring all of the subcontinent under Muslim rule. Aurangzeb made enemies of his Hindu subjects. Revolts were frequent. After his death, India fell into chaos. In 1739, Persian invaders attacked the helpless empire. Delhi was captured, and its treasures were seized. By 1750, the Mughul Empire had fallen apart.

WHO? WHAT? WHEN? WHERE?

1. Find the years of these events and arrange them into chronological order:

a. Akbar became ruler at Delhi 1556 (6)
b. Mahmud of Ghazni's raid 986 (1)
c. Tamerlane attacked Delhi 1398 (4)
d. Aurangzeb's reign 1658-1707 (8)
e. The Delhi Sultanate began 1206 (2)
f. Persians invaded Delhi 1739 (9)
g. Babur defeated the Delhi sultan 1526 (5)
h. The death of Firuz Shah Tughlak 1388 (3)
i. Shah Jahan became emperor 1628 (7)

2. Write sentences telling what effect each of these men had on India:

Mahmud of Ghazni p. 282
Firuz Shah Tughlak p. 283
Tamerlane p. 283
Aurangzeb p. 290
Babur p. 288
Akbar p. 288
Shah Jahan p. 290

3. Explain the importance of each of these places in India's history and tell where it is:

Delhi p. 283
Deccan p. 283
Fatehpur Sikri p. 289
Baluchistan p. 288
Persia p. 291
Kabul p. 288

4. Describe each of these:

Taj Mahal p. 290
Peacock Throne p. 290
Kutb Minar p. 284

5. Tell the meaning of each of these terms:

purdah p. 283
suttee p. 287
caste p. 287
joint family p. 287
Delhi Sultanate p. 283
Divine Faith p. 288
pro-Islam policies p. 290, 291

6. Find definitions for these words:

Turk	p. 281	Hindu	p. 287
Muslim	p. 281	Mughul	p. 288
Afghan	p. 281	Mongol	p. 288

QUESTIONS FOR CRITICAL THINKING

1. In your opinion, who was the greatest Muslim ruler of India? Explain your choice.

● **2.** What internal problems did the Muslim governments in India have? What caused these problems? What might have been a solution?

3. What were the best and the worst aspects of Muslim rule in India?

■ **4.** In what ways did Muslim rule change Indian culture? What ways of life did not change? Why?

5. Why has it been difficult for Muslims and Hindus to live together peacefully in India? How could this problem be solved?

ACTIVITIES

1. Draw a chart of all the members of a joint-family. How many generations could be living at one time? How many people could be included?

2. Class discussion: In what ways is India's joint family system like or unlike families in the United States?

3. Draw a map of India using arrows to show where invaders have come from. Use information from Chapter 3 as well as this chapter. Label the arrows. Also label the Deccan and main rivers, mountains, and cities.

4. Prepare a report on one of these: the Taj Mahal; the Peacock Throne; Muslim art; caste system in India today; or European contacts with India's Muslim rulers. If possible, show the class the books you have used to write your report.

● 2. Students are asked to examine the effects of cultural conflict.

■ 4. Students should show an understanding of why people cling to their old traditions and customs.

CHAPTER TEST **15**

SECTION ONE

1. What did the Muslim invaders of India have in common?
a. race, b. religion, c. nationality

2. Complete: Elephants were not good for use in battle because they often stampeded

3. True or false: The Muslim invaders made great changes at every level of Indian society.

SECTION TWO

4. The most important part of India's economy has always been:
a. trade, b. industry, c. farming

5. True or false: India's farms have always been owned by many small, independent landholders.

6. *Suttee* and *purdah* are examples of:
a. the high status of women in India, b. primitive farming methods, c. a male-dominated society

SECTION THREE

7. What two things did Babur, Akbar, Shah Jahan, and Aurangzeb have in common? ●

8. Akbar built Fatehpur Sikri.

9. Akbar brought large numbers of outsiders into government service.

10. True or false: Aurangzeb tolerated all religions in his empire.

SECTION FOUR

11. A major problem of Muslim rule was:
a. collecting taxes, b. choosing a new leader, c. finding artists to decorate buildings

12. Which of these is *not* a reason for the fall of the Mughuls?
a. corrupt officials angered the Hindu majority, b. invaders attacked from the north, c. Mughul nobles were weakened by rivalries

13. True or false: Aurangzeb successfully conquered all of India before his death in 1707.

● All were Mughul rulers of India and members of the same family.

CHAPTER
16

960 - 1800

China from the Sungs through the Manchus

Five marble bridges crossing the River of Golden Water lead to the Forbidden City, palace of the Ming emperors. Until the 20th century, no one outside the court could enter the Forbidden City. Inside, the Sons of Heaven, as the emperors were called, lived lives of luxury.

In Asia, Chinese civilization was the single greatest influence. From classical times, Chinese literature, philosophy, religion, and art affected the thinking of peoples throughout Asia. Chinese goods were traded widely in Asia and beyond.

A 13th-century European named Marco Polo returned after nearly twenty years in China and wrote a travel book which gave a vivid picture of China. The things he described were so fantastic that Europeans refused to believe him. For example, he wrote of black stones that burn like logs. "These stones," he said, "keep a fire going better than wood." For writing such things, Marco Polo was called the "prince of liars."

The fact that coal was still not widely used in 13th-century Europe is only one example of how far advanced China was. For more than 1,000 years, no other nation in Asia could match the greatness of Chinese civilization. Even when the empire became politically or militarily weak and was invaded by foreigners, the invaders adopted Chinese culture and were absorbed into the Chinese population. China's way of life remained unchanged and continued to be the oldest civilization in the world. This chapter tells how:

1. Chinese civilization continued under the Sungs.

2. City life differed greatly from peasant life.

3. The Mongols ruled in China.

4. Mings and Manchus maintained Chinese culture.

1 Chinese civilization continued under the Sungs

In the years after the Tang dynasty, the Chinese Empire was not as big as it had been. Large areas were lost in wars, and the danger of invasion was always present. But scientific advances were made and great works of art and porcelain were completed. Scholars studied history and developed ideas that lasted to modern times.

The Chinese Empire lost much territory. At its height, Tang China included lands from Korea and Manchuria west through Tibet and central Asia to the Jaxartes River. (See map on page 74.) Throughout this area, nobles and princes were vassals of the Chinese emperor. But the Chinese did not hold this territory long. In 751, Arabs intent on spreading Islam defeated ans. 1 the Chinese in central Asia. They took the province of Turkestan and converted the nomadic Turkic people living there.

The Tang dynasty came to an end in 906 after it was weakened by warfare on the borders and political corruption within the empire. Five weak dynasties followed the Tangs. Then, in 960, a strong new dynasty, the Sung, came to power. All through the years of Sung rule (960–1279), fierce nomadic tribes beyond the Great Wall were a constant danger.

Soon after the dynasty was established, a nomadic group from Manchuria began to fight its way into northern China. The Sung emperors believed they did not need to fight the nomads. They tried to appease them with bribes of money ans. 2 and silks. This only encouraged the nomads to ask for more. Then the Sungs tried to bribe one group of these barbarians to destroy another. This trick worked at first. But then the victors grew strong and turned against China. They captured the Chinese emperor and set up a Chin dynasty (not related to the earlier Ch'in) in northern China. The capital of the Chin Empire was Peking.

The Sung dynasty was not destroyed. The son of the captured emperor made a new capital at Hangchow in southern China. By 1127, there were two Chinese empires—the Chin in the north and the Sung in the south.

The fall of the Sungs in the north points up two themes in Chinese history. Chinese ans. 3 history can be seen as a succession of dynasties. ●

● Key Concept: the *dynastic cycle* in Chinese history.

Each, at its beginning was strong and prosperous. Then, rebellions and invasions troubled it, and corrupt and lazy officials further weakened it. At the end of each dynasty, it was overthrown. After a time, a new strong dynasty came to power. This process is called the *dynastic cycle,* and is a major theme in Chinese history. The story of the Sungs illustrates it well.

A second theme of Chinese history is *continuity.* Empires were established and then disappeared. Even foreign invaders came to rule the land. But Chinese civilization went on. In spite of the nomadic conquest in the north, for example, Chinese speech, writing, civil service, and ways of life remained unchanged.

New inventions improved the way of life. Starting with the late Tang age and going into the Sung, Chinese artisans and scientists developed inventions that improved farming.
ans. 4 Among these inventions were the horse collar, stirrup, and moldboard (the curved plate on a plow that turns the earth over). The cross bow and, later, gunpowder were inventions that gave the Chinese improved military strength.

At first, gunpowder was used only in religious ceremonies. The Chinese used this new explosive in great fireworks displays at festivals. Giant firecrackers went off with tremendous bangs, and rockets burst into shapes and colors.

Other inventions were mechanical clocks, a magnetic compass, and a seismograph to detect earthquakes. The Chinese developed an inoculation for smallpox and introduced the first adding machine, the abacus. The abacus is still in
● wide use throughout the world.

Scholars made contributions to Chinese civilization. Learned men wrote on botany, chemistry, and geography. Map making techniques improved. And history was studied as a science.

No people in the world have prized history ans. 5
more than the Chinese. It was a master subject ■
in their learning. They believed that history was not just a record of the past but it served another purpose too. It could be a warning and a guide by which people learned from past mistakes. Ever since the Han dynasty, it had been the custom to write an official history.

During the Sung age, many scholars wrote about history. Their writings told: (1) that history was important and why; (2) that it should be based on definite evidence, such as writings, government records, and biographies; and (3) that the historian should always be careful to be fair and not biased in his judgments. Many histories were written based on these rules. One such history covered events from 403 B.C. to 959 A.D. It took the author seventeen years to complete, and consisted of 294 written rolls.

Sung artists and craft workers created masterpieces. While the Tang age had been a time of great poets, the Sung period was one of great artists. Chinese painting reached a degree of perfection never again achieved.

The Chinese used a paintbrush in writing their language, and a distinctive style of painting grew from the special quality of lines made by the brush. The written characters are very complicated—some have twenty-five brush strokes. Certain writers were recognized as masters of the brush. They perfected their style by practicing brush strokes several hours a day. Because they wrote in ink on silk or special paper, artists had to be sure of every line they drew. They could not erase.

Chinese painting does not try to show exactly ans. 6
what the eye sees, as a photograph does. Paint-

● A student may be able to bring in and demonstrate an abacus. Or ask someone in the math dept.

■ Discuss the purpose of history today.

ers try to show the spirit of what they picture. So the Chinese painter believed that he had to spend days in thinking and looking at a scene until he understood its real meaning. Then he would paint it without looking at it. As one Chinese master told his students:

> Understand the character of what you paint. Look at the pine tree; it is like a wise scholar, dignified and stern; it is strong and constant and lives a long time. The willow, on the other hand, is like a beautiful woman, all grace and gentleness. The bamboo combs the hair of the wind and sweeps the moon, it is so bold that its shoots can break the hard ground as they push their way up; it is so gentle that it sways before every breeze. It is like wisdom itself. Keep the character of these things in your mind as you paint them.

Another art in which the Sung Chinese excelled was the making of porcelain. This type of pottery was made from a special white clay that had been mixed with powdered rock and sand,

"Bare Willows and Distant Mountains" was painted in ink on silk by Ma Yuan, a northern Sung artist.

Daily Life in Ming China

The Ming artist Chou-ch'en drew realistic pictures of street scenes in the early 1500s, where men such as these *(left)* amused passers-by with trained animals. In sharp contrast is the elegant scene from a silk scroll painting *(center)* in which a noble family welcomes friends to a birthday party in their manor house. The women preparing cloth *(right)* are engaged in one of "the most important jobs of the female." Others included: raising silkworms, preparing food, and studying.

moistened, and made into a smooth paste. The potter shaped this mixture and fired it in a kiln. The Chinese discovered unusual glazes and used them to give the surfaces of porcelain soft rich color. One piece of green-glazed porcelain was described as being "like curling disks of thinnest ice, filled with green clouds."

Many factories made porcelain plates, cups, bowls, candlesticks, and other objects. Later, when Europeans came to China, they set up shops that copied Chinese porcelain models. They exported their porcelain to Europe, and *china* has come to mean porcelain of an especially fine grade.

SECTION REVIEW 1

p. 295 **1.** How did the Chinese lose the western part of the Tang Empire?

p. 295 **2.** How did the Sungs try to keep the nomads out of China? What happened when their efforts failed?

p. 295, 296 **3.** Name and describe briefly the two basic themes of Chinese history.

p. 296 **4.** Name four inventions of the Sung period and tell how they improved Chinese life.

p. 296 **5.** Why was history important in China?

p. 296, 297 **6.** What were the Chinese trying to show in their painting? How did they go about it?

2 City life differed greatly from peasant life

Sung China in the 12th century has been described as the most advanced country in the world. Economically, the empire was prosperous. Towns and cities were centers of artistic and scholarly activity. However, the riches of trade, ideas, and the arts touched peasant lives very little. In both town and country, the family unit was very important in people's lives.

Foreign trade supported a large population. The empire had a population of at least

100 million. The people were roughly divided into five main classes: (1) peasants, (2) merchants, (3) soldiers, (4) mechanics and arti-
ans. 2 sans, and (5) scholars. The scholars were held in highest regard because they ran the government. Unlike medieval Europe, in Sung China soldiers hardly counted; they did not have high social standing.

ans. 1 Trade grew during the Sung period. In earlier centuries, foreign trade had consisted mainly of camel caravans traveling overland across central Asia with silk goods. In Sung times, the oceans became the highway of commerce. Many large ships, with crews of several hundred persons, carried cargoes to Korea, Japan, and South Asia. Chinese ships also sailed to Southeast Asia, the Persian Gulf, and the east coast of Africa. Exports included silks, art objects, and the highly prized porcelains.

As part of this business growth, paper money came into wide use and a kind of note similar to a modern check did away with the need to carry large amounts of money.

Cities were rich and comfortable. The prosperity of Sung life is best seen in its cities, especially the capital, Hangchow. It covered 8 square miles (20.8 square kilometers) and had a population of at least 1 million—much larger than the cities of Christendom.

One great central street led to the palace of the emperor. Scattered here and there were other fine buildings and palaces. The city also had many fine shops and restaurants. Most of the streets were paved, and a good garbage collection system kept Hangchow neat and clean.

Peasant life was poor. The luxury of the ans. 2
capital stopped at its walls. Beyond were the miserable villages where peasants worked from dawn to dusk. The peasants' tiny fields produced barely enough food to support a family. Their homes were mud huts with windows made of greased paper.

All farm work was done by hand by the members of the peasant family. Adults did the heavy work—digging, planting, hoeing, and harvesting. Children looked after the pigs and chickens, gathered firewood, and brought water from the well. During the year, a few feast days and festivals gave peasant families a little fun and relaxation.

There was very little contact between the ans. 2
peasants and the government. Officials collected

The Puzzle of the Ban Chieng Pots

Where did early people first learn to make bronze? This question is important because the use of bronze was a giant step forward in human development. Historians and archaeologists have for a long time believed that the first Bronze Age, and with it the rapid growth of civilization, began in Mesopotamia somewhere between 3000 and 2500 B.C. Recently, a startling discovery was made in Thailand that may change many ideas about the early history of humans.

In 1966, Stephen Young, the son of a former U.S. ambassador to Thailand, was carrying on research near the remote village of Ban Chieng [ban chē eng′]. One day while walking down a path that had been deeply rutted by heavy rains, he tripped over an exposed tree root. Trying to cushion his fall, he extended his arms. As he lay on the ground, his hands felt a number of round hard circles. They were the tops of clay pots, once deeply buried in graves.

A Thai princess, Pantip Chumbhot [pan′tip chùm bot′], heard of his discovery and financed a dig at Ban Chieng. She collected many pot fragments there, which she sent to the University of Pennsylvania. She had learned that a new method for dating pottery was being developed there.

This process, called *thermoluminescence,* heats pottery to a high temperature, at which point a faint ray of light is given off. By measuring its amount, scientists believe they can tell the age of the pottery. Tests at the university showed that the Ban Chieng pots were more than 4,000 years old.

More surprises came in 1973 when more funeral pots were unearthed. These were found with bronze tools and the stone molds from which they were made. Bronze cannot be dated; but the pots with them were found to be from 4000 to 3500 B.C. This was a thousand years earlier than the Bronze Age in Mesopotamia.

Did the use of bronze originate in Southeast Asia? Was this knowledge carried to the Middle East? If so, it would solve one of the mysteries of archaeology. No source of tin has ever been found in the Middle East, and this metal, mixed with copper, is needed to make bronze. There are rich sources of tin in Southeast Asia.

Some scholars do not believe that thermoluminescence is reliable, and research goes on. There is much argument over the meaning of the Ban Chieng finds. It is likely that these mysterious pots may provide new clues to human prehistory.

taxes and picked several men from each village who were forced to repair dikes, roads, and other public works. Peasants in their private lives were left alone. As one of their folk songs put it:

I begin to work when the sun rises;
I rest when the sun sets.
I dig a well for my drinking water;
I plow the field to provide my food.
Powerful as the emperors are,
What has that power to do with me?

The day-to-day life of the peasants in Sung China was not much different from that in feudal Christendom. But the Chinese farmers' lives remained almost unchanged down to the 20th century, while in Europe, farming life improved greatly over the centuries.

The family was the important unit of Chinese life. A family was made up of three
ans. 2 or four generations. It was based on the authority of the older generations over younger ones and of males over females. While the grandfather, if alive, or the father had the final word in all family matters, the eldest son had authority over younger brothers and all sisters. The grandmother had authority over her daughters, daughters-in-law, and granddaughters.

ans. 3 The Chinese family, with its tight organization, took on duties that governments took care of in many other countries. When differences arose between members of a family or between members of different families, the problem was not taken to an official. The families involved tried to settle the problem themselves. In this way, families did many of the things that police or judges would do in other communities.

At a time when there were no government pension systems, insurance, or health-care programs, the family took care of any relatives that needed help. In case of famine in a village, the better-off farmers were expected to help their neighbors, even if they belonged to other families.

● Discuss the good and bad points of Chinese family organization. Questions for Critical Thinking 4 asks students to compare Chinese and American family life.

All marriages were arranged by heads of families. There was little or no room for romance in the individual's life. It could happen that a young couple had never seen each other until the marriage ceremony. The idea of romantic love was not absent from Chinese thought. There are great love stories in Chinese literature. But love had nothing to do with people getting married.

Women had lower status than men. Like all people, the Chinese had order in their society. Some people were higher than others. One famous philosopher described the order in Chinese society when he wrote, "I am happy because I am a human and not an animal; a male and not a female; a Chinese and not a barbarian." Women were considered to be of much less importance than men. Many customs developed from this belief.

In a dispute between a wife and her mother-in-law (with whom she lived), the husband was expected to support his mother. When a man appeared in public with his wife, she walked ten steps behind.

Among the wealthy upper classes, the practice of foot-binding illustrates the inferior place of women in China. It began when a girl was about four years old. Her feet were tightly wrapped and gradually bent until the arch was broken and the toes were pushed under. These upper-class women, therefore, had very tiny feet. Tiny feet were considered to be beautiful, but their owners were crippled. Thus, the women were no more than ornaments in their husbands' homes.

The Sungs declined. The Sungs were never strong militarily. A little more than 150 years after they first came to power, other serious weaknesses developed in their government. Officials were more interested in their own comfort and wealth than in giving the people good government. Peasants were terribly burdened by very high interest rates on loans and by the forced labor they were required to give for public projects.

At this time, in 1069, the Sung emperor made a minor official named Wang An Shih [wäng′ än shē′] his prime minister. Wang An Shih was a brilliant scholar who had studied the governments of the "ancient rulers." He made broad reforms, some of which were a return to ancient ways, while others brought China "up to date."

Wang An Shih's government temporarily stopped decline. Wang An Shih believed he could get good officials by improving three areas: (1) the training of officials, (2) the control of their income and expenses, and (3) the selection process.

ans. 4 He made the civil service examinations more practical and improved the universities. He adjusted officials' salaries and made rules about exactly how much officials of certain ranks could spend on weddings, funerals, and entertainment. He believed these rules would prevent officials from taking bribes or otherwise getting rich from their positions, because they would not be able to show off their wealth.

● In addition, Wang An Shih began a *graduated income tax,* that is a tax that requires wealthy people to pay a greater percentage of their income than poorer people pay. This tax money was used to hire workers for government projects. Thus, he got rid of the hated forced labor. He introduced measures to give loans to farmers at low interest rates, and he controlled inflation with rules about how much things could cost and how much people could be paid.

● This point may need to be clarified. Show the difference between a graduated tax and a flat rate tax.

After the death of Wang An Shih in 1086, his reforms were scrapped and forgotten. The Sung Empire continued to decline until it met its end—the completion of this dynastic cycle—by foreign conquest in 1279.

SECTION REVIEW **2**

1. How were trade and business different in Sung China from Tang times? Name at least two ways. p. 299

2. Describe social order in Sung China. What groups of people were most important in the empire? In the family? p. 299, 301

3. Name at least three ways in which a Chinese family was like a government. p. 301

4. What were some of the methods Wang An Shih used to improve government? p. 302

3 The Mongols ruled in China

Throughout Chinese history, nomadic groups from central Asia had been breaking through the Great Wall. In the 13th century, a group called the Mongols succeeded in completely taking over China. They ruled for 100 years.

Genghis Khan united nomadic peoples. The people who are known in history as "the Mongols" did not all come from Mongolia. In a series of tribal wars, the famous warrior Genghis Khan [jeng′gis kän′] united many of the nomadic peoples of central Asia. This united group was known as the Mongols. ans. 1

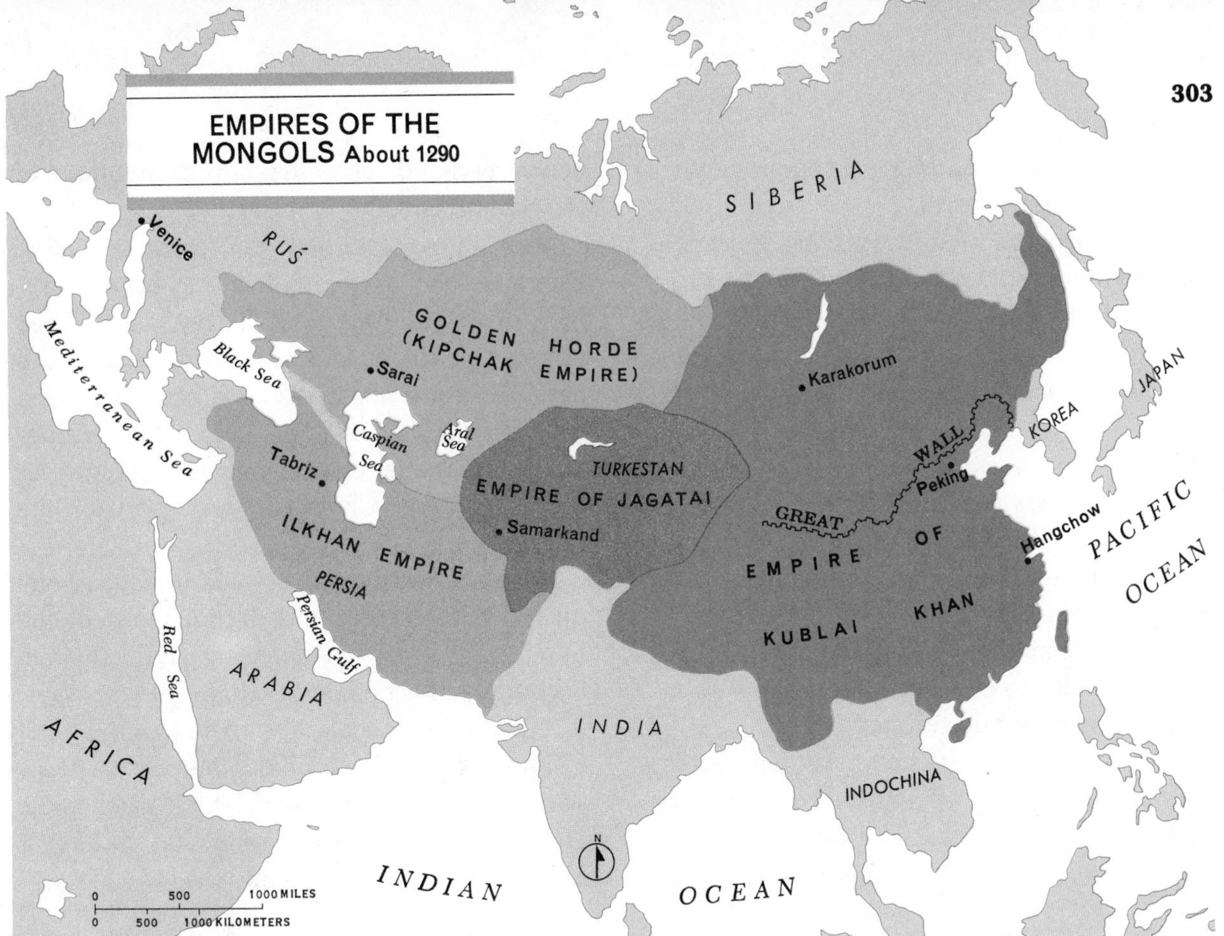

The civilized peoples had no chance against the cavalries of the nomads. Civilized peoples could not keep large cavalries because they used their land for farming. The nomads lived on the huge stretches of Asian *steppes*. They
ans. 1 used these vast, treeless plains as pastures for their horses. They kept great numbers of horses and were skilled riders. When the mounted Mongol army, with swords flashing, galloped into a village or town, it simply cut down everyone in its path.

In the first decade of the 13th century, Genghis's armies repeatedly attacked the Chin dynasty in northern China. The Mongols swept west as well as east. In the 1220s, they defeated Muslim empires in the area around the Aral and Caspian seas. And in 1223, they moved into Russia. For twenty years, Genghis Khan terrified and conquered peoples from southern Russia to Korea. His armies killed more than 5 million.

Kublai Khan became emperor of China. After Genghis Khan's death in 1227, the Mongols continued their conquests. In 1234, Genghis's successor brought the Chin dynasty to an end and established a Mongol dynasty in north China.

The greatest of Genghis's successors was his grandson Kublai Khan [kü'blī kän']. He became Mongol emperor in 1260. He conquered the Sungs in southern China in 1279. From that year he ruled both north and south China until his death in 1294.

At the height of their power, the Mongols controlled China, Russia, Persia, and central Asia. In theory, Kublai Khan was the only Mongol ruler, but actually the Mongol conquests were divided into four empires.

The Mongols showed great ability in governing the countries they conquered. Kublai Khan ans. 2 built roads, filled granaries with wheat for use in times of famine, and gave state aid to orphans and the sick. He also rebuilt the capital at Peking.

Marco Polo visited the Mongol court. A famous book, *The Travels of Marco Polo,* gives ans. 3 a great amount of information about Kublai Khan's empire. In 1271, when he was about seventeen years old, Marco Polo left his home town of Venice to travel with his father and uncle to the court of Kublai Khan.

The journey through central Asia and across the terrible Gobi took four years. Marco Polo became a favorite at the court of the Mongol emperor. He stayed in China for seventeen years, serving much of that time as an official of the government.

Marco Polo returned to Venice in 1295, where he had trouble convincing his countrymen of the truth of what he had seen. They thought his stories exaggerated the size of the population and wealth of China, and they called him "Marco Millions." However, other Europeans—missionaries and merchants—followed his route to distant China and brought back the same reports.

Under the Mongol rulers, life in China went on much as before, and the influence of the Sung period remained strong. Kublai Khan encouraged his people to adopt Chinese ways. ans. 4 In time, the Mongols absorbed much of the Chinese way of life. In China, this process of *assimilation* [ə sim′ ə lā′ shən] took place again and again. There is a saying that "China is a sea that salts all rivers that flow into it."

THE ADVENTURES OF MARCO POLO

Until the late 1960s, whites played the important roles in Hollywood movies. In this 1938 movie, Gary Cooper as Marco holds Sigrid Gurie, who has been made up to look Chinese. The splendor of the Mongol court impressed movie audiences almost as much as the real one had moved Marco Polo.

HISTORY IN THE MOVIES

SECTION REVIEW 3

1. Who were the Mongols? How were they able to
p. 302, conquer such a large territory?
303 **2.** How did Kublai Khan's rule help China?
p. 304 **3.** Who was Marco Polo? Why is he important in
p. 304 history?
4. What is assimilation? Before the Mongols lived in
p. 304 Chinese cities they had been nomads. How might
● that fact have helped them absorb Chinese culture instead of imposing their own on the Chinese?

4 Mings and Manchus maintained Chinese culture

In time, Mongol rule weakened, and the people began to revolt against their foreign masters. The Chinese continued to look on the Mongols as intruders, in spite of all the Mongol efforts to adapt themselves to Chinese life. Hung Wu, a leader of the discontented Chinese, gathered an army. He captured Peking in 1368 and drove out the Mongol rulers. China returned to the rule of a Chinese dynasty called the Ming, or "Brilliant" dynasty.

ans. 1 **Ming China prospered.** The Ming rulers tried to restore and strengthen all things Chinese. They cleared fields for farming and planted additional mulberry trees to provide food for silkworms. They increased trade with distant countries, and as a result, shipbuilding and navigation improved. Chinese ships sailed to the Philippines and other islands of the Far East, to India, and to Africa.

The Ming emperors made the capital of Peking into one of the finest cities in the world. With many palaces, temples, and walls, it was really four cities in one. Each was surrounded by a wall. In the center of Peking was the *Forbidden City,* in which only members of the royal family could live. Outside the Forbidden City was the Temple of Heaven, where the emperor prayed to the Supreme God for all of his people.

● If necessary, clarify the concept of assimilation. Point out that the Mongols were "assimilated" into Chinese culture.

Ming rulers limited contact with the West. After the downfall of the Mongols, Chinese contact with Europe stopped. Then, with the European exploration of the 15th century, it began again.

The Portuguese, eager for trade with the East, first sent representatives to Peking in 1520. This early contact did not work out well. The Portuguese plundered, kidnaped, and murdered, much to the horror of the Chinese, who called these Westerners the "ocean devils."

As a result, the government banned foreigners from China. However, it did allow the Portuguese to establish themselves at Macao [mə kou′], in southern China. Christian missionaries also came to the Far East. But they, like the merchants, did not always respect the wishes of the Chinese government. Thus foreigners continued to be unwelcome in China.

China tried not only to keep foreigners out, but also to keep its own people from leaving the

Delicately carved in jade, a farmer and a water buffalo plow a rice field. Manchu period.

ans. 4 country. Although Ming emperors of the 15th century had encouraged trade with other nations, those of the 16th century believed in a policy of isolation. They forbade almost all contact with the outside world. In 1619, the Ming emperor wrote to the tsar of Russia: "O Tsar, I neither leave my own kingdom nor allow my ambassadors or merchants to do so."

The Manchus overran China. Isolation,
ans. 2 together with government corruption and high taxes, weakened the Ming Empire. Several peasant uprisings occurred in the early 1600s.

Meanwhile, a nomadic tribe from Manchuria, the Manchus, started to expand their territory. They began breaking through the Great Wall and raiding the borders of Ming China. They conquered Korea in 1627.

Chinese glazed porcelains were among the most highly prized trade items in the world.

Discontent grew within China, and bands of robbers roamed the countryside. One powerful robber chief seized much territory. In 1644 he threatened the capital at Peking. The Chinese asked the Manchus to help them put down this chief. They did so. But then the Manchus took ans. 2
Peking for themselves and made their own prince the emperor of China. The new Manchu dynasty ruled from the capital at Peking until ans. 3
1912.

The Manchu Empire was huge. It included ans. 3
Mongolia, Manchuria, Korea, Indochina, Tibet, and eastern Turkestan, as well as China proper. The Manchus kept the Chinese system of government that had been set up by the Ch'ins. They divided the political jobs evenly between Chinese and Manchu nobles. The Chinese held most of the lesser offices.

Unlike the Mongols, the Manchus tried to keep their own customs and language. They forbade intermarriage with the Chinese. They made the Chinese wear *queues* [kyüz], or pigtails, as a sign of inferiority.

The first Manchu emperors were men of great ability. The first 150 years of their rule—to the end of the 18th century—was one of the most prosperous and peaceful in Chinese history. The rulers built roads and canals. They tried to stop famines and helped farmers clear new land.

Ch'ien Lung (1736–1795) was the last of the great emperors. He was hardworking, sometimes reading government reports until well past midnight. His scholarly interests aided schools and he was a supporter of the arts. In his ability to rule, he has been compared to the most outstanding rulers of his day: Catherine of Russia and Frederick the Great of Prussia.

Isolation was a weakness of Chinese policy. With Ch'ien Lung, the Manchu Empire reached its height. But the first signs of decline were present. The very peace and prosperity given by the Manchus led to a sharp increase in population. In 1710, it was 115 million and had doubled by 1793. This rapid increase had not been met by technical advances in agriculture and industry. By the end of the century, standards of living had begun to decline and there was growing unrest in the country. Added to
ans. 4 these problems was the Manchu policy of isolation that kept out of China good ideas developed in other countries.

China's rulers had little idea of the great advances in industry and science that were taking place in Europe. Chinese civilization was backward looking. It still regarded itself as the Middle Kingdom, superior to all other nations.

For example, in the 1790s, a high-ranking Englishman traveled to Peking to try to get special trading privileges for English merchants. The Chinese emperor refused to give them. He explained why in his letter to the English king:

● The stores of goods in the Celestial Empire are extremely plentiful. There is nothing We do not possess, so that there is really no need for the products of the foreign barbarians in order to balance supply and demand.

> However, the tea, silk, and porcelain produced by the Celestial Empire are indispensable to the different states of Europe and to your kingdom. For this reason, We have, in Our grace and pity, established Our official trading companies. . . . It has been Our wish that all your daily needs be properly supplied and that everyone share in Our overly abundant riches.

While there was good reason for the Chinese to believe in the superiority of their culture—for more than 1,000 years no other nation in Asia

● In discussing this excerpt, students may bring up a number of points on why it is practical to learn about other peoples and cultures. If so, relate these points to attitudes today.

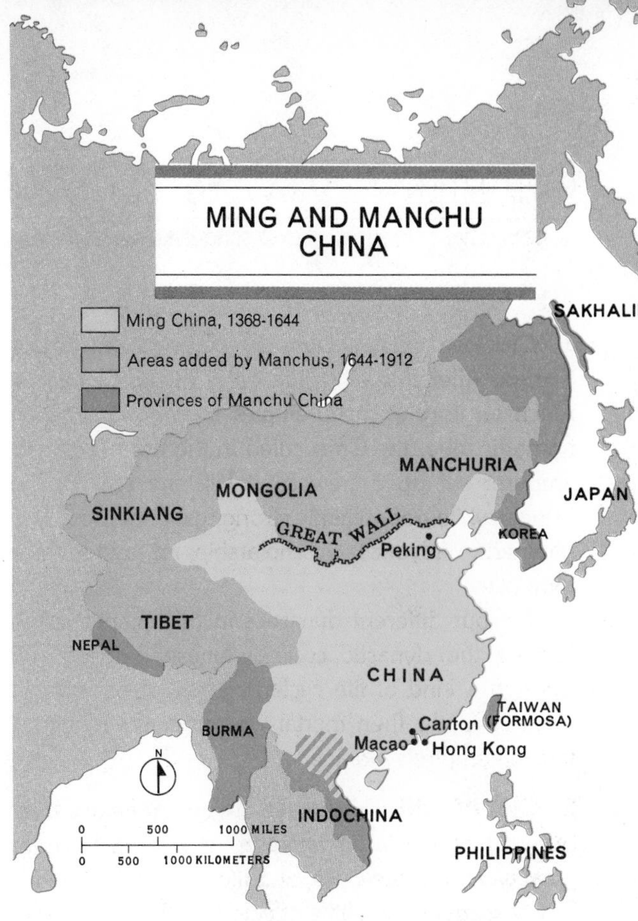

could match them—this reply illustrates an unreal attitude toward the outside world. This failure was to cause China much grief and serious problems in the 19th century.

SECTION REVIEW 4

1. How was Ming rule good for China? Give examples. p. 305

2. What three factors weakened the Ming dynasty? How did the Manchus take over? How does the history of Ming rule fit the pattern of the dynastic cycle? p. 306

3. Give the years of Manchu rule in China. What territories did they rule? p. 306

4. In which dynasty did the policy of isolation begin? Why did the Chinese limit their contact with foreigners? How is isolation a weakness in a civilization? p. 306, 307

CHAPTER REVIEW 16

SECTION SUMMARIES

1. Chinese civilization continued under the Sungs. After the fall of the Tang rulers, China lost much territory and the empire became divided. A nomadic tribe, the Chin, ruled in the north. A Sung emperor set up a new capital in the south. The Sungs, while not militarily strong, gave their country prosperity. Advances in scholarship, art, and science took place.

The four different dynasties in this chapter all illustrate the dynastic cycle. Chinese empires run through a kind of life cycle: from early promise to great strength, then mortal weakness and downfall in each empire's old age.

2. City life differed greatly from peasant life. Sung China was a thriving empire. Exports brought great wealth to the cities, and life was elegant there. But peasant life was little affected by the wealth and learning. Families provided much of the order and support in China; people relied on their families, not the government. Women had lower status than men.

A brilliant prime minister stalled the decline of Sung rule with reform. But with his death, corruption came back.

3. The Mongols ruled in China. Genghis Khan united the nomads of central Asia and conquered China. Mongol rule did not destroy Chinese civilization. In fact, the Mongols imitated and encouraged it. Marco Polo described Mongol China in a famous book.

4. Mings and Manchus maintained Chinese culture. As in the case of previous dynasties, the Mongols were ousted by a native Chinese government called the Ming. During Ming rule, Peking was rebuilt and trade flourished. But in less than 300 years, the Mings were overthrown by the invading Manchus. During the first 150 years of their rule, China had one of its most happy and prosperous periods. During the Ming and Manchu periods, antiforeign feeling grew. European traders were not welcome, European inventions and ideas did not come into the land.

WHO? WHAT? WHEN? WHERE?

1. In what years did these events happen:

a. The Tang dynasty fell. 906
b. The Sung dynasty came to power. 960
c. Nomads set up a dynasty in north China. 1127
d. Mongols conquered the Chin Empire. 1200
e. Kublai Khan conquered the Sung dynasty. 1279
f. A Chinese army drove out the Mongols. 1368
g. Manchus took over China. 1644
h. The Manchu dynasty ended. 1912

Which of the above dynasties were Chinese? Which were invaders? ●

2. Name the dynasties in which these events took place: ■

a. Trade was expanded to the Philippines and India.
b. Chinese men were forced to wear *queues*.
c. Marco Polo visited China.
d. Trade ships carried silks and porcelains to Southeast Asia, the Persian Gulf, and Africa.
e. The Forbidden City was built.
f. Roads were built, grain stored for emergencies, and orphans helped by the government.
g. Wang An Shih made reforms.
h. The emperor of China rejected an offer to trade with England.
i. The abacus was invented.
j. Genghis Khan's armies swept Asia.
k. The population of China reached 230 million.
l. Foreigners were banned from China because of Portuguese attacks.

3. Define these terms showing why they are important in China's history:

● The Tang and Sung were Chinese; the Chin, Mongol and Manchu were invaders.

■ 2. Sung d, g, i
Mongol c, f, j
Ming a, e, l
Manchu b, h, k,

CHAPTER TEST 16

dynastic cycle p. 296
porcelain p. 297
queues p. 306
isolation p. 306
"ocean devils" p. 305
assimilation p. 304

4. Tell the parts played by these people in China's past:

Wang An Shih p. 302
Genghis Khan p. 302
Hung Wu p. 305
Kublai Khan p. 303
Chi'en Lung p. 306
Marco Polo p. 304

QUESTIONS FOR CRITICAL THINKING

1. What is the meaning of the saying, "China is a sea that salts all rivers that flow into it"?
2. What factors explain the fall of the four dynasties in this chapter? What actions could have been taken to prevent their collapse?
3. Compare the relationships between the Chinese peasant and his government with that between the poor and the government of your country. What differences or similarities can you find?
4. What differences are there between Chinese family life under the Sungs and an average family in the United States today? What aspects of Chinese family organization would you like to see adopted by families today?

ACTIVITIES

1. You are Wang An Shih, and the President of the United States has just appointed you to improve the government. What reforms would you propose?
2. Using the Chinese painters' way of looking at nature, choose a tree or flower to study. Write a paragraph about what you feel is the character or spirit of your subject.
3. For discussion, debate, or role-playing: What were the advantages or disadvantages of China's voluntary isolation from the rest of the world? What might a conversation have been like between a Chinese emperor and a European visitor trying to set up communications between the two countries?

SECTION 1

1. China was divided when the ______ captured the northern area. a. Mongols, b. Chin, c. Sung
2. Which of these is not an invention of the Sung period? a. mechanical clocks, b. calendar, c. smallpox inoculations
3. Chinese artists tried to: a. make their paintings as realistic as photographs, b. capture the spirit of their subject, c. imitate western European art forms

SECTION 2

4. True or false: In the Sung society, soldiers were highly respected because they helped keep out invaders.
5. Traders in Sung China used: a. golden coins, b. a barter system, c. checks
6. Chinese families were run by: a. the oldest male, b. democratic methods, c. the mother and father

SECTION 3

7. North and south China were united in 1279 under ______ rulers. a. Chin, b. Chinese, c. Mongol
8. Which of these did *not* happen when the Sung dynasty fell? a. its high level of culture was destroyed also, b. life for the Chinese people went on as before, c. the new rulers adopted many Chinese customs
9. True or false: The Mongols lived on the steppes of central Asia.

SECTION 4

10. Under Ming rule, traders from Portugal were allowed to set up a post at Macao in southern China.
11. The Manchu emperor who has been compared to other great rulers of his time was: a. Hung Wu, b. Kublai Khan, c. Chi'en Lung
12. Which of these was *not* a problem during Manchu rule? a. increased population, b. isolation from new ideas, c. fighting between rivals for the throne

CHAPTER **17**

500–1750 A.D.

The Emergence of Japan

This proud figure is Minamoto Yoritomo, a military leader who made himself dictator of Japan in 1192. He took the title shogun and began a feudal age that lasted 700 years. In this wood sculpture he is sitting cross-legged, wearing the crown and clothes of court.

Yukio Mishima [yü kē ō mē′shē mä] was one of his country's most famous authors. His brilliant novels, plays, and short stories had given him an international reputation. One of his works, *The Sound of Waves,* was a prize-winning story about life in a fishing village.

● You might ask if your school or public library has this or other Japanese stories to use as extra assignments.

Mishima loved the old customs and traditions of Japan, especially the *samurai* [sam′ü rī′], or warrior, way of life from feudal times. He thought that after World War II his country had been copying foreign, Western ways that were corrupting its people. He lamented the decay of family ties, the decline of simple country living, and the strange "un-Japanese" behavior of young people in modern-day Japan. To counter these changes, Mishima formed a patriotic group called the "Society of the Shield." Its members were taught unswerving loyalty to the emperor, respect for old ways, body-building, and the art of combat.

Determined to call attention to these ideas in a dramatic way, Mishima and a few of his followers broke into the quarters of the commanding general of the Tokyo garrison of the Japanese army. They tied up the general, and then Mishima stepped out of his room onto a balcony to address the soldiers below. His plea to overthrow the government and to "return to the good old days" met with no response.

Feeling dishonored and a failure, Mishima acted in the manner of the samurai he admired. He plunged a dagger into his abdomen and gained the honorable death of seppuku [sep′pü′kü] more commonly called hara-kiri [har′ə kir′ē]. Mishima said he sacrificed himself "for the old beautiful tradition of Japan."

It is difficult for people in the Western world to understand Mishima's act without some knowledge of this ancient Japanese samurai tradition. It was curiously out of place in the commercial urban life of postwar Japan where the merchant and not the warrior commanded respect. In this chapter you will read how:

1. Japan's location influenced its history.

2. Early Japanese civilization borrowed from China.

3. Feudalism and a samurai warrior class developed.

4. The Japanese created distinctive home and family customs.

1 Japan's location influenced its history

Japan is a nation of islands. There are four large islands—called Hokkaido [hō kī′dō], Honshu [hon′shü], Kyushu [kyü′shü], and Shikoku [shi kō′kü]—and more than 3,000 small ones. In total land area, the country is about the same size as California.

The location of Japan has helped shape its ans. 1
people and history. About 100 miles (160 kilometers) of water separate it from Korea. It is 500 miles (800 kilometers) across the sea to mainland China. Japan has been far enough away from other countries to discourage invasion and to remain isolated when it chose to shut out the outside world. At the same time, the country has been near enough to the Asian mainland to be able to borrow from other civilizations, especially the Chinese, whenever the Japanese felt it desirable to do so.

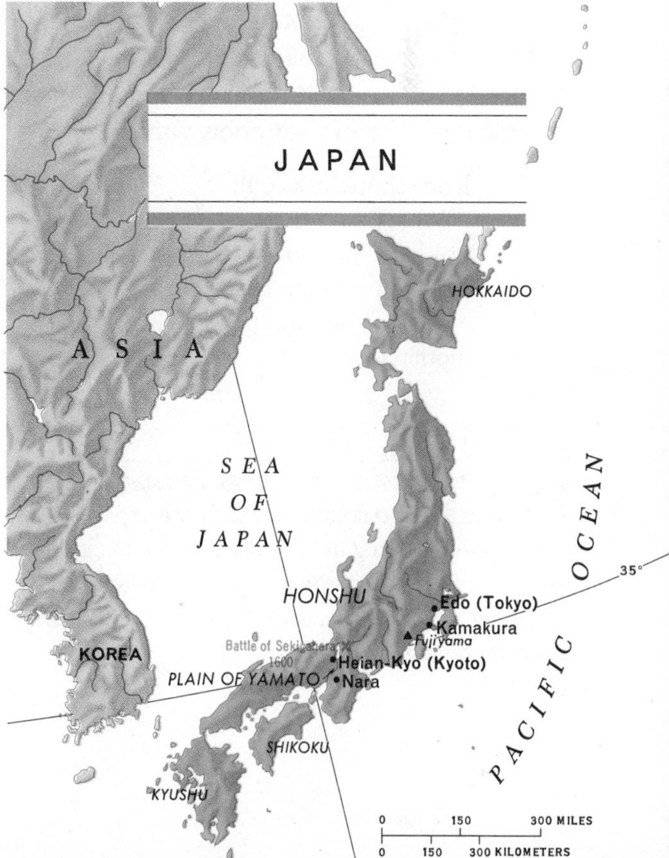

The sun goddess and the sea god create Japan in this 19th-century painting by Eitoku. Drops of water from the tip of the sea god's silver spear form the islands.

Japanese culture reflects a reverence for nature. Nature also has had a strong influence on Japanese life. Japan is a rugged, mountainous land noted for its picturesque scenery. One of the most impressive sights is Fujiyama (*yama* means mountain), a dormant volcano more than 12,000 feet (3,600 meters) high. In winter, it is snowcapped. In spring, its lower slopes are covered with cherry blossoms. The Japanese have developed a zest and appreciation for such wonders of nature that is reflected in all aspects of their culture. Japan's native reli-
ans 2 gion of Shintoism holds nature to be sacred, and shinto shrines have been built in many beautiful places throughout the country. The Japanese love of simple, natural beauty is also seen in their arts—in their style of architecture, sculpture, painting, and literature.

The Japanese call their land Nippon [ni pon′] or, especially in poetry, Yamato [yä′mä tō]. One of their poets wrote:

If one should ask you
  What is the heart
of Island Yamato—
It is the mountain cherry blossom
  Which exhales its perfume in the
morning sun.

SECTION REVIEW 1

p. 311 **1.** Name the two countries which are Japan's nearest neighbors. What are the distances between them and Japan? How has the sea protected Japan?

p. 312 **2.** What are two aspects of Japanese life that show a strong reverence for nature?

2 Early Japanese civilization borrowed from China

According to Japanese mythology, the islands were created and settled by a god and goddess. A divine grandson of the Sun Goddess was chosen as the ruler. In 660 B.C., one of his human descendants, Jimmu Tenno, was said to be the first Japanese emperor.

This belief in the divine origin of the emperor has played an important role in Japanese thinking. ● As one Japanese historian wrote:

> Great Yamato [Japan] is a divine country. It is only our land whose foundations were first laid by the Divine Ancestor. It alone has been transmitted by the Sun Goddess to a long line of her descendants. There is nothing of this kind in foreign countries.

Archaeology has revealed Japan's ancient past. Archaeological digging in the last thirty years has done much to fill in the gaps of knowledge about Japan's ancient history. People have lived in the Japanese islands for many thousands of years, probably from 30,000 B.C.
ans. 1 These early people hunted and fished and had a stone-age culture.

Around 250 B.C., a new people came to Japan, probably from northeastern Asia. These people were farmers who knew how to grow rice in flooded fields, using a farming method common in south China. They also knew how to weave cloth and use metals. Iron axes, knives, and hoes and bronze swords, spears, and mirrors have been found.

The first mention of Japan in writing appears in Chinese histories written at the beginning of the 1st century A.D. Japan is referred to as the "country of Wo," which is divided into 100 "countries" (that is, tribal groups). In a 3rd-century record, the Chinese say that the 100 "countries" of Wo were now grouped into 30, all ruled by a queen named Pimiko.

● Key Concept: the uniqueness of the homeland, the "fatherland", "mother England", the "middle kingdom", and the "land of the free" are examples.

A chief becomes emperor. Japanese contact with the mainland, particularly Korea, was strong from the 3rd through the 6th centuries A.D. Large groups of immigrants bringing new skills and ideas continued to move into the country. Among these immigrants were people with a strong warrior-tradition. These warrior people were skilled at fighting on horseback, and they rapidly populated the islands.

By about 500 A.D., one of these warrior chiefs, who ruled a small inland plain called Yamato, extended his rule over much of Japan and became recognized as emperor. The Yamato chief claimed descent from the Sun Goddess. His tokens of power—an iron sword, a curved jewel, and a bronze mirror representing the Sun Goddess—remain the symbols of the Japanese imperial family today.

As the Yamato chief and his descendants extended their rule, they spread the worship of the Sun Goddess. This faith, which later came to be called *Shinto* or "the way of the gods," held that ans. 2
nature had to be understood and reverenced. Many shrines were built during this early period in Japanese history to honor important features of nature, such as waterfalls, great groves of trees, and massive pieces of rock.

Japan learned from China. When the Yamato rulers became emperors, Japan had no written language and no architecture or art of any importance. The central government had little real power. China, however, had been developing a rich civilization for several centuries.

In the 6th century A.D., large numbers of Korean immigrants began crossing from the mainland. Educated Koreans brought with them the Chinese language with its character script. Skilled workers brought their arts and crafts.

Under the guidance of a great statesman, Prince Shotoku (574–622), Chinese ways were systematically copied. Prince Shotoku [shō tō′kü] ruled as regent for his aunt, Empress Suiko. In 600 A.D., he sent a large official delegation to China. In this delegation were a number of promising young men eager to study mainland civilization. They returned home as converts to Buddhism and champions of Chinese arts and institutions.

Prince Shotoku accepted Buddhism, as did the royal court. Buddhism gradually gained wide appeal. But Shintoism continued to be widely supported, and many Japanese practiced both faiths.

ans. 3 In addition to Buddhism, other borrowings from China included a calendar, ways of dress and cooking, and temple architecture. Chinese became the written language of the ruling class and scholars, who were then able to read the Chinese classics.

The Japanese tried to copy the efficient government of the Chinese. A law code similar to the Chinese one was drawn up, and strong efforts were made to extend the central government's power into the countryside as the Chinese had done. However, the Japanese rulers were never wholly successful in this extension of power. The Japanese rulers also made all land the property of the central government and established a taxing system.

Also following the Chinese example, the Japanese rulers decided to build a capital. Up to this time, Japan had no important political center. In 710, a capital city was built at Nara. Like the Chinese capital of the Tangs, it had fine palaces and Buddhist temples.

However, the Japanese did not adopt all ans. 3
Chinese ways. The Chinese examination system for selecting civil servants was not used because the Japanese believed that government officials should be chosen on the basis of birth and social rank. And unlike the Chinese, who believed that people could overthrow a bad ruler under the Mandate of Heaven, the Japanese thought that their divine emperor should never be overthrown. Thus, even though powerful families might gain actual political control, they always ruled behind the scenes. The emperor always remained honored in name as supreme ruler of Japan.

Japanese culture developed during the Heian Era (794–1156). In 784, Nara ceased to serve as the emperor's court and, after two moves, the capital was located in 794 at Heian-Kyo, which was later renamed Kyoto.

The founding of this new capital began what is known as the Heian [hā′än] period. During this time, Japan began to create its own kind of culture. It sent its last great embassy to Tang China in 838. By the early 900s, a distinct and new island civilization was being created in painting, architecture, and literature.

This flowering of cultural life was fostered by the emperor and his court in Heian. These nobles lived a sheltered life and hardly ever went out of the capital. They spent their days in ceremonies and festivities connected with court life and in endless pursuits of taste and culture.

Some of Japan's earliest prose literature was produced at this time. It was written almost entirely by women. One reason was that men of the court were taught to write in Japanese by using the complicated and cumbersome characters of Chinese. For formal writing, educated

Geography: A Key to History

East Asia's Bridgeland

While the Chinese influenced the Japanese, geographic features kept the two peoples separate; each developed a distinct culture. Ocean currents and winds made sea travel between China and Japan difficult. Instead, people traveled across Korea to get to China or Japan. Korea's culture reflects both China's and Japan's.

The dominant ocean current off East Asia is the *Kuroshio,* or Japan Current. It flows north from the sea between Indochina and the Philippines toward Japan. There is no major current that conveniently flows from Japan to China. Moreover, the Yellow Sea has many dangerous reefs and sandbars that hamper navigation.

East Asia, like India, experiences monsoon winds. These blow northwest from the Pacific in summer and southeast in winter. In doing so, they gave little help to sea travelers. Thus there was little sea contact between China and Japan until modern times, when steam power made it possible to move large ships against the current and against the wind.

Korea served as a land bridge between China and Japan. The Chinese first invaded Korea about 1122 B.C., settling near present-day Pyongyang. They introduced the growing of China's main crops, including rice and wheat. In later years, every major political change in China was felt in Korea. Chinese people who disagreed with the changes at home often fled to Korea.

During the Han dynasty, China sent troops to establish control in Korea. But these were pushed out by the forest tribes of Korea about the end of the Han period.

During the 1st century A.D., the Japanese invaded Korea, settling near present-day Pusan. They came across the Korea Strait in order to be near to Chinese culture. (Some anthropologists say the people of southern Korea and Japan are both descended from the same people. They think their ancestors came by sea, carried by the Kuroshio, from Taiwan and the Philippines.)

Throughout the past 2,000 years, the history of Korea has been marked by constant struggles between the Chinese and Japanese to control the country. In spite of this, the Korean people became unified and developed a unique culture.

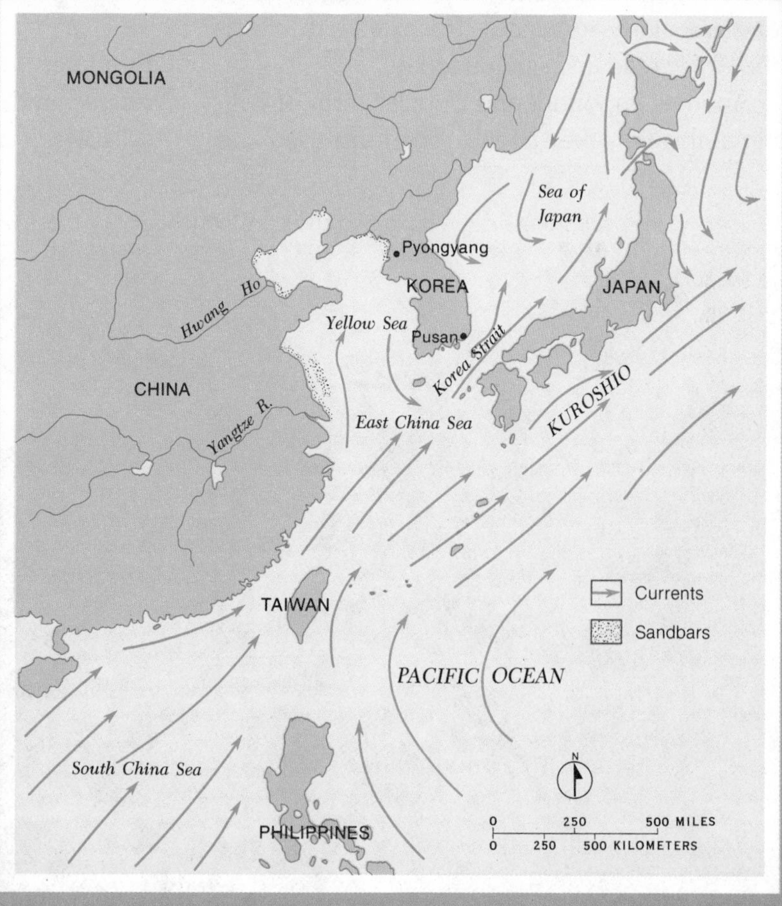

Japanese men wrote only in Chinese (much like the scholars of medieval Europe who ignored their native languages and wrote only in Latin).

Japanese women, however, did not learn to write in Chinese. Instead, they wrote in their native language using *kana.* Kana was actually a kind of alphabetic representation of the 47 syllables of the Japanese language. Kana developed in the 9th century.

Using simple kana, court women wrote di-
ans. 4 aries, letters, essays, and novels in abundance.
One of the most famous works of this period is the 11th-century *Tale of Genji* by Lady Murasaki. This novel—the first in any language—tells the story of Prince Genji, the "Shining Prince," and his many romances. It is a literary classic that is still read and studied today.

ans. 4 Another important and popular form of writing at this time was poetry. The form used was the *tanka.* It could only be five lines long and include a total of 31 syllables. The tanka was to remain the poetic model for 800 years. It is still a favorite form. Here are two early examples:

When spring comes
the melting snow
leaves no trace
Would that your heart too
melted thus toward me.

and:

I will think of you, love
On evenings when the grey mist
Rises above the rushes,
And chill sounds the voice
Of the wild ducks crying.

In a later period, the tanka became even more refined and compressed to three lines and 17 syllables. It was then called the *haiku* [hī′kü].

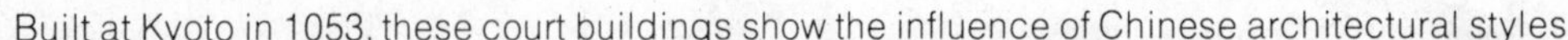

Built at Kyoto in 1053, these court buildings show the influence of Chinese architectural styles.

While the aristocrats in Heian were living lives of ease and comfort, Japanese outside the capital had rough and hard lives. Most were serfs, who worked a bare existence out of the land and had to give a large share of their crops to their local warrior-landlords. These landlords in turn had to pay heavy taxes to the tax collectors from the emperor's court to support the central government. The system gradually weakened when powerful court families and important local people got tax-free estates. As the taxing ability of the government declined, so did its power. By the middle of the 12th century, the emperor had authority in name only. He was in the hands of the warrior-landlords outside the capital who were fighting with each other for supremacy.

SECTION REVIEW 2

p. 313 **1.** How long ago do archaeologists think people first lived in Japan?

p. 313 **2.** What are the beliefs of Shintoism based on?

p. 314 **3.** What did the Japanese learn from China? Describe how Chinese culture was brought to Japan. In what two ways were Chinese and Japanese attitudes about government different?

p. 316 **4.** What were two literary achievements of the Heian period?

3 Feudalism and a samurai warrior-class developed

In 1156, outright civil war burst out between two great provincial landowning families. Each had its own loyal following of warriors, called samurai. These followers pledged complete loyalty to their lord. This allegiance was similar to the lord-vassal system of feudalism that grew up in Europe following the fall of Rome.

The Kamakura Shogunate (1192–1333) was founded. During the fighting, palaces were burned and people massacred. A leader named Minamoto Yoritomo [mē nä mō′tō yō rē tō′mō] came out on top. As victor, he was completely ruthless. He had his rivals killed, ans. 1 including his own brother. Yoritomo became the undisputed ruler and in 1192 had the emperor name him the *shogun* [shō′gun] or supreme general of the entire country. This office became *hereditary,* that is, passed down from father to son. Yoritomo's seat of government was at Kamakura, a small coastal town. The emperor remained a mere figurehead in Kyoto.

Under Yoritomo, Japan entered its feudal age, which lasted nearly 700 years. The feudal age was divided into three major periods: the Kamakura [kä mä kü′rä] Shogunate, the Ashikaga [ä shē kä′gä] Shogunate, and the Tokugawa [tō kü gä′wä] Shogunate. The samurai ans. 2 warriors were the most important class of people during the feudal period.

The key to the military and governmental power of the shoguns was the loyalty of the samurai class. Unlike European feudalism, the loyalty of the samurai knights was not a legal, contractual obligation. Instead, it was a moral tie. The samurai developed a code of conduct that came to be called *Bushido* [bü′shē dō], "the way of the warrior." Bushido stressed unswerving loyalty and a kind of spartan spirit of indifference to pain and hardship. Suicide by means of seppuku, or hara-kiri, was preferred to dishonor or surrender. Much of this code has survived to modern times in Japan.

A samurai wore very light armor that weighed no more than 25 pounds, which made him very agile on the battlefield. His main weapon was a sword. Many stories are told about the perfection of these blades: swords that could split a hair floating in space or slice through a stack of coins without leaving a scratch on the blade.

The Chinese tried to invade Japan. The Kamakura shoguns created order in Japan with samurai rule. But their greatest test came from overseas. The Mongol ruler of China, Kublai Khan, sent two invasions to conquer his island neighbor. The final attempt was made in 1281 when 150,000 soldiers carried in a great fleet were sent to conquer Japan. The Mongols were able to force a landing and the samurai fought desperately. When a great typhoon destroyed many of the Mongol supply ships, the invaders were forced to withdraw, thus losing many of their ships and soldiers. The Japanese gratefully called the typhoon the *Kamikaze* [kä′mē kä′zē], "the Divine Wind."

The Kamakura victory over the Mongols was its last great effort. Much treasure and strength had been spent defending the country. By the end of the 13th century, the power of the Kamakura shoguns was rapidly declining. The country broke into various feudal groups. In 1333, Kamakura rule ended. A new military group soon seized power and established the Ashikaga Shogunate.

Nobles struggled for power during the Ashikaga Shogunate (1394–1573). In the Kamakura period of Japanese feudalism, the shoguns ruled through their vassals, the samurai knights. In this second period, the shoguns did not control their vassals. For one reason, there were too many vassals to make the old system work. The power of the shogun hardly extended outside the capital, now back at Kyoto. Instead,

Warriors held the highest place in Japanese society and were admired for their skill and strength.

groups of samurai came to follow certain local nobles who were called *daimyo* [dī′myō], which meant "great name." The daimyo became absolute rulers on their lands. They had their own laws, which they could enforce over their followers. This system of regional rule was very similar to the type of feudal government that existed in Europe in the early Middle Ages.

During the period of the Ashikaga Shogunate, there was no effective central government in Japan. Daimyo struggled with each other for more power and territory. Local rivalries and wars raged over the country.

The arts flourished. Despite the turmoil, the country enjoyed one of its most productive eras in the arts. The Ashikaga period, like the Heian period long before it, was a golden age for Japanese culture. There were brilliant achievements in architecture, literature, and drama.

The *No* drama developed at this time. It was performed by two main characters and featured ans. 3

poetic passages chanted by a chorus. These ancient No plays are still performed today.

Another glory of this age was its painting. Beautiful landscapes, action-packed scenes of battle, and humorous drawings of people and animals were the chief subjects. The most famous artist of this time was a Buddhist monk named Sesshu (1420–1506). Many of his paintings have survived, including a magnificent landscape scroll that is 52 feet (about 15.6 meters) long.

ans. 3 The Ashikaga era is also important for its perfection of three typically Japanese arts. The first was flower arrangement. "Flower Experts" taught young women how to select and combine beautiful clusters for home decoration. The second art was the tea ceremony. This was held in a simple setting, in a room or tea house adjoining a garden. The tea was served with elaborate dignity amid quiet and thoughtful conversation. The third art was landscape gardening. Location was all-important for the garden, and the home had to form a single artistic unit. A well-developed garden usually had a little stream for a waterfall, then a bridge, and a small lake with its little island.

The Ashikaga period is also noted for another important event—the arrival of Europeans. In 1543, a group of Portuguese landed on a Japanese island. Within a few years, ship stops were frequent. Soon after, the famous Jesuit Saint Francis Xavier began preaching Christianity in the islands. At first, the newcomers were welcomed. Foreign trade increased. There was also important economic growth as handicraft industry advanced, farm production increased, and towns developed. There was a craze for all kinds of European gadgets, especially firearms. New plants, including tobacco and the potato, were introduced. Some Portuguese words—such as *pan* meaning "bread"—even found their way into the Japanese language.

During the end of the Ashikaga period in the late 1500s, fierce fighting continued between various noble groups. However, the larger and more powerful daimyo gradually began to win control over their weaker rivals. The field was finally dominated by two great rival groups. In 1600, the Battle of Sekigahara was fought between these two groups. The victor was Ieyasu [ē ye yä′sü], of the Tokugawa family.

Central government grew strong during the Tokugawa Era (1603–1868) In 1603, Ieyasu became shogun and master of a unified country (though the emperors still continued ans. 4
their unimportant existence in the old capital of Kyoto). The new shogun made all daimyo sign a written oath of loyalty to the central government. He exercised supreme military authority from his headquarters in Edo, a small coastal town, later known as Tokyo. The shogun made the daimyo live in Edo and spend every other year in the capital. Even when the daimyo left to go to their provincial homes, they had to leave the women of their family in Edo as hostages. The shogun also weakened the power of the daimyo in other ways. Thus, during this era, the central government grew strong again.

The first Tokugawa shogun also began a policy of isolating his country from foreign influence. This policy was continued by his successors. No Japanese were permitted to leave their homeland and those who had gone to other countries were not permitted to return. All foreign missionaries were expelled from the country or killed. Thousands of Japanese who had become Christian converts were executed. By 1638, Christianity had become virtually extinct in Japan.

By these measures, the Tokugawa created a conservative system of rule that resulted in peace for more than 250 years.

Changes came about in Japan. For a century, few important changes were noticeable in Tokugawa Japan. Japan remained a dominantly agricultural country. In the Tokugawa period, 8 out of 10 Japanese were farmer-serfs working on fiefs held by daimyo. But gradually, old feudal ways of life were challenged. During this period of peace, trade increased and cities grew in size. By the end of the 18th century, Tokyo's population had reached 1 million. As a result, the merchant and business classes became wealthy and influential. One of the leading families, the Mitsui, had a chain of stores in several cities by the 17th century. This chain became a leading company in modern Japan.

The wealth of the new business class helped it to support a new type of culture. Art and amusement were developed to please the city masses. The *Kabuki* [kä bü'kē] drama became popular. Unlike the dignified No plays, the Kabuki drama stressed violence, action, and melodrama. Its adventures of heroes and villains from stormy feudal times continue to be staged in modern times.

City people wanted art for their homes but could not afford costly paintings. To meet this demand, woodblock prints were produced. These colorful, inexpensive prints pictured beautiful women, actors, and scenes of everyday life in the streets, eating houses, and markets. Woodblock art reached the height of its development in the 18th century. Woodblock prints have been called "the world's first art for the masses."

By the end of the 18th century, Japan was ripe for great changes. The samurai had become poorer and out of place in the new commercial society, and young samurai became restless when they realized that the shogunate rule was out of date. Curious students obtained translations of books published in Europe and became eager to learn more about Western culture. The old feudal system was no longer able to meet the needs of the nation. It was swept away by the mid-19th century.

Visitors to the theater drank tea and ate rice cakes as the play sometimes went on all day.

SECTION REVIEW 3

p. 317 **1.** How did Yoritomo rise to power? Who was stronger, the shogun or the emperor?

p. 317 **2.** Who were the samurai? What did their code of conduct stress? How were they like the knights of feudal Christendom?

p. 318 319 **3.** Describe five developments in the arts that took place during the Ashikaga Shogunate.

p. 319 **4.** How did Ieyasu weaken the power of the daimyo? What other controls did the Tokugawa shoguns impose? What changes gradually weakened feudalism?

4 The Japanese created distinctive home and family customs

During their long history, the Japanese developed a unique way of life. In their homes and family lives, customs were quite different from those in other countries.

Ogata Korin (1658–1716) painted the fir-tipped island of Matsushima rising out of a foaming sea.

Japanese houses were simple. Houses were made of wood, since there was a shortage ans. 1 of stone. The homes were usually one-story to withstand the earthquakes that frequently occurred in Japan. Sliding panels made of heavy paper on wooden frames separated the rooms. These panels could be moved easily to make a room larger or smaller or to open it to the garden. The idea of "outdoors" and "indoors" was not as strong as in the Western world.

The homes had very little furniture—no chairs, beds, or sofas. Usually, the only piece was a low table for serving food. Meals consisted mostly of rice, fish, and vegetables, with a little seaweed and fruit. Very little meat was eaten. People sat crosslegged on cushions around the table.

Floors were covered with straw mats. These were protected by the custom of taking off sandals and clogs before entering a house. Heat came from a large earthware pot, the *hibachi* [hi bä′chē], that burned charcoal. Mattresses and blankets were kept hidden in cupboards and were spread on the floor at night for sleeping. Most rooms had no decoration except for a nook or alcove in which flowers could be

placed. On the wall of the alcove, there might be a single painting on paper or silk.

Houses had large tubs for very hot water. Whether rich or poor, everyone bathed daily. Before entering the tub, people washed thoroughly. The bath was mainly for relaxation.

The family in Japan, as in India and China, was the basic social unit. It was generally made up of a father and mother, their eldest son, his wife, and their children. The power of the father was unquestioned. Children were drilled in parental obedience. The head of the family represented it at all meetings and to some degree was responsible for the actions of its members.

The status of women changed. During the
ans. 2 earliest period of Japanese history, women enjoyed high political, social, and cultural status. In fact, during the Heian period, Japan had six empresses as rulers. At that time, women were the leaders in literary circles, and for one hundred years, all important authors were women. Laws protected the right of women to inherit and keep property. During Kamakura feudal days, samurai women were expected to have spartan virtues, and young girls were taught the use of weapons.

However, the trend was toward complete male supremacy. Women gradually lost their inheritance rights. By the Tokugawa period, they had become socially and legally inferior to men. Women were taught to serve men. Boys were valued more than girls. A wife did not share in her husband's social activities. This situation continued with little change well into the 20th century.

This gold lacquered box might have held a noblewoman's hairpins. Kamakura period, 14th century.

The artist Suzuki Harunabu caught the gust of wind that gave the laundress so much trouble.

SECTION REVIEW **4**

1. What materials were Japanese homes made of? p. 321
How were they furnished?

2. How did the role of women change in Japanese p. 322
society?

CHAPTER REVIEW 17

SECTION SUMMARIES

1. Japan's location influenced its history. The story of Japan has been greatly influenced by geography and climate. Beautiful rugged mountains, forested slopes, and varied landscapes created a strong love of nature among Japan's people. And the country's separation from the Asian mainland gave it protection from invasion.

2. Early Japanese civilization borrowed from China. In early stages of its history, Japan borrowed heavily from China. This was chiefly true in religion, government, and art. But by the 9th century when Japanese emperors had established their capital in Heian (Kyoto), Japan had begun to create its own special style of civilization. Poetic forms such as the tanka and haiku developed, and works of literature and painting were produced.

3. Feudalism and a samurai warrior-class developed. From the 12th through the mid-19th centuries, Japan's system of government was feudalism. There were three periods of feudal government—the Kamakura, Ashikaga, and Tokugawa—when the real ruler was the shogun. Emperors were mere figureheads but were respected because the Japanese thought them to be of divine descent.

During the early periods of feudal government, there was much discord and fighting between powerful noble families and their followers, the samurai. Finally, this civil war was ended by the advent of the Tokugawa Shogunate in 1603. The Tokugawa shoguns were able to control the unruly nobles and establish a strong central government. Japan was shut off from all contact with the outside world for more than 250 years. By the mid-19th century, a new merchant class had become powerful and influential in the cities. The old samurai class and feudal way of life seemed out of date. Japan was ready for sweeping changes.

4. The Japanese created distinctive home and family customs. During their long history, the Japanese people developed their own way of life. Japanese homes and furnishings were simple, and family life revolved around the father. The place of women in society changed over the years. From the Tokugawa period on, women had a lower status than men.

WHO? WHAT? WHEN? WHERE?

1. Match the years of each period with its name and arrange in chronological order:

Kamakura	1603–1868 Tokugawa (6)
Nara	1394–1573 Ashikaga (5)
Tokugawa	710–784 Nara (2)
Heian	500–710 Yamato (1)
Ashikaga	1192–1333 Kamakura (4)
Yamato	794–1156 Heian (3)

2. Match each of these events with the correct time period listed in question 1:

The Tale of Genji was written. Heian
Half of Japan's people became Buddhist. Yamato
Christianity was destroyed in Japan. Tokugawa
Yoritomo became the first shogun. Kamakura
Japanese culture became established. Heian
Portuguese traders came to Japan. Ashikaga
Official Japanese delegations went to China and brought Chinese culture to Japan. Yamato
A typhoon saved Japan from the Mongols. Kamakura

3. What do these terms mean to the Japanese?

shogun p. 317	Shinto p. 312
daimyo p. 318	Bushido p. 317
samurai p. 311	seppuku p. 317
kana p. 316	kabuki p. 320
Nippon p. 312	Kamikaze p. 318

CHAPTER TEST 17

QUESTIONS FOR CRITICAL THINKING

1. Why did the Japanese continue to support the emperor and his luxurious court after he had been reduced to a figurehead ruler?
2. Can you find a relationship between the art and life-style of the Japanese and the religious beliefs of Shintoism?
3. The main social unit of most early societies was the family. Has the family remained important in America today or has it been replaced? If so, by what?
4. Kabuki theater and woodcuts were produced for the public. What forms of art are enjoyed by "the masses" today?

ACTIVITIES

1. Draw or trace a map of Japan. Label these places:

Hokkaido
Honshu
Shikoku
Kyushu
Nara
Tokyo
Kamakura
Kyoto

2. Write a tanka or haiku following the rules included in this chapter. Find examples of Japanese tanka or haiku in your library and choose more than one favorite. Tell why you like them.
3. Find out about Japanese holidays and special celebrations. What events are important to the Japanese people and how are they celebrated?
4. Discuss the meaning of suicide in Japanese culture. First, reread the introduction to this chapter. Then find out the plot of the opera *Madame Butterfly*. Why did Mishima and Cio-Cio-san choose suicide?

● 1. (pp. 317 and 314) The Japanese emperors were considered to be divine.
2. (Use information on pp. 312, 316, 319, 321–22) Shinto is a form of nature worship. The simplicity of nature is imitated in home furnishing and in customs such as flower arranging.

SECTION 1

1. Japan is: a. a group of islands, b. a high plateau, c. one large island
2. Japan has been protected from invaders by its: a. high mountains, b. large size, c. sea barrier

SECTION 2

3. True or false: People probably began to live in Japan about 300 B.C.
4. Some of Japan's earliest prose literature was written by: a. Buddhist monks, b. women at the Heian court, c. Chinese immigrants

SECTION 3

5. The warriors of Japan's feudal families were called samurai.
6. The first shogun was: a. seppuku, b. Yoritomo, c. Kamakura
7. True or false: The Ashikaga Shogunate had great control over the noble families.
8. True or false: The Japanese have made an art of making and serving tea.
9. The most powerful person in Japan was the: a. daimyo, b. emperor, c. shogun
10. In 1638, the Christian religion was destroyed in Japan.
11. Business and trade grew under the Tokugawa shoguns.

SECTION 4

12. The head of a Japanese family was the: a. mother, b. oldest son, c. father
13. True or false: At one time, women in Japan were trained to use weapons like samurai warriors.
14. Stone was not used for building because: a. there is not very much stone in Japan, b. the ground is too soft, c. there are many earthquakes

3. The family structure has been weakened. Government services supply much of what was once a family responsibility.
4. Television, records, radio, motion pictures, books.

UNIT REVIEW 5 — TEST YOURSELF

1. Show whether the events described below took place in: a. India, b. China, or c. Japan

C The real ruler was a hereditary military ruler.
A Shah Jahan built a beautiful tomb to the memory of his dead wife.
B The people thought of themselves as living in the Middle Kingdom, superior to all other nations.
C An official delegation was sent to China to learn its customs.
C Water separates it on all sides from neighboring countries.
A Some Hindus adopted the custom of purdah.
C The emperor was considered divine and could never be overthrown.
B Civilization continued unchanged despite periodic invasions.
B The country was divided into two empires, with invaders ruling in the north.
A The people were divided into many castes.
C Women wrote most of the early prose literature.
B Invaders were assimilated into the culture of the country.

2. For each of the items below, choose the letter "T" if the statement is true for China, India, and Japan. Choose "F" if the statement is not true for all three.

T Women were considered less important than men.
F There was little contact between the peasants and the government.
T Families were run by the oldest male relative.
F Soldiers were an important group because of the many feudal wars.
F Mongols conquered the nations.
T Marriages were arranged by heads of families.
T People were divided into many classes.
F The ruler was of a different religion than most of the people.
T Christian missionaries made contact with the rulers.

3. Choose the correct ending for each statement:

The Delhi Sultans ruled India during the time that: a. the Mongols and the Mings ruled China, b. the Japanese began to adopt Chinese customs, c. the Taj Mahal was built
Who of these are remembered as good rulers? a. Yoritomo, b. Tamerlane, c. Wang An Shih
Which ruler forcibly isolated his nation from contact with the outside world? a. Prince Shotuku, b. Akbar, c. the Tokugawa shogun
Marco Polo visited: a. China, b. Japan, c. India
In the 16th century, the European nation that made contact with Asia was: a. England, b. Portugal, c. France
Which one was not a Muslim ruler? a. Mahmud of Ghazni, b. Ieyasu, c. Babur
The largest empire was that of the: a. Manchus, b. Mongols, c. Delhi Sultans
Which one was not an important reformer? a. Akbar, b. Wang An Shih, c. Ieyasu
In writing literature, Japanese women used: a. suttee, b. purdah, c. kana

4. Choose one of the following questions to answer. Be sure your answer includes examples that show you understand the subject. •

a. What is the dynastic cycle? How has it made China's history different from India's? From Japan's?

b. What is feudalism? How was feudalism in Japan like feudalism in western Christendom? How was it different? Consider both the similarities and differences in government and in the lives of ordinary people.

c. How does it make a difference to a country for it to have rulers who are from a different culture? (Use examples from what you have learned of India's history and of China's history in this Unit. Was the experience the same in both countries? Different? How?)

• Answers will vary.

Mr. WILLIAM
SHAKESPEARES
COMEDIES,
HISTORIES, &
TRAGEDIES.

UNIT 6

THE RISE OF THE WEST

If Martians had landed on Earth in the year 1200 and had looked for the most important civilization, they would not have picked Christendom. In 1200, the most advanced civilizations were in China, India, and the Middle East. Yet within 500 years, Christendom was transformed into modern Europe, the most powerful and influential civilization on Earth.

During the 500-year transition period, there were vast changes in government, philosophy, religion, art, weapons, and economic development. As Europeans established colonies and spread their culture overseas, an enlarged area of European civilization was created that came to be known as the West. The rise of the West, which no one could have predicted in 1200, was one of the remarkable happenings in human history.

How did the Europeans become so strong? An important part of the answer is that they organized themselves into large, rich, and powerful political units called *nations*. Kings of nations were ■ able to do things that feudal nobles could not, such as pay for expensive overseas voyages, support large armies, conquer lands and set up colonies, and build great navies to protect them.

The West also became the dominant civilization in the world because the peoples of Asia, Africa, the Middle East, and the Americas did not organize themselves into strong national states.

This unit tells the story of how the Europeans changed their political organizations and carried their culture around the world.

The printing press helped spread ideas throughout Europe.

■ The concept of a *nation* is important. Section 1 explains the term and all the Questions for Critical Thinking asks students to elaborate on it.

It is a story filled with conflict and violence. It begins when national monarchs used force to take power away from unwilling feudal nobles. It continues as these monarchs tried to take power away from each other. Great wars raged in Europe, some of them civil wars, others

	900	1000	1100	1200	1300
CHAPTER **18** **The Development of Nations**		Otto the Great invades Italy	Norman Invasion; Plantagenet's dynasty	Reign of Henry II; Magna Charta; Louis IX	Battle of Crécy
CHAPTER **19** **The European Renaissance**					Revival of learning begins; Petrarch born; Black Death
CHAPTER **20** **The Reformation and National Power**					Babylonian Capt
CHAPTER **21** **The Age of Exploration**					
CHAPTER **22** **The Formation of Latin America**					

international. As monarchs financed explorers, the violence spread to other continents. Every national monarch had the same purpose in mind—to make his or her own state as powerful as possible.

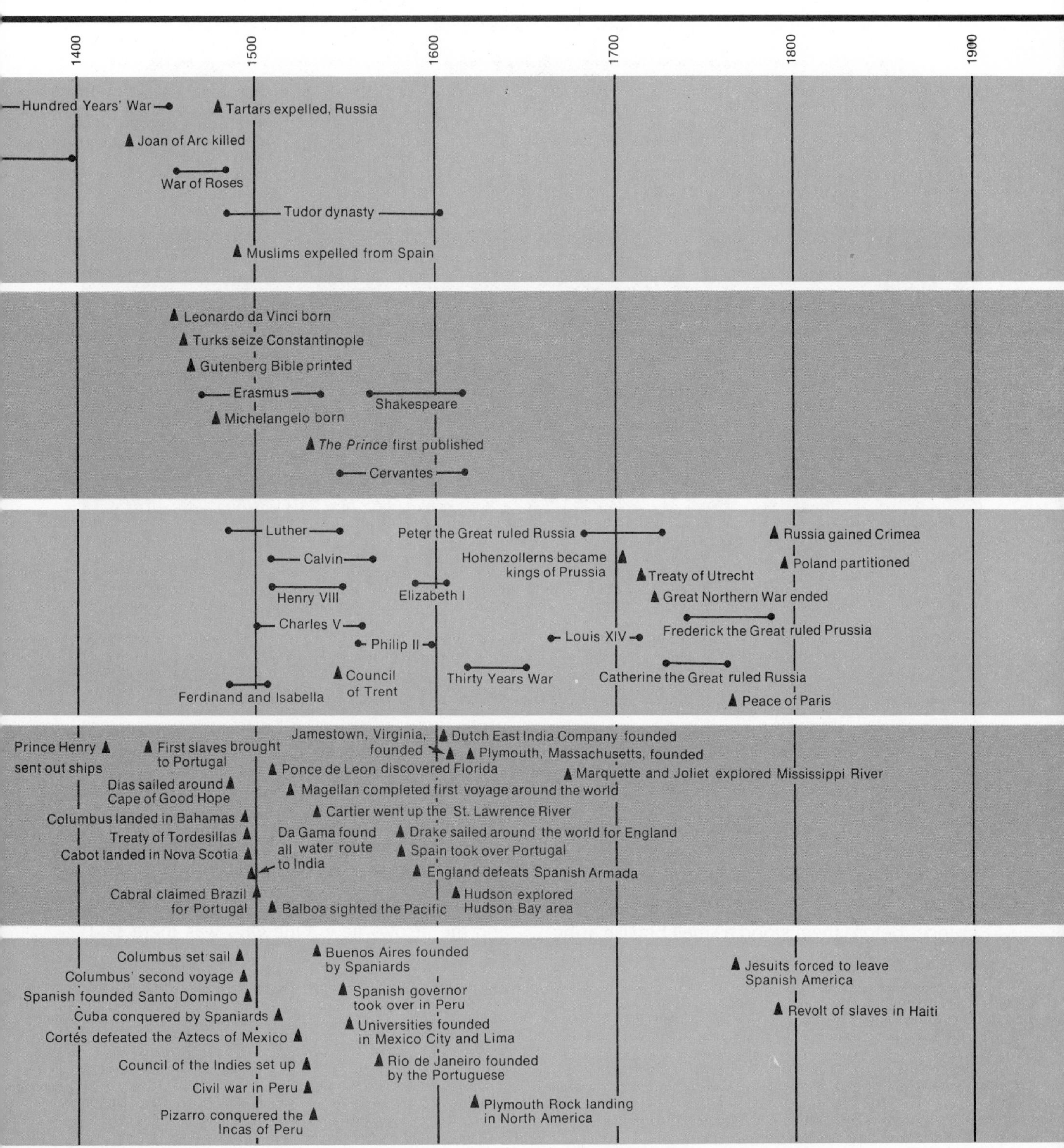
1400
1500
1600
1700
1800
1900
Hundred Years' War
Tartars expelled, Russia
Joan of Arc killed
War of Roses
Tudor dynasty
Muslims expelled from Spain
Leonardo da Vinci born
Turks seize Constantinople
Gutenberg Bible printed
Erasmus
Shakespeare
Michelangelo born
The Prince first published
Cervantes
Luther
Peter the Great ruled Russia
Russia gained Crimea
Calvin
Hohenzollerns became kings of Prussia
Poland partitioned
Treaty of Utrecht
Henry VIII
Elizabeth I
Great Northern War ended
Charles V
Frederick the Great ruled Prussia
Philip II
Louis XIV
Council of Trent
Thirty Years War
Catherine the Great ruled Russia
Ferdinand and Isabella
Peace of Paris
Prince Henry sent out ships
First slaves brought to Portugal
Jamestown, Virginia, founded
Dutch East India Company founded
Plymouth, Massachusetts, founded
Ponce de Leon discovered Florida
Marquette and Joliet explored Mississippi River
Dias sailed around Cape of Good Hope
Magellan completed first voyage around the world
Cartier went up the St. Lawrence River
Columbus landed in Bahamas
Treaty of Tordesillas
Da Gama found all water route to India
Drake sailed around the world for England
Cabot landed in Nova Scotia
Spain took over Portugal
England defeats Spanish Armada
Cabral claimed Brazil for Portugal
Hudson explored Hudson Bay area
Balboa sighted the Pacific
Columbus set sail
Buenos Aires founded by Spaniards
Columbus' second voyage
Jesuits forced to leave Spanish America
Spanish founded Santo Domingo
Spanish governor took over in Peru
Cuba conquered by Spaniards
Revolt of slaves in Haiti
Cortés defeated the Aztecs of Mexico
Universities founded in Mexico City and Lima
Council of the Indies set up
Rio de Janeiro founded by the Portuguese
Civil war in Peru
Plymouth Rock landing in North America
Pizarro conquered the Incas of Peru

CHAPTER
18

871–1552

The Development of Nations

This jeweled crown was made for the coronation of Otto I as Holy Roman Emperor in 961. It serves as a lasting symbol of the growth of strong kings during this time. It can be flattened for traveling, which was often necessary in the ever enlarging empires of the era.

On the afternoon of August 26, 1346, a large army of rain-soaked French knights rode across a muddy field near the village of Crécy [krā sē′], France. Before them stood a small English army of foot soldiers, archers with longbows, and knights without horses.

● The longbow was the secret weapon of the English. Six feet long, it shot steel-tipped arrows which were dangerous at 400 yards and deadly at 100.

French knights would not fight with commoners but English nobles fought at the side of peasant bowmen.

The showers ended. The French knights charged toward the outnumbered English. Suddenly, the English archers bent their longbows, and the arrows flew. One who was there said, "It was like snow." The heavy armor of the charging knights could not stop the deadly arrows. Many French fell, killed or wounded. But the army charged again and again. By midnight, more than a thousand French knights lay dead on the field. The English had lost only about fifty men.

This battle was only one of many between the English and French in the Hundred Years' War (1337–1453). But it held many signs for the future. When the English bowmen defeated the French knights, the end of the whole feudal system began. Armor was almost no help
ans. 3 against the longbow and cannon the English used. The battle at Crécy marked the first use of gunpowder in a field battle.

● The future also showed in the victors' new feeling about themselves. They were becoming English, not merely people of a certain village or followers of a certain noble. In other words, they were becoming loyal to their country. With their love of country, common language, customs, and growing central power, they were becoming a nation.

New weapons and a loyal people helped change the way lands and government were organized. The government of a national monarchy had more power. Its king ruled over more land and people than did the government of any local prince. The move toward strong national monarchies lasted into the 18th century. It started in western Europe. Later, it grew in eastern Europe. This chapter tells how:

1. Feudalism became old-fashioned.

2. England became one nation.

3. French kings built a national state.

4. Other European peoples made nations.

● Besides the glow of victory, the fact that all classes fought together also helped the growth of national pride in England.

■ Key concept: change occurred because the middle class was now strong enough to demand it and to help kings bring it about.

1 Feudalism became old-fashioned

During most of the Middle Ages in Europe, strong national governments were unknown. In France, at least 10 thousand separate pieces of land were in some way countries themselves. France had a king who in theory ruled over his nobles. But those nobles, who should have been loyal, often did just as they pleased.

Wider trade called for improved government. Times changed. By the year 1100, cities had begun to grow rather rapidly. Trade expanded, and the population grew.

The bourgeoisie disliked the lack of law and ans. 1
order that hurt business and threatened property. ■ They were unhappy with feudal obligations. And the different legal systems upset them. The nobility had their own courts, as did the Church. Church courts tried not only churchmen, but also students, crusaders, and churchmen's servants.

Trade and commerce needed safer and better ways to move about. A feudal noble could decide alone whether a highway that passed through his fief should be kept in good repair. He often charged huge tolls for use of a road or river through his land. Worse, people had no able police force to protect them. The rocky, muddy roads were full of bandits who attacked travelers. The situation called for a change.

Strong kings extended their power. Kings gained power at the expense of the Church and the nobles. Kings collected taxes from the grow- ans. 2
ing merchant class in exchange for protecting their property. This new source of wealth helped kings depend less on their nobles. Earlier, kings had relied on nobles who were their vassals to

bring in men for the armies. With more tax money, kings could pay *mercenaries*—professional soldiers and officers. Husky peasants could become good soldiers of the king. Almost all countries that began central national governments during this time followed this pattern.

ans. 4 As kings gained power, they built up their governments. They hired civil servants, that is, government workers, to handle money matters, military affairs, and legal problems. Advisers were hired to help kings rule their countries. The kings freed people in towns from many feudal duties. And kings reduced the tolls merchants paid and protected them along the roads. Kings also began to bring all the people under one set of royal courts. These courts tried to make the law the same for everyone. In sum, kings were building bigger, stronger units called *nations*.

A nation has three important characteristics. ans. 5
First, its central government is strong enough to ■
defend itself against enemies and keep order inside its borders. Second, a nation's people are set off from neighboring groups by language, religion, traditions, and way of life. Third, the people are loyal and proud of the group. Their feeling is called *nationalism* or *patriotism*.

■ See Question for Critical Thinking 2.

SECTION REVIEW 1

p. 331 **1.** Give three reasons the middle class disliked the feudal system.

p. 331 **2.** How did merchants' taxes help kings free themselves from nobles?

p. 331 **3.** What new tools of war changed medieval ways of fighting?

p. 332 **4.** Name four ways kings improved their governments as they gained power.

p. 332 **5.** What are the characteristics of a nation?

2 England became one nation

England began to build a strong centralized government as early as the 1000s. When the king of England died in 1066, William, duke of Normandy, stated his right to be king. Although a Frenchman, William had distant ties to English kings. He was not chosen, though. He then crossed the English Channel with an army whom he promised to reward with lands. In England, he defeated the new king, Harold, at the Battle of Hastings. William, who earned the name the Conqueror, became king of England.

William the Conqueror began a strong monarchy. As king, William the Conqueror was too strong to let his nobles challenge his power. He changed the feudal system so that it ans. 1
supported his own strong government. He made all nobles become his vassals, and he broke up the largest feudal holdings. He made all men of England bear arms for the king so that he did not have to rely on his nobles' armies.

William also added to his sources of money. He ordered a census of all the taxable wealth in his kingdom. These facts were gathered into the *Domesday Book,* which today gives an excellent picture of 11th-century England.

England was not one nation in 1066, and William did not make it one. But William did lay a firm base for a strong monarchy.

Henry II improved the legal system. William and the three kings who ruled after him are called the Norman kings. After them, England came under the rule of Henry II, a great-grandson of William's.

During the Hundred Years' War, sieges such as this one involved savage treatment of civilians in the town. A cannon, crossbows, and longbows are being used.

Hoping to win his quarrel with the Church, Henry II appointed his old friend Thomas à Becket as archbishop of Canterbury. But Becket did not give in to Henry. In a fit of anger, Henry asked, "Will no one rid me of this man?" Four loyal knights then murdered Becket in his own cathedral. Henry lost his battle over Church judicial rights and had to undergo a humiliating penance. This illuminated manuscript page shows the knights murdering Becket, who later was made a saint. Trips to his tomb became part of English life.

The reign of Henry II (1154–1189) was one of the greatest in English history. Henry was determined to unite all of England under his rule. He wanted all the people to look to him and to their national government for justice
ans. 2 and protection. Henry II made his royal law the law of the land. Because it was the same for everyone, it was fairer and better run than the many different kinds of law in use then. Over
● time, it came to be known as *common law*, because the whole country used it. It was based on custom and court decisions. Common law is used today in most of the United States and in nations and colonies that Great Britain began.

Henry II used an old custom of sending judges on regular tours all over the country. These traveling judges combined local legal customs with legal opinions from the king's court to form the common law. Judges who went from place to place were strangers in each district, so they were not open to bribes, threats, or feelings about friends. Each judge followed a *circuit*, or route. An important part of the English judicial system today, this practice also gave root to United States circuit courts.

● Key concept: Common law is the basis of much of the American system of justice.

■ An edited version of the film, *Becket*, may be available in some areas for school use.

The jury system also grew under Henry II. The first juries were people who came before a royal judge to accuse someone of breaking a law. They did not decide whether the person was guilty. From this early jury came the *grand jury* of today. The grand jury decides whether evidence against the accused is enough to hold that person for trial. About a century after Henry's time, another kind of jury came into use. It heard a trial and decided on guilt of the accused. This kind is called a *petit* (little), or trial, jury.

Henry II was an able, energetic man. He faced great problems that would have defeated others. The nobles—and even his sons—were against him.

The Church fought Henry's moves against its courts. Henry believed that Church courts were often too easy. He wanted all his subjects under one system of justice. His stand led to a well- ■
known quarrel with the Church. Thomas à Becket, archbishop of Canterbury, opposed Henry. So some of Henry's knights murdered Becket. Nobles and the Roman Church were greatly angered. Henry's cause was hurt. His

dream of equal justice for all English people was not realized until after the Middle Ages.

● **Magna Charta assured some rights.** Henry's youngest son John became king in 1199. He was a cruel, unreasonable ruler. In 1215, King John's nobles rebelled against his unjust rule. They forced him to agree to the *Magna Charta* [mag′nə kär′tə], or Great Charter.
ans. 3 This document limited John's power and protected nobles' feudal rights. The Magna Charta did not guarantee representative government. Taxation by the people's consent and trial by jury were not written in it. But these principles grew from the rights it did state.

The Magna Charta forced the king to make this promise: "To no one shall we sell, deny, or delay right or justice." He also promised to stop taking his vassals' property and forcing them to give him money.

The king could collect no money over that allowed by the old laws of feudalism except "by the common council of our kingdom." These words later grew to mean that the king could not raise any new taxes unless the people agreed through their representatives. American colonists used this principle in objecting to "taxation without representation."

Another clause of the Magna Charta declared:

> No free man shall be seized, or imprisoned . . . nor shall we pass sentence on him except by the legal judgment of his peers or by the law of the land.

These words were later taken to mean that all freemen had a right to trial by jury. Most English people were still serfs. But as more people became free, they also gained the rights promised to freemen in 1215.

● Key concept: The importance of the Magna Charta lies in two great principles: (1) the law is above the king and (2) the king can be forced to obey the law.

Parliament took shape under Edward I. Edward I (1239–1307) tried to bring the whole island under one rule. In 1284, he took over Wales. He also tried to take Scotland, but he could not defeat its freedom-loving people. These wars were costly, and Edward needed more money. So he collected extra taxes. The taxes were approved by the people's representatives in *Parliament* [pär′lə mənt].

English kings had long had a group of advisers made up of churchmen and nobles. In 1295, Edward called these great nobles and churchmen to meet with him. He also ordered the *sheriffs* (local officers of the law) to hold elections in their counties. Freemen chose two knights from each county. From each chartered town, called a *borough,* they chose two *burgesses,* or citizens. This group came to be known as the Model Parliament because later parliaments were modeled on it.

In time, the Church withdrew from Parliament. Nobles made up what became the House of Lords. Elected knights and townsmen made up what became the House of Commons. This second group was a *representative body.* That is, each member spoke for many people and voted in their interests.

Early kings called Parliament mainly to get ans. 4
money. But Parliament began to have other ideas. Its members hit on the idea of refusing to grant money until a ruler corrected wrongs. This means was called *redress of grievances.* Parliament drew up statements of demands called *bills.* These bills became laws, called *acts* or *statutes,* after the ruler signed them. So Parliament became a lawmaking, or legislative, body. In many countries, the word *parliament* has come to mean the highest lawmaking body. Thus, England has earned the name "Mother of parliaments."

Daily Life in Europe

These medieval book pages show how life was then. A woman holding a pet dog *(above)* buys a belt from a peddler. In a page from Chaucer's *The Canterbury Tales (above left)*, pilgrims are on their way to Saint Thomas à Becket's tomb in Canterbury. An illuminated prayer book *(below left)* called *The Book of Hours* shows French peasants planting grain in what is now downtown Paris. Behind them is the Louvre. It was then a king's storage place for money. Today, it is a famous museum. Three men *(below)* are village judges holding court out of doors.

The Wars of the Roses brought a new line of strong kings. ● In 1455, two branches of the English royal family began to fight over the throne. Those wars between the House of York and the House of Lancaster lasted thirty years. They were called the Wars of the Roses because the York emblem was a white rose and the Lancaster, a red rose. During these wars, many noble families of England were destroyed. In 1485,
ans. 5 Henry Tudor of the House of Lancaster won the throne. As Henry VII, he united the families and ■ began the Tudor dynasty. It ruled England until 1603.

The Tudor reign was a time of strong royal power. War had weakened the nobles. The king's judges carried out the common law. And a well-run group of civil servants helped govern the kingdom. England under the Tudors gained as a leader in European affairs. Culture flowered.

By the end of the Tudor reign, the English nation had become strongly rooted. All the people lived under common law. A national government ruled in all parts of the land. People thought of themselves as English. They were as one people, proud of their ruler and their country.

SECTION REVIEW 2

p. 333 **1.** How did William the Conqueror make the English monarchy stronger?

p. 334 **2.** Name three ways in which Henry II improved the legal system.

p. 335 **3.** What was the purpose of the Magna Charta? Name two modern democratic principles that are based on it.

p. 335 **4.** How did the rulers' needs for money change Parliament into a lawmaking body?

p. 337 **5.** Who was the first Tudor? Describe how Henry VII became king.

● Abler students may wish to read Shakespeare's *Richard III*.

■ Henry's queen was of the House of York.

3 French kings built a national state

France was far behind England in moving toward a national government. Central power ended after Charlemagne's death. A wholly feudal government grew around strong local princes. In the late 900s, the name France meant only a small section around Paris. What was vaguely thought of as a kingdom was really just a group of feudal states. As a result, the French kings' task of bringing their nation together was harder than that of their royal neighbors across the English Channel.

In 987, the French nobles elected Hugh Capet [kā′pit], Count of Paris, as king. Many of his feudal nobles were much more powerful than he. But the Capetian [kə pē′shən] family grew strong through wars and pacts with powerful nobles. The family ruled until 1328.

Kings strengthened the government. The ans. 1
Capetian kings first had to show that they were stronger than the nobles. The first king able to do that was Louis VI (Louis the Fat), who ruled from 1108 to 1137. He gained full control over his royal lands, called the *Ile de France*. His ● grandson, Philip II, won Normandy, Anjou, and other English holdings in France from King John. Year by year, Capetian kings pushed out from their capital at Paris to make Ile de France larger.

Like those in England, kings of France gave ans. 2
the people better government than had the feudal lords. Louis IX set up a system of royal courts. And he outlawed private wars and trial by combat. He told the people to ask his officials for help if nobles wronged them. In this way, he let all French people know that their government was important to their well-being. The

● A small area around Paris.

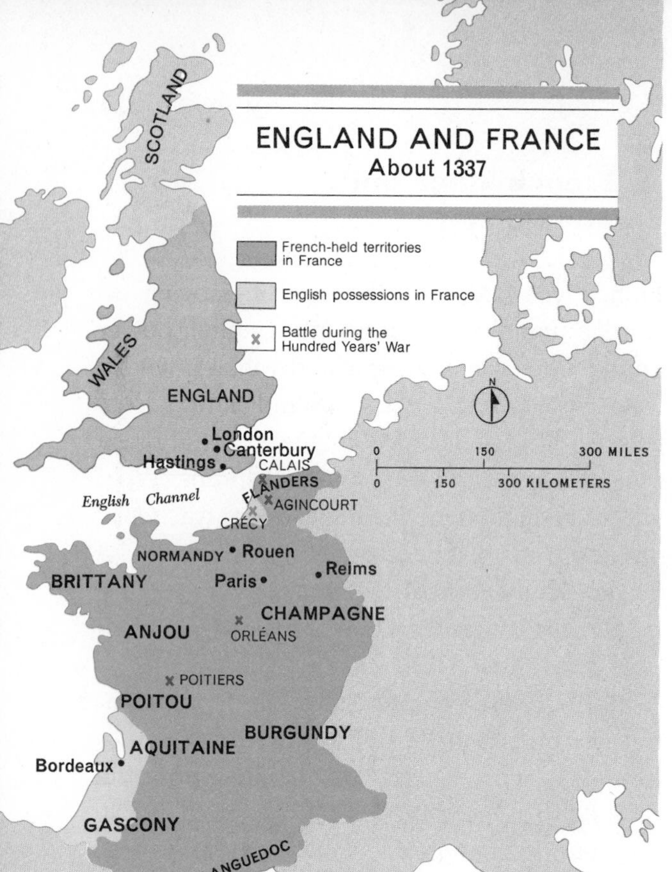

French, however, did not develop a strong parliament. The king, for example, did not have to ask the French parliament for approval of new taxes.

Louis IX was a true knightly king of the Middle Ages. He led his knights in the crusades. As a prisoner of the Muslims, he was brave and dignified. Peace and justice seemed to him far more important than conquests. The Church made him a saint after his death.

England threatened French freedom. French kings not only had worries at home but also often faced possible trouble with England. Some French lands still lay in English hands. Norman invaders under William the Conqueror had not given up their lands when they left France. So English rulers were vassals of the French kings. The English, though, believed themselves equals of their French lords. From the mid-1100s to the mid-1400s, the English and French were often at war.

● The city was saved. This victory was a turning point in the long conflict between France and England.

In 1328, the last Capetian king died without a direct male heir. Edward III of England had blood ties to the Capets through his mother. Therefore, he claimed the throne of France, but the French refused to accept him. That refusal was the excuse Edward needed to take an army to France in 1337. His move began a number of wars that in all became known as the Hundred Years' War. ans. 3

The fighting in all these wars took place in France, but the English often had the advantage of better generals and weapons. In 1346, Edward's troops, with longbows and cannons, crushed the French at Crécy. The next year they took Calais [ka lā′]. In 1415, under King Henry V, English longbows helped defeat a large French army at Agincourt. With this battle, England took back Normandy.

Joan of Arc inspired patriotism. Joan of Arc's story shows the French people's growing love of country. By 1425, it seemed that England would conquer and rule France. Then an amazing story unfolded. A simple country girl, Joan of Arc, "knowing neither A nor B," as she said, had visions and believed that she heard the voices of saints calling on her to rid France of English soldiers.

In 1429, she went to Charles, the uncrowned king, and asked for an army to save the city of Orléans. She promised to defeat the English and save the throne for him. Charles and his court doubted her. However, they themselves could not stop the English. They gave her the soldiers she asked for. ●

In shining armor, mounted on a white horse, Joan appeared to the French soldiers as a heaven-sent leader. Filled with new hope, they attacked the English like a thunderbolt. For a short time, Joan of Arc led her soldiers to victory after victory.

With her at his side, Charles was crowned king of France. Then Joan fell into the hands of the English. She was tried as a witch and burned at the stake in 1431.

ans. 4 The English could not destroy what Joan stood for. The French people treasured the memory of the simple peasant girl. Her love of country and her courage gave them a new sense of patriotism. Her loyal deeds helped a national spirit grow in France. People began to feel that France was united. No foreigner should be allowed to rule it. From this time on, the English fought a losing battle. By the end of the war in 1453, the English held only the city of Calais.

The French victory ended England's costly attempts to take France. Both nations now could turn to their own internal problems.

SECTION REVIEW 3

1. How did the Capetian kings grow strong? p. 337
2. How was French government improved? p. 337
3. Why did Edward III of England invade France in 1337? p. 338
4. Why were the French finally able to defeat the English? p. 339

4 Other European peoples made nations

While England and France were growing stronger and more unified, nations were beginning in other parts of Europe.

Portugal and Spain became separate nations. A Germanic tribe, the Visigoths, had

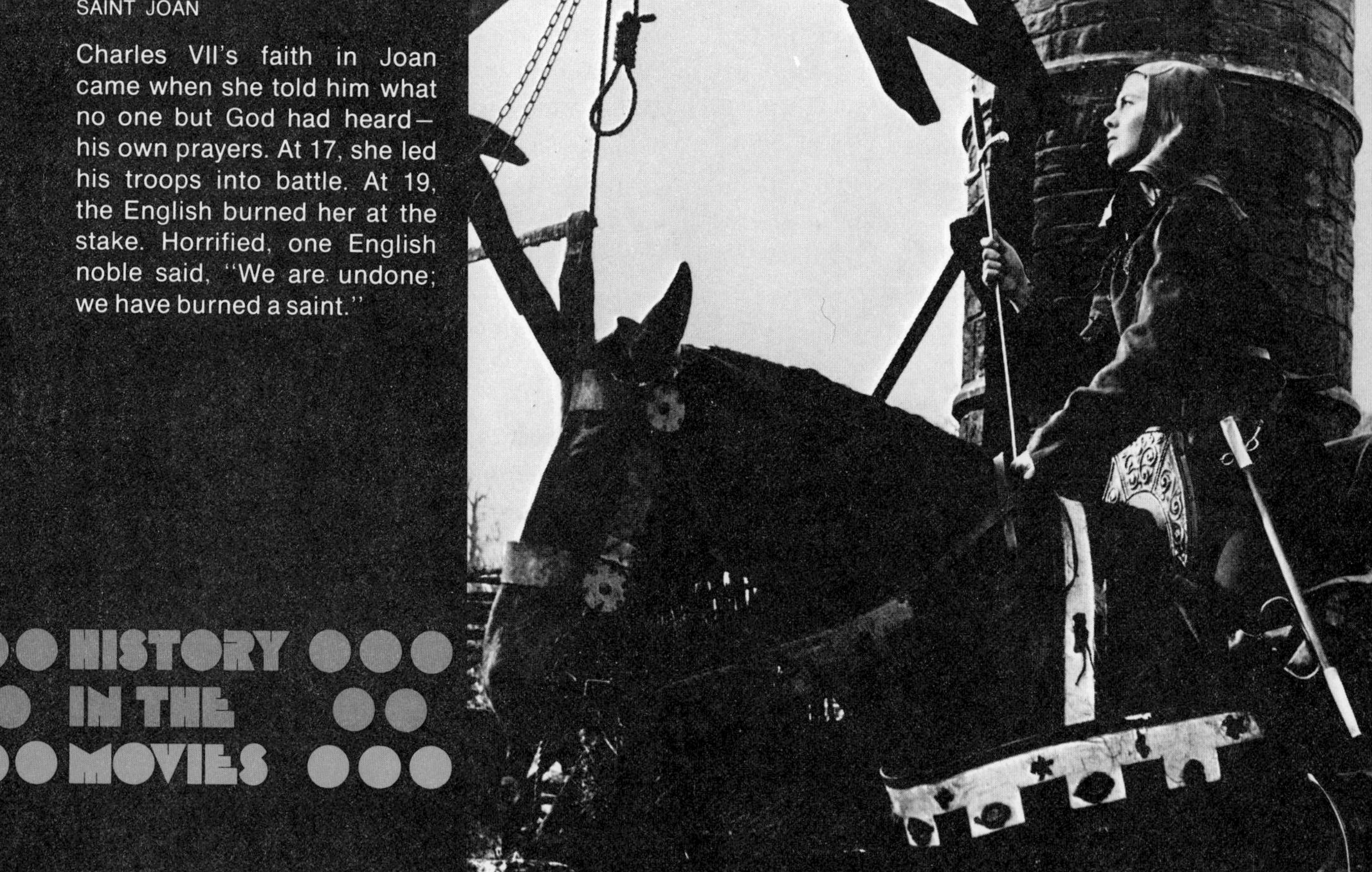

SAINT JOAN

Charles VII's faith in Joan came when she told him what no one but God had heard—his own prayers. At 17, she led his troops into battle. At 19, the English burned her at the stake. Horrified, one English noble said, "We are undone; we have burned a saint."

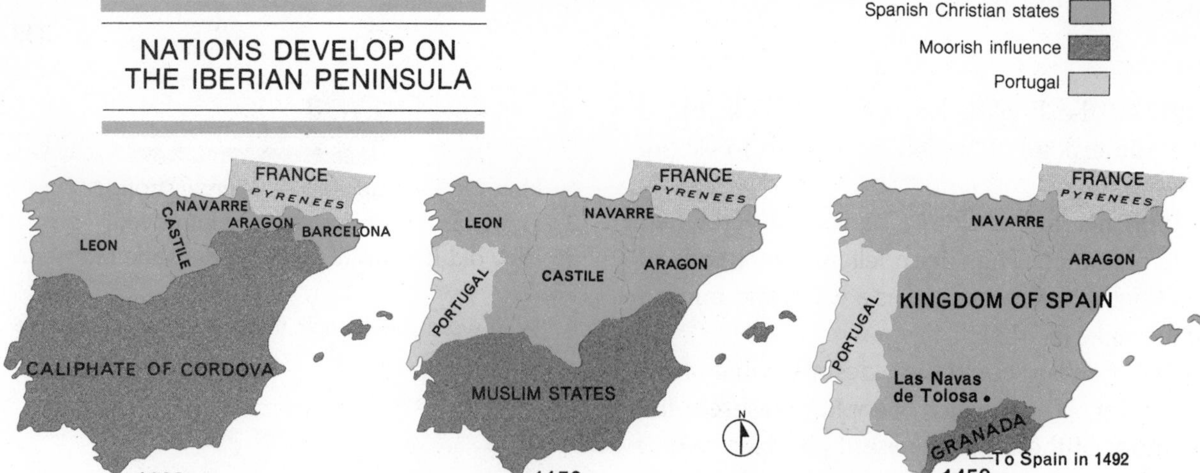

settled in the Iberian peninsula during the German invasions of the Roman Empire. Their kingdom lasted until early in the 700s. Then in 711, a group of Muslims known as Moors crossed the Strait of Gibraltar. They took most of the peninsula. A few Christians held out near the Pyrenees Mountains. Their groups were so small, though, that the Moors did not try very hard to defeat them.

The Moors built up a Muslim kingdom, the Caliphate of Cordova, that reached a high level of culture. In 1031, quarrels inside the kingdom caused it to break up into more than twenty
● small states. The breakup helped Christians in the north. They began a crusade to regain Spain for Christendom. Nobles from many parts of Europe came to help drive out the Moors.

Alphonso I of Portugal defeated the Moors in
ans. 1 his country in 1139. He declared Portugal an independent kingdom in 1143. Gradually, the Christian kingdoms of the northern peninsula drove back the Moors. After a major victory at Las Navas de Tolosa in 1212, only Granada remained in Muslim hands.

In 1469, Ferdinand, the future king of Aragon [ar′ə gon], and Isabella, later queen of Castile [ka stēl′], were married. This joined the two leading Christian kingdoms of the area. The *Reconquista* (reconquest) to drive out the
Moors began again. Finally in 1492, Ferdinand ans. 1
and Isabella took Granada. A united Spain was at last ready to become a strong nation.

● Use maps, above, to emphasize growth of Christian areas.

Other Europeans began to build nations. Nation making in medieval and early modern times fared best in western Europe, along the Atlantic coast. However, other national groups were forming elsewhere in Europe. In the north, Swedes, Norwegians, and Danes were becoming separate peoples. The Bohemians, a Slavic people, were united in the 11th century. One of their tribes, the Czechs, brought about that union. The Poles formed a strong group. Their lands became the Duchy of Poland. (A *duchy* is an area ruled by a duke.) The Magyar tribes of Asia settled on rich lands along the Danube River. They formed the kingdom of Hungary.

Russian rulers became powerful. A strong central government also grew in Russia. Russian rulers' power over their subjects was greater than that of rulers in any other European country. There was no parliament or Magna Charta ans. 2
in Russia to limit the power of Russian rulers.

The Russian nobles were weak and had no ar-
ans. 2 mies of their own. Towns had no special privileges. And the Orthodox church almost always favored the government. Very little, then, could stop ambitious leaders from becoming quite strong.

The beginnings of a Russian nation can be traced to two fierce but able rulers, both named Ivan. The first was Ivan III, sometimes called Ivan the Great. The second was his grandson Ivan IV, usually known as Ivan the Terrible.

ans. 3 Ivan the Great ruled from 1462 to 1505. He was a grand duke of Moscow. Slowly but surely he took over one small Russian feudal state after another. Finally, he ruled most of the Russian people.

Ivan also had to face foreign enemies. One, the Mongols, had conquered much of Russia in the 1200s. In 1480, Ivan stopped paying tribute to them. They then sent an army against him. For weeks, the two armies faced each other across a small river, but both decided to withdraw. Ivan's stand ended the two centuries of Mongol rule over Russia.

Ivan the Terrible moved between prayer and cruelty. In a rage, he killed his son with a pointed staff.

Next, Ivan III attacked the Polish-Lithuanian kingdom. It had taken over the western Russian regions while the Mongols held the country's middle and eastern lands. In two military campaigns, Ivan won back some border areas.

Under Ivan the Terrible (1533–1584), the Russians pushed into the eastern *steppes,* or plains. They defeated the nomadic tribes who lived there. Vast lands then came under the rule of Moscow's grand duke. In 1552, Russian soldiers took Kazan on the eastern steppes. (See map on page 179.) It was one of the chief cities of the Mongols.

The two Ivans moved toward a united Russia and a strong central government. They took the title *tsar* [zär], meaning caesar. And they called themselves the new Orthodox Christian emperors of the east. In uniting Russia, the tsars were becoming absolute rulers.

The Russian people paid a terrible price for ans. 3
the growing power of the Moscow rulers. The few towns that had governed themselves, such as Novgorod, lost freedom. Ivan the Terrible had thousands of Russian princes and landowners killed. Terror forced the *boyars,* Russian nobles, to obey Tsar Ivan's will. Loyal nobles were rewarded with lands. Heavier and heavier taxes and other duties forced Russian peasants into slavelike serfdom at the very time serfdom was ending in western Europe. ●

By the time Ivan the Terrible died in 1584, unrest was widespread. The country burst into an awful civil war. Russia then entered what is known as the Time of Troubles.

● Serfdom in Russia continued until 1861.

Nation making failed in Germany and Italy. By 850 A.D., the people of East Frankland were calling themselves Germans. Their language was becoming different from that spoken in West Frankland (France). German kings set out to bring their country under a strong central government. All went well for a time. The German tribes defeated Hungarian and Slav raiders from the east. Many German nobles promised to obey and serve their kings.

Shortly after 900, Henry the Fowler, a Saxon noble, became the German king of East Frankland. He was able to force his powerful nobles to be loyal to him. But each noble, master in his own lands, still raised his own army and joined with others to gain power.

Henry's son, Otto the Great, became one of the strongest kings of Germany. First, he defeated the Hungarians at the Battle of Lechfeld in 955. Then he began to move out eastward into the lands of the Slavs. (Through history, Germans often moved against these people. Possibly 60 percent of modern Germany once belonged to the Slavs.)

After his victory over the Hungarians, Otto was thought to be the strongest king in Europe, and his country, the most powerful. But Otto the Great made a mistake that had far-reaching effects. Instead of making himself supreme at home, he turned his attention toward Italy. In 962, Otto marched into the Italian peninsula and had the pope crown him as a new Roman emperor. From this time on, German emperors thought of themselves as rulers like the Roman caesars. The lands they ruled came to be called the Holy Roman Empire, although it was never really an empire.

ans. 4 Setting up the Holy Roman Empire was a sad mistake. German emperors wasted their time, money, and armies fighting to take all of Italy. At home, nobles regained power. Germany was only a collection of free cities and tiny feudal states. The emperor had little power. Seven of his feudal vassals became very important. They claimed the right to elect the ruler, and were called *Electors*.

• Possible discussion topic: Why do so many rulers wish to be thought of as heirs of the ancient Roman Empire?

Some of Germany's greatest kings were drawn to the idea of ruling an Italian empire. Frederick Barbarossa ("redbeard"), who began the Hohenstaufen dynasty, hoped to bring back the glory of Charlemagne. He wanted to unite Germany and Italy into one strong empire under his rule. He was crowned emperor at Rome in 1155. But he spent much of his reign, which lasted until 1190, in wasteful fighting. The liberty-loving Italian cities, supported by the papacy, completely defeated his efforts.

The grand ambitions of the German emperors destroyed more than the hope for a unified nation at home. Their desires also hurt Italy. German emperors were always interfering there. Instead of one nation, there were the Papal States, the kingdom of Naples and Sicily, and city-states—Venice, Milan, Florence, Genoa, and others. Each city-state controlled the land around it and had its own army and ambassadors. Because they disliked one another and were always warring, Italy could not become a nation. Neither Italy nor Germany became united kingdoms until the 1800s.

SECTION REVIEW 4

1. How did Spain and Portugal become nations? How was nation making there different from the French and English experiences? p. 340

2. List conditions in Russia that helped rulers grow very strong. p. 340 341

3. How did Ivan III and Ivan IV enlarge Russia? p. 341

4. How did the German kings' ambitions hurt nation making in both Germany and Italy? p. 342

CHAPTER REVIEW 18

SECTION SUMMARIES

1. Feudalism became old-fashioned. Modern European nations began during the late Middle Ages. As the population grew, cities grew, and trade expanded. Feudalism no longer worked well as a form of government.

Kings gained more power over feudal nobles. New ways of warring also made mounted knights less important. As kings became stronger, they improved their national governments. Countries were better run, and court systems were fairer.

2. England became one nation. After the Norman conquest in 1066, England became a strong kingdom. William the Conqueror made his central government the supreme authority. Henry II helped advance common law and trial by jury. King John signed the Magna Charta, which guaranteed basic rights to freemen. Under Edward I, Parliament began to change, slowly but steadily, into a representative lawmaking body. As a result, England as a nation started to move toward representative government. After a confused time, the Tudors came to power. They began a great era.

3. French kings built a national state. In France, the Capetian kings took power from the nobles and improved government. In this way, the kings' holdings gradually grew. The Hundred Years' War began because of English claims to the French throne. England won several victories early in the war. Under Joan of Arc, France took back lost territory. The war helped both nations. The question of English claims in France was settled. Patriotism rose, and feudal ways of warring ended.

4. Other European peoples made nations. In Spain and Portugal, Christians fought for centuries to get rid of Moors. Portugal gained liberty in the 12th century. Over 300 years later, Spain's most important Christian kingdoms were joined when Isabella of Castile and Ferdinand of Aragon married. Under them, in 1492, the Christians finally pushed out the Moors. Spain became a unified nation.

Several regions of northern Europe had become nations by 1500. Under Ivan III and Ivan IV, Russia freed itself from Mongol rule. Strong German kings, especially Otto the Great, made a promising start in joining German states. However, the German kings made a mistake in setting up the Holy Roman Empire. They tried but could not rule Italy. Neither Germany nor Italy gained political unity.

WHO? WHAT? WHEN? WHERE?

1. Match these events with the correct time period:

a) 801 – 1000 c) 1201 – 1400
b) 1001 – 1200 d) 1401 – 1600

The *Reconquista* was completed. d
William of Normandy conquered England. b
Otto the Great was crowned emperor by the pope. a
Edward I formed the Model Parliament. c
King John signed the Magna Charta. c
Mongol rule of Russia ended. d
The Hundred Years' War ended. d
The Tudor dynasty began. d
Russian rulers took the title tsar. d
Portugal became independent of Moorish control. b

2. Tell what happened at each of these places:

Wales p. 335 Aragon p. 340 Las Navas de Tolosa p. 340
Crécy p. 330, 8 Kazan p. 341 Danube River p. 340
Lechfeld p. 342 Hastings p. 333 Agincourt p. 338

3. Name the homeland and achievements of these people:

Edward I p. 335 Joan of Arc p. 338
Henry II p. 333 Ivan the Great p. 341
• Ferdinand and Isabella Otto the Great p. 342
Louis IX p. 337 Hugh Capet p. 337

• p. 340

4. How did each of these help end feudalism? p. 331 332

new weapons	mercenaries
taxes	civil servants
bourgeoisie	kings

5. How did each of these cause problems for people during the later Middle Ages? p. 331

Church courts	lack of police
feudal dues	lack of central government
transportation	

QUESTIONS FOR CRITICAL THINKING

1. Why did growing business and trade need strong central governments?
2. In what ways does the United States today have or not have the features of a nation as described in Section 1?
3. Compare the ways England and France or Spain and Russia became nations. What were the differences and similarities?
4. Why could an area not become a strong nation under the feudal system?

ACTIVITIES

1. If newspapers had existed at the time, they might have used headlines such as these. Give the meaning of the italicized words.
Bourgeoisie Growing in European Cities
King Recruits *Mercenaries*
Borough Election for *Burgesses* Held
Parliament Withholds Funds—Insists on *Redress of Grievances*
Tsar Reports Mongol Losses to *Boyars*

2. Role-play a conversation between Otto the Great and the pope, in which Otto convinces the pope to crown him emperor.
3. Write a *Domesday Book* entry on yourself. Include things such as records, clothes, books, jewelry, and bikes. p. 333

● Instead of unrelated sentences you might have students write short paragraphs using the terms in questions 4 & 5.

■ Or, for Activity 1, have students write short news stories or interviews on the subjects of the headlines.

CHAPTER TEST 18

SECTION 1

1. Which of these was not a problem caused by feudalism? a. many small independent areas, b. strong kings, c. rival nobles.
2. True or false: Mercenaries were government officials from royal families.
3: True or false: Mounted knights could be defeated by archers with longbows.

SECTION 2

4. The English began to bargain with their rulers through a representative body called Parliament.
5. After the Wars of the Roses, English rulers were members of the Tudor family.
6. Magna Charta: a. limited the power of English rulers, b. established Parliament, c. guaranteed representative government.

SECTION 3

7. True or false: All the people of France elected Hugh Capet as king.
8. True or false: Louis IX told the people to appeal to his officials when nobles wronged them.
9. Joan of Arc was a: a. leader of French armies, b. nun, c. peasant who became queen
10. True or false: The French and English kings had to bargain with parliaments for more taxes.

SECTION 4

11. Mongol rule of Russia was ended by: a. Otto the Great, b. Ivan the Great, c. Ivan the Terrible
12. Alphonso I: a. married Isabella, b. declared Portugal an independent kingdom, c. was beaten by the Moors
13. The Holy Roman Empire was: a. a bad idea begun by Otto the Great, b. a strong, unified nation, c. strengthened by Frederick Barbarossa

For Activity 2, students may need to review Ch. 7 material on the fall of Rome to Germanic tribes.

1300 – 1650

CHAPTER **19**

The European Renaissance

Courtesy Gallery Denise René

In the Renaissance, individuals became important. No longer was art made anonymously by monks in cloisters. Wealthy and powerful people, such as Lorenzo de' Medici, patronized artists. The fame of both patron and artist grew. De' Medici's bust is by Verrocchio.

● March 25, 1436, was an exciting day for the people of Florence in northern Italy. They were dedicating a cathedral, begun in the late 1200s and just finished. Church officials, state leaders, artists, writers, musicians, and other well-known people of the time were there. They had journeyed to the proud city to see the cathedral christened Santa Maria del Fiore (Saint Mary of the Flower).

A long parade moved through the banner-lined streets. A person who was there wrote that a great band of musicians led the parade.

● Explain to students that cathedrals took many years to complete because everything was made by hand. Artisans worked to glorify God rather than to fulfill a contract. Some students may be interested in *Cathedral*, by David Macaulay, which describes the building of a gothic cathedral in the 13th century.

"[Each carried] his instrument in hand and [was dressed] in gorgeous cloth of gold garments." Following them were choirs. They "sang at times with such mighty harmonies that the songs seemed to the listeners to be coming from the angels themselves." Then came the pope, wearing white robes and a crown. Seven cardinals in bright red and thirty-seven bishops and archbishops in purple came next. Behind them walked city officials and heads of guilds.

The rich citizens of Florence filled the streets and crowded into the cathedral. Their eyes and thoughts were on its grand dome that crowned the cathedral and gave the city a brand-new skyline. Everyone felt that a new era had begun.

In many ways it had. As trade had improved, city life had grown rapidly in northern Italy. Florence and other rich urban centers dominated northern Italy in the 1400s. The wealth of these cities supported much creative activity. From it came some of the greatest art, architecture, and literature the world has known. A new questioning spirit led to a revival of learning.

These changes—a new birth of learning and a great creative flowering—are known as the *Renaissance* (a French word that means rebirth). The word also names the time during which these changes took place. The ideas and influence of the Renaissance [ren′ə säns′] spread from Italy to most European countries. The western world was moving from medieval to modern times. This chapter tells how:

1. The Renaissance began in Italy.

2. The Renaissance focused on the individual.

3. Italians created art masterpieces.

4. The Renaissance spread to other countries.

1 The Renaissance began in Italy

Gradually, Renaissance ideas spread through most of Europe. However, the center of the Renaissance, the place it lived longest, was northern Italy. It began there because the city-states of northern Italy were the first to gain from greater trade and political independence.

New wealth supported art and learning. Most of the trade routes from the East, whether by sea across the Indian Ocean or overland ans. 1
through Asia and the Middle East, met at the ■
eastern end of the Mediterranean Sea. Italian merchants bought goods there and took them to ports in northern Italy. From there, the goods were carried across the Alps into northern Europe. The main goods were pepper, ginger, cinnamon, clove, and jewels. These were easy to carry because they did not take up much space. And they were very valuable.

Northern Italy was divided into a number of city-states. In plan, they were like the city-states of ancient Greece. Each was made up of a city and an amount of land around it. Growing trade brought great riches to these cities. The most important were Venice, Florence, Milan, and Genoa. Venice, "Queen of the Adriatic," was built on 117 small islands. Its power and wealth came from the sea. As early as 1500, Venetian merchants had a fleet of 3,000 ships. Florence was known for its cloth industry. Its workers numbered about 30 thousand.

Italian bankers and merchants grew rich from ans. 2
trade. New wealth allowed them to enjoy free time. They could study and learn to understand the arts. They invited artists and philosophers to live and work in their palaces. Therefore, the Renaissance took place mostly among the rich because only they could fund it.

■ See the map on p. 347.

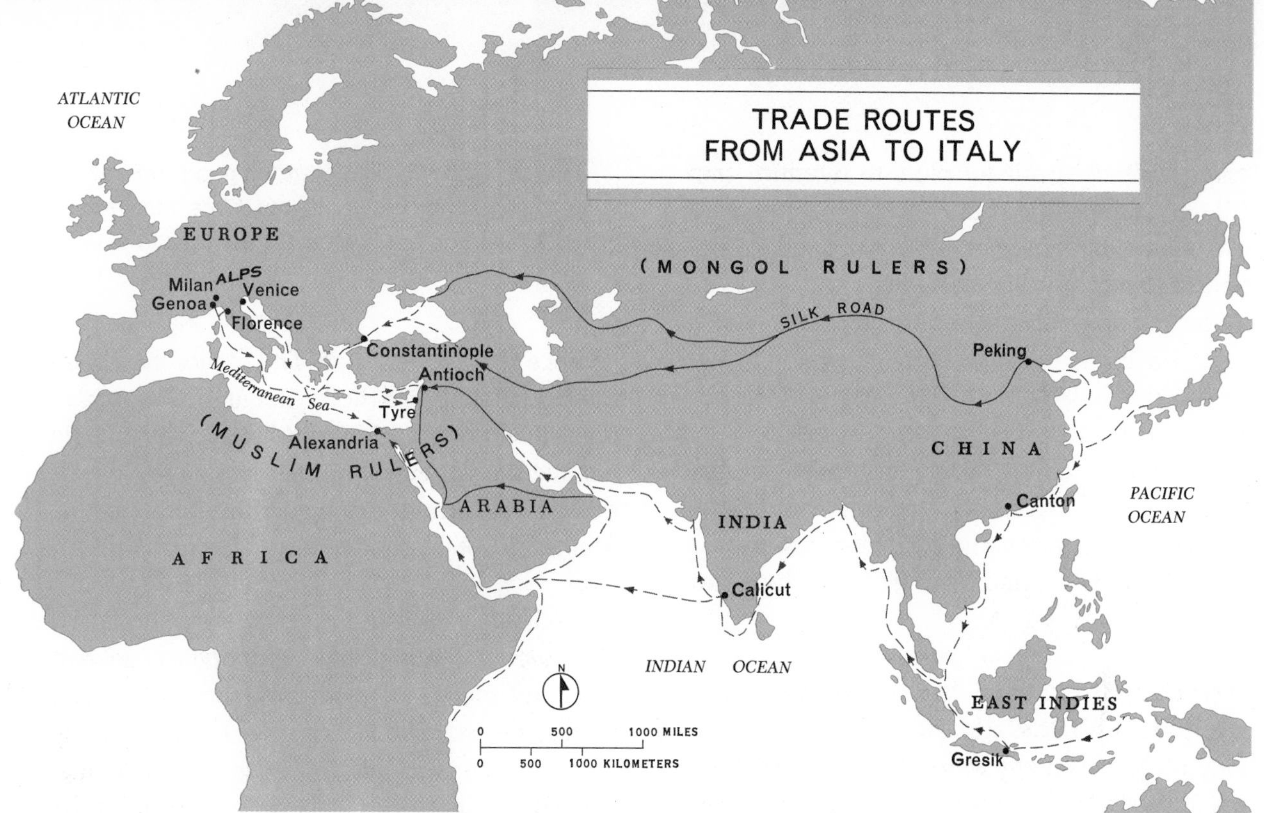

Italian rulers also led in helping artists and writers. The reward was glory, not only for rulers' families but also for their cities. The Este family, rulers of Ferrara, supported such painters as Leonardo da Vinci, Raphael, and Titian. The Medici [med′ə chē] family of Florence were patrons of artists Donatello and Michelangelo, among others. The popes, too, played an important role. Leo X, himself a Medici, made Rome a great center of art and learning.

Political conditions helped individualism. German kings during the Middle Ages wanted to join Italy and Germany together as the Holy Roman Empire. The popes, however, were strongly against this idea. They did not want their power weakened. Both sides—Germans
ans. 3 and popes—wanted the Italian city-states as allies. So both gave the city-states special privileges, such as electing their own officials, making their own laws, and raising taxes. As a result, a republican form of government grew up in most of the cities.

Since there was no central government in Italy, each city became a law unto itself. Quarrels broke out between groups of wealthy merchants. Often, noble families joined in the feuds. ● Such fights were bad for business. Because people needed law and order, a class of despots arose in the 1300s. These daring men gained power by force and trickery. Most of them were interested in the people's well-being. Therefore, they gave their cities well-run government. Some despots, such as those of the Medici family of Florence, had been bankers and merchants. Others, such as the Sforzas of Milan, began as leaders of private bands of soldiers called *condottieri* [kon′dôt tye′rē].

Italian despots came to power because they were strong, clever, and able. Those who ruled after them had to equal these qualities. Otherwise, they soon lost power. Once on top, a ruler

● *Romeo and Juliet* gives an example of two families at war during this era.

always watched out for plots to overturn him. Life in 14th-century Italy was dangerous. People were well trained in the use of daggers, poisoned drinks, and timely "accidents."

In such an atmosphere, the old medieval idea that the individual was not important turned
● upside down. Now the individual was all-important. Old bars against freedom of thought and deed broke down. People began to express their own ideas about life and art. They started to speak out against long-held customs and beliefs. And they found new glory in their own strengths.

Machiavelli excused the use of force and tricks in politics. In the Middle Ages, writings on government were rare. Most of them only described the desired traits of a ruler. These guidebooks were well meaning and dull.

In 1532, five years after the author had died, a small book by Niccolò Machiavelli [mak′ē-ə vel′ē] was published. It, too, gave advice on how to act as a ruler. But it was quite different
ans. 4 from the medieval guides. It became one of the best-known works ever written.

Machiavelli was born in Florence in 1469. He served his city for many years as a diplomat and government officer. When he left public life, he wrote *The Prince.* The book is a set of rules. With them, a strong ruler could build a unified Italian government. He could fight off other newly powerful European nations.

ans. 4 Machiavelli explained the political facts of life as he saw them. To get power and stay in power, a ruler had to forget ideals. Machiavelli had learned that by nature humans are not good, kind, loyal, or honest. So he advised:

> A wise ruler . . . cannot and should not observe faith when it is to his disadvantage and the causes that made him give his promise have vanished. If men were all good, this advice would not be good, but since men are wicked and do not keep their promises to you, you likewise do not have to keep yours to them.

Since it was published *The Prince* has been closely studied and hotly debated. For some, Machiavelli was a clever judge of why people behaved as they did. He saw what others missed. To others, he was immoral, since he seemed to pay no attention to religious teachings.

Machiavelli believed that the state should be all-powerful. He said that every political act had only one means of measure—success. In *The Prince,* he seemed to approve the use of any possible means to get and keep power. Lying, cheating, and murder were acceptable if a ruler needed them to gain his ends. The rights of citizens were only those that the ruler allowed for the benefit of the state. People were viewed simply as clay to be molded by the ruler. Machiavelli felt that the state must be stable at

Niccolò Machiavelli

● Key concept: the emphasis on individual abilities was a new idea for medieval Europeans.

all costs. That thought became a blueprint for strong, united nations.

SECTION REVIEW 1

p. 346 **1.** How did geography help northern Italy become the home of the Renaissance?

p. 346 **2.** Name three kinds of people who were patrons of the arts. To what class did they belong?

p. 347 **3.** In what ways did the Italian city-states gain from the Holy Roman Emperors and the popes?

p. 348 **4.** How is Machiavelli's *The Prince* different from earlier books on government?

2 The Renaissance focused on the individual

ans. 1 A new movement called *humanism* began in
● 14th-century Italy. The humanist way of looking at life is marked by an interest in people. The beauties and chances of life on Earth are important. Humanism taught people to live a full life and welcome new experiences. Humanists wanted people to have better lives in this world, rather than waiting for the next. The new movement was closely tied to a returning interest in classical learning. Humanists felt that the writings of Greece and Rome best told their ideas. It was for this renewed interest in ancient writings that the word *Renaissance* was first used.

Petrarch and Boccaccio were early humanists. Humanism owed much to the Italian writer, Francesco Petrarca, known as Petrarch [pē′trärk]. This writer, born in 1304, resented his father's desire to have him become a lawyer. For comfort, he began to read the Roman writers Cicero and Vergil. One story tells that Petrarch's father once threw the boy's books into the fire. The youth cried so much, though, that his father grabbed them back.

● Key concept: the emphasis of the humanists on happiness in this life had far-reaching effects on our world outlook.

Petrarch gave his life to a study of classical ans. 2
writers. From his study came a new approach to life. He found that the Romans had believed this world was important. That was clear in their writings about love, nature, and everyday life.

Petrarch and later humanists tried to gather the actual writings of ancient authors. They studied Greek and Latin. And they spent much money and time trying to find old manuscripts. They tore apart ruins. They sent agents to Constantinople to buy what they could. Monasteries were searched for the prized pieces of parchment. Greek manuscripts became more plentiful after 1453, when the Turks took Constantinople and many Greek scholars escaped to Italy.

Petrarch wrote in Latin, imitating the works of Cicero and Vergil. But it was a group of sonnets written in Italian and inspired by his love for a woman named Laura that made him one of the greatest lyric poets of all time. Of his love for her he wrote:

> If this should not be Love, O God, what shakes me?
> If Love it is, what strange, what rich delight?

Another noted humanist was Giovanni Boc- ans. 2
caccio [bō kä′chē ō], who wrote both poetry and prose. In 1348, the terrible plague known as the Black Death struck Florence, where Boccaccio lived. Thousands died from the awful disease. Boccaccio made this time the setting for the *Decameron*. In it, seven young women and three young men escaped the plague by living in a lonely country house. To pass the time, they tell the tales that make up the book. Many of the stories mirrored the spirit of the times by making fun of feudal customs.

Education aimed at "the complete man."
ans. 3 In medieval times, education had two chief uses. It trained priests for preaching and scholars for debating with other scholars. During the Renaissance, people decided that education had more uses. Its goal, still aimed mostly at ● men, became that of making people well rounded.

The ideal Renaissance aristocrat was well-mannered and witty. He had learned enough to understand good literature, painting, and music. The so-called Renaissance man was well formed in body and good at sports. In the arts of war he was a brave and able soldier. In *The Courtier,* Baldassare Castiglione [käs′tē lyô′ne] outlined this all-around person. Castiglione was himself a scholar, poet, and courtier (a person in service to a ruler).

To reach the goals of Renaissance education, Italian schools taught less theology and more literature, especially Latin and Greek. The humanists, who taught Greek and Latin language and literature, gained great respect. People journeyed far to hear their lectures. Rich men and rulers took humanists into their homes to teach their sons and daughters.

Earthly life was quite important to humanists, but most of them remained religious. Those who spoke against the Church believed in reform, not revolt. Humanist scholars carefully translated Greek and Hebrew sources of the Bible.

Renaissance people used many talents. Renaissance ideas about the individual gave people faith in their own powers. They were eager to search for new continents. They wanted to learn the secrets of nature. They questioned the authority of the Church and showed their love of life in literature and art.

● Students should understand that education was limited to upper-class people, mostly males. While the term "Renaissance man" means a well-rounded person, it was rarely applied to women. Invite student discussion: how is a society different when only a small group of people are educated?

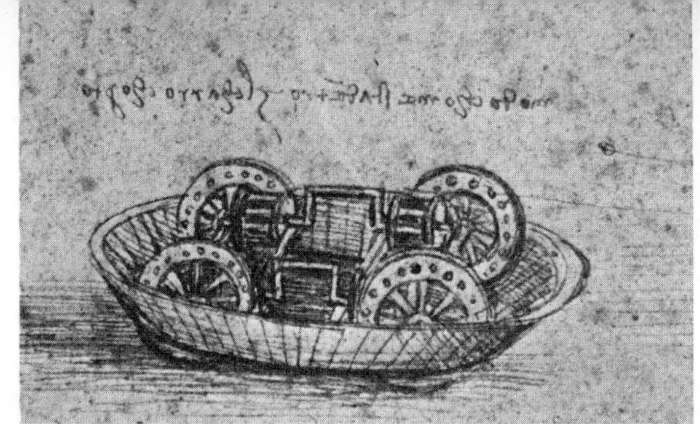

Leonardo da Vinci was the spoiled and pampered son of a well-to-do Florentine. In 1482, at age 30, he left Florence for Milan and the court of Ludovico Sforza, one of the most powerful princes in Italy. Leonardo wrote to the prince, describing himself as a siege engineer, demolitions expert, military architect, sculptor, and painter. And, said Leonardo, he would be happy to demonstrate his skills in the prince's park. He got the job. These pictures are some of Leonardo's war tools. The two top drawings are a tank. Second from the bottom right is an airplane. Most of Leonardo's ideas, such as the airplane, were not built until centuries later.

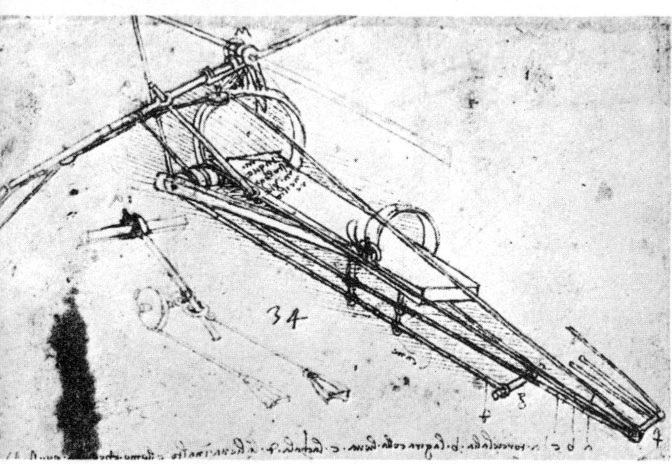

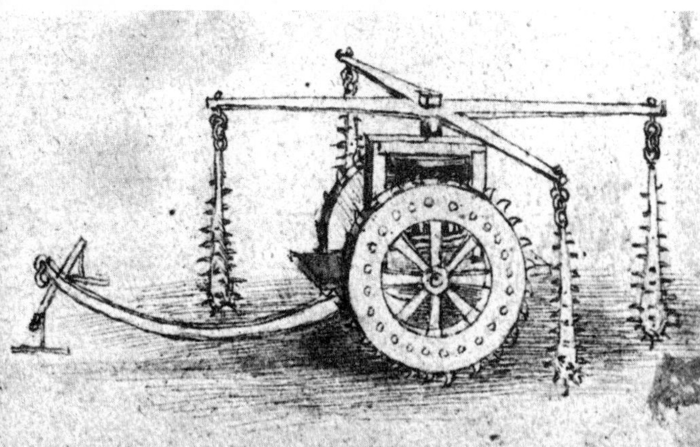

Rarely has the world seen so many people with so many talents. Not only could Renaissance people do many different things. They also could do them quite well.

Leonardo da Vinci [lē′ə när′dō də vin′chē] ans. 4 (1452–1519) was a genius who was an example of this many-sided person. He was one of the greatest painters of all time. He studied geology, chemistry, and anatomy and designed buildings, canals, and weapons.

Leonardo da Vinci left over 5,000 pages of notes and drawings. Besides human figures, he sketched cannons, engines, flying machines, and hundreds of other devices. Some were not made until centuries later. Leonardo left many tasks unfinished, but people marveled at his many skills. They admired him almost as if he were more than human.

Some Renaissance people went too far in making the individual all-important. They turned away from the group. They cared not at all for laws or morals. Anything a person could get away with seemed to be all right.

Benvenuto Cellini [chə lē′nē] was an example of this type of person. He was a great artist in metalwork and sculpture, and he wrote well. But he was also a liar, braggart, and murderer. In his autobiography, he wrote honestly of his adventures, which reveal his cool ruthlessness.

SECTION REVIEW **2**

1. What is humanism's outlook on life? Why did humanists study Greek and Roman classics? p. 349

2. What did Petrarch learn from the works of ancient Romans? How did Boccaccio mirror his time? p. 349

3. How was education during the Renaissance different from that of medieval times? p. 350

4. Name three talents that made Leonardo da Vinci a Renaissance man. p. 351

You might allow time for a discussion of illustrations on this and on the facing page.

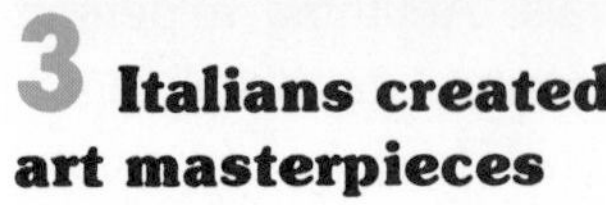

3 Italians created art masterpieces

ans. 1 During the Middle Ages, religion had moved people to build beautiful churches. Artists and sculptors did not sign their works because it was the subject of the work, not the individual creator, that was most important. Artistic works showed Church teachings, human suffering, and the joys of life after death.

● During the Renaissance, artists wanted to show how people and nature really were in life. Their new ways of painting and sculpting showed people as real individuals.

Florence led the way. Changes in the art of painting began early in the 1300s. The man who started the new style was the Florentine Giotto di Bondone (1266–1336). He was the first European artist to make figures appear to move, to be alive. Giotto [jot′ō] decorated the walls of churches with *frescoes*—paintings on wet plaster. Most of these were scenes from the life of Jesus. ans. 2

In the years after Giotto's death, Florence became the art center of Europe. Possibly only ancient Athens ever equaled it in numbers of artists in one place.

The Florentines learned to draw human figures accurately. They tried to make feelings and ideas show in the face and body. They used light and shadow to point up scenes. And they mixed new colors. Possibly most important, they figured out a way to make viewers feel as if they were looking *into* a painting instead of *at* it. Things appeared to be seen from a distance.

● Art mirrored the individualism and realism of the times.

■ Encourage students to look for these qualities in the art included in this chapter.

Painting of the Italian Renaissance was more realistic than that of the Middle Ages. In Giotto's "Lamentation over the Dead Christ," *(above)*, the figures have a solidity and roundness not found in medieval painting. Uccello set about discovering scientific principles of perspective. His painting "The Hunt" *(left)* does just this. The geometric arrangement of trees and careful placement of men and animals create a three-dimensional quality.

This way of making a painting seem real is called *perspective*.

A Florentine artist well known for this kind of painting was Paolo Uccello [üt chel′lō] (1397–1475). His paintings were often crowded with people. But he placed them carefully and gave them different sizes. In this way, he made a pleasing sense of perspective.

Some of the most important figures in the history of Western art lived during the Italian Re-
ans. 3 naissance. Michelangelo [mī′kl an′jə lō] was a great sculptor, painter, and architect. He was even a fair poet. He was born Michelangelo Buonarroti, near Florence in 1475. At thirteen, he became a helper to a painter and learned to make frescoes. For a number of years, Lorenzo de' Medici, ruler of Florence, helped Michelangelo carry on his studies.

● Draw attention to the *Pieta,* p. 354. Michelangelo was in his twenties when he created it.

Michelangelo liked sculpture better than
painting. Many of his painted figures have the 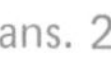 ans. 2
solid feeling of statues. He often said, "It is only well with me when I have a chisel in my hand." ●
But people always wanted him to paint. Pope Julius II asked Michelangelo to paint frescoes on the walls and ceiling of the Sistine Chapel in the Vatican, the seat of Church government. He painted lying on his back on a scaffold most of the time. The huge task of picturing the Bible story of Genesis from the Creation to the Flood took four years. Michelangelo lived only for his art and had little interest in money or comfort. Those who knew him said he took no pleasure in eating or drinking. He was satisfied with a little bread, a bit of cheese, a bed, and a workshop. He slept in his clothes to save time. Hard work made his sides and back misshapen.

Raphael [raf′ē əl], born in 1483, was most famous as a painter of religious subjects. Raphael was a great favorite of two popes. For Julius II, he painted several frescoes in the Vatican. Leo X appointed Raphael chief architect of St. Peter's Church.

Venice rivaled Florence as an art center. By the 1500s, Venetian painters had made their own traditions. They were most noted for their use of rich, glowing colors. Giovanni Bellini [be lē′nē], born about 1430, came from a family of famous painters. His style was soft and gentle. Two of his pupils became well
ans. 2 known. Giorgione [jôr jō′nā] painted many scenes from Greek and Roman mythology. Titian [tish′ən], born Tiziano Vecellio in 1477, painted scenes and people from the world around him. Another important Venetian was Tintoretto [tin′tə ret′ō]. His use of light and space made his paintings very dramatic.

Sculpture and architecture flourished. An outstanding sculptor of the early 1400s was
the Florentine Donatello [don′ə tel′ō]. He was ans. 2
the first sculptor of this time to show that he knew human anatomy. Possibly his best-known work is his grand statue of the Venetian general, Gattemelata. This statue was the first large-sized figure on horseback since Roman times. In the general's face, Donatello caught the spirit of the Italian despot—proud, powerful, and cruel.

In a class by himself was Michelangelo. Great as he was with brush and paint, he was even greater with chisel and stone. In his statue of the Biblical David, the sculptor showed how he saw

Michelangelo was the greatest sculptor of the Renaissance. He combined the classical Greek idea of the human form with his own personal view of its grace and power. He carved this statue when he was only in his twenties. Called the "Pieta," it is Mary mourning over the body of Jesus. Note that the figure of Mary is very young and quite large in relation to the figure of Jesus.

When nearly ninety, Michelangelo would carve all night, wearing a cardboard cap to which he attached a candle. He felt he could not work enough hours to do all that he dreamed of.

the ideal young hero. David is shown with a fine head, classic features, and flowing body. Michelangelo also carved figures for the Medici chapel and for the tomb of Pope Julius.

Italian Renaissance architects used Greek and Roman models for their buildings. However, building uses, churches, and palaces were different from those of classical times. So different treatments of Greek and Roman pillars and domes were needed. Therefore, Renaissance architects adapted their models to suit their own times. As a result, their work was new and had great beauty.

Several buildings were group efforts. Ten different architects worked on one of the greatest Renaissance buildings, the church of St. Peter in Rome. It is the largest Christian church in the world. Michelangelo designed its huge dome.

SECTION REVIEW 3

p. 352 **1.** In what ways was Renaissance art different from art in the Middle Ages?

p. 352 354 **2.** For what kinds of art did Giotto, Raphael, Donatello, and Titian become known?

p. 353 **3.** Why could Michelangelo be called a Renaissance man?

4 The Renaissance spread to other countries

From its beginnings in Italy, the Renaissance spread to many parts of Europe. Scholars and artists from the north journeyed southward to study with Italian masters. They took home new feelings and ideas. The Renaissance also spread through books printed by means of a new invention—movable type.

Printing helped spread the Renaissance. During the Middle Ages, people had written on *parchment* and on *vellum*. Parchment, made from sheepskin or goatskin, was expensive. One book might take the skins of twenty-five sheep. Vellum, made from calfskin, cost even more.

In the early 1100s, Europeans learned about paper from the Moors in Spain. The Moors knew about it through the Arabs. They, in turn, had learned of it from the Chinese.

Paper was less expensive than parchment or vellum. However, books were still expensive because they were written by hand. When the

Medici family in Florence wanted 200 books for their library, forty-five skilled copyists worked two years to make them. Under such conditions, even large libraries had only a few hundred books. Many people never saw a book, much less owned one.

The use of printing to make copies of books or pictures did not appear in Europe until the late Middle Ages. The first printing in Europe, like that in China, was block printing. Letters, words, or pictures were carved into blocks of wood. Then the blocks were inked and pressed down on paper. In late medieval Europe, wooden blocks were often used for printing playing cards and saints' pictures.

The Chinese invented movable type. Whether it came directly to Europe from the Chinese is not known. Credit for the first use of movable type in Europe is generally given to a German, Johann Gutenberg [güt′n bėrg′]. Possibly the first European book printed with movable type was the Gutenberg Bible, finished about 1456. By the end of the 1400s, eighteen countries had printing presses with movable type. European presses had printed 8 million books by the early 1500s.

ans. 1 The invention of movable type had important results. Books could be made rapidly and in great quantities. And the cost was much less than that of hand copying. The new books were far more accurate, too. Before printing, two exact copies of a book could not be made. Copyists always made mistakes. More important, printing made books available to a large number of persons.

Printing helped spread the Renaissance spirit. Italian books were sent all over Europe. The new movement in the rest of Europe was called the *Northern Renaissance.* It changed as each country added some ideas of its own.

● Note the difference between Italian and northern humanists.

Northern humanists looked at social and religious problems. ● Most humanists in ans. 2 northern Europe were more serious and interested in learning than were those in Italy. Italian humanists were interested in their own gains and expressions of self. Northern humanists cared about social problems. Religion and ethics, questions of right and wrong, were important.

Erasmus [i raz′məs], a Dutch scholar born about 1466, is often thought to be the greatest humanist. A priest, he spent much time studying Greek and Latin writings. He wrote many books, all in Latin. His satire *The Praise of Folly,* published in 1511, lashed out at the evils of the time. Erasmus attacked superstition, warlike princes, and false priests. He took to task scholars who wasted time with silly problems. Erasmus also used Greek sources for a Latin translation of the New Testament. He showed that the Bible used at the time had many errors.

All his life, Erasmus fought against ignorance, stupidity, and vice. He kept up a huge correspondence with learned people around Europe. In that way, he helped spread humanistic ideals. When he died in 1536, he left behind a large number of writings that later thinkers could study.

A group of English scholars who studied medicine and Greek in Italy brought humanism to England. On their return, these English humanists gathered at Oxford University. There they became known as the *Oxford Reformers.* As teachers, preachers, and authors, they tried to bring the new learning to England. One of their students, Sir Thomas More, became a great humanist. He carried on a life-long correspondence with Erasmus. More became a lawyer and served in many government posts under King Henry VIII. His best-known book, *Utopia*

(Nowhere), described a perfect society that was not real. However, people could compare it with their own society. This backdoor attack on society's evils later led to new laws that helped the poor.

Northern artists started different styles. Painters in the Low Countries (now Belgium and the Netherlands) began early to break away from medieval ways. They started painting in new ways even before Italian Renaissance art reached northern Europe. Among the first was
ans. 3 Jan van Eyck [van īk], born about 1380. He painted realistic landscapes and portraits. He very carefully showed trees, grass, and flowers as they appeared in nature. It was also Van Eyck who invented oil paints.

For Rembrandt, a person's true beauty was within. This drawing of his mother is a fine example of Rembrandt's efforts to portray people as individuals.

The skill of Italian painters impressed artists in northern Europe. Even more, they admired the Italians' use of perspective and mastery of anatomy. One of the earliest to study in Italy was the German Albrecht Dürer [dʏ'rər]. He first visited Italy about 1494. The artists' high social level there amazed him. He noted, "Here I am a lord, at home a parasite." Dürer's work put together medieval and Renaissance styles. He made a great number of woodcuts and engravings to illustrate the new printed books.

German artist Hans Holbein [hōl'bīn] the Younger (1497–1543) was appointed court painter to King Henry VIII of England. He became known for his lifelike portraits of the royal family. He also painted portraits of the humanists Erasmus and Sir Thomas More.

The Flemish artist Pieter Brueghel [brœ'gəl] (1525–1569) spent his life painting country landscapes and hearty scenes of peasant life. The Low Countries also were home to two of the greatest 17th-century painters. Peter Paul Rubens was known for his large, dramatic canvases. Rembrandt van Rijn was able to show character so well that his works have been acclaimed as among the best of all time.

Renaissance literature reached its height in Shakespeare and Cervantes. The English poet Chaucer is often thought of as the first writer of English Renaissance literature. He and the Oxford Reformers laid a base for English writers of the late 16th and early 17th centuries. On that base, they built a literature equal to any nation's written art.

Queen Elizabeth I, like many rulers of the time, helped and inspired writers. The greatest writer in the Elizabethan age—one of the greatest in world literature—was William Shakespeare (1564–1616).

● Can you bring in some of the art books available to show interested students examples of Italian and Renaissance art?

In 1434, the Flemish Jan van Eyck painted the wedding portrait *(opposite)* of Giovanni Arnolfini and Jeanne Cenami. Arnolfini was an Italian banker who lived in Flanders. Van Eyck showed a person's inner being by highlighting the uniqueness of each individual face and by placing people in their setting. Note the wooden shoes for walking in muddy streets, the beautiful brass chandelier, and the mirror that so incredibly shows the whole picture in reverse. Above the mirror, the artist wrote: "Jan van Eyck was here."

A century later, Pieter Brueghel the Elder in "Peasant Wedding" *(right)* showed his interest in the universality of human customs rather than individual personalities.

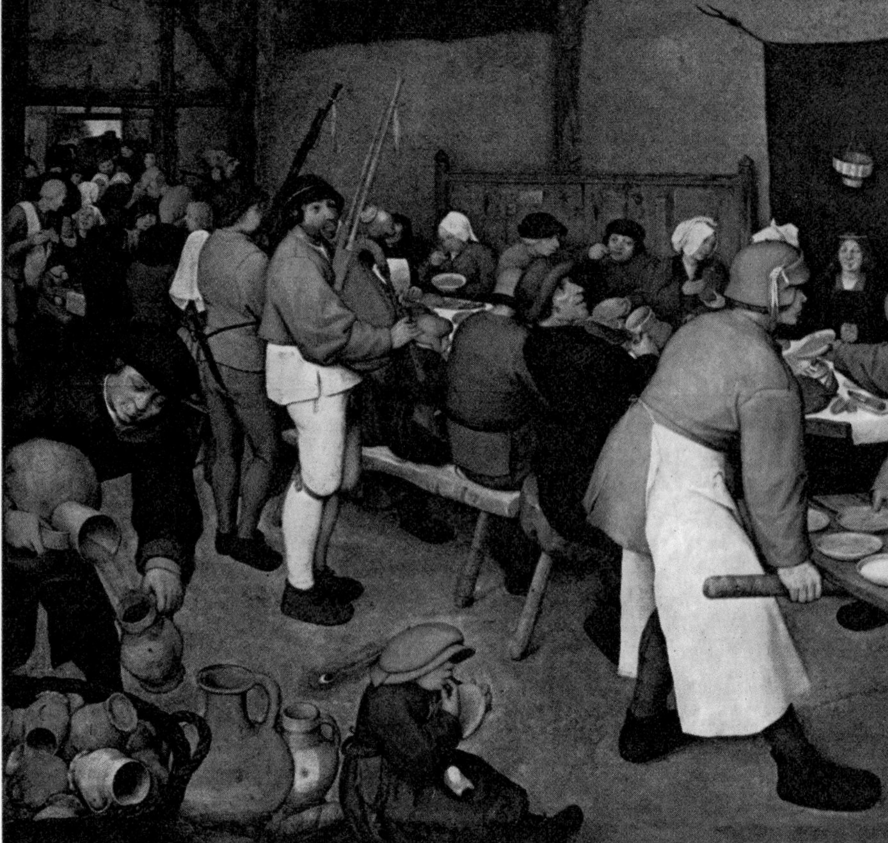

ans. 4 Shakespeare's plays are part of the literary heritage of all English-speaking people. He had a deep understanding of human beings. Some of the people he made so real are Hamlet, Lady Macbeth, Julius Caesar, Portia, and Falstaff. Hundreds of sayings have come from his rich writing into everyday English speech.

In France and Spain, humanists wrote about the evils of their day. An important author was the Spaniard Miguel de Cervantes [sər van′-tēz]. He wrote the novel *Don Quixote.*

Toward the end of the 1500s, when Cervantes wrote *Don Quixote*, feudalism and knighthood were out of fashion. But the codes of chivalry still appealed to many people in Spain. Cervantes's hero, Don Quixote [kē-hō′tē], was a poor but proud Spanish gentleman who loved to read knightly romances. At fifty, he made a suit of armor. Then he took his old horse and went to seek adventures. His servant Sancho Panza went with him. Cervantes's novel is a Renaissance work in two ways. First, it clearly shows Spanish life at the time. Second, it laughs at the ideals of knighthood and chivalry in the funny adventures of Don Quixote. His deeds were absurd, but Cervantes admired his hero's ideals of bravery and goodness. However, Cervantes seems to have felt that these ideals were no longer respected in the world as he knew it.

SECTION REVIEW **4**

1. What were two results of the invention of movable type? p. 356
2. How did northern European humanists differ from those in Italy? How did Erasmus and More use northern humanist ideas? p. 356
3. For what were Van Eyck, Dürer, Brueghel, and Rembrandt known? p. 357
4. In what ways were Shakespeare and Cervantes great Renaissance writers? p. 358

CHAPTER REVIEW 19

SECTION SUMMARIES

1. The Renaissance began in Italy. Italian city-states were well placed on the trade routes between East and West. The new wealth that trade brought allowed merchants and rulers to help artists and writers. Out of this new wealth came the Renaissance.

2. The Renaissance focused on the individual. Italian humanists, such as Petrarch and Boccaccio, raised much interest in the classic writings of Greece and Rome. Renaissance humanism taught that the individual was important. People admired the many different talents of such humanists as Leonardo da Vinci.

3. Italians created art masterpieces. The greatest showing of the Renaissance spirit took place in art, especially painting. Well-known Italian artists of the time are Giotto, Raphael, Michelangelo, and Titian.

4. The Renaissance spread to other countries. People, together with books printed from movable type, spread the ideas of the Renaissance. The writings of Italian humanists influenced two great European scholars, Erasmus and Sir Thomas More. But northern writers were more interested in social problems than were Italians. Northern painting also gained from the Italian Renaissance. Among northern artists were Dürer, Holbein, Brueghel, Rubens, and Rembrandt.

In England, the Renaissance blossomed in the Elizabethan Age. The greatest of the writers then was Shakespeare. Cervantes in Spain wrote *Don Quixote*. This memorable figure in fiction seems to show the end of the medieval era.

WHO? WHAT? WHEN? WHERE?

1. Arrange the following events in chronological order:

Publication of *The Prince* 1532 (6)
The Black Death hit Florence. 1348 (2)
Birth of Michelangelo 1475 (4)
Printing of the Gutenberg Bible 1456 (3)
Publication of *The Praise of Folly* 1511 (5)
Birth of Giotto 1266 (1)

2. What contribution did each of these persons make to the Renaissance?

Shakespeare p. 358	Erasmus p. 356
Lorenzo de' Medici p. 353	Gutenberg p. 356
Boccaccio p. 349	Donatello p. 354
Petrarch p. 349	Machiavelli p. 348

3. Arrange the following artists' names under the headings Italian Renaissance or Northern Renaissance:

Leonardo da Vinci Ital.	Titian Ital.
Dürer Northern	Brueghel Northern
Jan van Eyck Northern	Rembrandt Northern
Giotto Ital..	Michelangelo Ital.

4. With what city was the Medici family identified? The Este family? Name an artist that each family helped. ●

5. Define these terms and tell why they were important to the Renaissance:

Oxford Reformers p. 356	patrons p. 347
despots p. 347	Renaissance man p. 350
condottieri p. 347	movable type p. 356
frescoes p. 352	perspective p. 352

6. Match these men with their works:

Utopia a.	Cervantes d.
The Prince b.	More a.
Decameron c.	Erasmus e.
Don Quixote d.	Castiglione f.
The Praise of Folly e.	Boccaccio c.
The Courtier f.	Machiavelli b.

● 4. Medici were in Florence; Donatello and Michelangelo Este were in Ferrara; da Vinci, Raphael, Titian.

CHAPTER TEST 19

QUESTIONS FOR CRITICAL THINKING

1. What is your opinion of Machiavelli's advice to rulers during the Renaissance? What should be the standards of behavior for a government official? A business person? A high-school student?

2. Compare the purposes of education during medieval times, the Renaissance, and the present. Is the idea of a well-rounded person useful today? Explain.

3. In what ways was the Renaissance a break with the past? Are humanist ideals out of date today? Why or why not?

ACTIVITIES

1. Discuss what would happen if all printed matter were destroyed overnight. What changes would take place immediately? Over a long period of time? What would you miss most? Least?

2. Write a guidebook for United States Presidents. ● Have one person write on the board any and all ideas from the class—without discussion. After all ideas are on the board, discuss the value of each. Talk about ways the guidebook could be put together.

3. Use the pictures in this book to compare the artistic styles of different periods or areas. Some might be medieval, Indian, Greek and Roman, Italian and Northern Renaissance, modern. What kind of subject matter did the artists choose? Why? What are the differences between the styles? Which do you like best? Why?

4. One of the Renaissance artists is a friend of yours. Write a description of that person, including your opinion and the opinions of others.

5. Pretend that the class is a traveling Renaissance troupe of actors, musicians, and storytellers that is performing in a city marketplace. Include events of the day, famous people and their doings, fashions, religious events, and so forth in the performance.

● This exercise invites students to be modern-day Machiavellis. Their guidebook could be called *The President* as Machiavelli's was called *The Prince.*

SECTION 1

1. Northern Italy was a key point in trade between __Asia__ and __Europe__.

2. True or false: A strong central government in Italy gave rise to despots.

3. True or false: Italian workers and peasants helped support Renaissance artists.

4. Machiavelli's means of measuring political acts was: a. money, b. success, c. ethics

SECTION 2

5. Humanism stressed: a. religion, b. discipline, c. the individual

6. True or false: Petrarch was a sculptor.

7. Education during the Renaissance was aimed at making people __well-rounded__.

8. A good example of the Renaissance man was __Da Vinci__.

SECTION 3

9. True or false: Florentine artists used perspective to make scenes look real.

10. Venetian painters were masters in the use of __color__.

11. Michelangelo the artist was a __sculptor__, __painter__, and __architect__.

12. Italian architects based their buildings on __Greek__ and __Roman__ models.

SECTION 4

13. Which of these did not help the spread of Renaissance ideas? a. travel, b. parchment, c. movable type

14. True or false: Northern humanists were more interested in themselves than were the Italian humanists.

15. Albrecht Dürer combined __Medieval__ and __Renaissance__ styles of art.

16. The __Oxford Reformers__ laid a base for later English Renaissance writers.

CHAPTER 20

1309–1795

The Reformation and National Power

Elizabeth I of England was a giant in an age of giants. She gave England a stable government for forty-five years. During her rule, England became master of the seas and people such as Shakespeare flourished. Elizabeth's name stands for the flowering of English achievement.

> Out of love for the faith and the desire to bring it to light, the following propositions will be discussed at Wittenberg under the chairmanship of the Reverend Father Martin Luther, Master of Arts and Sacred Theology . . . those who are unable to be present and debate orally . . . may do so by letter.

This chapter enlarges on the changes that took place in Europe as a result of the new questioning spirit of the Renaissance.

Thus Martin Luther, a German priest, began an important document. He nailed it to the door of the Castle Church of Wittenberg on October 31, 1517. It was a custom of the time for debates to be announced in this way. His document, written in Latin, attacked the sale of *papal indulgences,* which freed sinners from punishment after death. Luther and many others felt the Church of Rome abused this practice. His protest began the great movement that is called the Reformation.

The Reformation had two basic phases. One was the Protestant Reformation and the other was the Catholic, or Counter, Reformation. In both, leaders tried to bring Christian practices closer to Christian ideals. Roman Catholics believed that reforms had to take place within the Church. But they would not allow changes in church law. Protestants believed that there could be no reforms without major changes in church law. So they set up their own churches. They rejected the authority of the pope and his right to interpret the Bible for all Christians.

The events of the Reformation were closely tied to political and social conflict. Kings and princes used religious differences to gain political ends. As the power of nations grew, it seemed this might upset the balance of power in Europe. During the 1600s and 1700s, wars were fought to prevent any one nation from becoming too strong. This chapter tells how:

1. The Catholic Church lost power.

2. The Reformation divided Europe.

3. Religious differences mixed with political conflicts.

4. France became Europe's leading power.

5. Strong rulers helped Russia grow.

6. Prussia became a powerful new state.

● Key Concept: many of the early reformers wanted simply to return to traditional Christian ideals

1 The Catholic Church lost power

The medieval period had been truly an Age of Faith. The Catholic Church reached the height of its political power in the 12th and 13th centuries. The Church began to lose some of its power after the reign of Innocent III.

Reformers tried to improve the Church. In the later Middle Ages, weaknesses arose within the Church. Some of the clergy led immoral lives, forgetting their religious vows and duties. Many grew worldly. Some popes, for example, became involved in Italian politics. Furthermore, the growing wealth of the Church led to corruption. Men bought positions in the Church—a practice known as simony—so they could enjoy ease and luxury. ans. 1

Many reformers tried to purify the Church. They wanted to return to its old ideals of poverty and service. Among the 13th-century reformers were the Franciscans and the Dominicans. In the 14th century, John Wycliffe, an Englishman, criticized Church ceremonies as formal and empty. He also translated the Bible from Latin into English so that common people could read it. Wycliffe's views influenced John Huss, a Czech who was burned at the stake in 1415 for criticizing the Church. Huss became a martyr, and his ideas did not die out. ● ans. 2

The Renaissance spirit of free inquiry led to further questions about religion. Erasmus criticized religious hypocrisy and the worship of images. Like most humanist critics, he felt that the Church could reform itself from within.

New forces challenged the Church. Forces outside the Church also weakened it. Kings who were gaining more power did not want popes

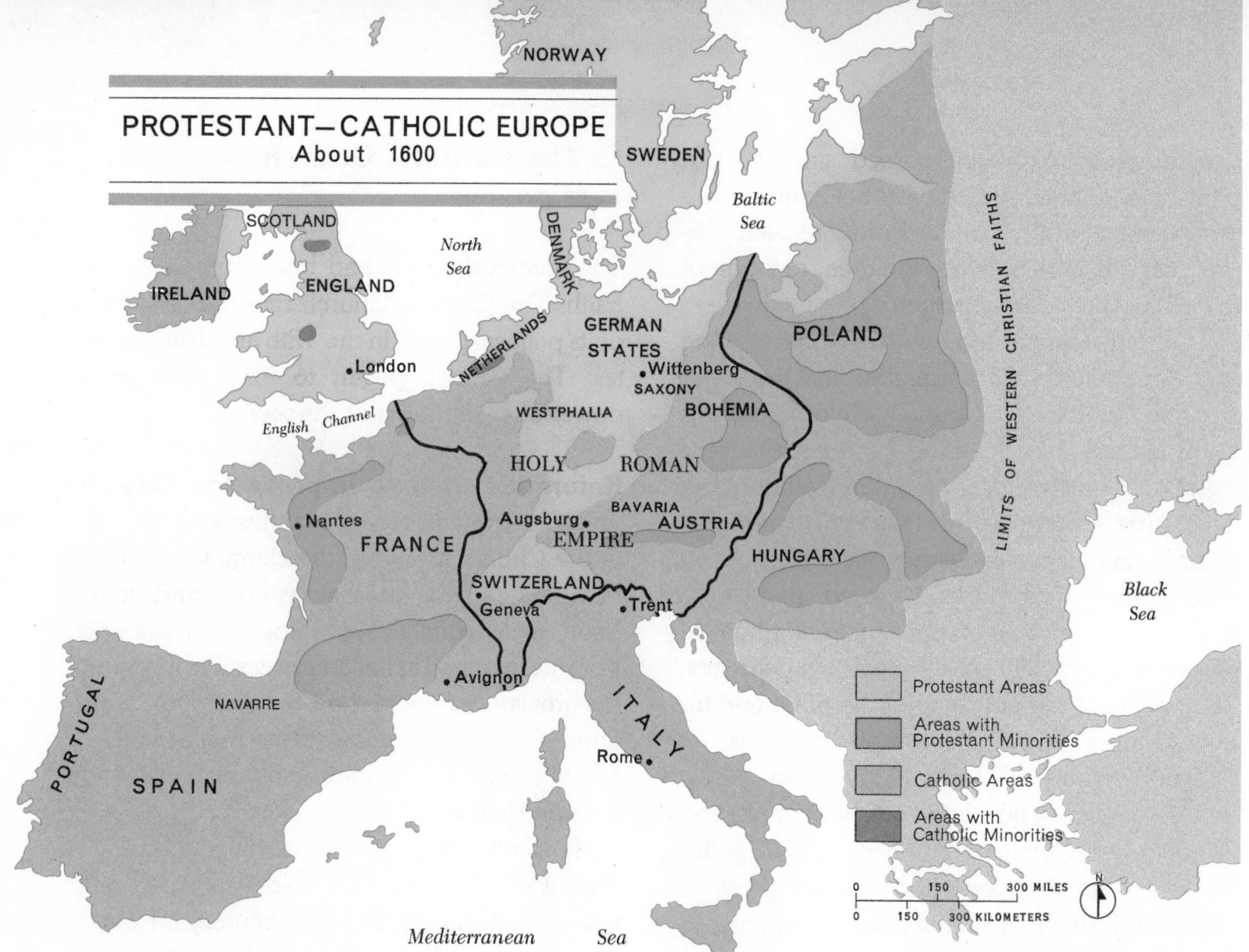

ans. 3 dictating to them. People did not like the rules and commands of foreign churchmen or the fact that most of the money they gave the Church went to Rome. Some people began to think it might be better to have a national church, run by their own country.

Another force that challenged the Church was the growth of business and commerce. The rising merchant class did not like the Church laws forbidding the lending of money at interest. In addition, many of them welcomed any movement that could help them obtain the kind of wealth the Church had.

The Church was split. Several rulers defied the authority of the pope. Philip IV of France went further. In 1309, he forced the pope to ans. 4
leave Rome and live in Avignon [ȧ vē nyôɴ′], France. This was called the Babylonian Captivity, and it lasted 65 years. It was named for the time when the ancient Hebrews were prisoners of the Babylonians.

In 1378, the Great Schism actually split the papacy. Italian cardinals elected an Italian pope, who ruled at Rome. French cardinals chose a French pope, who kept his court at Avignon. Each pope claimed to be the only true head of the Church. Each enjoyed the support of several European rulers.

Finally, a majority of cardinals deposed both popes and elected a third in 1409. But neither of the deposed popes would leave, so the three

became rivals. The dispute ended with the election
ans. 4 tion of a fourth pope in 1417. By that time, however, the long conflict had greatly lowered the standing of the papacy.

SECTION REVIEW 1

p. 363 **1.** What were some of the weaknesses of the Catholic Church in the late Middle Ages?
p. 363 **2.** Who tried to reform the Church in the 13th and 14th centuries? What did John Wycliffe do?
p. 364 **3.** Why did kings, merchants, and others resent the power of the Church?
p. 364 **4.** What were the Babylonian Captivity and the
365 Great Schism? What effect did they have?

2 The Reformation divided Europe

Conditions in Germany were especially good for opposing the popes. Being so far away, the Church had difficulty keeping its control and collecting money from the hundreds of independent German states. All that was needed to bring about a revolution against the Church was a strong leader.

Luther objected to the sale of indulgences. Martin Luther was born of German peasant parents in 1483. His father hoped he would be a lawyer. But Luther became a monk and a professor of religion at the University of Wittenberg. There he studied the problem of salvation, or how to save one's soul from hell.
ans. 1 Luther believed that salvation was a matter between an individual and God. Salvation was based on faith alone, an idea called *justification by faith.* He felt that it did not require the help of priests or good works—the showing of faith by doing the right things and taking part in Church ritual.

● Two new views of salvation are presented in this section, Martin Luther's on p. 365, and John Calvin's on p. 367.

Luther's views brought him into direct conflict with the Church. This conflict came to center around the granting of indulgences. The Church granted indulgences to sinners on condition that they confess their sins, truly repent, and give a special donation. Gradually, the Church came to rely on the sale of indulgences when it was in need of money.

Luther objected strongly to these sales, especially when Pope Leo X sent an agent to Wittenberg to raise money for the completion of St. Peter's Church in Rome. Luther felt that indulgences had no value because sins could be forgiven only by faith in Christ's sacrifice. In 1517 Luther nailed up his list of statements against the sale of indulgences. These Ninety-five Theses, as they were called, caused a great stir.

Luther started his own church and led the Reformation. Luther kept attacking the Church of Rome in his sermons and writings. In 1521, the pope excommunicated him and later his life was endangered. German princes came to Luther's aid, however. He soon began to organize a new church. His writings were copied on the new printing presses and were widely read.

Luther taught that every individual had a direct relationship with God. People were able to interpret the Bible for themselves. In some ways, however, Luther disappointed the humanists. He did not listen to ideas different from his own. Once he had set up his own church, he felt that everyone else who broke with the Roman Catholic Church should accept his beliefs, which came to be called Lutheranism, and won many followers in Germany.

Civil War broke out. The Holy Roman Emperor, Charles V, and other Germans remained Catholic. Disputes between the two religious groups led to a civil war. When Catholic leaders tried to restrict Lutheran practices in Catholic areas, several Lutheran princes protested. This protest gave rise to the word *Protestant.*

Finally, an agreement called the Peace of Augsburg was reached in 1555. It said that each ● prince could choose between Catholicism and Lutheranism. His subjects would then follow his choice.

Luther's ideas spread to many other parts of Europe, particularly Scandinavia. There Protestantism gained the support of the governments of Denmark (which included Norway at that time) and Sweden.

● Point out that subjects of a ruler were bound to follow the religion he chose.

Martin Luther *(above left)* was the central figure of the Reformation. In this workroom in Wartburg Castle *(above)*, Luther finished translating the New Testament into German. He did the monumental job in only eleven weeks. Later, he translated the Old Testament. More than any other single work, Luther's Bible established modern German. He spent most of a year in Wartburg Castle, protected by the elector of Saxony. Luther needed protection because Emperor Charles V had declared him an outlaw.

The enamel picture *(above right)* shows a preacher speaking to a Geneva, Switzerland, congregation. The man at far right is John Calvin. The words at the top are a quote from the Lord's Prayer.

Hans Holbein the Younger made this drawing of England's Henry VIII *(right)*. Henry broke with the Catholic Church for political reasons more than religious ones. He wanted a divorce in hopes that another wife might give him the son he wanted as an heir.

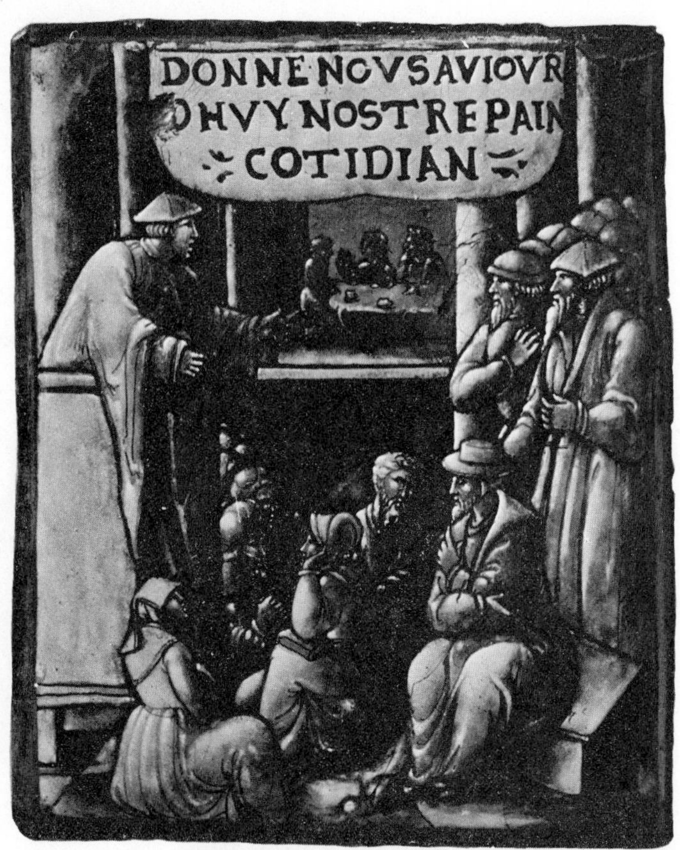

Calvinism became important. Other Christian reformers also set up separate churches. John Calvin, born in 1509, was a French lawyer and scholar. He had had to flee from France because of his Protestant ideas. In 1536, he visited the city of Geneva (in present-day Switzerland). When the people there asked him to stay and organize a church, he did so.

Although Calvin had been inspired by Luther, he disagreed with him on certain matters. One ans. 2 of Calvin's important ideas was that of *predestination.* This meant that God had already decided who was to be saved and who was to be damned. There was nothing a person could do to change this decision. Since nobody knew how God had decided in each case, a person's purpose in life, according to Calvin, was not to work out his salvation but to honor God. Calvin set forth his ideas in a famous book, *The Institutes of the Christian Religion.*

At Geneva, Calvin set up a theocracy. It strictly controlled not only church affairs, but also politics, education, amusements, and family life. Calvinism taught that one's work was actually part of one's religious life. Hard work, moral living, and thrift were believed to be the Christian virtues. A moral life and wealth were looked upon as signs that a person was predestined to salvation. These ideas are still very much a part ● of the Protestant work ethic.

Other new churches were soon set up, based on the Calvinist model. The Swiss Reformed and Dutch Reformed churches were two examples. So was the Presbyterian Church, begun by John Knox in Scotland. In France, Calvinists were known as *Huguenots* [hü′gə notz].

England broke with Rome. Protestantism was also felt in England. But most of the English remained loyal to the Catholic Church. King

● These ideas may be used to provoke discussion on the ways in which our society reflects these values today.

Henry VIII even wrote a pamphlet in 1521 attacking Luther. For this the pope rewarded him with the title "Defender of the Faith."

ans. 3 Soon afterward, however, Henry quarreled with the pope. He wanted the pope to dissolve • his marriage to Catherine of Aragon. When the pope refused, Henry chose a new archbishop of Canterbury. In 1533, the archbishop ruled that Catherine was not Henry's lawful wife. This left Henry free to marry Anne Boleyn, who he hoped would produce a male heir.

In 1534, the king had Parliament issue the Act of Supremacy. This made Henry VIII head of the Church in England. Henry also abolished monasteries and took over much of the Catholic Church's property. He made few changes in the religion. But his son, Edward VI, adopted several Protestant reforms.

Henry's daughter Mary became queen in 1553. A loyal Catholic, she severely persecuted English Protestants. This led people to call her "Bloody Mary." Elizabeth I, who succeeded Mary, brought back moderate Protestantism. Parliament then passed laws that began a national church of England. The head of this *Anglican* Church, as it is often called, is the king or queen of England, not the pope.

Most English people were happy with the Anglican Church. But some objected because it still used certain Catholic sacraments. They wanted the Church of England to be so pure in its Protestantism that they were called Puritans. Unhappy in England, many of them left and took Puritanism to the colonies in America.

Roman Catholics began a Counter Reformation. After seeing the spread of Protestantism, the Roman Catholic Church tried to win people back with the Counter Reformation. One part of the program was the founding of several new religious groups to help strengthen ans. 4
the Church. Most famous was the Jesuit order, which became known for excellent teaching and missionary work.

In 1542, Pope Paul III called the Council of Trent to deal with Church problems and suggest reforms. Delegates, meeting from 1545 to 1563, upheld all existing Roman Catholic doctrine. However, they ended such things as simony and the abuse of indulgences. They also improved church administration and education and reformed life in the monasteries.

The Counter Reformation, especially the work of the Jesuits, was very successful. By the 17th century, the Roman Catholic Church had stopped the spread of Protestantism in France. It won back Hungary and Poland, and kept Catholicism strong in Bavaria, Austria, Ireland, and the southern Netherlands.

The effects of the Reformation were widespread. • The Reformation strengthened new ans. 5
nations, kings, and the middle class. They gained from the limitation of papal power and from the Church wealth they seized.

The Reformation also helped democracy and representative government. The importance of lay people in church government increased, particularly among Calvinists. This idea of self-government carried over into political affairs. Calvinism also glorified work, thrift, and profits. Thus, the middle class gained new dignity and power.

In addition, the Reformation encouraged education, and in the long run, it aided religious toleration and freedom. But it had split the thousand-year-old unity of western Christendom. Protestants and Catholics were all Christians. But they no longer belonged to the same church organization. Northern Europe became mostly

• The ways in which the Reformation affected political change in Europe should be emphasized.

Protestant and southern Europe stayed mostly
ans. 5 Catholic. The same division still exists.

SECTION REVIEW 2

p. 365 **1.** What ideas of Martin Luther's brought him into conflict with the Church?

p. 367 **2.** What were the main beliefs of Calvinism? Name four countries to which it spread.

p. 368 **3.** How did England become Protestant?

p. 368 **4.** What were three important features of the Counter Reformation? Describe its success.

p. 368 **5.** What were some of the effects of the Reforma-
369 tion?

3 Religious differences mixed with political conflicts

For a long time, Protestants and Catholics were bitter enemies. They fought a series of wars from 1550 to 1650. Often, religion got mixed up with politics in these wars.

Spanish power threatened Europe. King Charles, a member of the Hapsburg family of Austria, ruled Spain from 1516 to 1556. He was
the strongest ruler of Europe. Through his ans. 1
mother and father Charles had inherited the Low Countries, southern Italy, and Austria. At the age of 19, he got himself elected Holy Roman Emperor Charles V. Thus by 1519, his control reached into central Europe as well.

The threatening power of Charles V led to the rise of a new idea in European politics. It was
called the *balance of power,* which meant that ans. 2
no one country should have overwhelming power over other countries. Countries constantly shifted alliances to keep this balance.

In 1556, Charles abdicated. His health was failing and he was tired of trying to hold his vast empire together. Austria went to his brother Ferdinand I, who became Holy Roman Emper-

The Armada was defeated by the smaller, faster English ships, bad planning, and storms in the English Channel.

or in 1558. Spain and the rest of the lands went to his son Philip II.

England defeated Spain. Philip wanted to strengthen his own rule and defend Catholicism. He saw Protestant England as his chief enemy. The English queen, Elizabeth I, was hostile to Spain. She even allowed English pirating of Spanish treasure ships.

ans. 3 In 1588, Philip sent out the Spanish Armada, a fleet of over 130 ships. It was to attack England and to prepare the way for an invasion. But the ships of the English navy were smaller and faster. And they were expertly sailed by such bold captains as Sir Francis Drake, John Hawkins, and Martin Frobisher. The Armada was defeated in the English Channel.

Elizabeth gained two important results from this battle. England remained free and Protestant, and it proved itself as a sea power. Under Elizabeth, England became an important naval power in Europe.

Civil war broke out in France. Meanwhile
ans. 4 in France, Huguenots were fighting Roman Catholics. At issue was which group would control the throne. During most of this time, France was ruled by weak kings. However, a regent, Catherine de' Medici, had great power. (A regent is a person who rules until the rightful ruler is able to.) Catherine's hatred of Protestantism was intense, and she planned to kill all Huguenots. In 1572, the bloody St. Bartholomew's Day Massacre took place. At least 10 thousand Huguenots were slain, but Protestantism was not stamped out in France.

In 1589, French King Henry III was assassinated. Henry of Navarre, leader of the Huguenot party, was heir to the throne. But French Catholics and Philip II of Spain denied his right to be king. With the aid of Elizabeth I of England, Henry became king in 1594. But he had to become a Catholic before he could be crowned. He was the first of the Bourbon dynasty.

Although Henry IV became a Catholic, he did not forget the Huguenots. In 1598, he issued the Edict of Nantes. This edict protected the liberties of the Huguenots. Thus, France became the first large country to permit more than one form of Christianity within its borders.

Another war lasted thirty years. Of all the areas in Europe, the German states of the Holy Roman Empire were most sharply divided be-

Catholics and Protestants committed terrible atrocities against each other. Here a French "holy league" looks for Huguenots to kill for heresy.

tween Catholics and Protestants. These states fought each other between 1618 and 1648 in a bitter struggle known as the Thirty Years' War. The war lasted so long because power politics became mixed up with religious issues.

ans. 5 The fighting began when a Catholic Hapsburg prince was chosen king of Bohemia in 1618. Many Bohemians were Protestant. Afraid of Catholic rule, they started a civil war and got a Protestant elected ruler of Bohemia. In the meantime, the Catholic Hapsburg prince became Holy Roman Emperor Ferdinand II. With the help of Catholic German princes and Catholic Hapsburg Spain, he fought Bohemia and won it back to Catholicism.

It now looked as if Ferdinand II would try to defeat all the German Protestant states. His goal was to set up a powerful unified empire under Hapsburg rule. The nations bordering on the empire were afraid this would upset the balance of power. Protestant Denmark was the first to declare war. Germany became a battleground.

When Ferdinand's armies defeated the Danes, Protestant Sweden became alarmed and entered the war. The Swedes got money from the French. Even though France was a Catholic country, it was more afraid of the growth of Hapsburg power than of Protestantism. The Swedes were led by their king, Gustavus Adolphus. He stopped the advance of the Hapsburgs, but was himself killed in battle.

As the war dragged on, the French too sent an army into German territory. After bloody fighting, the French and their allies won a major victory. The war ended in 1648 with the Peace of Westphalia. What began as a religious strug-

gle in 1618 had ended as a war to stop the Hapsburgs from dominating Europe. In this sense, the Thirty Years' War was fought to maintain the balance of power in Europe.

The Thirty Years' War had many important results. First, Germany remained divided between Protestants in the north and Catholics in the south. Second, hundreds of small German states kept their independence. Thus, Germany remained politically disunited for more than two centuries. Third, the war meant the end of an old medieval dream—a united Holy Roman Empire under the Catholic Church. In its place would be a modern Europe made up of independent states, each jealous of its own power.

SECTION REVIEW 3

p. 369 **1.** How did Spain become rich and powerful in the 16th century?

p. 369 **2.** What does balance of power mean and how was it kept?

p. 370 **3.** Why did Philip send out his Armada in 1588? What two goals were gained by Elizabeth I when the Spanish Armada was defeated?

p. 370 **4.** What caused the civil wars in 16th-century France? Why was the Edict of Nantes important?

p. 371 **5.** In what ways was the Thirty Years' War a religious struggle as well as a political war against Hapsburg domination of Europe? What were three long-lasting results of this war?

4 France became Europe's leading power

The Thirty Years' War also led to the decline of Spain and the rise of France as the strongest nation in Europe. Ever since the time of Charles V in the mid-16th century, France had been surrounded by Hapsburg Spain and Hapsburg Austria. France had felt its security was in danger. Now that danger was gone, the way was open for French power to grow.

Two cardinals helped make France strong. In 1610, Henry IV was assassinated. His wife became regent for their young son, but she mismanaged the country. Soon, an ambitious churchman named Richelieu [rish′ə lü] began to help her rule. In 1622, Richelieu was made a cardinal in the Catholic Church. Two years later, he became the chief minister of France. Even when Henry's son Louis XIII was old enough to reign, he found he could not get along without Richelieu. Louis allowed him almost absolute control over France.

Richelieu had two major aims. The first was to ans. 1
strengthen the power of the French king. The second was to make France supreme in Europe. To accomplish the first goal, he issued orders that took away political rights from the Huguenots and power from the nobles. To reach the second goal, Richelieu took France into the Thirty Years' War. France came out the strongest nation in Europe.

Richelieu was harsh and made the common people pay heavy taxes. When he died in 1642 they rejoiced. Louis XIII died a year later. His son Louix XIV became king at the age of four. Richelieu had trained Jules Mazarin, an Italian-born cardinal, to be his successor. Until Louis XIV was 22 years old, Mazarin actually ran the government. He followed Richelieu's policies, and France continued to grow strong.

Louis XIV was one of the most powerful French kings. Louis XIV ruled France from Mazarin's death in 1661 until 1715. He has

Louis XIV was a pool shark who rarely lost. Pool and gambling were the king's favorite indoor sports.

been called the perfect example of an absolute ruler with unlimited power. His motto was "L'État, c'est moi" (The State, it is me). Louis believed in the divine right of kings. He enjoyed playing the part of God's agent on Earth.

Louis was intelligent and worked hard at being king. His capable economic adviser, Jean Colbert [kôl ber′], helped France become strong through overseas growth. Colbert set up rules to improve the quality of French goods so that more people would buy them. To compete with the powerful Dutch and British East India trading companies, the French East India Company was begun in 1664. Louix XIV also added to the powers of the *intendants,* appointed officials who carried out his orders in the country. Also, he reorganized the French army and strengthened the navy.

Some of Louis's policies were unwise. Louis was a strong believer in Catholicism. He felt that non-Catholics would not be loyal to the king and would weaken France. In 1685, he cancelled the Edict of Nantes and took away freedom of worship from the Huguenots. Thousands fled to Prussia, England, and the British colonies in America. This hurt French trade and industry in which Huguenots were active.

In other areas, too, Louis's policies were unwise. *Le Roi Soleil,* or Sun King, as Louis XIV

The 18th-century wars among European nations led to battles in their colonies all over the world. The two-month seige of French Quebec by the British *(above)* was one.

was often called, demanded great luxury as well as power. He built a lavish palace at Versailles, a village about ten miles (16 kilometers) outside
ans. 2 Paris. There he surrounded himself with nobles who did nothing but serve and amuse him. ● Louis thus strengthened his power by making the nobles dependent on him. In this way, he kept them under his control.

The luxury and waste of Versailles cost the French taxpayers dearly. In addition, by moving from Paris to Versailles, Louis cut himself and his successors off from contact with the French people. Although this had serious results for the kings who came after him, Louis XIV gave France more unity and a stronger central government than ever before.

● You might discuss Louis XIV's methods of strengthening his rule.

Louis's wars weakened France. Louis had ans. 3
the strongest army in Europe. His ambition, like Richelieu's, was to make France the most powerful state on the continent. Thus France fought with other European nations in four long wars that lasted nearly fifty years.

Louis had two specific goals: to gain more territory to the north and east of France and to have a French prince become king of Spain and control Spain's huge overseas empire. From 1667 to 1714, the other European states made alliances to fight Louis and prevent him from upsetting the balance of power.

In the first three wars, Louis won a few border territories, but only after heavy losses in men and money. The fourth war was the longest and most costly. It grew out of a conflict over who was to succeed to the throne of Spain. Called
● the War of the Spanish Succession, it lasted from 1701 to 1714. The Spanish king, a Hapsburg, had no heirs. Shortly before he died in 1700, he signed a will under French pressure. In it, he named Louis's grandson, Philip, as his successor. He left Philip all Spanish territories in Europe and overseas.

The other European states had wanted to put a Hapsburg, Archduke Charles, on the Spanish throne. But in 1711, Charles inherited the Austrian throne and was in line to become the next Holy Roman Emperor. If he were made king of Spain as well, the Hapsburgs would control too much of Europe. The allies became divided on what to do. This led to a compromise peace with Louis.

The Treaty of Utrecht in 1713 ended the War of the Spanish Succession in Europe. Another treaty in 1714 ended the colonial conflict. Louis's
ans. 4 grandson, Philip, stayed on the Spanish throne. But he and Louis had to promise that the same king would never rule both France and Spain. Spain kept its overseas empire. But land that the Spanish Hapsburgs controlled in Italy and in present-day Belgium went to the Austrian Hapsburgs. And Spain lost Gibraltar, which England had captured during the war. England also took over some French colonies in Canada. In this way, France was stopped from dominating Europe, and the balance of power was kept.

Louis's wars and life of luxury left France with an empty treasury and a large debt. As he grew older, Louis doubted the wisdom of his many military adventures. On his deathbed in 1715, he warned his heir: "Try to preserve peace with your neighbors. I have been too fond of war."

SECTION REVIEW 4

1. What were Richelieu's aims? What did he do to accomplish them? p. 372

2. How did the royal court at Versailles strengthen Louis's absolutism, but weaken France? p. 374

3. In what ways did Louis XIV make France a stronger country? p. 375

4. How did the peace treaties after the War of the Spanish Succession keep a balance of power in Europe? p. 375

5 Strong rulers helped Russia grow

At the end of the 16th century, Russia was swept by great unrest. It was called a Time of Troubles because all government had broken down. The old ruling family did not have a male heir, and the peasants rose up in rebellion. Armies from Poland and Sweden took advantage of Russia's weakness. For a short time, Poles ruled Moscow. But the Russians finally drove out the invaders and brought some order. The Time of Troubles ended in 1613 when a popular assembly chose a young nobleman named Mikhail Romanov as tsar. The Romanovs built Russia into a great empire and ruled until 1917.

Peter the Great westernized Russia. Mikhail's grandson, Peter I—usually called Peter ■
the Great—came to the throne in 1682. He was ans. 1
determined to make Russia a strong, modern state by copying European technology. He created a small navy and modernized the army. He

● The causes and results of this war may need to be clarified.

■ Discuss what students feel might have been advantages or disadvantages of Peter's modernization program.

brought to Russia many European scholars, craftsmen, and engineers. They introduced European fashions and customs to Russia's upper classes. More important, they helped Peter set up scientific institutions, reform the calendar and alphabet, and start new industries.

Peter the Great, like most other European rulers of the time, believed firmly in absolutism. He removed all traces of local self-government. And he put the Russian Orthodox Church completely under his control. Peter also made all Russians serve the state. This was hardest on the peasants who had to pay heavy taxes. Serfdom grew worse, and there were many peasant uprisings in Peter's time.

Peter extended Russian boundaries. Peter the Great and later Russian rulers had a major goal in foreign affairs, to obtain "windows on the West." These were seaports on the Black Sea or Baltic Sea that would enable Russia to trade with western Europe by water. To gain ans. 2
such "windows," Peter waged war against the Swedes, who controlled much of the Baltic region. As a result, Russia was at war for most of the years that Peter ruled.

In these wars, Peter twice fought the Ottoman Turks, but without much lasting success. However, his Great Northern War against Sweden, for which he allied with Poland, Saxony, and Denmark, was successful. In 1703, Peter laid the foundations of St. Petersburg (now Leningrad), his new capital, on a region of the Baltic shore he had captured from Sweden. In 1709, the Russians won a smashing victory over the Swedes at Poltava in southern Russia. When

After the Russians overran Poland, Catherine the Great magnanimously tried to return his sword to the defeated Polish leader.

Catherine was very intelligent, practical, energetic, and an able administrator. And she possessed an iron will. She believed she could overcome any obstacle, and usually she did. For the first time since Peter the Great, Russia had a ruler who worked day and night, paying personal attention to even the smallest matters.

the Great Northern War ended in 1721, Sweden had lost nearly all of its possessions along the eastern shore of the Baltic. Russia had gained ● its Baltic "window" and had also become the dominant power in northern Europe.

Catherine the Great continued Peter's policies. Several weak rulers followed Peter the Great. Finally in 1762, Catherine II, a German princess, seized the throne from her mentally unfit husband, Peter III. Catherine was gifted and well educated. She thought of herself as
ans. 3 an enlightened ruler. She continued Peter's westernization policy by improving schools and modernizing laws. But the condition of the peasantry actually became worse. Catherine made serfs of more than a million peasants who had been free. They lived in the newly conquered areas in the south of Russia.

Catherine goaded the Turks into war in 1768. By 1774, she had won back the part of Azov which had been lost by Peter the Great. She also won free access to the Black Sea and the right to protect Christians living within the Ottoman Empire. A few years later, Catherine seized the Crimea. This brought about a second war with the Turks in 1787. A treaty signed in 1792 gave Russia ownership of the Crimea and other Turkish lands north of the Black Sea. During the same period, Russia took over some Polish lands. It was for all these conquests that Catherine was called "the Great."

● Use the geography essay on p. 378 to emphasize importance of a "window" to the west for Russia.

SECTION REVIEW **5**

1. How did Peter the Great try to westernize Russia? How did he strengthen Russian absolutism? p. 375

2. What were the goals of Peter's wars? How successful were they? p. 376

3. How did Catherine the Great affect the westernization of Russia? The condition of the serfs? The growth of Russia? p. 377

Geography: A Key to History

Russia and Ice-free Ports

Throughout history, a nation with good seaports has had an advantage in carrying on trade. In general, trade by water has been easier, cheaper, and often faster than trade by land. Even today, water is the most efficient way to carry bulky goods, such as ore.

Russia has the longest seacoast of any country in the world, yet it has had few usable seaports. Waters along most of Russia's Arctic coast are frozen over nine to ten months of the year. Murmansk is the only Arctic port that is ice-free year-round. Its usefulness has been limited because the seas tying it to western Europe are often stormy and treacherous.

The desire for ice-free ports was a major reason behind several Russian wars. In particular, Russian leaders fought to gain ports on the Baltic Sea, because the Baltic offers an open route to the Atlantic Ocean and western Europe.

One of the most important Baltic ports was Riga, near the mouth of the Western Dvina River. Medieval trade routes linked Riga with Europe and the Mediterranean. And the Western Dvina linked Riga with Russia's interior.

From 1557 to 1582, Tsar Ivan IV tried to conquer Riga and Narva, another Baltic port. He wanted to link Russia's internal trade routes with the Baltic Sea. After some initial successes, he was defeated by Polish and Swedish forces. Further attempts to win control of the Baltic ports were made by Tsar Peter the Great. In 1703 he built the city of St. Petersburg on the Gulf of Finland, hoping to open a new avenue to the West. As a result of the Great Northern War (1707–1721), Peter became master of the eastern shores of the Baltic. When Russia acquired Finland in 1809, it gained still more outlets to the Baltic.

Russia's leaders have also looked south, to the Black Sea. Russia fought the Turks to gain access to the Black Sea. Then it tried to win control of the straits leading from the Black Sea to the Mediterranean.

In the 19th and 20th centuries, Russia looked eastward. It fought Japan more than once in its search for an ice-free port on the Pacific.

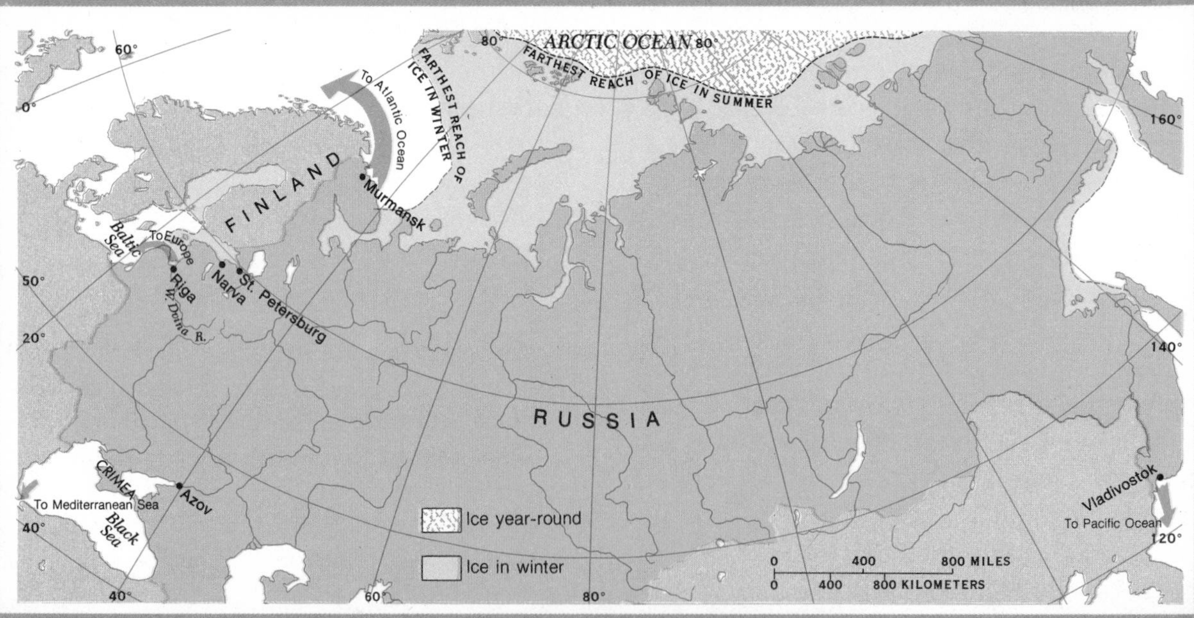

6 Prussia became a powerful new state

During the late Middle Ages, a new state began to take shape in northeastern Europe. This state, later called Prussia, owed its rise to the Hohenzollern [hō′ən zol′ərn] family. The Hohenzollerns were capable rulers who obtained both land and power through clever diplomacy. By the end of the Thirty Years' War, they had become the most important Protestant rulers in the German states. By 1701, they were kings of Prussia.

Frederick William and his son brought about many changes. Frederick William I, the second king of Prussia, was an absolutist who ruled from 1713 to 1740. He made Prussia
ans. 1 into a strong military state by tripling the size of its army. He also greatly improved the efficiency of both the army and the Prussian government.

ans. 2 His son, Frederick II, had many interests other than war. He enjoyed history, poetry, and music. He was also interested in the ideals of the Enlightenment. Frederick II abolished torture in criminal cases and reformed the civil courts. He granted religious toleration to all people in Prussia. He also worked hard to improve the government, industry, education, and living conditions of his people.

Frederick II made Prussia a great power. Frederick's major goal was to increase the power of Prussia. Shortly after he became king, Frederick invaded the Austrian territory of Silesia. This area was rich in farmland and industries. He thought he would succeed because Prussia had a stronger army than Austria.

At the time of Frederick's attack, the Austrian emperor had just died. Several heads of European states, including Frederick, had signed a pledge that they would respect Austrian boundaries and acknowledge the young Austrian princess, Maria Theresa, as the rightful heir to Austria. Frederick's attack broke the agreement. It also threatened the balance of power in Europe. The European states struck back in a war known as the War of the Austrian Succession. This war

Non est potestas Super Terram quae Comparetur ei Iob. 41. 24.

This picture is the first page of Thomas Hobbes's book *Leviathan.* The book was printed in 1651. The picture is a symbol of the complete control of an individual's rights by an absolute ruler. The body of the monarch is made up of tiny human figures. A pessimist and cynic, Hobbes believed that people are basically cruel and selfish. He felt that only an absolute ruler could bring peace and security.

became worldwide as the fighting extended to the overseas empires of the countries involved.

The war, which began in 1740, finally ended in 1763 with the Peace of Paris. A compromise, it allowed important shifts in the balance of power. Frederick got Silesia, and Prussia doubled in size. It is for this victory that Prussians called Frederick "the Great." Overseas, the
ans. 3 English had defeated France in North America. They gained Canada and all lands east of the Mississippi. England was also left free to conquer India. England therefore came out of the war as the greatest colonial power in the world.

Frederick the Great still wanted more land. His chance came in 1772. Prussia, Russia, and Austria forced a weak Poland to give up land to each of them. In the 1790s Poland was sliced up twice more by these greedy neighbors. Poland then disappeared as an independent nation until after World War I.

SECTION REVIEW 6

1. How did Frederick William I and Frederick II make Prussia a strong state? p. 379

2. Why was Frederick II called an "enlightened" monarch? Why was he called "the Great"? p. 379 380

3. Why were North America and India involved in the War of the Austrian Succession? p. 380

THE DISAPPEARANCE OF POLAND
1701–1795

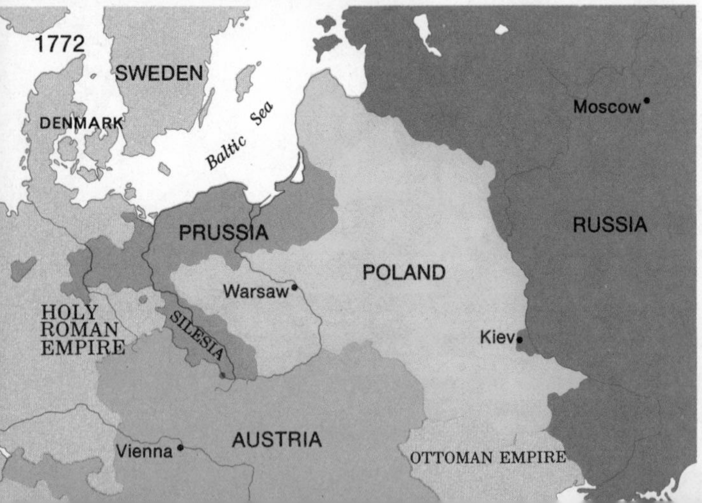

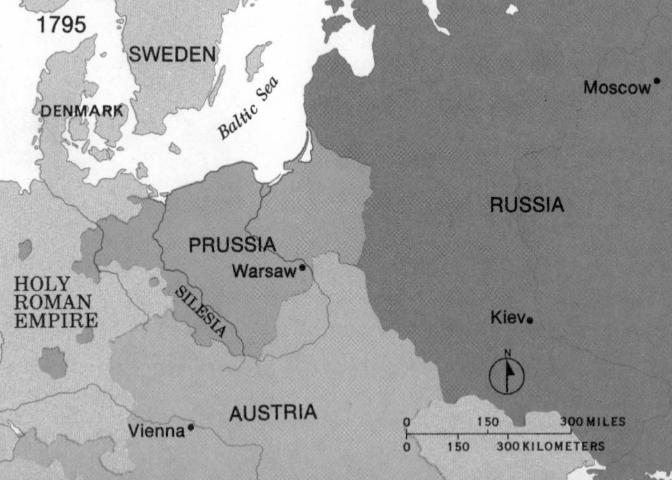

CHAPTER REVIEW 20

SECTION SUMMARIES

1. The Catholic Church lost power. The Protestant Reformation that swept Europe in the 16th and 17th centuries greatly reduced the power of the Catholic Church. The Reformation had several causes. Corruption had weakened the Church from within, which led to criticism and attempts to cleanse the Church by many reformers. New events from outside also reduced Church authority. Europeans began to resent papal control. Merchants wanted to be free of religious restrictions on trade.

2. The Reformation divided Europe. The Reformation started in Germany in 1517 when Martin Luther criticized the sale of indulgences by the Church. In Geneva, John Calvin began a new sect of Protestantism. Calvinism inspired the French Huguenots, the English Puritans, the Scottish Presbyterians, and others. England broke with Rome after a quarrel between Henry VIII and the pope. And the English began the Anglican Church. As Protestantism grew, the Catholic Church began the Counter Reformation to regain lost ground. New religious orders and reforms helped do this. But the Reformation had shattered the religious unity of western Europe. It aided both royal power and the spirit of democracy in some countries.

3. Religious differences mixed with political conflicts. European countries were involved in several wars between 1550 and 1650. Under Charles V and Philip II, Spain enjoyed its greatest glory. Jealous nations tried to check Spain to keep a balance of power. That balance shifted when England defeated the Spanish Armada in 1588. Civil war between Protestants and Catholics weakened France. But the Edict of Nantes gave Protestants some religious freedom. Religious fighting reached its peak in the Thirty Years' War. France grew at the expense of the Hapsburgs.

4. France became Europe's leading power. Cardinals Richelieu and Mazarin started France on the path to greatness. Louis XIV, a "perfect" absolute ruler, unified France and made it the leader of Europe. But his excessive spending on luxuries and wars later weakened France.

5. Strong rulers helped Russia grow. Peter the Great used his absolute power to modernize Russia and expand its territory. He gained a "window" on the Baltic Sea and built St. Petersburg. Catherine the Great was an "enlightened" ruler who also adopted some Western ways. She too increased Russia's size and power by gaining access to the Black Sea and seizing the Crimea and parts of Poland.

6. Prussia became a powerful new state. Under Frederick William I and Frederick the Great, Prussia became a strong military state. Frederick the Great was enlightened, but he too wanted to increase Prussia's size. Prussia and other European powers became involved in the War of the Austrian Succession, which was also fought in overseas colonies. The Peace of Paris gave Silesia to Frederick. Later, he also took some of Poland. England emerged from the war as the greatest colonial power.

WHO? WHAT? WHEN? WHERE?

1. Arrange these events in chronological order:

St. Bartholomew's Day Massacre 1572 (5)
War of the Spanish Succession 1701–14 (8)
Ninety-five Theses 1517 (2)
Edict of Nantes 1598 (6)
Catherine the Great became empress 1762 (9)
John Huss was burned at the stake 1415 (1)
Peace of Augsburg 1555 (4)
English Act of Supremacy 1534 (3)
Richelieu became chief minister of France 1624 (7)

2. How did these men influence the Reformation?
p. 363
John Wycliffe Henry VIII p. 368 Martin Luther p. 365
Erasmus p. 363 Philip IV p. 364 John Huss p. 363

3. How were these women involved in Protestant-Catholic conflicts?

Catherine of Aragon p. 368 Anne Boleyn p. 368
Elizabeth I p. 368, 370 "Bloody Mary" p. 368
Catherine de' Medici p. 370

4. Name the nationality of these persons and tell what important contribution each made:

Henry IV p. 370 Henry VIII p. 368
Catherine II p. 377 Peter I p. 375
Cardinal Richelieu p. 372 Frederick the Great p. 379

5. Explain how the Catholic Church was hurt by: a. the Great Schism, b. the Babylonian Captivity, c. simony, d. the sale of indulgences. a. p. 364 b. p. 364 c. p. 363 d. p. 365

6. Define "balance of power" and "window on the West." pp. 376, 378

QUESTIONS FOR CRITICAL THINKING

1. What were the major results of the Reformation? Include political and social changes.
2. Why could the 1600s be called the "French century"?
3. What nation will be associated with the 20th century? What makes a nation become "great"?

ACTIVITIES

1. Make maps or charts that show the 17th- and 18th-century shifts in alliances as Europe tried to maintain a balance of power.
2. Suggestions for role playing: a. Europeans of the 1700s discussing the effect of the Reformation on their lives, b. Peter the Great "Westernizing" his people, c. Mary Tudor and Elizabeth I discussing religion

CHAPTER TEST **20**

SECTION 1

1. The Great Schism split the papacy.
2. Simony was the practice by which important positions in the Church could be bought.
3. True or false: Merchants favored Church laws forbidding the charging of interest on loans.

SECTION 2

4. Match the 16th-century religion with the proper doctrine: a. Catholic, b. Lutheran, c. Calvinist.
Faith alone will ensure salvation. b.
Life's purpose is to honor God. c.
Faith and good works are necessary for salvation. a.
5. True or false: After the Peace of Augsburg, individuals could choose their own religion.

SECTION 3

6. The conflict between Philip II and Elizabeth I was based on: a. religion, b. politics, c. neither
7. True or false: Henry IV was the first Protestant king of France.

SECTION 4

8. True or false: The Treaty of Utrecht put a French prince on the Spanish throne.
9. Louis strengthened France by: a. building Versailles, b. strengthening the *intendants,* c. wars

SECTION 5

10. Peter the Great: a. increased religious freedom, b. got a "window" on the Baltic, c. lost much territory to Sweden
11. Catherine the Great fought: a. the British, b. the Swedes, c. the Turks

SECTION 6

12. After 1763, the world's greatest colonial power was: a. France, b. England, c. Prussia
13. True or false: Frederick the Great kept Prussia out of the War of the Austrian Succession.

1415–1673

CHAPTER

21

The Age of Exploration

European exploration was made possible in part by better ships and sailing methods. The geographer above works in his study with the tools of his trade close by. In the foreground, a loadstone (magnetic rock) floats in a bowl of water. A loadstone was an early form of compass.

After two months of sailing west across an unknown ocean, the crew was scared. They did not know where they were, the ocean seemed endless, and some wanted to turn back. But the admiral would not hear of it. Then, at 10 o'clock one night in October:

● Columbus' sea diary and other primary sources may be available in the school library.

the Admiral . . . being on the castle of the poop, saw a light, though it was so uncertain that he could not [be sure] it was land. He called Pero Gutierrez . . . and said that there seemed to be a light, and that he should look at it. He did so, and saw it. . . . It seemed . . . to

> be an indication of land; but the Admiral [wanted to make] certain that land was close. . . . At two hours after midnight . . . land was sighted [by a sailor named Rodrigo de Triana] at a distance of two leagues [six miles]. . . . The vessels were hove to, waiting for daylight; and on Friday [October 12] they arrived at a small island. . . . Presently they saw naked people.

The admiral was Christopher Columbus. The words came from the journal of his first voyage in 1492. His landing on that island in the Bahamas marked the beginning of one of the most important periods in history. It opened the way for Europeans to discover a whole New World that they had never dreamed existed. It set off an Age of Exploration that led to the building of colonies and a great increase in world trade. That in turn helped bring about the rise of capitalism and major changes in the economic and cultural lives of Americans, Africans, and Asians as well as Europeans. Chapter 21 tells how all this came about:

1. Europeans found lands unknown to them.

2. The world proved to be round.

3. Europeans built overseas empires.

4. The new discoveries brought many changes.

1 Europeans found lands unknown to them

A European desire for new trade routes and better navigation tools led to a great period of exploration from 1450 to 1650. During this Age of Exploration, Europeans found many lands that had been unknown to them.

Europeans wanted new trade routes. In the late Middle Ages, there was a growth in trade between Europe and the East. European ● trade was particularly heavy with India, China, and the East Indies. All such trade used both sea and land routes. Goods passed through many hands. Of course, each handler wanted to make a profit. Italian merchants made the largest profits of all because they had almost complete control over the Mediterranean part of the journey. Because of this, Europeans outside of Italy paid high prices for spices, silks, and jewels from the East. ans. 1

The upper classes of Europe were eager to buy imported goods. But they did not want to pay the high prices charged by the Italians. Merchants in other countries saw that there might be a way to change this. Costs would be much lower if goods could be shipped in a single sea voyage instead of in several stages across both land and sea. For these reasons, England, Portugal, France, Spain, and the Low Countries were interested in breaking the Italian monopoly. They wanted to trade directly with the East ■ themselves. Thus they began to search for all-water routes to the East. They were aided in their search by better compasses (to tell direction), astrolabes (to show the ship's latitude), and coastal maps.

Prince Henry aided the Portuguese. One of the first nations to set out beyond the Mediterranean Sea was Portugal. It owes much to a member of its royal family, Prince Henry the Navigator. Henry wished to expand Portuguese control and spread the Christian faith. He did

● As a refresher, the map on p. 347 can be used to show these trade routes, or use a large globe.

■ Key concept: trade spurred early explorations.

Christopher Columbus

ans. 2 not travel himself, but used his wealth to pay for the work of others.

Prince Henry opened a naval school and hired the best captains and mapmakers he could find. Beginning about 1415, he sent ships out year after year. They discovered the so-called Gold Coast of Africa (now part of Ghana), the Azores, the Cape Verde Islands, and the Madeiras. In 1441, a Portuguese sea captain brought the first African slaves to Portugal, beginning a brutal slave trade that marked the Western world for 400 years.

In 1460, Prince Henry died. He had given the Portuguese a good start in the field of discovery. Bartolomeu Dias picked up where Henry left off. In 1488, he sailed around the southern tip of Africa, giving it the name Cape of Storms. His voyage proved that a sea passage south of Africa did exist. This news pleased the king of Portugal so much that he renamed the point the Cape of Good Hope.

Columbus found the New World. Spain joined the search for an all-water route to India. Christopher Columbus was sure that he could reach the East by sailing west. Like many men of his time, he was certain that the world was round. But he believed the circumference of the ans. 3
earth to be much less than it actually is. Columbus thought, therefore, that a route westward to India would be shorter than an eastward route around Africa. Spain gave Columbus three ships for his exploration.

Columbus kept his ships pointed westward and landed on one of the Bahama Islands on October 12, 1492. Columbus went on to discover many other islands and even once reached the mainland of South America. Some historians say that Columbus always believed that he had found an outlying region of Asia rather than a New World. In their opinion, this is why he called the islands the Indies and their inhabitants Indians.

The pope divided new lands between Spain and Portugal. Three papal decrees in ans. 4
the 1450s gave Portugal a monopoly on African exploration and trade. To confirm its rights to newly discovered lands and to prevent conflicts with Portugal, Spain asked Pope Alexander VI which areas of the world it might claim. In 1493, the pope drew an imaginary north-south line, called the *papal line of demarcation.* The line went through the Atlantic Ocean 100 leagues (about 250 miles or 400 kilometers) west of the Azores. All newly discovered lands west of the line were to go to Spain. However, Portugal would not agree to this. So envoys from both

Who Really Discovered America?

The first discoverers of America were the ancestors of the American Indians – prehistoric people who crossed the Bering Strait between 10 and 30 thousand years ago. But the rest of the world did not know about the Americas until relatively recently.

Most of us believe that America was discovered by Christopher Columbus in 1492. But some scholars claim they have found evidence that long before Columbus, people from different parts of the world discovered the Americas. For example, there is evidence in Viking stories, called sagas, that Vikings, led by Leif Ericson, crossed the North Atlantic Ocean around 1000 A.D. and reached lands today called Newfoundland. Archeological discoveries support the sagas.

Other scholars say there is evidence that an Irish monk, Saint Brendan, came to Newfoundland in the 6th century to convert the Indians to Christianity. Some claim that a Welsh prince reached present-day Alabama in 1170, and support their theory by pointing to similarities between certain Welsh words and those of some Indian languages.

The predecessor of Mansa Musa, the 14th-century king of the African state of Mali, set out to prove one could sail west around the world. He never returned. Two hundred years later, the Spanish conquistadores, though they had never heard this story, were certain they found descendants of Africans living in Central America.

And there are Chinese scholars who, because of similarities between Aztec and Chinese language, myths, and coins, believe a Buddhist monk reached Mexico in 459 A.D,

The most recent theory is that Phoenicians, who are known to have traveled to Spain and Britain in the 600s B.C., established a colony in North America. The evidence is a collection of 400 grave markers found near Philadelphia. A Harvard scholar, Barry Fell, has worked 40 years to translate the inscriptions on them. He is sure the language is Iberian Punic.

Do all these theories mean Columbus is not important to history? No matter who reached America first, Columbus brought his discovery of land in the West to the attention of Europe. And he did it when Europeans were prepared to explore and to establish colonies.

According to Dr. Fell, the name on this stone is *Qas,* meaning "Blondie."

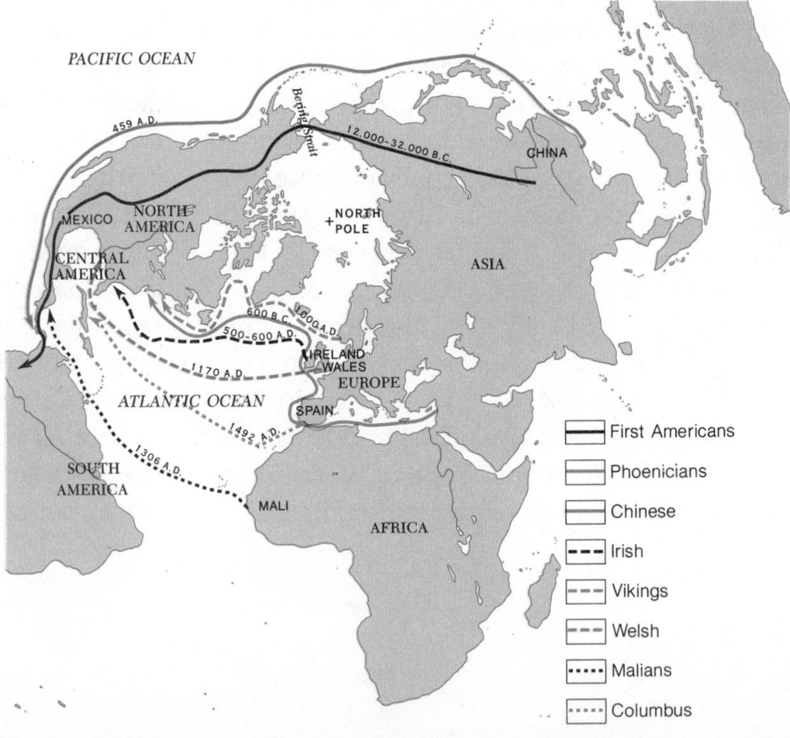

countries met in 1494 and drew up the Treaty of Tordesillas. This treaty moved the line 270 leagues farther west and gave Portugal the claim to what later became Brazil.

Da Gama sailed to India. While the Spaniards were voyaging westward looking for India, the Portuguese kept up their search for a southern route around Africa. In 1497, Vasco da Gama rounded the Cape of Good Hope and sailed north along the east coast of Africa. His small fleet entered the Muslim-dominated Indian Ocean.

After some trouble with the Muslims of Mombasa, da Gama was able to hire an outstanding Arab guide. With this expert, he headed across the Indian Ocean and reached the city of Calicut, India, in May, 1498.

The Hindus at Calicut were friendly. But the Muslims there had a monopoly on the spice trade. They saw da Gama as a threat and plotted to have him killed. However, da Gama escaped with a small cargo of cinnamon and pepper to take home.

ans. 5 Da Gama was greeted wildly on his return to Lisbon in September, 1499. The goods he brought back sold for sixty times the cost of the trip. However, he had lost nearly two-thirds of his crew as a result of scurvy. Yet da Gama had found the first all-water route from western Europe to India. He had found a way to bypass the trade monopoly of the Italians.

SECTION REVIEW 1

p. 384 **1.** Explain why goods imported from the East cost so much in Europe. What could European countries do to change this?

p. 385 **2.** How did Prince Henry help Portugal in the field of exploration? Why was Dias's voyage important?

3. In what way was Columbus's knowledge of geography wrong? What areas in the New World did he discover? p. 385

4. What part did the Catholic Church play in the Age of Exploration? p. 385

5. Why was da Gama treated as a hero when he returned to Portugal in 1499? p. 387

2 The world proved to be round

The voyages of Dias, Columbus, and da Gama excited many Europeans and led to other journeys. Eventually these journeys proved that the world was round. One could reach the East by sailing west.

America is found to be a new continent. One of the first to realize that the newly discovered lands to the west were not part of Asia was Amerigo Vespucci [ves pü'chē], an Italian. He made four voyages to the New World between 1497 and 1503. He believed that he was the first European to set foot on the South American mainland. Vespucci succeeded in spreading the idea that a new continent had been found. Thus, a German geographer named the new lands America after him. Some historians have doubts about Vespucci's claims, but the name, of course, has remained. ans. 1

Meanwhile, in 1500 Pedro Cabral put forward the Portuguese claim to Brazil. And in 1510, Vasco de Balboa began the first Spanish settlement on the American mainland at the Isthmus of Panama. Three years later, Balboa became the first European to gaze out at what he called the South Sea. Magellan later gave this great ocean the name Pacific, from the Latin word meaning "peaceful." ans. 2

Spaniards searched for gold. Other Spaniards continued to explore many parts of the Americas, mostly in search of gold. In 1513, Juan Ponce de León, while seeking a "Fountain of Youth," discovered Florida. Between 1539 and 1542, Hernando de Soto explored the southeastern part of the United States. He may have been the first European to sight the Mississippi River. In 1540, Francisco de Coronado moved into the southwestern United States. There he discovered the Grand Canyon and marveled at the buffalo herds roaming the plains.

Magellan circled the world. Ferdinand Magellan was Portuguese. But like Columbus, who was Italian, he got support from the king of Spain and set out in 1519 to reach India by sailing west. He had to put down several mutinies, and he lost many men and one of his five ships. Yet by 1520, Magellan rounded the southern tip of South America. His ships then had to edge their way through the narrow strait since called the Strait of Magellan. Because they ● were so close to the South Pole, ice formed on the sails and rigging. One ship returned to Spain. However, Magellan forced the rest of his frightened sailors onward.

Once in the Pacific, food and water became scarce. The crew suffered terribly. Finally, in March, 1521, Magellan reached some islands, which he named the Philippines in honor of King Philip of Spain. There he and several crew members were killed in a battle with the natives.

Two other ships were later lost. But one, the *Victoria,* pushed on. Loaded with a rich cargo of spices, it crossed the Indian Ocean, rounded Africa, and anchored at Seville, Spain, in September, 1522. After three years and twelve days, with only 18 out of 243 sailors left, the first ship to go around the world had returned.

Many explorers looked for a Northwest Passage. Most people, however, were still more interested in getting to the East than in exploring the Americas. The Spanish and Portu- ans. 3 guese controlled the southern regions of the Americas. Thus northern European countries tried for years to find a route to the East by going around or through North America.

As early as 1497, John Cabot, an Italian, was ans. 4 sent out by King Henry VII of England. He landed on the coast of Nova Scotia, Canada, and claimed the area for the king. Cabot was the first European since the Norsemen to set foot on the mainland of North America. Most important, his discovery gave England a claim to the ■ whole rich continent.

Jacques Cartier, sailing under the flag of France, made his way up the broad St. Lawrence River in 1534. He had hopes of reaching China. Instead, he claimed all of eastern North America, which he called New France. England also claimed the same area.

Other explorers continued searching for a Northwest Passage. One of the most famous English sea captains, Sir Francis Drake, combined exploration with piracy. In 1577, he sailed through the Strait of Magellan and north along the west coast of the Americas as far as California. On the way, he seized gold and silver from Spanish ships. He sailed northward, possibly as far as Vancouver Island. Not finding a western exit from the Northwest Passage, he headed back south. Then he journeyed home via the East Indies. He reached England in 1580, becoming the first Briton to sail around the world. His voyage brought a profit of 4,700 percent. It proved to many who had thought

● Some students may need help in understanding this idea.

■ The European rulers were able to lay claim to as much land as their armies were able to protect. As Christians they felt they had the right to take the land of the pagan peoples they conquered.

Most of the early French settlers in North America made their living by trapping or fishing. They traded or exported dried codfish and valuable beaver pelts to other colonists and Europe.

otherwise that the small English ships were well made. Henry Hudson also searched for a Northwest Passage. Working for the Dutch, he explored the Hudson River and Bay area in 1609. In 1610, he sailed for the English in search of a Northwest Passage. His mutinous crew made its way back to England, but Hudson was never heard of again.

SECTION REVIEW 2

p. 387 **1.** Where did the name America come from?

p. 387 **2.** What was important about the voyages of Cabral? Balboa? Magellan?

p. 388 **3.** Why were the Europeans looking for new trade routes?

p. 388 **4.** What happened as different European kings sent out explorers to find a Northwest Passage? Who were some of these explorers?

● Use the map on pp. 390-91 to point out the areas colonized by Europeans.

■ Key concept: the importance of colonies as sources of wealth and power, and as causes of rivalries between European nations.

3 Europeans built overseas empires

After their first discoveries, the Europeans began ● to take control over the areas they claimed. It was because they had superior weapons, such as cannons and guns, that so few Europeans could conquer so many natives. Once control was gained, the area was thought of as a colony belonging to the mother country. Europeans looked upon their colonies as a source of wealth. ■ There was great competition among countries to get as many colonies as possible.

Portugal established a far-flung trade empire. The Portuguese overseas empire was ans. 1 based on trade. Portugal set up trading posts on the east and west coasts of Africa, in India,

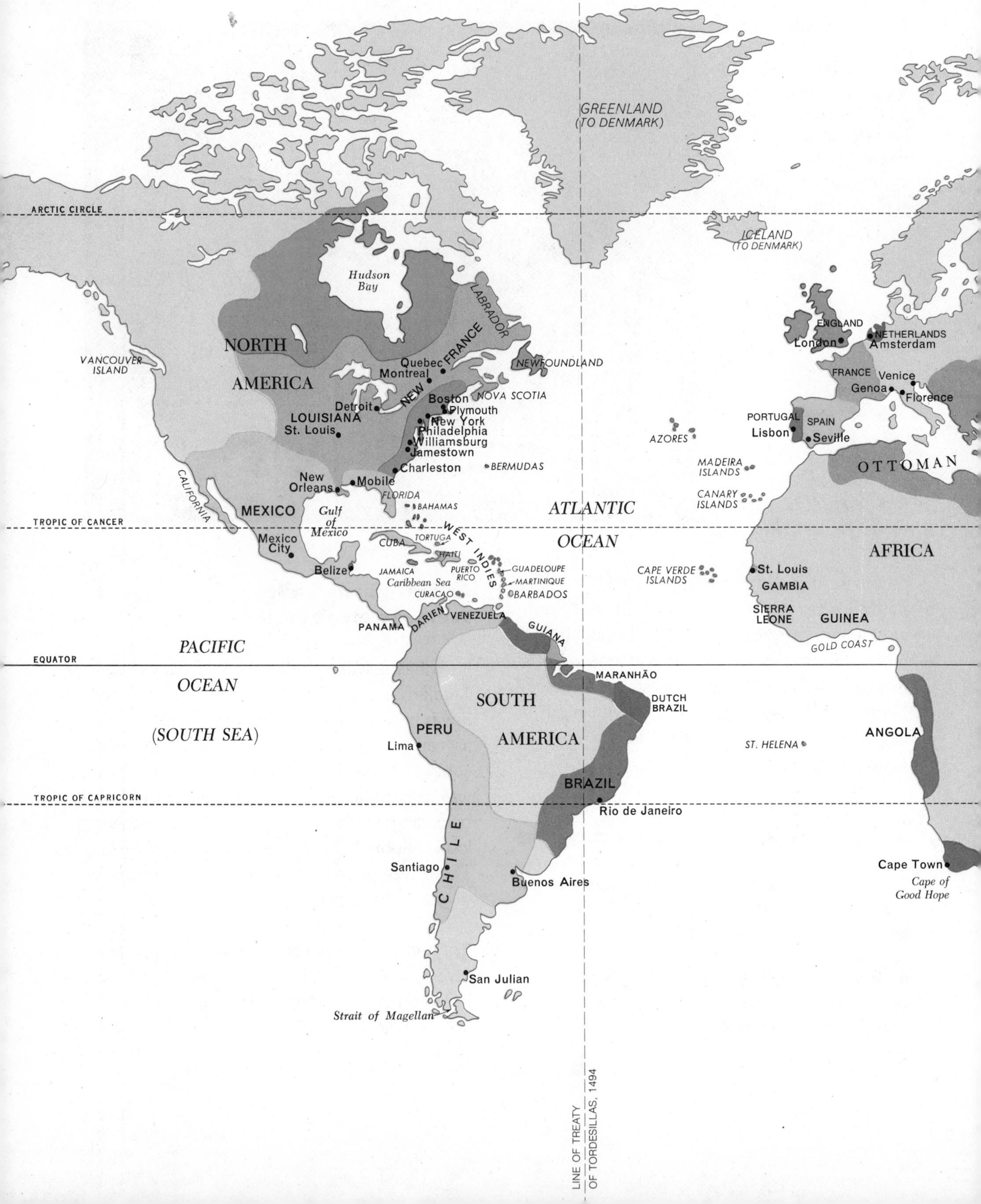

GREENLAND (TO DENMARK)
ARCTIC CIRCLE
ICELAND (TO DENMARK)
Hudson Bay
LABRADOR
NORTH AMERICA
NEW FRANCE
VANCOUVER ISLAND
Quebec
Montreal
NEWFOUNDLAND
ENGLAND
London
NETHERLANDS
Amsterdam
FRANCE
Venice
Genoa
Florence
Boston
NOVA SCOTIA
Detroit
Plymouth
LOUISIANA
New York
St. Louis
Philadelphia
Williamsburg
Jamestown
Charleston
BERMUDAS
PORTUGAL
Lisbon
SPAIN
Seville
AZORES
MADEIRA ISLANDS
OTTOMAN
CALIFORNIA
New Orleans
Mobile
FLORIDA
BAHAMAS
CANARY ISLANDS
ATLANTIC OCEAN
MEXICO
Gulf of Mexico
TROPIC OF CANCER
WEST INDIES
Mexico City
CUBA
TORTUGA
HAITI
AFRICA
Belize
JAMAICA
PUERTO RICO
GUADELOUPE
MARTINIQUE
BARBADOS
Caribbean Sea
CURACAO
CAPE VERDE ISLANDS
St. Louis
GAMBIA
SIERRA LEONE
GUINEA
PANAMA
DARIEN
VENEZUELA
GUIANA
GOLD COAST
PACIFIC OCEAN
(SOUTH SEA)
EQUATOR
MARANHÃO
SOUTH AMERICA
DUTCH BRAZIL
PERU
Lima
ST. HELENA
ANGOLA
BRAZIL
TROPIC OF CAPRICORN
Rio de Janeiro
CHILE
Santiago
Buenos Aires
Cape Town
Cape of Good Hope
San Julian
Strait of Magellan
LINE OF TREATY OF TORDESILLAS, 1494

MAJOR EMPIRES
About 1700

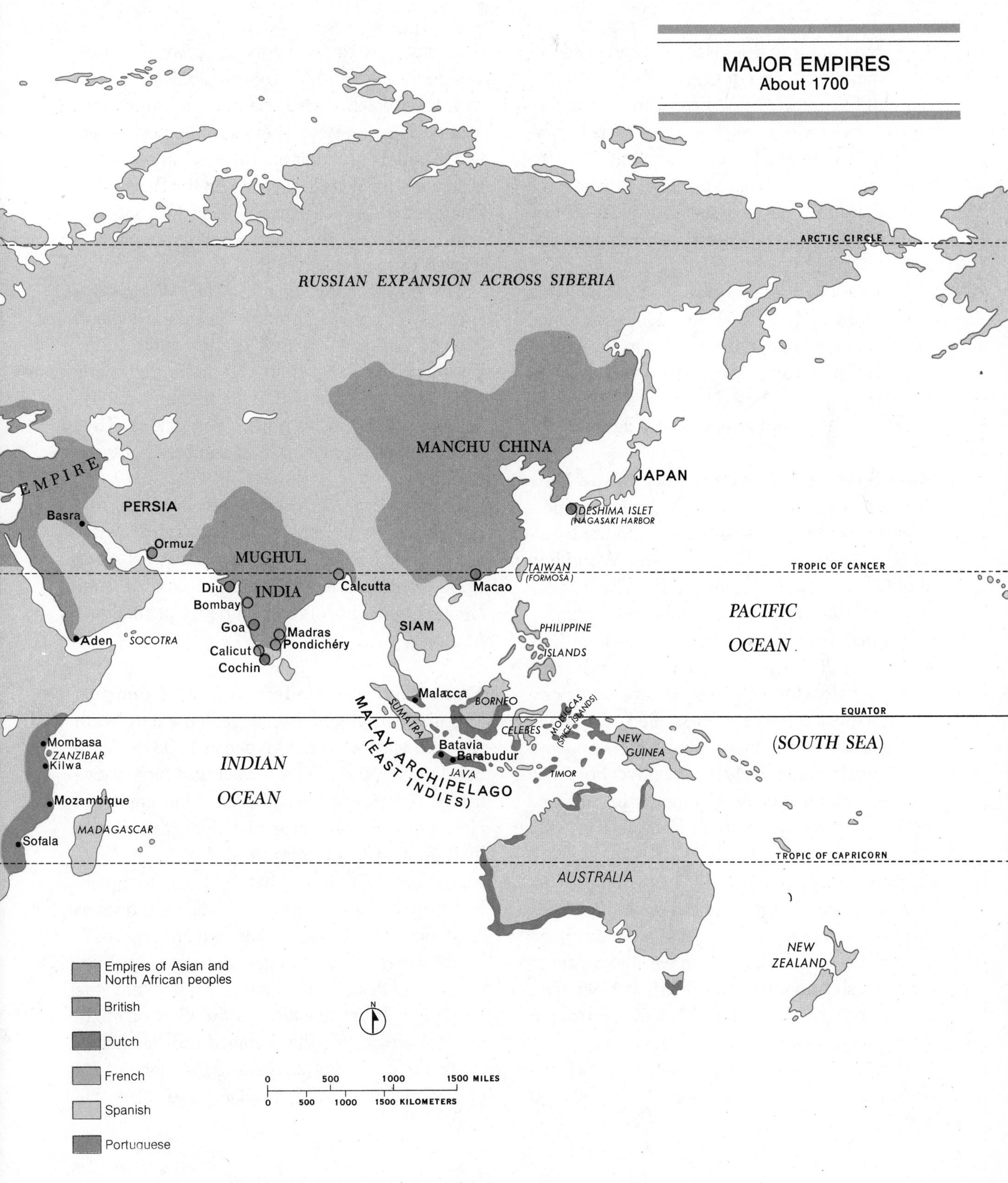

ARCTIC CIRCLE
RUSSIAN EXPANSION ACROSS SIBERIA
MANCHU CHINA
JAPAN
DESHIMA ISLET
(NAGASAKI HARBOR)
EMPIRE
PERSIA
Basra
Ormuz
MUGHUL
INDIA
Diu
Bombay
Goa
Madras
Pondichéry
Calicut
Cochin
Calcutta
Macao
TAIWAN
(FORMOSA)
TROPIC OF CANCER
SIAM
PHILIPPINE
ISLANDS
PACIFIC
OCEAN
Aden
SOCOTRA
Malacca
BORNEO
SUMATRA
MALAY ARCHIPELAGO
(EAST INDIES)
CELEBES
MOLUCCAS
(SPICE ISLANDS)
NEW
GUINEA
EQUATOR
(SOUTH SEA)
Batavia
Barabudur
JAVA
TIMOR
Mombasa
ZANZIBAR
Kilwa
INDIAN
OCEAN
Mozambique
MADAGASCAR
Sofala
TROPIC OF CAPRICORN
AUSTRALIA
NEW
ZEALAND
Empires of Asian and North African peoples
British
Dutch
French
Spanish
Portuguese
N
0 500 1000 1500 MILES
0 500 1000 1500 KILOMETERS

Java, Sumatra, the Spice Islands, and in southern China and also founded the colony of Angola. Except in Brazil, however, Portuguese merchants sent out only enough settlers to protect their commerce by controlling native rulers. Portugal was too small a country to spare the people. Besides, most of its territory lay in hot, humid lands with climates that Europeans disliked.

Spain took over Portugal and its overseas possessions in 1580. The Portuguese regained their independence in 1640. But in the meantime, the British and Dutch had seized much of the Portuguese empire. During the rest of the 1600s, Portugal's overseas power declined.

Most Spanish possessions lay in the New World. Except for the Philippines, most
ans. 2 Spanish overseas possessions were in the Western Hemisphere. By 1575, the New World had about 200 Spanish settlements. There were about 160 thousand Spaniards living in them.

Because Spain was much stronger than Portugal, it could set up more colonies and could better develop the colonies' natural resources. Also, Spain's colonies were settled by people who planned to stay there. Thus European ways of living were more easily transplanted. For these reasons, Spain's colonial empire in America lasted much longer than did Portugal's in Asia.

England began to seek colonies. Two events encouraged the English to also look for colonies overseas. The first was Drake's voyage around the world. The second was the defeat of the Spanish Armada by the British in 1588. This victory proved that England had become a strong naval power.

The first successful English settlement on the
ans. 3 American mainland was made in 1607 at Jamestown, Virginia. Plymouth, Massachusetts, was founded in 1620. Other colonies followed shortly. England also claimed a large area around Hudson Bay. There it set up posts to aid its fur traders. In addition, the English settled on islands in the West Indies and on the Bermudas. They seized Jamaica from Spain in 1655. By 1640, about 60 thousand English people had moved to the New World.

The English colonies in the New World grew strong. This was partly because England allowed religious minorities to settle there. These groups had a spirit and desire that made them ideal colonists. In addition, many English colonies were run by private companies. They allowed their settlers at least some self-government.

England became interested in the East, too, particularly as the power of Portugal declined. The British East India Company was set up in 1600. England later gained control of such wealthy trading posts as Bombay, Calcutta, and Madras.

France sent out traders and missionaries. The first permanent French settlement in North America was made at Quebec in 1608 by Samuel de Champlain. This armed post high above the St. Lawrence River became the capital of New France. Farther up the river, the French built another fort at Montreal.

Fur was to France what gold was to Spain. Fur trappers were among the first Europeans to explor the Great Lakes region. In 1673, Louis Joliet, a fur trader, and Jacques Marquette, a Jesuit missionary, found that the Mississippi River flowed into the Gulf of Mexico. Robert de la Salle followed the Mississippi to its source in 1682. De la Salle claimed for France all the surrounding land and rivers. He called the territory Louisiana in honor of King Louis XIV. The French set up small outposts along the shores of the Great Lakes and the Mississippi. These included ones at Detroit, St. Louis, and New Orleans.

Few French people, however, were willing
ans. 3 to settle in North America. The Huguenots were not allowed to go. This was because France, like Spain, excluded non-Catholics from its colonies. More French did settle in the warm Caribbean colonies of Martinique, Guadeloupe, Tortuga, and Haiti.

The Netherlands set up many colonies. The Netherlands, like Portugal, was a small
country that built a large, wealthy empire. Dur- ans. 4
ing their long fight for freedom from Spain, between 1567 and 1648, the Dutch built a strong navy. As Portugal came under Spanish control during this same period, the Dutch took over much of the Portuguese East Indian spice trade. The Dutch East India Company was founded in 1602. The Dutch made settlements on Java, Malacca, and at the Cape of Good Hope. They seized the Spice Islands (the Moluccas) in 1667.

In the New World, the Dutch settled Curaçao and other islands in the West Indies. They also set up Dutch Guiana on the coast of South America. They bought the island of Manhattan

Explorations made goods such as mirrors, window glass, and fine fabrics more available in Europe.

from the Indians in 1626 for about 25 dollars. They then began a colony, New Netherland, along the Hudson River. In 1664, the English seized this colony and renamed it New York.

SECTION REVIEW 3

p. 389 **1.** Why did the Portuguese establish an empire? Why was Portugal unable to hold on to its overseas possessions?

p. 392 **2.** In what ways was Spain's overseas empire different from Portugal's?

p. 392 393 **3.** What areas did England and France claim? Why did more English than French settle in the New World?

p. 393 **4.** How did relations between Spain and the Netherlands affect the Dutch empire? What areas belonged to the Dutch?

4 The new discoveries brought many changes

Through their discoveries, Europeans came into contact with lands and peoples different from their own. They learned about new foods, animals, and drugs, and about the true geography of the world. World trade grew rapidly. Large amounts of gold and silver were shipped back to Europe from the colonies. This led to a *Commercial Revolution* that brought great changes. These included new business methods, an increase in prices, and the growth of modern capitalism.

The expansion of European influence also spread Christianity and Western ideas to many parts of the world. Europeans interfered with the cultures of many native peoples. They tried to force these native peoples to become Christians and to adopt European ways. The most harmful effect was the growth of the slave trade. This new form of slavery was based on racist ideas.

World trade increased. The discovery of new trade routes ended the long monopoly enjoyed by the Italians. Proud and wealthy cities like Genoa, Venice, and Florence declined. Trade moved from the Mediterranean to the north Atlantic ports of London, Amsterdam, Bristol, and Antwerp.

The amount of trade grew rapidly. From Asia came larger shipments of spices, gems, paper, ivory, porcelain, textiles, and new items such as tea and coffee. The Americas shipped potatoes, tobacco, cocoa, and corn, which were also new to Europe. Canada exported furs and codfish. New England sent lye, ship timbers, pitch, and turpentine. From the West Indies came sugar, molasses, rum, and indigo. Africa sent hardwoods, ivory, gold, and ostrich feathers.

The slave trade grew and became racist. Slavery had existed in Africa and Asia for centuries. Long before the coming of Europeans, Arabs in East Africa traded in slaves. There were slaves in the ancient Greek and Roman Empires. In medieval Christendom there were a few slaves, who were used as servants, barbers, or musicians. This ages-old slavery had nothing to do with race. Black people in Africa were captured and sold into slavery by other blacks. People of any race captured in war could be made slaves. For a ransom, they could sometimes be freed. A free person could often choose to become a slave to escape paying heavy taxes; he or she could buy back freedom later. However, after the Europeans entered the slave trade, the trade grew and attitudes toward slaves gradually changed.

With the European colonization of the Amer-

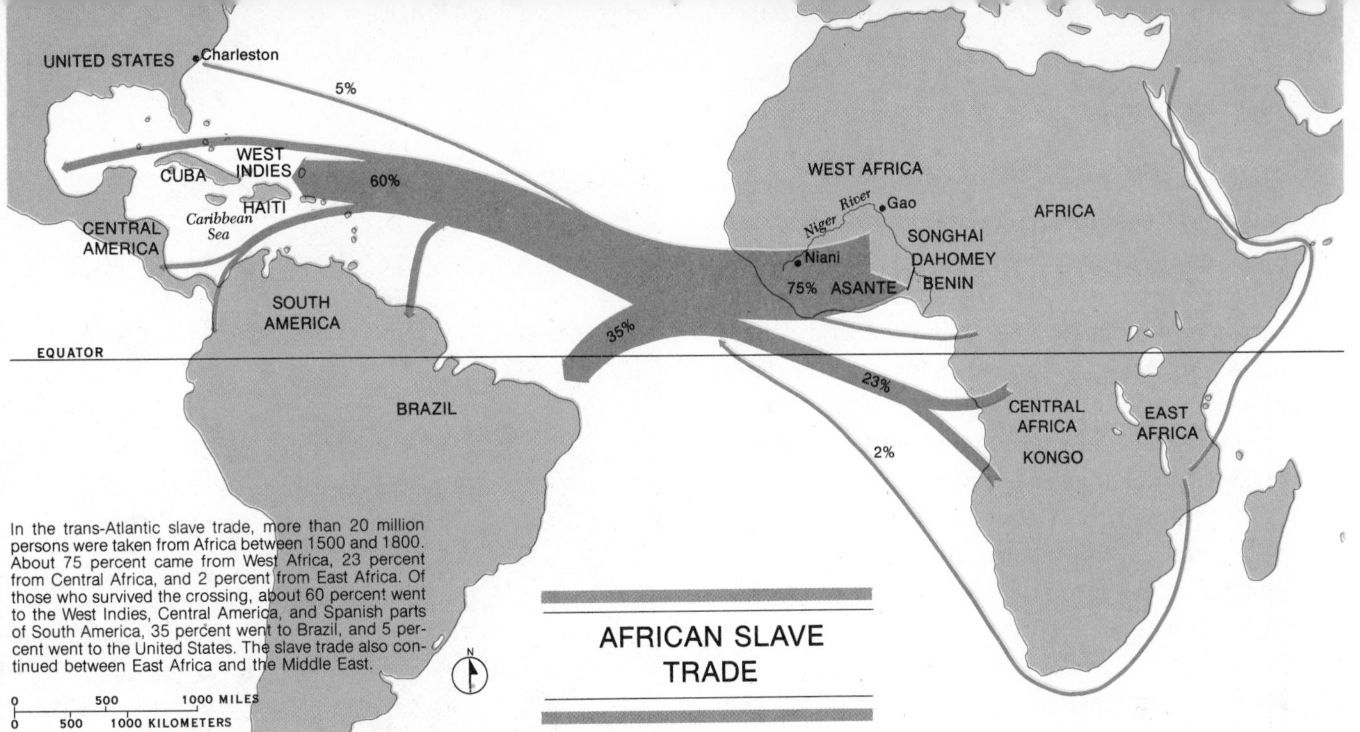

In the trans-Atlantic slave trade, more than 20 million persons were taken from Africa between 1500 and 1800. About 75 percent came from West Africa, 23 percent from Central Africa, and 2 percent from East Africa. Of those who survived the crossing, about 60 percent went to the West Indies, Central America, and Spanish parts of South America, 35 percent went to Brazil, and 5 percent went to the United States. The slave trade also continued between East Africa and the Middle East.

icas came large new markets for slaves. Altogether, about 20 million Africans were shipped to the Americas. Generally, they were rounded up by other Africans and sold to European slavers on the coast. The slaves traveled in filthy, crowded ships. Conditions on these slave ships were so bad that one fourth of the slaves died on the voyages. The survivors were forced to work in gold and diamond mines and on plantations that grew sugar, cacao, cotton, tobacco, and coffee.

ans. 1 Gradually many Europeans began to believe that blacks were born to be slaves. Both ● Catholics and Protestants tried to use the Bible to prove that black people were an inferior race and it was morally right to make them slaves. Slavery stopped being a temporary legal condition and became a permanent condition based on birth and African origin. For many Europeans, skin color became a sign of inferiority, and in this way slavery helped contribute to the growth of racial prejudice in the United States in modern times.

● Explain that this was an attempt by the Europeans to convince themselves they were not doing anything wrong in enslaving Africans.

■ Remind students that Italians learned of many of these practices from the Muslims they did business with.

Merchants learned new business methods. As European merchants grew rich, they looked for ways to protect, invest, and borrow money. Italians were the first European bankers. They had begun handling the money income of the popes as early as the 1100s. Banking did not become a big business until the 16th century, however. Checks, bank notes (a ■ form of paper money), and bills of exchange (a receipt for payment of goods in one city that was exchanged for similar goods in another city), all came into widespread use.

The growth in trade also led to the rise of insurance companies in the late 17th century. Merchants banded together and contributed to a common fund. Out of this, an owner would be paid for losses from fire, shipwreck, or piracy.

Another new idea was the joint-stock company. A person could gain part ownership in this type of company by buying one or more shares. If the company made a profit, each shareholder received part of the profit, called a dividend. If there were no profits, the value of the shares went down. Such companies made it possible to gather together much larger amounts of money than any single merchant could. Thus they were able to finance great fleets of trading ships. The Dutch East India Company and the British East India Company were both joint-stock companies.

Along with these companies came the growth of stock exchanges. There people could buy and sell their shares of stock. These exchanges also acted as barometers of business. The rise and fall in the price of stocks showed whether business was good or bad.

Modern capitalism was born. All of the business changes just described were signs of the beginning of modern capitalism. Capitalism ans. 2 is an economic system in which private individuals or companies, not the government, own the businesses. The goal is to make as much profit as possible by being efficient and competing with others.

Capitalism developed most strongly after 1500 in businesses that needed large amounts of money to operate. These included sugar refining, coal mining, iron manufacturing, large-scale cloth production, and especially, the outfitting of fleets for overseas trade. The people who worked in these businesses were wage earners. Unlike the members of medieval guilds, they did not own their materials or machines.

During the Middle Ages, people had dealt more in goods, services, and land than in money. The growing supply of gold and silver, however, allowed Europeans to coin more money. This made it easier to save or reinvest. Merchants and bankers could use the huge profits they made in trade to reinvest in joint-stock or other companies. Thus, this period became known as one of mercantile capitalism.

This middle-class couple are examples of the success of capitalism in Europe. Note the books, money, glass bottle, and mirror that surround them.

Prices rose in Europe. As we know, the Spaniards shipped great amounts of the gold and silver they found in Mexico and Peru back to Spain. There it was used to buy luxury goods and weapons from other European countries. In this way, Spanish gold and silver moved into the rest of Europe. It enabled people to buy more goods. However, goods could not be produced fast enough to keep up with the demand for them. The result was inflation, a rise in prices, all over Europe, especially after 1550. Prices kept rising for about 100 years.

This long-run inflation hurt some people and helped others. Merchants in the towns became richer because the goods they owned increased in price. But the working classes suffered because their wages remained low. They bought less as prices rose. European rulers found it more expensive to buy guns and uniforms for their new national armies. When they tried to raise taxes, the parliaments opposed them. In this way, inflation added to the problems of government in the 17th century.

European countries followed mercantilist
ans. 3 **policies.** The economic policies followed by most European countries in this period were called *mercantilism.* A mercantilist country believed that it would be rich and strong if it exported more than it imported. That way, more gold and silver would flow into the country than out of it. This is known as a favorable balance of trade. To maintain it, each country tried to sell as much as it could to other countries and to buy as little as it could in return. A mercantilist government aided export and shipping companies with money. This reduced the cost of goods they sold abroad. It also helped set up many new industries to make products at home that had been bought from other countries in the past. Thus, a country did not have to depend on others for as many materials.

Colonies were very important to mercantilist nations for several reasons. First, they could supply raw materials and slaves. Second, they were used by the mother country as closed markets in which to sell its manufactured goods. Foreign ● traders were kept out. Colonies were not allowed to produce anything the mother country exported. Third, some colonies were good ports or controlled vital waterways.

Mercantilists looked upon business between nations as a kind of economic war. A business deal could not benefit both sides. One had to gain, the other lose. The system led to hard competition among nations, to struggles over colonies, and to war. Many of the conflicts in the period from 1650 to 1800 can be explained partly or completely in terms of the mercantile policy.

The daily life of Europeans changed. In the period between 1500 and 1750, ways of life in Europe changed more than they had in the preceding 1,000 years. A rising standard of living allowed more people, especially the merchant class, to live comfortably.

New kinds of timber, such as mahogany from the West Indies, meant better houses and furniture. For instance, chairs began to replace stools in many homes. Window glass, carpets, and wallpaper came into use. Feather beds, pillows, and mirrors also became more common. Textiles, particularly cotton and linen, became cheaper. People began to have more clothes, to wear underwear, and to use handkerchiefs. The use of forks, napkins, and delicate china improved table manners.

There was more variety in food. Europeans learned to eat potatoes, oranges, lemons, strawberries, pineapples, bananas, and peanuts. Sugar replaced honey as a sweetener. The growing popularity of coffee led to the development of coffee houses. These became centers for literary and political discussions. Lloyd's of London, the insurance company, began as a coffee house. Tobacco also became popular among men and women. Like coffee and tea, tobacco was said to have healing powers.

A revolution in world ecology took place. ■
The sailing ships of the Age of Exploration ans. 4
tied all parts of the world together for the first time in human history. They carried not only people, but plants and animals from one part of the world to another. This brought about the

● Check to see if students understand that this policy in the long run would be harmful to the colonies.

■ The revolutionary results of the Age of Exploration are still affecting us today.

greatest change in ecology (the distribution of plant and animal life) the world has ever known.

The coffee bean, which was native to the Middle East, was brought to Java in the east and to South America in the west. Today, South America produces more than four-fifths of the world coffee crop. From the Americas, the sweet potato was brought to Asia. Manioc (a plant with a large starchy root from which tapioca is made) was brought to Africa. These plants greatly increased the food supply on both continents. The potato and Indian corn (called maize) brought from America later did the same for Europe. Maize spread to other continents, especially Asia. Today it is the third largest food crop in the world, after wheat and rice.

But the greatest change took place in the New World. The Europeans brought wheat, rye, oats, and rice. All of these were unknown in the Americas. Today the United States is the world's largest producer of wheat. Except for the llama, the peoples of the Americas had no beasts of burden or farm animals. The Europeans brought the horse, the donkey, and the mule to carry heavy loads. They brought cattle for meat and milk, the ox to pull the plow, as well as the pig, the goat, wool-bearing sheep, and barnyard chickens. From Asia, the Spanish brought sugar cane to the Caribbean. There it became the single most valuable crop. Cuba today is a leading producer of sugar. Unknowingly, the Europeans of the Age of Exploration started an ecological revolution that is still with us.

SECTION REVIEW **4**

1. How did the slave trade change the feelings of Europeans toward slavery and black people? p. 395
2. What is capitalism? How and when did it get started? p. 396
3. What was the main goal of mercantilism, and how did colonies contribute to this goal? p. 397
4. How did world ecology and eating habits change as a result of the Age of Exploration? p. 397 398

Explorations made coffee *(left)*, chocolate *(center)*, and tea *(right)*, common foods in European life.

CHAPTER REVIEW 21

SECTION SUMMARIES

1. Europeans found lands unknown to them. The great era of European exploration began late in the 15th century. With the rise of overseas empires, it brought about a Commercial Revolution. At the beginning of this period, Europeans were mainly interested in finding new trade routes to the East. They hoped to break the Italian monopoly on east-west trade. Improvements in sailing aided their search. With the help of Prince Henry, Portuguese sea captains began to explore the coast of Africa trying to find a southeastern route to India. Although Columbus failed to reach India by going westward, he made the much more important discovery of a New World. Later da Gama reached India by sailing around Africa.

2. The world proved to be round. Meanwhile, Vespucci spread the idea that America was a new continent, not part of Asia. This was proved in 1521 when Magellan's ships reached the East by going west.

The New World soon became important. Spaniards fanned out in search of gold. English, French, and Dutch explorers looked for a Northwest Passage. Each country staked out claims.

3. Europeans built overseas empires. The countries of Europe were quick to use their newly claimed territories. Portugal, France, and the Netherlands used them mainly for trade. The French built up a fur trade and the Dutch a spice trade. Spain and England also sent people to settle in their colonies, particularly in the New World. England allowed anyone to go, but Spain and France allowed only Catholics. Competition among Europeans for trade and colonies became intense. Portugal lost much of its empire to others.

4. The new discoveries brought many changes. The Age of Exploration led to a great increase in trade and in the supply of gold and silver. This in turn caused important changes that became known as the Commercial Revolution. The changes included the development of banking, insurance, joint-stock companies, and stock exchanges. These led to modern capitalism. With it, there was a growth in industry, a rise in prices, and a higher standard of living for Europeans. The policies of mercantilism and the exploitation of slaves and colonies helped make such changes possible.

For the world as a whole, there was a great redistribution of ideas, people, plants, and animals. Native cultures broke down as Europeans imposed Christianity and Western ways. World ecology changed as new food plants and animals were introduced everywhere. Daily life changed for many peoples. It was better for some and worse for others, mainly the slaves. Both a cultural and an ecological revolution took place between the 15th and 17th centuries.

WHO? WHAT? WHEN? WHERE?

1. Match the time periods with the events described: a. 1400–1450 b. 1451–1500 c. 1501–1550 d. 1551–1600 e. 1601–1650 f. 1651–1700

The Dutch bought Manhattan for $25. e.
Europeans first settled on the American mainland c.
Africans were first brought to Portugal as slaves a.
The first person sailed around the world c.
Columbus sighted land in New World b.
England claimed North America b.
The Papal line of demarcation was drawn b.
Portuguese first explored the African coast a.

2. In 1700, what European countries had colonies or trading posts in these areas? map 388-389

North America	Japan	China
South America	East Indies	India
Africa	West Indies	

3. Tell what flag these explorers sailed under and name the areas they explored:

Cabot p. 390 Dias p. 385 Cabral p. 387
Cartier p. 390 Marquette p. 392 Drake p. 390
da Gama p. 387 Columbus p. 385 Ponce de León p. 390

4. Tell how these terms relate to the Age of Exploration:

joint-stock company p. 396 profit p. 395, 396
p. 397 favorable balance of trade stock exchange p. 396
dividend p. 395 capitalism p. 396
mercantilism p. 397 closed markets p. 397

QUESTIONS FOR CRITICAL THINKING

1. In what ways is the Space Age similar to the Age of Exploration?
2. Why was it possible for Europeans, who were few in number, to win control over large areas of the world?
3. What were the most important changes in people's lives brought about by the events of the Age of Exploration?
4. As overseas empires were built and capitalism took hold, why did the merchant class become more important in deciding government policies?

ACTIVITIES

1. Choose five people from this chapter and make up "quotes" for them. Read them to the class and see if the class can guess who made the statements.
2. Research the types of ships used by early explorers and report on their size, equipment, speed, and so forth. Illustrate with pictures.
3. Find the country of origin of your favorite foods or of everything you eat in one day.
4. Read a primary source account from the Age of Exploration. This could be a diary, letters, or autobiography written by an explorer. Find out what it was like on the ship and how the sailors felt.

QUESTIONS FOR CRITICAL THINKING

1. Some possible answers are: fear of the unknown, bravery of explorers/astronauts, possible benefits to society, new 'worlds' to explore.
2. The map on pp. 390-91 shows Spain controlled more area, but England eventually gained more wealth.
3. Answers will vary. New foods, new lands, knowledge, wealth should be included. The change brought about in the lives of many Africans should not be ignored here.

CHAPTER TEST 21

SECTION 1

1. Early trade between the East and Europe made the __c__ rich. a. Spanish bourgeoisie, b. English and French kings, c. Italian merchants
2. True or false: European peasants demanded imported goods at lower prices so European governments searched for all-water routes to America.
3. Prince Henry the Navigator aided the explorations made by __c__. a. England, b. Spain, c. Portugal

SECTION 2

4. Match the explorer with his achievement: a. Vespucci, b. Cabral, c. Balboa, d. Coronado.
Claimed Brazil for Portugal. b.
First European to see the Pacific Ocean. c.
Explored the southwestern United States. d.
Had America named for him. a.
5. Who led the first successful expedition to sail around the world? a. Drake, b. Magellan, c. Cabot
6. Which one did not seek a Northwest Passage? a. England, b. Spain, c. France

SECTION 3

7. True or false: Europeans greatly outnumbered the armies of the people they conquered.
8. Which of these nations did not settle abroad in large numbers? a. Spain, b. Portugal, c. England
9. Which of these nations allowed religious minorities to settle in its colonies? a. England, b. Spain, c. France

SECTION 4

10. Which was not exported by Europeans *to* the colonies? a. pigs, b. gold, c. cattle
11. True or false: Spain became rich and powerful through the manufacture of luxury goods which it sold to the rest of Europe.
12. Which was not a part of mercantilism? a. favorable balance of trade, b. colonies, c. aiding peasants

1492–1800

CHAPTER **22**

The Formation of Latin America

The arrival of the Spanish and Portuguese in Latin America led to a mixing of three cultures: European, African, and Indian. This painted wooden bottle from about 1650 shows the mix. Done in Inca style, it has three figures: an African drummer, a Spanish trumpeter, and an Indian official.

On November 8, 1519, a Spanish soldier of fortune named Hernando Cortés became the first European ever to come face to face with the king of the Aztecs, Montezuma. The great meeting between Cortés and Montezuma was thus described by a Spanish eyewitness:

This introduction should give students an idea of the grandeur of the Aztec civilization.

We proceeded by the grand causeway which is eight yards wide, and runs in a straight line to the city of Mexico. It was crowded with people, as were all the towers, temples, and causeways, in every part of the lake, attracted by curiosity to behold men, and animals, such as

> had never before been seen in these countries. . . . We were met by a great number of the lords of the court in their richest dress, sent [ahead by] the great Montezuma, to bid us welcome. After waiting . . . some time, . . . Montezuma . . . approached, carried in a most magnificent litter, which was supported by his principal nobility. . . . Montezuma [left] his litter, and was borne in the arms of the princes . . . under a canopy of the richest materials, ornamented with green feathers, gold, and precious stones that hung in the manner of a fringe; he was most richly dressed and adorned, and wore buskins [half-boots] of pure gold ornamented with jewels. . . .
>
> When Cortés was told that the great Montezuma approached, he dismounted from his horse and advanced toward him with much respect; Montezuma bid him welcome, and Cortés replied with a compliment.

That first friendly meeting between Montezuma and Cortés turned out to be one of the most important events in the history of the Americas. It opened the way for Spain's conquest of Mexico, Central America, and the rich land of the Incas in Peru. Within a very short time, Spain ruled a huge colonial empire that stretched from Florida to Argentina. Portugal, meanwhile, took over Brazil.

The coming of Europeans to the Americas changed the course of history. Gold and silver from the Americas changed all of Europe, as did potatoes and corn. Even more important was the fact that Europeans came to the New World to settle permanently. The culture they brought with them blended with the culture of the Indians. There was a further blending as millions of Africans were brought over to work as slaves. During a period of three centuries, the mix gave rise to a new Latin American civilization. This chapter tells how:

1. Europeans conquered and colonized the Americas.

2. Spain controlled a large empire.

3. Indians and Africans were the main source of labor.

4. A Latin American civilization arose.

● The motivations of the conquistadores included adventure, gold, and desire to convert the Indians to Christianity.

1 Europeans conquered and colonized the Americas

On his second voyage across the Atlantic in 1493, Columbus brought 1,500 Spaniards with him. It was the first step in the settlement and conquest of the Americas by Europeans. It laid the basis for the Latin America we know today.

Cortés searched for gold. More than 125 years before the Pilgrims landed at Plymouth Rock, the Spanish in 1494 founded the city of Santo Domingo. This city is the capital of today's Dominican Republic. By 1514, the Spanish had conquered the island of Cuba. Five years later, the Spanish governor of Cuba heard rumors of gold on the mainland. He chose 33-year-old Hernando Cortés [kôr tez′], who had helped him conquer Cuba, to lead a daring expedition into Mexico.

Cortés was the son of well-to-do Spanish parents. He was one of the first, and greatest, of the conquistadores [kon kwis′tə dôr′ ēz] (conquerors) who came to the New World in search of ● adventure and gold. He was bold and ambitious, but also just and well liked as a leader. With 11 ships, 500 soldiers, 100 sailors, 16 horses, several small cannons, and gunpowder, he set sail for the coast of Mexico in 1519. Since ans. 1 the Mexican Indians had never seen cannons or horses before, Cortés had a great advantage when fighting them.

He also had good luck. Off the Mexican coast, he rescued a shipwrecked Spanish priest. This priest had been made the slave of a Mayan Indian chief. He had learned the Mayan language and now joined Cortés as an interpreter. The Mayan chiefs, frightened by the cannons and horses, gave Cortés a gift of 20 slaves. One of them was a young Aztec woman named Malinche [mä lēn′chā] who spoke Mayan and Nahuatl [nä′wä təl], the language of the Aztecs. The priest also taught her Spanish. Through her, Cortés spoke directly to Aztec and Mayan leaders. She acted as a diplomat and informant. Malinche even saved Cortés's life when she discovered an Indian plot to kill him.

Spanish troops and their Indian allies attack the main gate of Tenochtitlan. The drawing is from an Aztec manuscript that was made in the 1500s.

Cortés sailed northward until he discovered a good harbor where he founded the town of Vera Cruz. He learned that the Aztecs ruled the tribes of eastern Mexico. The Aztecs forced these tribes to send them tribute and humans for sacrifices. The tribes hated this, but warned Cortés that the Aztec king, Montezuma, was too powerful to be defeated. Some of Cortés's men wanted to return to Cuba to get more soldiers. But Cortés ordered all his ships burned. The men then had no choice but to march inland with him.

The Aztecs were defeated. The coastal Indians joined forces with Cortés. Others also joined Cortés as he moved inland and fought hard battles against independent tribes. Montezuma knew of Cortés's advance, but could not decide what to do. At first, he sent presents of gold to Cortés because he believed him to be an ancient Aztec god that was supposed to return one day.

● Montezuma had thousands of armed Aztec warriors at his command. He could have ordered them to attack Cortés's 400 men. Instead, he decided to welcome the Spaniards to Tenochtitlan, the Aztec capital. Once inside the city, Cortés took Montezuma as a hostage. A short time later, one of Cortés's captains invited Aztec nobles to a feast and murdered them. The Aztecs rose up in anger against the Spaniards. Montezuma was killed, but the Spaniards lost more than half their men getting out of Tenochtitlan.

Cortés soon received fresh supplies, cannons, and gunpowder from Cuba. He was also able to get more Indian allies. Then he laid siege to Tenochtitlan for three months, cutting off the water supply. The Aztecs were further weakened by hundreds of deaths from smallpox. The Spaniards had unknowingly brought this disease with them. Finally in August, 1521, the Aztecs surrendered. Tenochtitlan was renamed Mexico City.

● The Aztecs had large armies but were conquered because of a combination of factors, as explained in this section.

Pizarro conquered the Incas. Ten years after the fall of the Aztecs, another conquistador made his mark. His name was Francisco Pizarro [pi zär′ō]. He set out to find the rich Inca empire he had heard existed in Peru. Pizarro, the son of a soldier, wanted to be rich and important. Late in 1530, he set sail from Panama with his brothers, whom he had recruited, and some soldiers.

Like Cortés, Pizarro also had some good luck. ans. 2
In 1524, a civil war had broken out among the Incas. Two brothers were fighting each other to be ruler. Atahualpa [ä′tä wäl′pä] won, but the fight weakened his empire. Pizarro met Atahualpa high in the Andes Mountains in 1531. He attacked with guns and cannons. Thousands of Incas were killed, and Atahualpa was taken prisoner. Not a single Spaniard was even badly wounded.

Atahualpa soon realized that the Spaniards wanted gold. He offered to buy his freedom by filling a large room with gold, then filling it twice more with silver. But after paying this ransom, Atahualpa was killed anyway. Pizarro and his men wanted to be masters of Peru.

Pizarro, his brothers, and about 150 Spanish soldiers divided up the treasure. But the men became greedy and began to fight among themselves. This kept Peru in chaos. Yet the rule of the Pizarro brothers lasted sixteen years. In 1547, a royal governor with Spanish troops took over.

Spanish rule reached other areas. Both Cortés and Pizarro later sent out small groups of

Spanish troops to widen their control. Cortés's men pushed into Central America. Pizarro moved into present-day Ecuador and Chile. The Indians in Chile fought hard. But they were also weakened by smallpox, and were no match for the horses, muskets, and cannons.

Another of Pizarro's men led a group into a rich valley in present-day Colombia. It was ruled by an Indian king named Bogotá [bō′gə tä′]. There the Spaniards found houses decorated with gold and children playing "marbles" with emeralds. Once again they took control.

In the mid-1530s, a rich Spanish noble led an expedition across the Atlantic at his own expense. He sent a dozen ships, 1,500 settlers, and several hundred cattle and horses. They landed at the mouth of the Plata River. There they founded a town named Buenos Aires [bwā′nəs er′ēz], now the capital of Argentina.

Portuguese settled on Brazil's coast. While the Spaniards rapidly took over a huge area from Mexico to Chile, the Portuguese did very little with their claim to Brazil. They were much more interested in the large profits they were making from the spice trade with Asia. By
ans. 3 the 1530s, however, the king of Portugal feared that Spain might try to take over the coast of Brazil. To prevent this, he offered large grants of land to rich Portuguese nobles. In return, the nobles had to set up colonies at their own expense. By the mid-1500s, there were 15 armed towns along the Brazilian coast. The king of Portugal sent out a governor general. He also sent a thousand colonists and Jesuit missionaries to convert the Indians to Christianity. In 1565, the Portuguese founded the town of Rio de Janeiro [rē′ō dā zhə ner′ō].

In general, the Portuguese settlement of Brazil was slow and peaceful. This was largely because there was no organized Indian state to fight ans. 4
against. By 1600, there were nearly 100 thousand people living in the Portuguese towns of Brazil. A fourth of these people were black slaves who had been brought over to work on the sugar plantations. Sugar became Brazil's major export.

SECTION REVIEW **1**

1. List four advantages that helped Cortés defeat the Aztecs. p. 403

2. Describe how Pizarro conquered Peru. p. 404

3. Why did Portugal finally begin to settle its lands in Brazil? p. 405

4. Why was Spain's colonization different from Portugal's? p. 405

2 Spain controlled a large empire

ans. 1 Spain's empire in America was different from most other empires in history. It lay far away, across the Atlantic. It included islands as well as a huge area on the mainland. Cities and towns were sometimes thousands of miles apart. They were separated by mountains, deserts, and tropical rain forests. Travel from place to place was very hard. Spain had to find a way to govern this empire that was many times larger than itself.

The king ruled through a Council and viceroys. In 1524, Charles I set up a Council of the Indies to help him govern the colonies. The Council met in Spain, but acted as a kind of legislature for the colonies. ans. 2 It drew up a code of laws to control colonial life for the benefit of the mother country. As time passed, new laws were added. By 1681, there was such confusion that all the laws had to be reorganized into a simpler code.

● The administration of Spain's American colonies was regulated by the Spanish government through Spanish officials.

Viceroys were appointed for New Spain and Peru. These men ruled in the king's name. The viceroy of New Spain lived in Mexico City. He controlled all Spanish possessions in North and Central America and the Caribbean islands. The viceroy of Peru lived in Lima. He was in charge of all Spanish possessions in South America. In the 18th century, Spain di-

Daily Life in Latin America

The picture at *left* is a Brazilian town of the 1600s. It is designed much as were towns in Portugal. Note the large church in the center. At *right bottom* is an upper class family walking to church in Rio de Janeiro, Brazil. The family's slaves follow behind. Portuguese women and their slaves spent large amounts of time together. As a result, the music, language, and folklore of the Africans intermingled with that of the Portuguese. At *right top* is a picture of Porto Bello, in what is now Panama. From 1561 to 1748, Porto Bello was one of the three main stops that Spanish ship convoys made. It was a small, sleepy, disease-ridden town that came alive when ships arrived. Then the 40-day fairs attracted merchants from as far away as Chile and Argentina.

vided Peru into two viceroyalties. There was New Granada, with its capital at Bogotá, and La Plata, with its capital at Buenos Aires.

ans. 3 **Spanish nobles governed the colonies.** The Council of the Indies always chose nobles born in Spain to serve as officials in the colonies. Church leaders, such as bishops and archbishops, were also from Spain. Most of these officials were corrupt. They often returned to Spain richer than when they had left.

All Spanish-born officials looked down on everyone else, even on very rich settlers who happened to have been born in the New World. The permanent settlers hated this high-and-
ans. 4 mighty attitude of the *peninsulares* [pā nēn′ sü-lä′rās], as they called the officials born in Spain. They were angry at being denied important jobs in government. It made no sense to them since they all had a similar background. Spain ● permitted only Spanish Catholics to settle in the colonies. This was quite different from the policy followed in the English colonies of North America. There people of almost any religion and nationality were allowed to settle.

● Key concept: the class structure in Latin America resulted from these colonial policies.

Creoles and mestizos had lower social standing. Children whose parents were Spanish but who were born in the colonies were called *creoles* [krē′ōlz]. They had a lower social rank than their parents, even if they were very rich. Creoles often copied the manners and

Llamas carry heavy silver ore down the mountain in Potosí, Bolivia. It was one of the world's richest mines.

dress of the peninsulares. They sometimes tried to pass themselves off as Spanish-born.

In the early years after the conquest, very few Spanish women came to Mexico or Peru. Many Spanish soldiers married Indian women. The children born of these marriages were called *mestizos* [mə stē′zōs]. They had even lower social standing than the creoles. And mestizos had a difficult time. Most of them did not own land. They worked either as farmers on rented land, or as shopkeepers, craftspeople, or soldiers. But, the mestizos were soon the largest racial group in colonial Latin America.

SECTION REVIEW 2

1. Why was it hard for Spain to rule its new empire? p. 406

2. Who wrote laws for the colonies? Who ruled the colonies? p. 406

3. What religious requirements did Spain make on its colonial settlers? p. 407

4. Name and describe the three social groups in the Spanish colonies. p. 407

5. What advantages or disadvantages did each of the three social groups in the Spanish colonies have? Which group soon became the largest? p. 407 408

3 Indians and Africans were the main source of labor

ans. 1 The greatest kind of wealth in the Spanish colonies was land. After the Aztecs and Incas were defeated, the conquistadores took away their land and divided it up among the Spanish soldiers. The creole children of these soldiers soon became the landed aristocracy. The Catholic Church also came to own very large amounts of land. But to make the land produce crops took a great deal of manual work. Finding that labor became the biggest problem facing the Spanish colonists.

Indians were forced to do heavy work. At first, the Spanish colonists had the Indians till the fields for them. The Indians also had to work in the rich silver mines that were discovered in Mexico and what is now Bolivia. Entire villages of Indians were assigned to a landowner. They not only had to work on his lands, but also pay
ans. 2 tribute to him. For his part, the landowner was supposed to protect the Indians and convert them to Catholicism. In practice, he often treated them like slaves.

This system of forced labor was called the *encomienda* [en′kō mē en′də]. The Spanish government tried to reform the encomienda in the 1540s. But the viceroys and creole landowners ignored the reforms. Indians died by the thousands on the plantations and in the silver mines.

ans. 3 Not only did the Indians receive very cruel treatment, they also suffered terribly from European diseases such as smallpox. ● This led to perhaps the greatest population disaster in history. Before the Europeans came, there were about 15 to 25 million Indians in Latin America. Within a single century, the population shrank to about 4 million. This helps explain why lack of workers continued to be a major problem in the colonies.

The Church tried to protect the Indians. After Mexico and Peru had been conquered, many missionaries came to the New World to convert Indians to the Catholic faith. They also set up schools, founded hospitals, and explored frontier areas. Some missionaries tried to protect the Indians against creole owners, but they did not have much success.

The most famous defender of the Indians was Bartolomé de las Casas. ■ He was a Spanish priest who spoke out against the cruel treatment of Indians by the Spaniards. Charles I chose him to be "Protector of the Indians." Charles also supported other missionaries who tried to help the Indians. The efforts of the Church at least stopped the creoles from working so many Indians to death.

Jesuits created missions in Paraguay. The most successful missionaries were the Jesuits. They set up mission villages among the Guarani [gwä′rä nē′] Indians in Paraguay. They taught the Guarani how to grow grapes, oranges, olives, sugar cane, and corn. They also showed them how to raise livestock. The Jesuits learned the Guarani language and taught the Indians how to write it. The Indians learned how to work printing presses and print books in their own language. Today, Guarani is still widely used in Paraguay.

However, Portuguese slave raiders from Brazil kept attacking the Jesuit missions. They kidnaped some 60 thousand Guarani and sold them into slavery. Later, Spanish landowners also tried to use the Guarani for forced labor. This led the Spanish government to change its

● The Indians were vulnerable to European diseases because of the lack of previous contact with outsiders.

■ Students may be interested in Las Casas' history of this period.

policy. In 1767, it ordered all Jesuits to leave Spanish America. The mission villages in Paraguay fell apart.

Many Indians were converted to Christianity. Although the Jesuits were forced out, other missionary groups remained. In addition, the Catholic Church and its priests worked among the Indians. The priests also, of course, served the colonists.

Through these people, great numbers of Indians were baptized into the Catholic faith. Most, however, did not completely give up their old religions. They often blended their own rituals with Catholic customs and festivals. Sometimes, they simply gave Christian names to Indian gods. They built churches where old temples had once stood. In this way, Catholicism among the Indians of Spanish America developed an unusual form. Today in Peru, Ecuador, and Guatemala, Indians in Catholic churches use their own languages to say prayers that were used in the past for ancient gods.

African slaves were brought to Spanish America. As we have seen, there was a great loss of Indian population from European diseases and overwork. However, the large plantation owners in the West Indies and Brazil still needed thousands of field hands to do hot, back-breaking labor. The Spanish government therefore allowed them to import slaves from Africa. Altogether, over 11 million people were shipped across the Atlantic to Spanish colonies. About 2 million of them died on the way because of terrible conditions on the ships.

Slaves were used mostly in the Caribbean.
ans. 4 Most slaves worked on the sugar plantations of the Caribbean islands. By the mid-1600s, sugar cane had become the major crop of the islands. Slaves also worked on mainland plantations and on those where cacao, rice, cotton, and tobacco were grown. African slaves also did the heavy labor in mines. They worked on the docks in the port cities, and were used as personal servants as well.

Slavery on the Caribbean sugar plantations was brutal. Owners were interested only in profits. They did not care how slaves were treated. They often worked slaves to death and then bought new ones. This was cheaper than treating them better so they would live longer. Men and women, young and old, slaved 18 hours a day during the sugar harvest. The work done by women was so heavy that very few of their babies were born alive. Those that did live seldom survived to become adults.

Brazilian slaves were treated differently. African slaves also worked on the sugar plantations along the Brazilian coast. The Portuguese government also had allowed slaves to be imported. This was because they found that the Brazilian Indians were food gatherers and did not know much about plowing and planting.

Slaves in Brazil suffered just as those in the Caribbean islands did. But the Portuguese looked upon slaves as people with souls. They therefore converted the slaves to Christianity. Brazilian slaves attended church and took part in religious ceremonies.

Some Brazilian slaves became skilled workers and craftspeople. A few were able to buy their freedom. Some were freed when their masters died. Children of Portuguese masters and African mothers were often given their freedom at birth or when they grew up. Some slaves were taught to read and write and were even sent to study at universities in Portugal. Slaves in

The Catholic Church approved of marriages between Spaniards and Indian nobles. This picture is the announcement of such a wedding. The Incan bride and Spanish groom each wear native dress.

Brazil also had a legal right to earn money and inherit land.

There were many slave rebellions. Although slaves were watched carefully, many rebellions broke out. Most rebellions were brutally put down. However, some slaves managed to escape to freedom. Runaway slaves in Cuba fled to the hills inland, where they lived for many generations. On the French-owned island of Haiti, slave conditions were particularly horrible. In the 1790s, Haitian slaves rose up in the largest and most successful slave revolt in the Americas. Haiti became the first independent black government in the Western Hemisphere.

SECTION REVIEW **3**

1. How did the Spanish colonists become wealthy? p. 409
2. What were the colonists and the Indians supposed to do for each other? Who benefited most? Why? p. 409
3. Why did many Indians die after the conquest? p. 409
4. Describe the differences between slavery on the Caribbean islands and in Brazil. p. 410

4 A Latin American civilization arose

Spain and Portugal held on to their empires in the Americas for more than 300 years. During that period of colonial rule, three different peoples and cultures—Indian, African, and Spanish and Portuguese—blended together. The mixture gave rise to a new civilization called Latin American.

There was mixing of races. In spite of slavery and racial prejudice, whites, blacks, and Indians could mix and intermarry in the Spanish and Portuguese colonies. It was easier to mix in Latin America than it was in the English colonies of North America. Today, more than 50 million Latin Americans are descended from African slaves. In Mexico, much of the population is a mixture of Spanish and Indian.

The greatest amount of mixing took place in ans. 2
the towns of Brazil. On Brazilian plantations masters and slaves were still clearly divided. But black and white children played together and received religious training. Masters and slaves together took part in religious services. In Brazil, color lines became less sharp than anywhere else in the Americas.

Indian and African influences were strong. Both Indians and Africans played an important part in the growth of Latin American culture. They made major contributions in music, painting, literature, politics, and cooking. Even the Catholic faith was influenced by Indian and African religious ideas and customs.

ans. 1 Examples are easy to find. Sculptures and wall paintings in Spanish-American churches were often done by native artists. These artists usually showed Jesus as having Indian features. Latin American music was an interesting blend. It was made up of ancient Indian drums and pipes, new rhythms and dances brought by Afri-

Art and Literature in New Spain

Below left is the kitchen that once served a colonial Mexican monastery. Beautiful tiles like the ones shown are still made and highly prized. *Below right* is the ceiling of one of the most splendid churches in New Spain. The style is European but the figures are Indian. *Below center* is Sister Juana Inés de la Cruz (1651–1695), a Mexican. She was not only the greatest poet in all of colonial Latin America but also the greatest feminist. Overcoming great pressures against scholarly lives for women, she devoted her life to study and writing. As a teenager, she astounded scholars with her knowledge. The viceroy said that she answered every question put to her "like a royal galleon beating off the attacks of a bunch of row boats."

can slaves, and Spanish and Portuguese folk songs and religious chants. In this way, the traditions of three continents were blended into a new Latin American music.

The dominant influence was European. Since Spain and Portugal were the conquerors, they forced their culture upon everyone else. ● Spanish and Portuguese replaced hundreds of Indian languages. Catholicism replaced many Indian beliefs. With only two major languages and one religion from Mexico to Argentina, Latin America gained cultural unity.

European settlers brought many different vegetables and animals to the Americas. They also introduced the plow, the potter's wheel, and the metal fishhook. They taught European methods of farming and weaving. Just as important, the European settlers brought with them their legal systems, their form of government, and their idea of private property.

ans. 3 Spanish aristocrats in the Americas lived mainly in the many new towns and cities that were founded. Most cities were copied after ones in Spain. The new towns had a central plaza in front of a large Catholic church, with the streets laid out in squares.

In 1620, when the Pilgrims were just landing at Plymouth Rock, there were already 4,000 stone houses in Lima, Peru. Spanish nobles lived in these great mansions, which had balconies that looked out over the streets. Rich Peruvians (creoles) dressed in the latest European fashions. They drove around Lima in fancy open carriages. The city had an aqueduct that carried melted snow down from the mountains. Poor people, though, still had a hard life. However, a visiting European scholar wrote that it was no worse that the life of poor peasants or city dwellers in Europe.

● In areas where European control was weakest Indian culture has remained the dominant one up to the present. Many Indians in southern Mexico, Central America, and Bolivia do not speak Spanish. They consider the Spanish-speaking "city people" foreigners.

Schools and universities were set up. The Church controlled all levels of education in the colonies, just as it did in Spain and Portugal. Priests ran a few primary schools, but there were no high schools. Education was only for the upper classes. Only about 10 percent of the people could read and write.

In the 1550s, however, two universities were started. One was at Mexico City, and the other was at Lima. Today, they are the oldest universities in the New World. By the end of the 18th century, there were 25 colleges and universities in Spanish America.

The social status of women was low. Universities and colleges were attended mostly ans. 4
by young men. For the most part, Spaniards and Portuguese felt that women did not need higher education. A woman's main role was to have children. Poor women and slaves also had to do heavy work. Women whose husbands were landholders carried out the family's religious duties. A plantation owner respected his wife, but she was supposed to remain in the background. This attitude that gave women an important role in the home but a much lesser one in public life became part of Latin American culture. It has lasted into the 20th century.

SECTION REVIEW 4

1. Give specific examples to show how Latin Amer- p. 413
ican culture is a mixture of Indian, African, and European cultures.

2. In which colony did blacks and whites get along p. 412
the best? Give examples.

3. Describe the lives and education of rich Span- p. 414
iards in the cities.

4. In what ways were women in the colonies not p. 414
considered to be equal to men? How long did this feeling toward women last?

CHAPTER REVIEW 22

SECTION SUMMARIES

1. Europeans conquered and colonized the Americas. The formation of present-day Latin America began with the arrival of Spanish conquistadores in the early 16th century. Within a very short time, Spain took over all the territory from Mexico to Argentina. The only exception was Brazil which was claimed by Portugal.

One of the best-known conquistadores was Cortés, who defeated Montezuma and the Aztecs in 1521. Another was Pizarro, who conquered the Incas of Peru in 1531. Spain then owned the gold, silver, and other riches of the New World. Meanwhile, the Portuguese began to build rich sugar plantations in Brazil.

2. Spain controlled a large empire. To rule over its huge empire, Spain created a Council of the Indies at home. Viceroys were sent out to represent the king in the colonies. Spanish settlers born in the colonies, called creoles, hated the fact that high government positions were given only to nobles born in Spain, called peninsulares. Mestizos, people of mixed Indian and Spanish background, had even lower social standing.

3. Indians and Africans were the main source of labor. The colonies provided two major kinds of wealth. One was the plantations that grew sugar cane, especially in the West Indies. The other was the silver mines in Mexico and present-day Bolivia. At first, the plantation and mine owners used Indian forced labor to do the heavy work. The Church tried to protect the Indians. But the Indians died by the hundreds of thousands because of cruel treatment and disease.

Then large numbers of African slaves were shipped to the New World to work the mines and fields. Slavery was most brutal in the West Indies. It was a little less cruel in Brazil. There the Portuguese converted slaves to Christianity and gave them certain rights. From time to time, there were slave rebellions.

4. A Latin American civilization arose. During the 300 years that Spain and Portugal had their colonies in the Americas, there was a good deal of mixing between Indians, Africans, and Europeans. Their cultures blended and a new Latin American civilization grew up. Each of the three peoples made important contributions to life in the New World.

WHO? WHAT? WHEN? WHERE?

1. Find the years for these events and list them in chronological order:

Rio de Janeiro founded 1565 (10)
Cuba conquered 1514 (3)
Universities started at Mexico City and Lima 1550's (9)
Columbus's second voyage 1493 (1)
Arrival of Pizarro in Peru 1531 (7)
Cortés chosen to explore Mexico 1519 (4)
Jesuits forced to leave South America 1767 (11)
Aztecs surrendered to Cortés 1521 (5)
Santo Domingo founded 1494 (2)
Inca civil war 1524 (6)
End of Pizarro's rule in Peru 1547 (8)

2. Tell who these groups were and what each did in Latin America:

Jesuits p. 409
peninsulares p. 407
creoles p. 407
mestizos p. 408
Africans p. 410
Indians p. 409
viceroys p. 406
conquistadores p. 402

3. Name the modern countries where each of these was located:

Tenochtitlán Mexico
Inca empire Peru
Plata River Arg.
Buenos Aires Arg.
silver mines Mexico, Bolivia
Guarani missions Paraguay
the first colonial universities Mexico City, Lima, Peru

4. How did each of these affect the Indians or blacks of Latin America?

encomiendas p. 409
disease p. 409
missionaries p. 409, 410
baptism p. 410
slavery p. 410
intermarriage p. 408, 412
silver and sugar p. 409, 410
education p. 414

5. Write sentences telling the importance of these people:

Cortés p. 404
Atahualpa p. 404
Montezuma p. 404
Bartolomé de las Casas ●
Malinche p. 403
Pizarro p. 404

QUESTIONS FOR CRITICAL THINKING

1. What might have been the thoughts of Montezuma and Atahualpa toward the conquistadores? Why did Malinche help Cortés?

2. Why were the efforts of Catholic missionaries to protect the Indians not very successful?

3. How did the Indians keep their traditional religious beliefs alive?

4. What are some attitudes or feelings of Latin Americans today that began in colonial times?

5. In what ways was Spanish or Portuguese colonialism different from English colonialism in North America?

6. Why did the Spaniards and Portuguese think it was important to convert the Indians?

ACTIVITIES

1. On maps of the Western Hemisphere, trace the routes of Cortés and Pizarro in their conquests.

2. Debate or have a panel discussion on whether or not the Spanish conquest was a good thing for Latin America, using today's point of view.

3. In groups of four or five, act out scenes from the conquest and colonial times. Examples: Cortés's reaction to the first Indians he met in Mexico; Montezuma's decision to allow Cortés to enter Mexico; Jesuit vs. landowner attitudes toward the Guarani.

● p. 409

CHAPTER TEST **22**

SECTION 1

1. The first European settlers in the Americas were brought by: a. Cortés, b. Columbus, c. the English

2. True or false: Cortés was able to defeat the Aztecs because he had more soldiers than the Indians had.

3. Brazil's most important export by 1600 was: a. slaves, b. silver, c. sugar

SECTION 2

4. The Council of the Indies was: a. the lawmaking body for the colonies, b. an Aztec ceremony, c. a court located in Mexico

5. Colonial officials were chosen from: a. peninsulares, b. creoles, c. Jesuits

6. The largest racial group in Latin America is: a. white, b. mestizo, c. black

SECTION 3

7. True or false: The greatest source of wealth in the Spanish colonies was the silver mines in Mexico and Bolivia.

8. There was a shortage of workers in the colonies because: a. there had never been many Indians there, b. the Spanish government refused to allow the Indians to work, c. millions of Indians died from diseases brought in by the Spanish.

9. Slavery was especially cruel in: a. Brazil, b. the Caribbean islands, c. Mexico

SECTION 4

10. True or false: Pictures of Jesus in Latin American churches often have Indian features.

11. Education in the Spanish colonies was: a. controlled by the Catholic Church, b. open to all social classes, c. available to women

12. True or false: Life for the poor Indians and mestizos in Latin America was much worse than life for the poor in Europe.

UNIT REVIEW 6 — TEST YOURSELF

1. Match these events with the proper year: 1066, 1215, 1348, 1492, 1517, 1588, 1607, 1740.

Luther's 95 Theses 1517
Columbus landed in the Bahamas 1492
Jamestown founded 1607
Spanish Armada defeated 1588
The Battle of Hastings 1066
The Black Death 1348
The War of the Austrian Succession began 1740
Magna Charta 1215

2. Match these names with the identifying phrase:

Leonardo da Vinci N	Calvin E
Mazarin C	Malinche K
Bartholomeu Dias L	William the Conqueror G
Peter the Great J	Atahualpa M
Hudson H	Otto the Great O
Gutenberg D	Pizarro A
Shakespeare F	Erasmus B
	Balboa I

A. Spanish conqueror of Peru
B. Great humanist
C. Controlled France
D. Movable type
E. Doctrine of predestination
F. English author of plays
G. English king of French nationality
H. Searched for a Northwest Passage
I. First explorer to reach the South Seas
J. Modernized and westernized Russia
K. Cortés's interpreter and informant
L. Found a sea route around the southern tip of Africa
M. Tried to buy freedom with roomfuls of gold and silver
N. A Renaissance genius
O. Became Roman emperor in 962

3. True or false:

A. One of Henry II's legal developments was Magna Charta. F
B. Joan of Arc led France to victory during the Reconquista. F
C. The Renaissance began in Italy because of its good trade location. T
D. The first book printed on movable type in Europe was *The Prince.* F
E. Martin Luther objected to the sale of papal indulgences. T
F. The Peace of Augsburg allowed people to choose their religion. F
G. The Spanish Armada won a great victory. F
H. In 1493, the pope divided the New World between Spain and Portugal. T
I. Colonies were very important to mercantilism. T

4. Fill in the blanks with the correct book title:

A. In *The Prince*, the author seemed to approve the use of any possible means to get and keep power.
B. ● _______ laughs at the outmoded ideals of knighthood and chivalry as practiced in Spain.
C. The perfect society which did not exist was described in *Utopia*.
D. The *Decameron* tells of a group of young people escaping from the plague in a lonely country house.

5. Give the meaning and origin of each quote:

"No free man shall be seized, or imprisoned . . . nor shall we pass sentence on him except by the legal judgement of his peers or by the law of the land." Magna Charta

"L'État, c'est moi." Louis XIV – "The State is me."

"Try to preserve peace with your neighbors. I have been too fond of war." Louis XIV Meanings will vary

● *Don Quixote*

Unit 7
REVOLUTIONARY CHANGES IN THE WEST

When people change their ways of life in a rather short time, we call that a revolution. Probably no other people in the world had so many changes in their life-styles as did those of the Western world in the four centuries between 1500 and 1900. A person living in Western Christendom in 1500 was not so different from one living there in 1100. Four hundred years separated the two, but still they could have understood each other. However, a person in 1900 was so different from one in 1500, that even though they both might be Christians, they could not possibly have understood each other.

Every area of life changed, as did the ways people thought about themselves and the world they lived in. A person in 1500 was sure that the sun moved around the earth and that humans were at the very center of the universe. A person in 1900 knew that the earth moved around that same sun and that humans lived on one small planet among millions in the universe.

The organization of Western governments changed as large numbers of people came to believe that living in a democracy was better than living in a monarchy, that a united, independent country was better than a divided country or a colony. Westerners invented new machines for making the clothes they wore and the things they used, and they found new sources of power—first steam, then electricity—to run them. People learned how to grow

Machines, scientific discoveries, and new technology greatly changed people's lives.

● Discuss student's ideas of some other revolutionary changes that have occurred.

new foods and how to grow more of their everyday foods. The larger food supply led to a much greater population, and large numbers of people looked for work in industrial towns. Cities grew so fast that by 1900, the age-old rural, agricultural civilization of the West had become an urban, industrial one.

It is easy to say, looking back, that all of this change was progress, that life in the West was improving. Certainly, it was. But life did not improve for everyone, and progress did not take place everywhere at the same time. Changes upset people's lives. Some Westerners thought that new ideas threatened the old

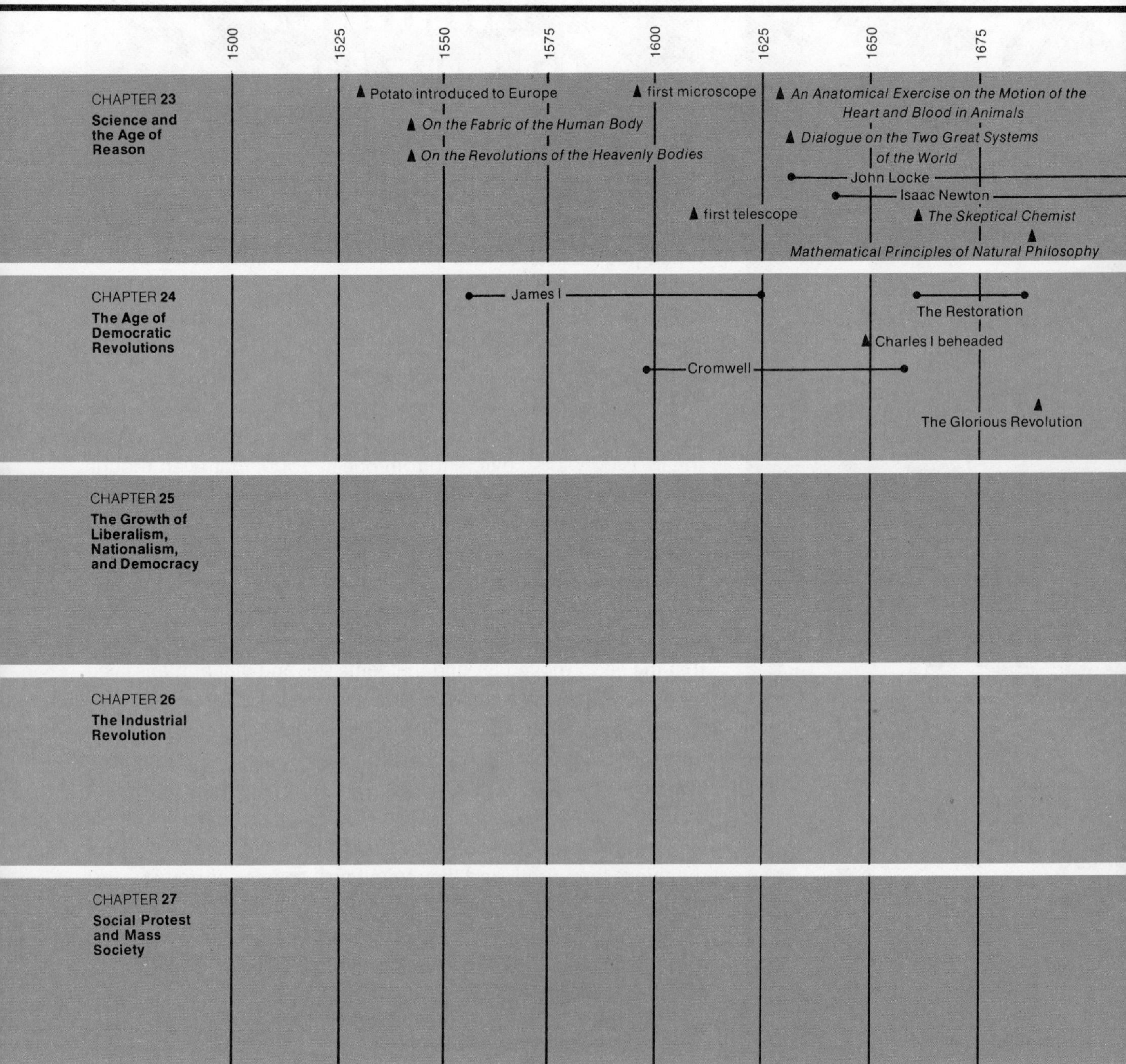

beliefs that made them feel secure. Others thought that conditions in the new industrial cities only made life worse. They argued and fought against change. As a result, these centuries were full of anger and violence as people searched for ways to learn to live with all the changes.

In 1900, the struggle was still going on. But between 1500 and 1900, life in the West changed so much that a new word was needed to describe this period. Historians have called it the *modern era*. We in the 20th century are still living in the modern era.

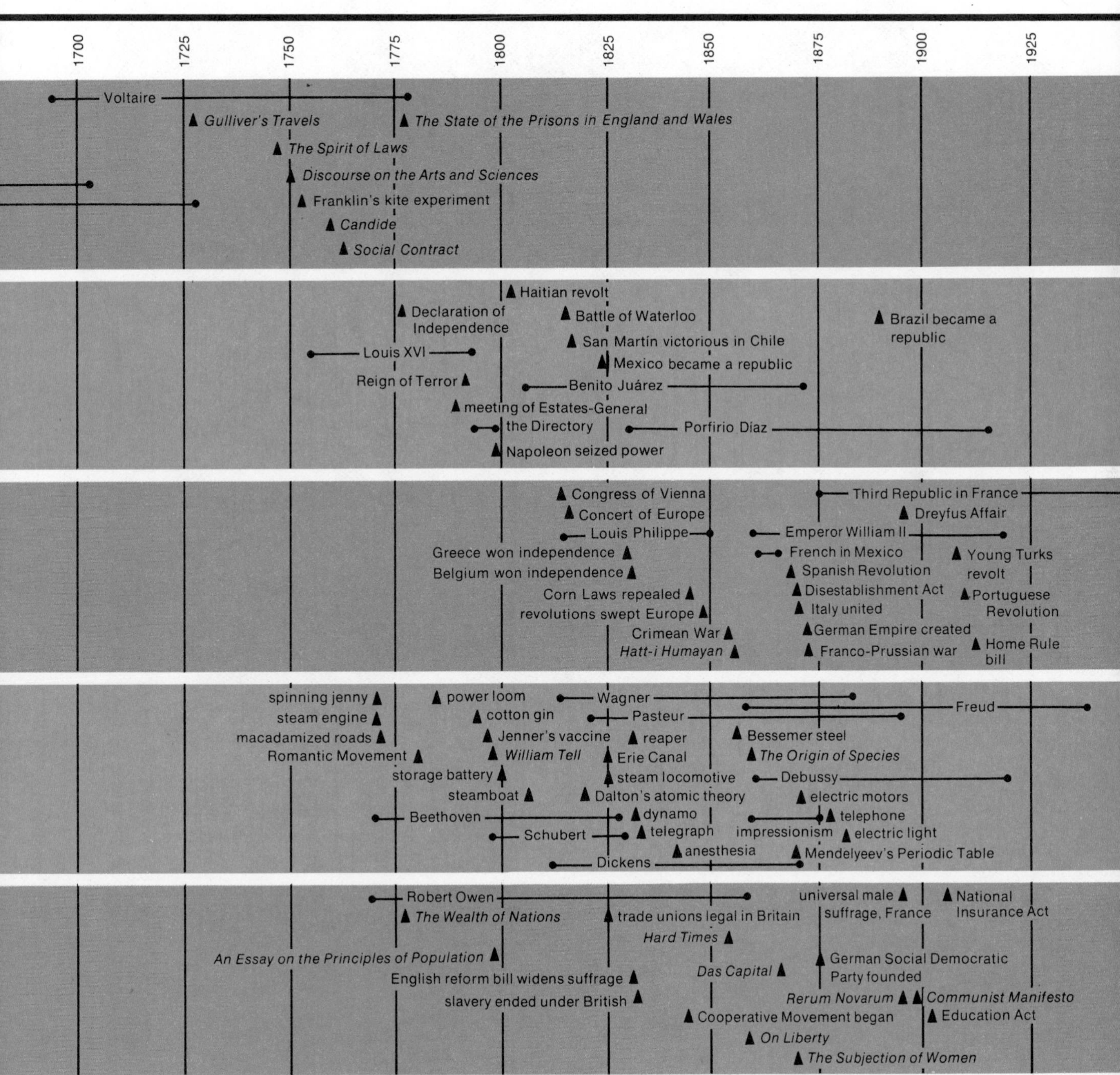

CHAPTER **23**

1500 – 1789

Science and the Age of Reason

The astrolabe was an instrument sailors used. A sailor held it up in front of his eye until he could see a star along the line formed by the instrument's movable hands. The angle between the horizon and the star would give him the ship's position. This astrolabe was perfected by Galileo in 1564.

In 1684, a scientist was working hard on what would become one of the best-known scientific books of all time. His secretary described how the scientist worked:

> I never knew him to take any recreation or pastime, either in riding out to take the air, walking, bowling, or any other exercise whatever, thinking all hours lost that were not spent in his studies. . . . He very rarely went to dine in the [college] hall . . . , and [when he did] if he has not been [re]minded would go very carelessly, with shoes down at heel, stockings untied,

> surplice on, and his [hair] scarcely combed. [The few] times when he [decided] to dine in the hall, [he] would turn to the left [instead of to the right where the dining hall was] and [would find himself] out [in] the street. . . . When he found his mistake [he] would hastily turn back, and then sometimes instead of going into the hall, would return to his [room] again.

The man was Sir Isaac Newton, who discovered the laws of gravity and ended a scientific revolution that had been going on for 150 years.

Most important in history is an understanding of how people have changed their ideas about themselves and the world they live in. Perhaps nothing has done more to change those ideas than the advances in science — the study of nature — that began in the Western world toward the end of the 15th century. By 1800, educated people in the West were thinking about nature in a way far different from the way people thought in 1500. The steps to this new way of thinking made a *scientific revolution.*

The scientific revolution was a result of both new information about nature and a new way of gathering it, based on experiment and reasoning. Together, these factors entered into every area of thought and action — religion, government, literature, and social and economic life. Thus, the time of the scientific revolution was also an age of reason. This chapter tells how:

1. Scientists worked out new theories about the universe.

2. Several branches of science moved forward.

3. Medical knowledge grew.

4. The scientific method was used in many fields.

1 Scientists worked out new theories about the universe

The ancient Greeks had tried to explain nature by its appearance rather than by experimenting and carefully watching what happened. As a result, they were sometimes wrong. For example, the Greek astronomer Ptolemy believed that the earth did not move because it did not seem to move. He thought that the earth stood still at the center of the universe and that the sun, moon, stars, and planets moved around it. That was the way he saw it.

For more than a thousand years, most people in Christendom accepted Ptolemy's view of the universe, the *geocentric* (earth-centered) ans. 1 theory. The Church used Ptolemy's ideas because they fitted in so well with Christian teachings. People, the Church said, lived to serve God and were the center of God's attention. Since God had made the universe to serve people, certainly the home of people, the earth, also had to be at the center.

A scientific method began to develop. By the end of the Middle Ages, some thinkers began to doubt Ptolemy's theory because so many ideas had been added. They believed that God had simpler ways of explaining how nature worked. Others thought that a new way was needed to learn about nature. As early as the 15th century, Leonardo da Vinci wrote: "Those sciences are vain and full of errors which are not born of experiment, the mother of certainty. . . ."

In the 16th century, the English philosopher ans. 2 Sir Francis Bacon urged that all scientists experiment, carefully observe, and then write what happened in the experiment. Information gathered this way and used with intelligent reasoning led to logical explanations that others could test by repeating the experiments.

Today, this scientific method is the basis of all science. In the 16th and 17th centuries, it changed people's way of learning so much that it caused a revolution in their thinking.

Copernicus questioned an old belief. In the 16th century, Nicolaus Copernicus, a Pole, developed his own ideas about the way the sun and the planets move. In his view, the sun is the center of the solar system, and the earth and planets move around it. Then, too, the earth turns on its axis every twenty-four hours as it makes its yearly trip around the sun.

ans. 1 Copernicus set forth his *heliocentric* (sun-centered) theory in a book, *On the Revolutions of the Heavenly Bodies.* He did not publish it until 1543, twenty years after he wrote it, because he knew his ideas would upset people who accepted Ptolemy's view.

The Copernican theory really got little attention at first. Almost no one believed it. Even astronomers found it hard to accept. First, they ● had not seen the stars in different places at different times of the year, as Copernicus had said they would. Second, he did not explain some points very well. For example, why did things not fly off the earth if it was in motion? As answers to these questions were found, more people thought that the Copernican theory might be true.

Kepler improved the Copernican theory. The first professional astronomer to openly agree with Copernicus's views was the German ans. 3 Johannes Kepler. During the early 17th century, he formed three laws of planetary motion: (1) a planet moves, not in a circle, but in an oval path called an ellipse, while the sun stays in place; (2) a planet speeds up when it comes closer to the sun; and (3) the amount of time a planet takes to move around the sun depends on how far away it is from the sun.

One question that Kepler could not answer was why the planets remained fixed in their paths and did not fly off into space.

Galileo made important discoveries. The ■ heliocentric theory received more help from the ans. 3 Italian astronomer Galileo. Born in Pisa, Italy, in 1564, Galileo later became a mathematics teacher at the university there.

In his laboratory, he rolled weights down an inclined plane to disprove Aristotle's theory that a body's weight decides how fast it will fall. Galileo showed that bodies of different weights fall at the same speed in the absence of air. (The story that he dropped the weights from the Leaning Tower of Pisa seems to be a legend.)

Galileo went from Pisa to the University of Padua, where he heard about the invention of the telescope in the Netherlands. He later built one and with it saw mountains on the moon, stars of the Milky Way, and other wonders. Galileo became convinced that Copernicus's ideas were correct. One reason was Galileo's discovery of the moons that move around Jupiter. They proved that not all heavenly bodies move around the earth. So, Galileo reasoned, some planets might move around the sun.

Galileo did not say anything about his ideas because in 1616 the Church had told him not to teach or defend the heliocentric theory. But in 1632, in his *Dialogue on the Two Great Systems of the World,* he seemed to say that the Copernican theory was true. As he had feared, he was called before the Inquisition in 1633 and closely questioned. Finally broken, Galileo, almost seventy years old, agreed to say that the

● See if students can answer these objections to the geocentric theory.

■ Key concept: the discoveries of scientists were based on the work of those who had come before them.

earth does not move around the sun. (Legend says that after he publicly denied that the earth moves, Galileo whispered to himself: "But it does move!")

Newton brought together scientific knowledge. Born in England in 1642, the year that Galileo died, Isaac Newton became one of the greatest scientists the world has ever known. His work climaxed the movement that had begun with Copernicus.

Newton taught mathematics at Cambridge University. While still in his twenties, he worked out the system of advanced mathematical figuring called calculus.

Newton's most important work, however, was in discovering a mathematical formula that explained gravity. Every planet, he said, has a force called *gravity* that pulls things toward it. The strength of a planet's gravitational force depends on the planet's mass (its size and weight) and how far it is from another object. Since the earth has more mass than the moon, its gravity is stronger; things weigh more on the earth than they do on the moon. Gravity is the reason planets stay in orbit. The sun's gravity holds the earth near it and keeps it from flying off in space. With this explanation, Newton was able to answer some of the unanswered questions about the heliocentric theory.

Newton called his formula the *law of universal gravitation.* In *Mathematical Principles of Natural Philosophy* (1687), he explained his ideas. It is one of the greatest scientific books ever written. Without Newton's discoveries, 20th-century scientists could not have sent astronauts to the moon.

SECTION REVIEW 1

1. Explain the geocentric theory and the heliocentric theory. Which theory did the Church support? p. 423 424
2. What are the four steps of the scientific method? In what way was Bacon's method different from the way other people of his time learned about nature? p. 423
3. What discoveries did Kepler and Galileo make that helped prove Copernicus correct? How did the Church react to Galileo's book? p. 424 425
4. Describe Newton's most important contribution to science. What did Newton's law explain? p. 425

Discoveries in science led to a new era in Western thought. In this painting, family members and friends study an orrery, a mechanical model of the solar system. In the Age of Reason, ordinary people could become scientists and inventors.

Did the Potato Change History?

For centuries, the population of Europe stayed at the same level. Then suddenly in the 1750s, it began to grow very fast, and by 1850 it had doubled. Such a fast increase changed the conditions of life not only in Europe but also in the whole world as millions of Europeans moved to other areas. Historians have called this sudden growth Europe's "population explosion."

Why did it happen? Historians are not sure. Many used to think it was because the death rate went down sharply in the 18th century. However, new research has shown that the death rate was not much lower in the 18th century than it had been before. Instead, the evidence shows that between 1750 and 1850 the birthrate rose among Europeans. Famine and disease still killed off many people because farming did not improve much, and advances in medicine were slow. Yet more people were born and stayed alive than at any earlier time in Europe's history.

How was this possible? To feed so many more people, much more food was needed, more than Europeans had ever had before. How did they get the extra food? That was the mystery.

Could it be that Europeans found new kinds of food? Some historians think so. They say Europeans learned to grow two new vegetables brought over from the New World—potatoes and corn. They are nutritious, easy to cultivate with hand tools (especially the potato), and can be grown in large amounts on only a small piece of land.

The Conquistadors had brought the potato to Europe from Peru in the 1530s. But not until the mid-18th century, did peasants in Europe get over their fear that the potato was poisonous. After that, it quickly became the main food of lower-class people, since a single acre of potatoes could feed a family of six, plus one farm animal, for nearly a whole year. As a result, more children lived to become adults and have children themselves. Thus, the population grew.

The potato may be the "missing link" to explain Europe's population explosion, and it may very well have changed history.

In his painting "The Potato Eaters," the 19th-century Dutch painter Vincent Van Gogh showed a passionate sympathy for the weary peasants who gathered together for their evening meal.

2 Several branches of science moved forward

The 16th and 17th centuries saw great advances not only in astronomy but also in chemistry and physics. Physics is the study of matter and energy, chemistry the study of substances.

● **Improved mathematics and new tools helped scientists.** Modern mathematics began in Christendom after 1100 A.D., when merchants and scholars started to use Arabic (really Indian) numerals. The decimal system was perfected, and mathematical symbols, such as +, ÷, ×, =, and $\overline{)\quad\quad}$, came into use.

ans. 1 Early in the 17th century, John Napier, a Scot, invented logarithms, a short way of doing calculations with very large numbers. Because logarithms reduced the time needed to solve hard problems, Napier in a sense doubled the working lives of his fellow mathematicians. In France, mathematician and philosopher René Descartes [rə nā′ dā kärt′] developed analytic geometry.

ans. 2 By the 17th century, the work of science was becoming exact because of new and more accurate tools for measuring and observing. In refracting telescopes, first made in the Netherlands about 1608, the image was focused by a lens. Because it was so long, the tool was hard to use. In 1668, Newton made a better one. The image in his reflecting telescope was focused by a mirror.

In 1645, Evangelista Torricelli [e vän′je-lē′stä tor′i chel′ē], a student of Galileo's, made the mercury barometer to measure air pressure. The barometer is used in forecasting the weather.

Later, a German physicist, Gabriel Fahrenheit [far′ən hīt], made the first mercury thermometer. It showed freezing at 32° and boiling at 212°, higher than earlier alcohol thermometers that measured temperatures only to 173°F. A Swedish astronomer Anders Celsius [sel′sē əs] used another scale that read 0° at freezing and 100° at boiling when he invented the centigrade thermometer.

German physicist Otto von Guericke [gā′ri-kə] invented the first air pump capable of creating a vacuum. To show how strong atmospheric pressure is, Guericke pumped the air out of two hollow metal hemispheres. Only the pressure of the air on the outside held them together. To pull the hemispheres apart, sixteen horses were needed.

Galileo was one of the first to study the pendulum. His notes about its movements were used later in building clocks. In 1656, Dutch astronomer Christian Huygens [hī′gənz] built the first useful pendulum clock. Using this, scientists could correctly measure small units of time.

Experiments began modern chemistry. Long a mix of fact and magic, the study of chemistry had no scientific base until the middle of the 17th century. Medieval alchemists believed, as had the Greeks, that all matter was made of four elements—earth, fire, water, and air. Also, things that burned were thought to contain a strange substance, *phlogiston* [flō-jis′tən], that made fire possible and was given off in burning.

The first person to use the scientific method in chemistry was Irishman Robert Boyle. In *The Sceptical Chemist* (1661), he attacked alchemists and the theory of the four elements. He ans. 3
proved that air could not be an element because it was a mix of several gases. Boyle said that an *element* is a substance that cannot be broken down by chemical means. A century later, Eng-

● A student or math teacher might be invited to give short demonstrations of these math symbols and methods.

lish scientist Henry Cavendish proved that water could not be an element because it was made up of hydrogen and oxygen.

ans. 3 Joseph Priestley, an English minister, identified several chemical substances, including ammonia and carbon monoxide. In 1774, he discovered an element he called "dephlogisticated air." Antoine Lavoisier [än twän′ lä vwä-zyā′], who worked about the same time in France, proved that a burning substance does not give off phlogiston. Instead, it combines with "dephlogisticated air," which he called oxygen.

Physicists studied magnetism and electricity. The first section of this chapter described some important works of Galileo and Newton in the branch of physics that is concerned with motion, sound, and light. Another branch of physics, the study of magnetism and electricity, owes much to William Gilbert, a doctor to Queen Elizabeth I of England. Gilbert's book *On the Magnet* (1600) explained how a compass needle acts by describing the earth itself as a large magnet.

ans. 4 Gilbert also studied static electricity. Ever since the time of the Greeks, thinkers had been puzzled by the power of amber, which when rubbed picked up bits of feathers or paper. Gilbert found that several other substances, such as sulfur and glass, behave in the same way. For them, he coined the word *electric* (from the Greek word for amber, *elektron*).

Scientists next made machines to produce the force that Gilbert had studied. One was a globe of sulfur mounted on a turning axis. When rubbed with a cloth, it gave off sound and light. With it, an electric current could be sent from one end of a thread to the other. Scientists also found a way to store electricity in the Leyden [līd′n] jar, an early form of condenser.

• Some students may enjoy researching and reporting on early medical practices.

The first important American scientist, Benjamin Franklin, believed that lightning was exactly like the static electricity in a Leyden jar. In 1752, he tested his idea by flying a wire-tipped kite during a thunderstorm. Electricity went through the rainsoaked string to a key tied to it. When Franklin put his hand near the key, he instantly felt a shock. The experiment was dangerous, but it proved Franklin's idea and led to his invention of the lightning rod to protect buildings.

SECTION REVIEW **2**

1. How did the new discoveries of the 17th century make mathematics easier? p. 427

2. How was the work of scientists helped by the inventions of Newton, Torricelli, Fahrenheit, Celsius, Guericke, and Huygens? p. 427

3. What discoveries of Boyle, Cavendish, Priestley, and Lavoisier proved that the alchemists of the Middle Ages were wrong? p. 427 428

4. What did Gilbert and Franklin contribute to the study of electricity? p. 428

3 Medical knowledge grew

Modern medicine began with Philippus Aureolus Paracelsus [par′ ə sel′səs], a 16th-century Swiss doctor who joined chemistry with medicine. He told the alchemists that they should aim ans. 1
to make medicines, not gold. He threw out such remedies as powdered Egyptian mummy and •
crushed sow bugs. Instead, he asked for experiments with chemical drugs to test their effects.

Vesalius began the study of anatomy. Another important person in the history of medicine was Brussels-born Andreas Vesalius [və sā-

William Harvey *(above)*, the doctor who discovered how the body's circulatory system works, is pictured with a drawing of the heart and blood vessels propped beside his portrait. *Right* is an early microscope from about 1660.

lē əs]. When he studied medicine at Louvain and Paris, he became angry with his teachers. Instead of examining the human body them- ans. 2 selves, they just read about it in the works of Galen, a 2nd-century Greek doctor. To learn anatomy on his own, Vesalius gathered dead bodies, sometimes robbing the gallows. He got into trouble with the law for this but escaped to Padua. His work there helped to make that city the most important center for medicine in Europe.

In 1543, Vesalius published a book, *On the Fabric of the Human Body.* It was the first to correctly describe the anatomy of the human body. Fellow teachers, jealous of Vesalius, bitterly attacked his ideas. He left university life while still in his thirties and became the personal doctor of the Holy Roman Emperor, Charles V.

Harvey explained blood circulation. William Harvey, an English doctor, made great discoveries in *physiology,* the study of how the human body works. He watched his patients closely and experimented with fish, frogs, and birds to find out how the heart works and whether the blood moves in a continuous stream. In 1628, he wrote *An Anatomical Exercise on the Motion of the Heart and Blood in Animals.* This thin, 72-page book explained for ans. 3 the first time how the heart pumps blood through the body.

Inventions aided diagnosis and treatment. Galileo may have helped invent the microscope, because he put lenses together to get large magnification. However, a Dutch eyeglass maker, Zacharias Janssen [zak′ ə rī′ əs yän′- ans. 4 sən], built the first microscope about 1590.

In the 17th century, Anton van Leeuwenhoek [lā vən hük′], also Dutch, first saw bacteria.

Leeuwenhoek made his own microscopes to see the wonders he described—red blood corpuscles, bacteria, yeast plants, and other tiny forms of life. But he never knew how important they are in human health.

SECTION REVIEW **3**

p. 428 **1.** How did Paracelsus try to change the medical practices of his day?

p. 429 **2.** How was Vesalius's way of studying anatomy different from that of his teachers?

p. 429 **3.** What did Harvey discover about the human body?

p. 429 430 **4.** How did Janssen and Leeuwenhoek help the study of medicine?

4 The scientific method was used in many fields

ans. 1 Scientists' discoveries showed that the physical universe was a well-ordered machine, working according to the laws of nature. Many thinkers ● reasoned that people also must be governed by some natural laws. They only needed to discover these laws. They could use the new scientific methods, just as astronomers had in discovering the laws that governed the heavens. These thinkers believed that they could use reason to discover how human societies worked. Then they could improve the ways that people live together. They had great hope for the future. Descartes declared:

> If we use the proper methods, we shall be able to outstrip our ancestors. The Golden Age is not behind us. Not only is progress possible, but there are no limits that can be assigned to it in advance.

● Point out that social scientists today attempt to study different cultures through scientific observation.

■ Key Concept: the *social contract* theory is a cornerstone of modern democratic governments.

This time of thought guided by scientific reasoning is called the Age of Reason. It lasted from 1628 to about 1789, or from the year Harvey announced his discovery of blood circulation to the French Revolution. It was an age in Europe when many thinkers looked at governments, religions, and the arts in relation to natural law. This whole effort to understand and improve society is called the Enlightenment.

The ideas of Locke and Montesquieu influenced government. The person who perhaps most influenced the Age of Reason was John Locke, an English philosopher born in 1632. Like many persons of his time, Locke believed that progress was certain if people would use their minds and follow reason.

In writing about government, Locke said that ans. 2 people had certain natural rights, chiefly to life, liberty, and property. When the people set up a government, he said, they gave it the power to protect these rights. He called this agreement between the people and the government a *social contract.* ■ If a government did not protect their rights, Locke said, the people could set up a new government.

Locke's social contract theory was eagerly studied in Europe and America. American revolutionaries used his ideas in their Declaration of Independence and later in the United States Constitution.

Another thinker who used reason in the study of government was a French noble and judge, the Baron de Montesquieu [mon′tə skyü]. His most important work was *The Spirit of Laws* (1748). This 20-year project was a study of laws and constitutions from ancient times to his own. Because of the book, Montesquieu is called a founder of political science, the scientific study of government. His writings on the division of powers among the three parts of government—executive, legislative, and judicial—guided the people who drew up the United States Constitution.

Voltaire attacked intolerance. François Arouet, born in Paris in 1694, later gave himself the name Voltaire [vol tār′]. A writer with a sharp and biting wit, Voltaire had no patience with fools.

Voltaire's attacks on the folly of his time often got him into trouble. Once he was held for eleven months in the Bastille prison in Paris. Voltaire wrote several books and over fifty plays. His best-known work is the satire *Candide* [kän-dēd′] (1759), which makes fun of the idea that this is "the best of all possible worlds."

Voltaire strongly influenced religious tolera- ans. 3
tion. He accepted the teachings of a new religious movement, *deism* [dē′iz′ əm]. The deists believed that God made the universe, set it up to work by natural laws, and then left it alone. The deists believed that God stayed out of people's daily lives and praying for help was useless. Therefore, rituals were not important, and religious differences were silly. Because Voltaire bitterly attacked the wrong acts he saw in organized religion, he was called an *atheist* [ā′thē-ist], one who believes there is no God. But he saw a need for religious beliefs. He once said,

Wealthy women in 18th - century Europe wore silks and brocades and were much decorated with lace, furs, and feathers. The men wore wigs, silk coats, silk stockings, and gold-braided hats. Humorists made fun of the extravagant dress styles and often equally outrageous manners. The illustrator of the two ladies at the opera *(right)* proved that costly dress doesn't make a person beautiful. Voltaire *(below)* wrote books that exposed the weaknesses of his day.

"If there were no God, it would be necessary to invent one."

Voltaire hated intolerance. He directly entered into several cases of religious persecution to gain justice. He is thought to have said: "I do not agree with a word you say, but I will defend to the death your right to say it."

Rousseau praised freedom. Jean Jacques Rousseau's thinking about the new ideas of his time was emotional rather than reasoned. He was born in 1712 in Switzerland. His French mother died when he was a baby, and then relatives cared for him. Rousseau [rü sō′] was apprenticed to a lawyer and then to an engraver, and then he ran away. For twenty years, he led a hand-to-mouth life as servant, tutor, music teacher, and writer.

In 1750, an essay that won a contest suddenly made Rousseau well known. This *Discourse on the Arts and Sciences* stated that before people were civilized they had been pure and good. Social organization had spoiled them, and they could become pure and good again only by getting "back to nature." This idea of honor in the simple life became very popular in France. The queen had a peasant village built, where she and her ladies played at being milkmaids.

One of Rousseau's most important books was *Social Contract* (1762). Like Locke, Rousseau thought that people had a contract with their government. But he did not accept the idea of revolution. Instead, he believed that the General ans. 4
Will—what is best for the state—kept order among people. Rousseau believed that free and democratic elections would show the General Will. However, people have used his ideas as an excuse for dictatorships, saying that one person of great talent can decide the General Will for all the people.

Diderot's encyclopedia helped spread the new ideas. Denis Diderot [dē′də rō] of France took on a giant task when he decided to put all of the new learning and ideas of the Enlightenment into an encyclopedia. He wanted his books to speak for tolerance and against superstition and the unjust ways of the time, as

Both the buildings shown here were built in England about 1670. The house on the *left*, with ornamental woodwork, is a rare example of this form of decoration. At the London inn on the *right*, plays were performed in the courtyard and coaches started from here to take passengers to vacation spots in the south of England.

well as to give facts about all branches of learning. Many important writers, such as Voltaire, Montesquieu, and Rousseau, sent articles to Diderot. He spent thirty years preparing the encyclopedia. The thirty-five large books, published between 1751 and 1772, greatly aided the spread of the new ideas of the Enlightenment. Thousands of sets were printed in France, and many editions appeared in other parts of Europe.

Reformers wanted to improve human well-being. The Age of Reason awakened concern for the well-being of all people. Religious liberty spread, and many improvements were made in public health and in the care of the sick and the insane.

Prisons also needed attention. Jails had always been dirty places governed by cruel laws. For example, in England, which had better prisons than did most countries, jailers got no salaries. They depended for their living on money that prisoners paid as "board." Some persons cleared of crimes could not leave jail until they had paid their board bills.

Such conditions improved partly because of John Howard, a county sheriff who led a reform movement. His book, *The State of the Prisons in England and Wales* (1777), pointed out the need for better prison administration. Prisons, Howard wrote, should not be used for punishment alone. Rehabilitation or reform of the convicts should come first.

Education also was reformed. The cruel discipline that was then common eased a little. And schools were opened for the lower classes.

Rousseau's ideas were important to education. He thought that children should not be treated as small adults but should be allowed to express themselves in their own ways.

● Students might be encouraged to read *Gulliver's Travels* to see if they can recognize its satire.

The arts were refined. Reason ruled not only scientists and scholars but also writers, painters, and musicians. The artists of the 18th century were proud of their rational control and tried to follow certain rules in their works. Many admired and imitated the arts of Greece and Rome. Their work was called *neoclassic* (*neo* means "new").

The Age of Reason was noted for satire. The best-known poet of the time was Alexander Pope of England, whose elegant verses showed up the foolish ways of society. Jonathan Swift's book *Gulliver's Travels,* written in 1726, has the ● form of an adventure story. Children enjoy the tale. But to adults it is a bitter satire on the meanness of human quarrels, wars, and vices.

Other kinds of writing benefited from the emphasis on reason and clarity. An early work in the novel form was Daniel Defoe's adventure story, *Robinson Crusoe.* But many people think the first novel was Samuel Richardson's *Pamela,* the romantic adventures of a servant girl. Today, it would be called soap opera. Another early novel was Henry Fielding's *Tom Jones,* a fascinating picture of 18th-century England. Important in the writing of history was Edward Gibbon's six-book study, *Decline and Fall of the Roman Empire.*

France had three dramatic writers. Pierre Corneille [kôr nā′] and Jean Racine [ra sēn′] used stories from classical mythology in their tragedies. The witty comedies of Molière [mô-lyer′] mocked false airs, mostly among doctors, lawyers, and the newly rich bourgeoisie.

Music in the 18th century, like literature, was balanced, controlled, and refined. England and France were known for literature in the Age of Reason, but the greatest musicians then came from Germany and Austria. Religion was important in the works of Johann Sebastian Bach

Artists in the Age of Reason had a view of life often criticized as sentimental. The family gathered to hear the musician in Antoine Watteau's painting "The Music Party" *(above center)* hasn't a care in the world. Not only the upper classes were shown this way. The German engraving of peasants in their simple cottage *(above left)* shows the love of family members for one another. It ignores the realities of their harsh life. Contrast this picture with Van Gogh's view 100 years later (see page 426). In the delicate German porcelain *(above right)*, a boy gives his mother a birthday bouquet as his sister and maid look on. *Robinson Crusoe (below)* was a romanticized version of the real experiences of a British sailor in the untamed wilderness.

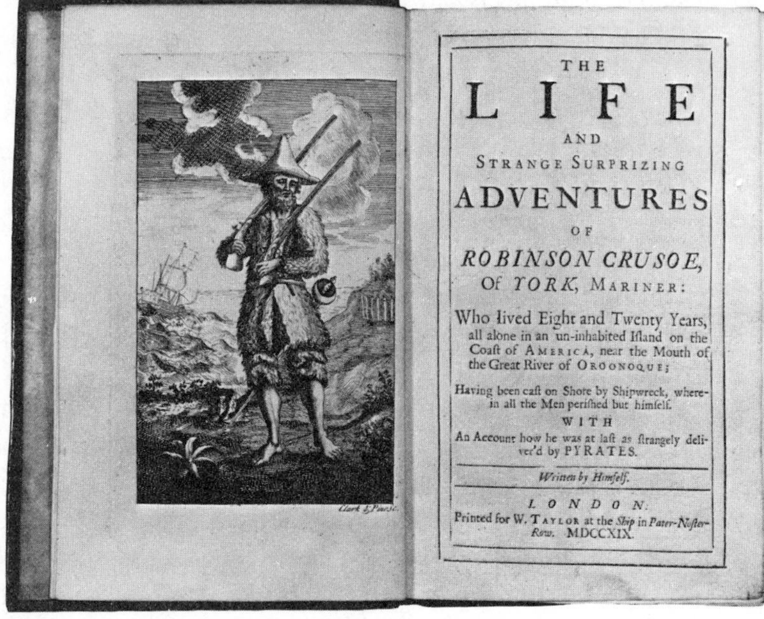

THE
LIFE
AND
STRANGE SURPRIZING
ADVENTURES
OF
ROBINSON CRUSOE,
Of *YORK,* MARINER:
Who lived Eight and Twenty Years, all alone in an un-inhabited Island on the Coast of AMERICA, near the Mouth of the Great River of OROONOQUE;
Having been cast on Shore by Shipwreck, wherein all the Men perished but himself.
WITH
An Account how he was at last as strangely deliver'd by PYRATES.

Written by Himself.

LONDON:
Printed for W. TAYLOR at the *Ship* in *Pater-Noster-Row.* MDCCXIX.

[bäk] and George Frederick Handel, who composed the *Messiah.* The Austrian musician Franz Joseph Haydn [hīd′n] wrote chamber music and started a new form of music, the symphony. His gifted pupil, Wolfgang Amadeus Mozart [mōt′särt], wrote more than 600 musical compositions, among them such operas as *Don Giovanni* and *The Marriage of Figaro.*

In architecture, the grand baroque form seen in Louis XIV's palace at Versailles gave way to a more delicate form called rococo [rō kō′kō]. Both of these forms lost favor after 1750. The quiet neoclassicism that followed can be seen in such buildings as St. Paul's Cathedral in London and Mount Vernon, George Washington's home.

SECTION REVIEW **4**

1. How did scientists in the Age of Reason influence other thinkers? p. 430

2. In Locke's "social contract," what are the natural rights of people? What is the purpose of government? How were his ideas accepted in Europe and America? p. 430

3. What were Voltaire's objections to organized religion? How did he support the idea of freedom of speech? p. 431

4. How was Rousseau's *Social Contract* different from Locke's? What were his ideas about education? p. 432

5. What improvements were made during the Age of Reason in religion, health, prisons, and education? p. 433

CHAPTER REVIEW 23

SECTION SUMMARIES

1. Scientists worked out new theories about the universe. A new era in Western thought began in the 16th century with the development of experimental science. One of its most important changes was a new view of the solar system. Some men of the Middle Ages had questioned Ptolemy's theory that the earth was at the center of the universe. Copernicus went further by proposing a new heliocentric theory. His ideas received little attention at first, but scientists later improved on them. Kepler's laws of planetary motion aided the heliocentric theory, and some of Galileo's discoveries helped, too. But the Church forced Galileo to renounce his views. The so-called Copernican revolution ended with Newton. He brought together earlier discoveries in the law of universal gravitation.

2. Several branches of science moved forward. New mathematical tools (logarithms, calculus, and analytic geometry) and means of measurement (clocks, barometers, and thermometers) aided scientists. Chemistry became a science with the work of Boyle, Priestley, and Lavoisier. Learning in physics owed much to the discoveries of Galileo, Newton, Gilbert, and Franklin.

3. Medical knowledge grew. Medical science, too, took great steps forward because of the work of Paracelsus, Vesalius, and Harvey. New tools, such as the microscope and thermometer, aided doctors.

4. The scientific method was used in many fields. Locke and Montesquieu applied the scientific method to government. Voltaire and Rousseau looked at morality, religion, and education. Diderot helped spread the new ideas with his encyclopedia. Reforms began in several fields. Reason also ruled in the arts, as seen in the satires of Pope, Swift, and Molière, the formal music of Haydn and Mozart, and the quiet balance of neoclassic architecture.

WHO? WHAT? WHEN? WHERE?

1. Tell who was responsible for these scientific achievements and during which time span: a. 1501–1600, b. 1601–1700, or c. 1701–1800.

discovered oxygen Priestly (C)
invented logarithms Napier (B)
developed the scientific method Bacon (A)
discovered three laws of planetary motion Kepler (B)
built the first microscope Janssen (A)
first saw bacteria Leeuwenhoek (B)
described the human anatomy Vesalius (A)
explained the circulation of blood Harvey (B)
proved lightning was electricity Franklin (C)
explained the law of gravity Newton (B)
developed the heliocentric theory Copernicus (A)
invented the reflecting telescope Newton (B)

2. How did each of these people try to change the idea of his time?

Locke p. 430
Vesalius p. 428
Voltaire p. 431
Swift p. 433
Howard p. 433
Diderot p. 432
Montesquieu p. 430
Bacon p. 423
Rousseau p. 432

3. Tell how Copernicus, Galileo, Kepler, and Newton each added something new to our knowledge of the solar system. p. 424, 425

● **4.** What common interest did Fahrenheit and Celsius share? William Gilbert and Benjamin Franklin? Joseph Priestley and Antoine Lavoisier?

5. Describe the accomplishments of these people:

Mozart p. 435
Harvey p. 429
Gibbon p. 433
Bach p. 433
Fielding p. 433
Defoe p. 433

6. Give the meaning of these terms:

scientific method p. 423
oxygen p. 428
element p. 427
General Will p. 432

● 4. Fahrenheit and Celcius were interested in temperature, Gilbert and Franklin in electricity, and Priestly and Lavoisier in chemistry.

ACTIVITIES

1. In groups, write and act out what you think a debate between supporters of the heliocentric and geocentric theories in the 16th century would have been like.

2. Choose the person you feel made the most important contribution to the world during the Age of Reason and report on his life by researching biographies or encyclopedias.

● **3.** Bring to class examples of some of the inventions discussed in this chapter, tell how they were invented, by whom, and what their uses are. Examples are: barometer, telescope, microscope, pendulum clock, thermometers (Celsius and Fahrenheit), Leyden jar.

4. Listen to recordings of music from the 18th century. Try to recognize or appreciate why this music is considered important. Find pictures that show the art or architectural forms of the period.

QUESTIONS FOR CRITICAL THINKING

1. What do you think is meant by the saying: "I do not agree with a word you say, but I will defend to the death your right to say it"? In what ways is this principle followed in our society?

2. In what ways do you agree or disagree with Rousseau's view that people were pure and good before civilization began but have been spoiled by social organization. Explain your answer.

3. Thinkers of the Enlightenment worked to correct the superstition and intolerance of their time. What are the wrongs of our time that should be changed?

4. How did the discoveries, inventions, or new ideas of the 17th and 18th centuries change the lives of people? Why did some people object to or refuse to believe some of the new discoveries?

5. What is the importance of experimentation in testing new ideas?

● In some cases, pictures of these items may be easier to obtain or a visit to the science lab in school might be arranged.

CHAPTER TEST **23**

SECTION 1

1. The scientific method was developed by: a. Ptolemy, b. Bacon, c. Copernicus

2. The heliocentric theory was the work of: a. Copernicus, b. Galileo, c. Ptolemy

3. Newton's laws explained: a. the geocentric theory, b. magnetism, c. gravity

SECTION 2

4. Refracting telescopes were: a. too long, b. inaccurate, c. too expensive

5. True or false: On Celsius thermometers, 32° represents the freezing point.

6. Joseph Priestley discovered: a. air, b. phlogiston, c. oxygen

SECTION 3

7. Alchemists tried to: a. cure diseases, b. make gold, c. dissect corpses

8. True or false: Anton van Leeuwenhoek did not understand the importance of his discoveries.

9. The first person to explain how the heart pumps the blood through the body was: a. Harvey, b. Howard, c. Charles V

SECTION 4

10. The Age of Reason lasted from: a. 1503 to 1656, b. 1756 to 1900, c. 1628 to 1789.

11. True or false: Locke believed people had the right to change their government if it did not protect their rights.

12. The first novel was: a. *Robinson Crusoe,* b. *Pamela,* c. *Gulliver's Travels*

13. The first encyclopedia was put together by: a. Diderot, b. Montesquieu, c. Fielding

14. True or false: The rococo form of architecture was replaced by the grand baroque.

15. The symphony form of music was created by: a. Mozart, b. Handel, c. Haydn

CHAPTER
24

1603–1889

The Age of Democratic Revolutions

In the Age of Democratic Revolutions, people in many countries fought for self-government. Simon Bolivar, the central figure on the white horse in the foreground, led the fight in South America for freedom from Spanish rule.

In 1782, a twenty-year-old upper-class Hollander from Rotterdam visited the United States and met George Washington. He was not impressed. He did not believe the American union would last, and he did not think Europeans should do what the Americans had done. The Europeans paid little attention to him. Nearly ten years later, in 1791, he wrote:

> Two great parties are forming in all nations. . . . For one, there is a right of government, to be exercised by one or several persons over the mass of people, of divine origin

● This is a good primary source of the conflicting opinions toward government in 18th-century Europe.

> and to be supported by the church, which is protected by it. These principles are expressed in the formula, Church and State.
>
> To this is opposed the new system, which admits no right of government except that arising from the free consent of those who submit to it, and which maintains that all persons who take part in government are accountable for their actions. These principles go under the formula, Sovereignty of the People, or Democracy.

The principles that the Hollander described formed over a long time. The ideas came from revolutions in England in the late 17th century, in North America and France in the late 18th century, and in Latin America in the early 19th century. Each was different and had different causes. But they were all fought for democratic ideas, and they changed the Western world. That is why some historians call this time the "age of democratic revolutions."

During the age of democratic revolutions, these ideas spread through all of the Western world as first the English, and then North Americans, French, and Latin Americans tried to change their ways of government. This chapter tells how:

1. Parliament triumphed in Britain.

2. North American colonies fought for independence.

3. The French Revolution changed society and government.

4. Napoleon became ruler of France.

5. Latin American colonies became independent nations.

● Key Concept: the divine right of kings, the feudal belief that kings were ruled only by God.

1 Parliament triumphed in Britain

The English kings never were as powerful as those on the European continent because Parliament was important in England. Without its consent, an English ruler could not make new laws, repeal old ones, or impose new taxes.

James I raised an important issue. Trouble began when Elizabeth I died in 1603, and James, king of Scotland, then became king of England also. He was the first Stuart king.

James strongly believed in the divine right of ● kings. Therefore, he believed that no one could ans. 1 stop him from doing as he wanted. Since the English Parliament by tradition checked royal power, James's ideas were unwise. He was in constant need of money, and Parliament showed its anger by refusing to give him funds. This constant battle raised an important issue—whether the king or Parliament had supreme power. In addition, two classes of people had become important in 16th-century England. One, the gentry, was made up of landowners who ranked just below the nobility. Merchants and manufacturers made up the other. Through their representatives in the House of Commons, both groups tried to gain more political power at the king's expense.

Religion made the problem worse. Roman Catholics still hoped to make England a Catholic country again. But Calvinist Protestants wanted a pure Anglican Church free of all remaining Catholic Church influence. Many of these Puritans were members of the gentry and middle class as well as being Parliament members who wanted more political power.

Charles I brought civil war. When James died in 1625, his son took the throne as Charles

I. Parliament, with many Puritan members, was just as suspicious of Charles as it had been of his father and refused to vote him the money he wanted. Charles tried to raise money by forcing his subjects to make payments to the government. Rich men who would not pay were put in prison, and poor men were sent to the army. When Parliament tried to stop such tactics, Charles dismissed it in 1629 and ruled alone for the next eleven years. Greatly in need of money to put down a Scottish rebellion, Charles finally recalled Parliament in 1640. Its members refused to vote any money unless Charles agreed that Parliament must meet at least once every three years and the king could not levy taxes without Parliament's consent.

Charles did not want to give up any of his power. In 1642, he led a band of soldiers into the House of Commons and arrested five of its leaders. Civil war then began.

Charles's wartime supporters, called Cavaliers, included most of the nobles and large landowners. The men of Parliament and supporters of the Puritans were called Roundheads because they cut their hair short. Oliver Cromwell, a devout Puritan, became the leader of the Roundheads. After four years of fighting, Cromwell's army won, and the king surrendered. In 1649, Parliament had Charles beheaded.

Parliament's power grew and political parties developed. Parliament then declared England to be a Commonwealth, and Cromwell eventually took control of the government. In 1653, he ended Parliament and became Lord Protector. Continued arguing between the wartime factions forced Cromwell to rule as a strict Puritan and military dictator, even though he believed in more freedom than the Puritans would allow.

In a 1643 cartoon *(right)*, long-haired Cavaliers and short-haired, Puritan Roundheads are shown sicking their dogs on each other. The Roundheads won, and Oliver Cromwell *(above)* became Lord Protector of England.

When Cromwell died in 1658, no one was ans. 2
strong enough to replace him. By then, too, most English people were fed up with strict Puritanism. In 1660, Charles's son, an exile in France, became king by agreeing to share power with Parliament.

Charles II was a clever, fun-loving king. His subjects called him the Merry Monarch. His 25-year reign was known as the Restoration, because during it the monarchy was restored. Since Charles had no legal heirs, his legitimate successor was his brother James, a strong Roman Catholic who believed in the divine right of kings.

A group in Parliament called Whigs tried to keep James off the throne. Whig supporters were the strongly Protestant middle class and merchants of London, as well as the upper nobility who saw a chance to become stronger under a weak king. Opposing the Whigs were the Tories (tôr′ēs). Tory supporters were lower nobility and gentry, who did not trust the London merchants and were loyal to the king. When Charles died, James became king.

ans. 3 **The Glorious Revolution confirmed the power of Parliament.** James II wanted more authority for himself and for the Catholic Church. Thus, he soon angered almost everyone, including the Tories. In 1688, when the king's wife bore a son, Tories and Whigs, afraid of a long line of Catholic kings, offered the crown to James's older daughter Mary, wife of William III of Orange, Dutch ruler and strong Protestant. In November, 1688, William and Mary landed in England at the head of a large army. James escaped to France, and William and Mary became the new rulers of England and Scotland. This new show of parliamentary power is known as the Glorious Revolution.

Parliament passed several important measures, usually called the Revolution Settlement. One, the Bill of Rights of 1689, guaranteed freedom of speech in Parliament, which would meet more often. And the king could not interfere with the election of its members. The people gained the right to *petition* (ask the help of) the government. Excessive bail was not allowed. And no army could be raised without Parliament's consent. Another part of the Revolution Settlement was the Toleration Act. It gave religious freedom to some Protestant groups. A third measure, the Act of Settlement of 1691, said that no Roman Catholic could rule England.

In making the king subordinate to Parliament, the Glorious Revolution was a great victory for the principles of parliamentary government and the rule of law. But it was a limited victory. Since ● members of Commons received no pay, only landowners with large incomes could serve.

Cabinet government developed under a new royal line. The last of the reigning Stuarts, Anne, died in 1714, leaving no heirs. ans. 4 The Act of Settlement had said that the monarch's closest Protestant relative would take the throne. Thus, a German second cousin became George I of England and began the Hanoverian dynasty. He spoke no English and spent much time in Germany.

Since he knew little about England, George I depended on a group called a *cabinet* to help him rule. These people were members of Parliament, mostly ministers in charge of government departments. During George I's reign, the cabinet began to make policy.

For half a century after 1714, the Whigs controlled the House of Commons. George I and George II, who ruled from 1727 to 1760, chose their ministers from the Whig party. Robert Walpole, head of the party from 1721 to 1742, served as the principal minister—a position later called prime minister.

Walpole always chose his cabinet members from the Whig party to be sure his policies would be supported in the House of Commons. When he lost support in Commons in 1742, he resigned as prime minister. Since then, British prime ministers and cabinets have been drawn from the majority party in Parliament.

● And, of course, at this time only large landowners had voting rights.

■ The relative freedom of American colonists from class restraints could be noted.

SECTION REVIEW 1

1. What were two serious conflicts between James I and Charles I and their English subjects? p. 439

2. Why did the English bring back the monarchy after Oliver Cromwell died? p. 440

3. Why did Parliament force James II to give up his throne? How did the Glorious Revolution show Parliament's strength? How was it a victory for wealthy English landowners? p. 441

4. How did a German come to be king of England? What were the powers of the cabinet and prime minister? p. 442

2 North American colonies fought for independence

While England was dealing with its troubles at home, its colonies in North America were growing and prospering. For over a century after Jamestown was founded in 1607, the colonists went their own ways with little notice from the mother country.

The colonies and England grew apart. Many colonists had left Europe to escape religious persecution, debts, or to find jobs. Settlers came from England, Scotland, Germany, the Netherlands, France, and Ireland. In the colonies, ans. 1 people depended more on themselves and less on inherited social place and privileges. ■ They were proud to be independent farmers, artisans, and merchants.

The American colonists also enjoyed a large degree of self-government. Every colony had its own representative assembly, which could put pressure on the governor by threatening to hold back money.

In the Declaration of Independence, American colonists explained their reasons for breaking away from England.

The English tightened their control. For many years, England did little to regulate the North American colonies. But in 1763, after England defeated France in a worldwide struggle for empire, the English government began a new policy.

The colonists in North America had done little in the war on their continent. It was won largely with British troops, ships, and taxes. British troops also protected the colonists against Indians. England reasoned that the colonists
ans. 2 should share the costs. So England enforced old laws and passed new ones to raise money.

Between 1765 and 1774, the colonists strongly opposed every effort to make them pay more taxes. In 1774, to teach the colonists a lesson, the British Parliament passed the so-called Intolerable Acts. These acts closed Boston harbor to shipping, which meant economic ruin, and took back the charter of Massachusetts, which ended local self-government. The dispute had been about taxation; now it was about the right to self-government.

American colonists won their freedom. Fighting started in April, 1775. At first, only a few colonists wanted full independence. As fighting went on, however, feelings grew stronger because the British government seemed unwilling to give in at all. Finally, on July 4, 1776, representatives of the colonies signed the Declaration of Independence. ●

What had begun as an American fight for freedom soon became a worldwide conflict for empire among the European countries. France, Spain, and the Netherlands declared war against England to gain back territories lost in 1763 and earlier. The French fleet and 6,000 troops helped the American colonies win. In 1783, a peace treaty was signed, and England recognized the thirteen colonies as independent. England did not lose any other colonies, however. The English navy, in a striking comeback in the final year of the war, defeated the fleets of France and Spain.

The American Revolution had important results. Independence did not lead immedi- ans. 3
ately to democratic government, but the seeds were well planted. The Revolution ended inherited titles and helped make people equal under the law.

The colonies eventually created a republic of a federal type, that is, a group of separate states, each giving up some governing rights to become united under a central government.

The Americans believed strongly in written constitutions and in limiting the powers of government. Besides the federal Constitution, all thirteen states had written constitutions that

● Key concept: the Declaration of Independence was written to justify the actions of the revolutionaries to the world, to win world support.

separated legislative, executive, and judicial powers, and included a bill of rights.

The American colonists' revolt became a symbol and source of inspiration to all peoples seeking freedom, especially in Latin America.

SECTION REVIEW 2

p. 442 **1.** Name three ways that life in the North American colonies was different from life in England.

p. 443 **2.** Name three actions of the English government that caused the colonists to declare their independence.

p. 443 **3.** What were four results of the American Revolution? Describe the new kind of government set up by the Americans.

3 The French Revolution changed society and government

The success of the American Revolution encouraged French people who wanted far-reaching changes in their own nation. Discontent there had been growing for a long time.

● **Inequality bred discontent.** French society ans. 1 was still divided along feudal lines. Every person belonged to one of three classes, or "estates." In the First Estate was the clergy, the Second Estate was the nobility, and the Third Estate included everyone else. Within this society, called the Old Regime, the estate decided a person's status, civil rights, and privileges. The clergy and the nobility were each less than one percent of the population. But the clergy owned ten percent of the land, and the nobility had all the best posts in the government and army.

The Third Estate was itself divided into three groups. On the top level were the bourgeoisie—lawyers, doctors, merchants, and business people. Below the bourgeoisie was a small group of city wage earners—skilled artisans, servants, and laborers. Some of them were near starving and could become a violent mob.

Over eighty percent of the French people were peasants, the largest part of the Third Estate. Although they owned forty percent of the land and serfdom had almost disappeared, they still had to pay certain feudal dues, which they saw as unfair.

● Remind students that France had not developed parliamentarian government as had England. Grievances in France were voiced by many people for a long time without the government hearing them.

Weak kings failed to reform taxes. The greatest single problem France faced was the unfair tax system. The First and Second Estates were excused from most taxes by law. The heaviest burden, then, fell on the peasants, who had the least money.

Louis XV, who ruled from 1715 to 1774, was not a strong leader. He knew about the unrest among the people, but seemed not to care.

Louis XVI, who was only twenty when he became king in 1774, really wanted to govern well. However, he did not have a forceful personality, nor will power, and he was afraid to stand up to the important people he dealt with.

France neared bankruptcy. During Louis XVI's reign, the French government soon neared bankruptcy. Three-fourths of the total budget was marked for military business and payments on the public debt.

In the late 1770s and in the 1780s, government officials tried to solve the money crisis by taxing the wealthy classes. They failed, however, because the nobility said new taxes could be approved only by the Estates-General. The Estates-General, made up of representatives from each of the three estates, had not met since 1614. Unable to collect taxes or borrow money,

Louis agreed to have the Estates-General meet in 1789.

Conflicts between the Estates-General and the king led to revolution. The first meeting of the Estates-General in 175 years could not agree on a method of counting votes, the Third Estate wanting to be counted equally with the other two groups. After weeks of ar-
ans. 2 guing, the Third Estate (bourgeoisie) declared itself a National Assembly. The members met on an indoor tennis court, where they swore to
● write a new constitution for France. Their "Tennis Court Oath" was the first act of revolution, for the Third Estate had no legal right to become a lawmaking body.

Meanwhile, the peasants and the workers suffered from bad harvests and depression. Food was scarce, prices were high, and unemployment was widespread. When the king threatened the Assembly, crowds in Paris started to
■ look for weapons. On July 14, the crowd stormed the Bastille [ba stēl′], a prison. Then they marched on the Town Hall, murdered the mayor of Paris, and set up a new city government. The king accepted the new government and ordered his troops to leave.

In the countryside, the peasants thought the nobles would attack them. They refused to pay taxes, attacked the nobles' manor houses, destroyed the records of feudal dues, and burned some manors to the ground.

The National Assembly set up a constitutional monarchy. The National Assembly was alarmed by the spreading disorder. On August 4, it boldly ended feudalism. The Assembly then started to create a new kind of government for France. For the next two years, it worked on a constitution that would include the principles of liberty, equality, and natural rights. The constitution favored the bourgeoisie. Only men who owned property could be elected to the new Legislative Assembly. The nobility lost all its privileges, and all people were said to be equal before the law. The king could delay new laws, but he could not veto them. The government took over Church lands, and also took control of the clergy. Louis XVI did not like the new constitution, but he had to accept it.

Foreign war led to a "second" revolution. ●
When a Legislative Assembly was elected in October, 1791, France became a constitutional monarchy. This government lasted only eleven months, chiefly because of war with other coun-
tries. The revolution alarmed the monarchs of ans. 3
Europe, who feared that the principles of liberty, equality, and natural rights would weaken their own powers. Also, the *émigrés,* French nobles who had left in 1789, persuaded the kings of Austria and Prussia that it was their royal duty to restore the monarchy in France. The revolutionaries thought they would be attacked. In April, 1792, the Legislative Assembly declared war on Austria.

As war fever rose in France, suspicion of the king mounted. In August, 1792, the Assembly suspended the monarchy, put the royal family in prison, and ended its powers. Paris was in panic. In September, a provisional government ordered that over 1,000 royalists be executed.

The Legislative Assembly was set aside. A new National Constitutional Convention, elected on the basis of universal male suffrage, was to draw up a more democratic constitution. War hysteria and the people's dislike of the 1791 constitution had caused the uprising in August, 1792, and the September Massacre. Together, they were a "second" revolution.

● Emphasize and discuss in what ways this was a revolutionary act.

■ This prison had long been a hated symbol of repression to the people of Paris although it had not been used for a long time.

● Now is a good time to explain the terms radical and moderate.

France became a republic. Beginning in September, 1792, France was ruled by the National Constitutional Convention, usually called the Convention. It declared France a republic and stated that it would spread the ideas of "liberty, equality, and fraternity" over Europe. French armies swarmed over the Austrian Netherlands (Belgium) and the area south of the Rhine. By 1793, France was at war with almost all of Europe.

As the war went on, the revolution in France became more extreme. In January, 1793, Louis XVI went to the *guillotine* [gil′ə tēn′], the dreadful machine that had beheaded so many people during the revolution.

The situation in 1793 was bad. Food was scarce, and prices were high. In the west, conservative peasants rebelled against the Convention. In June, 1793, a Parisian mob entered the Convention and seized the moderate leaders. Then the extreme radicals took over.

Radicals started a Reign of Terror. The Convention elected twelve members to be a Committee of Public Safety led by Maximilien de Robespierre [rōbz′pyer], a young lawyer. To stop any possible counterrevolution, the ans. 4
Committee started a Reign of Terror.

Between August, 1793, and July, 1794, more than 40 thousand persons were executed. The queen, Marie Antoinette, was among the first, and the moderates soon followed. Thousands of others, regardless of class, were put in prisons.

Meanwhile, the war had to be won. The Committee started a program of price controls and also began a national draft. These programs were the first attempt in modern times to bring together all the resources of a country for war. By the spring of 1794, France had the largest army in Europe. Unlike others, it was a citizen army with a strong feeling for its country.

By summer 1794, this citizen army, whose leaders were young officers just up from the

lower ranks, won several battles. Although the war lasted until 1797, the country was saved. The harsh rule of the Committee of Public Safety no longer had a purpose. In July, 1794, Robespierre and his followers went to the guillotine. The Reign of Terror ended.

ans. 5 **Conservatives set up the Directory.** The bourgeoisie were in power again, and they wanted to return to a moderate republic. In October, 1794, a new constitution ended the Convention, and set up a government known as the Directory. In the new government, a two-house legislature was responsible for electing a

The French Revolution turned the old order upside down. The king was executed in a public square *(left);* the murdered revolutionary (Marat, *right*) became a martyr; and French peasants *(below)* gained new dignity—equality before the law.

governing body of five men called directors. However, the Directory became corrupt and inefficient, and seemed unable to solve the country's problems. The time was ripe for a strong leader to seize power.

SECTION REVIEW 3

p. 444 **1.** Describe the class structure of the Old Regime. What groups belonged to each estate, and what percentage of the total population made up each estate?

p. 445 **2.** How was the National Assembly formed? Why was this an act of revolution?

p. 445 **3.** What were the causes of the "second" French Revolution?

p. 446 **4.** What was the purpose of the Reign of Terror? What did the Committee of Public Safety accomplish?

p. 447 **5.** What was the Directory?

4 Napoleon became ruler of France

A strong leader appeared—Napoleon Bonaparte [nə pō′lē ən bō′nə pärt]—a lieutenant of artillery in Louis XVI's army. Because he belonged to the lesser nobility, Napoleon could not hope to rise much higher. But the revolution opened the door to fame and power.

By 1797, Napoleon was leading the French army in northern Italy. After several brilliant victories there, he crushed the Austrians. He was only twenty-eight years old and already a hero.

Napoleon's ambition had no limits. Well aware of the growing dislike for the Directory, he waited for an opportunity to seize power. Meanwhile, he thought of a bold plan to hurt England by taking Egypt and then striking at India. Napoleon landed in Egypt in 1798, but the English fleet destroyed his transport ships and cut off his army.

Napoleon returned to France and made his Egyptian defeat seem a great triumph. Many people saw him as France's savior. He and his followers moved quickly and overthrew the Directory by force on November 9, 1799.

Napoleon became a dictator. The new ruler of France had a sharp mind and a remarkable ability to understand problems and make quick decisions. Napoleon had read deeply in history and law as well as military science. People were dazzled by his qualities.

Although he rose from the revolution, Napoleon planned to rule as a dictator. The new constitution included a legislature and three consuls. But as First Consul, Napoleon had all the real power and claimed to represent the interests of the whole country. Napoleon then turned to military affairs. He forced Austria to make peace in 1801 and England in 1802.

In his first five years as ruler, Napoleon carried ans. 1
out several important reforms in France. He increased the power and efficiency of the national government. He offered a stable life and order in France to all willing to work for him—royalists and republicans alike.

In many ways, Napoleon finished the work of the revolution. No privileges were allowed, promotion in government or the army was based on proven ability, and the tax system was reformed. Probably Napoleon's best known work was in modernizing French law. The *Code Napoleon* firmly set forth the principle of equality before the law.

Napoleon savagely put down all opposition. But even without political liberty and true representative government, the people liked him

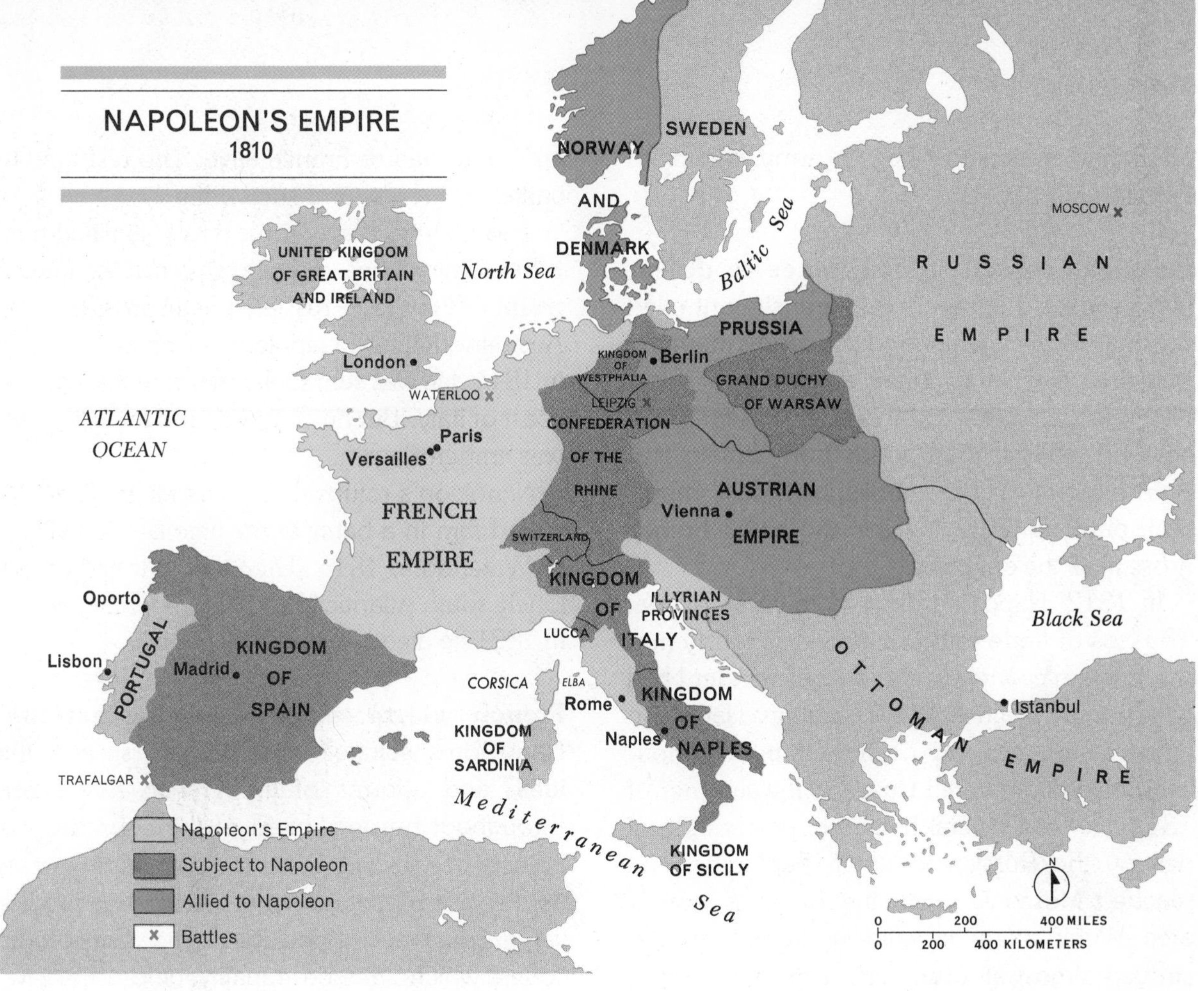

because he could offer order, stability, and efficiency. In 1804, he had himself crowned Napoleon I, Emperor of the French.

Napoleon made himself master of Europe. Napoleon ruled France for fifteen years—five years as First Consul and ten as emperor. Driven by his ambition to rule all of Europe, he spent fourteen of those years at war. By 1805, a group of countries including Britain, Austria, and Russia had allied against France. Napoleon defeated the Austrian and Russian armies with amazing speed.

Only England with its navy continued to fight the emperor. In 1805, Lord Horatio Nelson destroyed the French fleet in the Battle of Trafalgar. That victory proved British naval supremacy and protected England from invasion.

● Use maps to show how Napoleon might have stopped ships from reaching England.

From 1806 to 1812, Napoleon controlled most of the continent. Since he could not defeat ans. 2
the British navy, he decided to wreck England in economic warfare. He declared all of Europe ●
closed to British goods, and even Russia agreed to the plan. However, Napoleon's policy failed. The biggest reason was that the British found other markets, chiefly in Latin America.

To control ports on the Iberian Peninsula, Napoleon invaded Portugal, placed his brother Joseph on the Spanish throne, and stationed a French army in Spain. The Spanish people fought back. The English took advantage of this revolt, invaded Portugal and then Spain, and by

1813 had driven the French army back into France.

European powers joined forces to defeat Napoleon. People in the French-controlled nations were angered by Napoleon's demand that they give him money and soldiers. Also, Napoleon's economic blockade caused shortages of manufactured goods from Britain that French factories could not supply. Most important, patriotic feeling against the hated French arose in all the countries.

In 1812, Napoleon decided to crush Russia. The loss of trade with Britain had seriously hurt the Russian economy, and Tsar Alexander I had begun trade again in 1810. An angry Napoleon gathered a huge army of more than 500 thousand men and entered Russia in the summer of 1812. He won several battles, but he could not destroy the Russian army. In September, he reached Moscow, which the Russians evacuated. Within a few days, fire broke out and destroyed almost all of the city. After five weeks,
ans. 3 Napoleon ordered a retreat. Then the cruel Russian winter set in. Only 30 thousand of his army returned to France alive. The rest died in battles, blizzards, and snowdrifts.

This blow to Napoleon's power finished him. From all directions, enemies struck at the French tyrant—Russians, Prussians, Spaniards, English, Austrians, Italians. Napoleon's empire crumbled in 1814. He was sent to the island of Elba off the coast of Italy. But he escaped, and for 100 days, was emperor again.

Napoleon's return united the allies. They defeated him in a battle at the little Belgian village of Waterloo in 1815. Then they put him on the lonely south Atlantic island of St. Helena, where in 1821 he died.

In this British cartoon, Napoleon is playing chess on a map of Europe. His coach is Death.

French reform influenced other nations.
Napoleon's soldiers and officials spread the •
ideas and reforms of the French Revolution
throughout Europe. In all of the countries the ans. 4
French conquered, constitutions were drawn up. Feudalism, the manorial system, and medieval guilds were wiped out. The Napoleonic codes, which stressed equality before the law, directed the courts.

Church lands were seized, and the Church came under the state. Religious freedom for non-Catholics became the law. Taxes were reformed, and the metric system of weights and measures was used. Even after Napoleon was gone, most of these reforms remained.

SECTION REVIEW **4**

1. What reforms did Napoleon make in his first five years as ruler of France? p. 448
2. What was the purpose of the economic blockade of Britain? Why did it fail? p. 449
3. What were the two most important events that led to Napoleon's exile? p. 450
4. Name six reforms that the French made in European governments. p. 450

• Discussion topic: ask students why European countries fought Napoleon even though he began needed reforms.

5 Latin American colonies became independent nations

The Age of Democratic Revolutions also affected the Latin American colonies. In the 300 years that Spain and Portugal had ruled Latin America, a new civilization had arisen. But many wrongs had grown along with it.

Discontent grew among the Creoles. One wrong, the colonists thought, lay in the restrictions Spain placed on trade and manufactured goods. Another arose from Latin American society itself. Classes based on birth and background were very important.

ans. 1 At the top were the Spanish-born officials, the peninsulares [pā nēn′sü la′rās], who held all the important political and military posts. Below them, the colonial-born white aristocracy, the Creoles [krē′ōlz], lived like feudal nobles on the income from their lands. At the bottom were millions of Indians, blacks, and mixed peoples—mestizos (white and Indian) and mulattoes (white and black). Most of them lived like serfs or slaves. They did all the hard labor, which to the aristocracy was degrading.

The Creoles wanted to control their own affairs, but colonial rule placed all power in the hands of the peninsulares. Wealthy and well educated, many Creoles knew the works of
● Locke, Voltaire, and Rousseau, as well as the political ideas of the Enlightenment.

In the 1780s, encouraged by the North American example, colonists rebelled in Peru, Colombia, Ecuador, and Venezuela. One reason they failed was that unlike the North Americans whom France helped, Latin Americans fought alone. The only successful uprising in the 18th century was that on the western side of the island of Hispaniola. There, in 1794, Toussaint

● Have students compare Latin American colonists with North American colonists.

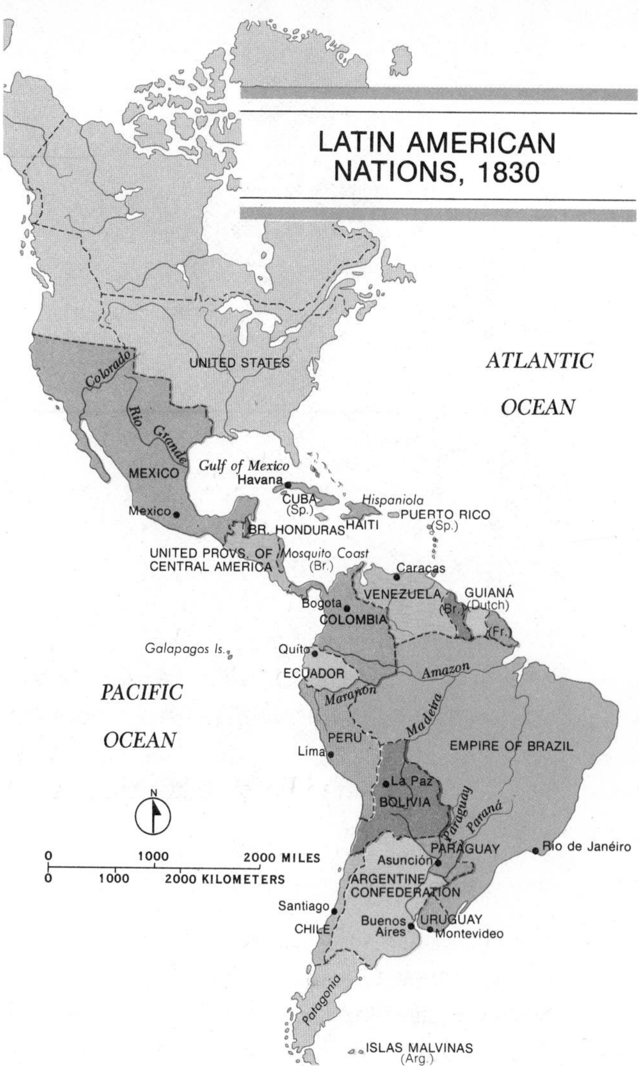

l'Ouverture [tü sᴀɴ′ lü ver tʏr′], a freed black slave, led a rebellion against the French. Toussaint was captured, but his successor led the Haitians to independence in 1803.

Successful revolts freed South America. When Napoleon took control of the Spanish ans. 2
government in 1808, the Spanish American colonists would not accept the new French regime. Revolts broke out all over the empire from Mexico to Argentina. The Spanish king returned to the throne in 1814 determined to bring back Spanish control, but the drive toward freedom had already gone too far.

Pierre Dominique Toussaint l'Ouverture, black leader of the Haitian independence movement.

● The greatest leader was Simón Bolívar [bō lē′vär], called "the Liberator" and "the Washington of South America." Born in 1783, Bolívar fought for more than 20 years to win freedom for the area that became Venezuela, Colombia, Panama, Bolivia, and Ecuador.

Another hero, José de San Martín [sän′ mär tēn′] was fighting in Spain against the French in 1811 when he learned that Buenos Aires had revolted. He went home and led armies against the Spanish in Argentina and Chile.

In 1821, San Martín entered Lima. There, he and Bolívar talked about how best to drive the Spanish from the rest of Peru. They disagreed, and San Martín unselfishly turned his army over to Bolívar and went to France. By 1826, Bolívar and others like him, inspired by the United States of North America, dreamed of a kind of united states for all of Spanish America. Their dream never came true.

Foreign powers held interests in Latin America. After Napoleon was defeated in 1814, the big powers of Europe began to worry about the Spanish American revolts. Most European nations wanted to either return the colonies to Spain or take over control themselves. But the United States and Great Britain opposed both ideas.

The British favored a joint declaration to warn Europeans to stay away from America. But 

United States President James Monroe alone issued the Monroe Doctrine in 1823. Monroe warned that the United States would not allow any European country to enter the affairs of the Western Hemisphere. Europe accepted this warning, knowing that the British navy stood ready to back up the Americans.

Mexico fought to win and keep its freedom. ans. 4 ■ In Mexico in 1810, Father Miguel Hidalgo led Indians and mestizos in revolt against the Spanish. Although he soon died, his movement grew under a lieutenant, Father José Morelos. The group took several cities, and in 1813 Morelos called a congress that declared Mexico free. He was captured and shot, but in 1824 Mexico became a republic.

In the years that followed, many people fought to rule Mexico. In 1834, Antonio Lopez de Santa Anna made himself ruler. While he ruled, Mexico lost half its land to the United States in the Mexican War (1846–1848).

Mexicans who wanted reforms grew strong during the 1850s, and in 1861 their leader, Benito Juárez [hwär′es], an Indian, became president. He wanted the Church to give up

● Students may wish to research the lives of Bolivar and San Martin.

■ Hidalgo and Morelos were creole priests.

Miguel Hidalgo *(left)* was a small-town priest who, in 1810, urged his townspeople to take back the land the Spaniards had stolen from their ancestors. Benito Juarez *(right),* the next champion of people's rights, was the first Indian to serve as head of state in Latin America since the European conquest.

Newly independent Mexico was not strong enough to keep its lands. In 1835, English settlers in Texas won independence from Mexico with the help of the United States. In 1845, the United States annexed Texas; and in 1846 it declared war on Mexico *(below)*. By 1848, Mexico had lost half its territory to the United States.

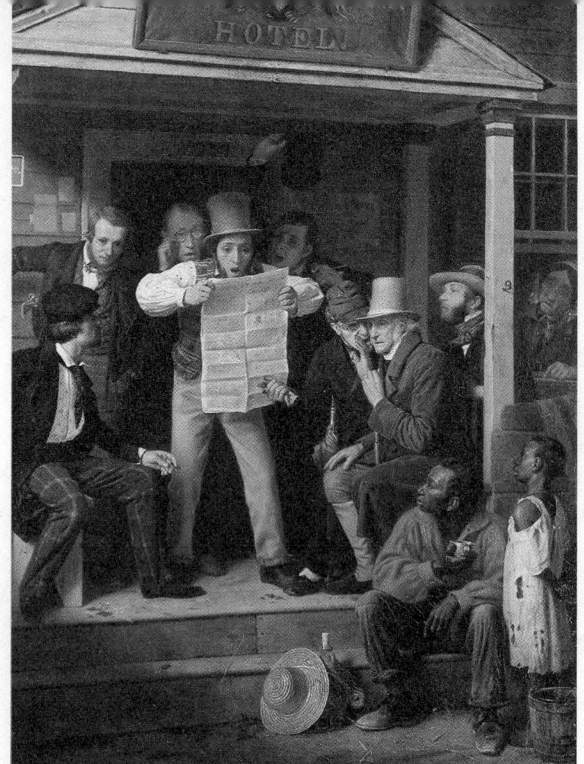

Richard Caton Woodville painted this American daily life scene: "War News from Mexico."

some land and the army officers to give up some privileges. Many upper-class Creoles became alarmed, and civil war broke out. To pay for the war, Mexico borrowed large sums of money in Europe, but it could not repay the debts. So ● in 1862, France sent troops to take over the country. The French ruled Mexico until 1867, when they were overthrown. Juárez again became president. Once more, he tried to carry out such reforms as democratic elections and free compulsory education, but lack of money held him back. He died in 1872. The next ruler was Porfirio Díaz, a mestizo army general, who set up a dictatorship that lasted until 1911.

Brazil gained its freedom peacefully. When Napoleon's troops entered Portugal in 1807, the Portuguese royal family fled to Brazil, which became the seat of the Portuguese Empire. Soon afterward, the king made Brazil a self-governing dominion. When he went back to Portugal in 1821, his son Dom Pedro, who had stayed to rule Brazil, made the country an independent empire.

When the slaves were freed in 1888 without compensation to their owners, the Brazilians were angry. In 1889, they forced the emperor to step down and then set up a federal republic.

Internal problems slowed progress. The Creoles who led revolts in South America were more interested in power for themselves than in any real change in the social or political system. So the pattern of life did not change, especially for the lower classes. ans. 5

Since Spain and Portugal had not allowed self-government in their colonies, the people had no political training. Very few Latin American republics were able to keep stable democratic governments. Many had corrupt dictatorships.

Sectional, racial, and class divisions made more government problems. At the time of independence, four fifths of the people were poor, uneducated Indians, blacks, mestizos, and mulattoes. Many knew neither Spanish nor Portuguese. And jealousy and distrust made cooperation among themselves and among the whites almost impossible.

SECTION REVIEW **5**

1. Describe the class divisions of Latin American society in the early 19th century. p. 451
2. What event gave the Latin Americans the chance to rebel against their governments? p. 451
3. What was the Monroe Doctrine? p. 452
4. Describe the ways in which Mexico and Brazil gained their independence. p. 452
5. Give three reasons Latin America did not set up stable democratic governments after independence. p. 454

● The story of French rule in Mexico, through Maximillian and Carlotta, is shown in the film *Juarez.*

CHAPTER REVIEW 24

SECTION SUMMARIES

1. Parliament triumphed in Britain. In England, trouble began when the Stuarts came to the throne. Their challenge to the power of Parliament and Puritanism led to civil war. Oliver Cromwell brought victory to Parliamentary forces, and the king was executed in 1649. Cromwell became Lord Protector, but when he died the monarchy returned.

Mistrust of the Stuart kings rose again, and in the Glorious Revolution of 1688 the crown was given to the Protestant William and Mary. Parliament made it clear that from then on the English ruler was the representative of a strictly limited monarchy. In the next fifty years, the development of a new kind of executive and the cabinet system were England's contribution to the concept of democratic government.

2. North American colonies fought for independence. Meanwhile, England's North American colonies refused to pay more taxes for their defense and wanted more home rule. Tempers rose, and fighting started in 1775. A year later, the colonists declared their independence, and with the help of France and other European countries, the Americans won their freedom. The Americans set up a constitutional republic that became an example for others.

3. The French Revolution changed society and government. One of the countries that followed America's lead was France. There, anger grew over the inequalities of the class system and the way of taxing, which was causing bankruptcy. When King Louis XVI called a meeting of the Estates-General in 1789, it made itself the National Assembly and drew up a new constitution for a limited monarchy. But foreign war led to a more radical government, the killing of the king, and a Reign of Terror in France.

4. Napoleon became ruler of France. France began to win the war, and the Terror ended. But the weak government allowed Napoleon Bonaparte to take power.

Napoleon made himself dictator of France. He also brought together many of the revolutionary reforms in France. His military victories made a large European empire. But by 1814, the combined attacks of the other European powers had broken it. However, Napoleon's most important legacy was the spread of certain ideas of the French Revolution throughout Europe.

5. Latin American colonies became independent nations. The overseas empires of Spain and Portugal were the oldest and largest of any European country. Although Spain ruled strictly, its New World colonies revolted after Napoleon took Spain, and finally won their freedom. Brazil, though, grew slowly and became independent only late in the 19th century. Many internal problems slowed progress in the area—unstable governments, class and racial divisions, illiteracy, and poverty.

WHO? WHAT? WHEN? WHERE?

1. Identify these people by telling what part they had in their country's revolution:

Oliver Cromwell p. 440	Robespierre p. 446
Louis XVI p. 444	Dom Pedro p. 454
● Toussaint l 'Ouverture	William and Mary p. 441
San Martín p. 452	Napoleon Bonaparte p. 448

2. Define each of these terms by describing their importance in the French Revolution:

Tennis Court Oath p. 446	citizen army p. 446
Reign of Terror p. 446	Bastille p. 445
Committee of Public Safety p. 445	

● p. 451

CHAPTER TEST 24

3. Define each of these types of governments:

Legislative Assembly p. 440 cabinet system p. 442
Convention p. 446 federal republic p. 443
Directory p. 447

ACTIVITIES

1. Discuss the causes of the revolutions studied in this chapter. How might the rulers have prevented violence?

2. Revolutions inspire songs. "Yankee Doodle" came out of the American Revolution. The musical "1776" deals with the Declaration of Independence. The musical "Marat Sade" has many songs that express the anger of the French city mob before the French Revolution. Use the library to find other revolutionary songs from a revolution discussed in this chapter.

3. Based on this chapter, pretend you are a citizen of one of the countries that experienced a revolution. Prepare a political cartoon either for or against the revolution. Display all cartoons on the board and have class members cast ballots indicating (a) which country the revolution took place in and (b) whether the cartoonist is for or against the revolution.

QUESTIONS FOR CRITICAL THINKING

1. In what ways can Napoleon Bonaparte be considered a "Son of the French Revolution"?

● **2.** Why were the ideas of Locke, Voltaire, and Rousseau important in the independence movements of Latin America?

3. To what extent did the revolutions studied in this chapter succeed or fail in accomplishing what the revolutionaries set out to do?

4. Why did the colonists' success in winning the American Revolution have much to do with independence movements of other peoples?

● Discuss in what ways these ideas were important in the American and French revolutions.

SECTION 1

1. Which of these was not a cause of conflict between English rulers and their subjects? a. religion, b. divine right, c. feudal dues

2. The Glorious Revolution took place when: a. Charles I was beheaded, b. Cromwell became ruler, c. William and Mary came to rule England

SECTION 2

3. True or false: For a long time, England allowed the American colonists to run their own affairs.

4. Without the help of ______ the American Revolution might have failed. a. Ireland, b. France, c. Russia.

SECTION 3

5. In the Old Regime, most of the people were: a. nobles, b. bourgeoisie, c. peasants and serfs

6. France was declared a republic by the: a. Directory, b. Convention, c. Estates-General

7. Robespierre led the: a. Legislative Assembly, b. Directory, c. Committee of Public Safety

SECTION 4

8. Napoleon was a member of the: a. lesser nobility, b. bourgeoisie, c. peasants, d. serf class

9. Which of these was not a reform made by Napoleon? a. fair tax system, b. democratic government, c. improved laws

SECTION 5

10. The people that most wanted to change the government of Latin America were the: a. priests, b. peninsulares, c. Creoles

11. True or false: The revolutions in Latin America established stable democratic governments.

12. True or false: Brazil gained its independence through a bloody war that lasted many years and that continued the Portuguese monarchy there into the 20th century.

1815–1914

CHAPTER **25**

The Growth of Liberalism, Nationalism, and Democracy

In 1814, the European nations that had beaten Napoleon held a meeting called the Congress of Vienna to make Europe stable. This German cartoon shows them dividing up the German states like slices of a pie. The map on page 459 shows the changes the Congress made.

It was March, 1848. In an Austrian château not far from Vienna, an old man was alone with his host. Again and again on a violin he played the "Marseillaise," the revolutionary French national anthem. The old man was Prince Metternich, who until a few days before had been one of the most feared and hated men in Europe. Now, after more than 40 years as the Austrian foreign minister, he had lost power because of an uprising in Vienna.

In many ways, the events of 1848 grew from the French revolutionary ideals of liberty, equality, and fraternity. They became known all over Europe and gave rise to three movements: (1) liberalism, which stressed progress and reform; (2) nationalism, which looked to give people of similar culture and traditions their own government; and (3) democracy,which moved toward giving a voice in government to more of the people than a small ruling class.

The political history of 19th-century Europe is mainly the story of how these three movements changed governments in Europe and around the world. It is a story full of fighting, for the number of liberals, nationalists, and democrats in Europe was small in the early 1800s. Governments feared radical changes would bring them down. Clashes often became revolutions, but most of them failed.

In the late 1800s, liberalism became strongly influenced by democracy. Democracy, though revolutionary in 1815 and radical in 1848, was by 1914 the most desired form of government. It gained ground fastest in western Europe and slowest in eastern Europe. But wherever people accepted it, political life changed.

The political map of Europe in 1914 was quite different from the map of 1815. Because of nationalism, two new great powers, Germany and Italy, were born. And in some way, liberalism and democracy had brought mass politics to most countries. This chapter shows how:

1. Governments resisted change.

2. Continental Europe was politically changed.

3. Democracy advanced in western Europe.

4. Reforms came slowly in southern and eastern Europe.

● Key concepts: Liberalism, nationalism and democracy were ideas which greatly affected 19th century Europe.

■ Discuss: How do people bring about change? Who *resists* change. Define conservative, moderate and radical attitudes.

1 Governments resisted change

After Napoleon was defeated, the people of Europe, sick of war, wanted long-term peace and stable lives. To gain these ends, the allies who had won the war met in Vienna for peace talks.

The Congress of Vienna tried to bring stable life. The Congress of Vienna began in September, 1814. The Congress had two chief tasks. First, it had to balance off the powerful states of Europe. Second, it had to find a way to peacefully settle fights among the great powers. More than twenty years of revolution and war had led to great changes in the map of Europe. The statesmen who met to redraw it faced a very hard task.

There was, first of all, the matter of containing France, which was still considered the main threat to the peace of Europe. Small buffer states were created along its borders. ans. 1

In Germany, Napoleon had set up the Confederation of the Rhine with thirty-eight states. The Congress turned this into a German confederation with thirty-nine states.

Almost half of Saxony was given to Prussia and nearly all of Poland to Russia. The Vienna peacemakers knew that no treaty can make a perfectly sure peace. So they tried to find a way to settle disagreements between countries before war started.

In November, 1815, Austria, Russia, Prussia, and Britain set themselves up as a group called the Concert of Europe, which would meet at certain times to guard the Vienna settlement and keep peace. (In 1818, France joined the group.) The Concert of Europe was the first international group to try to deal with European affairs.

The Great Powers opposed liberalism and nationalism. After 1815, liberalism and nationalism became dangerous to the peace made at Vienna. Both movements grew most rapidly in the cities, where the growth of commercial, industrial, and professional classes was fastest. From these city middle classes came leaders and support for liberal programs and nationalistic movements in the 1800s.

Some liberals wanted a monarchy, some a
ans. 2 republic. But all agreed on the need for parliaments that spoke for the people. Nineteenth-century liberals did not believe everyone should have a voice in government. However, by seeking to give a vote to every adult male who owned property, they aimed to broaden the base of government. Liberals believed that governments should protect the rights to speak, write, and gather freely. They believed that all persons should be treated as equals before the law.

Nationalists often favored liberal programs, but their main goal was self-rule. They said that all people who shared a language, customs, and culture had the right to decide their own form of government. In order to do that, they needed *self-determination,* that is, freedom from outside rule.

Nationalists felt that all true patriots should work for self-rule or for unification of a divided country. For example, nationalists in Hungary wanted freedom from Austrian rule, and German patriots did not like the disunity of the German Confederation.

The men who drew up the Vienna settlement almost completely ignored nationalistic feelings. The stand of the Great Powers was stated publicly by Metternich. He said that the Great ans. 1 Powers could rightly move to put down revolutions. In 1820 and 1821, Austrian troops crushed liberal revolts in Italy. In 1823, French troops put down a liberal revolt in Spain.

Liberalism and nationalism made gains in the 1800s. In 1821, Greek nationalists rose against the Ottoman Turks. In 1827, England, France, and Russia joined the fight to gain Greek freedom from Turkish rule. Outnumbered by better and larger forces, the Turks lost. A peace treaty was signed in 1829, and the next year Greece became independent. The new country caused the first important change in the political map of Europe since the Congress of Vienna.

In France, feeling had been turning against King Charles X because he opposed the constitution. In the general election of 1830, a large ans. 3 number of liberals won. Charles tried to put aside the elections, and revolution broke out. Charles X went into exile in England.

The wealthy middle classes then became leaders in the revolution. The crown was offered to Louis Philippe [lü′ē fə lēp′], Duke of Orleans, who promised to honor the constitution of 1814.

Louis Philippe's reign, called the July Monarchy, was a victory for the liberals. Censorship was ended, and trial by jury was guaranteed. More people were allowed to vote. However, voting was limited to men who owned large amounts of property. The king himself had been a successful businessman in his own right, and he protected private property and helped businesses. Merchants, bankers, and industrialists liked these policies, but radical democrats felt cheated. They became more and more unhappy with a government that seemed to work only for the wealthy classes.

Street fighting in Paris in 1848 led to the abdication of King Louis Philippe and the creation of a new French republic.

Revolution also broke out in Belgium, under Dutch rule since 1815. Late in August, 1830, Belgian nationalists and middle-class liberals rose against the Dutch and declared Belgium a free country. The Belgians held national elections and drew up a constitution that was more liberal than any other in Europe at the time.

In 1831, all five Great Powers (Russia, Prussia, Austria, Britain, and France) signed the Treaty of London. It accepted Belgian independence and stated that Belgium must always remain neutral. The treaty was not fully in force until 1839, when the Dutch signed it.

ans. 3 Great Britain was the only major western European country to escape violent revolution in the 1830s. However, two important changes were made when Parliament passed the Reform Bill of 1832.

First, the amount of property a man needed in order to vote was lowered. Thus, the number of voters grew by over fifty percent. Second, the voting districts for the House of Commons were changed to give a voice to the new industrial towns. Political power no longer belonged only to the large landowners. From 1832 on, power was divided among members of the upper middle class—merchants, manufacturers, and business and professional people.

British reformers made some gains. In Britain, many working people remained unhappy. They felt cheated politically by the 1832 Reform Bill, which did not give them the right to vote. The factory owners kept wages low, would not allow strikes, and tried to stop social legislation. Two movements drew much working-class support.

One, the Anti-Corn Law League, wanted to remove the protective tariffs that kept the price of grain, and thus bread, high. The League was well run and had money. Its cause was aided by failing businesses and crops in the mid-1840s.

Under pressure, Parliament ended the Corn Laws in 1846. This marked a turning point of political power in England. For the first time the middle and working classes won over the landowning upper class.

Another reform movement, known as Chartism, took its name from the People's Charter (or petition) of 1838. It called for broad reforms. These included universal male suffrage, ● the secret ballot, and an end to the need to own property in order to hold seats in the House of Commons. Between 1838 and 1848, the chartists sent the House of Commons three petitions signed by millions. All three were turned down. But the movement was strong, and within fifty years, the reforms became law.

Revolutions shocked Europe in 1848. The rumblings of the 1830s furthered the liberal cause. However, only in western Europe, west of the Rhine River, did industrialism and liberalism grow rapidly. East of the river, feudalism and autocracy changed little. However, both sides of the imaginary line had many discontented groups.

In western Europe, especially in Britain and France, the bourgeoisie enjoyed a kind of golden age. The lower classes had no political power, and the middle-class governments would not pass laws to help them. To the east, the major unhappy groups were nationalists and liberals. The desire for unification grew stronger in Germany and Italy. In the huge Austrian Empire, Czechs, Magyars, and Croats all wanted freedom from German control. Liberals, put down in 1820 and again in 1830, still wanted constitutional, representative government, civil liberties, and an end to serfdom.

● Explain universal male suffrage. Also explain why it would have been wise for European rulers to grant this right to vote (other recourse for change is revolution).

In the mid-1840s, a business depression caused a great loss of jobs in the area from Britain to Silesia. Also, potatoes and wheat—those staple foods of the lower classes—were scarce, and prices were high. Potato blights swept across Europe from Poland to Ireland in 1845 and 1846. In 1846, the grain crops also failed, and famine was widespread. Economic distress, then, joined political discontent to cause a wave of revolutions in 1848.

The major powers in these revolts were France, Austria, Prussia, and the states of the German Confederation. In France, the king was removed, and a constitutional republic in which all adult males could vote was set up. Prince Louis Napoleon, nephew of Napoleon Bonaparte, was elected president in December, 1848. All other revolutions failed. Liberals and
ans. 4 nationalists could not agree, and armies loyal to the monarchies put down the uprisings. The only gains were in the Austrian Empire, where liberals won an end to serfdom and in 1867 Hungarian nationals got self-government. From then on, the empire was called the Austro-Hungarian Empire.

SECTION REVIEW 1

p. 458 460 **1.** What steps did the Congress of Vienna take to protect the balance of power in Europe? How did the Concert of Europe hope to keep the peace?

p. 459 **2.** What were the main goals of liberals and nationalists in the 19th century? Why did nationalistic movements cause fighting in Europe?

p. 460 461 **3.** Describe the changes in government that took place in France, Belgium, and Britain in the 1830s. What class benefited most from the changes in France and Britain?

p. 462 **4.** What were two reasons that revolutions failed in 1848?

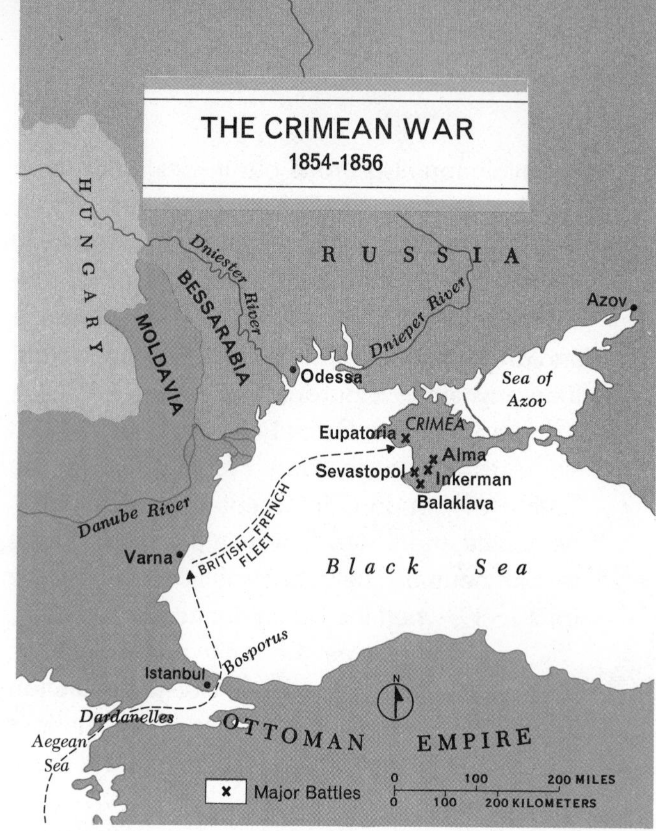

2 Continental Europe was politically changed

Although the 1848 revolutions tore almost all of Europe apart, the major countries did not war with one another. However, the revolutions brought forward a new kind of politician and state leader. These people were willing to use any way, even force, to push their national interests. This new spirit, known as *Realpolitik*, led to political changes in Europe. ●

The Crimean War had important results. The new spirit of *Realpolitik* can be seen in the Crimean War. The first big armed clash in Europe after 1815, it pitted France and Britain against Russia. All three countries had interests ans. 1
in the Middle East and were seeking gains in the

● Use Activity 1 to clarify the meaning of Realpolitik. Discuss how the Crimean War was an example.

Ottoman Empire. The Crimean War began in 1854, when Britain and France, in order to stop any Russian moves into the Middle East, joined forces with the Turks.

Almost all of the fighting took place in the Crimea, a Russian peninsula that sticks out into the Black Sea. After a long siege and heavy losses, the British and French won in 1855.

In 1856, the warring countries gathered at Paris for a peace conference. The treaty hurt Russia in several ways. Worst of all was that no one could keep battleships on the Black Sea. Russia was hurt most by this, because it now had an undefended southern border. From then on, Russia's first aim was to change the Black Sea clauses and get back military rights there. Russia could no longer be counted on to defend the existing balance of power, since this balance was not to its favor.

During the Crimean War, an English nurse, Florence Nightingale, brought about a complete change in the care of the wounded. She reorganized military hospitals and greatly reduced the death rate.

France became a dictatorship. After his election as president of the French Second Republic, Louis Napoleon worked to gain more power for himself. In a *coup d'état* [kü'dā tä'] he overturned the constitution. The next year, the people voted him Emperor Napoleon III.

Unlike his uncle, Louis Napoleon had no great ability in war or administration. But he was a clever politician. Although his methods were often unfair, he could turn the public's feelings in any direction. The parliament in France had no real power.

Napoleon III did help France economically.
Railroad building was greatly expanded. Iron ans. 2
ships replaced wooden ones. And in 1859, a French company began the ten-year task of building the Suez Canal.

Baron Georges Haussman, a city planner, laid out a new Paris of broad streets, public parks, and great buildings. For the peasants, Napoleon III set up model farms. For the workers, he legalized strikes. Asylums and hospitals were built. Medicine was free to the poorest classes.

Had Napoleon stayed with problems at home, he might have remained on the throne a long time. Instead, he decided to make France a great power in world politics. By 1854, he had led France into the Crimean War. Other military adventures followed.

One of Napoleon's most disastrous projects was in Mexico. Mexico had borrowed heavily from outside investors. In 1861, it stopped paying its foreign debt. France, Spain, and Britain sent troops to force President Benito Juárez to pay. Spain and Britain soon left, seeing that Napoleon had ambitious plans.

● Napoleon sent more troops to take Mexico City. Then in 1863, he made an Austrian archduke, Maximilian, emperor of Mexico. Maximilian meant well but depended on French troops to protect his government against the angry Mexicans.

The United States was then fighting its own civil war and could do nothing against the French. By 1866, the war was over, and the Americans told the French to leave. Napoleon, who needed his forces in Europe, deserted

After the French left Mexico, Maximilian tried to stay on as emperor. He took the small army he had left and marched north to meet Juárez. His army was defeated, and he was captured. Edouard Manet's painting shows his execution.

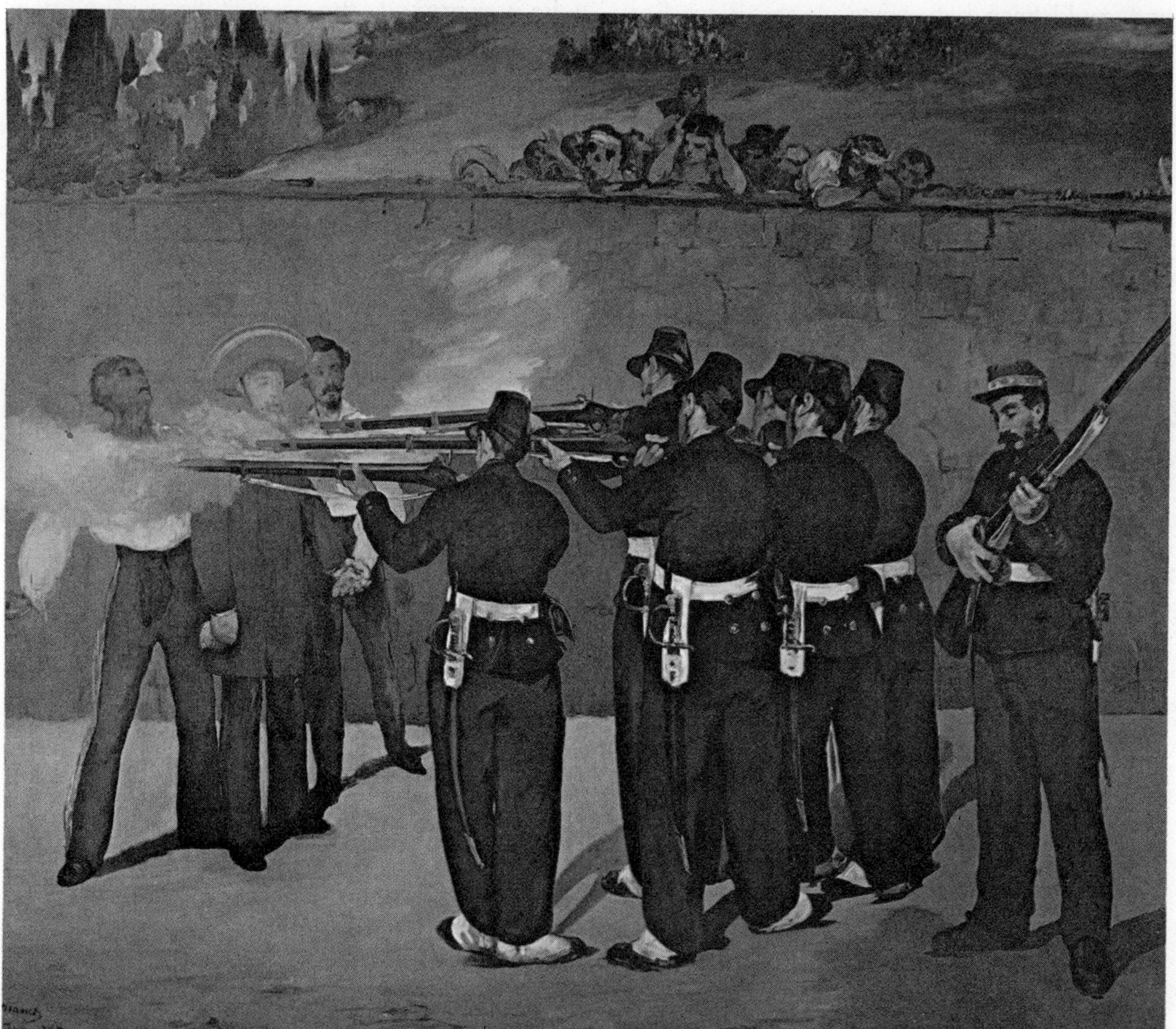

● Point out that Napoleon ignored the United States' "Monroe Doctrine".

Maximilian. In 1867, Mexican soldiers captured and shot him.

Italy was unified. In 1859, Italy was still divided into several large and small states. Ever since the French Revolution, Italian nationalism had been growing. It showed in the writings of such patriots as Giuseppe Mazzini. More generally, it showed in the *Risorgimento* [rə sôr ji men′tō], or resurgence, a movement among middle-class liberals who wanted Italian unity.

The events of 1848 showed that brave men and high dreams were not enough. Without the power to remove Austria from northern Italy, the dream of unity could not come true. Count Camillo di Cavour [kä vůr′] understood this fact better than did most Italians. In 1852, the count became prime minister of the Kingdom of
ans. 3 Sardinia. He made Sardinia, already politically and economically ahead of the other Italian states, a model of progress. It was the natural leader in unifying Italy.

Cavour was a clever man who knew that Italy could not gain unity without outside help. He won the aid of Napoleon III, who liked to think of himself as the champion of nationalism. In 1859, Cavour forced the Austrians into declaring war.

The French and Sardinian armies together easily defeated the Austrians. Revolutions broke out all over northern Italy. Napoleon III was afraid that the movement had gone too far. He angered Cavour by making peace with Austria.

The revolutions did not stop. By 1860, all of northern Italy except Venetia had joined with Sardinia. Then Cavour made peace with Austria.

The Papal States and the Kingdom of the Two Sicilies remained outside the Italian union.

At this point, a hot-tempered leader, Giuseppe Garibaldi [gar′ ə bôl′dē], took matters into his own hands. In May, 1860, with an army of about 1,100 men, he took the Kingdom of the Two Sicilies. Cavour persuaded Garibaldi to allow the Two Sicilies to join Sardinia. In 1861, only a few months before Cavour died, the Kingdom of Italy became real. Victor Emmanuel of Sardinia became king. The final steps in forming modern Italy were taken in 1866 and 1870, when Venetia and Rome were added.

The German Empire was formed. Politically, the Germany of 1862 was not much different from the Germany of 1815, that is, a batch of states inside the frame of the loose German Confederation. But socially and economically, important changes had taken place.

In 1834, the Prussians set up the *Zollverein* [tsôl′fer īn′], a union to deal with tariffs. Later, most of Germany (except Austria) joined it. To many German nationalists, greater economic unity pointed to political unity. They looked to Prussia to show the way.

Prussia, however, was not interested in German nationalism. It wanted to increase its own strength and importance within the Confederation, especially at the expense of Austria. This goal required a larger army, but the liberal Prussian parliament refused to allow new taxes that would pay for the army. At this point, in 1862, King William I of Prussia made Otto von Bismarck his prime minister, or chancellor.

● This tariff union aided German trade and industry.

It was a fateful move. Bismarck, a conservative landowner, had an iron will. He was a clever man who cared not at all about the public or its feelings. But he was deeply loyal to the Prussian monarchy.

As prime minister, Bismarck simply forgot about the liberal Prussian parliament and went ahead with the army. He ordered taxes collected without consent of parliament. The obedient ans. 4

people of Prussia did not revolt, and parliament's protests were ignored. Bismarck stated that the issues of the day would be decided not by speeches and votes, but "by blood and iron." Bismarck showed what he meant by quickly winning two wars. In these, he strengthened Prussia at the expense of Austria and Denmark.

ans. 4 Bismarck next turned his attention to southern Germany, where Prussia was disliked. He felt that only war with France would bring the southern states to the northern side—first as friends in war, and later joined politically.

A chance for war came in 1870 when Spain needed a king and France would not agree to Bismarck's choice. The Franco-Prussian War lasted only six months. During that time, Napoleon III's government collapsed.

Paris was besieged for 130 days. When it fell, Prussian troops marched into Paris. In the peace treaty that followed, Prussia took the French border provinces of Alsace and Lorraine. The French never forgot their shame at the hands of the Germans.

On January 18, 1871, while Paris was still under siege, the German Empire was created with William of Prussia as its emperor. The new empire soon became the strongest power in continental Europe.

SECTION REVIEW 2

p. 462 **1.** In what way was the Crimean War an example of *Realpolitik?*

p. 463 **2.** In what ways did Louis Napoleon improve France? How did he weaken France?

p. 465 **3.** What acts of Cavour and Garibaldi helped form modern Italy?

p. 466 **4.** How did Bismarck get the larger army that Prus-
467 sia needed? How did he get the south German states to join Prussia?

● Point out and discuss how these reforms followed the extension of voting rights.

3 Democracy advanced in western Europe

Between 1871 and 1914, the countries of western Europe grew socially, economically, and politically. The changes were very great, but important problems in these same areas remained.

Britain made many reforms. The economic, social, and political leader in these years was, again, Britain. For most of the time the reigning monarch was Queen Victoria. She became a symbol for an age of wide political power and great well-being. In the 1850s, the Whig and Tory parties became the Liberal and Conservative parties. William E. Gladstone led the Liberals, and Benjamin Disraeli [diz rā′lē], the Conservatives. The two alternated as prime minister from 1868 to 1880. After Disraeli died in 1881, Gladstone ruled politics until he retired in 1894.

Both parties put forward bills to extend voting ans. 1
rights. After 1884, most male adults had the right to vote. Under Gladstone and Disraeli, state-run public education was begun, the secret ballot became law, labor unions gained more freedom, and a workmen's compensation law ●
was passed.

After 1900, important changes took place in British politics. The rise of the Labour party led the Liberals, who wanted to keep the workers' votes, to start social welfare legislation. The Liberals held the government from 1905 to 1916. Led by Herbert Asquith and David Lloyd George, they passed laws that set up old-age pensions, unemployment insurance, and minimum wage laws.

Lloyd George's budget in 1909 was based on the idea that taxes on the incomes of rich people should be higher than those for poorer people. The House of Lords reluctantly agreed under pressure from the House of Commons and the king.

The so-called Irish Question was a difficult problem for England. The Roman Catholic Irish did not want to pay taxes to support the Anglican Church in Ireland. They also disliked England's political rule and a land system that kept the Irish poor. With the Disestablishment Act of 1869, Gladstone stopped Irish tax money from going to the Anglican Church in Ireland. He also

Queen Victoria, during her long reign from 1837 to 1901, became the symbol of a stable and powerful England. She is shown on this page with the two political leaders on whom she depended for advice in most affairs of state: the Liberal Gladstone, *left,* and the Conservative Disraeli, *right.*

made a start on land reform, giving peasants more rights over the land they farmed.

These economic measures helped the Irish. But at the same time, politics became the trouble point. The Irish had a strong leader in Charles Parnell. He favored Home Rule, that is, self-rule for Ireland.

Parliament finally passed the Home Rule bill in 1914. But the largely Presbyterian northern Irish population of Ulster objected. The problem was put aside during World War I. When the war ended, however, fighting broke out. In 1922, a compromise plan made southern Ireland (Eire) free and allowed Ulster to stay in the United Kingdom. But friction between Protestants and Catholics in Ulster has repeatedly produced bloodshed.

France moved into a Third Republic. After the fall of the Second Empire and defeat in the Franco-Prussian War, the French elected a National Assembly to make peace with Germany and decide what form of government France would have. The Assembly in 1875 set up a republic. It had a president, premier, and cabinet responsible to a two-house legislature. The lower house (the Chamber of Deputies) was elected by universal male suffrage. The Third Republic lasted until 1940—longer than any other government since 1789.

The Third Republic was often attacked by ans. 2
people who wanted to bring back the monarchy. The 1880s and 1890s were filled with crises, the climax being the Dreyfus case. Alfred Dreyfus, a Jew, was a French army officer. In 1894, a military court convicted him of treason. When evidence later showed that the real traitor was a Catholic aristocrat, public feeling divided sharply. Enemies of the Third Republic (the officer corps, monarchists, and the Church) were strongly against reopening the case. They said that to do so would weaken military authority.

In Ireland, economic problems were severe. Many peasants were evicted because they couldn't pay the rent.

British cartoon shows Bismarck being dismissed from his command of the ship of state by William II.

Pro-Republic forces finally won. When a civil court pardoned Dreyfus in 1906, the civil government was proven to be stronger than the • army. The Dreyfus Affair became an example that any person of any race or creed could get justice in a democracy.

The Republic in 1914 still had enemies. But most French people favored it. However, many political parties existed. Public feelings about issues often were divided. Fifty government ministries rose and fell between 1871 and 1914. Other problems occurred as an unhappy working class called for reforms.

• Abler students might like to research this case.

Germany made some reforms. Between 1871 and 1890, Chancellor Bismarck led the German Empire. He built it as a union of monarchies in which Prussia had the strongest voice. The empire had a constitution and a lower house (Reichstag) elected by universal male suffrage. But real power lay with the chancellor and the aristocratic upper house (Bundesrat).

Bismarck's strong nationalism made him question other Germans who did not bow to the state. During the 1870s, he attacked the Roman Catholic Church in Germany and cut sharply into Catholic education and freedom of worship. After a few years, Bismarck ended these attacks. He felt that the Catholic Church was no longer a threat. Also, he wanted Catholic support for his drive against socialism.

German industry grew rapidly and so did the German working class. Many workers became interested in socialism. When the Social Democratic party was organized in 1875, Bismarck became alarmed. Beginning in 1878, Germany passed many laws against socialism, but was unable to destroy it.

In the 1880s, Bismarck tried to draw workers away from socialism with a sweeping state program of social insurance. It was the most forward-looking program of its kind in Europe, but it did not destroy socialism. In 1890, Bismarck quarreled with the new emperor, William II, and was forced to retire.

William II was 29 when he became emperor in 1888. He reigned until 1918. An ambitious man with grand ideas about his own power, William II wanted to become a world leader. Thus, he began an aggressive foreign policy. In

Germany, he ended the antisocialist laws and furthered social insurance. However, he refused to allow greater political democracy. The Social Democrats grew stronger. By 1912, they were the largest single party in the Reichstag.

SECTION REVIEW 3

p. 467 **1.** List nine social reforms begun in Britain. In what year was each started? What was the Irish Question?

p. 469 **2.** Who were the enemies of the Third Republic? Why was the Dreyfus Affair an important test for French government?

p. 470 **3.** Why did Bismarck fight socialism? What policy did William II follow toward the working class in Germany?

4 Reforms came slowly in southern and eastern Europe

Outside the industrial center of western Europe
were less economically advanced countries,
such as Spain, Portugal, Italy, Austria-Hungary,
the Balkans, and the Ottoman Empire. Their
ans. 1 economies were chiefly agricultural. Unlike the
● industrial countries, they had few large cities,
railroads, or factories and more poverty, illiteracy, and disease. The rich and poor classes were sharply divided, the middle class was small, and governments were not stable.

Spain and Portugal lacked stability. During the late 19th century, Spain had no effective government. A revolution in 1868 had deposed the corrupt queen. But opposing groups could not agree on the next step. Monarchists were split, and republicans did not want a monarchy at all. Both the army and the Roman Catholic Church often intervened in politics.

Finally, in 1876 Spain became a constitutional monarchy. The right to vote was given only to male property owners, however. And Parliamentary rule had no meaning. The government remained corrupt and ineffective. The Spanish-American War against the United States reduced the size of the empire and emptied the treasury. In Spain, growing anger among peasants and workers led to radical social ideas. As the 20th century opened, Spain was faced with rising violence.

Violence in the neighboring monarchy of Portugal equaled that in Spain. Between 1853 and 1889, Portugal moved toward parliamentary government. But then the government returned to a monarchy that favored the established nobility. A revolution in 1910 overturned the hated monarchy, and Portugal became a republic. Stable government was impossible, however, as political parties fought for power.

Italy had great problems. Unification did
not erase Italy's old problems. Sectional hatreds ans. 2
were strong. People were illiterate, and education was backward. The land system and tax structure were unfair. And the people had very little experience in parliamentary government.

Even though Italy was a constitutional monarchy, only men of education and property could vote. Out of 20 million people, only 150 thousand had voting rights. Politicians cared more about being elected than about making reforms.

Economic problems became so great in the 1890s that riots broke out in several Italian cities. In 1911, suffrage was given to all men over age thirty. This act, though, only led to larger extremist parties. To escape such conditions,

● Discuss how these conditions would effect the growth of democracy.

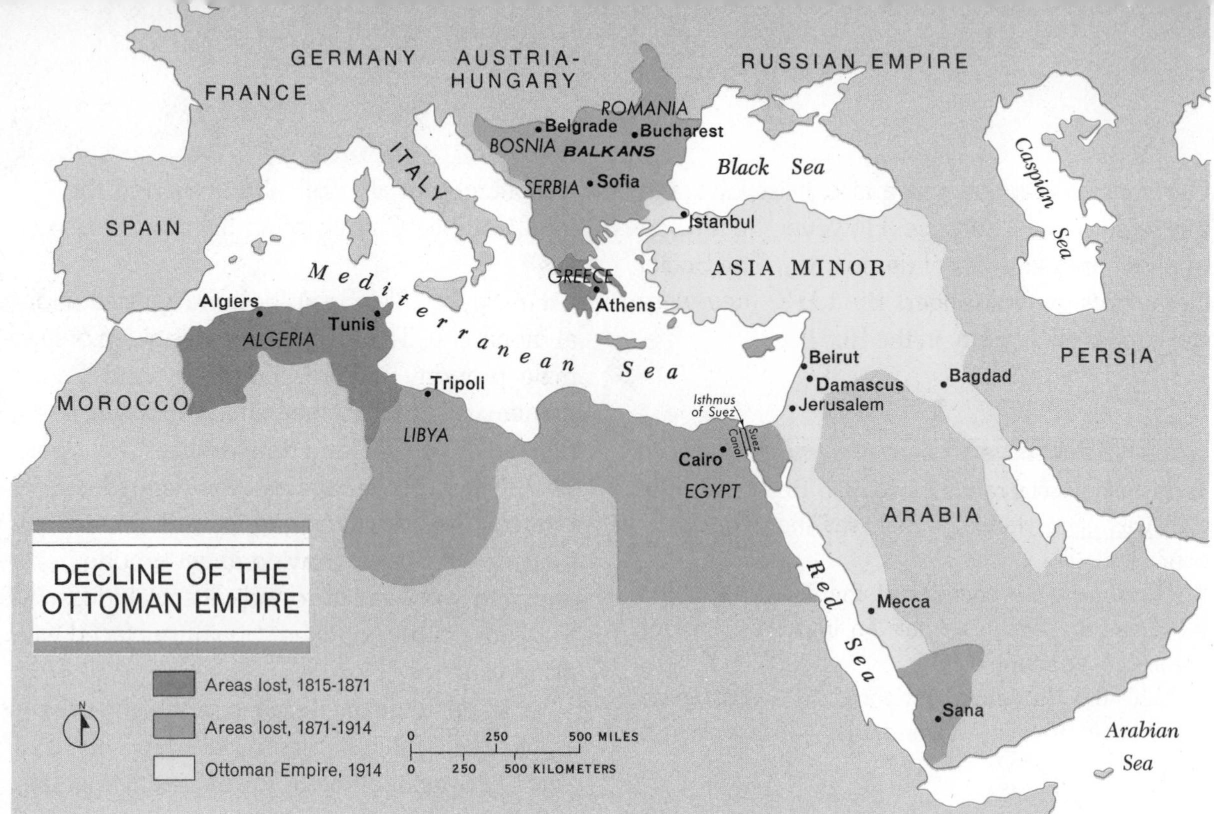

thousands of young Italians moved to other countries.

Minority groups threatened Austria-Hungary. The greatest problem that Austria-Hungary had after 1870 was one of nationalities.
ans. 3 The empire held so many different national groups that it was hard to find a policy that all would accept.

By the end of the century, the Magyars of Hungary began to push for full independence from Austria. Inside Hungary, the Magyars made up less than half the population. But they ran the government, and they were unfriendly toward the other nationalities in Hungary such as Romanians, Slovaks, and Serbs.

In Austria, Germans ruled the political, economic, and cultural life. The Czechs wanted to end German domination and have their own government. They were proud of their history and their cultural and economic advancement. The Emperor Francis Joseph tried to please all the nationalities and failed to please any. His failure finally led to the end of the empire.

The Ottoman Empire grew weaker. The ans. 4
Ottoman Empire had even more nationalities than Austria-Hungary. And it also had several religions. Most of its people were Muslims. But Jews and Christians, both Roman Catholic and Greek Orthodox, also lived there. Turks and other Muslims, the two most powerful groups, held all of the army and government posts.

The Ottoman Empire lagged far behind western Europe in economic and political development. For over two centuries, it had been ailing. Slowly, peoples on the borders of the empire broke away from Turkish rule.

By the end of the Crimean War, the Turks had lost most of their power over southern Russia, the Crimea, Romania, Serbia, Greece, Arabia, Egypt, and Algeria. Defeat in war pointed up Turkish weaknesses and showed the need for reform and reorganization.

In 1856, the Turkish government issued the *Hatt-i Humayun* [hat′i hu̇ mä′yün], the most important Turkish reform of the 19th century. It promised that people would be equal before the law and that torture would end. A fairer tax system would be used. And the corruption in public office would end. A constitution in 1876 provided for parliamentary government.

These changes met powerful resistance. The ruling sultan from 1876 to 1909, Abdul Hamid II [ab′du̇l hä mēd′], was strongly against reform. He dismissed parliament and began a reign of terror.

In 1877, war broke out between Turkey and Russia. This time they fought over Turkish lands in the Balkans. The Turks were defeated and lost more Balkan land. Abdul Hamid's rule did not soften, and the nationalistic peoples of the Balkans went on fighting. A revolution in 1908 brought a reforming group, the Young Turks, to power. They restored parliament but could not stop the rise of nationalism in the Balkans.

SECTION REVIEW 4

1. Name four problems that prevented Spain and Portugal from setting up democratic governments. p. 471

2. Why was it hard for parliamentary government to work well in Italy? p. 471

3. In what ways did the many national groups in Austria-Hungary cause problems in governing that empire? p. 472

4. What problems did the Ottoman Empire have? What reforms were tried? p. 472

The victorious Young Turks march through the streets after forcing Abdul Hamid II from his throne.

CHAPTER REVIEW 25

SECTION SUMMARIES

1. Governments resisted change. After Napoleon Bonaparte's defeat, European leaders met at the Congress of Vienna to return the balance of power and make a new map of Europe. The Great Powers also tried to find a way to stop wars before they started. The Concert of Europe was formed to keep peace. After 1814, liberalism and nationalism led to fighting in Spain and Italy, but these revolts were quickly crushed. The Greeks, though, finally won their independence. In 1830, the French rose against the backward monarchy. The Belgians won their freedom from the Dutch Netherlands. Outbreaks in German and Italian states and in Poland were put down. Britain escaped revolution by making changes. In 1848, people rose all over Europe. The French again were first. After a bloody civil war, they wrote a new constitution. Other 1848 revolts in Europe failed. In the Austrian Empire, though, serfdom was ended and Hungary won self-rule.

2. Continental Europe was politically changed. In the second half of the 19th century, nationalism and the growth of democratic institutions brought many political changes in Europe. A new idea about power politics was known as *Realpolitik*. Emperor Louis Napoleon brought well-being to France. But he led his country into bad foreign adventures. Count Cavour, the Sardinian prime minister, led a drive that brought about the unification of Italy. Otto von Bismarck led Prussia through wars with Denmark, Austria, and France. From these wars came a new German Empire.

3. Democracy advanced in western Europe. Beginning about 1870, several forward-looking countries of western Europe made great social and economic gains. England, led by Gladstone, Disraeli, and Asquith, made many liberal and democratic changes. Troubled southern Ireland finally gained its freedom. France under the Third Republic was not politically stable, but its people were safe and at peace. And the government survived internal attacks. The German government lost its campaigns against the Roman Catholic Church and the socialists. The growing German working class gained social benefits.

4. Reforms came slowly in southern and eastern Europe. Bad governments stopped Spain and Portugal from equaling the forward steps of the countries to the north. Italy could not overcome hard economic and social problems. Austria-Hungary did little to please the unhappy nationalities inside its borders. In the failing Ottoman Empire, a weak government could not subdue the Balkans.

WHO? WHAT? WHEN? WHERE?

1. Arrange these events in chronological order:

Greece won freedom 2
unification of Germany 7
Treaty of London 3
Crimean War 5
Congress of Vienna 1
serfdom abolished in Austrian Empire 4
unification of Italy 6

2. Identify these terms, telling how they helped liberalism and democracy to grow:

Risorgimento p. 465
Corn Laws repealed p. 461
Chartism p. 461
Male suffrage p. 459
Hatt-i Humayun p. 473
constitutional monarchy p. 471
Home Rule p. 469

3. Tell in what country each of these people lived and why each was important:

Bismarck p. 466
Metternich p. 460
Louis Napoleon p. 463
Francis Joseph p. 472
Gladstone p. 467
Disraeli p. 467
Queen Victoria p. 467
Maximilian p. 464
Emperor William II p. 470
Cavour p. 465
Parnell p. 469
Abdul Hamid II p. 473

CHAPTER TEST 25

4. Explain the meanings of these terms and give an example of each from this chapter:

nationalism p. 459, 465 — liberal p. 459, 461, 467
democracy p. 458, 459, 460 — conservative p. 466, 469
republic p. 469 — moderate p. 461

QUESTIONS FOR CRITICAL THINKING

● **1.** Would you be willing to live under a dictatorship if the ruler gave the people enough food, homes, and jobs?

2. Why did Bismarck and Louis Napoleon make many reforms even though they ruled as dictators?

3. Why did people in the countries that became industrialized ask for social reforms before people in the nonindustrialized countries did?

4. What were the biggest problems Italians and Germans faced in unifying their countries? Why did Germany become a Great Power while Italy did not?

5. Why was Britain so often the first country to make important social reforms?

ACTIVITIES

1. Have a class discussion on whether the spirit of *Realpolitik* is still alive in the world today. Use current news reports for research.

2. Do outside research on the Crimean War. What mistakes did the governments make? Why were they fighting? What happened in the "Charge of the Light Brigade"?

■ **3.** Liberals in 19th-century Europe worked for prison reforms, improved health care, improved working conditions. If you were a liberal today, what social changes would you work for? Write a petition to your government official urging your changes.

● QUESTIONS FOR CRITICAL THINKING

1. Ask students to think about the value of freedom versus security.

3. Students should show that they understand political reforms are (*often*) of lesser importance to hungry people.

SECTION 1

1. The purpose of the Congress of Vienna was to: a. unify Germany, b. strengthen France, c. keep a balance of power

2. True or false: The Great Powers of Europe in 1815 encouraged nationalism and liberalism.

3. In the early 1800s, the right to vote was meant for: a. all citizens, b. all men, c. men who owned property

SECTION 2

4. As a result of the Crimean War, which nation lost power? a. Russia, b. Turkey, c. France

5. The movement to unify Italy was called: a. *Realpolitik*, b. Risorgimento, c. *Zollverein*

6. True or false: Bismarck wanted a war with France to create unity among the German states.

SECTION 3

7. A great liberal leader in British government was: a. Gladstone, b. Dreyfus, c. Disraeli

8. Home Rule meant: a. the right to vote, b. freedom for Ireland, c. independence for Italy

9. True or false: Bismarck destroyed socialism in Germany by making many reforms.

SECTION 4

10. Which of these caused problems in Spain and Portugal? a. large industrialized cities, b. large middle class, c. conflicts between rich and poor

11. Which country's problems were caused by the many nationalities within its borders? a. Portugal, b. Italy, c. Austria-Hungary

12. In which country were there people of many different religions? a. Spain, b. Italy, c. Turkey

■ Activity 3. Have students define conservative and moderate stands on issues.

CHAPTER 1700-1900

26 The Industrial Revolution

A model of Watt's steam engine. Watt needed a way to measure the work his engine could do. He studied horses and developed the measurement of horsepower. Later scientists named the metric unit of power after him. One horsepower equals 746 watts.

● A scientific revolution changed people's ideas about nature. Democratic revolutions changed their ideas about government. At the same time, a quiet revolution in business and industry was beginning to change the ways people lived and worked. Very few people then—not even the inventors—fully understood how new machines would change people's lives.

● Use the timeline at the beginning of the unit to show how these changes overlapped in time. The timeline would help in completing Activity 2 also.

In November, 1774, a young inventor wrote to his father:

> The business I am here about has turned out rather successful, that is to say, the fire engine I

have invented is now going and answers much better than any other that has yet been made, and I expect that the invention will be beneficial to me.

The letter writer was James Watt, a Scottish instrument maker. His "fire engine" was a steam engine that would become known around the world. When James Watt wrote that letter, he could not have known that he would become one of the most important leaders in a huge industrial revolution.

In 1763, a fellow teacher at the University of Glasgow asked him to repair a model steam engine. Watt noticed that the engine wasted a great deal of fuel. He talked about the waste with several teachers at the university. No one could think of any useful solution. For months, Watt thought about the engine. He found an answer in 1765. For years after that, however, he worked on technical points. Finally, he took out a patent on his improved steam engine.

The use of steam power in industry helped change the world. The steam engine later reduced or replaced old energy sources—horses, oxen, water, and people.

By 1819 when James Watt died, steam-powered machines were replacing hand tools in British industry. Goods made in factories shared markets with goods made in the home. During the 1800s, industrialization spread to the rest of western Europe and across the seas to the United States and Japan.

Industrialization went along with progress in science and medicine. New discoveries in these fields brought better health and more comfort. They also changed people's ideas about human beginnings, development, and feelings about one another. Literature, art, music, and architecture also showed the great changes of the 1800s. This chapter tells how:

● The effect of rapid industrialization on the workers is told in Chapter 27.

1. The Industrial Revolution changed the Western world.

2. Science and medicine progressed rapidly.

3. The arts showed great energy.

1 The Industrial Revolution changed the Western world

Historians once viewed the changes that began in the late 1700s as *the* Industrial Revolution. They decided that it was a "cataclysm followed by a catastrophe." That is, new machines suddenly appeared and began the factory system, which cruelly used men, women, and children. ● All these things were supposed to have happened in just a few decades.

It is now known that this picture was not a really true one. The most important point about the so-called Industrial Revolution is the way that power-driven machinery took the place of hand tools in manufacturing. Thus, it had no certain beginning and has not yet ended.

Many new inventions appeared in the 18th and 19th centuries. They came from hundreds of years of work and discovery in many countries. The search for new machines and new kinds of power to run them still goes on.

However, the idea of an Industrial Revolution is a useful one. It shows that in a rather short time—about 200 years—the Western economy grew very rapidly. This great speedup was first seen in England between about 1760 and 1830. It began in Germany in the 1860s, the United States in the 1870s, and Russia in the 1890s. Many parts of the world have not yet had an industrial revolution.

ans. 1 **Several conditions in England favored industrialization.** First, England had good natural resources. The land held rich deposits of coal and iron. From short, swift rivers came the water power to keep machines moving. Ships that carried finished goods around the world moved easily in and out of British harbors. English wool and cotton from the colonies were the raw materials for a growing textile industry.

Second, England had a large labor force. In the 1700s, England's population had doubled. New ways of farming meant more food to feed the larger numbers of factory workers in the cities. Also, the British were leaders in inventing machines and in training people to use them. As a result, the workers were more skilled and educated than were workers on the continent.

Third, resources and a good labor force were put together by business people who had the money (capital) to buy the new machines and build the new factories. For centuries, the English had been building up capital from farming, handwork, and overseas trade. Some of that money went into joint-stock companies. After 1750, business people and landowners put back into companies even more of their gains. Therefore, businesses had money to buy equipment for a large number of new workers.

Fourth, markets were waiting for the finished goods. British goods found markets at home. There, the greater numbers of people needed much more food, clothing, and housing. Colonies abroad also were markets. And the Napoleonic wars increased the need for homegrown food and iron and steel goods.

Fifth, the government of 18th-century England helped industrialism grow. During the 1600s, trade was slow. The English government felt that any great business changes would hurt the economy. Therefore, government rules held down businesses. Profits were heavily taxed. And any inventions that might put people out of work were not allowed.

In the 1700s, however, markets opened. Foreign and home trade grew rapidly. Businesses were freer. Taxes on profits were lower. And the manufacture of new machines was actually wanted.

The English Parliament allowed great changes in the landholding system so that roads and canals could be built. And it gave patents to protect inventors' work. The British navy protected merchant sailors around the world. At home, a well-run legal system kept the roads free of robbers and promised justice for business people in the courts.

Finally, British society was rather mobile. That is, a poor person who worked hard and saved money might become wealthy. That person or a family member then could marry a landowner or a noble. Thus, business and industry grew because talented people could better themselves in it. The upper classes had long been in trade. The oldest son of a family took his father's noble title. The younger sons often turned to business. So work was not looked down upon.

Machines for the textile industry helped begin the factory system. Most goods before the late 1700s were made with hand tools in small shops or in people's homes. The domestic system, or cottage industry, was quite often used in textile manufacture. Managers handed out the raw materials. Workers spun the yarn and wove the cloth at home.

In the early 1700s, new city dwellers and markets abroad wanted so much cotton cloth that workers could not meet the need. In 1733, English weaver John Kay made a flying shuttle,

● You can use the geography essay on p. 479 to help make this point.

■ Invention are sometimes developed in response to an existing need. Sometimes inventions create needs (cotton gin created a need for more slaves).

Geography: A Key to History

Resources and Industrial Development

Industrial development cannot take place just anywhere. It needs a place where raw materials and power can be easily obtained, where a large population is available to work in industry, where money is available to invest in machines and factories, and where the markets for goods can be easily reached. Conditions in 18th-century England met all of these requirements, and it was in England that the Industrial Revolution began.

England's development as an industrial nation was greatly aided by the presence of mineral resources. England had rich, well-placed coal fields and iron ore deposits. Coal was used to convert iron ore into iron or steel and to provide power for machines.

Both coal and iron ore are costly and bulky to ship. In England, shipping costs were kept low because business people built industrial centers near the coal and iron mines. Manchester, Sheffield, and Birmingham became great industrial cities.

Some raw materials and finished goods, however, had to be shipped between ocean ports or inland areas and the centers of industry. A low-cost system of transportation was needed. Canals and, later, railroads were constructed to link port cities such as Liverpool and London with the industrial cities. Thus, England gained an early lead in industrialization.

France and Germany also had deposits of coal and iron ore. These were linked by a network of rivers, canals, and railroads, and the two countries became the industrial leaders in continental Europe. In North America, the northeastern United States became similarly industrialized.

Certain other places lacked one or more of the resources that favored industrial growth. South America had almost no coal. It did have rich deposits of iron ore, but many of them were hard to reach. Africa also lacked coal; so did the Mediterranean region of Europe. These circumstances help explain why some places did not become industrialized. Since the 1930s, other mineral resources have become increasingly important. Today, industrialization is taking place in areas that were once thought of as unsuitable.

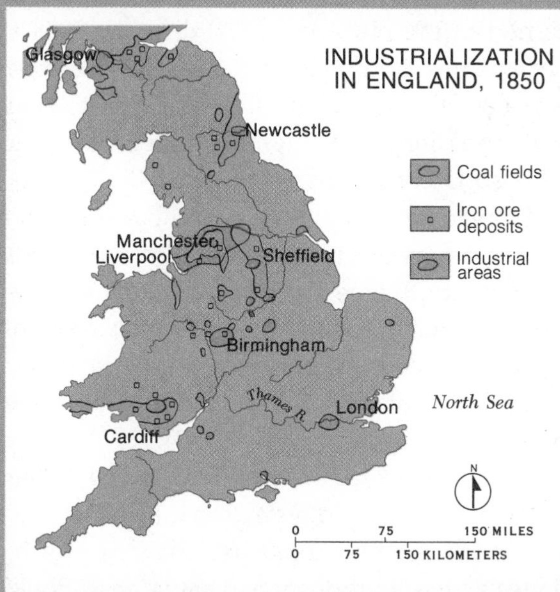

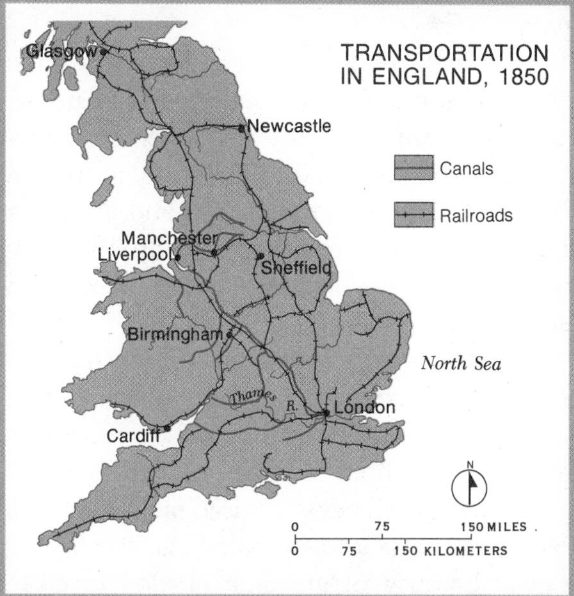

HISTORY IN THE MOVIES

OLIVER!

The Artful Dodger picks a pocket while his friend watches for trouble. Such events were not uncommon in 19th century England, where children sometimes had to steal to survive. These horrible lives were vividly described in Dickens's *Oliver Twist,* which was the basis for this movie musical.

which cut weaving time in half. Now the problem was that spinners could not supply enough yarn.

Then in 1769, two important inventions, the spinning jenny and the water-powered frame, provided yarn faster. By 1779, jenny-spinner Samuel Crompton had found a way to use the best parts of the spinning jenny and the water frame together in one machine. By 1830, his water-driven spinning mule had become a steam-driven machine.

These inventions ended the "famine in yarn." For a while, the weavers caused a jam. But by 1800, Edmund Cartwright's power loom was at work throughout England.

The new machines were used most in making cotton cloth. Raw cotton came into the market slowly because of the time needed to clean seeds from the cotton bolls. When New Englander Eli Whitney went to Georgia in 1793, he learned of the problem. In 10 days, he built a machine, the cotton gin, that could clean cotton as fast as 50 pairs of hands. By 1820, cotton led all exports from the southern United States. It was also Great Britain's chief import.

Manufacturers lowered costs by grouping machines together in factories close to sources of power. Both time and money were saved because workers no longer had materials brought to them. Instead, workers went to the factories. There they kept set hours and did not waste raw materials.

The so-called factory system allowed better control of quality and a steadier rate of production. Manufacturers could use such new techniques as mass production. That is, they could make large numbers of the same sizes by dividing labor in a way not possible in the domestic system.

Iron and steel manufacture was improved. The many new machines called for larger amounts of iron. Most early iron-making was done with charcoal, which was slow and costly. (Also, making charcoal was destroying English
ans. 2 forests.) In 1735, Abraham Darby began to make iron ore with coke—purified coal. The iron industry then moved from forest areas to coal regions.

In the 1780s, Henry Cort, a contractor for the British navy, made two discoveries. By "puddling," or stirring, molten iron with long rods in a furnace, he could quickly burn off many impurities and make a large amount of wrought iron. Also, by passing hot iron through heavy rollers he could squeeze out further impurities and make iron sheets.

In 1856, Sir Henry Bessemer found a way to burn off impurities in molten iron to make steel, which was stronger and generally more useful. Ten years later, an Englishman, Sir William Siemens, and a Frenchman, Pierre Emile Martin, built an open-hearth furnace for making a greater range of steels.

Great steel centers grew up near large reserves of coal and iron ore in northern England, the Ruhr valley in Germany, and the Pittsburgh area in Pennsylvania. The many tons of iron and steel these centers turned out were then used to make bigger machines with more parts. Farmers in the western United States used machines instead of people to grow food on many acres of rich soil. Cyrus McCormick's horse-drawn grain reaper and Hiram and John Pitts's threshing and winnowing machine appeared in the 1830s. John Deere built an all-steel plow in 1847. In the 1880s, the reaper and thresher became one machine, the combine. Farm machines such as these helped open up the huge plains of America and, later, of Europe.

Transportation became faster and cheaper. Moving about in the early 1700s was little different from getting around during the Middle Ages. Roads were bad, and traveling on horseback was slow and uncomfortable.

The work of two Scottish engineers, Thomas Telford and John McAdam, greatly improved
travel after 1770. Both worked for better drain- ans. 3
age of roads and the use of layers of crushed rock. McAdam's money-saving plan, known as macadamizing, formed the base for all modern road building.

Waterways also changed. Rivers were made deeper to accept large ships. And in 1761, one of the first modern canals was dug. The Duke of Bridgewater built the seven-mile (4.2-kilometer) canal to link some of his coal mines with the city of Manchester. This watercourse worked so well that the price of coal in Manchester dropped by 80 percent. After that, canal-building began all over England. By 1830, the country had one of the best inland waterway systems in the Western world. In the United States, the Erie Canal was finished by 1825.

Meanwhile, the steam engine had appeared. Taking his ideas from work done in the 1600s, an Englishman, Thomas Newcomen, invented a steam engine. From about 1705 on, Newcomen engines were widely used for pumping water out of mines. It was a model of one of these engines that James Watt repaired in 1763. His new engine, patented in 1769, was much more efficient than Newcomen's. In 1781, Watt found a way to suit the engine to rotary motion. Then it could be used to run machines.

● The chapter opener p. 476 gives more information on Watt's invention.

In the mid-1700s, donkeys pulled carts on iron rails around English coal mines. Richard Trevithick, an English mining engineer, thought that a steam engine on wheels would be better than animal power. Trevithick built two such engines in the early 1800s, but they were used only at mines.

In 1825, mining engineer George Stephenson built a locomotive that could do the work of 40 teams of horses. When a group of business people decided to build a railway between Liverpool and Manchester, they offered a prize for the best locomotive. Stephenson won the prize in 1829 with his Rocket. It pulled a train 31 miles (18.6 kilometers) at an average speed of 14 miles (8.4 kilometers) an hour.

Stephenson set off a railroad-building boom in England that reached its peak in the 1840s. By 1850, the most important routes were built, and freight trains ran steadily. Western Europe and the United States began building railroads in the mid-1800s.

Until about 1880, most ships still used wind and sail. A good supply of wood from the Americas and, after the 1830s, the use of iron hulls kept building costs low. Therefore, sailing vessels could offer very low rates.

In 1838, a British ship, the *Sirius,* crossed from Liverpool to New York under steam alone in 18 days. By 1850, fast ocean-going steamers ran at uniform times. They did a good business in mail and passenger traffic. But only after such inventions as the screw propeller did steamers begin to take the place of sailing vessels for carrying cargo.

Capitalism changed. During the Commercial Revolution, trade and commerce gave rise

Traveling in the 1800s
The Industrial Revolution changed transportation. In 1807, Fulton's steamship *Clermont (left)* made its first voyage up the Hudson River. It took 32 hours to go 150 miles (240 kilometers) from New York to Albany. After the Erie Canal *(below)* was completed in 1825, freight and passengers could go from New

to mercantile capitalism. As industrialism grew in the 1700s, capitalism changed to suit new kinds of business. Called industrial capitalism, it was usually based on small companies managed directly by their owners.

Some industries, such as railroads and iron and steel companies, needed huge amounts of capital to buy machines and tools. No one person had so much capital. Therefore, some kind of joint firm was needed.

ans. 4 The joint-stock companies that had formed during the Commercial Revolution had generally been used for overseas trade and colonization. They were also closely limited by government charters. During the 1800s, a looser kind of group, the corporation, was born. It could own property, and bring and defend suits at law. And it continued even though shareholders and directors changed.

By the end of the 1800s, many large businesses were corporations. They were managed not by their owners but by salaried people who used other persons' money. Banks and financiers became quite important because of the large amounts of capital needed. Therefore, in terms of economics, the time after 1850 is known as finance capitalism.

SECTION REVIEW **1**

1. What six conditions favored industrialization in England? p. 478

2. How was iron and steel manufacture improved? What effect did this have on agriculture? p. 481

3. What advances in transportation took place? What effect did they have? p. 481

4. What is the difference between a joint-stock company and a corporation? p. 483

York to Chicago or New Orleans on barges pulled by mules. Railroads provided faster transportation than ever dreamed of. By the end of the century, Western Europe and the United States were crisscrossed with rail lines. *Opposite* and *below* are upper-class passengers and coaches of the Liverpool—Manchester lines in England.

2 Science and medicine progressed rapidly

Industrialism grew fast because people became more willing to work in new ways. That willing spirit also led to important discoveries in science and medicine. In the 1800s, most Europeans were sure that science was the key to unlocking nature's secrets. Then all the dreams of material progress would come true.

Chemists and physicists made important discoveries. Chemistry got a new base because of the work of John Dalton, an English ans. 1 schoolteacher in the early 1800s. Dalton, like the Greek philosopher Democritus, believed that all matter is made of tiny pieces called atoms. He thought further that all atoms in any one chemical element are alike. And he thought that each element's atoms have a weight different from any other's atoms. Dalton said that in chemical compounds, atoms join into units (now called molecules). He made up a kind of chemical formula to describe them.

During the next 50 years, chemists discovered more elements and improved the ways of joining them. In 1869, Russian Dmitri Mendelyeev [men′də ā′əf] drew up the Periodic Table. In it, he put into families by atomic weight all the known elements (62 then). With this chart, he showed gaps where other elements might be and later were found.

Important discoveries in physics helped prove that electricity, magnetism, heat, and light were closely connected. In 1800, Alessandro Volta made one of the first batteries. Hans Christian Oersted [ėr′sted] of Denmark discovered electromagnetism in 1820. He found that electric current flowing through a wire would move a compass needle that lay next to it.

Further work on the connection between electricity and magnetism was done by English scientist Michael Faraday. In 1831, he showed that electric current could be made by moving a wire through the lines of force of a magnetic field. From Faraday's discovery, the first dynamo, came the electric generator.

In the 1860s, Scottish scientist James Clerk Maxwell made up exact mathematical equations to explain Faraday's work. With Maxwell's equations, physicists showed that radiant heat and other invisible kinds of radiation were also electromagnetic waves.

In 1885, German Heinrich Hertz found and measured the speed of what were later called radio waves. Another German, Wilhelm Roentgen [rent′gən], in 1895 discovered rays that could pass through solids. He called them X rays. While looking for rays like these, Pierre and Marie Curie discovered the element radium in 1898. Their discovery of this radioactive element was a high point in the new field of atomic physics.

New scientific discoveries led to inventions. In 1832, in the United States, Samuel Morse made the first electric telegraph. Another American, Alexander Graham Bell, patented the telephone in 1876. And American Thomas A. Edison made the first useful electric light in 1879. Italian Guglielmo Marconi's wireless telegraph began service across the English Channel in 1898. Three years later, messages were sent across the Atlantic. All these inventions brought together the new worldwide economy and helped cities grow.

Many of the discoveries of pure science helped solve industry's problems. During the 1800s, chemists broke down nearly 70 thousand chemical compounds. From this work

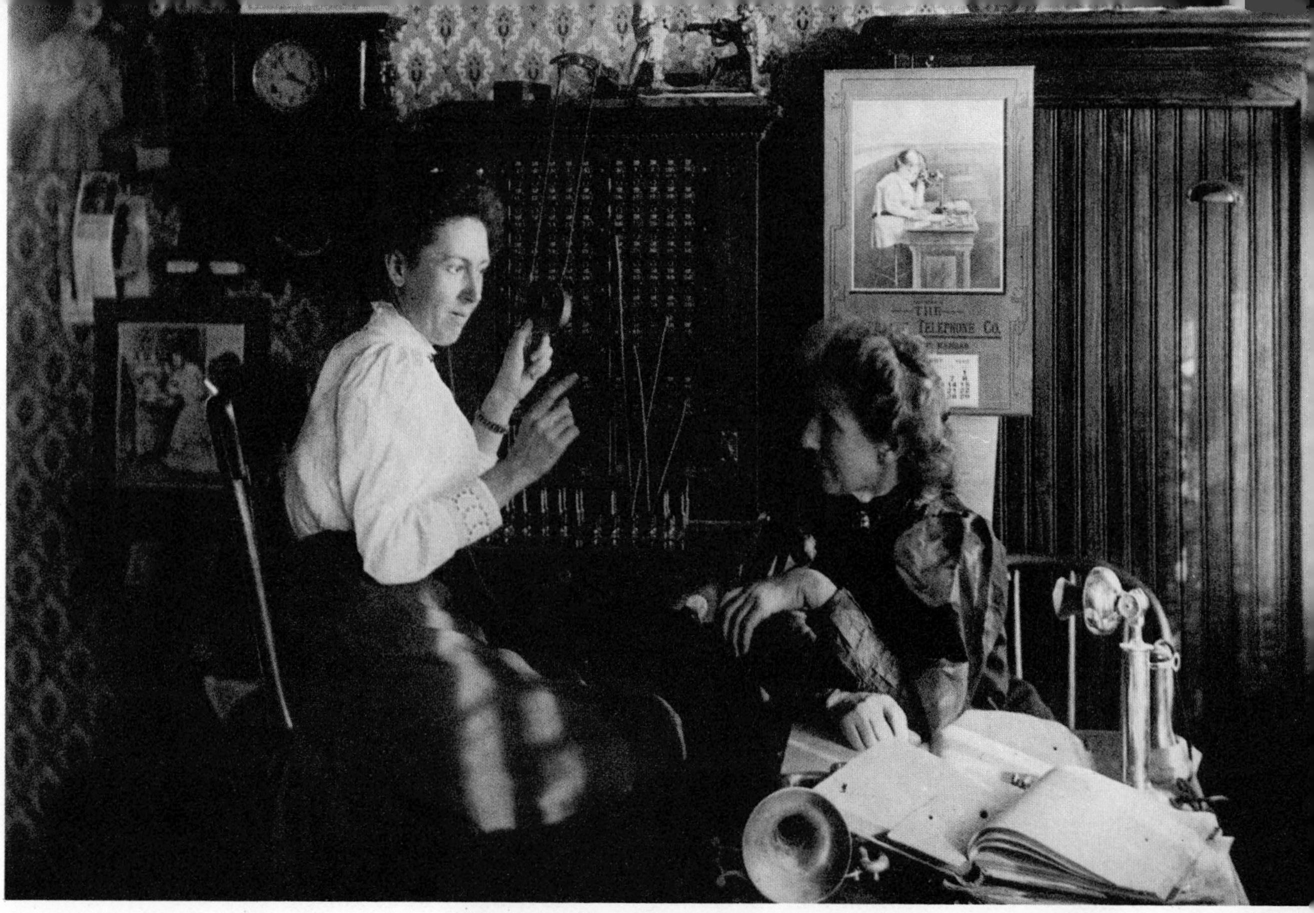

Alexander Graham Bell invented the telephone in 1876. The photograph *opposite* was taken when he completed the first long-distance call, between New York and Chicago. By 1910, the scene *above* was common across the United States as telephone operators connected each call by hand.

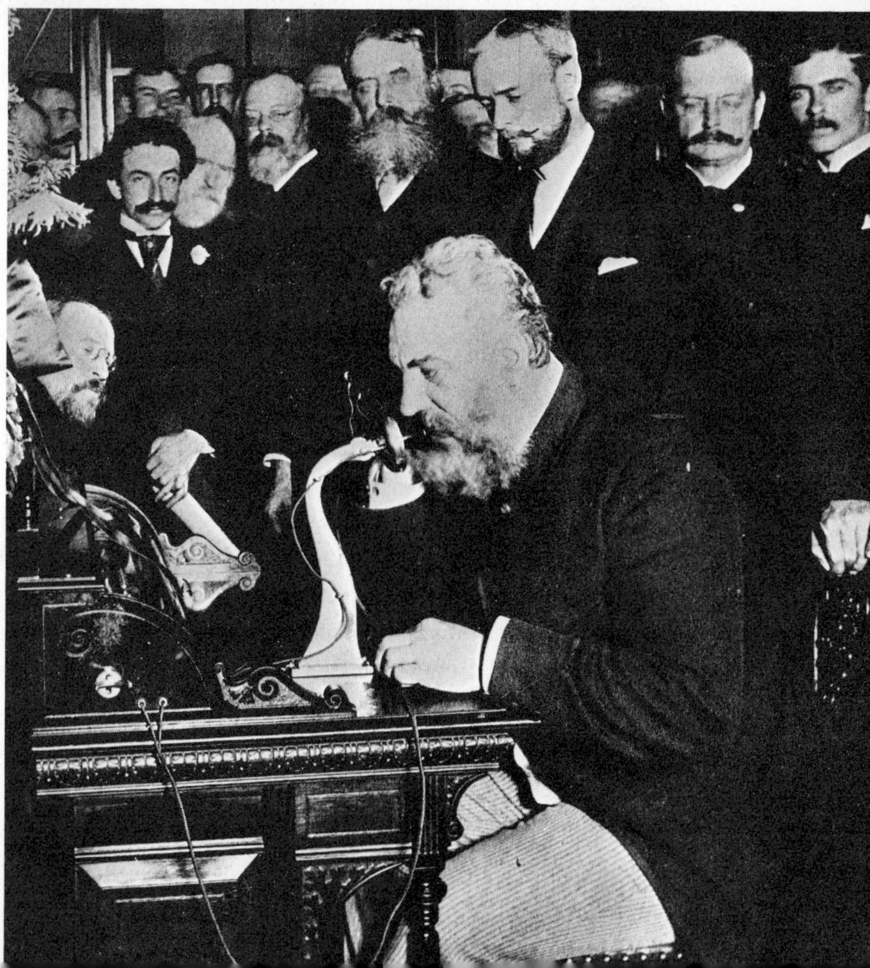

came portland cement, vulcanized rubber, synthetic dyes, and many other products.

Building on the work of Faraday and others, inventors made electric generators that turned out steady amounts of electricity cheaply. Soon, electricity was used to power trolley cars, trains, and ships. Engineers quickly made electric motors to power machines in factories.

Rich natural resources were turned into power. Fuel gas had been known since ancient times. However, it was not commercially made
ans. 2 and used until the late 1700s. Then English and French scientists made it useful for lighting. London, in 1807, became the first city to light streets with gas.

Petroleum gave rise to a new industry in the middle 1800s. The United States soon took the lead. At first, petroleum was used chiefly for lubrication and for making kerosene. Then in the 1860s and 1870s, scientists in France, Germany, and Austria began to build internal combustion engines. The more advanced of these engines used gasoline for fuel.

From then on, the by-product gasoline became petroleum's most important use. Gasoline engines were made lighter and finally powered the automobile.

Another type of internal combustion machine, the diesel engine, was patented in 1892. It ran on fuel oils instead of gasoline. The engine was widely used in ships and locomotives. It was heavier than the gasoline engine, but it was cheaper to run.

● **Medical research helped people live long-
ans. 3 er.** English physician Edward Jenner gave modern medicine a great push when he used vaccination to protect against smallpox. For centuries, the disease had been feared and often was deadly. In 1796, he inoculated a boy with the virus of cowpox (a mild form of smallpox). When the boy was later inoculated with smallpox, he did not become ill.

Surgery gained from new discoveries in chemistry. Until the mid-1800s, operations were painful and patients were held down by force. In 1846, W. T. G. Morton, a Boston dentist, publicly showed the value of ether during an operation at Massachusetts General Hospital. News of his work helped an Englishman, Sir James Simpson, who taught medicine at the University of Edinburgh, to discover chloroform. Anesthetics made surgery painless and made medical research on living animals possible.

Operations became less feared. However, surgery was still very often fatal because of infection. Sterilization was unknown. Surgeons wore their operating coats for years before washing them. Most of them did not understand the cause of infection.

It was French scientist Louis Pasteur who finally proved that microscopic organisms cause infectious diseases. In the 1850s, Pasteur began a study of fermentation. He found the cause to be certain bacteria. His heating process (later named pasteurization) slowed down fermentation. In other studies, Pasteur discovered several vaccines, including the one for rabies.

German scientist Robert Koch discovered each of the germs that cause eleven diseases, including tuberculosis and cholera.

Working with the new germ theory of disease, English surgeon Joseph Lister searched for a chemical antiseptic. He wanted to destroy bacteria and make surgery safe as well as painless. In the 1860s, he found that a mild carbolic acid solution was best for sterilizing hands, instruments, wounds, and dressings. Lister's discoveries are said to have saved more lives than were lost in all the wars of the 1800s.

● Discuss the differences between medical care before and after these advances.

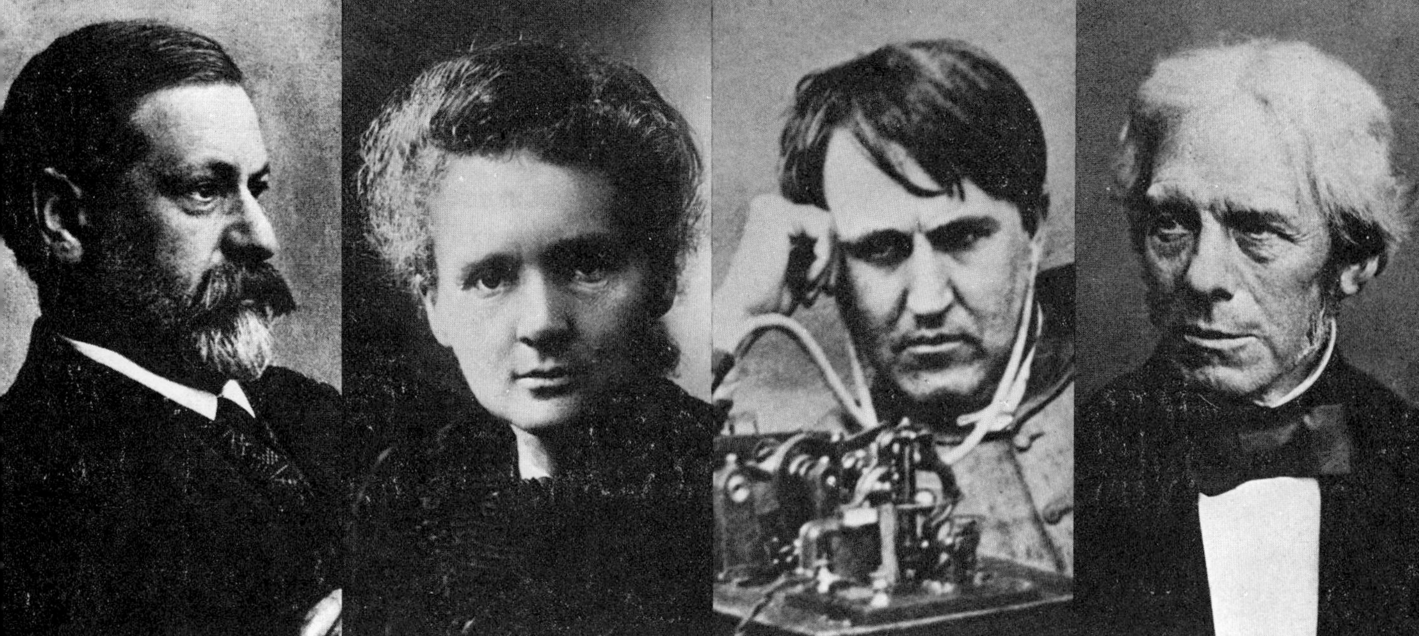

SIGMUND FREUD MARIE CURIE THOMAS EDISON MICHAEL FARRADAY

Like the discoveries in modern agriculture and industry, discoveries in medicine helped people live longer. Because of these discoveries, cities could grow, and city dwellers could live healthy lives.

Biology changed ideas. Ever since the ancient Greeks, there were philosophers who believed that the earth and living things had evolved from simple to complex forms. In the 19th century, the English naturalist Charles ● Darwin developed a theory to explain why there was such a variety of plant and animal types and why some types had disappeared ans. 4 while others lived on. He suggested that, because animals multiply faster than their food supply, they are always fighting to live. Those that live must be in some way better fitted to live in their environment than are those that die. So the fittest live on to bring forth another generation that is adapted in the same way. Darwin called nature's way of choosing "the principle of natural selection."

These three ideas—the fight to live, the survival of the fittest, and natural selection—formed the base of Darwin's theory of evolution. For more than 20 years, he carefully gathered facts to support his theory. In 1859, his findings appeared in *The Origin of Species by Means of Natural Selection.*

Darwin's theory said that, in a way, all living things evolved from simpler forms over the ages of time. In *The Descent of Man* (1871), Darwin wrote that human beings and apes had the same ancestor.

Just as the 16th-century scientists had touched off a storm of protest when they said the earth was not the center of the universe, Darwin's ideas were the topic of arguments all over 19th-century Europe. The churches felt he went against the Bible's story of creation.

The defenders and enemies of Darwinism fought for half a century. Finally many persons, even church people, came to feel that science dealt with some parts of human life and religion with others. They decided that people could accept both Darwinism and Christianity.

What Darwin did not explain well was the way in which characteristics are passed on. Gregor Mendel, an Austrian monk, did pioneering

● Some students might like to do additional research into Darwin's work on the Galapagos Islands, where he made his first observations of natural selection.

MARY SHELLEY | CHARLES DICKENS | GEORGE ELIOT | PERCY BYSSHE SHELLEY

work in that field. His careful work with plants showed that passed-on characteristics are carried by tiny things now called genes. Mendel's laws of heredity did not become widely known when he first stated them in the 1860s. Later, they became the base of the science of genetics.

Psychology became a science. Modern psychology, the science of human behavior, grew from the work of doctors who studied people's conscious lives. They were quite interested in the ways the senses worked. In the 1890s, Russian Ivan Pavlov went much further. In his experiments, he gave food to a dog while he rang a bell. Food and bell became very closely joined in the dog's mind. Finally, the dog watered at the mouth when a bell was rung, even when no food was present.

Pavlov's work with dogs changed scientists' ideas about people. Many of them took the view that people often acted in response to stimuli. •

Most important of all was the work of a Viennese doctor, Sigmund Freud. He believed that people often act because of unknown needs and desires. In the 1890s, he used psychoanalysis to bring out hidden motives. Freud's theory explained how these hidden motives worked. As a result, people began to learn about the impulses that direct their behavior. Freud's ideas gave understanding of human beings a new direction and provided new ways of treating mental illness.

• See if students can think of any examples of this response in animals or humans.

SECTION REVIEW 2

1. What chemical advances did John Dalton and Dmitri Mendelyeev make? p. 484

2. How did discoveries about natural gas change transportation? p. 486

3. How did discoveries about antiseptics, vaccination, anesthetics, and fermentation change medical knowledge? p. 486

4. What was Darwin's theory of evolution? p. 487

3 The arts showed great energy

Literature and the fine arts in the 1800s were very much alive. Here, too, industrialism clearly

EDGAR ALLAN POE JOHANNES BRAHMS PETER ILICH TCHAIKOVSKY GIUSEPPE VERDI

was felt. Some writers and artists firmly turned their backs on their own fast-moving, mixed-up world. They favored a dream life, the strange, or the past. Others tried to understand and describe the forces that were changing society.

As the middle class grew in size and power, it became more important as a sounding board for creative works. Artists, writers, and musicians no longer depended on wealthy patrons. As a result, they were freer in using their own ideas in many different art forms.

Romanticism ruled the early 1800s. Toward the end of the 1700s, people began to turn against the firm hold of reason that had marked the Enlightenment. Several artists and thinkers took a different view, called *romanticism*. ●

ans. 1 Romantics believed that people must pay attention to feelings they did not fully control. Feelings of love and the touch of beauty or religion, they said, could not be explained in rational terms alone. Romantics believed above all that art must mirror the artist's self in the artist's own way. Romanticism was, in another sense, a turning away from the ugly and materialistic side of the new industrial society.

● The various artistic movements of this period may need careful clarification for some students. They may be best taught by having students experience typical works either through museum visits or library research.

In literature, writers let their imaginations run freely. Liberty was an important theme. A German movement known as *Sturm und Drang* (Storm and Stress) praised inner direction and defiance of power. Among its members was Johann Friedrich von Schiller. His drama *William Tell* dealt with the Swiss fight for freedom. Johann Wolfgang von Goethe in the early 1800s wrote the epic human drama *Faust*. English poets Lord Byron and Percy Bysshe Shelley also showed a spirit of rebellion.

Romantics believed that beauty should rule life, as English poet John Keats wrote in "Ode on a Grecian Urn."

> "Beauty is truth, truth beauty,"—that is all
> Ye know on earth, and all ye need to know.

An important romantic theme was nature. However, nature was not orderly and mechanical, as 18th-century thinkers pictured it. Instead, it had a wild beauty.

The romantics thought, as did the French social philosopher Jean Jacques Rousseau, that simple (primitive) people were noble and good because civilization had not spoiled them. So romantics became quite interested in myths, fairy tales, and folk songs. Some collections of these stories and songs, such as the Grimm brothers' fairy tales, are treasures of the Romantic Movement.

Because reason was not enough, some romantics took their ideas from unknown worlds, such as dreams. Examples are English Samuel Taylor Coleridge's poem, "The Rime of the Ancient Mariner" (1797) and American Edgar Allan Poe's poetry.

Interest in the strange led the romanticists back to the Middle Ages, which they saw as a golden time of brave and just deeds, romance, and adventure. Such feelings are written into the novels of the Scotchman Sir Walter Scott and the French author Victor Hugo.

Painting, like literature, mirrored romantic ideas. French Eugene Delacroix [də lä krwä′], a master of color, painted strange scenes. Some of his subjects came from the revolts of the 1820s and 1830s. Painters in England, like poets, found subjects in nature. The works of John Constable and J. M. W. Turner were fresh and dramatic. Other landscape painters of the time thought these works revolutionary.

Romanticism in architecture was seen in a return to the Gothic style of the Middle Ages. In France and Germany, much work was done in repairing medieval buildings. In England, churches, houses, and public buildings were covered with pointed arches, flying buttresses, and turrets.

Romanticism in music, as in the other arts, meant a break with old forms. Composers added to 18th-century forms in order to say more with their music. For example, the symphony became much longer and had more parts. The orchestra grew in size, and many instruments were made easier to play. The piano, which allowed changes in tone, took the harpsichord's place. All of these changes appeared in the music of Ludwig van Beethoven. His grand symphonies and chamber music bridged classicism and romanticism.

The romantics' music was quite emotional. Franz Schubert wrote hundreds of songs that covered a wide range of feelings. Romantic music was marked, too, by the use of subjects from folk music. And the solo performer became very important. Two composer-pianists who used folk subjects in their works were Frédéric Chopin [shō′pan] and Franz Liszt.

Later movements turned against romanticism. In the mid-1800s, some overdone romantic art caused people to turn against its ideals. Much of the art had become simply poured-out feelings.

In literature, realism became a popular form. Realists, like the romantics, knew about the bad social conditions of their times. But as romantics ans. 2 tried to run from life, realists tried to show it as it was. Possibly the best known of these was an Englishman, Charles Dickens. His pictures of ● poor and put-upon people called attention to needed reforms. *Oliver Twist* showed the hard lives of children in workhouses and slums. *Nicholas Nickleby* and *David Copperfield* pointed out wrongs in education. *Bleak House* dealt with the social evils of the legal system.

In France, Honoré de Balzac wrote more than 90 novels for a series, *The Human Comedy*. The stories presented a searching picture of lower- and middle-class French life. Many of his novels attacked greed and social climbing.

Humorist Mark Twain described American middle-western and frontier life. At the same

● An excerpt from Dicken's *Hard Times* opens Chapter 27.

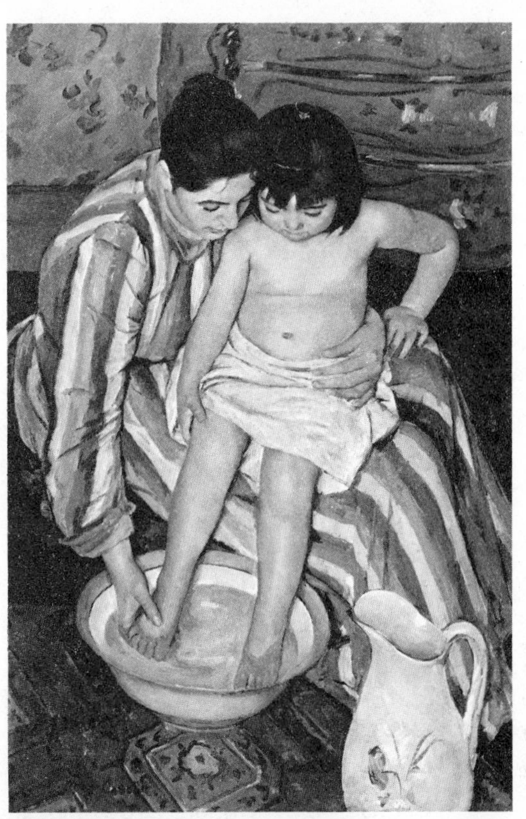

Romantic landscape artist John Constable painted the English countryside. "The Hay Wain," *above,* was painted in 1821. The French impressionist Claude Monet used short, choppy strokes to capture the appearance of sunlight on the water in "The Frog Pond," *below,* painted in 1869. American Mary Cassatt joined the impressionists in Paris and spent a long career painting. The theme of mother and child was a favorite of hers. "The Bath," *opposite,* was painted in 1892.

time, his writings made clear the evils of slavery and other social wrongs.

A Norwegian, Henrik Ibsen, wrote realistic drama in a new way. Through it, he presented many problems that until then could not be talked about in public. In his well-known play *A Doll's House,* he attacked marriage without love as immoral.

Other realistic writers centered their works on the characters they drew so well. In *Madame Bovary,* French Gustave Flaubert [flō bär′] described a weak woman whose downfall was romantic love. The works of two Russian novelists show deep understanding of the self. Feodor Dostoevski [dos′ tə yef′skē] wrote *Crime and Punishment.* Leo Tolstoy wrote *War and Peace* and *Anna Karenina.* English authors William Makepeace Thackeray, George Eliot (Mary Ann Evans), and Robert Browning showed keen insight into personality and deep interest in their characters' lives.

The naturalist group of writers tried to describe life as scientists would. They thought that writers should tell their stories without comment or feeling. From 1871 to 1893, a Frenchman, Émile Zola, wrote about families in 20 novels that are almost like a doctor's case books.

In painting, Gustave Courbet [kür be′], son of a French peasant, spoke for realism. He believed in painting people and places as they were. He once stated that he did not paint angels because he had never seen one. Courbet stirred other painters to break with the romantic and begin a movement known as impressionism.

ans. 3 The impressionists worked out new ways to put light and color into their paintings. They tried to present a single moment in time, before their own feelings changed it. French painters in this style were Claude Monet, Edgar Degas, and August Renoir.

Other artists, though, turned away from impressionism. In France, Paul Cézanne [sā zan′], led post-impressionists in the study of form and space. Dutch artist Vincent van Gogh used bright colors and bold outlines to show his strong feelings about people and places.

Architects in the time of realism left Gothic ans. 4
models in favor of more original styles. New building materials such as steel, reinforced concrete, and strong glass, helped in making the changes. In the United States, Louis Sullivan based his work on the idea that buildings must suit their functions. A modern bank, he said, should not look like a Greek temple. A warehouse was *not* a medieval castle. Sullivan was an early builder of skyscrapers, which put together new materials and new designs.

Music in the late 1800s showed several influences. German composer Johannes Brahms remained a romantic in his symphonies. Italian Giuseppe Verdi, also a romantic, composed such operas as *Rigoletto, La Traviata,* and *Aida.* Strong nationalist feeling is clear in the work of German Richard Wagner. His music dramas are based on German folk tales. Russians made up a school of nationalist composers. Peter Ilich Tchaikovsky and others drew on Russian folk music in their compositions. The French composer Claude Debussy, an impressionist, filled his music with bright, shimmering effects.

SECTION REVIEW **3**

1. What was romanticism? p. 489
2. How was realism different from romanticism? p. 490
3. Describe the style of painting known as impressionism. p. 492
4. How did architectural styles change? p. 492

CHAPTER REVIEW 26

SECTION SUMMARIES

1. The Industrial Revolution changed the Western world. The Industrial Revolution began in England, where conditions were quite favorable. The rise of industrialism was aided by a doubling of population, which meant workers for the new factories. Economic life was changed by new inventions and methods. In the important textile industry in England, a rapid move from hand to machine work began the factory system. Especially important were changes in iron and steel manufacture and farming by machines. Improved transportation—better roads, canals, railroads, and steamships—knit regions more closely together. Capitalism itself changed to suit new conditions. Old ways of organizing business gave over to industrial and then finance capitalism.

2. Science and medicine progressed rapidly. Meanwhile, the scientific spirit spilled out an ever flowing stream of new discoveries to add to people's knowledge of the world. Dalton's work began a chain of discoveries in chemistry and physics that brought great changes in a few decades. Inventors such as Morse, Bell, Edison, and Marconi helped make a line of communications that would ring the world. Others found new power sources, such as gas and petroleum. In medicine, one of the greatest changes came with Pasteur's germ theory of disease. Because of it, age-old enemies, such as tuberculosis, were defeated. New chemicals helped make surgery painless as well as safer. The theories of Darwin, Mendel, and Freud opened up other fields for scientific study.

3. The arts showed great energy. The ongoing changes of the time were mirrored in literature and other arts. The ordered neoclassicism of the Age of Reason gave way to romanticism. Most of the arts felt its hold until the mid-1800s. From then on, a large number of forms and movements rose and fell. Among them were the literary realism of Dickens, Flaubert, and Zola; the impressionistic painting of Monet and Renoir; Sullivan's functional architecture; and Tchaikovsky's nationalistic music.

WHO? WHAT? WHEN? WHERE?

1. Find the period in which each invention, discovery, or book listed below appeared:

a. 1751–1800
b. 1801–1850
c. 1851–1900

Coleridge's "Rime of the Ancient Mariner" a.
Deere's all-steel plow b.
Edison's electric light c.
macadamizing a.
Pasteur's rabies vaccine c.
Morse's telegraph b.
Flaubert's *Madame Bovary* c.
Watt's steam engine a.
spinning jenny a.
Dickens's *Oliver Twist* b.
Darwin's *The Origin of Species by Means of Natural Selection* c.

2. What contribution did each of these people make?

McCormick 481	Jenner p. 486	Koch p. 486
Bessemer p. 481	Roentgen p. 484	Lister p. 486
McAdam p. 481	Marconi p. 484	Mendel p. 487
Freud p. 488	Cartwright p. 480	Faraday p. 484
the Curies p. 484	Whitney p. 480	Mendelyeev p. 484

3. Tell whether these writers were romanticists, realists, or naturalists and explain why each is so classified:

Dickens p. 490	Eliot p. 492	Twain p. 490
Ibsen p. 492	Balzac p. 490	Scott p. 490

CHAPTER TEST 26

● **4.** Which of these were romanticists, realists, impressionists, or post-impressionists?

Delacroix	Courbet	Constable
Cézanne	Renoir	Monet

5. What kind of music did each of these composers write?

p. 490 Beethoven	Liszt p. 490	Brahms p. 492
p. 492 Tchaikovsky	Verdi p. 492	Chopin p. 490

QUESTIONS FOR CRITICAL THINKING

■ **1.** Why did the Industrial Revolution begin in England and not Germany or Russia?

2. Why did Charles Darwin's theories make religious leaders angry? How do some religions feel about the theory of evolution today? How do you feel about it?

3. Is the Industrial Revolution still going on today? If so, name recent developments.

ACTIVITIES

1. Report to the class on the life of the person you feel was the most important of this period. Include your ideas of why that person achieved what he or she did.

2. Write a diary of a 19th-century person. Include reactions to new developments and inventions and how these changed life.

3. Find pictures of paintings done in the different styles mentioned in this chapter. Write short paragraphs describing the differences in the paintings you have chosen.

4. Read passages to the class from one of the books named in this chapter. Read parts that show that the author was a romanticist, realist, or naturalist.

● 4. Delacroix and Constable were romanticists; Courbet, a realist; Renoir and Monet, impressionists; and Cezanne, a post-impressionist.

■ 1. See p. 478. Germany and Russia lacked the third, fourth, fifth and sixth factors mentioned

SECTION 1

1. True or false: By 1900, all nations had gone through an industrial revolution.

2. Which of these is not a reason the Industrial Revolution began in England? a. good natural resources, b. colonies to buy products, c. shortages of workers

3. Name the inventor who worked in the textile industry: a. Deere, b. Newcomen, c. Cartwright

4. Which of these discoveries happened first? a. the open-hearth furnace, b. the making of steel, c. "puddling" molten iron

5. Industrial capitalism was based on: a. small companies run by their owners, b. large corporations run by salaried managers, c. trade between weak nations

SECTION 2

6. One of the first batteries was made by: a. Watt, b. Roentgen, c. Volta

7. Morse's, Bell's, and Marconi's inventions improved: a. transportation, b. communication, c. agriculture

8. True or false: Before 1850, surgeons did not wash their operating coats often because they did not know about germs.

9. The scientist who proved that germs cause diseases was: a. Pasteur, b. Lister, c. Koch

SECTION 3

10. The artistic style that encouraged writers to express their own feelings was: a. realism, b. naturalism, c. romanticism

11. True or false: The novel *Oliver Twist* deals with the evils of slavery in France.

12. True or false: Louis Sullivan designed buildings to suit their functions, not to look like Greek temples or medieval castles.

1800–1914

CHAPTER 27

Social Protest and Mass Society

This backyard view of workers' houses in London was engraved by the French artist Gustave Doré for an 1830s book, *London—A Pilgrimmage* by Blanchard Jerrold. The view across rooftops and through the arch of a railroad bridge is one that could be seen from a train window.

It was a town of red brick, or of brick that would have been red if the smoke and ashes had allowed it; but as matters stood it was a town of unnatural red and black, like the painted face of a savage. . . . It had a black canal in it, and a river that ran purple with ill-smelling dye, and vast piles of buildings full of windows where there was a rattling and a trembling all day long, and where the piston of the steam-engine worked monotonously up and down, like the head of an elephant in a state of melancholy madness. It contained several large streets all very like one another, and many small streets still more like one another, inhabited by people

> equally like one another, who all went in and out at the same hours, with the same sound upon the same pavements, to do the same work, and to whom every day was the same as yesterday and tomorrow, and every year the counterpart of the last and the next.

This picture of a dirty, ugly industrial town and the deadly sameness of the lives of its people appeared in Charles Dickens's novel *Hard Times* (1854). ●

Dickens was one of several writers who managed to awaken the social conscience of the English people. Many others—social critics, church leaders, and well-doers—spoke out against the social evils of their time. This social protest movement covered Europe. Its roots were in the 1700s. Three great revolutions had centered attention on social problems.

The first was the intellectual movement known as the Enlightenment. It started the idea that social institutions must be studied to learn whether they did or did not help people in their natural right to seek life, liberty, and happiness.

The second was the French Revolution. It showed how the direct acts of the people could destroy the old feudal system and put in its place a republican government.

The third was the Industrial Revolution. In the long run, the steam engine, the factory, and the railroad changed society much more than had the French Revolution.

The rather swift change caused huge problems. For example, the new technology led to greater wealth. But many people thought that wealth was not fairly shared by everyone. Many stayed very poor, and others became very rich. The desire to share in the wealth brought bitter words and stronger social protest.

The three revolutions were all part of an even larger change. European society was turning into the first *mass civilization* the world had ever seen. And it took several forms.

A mass market grew for manufactured goods. Millions of new voters changed small political parties into huge, nationwide groups. Workers built labor unions with millions of members. Compulsory public schools began to educate millions of children. Mass-circulation newspapers appeared for the first time. Mass public transportation systems were built in all large cities. Mass spectator sports were born. In short, life as we know it today in the Western world—mass urban living—took shape in the late 1800s. This chapter tells how: ■

1. Urbanism and industrialism raised many problems.

2. Socialists asked for far-reaching changes.

3. An age of mass politics began.

4. An urban mass society grew.

1 Urbanism and industrialism raised many problems

The Industrial Revolution's strongest critics saw many evils. Those they marked as the seven deadly sins were: unhealthy, dangerous factories; impossibly long working hours; child labor; unjust use of women; low wages; slums; and repeated loss of jobs.

Growing cities had many different problems. In 1800, Europe was a giant farming community. No city anywhere held as many as a million people. By 1900, though, most western Europeans lived in great urban areas. Five

● *Hard Times* also contains a striking description of a public school of that time.

■ Key concept: mass civilization; explain the concept of mass civilization by adding to information above if necessary

Industry hired many children to work long hours for very little money. Children—some so small they had to climb onto the frames of the machines to reach their work—labored from 5:30 in the morning to 8 at night with only 40 minutes off for meals. Though they earned very little, their wages were needed by their families.

cities held over a million people. London alone had more than 6 1/2 million.

ans. 1 Rapidly growing old cities and those newly built brought many problems. Streets often were unpaved. Lighting was poor. Water supplies were too small. London had no police force until 1829. In 1838, the industrial city of Birmingham still used pigs to get rid of garbage from its 170 thousand people. Tuberculosis and epidemics of typhoid fever and other diseases ● ended many lives.

In view of today's standards, living conditions in the great industrial towns of the mid-1800s certainly were terrible. But city living then was better than it had been in the mid-1700s. And English industrial towns in the mid-1800s were less crowded and no dirtier than the great nonindustrial towns of other countries. Part of the blame for the large amount of disease in cities can be laid on the laws of the time. Because people had to pay taxes on windows and bricks, few were used in buildings. The buildings of the day were dark, airless, and fire hazards. Taxes on tiles slowed the laying of drains and sewers.

Workers labored under hard conditions. Working conditions in factories, mills, and mines were unhealthy and dangerous. With few safety devices on machines, there were many accidents. An injured worker almost never received compensation for loss of a leg or an arm.

Men, women, and children worked from 12 to 15 hours a day. In 1835, about a third of the factory workers in the cotton industry in England were young people. Half of them were under 14 years old.

Industrialization should not be blamed for all the social problems of the 19th century. Women and children, for example, quite often worked on farms and in cottage industries. The most cruelly used workers were in country villages, not in the growing manufacturing towns. In the towns, the worst working conditions were in small shops in cellars or garrets, not in factories that used steam power.

Servants' wages were lower than those of factory workers. Real wages remained low for unskilled factory workers. But they rose well for the large and growing numbers of skilled workers. Both diet and clothing improved.

Suffering and poverty were still there. But the hard conditions were not new and were not there simply because industrialism had arrived. What was new was an angry public awakened to the terrible conditions and a growing social consciousness that called for something to be done about them. This force was felt strongly first in England.

Business leaders favored the laissez-faire system. The Industrial Revolution made its own leaders. These bold middle-class men owned the railroads, mines, and factories that were so greatly changing the life of the times. They believed that government should in no ans. 2
way hold down business. And they favored the ideas of *laissez-faire capitalism.* (*Laissez-faire* [les′ā fār′] is French for "let do." In business, the term came to mean "let them do as they please.")

Adam Smith, a Scottish teacher, was the first important person to write favorably about capitalism. In *The Wealth of Nations* (1776), Smith stated that nations could gain wealth by removing such trade restrictions as tariffs. Then supply and demand could govern the exchange of goods.

Over twenty years later, Thomas Malthus, an English economist, made the laissez-faire idea

● In contrast the American Indian of 1492 had none of these problems.

much stronger with *An Essay on the Principles of Population* (1798). Malthus placed the blame for poverty on the growing population. If it went on growing, it would be larger than its food supply. Malthus's answer was that people should marry later in life and have fewer children. He believed, too, that social reforms would not help. They would simply lead to a larger population.

Both Thomas Malthus and Adam Smith wrote at a time when English society was still largely agricultural. In the early 1800s, English banker and economist David Ricardo put together Smith's free-trade ideas and Malthus's population theories and applied them to the new industrial society.

It was useless to try to improve workers' ● wages, Ricardo said. Wages were governed by an "Iron Law." That is, when population grew, the labor supply would grow, too. As more workers competed for jobs the jobs would go to those who would work for less. Workers would be poorer and so fewer of their children would survive to adulthood. The labor supply would then go down and wages would rise. Workers would have more children, and the labor market would again be too full. So, Ricardo reasoned, government efforts to improve the lot of factory workers were bad. Instead of interfering with the law of supply and demand, the government should practice laissez-faire.

Members of the new industrial capitalist class ans. 2
eagerly accepted and strongly supported laissez-faire. Supply and demand alone, they said, would control the production of goods and their selling prices. Consumers would have fair wages and prices and improved goods. And businesses could be sure of having good profits. Industrial capitalists cared little that laissez-faire did not always bring fair wages or just prices. For most of the 1800s these ideas were the accepted social philosophy of the growing middle class.

Many voices spoke out for reform. The most important piece of political legislation in ans. 3
19th-century England was the Reform Bill of 1832. It gave seats in the House of Commons to the new industrial towns of the north. By extending the right to vote, it gave a share of political power to the new business class.

Those who spoke for business in the Reform Parliament then used their new power to end

Before marriage, many young women from farms worked in the textile mills of Lowell, Massachusetts.

● Allow time for students to give their opinions of Malthus' and Ricardo's theories.

slavery in the British Empire (1833). They felt that slavery was morally wrong. In 1835, their power helped to reduce the upper-class landowner's hold on city government and to gain a hold for the new industrialists.

● These reforms helped the industrialist Whig
ans. 3 party. So the Tory party, originally the party of the landowning class, took up the workers' cause. They set up parliamentary groups to look into conditions in the factories and mines. The awful state described in their reports caused public anger. Between 1833 and 1847, the Tories pushed through acts that regulated the use of children and stopped the use of women, girls, and young boys in mines. A 10-hour workday also was set.

The drive toward reform involved, besides Charles Dickens, philosophers Jeremy Bentham and John Stuart Mill. Bentham made known the phrase "the greatest happiness for the greatest number." He said that the true test of any institution was its usefulness to society.

■ Bentham's pupil, Mill, championed personal liberty. His essay *On Liberty* (1859) is a defense of individual freedom. He did not accept laissez-faire and thought that social laws were needed. Mill's ideas on liberty and his humane, practical ideas about problems have been used down to the present day.

SECTION REVIEW 1

p. 498 **1.** What were some of the problems caused by the quick growth of cities and factories?

p. 498 **2.** In laissez-faire capitalism, what is the relationship
499 of government to business? How did Smith, Malthus, and Ricardo help form the middle-class belief in laissez-faire?

p. 499 **3.** What reforms did the Whigs and Tories make?
500 What conditions did people such as Dickens, Bentham, and Mill try to change?

● Point out how both parties supported reforms after voting rights were extended to workers.

■ Contrast Bentham's and Mill's ideas with laissez-faire philosophers (p. 499).

2 Socialists asked for far-reaching changes

Throughout the 1800s, many plans were offered to help workers and society in general. Some thinkers believed that the workers should own, manage, and control all means of production. Others thought that the government should have that power. These systems of social organization came to be called *socialism*. The persons who believed in them were known as *socialists*.

Many kinds of socialism arose in the early 1800s. Each offered its own plan for making over society.

Early socialists hoped to build a better world. The first to deal with the problem of how to change society were a number of early 19th-century thinkers and writers in France and England, who each had different ideas. In general, early socialists in England and France dreamed of a community based on the princi- ans. 1
ples of cooperation and economic planning. They hoped that from their model communities all people would discover the good in socialism and would want the same kind of life. These early socialists wanted to bring about a good society through persuasion.

One of the best known of the early socialists was the Englishman Robert Owen. The textile mills he owned in New Lanark, Scotland, had 2,000 workers, 500 of whom were children.

Owen took charge of the mills in 1800. He wanted to improve the living and working conditions of his people. He raised wages, and built schools and new houses. No workers were under 11 years old. As life improved, crime and disease were almost wiped out. And Owen's mills still made a profit.

Owen's ideas led to the founding of the Cooperative Movement. In 1844, a group of linen workers of Rochdale, England, gathered a sum equal to $140 and started a store. They were able to purchase goods at the store for fair prices and they shared the profits.

Other cooperative stores, or consumer co-ops, were formed elsewhere in Europe. Co-ops grew quite strong in England and in Scandinavia, where they owned and operated factories as well as retail stores. In the United States, storage and marketing co-ops became important among farmers.

Karl Marx brought a new kind of socialism. Karl Marx thought the early socialists were just dreamers. He offered what he believed was the true solution to society's ills. The name he gave to his ideas was *scientific socialism.*

Marx was born in 1815. He attended school in Germany, and then went to France as a journalist. There he met Friedrich Engels. They became friends for life.

In 1848, Marx and Engels wrote the *Communist Manifesto.* The pamphlet stated most of the ideas of Marxian socialism and set forth a whole plan for social revolution. The *Manifesto* drew little interest when it first appeared. But it would become one of the most important papers of modern history.

Also in 1848, Marx joined in the February revolution in Paris and the uprising in Germany. When these revolts failed, Marx escaped to London. There he began the first of three books that made up *Das Kapital,* his major work. The first book appeared in 1867. He died in 1883, before he could finish the third book. Engels completed the work for him.

Karl Marx was a revolutionary who believed that the capitalistic system was doomed. Capitalism would be destroyed, he believed, in a revolution. The workers – Marx called them the *proletariat* [prō′ lə tar′ē ət] – would tear control from the middle-class bourgeoisie. Too, Marx claimed that the socialist revolution must happen. He was sure of its coming because of the answers that he gave to two important questions: (1) Why do changes take place in history; and (2) How does the capitalist system work?

His answer to the first was that changes happen mostly because of changes in the economy. He stated that groups (he called them *classes*) who decide the ways goods are made and distributed are the ones who control the society. So they decide its laws, government, religion, and culture.

ans. 2

When new groups find new ways of making or distributing goods, they become rich and strong. They begin to speak against the older ruling groups. Then a fight for control breaks

In New Harmony, Indiana, a community of 2,000 people tried to live by Robert Owen's principles.

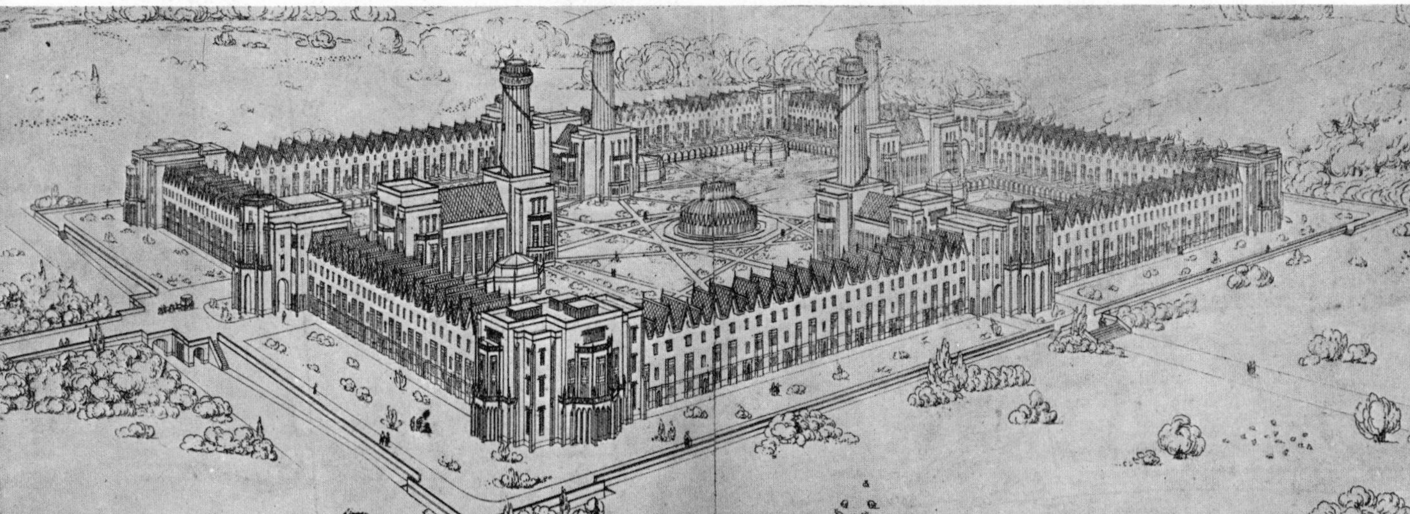

Käthe Kollwitz's lithograph of a workers' protest seems to illustrate Marx's theory of class struggle.

out. That is when a revolution takes place. The new groups then take over control from the old ruling groups.

Marx called the process *class struggle*. He said that all important changes in history have come about through class struggle. The *Communist Manifesto* declared: "The history of all hitherto existing society is the history of class struggles."

Marx used the French Revolution to show how class struggle works. That, he said, was when the capitalist (bourgeois) class of merchants and bankers overturned the feudal regime of landowners. The bourgeoisie had been kept out of power. Now it ruled.

Industrialization, though, had begun to make a new lower class—the workers. So a new class struggle would begin. In the revolution, the workers would take control. The workers would destroy the capitalist system. They would control all the means of production and distribution themselves. Then no group would ever again be lower than another. A classless society would be born, and the class struggle would stop.

Marx based his belief in a coming workers' (socialist) revolution on his answer to the second question: How does the capitalist system work? In *Das Kapital* (German for *capital*), he made a very careful study of capitalism.

Marx began his work with his *labor theory of value.* He stated that the value of any product depends on the amount of work needed to make it. For example, making a piano might use 1,000 hours of labor. If the workers had been paid at the rate of $1.00 an hour, the *real value* of the piano would be $1,000. If the manufacturer sold it for $2,000, the extra $1,000 was *surplus value.* That really belonged to the workers, because they had made the real value of the product through their work. Instead, this surplus value was profit in the manufacturer's pocket.

Logically, in this system, Marx said, the poor
● would become poorer and the rich richer as wealth settled into a few hands. Meanwhile, goods would pile up because the workers would be too poor to buy them. Then businesses would fail, factories would close, and millions would lose their jobs. Finally, after several depressions, capitalism would fall. Then the workers would take control, destroy the capitalistic system, and set up a socialist society.

Marx's ideas were attacked. Marx's ideas about changes in history taught many people that economic forces are important. In the late 1800s and early 1900s, wealth did settle into a few hands. Industry did grow ever larger. And several depressions did hurt business and workers. Yet, the events of history have shown that Marx was a poor prophet.

In his own day, and long after, Marx's ideas have been widely attacked. Most historians be-
ans. 3 lieve that Marx's ideas about historical forces are too simple, that events do not happen because of economics alone. People also act for other reasons—patriotism, religion, political loyalties.

Class struggle as a theory of historical change has serious faults. Many events in history show that people in several classes fight together against a common enemy. The world wars of modern times have shown that nationalism is sometimes a stronger force than class feelings.

Economists have shown that Marx's labor theory of value is not wholly correct. The cost of making a product is not just in the labor needed to make it. The manufacturer's costs in the factory, in materials, in workers' wages and benefits, and in storing, transporting, and advertising the product are also part of the cost. Then too, the general conditions of supply and demand help to decide the price of a product. For example, an oversupply of an item can send the selling price down. It may even fall below the cost of the work that went into it.

History did not bear out Marx's predictions. In the final years of the 1800s, conditions for the workers improved. Wages rose, and workers could buy the products made in the factories and mills. To be sure, some of the rich did become richer, but most of the poor did not become poorer. Instead, the general standard of living rose to heights never before reached in history.

● Point out that Marx lived at a time when working conditions were very harsh.

SECTION REVIEW 2

1. What kind of society did early socialists want to have? What successes did they have? p. 500

2. What was Marx's "class struggle"? What was his labor theory of value? p. 501

3. What were some arguments used against Marx's ideas? In what ways were his predictions incorrect? p. 503

3 An age of mass politics began

In the years between 1870 and 1914, Western civilization was becoming a mass urban, industrialized society. No other like it had ever been seen before in all of human history. This great change came at the same time that the age of mass politics began. We are living in that age.

Many countries began universal male suffrage. The most important political change in the half-century before World War I came in the new right of all men to vote. All property requirements were ended. Voting rights had become the chief symbol of democracy, and people fought long, bitter battles to get them. For a long time, property-owning classes turned away every effort to give men without property the right to vote.

France, in 1871, was the first country to allow all men to vote. Switzerland followed three years later. By 1884, Britain had allowed all male householders (homeowners) to vote. But not until 1918 could all Englishmen vote. In the 1890s, the Netherlands, Spain, and Norway removed property restrictions. Portugal, Sweden, and Denmark did so after 1900. Germany had granted the right by 1890, but Italy not until 1912.

The millions of new voters changed political ans. 1
parties into mass organizations. In the early 1800s, when only property owners could vote, political parties were small groups of upper-class men. Politicians did not ask for votes. In the late 1800s, though, more people had voting rights. Then a politician had to cover a whole district to meet people, make speeches, and win votes. Campaigns became costly. So politicians needed large parties with many dues-paying members to pay the bills. Today mass political parties and costly election campaigns are an expected part of political life in the Western world.

Women fought for legal rights. The general feeling toward women in the 1800s had two sides. Male-run society did not think highly of ans. 2
women's intelligence. But at the same time women were looked on as the base of the home and family. It was feared that if women had a

Winning the Vote
As new groups of people struggled to gain a voice in their government, their fight was not always recognized as legitimate. These cartoons seem to say that common men are too ignorant and rowdy *(left)* and women too foolish *(right)* to be trusted with important decisions. In spite of such views, both groups eventually won suffrage.

part in public business they would not care for their families. Then the cornerstone of all civilized life, the home, would fall apart. In Britain and France, women were not allowed to own property. When a woman married, any property she had became her husband's. Women could not start divorce proceedings, had no legal claim on their children, and could not vote.

In the mid-1800s, reformers in Europe and the United States began to call for equal legal and political rights for women. Most of the leaders were intelligent, middle-class women, such as the American Susan B. Anthony.

English philosopher John Stuart Mill helped the women's cause. In *The Subjection of Women* (1869), Mill stated that men taught women to believe from childhood that submission was a part of woman's nature. Then men could rule them more easily. As long as women had low legal and social status, he said, no one would ever know their true nature and abilities. He wrote:

> What we now call the nature of women is an eminently artificial thing—the result of forced repression. . . . It may be asserted without scruple, that no other class of dependents have had their character so entirely distorted from its natural proportions by their relations with their masters.

But public feeling was hard to change and progress was slow. Gradually, women were able to find jobs outside the home. Florence Nightingale, an English nurse during the Crimean War (1854–1856), helped to open nursing to women. Later, women entered some universities, especially in Italy and Switzerland. In the United States, where workers were needed, large numbers of women became factory workers, teachers, and secretaries.

By the end of the 1800s, women in most Western countries could by law own property. But the right to vote was still denied them.

The earliest voting rights for women were gained in the frontier areas. Women there were

American social worker Jane Addams established Hull House to service a slum neighborhood in Chicago.

ans. 2 more equal and had greater freedom. The first was New South Wales in Australia (1867). Wyoming in the United States followed (1869), and then New Zealand (1886). The first European country to allow women to vote was Norway (1907).

But the major countries held back. Only after World War I were women allowed to vote in ● Great Britain (1918). There, Emmeline Pankhurst and her two daughters led a long mass political fight to gain that right. The United States gave the right in 1920. Most other European countries followed after that.

Governments made social reforms. The kinds of reforms that western European governments made in the years after 1870 showed the influence of the new voters. The politics of all European states paid more attention to social problems. Big towns and mechanized industry meant more voters in the industrial wage-earn-  ans. 3
ing classes. These voters were the people who wanted government to move into social affairs.

The British government had already passed bills to regulate working conditions in factories, mines, and mills. So it began to work in new fields. In the 1870s, it passed laws to govern housing and public health. In 1902 the Education Act ended the work of building a national system of primary and secondary education.

When the new Liberal party came to power in 1905, it made even stronger reforms. It granted legal holidays with pay and passed the National Insurance Act of 1911. That act required contributions from employers and workers, and gave the whole working population guaranteed income during absence from work due to sickness. And certain kinds of workers got unemployment insurance.

Britain had copied from Germany, which, in the 1880s, was the leader in social legislation. The German government hoped to weaken socialism by passing laws aimed at the three most common problems of urban industrial life—sickness, accident, and old age. Later, workers got free medical and hospital care. Factory codes and child labor laws came in 1914.

In France, where industrialization and urbanization came more slowly, social legislation also was slower. Laws passed in the 1890s limited women to a 10-hour workday and provided in part for pensions and accident insurance. The 10-hour workday was made general in 1900. In 1906, a six-day work week was made legal.

Many other countries followed the leads of Britain, Germany, and France. By 1914, nearly every European country except Russia and the

● Abler students might be assigned to do research on the women's suffrage movement in England or the U.S.

The Salvation Army, a religious organization founded in England in 1865, gave food and shelter to the poor.

Balkan states had rather good factory codes and labor laws. Minimum standards for house and street building and the public preparation of food and drink also had been set.

Trade unions were formed. Modern trade unions are workers' groups that may legally bargain, one or more at a time, with employers for better wages and working conditions. Trade unions did not exist before the 1800s.

ans. 4 Business people and industrialists were bitterly against such workers' groups. They said they had the right to run their own businesses in their own ways. Trade unions would interfere with that right. Every European country in the early 1800s had laws against trade unions.

During most of the 1800s, workers fought a hard battle to make unions legal. The first country to act was Britain, in 1825. Countries on the continent held out much longer. In most countries, unions became legal only after 1860.

In the mid-1880s, trade unions changed. Until then, most unions were made up of skilled workers—mechanics, carpenters, printers. After that time, huge numbers of unskilled or semiskilled workers in whole industries, such as steel, banded together into country-wide unions.

These new unions came into being after a series of long and bitter strikes in the 1880s and 1890s in Belgium, England, France, and Germany. When a dock workers' strike in 1889 shut down the port of London, business people realized that they could not ignore workers' demands for better working conditions. The large industrial unions learned that they could get better results with strikes than with negotiations. As a result, in the years before World War I, the whole union movement became more aggressive.

Socialists formed political parties. Workers also tried to improve their lot by forming political parties. The socialists chiefly took the lead. The first party was the German Social Democratic Party, founded in 1875. Soon after, socialist parties like it were formed in Britain, France, and most other countries of western Europe. Their ideas were Marxist, but not revolutionary. Wherever representative government and democracy were strong, workers used their parties to elect people who would work inside the system for reforms.

ans. 5 The countries of eastern Europe had no parliaments. Political parties and trade unions there were outlawed. Strikes were thought a crime against the state. Those countries had no orderly way to bring about reform. And it was there that Marxism remained strongly revolutionary. Russia was one of these countries.

SECTION REVIEW **3**

p. 504 **1.** What changes took place in the way political campaigns were run from the early to the late 1800s? What was the reason for these changes?

p. 504, 506 **2.** Why had a male-run society been against women's participation in politics and public activities? What countries were first to allow women to vote?

p. 506 **3.** What new groups of voters asked their government to make laws regulating businesses? What were some of these new laws?

p. 507 **4.** What problems did workers have in organizing trade unions? What has been the goal of trade unions?

p. 508 **5.** Why were the followers of Marxist socialism in eastern European countries more in favor of revolutionary tactics than those in western Europe?

● Discussion topic: ask students in what ways their opinions or lives are affected by their education.

4 An urban mass society grew

The beginning of mass politics was only one sign of the growing mass civilization. Other signs were new social institutions and new ideas about government's role in society.

Public education was developed. Until about 1870, large numbers of Europeans could not read or write. Clearly, society needed people with at least a basic education to run ans. 1
modern factories and cities. So governments began to set up public school systems for children between the ages of 6 and 14.

Between 1871 and 1914 every Western country started a system of public education. On the lowest level, education was made compulsory and free. This was the only way to wipe out illiteracy. At the same time, higher-level schools grew in size and number. From them came engineers, doctors, teachers, technicians, and administrators to fill growing needs.

Ever since the Middle Ages, the Church had had the job of educating Europeans. So in most countries, bitter fights between church and state broke out over the control of education. The worst of these took place in France and Germany. Finally, though, the state won out.

Public education grew so rapidly that Prussia spent 30 times as much on primary education in 1901 as it had in 1871. England spent twice as much in 1914 as it had in 1900. Public educa- ●
tion became the greatest single force in shaping public opinion and in teaching people how to live in an industrial civilization.

New kinds of newspapers began. Public education made a mass reading public for the first time in history. So mass-circulation newspapers were begun to serve a new need.

ans. 2 The reports in these newspapers were called yellow journalism (named for a cartoon, "The Yellow Kid," carried in a New York paper). Earlier newspapers had reported mostly national and international news. Yellow journals reported murder, robbery, and scandal, in big, bold headlines. These stories, in a newspaper that cost only a penny, attracted large numbers of readers and advertisers. Begun in the United States in the 1880s, this type of newspaper quickly spread to other countries.

Another feature of the new yellow journals was sports news. During the late 1800s, mass spectator sports appeared. Games until then had been entertainment for the rich. But when paid public contests started, "games" became "sports."

In the 1870s, soccer became a spectator sport. To this day, it has remained the most popular sport in Europe. Shortly afterward, boxing and baseball became spectator sports. By 1876, the United States had enough professional baseball teams to organize the National League.

Local government grew rapidly. While national governments were making social security systems for workers, local governments were finding ways to make crowded cities livable. Between 1870 and 1914 there were great changes in city living. Modern urban life was born in this time.

Forward-looking mayors of industrial cities ans. 3
led the way in adding new services. In England by 1900, nearly every large town owned its gas and water supplies. The cities built schools, libraries, hospitals, museums, parks, and art galleries. City-run police and fire departments pro-

A school for poor boys in London. From the *Illustrated London News* for April 11, 1846.

tected the people. And the cities lighted the streets, collected the garbage, and disposed of the sewage. By 1914, most large cities on the continent had these services as well as city-owned public markets, laundries, slaughter-houses, and employment agencies.

Cities had to find a way for great numbers of people to move cheaply and quickly from one part of the city to another. Streetcars came into use in the 1860s. At first, horses pulled them. Later, in the 1880s electricity powered them.

In very large cities, underground railroads (subways) were built. London, in the 1860s, had the first subway. Boston built one in 1895, Paris in 1900, and New York in 1904. Many cities, especially in the United States, saved money by building elevated railroads. These, together with subways, made good, cheap public transportation.

The cost of government rose. The new national social security systems and city services cost a great deal of money. Taxing was the only way to get the large amounts needed. In 1870, no country in Europe had sales or income taxes. (Today, these two taxes are among the biggest sources of government income.) Money that governments needed came mostly from tariffs and from taxes on property.

As the costs of government rose, these taxes did not bring in enough money. Reformers said that new taxes were needed. They favored a progressive income tax (a higher tax on big incomes and a lower tax on small incomes). But many people, mostly in the middle and upper classes, were strongly against such a tax. The British government tried to push an income tax through Parliament in 1909. That move caused a constitutional crisis that lasted for two years. The tax was finally passed in 1911. By 1914 most European countries and the United States had begun the income tax. France, however, did not have one until 1917.

Middle-class views changed. By 1914, a century of social and political change had brought about another important change. The strong laissez-faire feeling of the early 1800s ans. 4 was weakening. People still valued the freedom, dignity, and worth of the individual. But they came to believe that the state should look after the welfare of its people.

The Catholic Church supported this new feeling about government. In 1891, Pope Leo XIII issued a mass-circulated letter, *Rerum Novarum* (of modern things). It defended private property as a natural right. But it pointed out that capitalism had failed to give social justice to the working class. Poverty, insecurity, and degradation were called unjust and unchristian. Socialism, the document said, was Christian when it tried to remove these evils. Only in denying God was socialism unchristian. *Rerum Novarum* asked that Catholics form their own socialist parties and labor unions in order to seek a greater measure of social justice.

SECTION REVIEW **4**

1. When and why was public education developed? p. 508

2. What changes took place in newspapers and public games in the 1800s? What were the first popular spectator sports in Europe and America? p. 509

3. Name some of the ways in which city life changed between 1860 and 1914. How did city governments pay for the greater services they provided? p. 509

4. How had middle-class views of laissez-faire changed by 1914? In what way did the Catholic Church support this change? p. 510

CHAPTER REVIEW 27

SECTION SUMMARIES

1. Urbanism and industrialism raised many problems. The rapid spread of industrialism upset many lives. Workers flocked from farms to cities. Crowded, unhealthy housing and poor water supply were problems of city dwellers. Conditions in factories and mines were bad: men, women, and children worked long hours for little pay. But still, the worker's lot in the 1800s was improved over the 1700s. Wages for skilled workers rose, and food and clothing were better. The middle class favored laissez-faire capitalism. Economists Smith, Malthus, and Ricardo supported the laissez-faire theory. Mill spoke for personal liberty. He wanted changes in laissez-faire policies and social laws.

2. Socialists asked for far-reaching changes. Some reformers wanted great social changes. Early socialists tried model communities based on cooperation and economic planning. Workers in the Cooperative Movement owned stores and factories, and shared the profits. Karl Marx began a different form of socialism. In the *Communist Manifesto,* he and Friedrich Engels said that the workers would revolt against the middle class and take over industry and government by force. The revolution, they said, must come because the capitalistic system was doomed. The worker's lot did not grow worse as Marx had predicted. Instead, after 1870 the general standard of living rose higher than ever before.

3. An age of mass politics began. Democracy took great strides forward with universal male suffrage and, later, legal and political rights for women. Labor unions became legal and gained members and power. Socialists worked with governments to reach their goals through reform laws. Only where democratic government was weak or did not exist, as in Russia, did revolutionary Marxism remain strong.

4. An urban mass society grew. In the 50 years between 1870 and 1914, a mass urban civilization came into being. Countries began compulsory public education. Cities began new services for millions of people. Cheap newspapers reached a mass reading public. Political parties became huge organizations. As governments grew, costs rose. New kinds of taxes were invented to pay for them. Most important was the progressive income tax. Over time, middle-class views on government changed from a belief in laissez-faire to a belief in a social state.

WHO? WHAT? WHEN? WHERE?

1. Give the years in which these social changes happened:

The 10-hour workday was established in England. 1833–47
All English men were allowed to vote. 1918
Male suffrage began in Italy. 1912
Women were given the vote in Norway. 1907
Women were allowed to vote in the United States. 1920
Child labor laws were written in Germany. 1914
Trade unions became legal in Europe. after 1860
Public schools were begun in the West. 1871–1914
The first subway was built in London. 1860s
A progressive income tax was adopted in England. 1911
Pope Leo XIII urged Catholics to seek social reform. 1891

2. Who were the authors and what were the subjects of these works?

Rerum Novarum Pope Leo XIII p. 510
The Wealth of Nations Adam Smith p. 498
An Essay on the Principles of Population Malthus p. 499
The Communist Manifesto Marx and Engels p. 501
On Liberty Mill p. 500
Das Kapital Marx p. 501
The Subjection of Women Mill p. 505

● **3.** What were the main ideas of: a. laissez-faire capitalism, b. Marxism, c. early socialism

● a. Governments should let businessmen do as they please.
b. Workers would eventually take over the means of production.
c. Communities should be based on cooperation and economic planning.

CHAPTER TEST 27

4. What countries passed laws or reforms to regulate these areas?
women's rights in society p. 505, 506
women and child workers p. 500.
the length of the workday p. 500.
medical care for workers p. 506
the rights of workers to organize and strike p. 507

QUESTIONS FOR CRITICAL THINKING

1. Why did so many people move from rural areas to work in the unsafe and unhealthy conditions of early factories?
2. Do you agree with the arguments Malthus and Ricardo made for laissez-faire? Explain your thinking.
3. What are some forces in the United States today that unite people to work for certain goals? Which are based on class, ethnic, religious, or other interests?
4. To what extent do you feel Marx's analysis of history as "class struggle" is correct? Give examples of conflicts in the past and their causes.
5. Which of the reforms mentioned in this chapter made the most important changes in society? What reforms do you feel are still needed?

ACTIVITIES

1. Find out the local, state, or federal laws that protect children today. Do you agree with them?
2. Discuss the role of women in society today. Do research to find the numbers of women employed, salaries, life span, and so on. Are special laws needed to protect women today?
3. Find out the expense involved in making a particular product, perhaps by visiting a local manufacturer.
4. Collect news clippings about union activities, or interview union members to determine the importance of unions today. Interview an employer to find out management's views on the need for unions.

SECTION 1

1. True or false: Early factory workers worked in worse conditions than anyone else in Europe.
2. Laissez-faire capitalism meant that: a. laws should be passed to regulate business practices, b. governments should let business owners run their businesses as they wished, c. workers should run the factories
3. An important reformer of the 1800s was: a. Malthus, b. Smith, c. Mill

SECTION 2

4. Which group believes that the means of production should be in the hands of the workers? a. socialists, b. trade unions, c. capitalists
5. Marx believed that all conflicts are caused by: a. religion, b. nationalism, c. class struggles
6. True or false: Working conditions worsened in the late 1800s.

SECTION 3

7. The first nation to allow all of its male citizens to vote was: a. England, b. France, c. United States
8. True or false: Women were first given voting rights in the large industrialized nations.
9. Social reform laws were passed because __c__ wanted them. a. businessmen, b. communists, c. workers

SECTION 4

10. By 1914, education, transportation, and protection were being provided by: a. cooperatives, b. city governments, c. factory owners
11. True or false: A progressive income tax is one that taxes rich and poor the same.
12. In *Rerum Novarum* the Catholic Church supported: a. social reform, b. communism, c. laissez-faire capitalism

● QUESTIONS FOR CRITICAL THINKING
1. p. 498, Conditions for farm laborers were even worse than for city workers.
2. Students could contrast these theories with those of Mill or Bentham.
3. Possible answers are political parties, community organizations, churches and social clubs, PTA; ask for names of specific organizations.
4. Students could refer to previous chapters.

UNIT REVIEW 7 — TEST YOURSELF

1. Match the person with the idea or development for which each is known:

a. Mendel	h increased cotton production
b. Marx	g Commonwealth of England
c. Bolívar	a genetics
d. Cavour	i laissez faire
e. Copernicus	f natural selection
f. Darwin	c liberation of South America
g. Cromwell	b class struggle
h. Whitney	k Prussian strength
i. Smith	d Italian unity
j. Louis Philippe	e heliocentric theory
k. Bismarck	j July monarchy

2. Fill in the blanks with the words from the list below that best complete the sentences: Socialism, nationalism, Risorgimento, Realpolitik, coal, iron, gold, combine, spinning jenny, steel plow, anatomy, astronomy, social contract, civilization, Roundheads, Cavaliers, creoles, and peninsulares.

Vesalius published the first accurate book on anatomy.

Locke's social contract theory supported the idea of government by the people.

The two opposing groups in the English civil war were the Roundheads and the Cavaliers.

The creole class led the revolutions in South America.

England's rich deposits of iron and coal helped its industrial development.

Two machines that improved farm production in the plains areas of America and Europe were steel plow and combine.

Romantics believed that primitive peoples were noble and good because Civilization had not spoiled them.

The Risorgimento was the Italian nationalist movement.

Bismarck tried to destroy socialism by giving the people a program of state health insurance.

3. Match each term with its definition:

c socialism	a trade unions
h impressionists	b divine right
e laissez faire	g naturalists
d scientific method	f social contract

a. Groups of workers that may legally bargain with employers for better wages and working conditions.

b. The belief that a king's power comes from God.

c. A system of government in which the state controls the means of production.

d. A way of finding answers by experimentation and observation.

e. Business term for "let them do as they please."

f. The belief that a ruler's power comes from the people.

g. Writers who tried to describe life as scientists would.

h. Painters who worked out new ways to use light and color.

4. List these people as leaders in: a. government, b. the arts, c. science, or d. social philosophy and reform

d Anthony	b Beethoven
a l 'Ouverture	a Lavoisier
b Tolstoy	b Degas
c Pierre and Marie Curie	d Pankhurst
d Verdi	d Robespierre
a Metternich	d Smith
b Ibsen	a Díaz

5. Identify the authors of these quotations, and tell what each statement is about and why it was made:

"The history of all hitherto existing society is the history of class struggles."

"But it [Earth] does move!"

"If there were no God, it would be necessary to invent one."

Karl Marx: to justify socialism
Galileo: after denying the theory that the Earth moves around the sun
Voltaire: expressing the importance of religion

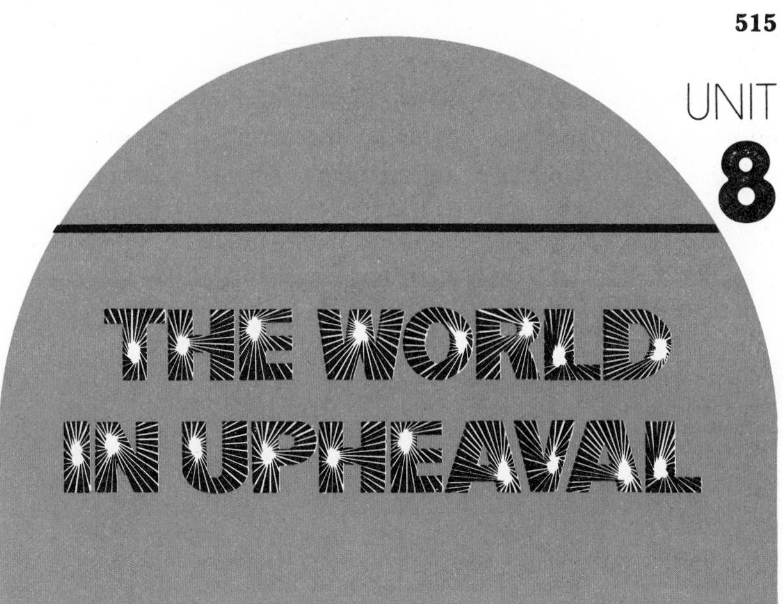

UNIT 8

THE WORLD IN UPHEAVAL

At the beginning of the 20th century, the countries of the West were the richest, most powerful, and most technologically advanced in the world. Their empires, trade, and influence reached around the globe. No one in 1900 would have believed that the world was about to go through fifty years of upheaval that would bring an end to Western dominance.

Why was the first half of the 20th century a time of such turmoil? The answer lies in the changes that were taking place everywhere. The changes came so quickly that they were hard to adjust to. In particular, national and economic rivalries led to the two world wars.

Wars often create more problems than they solve. In Europe, World War I opened the door to revolution in Russia. Out of this arose the first communist nation in history. War also opened the way for the rise of totalitarianism in Germany, Italy, and Japan. The governments of these states had total control over their citizens. They were nationalistic dictatorships that used terror to protect the rule of a single party. When these countries tried to expand their power to neighboring states, tensions built up and exploded into World War II.

Meanwhile, the idea of national independence spread among the peoples of Asia, Africa, and the Middle East. In these areas, strong resentment was building up against imperialism. World War I increased this resentment. World War II completely shat-

The atomic bomb's mushroom cloud brought terror to the world.

tered the old empires and led to a tripling of the number of independent states in the world. Everywhere, nationalism became the single most powerful force of the 20th century. It, more than anything else, explains why the world has been in upheaval for so much of this century.

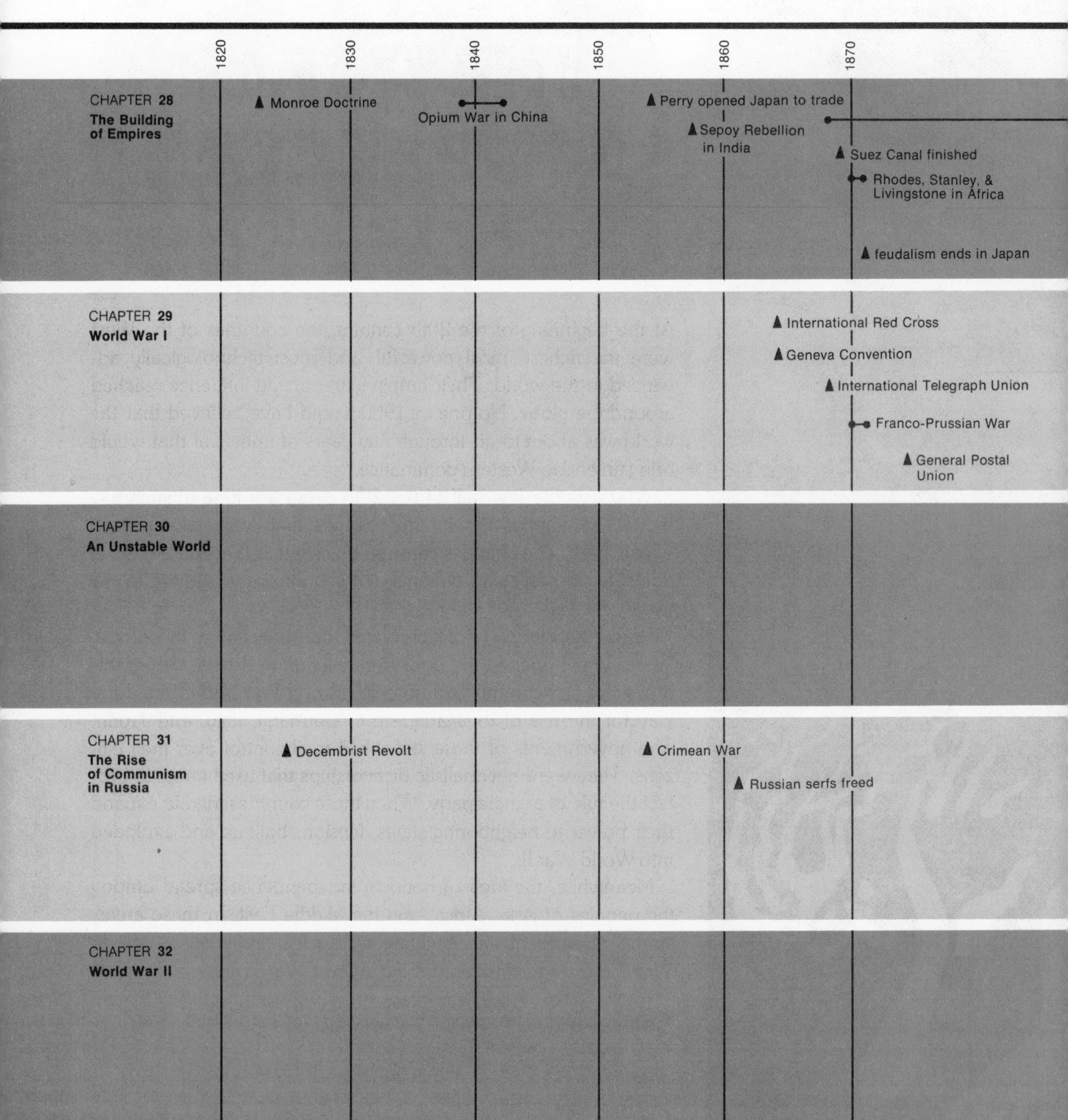

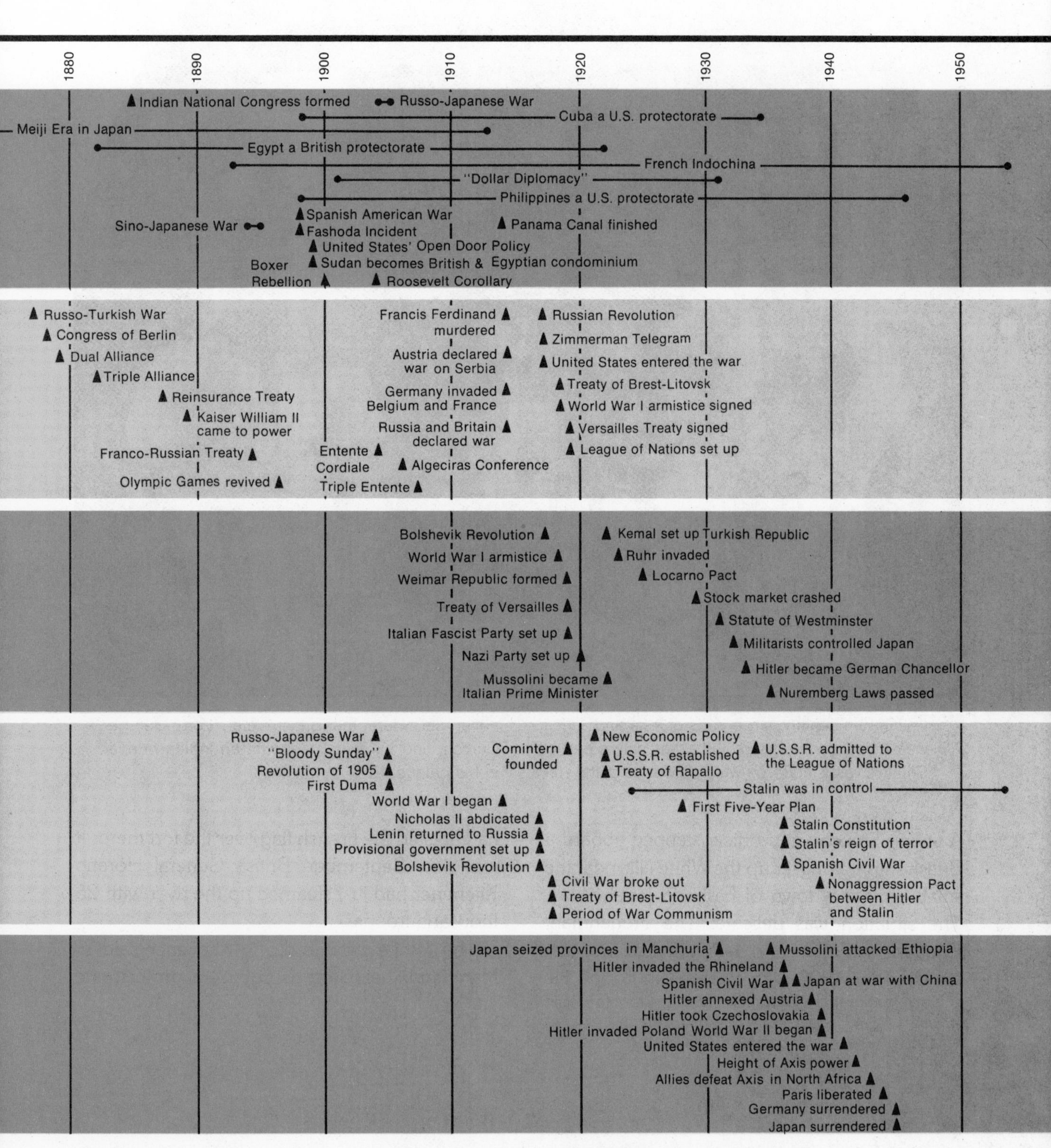

1880
1890
1900
1910
1920
1930
1940
1950
Indian National Congress formed
Russo-Japanese War
Cuba a U.S. protectorate
Meiji Era in Japan
Egypt a British protectorate
French Indochina
"Dollar Diplomacy"
Philippines a U.S. protectorate
Spanish American War
Sino-Japanese War
Fashoda Incident
Panama Canal finished
United States' Open Door Policy
Sudan becomes British & Egyptian condominium
Boxer Rebellion
Roosevelt Corollary
Russo-Turkish War
Congress of Berlin
Dual Alliance
Triple Alliance
Reinsurance Treaty
Kaiser William II came to power
Franco-Russian Treaty
Olympic Games revived
Francis Ferdinand murdered
Austria declared war on Serbia
Germany invaded Belgium and France
Russia and Britain declared war
Entente Cordiale
Algeciras Conference
Triple Entente
Russian Revolution
Zimmerman Telegram
United States entered the war
Treaty of Brest-Litovsk
World War I armistice signed
Versailles Treaty signed
League of Nations set up
Bolshevik Revolution
World War I armistice
Weimar Republic formed
Treaty of Versailles
Italian Fascist Party set up
Nazi Party set up
Mussolini became Italian Prime Minister
Kemal set up Turkish Republic
Ruhr invaded
Locarno Pact
Stock market crashed
Statute of Westminster
Militarists controlled Japan
Hitler became German Chancellor
Nuremberg Laws passed
Russo-Japanese War
"Bloody Sunday"
Revolution of 1905
First Duma
World War I began
Nicholas II abdicated
Lenin returned to Russia
Provisional government set up
Bolshevik Revolution
Comintern founded
New Economic Policy
U.S.S.R. established
Treaty of Rapallo
U.S.S.R. admitted to the League of Nations
Stalin was in control
First Five-Year Plan
Stalin Constitution
Stalin's reign of terror
Spanish Civil War
Civil War broke out
Treaty of Brest-Litovsk
Period of War Communism
Nonaggression Pact between Hitler and Stalin
Japan seized provinces in Manchuria
Mussolini attacked Ethiopia
Hitler invaded the Rhineland
Spanish Civil War
Japan at war with China
Hitler annexed Austria
Hitler took Czechoslovakia
Hitler invaded Poland World War II began
United States entered the war
Height of Axis power
Allies defeat Axis in North Africa
Paris liberated
Germany surrendered
Japan surrendered

CHAPTER 28

1820-1914

The Building of Empires

In the 19th century, large parts of Asia and Africa were ruled by foreigners. India was only a part of Britain's vast empire, on which, it was said, the sun never set. Here the British ruler, Lord George Curzon, and his wife meet with an Indian prince in his palace.

A young French army officer stepped aboard a British ship waiting far up the White Nile near the small Sudanese town of Fashoda [fə shō′də]. The situation was delicate. The Frenchman, Captain Jean Marchand, had marched into that town in July, 1898, with 120 African troops. He had hoisted the French flag over the fort there. It was now September. British General Horatio Kitchener had just steamed up the river with 25 thousand troops.

The White Nile territory, Kitchener said to Marchand, belonged to Egypt—a protectorate

The material in this chapter continues the development of events from Units 4 and 5 as well as Chapter 21.

of Britain. The French had no business there. Marchand replied that he could not retreat without orders from his government. Although there were far more British forces than French, Kitchener decided it would be enough of a stand to raise the Egyptian and British flags south of the fort. Then, the two men referred the problem back to their home governments. Eventually, France backed down and ordered Marchand to remove his troops.

Why were two of the great powers of Europe willing to risk a war over this steaming little town on the White Nile? What brought them to Africa in the first place? The answers to these questions ● depend on an understanding of the imperialism that flourished between 1870 and 1914. During this period, several economic conditions made European nations become interested in colonies. (1) Rapid industrialism and a rising standard of living created the need for more raw materials. Many of these came from tropical areas. (2) Competition among industrial countries led each to raise its tariffs on imported goods and to look abroad for new export markets. (3) The less developed areas of the world offered not only markets for goods but also places for investment. Stock in Algerian railways and Dominican sugar plantations might yield returns as high as twenty percent a year. To protect their investments, Westerners wanted their home governments to take control of the foreign lands.

The growth of European empires was also helped by strong nationalistic rivalry among the Western countries. Two new European states—Germany and Italy—eagerly entered the race for colonies. Each felt it was in the interest of national security to see that certain areas did not fall into enemy hands. The greatness of a nation came to be measured by its colonial possessions. Indeed, conflicts over imperialistic claims were an important cause of World War I.

● This is a good treatment of the reasons for 19th century imperialism.

Among Europeans, national pride was mixed with religious and humanitarian motives. Westerners often thought of their civilization as better than those of Asia and Africa. Missionaries, doctors, and colonial administrators believed they carried what the English poet Rudyard Kipling called the "white man's burden"—a duty to improve the natives' lives. This attitude led to certain reforms in some areas. Westerners helped end slavery, relieve famine, improve health and education, and advance justice. Too often, however, their superior attitude made enemies of the native peoples. And many Europeans who talked of noble purposes were more interested in profits. This chapter tells how:

1. **India lost its independence.**
2. **Foreign powers exploited China.**
3. **Japan became a world power.**
4. **Many nations gained influence elsewhere in the East.**
5. **Africa was carved into many colonies.**
6. **Imperialism grew in Latin America.**

1 India lost its independence

In the 17th century, Aurangzeb, the great-grandson of Akbar, had brought almost all of India under Mughul control. After his death in 1707, the Mughul Empire was torn with unrest. Within forty years, it fell into chaos.

The British won control. By this time, England and France had strong trading interests in

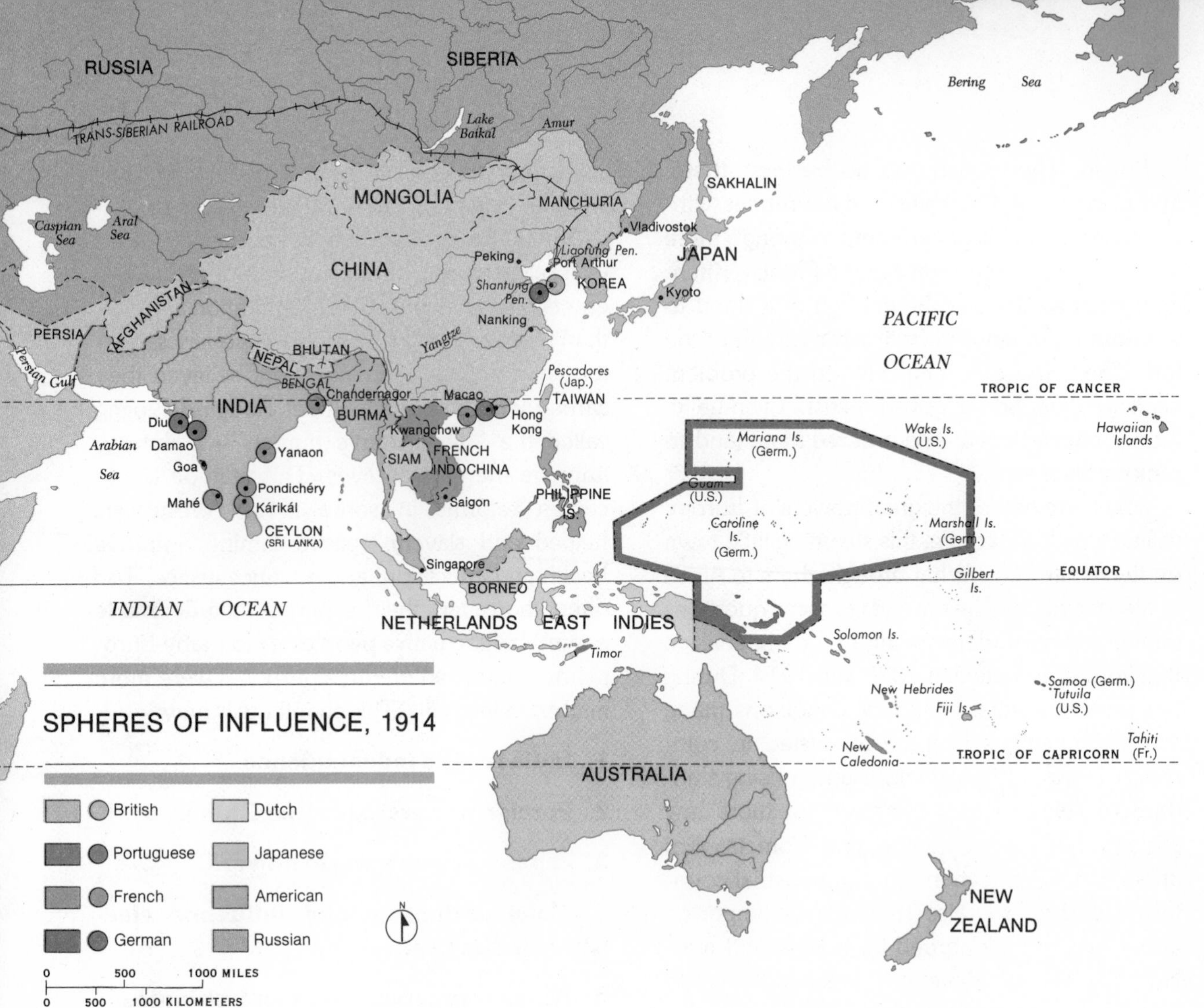

India. Mughul rulers had allowed the British East India Company to make several small settlements. These settlements, called factories, were rented to the English. They were armed, but used chiefly for storage and trading.

The French East India Company also set up trading posts along the east coast in the late 1600s. Competition between the two groups of traders grew stronger as Mughul rule grew weaker.

During the 18th century, when England and France were at war in Europe and North America, their quarrel spread to India. At first, the French were the winners. Then during the Seven Years' War (1756–1763), the English, led by the brilliant Robert Clive, defeated the French. They were then masters of Bengal. This region became the cornerstone of the British Empire in India. ans. 1

Company rule was limited. The British government decided that it did not want the East India Company to have political power. The India Act of 1784 gave power over the Company to a Board of Control whose president was a cabinet member. The British gov- ans. 2

• Additional information about these trading companies can be found in Ch. 21.

ernment also chose the highest Company official in India, the governor general. In 1814, Parliament took away the Company's trade monopoly in India. In 1833, its China trade monopoly was also taken away.

However, the East India Company remained active. As the Mughul Empire fell apart, the company extended British control over more and more territory. It sometimes did this by conquering lands directly. Or it arranged alliances with local rulers who accepted Company protection. By the mid-19th century, all of India had come under British control.

Indian dissatisfaction grew. Indians resented British missionaries and policies. They were alarmed by the expansion activity of the Company in the mid-1800s. In 1857, a rumor spread among the native troops, or sepoys, serving the British. The rumor said that new rifle cartridges — the ends of which had to be bitten off — would be greased with beef and pork fat. Hindus thought cows to be sacred. Muslims considered pigs unclean. Both groups were very angry. They rose in mutiny and killed many Europeans. However, the Sepoy Rebellion did not have the support of the people. The British were able to end the rebellion by late 1858.

As a result of the Sepoy Rebellion, however, ans. 3
the British Parliament abolished the East India Company in 1858 and set up a new cabinet post, Secretary of State for India. A viceroy was chosen to rule within India. The British divided India into two parts, British India, which was ruled directly by the British, and Indian India, which was ruled by native princes who were in charge of their own internal affairs.

In British India, the viceroy had full power. In 1861, legislative and executive councils that included some Indians were set up to help him. All the members were appointed rather than elected. An able Indian civil service was developed. Although the British did hold all top positions, Indians slowly filled most of the middle and lower posts.

British administration had mixed results. ans. 4
Probably the most important thing that the British did was to unify India. Now almost all of

Fierce fighting broke out in Delhi, where the sepoys claimed the last Mughul emperor was their real leader.

the subcontinent had come under one authority. The use of English as the official language helped, since before this, there had been no single language all educated Indians could speak.

The British in India also stopped bands of robbers, reduced the dangers of travel, and protected life and property. They outlawed suttee (the suicide of a widow on her husband's funeral pyre) and the killing of infant girls. They also improved medical facilities, added miles of railroad and telegraph lines, and built extensive irrigation works.

The picture had a dark side, too. Because of such improvements, the population grew rapidly and food supplies could not keep up. Thus, for many, the living standard became worse. One bad harvest was enough to cause famine. Poverty was and still is a major problem in India.

Another heavy blow was the end of the centuries-old handicraft system. With the growth of British industry, India became a market for cheap manufactured goods, especially cotton textiles. The Indians' handwoven cloth could not sell as cheaply as imported cloth. And the
■ Indians were not allowed to sell their cloth to other countries. Thus, they were forced to depend more and more on agriculture for earning a living.

Yet, a small group of Indian intellectuals arose. They were trained in British schools in the Indian cities. There they were taught English history as well as language. What they learned about the liberal traditions of 19th-century Europe brought out their own desire for self-government. In 1885, a group of primarily Hindu leaders formed the Indian National Congress. In 1906, a group of educated Muslims formed the Muslim League. Both groups had as their common aim representative self-government for India. Indian nationalism grew steadily in strength.

■ Colonial powers did not allow their colonies to trade with other countries because the colonies were needed as markets for goods from the mother country.

SECTION REVIEW 1

1. How did the Seven Years' War affect British and French interests in India? p. 520

2. Why and how did the British government reduce the powers of the British East India Company? p. 520

3. How did British rule in India change after the Sepoy Rebellion? p. 521

4. What improvements did the British bring to India? What problems were caused by British rule? p. 521

2 Foreign powers exploited China

In the mid-17th century, the Manchus set up a new dynasty in China. For many years, they were in charge of a huge, rich empire. However, decline began about 1800. The population grew rapidly. Agriculture could not keep up. Not enough food and increasing poverty caused discontent. By the mid-19th century, Manchu leadership was in serious trouble. Rebellions broke out in many parts of the country.

Europeans used force to win trading rights. Europeans had begun some trade with Ming China in the mid-16th century. But the Manchus cut it back. With the rise of industrialism in Europe, however, Westerners tried again to increase the amount of trade with China. Friction grew as the two very different civilizations came into greater contact.

Open warfare broke out in 1839. Basically, ans. 1
war came because the Manchus would not allow the British to have regular trade with China. On the surface, however, the cause was opium. The British East India Company had been importing opium into China in return for Chinese tea and silk. Although there was a law against

Before 1842, European and American merchants in China could not go outside a small area of the harbor.

this importation, the Manchus had not enforced it for years. Many Chinese were becoming addicted to the drug. They were turning to robbery to get money to buy opium and were neglecting their farms. Chinese leaders were very concerned about this. One day, a Cantonese official seized a large amount of the drug and destroyed it. The British protested, but talks failed.

The Opium War lasted three years. The Chinese, without a navy, were no match for the British. The conflict ended with the Treaty of
ans. 1 Nanking in 1842. The Chinese gave Hong Kong to the British. They paid damages for the opium they had destroyed. They also agreed to a fair tariff on trade. Most important, the Chinese were forced to open five port cities to trade. The Treaty of Nanking marked the real opening of ● China. Soon, other Western countries got similar trading rights.

● This treaty was one of a series known as "unequal treaties" because China was repeatedly forced to give up more privileges without getting anything in return.

Foreign traders, however, were well aware of the weakness and corruption of the Chinese government. The traders often abused their rights. In 1856, war again broke out. This time, a combined English-French fleet sailed to the Chinese capital, Peking. They forced the emperor to flee and burned the beautiful summer palace. The treaties signed in 1858 and 1860 ans. 2
marked another defeat for the Chinese. The Manchus opened eleven more ports. They legalized the opium trade. They agreed to receive Western diplomats and to protect Christian missionaries. China also gave foreigners the right of

extraterritoriality. That is, foreigners were excused from trial in Chinese courts. They were subject only to the courts of their home country.

ans. 3 The weakness of China was now clear to all. Foreign powers quickly moved in to carve up the "Chinese melon." They set up *spheres of influence.* In China, these were regions where the economic interests of another country were supreme. Within its sphere, a country had rights to specific tracts of land called *concessions.* It more or less controlled these concessions and enjoyed extraterritoriality there. Russia had concessions in the north of China, Germany on the Shantung peninsula, and France in the south.

The race to gain concessions from the Manchus caused the United States to state its Open Door Policy in 1899. The United States feared that China might be completely divided up into spheres that would shut out American trade. It therefore proposed that countries having such spheres should permit all nations to compete in them on equal terms. Several countries agreed to the American plan. This helped keep China together territorially. It also assured Americans a chance to trade in China.

The Chinese deeply hated the exploitation of ans. 4
their country by foreigners. Their Manchu rulers held tightly to traditional Chinese customs and resisted change to Western ways. Many people joined the secret Society of Harmonious Fists (or "Boxers") which opposed all Westerners. In 1900, the Boxers revolted. They destroyed railroads, burned bridges, and killed Europeans. The Boxer Rebellion was quickly put down by a combined force of Europeans, Americans, and Japanese. Afterwards, stricter controls were placed upon the Chinese government. However, there remained a group of Chinese who believed that change in their own government was needed in order to get rid of European control. They began a revolutionary movement that spread rapidly through the country.

Led by a German count, the colonial powers squashed the Boxer Rebellion in a swift show of strength.

SECTION REVIEW 2

p. 522 **1.** What were the causes of the Opium War? How
523 did the British profit from the Treaty of Nanking?

p. 523 **2.** What did the foreign powers win from the Manchu government in the treaties of 1858 and 1860?

p. 524 **3.** What were "spheres of influence" in China? What was the Open Door Policy of the United States?

p. 524 **4.** What action did some Chinese take to show their opposition to foreign imperialism?

3 Japan became a world power

About forty years before the Manchus became all-powerful in China, the Tokugawa [tō′kü gä′wä] clan had won control of the shogunate in Japan. With their strong leadership, Japan was unified under a stable political system. Foreigners were expelled, and Christianity was outlawed. Japan enjoyed a long period of peace, prosperity, sound government, and little contact with the rest of the world.

ans. 1 Tokugawa rule, however, had major weaknesses. The peasants had to pay high rents. There were several peasant uprisings in the mid-18th century. The noble class went deeply into debt. And many noble families were jealous of shogunate rule.

The United States opened Japan to trade. Since the early 1800s, American whaling ships had sailed in the northern Pacific. And clipper ships trading with China sailed near Ja-
ans. 2 pan. American shippers were interested in Japan because they needed places where they could stop for food, fuel, and water. They also wanted protection for their sailors. Those who had been shipwrecked on Japanese shores had been badly treated.

In 1853, the American government sent Commodore Matthew Perry and four ships to Japan. Perry brought a message from President Millard Fillmore, requesting that the Japanese open their country to foreign trade. Then he left, promising to return the following spring for an answer.

In February, 1854, Perry returned with ten ships. He carried many presents for the Japanese officials. There were books, guns, clocks, perfume, sewing machines, and even a small locomotive. The Japanese were impressed by the gifts and by Perry's dignity and show of ● force. They agreed to the Treaty of Kanagawa. This treaty opened two Japanese ports to American ships and provided better treatment for shipwrecked sailors. In 1858, a second treaty opened more ports and set up diplomatic relations between the two countries. It also granted extraterritoriality to American citizens in Japan. Soon afterward, other Western nations worked out similar treaties. The door seemed to be open for large-scale foreign influence in Japan.

The Japanese adopted new ways. Japan, however, did not go the way of China. Unlike the Chinese rulers, the Japanese decided that their country could survive only by adopting some Western ways. One of the first changes was in the shogunate itself. The Treaty of Kanagawa ■ had caused antiforeign demonstrations. The Tokugawas were blamed for these as well as for the poor conditions of the past hundred years. In 1867, strong noble leaders forced the shogun to give up his powers. The next year, the emperor was restored to power. The capital was moved from Kyoto to Tokyo. Emperor Mutsuhito, a youth of fifteen, adopted *Meiji*

● Point out that Japan had reached a high level of civilization (Ch. 17) and was probably more impressed by the weapons than by the gifts.

■ Young samurai visited the U.S. and became more dissatisfied with Tokugawa rule. Dissatifaction eventually led to revolution in 1868.

[mā'jē] (meaning "enlightened peace") as the name of his reign.

During the forty-five years of the Meiji Era, Japan was changed into a powerful modern state. It became the first industrialized country of Asia. However, the great changes in political, social, and economic affairs were carefully con-
● trolled. Japanese leaders sent their own people to study all the major Western powers. The leaders then adopted only what they thought would be good for Japan.

ans. 3 In 1871, the emperor ended feudalism. In 1889, he set forth a constitution like that which Bismarck had written for the German Empire. Although it provided for a two-house legislature, the emperor remained supreme. Only the lower house was elected. And only about 1 percent of the people could vote. Military leaders had great power in the government. The army and navy were strengthened. The army was based on the German model and the navy on the British. Compulsory education was introduced and illiteracy was almost wiped out. The government adopted new laws and a new judicial system, patterned after Western ones. All foreign rights of extraterritoriality were gone by 1899.

● Japan had followed this same practice in the 6th and 7th centuries when certain Chinese institutions were systematically adopted (Ch. 17)

Perhaps even more surprising than the political changes were those in economic life. Japanese leaders knew that Western strength was based on industrial power. Thus, they pushed ahead with a major program to make Japan strong industrially, too. At the time of the Meiji Restoration (1868), there were almost no factory workers in Japan. By 1900, there were a half million.

Because money to invest was scarce, the government had to give loans to private business. The government also entered directly into the building of railroads, factories, shipyards, and telegraph and telephone systems. Japan developed a "mixed" system of private and governmental enterprise led by a few rich families that made up an economic ruling class.

The Japanese opened their ports to American and European merchants in the late 19th century. In the scene *above left,* Westerners and Japanese gather together in a merchant's house at Yokohama, a major trading port. *Above right* is a Japanese drawing of a Dutch merchant family at dinner. The Japanese, who did not use chairs or forks, were amused by these oddities. They also thought the Dutch manners at dinner were unrefined.

Japanese ambitions led to foreign aggres-
ans. 4 **sion.** In becoming a modern industrial state, Japan also became imperialistic. A rapid rise in population grew out of better sanitation and medical services. In the Meiji Era alone, the population grew from less than 30 to over 50 million. The nation could not grow enough food for its people. It also lacked raw materials and markets for its manufactured goods. Japan saw the Asian mainland as a way to get around these troubles. As early as 1876, the Japanese had obtained trading privileges in Korea. This angered the Chinese and later led to the Sino-Japanese War of 1894–1895. By defeating China in this war, Japan made its first major gain of territory beyond its own borders.

The Treaty of Shimonoseki gave Japan the islands of Taiwan and the Pescadores [pes′ kə dôr′ēz]. It also gave them the Liaotung [lyou′du̇ng′] peninsula of Manchuria. Meanwhile, the Russians were expanding into Man- ans. 5
churia, too. They had long wanted Liaotung because at its southern tip lay Port Arthur. This was one of the finest harbors in East Asia because it could be used in all seasons. Backed by France and Germany, Russia forced Japan to return Liaotung to China. Soon afterward, Russia leased the peninsula and harbor for itself through a treaty with China. This move and other Russian moves in Korea angered Japan.

Talks between Japan and Russia over Korea and Manchuria broke down in 1904. Fighting began when Japan, without declaring war, attacked the Russian fleet at Port Arthur. Much to the surprise of the West, Japan won the Russo-Japanese War. This was the first time in modern

● history that an Asian country had defeated a European country. With the Treaty of Portsmouth (1905), Japan took back Liaotung and Port Arthur. Japan also got a sphere of influence in Korea, and won the southern half of the Russian island of Sakhalin. Five years later, Japan openly took over Korea. Almost overnight, Japan had become a major world power.

SECTION REVIEW 3

p. 525 **1.** What were three serious weaknesses of Tokugawa rule?

p. 525 **2.** Why did the United States want to set up closer contacts with Japan? How did they accomplish this?

p. 526 **3.** What Western practices were adopted by the Japanese?

p. 527 **4.** Why did Japan become imperialistic? What lands did Japan gain from the Treaty of Shimonoseki?

p. 527 **5.** Describe the causes and results of the Russo-Japanese War.

4 Many nations gained influence elsewhere in the East

We have already seen how India and China became victims of European imperialism. Thus, it should not be surprising that smaller countries in Asia, as well as many islands in the Pacific, would also come under Western rule. In the Pacific region, however, European imperialists found a new rival, the United States.

European powers expanded into several regions of Asia. For a long time, Russia had been building up its settlements in Siberia. When China became open to Western exploitation in the mid-19th century, the Russians also stepped in there. The Russians were always in search of warm-water ports. Thus, they moved to secure a large coastal area north of Korea where they founded Vladivostok in 1860.

In 1890, Russia began building the Trans-Siberian Railroad. China gave permission for the line to cross Manchuria. The Russians, however, failed to keep possession of the Liaotung peninsula after the Russo-Japanese War. This was a major blow to their imperialistic plans in that area. ans. 1

Meanwhile, Russian imperialists were also moving into southwestern Asia. This worried the British. They feared that Russia might reach the Persian Gulf and interfere with their shipping route to India and the East. The British were also upset that in central Asia the Russians had reached the borders of Afghanistan. Such a position threatened India. In 1907, Britain and Russia signed an agreement promising that neither country would take over Afghanistan. Persia was divided into spheres of influence, with Russia controlling the north and Britain controlling the south. ans. 1

In Southeast Asia, Britain and France were the two chief rivals. The French first moved into the area in the late 18th century. By the mid-1800s, however, hostile Asian feelings led to attacks on French missionaries. A French fleet attacked and captured Saigon in 1860. During the next twenty years, France set up protectorates in Cochin-China, Cambodia, and Annam. These areas had always paid tributes to China. China tried but was not able to get rid of the French by force in the 1880s. In 1893, the French took over Laos [lā'os]. They grouped all these areas together to form the French colony of Indochina. It was nearly fifty percent larger than France itself. ■ ans. 2

● Ask students what effect this victory of the Japanese might have had on the western attitudes towards Japan.

■ The one area that escaped imperialism was Siam. Students might be familiar with the film *The King and I* which describes the reforms made by the Siamese government.

Burma meanwhile had come under British influence. Conflicts along the Indian border had touched off small wars. As the winner of these wars, Britain was able to take over more and more land. Burma was formally added to India in 1885. Other possessions of the British in this area were Ceylon (present day Sri Lanka), Singapore, and northern Borneo.

One other important European power in this region was the Netherlands. It controlled the East Indies. As with the British in India, a private trading company (the Dutch East India Company) ruled for many years. Then in 1798, the home government took over. It made the territory a colony called the Netherlands East Indies. The Dutch made large profits from their colony. They shipped its spices, tobacco, sugar, coffee, and tea to Europe. They built schools, but made sure that the schools used native languages. This system preserved native cultures. More importantly, it delayed the spread of anticolonial ideas such as nationalism and democracy.

Pacific islands came under foreign rule. In the late 19th century, there was a rapid development of ocean transportation. This was followed by a great increase in shipping. Naturally, many of the thousands of islands in the Pacific became important ship stops. ans. 3

Britain, the greatest naval power, held Australia, New Zealand, and many Pacific islands. These included Fiji and the southern Solomons. Other nations followed this example. The Germans got the northern Solomons. They also bought some islands from Spain. Meanwhile, France secured Tahiti.

The United States, too, was interested in Pacific islands. During the 19th century, Americans and Europeans settled in the Hawaiian Islands. There they set up a thriving export trade in sugar. By the 1880s, Americans dominated the government, although Hawaii was still technically independent.

Hawaiian sugar planters wanted the islands to become part of the United States. When the Hawaiian queen refused, she was overthrown.

French troops stormed Saigon in Cochin China (now Vietnam) after a missionary was murdered in 1858.

AFRICA IN 1914
EUROPE
ASIA
Black Sea
Caspian Sea
Mediterranean Sea
Persian Gulf
Red Sea
ARABIAN PENINSULA
Madrid
Rome
Athens
Gibraltar
Tangier
SPANISH ZONE
Oran
Algiers
Tunis
TUNISIA
Madeira Is. (Port.)
Casablanca
MOROCCO
ALGERIA
Tripoli
Bengazi
Alexandria
Port Said
Suez Canal
Cairo
Agadir
IFNI
Canary Is. (Sp.)
LIBYA
EGYPT
(BRITISH PROTECTORATE)
Aswan
Nile River
RIO DE ORO
SAHARA DESERT
FRENCH WEST AFRICA
ANGLO-EGYPTIAN SUDAN
(CONDOMINIUM)
Omdurman
Khartoum
Asmara
ERITREA
ADEN
Socotra (Br.)
Timbuktu
Senegal River
Niger River
Dakar
Bathurst
GAMBIA
PORT. GUINEA
Bissau
Lake Chad
FRENCH EQUATORIAL AFRICA
Blue Nile River
Djibouti
FRENCH SOMALILAND
BRITISH SOMALILAND
Freetown
SIERRA LEONE
LIBERIA
Monrovia
IVORY COAST
GOLD COAST
Accra
TOGOLAND
DAHOMEY
Lagos
NIGERIA
Fashoda
ABYSSINIA
Addis Ababa
(ETHIOPIA)
ITALIAN SOMALILAND
White Nile
Lake Rudolf
CAMEROONS
Buea
Fernando Po (Sp.)
Gulf of Guinea
RÍO MUNI
Principe (Port.)
St. Thomas (Port.)
Annobon (Sp.)
EQUATOR
Ubangi River
Congo River
UGANDA
BRITISH EAST AFRICA
(KENYA)
Mogadiscio
Stanleyville
Entebbe
Lake Victoria
Nairobi
Mt. Kilimanjaro
FRENCH CONGO
BELGIAN CONGO
Brazzaville
Léopoldville
CABINDA
Boma
ATLANTIC OCEAN
GERMAN EAST AFRICA
(TANGANYIKA)
Pemba
Zanzibar
Dar es Salaam
Amirante Is. (Br.)
Ascension (Br.)
Loanda
Lake Tanganyika
Lake Mweru
Lake Nyasa
NYASALAND
Comoro Is. (Fr.)
Benguela
ANGOLA
(PORT. WEST AFRICA)
NORTHERN RHODESIA
Mozambique
Blantyre
PORTUGUESE EAST AFRICA
MADAGASCAR
Tananarive
St. Helena (Br.)
Zambezi River
Salisbury
Victoria Falls
SOUTHERN RHODESIA
Beira
GERMAN SOUTHWEST AFRICA
Windhoek
WALVIS BAY
BECHUANALAND
Limpopo River
TRANSVAAL
Pretoria
Johannesburg
Lourenço Marques
ORANGE FREE STATE
SWAZILAND
Orange River
UNION OF SOUTH AFRICA
Bloemfontein
NATAL
Durban
BASUTOLAND
Cape Town
Port Elizabeth
Cape of Good Hope
INDIAN OCEAN
France
Italy
Great Britain
Germany
Portugal
Belgium
Spain
N
0 250 500 1000 MILES
0 250 500 1000 KILOMETERS

In 1898, Congress took over the Hawaiian Islands. In 1959, Hawaii became the 50th state of the union.

Meanwhile, in the Spanish-American War of 1898, the United States acquired Guam and the Philippines, which had been Spanish possessions in the Pacific. When the war ended, the
● United States decided to keep the islands because of their economic and strategic value. The Filipinos fought for independence. However, after three years of hard fighting, they were finally defeated by the Americans. Military rule was set up. In 1902, the United States provided civilian rule and began to prepare the Philippines for self-government.

SECTION REVIEW **4**

p. 528 **1.** Name four areas in Asia that came under Russian rule in the 19th century. Why did these advances cause conflicts with Britain?

p. 528 **2.** Which areas came under British, French, and Dutch rule?

p. 529 **3.** Why did the islands of the Pacific become important in the late 19th century? How did the United States get control of Hawaii?

5 Africa was carved into many colonies

Nowhere did imperialism move with such speed as in Africa. Only a tenth of its huge land area was under European control in 1875. Within twenty years, only a tenth was free of such control.

France and Britain gained control of North Africa. Africa north of the Sahara had been

● Another view of the motives of the U.S. in keeping control of the Philippines may be found in C.S. Olcott's *The Life of Wm. McKinley,* Houghton Mifflin Co., 1916, pp. 110-111.

conquered by the Turks in the 15th century. It was made part of the Ottoman Empire. By the ans. 1
19th century, however, Turkish power was declining. The nations of Europe then saw a chance to extend their influence.

The first important European move into Africa was made by the French. They invaded Algeria in 1830, both for prestige and to stop Algerian pirates who attacked French ships. For many years, no other European state showed much interest in North Africa. Then in 1869, a French company finished building a canal across the Isthmus of Suez. The Middle East again became, as it had been in ancient times, a great crossroads of world trade.

In 1875, the British government bought a ans. 2
large bloc of shares in the Suez Canal Company. The canal was a vital link in Britain's lifeline to India, Australia, and New Zealand. When internal fighting broke out in Egypt in 1882, Britain sent in a military force. This force reduced the country to the status of a British protectorate.

The British next moved into the Sudan. They hoped eventually to control land from Cairo in the north to Cape Town in the south. But their immediate goal in the Sudan was to put down a native revolt. The first try ended in defeat when General Charles Gordon was killed by Sudanese forces at the battle of Khartoum [kär tüm′] in 1885. Thirteen years later, General Kitchener avenged Gordon's death by defeating the Sudanese at Omdurman. The following year, Britain and Egypt made the Sudan a *condominium,* that is, they made it an area jointly ruled by both countries. In fact, Britain was the stronger power.

Meanwhile, France had been actively developing Algeria. French influence was also being felt in Tunisia [tü nē′zhə] and Morocco. The

French had dreams of controlling the northern half of Africa, from Dakar on the west to French Somaliland [sə mä′lē land′] on the east. One step in carrying out this plan was Captain Marchand's expedition, which led to the Fashoda Incident described at the beginning of this chapter. The result was that the French were blocked by the British in the upper Nile region. But France continued to move into central and western Africa.

The rest of Africa was explored by Europeans. For centuries, only the coasts of Africa South of the Sahara were familiar to Europeans. In the early 1800s, however, many European explorers began to study the interior of Africa. One of the most famous was David Livingstone, a Scottish missionary. Between 1851 and 1873, he made several journeys. His writings increased interest in Africa and opposition to the slave trade.

Livingstone began his last journey in 1866. He was not heard from for several years, and many people feared that he was lost. In 1869, the New York *Herald* sent its best reporter, Henry M. Stanley, to Africa to "find Livingstone." He suffered great hardships in his search. Finally one day in 1871, he came into a village on Lake Tanganyika [tang′gə nyē′kə]. There stood a lone white man. In Stanley's words:

> As I advanced slowly toward him I noticed he was pale, looked wearied, had a grey beard, wore a bluish cap with a faded gold band around it, had on a red-sleeved waistcoat, and

Stanley and his force, armed with guns, fight off the Avissiba. From *In Darkest Africa* (1890), Stanley's book about his explorations.

a pair of grey tweed trousers. I would have run to him, would have embraced him, only I did not know how he would receive me; so I walked deliberately to him, took off my hat, and said: "Dr. Livingstone, I presume?" "Yes," he said with a kind smile, lifting his cap slightly. "I thank God, Doctor, I have been permitted to see you."

Stanley tried to persuade Livingstone to give up his work and return to Europe. But Livingstone refused and died in Africa two years later.

Meanwhile, Stanley became an explorer in his own right. During his journeys, he learned that Africa offered vast possibilities for commerce. Stanley returned to Europe to seek financial backing. With money from King Leopold II of Belgium, he founded a private company called the International Congo Association.

Western powers divided Africa. The International Congo Association rapidly began to divide the former African state of Kongo. In this region were many tribes who lived by farming or cattle raising. Stanley returned to the Congo in 1879. Within a few years, he made over 400 treaties with the native chiefs of these tribes. Stanley did not explain to the chiefs that by placing their marks on bits of paper in return for guns and cloth, they were giving their land to the Congo Association. Stanley gained huge tracts of land by these methods. This area came to be known as the Belgian Congo. ans. 3

Other explorers also used Stanley's methods and got huge areas of land for their countries.

In this 1880 photograph, French colonial administrators and African leaders discuss the government of Brazzaville (in the present-day Congo).

France took a vast area on the Congo River and important colonies in West Africa. Germany got slices of territory on the east and west coasts. The Italians made claims along the Red Sea. They were defeated soundly by the Abyssinians (later known as Ethiopians) in 1896 when the Italians tried to occupy their country.

The British, too, were active in this part of Africa. Cecil Rhodes went to South Africa in 1870. He made a fortune there in the diamond and gold mines. Rhodes was also important in Britain's gaining Bechuanaland [bech′ü ä′nə land′] and Rhodesia [rō dē′zhə]. Altogether, Britain ruled more than a dozen colonial areas.

By 1914, most of Africa had been taken over by European powers. Only Liberia and Abyssinia remained independent. The coming of Eu-
ans. 5 ropeans brought mixed results in Africa. On the one hand, they did away with slavery and tribal warfare in some areas. European help was also important in fighting disease and illiteracy and in building cities, roads, and industries.

On the other hand, Europeans wanted African labor most of all. Europeans used the Africans cruelly. Many were uprooted from their tribes and villages. Often their lands were taken over. They were made to pay heavy taxes and to supply forced labor. Some of the worst crimes took place in the Congo. There European overseers handed out brutal punishments in order to get greater rubber production. Execution, whipping, and torture were common.

Conditions slowly got better in the 20th century. A small Westernized class of Africans formed. They were angry about the treatment their peoples had received from the Europeans. These Africans formed the heart of a nationalistic movement that gathered strength as the years passed.

● The interrelationship of these factors may need to be a clarified for some students.

SECTION REVIEW 5

1. How was North Africa affected by the decline of the Turks? The construction of the Suez Canal? p. 531

2. How did Britain gain control over Egypt and the Sudan? p. 531

3. Describe how Livingstone, Stanley, and Rhodes opened up Africa to European powers. p. 533 534

4. What areas of Africa were possessions of Great Britain, France, and Germany by 1914? p. 530

5. How did European imperialism affect the peoples of Africa? p. 534

6 Imperialism grew in Latin America

Foreign interest in Latin America generally centered around economic matters. Colonization and direct rule were less common than in Africa and Asia.

Foreign investments led to trouble. Latin
America offered many important resources, in- ans. 1
cluding silver, gold, oil, rubber, platinum, tin, and copper. American and European investors were quick to make use of these resources. In the late 1800s, they spent billions of dollars to dig mines, sink oil wells, and build railroads and public utilities. These developments helped the countries in which they were made, but they also caused major problems. Corrupt local officials often made dishonest deals with foreign investors. And the investors made huge profits at the expense of the common peoples. ●

Another problem was that Latin-American governments were very unstable. Revolutions often caused changes of rulers. The new rulers would sometimes take over foreign property

Theodore Roosevelt and his company, the Rough Riders, were U.S. heroes when they helped defeat the Spanish in Cuba.

without payment. When this happened, the foreigners called for help from their homelands.

The United States used the Monroe Doctrine to intervene. The idea of large-scale European interference to protect their investments in Latin America worried the United States. The Monroe Doctrine had long been used by Americans to protect Latin America
ans. 2 from Europeans. In the 1890s, the United States
used the Monroe Doctrine in other ways.

For one thing, America began to act as a negotiator in disputes between Latin-American countries and European powers. More importantly, the United States now claimed that it had the right to intervene in Latin America itself to protect its own interests. The Spanish-American War of 1898 made this claim even clearer.

The Spanish-American War broke out. During the late 19th century, Cuba and Puerto Rico were swept by revolutions. These two countries were all that remained of Spain's New World empire. Both islands now wanted their
independence. Americans supported this desire ans. 3
and grew angry that the Cuban and Puerto Rican rebels were treated so harshly by the Spanish. These American feelings were backed up by other facts: (1) Americans had invested some $50 million in Cuba, (2) Cuba was the largest supplier of American sugar, (3) Cuba was strategically important because it controlled the entrance to the Gulf of Mexico.

It was clearly in the interest of the United States that Cuba be friendly and stable. To many Americans, this meant that Cuba should be free of Spanish rule. Thus, when the American battleship *Maine* was mysteriously sunk in ●

● Discuss what groups may have had motives to blow up the *Maine.* Spain? the Cuban rebels? Pro-war Americans?

Havana Harbor, those same Americans quickly blamed Spain and wanted to go to Cuba's aid. In 1898, the United States declared war and defeated Spain in less than five months.

As a result of the Spanish-American War, the United States took over Puerto Rico as well as the Philippine Islands in the Pacific. The war was supposed to have been fought for Cuba's freedom. Although Cuba was allowed to set up an independent government, the United States placed several limits on the new government. America kept the right to intervene in the foreign and domestic affairs of Cuba. The United States could also build naval bases on the island. In effect, Cuba became an American protectorate.

During the next twenty years, the United States actively intervened in Cuban affairs several times. Not until 1934 did the American ● government give up all such rights. Even then, the United States kept its naval base at Guantanamo [gwän tä′nə mō] Bay.

Dollar diplomacy characterized the early 20th century. In the thirty years after the Spanish-American War, American investments in Latin America reached new heights. The United States government worked closely with investors to get favorable terms for them. These joint efforts of government and business were often called "dollar diplomacy."

Theodore Roosevelt, President from 1901 to 1909, was a major figure in dollar diplomacy. He strongly favored the canal that the United States planned to build across the Isthmus of Panama. This area, however, belonged to Colombia. When revolution broke out there in 1903, President Roosevelt sent American marines to the scene. They kept Colombian troops from putting down the Panamanian rebels. Two weeks later, the United States formally recognized the new Republic of Panama. The United States then arranged a perpetual lease on a canal zone 10 miles (16 kilometers) wide. Panama, like Cuba, became an American protectorate. The Panama Canal, which had great strategic value for the United States, was finished in 1914.

Meanwhile, in 1904 Roosevelt stated his famous corollary to the Monroe Doctrine. The United States, he said, would be forced to take on the duties of international policeman in the Western Hemisphere.

During the era of dollar diplomacy, the Roosevelt Corollary was used to justify repeated American intervention in Central America and the Caribbean. In 1905, for example, the Dominican Republic went bankrupt. The United States took over the Dominican Republic's customs collections and made sure all its creditors were paid. The United States also stepped into Nicaragua [nik′ə rä′gwə] and Honduras [hon dür′əs] to set finances in order and to protect American investments. In 1915, internal trouble broke out in Haiti. American marines were sent to restore order. They remained in that country for almost twenty years.

Many people in the United States did not favor these imperialistic moves. They knew of the growing Latin-American resentment toward the ■ United States. Such feelings helped modify dollar diplomacy by the 1930s.

SECTION REVIEW 6

1. What three conditions in Latin America invited imperialism? p. 534

2. How did the American government change the meaning of the Monroe Doctrine in the 1890s? p. 535

3. What were three reasons that the United States entered the Spanish-American War? How did the United States keep control over Cuba after the war? p. 535

● The United States also kept Puerto Rico, and Puerto Ricans became U.S. citizens by birth in 1917.

■ Discuss how the feelings of Latin Americans toward the U.S. might have been affected by dollar diplomacy.

CHAPTER REVIEW 28

SECTION SUMMARIES

1. India lost its independence. Between 1870 and 1914, many Western countries extended their rule over foreign areas. The greatest interest was in underdeveloped areas. This movement, known as imperialism, had several causes and took many different forms. As early as the 18th century, the British had defeated the French in India. The British were then able to take over more land at the expense of the weak Mughuls. Rule by the East India Company was replaced by British government control after the Sepoy Rebellion of 1857.

2. Foreign powers exploited China. China under the Manchus had grown poor and weak by the 19th century. After the Opium War in 1839, the British gained important trading rights. Later, other foreign powers began to divide China up into spheres of influence. Several defeats left China helpless at the hands of Britain, France, Germany, and Russia. The United States also tried to get a foot in through its Open Door Policy. China held together, but the Boxer Rebellion and revolutionary groups showed how much the people hated foreign control.

3. Japan became a world power. The Japanese were brought into closer contact with the outside world by the United States. Japan, however, did not give in to Western domination. Instead, the Japanese began a major modernization program. The feudal shogunate was ended. A constitution was put into effect. Reforms were brought about in education and law. Most far-reaching was the rapid change from an agricultural to an industrial economy. As a result, Japan became a major power and itself turned to imperialism.

4. Many nations gained influence elsewhere in the East. Imperialism was also seen in other parts of Asia. Manchuria and Mongolia came under Russian influence. So did central and southwestern Asia. Indochina became a French protectorate. Burma was added to the British list. The Dutch ruled an island empire in the East Indies. Pacific islands were snapped up by Britain, Germany, France, and the United States.

5. Africa was carved into many colonies. Africa was quickly divided up. The French and the British each took parts of North Africa. Meanwhile, explorers moved into the interior south of the Sahara. By the end of the 19th century, all but two states of Africa had lost their independence. Britain and France controlled the most area. However, large portions went to Belgium, Germany, and Portugal. Italy also had some claims.

6. Imperialism grew in Latin America. In Latin America, the United States played a dominant role, especially after the Spanish-American War. It took over Puerto Rico and turned Cuba into an American protectorate. The policy of dollar diplomacy led to American intervention in Panama, Nicaragua, and Haiti.

WHO? WHAT? WHEN? WHERE?

1. Give the years in which each of these events occurred and arrange them in the correct chronological order:

Maine exploded in Havana Harbor. 1898 (7)
The Opium War broke out. 1839 (1)
The United States annexed Hawaii. 1898 (8)
Japan won the Sino-Japanese War. 1895 (6)
The Suez Canal was begun. 1869 (4)
The United States announced the Open Door Policy. 1899 (9)
Laos was seized by the French. 1893 (5)
The Russo-Japanese War ended. 1905 (11)
The British East India Company was abolished. 1858 (2)
The Boxer Rebellion was ended. 1900 (10)
The Meiji Restoration began a new era in Japan. 1868 (3)

CHAPTER TEST 28

2. What were the terms of each of the treaties listed below? Name the wars that ended with three of the treaties.

Treaty of Nanking p. 523	Treaty of Shimonoseki p. 527
Treaty of Kanagawa p. 525	Treaty of Portsmouth p. 528

3. Tell how each of these people helped in the development or the takeover of a colonial area:

Henry M. Stanley p. 532	Horatio Kitchener p. 531
Cecil Rhodes p. 534	Charles Gordon p. 531
Leopold II p. 533	Commodore Perry p. 525

● **4.** What were the causes of each of these movements: Muslim League, Indian National Congress, Sepoy Rebellion, Society of Harmonious Fists?

5. Explain each of these terms:

extraterritoriality p. 524	spheres of influence p. 524
p. 524 the Open Door Policy	imperialism p. 519
protectorate p. 528	Roosevelt Corollary p. 536

QUESTIONS FOR CRITICAL THINKING

■ **1.** What were the motives of imperialistic nations in taking over lands in Africa and Asia?

2. Why was Japan able to become an industrialized nation within fifty years?

3. Why was Japan's victory over Russia so surprising to the West?

ACTIVITIES

1. On a large wall map of the world, use colored string and pins to connect the imperialistic nations with the areas they ruled.

2. Prepare two maps of Africa, one showing the extent of foreign rule in 1875 and the other showing the extent of foreign rule in 1914.

3. Debate or discuss the harm and the good done by imperialistic rule.

4. Use the Atlas of the Modern World (pages 691–698) to find what areas are still under colonial rule in the world today.

● 4. p. 522, 522, 521, 524

■ QUESTIONS FOR CRITICAL THINKING

1. Ask for motives displayed in specific areas.

2. The government was able to force adoption of changes to institutions which promoted industry.

SECTION 1

1. True or false: Indians were allowed to take part in the government of India under British rule.

2. Britain's most important contribution to India was: a. education, b. industry, c. unification

SECTION 2

3. The Open Door Policy was a plan of: a. the United States, b. Britain, c. China

4. True or false: The Boxer Rebellion was caused by British sales of opium to the Chinese.

SECTION 3

5. True or false: The United States won the American-Japanese War, opening Japan to foreigners.

6. Which of these was *not* a Western idea adopted by the Japanese? a. legal system, b. compulsory education, c. democratic government

SECTION 4

7. Three European powers in Southeast Asia were Britain, France, and: a. Germany, b. the Netherlands, c. Italy

8. True or false: In their colonies, the British allowed the native languages to be used in schools.

SECTION 5

9. Imperialism moved most quickly in: a. Africa, b. Asia, c. Latin America

10. Under the rule of imperialism, tribal societies in Africa were: a. strengthened, b. weakened, c. destroyed

SECTION 6

11. True or false: The Monroe Doctrine was used by the United States to justify its interference in Latin America.

12. As a result of the Spanish-American War, the United States annexed: a. Mexico, b. the Philippines, c. Spain

3. (p. 527) No Asian nation had defeated a western nation before. (In this era.)

1914–1920

CHAPTER 29

World War I

The nations of Europe played a deadly game that led, in the end, to World War I. A Spanish cartoonist showed it as a game of billiards played by national leaders with rifles and swords for cues. The table is covered by a map of Europe, and bombs are stacked under it.

> A friend came to see me . . . he thinks it was on Monday, August 3 [1914]. We were standing at a window of my room in the Foreign Office. It was getting dusk, and the lamps were being lit in the space below on which we were looking. My friend recalls that I remarked on this [scene] with the words: "The lamps are going out all over Europe; we shall not see them lit again in our time." ●

● You might explain to students the meaning of this metaphor.

These were the sad words of Sir Edward Grey, the foreign secretary of Great Britain. Europe was heading into a long and deadly war. This was the Great War that drew into it not only the major powers of Europe, but also those of America and Asia as well.

The Great War, or World War I as it was later known, lasted for more than four years. Many think it was the single most important event of the 20th century. It was the beginning of Europe's decline as the center of world power and influence after 400 years of leadership. By the time the war ended, millions of people on both sides had been wiped out. Britain and France had been greatly weakened. The Hohenzollern, Hapsburg, and Romanov dynasties had fallen apart. Communists had taken over in Russia. Anticolonialism had grown stronger in Asia, the Middle East, and Africa. Finally, the United States had come forth as the most powerful nation in the world.

Nobody in Europe in 1914 could have guessed these results. This turned out to be the first *total* war in history. It was fought by mass armies. It involved people at home as well as soldiers at the front. And for the first time, weapons of mass destruction were widely used. These included the machine gun, the tank, the airplane, and the submarine.

● Why was the war fought at all? There is no simple answer. Basically, the European nations could not find a peaceful way to adjust to the great changes that had taken place since 1870. One of those changes was the rapid spread of industrialization, especially in countries such as Germany. This resulted in hard competition for trade, markets, and colonies. Another change was the growth of intense nationalism. This took place among both the old and new powers. When a new nation such as Germany, for example, tried to increase its power by building up a strong navy, an older nation such as Britain saw the new nation as a threat. An armaments race thus began. This came on top of the rivalries that already existed for colonies and for friendly allies. At the same time, the struggles of discontented peoples in the Balkans often broke out in fighting. Year by year, tensions built up in Europe. People began to feel that some day war would probably come. Thus we shall learn in this chapter how:

● Be sure your students understand each of these factors.

1. Disputes and alliances increased tensions.

2. Some forces promoted peace while others worked for war.

3. A Balkan crisis brought general war.

4. The world went to war.

5. The victors tried to build a lasting peace.

1 Disputes and alliances increased tensions

During the late 19th century, national rivalries in Europe became more and more dangerous to general peace. Each country looked for ways to provide itself with safety from enemy attack. One way was to form alliances against possible ans. 1
enemies. Another was to build up armaments. A third was to gain control of colonies because many people thought that colonies added to a country's strength.

Imperialism in Africa and Asia caused conflicts. In many places around the world, the imperialistic interests of different countries clashed. In Morocco, for example, Germany threatened French power. The first Moroccan crisis took place in 1905. It led to a diplomatic victory for France after a conference of European powers at Algeciras, Spain, in 1906. Six years later, the Germans again challanged the French. A German gunboat tried to enforce the Kaiser's protest against French activity in Morocco. This time, Britain's support of France forced Germany to yield.

Britain and France were not always allies, however. They came close to war in the 1898 Fashoda Incident described in Chapter 28. Britain also clashed with Dutch settlers called Boers in South Africa. There, Britain came out the winner after the Boer War in 1902.

Britain was also involved with Japan and Russia in Asian rivalries. For centuries, the Russians had been trying to get a warm-water port. They needed an outlet to the sea that would be open all year; Russia's own coasts were blocked by ice most of the time. In 1877, Russia declared war on the Ottoman Empire in hopes of gaining control of the Dardanelles. The Russians said that they were just rescuing their fellow Slavs in the Balkan part of the Ottoman Empire from Turkish cruelties. After months of hard fighting,

A German cartoon of Britain's empire shows it sprawled across three continents—a foot in Great Britain, another in Africa, and hands in Egypt and India.

the Russians won this Russo-Turkish War. They were then in a position to get to the warm-water ports of the Mediterranean Sea.

But Great Britain was alarmed at these Russian gains. They threatened British sea power in ● the Mediterranean and brought Russia close to the Suez Canal. The canal was the vital link in the sea route to India. To protect the canal, the British prime minister, Benjamin Disraeli, asked for the help of other European countries. In July, 1878, representatives of all the Great Powers met at the Congress of Berlin. The most important result of the Congress was to block Russia from further gains.

The actions taken at the Congress, however, did not halt Russia's drive for greater empire. Blocked in Europe and the Middle East, Russia in the 1890s turned to Manchuria. This move angered Japan since Russia had opposed Japanese control over Korea. Both Manchuria and Korea belonged to China. But China was too weak to stand up for its rights. Thus, the rivalry led in 1904 to the Russo-Japanese War (Chapter 28) in which the Russians were defeated by Japan. Japan's victory had a great effect on the peoples of Asia. It led them to believe that they would one day be able to throw off Western imperialist rule.

Bismarck's alliances frightened Europe.
After France was defeated in the Franco- ans. 2
Prussian War of 1870–1871, the German prime minister, Bismarck, feared that the French might seek allies in a war of revenge. France, after all, had lost the valuable provinces of Alsace and Lorraine. He began to make alliances for Germany, mainly to isolate the French. Bismarck's most important alliance was with Austria in 1879. Called the Dual Alliance, it lasted until 1914. In 1882, Italy joined Ger-

● Point out that because Great Britain is a small island it cannot produce enough food or raw materials to survive. Therefore its naval strength was vitally important.

many and Austria, thus setting up the Triple Alliance. The members of the Triple Alliance promised that if any one of them should be attacked, all three would fight together.

Through very skillful diplomacy, Bismarck was also able to bring Germany and Russia together. This took the form of the so-called Reinsurance Treaty of 1887. Germany promised its support to Russia in certain Balkan matters. And Russia promised neutrality in the event of a French attack on Germany. These agreements served to carry out Bismarck's basic plan: the isolation of France. There was no major country left on the continent of Europe with whom France could make an alliance.

The kaiser changed German policy. In 1890, young Kaiser William II caused Bis-
ans. 3 marck to resign from office. Contrary to Bismarck's policy of friendship with Russia, the kaiser stopped making loans to the tsar. The treaty between Germany and Russia was allowed to die. And the kaiser joined Austria in a promise to defend their common interests in the Balkans against the Russians.

The Russians now had to look to other great powers for alliances and loans. France eagerly grabbed the chance to ally itself with Russia. Both countries feared Germany. France had made an amazing recovery from its defeat of 1871. It had built a strong army and was again prosperous. It loaned Russia millions of francs. Russia used this money to purchase arms and build the Trans-Siberian Railroad. In 1894, France and Russia signed a military alliance.
ans. 4 Thus, Europe was split into two armed camps.

Great Britain began to seek allies and expand its navy. Great Britain was in neither camp. Protected by its great navy, Britain lived in what was called "splendid isolation." Its rich colonies circled the earth. Its strong navy brought a feeling of security to the home islands and colonies. Great Britain did not want to be tied down to alliances so long as no European nation threatened its interests.

By 1900, however, Great Britain decided that it needed allies. After all, Germany was building a merchant fleet and a navy to outstrip English sea power. In addition, Kaiser William's warlike speeches upset the British as much as his actions. Britain feared that an enemy blockade would put it in danger of starvation. This was because Britain imported most of its food. Thus, to keep control of the seas, Britain felt it had to build twice as many ships as Germany. At the same time, German industry rivaled that of Great Britain. The two nations competed in world markets.

Because of mutual distrust of Germany, Great Britain wanted to make an alliance with its old rival, France. In 1904, the British and French signed an agreement called the *Entente Cordiale* (French for "friendly understanding"). ● After this, France worked to bring Russia and Great Britain closer together. By 1907, Russia joined France and Britain in the second of the great European alliances, the Triple Entente.

● This was not a military agreement but a symbol of the "friendly understanding" between the two nations.

SECTION REVIEW 1

1. What were the three ways European nations tried to protect themselves from attack in the late 19th century? p. 540

2. Why did Bismarck try to isolate France after the Franco-Prussian War? What nations were allied with Germany by 1887? p. 541

3. What did Kaiser William II do that caused Russia and Britain to become allies of France? p. 542

4. Why were the Triple Alliance and Triple Entente a threat to peace in Europe? p. 542

2 Some forces promoted peace while others worked for war

We have seen some of the rivalries that were building national tensions. On the international level, however, there was growing economic and political cooperation. These forces favored peace. Unfortunately, they could not stop the tide of war.

The world economy needed peace. By the early 20th century, the nations and peoples of the world had become economically interdependent. European capital and know-how had helped speed the economic growth of Asia, Africa, and the Americas. For example, money borrowed from Britain helped build the American railway system, as well as railroads in Argentina and eastern Europe.

Peace meant that raw materials could be bought and finished goods sold throughout the world. Large companies could set up offices, factories, and plantations in foreign countries. Telephones, telegraphs, and cables could be used for quick communication. Railroads and steamships could carry products anywhere without danger. Most important of all, the industrialized countries, while political rivals, were also each other's best customers for manufactured goods. Prosperity built on international trade would be destroyed by war. Because of this, many people in business and politics worked for world harmony.

International organizations were formed. World organizations were another force fa-
ans. 1 voring peace. In 1868, twenty nations set up the International Telegraph Union. In 1874, the General Postal Union was formed. International agreements were also reached on such matters as weights and measures, underwater cables, navigation of international rivers, and protection of wildlife. The Greek Olympic games were revived in 1896. This event, held every four years, brought together people from nearly every country of the world.

In the Western Hemisphere, the Pan-American movement encouraged cooperation among American nations. Trade was promoted, and an organization was set up which became known as the Pan American Union.

The International Red Cross was founded to help lessen the hardships of war. The Geneva Convention of 1864 was a set of agreements reached at the first meeting. It became a model for other international agreements covering victims of warfare at sea, prisoners of war, and civilians during wartime. National Red Cross societies also gave peacetime aid to disaster victims and others.

In spite of the growth of international organi- ans. 2
zations and trade, fear and suspicion spread among rival European countries between 1900
and 1914. Every Great Power believed its own ans. 3
security depended on maintaining the alliance to which it belonged. That meant it had to support an ally if that ally got into a dispute with a rival. Allies of the rival would do the same. In this way, a local crisis anywhere in Europe could easily blow up into a general war among all the Great Powers.

SECTION REVIEW **2**

1. Give three examples of international cooperation before World War I began. p. 543

2. Why did the Great Powers feel that they had to support their allies? p. 543

3. How was it possible for a small local conflict to quickly become a widespread war? p. 543

3 A Balkan crisis brought general war

Just such a local crisis broke out in the Balkans in 1914. By then, relations between Serbia and Austria had reached a breaking point. Serbia, supported by Russia, wanted to unite with the Serbs living in the Austro-Hungarian Empire and create a Greater Serbia. Austria, supported by Germany, did not want to see that happen.
ans. 1 Austria feared that if Serbia did unite, all the other minority Slav groups living in the empire would also demand self-rule. The empire would then collapse. To save it, Austrian leaders felt they had to destroy Serbia as an independent nation.

The archduke of Austria was murdered. In June, 1914, Archduke Francis Ferdinand, heir to the Austrian throne, visited the Balkan city of Sarajevo [sär′ ə yā′vō]. As Archduke Ferdinand rode through the streets in an open car, a young man sprang forward. He fired a gun and killed both the archduke and his wife.

Count Leopold von Berchtold, the Austrian foreign minister, suspected that the crime was of Serbian origin. At once, he took steps to prevent Serbia from being a center for anti-Austrian propaganda. He sent a letter to Kaiser William II of Germany which was signed by the Austrian emperor, Francis Joseph I. In the letter, Berchtold asked for German help. The kaiser gladly ans. 2
agreed because he was eager to keep Austria as an ally. He also believed that the conflict could be kept within the Balkans. The kaiser's reply placed no limits on the amount of help Austria could expect from Germany. It became known as the "blank check."

With such strong support, Berchtold sent a message to Serbia on July 23, 1914. He warned that all anti-Austrian activities in Serbia must be stopped. He also said that Austro-Hungarian officials should be used to end such activities. Finally, all Serbian officials guilty of anti-Austrian propaganda should be dismissed.

■

Austria declared war on Serbia. Berchtold gave the Serbs forty-eight hours to reply to this ultimatum, as it was called. Should they refuse, he was sure that Austria could defeat Serbia in a local war. Furthermore, because Germany was an ally of Austria, he believed other nations would be afraid to help Serbia.

The Serbs did agree to some of the Austrian demands. But they felt they would lose their independence if they agreed to all of them. Serbia called on Russia for help. The Russians pledged support. Thus, a local war was in danger of blowing up into a big war.

As tension mounted, Sir Edward Grey, the ans. 3
British foreign secretary, tried to arrange talks ●
between Serbia and Austria. But meanwhile,

● The German kaiser made repeated attempts to restrain Austria—until the Russians began mobilization.

■ Have students compare this map of nationalities in eastern Europe with the map of Europe after World War I on page 552 to see how different nationality groups achieved independence.

Berchtold convinced the Austrian emperor that war was the only way to deal with the Serbs. He paid no attention to Grey's proposals for peace. German military leaders also encouraged Berchtold. On July 28, 1914, Austria declared war on Serbia.

Alliances brought other nations into the war. Even at that stage, more pressure from the German chancellor might have opened a path for a peaceful settlement. However, on ● July 30, mobilization of the Russian army began. This ended further tries at negotiation.

The Russians felt they should help their fellow Slavs, the Serbs. They also knew that a Serbian

● This was very significant because it can take more than a week to prepare an army for war. When Russia mobilized Germany had to do the same or risk being caught unprepared.

defeat would be a major blow to Russia's standing as a Great Power. When France assured Russia of support, Tsar Nicholas II gave in to the advice of his war-hungry generals.

News of Russian mobilization and French ans. 4
support caused alarm in the German capital. It looked as if Germany would have to fight on two fronts: France on the west and Russia on the east. Germany at once demanded that Russia halt war moves and that France stay neutral. These nations refused. On August 1, Germany declared war on France. The Germans demanded that their troops be allowed to cross Belgian frontiers on the way to the French front. Belgium refused and looked instead to Britain and

France for help. Germany ignored the refusal and sent its troops across Belgium anyway.

Great Britain, as a member of the Triple Entente, was not bound to help France or Russia in a war. But in entering Belgium, Germany had broken a 75-year-old international treaty that guaranteed Belgium's neutrality. The violation
ans. 4 angered Britain, who was a party to the treaty with Germany. It also made the British fearful because Germany might gain control of the North Sea coast and thus threaten the British Isles. Therefore, on August 4, Great Britain declared war on Germany.

SECTION REVIEW 3

p. 544 **1.** Why did the Austrian government feel threatened by Serbia before the death of the Archduke?

p. 544 **2.** What demands did Austria make on Serbia after the murder of Francis Ferdinand? How much help did Germany promise Austria?

p. 544 **3.** What steps were taken to prevent a war after Austria's message to Serbia?

p. 545 **4.** Why did Germany declare war on France? Why
546 did Great Britain declare war on Germany?

4 The world went to war

In August, 1914, at the start of the war, only six nations were fighting. On one side were the Allies—Great Britain, France, Russia, and Serbia. Opposing them were the Central Powers—Germany and Austria. The strength of the Central Powers grew when the Ottoman Empire joined in October, 1914, and Bulgaria a year later.

Although Italy was an ally of Germany and Austria in the Triple Alliance, it felt no real friendship for Austria. When the war began,

Be sure to allow time to study the photos included in this chapter. They can be used as primary sources for discussion, reports, or to motivate research.

In the Battlefields

The misery of World War I warfare had no equal. The military forces were deadlocked from very early in the war, yet the leaders could not accept any compromise to all-out victory. Armies found themselves fighting for months over possession of a few miles of mud, trenches, and barbed wire. As hundreds were killed and wounded, new troops, barely trained, were sent to the battlefields. *Above left:* young, untrained, scared, and far from home, two soldiers face certain death. *Below left:* inside a trench, soldiers found little shelter from bombs, hand grenades, and machine-gun fire. *Above right:* fighter-bombers were first used in World War I. *Below right:* an American and French ammunition train rushes supplies to the front.

Italy declared it would stay *neutral*, meaning it would not choose one side or the other. For several months, the Allies and the Central Powers each tried to win Italy to their respective sides. In April, 1915, after promises of territory in Austria and Africa, Italy joined the Allies.

Japan had already joined the Allies in 1914. In 1917, China declared war against Germany and Austria. By the end, thirty-one countries had entered the war. It lasted more than four years and drew more than 61 million people into military service.

Because the kaiser had decided to make Germany the most powerful country in the world, many in the Allied nations felt that Germany was chiefly at fault for causing World War I. They felt that Germany had encouraged Austria's dispute with Serbia. Also, Germany had brought the other countries in by declaring war on France and by marching through neutral Belgium. Actually, however, each of the Allies had a reason for wanting war with Germany. All shared in the blame.

The Allies held firm. By striking fast
ans. 1 through Belgium, Germany tried to deal France a quick blow. The highly trained German troops almost reached Paris before the French stopped them. The French were aided by a hasty Russian offensive on the Eastern Front. This made the Germans shift large numbers of troops from west to east. The French then forced the weakened Germans back at the Marne River. This ended German hopes for a quick victory.

● From 1915 to 1917, bitter fighting on the Western Front raged back and forth. The Allies and the Germans built trenches. Neither side made major advances. The war became a stalemate. Great battles were fought, and many were killed. But very little territory changed hands.

● The poetry of Rupert Brooke and Wilfred Owen could be used to add a deeper understanding of the realities of war.

■ For the first time the entire populations of the warring nations were involved in the war effort.

Technology gave both sides deadly weapons. Weapons had become more powerful than ever before in history. Battles were fought ■ in the air and under the sea, as well as on land and on sea. Germany attacked British battleships with submarines. Early in the war, both Germany and the Allies used airplanes for spying. By 1917, both had developed fighter and bomber planes. Each side bombed targets hundreds of miles from their home air bases.

The British introduced tanks. Later, the Germans used them. Sea and land mines, torpedo boats, hand grenades, flamethrowers, machine guns, and many other weapons were created or improved by technological advances. Giant guns, such as the German "Big Bertha," fired shells more than 75 miles [120 kilometers].

The Central Powers won victories in the east. On the Eastern Front, the Russians kept a large part of the German army busy. The Russian invasion of East Prussia in 1914 drew German divisions from the Western Front. However, after the Germans made a successful counterattack there, the Russians drew back. Further defeats took away the Russian will to fight. Russian losses, mounting into the millions,
were even greater than those of the French and ans. 1
British. Although they continued to resist the Germans and Austrians, for the most part the Russians fought only a defensive war.

In 1915, the British and French tried to use the Dardanelles to send supplies to Russia. But these plans failed. Later in 1915, Austria and Bulgaria defeated Serbia and occupied it. This victory gave the Central Powers control of an unbroken line from Berlin to Istanbul.

Germany stepped up naval warfare. During the first months of the war, Allied ship-

ping was heavily damaged by the German navy.
ans. 2 Early in 1915, Germany stated that all the waters around the British Isles would be treated as a war zone. Any enemy ship—including merchant ships—found in this zone would be attacked. Britain fought back by ordering a blockade of Germany and seizing all goods headed for German ports.

ans. 1 By 1916, the British blockade caused a great shortage of food supplies in Germany. Later in the year, Germany added more submarines. With their help, German light cruisers were able to slip through the blockade to raid Atlantic shipping. Britain speeded up shipbuilding and developed depth bombs. But German naval warfare—especially submarine warfare—was very effective. By the early part of 1917, supplies of food in England were running low, and the country was close to starvation.

In March, 1917, the people of Russia revolted against the tsar. They set up a new government that tried to carry on the war. But from that time on, Germany had little to fear from Russia.

The United States joined the Allies. One month later, the United States entered the war. Since August, 1914, the United States had tried ● to stay neutral. As the war dragged on, however, German submarines attacked American ships carrying supplies to Britain and France. The Americans said that as neutrals, they had freedom of the seas and could go anywhere. The Germans felt that they could not let supplies reach their enemies. In 1915 and 1916, German submarine attacks caused the loss of hundreds of American lives. President Woodrow Wilson warned the Germans to stop the attacks. But the Germans felt they were in a life-and-death struggle and ignored the warning. Then on January 31, 1917, Germany announced "unrestricted submarine warfare." This meant that all ships headed toward Britain and France would be attacked without warning. In the next two months, several American ships were sunk.

● The U.S. shared stronger ties of common traditions and friendship with Britain and France. There was also fear for the safety of the U.S. should Germany win the war.

Late in March, British agents got hold of a telegram sent to Mexico by Alfred Zimmermann, the German foreign secretary. It asked Mexico to ally itself with Germany and help fight the United States. Besides financial aid, Zimmermann promised that Mexico would recover Texas, New Mexico, and Arizona when the Allies were defeated.

German submarine warfare and the Zimmermann telegram raised pro-war feelings in the United States to a feverish pitch. President Wilson gave up his efforts to end the war through negotiation. He urged that the United States enter the war at once. On April 6, 1917, Congress declared war on Germany.

Russia got out of the war. At the same time that Russian soldiers were fighting in the battlefields of World War I, the Russian people were fighting the tsar's forces in the capital. A revolution in November, 1917, left Russia under Bolshevik party leadership.

By this time, the Russians were sick of the war that had cost them so many lives and severe food and fuel shortages. Their leader, Vladimir Ilyich Ulyanov (better known as Lenin), offered to make peace with Germany. On March 3, 1918, the Bolsheviks and the Germans signed the Treaty of Brest-Litovsk. Through this treaty, Russia lost a third of its people, nine-tenths of its coal mines, and all of the great Caucasian oil fields to Germany. As a result, Germany greatly increased its power. Even more important, Germany no longer needed to fight on two fronts.

The tide turned for the Allies. While Russia was crumbling, the first troops from the United States landed in France. German leaders tried hard to win the war before the American army could get into action. Following the Brest-Litovsk treaty, they sent almost every German soldier to the Western Front. There they began
ans. 4 a huge attack in the spring of 1918. But it failed as American, British, and French troops were able to stop the Germans. Later, American troops under General John J. Pershing carried out brilliant offensives in France.

In the fall of 1918, it became clear that Germany could not win. One by one, Germany's allies quit. On November 3, German sailors mutinied at Kiel. Four days later, a revolution broke out in Germany. A republic was founded, and the kaiser fled to Holland. Thus ended Hohenzollern rule and the Second German Reich.

Leaders of the new German government agreed to an armistice. They asked that the peace settlement be based on the Fourteen Points that President Wilson had set forth in a speech to Congress on January 8, 1918. Some of the points were: an end to secret agreements, freedom of the seas in peace and war, reduction of armaments, the right of nationality groups to form their own nations, and an association of nations to keep the peace. In other speeches, Wilson called for a negotiated peace with reasonable demands on the losers. The Allies also agreed to model the peace settlement on the Fourteen Points. However, there was some feeling that Wilson's terms would be too easy on Germany.

Early in the morning of November 11, 1918, the war was ended. In a railroad car in the Compiègne [kon′pyen′] Forest in northern France, two German delegates met Allied officials to sign the armistice.

On the Home Fronts
In the first two years of the war, the public in the warring countries was very enthusiastic. Everyone rallied behind the war effort, making personal sacrifices and changing life-styles so that materials and money could go to making weapons and military supplies. Women who had never worked outside their homes joined the Red Cross *(above)* and other volunteer organizations.

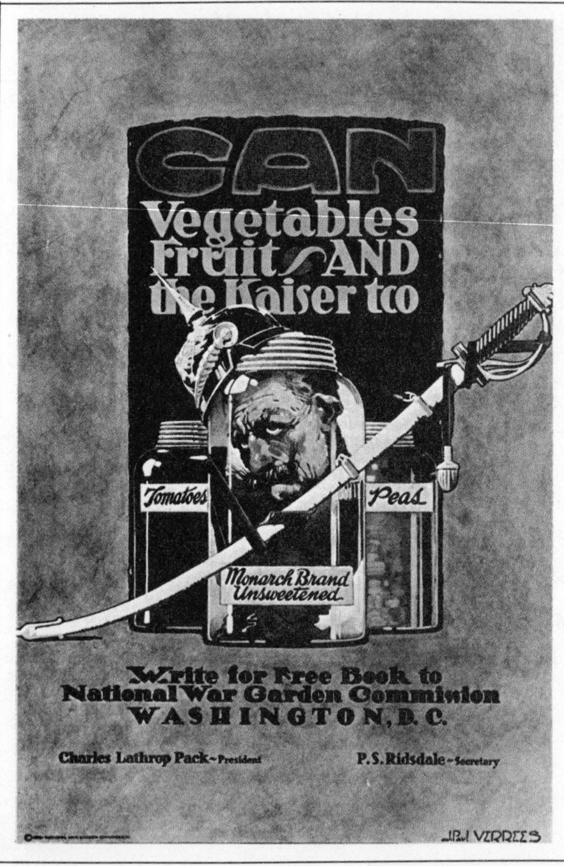

As more and more men left industrial jobs to fight in the war, women learned to take over. The women *below right* are learning to repair cars. One woman writer of the day feared that such training would unsuit them for "American Family Life." The poster *below left* urges Americans to grow and can their own food as one way to "can the Kaiser."

SECTION REVIEW 4

1. What successes did the Allies and the Central Powers have between 1914 and 1917? p. 548 549
2. Describe the actions taken in the naval warfare of Britain and Germany. p. 549
3. What made the United States enter the war? p. 549
4. What events led to victory for the Allies? Why did the Germans want the peace settlement to be based on the Fourteen Points? p. 550

5 The victors tried to build a lasting peace

No previous war in the world's history had caused such widespread horror. More than 10 million were killed in battle. Twenty million more were wounded. And 13 million civilians died from famine, disease, or war injuries. In addition, the cost of the war was estimated at more than $350 billion.

Three leaders dominated the Paris Peace Conference. After the armistice was signed, the Allied Nations met at Paris to discuss peace terms. Contrary to Wilson's wishes, the defeated countries were not allowed to send representatives to the peace conference. Thus the so-called Big Three dominated the meeting. They included President Wilson, David Lloyd George, prime minister of Great Britain, and Georges Clemenceau [klem′ən sō′], premier of France. ans. 1

Woodrow Wilson was a great idealist. He stated the hopes of people everywhere when he said that the conflict had been fought "for . . . democracy . . . for the rights and liberties of small nations . . . for . . . free peoples . . . to make the world itself at last free." At the conference, Wilson upheld his Fourteen Points. Above all, he wanted to see a League of Nations set up to keep the peace. To get the others to agree to this, he had to compromise.

Lloyd George wanted Great Britain to take control of Germany's colonies. He also wanted the German navy destroyed and Germany to pay for the cost of the war.

Georges Clemenceau, known as the "Old Tiger," had led France during the darkest hours of the war. He was mainly interested in making France safe from attack by making Germany as weak as possible. He wanted France to rely upon its alliances and the traditional balance of power for security. Clemenceau placed little faith in a league of nations. However, when Wil-
ans. 2 son gave in on many details, Clemenceau and Lloyd George agreed to make the creation of the League of Nations part of the Versailles Treaty.

Germany lost territory and wealth. When the German delegation arrived to sign the Treaty of Versailles, they found its terms harsher than they had expected.

The Germans were very angry at a war-guilt clause, Article 231, which placed the entire blame for the war on Germany and its allies. In addition, they were unhappy that many of Wilson's Fourteen Points were missing or were weakened by changes. The first delegates from Germany refused to sign the treaty. To avoid occupation by Allied soldiers, however, a second delegation signed it on June 28, 1919.

ans. 3 In the treaty, France won back the provinces of Alsace and Lorraine. The German territory west of the Rhine, called the Rhineland, was to become a buffer zone between the two enemies. It was to be occupied by Allied troops for at least fifteen years. Wilson and Lloyd George promised to protect France against possible future German attack. France was also given the rich coal mines of the Saar. But the Saar was to be administered by the League of Nations. After fifteen years, the Saarlanders could vote to have their region go back to the German government or remain under the French. In 1935, they voted to become a part of Germany again.

In March, 1917, Poland had become inde- ans. 3
pendent of Russia. Through the Versailles Treaty, it won a broad stretch of land from ●
Germany. This region became known as the Polish Corridor. It gave Poland an outlet to the Baltic Sea. The Polish Corridor also divided Germany, isolating its province of East Prussia.

The Versailles Treaty gave German colonies in Africa and in the Pacific to the League of Nations. The League in turn placed them under the control of the Allied Nations. These lands, ■
known as mandates, were given mainly to Great Britain and France. Some also went to Japan, South Africa, Australia, and New Zealand.

In the treaty, the Allies required that Germany repay the cost of the war. They wanted an immediate payment of $5 billion in cash. Two years later, they billed Germany for $32 billion, plus interest.

The treaty reduced German military power and permitted Germany an army of no more than 100 thousand men. The navy was allowed only six warships and some other vessels and no submarines or military airplanes.

The Germans were not alone in thinking such peace terms unjust. Even David Lloyd George was in doubt about the justice of the Versailles Treaty. President Wilson hoped that his dream, the League of Nations, could keep the peace. He thought that the League would be able to correct unjust features of the treaty later.

● Much of this land had been taken from Poland by Germany in the 18th century.

■ There were 3 classes of mandates, based on their ability for self-rule. A report on their administration was to be made once a year to the League.

The Versailles Treaty. Seated center are Clemenceau (with mustache), Lloyd George (right), and Wilson (left).

New independent nations were formed. ans. 4 Four empires had fallen apart in the course of World War I—the German, the Austro-Hungarian, the Ottoman, and the Russian empires. Based partly on secret agreements made during the war, the Allies drew up a series of peace treaties that broke up these empires. The Allies reorganized the land lost by Russia to Germany. From the western portion of the old Russian Empire came five new nations: Poland, Finland, Latvia, Lithuania, and Estonia.

The defeated Austro-Hungarian Empire was also broken up into several new countries. Austria and Hungary became two independent republics, as did Yugoslavia and Czechoslovakia. Some Austro-Hungarian land also went to Poland, Italy, and Romania.

The Ottoman Empire, too, was divided up. Syria, Iraq, and Palestine became mandates. The first was ruled by France; the last two by Britain. These mandates were promised independence at a future time.

The creation of the new states helped to fulfill one of Wilson's Fourteen Points. This was the right of *self-determination,* or the right of peoples to form their own nations. However, re-

drawing the map of Europe again brought some groups under foreign control. For example, Austrians living in the Tyrol came under the rule of Italy. Other German-speaking Austrians (the Sudetens) were placed under Czechoslovakian rule. Some Germans lived in the new Polish Corridor, and certain Hungarians came under Romanian control. Few of these peoples were happy about the changes made in their lives. Their discontent was a dangerous sign for the future of Europe.

SECTION REVIEW **5**

1. Who were the major participants at the Paris Peace Conference? What were the goals of each of the Big Three? p. 551

2. How did the League of Nations come to be part of the Treaty of Versailles? What was the League intended to do? p. 552

3. What were the major terms that the treaty imposed on Germany? p. 552

4. What four empires fell apart during the war? p. 553

CHAPTER REVIEW 29

SECTION SUMMARIES

1. Disputes and alliances increased tensions. In the late 19th century, there was growing economic cooperation among the Western nations. Progress and prosperity were made possible in part by peace. Yet a general mood for war began to take hold after 1900. National rivalries and colonial interests caused tensions. These led to an armaments race which added further fuel to the fire.

Nations tried to find security by joining various alliances. Under Bismarck, the German Empire set up the Triple Alliance with Austria-Hungary and Italy. To balance this, France, Russia, and Great Britain formed the Triple Entente. Such alliances meant that a local crisis could easily blow up into a general war.

2. Some forces promoted peace while others worked for war. Along with more economic interdependence, there was growing political cooperation. Several new international organizations were formed. But fears and insecurities caused the mood for war to grow stronger than the desire for peace.

3. A Balkan crisis brought general war. In 1914, the murder of Archduke Francis Ferdinand of Austria at Sarajevo led to war between Austria and Serbia. The war at once involved Russia, a friend of Serbia, and Germany, a partner of Austria. France and Great Britain soon joined Russia.

4. The world went to war. From 1914 to 1917, France and Britain fought bitterly against Germany on the Western Front. The British blockade in the North Sea prevented trade between Germany and neutral nations. This reduced food supplies in Germany. But German submarines sank so much Allied shipping that the British were also lacking food.

In 1917, the Bolsheviks gained control of Russia and made a separate peace with Germany. That same year, the United States declared war on the Central Powers. This was only after Germany began unrestricted submarine warfare and encouraged Mexico to attack the United States. In 1918, thousands of American soldiers joined the French and British in France. Together, the Allies pushed the Germans back and forced the Central Powers to ask for peace.

5. The victors tried to build a lasting peace. President Wilson's Fourteen Points set forth a basis for peace. But Wilson's points were not entirely acceptable to the other Allies. Agreement was reached, however, on Wilson's new international organization, the League of Nations.

The major part of the Versailles Treaty took away German territory, wealth, and military strength. Other treaties with the Central Powers set down the boundaries of new states. Some nationality groups gained independence. But others were unhappily placed under foreign control. The war had ended four major empires. It brought about the greatest change in the political map of Europe since 1815.

WHO? WHAT? WHEN? WHERE?

1. Place these events from World War I in the correct chronological order: 5 Germany began unrestricted submarine warfare. 1 Archduke Francis Ferdinand was murdered. 6 Treaty of Brest-Litovsk was signed. 2 Germany promised a "blank check" to Austria. 7 Armistice that ended World War I was signed. 4 England declared war on Germany. 3 Russia mobilized for war.

2. Describe the part played by each of these people in the 1914 crisis between Austria and Serbia: p. 544

Leopold von Berchtold	William II
Francis Joseph I	Edward Grey

CHAPTER TEST 29

● **3.** Use each of these terms in a sentence describing events that happened in World War I:

Central Powers	Allies
Western Front	armistice
naval blockade	neutral
Zimmermann telegram	Bolsheviks

4. Explain how each of these terms related to the peace agreements of World War I:

war-guilt clause p. 552	self-determination p. 553
mandates p. 553	Fourteen Points p. 552
buffer zone p. 552	compromise p. 552

QUESTIONS FOR CRITICAL THINKING

■ **1.** Why were the great powers of Europe unable to stop the Serbian crisis from expanding into a world war?
2. Why do you think the Germans used unrestricted submarine warfare even though they knew it might bring the United States into the war?
3. How might World War I have been prevented?

ACTIVITIES

1. Prepare a report on the new methods of warfare used in World War I. Tell how this war was different from previous wars.
2. Choose parts and role-play the debates at Versailles both before they are presented to the Germans and afterwards. Parts include: Wilson, Clemenceau, Lloyd George, and a German delegation led by the German foreign minister.
3. Draw a political cartoon for the editorial page of a British newspaper the day after Archduke Ferdinand was shot.

● Require students to write these sentences in their own words.

■ QUESTIONS FOR CRITICAL THINKING
1. Some reasons are: the alliance system, the mutual suspicion and feeling that it would be a quick war.
2. p. 547

SECTION 1
1. True or false: After the Franco-Prussian War, France joined Germany and Austria in the Triple Alliance.

2. Who stopped Germany's friendship with Russia? a. Bismarck, b. William II, c. Nicholas II

SECTION 2
3. True or false: Money borrowed from Britain helped build the American railway system.
4. Which of these factors did not cause fear and distrust among the Great Powers before the war: a. trade agreements, b. arms buildup, c. colonial rivalries, d. national interests

SECTION 3
5. In 1914, Serbia wanted to: a. become part of Russia, b. become free from Germany, c. unite all Serbs
6. Which is not a reason Great Britain declared war on Germany? a. alliance with France and Russia, b. Germany's violation of Belgium's neutrality, c. fear that Germany would control the North Sea

SECTION 4
7. Which nation changed sides from the Central Powers to the Allies? a. Japan, b. Bulgaria, c. Italy
8. Whom did the Allies blame for starting the war? a. Austria, b. Germany, c. Serbia

SECTION 5
9. The Big Three were the United States, Britain, and: a. Germany, b. Russia, c. France, d. Austria
10. True or false: After World War I, new nations were created so that no national group was under foreign control.

3. Answers will vary. Good discussion topic.

Activity 3. Discuss the purpose of political cartoons and go over possible British reactions to the shooting.

1919 – 1939

CHAPTER 30

An Unstable World

The Nazis preached that Germans belonged to a "super race" of people who were destined to rule the world. "Peace," they said, "is for weaklings," and they trained their young women to be strong and bear children to fight in "the victorious battles of the Fatherland."

● Fascism rejects democracy and the idea of majority rule in human society. It declares that men are unequal and cannot be made equal by universal suffrage. We believe that this is the century of authority, a century tending to the 'right,' a Fascist century. . . .

● Be sure to point out that this is a quotation from Mussolini.

Those were the words of Benito Mussolini [bə nē′tō mu̇s′ə lē′nē], the Fascist [fash′ist] dictator of Italy from 1922 to 1943. Mussolini was the first of the 20th-century fascist dictators, but not the last. Others came to power in Germany, Spain, and other European countries.

What had happened? Why was there a change in the general prewar trend toward democracy? A large part of the answer lies in the upsetting effects of World War I. In Russia, the war was one factor that made it possible for communists to seize power in Russia. In Eastern Europe, when the German, Austrian and Russian empires collapsed at the end of the war, many small independent countries came into existence. Most of them were economically weak, fiercely nationalistic, and had very little experience in democratic government. In Western Europe, although Britain and France remained strong democracies, they had to repay huge war debts to the United States. This was difficult for Britain, for example, because during the war it had lost many overseas markets and suffered a sharp drop in trade. The defeated countries also lost much of their foreign trade. They too had to make heavy payments, called *reparations,* to the winners.

All the countries faced major problems in trying to return to a peacetime economy after the war. Millions who had served in the armed forces found there were no jobs when they returned home. They became bitter and angry.

The postwar world became an unstable world. It was a world where extremist movements such as communism and fascism could grow. The worst economic depression in history struck in 1929. It was one of the long-range effects of World War I. Fascism in particular made further gains as a result of the depression. This chapter tells how:

1. World War I changed many nations.

2. The world economy fell apart.

3. Fascist leaders took control of weakened governments.

● This anti-democratic trend and its causes could be listed on the board as students name them for an introductory exercise.

■ Explain and discuss.

1 World War I changed many nations

Although the League of Nations was the idea of President Woodrow Wilson, the United States Senate refused to ratify the Treaty of Versailles which set up the League. Wilson's opponents in the Senate argued that the League ran against the Founding Fathers' advice to avoid "entangling alliances" with foreign countries. The League was a much weaker organization because the United States would not join. The League was not able to solve most of the problems left by World War I.

Fear of Germany continued. The most important problem in Western Europe after the war was the fear of a rebirth of German power. France was especially fearful. The French were very upset when the Americans refused to ratify the Versailles Treaty, as well as a treaty that promised them aid in case of a German attack. As a substitute for this protection, France signed alliances with several smaller countries in Europe in the 1920s.

The French also wanted to make sure that Germany carried out all the terms of the peace treaty. But in 1923, Germany claimed it could not continue to pay the heavy reparations. France, along with Belgium, sent troops to take over German coal mines and steel mills in the Ruhr area. The takeover failed because German workers went out on strike. Tension was high. The problem was settled in 1924 by a plan worked out by an American banker, Charles Dawes. The Dawes plan removed French and Belgian troops, lowered the amount of reparations, and gave Germany American loans.

In 1925, at the Swiss town of Locarno, the Germans signed an agreement with France,

Britain, Italy, and Belgium. Germany promised
ans. 1 not to try to take back territory lost after the war. The Locarno Pact also made the German Rhineland area a neutral zone between Germany and France. Germany promised not to keep troops or weapons there. This agreement made many people think that peaceful relations would now be possible between Germany and its neighbors.

ans. 2 **Many problems developed in Britain.** Britain came out of the war with a national debt ten times that of prewar days. British prosperity had depended mainly on foreign trade. Much of this trade was taken over during the war by companies in the United States and Japan. Mines, factories, and shops in Britain went into debt or shut down. Unemployment became widespread, especially among returning soldiers. There was a great need for better education, health care, and housing.

In 1926, discontent in the coal mines led to a general strike of all trade-union members. Although this strike lasted only a few weeks and was settled peaceably, conditions still did not improve for most workers. Unemployment remained the greatest single problem in Britain until the outbreak of World War II in 1939.

Meanwhile, important political changes took place between Britain and its empire. In the 19th century, a desire for self-government had been growing in British colonies populated by Europeans. By 1914, Canada, Australia, New Zealand, and the Union of South Africa had gained self-government for internal affairs. But Britain kept control of their foreign affairs. During the war, troops from these four countries fought in large numbers alongside the British. After the war, all four wanted complete independence. Each sent representatives to the Paris Peace Conference, and each was admitted to the League of Nations.

These Welsh coal miners marched to London to protest their continuing unemployment.

French soldiers and engineers guard a German locomotive during one of many outbreaks of violence.

In 1931, the British Parliament passed the Statute of Westminster. It created a Commonwealth of Nations completely free of Parliament's control. Many former colonies became voluntary members of the Commonwealth. They were united by loyalty to the British crown and by common traditions. Trade agreements also added to the unity of the Commonwealth.

France became unstable. Important financial problems arose in France when German reparations were not paid. Yet the country as a whole did well at first. Industry boomed, and there was full employment. Many tourists visited France, which also helped the economy.

ans. 3 A great depression in the 1930s ended French prosperity. Business and tourism fell off. Unemployment and the national debt grew. Public unrest also grew as France went through several changes of government.

● Point out that there were fascist sympathizers in many countries, not only Italy, Germany, Spain and Japan.

Extremist groups wanted to overthrow the republic. French fascists believed only a dictator ● could solve France's problems. French communists wanted a socialist government. A reform government tried to make changes in the mid-1930s, but it did not stay in power long. Unrest and strikes got worse in the late 1930s.

A republic was set up in Germany. Germany began the postwar years with a new national assembly that met at Weimar in January, 1919. The Weimar constitution included many democratic features: freedom of speech and religion, compulsory education of children, and freedom of association that protected labor unions. However, the president of the Weimar Republic was given certain emergency powers. These made it possible for a dictator to take over the government by legal means. Another big problem was that the system gave seats in the assembly to many small political parties. This kept any one party from gaining a majority. ● Therefore, the government was a *coalition* [kō′-ə lish′ən]. When no one party gets a majority of votes, a coalition government is formed of representatives from the different parties that received the most votes. This happens often in countries that have many political parties. These governments change often as the political balance among parties in the country changes.

The ruling group in the Weimar government was a coalition of socialist parties. Extremists on ■ both the Right (fascists) and the Left (communists) threatened the ruling group. They blamed the coalition for accepting the hated Treaty of Versailles. They declared that the socialists were traitors to their country. As the German economy grew weaker, people in Germany began to listen to these charges.

ans. 4 The heavy burden of reparations payments in Germany helped cause a wild inflation in 1922 and 1923. People had their life savings wiped out as prices skyrocketed. At the end of the war, an American dollar was worth about four German marks. By 1922, one dollar equaled 7,000 marks. In 1923, one dollar was worth millions, then billions, of marks. The German economy began to recover after 1924, only with the help of American loans.

Between 1925 and 1929, the Weimar Republic gained popular support. Industrial production reached prewar levels. Soon, it was second only to that of the United States. However, democracy in Germany remained shaky. A return of unemployment or inflation would help the extremists who were eager to overthrow the government.

Democracy was weak in most of eastern Europe. A number of things worked against the growth of strong democratic states in eastern and southern Europe. ans. 5 Many people in this area could not read or write. Nationality groups often argued and blocked lawmaking in the assemblies. The lack of modern industrial and agricultural methods kept living standards low.

Austria had been reduced in area to about the size of Maine. Many Austrians felt that only union with Germany could solve their economic problems. But this move was not allowed by the peace treaty. Neighboring Hungary had also been made smaller. It too started out as a democracy after the war. But by 1919, Hungary was being run by a dictator.

Poland, which had been wiped off the map at ● the end of the 18th century, was put back as a republic in 1918. But building democracy was difficult because wealthy landowners prevented reforms. In 1926, a Polish general took over the government. He slowly gained dictatorial power.

Only one of the postwar democracies in eastern Europe was a success: Czechoslovakia. This country had a strong president, Thomas G. Masaryk [mas′ə rik′]. Under him, foreign trade was encouraged, and industry boomed.

In southern Europe, the new state of Yugoslavia included people of two different Slavic groups, the Serbs and the Croats. They did not get along, and there was deep unrest. Before the end of the 1920s, a dictator was ruling in Yugoslavia, too.

Turkey made progress under a dictatorship. Because Turkey had opposed the Allies in World War I, it also had to accept great territorial cuts. Moreover, Turkey was placed largely under the control of the Allies. But in the early 1920s, Mustafa Kemal [müs′tä fä kə mäl′] and other patriots overthrew the sultan and set up a

● May need clarification.

■ The various political positions can be outlined at this point.

● You might briefly refer back to Chapter 20 to refresh student's memories of Poland's history.

Daily Life in the 1930s
Reginald Marsh captured the depression-weary spirit of the times in his 1932 painting of an American city street. William Gropper's cartoon (1933) shows businessmen shrinking from the unemployed.

republic. In 1923, the Allies recognized Turkey's independence. Kemal was elected Turkey's first president. He took the name Atatürk [at′ə-tėrk′], meaning "father of all the Turks." Kemal was a dictator, but he made many reforms and was *benevolent* (good to his people).

● The concept of a *benevolent dictator* should be discussed.

SECTION REVIEW 1

p. 559 **1.** What agreements were in the Locarno Pact?

p. 559 **2.** What conditions in postwar Britain caused unemployment and labor problems?

p. 560 **3.** What were some of the political and social problems in France during the 1930s?

p. 561 **4.** How did the Treaty of Versailles cause political and economic problems in Germany in the early 1920s?

p. 561 **5.** What problems and successes did the new democracies of eastern Europe have? Include Poland, Austria, Czechoslovakia, and Yugoslavia in your answer.

2 The world economy fell apart

By 1925, many people felt hopeful about the future. German inflation had slowed down, and the Locarno Pact had been signed. International trade was growing and so were new industries, such as mass-produced automobiles. It seemed as if the world was on the road to prosperity. However, there were major weaknesses in the world economy.

Agricultural prices fell during the 1920s. One of those economic weaknesses was in ● agriculture. After the war, the high wartime ans. 1 demand for wheat fell. At the same time, the use of more advanced equipment and techniques led to a huge rise in wheat production. As a result of the large supply and lower demand, the world price of wheat dropped sharply. By 1930, a bushel of wheat cost less than it had in 400 years. Wheat growers all over the world were facing ruin.

The growers of other crops were also troubled by overproduction. World prices for cotton, corn, coffee, cocoa, and sugar fell. Planters in Brazil, Africa, and the East Indies had to sell their crops at heavy losses. Farmers everywhere had less money to spend on manufactured goods. The farmers' problem became even worse when depression struck industry. Then city people had to spend less for food.

Industrial recovery depended on loans. A second weakness in the world economy was that much of the industrial expansion of the late 1920s was paid for with borrowed money. Running a business with borrowed money is known as *credit financing*. It becomes a problem ■ if the lender demands repayment and the borrower can't pay. Many European countries had received large private loans from the United States. This was especially true of Germany. If American lenders suddenly recalled their loans, industrial production would go down and many people would be out of work. Thus, the prosperity of Germany and the other European countries who had borrowed from the United States was insecure. It depended on the stability of the American financial system.

A financial crisis started a world depression. In October, 1929, prices on the New York Stock Exchange began to drop very quickly. Stock prices had been far above their normal ans. 2 levels because many people had bought stocks in hopes of making quick fortunes. Now these people began to fear that their gambles might not pay off. As they rushed to sell their stocks, prices fell.

The falling prices caused fear and even panic ans. 2 in the business world. Bankers called in their loans, and industrialists stopped expanding. American lenders recalled their loans from Europe. Businesses everywhere began to go bank-

● During the war, European nations had to import foodstuffs to feed their people and their armies.

■ Make sure students grasp this concept and the problems caused by it.

• rupt. Banks failed, and prices dropped all over the world. Between 1929 and 1932, world production fell by 38 percent. International trade shrank by over 65 percent. Unemployment went up everywhere. By 1932, one out of four Britons and two out of five Germans were out of work. It was the worst depression the world had ever known.

The world depression had important results. Every country felt the effects of the
ans. 3 depression. Each thought it could help itself by being less dependent on the world market and by protecting home industries. Every country thus began raising its tariffs, or taxes, on imported goods. The United States, the richest market in the world, passed the highest tariff in its history in 1930. High tariffs further reduced international trade.

The world depression also led to the growth of big government. The problems of mass unemployment were so great that people looked to their governments for help. Many governments began to take a much more active role in economic and social programs. In countries such as Italy and Germany, the world depression encouraged dictatorship. Moreover, because other countries were involved in their own problems, they were less willing to oppose acts of aggression by these fascist states.

SECTION REVIEW 2

p. 563 **1.** Why did the price of wheat fall sharply after World War I? What were the effects of this fall?

p. 563 **2.** Why did the price of stocks begin to fall in October, 1929? What effects did this have on the United States and Europe?

p. 564 **3.** Why did the depression cause countries to raise tariffs? How did the depression encourage dictators?

● The events following the crash should be carefully explained.

3 Fascist leaders took control of weakened governments

A *dictatorship* is a modern form of absolute government. A *dictator* is a person who seizes control of a government without claiming to rule through inheritance or free election. After World War I, several countries came under the rule of dictators. In Russia after the Bolshevik Revolution of 1917, a communist dictatorship was set ans. 1
up. It was based on government ownership of property and capital. Another type of dictatorship, fascism, permitted private ownership of property and capital. But it placed strict government rules on the people. Fascism arose first in

Mussolini *(below)* promised that a strong state could cure Italy's postwar ills, strengthen its economy, and rebuild national pride. The cost was individual freedom—even the freedom to think. *Below right:* fascist soldiers burn "subversive" books.

Italy, later in Japan and Germany. Both communism and fascism refused to allow opposing political parties. Each government used censorship, denied civil rights, and took complete control of people's lives. Communism and fascism became the strongest antidemocratic movements in the world.

Mussolini and the Fascists gained power in Italy. There was much unrest in Italy after the war. Many Italians were angry that Italy had received so little territory in the peace settlement. After all, 600 thousand Italian soldiers had died in the war. Also, Italy faced the same problems of business slowdown, unemployment, and high prices that existed in other countries. By the end of 1920, the cost of living was eight times higher than it had been in 1914. Many people found it difficult even to buy bread. They turned to the government for help. But the Italian parliament was split into many different parties. These parties could not cooperate with each other. Thus, the government had no strong leaders or programs.

As unrest grew, strikes broke out. Workers in northern Italy tried to take control of the factories. This scared middle-class people who were afraid of a communist revolution. In such a situation, many swung their support to the Fascist party headed by Benito Mussolini.

Before the war, Mussolini had been a social- ans. 2
ist. But he was thrown out of the party in 1914 when he favored Italy's entering the war. In 1919, he organized the Italian Fascist Party. He took the name fascist from the Latin word *fasces*. It meant the bundle of rods bound around an ax, which had been the symbol of authority in the Roman Empire. The Fascist par-

ty was made up mainly of out-of-work soldiers. They wanted action in place of the do-nothing policy of the government. They were a super-patriotic group that had a great devotion to Italy and to *Il Duce* [ēl′dü′chā], "the leader," Mussolini.

The Fascists wore black shirts as uniforms. They used the old Roman salute of the raised arm and followed strict military discipline. They beat up, tortured, and sometimes killed political opponents.

The aim of the Fascists was to gain political power. At first, Mussolini tried to do it legally through elections. But the Fascists did not win many votes. In September, 1922, some 10 thousand armed Fascists marched on Rome. They wanted to take over the government. The king, afraid of a civil war, invited Mussolini to become prime minister. In the next nine years, Mussolini used every means, including terror, to make himself dictator of Italy. The Fascist party became the only legal party in the country. The secret police arrested anyone who dared to criticize the Fascists.

By 1930, the world depression had increased the problems within Italy. Mussolini had begun many business and farm projects to provide jobs. But these efforts were not enough. Mussolini became tense. He felt that only some grand gamble, some successful military move, would enable him to keep his hold on the Italian people.

Military leaders won control in Japan. In the 1920s, democracy was making some progress in Japan. But the Japanese parliament had little power. It could not control the prime minister, who was responsible only to the emperor. Military leaders were nearly independent of the government, and they were eager for more

● See Questions for Critical Thinking, number 2, (p. 572). It could be used as a discussion topic re: the Fascist states.

power. They disliked democracy and disagreed with Japan's moderate policy toward China. ans. 3 After 1926, these militarists gained strength in parliament. They were supported by the peasants who blamed democracy for their poor living conditions.

By 1930, the effects of the depression were also being felt in Japan. Strikes gave the militarists a chance to seize more power. By late 1932, they were in control. Their main goal was to build up the most powerful army and navy in the Far East. They used murder to scare off political opposition. They justified their acts by glorifying Japan. They were supported by young ● men whose careers had been hurt by the depression. They also had the support of people with business interests in Manchuria who wanted a more aggressive policy toward China.

Military training in fascist countries began at an early age. These young Japanese boys, fully uniformed, raise their rifles in a salute.

Hitler and the Nazi party rose to power in Germany. As in other countries, the depression hit Germany in 1930. Unemployment rose sharply, and the Weimar Republic seemed unable to help.

Radical groups, such as communists and very right-wing factions, strongly opposed the Weimar Republic. They wanted revenge for the treatment that Germany had received at Versailles. The most stable element in the German population, the middle class, had been all but ruined by the inflation following World War I. The younger generation, disillusioned by this chaos, blamed the problems on the way their elders ran the country. Militarists blamed German defeat in World War I on liberals, pacifists, and Jews. There had long been deep-seated envy—and even hatred—of the Jews, who made up less than one percent of the population. Many Germans resented the fact that some Jews had achieved success as doctors, dentists, lawyers, authors, and musicians. It became popular to blame the Jews for Germany's troubles. Many Germans were willing to listen to anyone who made Jews the scapegoat for all the nation's ills.

● Students may need help understanding the meaning of the term "radical". It is correct, in the context of a republic, to describe communism or fascism as radical, because they each represent fundamental change in the form of government. Students should understand that *radical* is a descriptive term, not a pejorative one.

Adolf Hitler was born in an Austrian village in 1889. During World War I, he enlisted in the German army. While in a hospital recovering from war injuries, news of the armistice and the German defeat reached him. He felt great anger and shame for his adopted country. These feelings were mingled with frustrations in his personal life. He came to hate the new German government, Jews, and anyone associated with the Versailles Treaty.

In April, 1920, the National Socialist German Workers' party, or Nazi [nä′tsē] party, was formed. Its program, drawn up in part by Hitler, appealed to all discontented persons. As a public speaker, Hitler had a moving effect on German audiences. In 1923, he tried, but failed, to seize power in Bavaria. He was sent to prison for about a year. While in jail, he wrote the book *Mein Kampf* (My Struggle). The book was based on racist ideas. It presented a plan for aggression against other peoples and countries.

As the depression became worse, more and more people began to vote for Nazi representatives in the Reichstag, the German parliament. By 1932, the Nazis were the largest political party in Germany. In January, 1933, Hitler became chancellor (prime minister) of Germany. His government was known as the Third Reich ans. 4

Geography: A Key to History

Geopolitics and Nazi Power

Adolf Hitler's quest for power was aided by a geographic theory known as *geopolitics*. In one form, the theory was developed by Karl Haushofer, a retired general who taught geography at the University of Munich. Haushofer distorted the teachings of political geography to serve military purposes.

Haushofer's works on geopolitics described a nation as a living organism that has a life, a death, and a past from which it evolved. In order to live, he said, it must conquer other nations to gain needed *Lebensraum* [lā′bəns-roum′], or living space. Through a series of conquests, Germany had evolved from a group of small states to a great empire. It would continue to thrive if it continued to conquer, he said.

Haushofer taught that control of the land areas of Europe and Asia was the key to world conquest. He explained that whoever controlled the Heartland (an area extending from the southeastern Soviet Union to Mongolia) controlled the World Island (Europe, Asia and Africa) and thereby controlled the world. Haushofer backed up this idea with statistics that showed that the Heartland had the potential to be the greatest agricultural and industrial region in the world. The Heartland, he said, provided space for withdrawal of vital industries beyond range of possible attack. It was also a base from which armies could attack any country on the rim of the Heartland. He urged Germans to conquer all of eastern Europe and the Soviet Union.

Haushofer had great influence during the Hitler regime. His theories were taught in the schools and popularized in the press. They justified Nazi expansion as "natural" and necessary growth. Some geographers opposed his theories, pointing out that a nation is not an organism and that geography can only influence, not *determine*, human behavior. But these were unhealthy views to hold in Nazi Germany.

By the time the war ended, the study of geopolitics had fallen into disrepute because of Haushofer's distortions. He cast a shadow over the legitimate questions that political geographers ask, such as: What is the relationship, if any, between a country's greatness and its control of the seas, the air, or a particular chunk of land?

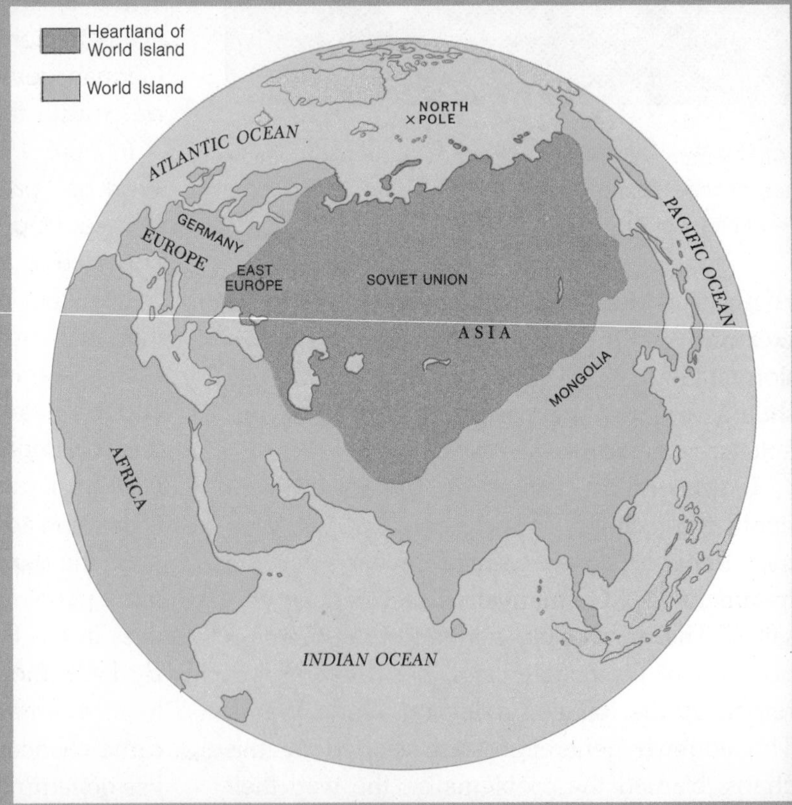

In postwar Germany, conditions were right for the Nazis to gain popularity. They distributed food to unemployed crowds *(above right)*, and their campaign against the Jews vented German feelings of humiliation. *Above left:* a Nazi stops a Jewish businessman on his way home and forces him to sweep the gutter.

[rīH]. (The First Reich, or empire, was begun
ans. 4 by Charlemagne in 800 and ended in 1806 by Napoleon. The Second Reich began in 1871 with the unification of Germany and continued until 1918, when Germany was defeated in World War I.) In 1934, Hitler stripped the Reichstag of all power. He also got rid of other parties, outlawed trade unions, set up labor camps, and threw out laws he did not like. On August 2, 1934, Hitler became Führer [fʏ'rər], or leader, of Germany.

ans. 5 **The Nazis preached the idea of a "super race."** According to the Führer, Germans were Aryans and were the "master race" or "super race." All other peoples, particularly Jews and Slavs, were inferior. Jews were to be killed, and Slavs were to be made into slaves. The Nazis began a carefully planned program to eliminate Jews from German national life. In 1935, with the infamous Nuremberg Laws, citizenship rights were taken away from Jews, and they were treated as unequal. Intermarriage of Jews and gentiles (non-Jews) was not allowed. Jewish businesses and services were boycotted. By 1938, tens of thousands of Jews had been put in concentration camps. Jewish children were not allowed to attend German schools. And in 1939, the regime eliminated all Jews from the economic life of Germany and forced them to live in ghettoes.

Hitler's idea of the German "super race" ans. 5
gave a sense of prestige to many Germans. They felt that Hitler was replacing weakness, defeat, and depression with strength, importance, and prosperity. Most Germans gladly accepted Hitler as their leader.

The Third Reich got ready for war. As they ans. 6
did in Italy and Japan, fascists in Germany tried to mold the minds of their citizens through a program that glorified war. Textbooks were rewritten and the press and radio were censored to carry out that program. Hitler said that Germany must have "living space." He began huge preparations for German expansion. Strict food-

rationing laws were put into effect to make Germany self-sufficient in case of war. A highway system was built so that troops could move rapidly. A huge stockpile of arms was also created.

Those German business leaders who in 1932 thought they could control Hitler found out too late that they could not. He had changed Germany into a police state. The government had total control over every area of life—the economy, schools, labor unions, newspapers, radio, and films. Such a system of total control is called *totalitarianism* [tō tal′ ə ter′ē ə niz′ əm].

Outside Germany, Hitler also had people fooled. Many people believed that their countries could deal with him. They felt that he only wanted to give Germany back its rightful place among nations. Some people in democratic countries admired Naziism for its discipline and its hostility to communism.

SECTION REVIEW **3**

1. Name the two forms of dictatorship described in this chapter. How were they similar? How different? p. 564

2. How did Mussolini come to power? What groups supported him? Why? p. 565

3. What group took over in Japan? How and with whose support? p. 566

4. Describe the steps by which Hitler came to power in Germany. p. 567 569

5. What was Hitler's idea of "master race," and why did many Germans accept it? p. 569

6. How did Hitler prepare his people to accept the idea of another war? Why didn't people inside or outside Germany oppose him when he first came to power? p. 569

In annual rallies at Nuremberg, Hitler stirred huge crowds with his fiery speeches. Here, in 1937, he declared he would not tolerate interference from the Church.

CHAPTER REVIEW 30

SECTION SUMMARIES

1. World War I changed many nations. The world that emerged in the postwar period was an unstable one. Every nation in Europe faced losses in business and trade along with high unemployment and inflation. In addition, suspicion among former enemies continued. The United States refused to ratify the Versailles Peace Treaty or join the League of Nations. Without American participation, European countries felt even less secure. In the mid-1920s, however, the Locarno Pact offered hope for peaceful settlement of disputes.

2. The world economy fell apart. The mood of optimism was soon wiped out by a world depression. It began in 1929 and proved to be the worst in history. Weakness was first seen in agriculture. The world prices of wheat and other crops dropped, and many farmers faced ruin. When the New York stock market crashed, American lenders began to recall European loans. Businesses failed, and people were out of work. All countries raised their tariffs, and international trade fell sharply.

3. Fascist leaders took control of weakened governments. These conditions helped the rise of extremist movements, particularly fascism. The older democracies were able to stay alive. But the newer ones, such as those of Italy and eastern Europe, turned to dictators. By 1933, Germany had become a Nazi dictatorship, and Japan had fallen under the control of militarists.

Mussolini in Italy and Hitler in Germany both set up police states. They outlawed all political parties except their own. They built totalitarian systems in which the state controlled everything. Citizens had no rights—only the duty to obey. The real aim of dictators such as Mussolini and Hitler was not to improve living conditions, but to expand their own power and that of the state.

WHO? WHAT? WHEN? WHERE?

1. Find the years in which these events took place and arrange them in chronological order:

Hitler became Führer of Germany. 1934 (12)
Poland became a republic. 1918 (2)
Prices fell sharply on the New York Stock Exchange. 1929 (10)
The Locarno Pact was signed. 1925 (9)
The Bolsheviks took over the government in Russia. 1917 (1)
Mussolini became dictator of Italy. 1922 (6)
The Nazi party was founded. 1920 (5)
A democratic constitution was adopted in Germany. 1919 (4)
France and Belgium took over the Ruhr. 1923 (8)
Turkey became a republic. 1922 (7)
The Italian Fascist party was organized. 1919 (3)
Militarists took control of Japan. 1932 (11)

2. Describe the governments that came to power in these countries after World War I.

France p. 560 Russia p. 564 Poland p. 561
Italy p. 565 Hungary p. 561 Turkey p. 561
Germany p. 560 Yugoslavia p. 561
Japan p. 566 Czechoslovakia p. 561

3. In what ways were these terms part of Hitler's plans for Germany?

"living space" p. 569 Reichstag p. 567
"master race" p. 569 Jews p. 569
Mein Kampf p. 567 dictatorship p. 564
Führer p. 569 Nazis p. 567

4. In what ways did these events cause problems for the industrialized nations after World War I:
decline in foreign trade p. 559
increased crop production p. 563
unemployment p. 559
credit financing by the United States p. 563
high tariffs p. 564

CHAPTER TEST 30

QUESTIONS FOR CRITICAL THINKING

● **1.** In what ways were the peace treaties of World War I to blame for economic problems in Europe?

2. Why were many people willing to accept a dictator when their countries were suffering hardships?

3. In what ways can the events described in this chapter be seen as leading to another world war?

4. What effect do you think the failure of the United States to join the League of Nations had on the events that followed?

5. How did the economic problems of the depression bring about political changes in the major countries of the world?

ACTIVITIES

1. You are a leader wanting popular support. Give a speech persuading the people to give you more power.

2. Find out what it was like to live during the depression. Ask older relatives or others to tell you what they remember. Or read firsthand accounts such as those in *Hard Times* by Studs Terkel.

■ **3.** Pretend that it is 1936, and all the class members live on the same block in Berlin. One day, a family on the block is arrested; nobody seems to know why. Divide into two sides: one who would help the family and one who would not. Hold a block meeting to decide what to do.

4. Using the *World Almanac*, graph the losses of human life during the war. Graph the total male population before and after the war.

5. Read newspaper and magazine articles of the postwar and depression period to find out how people in the United States were getting through this time.

6. Chose a leader such as Hitler, Mussolini, or Atatürk and read magazine or newspaper articles to find out how he was able to get popular support.

● QUESTIONS FOR CRITICAL THINKING
1, 3, and 5 can be useful in helping students to see that people have the ability to at least shape events — if they are aware of the potential problems.

SECTION 1

1. The nation that most feared Germany's recovery after World War I was: a. Austria, b. France, c. Britain

2. In the Locarno Pact, Germany: a. gave up the Ruhr to France, b. agreed to pay all reparations, c. promised not to keep troops in the Rhineland

3. True or false: Canada, Australia, and New Zealand first became self-governing under the Statute of Westminster.

4. Which of these countries had a successful democracy? a. Poland, b. Hungary, c. Czechoslovakia

SECTION 2

5. True or false: Increased crop production had bad results for farmers after World War I.

6. Many Europeans used ___c___ money to build and run their factories in the 1920s. a. German, b. British, c. American

7. The depression began in: a. 1925, b. 1917, c. 1929

8. Which was not a result of the depression? a. democratic revolutions, b. unemployment, c. high tariffs

SECTION 3

9. Which of these countries did not become a fascist dictatorship? a. Italy, b. Japan, c. Russia

10. The name "fascist" originated in: a. Poland, b. *Mein Kampf,* c. ancient Rome

11. True or false: Fascist rulers were able to seize power partly because people were frightened by the effects of the world depression.

12. In Japan, the group that came to power in 1930: a. wanted war with China, b. were communists, c. were socialists

13. Which of the following was not blamed for Germany's postwar troubles? a. the older generation, b. Hitler, c. Jews

14. A dictator rules: a. by inheritance, b. by election, c. by seizing power

■ This would be an especially meaningful activity if students could first view the film, (or read), *The Diary of Anne Frank.*

1796–1939

CHAPTER **31**

The Rise of Communism in Russia

At a time when artists in other countries were experimenting in abstract forms, Russian artists were encouraged to show realistically their social revolution. Ivan Chadre's bronze statue is a worker tearing a cobblestone from the street to use as a weapon in the uprising of 1905.

● Dear comrades, soldiers, sailors, and workers! I am happy to greet in your persons the victorious Russian revolution, and greet you as the vanguard of the worldwide proletarian army. . . . Any day now the whole of European capitalism may crash.

● Check to see if students understand the meanings of the vocabulary in this quote. For example, vanguard = leaders.

The speaker was Lenin, a bald, stocky man, who had led the Russian Bolsheviks for over ten years. The Bolsheviks were the radical Marxist group within the Social Democratic movement. Lenin, their leader, was in exile in Switzerland when revolution broke out in

Russia. In 1917, he was secretly returned to Russia with the aid of the German High Command. The occasion for his speech was his arrival in Petrograd on April 16, 1917.

The Germans hoped that Lenin and his followers would undermine the Provisional Government of Russia. This had been set up in March, 1917, after Tsar Nicholas II was forced to give up his throne. The Germans got their wish, but in a way they never expected. Lenin and his followers seized power in November, 1917. They set up the first Communist state in history. To understand why and how this happened we must look into Russia's past.

Russia in the 19th century was unlike any other country in Europe. It was a huge empire, nearly three times the size of the United States. It stretched from Germany to the Pacific Ocean. Within it lived 130 million people in 1900. But less than half of these people were Russians. There were other Slavs such as White Russians, Ukrainians, and Poles. There were also non-Slavs including Latvians, Lithuanians, Estonians, Finns, Germans, Jews, and many others.

● Ruling over this vast empire with its different nationalities, languages, and religions were the Romanov tsars. They were mostly autocrats who believed that only unlimited power could hold the empire together. After 1881, the tsars were generally opposed to major reforms.

The great majority of the peoples in the empire were peasants. They were poor and generally illiterate. Up until the mid-19th century most of them were serfs. Sometimes, the serfs would burst out in great fury against their landlords, the nobility. But tsarist troops always put down the outbursts with great brutality. The tsar felt he had to defend the nobles. He depended on them to help him rule the empire by serving as government and military officers.

● Some of this material may need to be clarified for some students.

■ Chapter 9 contains information regarding Russia's isolation.

Meanwhile, the ideas and economic changes ■ that had been taking place in Europe since the end of the Middle Ages had hardly touched ans. 1 Russia. Revolution came in 1917 because the tsarist government had been unwilling or unable to find a way to modernize this huge backward empire, and because, without a parliament, Russians had no way to obtain reforms in a peaceful, orderly manner. After that, Communist leaders faced the very same problems of modernization. They were able to build a modern, industrial country but did so in such a way that it took a terrible cost in human lives. Chapter 31 traces the process by which Russia became a Communist state:

1. Autocratic rulers weakened Russia.

2. Bolsheviks took control of Russia.

3. Stalin created a totalitarian society.

4. The Soviet Union tried to protect its security.

1 Autocratic rulers weakened Russia

To other Europeans of the time, the Russian Empire seemed distant, mysterious, and backward. The tsars had long ignored the deep desire of the Russian people for a better life. And the nobles continually objected to reforms that might weaken their power.

Tsars opposed constitutional rule. After the death of Catherine the Great in 1796, her

THE SOVIET UNION
In 1940

son, Paul I, became tsar. In 1801, he was assassinated.

Paul was succeeded by Alexander I, the most puzzling of all the Russian tsars. He said he hated despotism, but he did many cruel things. Growing dissatisfaction with Alexander led certain army officers to form secret societies. Many of these officers had come in contact with Western ideas during the Russian occupation of France after Napoleon's defeat. When Alexander died suddenly in December, 1825, these officers rebelled against the government. They had very little support from the people, and their uprising was easily put down. Yet the so-called Decembrist Revolt inspired later revolutionaries. It showed how ideas from the outside could spark a demand for reform.

After the revolt, Nicholas I became tsar. He felt that the only way to avoid future bloodshed was to be a strict autocrat. As one of his officials stated, "The tsar is a father, his subjects are his children, and children ought never to question their parents. . . ." Nicholas took personal control of everything. He censored the press and took away academic freedoms. He had police spies round up enemies and send them off to Siberia. However, Nicholas's bureaucracy was very corrupt and weak. As a result, the Russians suffered a terrible defeat in the Crimean War. Nicholas, a bitter man, died in 1855. ans. 1 ● ■

Alexander II brought about reforms. Alexander II was by nature as autocratic as his father. But the Russian defeat in the Crimean War led him to try reform. As he told a gathering of nobles in Moscow, "It is better to abolish serfdom from above than to wait until it begins to abolish itself from below." Thus in 1861, Alexander issued the Act on the Emancipation of the Peasants from Serfdom.

● See what the students think of this attitude toward government, as well as family structure.

■ Discuss censorship

Freedom for serfs came in Russia at the same time the slavery issue was being fought in the United States.

ans. 2 This act gave the serfs personal liberty and promised them some land of their own. The land was not given to them directly, however. Instead, it was placed under the rule of the local village or *mir.* The landlords were allowed to keep about half of their old estates. The freed serfs had to pay a "redemption" tax to the landlords for the other half. The tax lasted forty-nine years. Though no longer in bondage, the former serfs found that they were often worse off than before. In many cases, the land they got was poor. The well-to-do peasants were able to buy or lease the more fertile land. The others had to work the rest as farm laborers at very low wages. Thus, the life of the peasant remained hard.

Yet, freeing the serfs stands out as the single most important event in 19th-century Russia. It was the beginning of the end of power for the landed nobles. Emancipation brought free labor and industry, and a middle class arose.

There were other reforms in Russia in the 1860s and 1870s. Trial by jury was started. For the first time, law became a profession. More elementary schools were set up, and lower-class children were allowed to go to high schools. A form of local self-government known as a *zemstvo* [zemst′vō] was also set up in each district. The *zemstvo* had charge of schools, roads, health, and farming. But it was controlled mainly by the landowners.

These reforms raised hopes that Alexander II might even allow a constitutional government. ● But it soon became clear that he would not. Many educated people, particularly in the uni-

● Ask why a constitutional government was so much desired by the people.

Collection, The Museum of Modern Art, New York

Daily Life of Russian Peasants
Peasants owed much money to their former landowners and did not benefit from the technological revolution that changed the lives of farmers in Western Europe. In 1917 *(above)* they continue to wear homemade clothes and use homemade tools. Yet village life inspired the painting *(right)* by Marc Chagall.

versities, then became bitter. They formed small revolutionary groups. These groups began to assassinate government leaders. In 1881, they killed Alexander himself. But the murder of the tsar did not change the tsarist system.

The tsarist system grew stricter. The last two tsars were Alexander III, who ruled until 1894, and Nicholas II, who was tsar until 1917. Neither of them made any effort at meaningful reform. In fact, both rulers tried to turn back the clock. They brought back repressive measures and did away with some of Alexander's reforms. Censorship again became severe. Religious persecution was allowed. Many Jews were either terrorized or killed in terrible mob attacks called *pogroms* [pō gromz′]. Secret agents of the tsar incited revolutionary groups to murder officials. The agents then exposed the rebels to the police. Things got worse when low wages, long hours, and poor working conditions led to a wave of strikes in the 1890s. Yet both strikes and labor unions remained illegal in Russia.

Russia lost a war with Japan. In 1904, Russian imperialism in East Asia brought a clash with Japan. By 1900, Russia had dominated Manchuria and was eager to add Korea. ● Because Japan was thought to be weak, Russia did not try to avoid a war. As one official put it, a "little victorious war to stem the tide of revolution" would be most welcome.

Japan, however, decided to strike first. In February, 1904, the Japanese fleet attacked

● See the map on p. 573

Port Arthur. This was the Russian naval base on the tip of the southern Manchurian coast. As in the Crimean War, Russia was unprepared. Its army and navy suffered many defeats. The Russo-Japanese War ended with a peace treaty unfavorable to Russia that was signed in September, 1905.

The 1905 revolution warned the tsar. The Russo-Japanese War was very unpopular with the Russian people. This was partly because Russia lost the war and partly because the war effort prevented reform at home. During the war, a revolution broke out. It was touched off by "Bloody Sunday" on January 22, 1905. A large group of workers, carrying a petition to the tsar, was fired upon by troops in St. Petersburg. Several hundred unarmed workers were killed. News of this act aroused great anger against the government. A wave of strikes shut down the railroads, the telegraph system, and government offices. Councils of workers called *soviets* sprang up in the cities to direct the rebellion. Crowds carried red banners and posters demanding reforms. (Red was the traditional color of revolutionary socialism.)

Shocked by this outcry, Nicholas finally allowed ans. 3
a constitution in October, 1905. Civil rights were protected, and a national parliament, known as the Duma, was set up. At last it seemed that Russia had become a constitutional monarchy. But the Duma was very limited in its powers. The first two Dumas, which met in 1906 and 1907, were dismissed by the tsar when they asked for reform. The third and fourth Dumas did pass some reforms. But these Dumas had members who represented wealthy people much more than poor people.

More industrial growth in Russia did help some workers and the middle class. But peasants remained unhappy, and most factory workers were discontent. Peasants were desperately short of land, and factory workers had low pay and miserable living conditions.

Lenin addresses an enthusiastic crowd as Stalin (immediately behind him) and Trotsky (to the far right) look on.

SECTION REVIEW 1

p. 574 575 **1.** In what respects was 19th-century Russia a backward country compared to other European powers?

p. 576 **2.** Discuss the results and timing of the ending of serfdom in Russia.

p. 578 **3.** What led to the 1905 revolt? To what degree did it succeed? Fail?

2 Bolsheviks took control of Russia

World War I caused the tsarist system great trouble. The shock of defeat in battles against the Germans and the shortages of food and other goods made the masses rebellious. Their mood was similar to that of 1905. In 1917, after more than 300 years of rule, the Romanov dynasty was swept from power.

The tsarist government fell. Russia had entered the war patriotically in 1914. But the people lost interest as the number of dead and wounded mounted. Food and fuel supplies fell, and prices went up. The tsar proved to be a poor leader. He refused to allow the Duma any share in running the country.

In March, 1917, food shortages led to street ans. 1 marches in Petrograd, the capital. (St. Petersburg had been patriotically renamed Petrograd in 1914 in a wave of anti-German feeling.) Police and soldiers fought the crowds. But within a few days, the armed forces mutinied and joined the people. The uprising had become a revolution. Tsar Nicholas, at his army headquarters near the front, was forced to abdicate his throne.

Duma members soon formed a cabinet of middle-class liberals and set up a Provisional Government. Meanwhile, workers and soldiers in the cities formed soviets, as had been done in the 1905 revolution. The soviets soon took over local governments.

Workers and peasants, men and women, enlisted as volunteers in the Bolshevik army in 1917.

Russia's last royal family: Tsar Nicholas II, his wife, son, and daughters. Anastasia (see page 582) is far right.

The Provisional Government in Petrograd restored civil rights and promised free elections. It also continued the war, even though by now most Russians wanted to end it. This lost the Provisional Government much support, as did its refusal to approve land reform for the peasants and its delay in holding free elections. Indeed, peasants had already begun to seize estates and divide the land among themselves.

In July, 1917, Alexander Kerensky, a moderate socialist, became prime minister. He tried hard, but failed to win the people's support because he refused to stop the war or carry out land reforms. ans. 1

The Bolsheviks took over the government. Mounting unrest helped Lenin and his followers. They won a great deal of support by promising peace to the soldiers, land to the peasants, ●

● The Bolshevik slogan was "Peace, Land, and Bread!" Discuss the importance of this slogan.

and bread to the workers. Seeing a chance to seize power, they planned their moves carefully.

The right moment came in the fall of 1917. The Bolsheviks were still a small party. But they were able to take over the Petrograd and Moscow soviets. They formed a workers' militia called the Red Guard. Then on November 6 and 7, the Red Guard, joined by pro-Bolshevik soldiers and sailors, seized the central government by force. They captured important buildings in the capital and stormed the Winter Palace, the site of the Kerensky government. All the ministers except Kerensky were arrested. He escaped and tried to fight against Lenin. But he failed and later fled the country.

● Lenin's *coup d'état* was successful and daring. The Bolsheviks moved quickly to set up a party dictatorship and to adopt the name *Communist*.

The Communists faced many enemies. As the clear leader of the Communist party, Lenin became chief of state with unlimited power. He devoted his life to making Russia communistic. He began by applying Marxist principles to Russian society. In the early phase, known as "war communism," all private property went to the state. Industries, banks, railroads, and shipping were placed under government ownership. The landholdings of the Orthodox Church were taken away, and atheism was encouraged. To increase the food supply, however, the peasants were allowed to farm the land they had already taken over. But the peasants tried to hold back food from the cities because money was worthless and factory goods were not available. The Bolsheviks then sent soldiers and secret police to the villages to take the grain by force. The peasants again became angry and bitter.

ans. 2

● Explain the meaning of coup d'état, if necessary. But first see if students can grasp its meaning from the context.

In 1918, a furious civil war broke out against the Bolsheviks. It began after Lenin used armed sailors in January, 1918, to shut down the first freely elected Constituent Assembly in Russian history, because the Bolsheviks did not have a majority and did not want to give up power. Lenin wanted to establish a Communist dictatorship. Many Russians, from socialists to monarchists, were opposed to his dictatorship and fought against Lenin. They were joined by many non-Russian nationalities—for example, Ukrainians, Poles, Finns, Estonians, Latvians, Lithuanians—who saw a chance to break away from Russian rule. Fighting soon spread to almost every part of the old Russian empire. This Civil War lasted until 1920. It was worse for Russia than World War I. Famine and disease killed hundreds of thousands, and casualties were in the millions. Both sides committed terrible atrocities. Among the casualties were the ex-tsar, his wife, and their five children. They were all shot by the Bolsheviks in 1918.

Meanwhile, Lenin took Russia out of World War I by signing the separate peace treaty of Brest-Litovsk with Germany in March, 1918. Britain and France, still desperately fighting to defeat Germany, wanted to bring Russia back into the war. They therefore sent troops and supplies to Russia to help the opposition overthrow Lenin. The United States also sent troops but they took no active part in the fighting. Japan, seeking to dominate eastern Siberia, occupied Vladivostok [vlad′ə vos′tok] and other Pacific ports.

The Allies continued to take part in the civil war even after they signed an armistice with Germany in November, 1918. The Allies feared that communism would spread to the rest of Europe. Thus, they hoped to save Europe by

HISTORY IN THE MOVIES

ANASTASIA

In the 1920s, a Berlin woman began claiming she was Tsar Nicholas's daughter Anastasia. This 1956 movie scene shows the woman (Ingrid Bergman) being recognized by Nicholas's mother, the Empress Dowager, (Helen Hayes). In truth, the Empress Dowager refused to ever see the woman.

destroying Lenin's regime. Faced with civil war and Allied intervention, the Communist government seemed likely to fall.

Yet the Communists finally defeated their enemies. The opposition armies were widely scattered and uncoordinated. They were unable to win over many peasants because of the pro-landlord policy of the opposition generals. The Bolsheviks had also built up a superior army under Leon Trotsky, the Commissar for War. In addition, Allied intervention aroused Russian nationalism. All of these factors helped bring the Bolsheviks to victory. By late 1920, Communist rule was secure against internal enemies. But it enjoyed no great popularity.

Marxist principles were modified. To ease the strain of long years of war, the government in 1921 retreated from its policy of war communism. It introduced instead the New Economic Policy (NEP). The state still owned ans. 4
basic industries. However, private enterprise in retail trade and small business was allowed. "Nepmen" (as small businessmen were called) did well under the new policy. The peasants were also happier. Except for a tax on surplus grain, they were free to grow and sell their produce as they wished.

Under Lenin, the Communists laid the base for a powerful dictatorship. They built a strong, well-organized party. They made sure that the Communist party controlled the government and the economy. They used force and terror to put down all enemies. They taught the people the ideas of Marx and Lenin. And they made everyone become a worker for the state. In

1922, the Communist party created the Union of Soviet Socialist Republics (the Soviet Union) to take the place of the old Russian Empire. It consisted of four republics; after World War II it included fifteen union republics.

Stalin got rid of Trotsky. The death of Lenin in 1924 brought a bitter fight for power between Leon Trotsky and Joseph Stalin. Trotsky, a brilliant writer and speaker, was as well known as Lenin. Most people expected him to become
ans. 5 the new party leader. Stalin was not well known, but he was a shrewd politician. He used his post as party secretary to place his supporters in key jobs. The trend of the times also helped Stalin. The world revolution that Trotsky had talked about did not take place. Stalin, on the other hand, favored "building socialism in a single country." Russia should work by itself to become a workers' paradise. Then perhaps communist ideas might spread to other countries.

Stalin's policy was accepted at the Fourteenth Party Congress in 1925. Trotsky was dismissed from the party in 1927. Two years later, he was exiled. In 1940, he was murdered in Mexico, by an agent of Stalin.

SECTION REVIEW **2**

p. 579
580 **1.** What conditions led to the revolution in March, 1917? Why did the Provisional Government fall in November, 1917?
p. 581 **2.** How did Lenin make Russia communistic?
p. 581 **3.** Why did a civil war break out in Russia? Why did the Allies intervene?
p. 582 **4.** What was the NEP?
p. 583 **5.** How did Stalin defeat Trotsky after Lenin's death?
6. See if you can find out how it was that Trotsky was killed in Mexico, not in Russia.

3 Stalin created a totalitarian society

By the late 1920s, Stalin was clearly in charge of the Communist party. Yet, until the mid-1930s, he was careful to consult others and to act modestly. Officially he was not the head of the government, but in practice he was. His only title until 1941 was general secretary of the Communist party. In 1941, he became premier as well as party secretary.

In 1928, the NEP came to an end. The economy had gotten back to prewar levels. But the Marxist dream of a classless society had not come true. Stalin felt that the Soviet Union could not remain a great power unless it caught up with the West economically. As he explained:

> We were fifty to a hundred years behind the advanced countries. We must make up this lag in ten years. Either we do this or they will crush us.

Thus Stalin began a new policy, called the First Five-Year Plan. Its two major goals were rapid industrialization and the collectivization of agriculture. He believed that these goals could only be met by dictatorial controls. The huge amounts of money needed to build all the new plants and factories had to be squeezed out of the peasants. They would have to combine their small plots into large, collective farms. These farms would produce more by using tractors and other modern machines. The peasants would be forced to sell their crops at very low prices to the government. It would then export most of the crops to buy machines for the factories. In short, the peasants would have to pay the costs of industrialization. Their private land and other forms of private enterprise were again abolished.

Was Lenin a German Agent?

The great hero of the Soviet Union is Vladimir Ilyich Lenin, creator of the Soviet Communist state. For Soviet citizens, Lenin is like a god who could do no wrong. In the eyes of the Soviet government, to attack Lenin's character is a terrible sin and must not be allowed. Yet ever since 1917, various people, some of them historians, have charged that Lenin was not the great revolutionary he seemed to be. He did what he did, they say, only because he was paid by the Germans and followed their orders. Whenever this accusation against Lenin is made, the Soviet government is outraged and angrily denounces the charge as an outright lie.

Is there any evidence that Lenin really was a paid German agent? When World War II ended, the archives of the German government were opened up to historians. There they found definite proof that during World War I the German government had secretly sent money to support Lenin and the Bolsheviks, in hopes of undermining the Russian war effort.

Did receiving money from the Germans make Lenin a German agent? Some historians say it did and argue that the Germans not only gave him money, but also told him what to do. Most historians, however, say that getting money from the Germans is no proof that Lenin carried out German orders. They point out that the money came to Lenin from secret agents in Sweden and not directly from Germany. Therefore, Lenin may not even have known what the original source of the money was. Furthermore, they say, it is important to remember that Lenin was a fanatic revolutionary. It made little difference to him where he got money to support his revolutionary activities. His goal always stayed the same, and he made his own decisions.

Although there is no way for historians to be absolutely certain, most of them have come to the conclusion that Lenin was not a German agent. But they have no doubt that German money helped Lenin carry out the most important revolution of the 20th century. And the fact that Lenin got money from the Germans is still a sensitive issue in the Soviet Union. To this day, no Soviet historian dares to write about it in a history textbook.

Lenin's preserved body lies in a glass case. Every day, hundreds of people file by it to pay their respects.

If students ask why the Germans would have given money to Lenin: Germany was fighting the tsar's army in the war and by contributing to a revolution in Russia, Germany hoped to end the tsar's ability to fight Germany.

Of course, most peasants strongly objected to giving up their land, tools, and animals. Instead, many burned their grain and killed their livestock. The government felt it must crush this ans. 2 opposition. It shipped angry peasants to less fertile areas, where millions starved to death. Others were shot or sent to forced labor camps. Stalin called a halt to these brutal methods in 1930. From then on, propaganda and economic ans. 1 pressure were used instead. By 1936, about 90 percent of the peasants belonged to nearly 250 thousand collective farms.

In 1933, the Second Five-Year Plan began. Waste, inefficiency, and a shortage of skilled workers held up the Plan. But in the short span of twelve years, the Soviet Union became a first-class industrial power. The Third Five-Year Plan was cut short by World War II.

Life was "Stalinized." Under Stalin, ordinary citizens made some gains. The planned economy gave almost everyone jobs, and production increased. There was a drive to wipe out illiteracy and to enable more people to receive free tuition and scholarships at universities. ans. 2 State medical care, old-age pensions, and illness and accident insurance were put into effect. Women also gained almost complete equality with men. They were encouraged to enter the professions, especially medicine.

These gains, however, did not hide the steady "Stalinization" of Soviet culture. In the early ans. 2 Stalin years, writers, artists, and scholars were able to work freely so long as they were not outspokenly anti-Communist. But by the mid- ans. 3 1930s, the party leaders decided that the intellectuals had a part to play in building Communism. Thus, historians had to glorify Russian heroes of the past. Novelists had to show all Communists as pure idealists. Composers had to write melodies that the common people could enjoy.

Marxist theory was also changed to fit the needs of the state. The Communist motto, "from each according to his ability; to each according to his needs," was scrapped. Training and skill were rewarded with higher salaries, bonuses, and more social prestige. Soviet patriotism was admired, while the unity of the world's working classes was played down. The family also gained new importance. Childbearing was encouraged, and divorce laws were tightened. Atheism remained the official position on religion. The government did not stop harassing the Orthodox Church and other religious groups.

Stalin became the absolute dictator. In 1936, the "Stalin Constitution" was adopted.

In the 1920s, hardships forced the former bourgeoisie to sell their dresses in the open market at Leningrad.

Communists everywhere boasted that the Soviet Union was now the most democratic country in the world. In practice, however, the new constitution did not protect the basic freedoms of the individual. Those who hoped that there might be some loosening of totalitarianism were sadly mistaken. The Communist party still had all the political power. And behind the party stood Stalin. He was no longer willing to be first among equals. His drive for absolute power could not be stopped. His picture and his name appeared everywhere. He was always in the public eye as the "Great Marxist-Leninist."

ans. 4 Also, Stalin became suspicious of many of his old comrades. He had many, many party leaders arrested by the secret police on false charges of treason. After putting them through horrible tortures, he staged several public trials in Moscow from 1936 to 1938. Most of the people confessed and were executed at once, although there was no evidence of their guilt.

The same things happened to many others. They included army officers, government officials, scientists, writers, artists, and ordinary citizens. Hundreds of thousands were shot. Millions of others were sent to forced labor camps, never to be heard from again. Stalin unleashed a reign of terror upon the Russian people. He ruled as an absolute dictator. No one dared challenge him.

SECTION REVIEW **3**

1. What did Stalin's Five-Year Plans accomplish? p. 585
2. How did the Plans affect different groups? p. 585
3. How was Soviet culture "Stalinized"? How was Marxist theory revised during the 1930s? p. 585
4. Why did Stalin launch a 1930s reign of terror? p. 586

4 The Soviet Union tried to protect its security

Relations between the Soviet Union and the West were not very friendly in the 1920s and 1930s. Soviet leaders were sure that the capitalists wanted to crush the Soviet Union. Many

Daily Life in the Soviet Union
Under Stalin, the Communist government used many kinds of propaganda to make its people feel like part of a great system. The poster *(left)* was intended to show that Stalin loved all citizens, regardless of race. In the Ukraine, a newspaper was prepared on a truck in a farm field. This made the farmers feel they were an important part of a nationwide farming effort. In a government factory, workers voted to send a day's pay to help republican forces in the Spanish civil war. Thus workers felt they decided Soviet foreign policy.

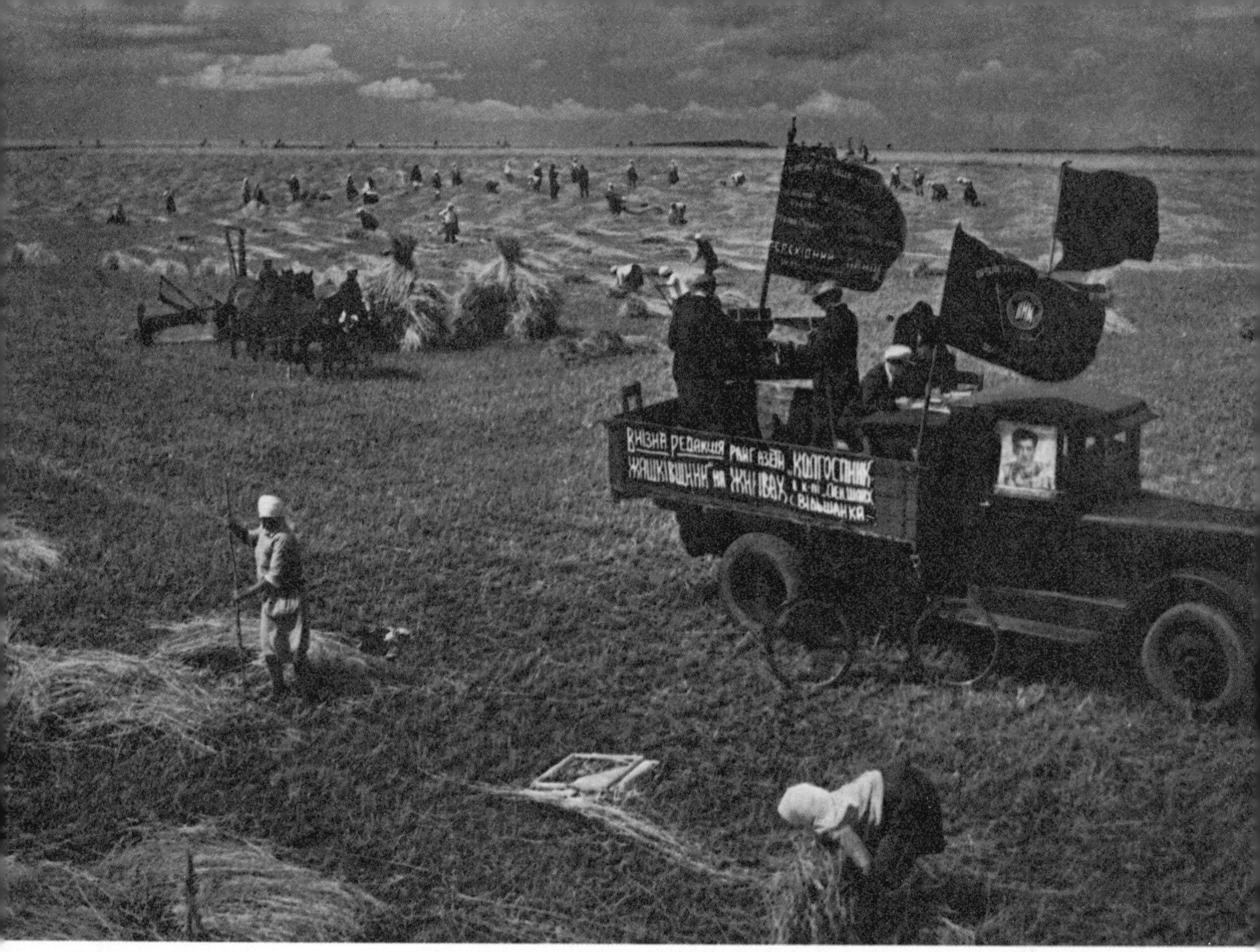

Виїзна редакція
на жнивах

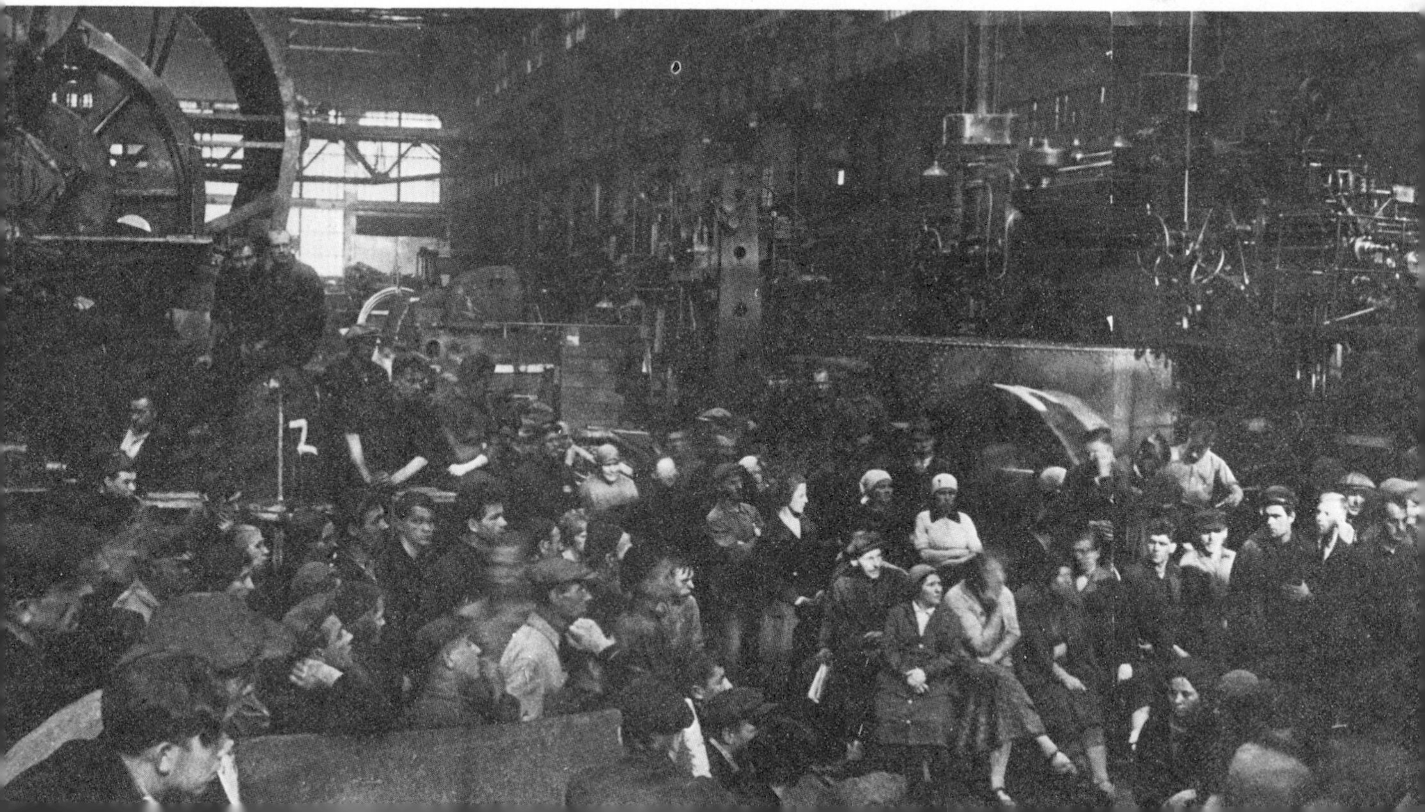

people in the democracies feared Marxist ideas of worldwide revolution. However, no government wanted to wage a war against the Soviet Union.

ans. 1 The Soviet Union constantly tried to stir up revolution abroad. Communist parties were founded during the early 1920s in most of the world's countries. These parties became members of the Communist International ("Comintern" for short), which was dominated by the Soviet Union. Although Stalin favored building socialism in his own country, he used the Comintern as a worldwide propaganda tool.

The U.S.S.R. tried to win friends. In the 1920s, Germany was the only friend of the Soviet Union in western Europe. Both countries were outcasts—Germany because it was a defeated power, the Soviet Union because of Communism. In 1922, they signed the Treaty
ans. 2 of Rapallo. Under it, Germany formally recognized the Soviet Union and in return, received full trading rights with the Soviet Union. That same year, but at a different place, a secret military agreement was signed. German officers were sent to help train the Red Army. In exchange, Soviet factories supplied arms to Germany. This was a violation of the Versailles Treaty, which said that Germany could not rearm.

Later in the 1920s, most of the major powers set up diplomatic relations with the Soviet Union. Britain and France did so in 1924, but the United States waited until 1933.

In East Asia, the U.S.S.R. also tried to win friends. Beginning in 1923, the Soviet Union aided the National People's party in its effort to unify China. In 1927, however, the National People's party, afraid of Communist control, rejected Soviet help. This dealt a sharp blow to Stalin's aim of revolutionizing China.

● Discuss this question: Should Britain and France have allied themselves with Russia before 1939?

Stalin failed to get collective security.
The 1930s saw a change in Soviet foreign pol- ans. 3
icy. By 1934, the "Rapallo spirit" with Germany was dead. Hitler, now in command, did not hide his hatred of communism and of the Soviet Union. Japanese designs on the Asian mainland also worried the Soviet Union. Faced with these dangers, Stalin felt that he must seek the good will of the western democracies. That is, he advocated a policy of collective security against the fascist dictatorships.

In 1934, the U.S.S.R. was admitted to the League of Nations. At the same time, the Comintern stopped inciting world revolution. Communists abroad were ordered to support anyone who would join in a common struggle against the aggressive dictators. This so-called Popular Front policy was successful in France in 1936 and 1937. The U.S.S.R. also sent military advisers and supplies to China in its fight against Japan. And it aided the anti-Franco forces in the Spanish Civil War, which broke out in 1936.

Yet Britain and France remained suspicious ans. 4
and distrustful of Stalin, the Communist dictator. Also, both countries wanted to avoid ●
offending Hitler. Thus, Stalin was forced to change his foreign policy. He reversed it when he and Hitler signed a nonaggression pact in 1939. Soon after that, World War II began.

SECTION REVIEW 4

1. What was the Comintern? How was it used by the Soviet Union? p. 588

2. What was the Treaty of Rapallo? What did each signer of the Treaty do? p. 588

3. Why did Stalin favor "collective security"? How did he try to achieve it? p. 588

4. Why did Stalin drop his policy of "collective security"? p. 588

CHAPTER REVIEW 31

SECTION SUMMARIES

1. Autocratic rulers weakened Russia. Although Russia was an important military and political force in 19th-century Europe, it remained an undeveloped country. The backward economy and government were in the hands of weak nobles and autocratic tsars. The majority of the people were poor, ill-treated peasants and serfs.

The first major reform came in 1861 when Alexander II freed the serfs. Freedom, however, did little to help the peasants economically. In 1881, Alexander II was assassinated. Under succeeding autocrats, Alexander III and Nicholas II, Russia grew weaker. In 1905, Russia suffered a terrible military defeat by the Japanese. Some reforms were made after that, but they were not very effective.

2. Bolsheviks took control of Russia. Russian participation in World War I finally destroyed the tsarist system. In March, 1917, the tsar was forced to abdicate. A Provisional Government of middle-class liberals took over. But the Provisional Government lost support and by November, Lenin and the Bolsheviks had seized power. A bloody Civil War broke out in 1918 when Lenin tried to establish a Communist dictatorship. The Bolsheviks took Russia out of World War I by signing the Treaty of Brest-Litovsk with Germany.

Lenin began a strict Marxist program while faced with the Civil War and Allied intervention. In 1921, however, he made a temporary retreat from communism with the NEP. The government kept control of basic industries but allowed some private farming and small business. The Union of Soviet Socialist Republics was established.

3. Stalin created a totalitarian society. After Lenin's death in 1924, Trotsky and Stalin fought for leadership within the Communist party. The victor was Joseph Stalin who began his own type of despotism. In 1928, Stalin initiated the first of his famous Five-Year Plans. Factory workers were strictly controlled, and peasants were forced to work on collective farms. In the process of collectivization and rapid industrialization, millions of people lost their lives. By the mid-1930s, the Soviet Union had made important economic gains. Its people, however, had to live in a police state with all activities carefully regulated. The Soviet Union had become a totalitarian society.

4. The Soviet Union tried to protect its security. In the 1930s, the U.S.S.R. began to take a more active role in world affairs. The Soviets gained diplomatic recognition from western countries. With the rise of Mussolini and Hitler, the U.S.S.R. searched for allies. When Britain and France turned down his bid for a defensive alliance, Stalin signed a nonaggression pact with Hitler in 1939.

WHO? WHAT? WHEN? WHERE?

1. In each group below, arrange the events in chronological order:

Events before the Revolution

a. The serfs were emancipated. 2
b. The Russo-Japanese War began. 3
c. The Decembrist Revolt took place. 1
d. The "Bloody Sunday" massacre occurred. 4
e. The first Duma met. 5

The Revolution

a. The Treaty of Brest-Litovsk was signed. 3
b. Kerensky became prime minister. 1
c. Lenin seized power. 2

The Establishment of the U.S.S.R.

a. Civil war began. 1
b. Trotsky was expelled from the Communist party. 4
c. The "Stalin Constitution" was adopted. 6
d. The New Economic Policy was begun. 2
e. The first Five-Year Plan was started. 5
f. Lenin died. 3

2. Explain how each of these people helped change tsarist Russia into the Soviet Union: p. 579-80

Lenin p. 581 | Alexander Kerensky
Leon Trotsky p. 582 | Joseph Stalin p. 582

3. What part in Russia's history was played by each of these:

Bolsheviks p. 580 | Decembrist Revolt p. 575
Duma p. 578 | soviets pp. 578-9

QUESTIONS FOR CRITICAL THINKING

1. What might Kerensky have done differently that would have prevented the Bolshevik takeover?
2. Compare the power of the tsar before 1905 with Stalin's in 1939. How were they alike? Different?
3. How might the U.S.S.R. of the 1930s have been different if either Lenin or Trotsky had been in charge rather than Stalin?

ACTIVITIES

● 1. Make up news headlines as they might have been written in Russia during 1917.
2. Role play interviews of Hitler and Stalin after the signing of the nonaggression pact of 1939. Members of the class should submit questions to be asked at a "news conference."
3. Write a letter from a Russian noble, worker, or peasant explaining the events of the revolution from that person's point of view.
4. Be a spokesperson for the serfs during the reign of Alexander I. Prepare your demands with reasons supporting them.
5. Follow-up on the mystery of Anastasia, the tsar's daughter. Was she killed or did she live? Present a case pro or con.
6. Analyze the Stalin Constitution and present its ideas to the class.

● 1. Tell students how many they are to write (3, 5, ?)
3. Assign particular viewpoints to specific students.

■ Discuss which of these reforms working people would value most highly, also artists.

CHAPTER TEST **31**

SECTION 1

1. Serdom was abolished in Russia by: a. Nicholas II, b. Alexander I, c. Alexander II
2. In the 1905 revolution, workers organized into groups called: a. Dumas, b. pogroms, c. soviets
3. True or false: Reforms made by Tsar Nicholas II most benefited the peasants and factory workers.

SECTION 2

4. Which of these reforms was made by the Provisional Government? a. land reform, b. increases in civil liberties, c. peace
5. "Peace, land, and bread" was promised by: a. Lenin, b. Kerensky, c. Trotsky
6. True or false: The United States sent troops to Russia during the Russian Civil War.

SECTION 3

7. Which of these was not a goal of the Five-Year Plans? a. to build factories, b. to make farming more efficient, c. to finance private businesses
8. Which of these was an improvement made by Stalin? a. full employment, b. artistic freedom, c. religious freedom ■
9. True or false: The "Stalin Constitution" made the Soviet Union on paper the most democratic government in the world.

SECTION 4

10. Communist parties all over the world were members of the: a. Rapallo Treaty, b. NEP, c. Comintern
11. Adolf Hitler and Stalin signed a nonaggression treaty in: a. 1934, b. 1936, c. 1939
12. To which of these countries did Stalin not send military aid in the 1930s? a. China, b. Japan, c. Spain

1939—1945

CHAPTER **32**

World War II

With the order that began World War II, Adolf Hitler sent Nazi troops into Poland. They destroyed towns and left hundreds of dead in their wake. Here a motorized detachment rides through a Polish town that has been repeatedly bombed by the Luftwaffe, the German air force.

If men wish to live, then they are forced to kill others . . . we National Socialists . . . aim . . . to secure for the German people the land and soil to which they are entitled on this earth. . . . Only the might of a victorious sword . . . will win soil for us. . . .

These words from Hitler's *Mein Kampf* became the basis for Nazi policy in Europe. They show Hitler's extreme nationalism and violence, along with his drive for expansion. Such forces helped push the nations of Europe into World War II in 1939.

Be sure to point out the photographs included in this chapter. They can be very useful in motivating discussion and for giving students an improved understanding of the events described.

But Adolf Hitler did not bring on World War II all by himself. There were other causes for the war, and some of them involved Japan. Although Japan was the most industrialized nation in Asia, it had almost no supplies of coal, iron, and oil. These had to be imported to keep Japanese factories going. This became more difficult as the world depression deepened and world trade shrank. Japan could not sell enough factory goods abroad to buy the raw materials that it needed. Unemployment became widespread. Under these conditions, Japanese militarists decided that only by conquering a vast empire in Asia could Japan survive as a great power. When the United States opposed this policy of expansion, Japan decided to use force.

In this way, the problems of Germany in Europe and of Japan in Asia were linked together in causing the second total war of the 20th century. As a result of that war, Germany was divided by the victorious allies. Japan lost all of its overseas empire.

The Soviet Union came to dominate all of eastern Europe. Western Europe lost its leading position in world affairs. It was weakened by the long war and by the rise of independence movements in overseas colonies. The United States and the Soviet Union emerged as the two super powers of the postwar world. Most importantly, World War II brought on the Atomic Age. For the first time in history, human beings had weapons that could destroy civilization. Since 1945, everyone on Earth has had to live with this possibility. Chapter 32 explains how:

1. **Tensions and fear grew again.**
2. **Peaceful relations ended.**
3. **War became worldwide.**
4. **The Allies won.**

• Use the map on p. 594 to point out the locations of Axis conquests.

1 Tensions and fear grew again

Only twenty-five years separated the beginnings of the two world wars. Both in 1914 and in 1939, war came after a build-up of tension and fear among the great powers. But in the case of World War II, tension spread in Asia and Europe.

Japan attacked China. Japanese militarists, as we have seen, were set on controlling China. In September, 1931, Japan seized several provinces in Manchuria. The Japanese then made Manchuria a puppet state called Manchukuo. They said that they would not give up this terri- ans. 1
tory, which was very rich in natural resources.

The Chinese retaliated by boycotting Japanese goods. They cut imports from Japan by 94 percent. In 1937, Japan began open warfare in China. Shanghai, Nanking, and other large cities fell to the Japanese. But the Chinese would not surrender. Instead, 50 million of them fled to the western part of China. They took machinery, farm equipment, and furniture in carts or on their backs. In late 1938, they set up a new capital for China at Chungking.

The League of Nations condemned the Jap- ans. 1
anese aggression. Its members—as well as the United States—spoke out against Japanese actions. But they were unwilling to use military force against Japan. Most of the Western countries were still suffering from the depression. They did not want to lose their trade with Japan.

Hitler and Mussolini caused tension in Europe. In 1935, Hitler openly stated that he ans. 2
was rearming Germany. Later that same year, Mussolini attacked defenseless Ethiopia. He wanted to build an Italian Empire in Africa. In 1936, Hitler sent German troops into the Rhine- •
land area north of France.

Between World Wars

Small-scale conflicts took place in many parts of the world. In 1931, Japan defeated the Chinese in Manchuria. In the picture *opposite*, a woman and boy stare numbly at the wreckage of their home in Chungking after a Japanese bombing attack. *Below* Ethiopian soldiers march to a front-line clash with Italian troops who invaded their country in 1935.

Hitler's moves were direct violations of the ans. 2 Versailles Treaty. And Mussolini's aggression was a challenge to the League of Nations. As with Japan, however, no effective action was taken against either dictator. Neither France nor Britain wanted to get into another war. Public opinion in both countries was strongly against war. But the failure to act only encouraged the two dictators, especially Hitler. Both felt that they could make more aggressive moves without being stopped by the western democracies. In October, 1936, Mussolini and Hitler formed an alliance known as the Rome-Berlin Axis, and Germany and Italy were called the Axis powers.

Fascism also gained control in Spain. Meanwhile, in 1931 the Spaniards had overthrown their monarch and set up a republic. The new government tried to deal with the problems of poverty, illiteracy, and social unrest. But it failed to control a strong fascist group that blocked the attempts to improve conditions. Led by General Francisco Franco, military chiefs ans. 3 revolted against the republic in 1936. The Spanish Civil War had begun. Franco's forces were joined by the fascists and extreme nationalists.

Thousands of people, known as Loyalists, ans. 3 rushed to the defense of the republic. They were aided by a communist group who felt their best interests would be served by fighting fascism. Volunteers from other countries also helped the Loyalists. For a while they were successful, but they lacked arms.

As in the Rhineland crisis, Britain, France, and other European states wanted to keep out of a war. Therefore, they followed a policy of strict neutrality, as did the United States. Such policies prevented the democracies from helping the Loyalists.

ans. 4 Mussolini and Hitler, however, sent arms and troops to aid Franco's Fascists. In March, 1939, the capital city, Madrid, was taken by Franco. This ended the republic. Many people feel that the neutral policy of the democratic states was largely to blame for the rise of yet another fascist dictatorship in Europe.

SECTION REVIEW 1

p. 592 **1.** Why did Japan seize Manchuria? Why didn't the League of Nations try to stop that war?

p. 592 **2.** What illegal actions were taken by the leaders of
594 Germany and Italy in 1935 and 1936? Why was nothing done to stop them?

p. 594 **3.** What groups fought on the side of the fascists in the Spanish Civil War? Who supported each?

p. 595 **4.** Name three fascist dictatorships in 1939.

2 Peaceful relations ended

Hitler's goal was to expand the power of Ger-
ans. 1 many until he controlled all of Europe. Britain and France, however, did not know that. They believed they could work out compromises to appease, or satisfy, Hitler. In this way they hoped to avoid war. But this policy of appeasement only proved to Hitler that the West was weak and that he could take whatever land he wanted. His aggression finally broke the uneasy peace of Europe.

Germany took over Austria. Hitler first ans. 2
planned to annex Austria, that is, add Austria to Germany. In February, 1938, he invited the Austrian Chancellor to his mountain hideaway in southern Germany. There Hitler forced the Chancellor to agree to include Nazis in the Austrian cabinet. In March, Hitler invaded Austria. Hitler's secret police, the Gestapo [gə stä′pō], took over Vienna. They began repressive measures against liberals and Jews. Thousands of persons, especially scientists, writers, and artists, fled the country to find safety.

By moving into Austria Hitler gained $100 million in gold, 7 million more citizens, and rich timber resources. Neither France nor Britain did anything more than protest this aggressive act.

Hitler next moved into Czechoslovakia. Hitler's next target was Czechoslovakia. He claimed that the 3 million Germans living in the Sudeten Mountains in Czechoslovakia were being oppressed by the Czechs. In the summer of 1938, he said that the Sudeten Germans must have self-rule. Hitler threatened war if his demands were not met. The Czechs turned to Britain and France for help. But the British, led by Prime Minister Neville Chamberlain, still wanted to avoid war at all costs. To do this, Chamberlain made two trips to Germany to talk to Hitler. Each time, Hitler's demands grew.

Chamberlain refused to accept the new terms and returned to London. He seemed to take a firm stand against Hitler. But then Hitler announced, "This is the last territorial claim I shall make in Europe." He asked Chamberlain and French Premier Edouard Daladier [da la dyā′] to meet with him and Mussolini in Munich on

September 29, 1938. They agreed. No one from Czechoslovakia or Russia (which had promised to protect Czechoslovakia) was at the meeting.

During the Munich Conference, Chamberlain and Daladier decided to sacrifice Czechoslovakia. They let Hitler take over the Sudetenland. In return, he promised to keep the peace. The

Use the map above to show in what ways World War II was truly a world war.

Czechs had no choice but to give in. Six months later, however, Hitler broke the promise he had made at Munich and took over the rest of Czechoslovakia. ans. 2

This brutal action finally convinced Britain and France that Hitler could not be appeased. They realized that his real aim was to dominate all of Europe. They therefore gave up their pol-

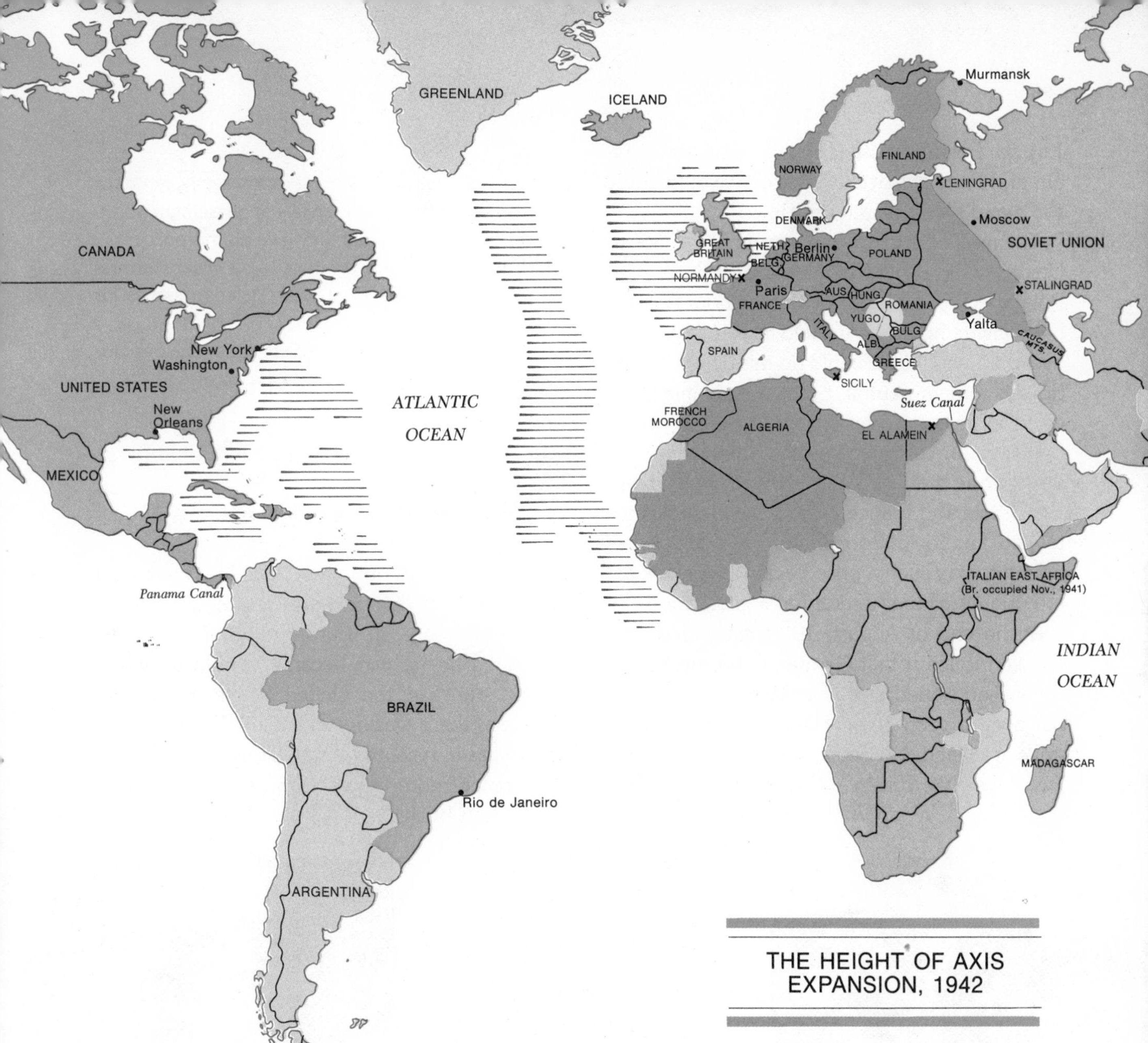

icy of appeasement and decided to oppose any further German demands.

Germany now demanded Polish territory. Hitler's next move was against Poland. The Treaty of Versailles had given Poland a corridor through Prussia. This gave Poland an outlet to the Baltic Sea at the port of Danzig. Danzig was declared a free or independent city under the protection of the League of Nations. About 90 percent of the corridor's population was Polish, but most of the people in Danzig were German.

In March, 1939, Hitler demanded that Danzig be given to Germany. He also said that the Nazis must be allowed to occupy a narrow strip of the corridor connecting Germany with East

Prussia. Poland refused, and this time both Britain and France warned Hitler they would come to Poland's aid if he attacked it.

ans. 3 The major question now was what the Soviet Union would do. Britain and France knew that Poland could not be defended without Russian help. Hitler, however, wanted to avoid fighting a two-front war. Hitler could do this by having the Soviets remain neutral. Stalin was mainly interested in protecting his western frontiers. Thus, he asked for control over the countries in eastern Europe that bordered on the Soviet Union. For Britain and France, that was too high a price to pay for Soviet cooperation. But Hitler was willing to pay such a price because he expected to conquer all that territory at a later time.

At the end of August, 1939, the world was shocked to learn that Germany and the Soviet Union had signed a pact agreeing not to go to war against each other. Hitler was now free to strike at Poland. On September 1, 1939, he did. Two days later, Britain and France declared war on Germany. World War II had begun.

SECTION REVIEW **2**

1. Explain Britain and France's appeasement policy toward Hitler. When did they give up this policy? p. 595

2. Name three areas taken over by Hitler's armies in 1938 and 1939. What were Hitler's motives for each take over? p. 595 596

3. What were Stalin's and Hitler's reasons for agreeing not to go to war against each other? p. 598

3 War became worldwide

When war broke out, it was mainly a European war. For more than two years, most of the fighting took place in Europe and the Atlantic Ocean. But the war became worldwide when Japan attacked the United States. From that time on, there was heavy fighting in the Pacific, as well as in Asia and Africa. Thus, World War II was much more truly a *world* war than World War I had been.

The Home Front
Like this weeping Frenchman, people from many nations watched Axis powers take over their countries while their own forces surrendered or went into exile. Once the war became worldwide, Allied posters, such as the one at right, appeared. The war totally ruled the lives of many civilians, especially Europeans. The cathedral in Coventry, England, which had been built during the Middle Ages, was completely bombed out by the Luftwaffe during the Battle of Britain. The Germans sought to destroy Coventry because it was a major industrial area. Meanwhile in London every night, thousands slept in the subways, which were used as an enormous bomb shelter.

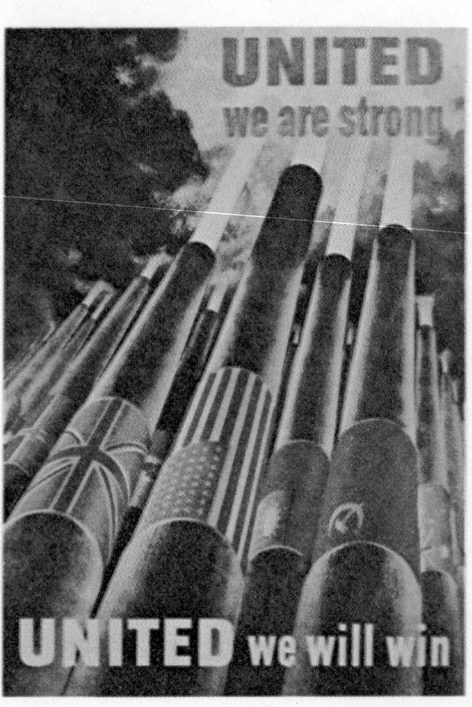

Eastern Europe was the first battlefield. In attacking Poland, Hitler struck very quickly. He used planes, tanks, and mechanized units. He called this a *blitzkrieg* [blitz′krēg′], which was a German word for "lightning warfare." The Poles were not prepared for that kind of warfare. In three weeks, they were totally crushed by the Germans.

As part of their agreement with Hitler, Soviet forces moved into eastern Poland, Latvia, Lithuania, and Estonia. The Soviet Union then ordered Finland to give up some of its land near Leningrad. When Finland refused, the Soviet Union attacked it in November, 1939. By March, 1940, Finland was defeated. It was forced to surrender the land the Soviet Union wanted for better protection of Leningrad.

The Germans conquered western Europe. After the defeat of Poland, Hitler made plans to crush France and Britain. First, he invaded and conquered Denmark and Norway in April, 1940. In May, he turned south and overran the Netherlands and Belgium. By conquering Belgium, Hitler had bypassed France's major defenses along the Maginot Line. The French army was cut to pieces. In June, 1940, France surrendered. That same month, Mussolini brought Italy into the war on the German side. Hitler was now in control of almost all of western Europe.

After the summer of 1940, Britain was left to stand alone against Germany. Hitler thought the British would be willing to make a compromise peace. But Winston Churchill, who had become prime minister in May, refused. Hitler then decided to attack Britain by sea. However, Hermann Goering [goe′ ring], commander of the German air force, convinced Hitler that the British could be bombed into surrender. Mass bombings of Britain began in August, 1940. The British fought back. For the next ten months, a terrible air battle raged in the skies over Britain. The Germans lost more than twice as many planes as the British. By May, 1941, Hitler knew that he had lost the Battle of Britain.

Hitler attacked the Soviet Union. As early as December, 1940, Hitler decided to invade ans. 1 the Soviet Union. He wanted to conquer the Soviets because of their rich grain fields and large supplies of oil, coal, and iron ore. Then he planned to turn back against Britain. Before moving into the Soviet Union, however, Hitler took control of the Balkans. He made alliances with Hungary, Romania, and Bulgaria. He also overran Greece and Yugoslavia early in 1941.

In June, 1941, German forces swept into the Soviet Union. By December, Germany conquered 600 thousand square miles (1.55 million square kilometers) of territory. The Soviets had lost more than 3.5 million soldiers and almost their entire air force. The Germans were close to Moscow and had surrounded Leningrad. For 900 days and nights Leningrad held out against constant bombardment. Nearly 1 million people died of starvation and disease.

Stalin had not believed that Hitler would break their 1939 treaty and so was not prepared ans. 1 for war. But despite terrible losses, the Soviet army was not destroyed. They still had huge reserves of manpower. Early in December, 1941, the Russians launched a counterattack to drive the Germans back from Moscow. The Germans were not prepared for fighting in the severe winter weather. They had no antifreeze in their tanks and wore only their summer uniforms. Many Germans froze to death in the −30°F. (−34.5°C.) weather. As the harsh winter had helped the Russians defeat Napoleon in 1812, it now aided the Soviets in their battle against Hitler. The German army was halted.

ans. 2 **Japan bombed Pearl Harbor.** On the morning of December 7, 1941, without warning or a declaration of war, Japan attacked the ● American naval base at Pearl Harbor in Hawaii. The Japanese also attacked the Philippines, British Malaya, and other places in Asia. The Japanese planned to build a great empire in Southeast Asia. Such an empire could supply ans. 2 Japan with oil, rubber, tin, and rice. It could also become a market for Japanese factory goods. Only the United States could stop Japan, because the European countries that had colonies in Asia were too busy fighting in Europe.

● Remind students of the Russo-Japanese War (p. 577) in which the Japanese also used surprise tactics.

The Japanese attacks destroyed much of the American Pacific fleet. They also brought the United States into the war. The United States declared war on Japan; then Germany and Italy declared war on the United States. By January 1, 1942, the United States, the Soviet Union, Britain, and twenty-three other nations had become allied to fight the Axis powers. (Japan had allied with Germany and Italy in 1936). The war was now worldwide.

SECTION REVIEW **3**

1. Why did Hitler want to conquer the Soviet Union? What losses did the Soviets suffer between June and December, 1941? What stopped the German advance in the Soviet Union? p. 600

2. Describe three steps by which Asia, America and Europe became linked in World War II. What were the reasons behind Japan's attack on Pearl Harbor? p. 600

4 The Allies won

In the spring of 1942, Axis power reached its greatest extent. By May, 1942, the Japanese had created an empire that included Burma, Malaya, French Indochina, the Dutch East Indies, Thailand, the Philippines, Hong Kong, the coast of China, and various islands in the South Pacific. Hitler controlled Europe from Norway to the Mediterranean and from the Atlantic coast to deep inside the Soviet Union. But 1942 was also the year the tide of battle began to turn against the Axis powers.

Hitler created a brutal New Order. Both Japan and Germany forced their conquered peoples to work for them. Hitler began to reorganize Europe for the benefit of the "master race." He called his scheme the "New Order."
ans. 1 It was a plan to make all of Europe serve Germany. Huge amounts of French food, Soviet grain, Czech weapons, and Romanian oil were shipped to Germany. Seven million foreign workers were brought to Germany as slaves.

In the conquered lands, the Nazis used ruthless terror to control the local people. The horrors of Nazi rule were most brutal against Poles, Russians, Czechs, Yugoslavs, and Gypsies. These were all considered to be "inferior" people. Over 3 million Soviet prisoners died in German prison camps.

Worst of all was the Nazi program of geno- ans. 2
cide, the murder of an entire people. This was carried out against the Jews of Europe. In the early years of the war, special Nazi execution squads shot hundreds of thousands of Jewish men, women, and children in Poland and the Soviet Union. Then, to speed up the slaughter, the Nazis built special death camps equipped with poison gas chambers and cremating ovens. Millions of Jews were rounded up all over Europe. They were crammed into sealed cattle cars and shipped to the death camps. By the end of the war, the Nazis had murdered nearly 6 million Jews, 1.5 million of them children. Jewish community life in Europe, which had existed for centuries, was totally destroyed.

Jews in Warsaw, Poland, in 1939 being rounded up and sent off to concentration camps by the Nazis.

The British defeated Axis troops at El Alamein, Egypt, in 1942. It was a decisive North African battle.

● **The tide of battle turned.** In June, 1942, a
ans. 3 great sea and air battle took place between the Japanese and the Americans at Midway Island in the South Pacific. When the battle ended, the Japanese had lost four large aircraft carriers and many trained pilots. The United States was able to restore the naval balance it had lost at Pearl Harbor. The tide of war had now begun to shift toward the Allies. Several months later, the Americans began to push the Japanese out of the South Pacific.

One month after the Battle of Midway, the Germans started another offensive in the southern Soviet Union. Their goal was to reach the Caucasus Mountains and cut off the food and oil supply to the central Soviet Union. By September, 1942, the Germans had reached the important city of Stalingrad on the Volga River. The Germans pounded the city and killed 40 thousand civilians. But the Soviets fought like tigers and held on. Although the German commander knew he could not win, Hitler refused to let him retreat and save the army. The Soviets brought up fresh reserves, surrounded the Germans, and crushed them. In January, 1943, the Germans at Stalingrad surrendered. It was their worst defeat of the war. They had lost an army of over 350 thousand men. From that time on, the Soviet Union took the offensive in eastern Europe and Germany steadily retreated.

A third important turning point of the war came in North Africa. By June, 1942, German and Italian troops had swept across North Africa to within 70 miles (113 kilometers) of Alexandria, Egypt. Their aim was to reach the Suez Canal and the rich oil fields of the Middle East. But in October, 1942, the British began a counterattack. By January, 1943, they had driven the Italians and Germans back 1,400 miles (2,258 kilometers) to the west. Meanwhile, in November, 1942, American and British troops landed in French Morocco and Algeria and

● Have students find Midway Island, Stalingrad, and N. Africa on a world globe.

pushed eastward. Squeezed by both sides, over 250 thousand German and Italian troops surrendered in May, 1943.

Italy declared war on Germany. After their North African victory, the path to Europe was open and the Allies invaded Sicily in July, 1943. Within two weeks, Mussolini was forced out of office and put in jail. A new government signed an armistice on September 8. They surrendered unconditionally to the Allies on the day before the Allies invaded Italy.

However, the new Italian government had very little real control. The Allied invasion met with stiff resistance from German forces and Italian supporters of Mussolini. On October 13, the new government of Italy declared war on Germany. But it was June 4, 1944, before the Allies could fight their way to Rome, and the Germans held northern Italy until the spring of 1945.

The Allies invaded France. An Allied invasion of France had been planned since 1942. The Allied leaders felt that a direct attack on Germany from the west was the quickest way to end the war. By 1944, some 1.5 million trained Allied troops were ready in Great Britain. Ships and landing craft were waiting at British ports. The Nazis did not expect the Allies to invade the Normandy coast. This part of the French coast lacked natural ports and had extreme tides. It was also defended by Hitler's "Atlantic Wall," which had many miles of underwater obstacles.

"Operation Overlord," under the command of General Dwight D. Eisenhower, moved across the English Channel on June 6, 1944. Six hundred ships battered German beach defenses. Paratroopers were dropped behind the German lines. Allied fighter planes outnumbered the German planes 50 to 1. After a week of fighting, the invasion army held a 60 mile (96 kilometer) strip of the Normandy beach. In July, the Allied armored divisions broke ans. 4
through the German lines. By August, Paris was liberated.

Germany surrendered to the Allies. By February, 1945, victory in Europe was in sight for the Allies. Roosevelt, Churchill, and Stalin met at Yalta in the southern Soviet Union to discuss peace terms. Agreements on territory and postwar control of Germany were made. In later years, this conference was criticized because of the concessions given to the Soviet Union.

A few weeks after Yalta, Soviet troops entered Berlin. German forces in Italy gave way to the Allies late in April. The final surrender of Germany took place on May 8, 1945.

A few days earlier, Hitler had committed suicide. In Italy, Mussolini had already been cap-

A Parisian rejoices at the liberation of her city by the Allies in September, 1944.

tured and shot by Italians. The Allied nations, too, had lost a leader. President Roosevelt had died on April 12, 1945. He was succeeded by Vice-President Harry S. Truman.

The Allies moved toward Japan. After the Battle of Midway in June, 1942, the United States began to attack the Japanese on island after island in the South Pacific, pushing steadily closer to Japan itself. American submarines caused heavy losses to Japanese shipping. American planes bombed the Japanese home islands. By 1945, Tokyo was in ruins. But the Japanese ignored American warnings of total
ans. 5 destruction. The United States wanted to avoid an invasion of Japan that would have meant the loss of hundreds of thousands of American soldiers. Instead, President Truman ordered that an atomic bomb be dropped. On August 6, 1945, the destructive force of 20 thousand tons of dynamite destroyed most of Hiroshima [hir′ ō shē′mə]. It wounded or killed more than 160 thousand persons.

On August 9, the Soviet Union declared war on Japan. Soviet troops invaded the Japanese-held areas of Korea and Manchuria. On the same day, a second atomic bomb was dropped on Nagasaki [nä′gə sä′kē]. President Truman warned that more bombs would follow unless there was an immediate surrender. Japan now asked for peace. On September 2, 1945, the Japanese signed the surrender. This ended a war that had lasted six years and one day.

SECTION REVIEW 4

1. How was Hitler's "New Order" put into practice? p. 601
2. What was the result of the Nazi program of genocide against the Jews? p. 601
3. How did the battles of Midway, Stalingrad, and in North Africa change the course of the war? p. 602
4. What events in Italy, France, and Germany led up to the surrender of Germany? p. 603
5. Why did the United States want to avoid an invasion of Japan? How were the Japanese forced to surrender? p. 604

Burned and maimed people wait for first aid in Hiroshima a few hours after the atomic bomb was dropped.

CHAPTER REVIEW 32

SECTION SUMMARIES

1. Tensions and fear grew again. In the 1930s, the leaders of Nazi Germany, fascist Italy, and militaristic Japan made aggressive moves. They broke treaties and bullied other countries. Japan attacked China. Hitler sent troops into the Rhineland. Mussolini moved into Ethiopia. Britain, France, and the United States did very little to stop them for fear that another world war would break out. They also did little to stop the victory of Franco's brand of fascism in Spain.

2. Peaceful relations ended. In 1938, Hitler became more aggressive. He annexed Austria to Germany. Then he got Britain and France to agree at the Munich Conference that Czechoslovakia should give up the Sudetenland to him. Six months later, he took over all of Czechoslovakia. In the spring of 1939, Britain and France then stopped their policy of appeasement and warned Hitler they would go to war if he tried to take territory from the Poles. Both Hitler and the western democracies wanted the help of the Soviet Union. But only Hitler was willing to pay Stalin's price. That price was Soviet control over the countries along its western borders. Germany and the Soviet Union signed a nonaggression pact in late August, 1939. On September 1, 1939, Germany attacked Poland. Britain and France declared war on Germany.

3. War became worldwide. By June, 1941, Hitler had conquered almost all of Europe, except Britain. He then attacked the Soviet Union. On December 7, 1941, Japan made a surprise attack on the American naval fleet at Pearl Harbor. Japan's plan was to cripple American naval power in the Pacific. Then the United States could not oppose Japanese expansion. By early 1942, Japan had conquered a huge empire in Southeast Asia.

4. The Allies won. The tide of battle turned against Japan, Germany, and Italy in 1942. The Americans defeated Japan at Midway Island. The United States then began a long campaign to push Japan out of the South Pacific. In the winter of 1942–1943, the Soviets won the great battle of Stalingrad. From that time on, the Germans steadily retreated. In North Africa, the British stopped the Germans and Italians from reaching the Suez Canal and the oil fields of the Middle East. In the spring of 1943, all German and Italian troops in North Africa surrendered. Later in 1943, Italy surrendered. In June, 1944, General Eisenhower led an invasion of Europe.

In April, 1945, Hitler committed suicide. Early in May, Germany surrendered. Japan surrendered in September, 1945, only after the United States had dropped atomic bombs on Hiroshima and Nagasaki.

● Sentences should be in students' own words so answers will vary. Require answers be based on actual events included in this chapter.

WHO? WHAT? WHEN? WHERE?

1. Find the month and year in which each event happened and arrange in chronological order:

An atom bomb was dropped on Hiroshima. 8/1945 (10)
Daladier, Chamberlain, and Hitler met at Munich. 9/38 (1)
France surrendered to Germany. 7/40 (4)
The U.S. won the battle of Midway Island. 7/42 (8)
The Battle of Britain began. 8/40 (5)
Japan surrendered to the Allies. 9/45 (11)
Hitler and Stalin signed a peace pact. 8/39 (2)
Britain and France declared war on Germany. 9/39 (3)
Germany surrendered. 5/45 (9)
Japanese bombers attacked Pearl Harbor. 12/41 (7)
German forces invaded the Soviet Union. 7/41 (6)

2. Write sentences telling about World War II events associated with each of these people: ●

Chamberlain	Eisenhower	Truman
Daladier	Stalin	Mussolini
Hitler	Roosevelt	Churchill

3. Tell who was involved in each of these and what the outcome was:

Midway Island p. 602	Battle of Britain p. 599
Pearl Harbor p. 600	Leningrad p. 600
Stalingrad p. 602	"Operation Overlord" p. 603

4. What countries were associated with each of these terms? What does each term mean?

appeasement p. 595	"New Order" p. 601
Gestapo p. 595	genocide p. 601
blitzkrieg p. 598	"Atlantic Wall" p. 603
Maginot Line p. 599	Allies map p. 596, 597

p. 596 5. Describe the conferences held at Munich in
p. 603 1938 and Yalta in 1945. What was the purpose of each conference? Why did some people disapprove of the decisions made at these meetings?

QUESTIONS FOR CRITICAL THINKING

1. How might World War II have been prevented?
2. Why is it important for students today to learn about what happened to the Jewish peple in Nazi Germany?
3. If the Japanese had not bombed Pearl Harbor, do you think the United States would have entered the war? Explain your answer.

ACTIVITIES

1. Interview your older relatives and friends about their lives during World War II. Ask about rationing, victory gardens, "C rations," and dog tags.
2. Prepare a news report on a World War II event (battle, siege, or conference) and present it to the class. Illustrate your report with maps and pictures.
3. Debate the use of the atomic bomb by the United States. Compare the effects of the atomic bombs on Japan with the effects of conventional bombs used in the Battle of Britian.

CHAPTER TEST 32

SECTION 1

1. Which of these did not lead to Japan's attacks on China in 1937? a. Japan's need for natural resources, b. China's refusal to buy Japanese products, c. League of Nations actions in Japan
2. In World War II, Germany and Italy were known as: a. the Great Powers, b. the Axis powers, c. the Allied powers
3. During the Spanish Civil War, the United States: a. remained neutral, b. sent aid to Franco, c. helped the Loyalists

SECTION 2

4. At the Munich Conference, it was agreed that Hitler could take over: a Czechoslovakia, b. Poland, c. the Sudetenland
5. The first countries to declare war on Germany in World War II were: a. Britain and the United States, b. the Soviet Union and France, c. Britain and France

SECTION 3

6. Hitler's method of warfare used in taking Poland was the: a. "New Order," b. *blitzkrieg*, c. Gestapo
7. In 1940, Britain's prime minister was: a. Churchill, b. Chamberlain, c. Daladier
8. True or false: Japan attacked Pearl Harbor to stop the U.S. from entering the war.

SECTION 4

9. True or false: Hitler's plan in Europe was to form a "New Order" in which all national groups would become German.
10. In which of these battles did the United States regain its naval superiority? a. Pearl Harbor, b. Normandy beach, c. Midway Island
11. True or false: In 1945, the Allied powers received the surrender of Hitler and Mussolini.

Questions 8, 9, and 11 require extra careful reading by students. For example, Hitler's plan in Europe was to form a "New Order", but in this plan, the different national groups were to serve the Germans not to become Germans.

UNIT REVIEW 8 TEST YOURSELF

1. Match the individual with his deed:

a. Masaryk
b. Hitler
c. von Berchtold
d. Truman
e. Mussolini
f. Kerensky
g. Chamberlain
h. Lenin
i. Perry
j. Wilson
k. Nicholas II
l. Livingstone

h Brought Japan into closer contact with the world
k Explored Africa and opposed the slave trade
i Favored a negotiated peace after World War I
a Led the only successful eastern European democracy after World War I
j Was the last tsar of Russia
d Ordered an atomic bomb dropped on Japan
b Tried to unite Europe under German rule
f Sacrificed Czechoslovakia to avoid war
g Used Marxist ideas to run Russian government
e Organized the Italian Fascist Party
c Asked for German help to fight Serbia

2. Which of these events was a direct cause of World War I?
The Japanese seized Manchuria.
The Bolsheviks took over Russia.
Archduke Francis Ferdinand was assassinated.
Hitler rose to power in Germany.

3. Which of these was not a problem after World War I?
Fear of German power
Germany's failure to pay heavy reparations
Great Britain's high rate of unemployment
A communist takeover in France

4. Which of these was not a reason for the rise of communism in Russia?
Tsar Nicholas II's refusal to end serfdom
The need to modernize Russian society
The autocratic rule of the Russian tsars
Hardships caused by World War I

5. Which of these was not a reason for European interest in colonies?
Industrial nations needed more raw materials.
The threat of foreign armies forced Europe to protect itself.
More markets were needed to sell manufactured goods.

6. Which event did not lead to World War II?
Britain and France's policies of appeasement
The Nazi-Soviet pact
Russia's attack on Poland
Japan's attack on Pearl Harbor

7. List these events in chronological order under the headings of: a. The Age of Imperialism, b. World War I, or c. World War II.
b The Zimmermann telegram was sent.
b,c German forces invaded Russia.
a The Russo-Japanese war ended.
c Russia defeated Finland.
a General Gordon was killed in Khartoum.
b Japan joined the Allies.
c Japan attacked the United States.
b The Bolshevik Revolution took place.
a English and French forces burned the summer palace at Peking.

8. Match the event with its geographic location:

a The Boxer Rebellion	d Cuba
b The Sepoy Rebellion	c Russia
c The Bolshevik Revolution	b India
d The *Maine* blew up.	a China
e Stanley found Livingstone.	f Hawaiian Islands
f Japan attacked Pearl Harbor.	g Japan
g First atomic bomb dropped in war	i English Channel
h Franco won the civil war.	e Africa
i "Operation Overlord"	j Balkans
j Archduke Francis Ferdinand killed	h Spain

E = mc²
Coca-Cola

UNIT

9

THE CONTEMPORARY WORLD

Everyone now alive is living in the contemporary world. This latest, or contemporary, period of human existence began after World War II. It is so different in various ways from all earlier periods that we sometimes forget how many of our unsolved problems today are carry-overs from the past. Every era has a mixture of the old and the new. (See, for example, the mystery "Can Time Stand Still?" on page 671.) What makes our era especially hard to understand is that so many parts of it are new.

The contemporary world is full of "firsts in history." It is the ● first time that human beings have had to live with the possibility of total annihilation through nuclear war. It is the first time that a few superpowers have dominated the entire world. It is also the first time that so many independent nations have existed around the globe.

Never before has the earth been so crowded with human beings. Never before have there been such wide differences between wealth and poverty among people and nations.

For the first time, too, human beings have set foot on the moon and actually seen what the earth looks like from outer space. And perhaps most important of all, for the first time human beings have begun to understand that the earth's resources, even air and water, are limited and that humans could destroy themselves by polluting their environment.

In the Space Age, our crowded planet faced new problems and new opportunities.

● You might have your students list other "firsts" of the contemporary world on the board.

We are aware of all this partly because, for the first time, we can reach any part of the world by jet plane in a matter of hours. In a matter of seconds, we can see and hear on television almost anyone or anything. This unit describes many of these new developments

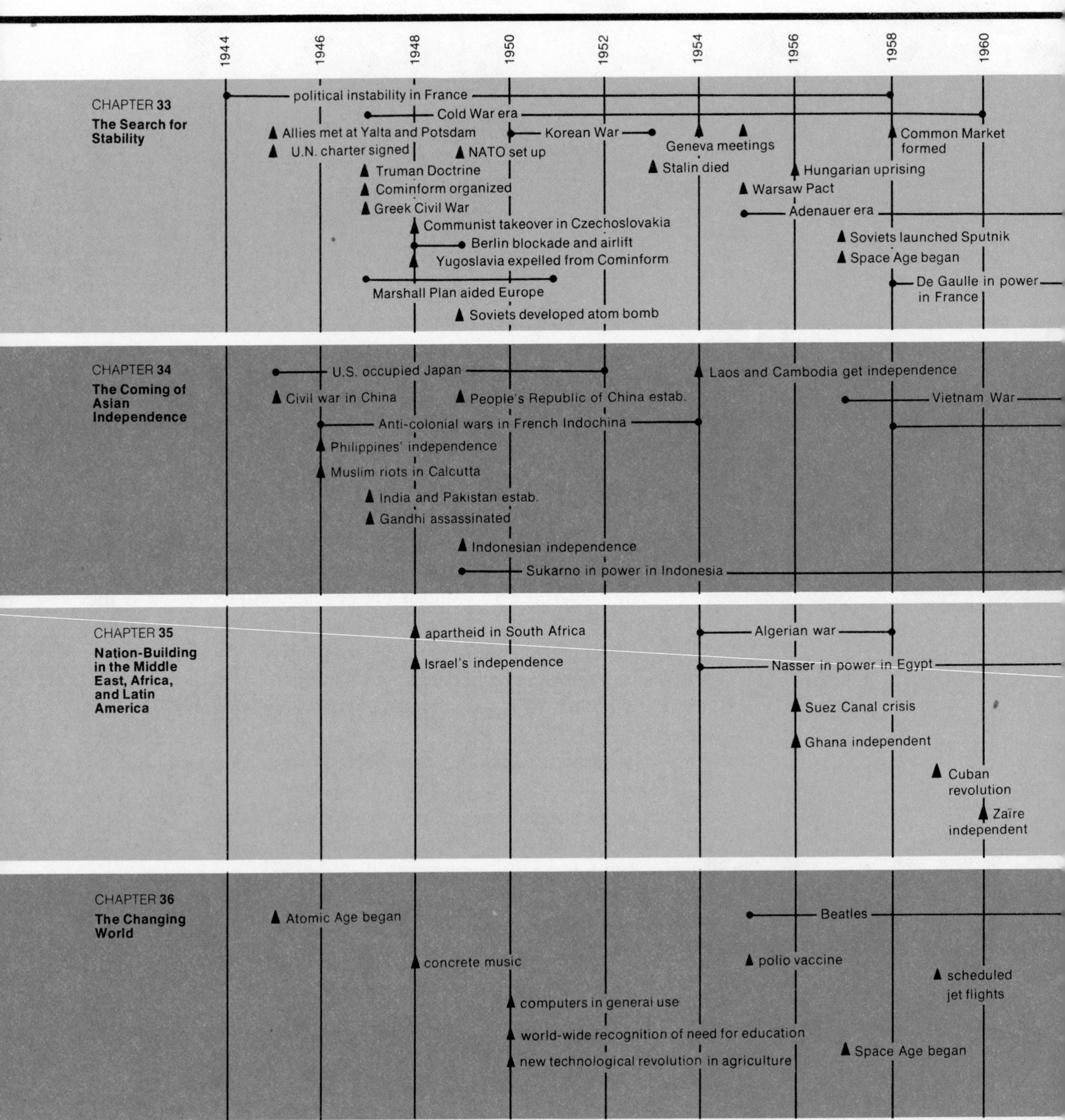

and some of the problems they have created. It also discusses the important older problems that are still with us. The combination of old and new problems are the unfinished business of this age, the challenges that people living today must meet.

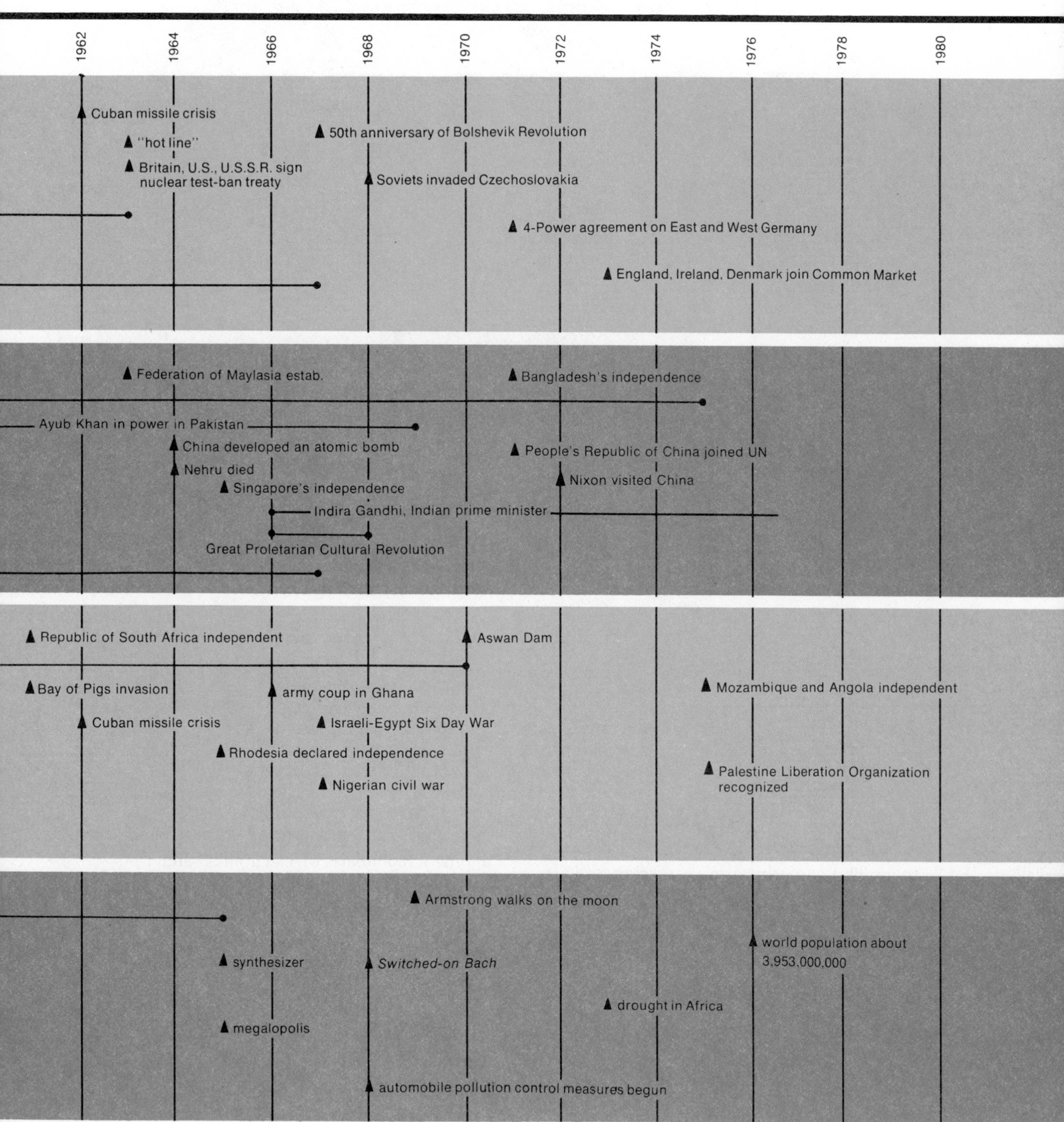

CHAPTER 33 — 1945–

The Search for Stability

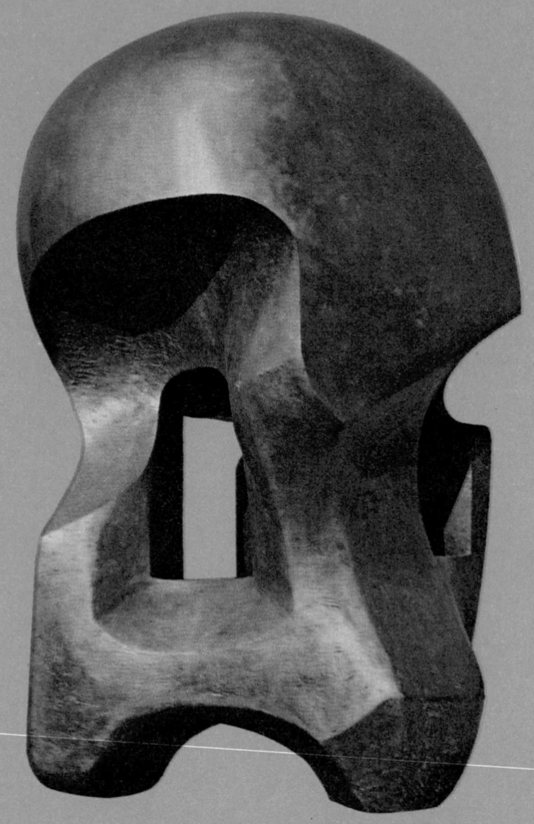

As in earlier centuries, artists of the 20th century made monuments to commemorate great events. On December 2, 1967, exactly twenty-five years after the first self-sustaining nuclear chain reaction, Henry Moore's bronze statue, "Nuclear Energy" was unveiled at the University of Chicago.

The news report of a terrifying event in October, 1962, reads like something from a science-fiction novel:

> Far down in the gray concrete vitals of the Pentagon, in the U.S. Air Force's "War Room," a handful of red-eyed, weary, uniformed men sat on a balcony, stared down into a plastic-trimmed nightmare of electronics, and pondered the fate of the world. Panoramic screens scanned U.S. outposts around the globe, bulb-clustered boxes showed troop movements, lighted maps flashed with blobs of color, each indicating a nuclear warplane or missile aimed

This news report is from "October, 1962—The Cuba Crisis: Nuclear War Was Hours Away," from *Newsweek*, 10/28/63.

and "cocked" at millions of human beings who lived on in ignorance of their peril.

The target: the Soviet Union. Detonation: hours away.

The report described an event in the Cuban missile crisis. It was because the Soviet Union put missiles in Cuba that the United States was ready for war. The crisis was settled peacefully, but it showed how the United States and the Soviet Union, who had been allies during World War II, had become fierce rivals afterwards. The crisis also showed how much nuclear weapons affected the postwar world. If the Cuban missile crisis had led to war—nuclear war—it could have meant the complete destruction of the human race. In such a war, there could have been no winners. That realization helped prevent a holocaust in October, 1962.

The threat of nuclear war and the strong rivalry between the Soviet Union and the United States were only two of many changes in international relations after World War II. These changes, which came very rapidly, made the world seem unstable and dangerous.

For more than twenty-five years after 1945, nations big and small, young and old, tried in various ways to find security for themselves. Slowly, a new pattern of international relationships came about that seemed to provide greater stability. This chapter describes the search for that stability as:

1. Nations went from World War II to the Cold War.

2. The Soviets dominated Eastern Europe.

3. Nations began a search for coexistence.

● Parents may be able to give personal recollections of this event.

■ Have students review the history of Russian-German conflicts in World War I and II.

1 Nations went from World War II to the Cold War

When the guns of World War II at last fell silent, large areas of Europe, Japan, and the Philippines and other islands in the Pacific lay in ruins. More than 30 million soldiers and civilians had lost their lives. Constant bombing had destroyed many cities and thousands of square miles of farmland. Millions of people had lost their homes. Rebuilding the world was a huge job, further complicated by international rivalries.

Wartime unity began to crack. Winston Churchill had called the alliance of the United States, Britain, and the Soviet Union a "Grand Alliance." True, these three countries cooperated reasonably well as long as their chief concern was to crush the Axis. But when it became clear that the war was nearing an end, each began to worry about its own national interests.

Serious differences among the Allies first became clear at the most important wartime conference—the meeting of Roosevelt, Churchill, and Stalin at Yalta in the U.S.S.R. in February, 1945. The three Allies signed the Declaration on Liberated Europe. In it, they agreed that the countries of Eastern Europe should solve their problems through freely elected democratic governments. After Yalta, however, Stalin made ans. 1
it clear that he would allow only communist governments in those areas occupied by the Soviet army. From the Russian point of view, the Soviet Union could be secure only by having friendly, communist countries on its western border.

The Allies' differences concerning Germany were even greater. Stalin was anxious that Germany should never again be strong enough to threaten the Soviet Union. Therefore, he wanted to make a harsh peace treaty with Ger-

many. Because Roosevelt and Churchill needed Stalin's help in the war with Japan, they agreed to a temporary plan. Germany was divided into four zones. Britain, the United States, the Soviet Union, and France each occupied and governed a zone. The capital city of Berlin was located within the Soviet zone, but it was occupied and administered jointly by the four powers. This "temporary" measure became, after the war, the basis of the "German problem."

Nearly six months after the meeting at Yalta, representatives of Britain, the United States, and the Soviet Union met again. The meeting was at Potsdam, a suburb of Berlin. The war in Europe was over. By this time, disagreements among the Allies had become much deeper. Many questions, such as the government and boundaries of Poland and the governments in Eastern Europe could not be resolved. Again only temporary measures could be agreed upon. All final peace treaties were postponed. In the meantime, Germany was being disarmed, demilitarized, and "denazified," that is, rid of Nazi influence and ideas.

The discussion concerning peace treaties with the defeated Axis powers dragged on and on. In February, 1947, treaties were finally signed with Bulgaria, Hungary, Italy, and Romania. All were required to make reparations to the Allies for damage caused by the war. They also had to agree to limit their armed forces. Some border changes were also made.

The negotiations over these treaties showed how much the former Allies had come to distrust each other. The Soviets tried to get the most favorable terms possible for Bulgaria, Hungary, and Romania. The U.S.S.R. was preparing those countries to become Soviet satellites. (*Satellite* is a word used to describe the technically independent nations that came under So-

● Locate these areas on the map of Europe on this page.

viet control in the years after World War II.) The Western powers worked equally as hard on Italy's behalf.

The distrust between the two sides grew deeper as they tried to solve the "German problem." The U.S.S.R. wanted heavy reparations from Germany in order to rebuild its own country. It wanted to change its occupation zone in Germany into another satellite. Britain and the United States, on the other hand, felt that Germany, with its rich industrial resources, should be allowed to grow strong again. Europe's economy depended on Germany's economy, they believed. But the Soviets felt they had suffered enough from their German neighbor. They were afraid to see Germany again grow strong. By early 1947, the "temporary" division of Germany took on a more permanent character. The possibility of a German peace treaty faded away.

The United Nations was established. In October, 1944, delegates from the United States, Britain, and the Soviet Union had met at Dumbarton Oaks, an estate in Washington, D.C. The delegates drafted a charter for a United Nations organization which was then approved in principle at Yalta in February, 1945. In June, 1945, representatives of fifty countries signed the charter at San Francisco. By October of that year, twenty-nine of these countries had ratified it, thus establishing the United Nations (UN) as a formal organization.

Two major UN bodies were created, the General Assembly and the Security Council. Every member country had a representative in the General Assembly. The Security Council had only eleven members. Five were permanent members and the other six were elected for two-year terms by the General Assembly.

The United States, the Soviet Union, Nationalist China, France, and Britain (then the great powers of the world) were the permanent members of the Security Council. The chief re- ans. 2
sponsibility of the Council was to keep peace in the world. Each of the five permanent members

At UN headquarters in New York City, diplomats meet to seek peaceful solutions to international problems.

could veto any decision. Thus, if the great powers disagreed, the Security Council could not work effectively as a peace-keeping agency.

ans. 2 At first, the General Assembly was less important than the Security Council. The Assembly had no power of enforcement. However, the Soviet Union used the veto so much that by 1950 it had paralyzed the Security Council. Then the General Assembly was given more power. It could authorize emergency action on its own if the Security Council was blocked by a veto.

Growth in UN membership also changed the General Assembly. In 1945, the UN had 50 members. By September, 1976, it had 143. Most of the new members were countries in Asia and Africa that had become independent after 1945. This meant that Asian and African nations had a majority of votes in the Assembly and a great deal more influence in UN affairs by the 1960s and 1970s.

The era of the Cold War began. The term *Cold War* was first used by American journalists in 1948 to describe the increasingly hostile relations between the Soviet Union and the United States. Between 1947 and 1953, the Cold War went through its first very tense phase.

The beginning came in March, 1947, when Britain decided that it would not be able to continue supplying aid to Greece and Turkey. At that time, Greece was going through a civil war in which the Greek communists, who had fought against the Nazis, appeared to be winning. Turkey was under very strong Soviet pressure to share control of two important straits, the Bosporus and the Dardanelles.

In the face of Britain's withdrawn support,
ans. 3 the United States government responded with the Truman Doctrine, a policy of supplying

military aid to Greece and Turkey. The Truman Doctrine became the basis of a new American policy to "contain" communism, that is, to prevent it from spreading beyond its already established borders.

However, more than guns were needed to contain communism. Europe needed political stability and economic health. In June, 1947, United States Secretary of State George Marshall announced a broad program of economic aid to all European nations, including communist countries. Stalin saw this program as an anticommunist move and refused to let the satellite countries participate. Therefore, only Western European countries received Marshall Plan aid.

When the aid program ended in December, 1951, the total cost had run to 13 billion dollars. Because of this extraordinary investment by the United States and the efforts of the European people, Western Europe made an astounding

Europe, 1948
Hunger was a major problem in the post-war world. The UN estimated that 60,000,000 people in Europe alone were in urgent need of help. Through photographs like the one at *left,* the UN asked everyone in the world to give a day's pay. In West Berlin, the problem became acute during the blockade. Ambulances *(right),* medical supplies, and food were flown into the city.

economic recovery and preserved its democratic institutions.

The Cominform and NATO were organized. After Stalin rejected the Marshall Plan in the summer of 1947, the Cold War became more intense. The communist parties of France, Italy, the Soviet Union, and the Soviet satellites organized the Cominform (Communist Information Bureau). The Cominform coordinated activities of various communist parties. In November, 1947, it supported a general strike by the communist-dominated trade unions in France. For a month, France seemed to be falling under the control of the French communists. Then the French government took strong measures and swung the country away from communism.

No sooner was the crisis in France over than the Western world was shocked by the news in February, 1948, that Czech communists had forcibly seized control in Czechoslovakia.

Meanwhile, the British and Americans, unable to get Soviet cooperation in reviving Germany, began setting up a separate West German government despite Soviet objections. In June, 1948, the Soviets tried to force the Western powers out of Berlin by placing a land blockade on the city. The West responded with a huge airlift. Airplanes flew food and fuel to the stricken city until May, 1949, when the Soviets lifted the blockade.

In September, 1949, West Germany became, officially, the Federal Republic of Germany. In October, East Germany became the German Democratic Republic.

These four events—the Greek civil war, the general strikes in France, the communist takeover in Czechoslovakia, and the Berlin blockade—convinced Western leaders that Stalin's aim

● Point out that communist parties exist in many noncommunist countries, including the U.S.

■ Explain that Soviets cut off supplies to the city, refer to the map on p. 614.

The Berlin Wall *(left)*, built by the East Germans, kept families and friends apart. Many, like 18-year-old Peter Fech, tried to escape across the wall. East Berlin soldiers shot him and brought him back *(above)*. He died later.

was to upset and conquer Western Europe. To guard against this danger, twelve Western countries signed the North Atlantic Treaty in 1949. The twelve countries were Belgium, Britain, Canada, Denmark, France, Iceland, Italy, Luxembourg, the Netherlands, Norway, Portugal, and the United States. In this treaty, they agreed to defend each other if attacked. They set up the North Atlantic Treaty Organization (NATO) with its own military force made up of units from each of the countries involved. Greece and Turkey joined NATO in 1952, and West Germany joined in 1955.

The Korean conflict broke out. In June, 1950, the Cold War suddenly expanded beyond Europe into Asia. Korea, like Germany, had been "temporarily" divided at the end of World War II. The Soviet Union controlled the northern part of the country. The United States controlled the southern part. The Soviets had set up a communist government in the north. They refused a United States proposal to hold elections in all of Korea under UN supervision. As a result, elections were held only in the southern part of the country, the new Republic of Korea.

ans. 4 In June, 1950, North Korea invaded South Korea. The United Nations called the invasion an "act of aggression." United States President Truman, taking advantage of a temporary Soviet boycott of the UN Security Council, persuaded that body to take quick military action. Altogether, sixteen UN members, including the United States, sent troops to Korea. Fighting was fierce. It increased in intensity when Communist China sent troops in November, 1950. The conflict continued until July, 1953. At that time, an armistice (temporary peace agreement) was signed. The armistice divided Korea much as it had been before the conflict began.

SECTION REVIEW 1

p. 613 **1.** Name two major issues on which the members of the Grand Alliance disagreed.

p. 615
616 **2.** What were the powers of the Security Council and General Assembly of the UN when it was first established? What changes were made and why?

p. 616
617 **3.** What were the purposes of the Truman Doctrine, Marshall Plan, Cominform, and NATO?

p. 619 **4.** Who fought on the two sides of the Korean War? What was the outcome of the war?

Soviet UN delegate Jacob Malik walked out of the Security Council because it would not seat the Communist Chinese delegation. He was still absent six months later, so he could not veto UN action in Korea.

2 The Soviets dominated Eastern Europe

The Soviet Union emerged from World War II having suffered enormous destruction. But it had the most powerful army in Europe, control over most of Eastern Europe, and growing influence as a superpower in world affairs.

The Soviet Union faced staggering problems in rebuilding itself. No country had
ans. 1 suffered more from World War II than had the Soviet Union. In addition to the millions of people who had lost their lives and the millions who were made homeless, one quarter of Soviet wealth in industry, schools, libraries, and other buildings had been wiped out.

The most important task facing the government was to rebuild the country and its economy. The Soviet government issued a new Five-Year Plan. Stalin wanted to rebuild all the wartime damage in only five years, from 1946 to 1950. In the next Five-Year Plan, from 1951 to 1955, he wanted to expand production beyond prewar levels.

These goals were only partly reached. By ans. 2
1953, the Soviet output of steel, coal, and electricity reached nearly double that of 1940. But consumer goods were scarcer than they had been in the 1920s.

Agriculture was in even worse shape. By 1953, production on the farms was only 10 percent higher than it had been in 1914 before the revolution. Meanwhile, the population had grown more than 20 percent larger.

The Soviets encouraged and supported communist revolutions in Eastern Europe. The Soviet government had political as well as economic goals. These included securing

M•A•S•H

In this movie scene, some doctors (Donald Sutherland, Elliott Gould, and Tom Skerritt) stage a zany party to forget their frustrations, fears, and boredom. First used in Korea, Mobile Army Surgical Hospitals were close to battle lines and thus saved many soldiers' lives. But the effect on the doctors was immense. Working in horrible conditions, they often healed soldiers only to have those same soldiers die in later battles.

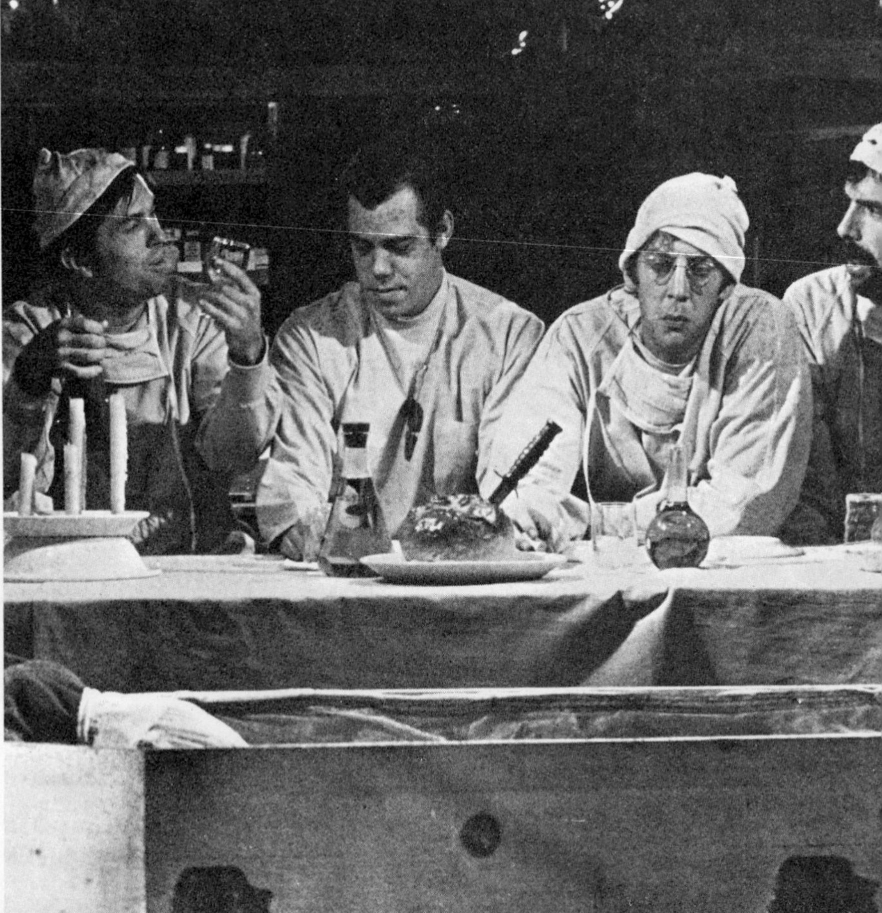

the country's western borders by strengthening the Soviet hold over Eastern Europe. In 1944 and 1945, Bulgaria, Czechoslovakia, Hungary, Poland, Romania, and Yugoslavia were brought under the control of the Soviet army. Peasants made up most of the populations of these countries, and their political parties were the only democratic ones there at the end of World War II. However, the major role in shaping the political life of postwar Eastern Europe was not these parties. It was the presence of the Soviet army of occupation. With it, the Soviets helped local communist parties in these countries bring about Soviet-style revolutions. By 1950, communist takeovers had occurred in Poland, Bulgaria, Romania, Hungary, and Czechoslovakia.

The one important exception was Yugoslavia. Led by a man called Tito [tē′tō], the Yugoslav Communist party set up a communist government without Soviet help. Tito had gained fame as a wartime leader against the Nazis. Yugoslavs united behind him in the cause of freedom.

Tito's independence angered Stalin. Determined to destroy Tito, Stalin expelled the Yugoslav Communist party from the Cominform in 1948. The Soviet Union also ended all economic aid. But Tito stayed in power. Since Yugoslavia was being shut off from the rest of the communist world, Tito slowly turned to Western countries for economic and military aid. Gradually, he relaxed some of the totalitarian government controls. He allowed private farming again. He also began workers' councils in industry and granted some civil rights to the people. Yugoslavia stayed a communist country, but it was independent of Soviet control.

Stalin's death led to important changes in the Soviet Union. Joseph Stalin died in March, 1953. His death touched off a struggle for power among the remaining leaders of the Soviet Communist party. In 1956, Nikita S. Khrushchev [krüsh chôf′] won the struggle.

In February, 1956, Khrushchev rocked the communist world with a speech that blamed Stalin for many crimes against the Soviet people. De-Stalinization became official govern- ans. 3
ment policy. This new policy changed several things. Most of the forced-labor camps were closed. The secret police became less violent. Writers got a bit more freedom in what they could write about. Cultural exchanges were begun with the West, and tourism was encouraged.

Khrushchev's policies showed important changes in Soviet society. The Five-Year Plans from 1945 through 1955 had built up heavy industry to make farm and factory equipment. But very few consumer goods—cars, TV sets, refrigerators, clothes—were produced. Shortages of such goods became critical as thousands of people moved from rural areas to the cities. By 1962, some 51 percent of the people lived in cities; in 1926, only 18 percent had lived there. The rapid growth of Soviet cities demanded greater productivity from individual workers. To achieve this great productivity, Soviet workers needed the incentive of being able to buy the things they wanted. Also, a new middle class of managers and professional people had arisen. They wanted a more comfortable life, as well as security and an end to the fear of war.

In the late 1950s and early 1960s, clothing and television sets became more available. A building program increased housing. Khrushchev also tried to raise farm production. But it barely kept up with population growth.

In spite of this lag, Khrushchev and other Soviet leaders continued to place emphasis on heavy industry, weapons, and space technology. The Soviets had already achieved big re-

sults in these fields. They had developed an atom bomb as early as 1949 and a hydrogen
ans. 4 bomb by 1953. They had launched the first satellite in orbit around the earth in 1957. In 1961, they put the first human being into outer space. In 1966, they made the first soft landing of instruments on the moon.

Relations with countries of Eastern Europe became less rigid. In May, 1955, the U.S.S.R. and the Eastern European satellite countries formed a military alliance called the Warsaw Pact. This pact was aimed at stopping NATO and Western plans to rearm West Germany. That summer, Khrushchev visited Yugoslavia in an attempt to heal the split with Tito. In February, 1956, Khrushchev said that communism could be achieved through ways other than those followed by the Soviet Union. These three events had a big effect on the satellite countries. Most of them were very nationalistic. They deeply resented Soviet control over their affairs. The satellites saw these events as a chance to end Soviet domination.

On October 23, 1956, an armed rebellion began in Hungary against the ruling Communist government. Savage fighting swept the Hungarian capital and broke the power of the Communist party. When a new regime took over and renounced its ties with the Soviet bloc, the U.S.S.R. acted. They were not willing to give up as much power as the satellites had
thought. Soviet troops poured into Hungary, ans. 5
crushed the rebellion, and restored Communist power. Thousands of people died in the fighting, and 200 thousand escaped to the West.

The Hungarian uprising made the Soviets again put political pressure on the satellite countries. Economically, however, Soviet policy eased. The Soviets stopped treating the satellites as colonies to be exploited. The satellites got more freedom to develop their economies to their own advantage rather than to that of the Soviet Union.

SECTION REVIEW **2**

1. How did World War II affect the Soviet Union? p. 620

2. In what ways did the new Five-Year Plans succeed? In what way did they fail? p. 620

3. What changes took place in the Soviet Union after Nikita Khrushchev became leader? p. 621

4. What were the Soviet Union's achievements in space technology? What shortages still existed in the Soviet Union in the 1950s and 1960s? p. 622

5. How did the Soviets react to the uprising in Hungary? How did relations between the Soviet Union and its satellites change after the uprising? p. 622

A truckload of Hungarian "Freedom Fighters" heads toward Budapest to face Soviet tanks. The Communist controlled radio announced that railroad workers had seen trainloads of Freedom Fighters taken as prisoners and shipped to Russia.

3 Nations began a search for coexistence

In the 1950s and 1960s, the United States and the Soviet Union built up their supplies of nuclear weapons. Their fear of each other turned into fear of both being destroyed. They found they had to accept each other's existence. It was this ● idea that led to competitive coexistence.

The Cold War began to thaw. The search for a basis of possible coexistence was a slow process. There were several trouble spots in the world. The Korean conflict had left a divided Korea. In Indochina, France had been fighting to keep its former colonial control ever since the end of World War II. In 1954, nineteen countries, including Communist China, met at Geneva, Switzerland, in an effort to reunite Korea and end the fighting in Indochina. However, the conference only created a short-lived peace in Indochina by dividing it into Laos, Cambodia, and North and South Vietnam.

In 1955, the United States, the Soviet Union, Britain, and France held a conference in Geneva that was hailed as a "meeting at the summit." No solutions were found to the major problems, but a spirit of friendliness improved the international climate briefly.

The "spirit of Geneva" was shattered by the Hungarian uprising of 1956 and its suppression by the U.S.S.R. The United Nations General Assembly condemned the Soviet Union for depriving the Hungarians of their freedom. The United States, however, refused to risk nuclear
ans. 1 war by sending troops to Hungary to help the anti-Soviet Hungarian "Freedom Fighters." This attitude showed Soviet leaders that the United States would not challenge their domination of Eastern Europe. Later in 1956, the Soviet Union joined the United States in the UN effort to end the Suez Canal crisis. Both superpowers realized that neither one wanted to start a larger war. Thus, 1956 became a turning point in the Cold War.

Relations between the Soviet Union and the United States improved. By 1959, Khrushchev had proved that he wanted better relations with the United States. Three summit meetings followed in the next three years. None of the important Cold War issues were worked out at any of them. But further efforts were made at direct contact. In 1961, Khrushchev started a private correspondence with ans. 1
President John F. Kennedy.

A setback in relations occurred in 1962, when ■ the Soviet Union gave Cuba nuclear missiles. In a tense showdown, President Kennedy made it clear that the United States would not let the missiles remain. Khrushchev finally withdrew the missiles in exchange for a pledge that the United States would not invade Cuba. Eventually, the Cuban missile crisis actually helped ease tensions. The possibility of a nuclear clash was a frightening and sobering experience to both superpowers.

To avoid accidental war, both countries in June, 1963, set up an emergency "hot line" of direct communication between Washington and Moscow. When war began between Israel and some Arab nations in 1967, the "hot line" was used to prevent any widening of the crisis.

Also important was the signing of a nuclear test-ban treaty by Britain, the Soviet Union, and the United States in July, 1963. It forbade nuclear tests in the atmosphere, outer space, and under water. Eventually, most of the other countries of the world signed. France and Communist China refused.

● Explain that this means two nations whose governments are enemies must learn to avoid armed conflict. Allow discussion.

■ This event is described more fully in the chapter introduction p. 612–613.

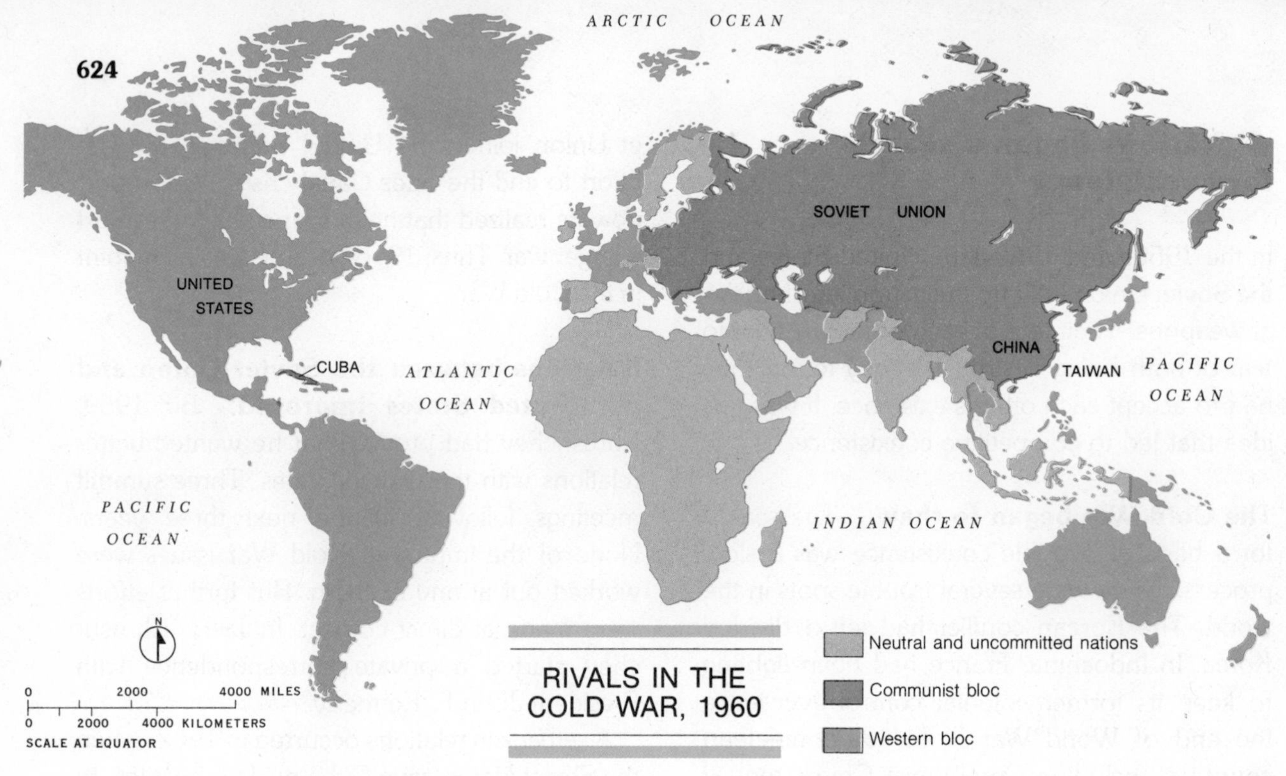

RIVALS IN THE COLD WAR, 1960

The test-ban treaty and the refusal of France and Communist China to sign it symbolized the three chief factors that relaxed Cold War tensions between the United States and the Soviet Union in the 1960s. One factor was the huge stockpile of nuclear weapons that each superpower had and the realization that the use of these weapons would mean the destruction of both nations. The second was the loosening of the alliance systems in Eastern and Western Europe. The third was a break in friendly relations between the Soviet Union and Communist China.

The communist world fragmented. A new drive for independence among the Eastern European countries began in the early 1960s. In ans. 2 dramatic defiance of the U.S.S.R., Romania announced that it would follow its own program of industrialization. The Romanians also gave diplomatic recognition to West Germany. The U.S.S.R. could do little about this situation since a great new problem was dividing the communist world.

In 1960, the Communist Chinese leaders began saying that Khrushchev's policy of coexistence with the West was ideological treason, that is, it went against basic communist beliefs. ● The Chinese were angry because the Soviets had refused to help China build an atomic bomb and had withdrawn almost all their industrial aid from China. Very quickly, the two countries became rivals in a struggle for leadership in the communist world.

Almost all the leaders of the Eastern European countries (except Albania) sided with the U.S.S.R. But they were dissatisfied with Khrushchev's handling of the Chinese.

The Soviet Union's retreat from Cuba in 1962 was another serious blow to Khrushchev's prestige. His policies at home, particularly those to increase food production, were not very suc-

● Ask students to name Soviet actions that are contrary to Marxist beliefs. (See Ch. 27) cessful either. Communist party opposition to him increased. Finally in October, 1964, he was removed from power.

New leadership took over in the Soviet Union. Aleksei N. Kosygin [kə sē′gin] succeeded Khrushchev as premier. Leonid I. Brezhnev [brezh′nef] became Communist party secretary. The Kosygin-Brezhnev leadership continued to push for coexistence. They claimed to speak for world communism. But by that time, the communist world was so fragmented that it was no longer clear what country spoke for world communism, or if it even existed.

In 1967, the Soviets celebrated the 50th anniversary of the Bolshevik Revolution. After a half century of Communist party rule, most Soviet citizens had come to accept the communist system as a fact of life. They were very proud of the industrial, scientific, and military achievements of their country.

However, a new generation of young intellectuals began to express open dissatisfaction with some parts of the Soviet system. Although strongly patriotic, they insisted on greater freedom of expression in literature and other arts. Because of their worldwide reputations, poets ● such as Yevgeny Yevtushenko [yef gyā′nyi yef′tü shen′kō] and Andrei Voznesensky [än drā′ē voz′nə sens′kē] were not punished for their critical outbursts. Writers who were not as well known, however, were put on trial, convicted, and sent to prison. The Communist party let it be known that freedom of expression was still severely limited. The Soviet government also tried to silence Alexander Solzhenitsyn [sōl′zhə nē′tsən]. He had become one of his country's most important writers in the 1960s. Scientist Andrei Sakharov [sä′kä rof], inventor of the Soviet H-bomb, spoke up for Soviet civil rights. Both stood their ground as critics of Soviet society. In 1974, however, Solzhenitsyn was expelled from the Soviet Union.

● Translations of the writings of a few of the more famous modern Russian poets and writers are available and could be used to aid in understanding Russian society.

Within Soviet-dominated Eastern Europe there were also limits to dissent. When Czechoslovakia tried to make its communist system more democratic in 1968, the Soviets led an armed invasion and put an end to the process.

Meanwhile, the problem of inefficient Soviet labor continued. In the 1970s, the Soviet economy needed to produce more food and greater quantities of better goods more cheaply. Neither of these aims was reached. In 1972 and again in 1975, the Soviets had to buy wheat from the United States to meet their food needs.

Western Europe reasserted its independence. Despite a decline in political influence after World War II, Western Europe was still an important economic region. It had a wealth of raw materials and one of the best-developed industrial systems in the world. With help from the Marshall Plan, Western Europe recovered economically from the war in about ten years. With prosperity, it once again took an active role in world affairs.

Britain, France, Germany, and Italy were the major West European countries. Less important were Belgium, Luxembourg, the Netherlands, and the Scandinavian countries. Following World War II, the traditions and institutions of democracy were either continued or reestablished. Particular problems varied from one country to another, as did the solutions.

Britain and France slowly achieved economic recovery. Throughout the postwar period, Britain's economic recovery was slow. British citizens enjoyed the highest standard of

living in their history in the 1960s; but the problems of low productivity, high imports, and in-
ans. 3 flation continued. In 1973, Britain became a member of the European Economic Community (Common Market), in hopes of stimulating the British economy.

Economic recovery in France was held back in the early postwar years by political instability. The large number of political parties prevented a lasting coalition government. In ten years, there were more than twenty cabinets. The French economy began to improve in the mid-1950s. But the French became bitterly divided over their government's continued involvement in Algeria, where a civil war began in 1958.

The return to power of General Charles de Gaulle in May, 1958, headed off civil war in France. He ended the Algerian war and gave that country independence. French prestige and influence were restored.

De Gaulle paid little attention to social reform at home. In 1968, workers and students paralyzed France for weeks with strikes. They demanded a change in government and widespread reforms. For a short time, France was close to revolution. The strikes ended when the workers got large wage increases and promises of reform. De Gaulle left office in 1969 and died a year later. His successor, Georges Pompidou, continued his policies.

By the mid-1970s, most French people wanted a more liberal policy at home and a more cooperative attitude toward France's European neighbors. They elected Valéry Giscard d'Estaing [vä lā′rē zhē skär′ des tan′] president in 1974. He began a far-reaching program of social and economic reform.

West Germany became Europe's most prosperous country. West Germany had the most spectacular economic recovery. German efficiency and hard work, combined with American foreign aid under the Marshall Plan, helped bring about the "economic miracle." From a beaten, devastated nation in 1945, West Germany emerged during the 1950s as the most prosperous country in Europe. A strong, stable, democratic government was begun by Konrad Adenauer [ad′n ou′ər]. In May, 1955, West Germany regained its full independence.

The "Adenauer era" ended in 1963 with his retirement. He had brought France and Ger-

Cultural exchanges helped relations in the 1970s. A U.S. table tennis team went to Communist China. Gymnast Olga Korbut, of the Russian Olympic team, performed for American audiences.

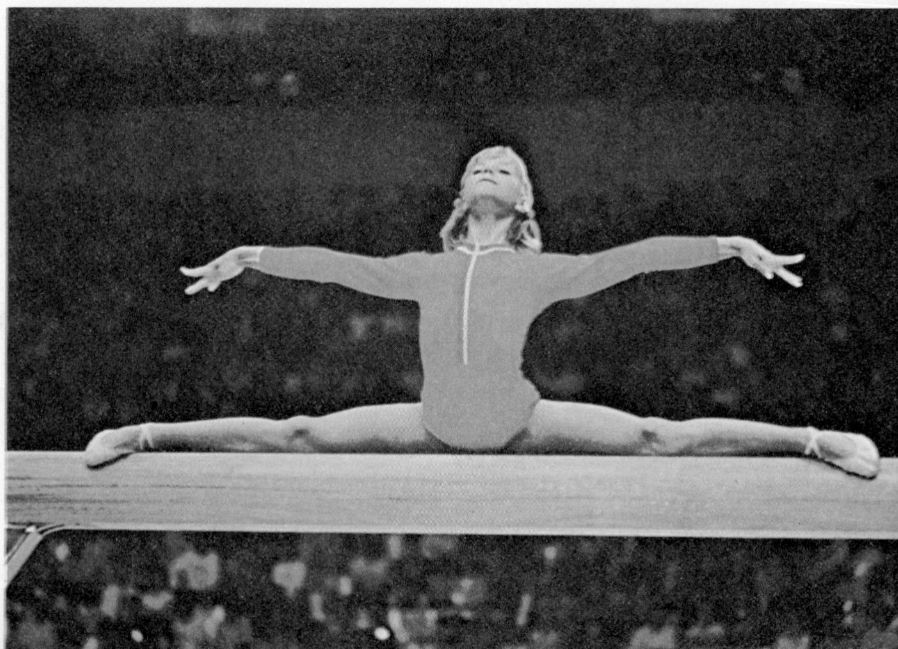

many together in a treaty of friendship. However, the most serious issue for Germans was the reunification of East and West Germany. After Adenauer's retirement, his party stayed in power for six more years. They followed a policy of strong resistance to East Germany and the Soviet Union.

In October, 1969, Willy Brandt [vil′ē bränt] became chancellor. He quickly moved to improve relations with Eastern Europe and the Soviet Union. In 1970, West Germany signed a treaty with the U.S.S.R. in which both sides renounced the use of force. Brandt also signed a treaty with Poland in which both countries accepted the postwar German-Polish border. These treaties laid the groundwork for a four-power agreement in September, 1971, between the United States, the Soviet Union, Britain, and France. The agreement made the status of West Berlin permanent and recognized its ties with West Germany. The East German regime was recognized as legitimate. The division of Germany, which had been a reality since the end of World War II, was now made legal. Brandt accepted this as the price for better relations with the Soviet Union and the countries of Eastern Europe.

The European Common Market was formed. The most dramatic development in Western Europe was the movement toward unity. In 1958, the European Economic Community (Common Market) was formed with six countries as members: Belgium, France, Italy, Luxembourg, the Netherlands, and West Germany. The goal of this organization was to create a common market in which goods would flow tariff-free across the borders of these coun-
ans. 4 tries. Such remarkable economic gains were made that by 1962, the European Common Market had become the largest single trading bloc in the world. It produced almost as much coal and steel as the United States and outproduced the Soviet Union.

● Students may need an explanation of this statement.

Throughout the 1960s, Britain made several efforts to join the Common Market. Each time, its application was blocked by President de Gaulle, who feared that Britain's entry would lessen France's influence in Europe. Only after de Gaulle's death in 1970 did French policy change. After long negotiations, Britain entered the Common Market in January, 1973. Ireland and Denmark joined in the same year, increasing the membership to nine countries.

With the revival of power and prosperity, Western Europe showed a new mood. It no longer was content to follow the lead of the United States as it had in the early years after World War II. Europe wanted to be its own master. In the late 1960s and 1970s, the United States found that its very success in helping bring about the recovery of Europe had created a new situation that required a careful readjustment of its foreign policy. ●

SECTION REVIEW 3

1. Describe three ways in which the Soviet Union and the United States have tried to ease tensions between the two countries. Why is it so important that war be avoided today? p. 623

2. Name five problems that led to Khrushchev's removal from power. What caused the split between Communist China and the Soviet Union? p. 624

3. How did Britain, France, and Germany deal with the need to improve economic conditions in the 1960s and 1970s? p. 626

4. How important was the Common Market for Europe? How did Europe's new prosperity change its relations with the United States? p. 627

CHAPTER REVIEW 33

SECTION SUMMARIES

1. Nations went from World War II to the Cold War. World War II ended in 1945. In that same year, the United Nations was founded to help keep peace in the world. Nevertheless, a Cold War developed that split the wartime Allies into communist and anticommunist camps. For twenty-five years, relations between countries in the two blocs were strained. At times, the world seemed on the edge of a third global war, as in the Cuban missile crisis of 1962.

2. The Soviets dominated Eastern Europe. Economically, the Soviet Union suffered greatly from World War II and recovered very slowly. But politically, the U.S.S.R. was one of the two strongest nations of the world in 1945. To secure its western borders and to spread communism, it encouraged and supported Soviet-style revolutions in Eastern Europe. For twenty-five years after 1945, the Soviet Union dictated the policies of Eastern European countries. Only Yugoslavia at first managed some degree of independence. When Hungary tried to shake Soviet control, the revolt was immediately crushed. But in the early 1970s, there were signs that Eastern European countries were gaining a little more freedom of action.

3. Nations began a search for coexistence. The first signs that the Cold War was beginning to thaw were seen at Geneva in 1954. The growing threat of nuclear destruction made coexistence necessary. To protect their countries from war, the Soviet Union and the United States set up an emergency "hot line" between their leaders. The Soviet Union lost some of its political leadership to Communist China, and a great rivalry grew up between the two. Many Western European countries joined the Common Market, which eventually became the world's largest single trading bloc. East and West Germany became legally separate countries.

● 3. The Truman Doctrine supplied military aid to Greece and Turkey. The NATO agreement was between Western nations for protection from Communist attacks.
The Cominform coordinated the activities of Communist parties. The Warsaw Pact was an alliance of Communist countries against NATO.

WHO? WHAT? WHEN? WHERE?

1. During which of the following time spans did each of these events occur:

a. 1945–1950	d. 1961–1965
b. 1951–1955	e. 1966–1970
c. 1956–1960	f. 1971–

The first human went into outer space. d.
The United Nations Charter was ratified. a.
Willy Brandt became chancellor. e.
The Common Market began. c.
Britain joined the Common Market. f.
Soviet soldiers crushed the Hungarian uprising. c.
The NATO pact was signed. a.
Algeria became independent. c.
Kosygin and Brezhnev replaced Khrushchev. d.
Russian missiles were installed in Cuba. d.
North Korea invaded South Korea. a.
The Truman Doctrine was formulated. a.
The term "Cold War" was first used. a.
Valéry Giscard d'Estaing became France's president. f.
United Nations membership reached 143. a.
Marshall Plan began. b.
An armistice was signed in Korea. f.

2. Explain the meanings of these terms in sentences written in your own words:

Cold War p. 616	Soviet satellite p. 614
hot line p. 623	Five-Year Plans p. 620

3. What were the purposes of the Truman Doctrine and NATO? Cominform and the Warsaw Pact? ●

4. How did the Marshall Plan and the Common Market help Western Europe recover economically?

4. The Marshall Plan (1947) gave economic aid to Western Europe. The Common Market allowed tariff-free trade among member nations.

CHAPTER TEST 33

QUESTIONS FOR CRITICAL THINKING

1. What hope is there that the UN might succeed in avoiding wide-scale war where the League of Nations failed?

2. Why did the Soviet Union under Khrushchev change its policy about the necessity for all communist countries to follow Moscow's rule?

3. Why did journalists label the era of conflicts between the U.S. and the U.S.S.R. a *cold* war?

4. Why did the United States formulate the Truman Doctrine and Marshall Plan to help Europe recover from the war?

5. How best can the United States "contain" communism today? Should it continue to try to do so? Why?

ACTIVITIES

1. Role-play committees from the United States and the Soviet Union attempting to convince a farmer in a poor country in Africa, Latin America, or Asia that either the United States or the Soviet Union has the best way of life.

2. Make a chart showing the accomplishments of the United States and the Soviet Union in the field of space exploration. (Ask your librarian for help in finding the latest information.)

3. Write a report on the UN, assessing its accomplishments and failures.

4. Find information in newspapers and magazines about the Strategic Arms Limitation Talks. Give an oral report to the class.

5. Go to the library and find information about the Marshall Plan. Find how much money some of the different European countries received and some of the specific things the money was used for. Report to the class on your findings.

SECTION 1

1. All the members of the United Nations are represented in the: a. General Assembly, b. Security Council, c. General Council

2. Which of these countries received aid from the United States under the Marshall Plan? a. all European nations, b. Greece and Turkey, c. only Western Europe

3. True or false: The West German government was set up by Britain and the U.S. despite Soviet objections.

SECTION 2

4. The Soviet army did not set up a communist government in: a. Poland, b. Hungary, c. Yugoslavia

5. True or false: In the 1950s and 1960s, a growing middle class demanded more consumer goods, thus weakening the Soviet military lead.

6. Open rebellion against domination by the Soviet Union broke out in: a. Cuba, b. East Germany, c. Hungary

SECTION 3

7. The United States and the Soviet Union came closest to the brink of war over: a. Vietnam, b. Korea, c. Cuba

8. True or false: A split appeared in the Communist world in the 1960s between Soviet communism and Cuban communism.

9. President de Gaulle blocked ___b.___ entry into the Common Market. a. West Germany's, b. Britain's, c. Italy's

10. In July, 1963, a nuclear test-ban treaty was signed by: a. France and the United States, b. the Soviet Union and France, c. the Soviet Union, the United States, and Britain

● QUESTIONS FOR CRITICAL THINKING

1. Larger membership and greater power of enforcement should be factors in most answers.
2. The satellites resented Soviet control.
3. Relations between the two countries were hostile without actual fighting.
4. To prevent war-damaged Europe from becoming Communist states.
5. Answers will vary. One way is to show the world a way of life that is better.

CHAPTER 34 1945–

The Coming of Asian Independence

After World War II, a communist revolution was successful in China. Many aspects of Chinese life changed. Here the Chinese people celebrate their new way of life in the square in front of the Gate of Heavenly Peace, an entrance to the Forbidden City.

One of the results of World War II in Asia was an almost complete collapse of Western colonialism. Within ten years, most of the Asian colonies were free.

The demand for independence in Asia had been building up for a long time. At the very beginning of the 20th century, an Asian nationalist told the people of his country:

> The point is to have the entire control in our hands. I want to have the key of my house, and not merely be a stranger turned out of it. Self-government is our goal. . . .

> What the New Party wants you to do is to realize . . . that your future rests entirely in your own hands. If you mean to be free, you can be free. . . .

Those words were spoken in 1907 by one of the leaders of the Indian nationalist movement. ● They could just as easily have been spoken by a nationalist leader in any Asian country under colonial control. In the fifty years that followed, the movement for independence transformed Asia. This chapter tells how:

1. India and China were leaders for independence.

2. India divided into three countries.

3. Countries of Southeast Asia became independent.

4. War and revolution transformed East Asia.

1 India and China were leaders for independence

The two oldest and largest civilizations in Asia, India and China, became the strongest leaders in the movement for independence. However, the situation in each country was quite different from that in the other.

ans. 1 **India demanded freedom.** During World War I, India loyally supported Britain. Almost a million Indian soldiers fought on the side of the British. Wealthy Indian princes made large financial contributions to the war effort. Indians hoped their loyalty and support would be rewarded by self-government. In 1917, Britain had promised to give self-rule to India in several stages. At the end of the war, the Government of India Act of 1919 gave certain powers to provincial legislatures but reserved other, more important ones for Britain. The Act disappointed most Indians.

The widespread dissatisfaction found a spokesman in Mohandas K. Gandhi [gän′dē]. This remarkable nationalist leader had been educated in Britain as a lawyer. He then set up a successful practice in South Africa, helping the Indians who lived there. Gandhi returned to India during World War I. He became the champion of the oppressed and lowly. ans. 2 He led a very simple and self-sacrificing life, following the strict ways of the Hindu faith. Millions of Indians began to look up to him as a holy man, or *mahatma* [mə hät′mə].

Gandhi strongly opposed the Government of India Act. Because he did not believe in violence, Gandhi led the people in a campaign of "nonviolent disobedience" to force the British ■ to give self-rule to India. Strikes and fasts and protest marches were the "weapons" of Gandhi's campaign.

Not all Indian nationalists believed in nonviolent resistance, however. In 1919, there was a wave of murder, looting, and arson. This violence reached its climax at the city of Amritsar. British soldiers fired at demonstrators. Many innocent people, including women and children, were killed or wounded. Gandhi and his followers in the Indian National Congress were shocked. They became determined to win complete freedom.

During the 1920s and 1930s, Gandhi launched several campaigns of nonviolent resistance against British authority. One of his methods was a boycott of British-made goods.

● Key concept: Asian nationalism. Return to this idea when discussing different independence movements in this chapter.

■ Explain and discuss *non-violent disobedience.*

Mohandas K. Gandhi, leader of the Indian independence movement

The British arrested him several times and put him in jail. While working for the independence of India, Gandhi tried to improve the life of the "untouchables," those Indians who belonged to the lowest caste of Indian society. He also tried to bring about cooperation between Hindus and Muslims. Gandhi believed that injustice could be wiped out through love and patience.

In the 1930s, the British met with Indian leaders to gradually prepare India for self-government. In 1935, the British Parliament passed a law that gave the Indian provinces self-government. From New Delhi, the capital, Indian members of the legislature then controlled all matters except those relating to defense and foreign affairs.

A revolution took place in China. During the late 19th century, China had been forced to give up some territory to Japan. At the same time, European powers were establishing spheres of influence in China and obtaining special economic privileges there. Young Chinese who resented this foreign influence organized secret societies to fight against it. Among these nationalists was Sun Yat-sen [su̇n′ yät′sen′].

● Ask students to give their opinions about the value of these principles in today's society—as well as in India during Gandhi's life.

Sun studied in Honolulu, Hawaii, for three years and later graduated from a medical college in the British colony of Hong Kong. For many years, he made plans to overthrow the tyrannical Manchu dynasty. His revolutionary activities forced him to flee China. For sixteen years, he worked among Chinese communities abroad to organize the Kuomintang [kwō′min tang′], or Nationalist Peoples Party. ans. 3

In 1911, Chinese revolutionaries overthrew the government. Sun then struggled against various warlords who wanted power for themselves. After a long conflict, Sun was elected president of China in 1921, and made plans to unify the country. He was not able to get aid from the Western powers, whom he had attacked for their imperialistic ambitions in China. Thus Sun turned to the Soviet Union for help. The Soviets sent him money, arms, and advisers.

Sun died in 1925. Although he had not unified the country, he was a source of inspiration to his followers. Sun's writings became guides for reform. One book, *Three Principles of the People,* became a guide for the Kuomintang. It called for nationalism and freedom from foreign control, government by the people and for the people, and economic security for all the Chinese.

Sun's place was taken by Chiang Kai-shek [chyang′ kī′shek′], a young military officer. In 1926, Chiang led his army northward. Two years later, he captured the government at Peking and united China. Shortly afterward, ans. 4 Chiang turned against the communist wing of the Kuomintang, which he was afraid was becoming too strong. He launched a surprise attack against the Chinese Communists and killed many of them. A small group of Chinese Communists led by Mao Tse-tung [mou′ tse′tung′] survived. From that time on, the Kuomintang and the Chinese Communists were bitter enemies.

Chiang's government was recognized by the Western powers as the official government of ● China. Chiang began removing the special privileges that foreign countries had forced China to give them.

SECTION REVIEW 1

p. 631 **1.** Why did Indians hope for independence after World War I? Why did the Government of India Act not satisfy their hopes?

p. 631 **2.** Describe the goals and work of Gandhi.

p. 632 **3.** What enemies did Sun Yat-sen fight in his struggles to unify China? What country sent him help?

p. 633 **4.** What group in the Kuomintang did Chiang try to eliminate? Who was its leader?

2 India divided into three countries

In 1945, Britain announced that India would be granted full independence not later than 1948. The delay of three years, the British hoped, would give Indians time to set up a workable government. But problems made the dream of one Indian government impossible.

India and Pakistan became free countries. Establishing a government for India was dif-

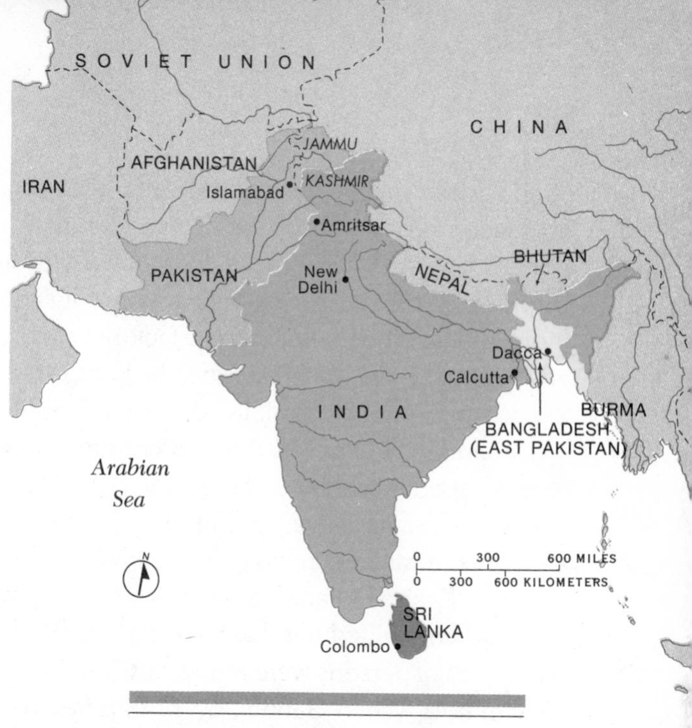

INDIAN SUBCONTINENT

ficult. India's population of about 400 million ■ people spoke more than fourteen different languages. They were also divided by wide extremes of wealth and poverty and deep religious differences. The Muslims made up 25 ans. 1 percent of the population. As a minority, they feared that the Hindus might follow a policy of persecution toward them. Therefore, they demanded an independent state of their own. In 1946, religious riots broke out. More than 12 thousand people were killed, mainly in the large city of Calcutta.

Because of these serious divisions, the British eventually accepted the idea of partition. In 1947, they established two countries. One country, India, was mostly Hindu, while the other, Pakistan, was mostly Muslim.

Geographically and economically, the division was an artificial arrangement. Pakistan was given two separate regions that were separated by 1,000 miles (1,600 kilometers). These two

● These special privileges were explained in Chapter 28.

■ You might discuss why these conditions made a stable democracy difficult.

regions were mainly agricultural. Jute, a strong fiber used to make rope, was a major cash export. Crops in Pakistan were so plentiful that a surplus of grain and other foods was produced. India, on the other hand, had the factories needed to process raw materials, such as jute. But it did not grow enough food. In addition, the political boundaries between the two countries cut across important canals and rivers.

Many Muslims moved to Pakistan, but some 40 million remained in India. Many Hindus also stayed in Pakistan. Fanatics on both sides began riots and committed horrible atrocities. In 1947, thousands of persons were massacred in Hindu-Muslim riots. When Gandhi, by 1948 a frail old man in his late seventies, tried to stop the terrible riots, he was killed by a religious fanatic.

Kashmir, a state along the extreme northern boundary of India, had been expected to join Pakistan, because most of its people were Muslim. But the Hindu ruler wanted to become part of India. As a result, fighting broke out between India and Pakistan. The United Nations intervened in 1949 and again in 1965, but the dispute continued.

India chose a democratic form of government. Of the two new states, India was the larger, with an area a third the size of the United States. The people of India were mostly poor, undernourished, and illiterate. Food shortages, even famine, were constant threats. And the population was growing at the rate of about 10 million per year.

The government introduced measures for family planning to slow down population growth. It also pushed a program of land reform to increase food production and industrialization

to diversify the economy and provide more jobs.

India originally chose to solve its problems under a democratic government. Through the leadership of the first prime minister, Jawaharlal Nehru [nā'rü], democratic institutions were modeled on those of England and America. The government practiced state planning through five-year plans such as the communist countries used. But it also allowed free enterprise and a multiparty system. The goal of the Indian government was a welfare state by means of gradual economic development.

Nehru died in 1964. During his term of office, important gains were made in food production and industrialization. But the living standard of most people remained practically unchanged because of the continuing increase in population.

In 1966, the ruling Congress party chose Indira Gandhi, Nehru's daughter, as prime minister. With the slogan of "Banish Poverty," she won the national election in 1967. Her government followed a policy of better distribution of wealth by moderate socialism. However, her programs were not very successful, and opposition to her government grew. Many of her political opponents were arrested. She began strict censorship, and allowed no criticism of her policies. Indira Gandhi became a strong authoritarian ruler. In 1977, she was voted out of office.

By the mid-1970s, some economic progress
had been made. But India was still largely a ans. 2
poor, rural country. In the countryside, most people lived in mud huts and made poor livings as tenant farmers. Large numbers of those who had no land and no skills moved to the cities. There they often found life to be much worse.

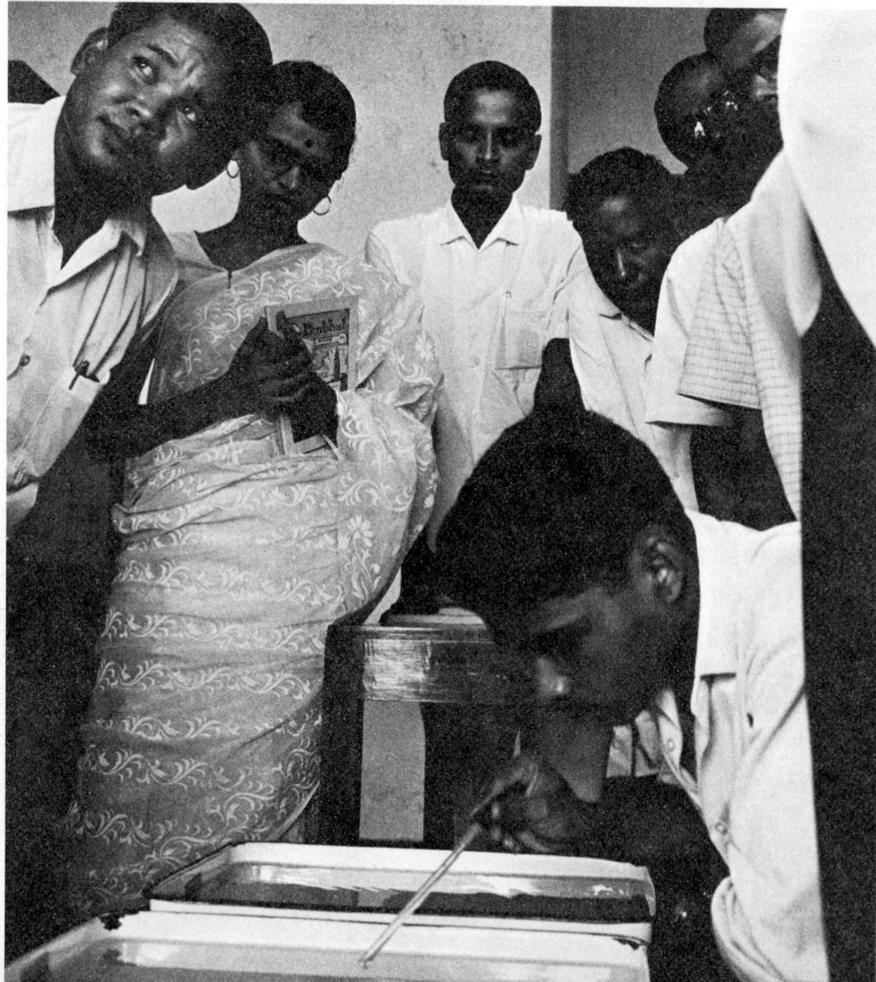

In India, the government set up programs to help solve problems of lack of food, water, jobs, and education. *Left:* Hundreds of men, women, and children carry earth to build a mile-long embankment. The embankment will hold water for irrigating the district, which is often stricken by drought. The project provided wages for the hard-hit people of the area. *Right:* University graduates are taking a two-year course at the Central Institute of Fisheries. They are learning both the administrative and technical aspects of the fisheries industry.

Military dictatorship developed in Pakistan. Unlike India, Pakistan suffered from political instability after independence. Corrupt politicians did not try to represent the people's interests. In 1958, a patriotic military leader, General Mohammad Ayub Khan [ä yüb kän′], seized control of the government. Politics in Pakistan became more stable under his dictatorial rule.

Like India, Pakistan was a poor country. Although it produced most of the world's jute, Pakistan had no processing mills until the 1950s. Pakistan also had few railroads or good roads. Some 80 percent of the people were farmers who barely made a living from their tiny plots of land. Only 20 percent of the people could read and write.

ans. 3 In the 1960s, encouraging economic progress was made. A land-reform program was started. Other reforms were made in education, the legal codes, and transportation.

After 1965, however, Ayub grew unpopular. In the poor and overcrowded eastern wing of Pakistan, corruption flourished. The middle class resented not having any share in political power. In 1969, riots broke out. Ayub was replaced, first by the leader of the armed forces, and later by a civilian.

In the 1970s, Pakistanis were only slightly better off economically than Indians.

Bangladesh fought for independence. In
ans. 4 the late 1960s, the eastern wing of Pakistan became increasingly resentful of its union with the western region. A major problem was its underrepresentation in the central government. The tie between the two regions was religion—Islam. But in all other ways, especially language and culture, the two regions were different. Most important, the westerners were wealthier than the easterners. West Pakistanis controlled the big industries. They held most of the important posts in the military, business, and civil service. The eastern region earned a large share of Pakistan's revenues from its exports of jute. The west, however, controlled how government money was spent.

These conditions led to the growth of East Pakistani nationalism. The eastern region demanded that a federal state be started. It wanted its own currency and control over taxation. The powers of the central government, it argued, should be limited to defense and foreign affairs.

In effect, these demands would have made East Pakistan almost self-governing. West Pakistan refused the demands. In 1971, the central government in West Pakistan ordered its army to attack the rebellious eastern region. Thousands were killed, and property was looted and burned. Several million refugees fled to India. East Pakistan proclaimed itself as the independent state of Bangladesh.

India supported Bangladesh and sent troops to help the new nation. In two weeks, the war was over. Not long after, Bangladesh was recognized as an independent country.

Bangladesh's victory brought political change. Pakistan, defeated and reduced in size, was no longer an effective rival. India became the most important power in the subcontinent. As a result, India gained influence in Asian and world affairs.

Bangladesh had an uncertain future. Most of its capital and other major towns had been destroyed in the war. Bangladesh had few natural resources and had to import millions of tons of rice and wheat yearly to feed its people. The most populated rural area in the world, Bangladesh had one of the poorest populations.

SECTION REVIEW 2

p. 633 **1.** Why did the British divide India into two countries?

p. 635 **2.** What problems still existed in India in the 1970s?

p. 636 **3.** What reforms improved conditions in Pakistan?

p. 636 **4.** Name five conditions that led to war between East and West Pakistan. What were two results of the war?

3 Countries of Southeast Asia became independent

Geographically, politically, and culturally, Southeast Asia is one of the most complex areas of the world. It extends southeast from Burma to Thailand, Laos, Vietnam, Cambodia, Malaysia, and Singapore. It also includes the Philippines and Indonesia.

Lying between the Indian and Pacific oceans, Southeast Asia has been important to sea traders for centuries. The region has also been important for its raw materials. After World War II, it was the world's largest exporter of natural rubber, dried coconut, quinine, kapok, rice, tea, pepper, and tin. It also produced important quantities of petroleum, iron ore, and bauxite, the source of aluminum.

Despite its rich natural resources, Southeast Asia remained mostly poor. Each country was chiefly agricultural and dependent on the export of one or two agricultural products.

Nationalism grew in Southeast Asia. Nationalism became a major force in Southeast Asia after World War I. During World War II,

Vietnam, in Southeast Asia, was a battle-ground for 25 years. *Above right:* Buddhist monks led a protest against the corrupt government in South Vietnam. *Above left:* American troops land by helicopter to help fight the North Vietnamese Communists. *Below left:* a mother and children struggle across a river to escape the bombing of their village.

when Japan occupied the entire region, nationalist feelings grew even stronger.

ans. 1 Japanese rule lasted only three years. But in that period, the Japanese allowed local leaders to take over important government posts. Near the end of the war, Japan trained local troops and officers to fight the Allies. After the Japanese surrendered and before the colonial powers could reestablish control, many of these popular local leaders took over and proclaimed the independence of their countries.

Nationalist governments all over Southeast Asia demanded recognition of their independence. When the colonial powers brought in troops to take back their old ruling positions, war often broke out.

In some cases, however, independence came ans. 2
without a struggle. The United States, faithful to a prewar promise, gave independence to the Philippines in 1948. Britain gave autonomy to Malaya in 1946. (Malaya gained complete independence in 1957. In 1963, it was renamed the Federation of Malaysia when British possessions in Singapore and on the island of Borneo were added to it. In 1965, Singapore separated from Malaysia and became an independent republic.) Britain gave independence to Burma in 1947.

In other areas of Southeast Asia, however, independence was won only after bitter fighting. The longest colonial wars were fought in Indonesia (formerly the Dutch East Indies) against the Dutch and in Indochina against the French.

Indonesia won its freedom. In Indonesia, the Dutch fought local nationalists for four years. Then in 1949, the Dutch finally granted independence to Indonesia.

Following independence, Indonesia had ●
many difficulties. Its population began to grow faster than its food supply. Exports dropped. Inflation increased, and food shortages climbed. Indonesia's president, Sukarno [sü kär′nō], followed a series of disastrous policies. Revolts ans. 3
broke out. Foreign properties were taken over. Some 50 thousand Dutch business managers and technicians, whose skills were needed to run the economy, were forced to leave the country. In 1963, supported by the army, Sukarno became absolute ruler for life. All opposition political parties were banned.

Sukarno became increasingly procommunist. He cooled relations with the West and

● This section may need to be clarified for some students.

strengthened them with Communist China. But then, in 1965, the army learned of a communist plot to take over the country. Thousands of communist sympathizers were killed. A military regime led by General Suharto eventually took over the government in 1967. Sukarno lost all political power and died shortly afterward.

The new government cut the ties with Communist China and restored relations with the West. It also began to revive the economy and develop the country's resources.

• **Indochina suffered continuing conflict.** After Japan was defeated in World War II, France tried to get back its control in Indochina. In 1946, however, it was forced to grant some self-rule to Laos and Cambodia. The status of Vietnam, the third political unit in French Indo-
ans. 4 china, remained unsettled. Various anticolonial groups opposed French rule. The most effective group was the Viet Minh [vē yet măn] led by Ho Chi Minh, a communist. In 1945, he proclaimed independence for the Democratic Republic of Vietnam.

The French refused to recognize Ho Chi Minh's government and fighting broke out in 1946. The war lasted until 1954, when the French were defeated. Later that year, agreements were signed at Geneva, Switzerland, that gave full independence to Laos and Cambodia and called for free elections in Vietnam. A temporary truce line was drawn at the 17th parallel dividing Vietnam between north and south.

Elections were never held. Ho's communist government controlled the north, and an anticommunist government controlled the south. In 1957, the communists in the north began guerrilla operations in the south to reunite the country. They were later supported by South Vietnamese communists, called Viet Cong. North Vietnam was supported by Communist China and the Soviet Union. The United States supported the government of South Vietnam in the belief that it would prevent the spread of communism into other parts of Southeast Asia.

• This sub-section contains a condensed treatment of the long series of events which led to U.S. involvement in Vietnam. Allow time for discussion.

The United States began sending men, money, and arms in the late 1950s to back up the unstable government in South Vietnam. By 1968, more than half a million United States troops were fighting in Vietnam. In the United States, there was increasing criticism of the war, particularly in the late 1960s. Thousands of Americans had died, billions of American dollars had been spent, and little had been accomplished. As a result of this growing pressure to end the war, the United States government began peace negotiations in 1968. In January, 1973, a cease-fire agreement was finally signed.

In 1975, the South Vietnamese government collapsed and the Viet Cong, or South Vietnamese Communists, took control. They began to work with the North Vietnamese to unify all of Vietnam under a single communist government. Meanwhile, the entire country faced an enormous job of rebuilding. After 30 years of continuous war, Vietnam had suffered great destruction. More than 2 million men, women, and children had been killed. Much of the countryside had been bombed and laid waste.

SECTION REVIEW **3**

1. How did the Japanese occupation of Southeast Asia help nationalist movements there? p. 639

2. Name two colonial areas that gained independence through fighting. Name two others that were given independence peacefully. p. 639

3. How did Sukarno's policies hurt Indonesia? p. 639

4. Why was there a war between North and South Vietnam? Which side did the United States support? Why? What was the outcome of the war in Vietnam? p. 640

4 War and revolution transformed East Asia

By the middle of the 20th century, important changes had taken place within the major countries of East Asia. Communist China, after passing through a period of revolution, became the largest and potentially the most powerful state of Asia. Japan, after its defeat in World War II, became one of the most highly industrialized countries in the world. Both Japan and China became interested in playing greater roles in world politics.

A Communist revolution triumphed in China. Late in 1945, war broke out between
ans. 1 the Nationalist government in China, led by Chiang Kai-shek, and the Chinese Communists, led by Mao Tse-tung. Mao had the support of the peasant masses. The Soviet Union aided him and the Chinese Communists by giving to them weapons and supplies taken from the defeated Japanese army after World War II.

The United States supported Chiang and the Nationalist government in their struggle against the Communists. But corrupt Nationalist leaders got control of much of the material the United States sent to Chiang. It was sold for private profit and ended up in the hands of the Chinese Communists. The United States tried to bring the two sides together. But the suggestion of a coalition government was turned down.

By 1948, Mao's forces controlled northeast China. The following year, cities of eastern and southern China, including Nanking, Shanghai, and Canton, fell to Mao's forces. In October, 1949, the Communists proclaimed the birth of the People's Republic of China.

In December of that year, Chiang and his remaining forces fled to the island of Taiwan. They set up the Nationalist Chinese government in exile. The Chinese Communists tried to destroy Chiang's government on Taiwan. However, they were blocked by the United States. Chiang died on Taiwan in 1975, and his son took over the government.

Chinese society changed greatly. The People's Republic of China, with some 600 million people, was the largest nation in the world. Like other communist countries, its government was a totalitarian dictatorship. All power was concentrated in the Communist party's Central Committee, which was led by Chairman Mao Tse-tung.

Mao was determined to transform China into a strict Marxist nation, communist in every respect. This effort to remake Chinese society was undertaken in a very short time. At first, Mao

The last traditional ruler of China, Empress Tz'u Hsi firmly controled China from 1862 to 1908.

Daily Life in Communist China Mao Tse-tung's ideas reached into every corner of Chinese life and his presence was felt even in the privacy of people's homes. The family *left* is eating dinner under Mao's picture. The arts in China celebrated China's cultural revolution. The Peking ballet troupe's "Red Detachment of Women" *(right)* tells of an early Communist uprising against the Nationalist government.

was very popular among the peasants. He re-
ans. 2 formed land ownership, lowered rents, and built schools. The Communists wanted to build up Chinese industrial and military strength as quickly as possible and to make China a strong power again.

However, terror became a basic tool of control. Mao admitted that his government executed thousands of people who opposed his programs. The Communists also set out to destroy Chinese family unity. They believed people's first loyalty should be to the community. They ● attacked the Confucian traditions of ancestor worship and denounced all ideological ties with the Chinese past.

Industrialization was strongly pushed in an attempt to achieve the "Great Leap Forward." To increase the amount of food produced, Communist leaders began *agricultural collectives* of several hundred farm families. Small farm plots ■ were consolidated, and planting and harvesting were controlled by the government. Other collectives mobilized people for road building and irrigation.

The next step was the establishment of *communes.* At first, these were made up of 4,000 to 5,000 farm and industrial families. Each commune was directed by political leaders who answered to the government. However, the commune system did not do well. In addition, bad weather and floods damaged crops and resulted in food shortages in 1959.

Faced with these setbacks in agriculture, Chinese Communist rulers greatly reduced the size of the communes in the early 1960s. They also slowed down the pace of industrial growth. More resources were put into agricultural improvement. As the population grew to a stagger-

● Ask students if they remember Shih Huang Ti who also tried to destroy Confucianism. (See Ch. 3)

■ Define collectives and communes if necessary. You might also discuss the concepts.

ing 800 million, the problem of food production continued to be critical.

Mao revived the revolutionary spirit. By the mid-1960s, though life was still hard, most Chinese were better off than they had ever been before. Food was rationed, but at least no one starved. Health conditions had improved. The average Chinese could buy small consumer goods, such as bicycles and sewing machines. In the face of this prosperity, Mao feared that the Chinese people were forgetting their revolutionary spirit and becoming too concerned with the "easy life." He feared that, like the Soviet Union, China might become "bourgeois."

ans. 2 In 1966, Mao began a purge of intellectuals whom he felt were lukewarm in their devotion to true Leninist communism. Mao called the purge the Great Proletarian Cultural Revolution. Later that year, schools were closed. Hundreds of thousands of teen-agers were organized into the Red Guards. They were told they were crusaders for a better China. The young people attacked teachers, party officials, and people in all walks of life who held to "old ideas, old culture, old customs, and old habits." The Red Guards also ordered all Chinese to rid themselves of "bourgeois" ways. Top leaders were executed, and "kangaroo courts" made people confess to nonexistent crimes.

As the great purge shook the nation, law and order began to break down. Violent uprisings broke out in some cities. There were clashes between peasants and Red Guards in the countryside. Some regional army commanders refused to obey commands from the central government. Ironically, the order and unity that had been so painfully imposed by the Communists was in danger of breaking down.

Late in 1968, Mao realized that the Cultural Revolution was out of control and stopped it. The army restored order. The Red Guards were disbanded. Schools were reopened and industry was revived. The year 1969 was one of national recuperation.

China changed its foreign policy. In the early years of the People's Republic of China, the government remained isolated from the rest of the world. For centuries, Chinese rulers had ans. 3
practiced policies of isolation. For more than 150 years before the Communist takeover, China had been humiliated by foreign imperialists. Hatred of foreigners was an important part of Chinese nationalism. This attitude largely explained the Chinese Communist attitude ● toward the West. In addition, many Western nations did not recognize the Communist government in China. The United States recog-

● You might discuss how much of Communist China's attitudes toward the West are like those of earlier China.

nized the Nationalist government on Taiwan as the legal government of all of China.

China's relations with the Soviet Union were also strained. Trouble began in 1958 on the China-Soviet border. By 1969, the Soviet Union had 500 thousand troops along the border. Various reasons were given for this quarrel. China denounced the Soviet Union for betraying true communism and thought the Soviets should be more anti-American. In addition, China wanted more military and economic aid from the Soviet Union than it had received. The Soviets refused and recalled all their technical advisers in the early 1960s.

China's nationalism led to a demand for the return of all Chinese territory taken by tsarist Russia in the 19th century. The Soviet Union ignored the claims but kept a close watch on the border. Nationalism also explained the Chinese effort to build up a nuclear force. The Chinese believed that the West respected only military force. Nuclear power was therefore the means by which China hoped to regain its place in world affairs. In 1964, China exploded its first atomic bomb. In 1967, it exploded its first hydrogen bomb.

An important change took place in China's foreign outlook during the 1970s. Under Premier Chou En-lai [jō′ en′lī′], government policy became more moderate. China tried to end its international isolation and to have more influence in world affairs. It was voted into the UN in 1971, replacing Taiwan as a member.

Relations between the People's Republic of China and the United States improved when President Richard Nixon visited China in 1972. In 1979, when Jimmie Carter was President, both countries established full diplomatic relations. The United States continued unofficial relations with Taiwan.

● Discussion topic: How should the future of Taiwan be settled?

Japan became a democracy. When World War II ended, Japan was reduced from an empire of 3 million square miles (7.8 million square kilometers) and 500 million people to four main islands of 142 thousand square miles (369.2 thousand square kilometers) and 80 million people. Many Japanese were hungry and ill-clothed. Cities, factories, and railroads had been bombed, and the economy had collapsed.

Allied troops, almost entirely from the United States, occupied the country. General Douglas MacArthur of the United States Army was commander of the Allied forces in Japan. His orders were to carry out complete disarmament and demilitarization, to develop democratic institutions, and to create a sound economy. The United States took a major role in determining Japan's future and provided aid totaling 2 billion dollars to accomplish its goals.

The seven-year occupation of Japan changed ans. 4
the history of that nation. In 1945, Japan could have moved toward either totalitarianism or democracy. Under MacArthur, Japan became the leading democratic country in East Asia.

The occupation authorities also carried out a land-reform program. The large landholdings of absentee landlords were divided up. Poor tenants thus became independent farmers. American authorities also encouraged trade unions. The Americans tried to break up the few monopolistic companies that controlled most of Japan's industry. But the campaign was not very successful and was later dropped.

Still, most of the occupation goals had been accomplished. As a result, the United States and forty-seven other countries (not including the Soviet Union) signed a peace treaty with Japan in 1951. The treaty restored Japanese independence. A security treaty, signed at the same time, allowed the United States to have military bases in Japan. It also committed the United States to defend Japan. The occupation ended in 1952. In 1956, diplomatic relations were restored between Japan and the Soviet Union. Shortly afterward, Japan was admitted to the United Nations.

Japan became a leading industrial power. Throughout the 1950s and 1960s, the country's new democratic system became firmly established, and remarkable economic growth
ans. 5 took place. By 1962, economic output had more than doubled. Manufacturing had quadrupled, and food was plentiful. Foreign trade was breaking records.

By 1975, the Japanese population reached 110 million. Cities had grown rapidly. The population of Tokyo reached 11.5 million, making it the largest city in the world. From 1960 to 1970, the production of goods increased 400 percent. Japan became third in world industrial production, behind the United States and the Soviet Union. It led the world in shipbuilding and was second in the building of cars and computers. Japan had achieved an economic miracle.

A number of factors contributed to Japan's economic growth. Money and effort were concentrated in economic development rather than in weapons and armies. Government policy favored tariffs on imports and aid to industry. In addition, Japan's work force was highly skilled.

Japan paid a high price for its industrial growth, however. Schools, housing, and garbage and sewage disposal had been neglected. Moreover, little thought had been given to the impact on the environment. Smog was almost a national disaster. People suffered from lung diseases. Birds and trees died from fumes. Certain kinds of fish disappeared from the seas. By 1970, the Japanese realized that there was great need to spend more money on the country's public services. In that year, the parliament passed strong laws against pollution.

Japan's 1946 Constitution made men and women equal. These newlyweds shop together for groceries.

Since 1945, Japan had exercised little influence in the world. By the mid-1970s, its economic achievements made it ready to take on a new role in world affairs. In 1972, Japan's prime minister paid an official visit to Communist China to restore friendly relations.

Japanese-American relations also changed. The United States bowed to Japanese pressure and returned the Ryukyu Islands to Japanese authority in 1972. However, the United States held on to military bases on the islands. The Japanese resented not being consulted about the surprise turnabout in American relations toward the People's Republic of China. But the main tension between the two allies was over trade relations. American business people did not like the high tariffs on products they exported to Japan. They asked for similar limits on Japanese goods imported into the United States. The Japanese needed American raw materials to keep up their economic growth. They did not like limits placed on their purchases.

People of good will in both nations worked for solutions to these problems. They believed that peace in the Pacific depended upon close cooperation between the United States and Japan. In 1975, relations improved. As a symbol of this, Emperor Hirohito that year made an unprecedented visit to the United States.

SECTION REVIEW 4

1. What two groups fought in the Chinese Revolution? Who led each? What foreign powers supported each? Which one won? p. 641

2. What changes in China did Mao's government make in the 1950s? What was the Cultural Revolution of the 1960s? p. 642 643

3. Why was China's foreign policy isolationist in the 1950s and 1960s? p. 643

4. What were three important results of the American occupation of Japan? p. 644

5. In what ways did Japan's economy grow? What problems resulted from that economic growth? What benefits? p. 645

A TV factory in Japan. By 1969, Japan was the world's largest producer of television sets.

CHAPTER REVIEW 34

SECTION SUMMARIES

1. India and China were leaders for independence. Nationalist movements grew strong in India and China in the late 19th century. Mohandas Gandhi used boycotts and nonviolent resistance against British rule. During the 1930s, Britain granted India a limited amount of self-government. Nationalists in China overthrew the corrupt Manchu dynasty and established a republic in 1912. Sun Yat-sen was the leading Nationalist. He was succeeded in 1925 by Chiang Kai-shek, who united the country. After 1927, he and the Chinese Communists became bitter enemies.

2. India divided into three countries. With independence, the former British colony of India split apart into two unfriendly states: India, mainly Hindu, and Pakistan, mainly Muslim. During a civil war in 1971, the eastern wing of Pakistan proclaimed itself the independent state of Bangladesh.

3. Countries of Southeast Asia became independent. Many countries in Southeast Asia gained their freedom following World War II. Some won it without fighting, such as the Philippines. Others, such as Indonesia and Vietnam, fought long, bitter wars to achieve independence. Even after independence and partition in 1954, war continued in Vietnam between communist and anticommunist forces. The United States entered the war, hoping to stop the spread of communism. But antiwar sentiment at home led it to withdraw and arrange a ceasefire agreement in 1973. Two years later, the anticommunist South Vietnamese government collapsed and was replaced by a Vietnamese Communist regime.

4. War and revolution transformed East Asia. In East Asia, China became a communist nation in 1949. It radically changed old institutions and emphasized industrial and agricultural development. In 1970, China began to end its international isolation. The following year, it was voted into the United Nations. Japan prospered in the years after World War II and became a democratic nation. By 1970, it ranked third in the world in industrial production. In the mid-1970s, both China and Japan were ready for new, important roles in world affairs.

WHO? WHAT? WHEN? WHERE?

1. List these events in chronological order under the proper area headings:

a. Indian subcontinent
b. Southeast Asia
c. China
d. Japan

Sun Yat-sen became president. 1921 c.
Pakistan became a republic. 1956 a.
American occupation of Japan began. 1945 d.
South Vietnamese government collapsed. 1975 b.
Gandhi was assassinated. 1948 a.
American occupation of Japan ended. 1952 d.
Tokyo became the world's largest city. 1970s d.
Communist China replaced Taiwan in the UN. 1971 c.
The United States began fighting in Vietnam. 1964 b.
Bangladesh became independent. 1971 a.
The Cultural Revolution began. 1966 c.
Ayub Khan seized power. 1958 a.
The Philippines became independent. 1946 b.
India and Pakistan were divided. 1947 a.
Asia's first hydrogen bomb was exploded. 1967 c.

2. Explain the importance of these national leaders:

Mohandas Gandhi p. 631
Sun Yat-sen p. 632
Chiang Kai-shek p. 633
Mao Tse-tung p. 641
Indira Gandhi p. 635
Ayub Khan p. 636
Sukarno p. 639
Ho Chi Minh p. 640
Suharto p. 640

3. What was the purpose of the Cultural Revolution? Who were the Red Guards? p. 642

p. 643 4. What was the "Great Leap Forward" in China? How were communes and collectives used?

5. Define these terms:

mahatma p. 631	bourgeois communism 643
p. 631 nonviolent disobedience	Viet Cong p. 640
Viet Minh p. 640	Kuomintang p. 632

QUESTIONS FOR CRITICAL THINKING

1. Which of the leaders mentioned in this chapter would you consider to be heroes? Why?
2. Why has it been so difficult for many nations to set up successful democracies?
3. What are some reasons that wars start? Give examples from this chapter.
4. Should the United States help people who are fighting communist forces? Why or why not?
5. Why did Communist leaders try to destroy the traditional customs and beliefs of the Chinese people?

ACTIVITIES

1. Write a short biography of a person mentioned in this chapter. Read your biography to the class.
2. Prepare a chart of the countries of Asia. List populations, average per person incomes, natural resources, types of government, gross national products, exports, and imports. Also note which countries were once colonies and when independence came.
3. Follow the presentation of the chart (activity 2) with a class discussion on the advantages and disadvantages each country has in dealing with the problems of today.

QUESTIONS FOR CRITICAL THINKING

1. Answers will vary.
2. Lack of experience with western democracy, social customs that are not democratic, and ethnic rivalries are some possible answers.
3. Answers will vary.
4. Opinion.
5. To ready them for rapid changes in their way of living.

CHAPTER TEST 34

SECTION 1

1. China was unified during the rule of: a. Sun Yat-sen, b. Chiang Kai-shek, c. Chou En-lai
2. True or false: China's Nationalist party began to fight for freedom from British colonial rule in 1926.
3. True or false: The Government of India Act of 1919 did not satisfy Indians because it reserved many important powers for Britain.

SECTION 2

4. Colonial India was divided into two nations because of problems caused by differences of: a. politics, b. race, c. religion
5. The first prime minister of India was: a. Mohandas Gandhi, b. Jawaharlal Nehru, c. Indira Gandhi
6. True or false: Indira Gandhi moved India away from democracy with repressive measures.

SECTION 3

7. True or false: Many problems in Southeast Asia are caused by the lack of natural resources in the area.
8. Native leaders in Southeast Asia began to take over government jobs during __b__ occupation. a. French, b. Japanese, c. American
9. Ho Chi Minh was leader of the: a. Kuomintang, b. Nationalist party, c. Viet Minh

SECTION 4

10. True or false: After the Communist victory, the Nationalist government of China moved to the island of Taiwan.
11. During American occupation, Japan became a: a. democracy, b. colony, c. dictatorship
12. True or false: The People's Republic of China is the world's most populous nation.

1945–

CHAPTER 35

Nation-Building in the Middle East, Africa, and Latin America

Nation-building in Africa was difficult and bloody as different peoples fought for self-government. In 1967, the Ibo people in Nigeria seceded and called their state Biafra. Thirty months of bitter fighting followed. Outnumbered, Biafra surrendered in 1970.

Nationalism is a European idea. In the 19th century, it became the most powerful political force of the Western world. Nationalism taught that every people had the right to shape their own future and that the best way to do so was through an independent nation. In the 20th century, this European idea spread to every part of the globe.

Two important developments helped speed up the growth and spread of nationalism. One was the creation of Western-type schools around the world that taught that freedom was good for all people, not just for Europeans. The other was deepening bitterness against Western control, whether it was political and military as in Africa and the Middle East or economic as in Latin America. These feelings were dramatically expressed in a poem by Patrice Lumumba, one of the black independence leaders in the Belgian Congo, now the country of Zaïre:

> The dawn is here, my brother! Dawn! Look in our faces,
> A new morning breaks in our old Africa.
> Ours alone will now be the land, the water, mighty rivers
> Poor African surrendered for a thousand years.
> Hard torches of the sun will shine for us again
> They'll dry the tears in eyes and spittle on your face.
> The moment when you break the chains, the heavy fetters,
> The evil, cruel times will go never to come again.
> A free and gallant Congo will arise from black soil,
> A free and gallant Congo—black blossom from black seed!

● However, nation-building in Africa, the Middle East, and Latin America turned out to be much more difficult than the winning of independence. Leaders in these areas had to overcome such problems as widespread poverty and illiteracy, tribal rivalries, and conflicts with neighboring states. This chapter tells how:

1. Nationalism transformed the Middle East.

2. Black Africa changed rapidly.

3. Latin America faced many challenges.

● Explain that liberation begins problems that new leaders must deal with.

1 Nationalism transformed the Middle East

After World War I, there were at least three major nationalist movements in the Middle East. One was Turkish (see Chapter 30), a second was Arab, and a third was Zionist.

The Arabs wanted total independence from Western control. The Zionists wanted to make a Jewish homeland in Palestine. After World War II, both Arabs and Zionists reached their goals. But the two came into sharp conflict.

Arabs in North Africa and the Middle East demanded independence. After World War I, the Arabs in North Africa and the Middle East wanted to be free of foreign control. During the 1920s, several underground movements in Tunisia, Algeria, and Morocco challenged French rule. But it was in Egypt that nationalism first exploded into violence. Egypt was a protectorate, that is, a weak country under the control of a strong one. Egypt was a protectorate of Britain.

After a delegation of Egyptian nationalists were denied permission to attend the Paris Peace Conference, Egypt rose up in revolt. Order was not restored until 1922, when the British agreed to end the protectorate. Egypt became independent. However, Britain kept the rights to have troops there, to run Egyptian foreign affairs, and to defend the Suez Canal.

In the Middle East, Arab resentment against the corrupt rule of the Ottoman Turks had been building up for a long time. When the Ottoman Empire entered World War I on the side of Germany, Britain tried to win over the Arabs in order to weaken Turkish power. In 1915 and 1916, Britain made vague promises of independence to the Arabs to spark a rebellion against

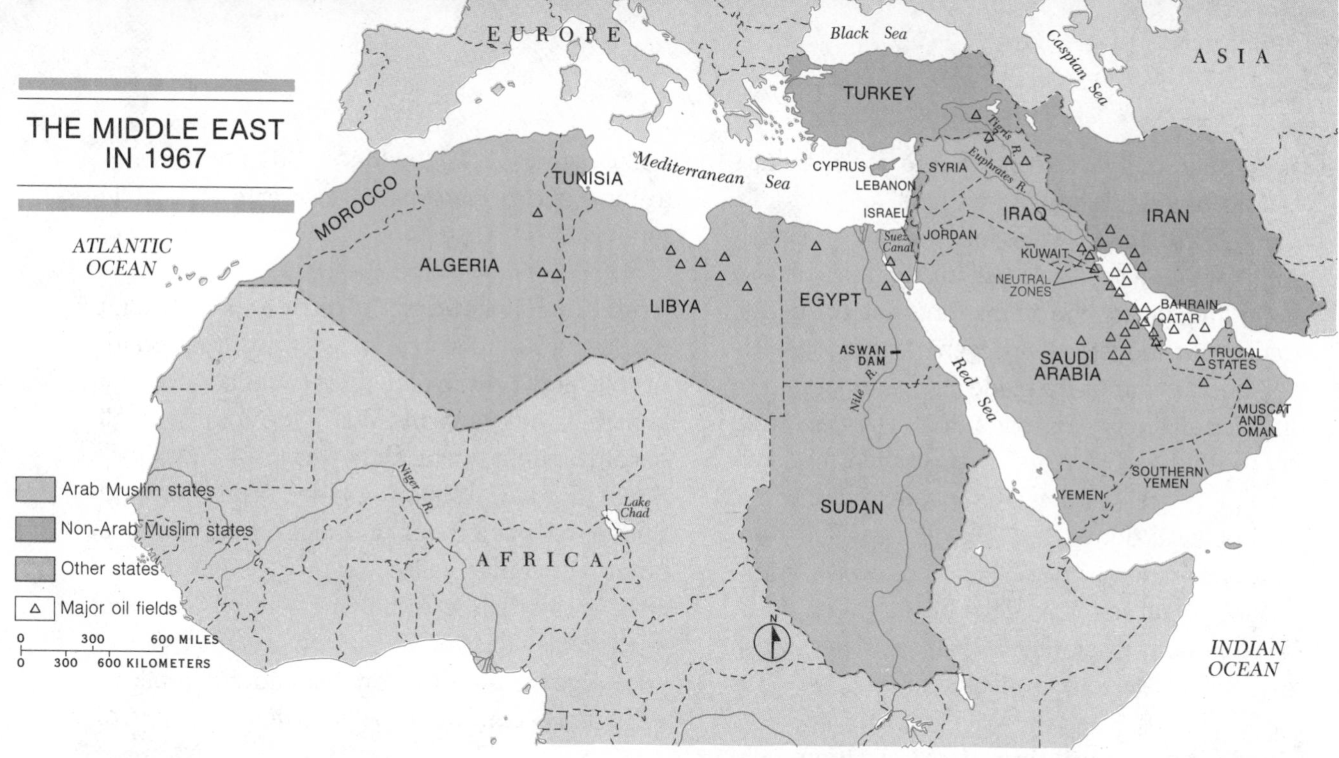

the Turks. In June, 1916, the attempt was successful when the Arabs revolted.

When the war ended, Arab leaders claimed self-government as their reward. But it soon became clear that Arab independence would be a victim of European power politics. During the war, Britain and France had made a secret agreement to divide the Middle East between them. After the war, the newly formed League of Nations made Syria and Lebanon French mandates. Iraq, Palestine, and Trans-Jordan were given to Britain to oversee. The Arabs felt that the mandates were poor substitutes for independence. In the years that followed, Arab hostility toward their European rulers grew.

Saudi Arabia and Iran become independent. The collapse of the Ottoman Empire in
ans. 1 1918 brought independence to several states in the Arabian peninsula. The most important was the newly created kingdom of the Hejaz [hē jaz′]. Its ruler was Abdul-Aziz, commonly known as ibn-Saud [ib′ ən sä üd′]. Ibn-Saud conquered the warring Bedouin tribes and controlled nearly all of the peninsula by 1926. In 1932, ibn-Saud changed the name of his kingdom to Saudi Arabia. In that same year, rich oil reserves were discovered there that added greatly to his power and prestige.

Clarify if necessary: *Muslim* denotes the religious beliefs, *Arab* defines a Semitic people of N. Africa and Arabia.

In 1921, Reza Shah Pahlavi took over Persia. A Muslim but not an Arab country, it became known as Iran, or Land of the Aryans. A strong nationalist, the shah fought against any foreign influence in Iranian affairs. He also became determined to modernize his country. The shah ans. 2
built schools, developed national resources, and supported the rights of women and other reforms. As the years passed, the shah became a despot. In 1941, he abdicated and his son, Muhammad Reza Shah Pahlavi, became ruler.

Jews established a homeland in Palestine. A source of continual strife in the Middle East was the state of Palestine. Jews and Arabs had lived in Palestine ever since biblical times. In 1917, the British, in the Balfour Declara- ans. 4

tion, said that a national home for the Jews would be established in Palestine.

In 1920, when Palestine became a British mandate, large-scale Jewish immigration began. Over the years, the immigrants set up farms, developed industries, and generally prospered.

Although the Arabs made up the larger part of the population in Palestine, they were alarmed by these developments. They viewed the Jews as "intruders" and feared possible economic and political domination. As refugees fled from Nazi Germany in the 1930s and Jewish immigration increased, the Arabs began to use guerrilla warfare to stop immigration. The British tried but failed to bring peace to the area.

World War II brought radical changes. In the area from Morocco in the west to Iran in the east, three political divisions developed—non-Arab Muslim states, Arab Muslim states, and Israel. (Also in a class by itself was Lebanon, which was half Christian and half Arab Muslim.) The drive for national independence in each was very strong and often led to violence. All this was made more complicated—and more dangerous—by the big powers who competed for influence in the area.

The two non-Arab Muslim states were Turkey and Iran. Democracy in Turkey was weak, threatened by serious economic problems and a large, conservative rural population opposed to further Westernization. Nevertheless, social reforms and industrialization continued.

In Iran, the shah pushed ahead with modernization and economic development. He used money from large oil profits to begin a program of reform in the 1960s. In the 1970s, he spent heavily on military equipment. Many people objected to his programs and his dictatorial rule. The secret police, called Savak, were especially hated. In 1979, the shah left the country and efforts were made to create an Islamic republic.

Arab Muslims ended colonialism. Among
the Arab Muslim states, only Egypt, Iraq, Saudi
Arabia, and Yemen had independence—at least
in name—before World War II. After the war, all
became independent. Between 1944 and 1956,
Syria, Jordan, Libya, Tunisia, Morocco, and ans. 3
Sudan all gained full independence. Various
other countries also achieved independence from their colonial masters without too much difficulty.

In Algeria, the situation was more complicated. France considered Algeria to be a part of

In Iran today, Muslim women in traditional veils are seen in modern shopping centers.

France, not a colony. And of ten million Algerians, one million were of European descent, mostly French settlers. Nearly all of the best land and most of the businesses were in French hands. The rest of the Algerian population, some nine million, were chiefly Arabs. They shared in little of the wealth. An Algerian nationalist movement developed, demanding independence. In 1954, civil war broke out. The French and the Algerians both used terrorism and torture. After four years of fighting, the French president, Charles de Gaulle, made peace with nationalist leaders. Algeria then was given its independence.

In Egypt, the army overthrew the corrupt rule of King Farouk in 1952. The plot was masterminded by a young colonel named Gamal Abd-el Nasser. In 1954, he became president. To help Egypt's poor, Nasser pushed through land reforms, increased the pace of industrialization, developed natural resources, and tried to achieve a more equal distribution of wealth.

One of Nasser's chief projects was a huge dam and power station on the Nile River near Aswan. The United States and Britain withdrew their offer to finance the dam in 1956 because Nasser bought Soviet military equipment. Nasser retaliated by nationalizing, that is, by taking ● over, the Suez Canal. This act caused an attack by Israel, Britain, and France in 1956. For a while, the world teetered on the brink of a major war. But quick action by the UN, supported strongly by the United States, kept the peace. Nasser kept control of the canal and the Soviets financed the Aswan High Dam, which was completed in 1970.

Oil increased the influence of Middle Eastern countries. Strong feelings of nationalism provided a basis for unity among the countries of the Middle East, especially the Arab world. But conflicting ambitions and political rivalries made unity impossible most of the time. There were also social differences. In most Middle Eastern countries, society was split into two groups. At the top were a few very rich merchants and landowners. At the bottom were many poor and powerless tenant farmers.

● It had belonged to Britain and France.

The discovery and development of very rich oil reserves in many of these countries, however, gave them the potential to develop their economies. The oil was also a strong bargaining point, particularly with Japan and Western countries whose industries could not run without oil from the Middle East. In the 1970s, this bargaining power grew when the oil-rich countries of the Middle East worked together and quadrupled the price of oil. Since they produced most of the world's oil, their influence in world affairs greatly increased.

Jews in Palestine founded Israel. A struggle began to develop between the Jews and the Arabs in Palestine. At the end of World War II, (ans. 4) the British withdrew and turned the problem over to the UN. In 1947 and 1948, seven Arab countries attacked Jewish settlements in Palestine. The Jewish forces not only held their own but gained important victories. The independence of Israel, as Jewish Palestine was now called, was recognized by the United States, the Soviet Union, and nearly fifty other countries in 1948.

But the end of hostilities in 1949 left the area in an unsettled state. The Arabs refused to sign a peace treaty recognizing the existence of Israel. Israel now controlled the larger part of what had been Palestine, including part of Jerusalem. Moreover, during the fighting, hundreds of thousands of Arabs had fled from their homes in

Jewish-held Palestine. These refugees were housed in makeshift camps run by the UN in nearby Arab lands. The misery of the Palestinian refugees and their nationalist feelings proved to be an explosive force into the 1970s.

Arab-Israeli tensions deepened. The raids by Arab terrorists and counterattacks by Israel were constant events in the 1960s. In 1967, Egypt's Nasser began a series of actions that led to war with Israel.

As Arab threats of war increased, Israel decided to strike the first blow. On June 4, 1967, the Israeli air force attacked Egyptian bases and destroyed their planes. Without air protection, the Egyptian army was completely defeated. Israeli troops overran the entire Sinai peninsula and reached the Suez Canal. The war was over in six days.

Egypt and Israel accepted a cease-fire agreement. But in the next few years, no progress was made toward lasting peace. Egypt's new leader, Anwar Sadat [än wär′ sȧ dat′], who came to power after Nasser's death in 1970, insisted that Israel withdraw from all the lands it had taken. Only then would Egypt agree to negotiate a peace treaty. For its part, Israel refused to withdraw until a peace was made in which the Arab states finally recognized Israel's legal existence.

In 1973, Egypt and Syria attacked Israel. The Israelis were driven back from the Suez Canal. But they won strategically important territory from the Syrians. A truce ended the fighting. In 1975, Egypt and Israel, with help from the United States, signed a peace agreement. The Suez Canal was reopened, and Israel gave up some occupied territory in the Sinai. But Syria and Israel seemed unable to reach an agreement. At the same time, Arab Palestinian guerrillas continued their terroristic activities against the Israelis in the hope of regaining land and creating an Arab Palestinian state.

By 1976, nearly 1 million Palestinian refugees lived in camps outside Israel's borders.

The deepening tensions were made more dangerous by the actions of the United States and the Soviet Union, who had conflicting interests in the Middle East. In the 1960s, the Soviet Union tried to eliminate American influence in the area. It built up a strong naval force in the eastern Mediterranean and gave Egypt large quantities of arms. For its part, the United States supported Israel with large amounts of financial and military aid. In 1972, a break in relations took place between Egypt and the Soviet Union. After that, Egypt built up a strong friendship with the United States. Syria, however, continued to rely on the Soviet Union.

In 1978, President Sadat of Egypt and Prime Minister Menachem Begin of Israel met with President Carter at Camp David in the United States. These discussions led to the signing of a formal peace treaty between Egypt and Israel in March 1979.

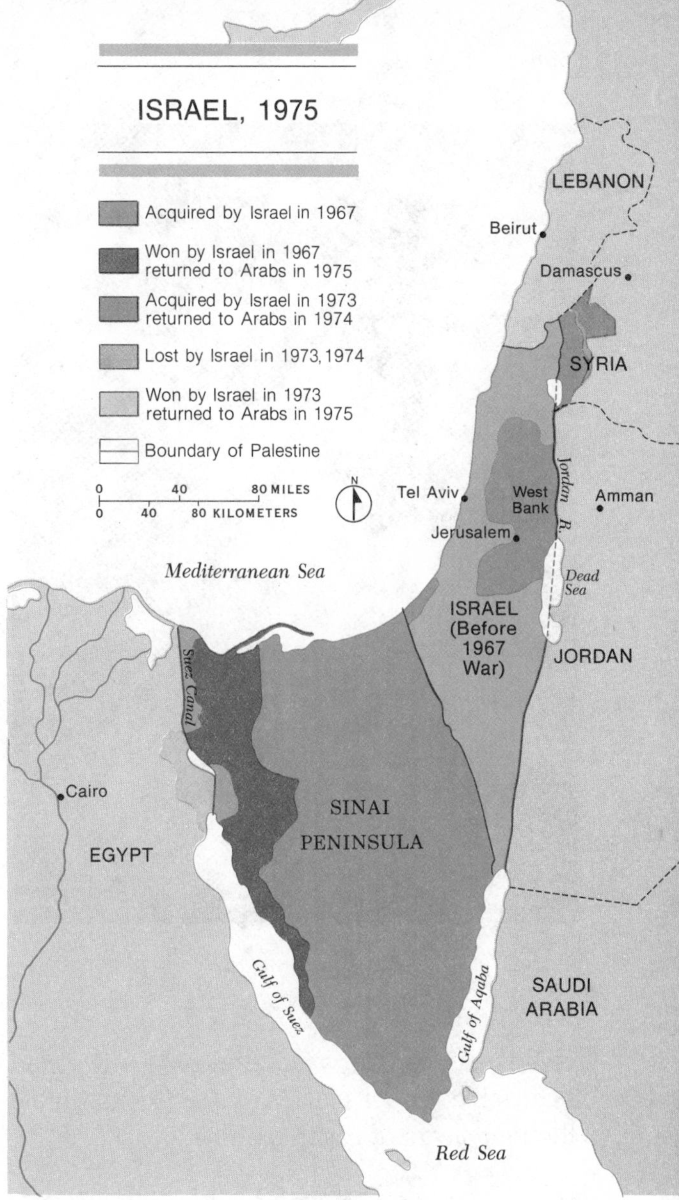

SECTION REVIEW 1

p. 651 **1.** When and how did Saudi Arabia win independence?

p. 651 **2.** What steps did the shahs of Iran take to modernize the country?

p. 652 **3.** Name seven Arab Muslim states that won independence after World War II.

p. 651 653 **4.** What events before and after World War II caused tension between the Jews and Arabs in Palestine? How have other nations added to the problem?

2 Black Africa changed rapidly

The spirit of nationalism that swept through the Middle East also reached black Africa, that part of Africa south of the Sahara and populated largely by black people. The progress of nationalism was extraordinary. In 1950, only four states on the entire African continent were free. By 1976, almost all were independent.

This rush into freedom created many difficulties. Under colonialist rule, countries in black Africa were not prepared for self-government. None of the new African states had any strong traditions of political unity. They had no common language other than their colonial language, usually French or English. Most people

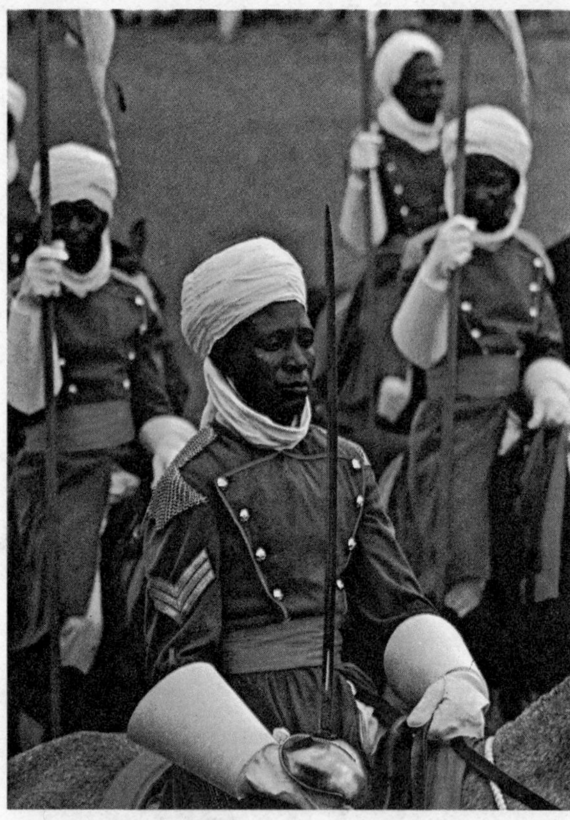

Independence celebration in Nigeria.

could not read or write. And only a few had been able to get university educations during the long years of European rule.

Ethnic rivalries threatened national unity. ● During the 19th century, European colonists, with little regard for African ways of life, created ans. 1 the political systems. Various ethnic groups, who had nothing in common, were often forced to live within one colonial unit. When colonialism ended, these artificial units were given independence. Ethnic rivalries often developed that threatened national unity. Over the years, some Africans educated in European ideas learned to think nationally, for instance as Kenyans, Ugandans, or Nigerians. But many still regarded themselves as tribal members, such as Hausa, or as members of a particular ethnic group, such as Arab Muslims. This ethnic loyalty often led to hostilities, feuds, and even civil wars in the new countries.

● Colonies, which later became nations, were created on political bases not according to ethnic territories. Discuss why this caused problems.

Tribal rivalries had tragic results in Zaïre [zä ir′], the former Belgian Congo. The Belgians suddenly gave the area independence in 1960. Patrice Lumumba [pə trēs′ lü mům′bə], Zaïre's young leader, could not hold the country together. Independence was soon followed by mutiny in the army, tribal feuds, attacks on white civilians, and secession of the rich mining province of Katanga [kə täng′gə]. United Nations troops restored order, but only after Lumumba had been killed. When the UN withdrew, violence broke out again. In 1965, an army officer, Joseph D. Mobutu [mō bü′tü], (in 1971, he changed his name to Mobutu Sese Seko) restored the authority of the central government. Unrest continued on a small scale, but tribal conflicts ended.

Serious tribal tensions also caused civil war in Nigeria. A West African country of 68 million people, it had more than 200 tribal groups. One tribe, the Ibo [ē′bō], were resented because of their success in commerce and the professions. A number of Ibos were massacred. In 1967, civil war broke out. The Ibo seceded from Nigeria and proclaimed the independent state of Biafra [bē ä′frə]. The war was bloody and desperate. In 1970, Biafra surrendered. Ethnic rivalries also threatened national unity in other countries, such as Sudan, Kenya, and Burundi.

The new African states searched for suitable forms of government. Nearly all the newly independent African states had governments patterned after Western models. Successful "government of the people," however, usually needs long experience, educated citizens, and a stable middle class. These ans. 2 conditions did not exist in African societies. By 1975, twenty-one out of the forty-four independent countries were ruled by a single party. Twelve had military governments, and only eleven had multiparty parliamentary systems.

In many countries of black Africa, the outward forms of democratic, representative government were kept. But a "strong man" with popular appeal became the actual ruler with all power concentrated in his hands. In a number of cases, the leader became a dictator. Kwame Nkrumah [kwä′mē nə krü′mə], the first prime minister of Ghana, was such a leader. In 1956, he led Ghana through a peaceful transition from colonialism to independence. But gradually, Nkrumah gagged the press and jailed opponents. He followed disastrous political and economic policies and would not permit any criticism of them. In 1966, outraged army officers took control of the government. Nkrumah died in exile.

Economic and social conditions improved slowly. Although many black African states were independent by 1960, economic and social conditions in Africa were far from promising. In 1959, the average per capita income in many ans. 3 black African countries was less than 100 dollars. Hunger was widespread. The death rate was high. Only about 50 percent of the children surviving infancy reached adulthood. The educational system was poor. Few countries had as many as 2 percent of their children in high schools. There were very few African doctors, scientists, agricultural specialists, and engineers.

In the 1960s and 1970s, social and economic conditions showed some improvement, espe-

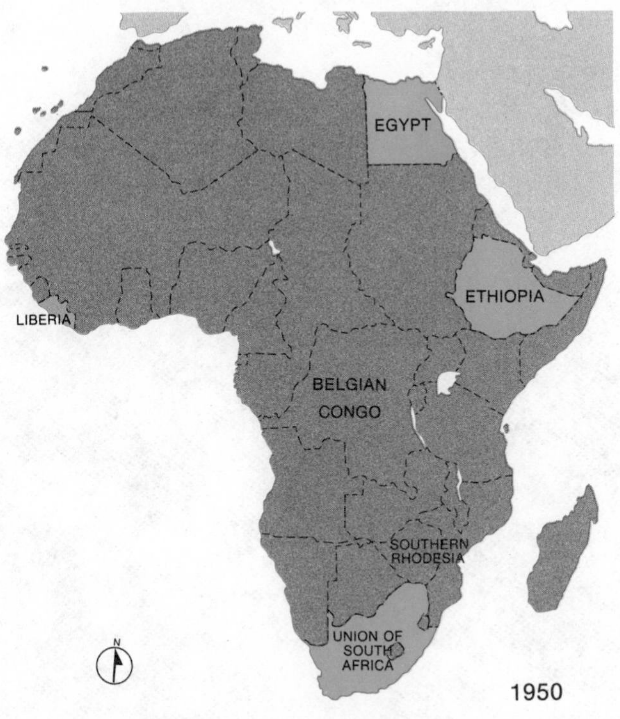

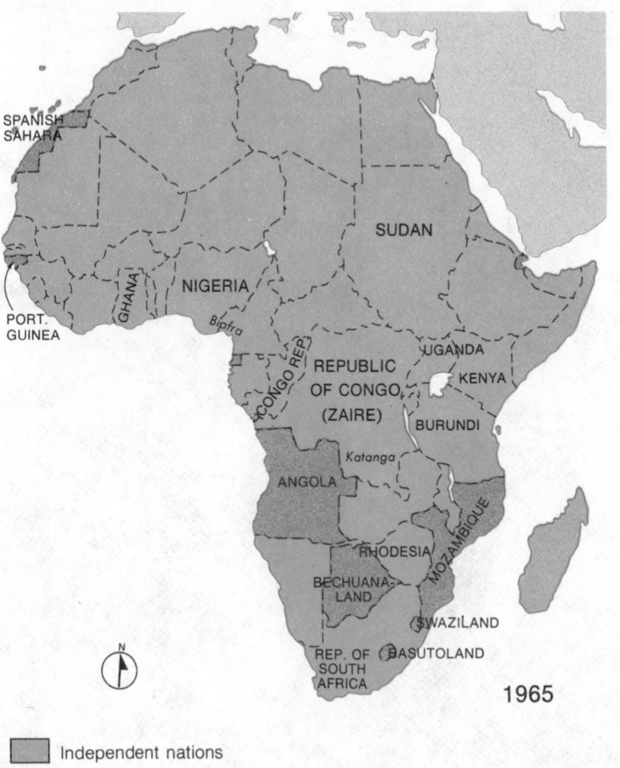

NATIONS EMERGE IN AFRICA 1950–1965

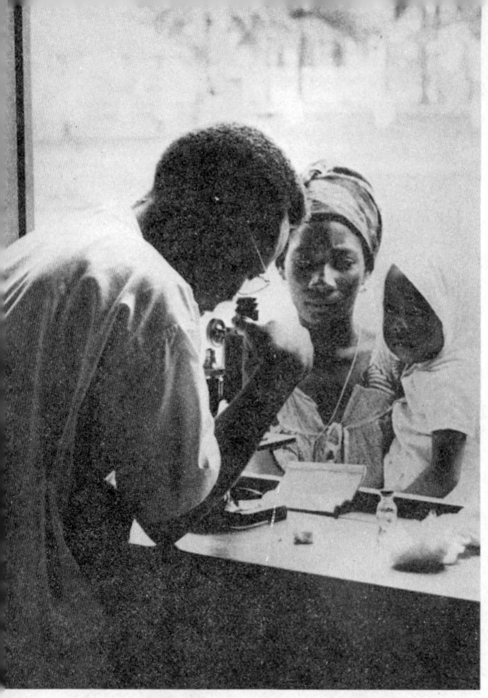

The World Health Organization, a UN agency, helped African governments set up health-care centers *(above)*, train doctors, control diseases, and improve sanitation.

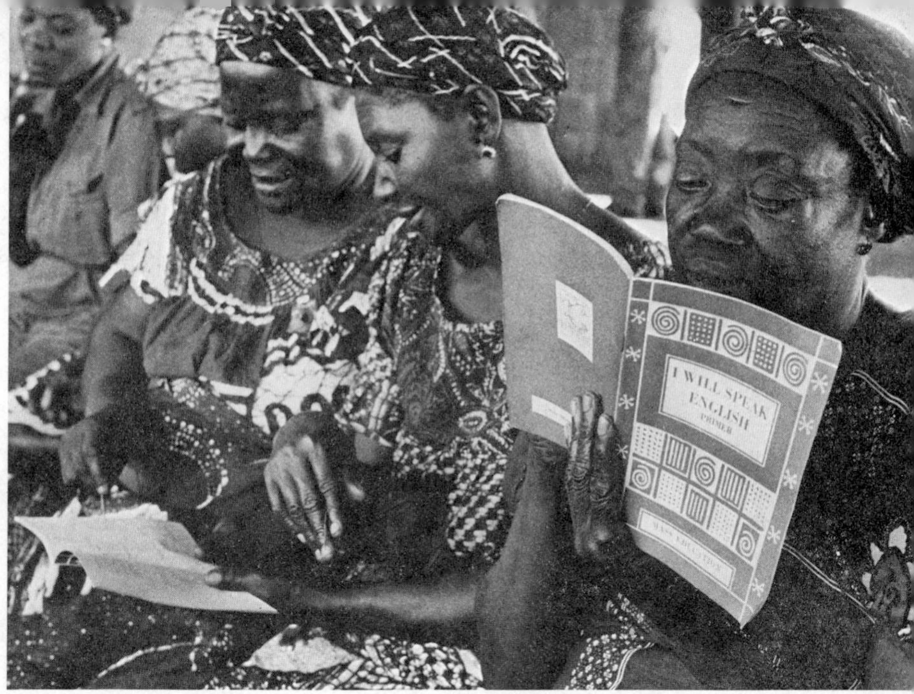

The new African states were short of educated people. Here women of Ghana learn to read as part of a literacy campaign by Nkruma's government.

In 1962, Burundi became independent peacefully—it had been a UN trust territory administered by Belgium. Elections were held *(below)* and all adults voted.

Geography: A Key to History

Economic Independence and Resources

Many nations have found that political independence does not bring with it economic independence. The usable mineral and water resources of the world are unevenly distributed, the lion's share being in western Europe and North America. Many of the new nations face big economic problems because of their lack of mineral resources.

The nations of Africa are a good example. The map shows the location of major mineral resources and economic activity. Compare this map with the political map of Africa on page 694 to see which nations have what resources. Most African nations have not become industrialized because they lack the resources to do so.

Compared with the rest of the world, Africa has few deposits of iron ore. Moreover, most of its iron ore is located far from its few sources of coal. (Heat from burning coal is needed to get iron from iron ore.) The ironworkers of ancient Africa burned charcoal to smelt iron from the ore. But this process takes too much charcoal to be profitable in producing large quantities of iron.

Electric power is needed for industrial development, and some parts of Africa have tremendous potential water power to produce it. However, the attempts to harness water power by building dams have brought ill as well as good. Where once streams flowed rapidly, now stagnant lakes form in back of dams—perfect breeding grounds for the mosquitoes and snails that carry debilitating diseases of humans.

The African continent has some minerals that industrialized countries want. But it is more profitable for an industry to buy ore and ship it to its refineries elsewhere than to ship in coal to use in refining ore.

Much of the economic activity in Africa is *extractive.* The Africans extract minerals from the soil, or hardwood trees from the forests, or palm oil fruit from trees. Many of these raw materials are shipped elsewhere to be processed or refined.

Some African countries are investing the money from their raw materials in refineries or other facilities that will bring more business into their country. For other African countries, such a course is impossible; they have few raw materials to sell, and so they have little or no money to invest.

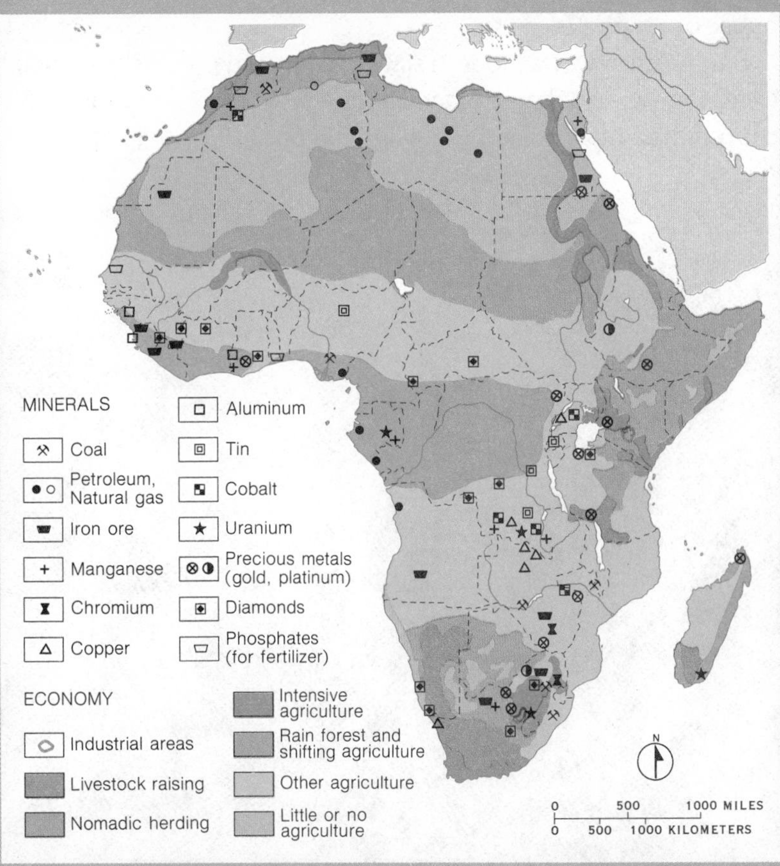

cially in those African countries that had good natural resources. Nigeria, for example, which had oil deposits, adopted a four-year plan in 1971 for economic development that called for spending almost 5 billion dollars. Exports quickly increased and the destruction caused by its civil war was repaired. In Zaïre, which had rich copper mines, the gross national product reached nearly 2 billion dollars by 1973.

White rule in South Africa was racist. South Africa was the most powerful African state economically and militarily. Its natural resources included diamonds and gold, and it was highly industrialized. Once a British colony, the country declared its complete separation from Britain in 1961 and took a new name, the Republic of South Africa.

South Africa was a modern state in every way except in race relations. Since its founding, the country had been ruled by a white minority.

In 1948, the government began a policy of ans. 4
apartheid [ə pärt′hīt]. This meant strict separation of races in all aspects of South African life. Blacks and "coloreds" (people of mixed racial descent) were not allowed to live in the same parts of town as white people. They could not go to the same schools, ride on the same trains, eat in the same restaurants, or even sit on the same park benches. To go from one area of the country to another, they had to carry "passes" and identification cards and follow strict regulations. They could work only at jobs no white people wanted.

Many political and religious leaders throughout the world protested these harsh racist laws. But their views had little practical effect.

In the early 1970s, South African foreign policy changed as it tried to win friends among its African neighbors. However, most black African countries remained hostile to the white minority government.

Johannesburg, South Africa, 1960. Black Africans line up for new work passes after burning theirs in a protest.

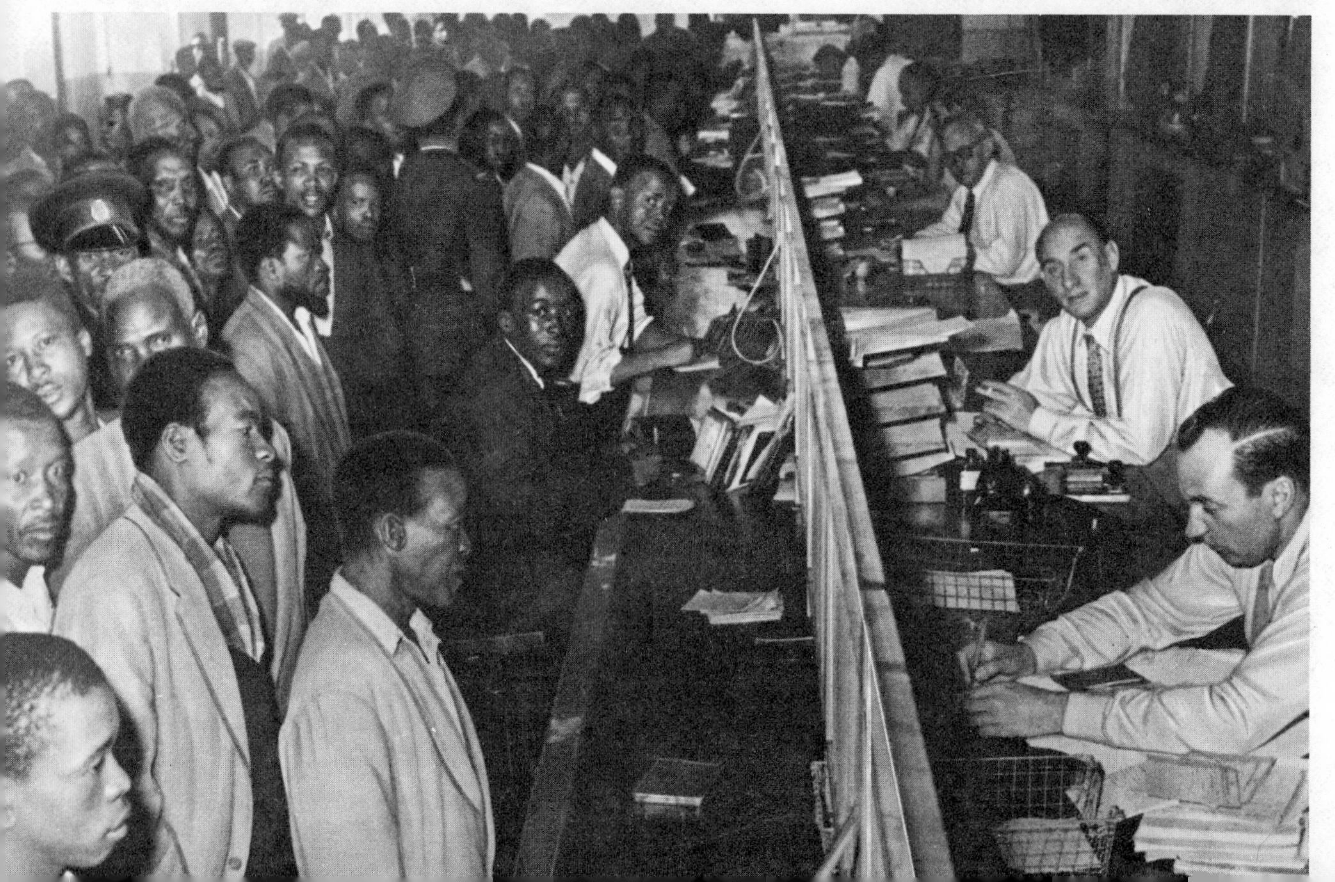

Rhodesia became a nation under white rule. The situation in Rhodesia was very much the same as in South Africa, though it had not been going on as long. In 1965, the British colony of Rhodesia, controlled by a small white minority, declared its independence. Great Britain insisted that it could not approve such action until full political rights were given to the black African majority. Rhodesia refused. The British then began a trade embargo, that is, the government made trade with Rhodesia illegal for British citizens. The United Nations joined the trade embargo. In the late 1970s, a guerrilla movement of black Rhodesians fought to overthrow the white-dominated Rhodesian government.

Angola and Mozambique fought for independence. In the large Portuguese territories of Angola and Mozambique, there was no legal race discrimination. Full rights of Portuguese citizenship went to Africans who became educated and "civilized" according to Portuguese standards. But few Africans had the opportunity to reach this status.

In the early 1960s, rebellions began in Angola and Mozambique, and the demands for freedom grew. In 1975, a left-wing revolution gave Portugal a new government. Mozambique and Angola then received their independence.

SECTION REVIEW 2

p. 656 **1.** How did tribal rivalries cause problems for the newly independent African states?

p. 657 **2.** What kind of government did the newly independent black African countries have? What problems were involved?

p. 657 **3.** List five economic or social problems that faced the new states.

p. 660 **4.** What conditions in South Africa and Rhodesia might cause serious problems in the future?

3 Latin America faced many challenges

Although most of Latin America became independent in the early 19th century, nation-building was slow and difficult. Like Africa and Asia, Latin America was one of the great economically underdeveloped regions of the world. After World War II, its history was a series of economic crises, political rebellions, and social upheavals.

Economic problems troubled many countries. Since colonial times, Latin America had had great extremes of wealth. At the top of society was a small, very wealthy landowning class. Almost everyone else was without land or property and very poor. They worked on the estates of the rich. Throughout the 19th and early 20th centuries, the economic condition, educational opportunities, and health of most of these people did not improve. Most never learned to read and write. Most suffered from disease and not having enough to eat.

One reason for the poverty was that Latin ans. 1
America did not develop strong economies. Few Latin American countries became industrialized. Most were agricultural economies based on the export of one major product. Others relied on the mining of one mineral resource.

In Colombia, coffee was the chief export crop. In Cuba it was sugar, in Nicaragua bananas, in Uruguay wool, in Chile copper, in Bolivia tin, and in Venezuela oil. The problem with having only one main product to export is that prices often go up and down without warning. Also, bad weather could ruin a crop and thus destroy the major national source of income for a year; minerals are eventually used up. Without a reliable source of foreign income, most Latin

American governments could not afford to modernize farming methods or develop industry that would provide new income and jobs for their people. Moreover, most Latin American natural resources were developed by United States companies. Though Latin Americans needed foreign capital, they deeply resented foreign control over their economies.

ans. 2 From the early days of independence, landowners had held political control in Latin America. They were supported by the Roman Catholic Church and by the military. There were frequent "revolutions" and changes in government as the wealthy classes fought among themselves. However, these revolutions did not really change the lives of most people. They remained poor.

A revolution changed Mexico. In the 20th century, there began to be exceptions to this rule. The first was the Mexican Revolution, which started in 1911. In this long, bitter fight, the poor landless people, led by the small middle class, overthrew the rich landholders.

The political party of the revolution, known as the PRI, has held power since that time. Its most radical phase occurred during the 1930s when, for example, oil companies owned by the United States were taken over by the PRI government. Since then, however, the party has generally followed a moderate policy of social and economic reform to improve the lives of the Mexican people.

ans. 3 The greatest advance in the Mexican people's standard of living was made after World War II. From 1946 to 1958, about 2.5 million acres (1 million square hectares) of new land were irrigated for farming. Using the new farmland and advanced technology, Mexico for the first time produced enough crops to feed its people. Up to then, it had had to import basic foods. Improvements in farming also allowed Mexico to export large quantities of sugar, beef, and coffee. Thus, Mexico earned more money to develop its own economy. In the mid-1950s, it began a program of industrial development. Within ten years, Mexico produced its own iron, steel, chemicals, and electrical goods. Government development of a large tourist industry also strengthened the economy.

At the same time, the government improved social conditions. Public health programs cut down the spread of disease. Low-cost housing gave homes to thousands of new city dwellers. Sanitation facilities provided pure drinking water to villages that had never had it before. And the government built new schools across the country.

By the mid-1970s, Mexico had the fastest growing economy in the Americas. More than a fourth of the Mexican people were middle class. In the late 1970s huge oil reserves were found in Mexico. Mexico also had one of the most stable governments in all of Latin America.

But many Mexicans were still poor. Unemployment was very high, and the population was growing very fast. Extending the benefits of economic and social progress to all its citizens remained Mexico's greatest problem.

Castro led a revolution in Cuba. Another country where revolution brought real change was Cuba. It was transformed from a corrupt dictatorship under Fulgencio Batista [bä tēs′tä] to a communist dictatorship led by Fidel Castro. ans. 4

After the revolution in 1959, Castro promised free elections, democratic government, and far-reaching social and economic reforms. At first, Castro had the support of the United States. However, he lost this support when free elec-

A popular hero of the early years of the Mexican Revolution was Emiliano Zapata. He led peasants in a fight against the rich landowners. Jose Clemente Orozco's painting "Zapatistas" *(right)* pictures the farmers' army. Land reforms were one of the changes the Mexican Revolution brought about.

Mexico's National Agricultural Institute is one of the largest in Central and South America. Here researchers, students, and farmers work to improve farming methods.

Collection, The Museum of Modern Art, New York

Soviet Premier Nikita Khrushchev and Cuban Premier Fidel Castro greet each other.

tions were not held, United States properties were taken over without payment, criticism was not allowed, and people opposing Castro were executed or jailed. Thousands of refugees fled to the United States and Latin American countries. Some of these refugees, with the help of the United States government, organized armed groups to invade Cuba and remove Castro from power. Their 1961 attempt at the Bay of Pigs in Cuba failed miserably. The invasion strained relations between the United States and Cuba even more.

Shortly afterward, Castro said that Cuba was a socialist state and his government a communist one. He then got economic aid from the Soviet Union. In 1962, the Cuban missile crisis occurred. Although the crisis passed, the United States continued to view Castro's government with suspicion.

Castro supported guerrilla and terrorist groups in other Latin American countries. These groups were a serious threat to many governments and to United States business interests in those countries. As a result, most Latin American countries joined the United States in a diplomatic and trade embargo against Cuba.

Economic conditions in Cuba steadily worsened in the late 1960s. However, Cuba made important social gains. Health and education improved. Land was distributed more equally between the rich and poor. And the export of sugar cane increased. By the mid-1970s, Cuba's relations with the United States and the countries of Latin America also improved.

Other Latin American governments sought economic independence. Unlike Cuba and Mexico, other Latin American countries did not go through radical revolutions. But there were many changes in government in the postwar era. Most resulted in military dictatorships.

In 1963, for example, a left-wing government took over in Peru. In 1965, a right-wing military government came to power in Brazil. In 1970, Chile had the unique experience of being the first country ever to elect a Marxist president, Salvador Allende [säl bä ᴛʜôr′ ä yān′dā]. In 1973, the situation reversed when a right-wing military government took power in a coup in which Allende and many others were killed.

What most of these governments had in common was a strong desire for economic development. In some cases, such as Brazil and Peru, they were successful.

Most of these governments were also strongly nationalistic. Almost all of them strongly resented economic domination by the United States.
ans. 5 In Chile, Allende nationalized the huge copper-mining industry, throwing out the United States companies that owned the mines and factories. Allende said this would give Chile its "economic independence." Peru, Venezuela, and Bolivia also took over American-owned companies in the 1960s and 1970s.

The United States supported the Latin American goal of economic development. In the early 1960s, it began a major program of economic aid. However, the United States deeply resented hostile actions such as the nationalization of American-owned companies. In the late 1960s and early 1970s, relations between the United States and Latin America were friendly but distant. A major step toward improving relations came in 1978, when the United States and Panama signed a treaty to turn over to Panama control of the Panama Canal.

SECTION REVIEW 3

1. Why didn't most Latin American countries produce great wealth from their natural resources and agriculture? p. 661

2. What groups controlled Latin American governments? Why did the frequent revolutions not bring about lasting changes? p. 662

3. Name three situations that were improved in Mexico after the 1911 revolution. p. 662

4. What kind of government did Castro set up in Cuba? How has his government helped Cuba? Hurt Cuba? p. 662

5. What countries nationalized United States industries? How did this affect relations between Latin America and the United States? p. 665

Troops patrol the streets of Santiago, Chile, during the strikes and rioting of 1972.

CHAPTER REVIEW 35

SECTION SUMMARIES

1. Nationalism transformed the Middle East. The most important change in the Middle East after World War I was the rise of nationalist movements among non-Arab Muslims, Arab Muslims, and Jewish Zionists. After World War II, Western colonial control collapsed. Newly independent Arab Muslim states clashed with the new Jewish state of Israel. Rivalry between the United States and the Soviet Union for influence in the Middle East made the Arab-Israeli conflict even more dangerous.

2. Black Africa changed rapidly. After World War II, a tide of anticolonial revolutions spread through Africa. Unfortunately, independence did not solve old problems. The national unity of many new African states was threatened by tribal rivalries, and one-party rule often developed. South Africa and Rhodesia, where white minority governments ruled a black majority, remained potentially explosive areas.

3. Latin America faced many challenges. Latin America, despite frequent changes in governments, was economically underdeveloped. This began to change in the 20th century. Mexico had a revolution and made great economic progress, especially after World War II. Cuba, after a communist revolution, also made gains. In the 1970s, other Latin American countries achieved better standards of living for their peoples. Nationalistic movements and communist ideas kept relations between the United States and Latin America cool.

WHO? WHAT? WHEN? WHERE?

1. Define these terms:

apartheid p. 660
embargo p. 661
nationalization of industry p. 665

2. Match the time period with the events listed below:

a. before 1950
b. 1951–1955
c. 1956–1960
d. 1961–1965
e. 1966–1970
f. after 1970

Civil war began in Nigeria. e
The Mexican revolution began. a
Allende became president of Chile. e
The Aswan High Dam was finished. e
Nkrumah was overthrown. e
Castro took over Cuba. c
Mozambique and Angola became independent. f
Mobutu restored order in Zaïre. d
Rhodesia declared itself a republic. e
The Suez Canal was reopened. f
Nasser became president of Egypt. b

3. Identify these leaders by nationality and describe when and how each came to power:

Joseph Mobutu p. 656
Patrice Lumumba p. 656
Fidel Castro p. 663
Gamal Abdel Nasser p. 653
ibn-Saud p. 651
Salvador Allende p. 664
Anwar Sadat p. 654
Kwame Nkrumah p. 657
Reza Shah Pahlavi p. 651

● QUESTIONS FOR CRITICAL THINKING

1. What are the major problems that the countries of black Africa must solve?
2. Why is the Middle East of such importance to the rest of the world?
3. What conditions are necessary for successful democratic government?

● QUESTIONS FOR CRITICAL THINKING
1. Some possible answers: tribal rivalries, poverty, illiteracy.
2. primarily because of its rich oil reserves
3. educated citizens, a stable middle class and experience in self-rule

CHAPTER TEST 35

4. What attraction does communism have for underdeveloped countries?
5. In what ways were the ideas of nationalism and democracy taught by the European powers to their colonies in the Middle East and Africa?

ACTIVITIES

1. Divide the class into committees. Then make lists of reforms that might be needed in a newly independent country. Now compare the list of each committee with those made by the others. Make one list of reforms that the whole class agrees are needed.
2. Use reference books to make charts or maps showing the natural resources of the newly independent African nations, nations of the Middle East, and Latin American nations. *Aldine's University Atlas* (Scott, Foresman) and *Goode's World Atlas* (Rand McNally) are both good sources for this information. It would be useful to find information for today and for twenty years ago. How has the knowledge of a region's resources changed?
3. Using the information from Activity 2, hold a class discussion on the potential for successful development of the countries involved. Some of the questions you might try to answer are these: Where are natural resources located in relation to each other? In relation to population centers? How does the transportation system affect a country's chances of becoming industrialized? What places have iron ore but lack coal? Do political boundaries separate sources of natural resources? How do these factors affect a country's chances of becoming industrialized?

● 4. Communism gives an explanation of the situation they are in and calls for land reforms and social reforms.
5. (From chapter intro.) Western-type schools in the colonies taught about the political and social ideals of the west.

SECTION 1

1. Which of the following is not true of Iran and Egypt? a. both are Arab, b. both are Muslim, c. both are in the Middle East
2. In which of these countries was there once a large European population? a. Saudi Arabia, b. Syria, c. Algeria
3. True or false: American-Egyptian relations became strong when the United States financed the Aswan High Dam.
4. Nationalists from which area demanded that Israel allow them to return to their lands? a. Syria, b. Jordan, c. Palestine

SECTION 2

5. Nationalism was threatened in Africa by peoples' loyalties to their: a. village, b. family, c. tribe
6. True or false: The Nigerian civil war gave Biafra independence.
7. Rhodesia and South Africa were controlled by their: a. white majority, b. black majority, c. white minority
8. True or false: In many countries of black Africa, a strong man with popular appeal became the actual ruler.

SECTION 3

9. True or false: The main cause of slow economic development in Latin America was its lack of natural resources.
10. The first Latin American country to elect a Marxist president was: a. Cuba, b. Brazil, c. Chile
11. The Bay of Pigs invasion and Cuban missile crisis involved Cuba and: a. Brazil, b. the United States, c. Peru
12. True or false: The Mexican revolution of 1911 led to great economic and social reforms there.

CHAPTER 36 1945–

The Changing World

The American architect R. Buckminster Fuller studied modern materials and design in order to make strong, economic structures. The geodesic [jē ə des′ik] dome is one of his most accepted works. This one is the American Pavillion at the Montreal World Fair (Expo '67).

"The Italian navigator has reached the New World," telephoned Arthur H. Compton, a scientist in Chicago, to a fellow worker in Boston one day in December, 1942.

"And how did he find the natives?"

"Very friendly," answered Compton.

This conversation referred, not to Columbus, but to an Italian scientist who had just completed one of the most important experiments in modern history.

In October, 1942, physicists at the University of Chicago went to work in a squash court under the stands of the university stadium. They built a sphere made of wood and graphite bricks in which pieces of uranium were placed. When ● finished, the sphere was a small atomic pile about 26 feet (about 7.8 meters) wide.

On December 2, a small group of scientists gathered around the pile to watch an experiment. Enrico Fermi, the "Italian navigator," was in charge of the project. He asked a fellow physicist to pull a cadmium rod a few inches out of the pile. As he did this, the reaction in the pile was measured. A mechanical pen traced a rising line on a graph. Then, it leveled off and stopped. For several hours, the rod was pulled out inch by inch. Each time, the line on the graph rose and stopped. At 3:20 in the afternoon, the rod was pulled out past a critical point and the pen climbed steadily *without leveling off.* Fermi and his fellow scientist had produced the first controlled atomic chain reaction—a series of splittings in uranium atoms that changed matter into energy. Later in the afternoon, the cadmium rod was pushed back into the pile. The reaction stopped. The success of the ex-
ans. 2 periment meant that for the first time the energy of atoms could be harnessed. Enrico Fermi had indeed reached a "New World"—the Atomic Age. This dramatic accomplishment was only one of many revolutionary changes in the 20th century. In this chapter, you will see how:

1. Science and technology changed the 20th-century world.

2. The arts reflected the changing world.

3. The gap between rich countries and poor countries widened.

4. The growth of cities created problems.

● If needed, perhaps a science teacher could speak to the class and explain this material.

1 Science and technology changed the 20th-century world

One reason for the rapid advance of science and ans. 1
technology in the 20th century was team research. In the past, scientists had worked alone or in small groups. This changed in the 20th century, when governments and private industries began to set up large research and development centers. There many hundreds of scientists worked together on a certain project and pooled their knowledge.

Another reason for the rapid pace was the great numbers of scientists involved. About 90 percent of all scientists ever born were living in the 1960s and 1970s.

New theories revolutionized physics. In 1900, people commonly believed that scientists had discovered all the important natural laws that governed the universe. But the world was really just at the beginning of a whole new era of discovery.

In 1905, a young German, Albert Einstein, published some scientific papers of great significance. In one paper, Einstein related matter to energy in a famous formula: $E = mc^2$ (energy equals mass times the velocity of light squared). This means that mass and energy are equivalent, and a small amount of matter can be transformed into a huge amount of energy. In another paper, Einstein outlined his Special Theory of Relativity. He stated that time and space, even gravity and motion, are dependent on or relative to the observer. He challenged the world to think in terms of a new, fourth, dimension—time—and no longer be limited to length, breadth, and thickness.

Meanwhile, other scientists were exploring the structure and behavior of atoms. In the

1930s, scientists succeeded in splitting the uranium atom. They predicted that the process could release large amounts of energy if properly controlled. Building on the discoveries of these scientists and on Einstein's formula of 1905, Fermi's international team of scientists was able to build a nuclear reactor.

ans. 2 The earliest use of nuclear energy was for weapons in World War II. Later, scientists found other important uses for atomic energy in such fields as medicine, agriculture, and space travel. Perhaps the most promising use of atomic energy was in generating electrical power.

Technology advanced rapidly. When the findings of laboratory scientists became available, technicians put them to work in the everyday world. Manufacturers adapted the internal combustion and diesel engines to ships, land transportation, and airplanes.

By mid-century, auto manufacturers in the United States and Western Europe were producing more than nine million automobiles each year. The auto industry had become the largest single employer in the United States economy. The car made it possible for ordinary people to travel for pleasure and employment. It helped people get to know places other than their own and broadened their perspective.

Twenty-five years after the Wright brothers made their first airplane flight in 1903, commercial aviation became a reality. World War II stimulated the development of more powerful engines, more lasting metals, and better instrumentation and design. In the 1960s, jet engines began to replace piston engines. By the 1970s, jet planes flying at more than 600 miles (960 kilometers) per hour were common.

If distance in the jet age was measured in hours, communication was reduced to a matter of seconds. The telephone and radio came into general use in the 1920s and 1930s. They made almost immediate communication possible between persons on opposite sides of the earth.

Air conditioning cooled and cleaned the air and helped people control the climate at home, at work, in school, in travel. A revolution in crop production was brought about through plant breeding, new forms of fertilizers, and insecticides. The productivity that resulted on American farms in the postwar period was so great that 5 percent of the population could raise enough food to feed the other 95 percent and still have a sizable amount left over. ●

Artificial materials called *synthetics* created an important industry. Bakelite, a heat-resistant plastic, and rayon, an artificial fiber, were produced commercially early in the century. Plastics became valuable in the manufacture of thousands of items.

Automation revolutionized business and industry. A basic development of the 20th century was automation—the use of machines ans. 3
to perform complex tasks with little human guidance. Automation became as important to the 20th century as mechanization was to the 19th century.

In the automobile industry, automated systems were used to put engine parts together. Other large industries, too, found it profitable to use such systems that did away with physical labor and tedious tasks.

By mid-century, automation took many forms. The most important perhaps was the computer, which was developed in World War II and came into widespread use in the 1950s and 1960s. Computers were able to store and produce information for every kind of business. They aided research. They made surveys. They

● The effects of the increased productivity of farms in the U.S. should be discussed.

Can Time Stand Still?

There are many stories and movies about scientists who invent machines that can take people back in time. This kind of science fiction has been very popular in the 20th century. It is an age when science has become so advanced that we can explore the mysteries of outer space, put people on the moon, and land instruments on Venus. However, one of the greatest mysteries of our era may be right here on Earth.

In the mid-1960s, a hunter in the southern Philippine Islands was tracking through dense rain forest when suddenly he came upon three men digging for roots with sticks. They were naked except for a little clothing made of leaves. Terrified at the sight of the hunter, they began to run away. But they stopped when he called to them in a friendly voice.

The hunter learned that these men were members of a small group of twenty-five people, including twelve adults and thirteen children. They called themselves the Tasaday [tä′sä dī′]. They lived in three caves, completely surrounded by jungle. The caves could not be seen from the sky or even from a few yards away.

One good book on the Tasaday is *Survivors of The Stone Age,* by Rebecca Marcus (Hastings House: 1975).

The Tasaday knew nothing about the world outside their small part of the forest. The only tool they had was a stone scraper. (Similar ones were the first tools used by humans some 50 thousand years ago.) They did not know how to hunt or plant crops. For food, they dug up wild yams with sticks, gathered wild berries and bananas, and caught small fish, crabs, and frogs. They knew how to use fire and cook food. But they did not have pottery or any way to carry water.

The hunter (and the anthropologists who later visited the Tasaday) learned that they are a gentle, happy people. Their spoken language—they have no writing—seems to have no words for "enemy," "war," or "murder." There is no way even of saying "bad." They have no remembrances of their own history and have no gods. Their greatest fear—understandable in a jungle environment—is of snakes.

Who are these people? How have they survived for so long without being discovered? Why have they not changed their way of life? How do they manage to be so tender and sharing with each other and to live so happily together?

Anthropologists have not yet found answers to these questions. The evidence seems to be that the Tasaday are a genuine stone-age people who have survived into the 20th century with their traditional way of life unchanged. If this is true, then for them, time actually did stand still for 50 thousand years.

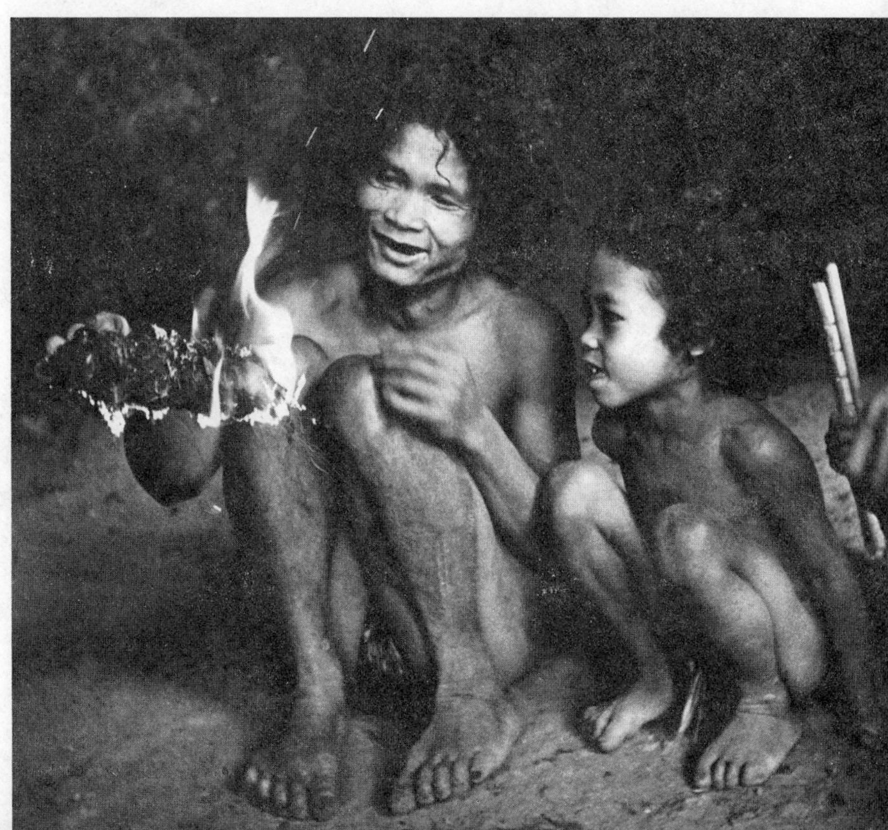

kept inventories and figured payrolls. They handled airline reservations, translated languages, planned school programs for teachers and students, and did thousands of other jobs. Without the calculation capacity of computers, exploration of outer space would have been impossible.

ans. 4 **The "Space Age" began.** The Space Age began in 1957 with the launching of the Soviet Union's *Sputnik*, the first artificial earth satellite. Within months, the United States also sent its first satellite aloft. In the 1960s, both the United States and the Soviet Union rocketed people into space and successfully brought them back. They placed smaller satellites into orbit to send back scientific, weather, and military information to Earth by means of radio and television. They launched satellites to Venus and Mars, and the Russians landed instruments on Venus.

To many, the most dramatic achievement came with the United States Apollo program to land people on the moon. In July, 1969, Neil Armstrong became the first human ever to set foot on the moon.

SECTION REVIEW 1

1. What were two reasons for the great increase in p. 669
scientific discoveries in the 20th century?

2. What new source of energy was developed in p. 669
1942? Name three uses for this new energy. 670

3. What is automation? Give two specific examples p. 670
of ways it has been used.

4. Describe the progress that has been made in the p. 672
exploration of space.

When Orville Wright flew the first motor-driven airplane at Kittyhawk, North Carolina, in 1903, he began a new age. By 1970, the number of people in the world who had flown in one year was well over 300 million.

2 The arts reflected the changing world

ans. 1 Advances in science and technology had a tremendous effect on the arts. Plastics, computers, electronics, acrylic paints—these and more gave new materials to artists, sculptors, and musicians. Photography and cinematography (movie making) became new art forms. Improvements in printing and television gave the communications arts immediate impact on millions of lives. The arts of the years after 1945 were alive with experimentation in new forms.

Artists used "mixed media." Artists of the postwar years made art objects out of many materials. No longer was the word *artist* synonymous with *painter.* Collages, mobiles, and constructions of all kinds were the new works of art. These works caused much controversy. Many people felt that the artists were not "serious." But mid-20th-century artists were as serious about learning how to use the new materials and techniques as artists of the Renaissance had been in learning perspective and the characteristics of oil paints.

The subject matter of contemporary art was immensely varied. Many artists were interested in the textures, shapes, colors, and movement of the materials they worked with. Their works were abstract. Others worked with scraps torn from newspapers, found objects, letters, and other pieces of *realia,* or real objects. When they combined these things, the work had a meaning beyond its composition. Still other artists

Air technology reached new heights in the 1970s. The British supersonic transport Concorde could fly from New York to London in three hours.

With her camera, Dorothea Lange composed pictures as beautiful and powerful as any painter with a brush. *Above:* "Hoe Culture, Eutah, Alabama." Although Willem De Kooning titled the painting *left* "Woman VI," it is a painting of paint, not of a woman. *Below* is Andy Warhol's "Campbell's Soup." He was fascinated by the symbols of modern culture. This can is 3 feet (90 centimeters) high.

Collection, The Museum of Modern Art, New York

Mirrors, lenses, and transparent plastics give Karl Gerstner's "Lens Picture," *above,* an optical effect of constant movement and change. Nicholas Shoffer's construction "Lux 2," *above right,* is electrically powered to move in sequence with colored lights. Alexander Calder's "Red Petals," *opposite,* is a 9-foot (27 meters) high mobile. Air currents keep its petals gently swinging. Roy Lichtenstein took the tough crude world of the comic strip and blew it up to outsize proportions. "Torpedo Los," *below,* is a serious painting.

worked with images. Automobiles, telephones, sandwiches, and soup cans turned up in their pictures.

The camera became the recorder of events. Artists did not need to draw things as they were because the camera could always show that. Photographers, too, experimented with their media. Their lenses magnified, shrank, or distorted the pictures they took. United States photographers of the Depression years, notably Dorothea Lange, had proved that the camera could be used to evoke emotions. With the advance of motion pictures, cinematographers, too, showed that movie making was an art.

Electronics revolutionized the music world. Electronic music began with the invention of electric organs and organlike instruments in the 1920s and 1930s. These instruments made possible a whole range of sounds. With the invention of the tape recorder, the field really took off.

ans. 2 Two French composers, Pierre Schaeffer and Pierre Henry, began to produce tape collages in 1948. Their "concrete music," as they called it, was composed of sound effects, musical fragments, and environmental noises of all kinds. With the tape recorder, not only could sounds of all kinds be brought together, but new sounds could be created by adjusting the speed or by playing the tape backwards.

Composers in Europe and the United States produced many tape compositions in the 1950s and 1960s. Then, in the 1970s, an invention that linked the tape recorder with the electric organ gave composers another boost. This invention, the *synthesizer,* made electronic composing much faster. The composer no longer had to record individual fragments of tape, back them up, and re-record on a different track, back up and record again to get the desired effect. The synthesizer, first developed by scientists at the RCA laboratories in Princeton, New Jersey, could be played like an organ. When Walter Carlos recorded his arrangement of some of 18th-century Johann Sebastian Bach's works on a Moog [mōg] Synthesizer, the result was a very popular album, *Switched-on Bach.*

In the United States, ethnic writers gained audiences as people came to appreciate the richness of a multi-ethnic society. As racial barriers gradually broke down, important black writers emerged. *Below left:* playwright Lorraine Hansberry; *center:* poet Gwendolyn Brooks; *right:* novelist James Baldwin.

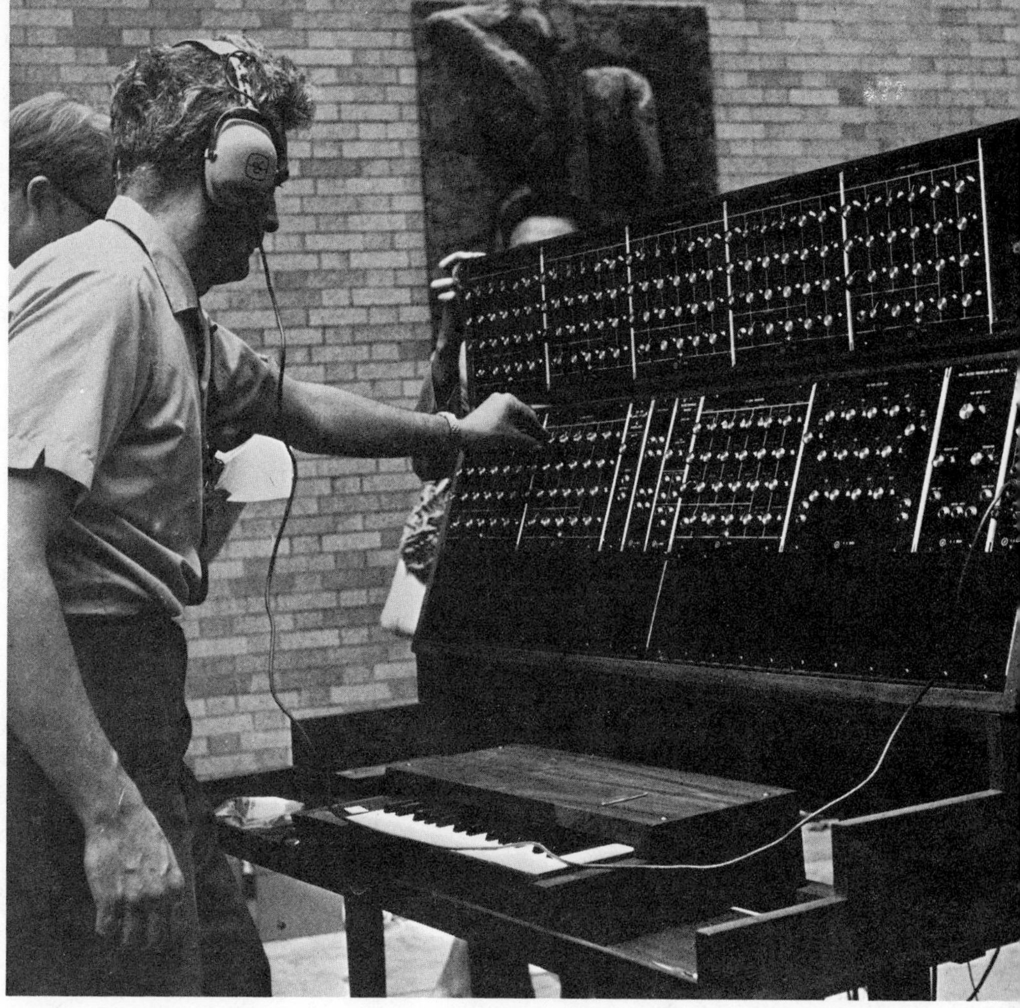

Robert Moog, who designed the best known of the electronic musical synthesizers, makes a final adjustment on his Moog Synthesizer before a jazz concert at New York's Museum of Modern Art in 1969.

Electronic developments were also responsible for bringing music to a mass audience. Radio, television, and hi-fidelity components made music instantly available to huge numbers of
ans. 3 people. Jazz and the blues, two forms developed by black musicians in the United States in the early part of the century, gained worldwide audiences in the years following the war. In the 1950s and 1960s, rock music, which also originated in the United States, gained international fame with performances by the British group, the Beatles. As the Beatles traveled, they in turn picked up the music of others. Through
● their albums, the musical sounds of India were played on home stereo sets as far away as Brazil or New Zealand.

● This interest in the music of India was part of the Beatles' quest for self-awareness. It led them and many others in the 1960s and 1970s to examine oriental philosophies and religions.

In the 1970s, another popular United States ans. 3
form, the country-and-western song, gained popularity abroad. Musicians in the Soviet Union, who were searching for the folk tunes of their ancestors, recognized the same simplicity in these melodies, lyrics, and arrangements.

SECTION REVIEW 2

1. Name three or four new materials available to p. 673
artists in the postwar years. Give an example of how a new material produced a new art form.

2. How can a tape recorder be a musical instru- p. 676
ment? Why was its invention important to the development of music in the years after World War II?

3. Name three forms of popular music that began p. 677
in the United States and gained worldwide appeal.

3 The gap between rich countries and poor countries widened

The continuing advance of science and technology brought about dramatic changes in the industrialized countries of the world. In the poor or developing countries, two other social revolutions, that of exploding populations and that of rising expectations, had an even greater effect. A result of these revolutions was that the poor countries became poorer, the rich countries richer.

The industrialized countries had stable governments and economies. Most of the
ans. 1 industrialized or technologically advanced countries of the world were located north of the equator. The United States, Canada, the countries of Europe, the Soviet Union, and Japan were counted among them. Australia, New Zealand, and South Africa were also considered industrialized. These countries were generally prosperous. Some were highly industrialized. Japan, the Soviet Union, the United States, and West Germany, for example, had many kinds of heavy industry. Other countries, such as Denmark, New Zealand, and Australia, were wealthy because of highly developed agriculture.

These countries did not always share the same political ideals. Their systems of government varied widely. Most of them, however, had stable governments that were acceptable to their citizens.

ans. 1 Generally, people in these countries also had adequate food and medical care and lived in comfortable homes. But there was still a minority in each country, and black majorities in South Africa and Rhodesia, that were poor, ill-fed, and ill-housed. Yet their standard of living was generally higher than that of the poor, ill-fed, and ill-housed in the other countries of Africa and in Asia and Latin America.

● Give students an opportunity to ask questions concerning this paragraph.

Technology transformed the economies of industrialized countries. One important type of advanced technology that came to be widely used was the system of scientific management, which organized labor efficiently so no time or action was wasted. It led to greater profits for employers and an increase in wages for workers. It also brought about a reduction in the cost of manufactured goods.

For example, the use of scientific manage- ans. 2
ment helped make automobiles available at relatively low cost. It also lowered the cost of ●
other factory-produced items, particularly household appliances. More and more ordinary people were able to buy them. The development of a mass market for consumer products greatly increased sales and profits for companies making such products. Increases in profits made it possible to increase wages in such industries. Increases in wages raised the standard of living for thousands of workers and, in turn, made it possible for them to buy such consumer goods. This expansion in production and consumption helped strengthen the economy of industrialized countries.

Technology transformed society. The work force gained greater economic security as wages increased. Workers made up the steadily growing middle class, which became an important market for business and industry. In the United States, Britain, France, and West Germany, the number of immensely wealthy people increased but at a much lower rate than the middle class. The proportion of poor dropped but did not disappear.

Dr. Jonas Salk put an end to one major world health problem when he developed a vaccine for polio.

Because of better health practices, fewer persons in the developed countries died in infancy or childhood. Moreover, adults lived longer than ever before.

None of the transformations caused by technology came easily. Everywhere in the rich countries deeply rooted social and political institutions had been and were being challenged. As society felt the impact of technology, new social issues arose. All industrial countries had to face problems such as the economic security of workers and the role of government in education.

Great differences characterized the poor
ans. 3 **countries.** Three quarters of the people of the world lived in countries that were poor. These countries were located in Asia, Africa, and Latin America. By and large, in these countries the per person income averaged less than 300 dollars a year. This low income provided such a limited tax base that there was little money available for school development, road building, public health services, and other community needs.

There were great differences among these countries in culture, religion, political systems, and population. Their forms of government varied from communist dictatorship to Western-style democracy. Their populations ranged from a half million people in Botswana to about 800 million people in China. Their religions included Buddhism, Islam, Hinduism, Confucianism, Taoism, Shintoism, and, to a much lesser degree, Christianity.

Poor countries shared some characteristics. Most of these countries, of course, had been affected to some extent by science and technology. They had some commercial farmers, some skilled industrial workers, and some highly efficient business executives.

However, these groups made up a very small
part of the population. In most of the poor coun- ans. 4
tries, farming had for centuries been the main means of earning a living. But the simple, traditional methods farmers used produced only enough food to feed their families—if no natural disaster occurred. There was little, if anything, left over to sell in the marketplace. In addition, many farmers had only small plots of land to till. Most had no technical training and no knowledge of market demand and business techniques. They were not accustomed to thinking in terms of profits and losses, of shifting from

one crop to another, or of trying out risky new methods.

Many of the poor countries were handicapped by a lack of natural resources. They did not have coal, iron, manganese, tin, and other raw materials basic to modern industry. Countries that were rich in natural resources, such as the oil-producing nations, often did not have the skills and money to develop them. They often had to rely on foreign companies to help develop their resources.

In many poor countries, too, there was a strong resistance to change. The upper classes measured social status in terms of land ownership, government position, or the professions. The business manager, engineer, mechanic, or farming specialist was given a much lower social status. One result was that in the 1960s, only 4 percent of the many students from poor countries studying abroad were interested in agriculture, the basic problem of their homelands.

No two nations were poor for quite the same reasons. The gap between the rich countries and the poor countries was a vast gulf not only in economic development but also in motives, attitudes, and social institutions.

Hunger became the chief problem. The most critical problem facing all poor countries was the threat of hunger. Every day during the 1970s, about 10,000 persons died as a result of malnutrition. Of every twenty children born in these countries, ten died before the age of one from a poor diet. Probably many more suffered permanent physical or mental retardation.

This terrible situation was the result of the population growing faster than food production. The gain in world population between 1900 and 1965 was greater than the total world population in 1900. In the late 1960s and early 1970s, food supply increased about 1 percent each year. But the world population increased by 2 percent.

The food-supply problem in South Asia and parts of Africa and Latin America was especially desperate. When drought struck large areas along the southern edge of the Sahara in the mid-1970s, hundreds of thousands of Africans died for lack of food.

Solving the population problem was not easy. To farm families in poor countries, children represented status. They were also sources of labor. Moreover, in countries where there was no such thing as social security, children were relied on to support their elderly parents. The same had been generally true in the rich, industrialized countries. There a voluntary drop in birth rates came only *after* a large degree of economic improvement was reached and people no longer felt a need to have large families.

One answer to the population explosion was ans. 4
family planning. Another was increasing food production. As most of the world's fertile land was already in use, the best way to do this was through the increased use of fertilizer. But that, too, presented some difficulties. The production of fertilizer depended upon having investment capital to develop mines, plants, and production facilities. Poor countries did not have the capital.

The revolution of rising expectations began. In the late 19th century during the height of imperialism, Western countries dominated most of Asia, Africa, and the Middle East. Even in politically independent Latin America, Western nations exercised control over the economy.

These regions were economically exploited for the benefit of the imperial powers. But with imperialism also came the first industrial capital to these areas. The Western powers built roads, railroads, docks, warehouses, and mines. These mainly benefited the economy of the Western ruling country, not that of the colony, because their purpose was to help get out raw material. Malaya supplied rubber to Western countries, Rhodesia copper, Sri Lanka tea, and Arabia oil. The same one-sided growth was true of Latin America.

Imperialism had another, very different, effect as well. Young people from Asia, Africa, and the Middle East who studied in England, France, Holland, and the United States discovered Western philosophies. They were attracted to the ideas of democracy, equality, and liberty, as well as socialism and communism. These young intellectuals included Ho Chi Minh of Vietnam, Jawaharlal Nehru of India, Sukarno of Indonesia, Chou En-lai of China, Ahmed Ben Bella of Algeria, and Kwame Nkrumah of Ghana. They returned home, fired with a passion to preach the new ideas and to work for independence.

Once the era of imperialism had ended and these countries gained their independence, they tried to rid themselves of poverty. They wanted the wealth, health care, and education opportunities that people in rich countries had. Economic development became an important matter for every poor country.

The movement toward economic progress was bound to be slow. Europe had had great resources with which to start its industrialization. But it did not feel the benefits of industrialism for almost a hundred years. The poor countries wanted to achieve their goals much faster. There was an awakening hope among the millions of people in these countries that social progress and a strengthened economy could and should be achieved in their own lifetimes. However difficult the task, the national leaders had to make every effort to raise living standards and thus satisfy the understandable expectations of the people.

The gap between rich and poor countries widened. In the 1960s and 1970s, the rich countries, for the most part, continued to grow rich at an increasingly faster pace. With the exception of the oil producers, the poor countries were barely holding their own. Some were even worse off than they had been ten years before.

It was as if both a rich woman and a poor woman were striving to advance economically. Because the poor woman had to spend nearly all she earned just to live, she had little left over to save and invest. Her condition improved slowly, if at all. The rich woman, on the other hand, spent only a small proportion of her income on daily necessities. She had a great amount left over for savings and, therefore, increased her total wealth easily. Her savings provided a growing fund for further investment. ans. 5 ●

By 1976, less than 30 percent of the world's population controlled 70 percent of its wealth. Average per capita national income in the United States grew from 2,559 dollars in 1960 to 5,523 dollars by 1976. In that same period, average per capita national income in the poor countries increased from 130 dollars to only 190 dollars. In 1976, some 900 million people lived on less than 75 dollars each per year.

Because the poor countries could not solve their problems by themselves, the rich countries had to come to their aid. They saw that it was in their own interest to do so. The United States provided the major share, although all rich countries made contributions. It was still not enough. In the mid-1970s, the poor countries became more vehement about the need for greater economic cooperation and assistance from rich countries.

● Have students show that they grasp this analogy by explaining it in terms of rich and poor nations.

Margaret Thatcher Leader of Britain's Conservative Party in the 1970s.

Francoise Giroud Publisher and France's Secretary of State for the Status of Women from 1974.

Women in Leadership
The 20th century saw a gradual breakdown in the centuries-old discrimination against women practised in many countries.

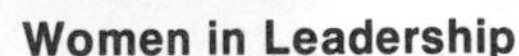

Indira Gandhi Prime Minister of India, 1966–1977

Marie Ngapeth United Nations delegate from the Cameroon, 1960s

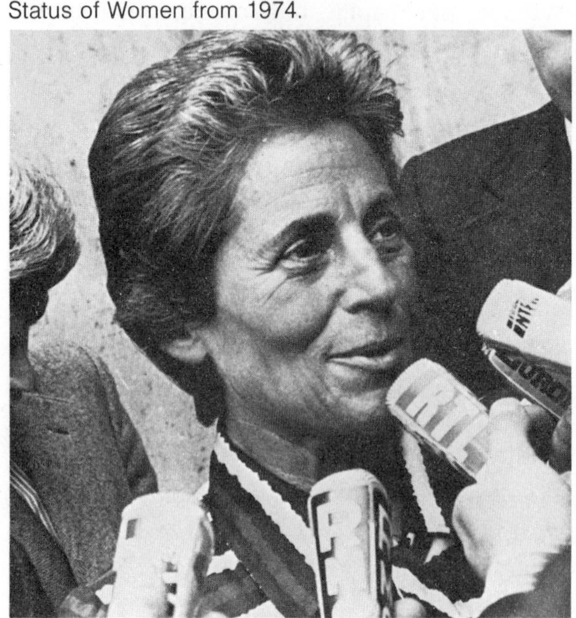

Golda Meir Prime Minister of Israel, 1969–1974

Eleanor Roosevelt United States delegate and chairman, UN Commission on Human Rights, 1946–1951

SECTION REVIEW 3

1. Which were the industrialized countries? What life-styles did their people share? p. 678

2. Give an example of how scientific management of a company or industry can raise the standard of living for the workers. p. 678

3. Which were the poor or developing countries? p. 679

4. What were some reasons that the poor countries could not solve the problem of feeding their populations? What two possible solutions are named in the chapter? p. 679 680

5. Why did the gap between rich and poor countries grow wider? p. 681

4 The growth of cities created problems

The rapidly increasing concentration of population in urban centers and the growth of metropolitan areas became worldwide in the 20th century. Millions of people faced urban challenges and opportunities.

The attraction of people to cities was nothing new in the 20th century. But the speed with which cities grew because of migration from rural areas was greater than at any other time, particularly in the United States and in countries of Western Europe. Each technological advance in agriculture in these countries after World War II made it possible for farmers to work more land ans. 1 with fewer hired hands. Each technological advance in industry tended to enlarge industrial complexes and to extend transportation and communication systems. These increases in urban areas created a demand for more workers than ever before.

Cities had various origins. Growing industrialization promoted urbanization. In 1900, only Britain had an urbanized society, with more than half its population in cities over 20,000. By mid-century, every industrialized country had become urbanized. Cities of more than one million people were rare in the 1800s. But in 1970, almost 100 cities had more than a million.

Many large cities also developed in countries that had no important industries. Argentina, Chile, and Venezuela had relatively little heavy industry. But a large proportion of the population in each of these countries was concentrated in cities. Cairo, Egypt; Calcutta, India; Mexico City, Mexico; and Teheran, Iran, grew to be among the most populated cities of the world, but not because of industrialization. In every case, these cities attracted thousands of villagers who hoped to find a better life there. Although often disappointed, they chose to remain in the cities because they had nothing better to go home to.

In the poor countries of the 20th century, cities had special problems. Most did not have the money to support large concentrations of people or to provide water, sanitation, electricity, housing, or schools. As a result, large slum areas sprang up. Between 1960 and 1975, the fastest-growing cities were in the poorer countries of the world. It was estimated that by the year 2000 there would be more than 25 cities with populations of more than 12.5 million. Of these, at least 18 would be in poor countries.

ans. 2 **The automobile reshaped the city.** With the widespread use of automobiles after World War II, suburban areas sprawled out from cities in all directions. Immense metropolitan areas developed in Britain, Holland, West Germany, and Belgium.

● Point out that many industries move out to suburbs because of cheaper land, taxes, and room to build large modern plants.

In the United States, areas between cities filled up with housing developments, suburbs, new towns, and new businesses. A continuous band of urban and suburban development stretched from New Hampshire to Virginia. Another band stretched from Los Angeles to San Diego in California. A band of this kind was called a megalopolis [meg′ə lop′ə lis].

It was predicted that 90 percent of all people in the United States would live on 10 percent of the land between 1990 and the year 2000. This possibility presented a host of new challenges to city planners and to local and state governments. Many local governments were not equipped to handle the flood tide of urban needs. They were forced to try to create more efficient governmental agencies. For such huge metropolitan regions, broad new approaches were required to deal with the use and development of natural resources, cultural activities, transportation, and government.

One challenge that needed urgent consideration was public transportation. By the late 1960s, the automobile was one of the most important means of transportation, particularly in the United States and Canada. Almost 65 percent of the urban workers regularly used automobiles in going to and from work. With greater use of automobiles, the number of passengers using public transportation dropped. And the drop in revenue resulted in reduced service. In Los Angeles, public transportation was almost completely replaced by private automobiles and an enormous system of freeways. The decline of public transportation made it difficult, and often impossible, for poor people in the inner cities to ● travel to jobs. This led to high unemployment in many American cities.

The rapid multiplication of automobiles also created problems of traffic congestion on city

With a population of over 12 million, Tokyo, Japan had more people than any other city in the world in the mid-1970s. Lying in the most industrialized area in the world and jammed with about 2½ million motor vehicles, the congested city also had one of the world's worst air pollution problems. To protect himself from the heavily polluted air, this motorcyclist wears a mask.

streets and on highways. In Britain, for example, the number of automobiles increased faster than highways could be improved to accommodate them.

ans. 2 **Pollution of air and water menaced health.** Automobiles became one of the main
ans. 3 causes of air pollution. But furnaces in apartment houses, office buildings, and industrial plants also discharged large amounts of pollutants. Automobile manufacturers sought new technology to eliminate pollution caused by cars. Cities began to regulate the use of heating fuels. But progress was slow. In the mid-1970s, air pollution in Tokyo, Japan, was so bad that people on the streets often wore face masks for protection.

Water pollution also became a major concern. City sewer systems in the United States dumped twice as much waste into major waterways and streams in the 1960s as the maximum considered allowable in 1955. One fourth of the waste was raw sewage. Cities needed to develop more effective ways than the conventional chemical methods used to treat water in order to assure a drinkable water supply in the future.

Technology, the product of human ingenuity, produced comforts of which people of earlier ages had never dreamed. But it also created serious new problems for people to solve.

SECTION REVIEW 4

1. What are some reasons people from farming areas have moved to cities? p. 683

2. List three major effects of automobiles on cities. p. 684 685

3. What were some of the problems that cities faced in the late 20th century? p. 685

CHAPTER REVIEW 36

SECTION SUMMARIES

1. Science and technology changed the 20th-century world. New theories and team research produced scientific advancement in the 20th century. Nuclear energy revolutionized both warfare and industry. Industry changed with the enormous production of automobiles and airplanes. In communications, agriculture, and synthetics, advances had an immediate impact on ordinary people. The Space Age began, and people reached out into the solar system for new information about Earth.

2. The arts reflected the changing world. Artists, like scientists, explored the new dimensions that new knowledge made possible. Works of art took many shapes. The subject matter varied from the material itself to the images of the culture. In music, electric organs, tape recorders, and synthesizers gave composers new instruments to work with. A mass audience all over the world listened to musical forms from the United States.

3. The gap between rich and poor countries widened. Science-based technology transformed the economies and societies in the rich countries. Scientific management and automation increased productivity. Millions of workers shared in this increase as wages climbed higher. It was not so for the poor and developing nations of Latin America, Asia, and Africa. Here low per-person income, lack of natural resources, rigid social structure, and years of imperial exploitation meant underdeveloped economies and severe hunger problems. Exposure to the developed nations of the West produced a revolution of rising expectations. Twentieth-century leaders worked for economic development, but it was clear that the poor nations could not achieve their goals without the aid of the rich.

4. The growth of cities created problems. In all countries, huge metropolitan areas were formed. The character and shape of cities gradually changed with the expansion of business and industry, with the use of the automobile, and with migrations to and from the inner cities. Problems of urban housing, employment, and health became critical for unskilled migrants from farms in the poor countries. Also, problems of pollution and mass transportation presented new challenges for all cities.

WHO? WHAT? WHEN? WHERE?

1. Find the years in which these events took place and list them in chronological order:

Scientists succeeded in splitting the uranium atom. 1942
"Concrete music" was first composed. 1948
The Wright brothers made their first flight. 1903
The Space Age began. 1957
Nearly 100 cities of the world had populations over one million. 1970
Albert Einstein published his Special Theory of Relativity. 1905
The Soviet Union launched the first artificial earth satellite. 1957
Rock music began to have a worldwide audience. 1950s, 60's
Neil Armstrong walked on the moon. 1969

2. Use each of these terms in a sentence to show you know what it means:

nuclear energy p. 670
automation p. 670
synthetics p. 670
mass audience p. 677
productivity p. 670
mixed media p. 673
synthesizer p. 676
blues p. 677
standard of living p. 678, 681
megalopolis p. 684

3. Explain the importance of these terms in relation to the growth of cities in the 20th century:

urbanization p. 684
water pollution p. 685
public transportation p. 684
air pollution p. 685
governmental agencies p. 684
slums p. 684

CHAPTER TEST 36

QUESTIONS FOR CRITICAL THINKING

1. How does the way you live today differ from the way that your great-grandparents lived in terms of health, education, consumer goods, and vocational opportunities? Is life better in every way now?
2. Why have the two social revolutions of exploding populations and of rising expectations affected the poor countries more deeply than the rich countries?
3. In what ways is it in the interests of the rich countries to come to the aid of the poor countries?
4. What do you think were the greatest technological or scientific advances of the 20th century? How did they change the lives of ordinary people?

ACTIVITIES

1. Form committees to investigate and report on ways in which the urban area nearest you is dealing with its problems.
2. Choose two of the following groups and prepare an oral report on how they help people in poor countries achieve a better way of life.

a. the World Bank
b. FAO
c. UNICEF
d. WHO
e. Foster Parents Plan
f. A.I.D.
g. CARE

3. Make a scrapbook of pictures of modern art or architecture. Find information about the artists or architects and the materials they used in their work.
4. Read Aldous Huxley's *Brave New World* or George Orwell's *Nineteen Eighty-Four.* Write a report on what the author feared about 20th-century life.
5. Use a tape recorder to make your own musical composition. Use some sounds other than those produced by standard orchestra or band instruments.

● QUESTIONS FOR CRITICAL THINKING
1. Answers will vary
2. Populations are increasing fastest in the poor countries, which cannot provide for their people who are demanding better ways of life.
3. Opinion. Two answers are: the possibility of wars which could involve the entire world and that we need their resources to keep our high standard of living.
4. Opinion. Answers will vary.

SECTION 1

1. True or false: There were more scientists alive in the 1960s and 1970s than had lived in the whole history of the world.
2. A nuclear reactor changes _matter_ into _energy_. ■
3. In postwar America, _b_ percent of the population were farmers: a. twenty-five, b. five, c. fifty

SECTION 2

4. A change in art forms after the war took place because of: a. disillusionment with two world wars, b. artists not being serious, c. new materials
5. True or false: People all over the world enjoyed listening to jazz, blues, rock, and country-and-western music.

SECTION 3

6. What fraction of the world's people live in poor countries? a. 1/2, b. 3/4, c. 2/3
7. Which grew faster in the 1960s and 1970s? a. food production, b. the world population
8. True or false: There are no industrialized countries in Africa.
9. True or false: None of the poor countries has a good supply of natural resources.

SECTION 4

10. A continuous band of urban and suburban development is called a _megalopolis_
11. Which of these was not directly caused by increased use of automobiles? a. air pollution, b. migration to cities, c. the decline of public transportation
12. Between 1960 and 1975, in which countries did cities grow faster? a. the rich countries, b. the poor countries

■ Answer is found in Ch. Introduction p. 669.

UNIT REVIEW 9 — TEST YOURSELF

1. Match the country with its identification.

H Mexico	B Hungary
J Ghana	F Vietnam
G Greece	D Bangladesh
I Angola	E Chile
C West Germany	A Japan

A. Regained control of Okinawa in 1972
B. In 1956, an armed rebellion here was put down by the U.S.S.R.
C. Recipient of a huge airlift by the U.S. in the late 1940s
D. Formerly East Pakistan
E. In 1973, the elected Marxist president was overthrown by a right-wing coup.
F. In the 1960s, United States troops fought here.
G. Benefited from the Truman Doctrine
H. Latin America's fastest growing economy
I. Became independent of Portugal in the mid-1970s
J. Kwame Nkrumah was president of this country.

2. True or false:

T A. Nationalism is a new factor that began in contemporary times.
T B. A few superpowers dominate the world today.
T C. Never before have there been so many people alive on Earth.
T D. There are fewer independent nations today than in earlier times.
T E. The gap between rich and poor nations is growing wider.
F F. The United States was the first nation to land a person on the moon.
T G. Today most of the world's fertile land is already being used.
T H. In the 1970s, nations in the Middle East became more important in world affairs.
F I. There are no areas of disagreement between China and the Soviet Union.

3. Match these people with their identifying statements:

Nikita Khrushchev G	Ho Chi Minh E
John F. Kennedy J	Mao Tse-tung K
Alexander Solzhenitsyn D	Anwar Sadat L
Willy Brandt C	Fidel Castro A
Chiang Kai-shek B	Albert Einstein H
Indira Gandhi I	Neil Armstrong F

A. Declared Cuba to be a socialist state
B. Led the Kuomintang against the Chinese Communists
C. Improved relations between West Germany and the Soviet Union
D. Was expelled from the Soviet Union for criticizing communism
E. Proclaimed the independence of Vietnam from French rule
F. Was first person to walk on the moon
G. Began the de-Stalinization of the Soviet Union
H. Developed the Special Theory of Relativity
I. Began strict censorship and arrested thousands of political opponents while prime minister of India
J. Forced the Soviet Union to take its missiles out of Cuba
K. Began the Great Proletarian Cultural Revolution in China
L. Became Egypt's president after Nasser's death in 1970

4. Place these events in chronological order:

United Nations membership reached 143. 7
An armistice was signed in Korea. 2
The Soviet Union put the first *Sputnik* into orbit. 3
The Cuban missile crisis occurred. 4
The Biafran civil war ended. 5
The conflict in Vietnam ended. 6
The Berlin airlift prevented a communist takeover. 1

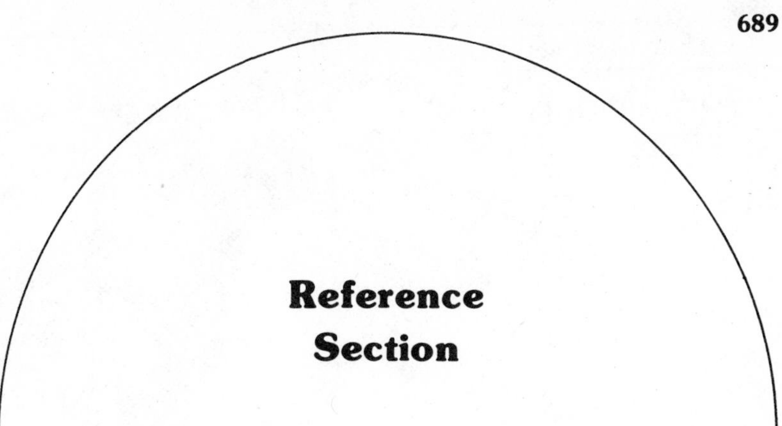

Reference Section

THE WORLD

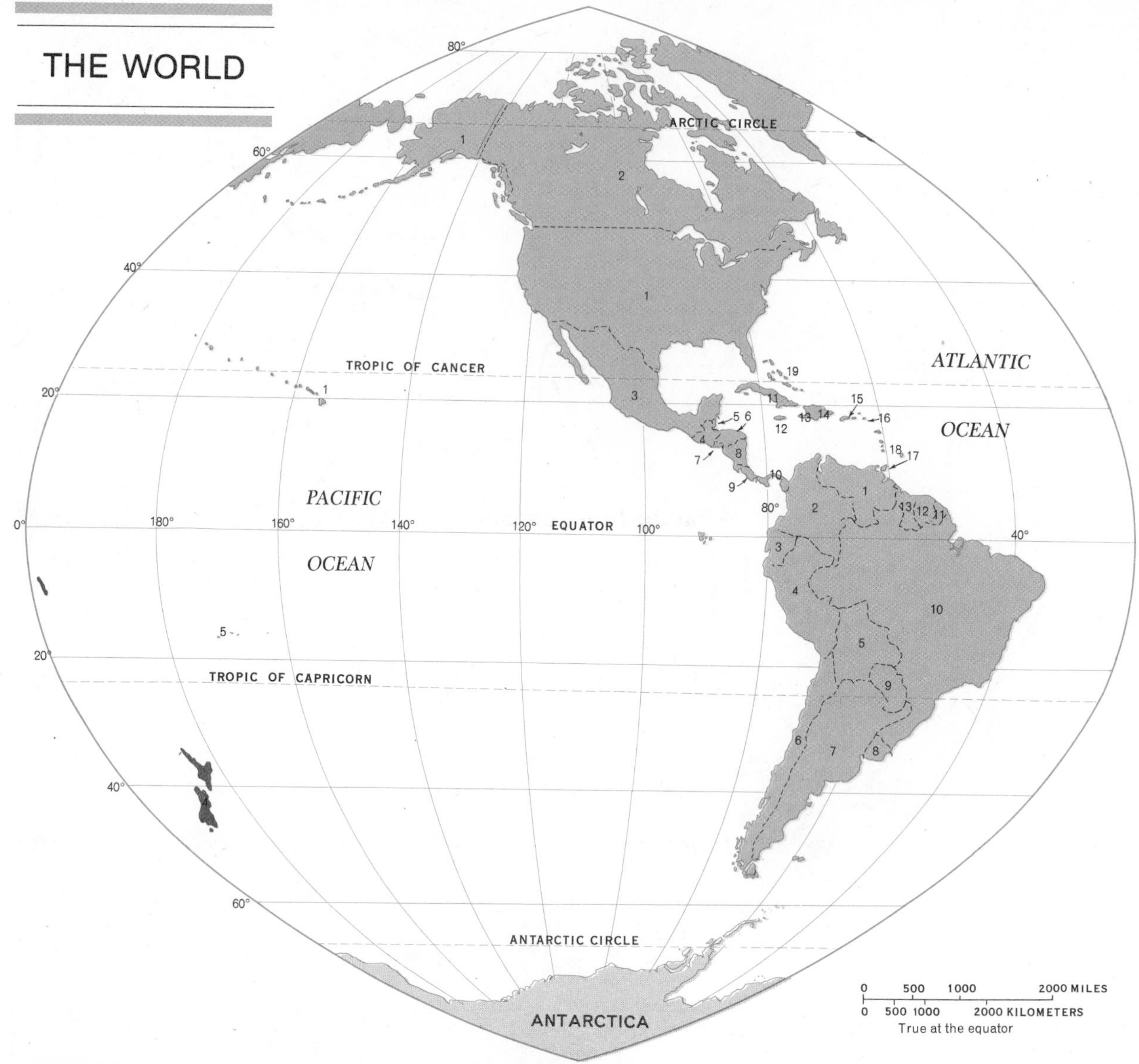

NORTH AMERICA

1. UNITED STATES
   ALASKA
   HAWAII
2. CANADA
3. MEXICO
4. GUATEMALA
5. BELIZE (Br.)
6. HONDURAS
7. EL SALVADOR
8. NICARAGUA
9. COSTA RICA
10. PANAMA
11. CUBA
12. JAMAICA
13. HAITI
14. DOMINICAN REPUBLIC
15. PUERTO RICO (U.S.A.)
16. VIRGIN ISLANDS (U.S.A.)
17. TRINIDAD AND TOBAGO
18. BARBADOS
19. THE BAHAMAS

SOUTH AMERICA

1. VENEZUELA
2. COLOMBIA
3. ECUADOR
4. PERU
5. BOLIVIA
6. CHILE
7. ARGENTINA
8. URUGUAY
9. PARAGUAY
10. BRAZIL
11. FRENCH GUIANA
12. SURINAM
13. GUYANA

AFRICA

1. ALGERIA
2. MOROCCO
3. MAURITANIA
4. SENEGAL
5. GAMBIA
6. GUINEA-BISSAU
7. GUINEA
8. SIERRA LEONE
9. LIBERIA
10. IVORY COAST
11. MALI
12. UPPER VOLTA
13. GHANA
14. TOGO
15. BENIN
16. NIGERIA
17. SÃO TOMÉ AND PRINCIPE
18. NIGER
19. CHAD
20. CENTRAL AFRICAN REPUBLIC
21. CAMEROON
22. EQUATORIAL GUINEA
23. GABON
24. CONGO
25. ZAIRE
26. ANGOLA
26, arrow. CABINDA (ANGOLA)
27. NAMIBIA (SOUTH-WEST AFRICA)
28. SOUTH AFRICA
29. LESOTHO
30. SWAZILAND
31. BOTSWANA
32. MALAGASY REPUBLIC
33. MOZAMBIQUE
34. RHODESIA
35. ZAMBIA
36. MALAWI
37. TANZANIA
38. BURUNDI
39. RWANDA
40. UGANDA
41. KENYA
42. SOMALI REPUBLIC
43. AFARS AND ISSAS (Fr.)
44. ETHIOPIA
45. SUDAN
46. EGYPT (A.R.E.)
47. LIBYA
48. TUNISIA

Map based on information available March 1, 1976

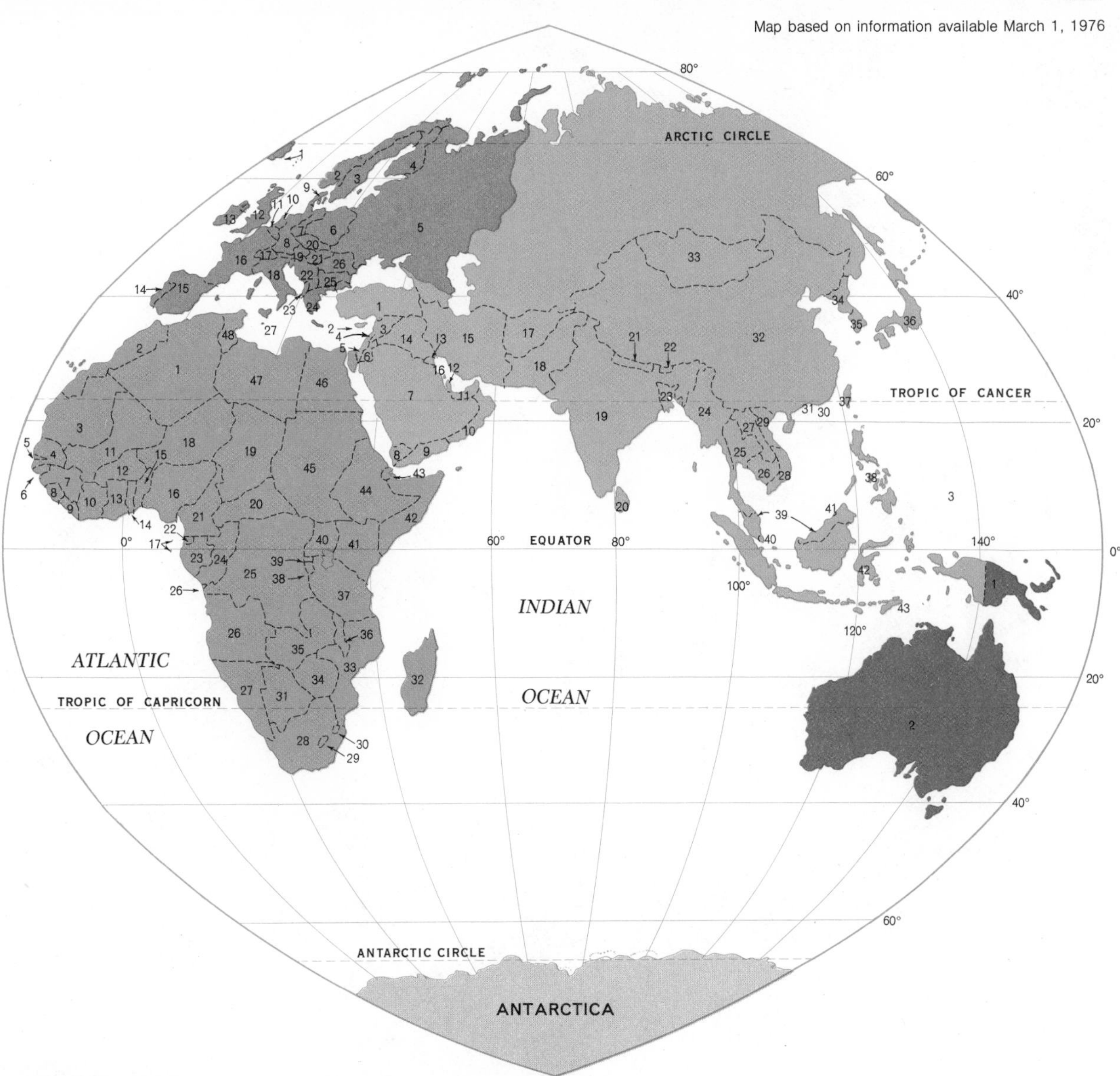

EUROPE

1. ICELAND
2. NORWAY
3. SWEDEN
4. FINLAND
5. UNION OF SOVIET SOCIALIST REPUBLICS
6. POLAND
7. EAST GERMANY
8. WEST GERMANY
9. DENMARK
10. NETHERLANDS
11. BELGIUM
12. UNITED KINGDOM
13. IRELAND
14. PORTUGAL
15. SPAIN
16. FRANCE
17. SWITZERLAND
18. ITALY
19. AUSTRIA
20. CZECHOSLOVAKIA
21. HUNGARY
22. YUGOSLAVIA
23. ALBANIA
24. GREECE
25. BULGARIA
26. ROMANIA
27. MALTA

ASIA

1. TURKEY
2. CYPRUS
3. SYRIA
4. LEBANON
5. ISRAEL
6. JORDAN
7. SAUDI ARABIA
8. YEMEN
9. P.D.R. OF YEMEN
10. OMAN
11. UNITED ARAB EMIRATES
12. QATAR
13. KUWAIT
14. IRAQ
15. IRAN
16. BAHRAIN
17. AFGHANISTAN
18. PAKISTAN
19. INDIA
20. SRI LANKA
21. NEPAL
22. BHUTAN
23. BANGLADESH
24. BURMA
25. THAILAND
26. CAMBODIA
27. LAOS
28. SOUTH VIETNAM
29. NORTH VIETNAM
30. HONG KONG (Br.)
31. MACAO (Port.)
32. PEOPLE'S REPUBLIC OF CHINA
33. MONGOLIA
34. NORTH KOREA
35. SOUTH KOREA
36. JAPAN
37. TAIWAN (NATIONALIST CHINA)
38. PHILIPPINES
39. MALAYSIA
40. SINGAPORE
41. BRUNEI (Br.)
42. INDONESIA
43. PORTUGUESE TIMOR

OCEANIA

1. PAPUA NEW GUINEA
2. AUSTRALIA
3. GUAM (U.S.A.)
4. NEW ZEALAND
5. TUTUILA (U.S.A.)

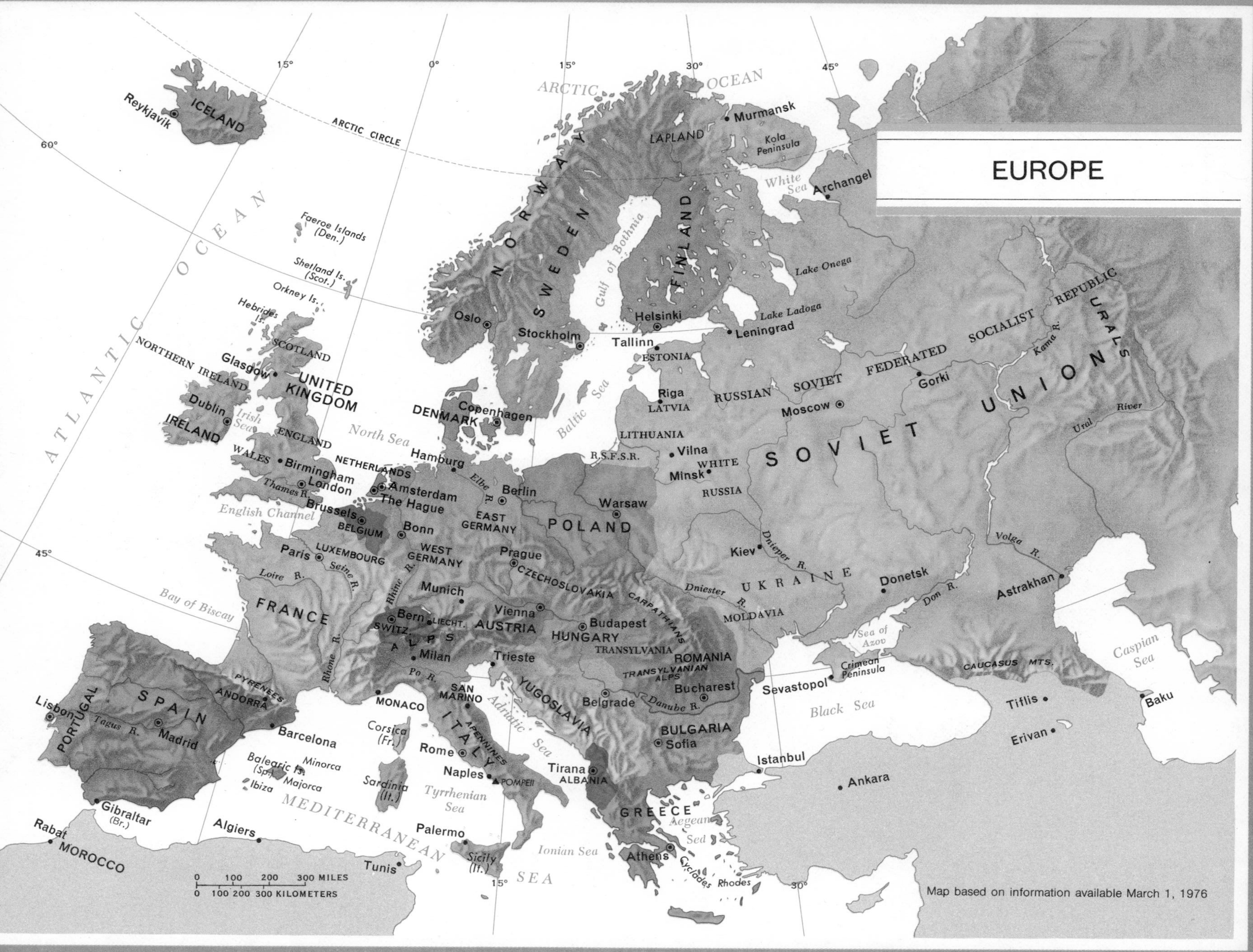
EUROPE
Map based on information available March 1, 1976
ARCTIC OCEAN
ATLANTIC OCEAN
ARCTIC CIRCLE
MEDITERRANEAN SEA
North Sea
Baltic Sea
Gulf of Bothnia
White Sea
Black Sea
Caspian Sea
Sea of Azov
Adriatic Sea
Ionian Sea
Tyrrhenian Sea
Aegean Sea
English Channel
Irish Sea
Bay of Biscay
Lake Ladoga
Lake Onega
ICELAND
Reykjavik
Faeroe Islands (Den.)
Shetland Is. (Scot.)
Orkney Is.
Hebrides Is.
UNITED KINGDOM
SCOTLAND
ENGLAND
WALES
NORTHERN IRELAND
IRELAND
Glasgow
Dublin
Birmingham
London
Thames R.
NORWAY
SWEDEN
FINLAND
LAPLAND
Oslo
Stockholm
Helsinki
Murmansk
Kola Peninsula
Archangel
DENMARK
Copenhagen
NETHERLANDS
Amsterdam
The Hague
BELGIUM
Brussels
LUXEMBOURG
FRANCE
Paris
Seine R.
Loire R.
Rhone R.
MONACO
Corsica (Fr.)
SPAIN
Madrid
Barcelona
Tagus R.
PORTUGAL
Lisbon
ANDORRA
PYRENEES
Balearic Is. (Sp.)
Minorca
Majorca
Ibiza
Gibraltar (Br.)
MOROCCO
Rabat
Algiers
Tunis
EAST GERMANY
WEST GERMANY
Berlin
Hamburg
Bonn
Munich
Elbe R.
Rhine R.
SWITZ.
Bern
LIECHT.
ALPS
AUSTRIA
Vienna
ITALY
Milan
Po R.
SAN MARINO
APENNINES
Rome
Naples
POMPEII
Palermo
Sicily (It.)
Sardinia (It.)
Trieste
POLAND
Warsaw
CZECHOSLOVAKIA
Prague
HUNGARY
Budapest
YUGOSLAVIA
Belgrade
ALBANIA
Tirana
GREECE
Athens
Cyclades
Rhodes
BULGARIA
Sofia
ROMANIA
Bucharest
TRANSYLVANIA
TRANSYLVANIAN ALPS
CARPATHIANS
Danube R.
Istanbul
Ankara
SOVIET UNION
RUSSIAN SOVIET FEDERATED SOCIALIST REPUBLIC
R.S.F.S.R.
URALS
ESTONIA
Tallinn
LATVIA
Riga
LITHUANIA
Vilna
WHITE RUSSIA
Minsk
UKRAINE
Kiev
Dnieper R.
Dniester R.
MOLDAVIA
Leningrad
Moscow
Gorki
Kama R.
Volga R.
Ural River
Don R.
Donetsk
Astrakhan
Crimean Peninsula
Sevastopol
CAUCASUS MTS.
Tiflis
Erivan
Baku
0 100 200 300 MILES
0 100 200 300 KILOMETERS

ASIA
ARCTIC OCEAN
PACIFIC OCEAN
INDIAN OCEAN
ARCTIC CIRCLE
TROPIC OF CANCER
EQUATOR
SOVIET UNION
SIBERIA
EUROPE
AFRICA
AUSTRALIA
MONGOLIA
GOBI (DESERT)
CHINA
MANCHURIA
TIBET
PLATEAU OF TIBET
TAKLA MAKAN (DESERT)
INDIA
PAKISTAN
AFGHANISTAN
IRAN
PLATEAU OF IRAN
TURKEY
SYRIA
LEBANON
CYPRUS
ISRAEL
JORDAN
IRAQ
KUWAIT
BAHRAIN
QATAR
UNITED ARAB EMIRATES
SAUDI ARABIA
OMAN
YEMEN
P.D.R. OF YEMEN
NEPAL
BHUTAN
BNGL.
BURMA
THAILAND
LAOS
VIETNAM
CAMBODIA
MALAYSIA
INDONESIA
PHILIPPINES
TAIWAN (FORMOSA)
JAPAN
NORTH KOREA
SOUTH KOREA
SRI LANKA
MALDIVES
SINGAPORE
BRUNEI (Br.)
PAPUA NEW GUINEA
WEST IRIAN
PORTUGUESE TIMOR
TURKESTAN
Moscow
Omsk
Chita
Magadan
Ulan Bator
Peking
Harbin
Pyongyang
Seoul
Tokyo
Yokohama
Osaka
Shanghai
Nanking
Wuhan
Chungking
Canton
Macao (Port.)
Victoria
HONG KONG (Br.)
Taipei
Manila
Quezon City
Hanoi
Vientiane
Ban Chieng
Bangkok
Pnom Penh
Saigon
ANGKOR WAT
Rangoon
Kuala Lumpur
Kuching
Kota Kinabalu
Djakarta
Makassar
Port Moresby
Dacca
Calcutta
Lhasa
Madras
Colombo
Bombay
New Delhi
Delhi
Amritsar
Islamabad
Karachi
Kabul
Tashkent
Teheran
Baku
Bagdad
Kuwait
Riyadh
Mecca
San'a
Aden
Muscat
Damascus
Beirut
Amman
Jerusalem
Ankara
Istanbul
Lake Baikal
Lake Balkhash
Aral Sea
CASPIAN SEA
BLACK SEA
RED SEA
Persian Gulf
ARABIAN SEA
Bay of Bengal
SOUTH CHINA SEA
EAST CHINA SEA
SEA OF JAPAN
SEA OF OKHOTSK
PHILIPPINE SEA
SULU SEA
CELEBES SEA
JAVA SEA
BANDA SEA
ARAFURA SEA
CORAL SEA
BARENTS SEA
KARA SEA
LAPTEV SEA
EAST SIBERIAN SEA
Lena R.
Aldan R.
Amur R.
Yenisey R.
Nizhnyaya Tunguska R.
Angara R.
Ob' R.
Irtysh R.
Ishim R.
Ural R.
Syr Dar'ya R.
Amu Dar'ya R.
Indus
Ganges
Brahmaputra
Yangtze R.
Hwang Ho R.
Tigris
Euphrates
URALS
CAUCASUS MTS.
PAMIRS
HIMALAYAS
WESTERN GHATS
EASTERN GHATS
KAMCHATKA PEN.
Sakhalin
Kurile Islands
Ryukyu Is.
Hainan
LUZON
BORNEO
CELEBES
SUMATRA
JAVA
MALAY PEN.
Novaya Zemlya
Franz Josef Land
New Siberian Islands
Wrangel Island
Andaman Islands (India)
Nicobar Islands (India)
Laccadive Islands (India)
Cape Comorin
Socotra (P.D.R. of Yemen)
0 500 1000 MILES
0 500 1000 KILOMETERS
Map based on information available March 1, 1976

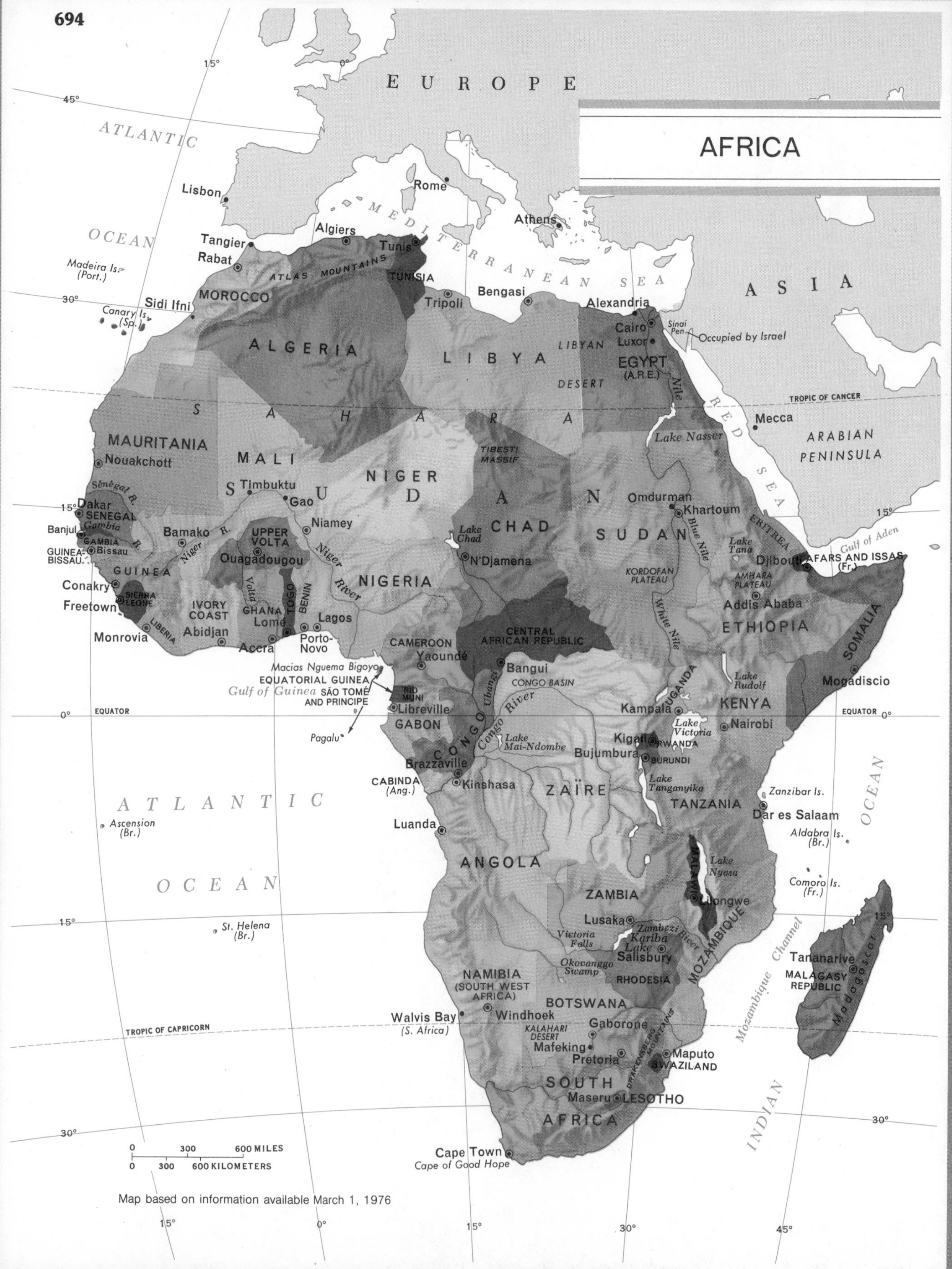
AFRICA
EUROPE
ASIA
ATLANTIC OCEAN
MEDITERRANEAN SEA
RED SEA
Gulf of Aden
ARABIAN PENINSULA
INDIAN OCEAN
Mozambique Channel
Gulf of Guinea
TROPIC OF CANCER
EQUATOR
TROPIC OF CAPRICORN
SAHARA
LIBYAN DESERT
KALAHARI DESERT
MOROCCO
ALGERIA
TUNISIA
LIBYA
EGYPT (A.R.E.)
MAURITANIA
MALI
NIGER
CHAD
SUDAN
SENEGAL
GAMBIA
GUINEA-BISSAU
GUINEA
SIERRA LEONE
LIBERIA
IVORY COAST
GHANA
UPPER VOLTA
TOGO
BENIN
NIGERIA
CAMEROON
CENTRAL AFRICAN REPUBLIC
EQUATORIAL GUINEA
RIO MUNI
SÃO TOMÉ AND PRINCIPE
GABON
CONGO
CABINDA (Ang.)
ZAÏRE
ANGOLA
ETHIOPIA
ERITREA
AFARS AND ISSAS (Fr.)
SOMALIA
UGANDA
KENYA
RWANDA
BURUNDI
TANZANIA
ZAMBIA
MALAWI
MOZAMBIQUE
RHODESIA
NAMIBIA (SOUTH WEST AFRICA)
BOTSWANA
SOUTH AFRICA
SWAZILAND
LESOTHO
MALAGASY REPUBLIC
Madagascar
Lisbon
Rome
Athens
Tangier
Rabat
Algiers
Tunis
Tripoli
Bengasi
Alexandria
Cairo
Luxor
Sidi Ifni
Madeira Is. (Port.)
Canary Is. (Sp.)
Sinai Pen.
Occupied by Israel
Mecca
Nouakchott
Timbuktu
Gao
Dakar
Banjul
Bissau
Bamako
Niamey
Ouagadougou
Conakry
Freetown
Monrovia
Abidjan
Accra
Lomé
Porto-Novo
Lagos
N'Djamena
Omdurman
Khartoum
Djibouti
Addis Ababa
Mogadiscio
Yaoundé
Bangui
Macias Nguema Bigoyo
Libreville
Pagalu
Brazzaville
Kinshasa
Kampala
Nairobi
Kigali
Bujumbura
Zanzibar Is.
Dar es Salaam
Aldabra Is. (Br.)
Comoro Is. (Fr.)
Luanda
Lilongwe
Lusaka
Salisbury
Tananarive
Windhoek
Walvis Bay (S. Africa)
Gaborone
Mafeking
Pretoria
Maputo
Maseru
Cape Town
Cape of Good Hope
Ascension (Br.)
St. Helena (Br.)
ATLAS MOUNTAINS
TIBESTI MASSIF
KORDOFAN PLATEAU
AMHARA PLATEAU
CONGO BASIN
DRAKENSBERG MOUNTAINS
Sénégal R.
Gambia R.
Niger R.
Niger River
Volta
Nile
Blue Nile
White Nile
Ubangi
Congo River
Zambezi River
Lake Chad
Lake Nasser
Lake Tana
Lake Rudolf
Lake Victoria
Lake Mai-Ndombe
Lake Tanganyika
Lake Nyasa
Lake Kariba
Victoria Falls
Okovanggo Swamp
0 300 600 MILES
0 300 600 KILOMETERS
45°
30°
15°
0°
Map based on information available March 1, 1976

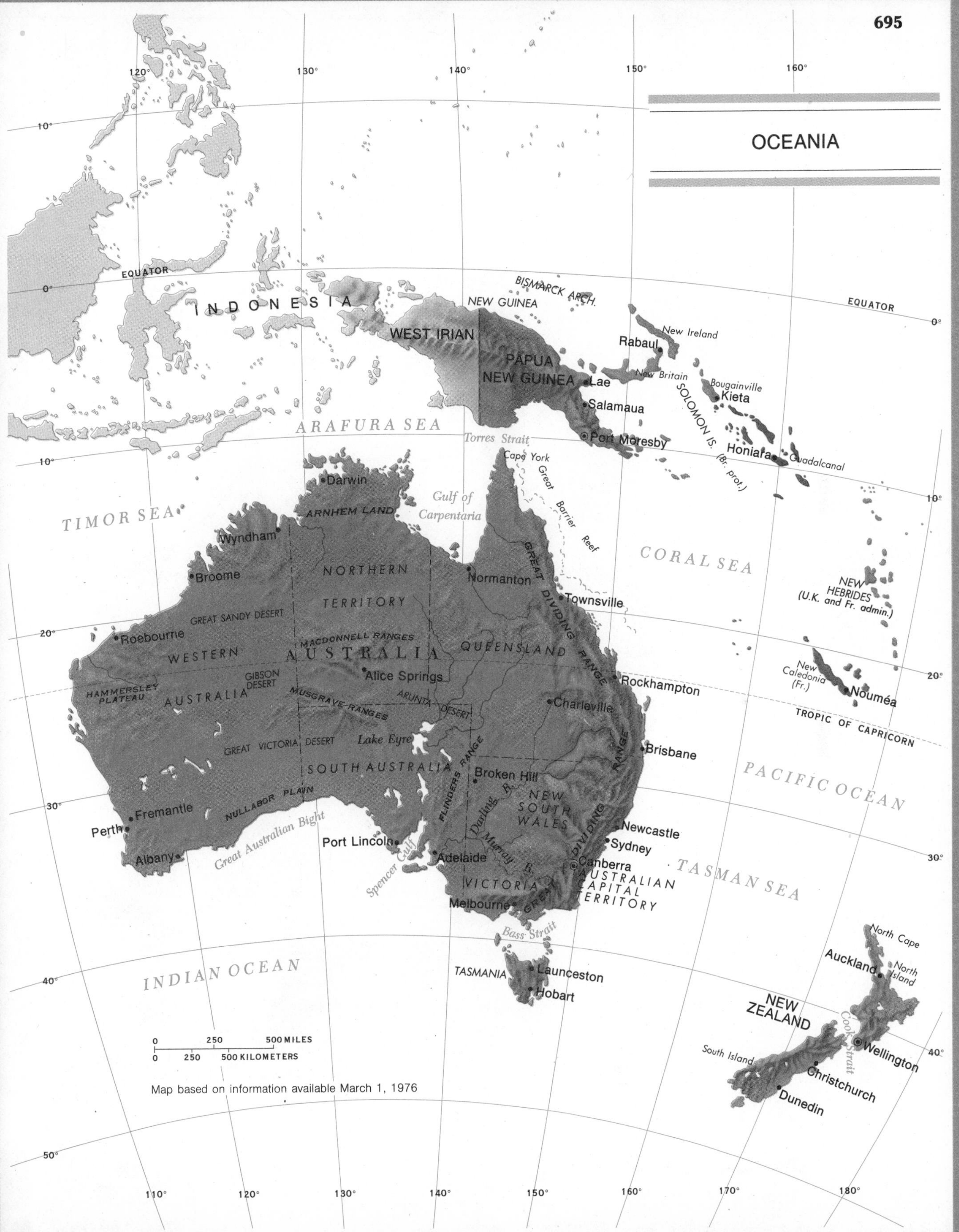
OCEANIA
INDONESIA
WEST IRIAN
NEW GUINEA
PAPUA NEW GUINEA
BISMARCK ARCH.
New Ireland
Rabaul
New Britain
Lae
Salamaua
Port Moresby
Bougainville
Kieta
SOLOMON IS. (Br. prot.)
Honiara
Guadalcanal
ARAFURA SEA
Torres Strait
Cape York
Great Barrier Reef
TIMOR SEA
Darwin
ARNHEM LAND
Gulf of Carpentaria
CORAL SEA
NEW HEBRIDES (U.K. and Fr. admin.)
Wyndham
Broome
NORTHERN TERRITORY
Normanton
GREAT DIVIDING RANGE
Townsville
GREAT SANDY DESERT
Roebourne
MACDONNELL RANGES
AUSTRALIA
QUEENSLAND
WESTERN AUSTRALIA
HAMMERSLEY PLATEAU
GIBSON DESERT
Alice Springs
ARUNTA DESERT
MUSGRAVE RANGES
Rockhampton
Charleville
New Caledonia (Fr.)
Nouméa
TROPIC OF CAPRICORN
EQUATOR
GREAT VICTORIA DESERT
Lake Eyre
Brisbane
SOUTH AUSTRALIA
FLINDERS RANGE
Broken Hill
Darling R.
NEW SOUTH WALES
PACIFIC OCEAN
NULLABOR PLAIN
Perth
Fremantle
Great Australian Bight
Port Lincoln
Spencer Gulf
Murray R.
Newcastle
Sydney
Albany
Adelaide
Canberra
AUSTRALIAN CAPITAL TERRITORY
TASMAN SEA
VICTORIA
Melbourne
Bass Strait
INDIAN OCEAN
TASMANIA
Launceston
Hobart
North Cape
Auckland
North Island
NEW ZEALAND
Cook Strait
Wellington
South Island
Christchurch
Dunedin
0 250 500 MILES
0 250 500 KILOMETERS
Map based on information available March 1, 1976

NORTH AMERICA
NORTH POLE
ARCTIC OCEAN
GREENLAND SEA
GREENLAND (Denmark)
ICELAND
ARCTIC CIRCLE
Baffin Bay
Baffin Island
Davis Strait
Godthaab
BERING SEA
Bering Strait
U.S.S.R.
Nome
BROOKS RANGE
ALASKA
ALASKA RANGE
Fairbanks
Anchorage
Aleutian Islands
KLONDIKE REGION
YUKON
Gulf of Alaska
Juneau
Victoria Island
NORTHWEST TERRITORIES
Mackenzie River
Great Bear Lake
Great Slave Lake
Lake Athabaska
Reindeer Lake
Hudson Bay
James Bay
ATLANTIC OCEAN
NEWFOUNDLAND
Labrador
Newfoundland
St. John's
QUEBEC
St. Lawrence R.
Gulf of St. Lawrence
NEW BRUNSWICK
Halifax
NOVA SCOTIA
BRITISH COLUMBIA
COAST MOUNTAINS
Queen Charlotte Islands
ALBERTA
SASKATCHEWAN
MANITOBA
Edmonton
Lake Winnipeg
CANADA
Lake of the Woods
ONTARIO
Winnipeg
Vancouver
Vancouver Island
Columbia River
Seattle
Portland
ROCKY MOUNTAINS
Quebec
Montreal
Ottawa
Toronto
L. Superior
L. Michigan
L. Huron
L. Ontario
L. Erie
Boston
Cape Cod
New York
Philadelphia
Washington
Chesapeake Bay
Cape Hatteras
BERMUDA (Br.)
PACIFIC OCEAN
CASCADE RANGE
SIERRA NEVADA
Great Salt Lake
UNITED STATES
Minneapolis
Missouri R.
Chicago
Detroit
Pittsburgh
Ohio R.
APPALACHIAN MTS.
San Francisco
Denver
St. Louis
Los Angeles
Colorado R.
Arkansas R.
Mississippi R.
Atlanta
Fort Worth
Dallas
Houston
New Orleans
Miami
THE BAHAMAS
Guadalupe (Mex.)
LOWER CALIFORNIA
TROPIC OF CANCER
Gulf of California
Rio Grande
SIERRA MADRE ORIENTAL
SIERRA MADRE OCCIDENTAL
MEXICO
Gulf of Mexico
Cape San Lucas
Tampico
Mexico
Veracruz
WEST INDIES
Havana
CUBA
Bay of Pigs
Guantanamo Bay
HAITI
Port-au-Prince
Santo Domingo
DOM. REP.
San Juan
PUERTO RICO (U.S.A.)
JAMAICA
Kingston
BELIZE
Belmopan
GUATEMALA
Guatemala
HONDURAS
Tegucigalpa
EL SALVADOR
San Salvador
NICARAGUA
Managua
San José
COSTA RICA
CANAL ZONE (U.S.A.)
Panama
PANAMA
CARIBBEAN SEA
CENTRAL AMERICA
SOUTH AMERICA
Cocos Islands (Costa Rica)
HAWAII
Kauai
Lihue
Niihau
Oahu
Kailua
Honolulu
Molokai
Kahului
Maui
Lanai
Wailuku
Kahoolawe
Hilo
Hawaii
HAWAIIAN IS.
PACIFIC OCEAN
0 75 150 MILES
0 75 150 KILOMETERS
EQUATOR
0 350 700 MILES
0 350 700 KILOMETERS
Map based on information available March 1, 1976

SOUTH AMERICA

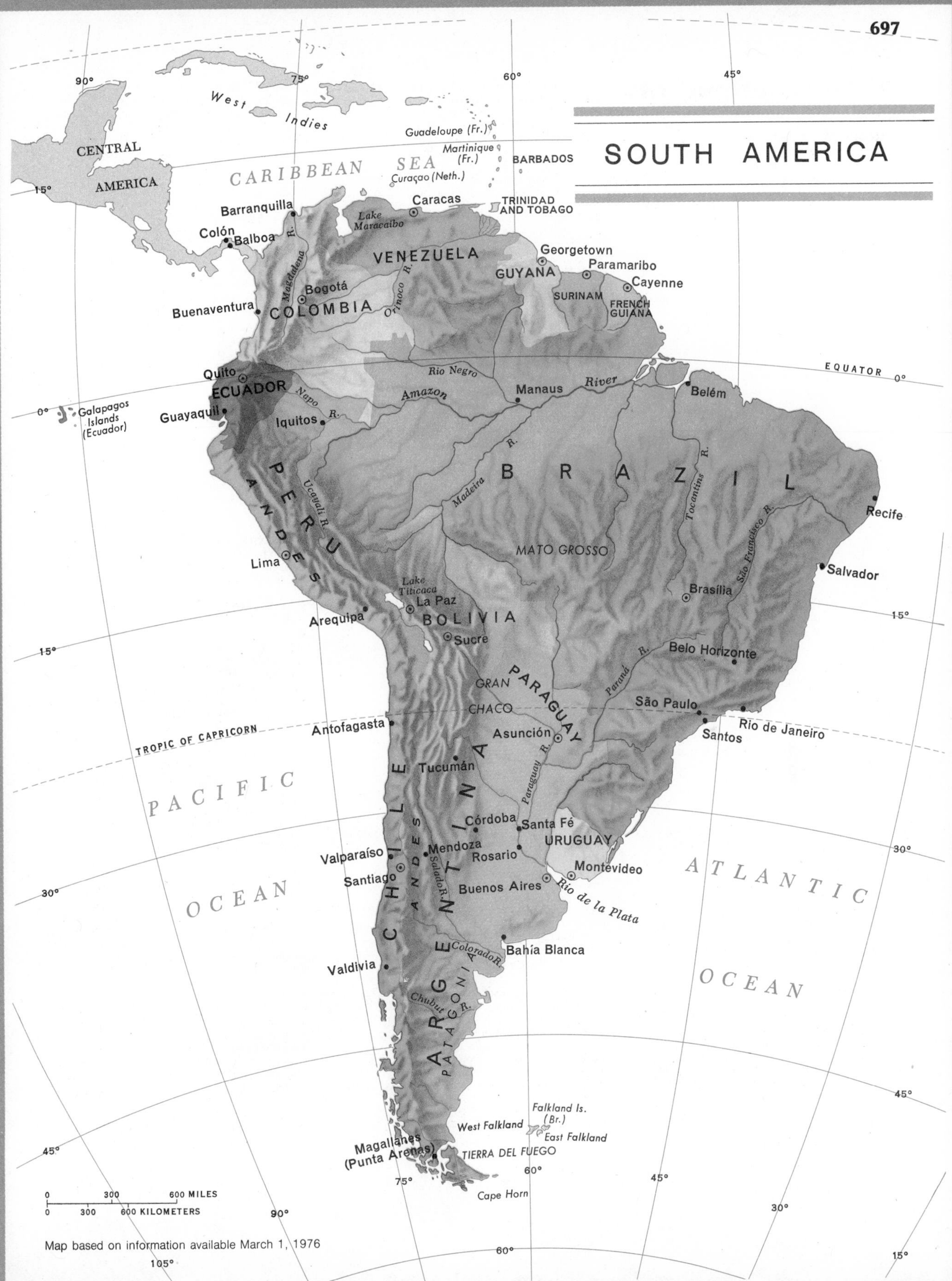

Map based on information available March 1, 1976

Acknowledgments

Quoted Material

1 From "History as Mirror" by Barbara W. Tuchman, *The Atlantic,* September 1973. (Boston: The Atlantic Monthly Company, 1973)
1 From *The International Dictionary of Thoughts* compiled by John P. Bradley, Leo F. Daniels, and Thomas C. Jones (Chicago: J. G. Ferguson Publishing Company, 1969).
20 From *The Literature of the Ancient Egyptians,* trans. by Aylward M. Blackman. (London: Methuen and Co. Ltd.).
28 From *The Book of The Dead,* Oliver J. Thatcher, ed., *The Ideas That Have Influenced Civilization,* Milwaukee, 1901.
32 C. H. Johns, ed., *Babylonian and Assyrian Laws, Contracts and Letters,* "Library of Ancient Inscriptions" (New York: Charles Scribner's Sons, 1904), pp. 44–67 *passim.*
38 *Herodotus,* trans., H. G. Rawlinson, rev. and annotated. A. W. Lawrence (London: Nonesuch Press, Ltd., 1935), p. 735.
44 Reprinted by permission of G. P. Putnam's Sons and Macdonald and Jane's Publishers Ltd. from *The Ancient Worlds of Asia* by Ernst Diez, trans. by W. C. Darwell. Copyright © 1961 by Macdonald & Co. (Publishers) Ltd.
58 From the *Bhagavad Gītā* trans. by Sir Edwin Arnold, (Boston 1885).
60 bottom Cited in H. G. Rawlinson, *India: A Short Cultural History* (London: Cresset Press, 1937).
62 Quoted in Percival Spear, *India: A Modern History,* (Ann Arbor: University of Michigan Press, 1961).
64 J. Legge, trans. and ed., "The Travels of Fa-Hsien," in *Chinese Literature* (London: Cooperative Publishing Co., 1900), p. 230.
66 Quoted in K. M. Panikkar, *A Survey of Indian History* (London: Meridian Books, Ltd. 1948), p. 130.
76 From *The World's Great Religions.* (New York: Time, Inc., 1957).
81 Quoted in Robert Payne, *The White Pony* (New York: The John Day Company, 1949), pp. 198–199.
85 From *The History of the Peloponnesian War* by Thucydides, edited by Sir Richard Livingstone. (New York: Oxford University Press, 1966).
86 Thucydides: *The Peloponnesian War,* trans., Rex Warner (Middlesex: Penguin Books, Ltd., 1954), pp. 118, 119.
93 From *Herodotus, History of the Persian Wars,* trans., George Rawlinson in *The Greek Historians,* Vol. 1, ed. Francis R. B. Godolphin, p. 378. (New York: Random House, Inc., 1942).
104 *Thucydides Translated into English,* Benjamin Jowett, ed. and trans., Vol. I (Oxford: The Clarendon Press, 1900), p. 16
134 A. J. Grant, trans. & ed., *Early Lives of Charlemagne* by Eginhard and the Monk of St. Gall. (London: Oxford University Press, 1922).
170–171 Marcus Nathan Adler, trans. *Itinerary of Benjamin of Tudela.* (New York: Philipp Feldheim, Inc.).
175 Quoted in J. F. C. Fuller, *A Military History of the Western World,* Vol. I, (New York: Funk and Wagnalls, 1954), p. 522.
177 *Procopius,* Vol. I, trans., Henry B. Dewing, Loeb Classical Library (Cambridge: Harvard Univ. Press, 1914), pp. 231–233.
179 Samuel H. Cross and Olgerd P. Sherbowitz-Wetzor (trans. and ed.), *The Russian Primary Chronicle* (Cambridge: Harvard University Press, 1930, 1958).
182 From *Medieval Russia's Epics, Chronicles, and Tales* translated and edited by Serge A. Zenkovsky. Copyright © 1963 by Serge A. Zenkovsky. Reprinted by permission of the publishers, E. P. Dutton & Co., Inc.
188 The Koran, trans. by M. M. Pickthall in *The Meaning of the Glorious Koran* (New York: Mentor Books, 1956), pp. 438–439. Reprinted by permission of George Allen & Unwin Ltd., London.
212 (top) From *A Literary History of the Arabs* by Reynold A. Nicholson. Published by Cambridge University Press, 1966. Reprinted by permission.
212 (bottom) From *Rubaiyat of Omar Khayyam* trans. by Edward Fitzgerald. (Boston: Houghton Mifflin, 1898).
231 "Hymn of Propitiation" from *People of the Small Arrow* by J. H. Driberg. Published by Payson & Clarke, 1930. Reprinted by permission of Routledge & Kegan Paul Ltd.
239 From *Narrative of Travels and Discoveries in Northern and Central Africa, In The Years 1822, 1823, and 1824* by Major Denham, Captain Clapperton and Doctor Oudney. (London: John Murray, 1826) p. 63.
244 From *Ancient African Kingdoms* by Margaret Shinnie. (New York: St. Martin's Press, Inc., 1965).
247 Quoted in *Discovering Our African Heritage* by Basil Davidson. (Boston: Ginn and Company, 1971), p. 119.
258 Hakluyt Society, *Works Issued by the Hakluyt Society,* 196 vols. London, 1847–1951.
281 Sir H. M. Elliot and John Dowson (eds. & trans.), *The History of India as Told By Its Own Historians* (London: Trubner & Co., 1871), III, 182–185.
297 Quoted in Elizabeth Seeger, *The Pageant of Chinese History,* (London: Longman Group Limited, 1934, 1947).
301 Quoted in Dun J. Li, *The Ageless Chinese.* (New York: Charles Scribner's Sons, 1971).
307 E. Backhouse and J. O. P. Bland, *Annals & Memoirs of the Court of Peking* (Boston: Houghton Mifflin Co., 1914).
311 Mikiso Hane, *Japan a Historical Survey* (New York: Charles Scribner's Sons, 1972).
312 From *An Outline History of Japan* by Herbert H. Gowen. (New York: Appleton-Century, 1927).
313 From *History of Japan I* by James A. Murdoch, 1964. Reprinted by permission of Routledge & Kegan Paul Ltd.
316 (top) From *A History of East Asian Civilization I* by Edwin O. Reischauer and John K. Fairbank. (Boston: Houghton Mifflin Company, 1960) p. 497.
316 (bottom) Reprinted from *The Manyoshu* (New York, 1965), page 283, by permission of Columbia University Press.
348 *Machiavelli: The Prince and Other Works,* trans. by A. H. Gilbert (Chicago: Packard and Co., 1941).
383–384 Hakluyt Society, *Works Issued by the Hakluyt Society,* 196 vols. London, 1847–1951.
401–402 Bernal Diaz del Castillo, *The True History of the Conquest of Mexico,* trans. by Maurice Keating, 1800.
422–423 From *Memoirs of the Life, Writings, and Discoveries of Sir Isaac Newton* by Sir David Brewster (Edinburgh: Thomas Constable and Company, 1855).
438–439 Quoted in R. R. Palmer, *The Age of the Democratic Revolution,* Vol. I, *The Challenge.* Copyright © 1959 by Princeton University Press; Princeton Paperback, 1969. Reprinted by permission.
476–477 Quoted in Paul Joseph Mantoux, trans. by Marjorie Vernon, *The Industrial Revolution in the Eighteenth Century,* (New York: Harper & Row, 1961).
505 Quoted in J. H. Hexter & Richard Pipes, *Europe Since 1500.* (New York: Harper & Row, Publishers, 1971).
539 Viscount Grey of Fallodon, *Twenty-Five Years,* Vol. II (New York: Frederick A. Stokes Company, 1925), p. 20.
551–552 Woodrow Wilson, *War and Peace: Presidential Messages, Addresses, and Public Papers* (1917–1924), ed. Ray Stannard Baker and William E. Dodd (New York: Harper & Brothers, 1927), I.
557 Benito Mussolini, *Fascism: Doctrine and Institutions* (Rome: Ardita Publishers, 1935)
573 Quoted in N. N. Sukhanov, *The Russian Revolution, 1917: A Personal Record,* Joel Carmickael, ed. (New York: Oxford University Press, 1955), p. 273.
591 From *Mein Kampf* by Adolf Hitler, translated by Ralph Manheim. (Boston: Houghton Mifflin, 1943).
630–631 Bal Gangadhar Tilak, *His Writings and Speeches* (Madras, India: Ganesh & Co., 1923).
650 From *Poems From Black Africa,* edited by Langston Hughes. Copyright © 1963 by Langston Hughes. Reprinted by permission of Indiana University Press.

Illustrations

The abbreviations indicate position of pictures on a page. *T* is top, *b* is bottom, *m* is middle, *l* is left, *r* is right.

2–3 Ron Bradford
6 By kind permission of The British Academy
9 The Cleveland Museum of Natural History
13 (t) Courtesy of The American Museum of Natural History (m,l) Soprintendenza alla Preistoria e All'Etnografia, Rome (m: m,r) Archives Photographiques (b) Courtesy of The Field Museum of Natural History, Chicago
15 National Museum, Denmark
17 Colorphoto Hinz, Basle
20 Larry Burrows, Time-Life Picture Agency. © Time Inc.
24 (t) Courtesy of The Oriental Institute, University of Chicago (m: b) The Metropolitan Museum of Art
25 (t) The Metropolitan Museum of Art (b) Courtesy of The Oriental Institute, University of Chicago
29 & 30 Hirmer Fotoarchiv, Munich
32 Museum of Arab Antiquities, Iraq
34 (t) Courtesy of The Trustees of The British Museum (m: seated harpist) Courtesy of The Oriental Institute, University of Chicago (m: cylinder seal & impression) The Metropolitan Museum of Art, Bequest of W. Gedney Beatty, 1941 (b: lady on stool) Musée du Louvre (b,r: Ningal) University Museum, University of Pennsylvania
36 Movie Star News
37 The Metropolitan Museum of Art, Harris Brisbane Dick Fund, 1954
38 Courtesy of The Oriental Institute, University of Chicago
40 (t) Embassy of India, Washington, D.C. (m) Courtesy of The Director of The National Museum, New Delhi (b,l) Pakistan National Museum (b,r) Courtesy Museum of Fine Arts, Boston
43 (t,l) Musée Cernuschi, Paris (t,r) Courtesy Museum of Fine Arts, Boston (b,l) Columbia University, East Asian Library (b,r)

Courtesy of The Field Museum of Natural History, Chicago
48–49 Ron Bradford
52 Shostal Associates, Inc.
56 Bernard Wolff/Photo Researchers
60 Johnston & Hoffmann, Calcutta
61 The Bettmann Archive
65 Courtesy of The Field Museum of Natural History, Chicago
66 Bill Cella/Photo Researchers
69 Andy Bernhaut/FPG
73 Nelson Gallery—Atkins Museum, Kansas City, Missouri (Nelson Fund)
77 (t,l) Courtesy of The Trustees of The British Museum (t,m: t,r) The British Library Board (b,l) Courtesy of The American School of Classical Studies (b,r) Courtesy of The Oriental Institute, University of Chicago
78 (t) Nelson Gallery—Atkins Museum, Kansas City, Missouri (Nelson Fund) (b) The St. Louis Art Museum
79 (t) Royal Ontario Museum, Toronto, Canada (b) The St. Louis Art Museum
80 Courtesy of The Trustees of The British Museum
82 (t) University Museum, University of Pennsylvania (b) Eugene Fuller Memorial Collection, Seattle Art Museum
85 Art Reference Bureau
89 (t) Hirmer Fotoarchiv, Munich (b) Editions d'Art, Albert Skira
93 Staatliche Museen zu Berlin, DDR, Antiken-Sammlung
94 (t) Editions d'Art, Albert Skira (b) Courtesy of The Trustees of The British Museum
95 (t,l) The Metropolitan Museum of Art, Fletcher Fund, 1931 (t,r) Alinari-Art Reference Bureau (b) Ashmolean Museum, Oxford
98 Movie Star News
102 Dr. Raymond V. Schoder
104 Embassy of Greece
105 Alinari-Art Reference Bureau
106 Dr. Raymond V. Schoder
109 Alinari-Art Reference Bureau
112 Giraudon
116 (t,l) Art Reference Bureau (t,r) Musei Capitolini (b) Alinari-Art Reference Bureau
117 (t) Alinari-Art Reference Bureau (b) Museu Nazionale, Naples
121 Alinari-Art Reference Bureau
122 Dr. Raymond V. Schoder
124 (l) The French Government Tourist Office (r) Anderson/Alinari-Art Reference Bureau
125 (L) Anderson/Alinari-Art Reference Bureau (r) Alinari-Art Reference Bureau
130–131 Ron Bradford
134 Photo: Andre Held, Ecublens (Switzerland)
137 Giraudon
138 Anderson/Alinari-Art Reference Bureau
139 Alinari-Art Reference Bureau
141 (t) Bodleian Library Colour Filmstrip Roll 159 B (b,l) Anderson-Art Reference Bureau (m,r) Courtesy of The Trustees of The British Museum (b,r) Courtesy of The Trustees of The British Museum
144 (l) The British Library Board (r) Kunsthistorisches Museum, Vienna
145 (l) Photo: National Museum of Ireland (r) Rheinisches Landesmuseum, Bonn
148 Photo: Bibl. Nat. Paris
151 Giraudon
155 The British Library Board
156 The Pierpont Morgan Library
157 (l) The British Library Board (r) Giraudon
159 Ewing Galloway
162 (t) Photo: Bibl. Nat. Paris (b,l) The British Library Board (b,r) Giraudon
166 Historical Pictures Service, Inc.
165 Movie Star News
170 Marc Riboud/Magnum
176 (t,l) Kunsthistorisches Museum, Vienna (t,r) Photo: Bibl. Nat. Paris (b) Biblioteca Nacional, Madrid
181 (t,l) Sovfoto/Novosti (t,r) Courtesy of The Newberry Library, Chicago (m) The Bettmann Archive (b) Photo: Bibl. Nat. Paris
185 Photo: Bibl. Nat. Paris
187 Edinburgh University Library
188 (l) Courtesy of The Smithsonian Institution, Freer Gallery of Art, Washington, D.C. (r) Edinburgh University Library
189 (l) Edinburgh University Library (r) R. B. Fleming & Co., Ltd.
193 Courtesy of The Oriental Institute, University of Chicago
195 Musée de L'Homme, Paris
196 (t,l) The British Library Board (t,r) The British Library Board (b) Photo: Bibl. Nat. Paris
201 Shostal Associates Inc.
203 Photo: Bibl. Nat. Paris
204 The Metropolitan Museum of Art, Rogers Fund
207 (t) Photo: Bibl. Nat. Paris (b) Erich Lessing/Magnum
209 (l) The Pierpont Morgan Library (r) The British Library Board
210 The Metropolitan Museum of Art, Rogers Fund, 1913
211 Reproduced by permission of The Director of The India Office Library and Records
213 Trans World Airlines Photo
218–219 Ron Bradford
222 University Museum, University of Pennsylvania
225 The French Government Tourist Office
229 Musee de L'Homme, Paris
232–233 Lepsius, Denkmaler . . . 1860
235 (l) By Courtesy of The Federal Department of Antiquities, Nigeria (r) Courtesy of The Trustees of The British Museum
238 Lee Boltin
241 Courtesy of The Newberry Library, Chicago
242 Courtesy of The Trustees of The British Museum
244 Courtesy of The Newberry Library, Chicago
247 Joe B. Blossom/Photo Researchers
248 Authenticated News International
250 Photograph by Ken Heyman
253 Courtesy of The Newberry Library, Chicago
257 George Holton/Photo Researchers
258 Dumbarton Oaks, Washington, D.C.
260 (l) David Muench (r) Museum of The American Indian, Heye Foundation
263 (l) Emil Muench (r) Museo Nacional de Antropoligia, Mexico
264 Wurtembergisches Landesmuseum
266 Reproduced from the collections of The Library of Congress
269 Movie Star News
270 (l:m) Courtesy of The Art Institute of Chicago (r) New York Public Lib.
276–277 Ron Bradford
280 Bernard G. Silberstein/FPG
285 (t) Shostal Associates, Inc. (b) Lawrence L. Smith/Photo Researchers
286 (t) Reproduced by permission of The Director of The India Office Library and Records (b,r) Musee Guimet, Paris
289 (l) Giraudon (r) Reproduced by permission of The Director of The India Office Library & Records
290 Alice & Nasli Heeramaneck Collection, N.Y.
294 Marc Riboud/Magnum
297 Ma Yuan: "Riverside Village on a Late Autumn Day," late 12th-early 13th century Courtesy Museum of Fine Arts, Boston
298 (l) Courtesy of The Field Museum of Natural History, Chicago (r) Detail, "Spring Festival on the River," Ming dynasty The Metropolitan Museum of Art
299 Emperor Hui-tsung: "Ladies Preparing Newly Woven Silk," Sung dynasty Courtesy Museum of Fine Arts, Boston
304 Movie Star News
305 Eugene Fuller Memorial Collection, Seattle Art Museum
306 The Metropolitan Museum of Art, Gift of Robert E. Tod, 1937
310 The Tokyo National Museum
312 Eitoku: "Izangi and Izanami Standing in Clouds and Creating Island out of the Sea Water," late 19th century Courtesy Museum of Fine Arts, Boston
315 The Brooklyn Museum, Lent by the Stephen Gano Collection
316 Sakamoto Photo Research Laboratory, Tokyo
318 Detail, "The Burning of the Sanjo Palace," 13th century Courtesy Museum of Fine Arts, Boston
320 Masanobu: Interior view of the Nakamura Theatre in Edo, 18th century Courtesy of The Art Institute of Chicago
321 Korin: Detail: "The Islands of Matsushima," Courtesy Museum of Fine Arts, Boston
322 (t) Harunobu: "Young Woman and a Shower," Courtesy of The Art Institute of Chicago (b) Courtesy Museum of Fine Arts, Boston
326–327 Ron Bradford
330 Kunsthistorisches Museum, Vienna
333 The British Library Board
334 The Pierpont Morgan Library
336 (t,r:b,r) The Bettmann Archive (t,l) The British Library Board (m) Giraudon
339 Movie Star News
341 Sovfoto
345 Detail, "Lorenzo de'Médici," Andrea del Verrocchio, National Gallery, Washington, D.C., Samuel H. Kress Collection
348 Alinari-Art Reference Bureau
350 (t) Courtesy of The Trustees of The British Museum (m:b) REPRODUCED BY GRACIOUS PERMISSION OF HER MAJESTY THE QUEEN
351 (t) Courtesy of The Trustees of The British Museum (2 m) Biblioteca Ambrosiana, Milan (b) REPRODUCED BY GRACIOUS PERMISSION OF HER MAJESTY THE QUEEN
352 Ashmolean Museum, Oxford
353 Civic Museum of Padua
354 Alinari-Art Reference Bureau
357 Courtesy of The Trustees of The British Museum
358 Kunsthistorisches Museum, Vienna
359 The National Gallery, London
362 Colonial Williamsburg Photograph
366 (l) Courtesy of the John G. Johnson Collection, Philadelphia (r) Luther-Film-Gesellschaft MBH
367 (t) Giraudon (b) Graphische Sammlung, Munich/Art Reference Bureau
369 The National Maritime Museum, London
370–371 Bulloz/Art Reference Bureau
373 Archives Photographiques
374 Peter Wenkworth Collection; Photograph by R.B. Fleming
377 Historical Pictures Service
379 Henry W. and Albert A. Berg Collection, The New York Public Library, Astor, Lenox and Tilden Foundations
383 The National Maritime Museum, London

385 Direzione Belle Arti del Comune, Genoa, Mario Agosto
386 Joseph D. Germano
391 Rare Book Division, The New York Public Library, Astor, Lenox and Tilden Foundations
393 Boymans-van Beuningen Museum, Rotterdam
396 Giraudon
398 The New York Public Library, Astor, Lenox and Tilden Foundations
401 Courtesy of the Trustees of the British Museum
403 Reproduced from the Collections of the Library of Congress
406 Montanus, . . . *Amerika* . . . , Amsterdam, 1673
407 (t) The Pierpont Morgan Library (b) Radio Times Hulton Picture Library
408 Courtesy, Hispanic Society of America, New York
411 José Casals/Nuestra Señora de Copacabana, Lima
412 Three Lions, Inc.
413 (l) Museo Nacional de Historia, Mexico (r) Shostal Associates
418–419 Ron Bradford
422 The Adler Planetarium, Chicago
425 Derby Corporation Museum and Art Gallery, England
426 Vincent Van Gogh: "The Potato Eaters," 1885, Courtesy National Museum Vincent Van Gogh, Amsterdam
429 (t) By courtesy of the Wellcome Trustees (b) Crown Copyright. Science Museum, London
431 (l) Nelson Gallery-Atkins Museum, Kansas City, Missouri (Nelson Fund) (r) The Pierpont Morgan Library
432 (l) A.F. Kersting (r) J. Chettleburgh
434 (t,r) Reproduced by permission of the Trustees of The Wallace Collection London (b) From Defoe's *The Life and Strange Surprizing Adventures of Robinson Crusoe of York, Mariner,* First Edition (t,l) The Metropolitan Museum of Art, Gift of Junius S. Morgan, 1923
435 Courtesy of the Trustees of the British Museum
438 Courtesy of the Pan American Union
440 National Portrait Gallery, London
441 Courtesy of The Newberry Library, Chicago
443 Courtesy of Historical Society of Pennsylvania
446–447 The New York Public Library, Spencer Collection
447 (t) A.C.L., Brussels (b) Giraudon
450 From *Caricature* by C.R. Ashbee, 1928
452 The Mansell Collection
453 (t:l, r) Culver Pictures (b) Reproduced from the Collections of the Library of Congress
454 National Academy of Design
457 Cartoon by Pecht, from *Der Weltkreig in Der Karikatur,* by Fuchs
460 Giraudon
463 The Bettmann Archive
464 Mannheim Municipal Art Museum, Germany
468 (t: b,l) Radio Times Hulton Picture Library (b,r) The National Trust, Hughenden Manor, Buckinghamshire, England
469 Culver Pictures
470 Cartoon of Bismarck entitled "Dropping the Pilot," from *Punch,* March 29, 1890
473 Brown Brothers
476 The Smithsonian Institution, Washington, D.C.
480 Movie Star News
482 (t) Black Star (b) Courtesy of the New York Historical Society
483 (t) London Electrotype Agency (b) Crown Copyright. Science Museum, London
485 (t) Kansas State Historical Society (b) Brown Brothers
487 (l) Brown Brothers (m,l) The Bettmann Archive (m,r) U.S. Dept. of the Interior, National Park Service (r) Crown Copyright. Science Museum, London
488 (l) The Curators of the Bodleian Library, Oxford (m,l: m,r: r) National Portrait Gallery, London
489 (l) Drawing from a picture by Oscar Halling (m,l: m,r: r) Historical Pictures Service
491 (t,l) John Constable: "The Hay Wain," 1821 The National Gallery, London (t,r) Mary Cassatt: "The Bath," 1891 Courtesy of The Art Institute of Chicago (b) Claude Monet: "La Grenouillere," 1869 The Metropolitan Museum of Art, Bequest of Mrs. H. O. Havemeyer, 1929. The H. O. Havemeyer Collection
495 "Over London-By Rail," illustration by Gustave Doré from *London—A Pilgrimage,* Blanchard Jerrold
497 International Museum of Photography at George Eastman House
499 Prints Division, The New York Public Library, Astor, Lenox and Tilden Foundations
501 Reproduced from the Collections of the Library of Congress
502 A. Von Der Becke & Son, Berlin
505 Reproduced from the Collections of the Library of Congress
506 Courtesy of the Chicago Historical Society
507 From Frank Leslies Illustrated Newspaper, December 14, 1867
509 London Electrotype Agency
514–515 Ron Bradford
518 Radio Times Hulton Picture Library
521 National Army Museum, England
523 Peabody Museum of Salem
524 FPG
526 Sadahide: "Foreign House on a Harbor," Courtesy of The Art Institute of Chicago.
527 From: *A Collection of Nagasaki Prints,* N.H.N. Mody, London, 1939
529 From a sketch sent by M.L. Roux, Secretary to the Admiral Rigault de Genouilly
532 From: *In Darkest Africa,* Henry M. Stanley, Vol. I, 1890
533 René Dazy
535 Reproduced by permission of The Library of Congress; photograph by Dinwiddie, 1898
539 Courtesy of The Trustees of The British Museum
541 From *Gott Strafe England,* Munich
546 both Courtesy Imperial War Museum, London
547 (t) U.S. Air Force Photo (b) The National Archives
550 (t) FPG (b) West Point Museum Collection, U.S. Military Academy
551 (t) FPG (b) The National Archives
553 Courtesy Imperial War Museum, London
557 Pressfoto: E. Thaler, Berlin
559 & 560 U.P.I.
562 (t) Reginald Marsh: "Tatoo and Haircut," 1932 Courtesy of The Art Institute of Chicago (b) William Gropper
564 Wide World
565–567 U.P.I.
569 (l) The National Archives (r) U.P.I.
570 U.P.I.
573 Sovfoto
576 Illustrated London News, 1861
577 (l) James Sawders, New Jersey (r) Chagall, Marc. *I and the Village.* 1911. Oil on canvas, 6′ 3 5/8″ × 59 5/8″. Collection, The Museum of Modern Art, NY Mrs. Simon Guggenheim Fund.
578 Sovfoto
579 Charles Kay
580 U.P.I.
582 Movie Star News
584 Tass from Sovfoto
585 U.P.I.
586 Swedish-American Line
587 (t) Sovfoto (b) Tass from Sovfoto
591 U.P.I.
593 (b) U.P.I. (t) Three Lions
598 (l) Wide World (r) West Point Museum Collection, United States Military Academy
599 (l) Fox Photos, Ltd., London (r) Courtesy Imperial War Museum London
601 H. Roger Viollet
602 Courtesy Imperial War Museum, London
603 & 604 Wide World
608–609 Ron Bradford
612 Photo by James L. Ballard
615 & 616 United Nations
617–619 U.P.I.
620 Movie Star News
622 U.P.I.
626 (l) Bill Stanton/Magnum (r) Tass from Sovfoto
630 U.P.I.
632 Allen & Unwin
634 U.P.I.
635 United Nations
638 & 639 U.P.I.
641 Courtesy of the Smithsonian Institution, Freer Gallery of Art, Washington, D.C.
642 Paris Match/Pictorial Parade
643 © Time Inc., photograph by John Dominis
645 Hiroji Kubota/Woodfin Camp
646 Courtesy of the Consulate General of Japan
649 Wide World
652 George Bellerose/Stock, Boston
654 Katrina Thomas/Photo Researchers
656 Marilyn Silverstone/Magnum
658 (t,l) WHO photograph by D. Henrioud (t,r) Marc Riboud/Magnum (b) United Nations
660 Wide World
663 (t) Orozco, Jose Clemente, *Zapatistas.* 1931. Oil on canvas, 45 × 55 Collection, Museum of Modern Art, New York. Given anonymously. (b) United Nations
664 Wide World
665 U.P.I.
668 Shostal Associates
671 John Nance/Magnum
672 United Air Lines
673 U.P.I.
674 (t) Hoe Culture Eutah, Alabama, July 1936. Reproduced from the Collections of the Library of Congress; photograph by Dorothea Lange for FSA (b,l) Willem De Kooning: "Women VI," 1953 Museum of Art, Carnegie Institute, Pittsburgh (b,r) Warhol, Andy. *Campbell's Soup.* 1965. Oil, silk-screened on canvas. 36 ⅛ × 24″. Collection, Museum of Modern Art, New York. Philip Johnson Fund.
675 (t,l) Karl Gerstner: "Lens Picture," 1962-64 Staempfli Gallery, New York (t,r) Nicolas Schoffer: "Lux 2," 1957 Courtesy Gallery Denise René (b,l) Roy Lichtenstein: "Torpedo . . . Los," 1963 Courtesy of Mrs. R. B. Mayer, Chicago (b,r) Alexander Calder: "Red Petals," Collection of Arts Club of Chicago
676 (l) Wide World (m) Courtesy of Harper & Row (r) Photograph by Mottke Weissman, Courtesy of the Dial Press
677 Wide World
679 The National Foundation for Infantile Paralysis
686 (t,l: t,r: b,l) Wide World (b,r) United Nations
683 U.P.I.
685 Martha Cooper Guthrie

Index

The index tells you where to find maps *(map)*, illustrations *(illus.)*, definitions *(def.)*, and pronunciations *(pron.)*. Pronunciations are respelled in the familiar Thorndike Barnhart pronunciation key. The table below shows the sound each symbol represents. For many foreign words in *History and Life*, the pronunciation given is not the local pronunciation but an Anglicized version, one acceptable to educated Americans.

a	hat, cap	j	jam, enjoy	th	thin, both
ā	age, face	k	kind, seek	TH	then, smooth
ä	father, far	l	land, coal	u	cup, butter
		m	me, am	u̇	full, put
b	bad, rob	n	no, in	ü	rule, move
ch	child, much	ng	long, bring		
d	did, red			v	very, save
		o	hot, rock	w	will, woman
e	let, best	ō	open, go	y	young, yet
ē	equal, see	ô	order, all	z	zero, breeze
ėr	term, learn	oi	oil, voice	zh	measure, seizure
		ou	house, out		
f	fat, if			ə	represents:
g	go, bag	p	paper, cup	a	in about
h	he, how	r	run, try	e	in taken
		s	say, yes	i	in pencil
i	it, pin	sh	she, rush	o	in lemon
ī	ice, five	t	tell, it	u	in circus

FOREIGN SOUNDS

Y as in French du. Pronounce ē with the lips rounded as for English ü in **rule.**

œ as in French peu. Pronounce ā with the lips rounded as for ō.

N as in French bon. The N is not pronounced, but shows that the vowel before it is nasal.

H as in German ach. Pronounce k without closing the breath passage.

S